WILLIAM BAIRD is professor emeritus of New Testament at Brite Divinity School at Texas Christian University.

HISTORY OF NEW TESTAMENT RESEARCH

HISTORY OF NEW TESTAMENT RESEARCH

VOLUME THREE: FROM C. H. DODD TO HANS DIETER BETZ

WILLIAM BAIRD

Fortress Press
Minneapolis

HISTORY OF NEW TESTAMENT RESEARCH

Volume 3: From C. H. Dodd to Hans Dieter Betz

Cover design: Tory Herman

Library of Congress Cataloging-in-Publication Data is available

Print ISBN: 978-0-8006-9918-5

eBook ISBN: 978-1-4514-2619-9

Manufactured in the U.S.A.

For Shirley Elizabeth Baird and Lisa Baird Parks

CONTENTS

Previous Volumes

Acknowledgments

This book was completed in the face of adversity. Beyond the problem of advancing age, I endured complications following surgery (July, 2009), requiring months of hospitalization and therapy. There was a period in which no work was possible, and I believed that I could never complete the project. In time, with the help of others, I was able to return to the task. My friend and gifted physician, Dr. Robert H. Kelly, guided me back to health. Research assistance—including mundane tasks like carrying books—was provided by a promising young scholar, Coleman A. Baker, PhD; some of his work was supported by a TCU Faculty Emeritus Grant. Institutional support was supplied by Brite Divinity School and the Mary Couts Burnett Library at Texas Christian University—especially the Circulation and Interlibrary Loan Departments. Friends and colleagues provided encouragement. For the last few years, I have enjoyed weekly lunch with my successor at Brite, M. Eugene Boring. Virtually everything in the book has been discussed with Gene, and benefited from his insight. From time to time, we are joined by Victor Paul Furnish who travels from Dallas. Both Gene and Vic read the manuscript and suggested revisions which have significantly improved the final product. Helpful suggestions were also made by my long-time friend and colleague, James O. Duke, who read the manuscript with great care. This book is dedicated to two women who have been important for my life: my wife, Shirley, and my daughter, Lisa.

Abbreviations

AAR American Academy of Religion

AARAS American Academy of Religion Academy Series

AB The Anchor Bible (commentaries)

ABD Anchor Bible Dictionary, ed. D. N. Freedman, 6 vols. (New York: Doubleday, 1992)

ABRL Anchor Bible Reference Library

AGSU Arbeiten zur Geschichte des Spätjudentums und Urchristentums

AGThL Arbeiten zur Geschichte und Theologie des Luthertums

AnBib Analecta biblica

ANTC Abingdon New Testament Commentaries

ANTF Arbeiten zur neutestamentlichen Textforschung

ASBT Acadia Studies in Bible and Theology

ASNU Acta seminarii neotestamentici Upsaliensis

ASOR American Schools of Oriental Research

ASV American Standard Version

ATANT Abhandlungen zur Theologie des Alten und Neuen Testaments

AThR Anglican Theological Review

ATLA American Theological Library Association

AYBRL Anchor Yale Bible Reference Library

BA Biblical Archaeologist

BCE Before Common Era

BETL Bibliotheca ephemeridum theologicarum Lovaniensium

BEvT Beiträge zur Evangelischen Theologie

BGBE Beiträge zur Geschichte der biblischen Exegese

BHT Beiträge zur historischen Theologie

BJRL Bulletin of the John Rylands University Library of Manchester

BNTC Black's New Testament Commentary

BRev Bible Review

BTB Biblical Theology Bulletin

BZ Biblische Zeitschrift

BZAW Beihefte zur Zeitschrift für die alttestamentliche Wissenschaft

BZNW Beihefte zur Zeitschrift für die neutestamentliche Wissenschaft

CBQ Catholic Biblical Quarterly

CBQMS Catholic Biblical Quarterly Monograph Series

CE Common Era

ConBNT Coniectanea neotestamentica or Coniectanea biblica: New Testament Series

CT Christian Testament (New Testament)

DAS Directory of American Scholars, 6th ed (New York: R. R. Bowker, 1974)

DBCI Dictionary of Biblical Criticism and Interpretation, ed. Stanley E. Porter (London: Routledge, 2009)

DBI Dictionary of Biblical Interpretation, ed. John H. Hayes, 2 vols. (Nashville: Abingdon, 1999)

2DH Two-Document Hypothesis

DJS Duke Judaic Studies

DMBI Dictionary of Major Biblical Interpreters, ed. Donald K. McKim (Downers Grove, Ill.: InterVarsity, 2007)

DRev Downside Review

DSS Dead Sea Scrolls

EBib Etudes bibliques

ed(s). editor(s), edited by, edition

EHPR Etudes d'histoire et de philosophie religieuses

EKKNT Evangelisch-katholischer Kommentar zum Neuen Testament

Enc Encounter

Eng. English

EpRev Epworth Review

ET English translation

ETS Evangelical Theological Society

EvQ Evangelical Quarterly

EvT Evangelische Theologie

ExpTim Expository Times

FF Foundations and Facets

For Forum

Fr. French

FRLANT Forschungen zur Religion und Literatur des Alten und Neuen Testaments

FTMTh Fortress Texts in Modern Theology

Ger. German

2GH Two-Gospel Hypothesis

HNT Handbuch zum Neuen Testament

HNTC Harper's New Testament Commentaries

HNTR History of New Testament Research, Vols. 1 and 2, William Baird (Minneapolis: Fortress, 1992, 2003)

HTKNT Herders theologischer Kommentar zum Neuen Testament

HTKNTSup Herders theologischer Kommentar zum Neuen Testament: Supplementband

HTR Harvard Theological Review

HTS Harvard Theological Studies

IB Interpreter's Bible, ed. G. A. Buttrick et al, 12 vols. (New York: Abingdon-Cokesbury, 1951-57)

ICC International Critical Commentary

IDB The Interpreter's Dictionary of the Bible, ed. George A. Buttrick, 4 vols. (New York: Abingdon, 1962)

IDBSup Interpreter's Dictionary of the Bible: Supplementary Volume

IKZ Internationale kirchliche Zeitschrift

Int Interpretation

IRev Iliff Review

JAAR Journal of the American Academy of Religion

JBL Journal of Biblical Literature

JBR Journal of Bible and Religion

JFSR Journal of Feminist Studies in Religion

JR Journal of Religion

JRASup Journal of Roman Archaeology Supplementary Series

JSHJSup Journal for the Study of the Historical Jesus: Supplement Series

JSHRZ Jüdische Schriften aus hellenistisch-römischer Zeit

JSNT Journal for the Study of the New Testament

JSNTSup Journal for the Study of the New Testament: Supplement

JSOT Journal for the Study of the Old Testament

JTC Journal for Theology and the Church

JTS Journal of Theological Studies

KD Kerygma and Dogma

KEK Kritisch-exegetischer Kommentar über das Neue Testament (Meyer-Kommentar)

KJV King James Version (Authorized Version)

KVR Kleine Vandenhoeck-Reihe

LBC The Layman's Bible Commentary

LQ Lutheran Quarterly

LXX Septuagint (Greek trans. of the OT)

MNTC Moffatt New Testament Commentary

MSS manuscripts

MT Masoretic Text

MTh Modern Theology

MThS Münchener Theologische Studien

MTS Marburger Theologische Studien

NASB New American Standard Bible

NAWG Nachrichten der Academie der Wissenschaften in Göttingen

NCB New Century Bible

NEB New English Bible

NFT New Frontiers in Theology

NHC Nag Hammadi Codices

NHMS Nag Hammadi and Manichaean Studies

NHS Nag Hammadi Studies

NICNT New International Commentary on the New Testament

NIGTC New International Greek Testament Commentary

NIV New International Version

NJBC The New Jerome Biblical Commentary, ed. Raymond E. Brown, Joseph A. Fitzmyer, and Roland E. Murphy (Englewood Cliffs, N.J.: Prentice Hall. 1990)

NLTh Nelson's Library of Theology

NovT Novum Testamentum

NovTSup Supplements to Novum Testamentum

NRSV New Revised Standard Version

NT New Testament

NTAbh Neutestamentliche Abhandlungen

NTAM New Testament Archaeology Monograph

NTD Das Neue Testament Deutsch

NThG Neue theologische Grundriss

NTL The New Testament Library

NTS New Testament Studies

NTTS New Testament Tools and Studies

NZSTRP *Neue Zeitschrift für systematische Theologie und Religionsphilosophie*

OPIAC Occasional Papers of The Institute for Antiquity and Christianity

OThM Oxford Theological Monographs

p(p). page(s)

PC Proclamation Commentaries

PHP Pendle Hill Pamphlets

RHPR Revue d'histoire et de philosophie religieuses

PMS Princeton Monograph Series

PTS Patristische Texte und Studien

PVTG Pseudepigrapha Veteris Testamenti Graece

ReL Religion in Life

RelSRev Religious Studies Review

repr. reprint, reprinted in

rev. revised, revised in

RGG Religion in Geschichte und Gegenwart, ed. K. Galling, 7 vols., 3d ed. (Tübingen: J. C. B Mohr [Paul Siebeck], 1957-1965); 9 vols.; 4th ed. (Tübingen: Mohr Siebeck, 1998-2005); ET: *Religion Past and Present* (Leiden: Brill 2007)

SAC Studies in Antiquity and Christianity

SBL Society of Biblical Literature

SBLBMI SBL The Bible and Its Modern Interpreters

SBLBSNA SBL Biblical Scholarship in North America

SBLCP Society of Biblical Literature Centennial Publications

SBLCPS SBL Confessional Perspective Series

SBLDS SBL Dissertation Series

SBLEJL SBL Early Judaism and Its Literature

SBLMS SBL Monograph Series

SBLRBS SBL Resources for Biblical Study

SBLSBS SBL Sources for Biblical Study

SBLSCS SBL Septuagint and Cognate Studies

SBLSSup SBL Semeia Supplements

SBLTCS SBL Text-Critical Studies

SBS Sources for Biblical Study

SBT Studies in Biblical Theology

SCHNT Studia ad corpus Hellenisticum Novi Testamenti

SD Studies and Documents

SDSSRL Studies in the Dead Sea Scrolls and Related Literature
SEC Studies in Early Christianity
SFSHJ South Florida Studies in the History of Judaism
SHAW Sitzungsberichte der heidelberger Akademie der Wissenschaften
SHR Studies in History of Religions (supplement to *Numen*)
SJLA Studies in Judaism in Late Antiquity
SJT Scottish Journal of Theology
SM Sermon on the Mount
SNTS Studiorum Novi Testamenti Societas
SNTSMS Society for New Testament Studies Monograph Series
SP Sermon on the Plain
StBS Stuttgarter Bibelstudien
STDJ Studies on the Texts of the Desert of Judah
SThK Systematische Theologie und Kirchengeschichte
SThU Schweizerische theologische Umschau
StudNeot Studia neotestamentica
SVTP Studia in Veteris Testamenti pseudepigrapha
SymBU Symbolae biblicae Upsalienses
TDNT Theological Dictionary of the New Testament, ed. G. Kittel and G. Friedrich, trans. G. W. Bromiley, 10 vols. (Grand Rapids, Mich.: Eerdmans, 1964-1976)
TF Theologische Forschung
TGST Tesi Gregoriana: Serie Teologia
ThEH Theologische Existenz Heute
ThSt Theologische Studien
ThTo Theology Today
TLZ Theologische Literaturzeitung
trans. translation, translated by
TRu Theologische Rundschau
TS Texts and Studies
TU Texte und Untersuchungen
TynBul Tyndale Bulletin
TZ Theologische Zeitschrift
UNT Untersuchungen zum Neuen Testament
USQR Union Seminary Quarterly Review
WBC Word Biblical Commentary

WMANT Wissenschaftliche Monographien zum Alten und Neuen Testament

WUNT Wissenschaftliche Untersuchungen zum Neuen Testament

YSR Yale Studies in Religion

ZNW Zeitschrift für die neutestamentliche Wissenschaft und die Kunde der älteren Kirche

Introduction

Written some two thousand years ago, the New Testament (NT) remains an exceptional document. For some, it is the most important book ever written; for others it is the basic record of the beginnings of a world religion. For some, it records the words of God; for others it is a historical witness to the Word made flesh. For all of these, the study of the NT is significant. The history of that study is a fascinating story in its own right, but for the serious student of the Bible, knowledge of that history is essential. New wine should not be put in old wineskins, and it is important to know the difference. Old mistakes ought to be avoided; new ventures find their point of departure in the old.

This account of the history of NT research has a history of its own. In response to a request to write such a history—and after months of preparing a prospectus—I signed (in 1984) a contract that promised a book of some 500 pages, to be completed within six years. As work on the project progressed, it became evident that the history could not be covered in a single volume, and as work on the second volume progressed it became apparent that a third volume would be needed. Volume 1, *From Deism to Tübingen*, reviewed research from about 1700 to around 1870. Volume 2 was intended to bring the account up to the period of the Second World War; my original plan had been to end the volume with the chapter on "the Zenith of Enlightenment Criticism." Lack of space, however, led to the assigning of this chapter to Volume 3. The subtitle of Volume 2, *From Jonathan Edwards to Rudolf Bultmann*, is somewhat misleading. Jonathan Edwards was presented as a precursor of nineteenth-century American research, and the treatment of Bultmann's work was limited to his history of religion and form-critical scholarship.

The working subtitle for Volume 3, *From Biblical Theology to Pluralism*, came increasingly to appear inadequate: "The New Biblical Theology" was not the first, but the second chapter; an earlier plan to investigate the multitude of new methods that emerged in the last half of the century had to be abandoned because of lack of space and time. Also, the original plan for Volume 3 included more scholars, but again space and time limitations made this impossible. Since no obvious point of termination was apparent, I made an arbitrary decision: the volume would include primarily scholars born before 1930. Although there are exceptions, virtually all of the scholars have retired, and (again with exceptions) their major works were written in the twentieth century. The subtitle, *From*

C. H. Dodd to Hans Dieter Betz, highlights the focus of the volume: the history of twentieth-century NT research in the Enlightenment tradition. Both Dodd and Betz are masters of historical criticism, and both are devotees of classical philosophy and rhetoric. Betz illustrates an important feature of the history rehearsed in this volume: the increasingly international character of NT research.

As in the previous volumes, the material is arranged more or less chronologically. Some of the chapters are ordered topically, but within the individual chapters chronological order is largely followed. As in the earlier volumes, "NT research" includes the whole discipline, from textual criticism to theology. Again attention is focused on the work of individual scholars, but in this volume cooperative research is also reviewed. The title *History of New Testament Research* is an overstatement. This is a history of NT research in *some* places by *some* scholars. Attention is given almost exclusively to research in northern Europe (Germany and Britain) and North America. With the exception of the work of Elisabeth Schüssler Fiorenza, feminist NT research has not been reviewed. The abundance of excellent NT research by women belongs mainly to the period beyond the limitations of this book. Scholars have been selected according to their importance for the ongoing history.

As to method, this book reviews and analyzes major works of major scholars. By major works I mean primarily books and collections of articles and essays. This method assumes that knowledge of these primary sources constitutes the essence of NT research: a knowledge that will have continuing value, irrespective of new movements and methods. The attempt has been made to present the works faithfully and sympathetically—a daunting task in view of the fact that many of the scholars are alive and potential readers of the volume. My efforts at evaluation, mainly in short summaries at the end of chapters, attempt to critique the material in terms of its own presuppositions and context and with the assistance, when available, of major secondary sources.

A new feature of this volume is the inclusion of accounts of personal experiences. Although urged by friends and colleagues to include these, I do so with reluctance, wary of the appearance of name dropping or being self-serving. Nevertheless, these experiences constitute oral tradition and have been, like the forms of the gospel tradition, reshaped by the retelling. Any scholar of my generation who has studied in the major university settings and in Europe can recount similar stories.

When English translations are available I have used them, only occasionally checking the original. Unless otherwise noted, the translations from German and French are mine. Quotations from the Bible are usually from the NRSV, although in contexts in which I am explicating commentaries I have often used the translation of the commentator. I have used "OT" for the Old Testament, since this is the usage of most of the scholars reviewed; this usage is not meant to imply any sort of supersessionism. For my part, I have attempted to use inclusive language, but in reporting the work of others (whose work antedated the identification of the problem) I have followed their usage.

The bibliography, as the title shows, is selective; it does not include all the references found in the notes, but contains only major works of the major scholars. The practice (in vols. 1 and 2) of distinguishing primary from secondary sources has not been followed. Major secondary sources about a scholar are listed alphabetically at the end of the section on that particular scholar. Biographical references for each scholar are found in the first note referring to the scholar's life and work.

Readers of volumes 1 and 2 may be surprised by the appearance of endnotes (placed at the end of chapters) rather than footnotes. This procedure represents a new program adopted by Fortress Press to make books as readily accessible for electronic publication as in print. For scholars (like myself) who prefer footnotes, a few suggestions may be helpful. There are a large number of notes, for example, almost three hundred in chapter 1. Many of these are mere references, including frequent use of "Ibid." Readers who wish to follow the main lines of the argument may wish at least initially to ignore the notes. On the other hand, there are some notes of major importance which develop arguments more extensively or present alternative positions in some detail. The concerned reader, when beginning a chapter, may wish first to scan all the notes, marking the longer notes for consideration as the chapter is read.

After almost thirty years of work on this project, I conclude with mixed feelings. I am relieved to be finished, but reluctant to end what has been an exciting adventure. The results in these volumes reflect only a fraction of the research and notes I have collected over the years. I am a slow, ponderous worker, taught to investigate all the sources—a clear impossibility. Others (whose names I could name) would have done this job better, but I am fortunate to have been afforded the opportunity. Though the task has sometimes been arduous, the work has mainly been an enjoyable challenge. I have approached each "new" subject with enthusiasm: I have heard of the scholar and read a bit, but now I have the opportunity to explore in detail, to investigate the primary sources!

Some reviewers have accused me of undue affection for the historical critical method. To that I can merely reply, *mea culpa*. I am well aware, of course, that the use (or abuse) of the critical method has been destructive for some, resulting in a depreciation of Scripture and loss of faith. For me the opposite have proved true. It has been the historical critical method that has sustained my faith and deepened my devotion to the New Testament, the book I have spent my life attempting to understand and to teach.

PART I

The Renaissance of New Testament Criticism

1

The Zenith of Enlightenment Criticism

Anglo-American Research in the Gospels

In 1939, international exhibitions were held on both American coasts: the New York World's Fair and the Golden Gate International Exposition in San Francisco. The fair in New York had as its theme "The World of Tomorrow." As visitors strolled by artificial pools and fountains and marveled at recent technological achievements like television they were moved by nostalgia for the fading Enlightenment. Trying to forget the tragedy of the First World War and the rise of totalitarianism, they embraced again that hope in progress, the uninhibited advance of human civilization. Representatives from sixty-three nations from around the globe came to New York, crossing geographical and political barriers to present their accomplishments in pavilions side by side: a final display of internationalism before the outbreak of the greatest conflagration in human history. Even before the exhibitors had torn down the temporary buildings, Hitler's troops had marched into Poland. The tomorrow of the new world never dawned.

In the period before and immediately after the Second World War, NT research shared the nostalgia for the Enlightenment. . The methods of empiricism and rationalism were continued and refined. Like the cooperative efforts of the exhibitions, scholars moved toward consensus. New Testament scholarship became increasingly international, and movements toward synthesis appeared. In Britain and America contributions were made to the study of the Gospels, seen in the work of Taylor and Cadbury. As in other disciplines—atomic physics, for example—NT research continued a development toward greater complexity. The NT scholar is called to become a virtuoso, a sort of Paganini of academia, mastering linguistics, textual analysis, exegetical imagination, historical reconstruction, and constructive theology. As

Paul said, "Who is sufficient for these things?" Some, like Charles Harold Dodd, were.[1]

In the period between the wars prominent British and American scholars studied the Gospels. They accepted the Two-Document Hypothesis (2DH) as axiomatic: that Matthew and Luke independently used as sources Mark and a collection of sayings called "Q." They were more cautious, however, in regard to other developments in continental scholarship. In response to the method of history of religion[2] they affirmed the significance of the historical setting but stressed Jewish rather than Hellenistic backgrounds. In response to eschatological interpretation they acknowledged the prevalence of apocalyptic forms but proposed revision of the eschatological substance. In response to form criticism they recognized the reality of the oral tradition but questioned the application and results of the method. The work of these scholars indicates the interconnected nature of the issues. Form criticism is concerned with the development of the tradition, and the tradition was concerned with Jesus, and Jesus had his setting in Judaism, and Judaism was concerned with eschatology. Is the tradition of Jesus recorded in the Gospels reliable? How is Jesus related to Jewish apocalyptic thought? Did Jesus understand himself as Messiah? To these and a host of related questions, British and American scholars turned.

REACTION TO FORM CRITICISM: VINCENT TAYLOR

VINCENT TAYLOR (1887–1968)

LIFE AND EARLY WORK

Vincent Taylor was born in Edenfield, Lancashire.[3] As to his academic preparation, Taylor did not begin his higher education until he was twenty-two, when he entered the Methodist theological school at Richmond. Taylor's academic degrees were awarded on the grounds of scholarly accomplishments after he left the classroom. On the basis of his book on the virgin birth he was awarded a PhD (1922), and in honor of a publication on Luke, a DD (1926), both from the University of London. In 1930, Taylor was appointed to the faculty at Wesley College in Leeds, where after six years he was named Principal, and where he remained until his retirement in 1953. In spite of his ministerial and administrative duties, Taylor had a passion for research, and he adhered to a self-imposed discipline, always producing at least a page a day.

Taylor's first major work was *The Historical Evidence for the Virgin Birth.*[4] He insisted on rigorous historical investigation. "Doctrinal presuppositions must be resolutely laid aside; there must be a common desire to ascertain the true facts of the evidence, whatever the results may be."[5] Taylor begins his investigation by reviewing texts outside of Matthew and Luke. He notes that no mention of the virgin of birth is found in the Gospel of Mark, the Pauline epistles, and Hebrews, and he concludes that the authors of these documents did not know the doctrine. Since it is not included in Acts, Taylor believes Luke did not consider the virgin birth a feature of early Christian preaching. Taylor analyzes the text of Luke and concludes that Luke's original account did not include the virgin birth. Later, after he learned of the doctrine, Luke, according to Taylor, added 1:34-35 and the parenthesis of 3:23. Turning to Matthew, Taylor believed the first two chapters were part of the original gospel, including the account of the virgin birth in 1:18-25. On the basis of his careful analysis of the details of these texts, Taylor concluded that the doctrine can be neither proved nor disproved by historical investigation. In his opinion, denial of the supernatural birth of Jesus does not destroy the faith expressed in the doctrine. "If, in the end, we must call poetry what they called fact," says Taylor, "it will not be because we are strangers to their faith. They too were bound by the spell of that Transcendent Face in which is the light of the knowledge of the glory of God."[6]

CRITICAL WORK ON THE GOSPELS

Taylor's major critical effort was devoted to the Synoptic Gospels. In regard to the problem of literary sources, he published *Behind the Third Gospel: A Study of the Proto-Luke Hypothesis*,[7] essentially a defense and expansion of the theory of B. H. Streeter.[8] According to Streeter, Luke had combined material he had collected at Caesarea, as companion of Paul, with the document Q, which he received after the death of Paul, to compose a gospel Streeter called "Proto-Luke." Later, acquiring a copy of Mark, Luke, in Streeter's opinion, added blocks of Markan material to Proto-Luke, resulting in the Gospel of Luke. In investigating this theory Taylor begins with the passion and resurrection narrative, where he finds material independent of Mark, and concludes that Luke used a non-Markan source to which he added Markan material. Late in his career Taylor revived this investigation, producing research that was published posthumously as *The Passion Narrative of St Luke: A Critical and Historical Investigation*.[9] The book is essentially a detailed analysis of the literary relationship between Luke 22–24 and Mark 14–16. Taylor proceeds through the texts, analyzing the linguistic and stylistic details, and reaches the conclusion that "the Lukan narratives of the Passion and resurrection were probably derived from an earlier non-Markan source or sources."[10] In this later work

Taylor concludes that Luke was not the author of this source, but that he found it, a written document, at Caesarea.

After the discussion of the passion narrative, *Behind the Third Gospel* presents Taylor's investigation of Luke's use of Mark in the narrative prior to the passion. Employing meticulous vocabulary and stylistic research, Taylor investigates the Lukan and Markan parallels and concludes that Mark does not provide the framework for Luke's narrative. Instead, Luke, according to Taylor, used another source as primary and added Markan material to it. This primary source Taylor identifies as Proto-Luke. "The Proto-Luke Hypothesis . . . posits a continuous non-Markan source, consisting mainly of Q matter and material peculiar to Lk., as the foundation and framework of the Third Gospel."[11] On the basis of this hypothesis Taylor affirmed the historical value of Proto-Luke, especially in the accounts of the passion and resurrection. "Here, indeed, it is everywhere comparable to Mk. as a competent witness, and where the two disagree it is Proto-Luke as a rule which preserves the better tradition." The value of Proto-Luke, Taylor believes, enhances the value of the Gospel of Luke.

> Too long we have looked upon the teaching peculiar to the Third Gospel as if it stood upon a lower plane of authentication than that of Mk. and Q. The Proto-Luke Hypothesis destroys this assumption; it throws back into the earliest stage of Gospel tradition the picture of a Christ whose compassion blesses the outcasts of society, and whose last words to man are a message of hope to a dying thief.[12]

Thus Taylor developed the Proto-Luke hypothesis beyond Streeter, making a credible case for the importance of Luke's special material (L), but his claim that the hypothetical Proto-Luke, rather than Mark, is the framework for the Gospel of Luke is questionable.[13]

Taylor's important contribution to form criticism is *The Formation of the Gospel Tradition.*[14] First published in 1933, the book was slightly revised in 1935 and frequently reprinted. In the preface Taylor asserts that form criticism furnishes "constructive suggestions which in many ways confirm the historical trustworthiness of the Gospel tradition." The method "forces us to read the Gospels in the closest connexion with the life and experience of the first Christians, and brings the Gospels and the Epistles into nearer relationships."[15] Taylor begins with a review of the work of Martin Dibelius, Rudolf Bultmann, and Karl Ludwig Schmidt.[16] He agrees that forms like those identified by these scholars are found in the Gospels, but he notes the difficulty of detecting the original form and determining the *Sitz im Leben*. He believes the form critics attribute too much creativity to the church and fail to recognize the continuing presence of eyewitnesses. "If the Form-Critics are right, the disciples must have been translated to heaven immediately after the Resurrection."[17]

Taylor proceeds to investigate the gospel material according to his understanding of the forms. Most important is his distinctive contribution to form criticism: the identification of the "pronouncement stories."

> Their chief characteristic . . . is that they culminate in a saying of Jesus which expresses some ethical or religious precept; the saying may be evoked by a question friendly or otherwise, or may be associated with an incident which is indicated in very few words. Prized because they gave guidance to the first Christians, these stories circulated as single units of tradition, or were combined in groups on a purely topical thread.[18]

He proceeds to the "sayings and parables," about which he writes: "I have no hesitation in claiming that the tradition of the words of Jesus is far better preserved than we have any right to expect, and with much greater accuracy than is to be found in the record of the words of any great teacher of the past."[19] In regard to "miracle stories" Taylor believes the tendency of the tradition is to shorten the accounts. Concerning the "stories about Jesus," he writes: "The result, then, for a study of the formal aspects of the Stories about Jesus is to strengthen confidence in their historical value."[20]

Taylor concludes with his reconstruction of the development of the gospel tradition: in the period from 30–50 CE, independent sayings and stories about Jesus were repeated in the interest of the practical needs of the community; from 50–65, individual elements were gathered into collections; from 65–100 Gospels were written: Proto-Luke (60–65), Mark (in Rome, 65–70), Matthew in Antioch or northern Syria (around 90). Thus Taylor embraces the method of form criticism but shrinks from the skepticism of its German practitioners. He recognizes the formative influence of the early community but attributes virtually nothing substantial to it. He believes that the tradition, oral and written, faithfully transmits the words and deeds of Jesus.

Taylor's *magnum opus* was his commentary on Mark.[21] He begins his lengthy introduction (some 150 pages) with a survey of the history of the Gospel of Mark in the early church. In reviewing nineteenth century criticism, Taylor notes the triumph of the Two-Document Hypothesis (2DH) and says that "in a modern commentary, it is no longer necessary to prove the priority of Mark."[22] Taylor believes the author was John Mark, who preserved the reminiscences of Peter. He thinks the Gospel was written in Rome, between 65 and 67 CE. As to sources, Taylor believes that, in addition to the tradition of Peter, Mark used written material: for example, an early collection of sayings. Mark presents his Christology, according to Taylor, in titles used for Jesus, especially "Son of Man" and "Son of God." "The sheer humanity of the Markan portraiture catches the eye of the most careless reader; and yet, it is but half seen if it is not perceived that this Man of Sorrows is also a Being of supernatural origin and dignity, since He is the Son of God."[23] According to Taylor the "messianic secret" is a creation not of Mark but of Jesus, and was designed to avoid popular misunderstanding of his messianic role. Mark's ordering of the narrative, in Taylor's opinion is, historically correct.

> In sum we may say that in Mark we have an authority of first rank for our knowledge of the Story of Jesus. Separated at the time of writing by little more than a generation from the death of Jesus, its contents carry us back farther into the oral period before Mark wrote to the tradition first of the Palestinian community and subsequently that of the Gentile Church at Rome.[24]

The commentary proper consists of over 460 pages, plus fifty pages of additional notes. The material is presented according to Taylor's understanding of the structure of the Gospel. The Greek text, a revised Westcott and Hort, is printed at the top of the page; the comments (actually notes on the text) are printed in double columns below. "Detached notes" or excurses are interspersed at the appropriate places. As an example of his exegesis, "The Confession of Peter and the First Prophecy of the Passion" (Mark 8:27-33) is of special concern to Taylor. In his introductory comment he identifies the form as a "story about Jesus," not a "legend," as Bultmann supposes. Taylor thinks it remarkable that popular opinion did not include an identification of Jesus as Messiah. In regard to v. 29, Taylor observes that use of ὑμεῖς in Jesus' question is emphatic, and Peter's response σὺ εἶ ὁ Χριστός is also emphatic. Regarding χριστός, Taylor notes that this word translates מָשִׁיחַ in the LXX, and that it is used for the Davidic Messiah in the Psalms of Solomon 17:32 and for the superhuman Son of Man in 1 Enoch 48:10. Commenting on this first and the repeated predictions of the passion, Taylor emphasizes Jesus' intent to instruct the disciples concerning the suffering Messiah. He also believes Jesus predicted his own resurrection, but with less precision than Mark's "after three days." According to Taylor, suffering was essential to Jesus' understanding of his teaching is based on a unique combination of the idea of the Suffering Servant of Isa. liii with that of the Son of Man."[25]

An example of Taylor's excurses is the "Detached Note on the Date of the Cleansing of the Temple," inserted after his introductory comments on Mark 11:15-19. Taylor argues against the Markan location of the event in passion week and offers reasons for an earlier date as presented in the Fourth Gospel, or according to Goguel's chronology in which the cleansing of the temple occurred during a visit to Jerusalem prior to the journey to Perea, a few months before the final trip to Jerusalem.[26] Among the additional notes appended at the end, "The Construction of the Passion and Resurrection Narrative" is of special interest. Taylor detects two strata of tradition, an early summary account and a later version characterized by Semitisms. "The hypothesis suggested is that Mark found an account of the Passion in Rome and expanded it by the aid of the Petrine tradition."[27]

All in all, Taylor's *Mark* is a monumental achievement. He attends skillfully to all the disciplines of critical exegesis—text criticism,[28] linguistics, and grammar—all in the service of historical reconstruction and theological meaning. He provides references to the LXX, rabbinic sources, classical literature, and a host of modern scholars. Taylor's work remained throughout the twentieth century a widely used and highly respected commentary.

NEW TESTAMENT THEOLOGY

Like Brahms, who did not attempt a symphony until after he was forty, Taylor undertook theological construction only after he had mastered the theory and practice of biblical criticism. In the preface to his first book on the atonement he wrote: "After devoting something like twenty-five years to the study of the problems of literary and historical criticism in connexion with the Gospels, and especially to the minutiae of source criticism, I am conscious of a strong desire to investigate some more vital issue, arising out of these studies, which bears intimately upon Christian life and practice."[29] As a result he produced two series of books on NT theology: a trilogy on the atonement and a second trilogy on Christology.

Taylor's first book on the atonement, *Jesus and His Sacrifice*, focuses on the passion sayings in Mark and L. Particularly important is Mark 10:45 ("the Son of Man came . . . to serve, and to give his life a ransom for many"), which Taylor takes to be an authentic word of Jesus, reminiscent of Isaiah 53. In L, Taylor stresses Luke 17:25 ("but first he must endure much suffering and be rejected by this generation"), a text in which Taylor believes Jesus identifies himself as the suffering Son of Man. Also important is the saying of Jesus: "For I tell you, this scripture must be fulfilled in me, 'And he was counted among the lawless'; and indeed what is written about me is being fulfilled" (Luke 22:37). According to Taylor this is the only explicit citation of Isaiah 53 in the teaching of Jesus, but it shows that Jesus understood his impending death according to the image of the Suffering Servant. In sum:

> Jesus looked upon His suffering and death as the fulfilment of a divine purpose, in which His will was at one with that of the Father, and in virtue of which He accepted an active vocation connected with the Rule of God. He thought of His death as a victorious struggle with the powers of evil, and interpreted His suffering, in relation to men, as representative and vicarious in a sacrificial ministry which involved participation in the consequences of human sin.[30]

In the second book, *The Atonement in New Testament Teaching*, Taylor finds evidence that the earliest tradition agrees with the teaching of Jesus concerning his role as Suffering Servant.[31] Taylor is anxious to show that the doctrine of atonement did not originate with Paul or the author of Hebrews but rather, he thinks, with Jesus, and that it was affirmed by the pre-Pauline Christians. To be sure, Paul developed the doctrine in his own way, stressing the necessity of Christ's death and affirming God's action in Christ as grounded in grace and received by faith. As to Hebrews, "The writer devotes all his attention to one cycle of ideas, the vicarious, representative, and sacrificial offering of Christ."[32] Drawing implications from his study of the texts, Taylor declares that atonement is the work of God, revealing God's love. He asks: "How can it be said that Christ, the merciful Son, was punished by the Father, that He died as man's substitute, or offered compensation to God for sin, if in all that He does for man, God is the moving cause of redemption and in it gives free course to His love?"[33] No, says Taylor, Christ's death is neither punishment for sin nor substitute for sinners; it is representative, vicarious suffering, best described as reconciliation.

Taylor's final book on the atonement, *Forgiveness and Reconciliation*, presents a systematic investigation of the major themes.[34] He begins with "forgiveness," which he understands as a prior condition of reconciliation. In investigating "justification" he gives primary consideration to Paul.[35] "In this doctrine, when it is said that God justifies men, the meaning is that he declares them to be righteous in His sight in virtue of spiritual conditions which to Him are valid, namely faith in Him as the Saviour and Redeemer of men."[36] "Reconciliation," a favorite term for Taylor, affirms the reconciliation of humans to God, not God to humans. "Fellowship" describes the result of reconciliation, seen in the NT ideas of knowing God and union with Christ. In accord with his Wesleyan heritage, Taylor stresses "sanctification." "Beyond doubt," says Taylor, "the New Testament teaches the absolute necessity of ethical and spiritual perfection, or, if we prefer the word, attainment. It knows nothing of a reconciliation with God which does not make this goal the object of passionate desire."[37]

Taylor's trilogy on Christology began with his book on *The Names of Jesus*.[38] With his usual thoroughness he investigates forty titles that are applied to Jesus in the NT. Most important are those used to convey messianic meaning. "Son of Man," according to Taylor, is the title Jesus chose to express his own understanding of messiahship. In the early part of his ministry, according to Taylor, Jesus viewed the Son of Man as the embodiment of the elect community, but in the latter part he identified himself as Son of Man, interpreted according to the idea of the Suffering Servant. Taylor discusses at length the famous Son-Father saying from Q (Matt 11:27 // Luke 10:22), which he accepts as authentic and as confirming the unique relation of Christ to God.

Taylor's second book on Christology is *The Life and Ministry of Jesus*, based on lectures given at Oxford.[39] At the outset he acknowledges that a biography of Jesus is impossible, but he believes careful study of the sources can produce a reliable account of the ministry of Jesus. Prior to the Galilean ministry the decisive event was the baptism by John, whereby "Jesus was conscious of being the Son of God in a unique sense."[40] Regarding the accounts of the Galilean ministry, Taylor is suspicious of the nature miracles and believes Jesus gave priority to preaching. "He clearly regarded his message concerning the Kingdom as of greater importance than his works of healing."[41] Convinced that the crowd misunderstands messiahship, Jesus, in Taylor's reconstruction, withdraws alone to Tyre to reflect on the meaning of his mission. The confession of Peter at Caesarea Philippi provides Jesus with the occasion for instructing the disciples in his new understanding: he is himself the suffering Son of Man. In regard to the resurrection narratives, Taylor acknowledges that legendary features have crept in, but he believes the fact of the resurrection is proved by the transformed lives of the disciples.

The third book of the trilogy, *The Person of Christ in New Testament Teaching*, deals explicitly with Christology.[42] In this book Taylor exegetes the christological expressions in the Synoptics, Acts, 1 Peter, Hebrews, and the Fourth Gospel, but he gives primary attention to Phil 2:6-11. Although this may be a pre-Pauline hymn, as Ernst Lohmeyer had argued, Taylor believes it embodies Pauline theology.[43] The main theme of the text is Christ's renunciation of his pre-incarnate equality with God in order to assume the form of a servant. The word ἐκένωσεν means that Christ emptied himself, and becomes the key term for the kenotic Christology that Taylor adopts. "The hymn speaks of the majesty of the glory of Christ's pre-incarnate life, His renunciation of his glory and His full acceptance of a human lot culminating in obedience unto death, and the exaltation which reveals all that is true of Him."[44] Taylor proceeds to present his interpretation of the Christology of the "great writers" of the NT: Paul, the author of Hebrews, and the writer of the Fourth Gospel. All these writers, according to Taylor, affirm the pre-existence and divinity of Christ; all affirm Taylor's version of kenotic Christology. "The Christology which seems most in accord with the teaching of the New Testament is the doctrine that, in becoming man, the Son of God willed to renounce the exercise of divine prerogatives and powers, so that in the course of His earthly existence, He might live within the necessary limitations which belong to human finitude."[45]

On the whole, Taylor is a significant NT scholar who enlisted meticulous historical critical analysis in the service of theological construction. He is remembered more for his critical work—his identification of the pronouncement stories, his commentary on Mark—than for his historical and theological reconstruction. Taylor's solution to the messianic question (Jesus' designation of himself as Son of Man-Suffering Servant) would continue to be popular with his British successors.

STUDIES IN LUKE-ACTS: HENRY J. CADBURY (1883–1974)

LIFE AND RELIGIOUS PERSPECTIVE

Henry J. Cadbury was born in Philadelphia into a household with solid Quaker foundations; the English branch of the family is noted for its production of chocolate candy.[46] At age nineteen Cadbury graduated Phi Beta Kappa from Haverford College. He studied classics at Harvard and received his MA in 1904. After working as a school teacher, he returned to Harvard to earn his PhD in 1914. He had begun teaching at Haverford in 1910, but in 1919 he resigned in reaction to an uproar created by a letter he had written to a Philadelphia newspaper lamenting American hatred of Germans. Cadbury joined the faculty of Andover Theological Seminary, which was at the time associated with Harvard. When Andover separated and moved to Newton, Massachusetts (1926), Cadbury accepted a position teaching biblical literature at Bryn Mawr. During this period he declined invitations from the divinity schools of both Harvard and Yale.[47] In 1934 he finally yielded to the call from Harvard, succeeding his mentor J. H. Ropes in the Hollis Chair of Divinity—the oldest endowed chair in America. Robert M. Grant, one of his students, said of Cadbury that "he encouraged his students to think their own thoughts, no matter how unlike his they might seem. He was honest, learned, and thorough, a thoughtful and sensible scholar."[48]

Cadbury was active in the Quaker peace movement.[49] He served two terms as chairman of the American Friends Service Committee (1928–1934; 1944–1960). On behalf of the Committee he accepted the Nobel Peace Prize in 1947, dressed in formal attire borrowed from the relief supply the Committee had collected for impoverished members of postwar European symphony orchestras. Cadbury served on the translation committee of the Revised Standard Version (RSV). After retirement from Harvard in 1954 he moved to Pendle Hill, the Quaker educational center in Pennsylvania. He lectured widely in America and Europe and was named president of both the Society of Biblical Literature (SBL) and the Studiorum Novi Testamenti Societas (SNTS). He traversed land and sea in the cause of peace, testifying before congressional committees and counseling with government officials. Cadbury died at ninety after suffering an injury from a fall down stairs.

Henry Cadbury was a devout Quaker and a person of deep, unpretentious faith.[50] In an unpublished paper on "The Relation of Jesus to Spiritual Life," he wrote: "But it is my privilege to speak here of a force for deepening spiritual life. . . . That force is Jesus Christ."[51] However, he resisted the efforts of some Quakers to promote Christocentric doctrine.

> We need to recognize that Christocentricity—if one must use the modern term—is also of various sorts, and not merely the doctrines so often associated with it. . . . Beside doctrinal centrality Jesus Christ can claim our loyalty in other and perhaps more fruitful ways. His teaching, as we can recover it, even if not given any more authority than the self-evident validity that he himself saw in it, continues to have an appeal outside Christianity.[52]

Cadbury's own religion affirmed an inner certitude of a rationally informed conscience—a commitment to truths that seem self-evident. This perspective is reflected in his view of the Bible. "Its value consists of its agreement with experience, or with Truth," says Cadbury. "What is true in the Bible is there because it is true, not true because it is there. Its experiences 'answer' to ours, that is, they correspond with ours."[53] The Quaker tradition also allows room for historical criticism. Although Quakers can cite chapter and verse in support of pacifism, they do not proclaim the absolute authority of the Bible. "With their belief in the continuing revelation of the Holy Spirit—the same Holy Spirit that inspired the Scriptures—Friends have appealed for the experience as well as for the knowledge of the Scriptures."[54] The Bible, as record of faith and witness to truth, calls for ethical response. When asked why he devoted so much effort to the work of the American Friends Service Committee, Cadbury replied, "I am still trying to translate the New Testament."[55]

WORK ON LUKE-ACTS

Cadbury's many books and articles on the NT give primary attention to Luke-Acts—a term he apparently coined.[56] His Harvard dissertation investigates *The Style and Literary Method of Luke*.[57] The purpose of the dissertation is to study the writer of Luke and Acts as an individual author within the Hellenistic milieu. In the first part Cadbury investigates the diction of Luke and Acts. He observes that Luke uses a large vocabulary, and that his Greek is closer to Attic than is sometimes supposed. Cadbury investigates the claim of W. K. Hobart (1882)—with refinements by Harnack, Zahn, and Moffatt—that the author of Luke-Acts made distinctive use of medical language. Listing the alleged medical terms, Cadbury notes their extensive use in Lucian, Josephus, and the LXX. In an excursus on Lucian, Cadbury shows that if we examine the seventy-five so-called medical terms that appear in the NT only in Luke-Acts, Lucian uses them twice as often as Luke does. Cadbury concludes:

> The style of Luke bears no more evidence of medical training and interest than does the language of other writers who were not physicians. . . . Of course the absence of marked medical traits does not prove that a doctor did not write Luke and Acts. . . . So Luke, "the beloved physician" and companion of Paul, may have written the two books which tradition assigns to him, though their Greek be no more medical than that of Lucian, "the travelling rhetorician and show-lecturer"; but the so-called medical language of these books cannot be used as a proof that Luke was the author, nor even as an argument confirming the tradition of his authorship.[58]

In a later essay Cadbury observes that "unlike the present medical profession the ancient physician scarcely had a technical vocabulary at all."[59] Over a decade later, with tongue in cheek, Cadbury published "Luke and the Horse-Doctors," in which he demonstrates that Luke's vocabulary has affinity with the language used by ancient veterinarians.[60] Little wonder the story circulated that Cadbury earned his doctorate by depriving St. Luke of his!

In the second part of his dissertation Cadbury investigated Luke's use of sources. Assuming the priority of Mark, Cadbury believed Luke's method of using sources can be derived from the way he used Mark. In regard to the arrangement of material, Cadbury concluded that Luke largely follows Mark. Luke tends to shorten Mark's dialogue and avoid his repetition. Cadbury believed that some of Luke's changes indicate his literary predilections: he avoids exaggeration; he more clearly identifies audiences; he adds applications. In general, Cadbury thought that Luke improves Mark's grammar and style. He concluded with data concerning Luke's use of nouns, pronouns, adjectives, adverbs, and prepositions. Cadbury's interest in the style of Luke-Acts continued throughout his career. Late in life he wrote "Four Features of Lucan Style," in which he notes elements of style that appear as pairs of opposites: repetition and variation, distribution and concentration.[61]

Henry Cadbury was one of the first English-speaking scholars to publish a response to form criticism. His essay, "Between Jesus and the Gospels,"[62] was written over a decade before the research on form criticism by Taylor. Cadbury reviews the work of Dibelius, Bultmann, and Schmidt,[63] and offers his own observations. Most important, the material of the Gospels has a history, and it was shaped by interests that were not primarily historical. Cadbury also agrees with the form critics that the order of the narrative in the Gospels is not reliable. "If there is any scheme in the gospel, any development or progression," says Cadbury, "it is Mark's, and not a residue of a primitive tradition. Tradition provided a great variety of memorabilia, but not the framework for setting them into a narrative."[64] Similarly, Cadbury believes the order of the sayings material is equally arbitrary. The Gospels are "patchwork quilts, coats of many colors."[65] However, in contrast to the German form critics, he rejects the thesis that much material has been imported into the tradition from foreign soil, insisting that "we need not ourselves plunge into monomaniac Panbabylonianism."[66] He also thinks the incidences of divergences, incongruities, and contradictions tend to confirm the general reliability of the tradition.[67]

Much of Cadbury's work on Acts was published in connection with the multi-volume *Beginnings of Christianity*.[68] When Cadbury moved to Cambridge to teach at Andover he was invited to participate in the project, and when Foakes Jackson withdrew, Cadbury joined Kirsopp Lake in editing the last two volumes. Cadbury contributed such essays as "The Composition and Purpose of Acts" and "The Identity of the Editor of Luke and Acts" to volume 2, and volume 3, *The Text of Acts*, included his collations of the Vulgate and Codex

Vaticanus and of the Peshitto and Vaticanus. The *Commentary* (vol. 4) was the joint work of Lake and Cadbury, and Lake, who acted as the final editor, notes that Cadbury's "interests are more specifically linguistic and literary."[69] Cadbury contributed ten notes to volume 5, *Additional Notes to the Commentary*.

Cadbury's typical linguistic and literary interests are displayed in his appendix to volume 2, "Commentary on the Preface of Luke."[70] Cadbury notes that Luke's preface is the only place in the Synoptics where conscious authorship and purpose are expressed. He writes that the preface reveals conventional Hellenistic literary motifs, for instance, a preface to the first volume of a multi-volume work that introduces the whole composition. Cadbury proceeds through the text of the preface, commenting on virtually every word; he treats textual, linguistic, and grammatical matters with great detail, all with reference to Hellenistic usage. For example, in regard to παρηκολουθηκότι ("after investigating," Luke 1:3), Cadbury says the basic meaning is "follow," but the usage is figurative, allowing various shades of meaning: (1) following what is read or said; (2) keeping in touch with a course of events; (3) actual presence or participation in events. In regard to v. 4, Cadbury asserts that the avowed purpose of the author was to present a defense of Christianity. In view of this apologetic purpose, "Theophilus was not a catechumen but an influential non-Christian . . . to whom this work is nominally dedicated or addressed with the intention of meeting incriminating reports or impressions by the presentation of exonerating facts."[71] In regard to the author, first person is used in the preface three times: "fulfilled among us" has no personal meaning; "handed on to us" means "we Christians who have received the tradition"; κ'αμοί ("I too") refers to the author himself, and identifies him with the "many" who have attempted to construct a narrative.

Among Cadbury's contributions to volume 5 (*Additional Notes*), his note on "The Hellenists" illustrates his penchant for rowing against the stream of scholarly consensus.[72] He observes that Ἑλληνιστής is not a common word in the Hellenistic age. It is derived from the verb ἑλλενίζω ("to practice Greek ways") and has no reference to language. Cadbury rejects the conventional interpretation of Acts 6:1 whereby the "Hellenists" are identified as Greek-speaking Jewish converts and the "Hebrews" as Aramaic-speaking Jewish Christians. He observes that Ἑβραῖοι is not used in the NT for language but to describe Jews in contrast to Gentiles. Noting that some manuscripts omit the word "Jews" from Acts 2:5, Cadbury contends that the original account of the crowd at Pentecost included Gentiles. According to him, Luke did not envisage a gradual development toward Gentile mission but believed Gentiles belonged to the divine plan from the beginning. "There is therefore no difficulty in supposing that Acts vi. 1 may have introduced a story . . . in which Gentiles and Jews already formed the two national divisions of the Jerusalem church."[73] According to Cadbury the Hellenists are Gentiles or "Greeks."

Cadbury's note on "The Titles of Jesus in Acts" employs philological and historical research in the service of theology.[74] He analyzes fifteen terms that are used for Jesus, including Lord, Son of Man, Son of God, and Savior. In regard to ὁ παῖς (the servant), Cadbury notes that this term is used four times in Acts 3 and 4—a usage not found elsewhere in the NT. He indicates that some interpreters take this term to represent primitive Christology while others glimpse an allusion to the Suffering Servant. His concluding comment is vintage Cadbury.

> Whether it is reminiscent of the figure in Second Isaiah, or whether it is rather a somewhat archaic term not so much redolent of a given section of Scripture as suggestive of the language in which the notable figures of sacred history are described, cannot be settled with certainty. It is sufficient here to warn against the too easy assumption of dependence on Second Isaiah's 'Ebed Yahweh.[75]

This note, like all of Cadbury's contributions to The Beginning of Christianity, is a model of historical critical research: meticulous attention to detail, rigorous research in the primary and secondary sources, imaginative reconstruction, and, typical of Cadbury's "principle of parsimony,"[76] a stubborn resistance to the temptation to draw conclusions unwarranted by the data.

Cadbury's most important contribution to NT research is *The Making of Luke-Acts*, first published in 1927 and reprinted as recently at 1999.[77] His purpose is "to give as clear, comprehensive and realistic a picture as possible of the whole literary process that produced Luke and Acts."[78] Cadbury affirms the importance of Acts as a historical source, "the only bridge we have across the seemingly impassable gulf that separates Jesus from Paul, Christ from Christianity, the gospel of Jesus from the gospel about Jesus."[79] Cadbury insists that the two documents, Luke and Acts, constitute a unity and must be viewed as two parts of a single work. The balance of the book investigates the four main factors involved in the composition of Luke-Acts.

First Cadbury discusses the sources used by the author. Before there were written sources, the tradition was transmitted orally. The material was of two types: narrative and sayings; these circulated in independent units and were eventually gathered into collections. According to Cadbury, Luke's primary written sources were Mark and Q. He is skeptical of the effort to secure apostolic authority for the Gospel of Mark on the basis of the tradition from Papias. As to date, Cadbury believes all that can be known is that Mark wrote before Matthew and Luke. In regard to Q, Cadbury believes it impossible to ascertain what was omitted from Q by Matthew or by Luke, and which evangelist more faithfully follows the order and wording of Q. He thinks the identification of Q with the Logia of Matthew and the hypothesis of a Proto-Luke represent risky scholarly conjectures.

In the second part Cadbury investigates Luke's literary method. As to language, he believes that Luke's usage is of higher quality than the rest of the NT but that it is essentially the vernacular Greek of the Hellenistic period. As to genre, Cadbury believes Luke-Acts cannot be classified as biography or history, though it is closer to history. Like Hellenistic writers, Luke includes speeches, letters, and canticles, all of which Cadbury thinks are largely Lukan compositions.

In the third part Cadbury considers the personality of the author as it is revealed in his language and style. Cadbury notes that Luke can adapt his style to fit the situation of his narrative. Luke, Cadbury observes, is fond of presenting persons in parallel and in pairs; he is able to create suspense and convey a sense of pathos; he is cosmopolitan and urban in perspective. As to theology, Cadbury notes Luke's apocalyptic eschatology and his stress on the resurrection. "No New Testament writer more often refers to the resurrection as predicted in Scripture or cites more texts in its support than does Luke."[80]

In the fourth part Cadbury turns to the purpose of the author. According to him Luke's purpose is to evoke faith in Christ; Luke understands the history he recounts as fulfilling the purposes of God. Luke, in Cadbury's opinion, offers a twofold apologetic: the legitimacy of Christianity in relation to Judaism and the innocence of Christianity in relation to Rome. For Cadbury the ending of Acts allows various hypotheses: Luke has run out of sources or out of papyrus, or attained his goal, or planned to write a third volume. As to the identity of the author, Cadbury observes that the tradition of Lukan authorship could have been fabricated from data in Acts. However, he believes the traditional argument is not without weight. In Cadbury's opinion scholarship cannot attain certainty about the date, place of writing, or identity of the author—matters he believes to be of secondary importance. "We do well also to realize how little our uncertainty about the author's identity interferes with our effort to make clear and complete the story which we have aimed to recover."[81]

In regard to historicity, Cadbury rejects the common notion that reliability is tied to the question of authorship; instead, he believes reliability should be evaluated in terms of the kind of literary investigation he has undertaken in this book.

> The main effect of our method of study upon the question of historicity will be, however, neither to verify nor to correct the data recorded in these volumes, but to give reality, interest and attention to the later stage of history which the making of Luke-Acts represents. Instead of trying to conceal our real ignorance with plausible speculation, obscurum per obscurius, we shall turn our minds from the hidden underlying facts to the more accessible fact of the creation of this significant literary production. That fact itself—the making of Luke-Acts—by its concreteness, its verifiable fitness to its historical setting, and its irrefutable revelation of its author's mind, times and heart can lend to our study of Scripture an element of historical certainty and human interest, which the more controversial and debatable subjects of date, authorship, inspiration, orthodoxy and accuracy do not permit.[82]

In sum, Cadbury's Making of Luke-Acts is a classic—one of the great books of twentieth-century NT research.[83] It is an original work that joins penetrating analysis with synthesizing wisdom. Cadbury shows that scholarship is not always in the wind and earthquake and fire, but in the still, small voice of unpretentious, meticulous research.

Cadbury's research on Acts is advanced in *The Book of Acts in History*.[84] In this book he investigates Acts in relation to its historical setting. In regard to the Greek background, Cadbury says that Luke is "undoubtedly the most Hellenic of the evangelists, and in secularity, in language, in approach to literature the nearest to a Greek man of letters that the early Church provides."[85] Concerning the Roman background he writes: "Just as the Book of Acts constantly presupposes and often mentions this Roman environment, so that book itself is a first-rate source for an impression of what contemporary life under Rome was like."[86] As to the Jewish background, Cadbury believes Luke provides significant information about the Jews of the Diaspora. In considering the Christian background he observes that Luke presents a Christianity different from Paul's, but he affirms the importance of Paul for early Christian history.[87] Just as *The Making of Luke-Acts* had investigated the prehistory of Acts, so in a final chapter of *The Book of Acts in History* Cadbury investigates the history of Acts after it was written. He notes that Acts was separated from Luke in the development of the canon but that, even though included in the canon, it was not widely known in the early church.

Throughout his career Henry Cadbury reflected on the practice of NT criticism, especially as it relates to Jesus. In *The Peril of Modernizing Jesus* he exposes the anachronism of portraying Jesus in modern garb. The impetus for modernizing, Cadbury thinks, arises from the assumption that Jesus has universal significance—that he and his message are normative for today. The peril can be avoided, according to Cadbury, by acknowledging one's presuppositions and by "painstaking historical research and imagination."[88] Objective historical research will confirm the Jewishness of Jesus—his apocalyptic eschatology, his antiquated worldview. Cadbury thinks that "Jesus' conformity to the mentality of his age spells at the same time his alienness to our own."[89] Although he acknowledges that Jesus viewed himself as Messiah, Cadbury does not believe Jesus claimed the sort of purpose and plan usually attributed to him. "What I wish to propose is that Jesus probably had no definite, unified, conscious purpose, that an absence of such a program is a priori likely and that it suits well the historical evidence."[90] Cadbury is also wary of finding in Jesus a normative religious experience. "Jesus himself made religious experience no aim or goal in his own life or in his teaching."[91] Jesus did not, according to Cadbury, claim a unique relation to God. "Even when God is mentioned Jesus does not make him central in his teaching. That teaching is about human conduct."[92] In short, no NT scholar since Albert Schweitzer had so audaciously questioned the relevance of Jesus.[93]

Cadbury's Shaffer Lectures at Yale were published as *Jesus: What Manner of Man.* "I have attempted here," says Cadbury, "to be more positive than in *The Peril of Modernizing Jesus* without myself ignoring the warning I have sounded in that volume."[94] Adopting the archaic language of the Authorized Version, Cadbury explores questions raised by the Gospels, such as "Is not this Jesus?" In response, Cadbury says that the personality of Jesus is difficult to assess, but he insists that Jesus' primary concern is human conduct. To "whence this Wisdom?" Cadbury replies that Jesus reasons from nature and affirms truth that is self-evident. To "why speakest thou in parables?" Cadbury answers that Jesus taught in parables because parables represent teachings derived from the observation of nature and people. "What is this? New teaching?" The newness in Jesus' teaching, responds Cadbury, is not its content but its urgency, its apocalyptic emphasis. To "how knoweth this man?" Cadbury replies that Jesus "was of such ethical maturity that his judgment was frequently right."[95]

According to Cadbury, "Jesus appeals to the hearer's powers of moral appreciation and response."[96] "By what authority?" According to Cadbury's answer, Jesus' authority was not external, but "due to a kind of self-validating character in the teachings themselves."[97] He concludes: "He is like all personality, an enigma. These chapters make no pretense of fathoming him. While he may help us understand ourselves and God, he is reported as having said, 'No one knows the Son, save the Father.'"[98] Thus Cadbury presents a minimalist Jesus whose religion is Jewish, whose passion is ethics, whose urgency is apocalyptic.[99]

Cadbury's work on Jesus reflects his lifelong preoccupation with the method and practice of criticism. Early in his career he contributed an essay to a volume on *Christianity and Modern Thought*, directed to the general reader and entitled "Critical Study of the New Testament."[100] In surveying the history of research he laments the persistent resistance to enlightened study of the NT.

> More than any other book the New Testament has had to wait and still must wait for enlightenment in many other fields of knowledge before receiving fair treatment. Presuppositions linger about it the longest, as the clouds cling longest to the highest peaks of the mountains. The truth about it has not often come to men by passive waiting, it has been won step by step with effort and struggle. The dust of strife has never been allowed to settle so that clear light could shine, but men have had to grope rather than see.[101]

In 1938 Cadbury described "The Present State of New Testament Studies."[102] This essay assesses developments in various areas of NT study: text criticism, archaeology, history of religion. "Progress depends . . . on the patient effort of imaginative minds, often in unseen and unconscious collaboration, freshly revolving and resolving the intricate data for the New Testament by trial and error, by ever new reference to material in the contemporary cultures, until a fragment of new probability emerges from the search."[103] Three years later, Cadbury envisioned "New Testament Study in the Next Generation," calling for removal of the debris of theories earlier exploded and warning against the illusion that everything new is good.[104] In 1960 his essay, "New Testament Scholarship: Fifty Years in Retrospect," contends that scholars have tried in vain to escape the apocalyptic element in the teaching of Jesus; realized eschatology he characterizes as "unrecognized wishful thinking." In regard to a biblical theology that neglects the historical Jesus, Cadbury exclaims: "How it is possible to claim so much for Christ as the one great divine event in history and be so indifferent about the problem of what in actual history we can know of Christ is a matter of surprise."[105]

In overview, Cadbury's assessment of criticism is ambivalent: he affirms historical criticism but eschews fads and extremes, fanciful conjectures and overconfident conclusions. Typical is his essay, "Some Foibles of New Testament Scholarship."[106] After rehearsing many of those already noted, Cadbury identifies the fundamental foible as "the way in which New Testament scholars have felt uncomfortable to leave questions unsolved. . . . [I]nstead of relying on precarious argument the scholar should make clear to the layman, who like nature abhors a vacuum, that we have not enough data to decide."[107] For Cadbury, critical orthodoxy is almost as abhorrent as theological orthodoxy. In his presidential address at the SNTS he questioned the widely-held consensus concerning the pseudonymity of the letter to the Ephesians. After analyzing the style and vocabulary of Ephesians in relation to the other Pauline letters he concludes that the differences are not great enough to prove a different author nor the similarities sufficient to prove the same author. Cadbury acknowledges that he has not considered theology in his assessment of the authorship of Ephesians, an issue he believes to be clouded by subjectivity. Thus the address discloses Cadbury's strength and also his weakness: his passion for objectivity and his antipathy for theology, the latter an element that is significant for the assessment of authorship.

In the history of NT research, Henry J. Cadbury represents a rare species. At a meeting of the SBL sometime in the early 1960s Professor Cadbury chose to sit with me (a young unknown) at lunch, when he could have dined with old friends and eminent scholars. Even more astonishing was his conversation. He wanted to know my views concerning the papers read in the morning session, and asked me what I had been reading that he should read!

As to Cadbury's research, few have followed the Enlightenment ideal of objectivity more faithfully. Edgar J. Goodspeed is said to have remarked about Cadbury that "the consciousness of even a single certainty would be an insupportable weight upon his mind."[108] At the very least Cadbury commends caution; the road of NT research is littered with shattered conjectures. Indeed, Cadbury's approach may appear to be primarily negative—a conspicuous indifference to Jesus and the NT. Nevertheless, he affirms the integrity of the historian in the quest for truth. The truth he seeks, of course, is not grandiose; Cadbury, like his portrayal of Jesus, is too humble for that. His truth is in the details, the fragments that make up the mosaic of human life and history.

LIFE AND TEACHINGS OF JESUS: T. W. MANSON (1893–1958)

LIFE AND WORK

Thomas Walter Manson was born in Tynemouth, Northumberland, of Scottish ancestry.[109] He studied at Glasgow (MA, 1912) and at Cambridge (1919–22). From 1922 to 1925 he worked as a tutor at Westminster College, Cambridge, and from 1932 to 1936 as professor at Mansfield College, Oxford, succeeding C. H. Dodd. Later Manson again succeeded Dodd at Manchester University, where he was Rylands Professor of Biblical Criticism and Exegesis from 1936 to 1958. Manson lectured widely in Europe and America and was named president of SNTS. Harold H. Rowley described Manson as "a man of great learning and of strength and grace of character, a Christian gentleman in every sense of the term, a man of highest integrity and loyalty."[110]

Manson's basic approach to the Bible is evident in his essay "The Nature and Authority of the Canonical Scriptures."[111] Most important, Manson believed the Bible to be a book that contains revelation. Compared with the two other great religions—Buddhism and Islam—Christianity, according to Manson, is the only religion with a valid claim to revelation. "Revelation . . . means primarily an act of God whereby He manifests His real nature to men."[112] In Manson's opinion, revelation reaches its zenith in "the personality and life of Jesus of Nazareth. . . . It is a revelation in terms of the highest category we can know—that of personality."[113]

RESEARCH IN THE GOSPELS

T. W. Manson's major work is *The Teaching of Jesus: Studies of Its Form and Content.*[114] Originally published in 1931, the book was slightly revised in 1935 and frequently reprinted. It makes two basic affirmations: the substance of the gospel is the person of Christ; the key to understanding the NT is the idea of the saving remnant. In the first part Manson treats preliminary questions. His distinctive contribution is his attempt to distinguish the various audiences to whom the teachings of Jesus were addressed: the disciples, the multitudes, the opponents. In regard to sources, Manson generally accepts B. F. Streeter's four documents.[115] Following the Papias tradition, Manson believes Mark preserves the tradition of Peter, but he rejects Papias's assertion that Mark did not write in order. Q is identified by Manson as the Logia written in Aramaic by Matthew.[116] M represents the Jewish perspective and is, according to Manson, of less value that Mark and Q. Manson accepts the Proto-Luke hypothesis and believes L represents oral tradition collected by Luke himself. Turning to the formal features of Jesus' teaching, Manson notes that Jesus taught in Aramaic and that his rhetoric echoes the poetic expressions of the OT. According to Manson, "A parable is a literary creation in narrative form designed either to portray a type of character for warning or example, or to embody a principle of God's governance of the world and men."[117] Manson believes all the parables "are governed by a single purpose—to show, directly or indirectly, what God is and what man may become, and to show these things in a way that will reach men's hearts if it is possible to reach them at all. And, when we come to think of it, the greatest and most effective parable of them all is his own life."[118]

The second part of the book discusses the content of Jesus' teaching. According to Manson the background of Jesus' teaching is to be found in the OT.[119] Manson believes Jesus gives primary attention to the doctrine of God, particularly the idea of God as Father, especially in the latter part of his ministry. "The result of this detailed examination of all four sources is to justify the general conclusion, suggested by Mk and Q, that Jesus rarely if ever spoke directly of God as Father except to his disciples and that he began to speak to them in this way only after Peter's Confession."[120] Manson believes the kingdom of God has been misunderstood in two ways: as a social order, and as an apocalyptic phenomenon. Analyzing the sources, he detects a shift: prior to the confession of Peter, Jesus speaks of the coming of the kingdom; after the confession he speaks of people entering the kingdom. This leads Manson to conclude that the kingdom is essentially a personal relationship to God, already present in Jesus, to be fully consummated in the future.

According to Manson the kingdom has three main aspects. First, it expresses the eternal sovereignty of God. In the post-exilic period the attempt to relate the sovereignty of God to the evil world led to the rise of apocalyptic, pushing retribution into a supernatural future and understanding the present according to a dualism. In Manson's view Jesus took up and advanced the older prophetic position: God's kingdom is already at work and its triumph in the future is certain.

Second, the kingdom is God's rule in the world. In Israel's history, the failure of the people to obey God led to the prophetic idea of the faithful remnant: the people in whom the kingdom of God is present. In Second Isaiah the remnant is presented according to the figure of the righteous servant who suffers on behalf of others. Manson believes this idea was appropriated by Jesus, and after the confession of Peter it was applied to Jesus' own mission. Manson understands the confession "as the watershed of the Gospel history. Indeed it is not too much to say that Peter's inspired declaration at Caesarea Philippi has changed the whole course of the world's history."[121] After the confession the presence of the kingdom in the world is expressed, according to Manson, in

Jesus' use of the title "Son of Man." Manson believes that the two incidents in Mark when the title is used prior to the confession (2:10; 2:28) represent the Aramaic *bar nasha*—an expression that simply means "man."[122] After the confession Jesus, according to Manson, uses the title Son of Man, like Servant of the Lord, to refer to the remnant.

> His mission is to create the Son of Man, the Kingdom of the saints of the Most High, to realize in Israel the ideal contained in the term. This task is attempted in two ways: first by public appeal to the people through the medium of parable and sermon and by the mission of the disciples: then, when this appeal produced no adequate response, by the consolidation of his own band of followers. Finally, when it becomes apparent that not even the disciples are ready to rise to the demands of the ideal, he stands alone, embodying in his own person the perfect human response to the regal claims of God.[123]

Jesus is himself the saving remnant. As Manson says elsewhere, "the ministry of Jesus is not a prelude to the Kingdom of God: it is the Kingdom of God."[124]

The third aspect of the kingdom is the final consummation. According to Manson, Jesus takes up the eschatology of the OT, which sees the end of history as the fulfillment of God's purposes, and gives it a new expression: "the final consummation is not a compensation for the sufferings of the faithful in the present, but the result of them."[125] On the basis of his investigation of the Son of Man sayings that refer to the future, Manson believes Jesus expected the eschaton to come with surprise and to include a universal judgment. Manson wrestles mightily with the problem created by Jesus' prediction that the kingdom would come with power before the death of some of his contemporaries. He concludes that Jesus is not infallible, that he shares the limitations of his own time, and that "the belief in the nearness of the Day of the Lord is not one of the unique features in the eschatology of Jesus but a belief which, like the belief in demons or the Davidic authorship of the Psalter, was the common property of his generation."[126]

T. W. Manson also published a significant work on *The Sayings of Jesus*—a work that is essentially a commentary on teaching material in the sources Q, M, and L.[127] Again he finds the center of the gospel in the person of Jesus. "The teaching of Jesus in the fullest and deepest sense is Jesus Himself, and the best Christian living has always been in some sort an imitation of Christ; not a slavish copying of His acts but the working of His mind and spirit in new contexts of life and circumstance."[128] In discussing the development of the tradition Manson notes that sayings were grouped according to topics and shaped to meet catechetical and apologetic needs of the church. Thus he recognizes form criticism, although two major features of his work—the identification of audiences and the acceptance of Mark's order—are antithetical to form-critical results. As to written sources, Manson stresses early dating: Q before 50, M around 65, and L around 60.

Examples of Manson's exegetical work can be seen in his comments on pericopes from M and L. In the section "The Teaching Peculiar to Matthew" (M), Manson interprets "The Last Judgement" (Matt 25:31-36). He views the whole text as presenting the apocalyptic drama of judgment and identifies the *dramatis personae*: the "king" is Jesus; the "brethren" (NRSV: "members of my family") are persons associated with Jesus; the "sheep" are Gentiles who helped; the "goats" are Gentiles who did not. According to Manson the "Son of Man" is the remnant—the corporate body of Jesus and his faithful associates, that is, the kingdom of God. The basis of judgment, in this view, is the response to the kingdom. "The deeds of the righteous are not just casual acts of benevolence," says Manson. "They are acts by which the Mission of Jesus and His followers was helped, and helped at some cost to the doers, even at some risk."[129]

In the section "The Teaching Peculiar to Luke" (L), Manson interprets "The Two Sons" (Luke 15:11-32). He sees the parable as a unity making two points: God's care for the sinner, and a rebuke to the censorious attitude of the righteous toward sinners. According to Manson the father represents God; the elder brother, the scribes and Pharisees; the younger brother, the publicans and sinners. In noting how the younger son is reduced to the lowest state and engaged in a most loathsome job, Manson cites the Talmud: "Cursed is the man who rears swine, and cursed is the man who teaches his son Greek philosophy."[130] Manson's sense of humor is also evident in his comment on the protest of the older brother. "The impression remains, however, that the chief reason why he never got so much as a kid to make merry with his friends was that he would not have known how to make merry if he had got it."[131] Manson concludes: "So the upshot of the matter is that the way of the father with the prodigal is God's way with sinful men and Jesus' way with publicans and sinners."[132]

In an essay on "The Life of Jesus," Manson acknowledges that a biography of Jesus cannot be written, but he argues that the main course of the ministry can be reconstructed by careful study of the sources.[133] In a lecture published some years later he discussed "The Quest of the Historical Jesus—Continued."[134] The essay and lecture lament the limits of form criticism: its failure to recognize the reliability of Mark's order and to give attention to the *Sitz im Leben Jesu*. Manson also depicts Schweitzer's historical Jesus as a "deluded fanatic."[135] However, he sees the quest of the historical Jesus as "still a great and most hopeful enterprise." The reason for the quest is clear: "But if God does reveal himself in history, it is there if anywhere that we must find him. . . . If God spoke through the life and death of Jesus it is vitally important to know as fully and as accurately as possible what sort of life and death became the medium of God's revelation."[136]

T. W. Manson's positive contribution to the quest is presented in his little book, *The Servant-Messiah*.[137] He begins with a survey of the messianic hope from the time of Antiochus IV to Hadrian, especially as expressed by the Jewish parties,[138] writing that "history shows that the Jews of Palestine were only too ready to welcome any promising champion of the cause of Israel and to take up arms in a holy war for the kingdom of God."[139] Manson believes the confident expectation of the Jews was confounded by John the Baptist's message of judgment and by Jesus' radical revision of the messianic hope. He contends that "the whole Ministry—the teaching of Jesus, his acts, and finally the Cross, are a standing denial of the current beliefs and hopes."[140] In investigating the historical material about Jesus, Manson begins with Q. From this primitive document he believes he can derive the principles that motivated the ministry of Jesus. Jesus' rejection of a political role, according to Manson, is evident in the temptation narrative. In contrast to apocalyptic thought, Manson believes Jesus affirmed the future already present in history in himself as Son of Man—a figure who combines the Servant of Second Isaiah and the Son of Man of Daniel. "That dream-figure the Son of man, who gives his life a ransom for many and comes in glory with the clouds of heaven, became historical reality on the day when Jesus of Nazareth, coming up out of the Jordan from John's baptism, took the first step on the road that led to Calvary."[141]

Turning to Mark, Manson attempts to reconstruct the course of the ministry of Jesus. It begins with the baptism, faces a crisis at the feeding of the multitude, and reaches a turning point at the confession of Peter. In the last phases of the ministry Manson detects two crucial events. The cleansing of the temple, which Manson locates at the Feast of Tabernacles prior to the final visit to Jerusalem, is an action whereby Manson believes Jesus clears out the court of the Gentiles to demonstrate that the way is prepared for Gentile participation in the kingdom.[142] The second crucial event, of course, is the crucifixion, the culmination of divine revelation.

> Jesus stood for something greater than the Empire or the Temple or the Law. He stood for the kingdom of God. In truth he was the

kingdom of God. In his Ministry he had shown the rule of God in action, what it offers to men everywhere and what it demands of them. In Pilate, Caiaphas, and the rest the lesser loyalties united against the kingdom of God incarnate in Jesus the Messiah; and so Jesus went to the Cross—and made it his everlasting throne.[143]

The ministry, however, did not end but continued in the church, the body of Christ, "the continuation of the incarnation."[144] "The Resurrection means above all just this," concludes Manson, "that Christians do not inherit their task from Christ, they share it with him. We are not the successors of Jesus, but his companions."[145]

NEW TESTAMENT CRITICISM AND THEOLOGY

Besides his work on the Gospels, T. W. Manson engaged in research on other parts of the NT. In "The New Testament and Other Christian Writings of the New Testament Period" he presents critical introductions to all the NT documents.[146] In regard to the Pauline epistles, Manson accepts the authenticity of 2 Thessalonians but believes it was written before 1 Thessalonians. He believes the Corinthian correspondence consists of four original letters and favors the south Galatian destination of Galatians. He tends to support Ephesus as the place of writing Philippians, though he does not believe Paul was in prison at the time.[147] Manson thinks the place of writing of Colossians and Philemon is Rome; he believes the problems related to Ephesians defy definite solution. As to Hebrews, Manson believes it was written before the destruction of Jerusalem, perhaps by Apollos.[148] In regard to the Catholic Epistles, Manson thinks 1 Peter was written by Peter with extensive help from Silvanus; 2 Peter he believes to be unquestionably pseudonymous. Manson thinks the Fourth Gospel and 1 John were written by the same author (probably John the Elder), the Apocalypse by another writer (possibly John the Apostle).

In an essay, "St. Paul's Letter to the Romans—and Others," Manson presents his distinctive understanding of the original form and destination of Romans.[149] He begins by presenting the data: the omission from some manuscripts of the references to Rome at 1:7 and 1:15; the location of the doxology in various editions at the end of chapters 14, 15, and 16. Manson believes Marcion's edition did not include chapter 16, and that Marcion cut off chapter 15. Chapter 16, according to Manson, was originally written to Ephesus. Manson thinks Paul originally wrote Romans 1–15, and at about the same time sent a copy of it along with a recommendation of Phoebe (chapter 16) to the church at Ephesus. Manson concludes that Romans circulated in three editions: Marcion's (chs. 1–14); Paul's original version to Rome (1–15); and the Ephesian version (1–16).

T. W. Manson also contributed to the study of NT theology. In his book *The Beginning of the Gospel*,[150] Manson insists that the person of Christ must be understood historically; his Christology is virtually identical with his historical Jesus. The essence of that Christology is seen in the fusion of the ideas of the Son of Man and the Servant of the Lord. In regard to ethics, Manson presented lectures at Manchester and at Colgate-Rochester Divinity School that were published posthumously under the title, *Ethics and the Gospel*. In these lectures he explicates the moral teaching of Jesus as presented in the Sermon on the Mount. In recognizing that the Sermon in its present form is a composition of the author of Matthew, Manson, anticipating redaction criticism,[151] comments, "We must not think of the evangelists as literary hacks producing gospels by stringing other people's work together; they were genuine composers, with gifts as authentic as those of the poet or the musician or the artist, and a good deal more important."[152] In any case, the Sermon is important, according to Manson, because it includes reliable material from Q. He believes the distinctive feature of the ethic of Jesus is the command to love as Jesus loved. "Christian ethics is certainly not slavish obedience to rules and regulations. It is active living, and therefore it has the power to go to the heart of every ethical situation that arises."[153]

Manson was especially concerned with the theology of ministry. In *The Church's Ministry*, originally lectures given at the University of London, he argues that the doctrine of ministry must be related to the doctrine of the church, and the church must be understood in relation to Christ. Ecclesiology, according to Manson, is a branch of Christology. Manson believes the ministry of the church is the continuation of the ministry of Christ. "The Body of Christ is the organism which He uses to carry out His purposes in the world in the same way that He used His physical body in the days of the ministry in Galilee and Judaea."[154] Manson traces the emergence of various forms and titles of ministry in the history of the early church and concludes that none of these can be identified exclusively as apostolic, and that no single doctrine of the ministry is absolute. The view of the church as body of Christ confirms the essential unity of the church, according to Manson, and such a view can affirm both hierarchical and free church understandings of ministry. One is not made a minister by the action of bishops, presbyteries, or congregations, but only by the call of Christ.[155]

A collection of T. W. Manson's essays on NT theology has been published as *On Paul and John: Some Selected Theological Themes*.[156] Among the essays on Paul, "Paul the Christian and Theologian" argues that the apostle was no systematic or philosophical theologian. "He is telling what God has done, is doing, and will do on the stage of world-history rather than what are the ultimate ideas and axioms in terms of which the universe may be explained."[157] An essay on "The Cosmic Significance of Christ" finds the background not in Greek cosmology but in the Jewish idea that the world is under the control of demonic powers. In this context Paul speaks of the redemption of the universe (Romans 8) and the cosmic significance of Christ (Colossians 1). In "The Significance of Christ as Saviour" Manson contrasts the Greek and Hebraic ways of viewing salvation: for the Greeks salvation is knowledge, and emphasis is placed on seeing; for the Hebrews salvation involves hearing and obeying. According to Manson, Paul understands humans to be enslaved to sin, a slavery that can be broken only by the action of God disclosed in Christ. God's action in Christ presents new revelation of God's nature as characterized by love, and it makes possible a response of faith and radical repentance. "The work of Christ," says Manson, "is thus something which affects the status of man before God and the moral condition of man in himself. It breaks the power of the evil forces that claim man, and it has a moral regenerating power in the life of man."[158] Thus Manson basically affirms the moral influence doctrine of atonement.

In the second part of this book Manson presents essays on the theology of John. The essay on "Johannine Themes" begins with a discussion of agape in the teachings of Jesus, Paul, and John. According to Manson, John stresses the love of God revealed in Christ and finds love grounded in the nature of God. Manson believes that John understands salvation as eternal life—a present reality. Salvation is accomplished, according to Manson, by God's action in Christ. Manson believes the sacrifice of Christ to be a disclosure of God's love, and he understands Johannine atonement essentially as revelation. "The foundation of all that John has to say about atonement is that it is a manifestation, the supreme manifestation of God's love (John 3.16)."[159] Manson believes that for John the blood of Christ signifies the death of Christ; the shedding of blood does not represent a magical transaction, but the ethical action of love—Jesus sacrificing his life for others, fulfilling the prophecy of Isaiah 53. In his work on NT theology Manson notes distinctions within the NT, but basically he finds that the theology of the NT is one—a theology Manson himself is happy to embrace.

On the whole, T. W. Manson's NT research combines faith and criticism. His faith rests on his recognition of the revelation of God in Jesus; his criticism provides the ground and meaning of that revelation. As heir of the critical tradition Manson affirms the priority of Mark and the existence of Q; as a person of faith he hears the witness of Peter in Mark and the voice of Matthew in Q. As critic he minimizes M; as a person of faith he maximizes L. Behind these written sources Manson, as critic, recognizes an oral tradition shaped by interests of the post-resurrection church. As person of faith Manson contends that the oral tradition is reliable, that the shaping did no distorting, that the source and criterion of the tradition is Jesus. As critic Manson is committed to the quest of the historical Jesus; as a person of faith he finds a Jesus who transcends the limits of history. Jesus speaks in apocalyptic language, but he is not an apocalyptist. Jesus is messiah, but a reinterpreted messiah. In the end, Manson presents a Jesus of faith—a Jesus who constitutes the unity of the whole NT.

A British Master of the Discipline: C. H. Dodd (1884–1973)

Life and Theological Perspective

Charles Harold Dodd was born in Wrexham, North Wales.[160] In 1902 he entered University College, Oxford, where he became an honor student in classics and philosophy. In 1907 he studied in Berlin and was impressed by Adolf von Harnack.[161] From 1908 to 1911 he pursued theological studies at Mansfield College, Oxford. Dodd was ordained to the Congregational ministry in 1912. In 1915 he was appointed Yates Lecturer at Mansfield, succeeding James Moffatt.[162] In 1930 Dodd was named Rylands Professor of Biblical Criticism and Exegesis at the University of Manchester, and in 1935 Norris-Hulse Professor at Cambridge—the first non-Anglican to hold a chair in divinity at either Cambridge or Oxford. After retirement in 1949 Dodd served as director of the project to produce a new translation, resulting in the New English Bible of the NT in 1961 and the whole Bible in 1970. In 1950 Dodd was visiting lecturer at Union Theological Seminary in New York. After returning to England he moved to Oxford, where he spent the balance of his life. He was a founding member of SNTS and served as its president, 1951–52.

Like Zacchaeus, Dodd was self-conscious about his small stature. W. D. Davies (in a recording made in 1986) told me that when, as a student, he would visit in Dodd's study, the furniture would be so arranged that he would sit in a low chair and Dodd would sit above him on a higher one. Dodd was notorious for his absentmindedness, once appearing for a lecture wearing one of his own shoes and one of his daughter's. He lectured with vitality and eloquence and was famous for his sense of humor, which even crept into his publications. In the introduction to his Romans commentary he gives the reason for a "clumsily made cut" at 16:23 as the "illimitable stupidity of editors."[163] From early in his career, Dodd's name was the subject of many limericks, for example:

There once was a scholar called Dodd,
whose name was exceedingly odd.
He said, if you please,
Spell my name with three D's
Though one is sufficient for God.

Dodd was devoted to ecumenicity, and served on the Faith and Order Commission of the World Council of Churches.

Dodd's theological perspective is characterized by three main features: natural theology, a theology of history, and Platonism. In regard to natural theology, Dodd notes parallels between NT ethics and Stoicism and observes that both assume a common understanding of the good, implying an idea of natural law.[164] About the parables, Dodd argues that Jesus draws lessons from nature that are self-evident, and in discussing Rom 1:19-21 he points out that Paul declares that Gentiles who have no special revelation can know the works of God in creation. In the Fourth Gospel, Dodd sees evidence of natural theology in the idea of creation through the Logos. "In Christ, therefore, man is confronted with that Word, Wisdom, or Law which is the law of his creation, the same which was partially disclosed to Israel in the Torah, and is known in some measure to all mankind, through conscience and reason, as the Law of Nature."[165] Dodd's distinctive "realized eschatology" assumes natural theology, the idea that God's presence and accessibility can be maintained within the structures of the world.

Dodd holds a distinctive theology of history.[166] He declares that Christianity is a historical religion; it affirms the revelation of God in history. Although revelation is progressive—an idea expressed in his earlier works[167]—Dodd believes that it finds its ultimate expression and norm in an event within history. "It takes the series of events recorded or reflected in the Bible, from the call of Abraham to the emergence of the Church, and declares that in this series the ultimate reality of all history, which is the purpose of God, is finally revealed, because the series is itself controlled by the supreme event of all—the life, death and resurrection of Jesus Christ."[168] Although Dodd views history as a process, he believes its beginning and end is beyond history.

History, therefore, as a process of redemption and revelation, has a beginning and an end, both in God. The beginning is not an event in time; the end is not an event in time. The beginning is God's purpose, the end is the fulfilment of His purpose. Between these lies the sacred history which culminates in the death and resurrection of Christ.[169]

Dodd rejects the idea of history as progress toward a divine goal.

> The Gospel does not speak of "progress," but of dying and rising again. The pattern of history is revealed less in evolution than in crisis. Once in the course of the ages the spirit of man was confronted, within history, with the eternal God in His kingdom, power, and glory, and that in a final and absolute sense. There was a great encounter, a challenge and response, a death and resurrection; and divine judgment and life eternal came into human experience.[170]

This idea of challenge and response, which Dodd borrows from Arnold Toynbee, understands history as transformed by spiritual power—the transcendent kingdom that comes into history and gives history meaning.

As an undergraduate Dodd fell under the spell of Plato and never recovered. His notion about the transcendent kingdom assumes Plato's idea of the eternal realm of reality. "In the history of civilizations," writes Dodd, "the great encounter is not unique but extremely rare, but this rarity must be taken as what Plato might have called a 'shadow' or 'image' of the idea of uniqueness which is the ultimate reality in the case, as the virtue of a good man is only the shadow of the Idea of the Good."[171] Dodd's Platonism is evident in his two Ingersoll Lectures on Immortality (1935, 1950).[172] Dodd says: "That which is completely real is beyond time."[173] For him, however, transcendental reality enters into history, so that historical events are not mere shadows of reality; they embody transcendent reality. Nevertheless, as W. D. Davies observes, Dodd's realized eschatology "was the contribution of a Platonist."[174]

EARLY NEW TESTAMENT RESEARCH

Dodd's inaugural lecture at Cambridge in 1936, *The Present Task in New Testament Studies*, surveys the scene and sets his agenda.[175] In regard to history of religion, Dodd recognizes the importance of historical backgrounds, but denies that parallels indicate derivation. As to form criticism, Dodd approves the method and affirms its focus on the development of tradition in relation to the history of the early Christian community. In a later essay he wrote: "The most important service, to my mind, which the form critics have rendered to our studies is their insistence upon the living situation in the history of the church."[176] The inaugural lecture also called for concerted attention to the Fourth Gospel. "If the solution of the Synoptic Problem was the most spectacular success of the nineteenth-century critics, the Johannine Problem represents their most signal failure."[177] Most important, Dodd hails the NT as "an organic unity," and says: "It is the task of New Testament study to understand this phenomenon for what it is in itself, in its characteristic unity as well as in its diversity."[178] In "Thirty Years of New Testament Study" (1950),[179] Dodd writes, "As the great tradition reveals itself afresh in its wholeness and essential unity, the yawning gap which earlier criticism left between the Jesus of History and the emergent Church disappears, and we begin to see that to make a separation between the historical and the theological understanding of the Gospels is to put asunder what God hath joined."[180]

Prior to his inauguration at Cambridge, Dodd had presented his understanding of *The Authority of the Bible*.[181] In the preface to the first edition he observes that criticism has destroyed the doctrine of infallibility, but in the process it has undermined biblical authority. His purpose is to examine the question of authority inductively from the perspective of the Bible itself. Dodd draws an analogy from science: just as our knowledge of science depends on experts, so also does our knowledge of religion. "In this sense we find a religious authority in the Bible—the authority of experts in the knowledge of God, masters in the art of living; the authority of religious genius."[182] Dodd explicates three classes of religious expertise in the Bible: the inspiration of individuals, the corporate religious experience, and the authority of the Incarnation. In regard to individuals, Dodd praises the prophets. They believed their message had come from God, according to Dodd, "because of its inherent truth and worthiness."[183] The authority of corporate experience is seen in the OT, which witnesses to "a process which taken as a whole reveals God."[184]

The ultimate expert in religion, in Dodd's view, is Jesus, so that the supreme expression of biblical authority is the Incarnation. Our knowledge of Jesus rests on historical critical study of the Gospels, and for Dodd the Gospels rest on reliable tradition. In a later publication he rejects Karl Ludwig Schmidt's theory that the order of the Gospel of Mark is arbitrary and unreliable.[185] "Thus," concludes Dodd, "it seems likely that in addition to material in pericope form, Mark had an outline, itself also traditional, to which he attempted to work, with incomplete success."[186] For Dodd it is not the words of Jesus but the person behind the words that constitutes his authority. Indeed, the truths Jesus and the Bible affirm are largely self-evident. Dodd says that "Jesus never told men anything about God but what they could see for themselves."[187]

Much of Dodd's early work focused on Paul. *The Meaning of Paul for Today* first appeared in 1920 and was reissued in paperback as late as 1957.[188] As sources for his investigation he accepts ten epistles (all except the Pastorals) as authentic. Basically, Dodd presents a liberal Paul: "the classic exponent of the idea of freedom and universality in religion."[189] According to Dodd, Jewish apocalypticism had a decreasing influence on Paul's thought. "As he grew older, the apocalyptic imagery of the earlier days tended to disappear at least from the foreground of his thought, and more and more his mind came to dwell upon the gradual growth and upbuilding of the Divine Commonwealth."[190] For the Jews, the commonwealth was nationalistic; they, according to Dodd, had "an outlook upon the world which bears the appearance of national arrogance run to an almost insane extreme."[191] By way of contrast, Dodd sees Paul's view of the commonwealth as universal.

Turning to the main features of Paul's gospel, Dodd investigates Paul's understanding of sin as a corporate condition that cannot be corrected by human effort. However, what humans could not do, God, according to Dodd, accomplished by sending the Son. For Paul, Jesus was the Messiah, and for Dodd the origin of that identification is to be traced to Jesus himself. "It seems at least highly probable that He was the first to link the thought of the Messiah with that of the ideal 'Servant of Jehovah' in the prophecies of the 'Second Isaiah'—the Servant who would suffer and die that others might know God."[192] Dodd believes Paul's doctrine of salvation is expressed in metaphors. For example, Paul used the metaphor of sacrifice. "So far, therefore, from the sacrifice of Christ being thought of as a means of soothing an angry Deity, it is represented as an act of God Himself to cope with the sin which was devastating human life."[193] Humans, according to Dodd, appropriate God's action in Christ by faith, an act of trust in God and acceptance of Christ as God's gift. Dodd stresses the continuation of justification into sanctification: life in the Spirit in which the believer makes moral progress, imitating Christ. When believers receive the gift of the Spirit they become members of the body of Christ. The motivating force within that community, according to Dodd, is love—the love of God directed toward all humanity. "That vision of a world made one and free was the inspiration of the apostle's life work."[194]

After studying and teaching the epistle to the Romans for more than a dozen years, Dodd produced a commentary on "the first great work of Christian theology."[195] In a short introduction he deals with critical issues, giving major attention to the question of integrity. After reviewing the evidence and refuting the argument that chapter 16 was originally a letter sent to Ephesus, Dodd concludes that the original epistle included chapters 1 through 16, and that the letter was later shortened and circulated in different editions. The occasion of the letter was Paul's projected visit to the Roman Christians on the way to Spain. "He therefore sets before them a comprehensive and reasoned statement of the fundamentals of Christianity as he understood it, which is at the same time an *apologia* for the principles and methods of his Gentile mission."[196] Dodd orders the material according to his understanding of the structure of the epistle. In format he follows the pattern of the Moffatt series: the text is presented in Moffatt's translation, followed by running commentary, with specific terms and phrases indicated in bold type.

In Rom 3:21-26, for example, Dodd finds the "Statement of the Doctrine of Justification." In interpreting this text he explicates the meaning of the major terms. For instance, "righteousness" employs courtroom language and presents an audacious idea: God acquits the guilty. "Ransom" is a term mainly used for freeing slaves and, according to Dodd, it can be used without reference to payment. The word *hilastērion*, which Moffatt translates "propitiation," should, in Dodd's opinion, be rendered "expiation." "In accordance with the biblical usage, therefore, the substantive (*hilastērion*) would mean, not propitiation, but 'a means by which guilt is annulled': if a man is the agent, the meaning would be 'a means of expiation' if God, 'a means by which sin is forgiven.'"[197] The reference to "blood" shows that Paul is using sacrificial language. According to Dodd these terms indicate that Paul is using three metaphors: the law court (justification), slavery (emancipation), sacrificial-ritual (blood), all representing what God has done in Christ in history. Dodd rejects the idea that God's justice is being satisfied or that Christ changed the attitude of God toward humans. "No antithesis between justice and mercy was in Paul's mind," says Dodd. "The justification of the sinner—his deliverance from the guilt of sin—is the conclusive proof of the righteousness of God."[198]

A special feature of Dodd's *Romans* is his treatment of chapters 9–11. He believes these chapters represent a separate treatise Paul had composed earlier and inserted here. Dodd also believes these chapters express Paul's universalism. "If we really believe in One God, and believe that Jesus Christ, in what He was and what He did, truly shows us what God's character and His attitude to men are like, then it is very difficult to think ourselves out of the belief that somehow His love will find a way of bring all men into unity with Him."[199] In general, Dodd's work on Paul can be characterized as conservative in criticism (accepting ten epistles as authentic) and liberal in theology (seeing Paul as champion of freedom and universalism, foe of the orthodox doctrine of atonement).

DISTINCTIVE FEATURES OF DODD'S RESEARCH

Already in the 1930s Dodd began to formulate his realized eschatology and his understanding of the kerygma. The first full expression of realized eschatology appears in his *The Parables of the Kingdom*.[200] Originally presented in 1935 as lectures at Yale, the book was slightly revised in 1960. Dodd's major concern is to counter Schweitzer's apocalyptic interpretation.[201] He selects the parables because he believes they constitute the most characteristic and authentic elements of the teachings of Jesus. Dodd agrees with Adolf Jülicher that the parables are not allegories, and that they provide essentially one point of comparison.[202] "At its simplest the parable is a metaphor or simile drawn from nature and common life, arresting the hearer by its vividness or strangeness, and leaving the mind in sufficient doubt about its precise application to tease it into active thought."[203]

The theme of the parables, according to Dodd, is the kingdom of God—a theme that has its background in the Jewish idea of the reign of God. In contrast to the Jews, who expected the rule of God over the whole world in the future, Jesus, in Dodd's opinion, preached a radical new idea: the kingdom has already come. Dodd says that "the 'eschatological' Kingdom of God is proclaimed as a present fact, which men must recognize, whether by their actions they accept or reject it."[204] He supports this interpretation by arguing that the words ἤγγικεν (Mark 1:15; literally, "has come near") and ἔφθασεν (Matt 12:28; literally, "has come") represent an Aramaic term that means "arrival." As to texts that seem to speak of a future coming, Dodd believes some of these have been added by the later church and others represent Jesus' visionary forecasts of the supernatural (not the historical) order. In regard to Mark 9:1, which most scholars translate "there are some standing here who will not taste death before they see the kingdom of God come with power" (RSV), Dodd renders as in the NEB, "there are some of those standing here who will not taste death before they have seen the kingdom of God already come in power." This text, according to Dodd, does not mean that in future some will see the kingdom coming, but that they will recognize in the future that the kingdom has already come.[205] "When He spoke of it in terms of the future, His words suggest, not any readjustment of condition on this earth, but glories of a world beyond this."[206]

Among those sayings that seem to refer to the future, Dodd gives special attention to Jesus' words about the day of the Son of Man. He thinks this refers to a supra-historical happening. However, he believes Jesus applied the title Son of Man to himself, thereby predicting his triumph over death. Jesus, in Dodd's opinion, understood this triumph as his resurrection, but the later church misconstrued the triumph as twofold: the resurrection *and* the future coming of the Son of Man. According to Dodd, "[t]he absolute, the 'wholly other,' has entered into time and space," but "[t]he historical order however cannot contain the whole meaning of the absolute. . . . The Son of Man has come, but also He will come."[207] However, according to Dodd the future coming will not be the apocalyptic event the church expected.

> There is no coming of the Son of Man in history "after" His coming in Galilee and Jerusalem, whether soon or late, for there is no before and after in the eternal order. . . . "The Day of the Son of Man" stands for the timeless fact. So far as history can contain it, it is embodied in the historic crisis which the coming of Jesus brought about. But the spirit of man, though dwelling in history, belongs to the eternal order, and the full meaning of the Day of the Son of Man, or of the Kingdom of God, he can experience only in that eternal order.[208]

Dodd proceeds to support his view by interpretation of particular parables. For example, he believes that the parables of crisis, such as the Thief in the Night (Matt 24:43-44; Luke 12:39-40) and the Ten Virgins (Matt 25:1-12), originally had to do with crises related to the ministry of Jesus, but that they were later changed into parables that address the delay and second coming of Christ. In regard to the parables of growth—for example, the Seed Growing Secretly (Mark 4:26-29)—Dodd argues that they refer to the growth of the kingdom during the ministry of Jesus. He concludes that the parables present the eschatology of Jesus. "It is realized eschatology."[209]

Without question, realized eschatology is a central, unifying feature of Dodd's total theological-historical project. While many reviewers agree that he has correctly disclosed a present or realized element in Jesus' understanding of the kingdom, most scholars accuse Dodd of heavyhanded exegesis—of depreciating the apocalyptic feature of Jesus' teaching, of attributing future eschatology to the church, and of transforming futuristic eschatology into Platonism.[210]

According to Dodd, Jesus preached the kingdom; the early Christians proclaimed the kerygma—the pattern of events in which the kingdom was present. Dodd believes the kerygma to be the central message of the NT, which constitutes its unity and confirms the reliability of its tradition. This view was articulated in lectures given at Kings College, London, in 1935, and published as *The Apostolic Preaching and Its Developments*.[211] He begins by examining the preaching of the early Christians. "The word here translated 'preaching,' *kerygma*, signifies not the action of the preacher, but that which he preaches, his 'message.'"[212] Dodd finds the locus classicus for this idea in 1 Cor 15:3-4. "The Pauline *kerygma*, therefore, is a proclamation of the facts of the death and resurrection of Christ in an eschatological setting which gives significance to the facts."[213] Paul says that he received the message from tradition—confirming Dodd's conviction that the kerygma had been formulated and widely proclaimed before Paul. Dodd outlines the content of the kerygma:

- The prophecies are fulfilled, and the new Age is inaugurated by the coming of Christ.
- He was born of the seed of David.
- He died according to the Scriptures, to deliver us out of the present evil age.
- He was buried.
- He rose on the third day according to the Scriptures.
- He is exalted at the right hand of God, as Son of God and Lord of quick and dead.
- He will come again as Judge and Saviour of men.[214]

Dodd finds this pattern confirmed by the speeches in Acts.

Dodd turns to the development of the kerygma in the NT. In the Gospels he detects a tendency to relapse into apocalyptic thought, but he believes an authentic line can be traced from Paul to Mark. "Thus the authentic line of development, as the expectation of an immediate advent faded, led to a concentration of attention upon the historical facts of the ministry, death, and resurrection of Jesus, exhibited in an eschatological setting which made clear their absolute and final quality as saving facts."[215] Dodd thinks Mark understood himself to be writing a form of the kerygma, expanding the historical details and writing commentary. Matthew and Luke tend to divert attention from kerygma and didache (teaching), but they, too, according to Dodd, present an interpretation of the facts.

> This, no doubt, means that we cannot expect to find in the Gospels . . . bare matter of fact, unaffected by the interpretation borne by the facts in the kerygma. But it also means that wherever the Gospels keep close to the matter and form of the kerygma, there we are in touch with a tradition coeval with the Church itself.[216]

Dodd believes the eschatological significance of the facts is explicated by Paul and John: "It is in the epistles of Paul, therefore, that full justice is done for the first time to the principle of 'realized eschatology' which is vital to the whole kerygma. That supernatural order of life which the apocalyptists had predicted in terms of pure fantasy is now described as an actual fact of experience."[217] John advances beyond Paul:

> Now for John the whole life of Jesus is in the fullest sense a revelation of His glory. . . . John therefore draws together two separate strains in the development of Christian thought: that which started from an eschatological valuation of the facts of present experience, and that which started from a similar valuation of the facts of past history. Accordingly, he has given to his work the form of a "Gospel," that is to say, of a restatement of the kerygma in historical terms.[218]

Although there are various expressions and interpretations, the kerygma comprises the unifying message of the NT. "With all the diversity of the New Testament writings, they form a unity in their proclamation of the one Gospel."[219]

Since the first element in the kerygma announces the fulfillment of prophecy, Dodd finds its background in the OT. In his book *According to the Scriptures*[220] he refers to the kerygma as "the ground-plan of New Testament theology."[221] In building on this ground plan the writers of the NT supported their ideas by use of the OT, so that material from the Hebrew Scriptures provided what Dodd's subtitle calls *The Sub-Structure of New Testament Theology*. This observation leads Dodd to investigate the hypothesis of "testimonies"—the theory that the early Christians used collections of OT material in support of their message. In contrast to Rendel Harris, who defended the existence of an early written document, Dodd argues that the testimonies were circulated orally.[222] He develops his thesis by investigating the use of fifteen OT texts, largely from Psalms and Isaiah, that indicate "that New Testament writers were working upon a tradition in which certain passages of the Old Testament were treated as 'testimonies' to the Gospel facts, or in other words as disclosing that 'determinate counsel of God' which was fulfilled in those facts."[223] Pursuing his thesis further, Dodd argues that the early Christians understood the texts of the testimonies in their larger context and interpreted them according to a hermeneutic that became fixed in the early tradition. These texts were interpreted, according to Dodd, in support of the main elements of the kerygma and for the development of NT theology. For example, texts about the Son of Man and the Servant of the Lord were incorporated into primitive Christology. For Dodd all the pieces of the puzzle—biblical testimonies, reliable traditions, factual kerygma, NT theology— fit together into a harmonious picture.

Fundamental to Dodd's understanding of the kerygma is his distinction between preaching (kerygma) and teaching (didache)—a distinction explicated in his book *Gospel and Law*.[224] Always alert to the appearance of patterns, Dodd finds evidence for the distinction in the NT. He notes, for instance, that the epistles usually begin with theology and later turn to ethics. This leads Dodd to the conclusion that ethics is response to proclamation. Thus features of early Christian ethics correspond to elements of the kerygma. For example, the proclamation that the kingdom has come brings a new ethical situation; the proclamation of Christ calls for imitation of his self-giving; the kerygma as expression of God's love demands that love become the motivating force in Christian life. In sum, "[w]e recall that the earliest form in which Christianity was presented to the world, so far as we can discover, was two-fold: it consisted of the proclamation (*kērygma*), which declared what God has done for men, and the teaching (*didachē*), which declared what God expects man to do."[225] With this book Dodd is anxious to correct what he considers an excessive emphasis in Reformed theology on grace to the neglect of law—the law of Christ, the ethical response to grace.

In overview, it is clear that Dodd's view of the kerygma is fundamental to his affirmation of the unity of the Bible, realized eschatology, and the factual basis of faith. Actually, "kerygma" has become with Dodd a loaded term; the word for gospel (εὐαγγέλιον) is used more often in the NT (seventy-six times) than κήρυγμα (nine times), and, contrary to Dodd, the word κήρυγμα a can signify the action of proclaiming as well as the content of the proclamation. Dodd tends to overemphasize the factual character of the proclamation, in spite of his insistence that the facts have their significance in an eschatological setting.[226] Moreover, critics have pointed out that Dodd's distinction between *kērygma* and *didachē* is too sharply drawn, and Dodd's theory concerning the testimonies has been subject to harsh criticism.[227] Of course, no one doubts that the early Christians supported their message with material from the OT, and virtually everybody welcomes Dodd's stress on NT ethics.

DODD'S MAJOR WORK: RESEARCH ON THE FOURTH GOSPEL

As the document that adopts realized eschatology and interprets the facts of the kerygma theologically, the Fourth Gospel is Dodd's favorite book. However, prior to his major works of the Fourth Gospel he also published a commentary on the Johannine epistles.[228] The distinctive feature of this commentary is Dodd's argument that 1, 2, and 3 John were not written by the author of the Fourth Gospel. He detects differences of vocabulary and style, but primarily he discerns differences in thought. "Eschatology, the Atonement, the Holy Spirit:

these are certainly no minor themes in Christian theology. In all three the First Epistle of John represents an outlook widely different from that of the Fourth Gospel."[229]

Dodd believes the three epistles were written by the same author, a disciple of the writer of the Fourth Gospel, possibly John the Elder, writing between 96 and 110. In his exegesis of the exordium of 1 John he contends that the author's use of "we" does not imply that he was himself an eyewitness of "what was from the beginning." "He speaks not exclusively for himself or for a restricted group, but for the whole Church to which the apostolic witness belongs by virtue of its *koinonia*, over against the world which being outside the *koinonia* has no knowledge of the incarnate Son, and therefore no knowledge of the Real God."[230]

Dodd's major work, *The Interpretation of the Fourth Gospel*, appeared in 1953, a weighty volume of 453 pages plus indices.[231] It is arranged in three parts: historical background, leading ideas, and argument and structure. As to the historical background, Dodd believes the setting within early Christianity is most important. He thinks the author knew the early kerygma and assumed realized eschatology.[232] According to Dodd the author directed his Gospel primarily to non-Christians. The world in which these readers live is permeated with Hellenistic syncretism.[233] To illuminate this syncretism Dodd turns first to the Hermetic literature, noting parallels to the Fourth Gospel. He says, surprisingly, that "it is surely clear at least that the Son of Man in the Fourth Gospel has more affinity with the Ἄνθρωπος of *Poimandres* than with the Son of Man of Jewish Apocalyptic."[234] Turning to Hellenistic Judaism, Dodd investigates Philo and notes the common idea of the Logos as medium of creation. Philo, however, could never have imagined the incarnation of the Logos. "This means that the Logos, which in Philo is never personal, except in a fluctuating series of metaphors, is in the gospel fully personal, standing in personal relations both with God and with men, and having a place in history."[235] In discussing rabbinic Judaism, Dodd notes the trend in scholarship away from Hellenistic toward Jewish backgrounds, one he heartily commends. Dodd acknowledges parallels between the Fourth Gospel and pre-Christian Gnosticism but emphasizes the distinctions. As to the Mandaean sources, Dodd believes they represent a much later form of gnostic thought and "have no value for the study of the Fourth Gospel."[236] He concludes: "Rabbinic Judaism, Philo and the *Hermetica* remain our most direct sources for the background of thought, and in each case the distinctive character of Johannine Christianity is brought out by observing the transformation it wrought in ideas which it holds in common with other forms of religion."[237]

The second part of this book deals with the leading ideas of the Fourth Gospel. By way of introduction Dodd observes that the author expresses his ideas in symbols or signs. Dodd, remembering Plato, says that a sign in the Fourth Gospel "refers, in the first instance, to timeless realities signified by the act in time."[238] Among the leading ideas Dodd includes "eternal life" (a quality of life that is already present), "knowledge of God" (a personal revelation in Christ), and "truth." About the latter he writes:

> To conclude: the use of ἀλήθεια in this gospel rests upon common Hellenistic usage in which it hovers between the meaning of 'reality,' or 'the ultimately real,' and 'knowledge of the real. . . . To 'know the truth' they must not only hear His words: they must in some sort be united with Him who is the truth. Thus even when the concept of knowledge of God is most fully intellectualized, it remains true that it involves a personal union with Christ, which goes beyond mere intellectual apprehension.[239]

The idea of "faith" is closely related to truth and knowledge. "Thus πίστις is that form of knowledge, or vision, appropriate to those who find God in an historic Person of the past, a Person who nevertheless, through it, remains the object of saving knowledge, the truth and the life."[240]

Most important are the ideas of the Fourth Gospel that present the author's understanding of Jesus. For this author the term "messiah" emphasizes Jesus as king. The author takes up the title "Son of Man" from the Christian tradition but gives it meaning in light of the archetypal man of Hellenistic thought, combining it with the idea of the Servant as representative of the people.

> Thus the term "Son of Man" throughout this gospel retains the sense of one who incorporates in Himself the people of God, or humanity in its ideal aspect . . . . In the Fourth Gospel . . . there is never any doubt that the evangelist is speaking of a real person, that is, of a concrete historical individual of the human race, "Jesus of Nazareth, the Son of Joseph" (i.45).[241]

The term "Son of God" expresses the unique relation of Jesus to God. "The relation of Father and Son is an eternal relation, not attained in time, nor ceasing with this life, or with the history of this world. The human career of Jesus is, as it were, a projection of this eternal relation (which is the divine ἀγάπη) upon the field of time."[242]

Dodd presents a very sophisticated analysis of the linguistic details and historical background of the idea of the Logos, where an ambiguity in regard to Jewish and Hellenistic sources is evident.

> The ambiguity which (from our point of view) enters into the Johannine conception of the Logos could be understood if we assumed that the author started from the Jewish idea of the Torah as being at once the Word of God and the divine Wisdom manifested in creation, and found, under the guidance of Hellenistic Jewish thought similar to that of Philo, an appropriate Greek expression which fittingly combined both ideas.[243]

The author of the Fourth Gospel, however, does not begin with cosmic speculation and fit Jesus in; he begins with faith in Jesus and describes him in Jewish and Hellenistic terms. "We start with faith in Jesus, which involves the recognition that the meaning which we find in Him is the meaning of the whole universe—that, in fact, that which is incarnate in Him is the Logos."[244]

In the third and last part of *The Interpretation of the Fourth Gospel*, Dodd examines the argument and structure. Most important, he dismisses all hypotheses of displacement and accepts the extant order as original. Dodd believes that the body of the Gospel is ordered into two main sections: the Book of Signs (2:1—12:50), and the Book of the Passion (13:1—20:31). The Book of Signs, according to Dodd, is divided into seven episodes. For example, the sixth episode, "Victory of Life over Death" (11:1-53) recounts the raising of Lazarus, which affirms the belief that eternal life is already present. Dodd believes that these episodes present a continuous argument with interrelated cross references, so that any attempt to rearrange the material would disturb the essential unity of the composition. The Book of the Passion, according to Dodd, is divided into two main parts: the farewell discourses and the passion narrative proper. In analyzing the passion narrative he notes differences from the Synoptics and contends that the Fourth Gospel rests on independent tradition. The author, Dodd believes, used historical tradition to present his theology.

> Here is something that happened in time, with eternal consequence. . . . It is an "epoch-making" event; in history things can never be the same again. But more: in it the two orders of reality, the temporal and the eternal, are united; the Word is made flesh. It is an event in both worlds; or rather, in that one world, of spirit and of flesh, which is the true environment of man. . . . Thus the cross is a sign, but a sign which is also the thing signified. The preliminary signs set forth so

amply in the gospel are not only temporal signs of an eternal reality; they are also signs of this Event, in its twofold character as word and as flesh. They are true—spiritually, eternally true—only upon the condition that this Event is true, both temporally (or historically) and spiritually or eternally.[245]

In sum, this is a monumental achievement enlisting philological, historical, and exegetical work with theological sensitivity—all in the service of a comprehensive understanding of the Fourth Gospel and its message.[246]

Written a decade later, Dodd's *Historical Tradition in the Fourth Gospel* is a sequel to the earlier book.[247] Another sizable tome (432 pages), this volume expands Dodd's perception of the historical tradition behind the Gospel of John. For Dodd the crucial question is: "Can we in any measure recover and describe a strain of tradition lying behind the Fourth Gospel, distinctive of it, and independent of other strains of tradition known to us?"[248] Compared to this question, Dodd considers the usual critical issues like authorship to be secondary. About the author he says: "It is not impossible to imagine that a Galilaean fisherman may have grown into the accomplished theologian whom we meet in the Fourth Gospel, but I find it difficult."[249] Dodd begins his quest for the tradition with an analysis of the narrative material, starting with the passion narrative. He carefully compares details of the narrative with the accounts in the Synoptics, discovering considerable agreement. Dodd argues that this agreement cannot be explained by literary dependence since sometimes John agrees with one and sometimes with another of the Synoptics, requiring a complex use of sources that would have been unfeasible. Dodd also analyzes material that is peculiar to the Fourth Gospel. Much of this material, he thinks, serves no theological tendency, so that it would not have been invented by the author.

To sum up: the evidence of the few passages which suggest *prima facie* literary dependence of the Fourth Gospel upon the others in the Passion narrative is not sufficient to prove such dependence. On the contrary there is cumulative evidence that the Johannine version represents (subject to some measure of "writing up" by the evangelist) an independent strain of the common oral tradition, differing from the strains of tradition underlying Mark (Matthew) and Luke, though controlled by the same general schema. Its apparent contacts with Jewish tradition, and the appreciation it shows of the situation before the great rebellion of A.D. 66, make it probable that this tradition was formulated, substantially, before that date, and in Palestine.[250]

Following the same procedures, Dodd examines the narrative material concerning the ministry of Jesus and reaches the same conclusion.

Turning to the sayings of Jesus, Dodd acknowledges that the dialogues and discourses of the Fourth Gospel are literary compositions, but he believes they incorporate earlier tradition. "In view of all this, there would seem to be a strong presumption that even where John is to all appearance composing most freely, there is, sometimes at least, an older tradition behind him."[251] Where sayings of Jesus in John have parallels in the Synoptics, Dodd argues for common tradition rather than literary dependence. Although the Fourth Gospel is sometimes supposed to contain no parables, Dodd points out that parables may be short parabolic expressions like the saying about a grain of wheat (John 12:24).

Jesus' predictions about the future are of major concern to Dodd. He finds two distinct traditions in the Synoptics: sayings about the resurrection and sayings about the *parousia*. According to Dodd the Fourth Gospel emphasizes neither, but instead speaks of departure and return. "The starting point would appear to be some oracular utterance of Jesus conveying, perhaps in figurative terms, the assurance that his death meant a separation which was only temporary and would be succeeded by restored relations with his followers, to their abiding satisfaction."[252] This original expression, Dodd believes, was later misconstrued to refer to the resurrection or to the *parousia*.

> In a word, I suggest that John is here reaching back to a very early form of tradition indeed, and making it the point of departure for his profound theological reinterpretation; and further, that the oracular sayings which he reports have good claim to represent authentically, in substance if not verbally, what Jesus actually said to his disciples—a better claim than the more elaborate and detailed predictions which the Synoptics offer.[253]

Dodd concludes: "The above argument has led to the conclusion that behind the Fourth Gospel lies an ancient tradition independent of the gospels, and meriting serious consideration as a contribution to our knowledge of the historical facts concerning Jesus Christ."[254]

Without question, Dodd's two volumes have made an enormous contribution to Johannine research.[255] To be sure, he found in the Fourth

Gospel support for his own historical-theological views: realized eschatology as original with Jesus, the kerygma as historical facts expressing eternal truths, the tradition about Jesus as reliable. No doubt these discoveries had been prepared by Dodd's presuppositions. No doubt, *The Historical Tradition in the Fourth Gospel* is an apologetic work. As Dodd acknowledges, the meticulous argument is cumulative, like adding feathers one by one until finally the scale is tipped. Some scholars have welcomed Dodd's identification of John's independent tradition and his affirmation of the historical reliability of the Fourth Gospel.[256] Others have criticized his method[257] or charged that he has overstated his case, for instance, that the tradition is early and Palestinian, or that John's eschatology is closer to Jesus than the Synoptics.[258] For some Dodd dismisses the problem of arrangement and literary sources too quickly, and the question of the relation to the Synoptics remains a matter of ongoing debate.[259] Nevertheless, Dodd gave a virtuoso performance, worthy of the accolades he has received.

Dodd's use of the tradition in the quest of the historical Jesus is evident in one of his last publications, *The Founder of Christianity*.[260] This book expands, on the basis of intervening research, his 1939 article on "The Life and Teaching of Jesus Christ."[261] Although he acknowledges that a biography of Jesus cannot be written, Dodd believes the main outline of the career of Jesus can be reconstructed. The Gospels are the primary sources for this reconstruction. Dodd believes Mark was the earliest gospel, used by Matthew and Luke, but John is also important because, as Dodd had argued in his earlier work, it rests on early, reliable tradition. Dodd begins with an investigation of the personal traits of Jesus. According to him, Jesus was a creative person whose teachings were vivid, drawn from real life. Dodd admits that Jesus used apocalyptic imagery but he claims that this was not essential to his teaching. His distinctive message, in Dodd's opinion, was that the long-awaited kingdom of God had actually come. In relation to that message Dodd believes Jesus had to recognize himself to be the "messiah"—a title he avoided. Instead, says Dodd, Jesus understood his mission in terms of the Servant of second Isaiah and adopted the title "Son of Man" in order to present his relation to the consummation of the kingdom beyond history. "In view of this, it follows that the total event of the earthly career of Jesus, as well as his action in details, is regarded in two aspects: on the one side it had effects in an actual historical situation; on the other side it had a significance reaching out into man's eternal destiny, and to be expressed only in symbol."[262]

Dodd proceeds to recount the story of the ministry of Jesus. It begins with Jesus' baptism. "For him, and not only for those who wrote about him, it was the act of God by which he was 'anointed' for his mission."[263] After an early ministry in Judea (attested by the tradition of the Fourth Gospel), Jesus carried on his mission to Galilee—a mission of preaching, healing, and disregarding the ritual rules of Judaism. According to Dodd the feeding of the multitude was decisive. He believes that Jesus understood the event to symbolize the messianic banquet of the kingdom, but the crowd, misunderstanding his role, wanted to make him king (John 6:15). This misunderstanding provoked Jesus to withdraw from Galilee, to travel in foreign areas, and to concentrate on teaching the disciples. Because of his intent to establish the new people of God, Jesus, according to Dodd, took his mission to the capital, to Jerusalem. Dodd believes Jesus made two trips to the Holy City toward the end of his career: a journey at the time of the Feast of Tabernacles and another at the time of the following Passover. Jesus was arrested, Dodd believes, because of his cleansing of the temple and his attack on the religious authorities. Before the Sanhedrin he was accused of blasphemy, before Pilate with insurrection—the claim to be king (most clearly presented in the Johannine tradition). After his execution Jesus appeared to his disciples but, in Dodd's opinion, the appearances cannot be fit into a continuous, consistent narrative. Besides, he says, the consequence of the resurrection—the changed lives of the believers—is more important than the "facts." Nevertheless, Dodd concludes, "We are dealing with a truly 'historic' event."[264]

Looking back over the work of Dodd makes it clear that he is one of the greatest NT scholars of the first half of the twentieth century. He mastered the skills and appropriated the methods. He was sensitive to the theological meaning and relevance of the NT. To be sure, his major ideas and the details of his argument have provoked insightful criticism. Yet the greatness of Dodd is not in the particulars but in his comprehensive synthesis. Combining natural theology with a theological understanding of history, he affirmed an eschatology that was realized in history and expressed in the kerygma—the central message of the NT. This comprehensive synthesis could include all in its perception: the tradition, the sources, the life of Jesus, the theology of Paul, the vision of John—one majestic stained glass window through which the light of God illuminated the ongoing life of humans.

SUMMARY

The research reviewed in this chapter reaches a high point—a zenith, as the title suggests. Here the methods developed in the nineteenth century were refined and enlarged. The scholarship summarized is Anglo-American, displaying an increasing maturity and independence from the German domination of the earlier era. Indeed, through much of the period relations between Germany and Britain/America were less than cordial. In NT studies the Anglo-Americans accepted form criticism with some qualifications but viewed the lessons of the history of religion school with suspicion. In the main the Germans were seen as skeptical and extreme; what was needed was calm, moderating balance.

Thus the Anglo-Americans accepted the priority of 2DH, proud of their Oxford ancestors and the legacy of Streeter.[265] The gospel accounts were generally reliable, not tendentious à la Wrede.[266] Although the sources did not provide material adequate for a biography, they offered orderly accounts of the main contours of Jesus' career. The resulting Jesus was similar to the liberal Jesus of the nineteenth century, a winsome teacher with universally valid ethical teachings. He was conscious of his messiahship and understood his vocation as Son of Man, assuming the role of the Suffering Servant. His message of the kingdom was primarily ethical, with stress on the present. Eschatological motifs, an element of the atmosphere of the times, were present, but not radical apocalyptic (à la Schweitzer).[267] Paul was of secondary importance—a "liberal Paul," possibly a universalist.

Little did the scholars at Oxford, Cambridge, and Harvard expect that virtually everything they accepted as established would come under attack in the rest of the century—the priority of Mark, the existence of Q, the historical Jesus, the Son of Man–Suffering Servant Messiah, the liberal Paul. Most of all, they did not anticipate the frontal attack that would aim to blow them out of the water: the militant message of the new biblical theology.

Notes

1. For personal reminiscences of some of the major figures in this chapter, see Amos N. Wilder, "New Testament Studies, 1920–1950: Reminiscences of a Changing Discipline," *JR* 64 (1984): 432–51.

2. In this volume the terms *Religionsgeschichte* and *religionsgeschichtliche Schule* are translated "history of religion" and "history of religion school." The "s" in "*religions-*" represents a genitive singular, not a plural.

3. See A. Raymond George, "Vincent Taylor," in Vincent Taylor, *New Testament Essays* (London: Epworth, 1970), 1–4; C. L. Mitton, "Vincent Taylor: New Testament Scholar," ibid., 5–30; Owen E. Evans, "Theologians of our Time: Vincent Taylor," *ExpTim* 75 (1963–64):164–68.

4. Vincent Taylor, *The Historical Evidence for the Virgin Birth* (Oxford: Clarendon, 1920).

5. Ibid., iii.

6. Ibid., 133.

7. Vincent Taylor, *Behind the Third Gospel: A Study of the Proto-Luke Hypothesis* (Oxford: Clarendon, 1926).

8. See *HNTR* 2:265–66.

9. Vincent Taylor, *The Passion Narrative of St Luke: A Critical and Historical Investigation*, ed. Owen E. Evans (Cambridge: Cambridge University Press, 1972).

10. Ibid., 119.

11. *Behind the Third Gospel*, 182. The text of Proto-Luke according to Taylor's reconstruction is published in his *The First Draft of St. Luke's Gospel*, "Theology" Reprints 1 (London: SPCK, 1927).

12. *Behind the Third Gospel*, 246, 274.

13. A succinct summary of Taylor's gospel criticism is presented in his book *The Gospels: A Short Introduction*, 7th ed. (London: Epworth, 1952), originally published in 1930 and revised in 1939. In this book Taylor argues that Q was written in Aramaic by Matthew; he believes the Fourth Gospel was written in Ephesus by a Jewish Christian who preserves the tradition of John the apostle.

14. Vincent Taylor, *The Formation of the Gospel Tradition* (London: Macmillan, 1957).

15. Ibid., vi.

16. See *HNTR* 2: 269–86.

17. *Formation of the Gospel Tradition*, 41.

18. Ibid., 63. This is the form Dibelius calls the "paradigm" and Bultmann the "apophthegm

19. Ibid., 113.

20. Ibid., 166.

21. Vincent Taylor, *The Gospel According to Mark: The Greek Text with Introduction, Notes, and Indexes* (1952; repr. London: Macmillan, 1957; repr. Thornapple Commentaries [Grand Rapids: Baker, 1981]).

22. Ibid., 11.

23. Ibid., 121.

24. Ibid., 148.

25. Ibid., 378.

26. See *HNTR* 2: 447.

27. Taylor, *Mark*, 658.

28. Late in his career Taylor published a useful student handbook, *The Text of the New Testament: A Short Introduction* (London: Macmillan, 1961).

29. Vincent Taylor, *Jesus and His Sacrifice: A Study of the Passion-Sayings in the Gospels* (London: Macmillan, 1937), vii.

30. Ibid., 270–71.

31. Vincent Taylor, *The Atonement in New Testament Teaching* (2d ed. London: Epworth, 1950). The book was first published in 1940 and slightly revised in the 2d ed. of 1945, with reprints in 1946 and 1950.

32. Ibid., 111.

33. Ibid., 172–73.

34. Vincent Taylor, *Forgiveness and Reconciliation: A Study in New Testament Theology* (London: Macmillan, 1941).

35. An exegetical investigation of Paul's thought is presented in Taylor's short commentary, *The Epistle to the Romans*, EPC (London: Epworth, 1955).

36. *Forgiveness and Reconciliation*, 62.

37. Ibid., 189.

38. Vincent Taylor, *The Names of Jesus* (London: Macmillan, 1953).

39. Vincent Taylor, *The Life and Ministry of Jesus* (New York: Abingdon, 1955).

40. Ibid., 60.

41. Ibid., 90.

42. Vincent Taylor, *The Person of Christ in New Testament Teaching* (London: Macmillan, 1958).

43. See *HNTR* 2: 463–66.

44. *Person of Christ*, 79.

45. Ibid., 387.

46. See Margaret Hope Bacon, *Let This Life Speak: The Legacy of Henry Joel Cadbury* (Philadelphia: University of Pennsylvania Press, 1987); Mary Hoxie Jones, "Henry Joel Cadbury: A Biographical Sketch," in *Then and Now: Quaker Essays: Historical and Contemporary*, ed. Anna Brinton (Philadelphia: University of Pennsylvania Press, 1960), 11–70; George W. MacRae, "Henry Joel Cadbury (1883–1974), in *Profiles from the Beloved Community*, ed. George Huntston Williams, George W. MacRae, and Paul D. Hanson (Cambridge: Harvard University Press, 1976), 13–21; Amos N. Wilder, "In Memoriam: Henry Joel Cadbury, 1883–1974," *NTS* 21 (1975): 313–17.

47. The archives at Yale Divinity School contain a letter (dated 1928) from B. W. Bacon (see *HNTR* 2: 300–5) to Amos N. Wilder, a prospective graduate student, later a professor at Harvard. In urging Wilder to come to Yale, Bacon wrote that he expected Cadbury to be his successor.

48. Quoted by Bacon, *Let This Life Speak*, 171.

49. See Henry J. Cadbury, "The Basis of Early Christian Antimilitarism," *JBL* 37 (1918): 66–94.

50. Besides his research in the NT, Cadbury published extensively in Quaker history, discovering and editing works by early Quakers like George Fox and John Woolman.

51. Quoted in Bacon, *Let This Life Speak*, 26.

52. Henry J. Cadbury, *The Character of a Quaker*, PHP 103 (Wallingford, PA: Pendle Hill, 1959), 27.

53. Henry J. Cadbury, *A Quaker Approach to the Bible* (Guilford, NC: Guilford College, 1953), 170.

54. Ibid., 9.

55. Quoted in Jones, "Henry Joel Cadbury," 52.

56. For survey and general assessment of Cadbury's NT research see Beverly Roberts Gaventa, "The Peril of Modernizing Henry Joel Cadbury"; Donald L. Jones, "The Legacy of Henry Joel Cadbury: Or What He Learned That We Ought to Know"; Richard I. Pervo, "'On Perilous Things': A Response to Beverly R. Gaventa," all in *Cadbury, Knox, and Talbert: American Contributions to the Study of Acts*, ed. Mikeal C. Parsons and Joseph B. Tyson, SBLBSNA (Atlanta: Scholars, 1992), 7–26, 27–36, 37–43.

57. Henry J. Cadbury, *The Style and Literary Method of Luke*, HTS 6 (Cambridge: Harvard University Press, 1920).

58. *Style and Literary Method*, 50–51.

59. Henry J. Cadbury, "The Medical Language of Hippocrates," *HTR* 14 (1921): 106.

60. Henry J. Cadbury, "Luke and the Horse-Doctors," *JBL* 52 (1933): 55–65.

61. In *Studies in Luke-Acts: Essays Presented in Honor of Paul Schubert*, ed. Leander E. Keck and J. Louis Martyn (Nashville: Abingdon, 1966), 87–102.

62. Henry J. Cadbury, "Between Jesus and the Gospels," *HTR* 16 (1923): 81–92.

63. See *HNTR* 2: 269–86.

64. "Between Jesus and the Gospels," 87.

65. Ibid., 90.

66. Ibid., 91.

67. Cadbury's early assessment of form criticism is confirmed in later writings; see his "Looking at the Gospels Backwards," *Studia Evangelica* 2, TU 87 (1964): 47–56; "Gospel Study and Our Image of Early Christianity," *JBL* 83 (1964): 139–45. These two essays are reprinted in Cadbury's *Behind the Gospels*, PHP 160 (Wallingford, PA: Pendle Hill, 1968).

68. *The Beginnings of Christianity. Part I: The Acts of the Apostles*, ed. F. J. Foakes Jackson and Kirsopp Lake, 5 vols. (London: Macmillan, 1920–33); see *HNTR* 2: 409–10.

69. *Beginnings of Christianity*, 4: vii.

70. Ibid., 2: 489–510.

71. Ibid., 2: 510.

72. Ibid., 5: 59–74.

73. Ibid., 5: 69.

74. Ibid., 5: 354–75.

75. Ibid., 5: 369.

76. Amos N. Wilder, "In Memoriam," 316.

77. Henry J. Cadbury, *The Making of Luke-Acts* (New York: Macmillan, 1927; repr. London: SPCK, 1958; Peabody, MA: Hendrickson, 1999). For a short appraisal of this book see the "Foreword" to the 1999 edition by Paul N. Anderson.

78. *The Making of Luke-Acts*, v.

79. Ibid., 2.

80. Ibid., 279.

81. Ibid., 360.

82. Ibid., 368.

83. E. F. Scott writes: "There is more genuine scholarship in it than in nine-tenths of the ostentatiously learned books that are being written today about the New Testament." (Quoted in Bacon, *Let This Life Speak*, 75–76).

84. Henry J. Cadbury, *The Book of Acts in History* (New York: Harper & Brothers, 1955).

85. Ibid., 53.

86. Ibid., 58.

87. Cadbury did not produce a major work on Paul, but published a few essays. A summary of the apostle's thought is presented in his "Concurrent Phases of Paul's Religion," in *Studies in Early Christianity*, ed. Shirley Jackson Case (New York: Century, 1928), 369–87. In this essay Cadbury follows his usual method: philological and literary analysis of the sources and inductive summary of results. Among Pauline themes, he believes that the mystical and ethical motifs assure the permanent value of Paul's thought.

88. *The Peril of Modernizing Jesus* (New York: Macmillan, 1937), 191.

89. Ibid., 83.

90. Ibid., 141.

91. Ibid., 187.

92. Ibid., 188.

93. In a later essay Cadbury addresses the obverse of modernizing Jesus: "The Peril of Archaizing Ourselves," *Int* 3 (1949): 331–37.

94. *Jesus: What Manner of Man* (New York: Macmillan, 1947), v.

95. Ibid., 73.

96. Ibid., 98.

97. Ibid., 119.

98. Ibid., 123.

99. Cadbury's interest in Jesus continued throughout his career. At seventy-nine he delivered a lecture at Haverford on *The Eclipse of the Historical Jesus*, PHP 133 (Wallingford, PA: Pendle Hill, 1964). In this lecture Cadbury advocates a quest that is free from presuppositions about Jesus' meaning for today and from a biblical theology that is more concerned with the kerygma than with the historical Jesus.

100. Henry J. Cadbury, "Critical Study of the New Testament," in *An Outline of Christianity: The Story of Civilization. Vol. 4, Christianity and Modern Thought*, ed. R. G. Parsons and A. S. Peake (London: Waverley, 1926) 280–301.

101. Ibid., 281.

102. Henry J. Cadbury, "The Present State of New Testament Studies," in *The Haverford Symposium on Archaeology and the Bible*, ed. Elihu Grant (New Haven: ASOR, 1938), 79–110.

103. Ibid., 106.

104. Henry J. Cadbury, "New Testament Study in the Next Generation," *JR* 21 (1941): 412–20.

105. Henry J. Cadbury, "New Testament Scholarship: Fifty Years in Retrospect," *JBR* 28 (1960): 194–98, at 195, 196.

106. Henry J. Cadbury, "Some Foibles of New Testament Scholarship," *JBR* 26 (1958): 213–16.

107. Ibid., 214.

108. Quoted by Amos N. Wilder, "New Testament Studies, 1920–50" (see n. 1 above), 444.

109. See Harold Henry Rowley, "T. W. Manson: An Appreciation," in *Studies in the Gospels and Epistles*, ed. Matthew Black (Manchester: Manchester University Press, 1962), vii–xvi; "Thomas Walter Manson, 1893–1958," in *New Testament Essays: Studies in Memory of Thomas Walter Manson*, 1893–1958, ed. A. J. B. Higgins (Manchester: Manchester University Press, 1959); Matthew Black, "Theologians of Our Time: Thomas Walter Manson," *ExpTim* 75 (1963–64): 208–11; C. H. Dodd, "T. W. Manson and His Rylands Lectures," *ExpTim* 73 (1961–62): 302–3.

110. "T. W. Manson," xv.

111. T. W. Manson, "The Nature and Authority of the Canonical Scriptures," in *A Companion to the Bible*, ed. T. W. Manson (New York: Scribner's, 1939), 3–12.

112. Ibid., 8.

113. Ibid., 9.

114. T. W. Manson, *The Teaching of Jesus: Studies of Its Form and Content* (2d ed. Cambridge: Cambridge University Press, 1935).

115. See *HNTR* 2: 265–66.

116. See T. W. Manson, "The Gospel According to St. Matthew," in his *Studies in the Gospels and Epistles*, 68–104; originally in *BJRL* 29 (1946).

117. *The Teaching of Jesus*, 65.

118. Ibid., 81.

119. See T. W. Manson, "The Old Testament in the Teaching of Jesus," *BJRL* 34 (1952): 312–32.

120. *The Teaching of Jesus*, 98.

121. Ibid., 210.

122. In his later essay, "The Son of Man in Daniel, Enoch and the Gospels," in *Studies in the Gospels and Epistles*, 123–45 (originally published in *BJRL* 32 [1950]), Manson abandons this interpretation and reads the earlier references in Mark as referring to Jesus and his disciples, that is, to the community, thus confirming his understanding of the Son of Man as remnant.

123. *The Teaching of Jesus*, 227–28.

124. *Studies in the Gospels and Epistles*, 9–10.

125. *The Teaching of Jesus*, 259.

126. Ibid., 283.

127. "Book II. The Sayings of Jesus," in H. D. A. Major, T. W. Manson, and C. J. Wright, *The Mission and Message of Jesus: An Exposition of the Gospels in the Light of Modern Research* (New York: Dutton, 1938), 299–639; repr. T. W. Manson, *The Sayings of Jesus* (London: SCM, 1949).

128. *Mission and Message*, 301.

129. Ibid., 534.

130. Ibid., 580.

131. Ibid., 582.

132. Ibid.

133. "The Life of Jesus: A Study of the Available Materials," in *Studies in the Gospels and Epistles*, 13–27; originally in *ExpTim* 53 (1942): 248–51.

134. *Studies in the Gospels and Epistles*, 3–12.

135. Ibid., 8. See *HNTR* 2: 231–35.

136. *Studies in the Gospels and Epistles*, 11.

137. T. W. Manson, *The Servant-Messiah* (Cambridge: Cambridge University Press, 1953).

138. See also T. W. Manson, "Sadducee and Pharisee: The Origin and Significance of the Names," *BJRL* 22 (1938): 3–18.

139. *The Servant-Messiah*, 35.

140. Ibid., 50.

141. Ibid., 64.

142. This interpretation is developed in Manson's book, *Jesus and the Non-Jews* (London: Athlone, 1955). Manson insists that "we must think of the Cleansing of the Temple not as a demand for a more spiritual and less materialistic attitude on the part of the Temple clergy, but as a demand to make room in God's house for the Gentiles to come and worship him in peace and quietness" (p. 12). Manson's purpose in this book is to contend that the restriction of ministry to Israel (Matt 10:5-6; 15:24) was only temporary. "I think that Jesus saw the immediate task as that of creating such a community within Israel, in the faith that it would transform the life of his own people, and that a transformed Israel would transform the world" (p. 18).

143. *The Servant-Messiah*, 88.

144. Ibid., 98.

145. Ibid.

146. In *Companion to the Bible*, 97–129.

147. See "The Date of the Epistle to the Philippians," *Studies in the Gospels and Epistles*, 149–67.

148. See "The Problem of the Epistle to the Hebrews," *Studies in the Gospels and Epistles*, 242–58, in which Manson describes Hebrews as "the Epistle of Apollos to the Churches of the Lycus Valley" (p. 242).

149. In *Studies in the Gospels and Epistles*, 225–41; repr. in *The Romans Debate*, ed. Karl P. Donfried, rev. ed. (Peabody, MA: Hendrickson, 1977), 3–15.

150. T. W. Manson, *The Beginning of the Gospel* (London: Oxford University Press, 1950).

151. See pp. 150–52, 332–40 below.

152. T. W. Manson, *Ethics and the Gospel* (New York: Scribner's, 1960), 46. See C. Fitzhugh Spragins, "Is T. W. Manson also Among the Situationists? A Prominent British New Testament Scholar Agrees—and Disagrees—with Situation Ethics," *ExpTim* 81 (1970): 244–47.

153. *Ethics and the Gospel*, 103.

154. T. W. Manson, *The Church's Ministry* (London: Hodder & Stoughton, 1948), 20–21.

155. See T. W. Manson, *Ministry and Priesthood: Christ's and Ours* (London: Epworth, 1958).

156. T. W. Manson, *On Paul and John: Some Selected Theological Themes* (Naperville, IL: Alec R. Allenson, 1963).

157. Ibid., 11.

158. Ibid., 62.

159. Ibid., 122.

160. For Dodd's life and work see F. W. Dillistone, *C. H. Dodd: Interpreter of the New Testament* (Grand Rapids: Eerdmans, 1977); Georg Strecker, "Charles Harold Dodd," *KD* 26 (1980): 50–57; W. D. Davies, "*In Memoriam*: Charles Harold Dodd, 1884–1973," *NTS* 20 (1974): i–v; George B. Caird, "C. H. Dodd," in *A Handbook of Christian Theologians*, ed. Dean G. Peerman and Martin E. Marty, enlarged ed. 1984 (repr. Nashville: Abingdon, 1992), 320–37; F. F. Bruce, "C. H. Dodd," in *Creative Minds in Contemporary Theology*, ed. Philip Edgcumbe Hughes (Grand Rapids: Eerdmans, 1966), 239–69; "Charles Harold Dodd: Curriculum Vitae; Biography of the Works of Charles Harold Dodd," in *The Background of the New Testament and Its Eschatology: In Honour of Charles Harold Dodd*, ed. W. D. Davies and David Daube (Cambridge: Cambridge University Press, 1956), xi–xviii; Ronald W. Graham, "C. H. Dodd: An Introduction to His Theology," unpublished manuscript, archives, Lexington Theological Seminary.

161. See *HNTR* 2: 122–35.

162. See *HNTR* 2: 293–98.

163. C. H. Dodd, *The Epistle of Paul to the Romans*, MNTC (New York: Harper & Brothers, 1932), xvi.

164. See C. H. Dodd, "Natural Law in the New Testament," in idem, *New Testament Studies* (Manchester: Manchester University Press, 1953), 129–42; William A. Beardslee, "Natural Theology and Realized Eschatology," *JR* 39 (1959): 154–61.

165. "Natural Law in the NT," 142.

166. See C. H. Dodd, *History and the Gospel* (New York: Scribner's, 1938; rev. ed. London: Hodder and Stoughton, 1964); "Eschatology and History," appendix to idem, *The Apostolic Preaching and Its Developments* (London: Hodder & Stoughton, 1936, repr. New York: Harper & Row, 1964), 79–96; *The Bible To-Day* (Cambridge: Cambridge University Press, 1946; repr. 1956); C. H. Dodd, "The Kingdom of God and History," in H. G. Wood, C. H. Dodd, et al., *The Kingdom of God and History* (Chicago: Willett, Clark, 1938), 15–38.

167. E.g., C. H. Dodd, *The Authority of the Bible* (New York and London: Harper & Brothers, 1929, 2d ed. 1938; repr. 1958).

168. *History and the Gospel*, 22.

169. Ibid., 118.

170. "Eschatology and History," 95.

171. Ibid., 91.

172. *The Communion of Saints: Being the Ingersoll Lecture on the Immortality of Man for the Academic Year 1934–35* (Cambridge, MA: Harvard Divinity School, 1935); *Eternal Life: Being the Ingersoll Lecture on the Immortality of Man, 1949–1950* (Cambridge, MA: Harvard Divinity School, 1950); repr. *New Testament Studies*, 143–73.

173. Ibid., 169.

174. "In Memoriam," iii.

175. C. H. Dodd, *The Present Task in New Testament Studies* (Cambridge: Cambridge University Press, 1936).

176. "Thirty Years of New Testament Study," *ReL* 47 (1978): 320–29, at 322.

177. *Present Task*, 22.

178. Ibid., 35.

179. See n. 176 above. Originally published in *ReL* 19 (1950) and in *USQR* 5, no. 4 (May 1950): 5–12, the essay was reprinted in *ReL* 47 (1978).

180. Ibid. (1978), 329.

181. C. H. Dodd, *The Authority of the Bible* (New York and London: Harper & Brothers, 1929; 2d ed. 1938; repr. 1958).

182. Ibid., 25.

183. Ibid., 96.

184. Ibid., 190.

185. See *HNTR* 2: 270–73.

186. "The Framework of the Gospel Narrative," in *New Testament Studies* (1953), 1–11. Dodd also published a short popular introduction to the four gospels: *About the Gospels* (Cambridge: Cambridge University Press, 1950), originally addresses presented on the BBC in 1949.

187. *The Authority of the Bible*, 291.

188. C. H. Dodd, *The Meaning of Paul for Today* (New York: Meridian, 1957).

189. Ibid., 19.

190. Ibid., 40–41.

191. Ibid., 44. In *History and the Gospel*, Dodd offers a more positive evaluation of Judaism: "Its faith in God is magnificent; its conception of His nature, character and claims is elevated; its ethical standards are singularly lofty, and certainly compare favourably with any other moral teaching current in our period, even that of the finer Stoics" (p. 81).

192. *The Meaning of Paul*, 86.

193. Ibid., 101.

194. Ibid., 159.

195. *The Epistle of Paul to the Romans* (see n. 163 above)), xiii.

196. Ibid., xxv.

197. Ibid., 55.

198. Ibid., 59.

199. Ibid., 186. Besides his Romans commentary, Dodd also contributed the sections on Ephesians, Colossians, and Philemon to *The Abingdon Bible Commentary*, ed. Frederick Carl Eiselen, Edwin Lewis, and David G. Downey (New York: Abingdon-Cokesbury, 1929).

200. C. H. Dodd, *The Parables of the Kingdom* (New York: Scribner's, 1936; rev. ed. 1961).

201. See *HNTR* 2: 229–37.

202. See *HNTR* 2: 158–59.

203. *The Parables of the Kingdom*, 5.

204. Ibid., 26.

205. Dodd's influence on the NEB is also evident in Matt 12:28 and Luke 11:20, where the term "already" is also inserted.

206. *The Parables of the Kingdom*, 54–55.

207. Ibid., 82.

208. Ibid., 83.

209. Ibid., 159. In the preface to the 2d ed. of his *Parables of the Kingdom*, Dodd acknowledges that the expression "realized eschatology" is "not very felicitous" (p. viii), and in a footnote in *The Interpretation of the Fourth Gospel* (Cambridge: Cambridge University Press, 1953; repr. 1954), 447, he commends the suggestions of "inaugurated eschatology" (by George Florovsky) and "sich realisierende Eschatologie" (by Joachim Jeremias). These phrases indicate that Dodd has come to the view that the kingdom has not come in a single event but comes in the ministry of Jesus, in future crises (like the fall of Jerusalem), and in the supra-historical future; see Dodd's *The Coming of Christ: Four Broadcast Addresses for the Season of Advent* (Cambridge: Cambridge University Press, 1951).

210. See Norman Perrin, *The Kingdom of God in the Teaching of Jesus* (Philadelphia: Westminster, 1963), 58–78; Richard H. Hiers, Jr., "Pivotal Reactions to the Eschatological Interpretations: Rudolf Bultmann and C. H. Dodd," in *The Kingdom of God in 20th Century Interpretation*, ed. Wendell Willis (Peabody, MA: Hendrickson, 1987), 15–33.

211. C. H. Dodd, *The Apostolic Preaching and Its Developments* (London: Hodder and Stoughton, 1936; repr. New York: Harper & Row, 1964).

212. Ibid., 7.

213. Ibid., 13.

214. Ibid., 17.

215. Ibid., 42.

216. Ibid., 56.

217. Ibid., 65.

218. Ibid., 69.

219. Ibid., 74.

220. C. H. Dodd, *According to the Scriptures: the Sub-Structure of New Testament Theology* (London: Nisbet, 1952; repr. 1953). The basic argument of this book is presented in short form in C. H. Dodd, *The Old Testament in the New* (Philadelphia: Fortress Press, 1963).

221. *According to the Scriptures*, 12.

222. See *HNTR* 2: 405–6.

223. *According to the Scriptures*, 57.

224. C. H. Dodd, *Gospel and Law: The Relation of Faith and Ethics in Early Christianity* (Cambridge: Cambridge University Press, 1951). Dodd's concern with ethics and the ethical implications of the gospel is also evident in his *Christ and the New Humanity* (Philadelphia: Fortress Press, 1965); this pamphlet includes two essays, "Christianity and the Reconciliation of the

Nations" (a lecture originally given in 1951), and "The Gospel and the Law of Christ" (a lecture given in 1946).

225. *Gospel and Law*, 66.

226. The eschatological setting is simply Dodd's realized eschatology, namely, that eternal reality enters into history, but the objective facts of history are essential to this eschatology. See William Baird, "What is the Kerygma: A Study of I Cor 15:3-8 and Gal 1:11-17," *JBL* 76 (1957): 181–91.

227. See John J. Vincent, "Didactic Kerygma in the Synoptic Gospels," *SJT* 10 (1957): 262–73; Stephen J. England, "The Tradition of the Life and Teachings of Jesus in the 'Kerygma,'" *Enc* 21 (1960): 81–92; Albert C. Sundberg, Jr., "On Testimonies," *NovT* 3 (1959): 268–81. Sundberg provides data to indicate that Dodd's identification of particular OT texts as constituting the Bible of the early church is mistaken; he also questions Dodd's notion of a harmonious early Christian hermeneutic.

228. C. H. Dodd, *The Johannine Epistles*, MNTC (New York and London: Harper & Brothers, 1946).

229. Ibid., liv.

230. Ibid., 16.

231. C. H. Dodd, *The Interpretation of the Fourth Gospel* (Cambridge: Cambridge University Press, 1953; repr. 1954).

232. See Jörg Frey, *Die johanneische Eschatologie 1: Ihre Probleme im Spiegel der Forschung seit Reimarus*, WUNT 96 (Tübingen: Mohr Siebeck, 1997), 247–51.

233. Dodd's research on Hellenistic backgrounds is presented in his book, *The Bible and the Greeks* (London: Hodder & Stoughton, 1934; repr. 1954). Here Dodd considers the religious vocabulary of Hellenistic Judaism and investigates the Hermetic literature as an example of the Hellenistic syncretism that influenced early Christianity.

234. *Interpretation of the Fourth Gospel*, 44.

235. Ibid., 73.

236. Ibid., 130.

237. Ibid., 133.

238. Ibid., 142.

239. Ibid., 177–78.

240. Ibid., 186.

241. Ibid., 248–49.

242. Ibid., 262.

243. Ibid., 278.

244. Ibid., 285.

245. Ibid., 439.

246. Dodd also contributed to a collection of essays on the Fourth Gospel: "The Prologue to the Fourth Gospel and Christian Worship," in *Studies in the Fourth Gospel*, ed. Frank Leslie Cross (London: Mowbray, 1957), 9–22. In this essay Dodd finds the foundation of Christian worship in the incarnation, the Word made flesh in whom the glory of God is revealed.

247. C. H. Dodd, *Historical Tradition in the Fourth Gospel* (Cambridge: Cambridge University Press, 1963).

248. Ibid., 8.

249. Ibid., 16.

250. Ibid., 150.

251. Ibid., 334.

252. Ibid., 418.

253. Ibid., 420.

254. Ibid., 423.

255. For a summary and analysis of Dodd's work and its influence see D. Moody Smith, *John Among the Gospels*, 2d ed. (Columbia, SC: University of South Carolina Press, 2001), 53–63.

256. See A. M. Hunter, "C. H. Dodd's Historical Tradition in the Fourth Gospel," *ExpTim* 75 (1963–64): 146–47; J. S. King, "There and Back Again," *EvQ* 55 (1983): 145–57.

257. See Donald A. Carson, "Historical Tradition in the Fourth Gospel: After Dodd, What?" in *Gospel Perspectives: Studies of History and Tradition in the Four Gospels*, ed. R. T. France and David Wenham (Sheffield: JSOT Press, 1981) 2: 83–145. Carson also notes the criticism that Dodd does not adequately engage in interaction with other scholars.

258. See Rudolf Bultmann, "The Interpretation of the Fourth Gospel," *NTS* 1 (1954–55): 77–91. Bultmann also criticizes what he considers to be Dodd's overemphasis on OT–Jewish backgrounds.

259. Dodd supports the position of Percival Gardner-Smith, *Saint John and the Synoptic Gospels* (Cambridge: Cambridge University Press, 1938). For a survey of later discussion of sources see Donald A. Carson, "Current Source Criticism of the Fourth Gospel: Some Methodological Questions," *JBL* 97 (1978): 411–29.

260. C. H. Dodd, *The Founder of Christianity* (New York: Macmillan; London: Collier-Macmillan, 1970).

261. In *A Companion to the Bible*, ed. T. W. Manson (New York: Scribner's, 1939), 367–89; to this volume Dodd also contributed "The History and Doctrine of the Apostolic Age" (pp. 390–417), a concise account of his understanding of the history and thought of the church in the first century.

262. *The Founder of Christianity*, 116.

263. Ibid., 123.

264. Ibid., 171.

265. See *HNTR* 2: 261–66.

266. *HNTR* 2: 147–49.

267. *HNTR* 2: 231–35.

2

The New Biblical Theology

The second quarter of the twentieth century was an era of crisis. World War I ended with ten million dead troops and a million civilian casualties. The Treaty of Versailles deprived Germany of 13 percent of its territory and 19 percent of its heavy industry. This devastation of land and economy prepared the way for the triumph of National Socialism and the dictatorial rule of Adolf Hitler. Dictatorships arose, too, in Italy and on the Iberian Peninsula. In Spain totalitarianism was attained by the Spanish civil war, grotesquely portrayed by Pablo Picasso's "Guernica." General Francisco Franco was aided by Hitler and Mussolini, who were warming up for World War II. The earlier war, the "Great War," had not ended all wars or made the world safe for democracy. Instead, the second World War surpassed it in scope and terror, heaping up thirty-five million casualties. Innocent noncombatants were targeted in a way that was unprecedented. Dresden, an architectural jewel with little strategic significance, was destroyed in two nights by eight hundred British Lancasters and three hundred American B-17s, leaving over one hundred twenty-five thousand bodies in the rubble. At Hiroshima more than seventy thousand people perished at the dropping of the first A-bomb, and in time that number was doubled by the radioactive fallout. The awesome mushroom cloud signaled the beginning of the atomic age. Human beings, mastering the elementary unit of matter, had within their grasp the power to destroy civilization.

Theologians responded to the crisis of the times with a theology of crisis. Earlier, Wilhelm Wrede and Albert Schweitzer had destroyed the Jesus of liberalism.[1] Now the whole liberal world—the Victorian world of peace, prosperity, progress, and politeness—had collapsed. In Germany some of the "Friends of the Christian World," a company of liberal theologians, became the foes of the prevailing culture and launched a new journal, *Zwischen den Zeiten*. This title venerated a dramatic speech, "Between the Times," by Friedrich Gogarten,[2] according to whom "[i]t is the destiny of our generation to stand between the times. We never belonged to the period presently coming to an end; it is doubtful whether we shall ever belong to the period which is to come."[3] The old world to which they did not belong was about to perish, and good riddance! In 1914, Karl Barth was shocked by the stance of ninety-three German intellectuals who signed a manifesto in support of the bellicose policy of Kaiser Wilhelm II—among them Barth's teacher, the doyen of liberalism, Adolf von Harnack. Barth's commentary on Romans became the bugle call to battle.

DIALECTICAL THEOLOGY AND DOGMATICS: KARL BARTH (1886–1968)

Barth, the herald of the new theological venture, believed he had sounded the alarm unaware. "As I look back upon my course, I seem to myself as one who, ascending the dark staircase of a church tower and trying to steady himself, reached for the banister, but got hold of the bell rope instead. To his horror, he had then to listen to what the great bell had sounded over and not over him alone."[4] In any event, Barth was destined to become the most important theologian of the twentieth century.

LIFE AND THEOLOGICAL DEVELOPMENT

Karl Barth was born in Basel, Switzerland, the son of an instructor in the college of preachers who was later a professor of church history at Bern.[5] The young Barth began his university studies at Bern (1904), but transferred to Berlin, where he was impressed by Harnack. After further study at Tübingen, Barth moved to Marburg (1908) and fell under the spell of Wilhelm Herrmann. While at Marburg, Barth worked as an assistant to Martin Rade, editor of the liberal journal *Die christliche Welt*. From 1911 to 1921 Barth served as pastor in the village of Safenwil (Aargau). He became increasingly disillusioned with liberalism and the Christian socialism he had earlier embraced. He began to read the Bible intensely, and discovered the strange world of the Bible, the world of God. In 1916 Barth began work on his Romans commentary, which was published in 1919 in an edition of only a thousand copies. Barth moved to Göttingen in 1921, where he assumed the chair of Reformed Theology. From 1925 to 1930 he served as professor of dogmatics and NT at Münster. In 1930 he moved to a similar position at Bonn, where he increasingly opposed National Socialism. He was the primary author of the Barmen Confession (1934), the statement of faith of the anti-Nazi Confessing church.[6] Barth was banished from Bonn because he refused to sign a loyalty oath and open his lectures with a salute to Adolf Hitler.

In 1935 Barth moved to Basel, where he lectured on dogmatics. He attracted students from around the globe and lectured widely in Europe, including the Gifford Lectures in Scotland. Barth was a devotee of the music of Mozart, and he presented the memorial address on the occasion of the two hundredth anniversary of the composer's birth.[7] "But the golden sounds and melodies of Mozart's music," wrote Barth, "have from early times spoken to me not as gospel but as parables of the realm of God's free grace as revealed in the gospel—and they do so again and again with great spontaneity and directness."[8] Barth retired in 1961, and in 1962 he spent seven weeks in the United States, where he lectured at Princeton and Chicago. He was a person of genuine humanity, noted for his sharp wit and sense of humor. His opponents considered him combative, though Barth himself said, "I am by nature a gentle being and entirely averse to all unnecessary disputes."[9]

BARTH'S THEOLOGY

Over Barth's desk hung a copy of Matthias Grünewald's "Crucifixion" from the Isenheim altarpiece. In the picture John the Baptist holds the Bible in one hand, and with the other he points to the suffering Christ. This is the role Barth adopts as his theological task.[10] His theology is usually described as developing in three stages. In the first, his thought was dominated by the liberalism he had learned from his teachers. In the second, he turned to dialectical theology—a turn provoked by the collapse of liberalism in the face of World War I. At this stage Barth proclaimed God as the subject and content of revelation. He stressed the gospel as objective, including concrete historical events as the positive grounds of revelation, a view that has been characterized as a "positivism of revelation" or "otherworldly positivism."[11] In the third stage, Barth moves to the mature theology of his *Church Dogmatics*—a move marked by his book on Anselm (1931).[12] About the change, Barth writes: "The positive factor in the new development was this: in these years I had to learn that Christian doctrine, if it is to merit its name and if it is to build up the Christian church in the world as she needs to be built up, has to be exclusively and conclusively the doctrine of Jesus Christ—of Jesus Christ as the living Word of God spoken to us men." Barth describes this development as "christological concentration."[13]

The theology of the second stage is often characterized as the "early Barth"—the Barth of the period of the commentary on Romans.[14] In this stage Barth, like a raging bull, goes on the attack. He assaults religion with its quest for religious experience—the futile attempt to bring God near, to manipulate God. According to Barth this kind of religion is in reality a revolt against God. Two kinds of theology, he says, deserve to be destroyed: one that reduces doctrine to anthropology, and one based on some antecedent system of thought. Barth believes all humans to be hopeless sinners, standing under the wrath of God. Release from this predicament depends totally and exclusively on the action of God. God reveals the impossible possibility: freedom from sin through the death and resurrection of Christ. This act of grace offers an indicative—the transformation of humans—and an imperative: obedience to God's love in love of neighbor. All of this Barth pours out in a rhetorical cascade of crises, offenses, and paradoxes.

Barth's break with liberalism is apparent in his debate with Harnack.[15] In response to Barth's *Epistle to the Romans*, Harnack charges him with the destruction of historical criticism. Barth, says Harnack, has turned the teaching chair into a pulpit. In response Barth declares that the task of theology and the task of preaching are one and the same. Harnack's essay, "Fifteen Questions to Those Among the Theologians Who Are Contemptuous of the Scientific Theology," contends that Christianity is a historical religion and must be interpreted by scientific historical research. "If the person of Jesus Christ stands in the center of the gospel, how," asks Harnack, "can the basis for a reliable and common knowledge of this person be gained other than through critical historical study, lest we exchange the real Christ for one we have imagined?"[16] Barth's answer assumes his radical view of faith.

> The reliability and common nature of the knowledge of the person of Jesus Christ as the midpoint of the gospel can be no other than that of a faith awakened by God. Critical historical study signifies the deserved and necessary end of the "bases" of this knowledge, which are not really bases, because they were not laid by God himself. He who still does not know ... that we no longer know Christ according to the flesh may let himself be told this by critical biblical science; the more radically he is terrified the better it is for him and for the subject matter.[17]

Later, in "An Open Letter to Professor Karl Barth," Harnack asserts that if Barth's method were adopted, the teaching of the gospel would be "exclusively handed over to revival preachers, who freely create their understanding of the Bible."[18] In answer, Barth declares:

> What I must defend myself against is not historical criticism, but rather the matter-of-course way in which one, still today, empties theology's task: Instead of that which our predecessors called "the Word" (the correlation of "Scripture" and "Spirit") one has placed this

and that which have been dug up by historical criticism beyond the "Scripture" and apart from the "Spirit," which one calls the "simple gospel," a gospel that can be called "word of God" only as a figure of speech, because it is in fact at best a human expression thereof.[19]

Harnack replies: "A scientific theological presentation can also inspire and edify, thanks to its object, but the scientific theologian who is bent on inspiration and edification brings strange fire upon his altar, for as there is only one scientific method, so there is also only one scientific task—the pure knowledge of its object."[20] To this Barth responds, "The concept of revelation is not a scientific concept."[21]

As noted above, the emergence of Barth's mature theology is evident in his book on Anselm (1931). "Among all my books," says Barth, "I regard this as the one written with the greatest satisfaction."[22] Barth believes that Anselm's theme, "faith seeking understanding," affirms that the content of faith is given by revelation, and that reason demonstrates the inner coherence of faith. Barth also recalls his theological shifts in his lectures on *The Humanity of God* (1956).[23] "What began forcibly to press itself upon us about forty years ago was not so much the humanity of God as His *deity*—a God absolutely unique in His relation to man and the world, overpoweringly lofty and distant, strange, yes even wholly other."[24] As the years went by, Barth came increasingly to believe that the deity of God had its meaning in history and in relation with humans. The humanity of God is disclosed in Christ, the mediator, revealer, and reconciler.

> In Jesus Christ there is no isolation of man from God or of God from man. Rather, in Him we encounter the history, the dialogue, in which God and man meet together and are together, the reality of the covenant mutually contracted, preserved, and fulfilled by them. Jesus Christ is in His one Person, as true God, man's loyal partner, as true man, God's.[25]

This understanding of the humanity of God entails, in Barth's opinion, an affirmation of the significance of humanity—a humanity not destroyed by the fall. Moreover, the humanity of God affirms the importance of human community. The church is "the place where God's glory wills to dwell upon earth, that is, where humanity—the humanity of God—wills to assume tangible form in time and here upon earth."[26] The shift in Barth's thought is also seen in the change of the title of the work that spanned his lifetime. In 1928 he published the prolegomena to Christian Dogmatics; in 1932 he published the first volume of Church Dogmatics.

Karl Barth's *Dogmatics* is one of the greatest works in the history of Christian doctrine.[27] The product of over thirty-five years of arduous research and reflection, Barth's work filled twelve large volumes, a thirteenth left unfinished at his death. To be sure, Barth seemed to think every thought that entered his mind was worth writing down, but profound thoughts they were. The daunted reader is swamped with detail and perturbed by repetition. Even to Barth himself the mammoth project appeared a little ridiculous.

> The angels laugh at old Karl. They laugh at him because he tries to grasp the truth about God in a book of Dogmatics. They laugh at the fact that volume follows volume and each is thicker than the previous one. As they laugh, they say to one another, "Look! Here he comes now with his little pushcart full of volumes of the Dogmatics!"—and they laugh about the men who write so much about Karl Barth instead of writing about the things he is trying to write about. Truly, the angels laugh.[28]

The content of the Dogmatics is arranged according to four main doctrines: The Doctrine of the Word of God, the Doctrine of God, the Doctrine of Creation, and the Doctrine of Reconciliation. The discussions of these doctrines are ordered into chapters, numbered sequentially throughout the entire work, and the chapters are divided into sections (§§), which are also numbered sequentially throughout the entire work. Each of these numbered sections begins with a proposition summarizing the argument that follows. The sections are divided into subsections. Material in smaller type presents expanded argument and exegetical evidence. Many segments of this gigantic work are crucial for understanding Barth's contribution to the history of NT research.

In explicating the Doctrine of the Word of God, Barth starts with "The Word of God as the Criterion of Dogmatics" (chapter 1). He begins by discussing "Church Proclamation as the Material of Dogmatics" (§3).[29] According to Barth the Word of God is expressed in three forms. First, the Word is preached; it is event, action of God. "The Word of God preached means . . . man's talk about God in which and through which God speaks about Himself."[30] Second, the Word is written. "The Bible is God's Word to the extent that God causes it to be His Word, to the extent that He speaks through it."[31] Third, the Word is revealed. "Revelation," says Barth, "in fact does not differ from the person of Jesus Christ nor from the reconciliation accomplished in Him. To say revelation is to say 'The Word became flesh.' "[32] As to the nature of the Word, Barth believes the revelation in Christ shows that it is personal Word and cannot be reduced to a human system. Through proclamation and Scripture, Christ becomes contemporary: God with us.

In chapter 2, "The Revelation of God," Barth insists that the God of revelation is the triune God.

> The God who reveals Himself according to Scripture is One in three distinctive modes of being subsisting in their mutual relations: Father, Son, and Holy Spirit. It is thus that He is the Lord, i.e., the Thou who meets man's I and unites Himself to this I as the indissoluble Subject and thereby and therein reveals Himself to him as his Lord.[33]

According to Barth, God the Father is the Creator; God the Son is the Reconciler. Barth believes such texts as Col 2:9 and Titus 2:13 affirm the deity of Christ. "To confess Him as the revelation of His Father," says Barth, "is to confess Him as essentially equal in deity with this Father of His."[34] Barth insists that Christ is the eternal Son. He does not become Son at his revelation; he is Son from eternity. His humanity is co-eternal with his divinity. God the Holy Spirit is God the redeemer.

Barth's doctrine of the Incarnation is more fully explicated in the second part of Chapter 2, "The Incarnation of the Word," in the second half-volume of *The Doctrine of the Word of God*.[35] In the first section (§13) he discusses "God's Freedom for Man." Here Barth contends that Jesus Christ is the objective reality of revelation. Barth believes the Synoptics begin with the humanity of the One who shows himself to be the Son of God by the resurrection, while John begins with the mystery of the God who takes on the flesh of humanity. "To sum up: that God's Son or Word is the man Jesus of Nazareth is the one christological thesis of the New Testament; that the man Jesus of Nazareth is God's Son or Word is the other."[36] In regard to "The Time of Revelation" (§14), Barth argues that the revelation in history was a miraculous event. He thinks that Jesus Christ was already revealed as the "expected One" in the Hebrew Bible, and that "on the basis of the covenant Jesus Christ had to be crucified."[37]

The next section (§15) investigates "The Mystery of Revelation." Barth believes the sign of the mystery is seen in the resurrection and the miraculous birth of Jesus. In a small print section he discusses the texts and problems regarding the doctrine of the virgin birth. He acknowledges that the doctrine is explicit only in Matthew and Luke, that the Sinaitic Syriac text of Matt 1:16

reads: "Joseph . . . begat Jesus," and that the genealogies of Matthew and Luke present Jesus as the son of David. In Barth's opinion the doctrine does not stand or fall on the basis of this evidence. "The final and proper decision is whether in accord with the demands of Church dogma this testimony is to be heard and heard as the emphatic statement of the New Testament message, or whether in defiance of Church dogma it is not to be heard, i.e., only to be heard as a sub-statement of the New Testament message which is not binding."[38] The doctrine of the virgin birth, according to Barth, affirms the freedom and sovereignty of God. It also "signifies the exclusion of sin in the sense of *peccatum originale*."[39] He concludes:

> The man Jesus of Nazareth is not the true Son of God because He was conceived by the Holy Spirit and born of the Virgin Mary. On the contrary, because He is the true Son of God and because this is an inconceivable mystery intended to be acknowledged as such, therefore He is conceived by the Holy Spirit and born of the Virgin Mary. And because He is conceived and born, He has to be recognised and acknowledged as the One He is and in the mystery in which He is the One He is.[40]

Barth believes that dogmatics is fundamentally Christology. His treatment of this crucial doctrine is found in the fourth main part of his *Dogmatics, The Doctrine of Reconciliation*.[41] Chapter 14 deals with "Jesus Christ, the Lord and Servant," and §59 discusses "The Obedience of the Son of God." The introductory proposition reads:

> That Jesus Christ is very God is shown in His way into the far country in which He the Lord became a servant. For in the majesty of the true God it happened that the eternal Son of the eternal Father became obedient by offering and humbling Himself to be the brother of man, to take His place with the transgressor, to judge him by judging Himself and dying in his place. But God the Father raised Him from the dead, and in so doing recognised and gave effect to His death and passion as a satisfaction made for us, as our conversion to God, and therefore as our redemption from death to life.[42]

The first subsection, "The Way of the Son of God into the Far Country" presents Barth's doctrine of the incarnation. Going into a "far country"—a phrase taken from the parable of the Prodigal Son—describes the incarnation of Christ in history. According to Barth the full humanity of the incarnate

Son does not compromise his divinity. Although exalted titles are used, Barth believes the NT avoids any taint of docetism; the Word became "Jewish flesh."[43] However, the humiliation and condescension of the Son (Phil 2:7) does not, according to Barth, alter or diminish his deity.

A second subsection discusses "The Judge Judged in Our Place" and is a presentation of Barth's doctrine of the atonement. In Barth's view the Son enters into the world and becomes sinner and enemy of God, taking the place of sinful humans. Barth asserts that Christ is Judge "for us," and explicates this phrase by investigating (in small print) the prepositions used in the NT: ἀντί, ὑπέρ, and περί. He continues:

> The passion of Jesus Christ is the judgment of God in which the Judge Himself was the judged. And as such it is at its heart and centre the victory which has been won for us, in our place, in the battle against sin. . . . As the passion of the Son of God who became man for us it is the radical divine action which attacks and destroys at its very root the primary evil in the world.[44]

Barth also emphasizes the obedience of Jesus Christ. In a long small print passage (of more than thirteen pages) he exegetes the Gospel narratives of the temptation and the agony in Gethsemane. In regard to the latter he insists that there was no real conflict between the will of Jesus and the will of God; Christ was only praying for some other way to fulfill God's will. A final subsection presents "The Verdict of the Father." Here Barth explores the question: Since the revelation occurred in history, how can Christ be present today? His answer: the resurrection, an event of a different kind that takes place in time and space and makes the event of Christ an eternal event, contemporary and universal. Barth concludes that "we can do justice to the Easter narratives of the New Testament only if we accept their presupposition that in the story which they recount we have to do with an 'act of God,' the act of God in which it was revealed to the disciples that the happening of the cross was the redemptive happening promised to them, on which therefore the community and its message were founded."[45]

BARTH AND THE BIBLE

Barth is, from start to finish, a biblical theologian.[46] The task of theology, he thinks, is to explicate the biblical revelation. His *Church Dogmatics* contains over twelve thousand references to the NT. In this magnum opus Barth presents more than seventy lengthy exegetical investigations and some two thousand shorter exegetical studies. His view of the Bible during his sojourn in Göttingen (1921–25) is published in *Das Wort Gottes und die Theologie*.[47] Reflecting the thought of the "early Barth," this book understands the Bible to be primarily concerned with the transcendent God.

> God is the new, incomparable, unattainable, not only heavenly but more than heavenly interest, who has drawn the regard of the men of the Bible to himself. He desires their complete attention, their entire obedience. For he must be true to himself; he must be and remain holy. He cannot be grasped, brought under management, and put to use; he cannot serve. He must rule. He must himself grasp, seize, manage, use. He can satisfy no other needs than his own. He is not in another world against this one; he submerges all of this in the other. He is not a thing among other things, but the Wholly Other, the infinite aggregate of all merely relative others. He is not the form of religious history but is the Lord of our life, the eternal Lord of the world.[48]

Barth's mature understanding is found in his *Church Dogmatics*, Chapter 3, entitled "Holy Scripture."[49] The proposition for §19, "The Word of God for the Church," reads:

> The Word of God is God Himself in Holy Scripture. For God once spoke as Lord to Moses and the prophets, to the Evangelists and apostles. And now through their written word He speaks as the same Lord to His Church. Scripture is holy and the Word of God, because by the Holy Spirit it became and will become to the Church a witness to divine revelation.[50]

In the first subsection Barth discusses "Scripture as Witness to Divine Revelation." The Bible, according to him, is not identical with revelation; it witnesses to revelation; it is written in human words by human beings. Barth argues that there is "no special biblical hermeneutics," but that biblical interpretation is simply "the special form" of the universally valid hermeneutic principle.[51] However, what makes biblical hermeneutics different is its theme: the history of Jesus Christ. This theme requires a circular understanding: the interpreter must know the subject, but the subject can only be known through the text. Barth belittles a false objectivity: "There is a notion that complete impartiality is the most fitting and indeed the normal disposition for true exegesis, because it guarantees a complete absence of prejudice. For a short time, around 1910, this idea threatened to achieve almost canonical status in Protestant theology. But now we can quite calmly describe it a merely comical."[52] According to Barth the text has only one meaning. "In exegesis, too—and especially in exegesis—there is only one truth."[53]

In the second subsection Barth discusses "Scripture as Word of God." According to him the church did not create but only confirmed the canon. The canon affirms the unity of Scripture, but Barth does not believe the canon is closed absolutely. For him the doctrine of Scripture is based on the Bible, and such texts as 2 Tim 3:14-17 and 2 Pet 1:19-21 indicate that the Holy Spirit is the author of Scripture. Barth presents a long discussion in small print in which he argues against the doctrine of infallibility. He says that "the vulnerability of the Bible, i.e., its capacity for error, also extends to its religious and theological content. . . . [T]he biblical authors shared the outlook and spoke the language of their own day." Between John and the Synoptics, Barth detects "obvious overlappings and contradictions."[54] "The Bible," says Barth, "is not the Word of God on earth in the same way as Jesus Christ, very God and very man, is that Word in heaven."[55] In §20, "Authority in the Church," Barth argues that Scripture has authority "because it is a record, indeed historically it is the oldest extant record, of the origin and therefore of the basis and nature of the Church."[56] Although it is the singular authority in the church, the Bible's authority is relative; it only represents divine authority. Scripture witnesses to the authority of Christ, the Lord of the church.

In §21, "Freedom in the Church," Barth includes a discussion of the interpretation of Scripture.[57] The obligation to interpret and apply Scripture, according to Barth, rests on all members of the church and "not upon a specialised class of biblical scholars."[58] As to method, Barth proposes three steps. The first, *explicatio*, involves literary and historical investigation. "I must try to hear the words of the prophets and apostles in exactly the same freedom in which I attempt to hear the words of others who speak to me or have written for me as in the main intelligible words. That means that I must try to hear them as documents in their concrete historical situation."[59] He continues: "For this purpose I use the methods of source-criticism, lexicography, grammar, syntax and appreciation of style."[60]

Already in his *Epistle to the Romans*, Barth had addressed the problem of criticism.

> The historical critical method of Biblical investigation has its rightful
> place. . . . But, were I driven to choose between it and the venerable
> doctrine of Inspiration, I should without hesitation adopt the latter.

. . . The doctrine of Inspiration is concerned with the labour of apprehending, without which no technical equipment . . . is on any use whatsoever. Fortunately, I am not compelled to choose between the two. Nevertheless, my whole energy of interpreting has been expended in an endeavour to see through and beyond history into the spirit of the Bible, which is the Eternal Spirit. . . . If we rightly understand ourselves, our problems are the problems of Paul; and if we be enlightened by the brightness of his answers, those answers must be ours.[61]

Throughout his career Barth remained suspicious of the pretended objectivity, excessive skepticism, and dearth of theological insight among most NT critics. He spoke, for example, of scholars "who to my amazement have armed themselves with swords and staves and once again undertaken the search for the 'historical Jesus'—a search in which I now as before prefer not to participate."[62]

The second step in exegesis, *meditatio*, goes beyond criticism to theological reflection. This step, according to Barth, involves the situation and perspective of the interpreter. It even makes use of philosophy. "If we hold up hands of horror at the very idea, we must not forget that without such systems of explanation, without such spectacles, we cannot read the Bible at all." We must assume "some philosophy or other" but there is no one, absolute philosophy.[63] The philosophical perspective is, according to Barth, subordinate to Scripture and must be controlled by Scripture. Most of all Barth believes one must wrestle with the subject matter until the interpreter is one with the author. As he had said in the preface to the second edition of the Romans commentary:

Intelligent comment means that I am driven on till I stand with nothing before me but the enigma of the matter; till the document seems hardly to exist as a document; till I have almost forgotten that I am not its author; till I know the author so well that I allow him to speak in my name and am even able to speak in his name myself.[64]

The third stage is *applicatio*—the use of the scriptural Word so that it becomes contemporary. Barth says that "instead of making use of Scripture at every stage, it is Scripture itself which uses us—the *usus scripturae* in which *scriptura* is not object but subject, and the hearer and reader is not subject but object."[65]

BARTH'S COMMENTARIES

Karl Barth's *Epistle to the Romans* was a theological scandal. In the preface to the sixth edition (1928) Barth observes that the book gave offense, and that he sends it out again because it continues to give offense. As he says in an early preface, "I had set out to please none but the very few, to swim against the current, to beat upon doors which I thought were firmly bolted."[66] The second edition (1922) is a total revision of the first, written because Barth had continued to read Franz Overbeck, Plato, Kant, Kierkegaard, and Dostoevsky—but most of all, Paul. "Paul knows of God what most of us do not know; and his Epistles enable us to know what he knew."[67] What Paul knew, according to Barth, is missed by scholars who heap up data from the history of religion. "I entirely fail to see why parallels drawn from the ancient world . . . should be of more value for an understanding of the Epistle than the situation in which we ourselves actually are, and to which we can therefore bear witness."[68]

In format the commentary totals over five hundred pages and offers no critical introduction. The material is ordered according to the chapters of the Epistle. The chapters are given titles and divided into subsections that are also titled. The exegesis is presented in running paragraphs, and the words and phrases under consideration are printed in bold type. Introductory paragraphs at the beginning of the major sections (chapters) often raise questions that anticipate the subsequent exegesis. A few examples can scarcely do justice to the force of Barth's rhetoric and the power of his theological insight.

In chapter 1, which he entitles "Introduction," Barth does not consider the possibility that Rom 1:2-4 reflects an early creedal formula, or that vv. 8-18 represent the conventional Pauline thanksgiving. Instead, he interprets the "gospel of God" according to his own theological perspective. "The Gospel," writes Barth, "proclaims a God utterly distinct from men. Salvation comes to them from Him, because they are, as men, incapable of knowing Him, and because they have no right to claim anything from him."[69] In regard to "The Theme of the Epistle" (1:16-17), Barth sees in Paul's declaration that he is not ashamed of the gospel an allusion to the futility of Christian apologetics. The problematic phrase "through faith for faith" (v. 17) Barth interprets as meaning from the "faithfulness of God" to the "fidelity of men." Barth describes the subsection 1:18-32 as "The Night." The cause of this darkness is the ungodliness of humans, their "rebellion against God." What can be known through God's creation (*contra* natural theology) is "the invisibility of God." "And what does this mean but that we can know nothing of God, that we are not God, that the Lord is to be feared?"[70] Failure to recognize that they can know nothing of God, according to Barth, is the reason humans are without excuse. The confusion between Creator and creation has tragic consequences.

> The distance between God and man had no longer its essential, sharp, acid, and disintegrating ultimate significance. The difference between the incorruption, the pre-eminence and originality of God, and the corruption, the boundedness and relativity of men had been confused. Once the eye, which can perceive this distinction, has been blinded, there arises in the midst, between here and there, between us and the 'Wholly Other,' a mist or concoction of religion.[71]

Barth entitles his exposition of Chapter 3, "The Righteousness of God." The subsection 3:21-31 is titled "Jesus." Barth sees in the phrase "but now" a reference to the ultimate crisis—a favorite word, usually printed KRISIS. "*But now* directs our attention to time which is beyond time, to space which has no locality, to impossible possibility, to the gospel of transformation, to the imminent Coming of the Kingdom of God, to affirmation in negation to salvation in the world, to acquittal in condemnation, to eternity in time, to life in death."[72] The righteousness of God, according to Barth, comes from outside; it is the forensic righteousness which the Judge pronounces—the righteousness revealed in Jesus.

> The faithfulness of God is established when we meet the Christ in Jesus. . . . [W]e meet truth of another order at one point in time, at one place in that time which is illuminated throughout by reality and by the answer of God. . . . Our discovery of the Christ in Jesus of Nazareth is authorized by the fact that every manifestation of the faithfulness of God points and bears witness to what we have actually encountered in Jesus.[73]

Barth translates ἱλαστήριον as "a covering of propitiation" and sees the "mercy seat" as an analogy for Jesus; he interprets the idea of covering (Kapporeth) paradoxically: atoning activity is "in Jesus covered as well as displayed."[74] This gift of God's righteousness can be received only by faith. "Credo, quia absurdum."[75]

Barth exegetes Romans 5 under the theme, "The Coming Day." Within 5:1-11, "The New Man," Barth discusses the textual variant in v. 1. He favors the reading ἔχομεν ("we have" peace) rather than ἔχωμεν ("let us have" peace) because he thinks the latter it is not as well attested and does not fit the context.[76] In discussing 5:12-21, "The New World," Barth rejects the traditional doctrine of original sin. He believes that the sin of Adam that brought death into the world was not a historical event. That event is, "like the righteousness manifested to the world in Christ, timeless and transcendental."[77] He continues: "The Fall is not occasioned by the transgression of Adam; but the transgression was presumably its first manifest operation."[78] In regard to 6:1-11, "The Power of the Resurrection," Barth emphasizes the uniqueness of the resurrection. He says that "the raising of Jesus from the dead is not an event in history elongated so as still to remain an event in the midst of other events. The Resurrection is the non-historical . . . relating of the whole historical life of Jesus to its origin in God."[79] In regard to Rom 7:14-25, Barth rejects the idea that Paul is presenting his personal biography prior to his conversion.

> Paul is not describing the situation before his conversion! . . . Paul describes his past, present, and future existence. He portrays a situation as real after the episode on the road to Damascus as before it. He is writing about a man, broken in two by the law, but who, according to the law, cannot be thus broken. Paul is thrust into a dualism which contradicts itself. He is shattered on God, without the possibility of forgetting Him.[80]

The "I" of the text, says Barth, is humanity; the time of the text is eternity; the "law" of the text is religion.

Romans 8:3-4 is of crucial importance to Barth. Here Paul describes God's act of "sending his own Son in the likeness of sinful flesh." Barth titles this subsection, Rom 8:1-10, "The Decision," and by this he means God's free, incredible, absurd action in sending the Son: "the scandal of historical revelation."[81] In this action God pronounces the death sentence on sin.

> This condemnation of sin dwelling in the flesh, this exposure of the true nature of the flesh, this parable of the Spirit, takes place . . . in the ever increasing deprivation and diminution of the life of Jesus, emphasized first in the Temptation, then in Gethsemane, and finally on Golgotha. In order that the condemnation might be perfected, the *kenosis* of the Son of God, this form of a servant, this impenetrable incognito, is not accidental but essential.[82]

The awesome doxological passage (11:33-36) that begins "O the depth of the riches and wisdom and knowledge of God!" Barth views as a summary of the whole document. "This means that the theme of the Epistle to the Romans—Theology, the Word of God—can be uttered by human lips only when it is apprehended that the predicate, *Deus revelatus*, has as its subject *Deus absconditus*."[83] For many reviewers the commentary was less an exposition of the thought of Paul in his historical context than the propagation of the theology of Karl Barth, accosting the Christendom of the twentieth century.[84]

In 1941 Barth published a *Shorter Commentary on Romans*.[85] It includes an introduction that discusses date and place of writing (58 CE from Corinth), and argues that the original long edition of Romans (chs. 1–16) was later circulated in shorter versions. In content this commentary gives more attention to historical interpretation and reduces the startling and paradoxical rhetoric of the earlier masterpiece. Barth continues to oppose the idea that Rom 1:18-21 supports natural theology. Chapter 11, he believes, implies universal salvation but, more important, it affirms the freedom of God. "Man's disobedience cannot confront God with an everlasting fact. God remains free as regards the disobedient just as he remains free as regards the obedient."[86]

Aftershocks from the tremor of Barth's *Romans* recurred in his commentary on 1 Corinthians.[87] Based on lectures given at Göttingen in 1923, the commentary is entitled *The Resurrection of the Dead*. Barth, in the foreword to the first edition (1924), explains that his approach departs from that of the historical critics. They usually see Chapter 15 as the last of a diverse list of subjects treated in the epistle; Barth views it as the theme and culmination of the whole letter.

> The chapter devoted to the Resurrection of the Dead does not stand in so isolated a relation to the First Epistle to the Corinthians as at first glance might appear. It forms not only the close and crown of the whole Epistle, but also provides the clue to its meaning, from which place light is shed on the whole, and it becomes intelligible, not outwardly, but inwardly, as a unity.[88]

This approach, of course, is typical Barth: preoccupation with theological interpretation, stress on the unity of the NT, and affirmation of the magnitude of the resurrection. Barth orders the material of this book in three parts: The Trend of I Corinthians I–XIV; The Resurrection Chapter; Explanation of I Corinthians XV. Attention is given to exegetical detail in the third part, where Barth arranges the text into sections and subsections according to his understanding of the structure of the chapter.

In the first part Barth presents an overview of the argument of 1 Corinthians. He sees in chapters 1–4 a contrast between the egocentric wisdom of humans and the paradoxical wisdom of God in the crucified Christ. In chapters 5–6 Barth finds a focus on ethics: Paul exhorts the Corinthian Christians to live in obedience to the imperative of the new being. In Chapter 7, in Barth's opinion, Paul is opposing the pride of sexual asceticism; in chapters 9–10, according to Barth, he insists that the gift of freedom must be subordinate to the command of love. In discussing the Lord's Supper (ch. 11) Barth, in contrast to a host of interpreters, believes Paul is little concerned with the tradition from the historical Jesus.

> For what we call the historical Jesus, a Jesus pure and simple, who is not the Lord Jesus, but an earthly phenomenon among others to be objectively discovered, detached from His Lordship in the Church of God, apart from the revelation given in the Jesus of the Church and at first to the apostles—this abstraction was for Paul (and not for him alone) an impossible idea. . . . But Paul is not now reflecting on what this Jesus, who was known after the flesh, might have said on the occasion of the Supper, but upon what Kyrios Jesus, the Lord of the Church said to him, Paul, when He made him His ambassador. The Lord does not live for him in the oldest, best-attested or most credible tradition—why should it be just the Lord who lives and speaks there?—but in His supreme present revelation to His Church, in concreto, in the herald's commission which it has become to Paul. He reported direct from the source: The Lord Himself is the tradition.[89]

In Chapters 12–14, Barth sees Paul attacking the excesses of religion and the human claim to special accomplishment. The theme running through all these chapters, as Barth points out in his overview of Chapter 15 (the second part of the commentary), is judgment on the religion that flourishes in Corinth and affirmation of the eternity of God, disclosed in the resurrection: "His absolute transcendence as Creator, Redeemer, and King of all things, of history."[90]

In the third part Barth proceeds to the exegesis of 1 Corinthians 15. He believes the list of appearances in vv. 3-7 has nothing to do with proof. The emphasis, according to Barth, is on the appearance *of Christ*, on revelation, not on the perception of the witnesses.

> As if this "positive" manner of asserting the resurrection of Jesus were not in fact the secret denial of the very thing which we would fain assert, the resurrection as the deed of God, whom no eye has seen nor ear heard, who has entered no human heart, neither outwardly nor inwardly, not subjective and not objective, not mystical nor

spiritistic and not flatly objective, but as a historical divine fact, which as such is only to be grasped in the category of revelation and in none other.[91]

Regarding 15:12-19, Barth contends that the resurrection of the dead, the general resurrection, is essential to the Christian faith. "If God is not God in our life, then He is also not that in the life of Christ. . . . If no dead are to arise except the One, then the resurrection of even this One is an offence dispensable, unimportant, a foreign dualistic element in a philosophy otherwise uniform."[92]

In discussing the cryptic reference to "baptism on behalf of the dead" (15:29) Barth writes that he believes Paul is alluding to vicarious baptism—an allusion indicating that Christ is Lord of the dead as well as the living. Barth believes that the "spiritual body" (15:44), though a new reality, the absolute miracle, has to do with corporeality. "To wish to be God's without the body is rebellion against God's will, is secret denial of God; it is, indeed, the body which suffers, sins, dies. We are waiting for our Body's redemption; if the body is not redeemed to obedience, to health, to life, then there is no God; then what may be called God does not deserve this name."[93]

The last verses of the chapter (50-58) affirm, says Barth, that God is God.

As God's gift, the victory, the "reality of the resurrection," is present; is valid word spoken to us, not to be forgotten, not to be dragged down into the dialectic of our existence, not to be restricted, not to be weakened, not to be doubted. But just for this reason everything depends upon this "victory" being and remaining God's gift "through our Lord Jesus Christ" present in hope. There is no presence of God fuller, more joyful and stronger than that in the eternal future; there is no having, possessing, and enjoying more real than in the words spoken with empty hands: "But thanks be to God," in which all right and all glory is given to Him with whom that which falls to us is abolished.[94]

All in all, Barth offers majestic rhetoric, powerful theology, and, according to some, questionable exegesis.[95]

Barth's commentary on Philippians is based on his lectures at Münster during the winter semester of 1926-27.[96] The commentary, consisting of some 120 pages in its English translation, provides no critical introduction. The material is ordered in titled sections according to Barth's understanding of the structure of the letter. The biblical text (in translation) is presented at the beginning of each section. Comments are in running paragraphs with phrases from the text printed in bold type. A few examples can illustrate Barth's exegetical accomplishment.

Barth says of the "Introduction" (Phil 1:1-2) that the mention of Timothy in the salutation does not indicate that he is co-author. He notes that the terms for "bishops" and "deacons" were used in Paul's day for municipal officials and leaders of guilds; in the church, their functions were administrative. The next section, "Copartners of Grace" (1:3-11), is identified by Barth as a conventional Pauline expression of thanksgiving. As to the textual variant in v. 3, Barth (contra Nestle-Aland) prefers the Western reading: εγω μεν ευχαριστω τω κυριω ημων, so that Paul is expressing thanks "to our Lord" rather than "to my God" (NRSV). Barth believes the "day of Jesus Christ" (v. 6) refers to both the future hope and the present coming of the Lord. "It is not the day of our death, our blessed departure from the world that forms the end," says Barth, "but the day of Christ Jesus, his victory in this world, its creation anew by him—the day of our death only in so far as it coincides for us with that day, and therefore so far as it means for us not *our escape*, but the *coming of the Lord* into the transitory world."[97] In discussing "Christ will be Magnified" (1:12-26), Barth concludes that the reference to the praetorium (1:13) proves that the letter was written from the Roman imprisonment.[98] In this situation of uncertainty one thing is absolutely clear for Paul: "The preaching of Christ is the axis and the whole question of whether one is for and against Paul is one of the questions that revolve around it. He holds to that axis. If he has only more or less confidence in men and their motive, he has *complete* confidence in him who is their Lord as well as his, and also in the work executed with strange tools by his hand."[99]

Philippians 2:1-12 is important for Barth's Christology. Within the context of the section "Children of God among a Perverse Generation" (1:27–2:16), Barth views these verses as an excursus: "a little compendium of Pauline testimony."[100] In regard to v. 6 he stresses Christ's equality with God. "This equality of Christ with God is so to speak the fixed, *ultimate* background, from which his road sets out and to which it returns."[101] According to Barth, Christ emptied himself of the form of God and took on human form by his own free will and without diminishing his deity. "What happens to the Man Jesus in his humiliation is only the reflection of what happens to God's Equal in his self-emptying. The death on the cross is indeed only the unfolding of the incarnation. There, on Golgotha, the meaning of the incarnation, the meaning of Bethlehem, breaks through and comes into view."[102]

Similarly, Christ's exaltation, according to Barth, does not remove his humiliation.

But what it says is, that precisely he who was abased and humbled even to the obedience of death on the cross is also the Exalted Lord. Notice that there is no mention of any reassumption of the "form of God." No, he who became Man and was crucified, whose abasement and humiliation is not by any means washed out or cancelled—it is he who is exalted, it is to him the great name is given, it is of *him*, as the Equal of God that he never ceased to be, but as the Equal of God who abased and humbled himself, that all that follows is said. There is no other Christ than this, God's Equal become Man.[103]

In general, Barth's *Philippians* gives more attention to historical criticism than his earlier commentaries. He deals with textual and linguistic details such as the wordplay on κατατομή and περιτομή (3:2-3); he notes the problem of the integrity of the epistle; he sees in 3:12-14 use of the metaphor of the stadium; he identifies the opponents as Judaizers. These exegetical details, moreover, are woven into a splendid tapestry of theological composition.

Barth's work on the Fourth Gospel is less well known. About this Gospel as a whole he wrote: "We might almost say that in the story of Jesus in the Fourth Gospel we have one long story of the transfiguration."[104] Barth lectured on the Gospel of John at Münster in 1925–26, and again at Bonn in 1933 with Nazis sympathizers in the audience. The lectures on John 1–8 were published posthumously, and from this publication the comments on chapter 1 were translated into English.[105] The English commentary comprises a little over 140 pages. Barth offers no historical-critical introduction. He has no interest in the "Johannine Problem" and assumes that the author was an eyewitness whom he calls an apostle. Barth arranges the material according to his understanding of the structure of the passage in three sections: 1:1-18, 1:19-34, and 1:35-51. Major attention is give to the first section—over 120 pages. A short introduction deals primarily with hermeneutics.

Conscientious expositors must be as free as possible from such things a religious or non-religious notions, from philosophical or ethical convictions, from personal feelings or reactions, from historical habits of thought, prejudices, and the like. They must have an ear simply for what the text says to them, for the new thing that it seeks to say in face of the totality of their previous subjective knowledge. . . . If we want to be truly objective readers and expositors of John's Gospel, however, we will not want to free ourselves from the fact that we are baptized, that for us, then, John's Gospel is part of the canonical scripture of the Christian church. . . . Canonical scripture, however, means scripture to which we stand in that relation from the very first, a Word that is spoken to us from the very first in the name of God and with the claim that it is saying something radically new, a Word which even before we could hear it has opened a dialogue with us, a dialogue which, because it is conducted in the name of God, we cannot escape.[106]

Barth's discussion of the Johannine Prologue (John 1:1-18) provides some examples of his exegesis. The distinctive feature of his interpretation of the Prologue is his idea that the Logos is identified as Jesus early in the passage; already in v. 2 the phrase οὗτος ἦν looks forward to the same phrase in v. 15, where reference to Jesus is clear. As to the term Logos, Barth notes various theories about the source, including the view that it was borrowed from Philo or the Mandaeans. For Barth these matters are of little moment. Whatever the background, the Word must be understood in John's terms. For John, according to Barth, the Logos does not determine the meaning of Jesus; Jesus determines the meaning of the Logos. The phrase "in the beginning" (v. 1) indicates that the Word was eternal; the Logos is God, the only God. In regard to the debate about punctuation in vv. 3-4, Barth rejects the view of Walter Bauer (followed in the NRSV): "and without him not one thing came into being. What has come into being in him was life, and the light was the light of all people." Barth believes this punctuation implies cosmic speculation that is foreign to the text. Instead he puts the period at the end of verse 3: "Everything was made by him, and without him nothing that is was made." Barth believes this punctuation and translation present the intention of the text: that the Logos, the Revealer, is the Creator of all things. The phrase "in him was life" is taken by most exegetes to refer to the general life of the creation, but Barth understands it as an expression of the soteriological–eschatological message of the whole Gospel: life is the work of the Redeemer. The saying that "the life was the light" indicates that the Redeemer is also the Revealer. Barth rejects the theory that vv. 6-8 constitute a later addition to an original source; instead, for him the historical witness of John is essential to the Evangelist's account.

For Barth, v. 14 is of utmost importance. "The concreteness, the contingency, the historical singularity of the eternal, absolute, divine Word is what is stated with this sentence."[107] In his view, coming in the flesh does not emphasize the coming of the Logos but describes the way the Logos came: in the flesh. In becoming flesh the Logos does not cease to be Logos: he is very God and very man. The Word is the subject of revelation; the flesh is the medium. "The so-called historical Jesus, abstracted from the action of the Word, is *not* revelation."[108] The word translated "lived" (ἐσκήνωσεν) indicates that the dwelling is temporary, expressing to Barth the once-for-all of revelation. The "us" among whom the Logos lodged includes those who saw him in the flesh (even people like Pilate and Caiaphas); the "we" who have seen his glory includes, as well as the first generation, those who behold their witness. In this verse Barth notes the first reference to the Logos as Son of God—the unique Son of the Father, the one full of grace and truth.

All in all, this is a very impressive demonstration of exegetical skill. Barth analyzes the text in its historical setting and attends to text-critical and exegetical detail, using the tools of linguistics and grammar. He refers to a host of secondary sources, including the works of Walter Bauer, Rudolf Bultmann, Heinrich Holtzmann, Theodor Zahn, Franz Overbeck, Wilhelm Heitmüller, Alfred Loisy, and Richard Reitzenstein. Barth also attends to the exegesis of the ancient and classical commentators, among them Clement, Augustine, Bengel, Schleiermacher, Luther, and Calvin. As always, theological exegesis dominates. Barth concentrates on the text, sees the details in relation to the comprehensive thought of the author, argues from context, and employs christocentric hermeneutics.

A critique of Karl Barth's massive theological system is quite beyond the scope and capability of this history. Even an assessment of his contribution to NT research is a formidable undertaking. Surely his most important contribution is his sheer, singular attention to Scripture. The fact that the most important theologian of the twentieth century was a biblical theologian is of monumental significance. For Barth the Bible is the primary witness to God's revelation in history. Barth, of course, is no biblicist; he draws a distinction between God's absolute revelation in Jesus Christ and the account of that revelation in Scripture. He also calls for a special way of reading Scripture, one that demands an unswerving attention to the content of the text. The text is read in terms of its own intrinsic understanding of truth. The center of that truth is the paradoxical event of Christ, the criterion of truth, perceived by faith, the gift of God.

The impetus Barth's work has given to biblical study is impossible to overestimate. To be sure, his relationship to the "achievements" of scientific criticism is ambiguous. On the one hand he affirms historical criticism as the appropriate first step in exegesis and often employs it with exceptional skill. On the other he attacks the critical establishment for its pretentious objectivity and its failure to go beyond the first step to the larger strides of theological interpretation and application. However, Barth's own theological exegesis sometimes appears to read fourth- and fifth-century Trinitarian and christological doctrine into first-century NT texts. His appropriation of exegetical results for his present theological task seems to ignore the necessity of historical distance, a fundamental presupposition of historical method. The question arises as to how historical criticism, with its assumption of the Enlightenment world view, relates to Barth's positivism of revelation and faith. The larger question—the question of the relation of historical critical exegesis to theological interpretation—will continue to occupy scholars throughout the twentieth century. This question, like the improvisations of Mozart, will become a theme with variations in the NT research of Rudolf Bultmann.

Theological Hermeneutics: Rudolf Bultmann (1884–1976)

Rudolf Bultmann is the most important NT scholar of the twentieth century. His research in *Religionsgeschichte* and form criticism, especially his monumental *History of the Synoptic Tradition*, has been reviewed in the second volume of this history.[109] In view of the mountain of work Bultmann amassed and the forest of secondary sources that has overgrown it, a necessary selectivity results inevitably in oversimplification.

Life and Work

On one occasion when in Marburg (1961–62) I remarked, in a conversation with Ernst Fuchs, that it seemed strange that no one had written a biography of Bultmann. He replied, "What's to write?" By that, of course, he meant that Bultmann's academic career had been rather conventional. Recently a superb biography has appeared, over five hundred pages long and covering every detail of Bultmann's life and work.[110] Rudolf Bultmann was the son of a Lutheran pastor, educated at Tübingen, Berlin, and Marburg. After teaching at Breslau and Giessen, he moved to Marburg in 1921 where he remained for the rest of his life. His youngest brother was killed in World War I, and during World War II his only surviving brother died in a concentration camp. Bultmann was a member of the anti-Nazi Confessing Church. Beginning his class lecture of May 2, 1933, he declared: "I have made a point never to speak about current politics in my lectures, and I think I also shall not do so in the future. However, it would seem to me unnatural were I to ignore today the political situation in which we begin our new semester."[111] Hitler had consolidated his power in March, and many Germans were hopeful about the possibilities for the future. Bultmann warned that the future possibilities also entailed dangers. In particular he scored the injustice that was already being done to German Jews. "If we have correctly understood the meaning and the demand of the Christian faith, then it is quite clear that, *in face of the voices of the present, this Christian faith itself is being called in question.* In other words, it is clear that we have to decide whether Christian faith is to be valid for us or not."[112]

After the war Bultmann lectured widely, including the Shaffer Lectures at Yale (1951) and the Gifford Lectures in Edinburgh (1955).

Early in his career Bultmann was influenced by dialectical theology, heralded by Barth's *Romans.* According to Bultmann, "the new theology correctly saw that Christian faith is the answer to the Word of the transcendent God which encounters man, and that theology has to deal with this Word and the man who has been encountered by it."[113]Bultmann became closely associated with Martin Heidegger, who served on the Marburg faculty from 1922-1928. In regard to Heidegger's existentialism, Bultmann wrote:

> I found here the concept through which it became possible to speak adequately of human existence and therefore also of the existence of the believer. In my efforts to make philosophy fruitful for theology, however, I have come more and more into opposition to Karl Barth. I remain grateful to him, however, for the decisive things I have learned from him.[114]

Bultmann and Barth had become acquainted during their student days at Marburg, and their friendship flourished through their association with the Friends of the Christian World and later in the circle that published *Zwischen den Zeiten.* Although they became increasingly alienated theologically, Bultmann and Barth carried on correspondence through much of their lives.[115] Barth could still maintain his sense of humor in response to Bultmann's essay on Romans 5. "In heaven (as the top floor of the mythological world-structure) we may perhaps seek out the apostle Paul together—in my case, of course, only after a longer excursion to W. A. Mozart—and ask him to explain to us what he himself ultimately had in mind."[116]

Bultmann, for his part, sent a greeting on the occasion of Barth's eightieth birthday. "From the depths of his heart your old friend wishes you good health and good courage for the new year of your life."[117]

BULTMANN'S THEOLOGY

Bultmann's theology is a synthesis of three major influences: liberalism and Enlightenment criticism; Reformation (Lutheran) doctrine as shaped by the Marburg neo-Kantians and Wilhelm Herrmann and reinterpreted by the early

Barth; and existentialist philosophy as expressed by Kierkegaard and developed by the early Heidegger.[118]

Bultmann's dedication to historical criticism is apparent in his contributions to history of religion and form criticism.[119] As he says, "I have endeavored throughout my entire work to carry farther the tradition of historical-critical research as it was practiced in 'liberal' theology and to make our recent theological knowledge the more fruitful as a result."[120] Indeed, Bultmann advocates radical criticism.

> I have never yet felt uncomfortable with my critical radicalism; on the contrary, I have been entirely comfortable. But I often have the impression that my conservative New Testament colleagues feel very uncomfortable, for I see them perpetually engaged in salvage operations. I calmly let the fire burn, for I see that what is consumed is only the fanciful portraits of Life-of-Jesus theology, and that means nothing other than 'Christ after the flesh' (Χριστὸς κατὰ σάρκα).[121]

Bultmann remained under the influence of the Lutheran piety of his home. As Barth writes, "Bultmann's work is inconceivable apart from his Lutheran background. . . . [T]hose who throw stones at Bultmann should be careful lest they accidentally hit Luther, who is also hovering somewhere in the background."[122] Bultmann, concerning his own method of interpretation, writes: "Our radical attempt to demythologize the New Testament is in fact a perfect parallel to St Paul's and Luther's doctrine of justification by faith alone apart from the works of the Law."[123] Bultmann, of course, was miles removed from Lutheran orthodoxy. Instead, his Lutheranism was influenced by Wilhelm Herrmann who, in turn, had been influenced by the Marburg neo-Kantian philosophers, Hermann Cohen and Paul Natorp.[124] These philosophers opposed metaphysics and stressed a non-objective understanding of the individual. Herrmann shared their aversion to metaphysics and affirmed the autonomy of faith.

From Luther, Bultmann inherited the theology of the word, and he developed that theology under the tutelage of Karl Barth. Bultmann had been associated with the liberal Friends of the Christian World, but he joined the dialectical theologians who founded *Zwischen den Zeiten*. Unlike Barth, Bultmann was not dramatically influenced by World War I. He wrote, "I do not believe that the war has influenced my theology."[125] For Bultmann the turn from liberalism to dialectical theology was a theological conversion: a turn from faith in the personality of Jesus to faith in the Christ of the kerygma.[126] He says that "*Jesus Christ confronts men in the kerygma and nowhere else.*"[127] About the new theological movement, Bultmann writes: "Theology whose subject is God can therefore have as its content only the 'word of the cross' (λόγος τοῦ σταυροῦ). But that word is a 'stumbling block' (σκάνδαλον) to men. Hence the charge against liberal theology is that it has sought to remove this stumbling block or to minimize it."[128]

Bultmann believed the new theology to be important for NT interpretation.

> The significance of 'dialectical theology,' therefore, does not consist in definite theological propositions presented to the investigator either for criticism or as the basis for exegesis. The insight into the dialectic of man's existence, that is, into the historical nature of man and of his statements, opens to the investigator a new road which is not a substitute for the old historical method, but which deepens it.[129]

As to Barth, Bultmann was one of the first to write a favorable review of *The Epistle to the Romans*. Barth's commentary, according to Bultmann, affirmed "the simple—Pauline—radicalism, which is clear about what faith means, and what grace means"; faith is miracle, a venture, "a leap into the void."[130] Bultmann, however, was critical of Barth's failure to understand Paul in his historical setting, a criticism repeated in his review of Barth's work on 1 Corinthians. In the latter case Bultmann insists that "exegesis must be developed on a basis of the most exact knowledge of the contemporary background and by means of careful and penetrating analysis of the content."[131] Nevertheless, throughout his career Bultmann remained loyal to the dialectical theology of the early Barth. When the two theologians met after World War II, Bultmann is reported to have responded to all Barth's queries, "I stand where you stood."[132]

Existentialist philosophy, the third main influence on Bultmann, is apparent in his accord with Kierkegaard and Heidegger. Bultmann affirmed the basic Kiekegaardian dialectic of the infinite qualitative difference between time and eternity. "God," says Bultmann, "is the absolutely transcendent One, the Eternal One, and his eternity is qualitatively different from everything of this world, to which the world of mind also belongs."[133] The influence of Heidegger dates from the association of philosopher and theologian at Marburg.[134] In a letter to Gogarten (October 19, 1924) Bultmann wrote that "during an afternoon each week I am now reading with Heidegger the Gospel according to St. John. I hope to learn all sorts of things from these meetings."[135] Above all, he learned the centrality of human existence—what Heidegger called *Dasein*—for theological understanding. Bultmann did not believe there was a final philosophy, nor did he believe that existentialism could provide the way to authentic existence. However, he did believe it provided the method whereby human existence could be analyzed.

On these three foundations—historical criticism, dialectical theology, and existentialist philosophy—Bultmann built a dazzling theological structure. Actually, every facet of Bultmann's thought reflects the interrelation of the total theological edifice, and from the vision of the whole each facet has its place and significance. In virtually everything Bultmann wrote since 1925 his theology appears in miniature.[136] Various writings, however, present his major themes. Above all, he intended to be a biblical theologian.

> Theology, therefore, is always exegesis inasmuch as it has access
> to revelation only through the witness of Scripture and seeks to
> grasp by exegesis what Scripture, understood as witness, says. In
> form, therefore, theology is always exegesis of Scripture. Its content
> speaks of revelation. But since revelation is the eternal event, judging
> or forgiving man, the object of theology is nothing other than
> the conceptual presentation of man's existence as determined by
> God—that is, as man must see it in the light of Scripture.[137]

Since Scripture is witness to revelation in history, history and eschatology are important themes for Bultmann. His understanding of these themes is explicated in his Gifford Lectures of 1955 on *History and Eschatology*. According to Bultmann the OT understood history from the perspective of eschatology, that is, as moving toward the end, toward the goal of God. For Paul, the end has already arrived but has not yet been consummated; humans live in the time between, in the "already" and the "not yet." Thus, in Bultmann's view, Paul interprets eschatology from the perspective of anthropology. Bultmann thinks John further clarifies this perspective by eliminating futuristic eschatology entirely. After a survey of efforts by philosophers to find meaning in history he concludes that history can only be understood from the standpoint of human existence. From this perspective he believes history calls humans to responsibility for the future, calls for decision. However, human beings, according to Bultmann, are not free to make the decision; freedom comes only by the gift of God. "According to the New Testament," says Bultmann, "*Jesus Christ is the eschatological event*, the action of God by which God has set an end to the old world. In the preaching of the Christian Church the eschatological event will ever again become present and does become present ever and again in faith."[138]

Closely related to his theology of history and eschatology is Bultmann's idea of revelation.[139] According to Bultmann revelation can be understood in two ways: as communication of knowledge or as an occurrence or event that puts humans in a new situation. The NT, he thinks, is concerned with the latter: the event of Christ that brings authentic existence. According to Bultmann this revelation can only be perceived on the basis of a pre-understanding, which in turn involves a self-understanding—an understanding of human limitations. "If we ask now about the concept of revelation in the New Testament, then we must ask, first of all, how man's limitation is understood there. And the answer is simple: *man is limited by death.* . . . And by the same token, the further answer is also simple: *revelation gives life.*"[140]

According to Bultmann's reading of the NT this life-giving revelation comes from the outside, by God's action in Christ in history, in the Word made flesh. The event occurs in the cross and resurrection whereby the saving action of God becomes an event in human existence, an event of faith. Thus, for Bultmann, revelation is not a communication of information. "What, then, has been revealed? Nothing at all, so far as the question concerning revelation asks for doctrines. . . . On the other hand, however, everything has been revealed, in so far as man's eyes are opened concerning his own existence and he is once again able to understand himself."[141]

Yet Bultmann also believes that revelation is revelation of God. "God is thus revealed as the One who limits man and who brings him to his authenticity in his limitation—namely, whenever this limitation is understood as God's limitation."[142] Moreover, the NT is revelation. "Therefore, the New Testament itself is revelation only insofar as it is kerygma or insofar as it 'preaches Christ' (Luther); and this means that there is a criterion for determining the extent to which the New Testament's statements speak as revelation."[143]

Since revelation occurs in Christ, Bultmann's understanding of Jesus is crucial to his theology. This is set forth is his remarkable *Jesus*, a book without parallel in the history of life of Jesus research.[144] It is Bultmann's first major work reflecting the influence of dialectical theology and existentialist philosophy.[145] In the introduction he explains his viewpoint and method. He insists that history cannot be understood objectively, but only from the inside, only in dialogue with history. Bultmann is not concerned with the biography of Jesus. "I do indeed think that we can now know almost nothing concerning the life and personality of Jesus, since the early Christian sources show no interest in either, are moreover fragmentary and often legendary."[146] Moreover, Bultmann is not concerned with the messianic consciousness of Jesus, and in his opinion Jesus did not believe himself to be the messiah. Bultmann is concerned with the message of Jesus, and to investigate this he follows the method of form criticism as formulated in his *History of the Synoptic Tradition*.[147]

Bultmann presents the message of Jesus in three concentric circles, moving from the larger, outer circle to the inner circle, the essential core of the message of Jesus. The outer circle encompasses Jesus' announcement of "The Coming Kingdom of God." With Johannes Weiss and Albert Schweitzer, Bultmann understands the kingdom as an apocalyptic concept.[148] It is the supernatural action of God that confronts humans with a decision.

> If men are standing in the crisis of decision, and if precisely this crisis is the essential characteristic of humanity, then every hour is the last hour, and we can understand that for Jesus the whole contemporary mythology is pressed into the service of this conception of human existence. Thus he understood and proclaimed his hour as the last hour.[149]

Within this circle of the kingdom is the second, smaller concentric circle: the teaching of Jesus concerning "The Will of God." As Jesus was viewed as prophet in the first circle, here he is seen as teacher. Like the rabbis, Jesus called for obedience to God's will, but whereas the obedience taught by them was formal, Jesus, according to Bultmann, demanded radical obedience—an obedience possible only in freedom.

> Radical obedience exists only when a man inwardly assents to what is required of him, when the thing commanded is seen as intrinsically God's command; when the whole man stands behind what he does; or better, when the whole man is in what he does, when he is not doing something obediently, but is essentially obedient.[150]

The command that must be obeyed is the absolute demand of love. This command is without objective content, without rules or ethical principles. "If a man really loves, he knows already what he has to do."[151] The command is absolute, allowing no neutrality, an either/or.

The third, innermost concentric circle focuses on Jesus' teaching about God: "God the Remote and the Near," a paradox that recurs throughout this final chapter. According to Bultmann, Jesus views God as the transcendent

God who is also Lord of history. God is remote and near in Jesus' idea of the kingdom as both future and present. "Thus if we wish to understand the message of Jesus, it is not possible to ignore the future character of the Kingdom of God nor to minimize the distance of God in the present. Instead, it is only possible to accept the paradox that the remote, future God is at the same time, precisely *because* He is the remote and future God, also God of the present."[152]

The miracles also show that the transcendent God is active in particular events. "God is distant, wholly other, in so far as everyday occurrences hide Him from the unbeliever; God is near for the believer who sees His activity."[153] Bultmann sees the same paradox in Jesus' belief in prayer, a practice whereby the omnipotent, remote God can be petitioned for daily bread. The idea of God as Father reflects the same paradox: God is the remote God who offers to humans an intimate relationship in faith. Finally, the paradox is seen in Jesus' idea of sin and forgiveness: in sin God is remote, for humans reject the claim of God; in forgiveness God is near, for God comes to humans in grace. Bultmann concludes:

> Thus it has finally become clear in what sense God is for Jesus God of the present and of the future. God is God of the present, because His claim confronts man in the present moment, and He is at the same time God of the future, because He gives man freedom for the present instant of decision and sets before him as the future which is opening to him by his decision, condemnation or mercy. God is God of the present for the sinner precisely because He casts him into remoteness from Himself, and He is at the same time God of the future because He never relinquishes His claim on the sinner and opens to him by forgiveness a new future for new obedience.[154]

In the last analysis "Jesus is therefore the bearer of the word."[155]

Closely related to his understanding of Jesus is Bultmann's Christology—another major theme of his theology. In his essay, "Die Christologie des Neuen Testaments," he argues that the NT views Jesus Christ as the eschatological event.[156] For Paul, according to Bultmann, Christology is proclamation. "Pauline christology, therefore, is nothing other than *the proclamation of the saving act of God which took place in Christ*."[157] Paul expresses this Christology in his doctrine of justification. In Bultmann's opinion this affirms Melanchthon's dictum: "to know Christ is to know his benefits." Bultmann finds John to be in essential agreement. "[F]or John, as for Paul, christology is proclamation, as is manifest from the fact that John—adopting a mythological term—calls Jesus *the Logos, the Word of God.*[158] The decisive feature of NT Christology, according to Bultmann, is the affirmation that the proclaimer (Jesus) became the proclaimed (Christ); the one who preached the Word is identified as the Word. "The proclaimer must become the proclaimed," argues Bultmann, "because it is the fact *that* he proclaimed which is decisive. The decisive thing is his person (not his personality), here and now, the event, the commission, the summons."[159]

Bultmann's Christology is further explicated in his lecture, "The Christological Confession of the World Council of Churches."[160] The Council, according to its confession, "is composed of Churches which acknowledge Jesus Christ as God and Saviour."[161] The question for Bultmann is whether this confession designates Christ's metaphysical nature or his soteriological significance. In answering the question he investigates christological titles used in the NT, noting that Christ is not named "God" in Paul and the Synoptics, and that the only certain designation of Christ's deity is Thomas's confession: "My Lord and my God" (John 20:28). In the Palestinian community Jesus is confessed as Messiah or Son of David—titles identifying him as the conveyer of eschatological salvation. The Hellenistic church confesses Christ as Lord or Son of God—titles that identify him as heavenly redeemer. According to Bultmann these confessions are not pronouncements about Christ's nature but about his significance. The titles identify Christ as the paradoxical event, calling humans to decision. Bultmann concludes:

> The formula "Christ is God" is false in every sense in which God is understood as an entity which can be objectivized, whether it is understood in an Arian or Nicene, an Orthodox or a Liberal sense. It is correct, if "God" is understood here as the event of God's acting. But my question is, ought one not rather to avoid such formulae on account of misunderstanding and cheerfully content oneself with saying that he is the Word of God?

Bultmann answers, "[H]e is the Word, and as such he is God."[162]

HERMENEUTICS AND CRITICISM: DEMYTHOLOGIZING

Both before and after his famous lecture on demythologizing, Bultmann reflected on hermeneutics. In his essay, "The Problem of Theological Exegesis" (1925) he questions the "objective" criticism of the liberals.[163] "Historical exegesis asks: 'What is said?' We ask: 'What is meant?'" Bultmann contends that historical and theological exegesis are inseparable.

[O]ne should emphasize that the separation of historical and theological exegesis is an untenable position for both and that no one has the right to tack a theological commentary on to a philological historical commentary. In the actual process of exegesis, the relationship of historical and theological exegesis cannot really be analyzed, since genuine historical exegesis rests on the existential encounter with history and therefore coincides with the theological exegesis.[164]

In a later essay on "The Problem of Hermeneutics" Bultmann argues that the interpreter must have a "life relation" to the text—what he often describes as pre-understanding.[165]

The presupposition of any understanding interpretation is a prior life relation to the subject matter that is directly or indirectly expressed in the text and that provides the objective in questioning it. Without such a life relation in which text and interpreter are bound together, questioning the text and understanding it are impossible.[166]

Recognition of this pre-understanding, for Bultmann, is not a retreat into subjectivity. "Here the 'most subjective' interpretation is the 'most objective,' because the only person who is able to hear the claim of the text is the person who is moved by the question of his or her own existence."[167] In an essay, "Is Exegesis without Presuppositions Possible?" he contends that "there cannot be any such thing as presuppositionless exegesis."[168] The interpreter begins with pre-understanding and from this pre-understanding puts questions to the text, which in turn addresses and modifies the pre-understanding; this is the hermeneutical circle.

Bultmann's notorious lecture, "New Testament and Mythology," was presented first to a group of pastors at Frankfurt and later at a theological conference in Alpirsbach.[169] Both audiences consisted of members of the Confessing Church. The date was 1941, a perilous time for Christians striving to understand the gospel in a threatening political situation. In this lecture Bultmann insists that demythologizing is necessary because the NT message of salvation is presented in the language of ancient cosmic myth—a language incredible to modern humans, demanding sacrifice of the intellect. A decade later he presented a fuller explication of demythologizing in his Shaffer Lectures.[170] He begins by considering the message of Jesus in relation to the problem of mythology. Since Jesus understood the kingdom of God in terms of apocalyptic eschatology, Bultmann believes the message of Jesus is expressed in mythological language and assumes a mythological worldview.

> We must ask whether the eschatological preaching and the mythological sayings as a whole contain a deeper meaning which is concealed under the cover of mythology. . . . This method of interpretation of the New Testament which tries to recover the deeper meaning behind the mythological conceptions I call demythologizing—an unsatisfactory word, to be sure. Its aim is not to eliminate the mythological statements but to interpret them.[171]

Myth must be interpreted, says Bultmann, because it presents the transcendent as objective; it misconstrues God's transcendence in terms of space and time. Instead, the relation to God must be understood existentially; myth, according to Bultmann, should be interpreted in relation to human existence. He discovers a warrant for demythologizing in the NT itself. Although Paul uses apocalyptic language, he believes the eschatological event had occurred in the death-resurrection of Christ. John, according to Bultmann's exegesis, completely abandons futuristic eschatology and sees the parousia in the event of faith. Moreover, Bultmann is convinced that demythologizing is necessary because modern humans cannot accept the primitive worldview with its three-storied cosmology and its belief in miracles. Modern humans, however, should not reject the message of the NT because its mythological form is in conflict with the scientific worldview. To do so would be to reject Christianity for the wrong reason. Demythologizing, on the other hand, "will eliminate a false stumbling-block and bring into sharp focus the real stumbling-block, the word of the cross."[172]

Bultmann proceeds to explicate demythologizing as a hermeneutical method. This method, according to Bultmann, is moved by the question of human existence in relation to God. From this perspective "the Bible becomes for me a word addressed personally to me, which not only informs me about existence in general, but gives me real existence."[173] The interpreter, according to Bultmann, brings to the text a pre-understanding—an understanding of human existence that presupposes some philosophical point of view. This observation leads him to explore the question of the "right philosophy." Although there can no perfect philosophy, Bultmann believes existentialism provides a method capable of understanding human existence. "Thus it follows that existentialist philosophy can offer adequate conceptions for the interpretation of the Bible, since the interpretation of the Bible is concerned with the understanding of existence."[174] Existentialism, of course, does not provide the solution to the human problem; salvation is offered only in the scandal of the cross.

Finally, Bultmann addresses questions that have been raised concerning demythologizing. Is it not still mythological to speak of God as acting? No, replies Bultmann: not if God's action is understood as action for human existence, seen in faith. Does not speech about the transcendent God require mythological language—symbols and images? No, says Bultmann: existential speaking about God is analogical. "Therefore, to speak in this manner is not to speak in symbols or images, but to speak analogically. For when we speak in this manner of God as acting, we conceive God's action as an analogue to the actions taking place between men."[175]

Does not existential interpretation reduce theology to subjectivity? No, says Bultmann: to say that God acts in human existence does not mean that God does not act elsewhere. "Thus, the fact that God cannot be seen or apprehended apart from faith does not mean that He does not exist apart from faith."[176] Does not demythologizing offer a timeless truth in place of God's action in Christ? No, says Bultmann: it affirms God's action in the concrete situation of history.

> For this "once for all" is not the uniqueness of an historical event but means that a particular historical event, that is, Jesus Christ, is to be understood as the eschatological "once for all." As an eschatological event this "once for all" is always present in the proclaimed word, not as a timeless truth, but as happening here and now. . . . The paradox is that the word which is always happening here and now is one and the same with the first word of the apostolic preaching crystallized in the Scriptures of the New Testament. . . . It is the eschatological once-for-all because the word becomes event here and now in the living voice of the preaching.[177]

Bultmann concludes that "demythologizing is the radical application of the doctrine of justification by faith to the sphere of knowledge and thought."[178]

Later essays by Bultmann respond to developments in the ongoing discussion of demythologizing. In "On the Problem of Demythologizing" (1952) he contends that debate about the definition of myth has not advanced the discussion.[179] In fact, Bultmannian scholars differ on this issue. Some detect development in Bultmann's definition. In his earlier writings he presents myth from the viewpoint of the history of religion school as a narrative recited in a cosmic drama (for example, the Gnostic redeemer myth). Bultmann also understands myth from the perspective of the Enlightenment as primitive cosmology in contrast to the scientific worldview. Later, under the influence of existentialist philosophy, he stresses myth as the objectifying understanding of existence.[180] In any event, objectification is crucial. As Bultmann says in a footnote to his original essay, "That mode of representation is mythology in which what is unworldly and divine appears as what is worldly and human or what is transcendent appears as what is immanent."[181] In a later essay on the same subject he takes up the question whether the understanding of myth as objectification implies that existentialist interpretation abandons the objective. No, Bultmann replies; existentialist interpretation interprets the objective.

> Therefore, it is quite clear that existentialist interpretation of history has need of objectifying observation of the historical past. Even if such observation cannot grasp the historical meaning of an act or an event, existentialist interpretation is equally unable to dispense with the (most reliable possible) determination of facts.[182]

In sum, it is clear that demythologizing is nothing other than existentialist interpretation, a method Bultmann had been using since the mid-1920s. Much of the controversy, no doubt, results from the terminology. To refer to the message of the NT as mythological seems to discredit the truth and authority of Scripture. The term "myth" also suggests that the background of the NT is to be found in pagan sources, tainting the purity of the stream of continuity from the OT to the NT. Although Bultmann has recognized that the term "demythologizing" is not satisfactory, its negative connotation is not insignificant for Bultmann's hermeneutics. Radical criticism, in the hands of Bultmann, is a tool for destroying the false ground of faith: cosmology, miracle, historicism, dogma, and every form of objectification. To be sure, Bultmann affirms the positive: he does not intend to eliminate the myth but to interpret it. His interpretation, however, is focused on the meaning of human existence. Although he believes this existence must be understood in relation to God, Bultmann moves anthropology to the center of the theological arena. Thus the christocentric and theocentric confession of the NT is pushed to the sidelines. In any event, for the history of NT research the major concern is Bultmann's use of his method in the interpretation of the biblical documents.

NEW TESTAMENT EXEGESIS

Bultmann's *The Gospel of John* is one of the greatest commentaries in the history of NT exegesis.[183] It said to have sold more copies than any other commentary on any NT book: by 1992, some forty-four thousand. In 1918, Rudolf Bultmann, a thirty-three-year-old associate professor at Breslau who at the time had published only one book and a few essays and reviews, was invited to write the new edition of the commentary on John for the prestigious Meyer series. The previous edition had been written by the venerable Bernhard Weiss, who was to have been succeeded by his son Johannes, but the younger Weiss (one of Bultmann's teachers) had died in 1914.[184] Bultmann, who proved himself sufficient to the task, spent twenty years on the project, which began to appear in installments in 1937 and was completed in 1941. During the twenty-year period Bultmann frequently lectured on the Fourth Gospel and offered seminars on Johannine problems. He also published essays on the religious-historical background of the Gospel and a seminal article on the eschatology of John.[185]

The commentary includes no historical-critical introduction. Details concerning backgrounds, sources, authorship, and the like are given within the commentary, and separate treatment, according to Bultmann, belongs to the science of introduction. The English edition adds an introduction by Walter Schmithals, gleaned from data within the commentary. As to sources, Bultmann believes the evangelist used three written documents: the passion narrative, the *Semeia* or signs source, and the *Offenbarungsreden* or revelation-discourses source.[186] Later, according to Bultmann, the work of the evangelist was revised by an ecclesiastical redactor. Bultmann believes nothing definite can be known about the author or the redactor, though the redactor (who added chapter 21) believed the Beloved Disciple had written the Gospel—an authorship Bultmann rejects. The redactor, in Bultmann's view, added futuristic eschatology and drastically revised the order of the original Gospel—an order Bultmann strives to recover. Bultmann's major rearrangements place chapter 5 after chapter 6 and chapter 14 after chapter 17. The complexity of his rearrangement can be seen in subsection C, in the third section of the first part of the Gospel, where Bultmann's order is: 9:1-41; 8:12; 12:44-50; 8:21-29; 12:34-36; 10:19-21.[187] He believed the original writing and later editing took place between 80 and 120, with considerable time between. Bultmann's commentary is mainly concerned with the original Gospel (prior to the redaction), a coherent work of a perceptive author who uses Gnostic imagery, abandons Jewish apocalyptic, and anticipates the theology of Rudolf Bultmann.

As to format, Bultmann's *Commentary on the Gospel of John* (a total of over 500 pages in German, over 700 in the English translation) is ordered according to Bultmann's rearrangement of the structure of the Gospel. After the prologue (1:1-18) he divides the material into two main parts: Chapters 2–13, "The

Revelation of the DOXA to the World," and Chapters 13–20, "The Revelation of the DOXA before the Community." The first part is divided into four sections: "The Encounter with the Revealer," "The Revelation as KRISIS," "The Revealer's Struggle with the World," "The Revealer's Secret Victory over the World." The second part contains two sections: "The Revealer's Farewell," and "The Passion and Easter." The sections are divided into subsections introduced by general comments. Detailed commentary is given verse by verse, with attention to terms, history of religion parallels, text criticism, linguistic and grammatical analysis. Sections in smaller print treat secondary issues and add details. Extensive footnotes provide additional details and include detailed references to ancient and modern sources. Although Bultmann gives scrupulous attention to critical and exegetical minutiae, his main concern is theology. Literal history is of little importance; the reference to "winter" (10:22), for example, indicates "that the end is near. The seasons of the year reflect the progress of revelation."[188] History of religion parallels, Heideggerian concepts, and dialectical doctrine are woven together into a seamless robe of theological interpretation.

Bultmann's exegesis of the prologue (John 1:1-18) provides a significant example of his way of working. In the introductory comments he discusses three topics. First there is a preliminary glance: the prologue is an overture, introducing the themes of the whole Gospel. Second, he treats the literary character of the prologue: it is a carefully crafted composition, an expression of cultic-liturgical poetry. Third is literary analysis: beneath the texts lies a written source: a hymn of the community of John the Baptist; this hymn belongs to the revelation discourses source.

The detailed comments are divided into two main subsections: first, "The Pre-Temporal Existence of the Logos" (1:1-4). Verses 1-2 present the relation of the Logos to God. Since the name Logos is introduced without explanation, Bultmann believes that he (the Logos) was known to the community of the Evangelist. "He is spoken of as a person in the language of mythology."[189] In regard to the meaning of Logos, Bultmann presents (in smaller print) a discussion of the religious background. He concludes that the source is neither the OT nor Stoicism but the mythological figure of pre-Christian Gnosticism.

> In Christian Gnosticism, the redeemer who becomes man was held to be Jesus. That is not to say that the idea of the incarnation of the redeemer has in some way penetrated Gnosticism from Christianity; it is itself originally Gnostic, and was taken over at a very early stage by Christianity, and made fruitful for Christology.[190]

Returning to regular print, Bultmann says that the phrase ἐν ἀρχῇ indicates that the Logos was before all time and does not belong to the world; the phrase describes "his absolute otherness."[191] The statements ὁ λόγος ἦν πρὸς τὸν θεόν and καὶ θεὸς ἦν ὁ λόγος, according to Bultmann, are mythological statements declaring that the Logos is equal with God. However, Bultmann believes this is not a simple identification but a paradox: God is only encountered in the Revealer.

Verses 3 and 4 express the relation of the Logos to the world. The statement "all things came into being through him, and without him not one thing came into being" indicates positively and negatively that all things without exception were created by the Logos. Concerning the punctuation of verses 3-4, Bultmann puts the period after οὐδὲ ἕν, so that ὃ γέγονεν begins a new sentence. This agrees with the NRSV: "All things came into being through him, and without him not one thing came into being. What has come into being in him was life." Bultmann believes the reference to "light" in verse 4 indicates the unity of revelation and salvation: a revelation that brings self-understanding. Jesus is the Light "in this eschatological sense in John; he is the Revealer, who gives man that particular understanding of himself in which he has the 'life'. . . . Creation is at the same time revelation, inasmuch as it was possible for the creature to know of his Creator, and thus to understand himself."[192]

The second section of the prologue, 1:5-18, presents "The Logos as the Revealer in History." Rather than saying that the darkness did not "overcome" the light (v. 5), Bultmann translates κατέλαβον as "understand"; the meaning is the same as "the world did not know him" (v. 10). Bultmann believes that verses 6-8 represent an interpolation the author has inserted into the source; he (the author) intends to refute the belief that John the Baptist was the Logos. Bultmann thinks that in verses 9-10 reference is made to the Logos in the world, anticipating verse 14. The distinction between ἴδια and ἴδιοι, according to Bultmann, is due to the translator of the source; the Aramaic would have used only one term. Bultmann believes both terms mean "his own" and refer to the world of humans; neither refers to Israel. As to the textual variant in verse 13 ("blood" [singular] rather than "bloods"), Bultmann rejects the singular and any allusion to the virgin birth; he accepts the plural as referring to believers who are children of God. This verse, according to Bultmann, was added by the evangelist.

In verse 14 the coming of the Logos, which has been anticipated in the previous verses, is now announced: the miracle of the incarnation of the Logos—the theme of the Gospel. "It is the *language of mythology* that is here employed. Just as the ancient world and the Orient tell of gods and divine beings who appear in human form, so too the central theme of the gnostic Redeemer-myth is that a divine being, the Son of the Highest, assumed human form, put on human flesh and blood, in order to bring revelation and redemption."[193] The myth, according to Bultmann, has two features: the event is otherworldly in origin; it occurs in the human sphere. The revelation of the Logos in the flesh is an offense to the idea of the Gnostic redeemer.

> It is in his sheer humanity that he is the Revealer. True, his own also see his δόξα (v. 14b). . . . But this is the paradox which runs through the whole gospel; the δόξα is not to be seen alongside the σάρξ, nor through the σάρξ as through a window; it is to be seen in the σάρξ and nowhere else. . . . The revelation is present in a peculiar hiddenness.[194]

Bultmann distinguishes the pronouns in verse 14: the "us" among whom the Logos dwells refers to humanity in general; the "we" who have seen his glory includes the eyewitnesses and the ongoing community.

> The "eye-witnesses" as such are considered not as those who stand guarantee for some later generation for the truth of the revelation, but as those who confront every generation anew with the offence that the δόξα must be seen in the one who became σάρξ. . . . Thus every generation is tied to the previous one, in whose proclamation the offence of the σάρξ γενέσθαι is renewed, because this proclamation does not pass on a timeless idea but transmits an historical event.[195]

Bultmann believes verses 17-18 were added by the evangelist and stress his understanding of the transcendence of God. "[T]he Evangelist rejects any concept of God by means of which God can be thought of as the object of human or suprahuman knowledge. God ceases to be God if he is thought of as an object. . . . That God is inaccessible, means that he lies beyond man's control."[196]

Bultmann understands 2:1-12, "The Miracle of the Epiphany" (along with the narrative of the cleansing of the temple), as the prelude to the first main part of the Gospel. Here he detects the use of the signs source, which, he thinks, uses language different from that of the revelation discourses. The evangelist, according to Bultmann, has adapted the sign. For example, Bultmann thinks he added verse 9b, which says that the steward did not know but the servants who had drawn the water knew—the typical Johannine theme of not knowing and knowing. Standing at the beginning of the signs source, this sign, according to Bultmann, presents an epiphany miracle based on the legend of the epiphany of Dionysus. For the evangelist the sign, in Bultmann's opinion, is symbolic of the whole ministry of Jesus: it presents the revelation of his glory.

Bultmann's exegesis of 6:1-59, "The Bread of Life," illustrates the complexity of his reconstruction and interpretation. The account of "The Feeding of the Multitude" (6:1-26) reflects the same tradition as the miracle recounted in Mark 6:30-52, but Bultmann believes the evangelist also makes use of the signs source. According to him the evangelist has added verses 14-15, which record the intent of the crowd to make Jesus king; the evangelist presents this misunderstanding in order to oppose traditional eschatology. Bultmann thinks the discourse on "The Bread of Life" (6:27-59) is based on the revelation-discourses source, but he believes the ecclesiastical redactor has added 6:51-58, rearranged the material, and misconstrued the bread of life as the Eucharist. The redactor, according to Bultmann, has also added references to futuristic eschatology (6:39, 54).

Bultmann's history of religion research is also seen in his long footnote (pp. 225–26) on the use of the formula ἐγώ εἰμι in Hellenistic sources. In his understanding of the discourse as presented by the evangelist he detects typical Johannine themes: dualism (v. 27); the exclusive revelation of the Father by the Revealer (v. 46); the purpose of the mission (vv. 38-40). "It reaffirms that in Jesus God acts, that his history is an event of revelation, that salvation depends on faith in him, and that faith in him is assured of salvation because God himself is active in this faith."[197]

The account of the raising of Lazarus is important for Bultmann's understanding of Johannine eschatology. John 11:1-44, "The Resurrection and the Life," is based, according to Bultmann, on the signs source. The introductory section (vv. 1-16) makes it apparent that Lazarus's illness is for the glory of God, and that going to Lazarus means that Jesus is going to his death. In the dialogue with Martha (vv. 17-27) Bultmann sees the clear presentation of the evangelist's eschatology: future resurrection is transformed into present resurrection. Jesus speaks as the Revealer: "I am the resurrection and the life."

> The promised ζωή therefore cannot be described concretely, nor can it be defined in its content . . . . Any representation of the "what" and "how" of the promised ζωή could only speak of human possibilities, and the highest of these would not be better than the most primitive in comparison with the promised ζωή, which as

eschatological reality—as ἀνάστασις καὶ ζωή—stands beyond human possibilities. Readiness for that means the ready acceptance of earthly death, i.e. the giving up of man as he now knows himself and now wants to be. For the world, therefore, the ζωή appears under the mask of death.[198]

As to the controversial report that Jesus "was greatly disturbed in spirit and deeply moved" (v. 33), Bultmann understands this as Jesus' anger in the face of the unbelief of Mary and the crowd. In verse 43 Jesus cries, "Lazarus, come out"; he speaks the word that accomplishes the miracle.

In the farewell discourses Bultmann rearranges the order of the material he believes to have been drawn largely from the revelation discourses. The passion narrative, which presents the crowning work of the Revealer, makes use, according to Bultmann, of a written source independent of the Synoptics. He believes the idea that Jesus carried the cross and the account of the distribution of his clothing are drawn from that source. On the other hand, he sees 19:26-27—Jesus' words to his mother and the Beloved Disciple—as added by the evangelist; the meaning, according to Bultmann, is symbolic: the mother represents Jewish Christianity, which overcomes the offense of the cross; the Beloved Disciple represents Gentile Christianity, which honors the mother (Jewish Christianity) from which it has come. Bultmann thinks 19:34-35 was added by the redactor, who sees the emission of blood and water as symbolizing Eucharist and Baptism.

The story about "Thomas the Doubter" (20:24-29) is put at the end of the Gospel because of its importance. Bultmann believes the confession of Thomas, "My Lord and my God" (20:28), to be wholly appropriate; the Logos has returned to the place of his origin; he is recognized as "God," as he was from the beginning (1:1). However, the appearance to Thomas, like all the Easter stories, is, according to Bultmann, a concession to·the weakness of humans. Thus Jesus' final word censures a faith that rests on sight.

> And if this critical saying of Jesus forms the conclusion of the Easter narratives, the hearer or reader is warned not to take them to be more than they can be: neither as narrations of events that he himself could wish or hope to experience, nor as a substitute for such experiences of his own, as if the experience of others could, as it were, guarantee for him the reality of the resurrection of Jesus; rather they are to be viewed as proclaimed word, in which the recounted events have

become symbolic pictures for the fellowship which the Lord, who has ascended to the Father, holds with his own.[199]

All in all, Bultmann's Gospel of John is a magnificent accomplishment, providing abundant linguistic and historical data for dissenters to write a commentary of their own. For him the Fourth Evangelist, meticulously distinguished from his sources and from the editorial work of the redactor, is the theologian of the NT—one who is both creation and creator of Bultmann's theology.[200]

Bultmann had a special affection for 2 Corinthians. According to one of his disciples, "[t]he theology of Bultmann is more strongly influenced by the theology inherent in Paul's Second Letter to the Corinthians than by any other letter or Gospel of the New Testament canon."[201] Bultmann himself wrote: "The lecture on Second Corinthians was particularly dear to me, and it was also my last lecture upon leaving my post in the summer semester of 1951."[202] Prior to the publication of his commentary on this epistle he had published a monograph on exegetical problems in 2 Corinthians.[203] This short work deals with 2 Cor 5:1–5; 5:11–6:2; 10–13; 12:1. Bultmann's commentary on 2 Corinthians was published posthumously.[204] The text is based on the manuscript he had used as a basis for his lectures during the period from 1940 to 1951. In 1954 he entrusted this manuscript to Erich Dinkler to serve as the basis for a commentary, but Dinkler was never able to complete the task. After twenty years it was decided to publish Bultmann's text with translations (by Dinkler) that introduce the sections of the commentary.

A few "Preliminary Remarks" note that this is the most personal of Paul's letters but that "Paul's person is at issue only insofar as he is bearer of the apostolic office, and the theme of the epistle is the apostolic office."[205] Attention is given to the most important issue of critical introduction: the original shape and situation of the Corinthian correspondence. According to Bultmann's reconstruction Paul wrote a total of four letters to Corinth. Letters A and B were combined into 1 Corinthians. The writing of these letters was followed by Paul's interim visit to Corinth, the so-called "painful" visit. Letter C, sometimes called the "tearful letter" (mentioned in 2 Cor 2:3–4; 2:9; 7:12) was delivered by Titus and consisted of 2 Cor 2:14–7:4 (6:14–7:1 is a non-Pauline interpolation), chapters 10–13, and chapter 9. Letter D, the final correspondence, consists of 2 Cor 1:1–2:13; 7:5-16, and chapter 8.

The exegesis of 2 Cor 5:11–6:10, "The revelation of ζωή as proclamation," is very important for Bultmann's kerygmatic theology. According to him verses 16-19 present "The basis for the proclamation in the saving event."[206]

Elsewhere Bultmann frequently decries the attempt to cling to the Christ "according to the flesh." Here he says, "The Χριστὸς κατὰ σάρκα is Christ as he can be encountered in the world, before his death and resurrection."[207] As to the grammar, Bultmann thinks that it makes little difference whether "according to the flesh" modifies "Christ" or the verb "know"--whether the fleshly Jesus is the object of knowledge or the action of knowing is "from a human point of view" (NRSV). In no way, according to Bultmann, can the former be construed to suggest that Paul had personal acquaintance with the historical Jesus. "The meaning is that not even Christ may be regarded as he can be met with in the world."[208] The reference to anyone who is "in Christ" (v. 17) describes the person who shares the event of God's action in Christ. "The ἐν Χριστῷ is thus not a formula of mysticism, but rather of eschatology, or it has an eschatological ecclesiological sense."[209] The idea of reconciliation (v. 18) assumes that humans have been enemies of God.

> Paul does not at all reflect on the idea of God's having to be reconciled; God himself has reconciled the world to himself, but that does not mean he has set aside its anger, but rather annulled the relationship of objective hostility and established peace through the forgiveness of trespasses. This is done through the death of Christ; in what way, is not said.[210]

The ministry of reconciliation, according to Bultmann, is the ministry of proclamation. "Thus the preaching itself belongs to the saving event."[211] This is emphasized in 6:2, where Paul sees the prophecy of Isa 49:8 fulfilled in the eschatological act of preaching.

> "Now," that is, the event in Christ is the eschatological event. . . . This "now" is present in the apostolic preaching at the moment the preaching encounters its hearers—even where it encounters them a second time, as it does the Corinthian community right now. The admonition, therefore, is that it receive the message μὴ εἰς κενόν by recognizing that Paul's word encounters it as Christ's and God's eschatological word, that it thus understand itself as a new creation, and with that achieve a proper understanding of the gospel and the apostle—the apostle whose activity belongs to the eschatological saving deed.[212]

NEW TESTAMENT THEOLOGY

Rudolf Bultmann's historical-critical, form-critical, history of religion, exegetical, and theological endeavors reached a towering theological synthesis in his *Theology of the New Testament*.[213] The product of a lifetime, this book appeared in installments from 1948 to 1953. The English translation was published in two volumes in 1951 and 1955. The second German edition (1954) printed the complete work in a single volume. Subsequent editions were reprints, though editions 5 through 8 (1965–80) included updated bibliographical material supplied by Bultmann and Werner G. Kümmel. The ninth edition (1984), by Otto Merk, adds data to the bibliographical paragraphs at the beginning of sections throughout the book and includes bibliographical appendices that incorporate such material as reviews of Bultmann's book. A reprint of the English translation, with the two volumes bound into a single paperback, and superbly introduced by Robert Morgan, appeared in 2007.

Bultmann's general view of NT theology is presented in the Epilogue to this work. The task of NT theology, he says, is to set forth the theological thoughts of the documents of the NT. Bultmann believes these thoughts can only be understood from the perspective of faith. "Therefore the theological thoughts of the New Testament can be normative only insofar as they lead the believer to develop out of his faith an understanding of God, the world, and man in his own concrete situation."[214] In this Epilogue he also traces the history of the study of NT theology from Lutheran orthodoxy to Adolf Schlatter. Most of the scholars reviewed, Bultmann believes, have failed to grasp the relation of theology to kerygma. Bultmann's own approach advocates the use of historical criticism in the service of theological interpretation. Most of all, the thoughts of the NT must be explicated in terms of existential self-understanding.

> For they claim to have meaning for the present not as theoretical teachings, timeless general truths, but only as the expression of an understanding of human existence which for the man of to-day also is a possibility for his understanding of himself—a possibility which is opened to him by the New Testament itself in that it not only shows him that such self-understanding is the reply to the kerygma as the word of God addressing him, but also imparts to him the kerygma itself.[215]

Part I deals with the "Presuppositions and Motifs of New Testament." In discussing "The Message of Jesus," Bultmann makes one of his most maligned and misunderstood statements: "*The message of Jesus* is a presupposition for the theology of the New Testament rather than a part of that theology itself."[216] Critics have taken this to mean that Bultmann considers Jesus to be unimportant, or that he thinks Jesus' teaching about God to be of little theological significance. Although he abandons the historical Jesus as the ground for faith, Bultmann considers the fact of the historical Jesus to be essential to the NT message. Although he is skeptical about a biography of Jesus, he reconstructs the teaching of Jesus and believes Jesus' proclamation of God to be of utmost significance. All this evident in his *Jesus and the Word*. For Bultmann, Christian theology cannot begin until the proclaimer becomes the proclaimed. This happens only after the death-resurrection of Jesus Christ, the event presupposed by every document of the NT.

> Christian faith did not exist until there was a Christian kerygma; i.e., a kerygma proclaiming Jesus Christ—specifically Jesus Christ the Crucified and Risen One—to be God's eschatological act of salvation. . . . Thus, theological thinking—the theology of the New Testament—begins with the *kerygma* of the earliest Church and not before.[217]

The message of Jesus, according to Bultmann, is eschatological: Jesus proclaims the kingdom of God—the apocalyptic intervention of God. The sign that God is breaking in is seen in Jesus himself and his message. Bultmann believes the message includes the demand of God, a call for radical obedience. The command that must be obeyed is the absolute demand of love. "Both things, the eschatological proclamation and the ethical demand, direct man to the fact that he is thereby brought before God, that God stands before him; both direct him into his Now as the hour of decision for God."[218]

Bultmann turns to an investigation of "The Kerygma of the Earliest Church." A crucial question is the relation of the message of the earliest church to the preaching of Jesus. The decisive factor for Bultmann is that Jesus, who had been the bearer of the message, has become the content of the message. At first he was proclaimed as the apocalyptic Son of Man, indicating that the proclamation remained within the framework of Jewish apocalyptic. The early Christians recognized Jesus as the messiah on the basis of belief in the resurrection; the scandal of the cross was overcome by the Easter faith.

Next, Bultmann discusses "The Kerygma of the Hellenistic Church Aside from Paul." According to this kerygma Jesus was proclaimed as judge and savior; his exaltation coincides with his resurrection. The message of the church was called εὐαγγέλιον and κήρυγμα and λόγος, and the acceptance of the message was called faith (πίστις). "In Christianity, for the first time, 'faith' became the prevailing term for man's relation to the divine; in Christianity, but not before it, 'faith' came to be understood as the attitude which through and through governs the life of the religious man."[219] In the Hellenistic setting the community developed a church consciousness. The church broke with Judaism and understood itself as the true people of God. Increasingly, Baptism and the Lord's Supper were viewed as sacraments. Jesus was increasingly confessed as Lord and Son of God. "[T]he term Kyrios used of Christ is derived from the religious terminology of Hellenism, more specifically from that of oriental Hellenism, in which Kyrios was the Greek translation of typical terms in various languages which denoted the deity as 'Lord.'"[220] According to Bultmann the Hellenistic church was influenced by Gnosticism.

> Gnosticism is not a phenomenon that first appeared within the Christian Church. It cannot be described as a speculative Christian theology under the influence of Greek philosophical tradition. It is not properly regarded as the "acute Hellenization" of Christianity, as Harnack in his time supposed. It has its roots in a dualistic redemption-religion which invaded Hellenism from the orient.[221]

For Bultmann the decisive question is: Will Hellenistic Christianity, though influenced by Gnosticism, avoid cosmic dualism and understand human history as genuine historical happening? The correct answer, he believes, will be provided by a recent convert, Paul of Tarsus. Thus Part II presents "The Theology of Paul."[222]

> The historical position of Paul may be stated as follows: Standing within the frame of Hellenistic Christianity he raised the theological motifs that were at work in the proclamation of the Hellenistic Church to the clarity of theological thinking; he called to attention the problems latent in the Hellenistic proclamation and brought them to a decision; and thus—so far as our sources permit an opinion of the matter—became the founder of Christian theology.[223]

According to Bultmann, Paul was reared in Hellenistic Judaism and responded to the kerygma of the Hellenistic church. Bultmann proceeds to investigate Pauline theology from the perspective of anthropology.

> Every assertion about God is simultaneously an assertion about man and vice versa. For this reason and in this sense Paul's theology is, at

the same time, anthropology. . . . The christology of Paul likewise is governed by this point of view. In it, Paul does not speculatively discuss the metaphysical essence of Christ, or his relation to God, or his "natures," but speaks of him as the one through whom God is working for the salvation of the world and man. Thus, every assertion about Christ is also an assertion about man and vice versa; and Paul's christology is simultaneously soteriology.[224]

"Therefore," concludes Bultmann, "Paul's theology can best be treated as his doctrine of man."[225] This conclusion, of course, is arbitrary. Following Bultmann's "vice versa," "one might equally well conclude that Paul's theology may best be presented as the doctrine of God," as Schubert Ogden observes.[226] The choice of anthropology as the organizing principle is made on the basis of Bultmann's own existentialist bias.

Bultmann arranges Paul's anthropology in two sections: "Man Prior to Faith," and "Man Under Faith." In the first section he investigates Paul's anthropological terms. Most basic is the word *soma* or "body."

> *Man, his person as a whole, can be denoted by* soma. . . . *Man is called* soma *in respect to his being able to make himself the object of his own action or to experience himself as the subject to whom something happens.* He can be called *soma, that is, as having a relationship to himself—as being able in a certain sense to distinguish himself from himself.*[227]

The terms *psychē, pneuma,* and *zoe* indicate that human beings can be the subject their own actions, able to know and to will. The terms "mind" and "conscience" suggest that humans are responsible for themselves. The term "heart" indicates that humans are moved by emotion.

> As the investigation of the term *soma* showed, man according to Paul, is a being who has a relationship to himself, is placed at his own disposal, and is responsible for his own existence. But this existence as his, as the investigation of the terms *psyche, pneuma, zoe, nous,* and *kardia* showed, is never to be found in the present as a fulfilled reality, but always lies ahead of him. In other words, his existence is always an intention and a quest, and in it he may find himself or lose his grip upon himself, gain his self or fail to do so. This brings the possibility that man can be good or bad.[228]

Whether humans are good or bad depends, according to Bultmann, on their relation to God; the false relation to God is characterized by the terms "flesh," "sin," and "world." "Flesh" can refer to mere corporeality, but to live "according to the flesh" (*kata sarka*) is to live in pursuit of the human, the transitory—to come under the power of sin. The punishment for sin is death, and for Paul (and Bultmann) sin and death are universal. Regarding Rom 5:12-19, Bultmann believes that Paul, under the influence of Gnosticism, presents the notion of inherited sin. However, in Paul's comparison of Adam and Christ the effect of Christ's obedience is not viewed as an inevitable necessity. "That suggests, then, that one should assume by analogy that through Adam there was brought about for Adamitic mankind the *possibility* of sin and death—a possibility that does not become reality until individuals become guilty by their own responsible action."[229]

The term "world," according to Bultmann, is not a cosmological but a historical term; it means the world of humans. Paul's phrase "this world" depicts the present evil age. Closely related to Paul's understanding of sin and world is his idea of law. Law presents the demands of God and, according to Bultmann, Paul views the whole OT as law. "To lead man into sin, therefore, is *the purpose of the Law in the history of salvation*, not only by arousing his desires to transgression but also by offering him the uttermost possibility of living as a sinner by perverting his resistance to the commandment into a striving after a 'righteousness of his own' through keeping the commandment." However, the law makes self-understanding possible, for it reveals to humans that they are sinners, destined for death.

In discussing "Man Under Faith," Bultmann argues that humans can escape the sentence of death only by God's gift of righteousness. According to him, Paul understood righteousness as forensic: God pronounces the sinner righteous. God's righteousness has been revealed in the saving action of God in Christ: the eschatological event. Righteousness stands in total opposition to the idea of human achievement and any hint of boasting. Bultmann, disclosing his anti-Judaism, declares: "'Boasting (in the Law)' is the fundamental attitude of the Jew, the essence of his sin."[230] In contrast, the attitude of faith recognizes that righteousness cannot be attained by human effort; it is a sheer gift. Grace is not an attitude but an act: God's action in the death and resurrection of Christ. "Jesus' death-and-resurrection, then, is for Paul the decisive thing about the person of Jesus and his life experience, indeed, in the last analysis it is the sole thing of importance for him—implicitly included are the incarnation and the earthly life of Jesus as bare facts."[231] Of course, the resurrection, for Bultmann, is not a fact of history but an event of faith whereby the scandal of the cross is appropriated as saving event.

To describe the significance of the salvation-occurrence Paul uses, in Bultmann's view, a variety of expressions. For example, Christ's death is presented as propitiatory or vicarious sacrifice—a cultic expression. Christ's death is also presented in analogy with the death of the deity in the mystery cults, or according to the redeemer of the Gnostic myth. "Clearly Paul found none of these thought-complexes and none of their terminologies adequate to express his understanding of the salvation occurrence."[232] Most important, for Bultmann, the salvation occurrence takes place in the proclamation: the eschatological "now" of salvation. "[T]he salvation-occurrence is nowhere present except in the proclaiming, accosting, demanding, and promising word of preaching. . . . The salvation-occurrence is the eschatological occurrence just in this fact, that it does not become a fact of the past but constantly takes place anew in the present."[233] The proclamation confronts humans with a decision.

> This is the decision-question which the "word of the cross" thrusts upon the hearer: whether he will acknowledge that God has made a crucified one Lord; whether he will thereby acknowledge the demand to take up the cross by the surrender of his previous understanding of himself, making the cross the determining power of his life, letting himself be crucified with Christ.[234]

Bultmann continues:

> [T]he proclaimed word is neither an enlightening *Weltanschauung* flowing out in general truths, nor a merely historical account which . . . reminds a public of important but by-gone facts. Rather, it is *kerygma*—herald's service—in the literal sense—authorized, plenipotent proclamation, edict from a sovereign. . . . So it is by nature, personal address which accosts each individual, throwing the person himself into question by rendering his self-understanding problematic, and demanding a decision of him.[235]

According to Bultmann, Paul's preaching of the word gathers people into community. They are received into the community by Baptism, and within the community they observe the Lord's Supper, which like Baptism is, in Bultmann's view, simply another mode of proclamation. The human response to proclamation is faith, and faith, says Bultmann, is primarily obedience. "'Faith'—the radical renunciation of accomplishment, the obedient submission to the God-determined way of salvation, the taking over of the cross of Christ—is the free deed of obedience in which the new self constitutes itself in place of the old."[236] The life of faith, according to Bultmann, is a life of freedom but, paradoxically, also a life of obligation: the one who is free has become a slave of Christ. This new life involves an indicative and an imperative; the person who has become a new being is called to act like a new being: "Become what thou art!"[237] At Baptism the believer receives the gift of the Spirit, and the Spirit empowers people for ethical obedience. Although freed from the law, the believer stands under the demand of love. The believer is freed from death, freed from the world and its powers. "In God, freedom, righteousness, and life have their cause, and it is in them that the glory of God as ultimate meaning and ultimate goal comes to it own."[238]

In Part III (volume 2 in the English edition) Bultmann presents "The Theology of the Gospel of John and the Johannine Epistles." The unknown author, according to Bultmann, is not a follower of Paul but an original thinker whose background is in gnosticizing Judaism. Bultmann begins with a discussion of the "Johannine Dualism." Following his penchant for anthropology, he first investigates the "World and Man." As in Paul, so here, Bultmann sees the world as the world of humans, under the power of sin. John's terms "light" and "darkness" have their meaning, according to him, in relation to human existence. "Each man is, or once was, confronted with deciding for or against God; and he is confronted anew with this decision by the revelation of God in Jesus. The cosmological dualism of Gnosticism has become in John a *dualism of decision*."[239] Bultmann believes the author's thought is characterized by determinism, although a determinism paradoxically understood: only those can come to God who are drawn by God, yet people are called to decide. This indicates that the decision of faith is not a human accomplishment, but instead is the work of God. The human striving for light and life perverts the creation into "the world," into darkness.

The solution to the problem is provided by the action of God: "The 'KRISIS' of the World." This crisis or judgment occurs in the sending of the Son; he is the light that comes into the world of darkness and death. To describe this event John borrows the language of Gnosticism but, according to Bultmann, John historicizes the myth of the redeemer. "The judgment, then is no dramatic cosmic event, but takes place in the response of men to the word of Jesus."[240] The coming of the Son is an offense; the Word comes in the flesh. "The Revealer appears not as *man-in-general*, i.e. not simply as a bearer of human nature, but as a *definite human being in history*: Jesus of Nazareth."[241] In the earthly life of Jesus, the glory of the Son is revealed: "the exalted Jesus is at the same time the earthly man Jesus; the 'glorified one' is still always he who 'became flesh.' In other words, Jesus' life on earth does not become an item of the historical past, but constantly remains present reality."[242]

According to Bultmann, John is the first to clearly understand the paradoxical character of revelation.

> He accordingly presents the fact that in Jesus God encounters man in a seemingly contradictory manner: in one direction by statements that declare that Jesus has equal dignity and rights with God, or even that God has abdicated His right to Jesus, so to speak. In the other direction, John declares that Jesus speaks and acts only in obedience to the will of the Father and does nothing on his own authority.[243]

Paradoxically, the glory of Christ is revealed in the crucifixion. Bultmann believes that John has telescoped all the events of redemption into one.

> As we have seen, the "facts of salvation" in the traditional sense play no important role in John. The entire salvation-drama—incarnation, death, resurrection, Pentecost, the parousia—is concentrated into a single event: the Revelation of God's "reality" (ἀλήθεια) in the earthly activity of the man Jesus combined with the overcoming of the "Offense" in it by man's accepting it in faith.[244]

The revelation is given in the Word, and the words of Jesus are assertions about himself; consequently he is called the Logos. "Thus it turns out in the end that Jesus as the Revealer of God *reveals nothing but that he is the Revealer.*"[245] John, according to Bultmann, is not concerned with transmitting details of the historical tradition about Jesus. "John . . . in his Gospel presents only the fact (*das Dass*) of the Revelation without describing its content (*ihr Was*)."[246]

As with Paul, so with John, Bultmann finds heavy emphasis on faith. Faith is hearing the proclaimed word in which "the Proclaimer himself is present."[247] Faith is decision about one's existence; it is *"transition into eschatological existence."*[248] The obedience of faith, according to Bultmann, is also obedience to the command of love—an imperative arising from the indicative: "Out of the love we have received arises the *obligation to love.*"[249] The life of faith, the new eschatological existence, is characterized by peace and joy and is empowered with the gift of the Spirit. The Spirit, whom John calls the Paraclete, is the substitute for Jesus who bears witness to Jesus.

That means that the knowledge bestowed by the Spirit is to have its activity in the *proclamation*, in *preaching*. It is in and through it that the Revelation time and again becomes event. . . . That is, the eschatological occurrence which took place in Jesus' coming and going is to continue to take place in preaching. This continuing eschatological occurrence is the Spirit's activity in preaching.[250]

For Bultmann the high point of NT theology has been reached. He also reaches a high point in his own literary expression: quotations from the biblical texts are artfully woven into his rhetoric, so that the NT speaks through the words of Bultmann and Bultmann speaks through the words of the NT.

Part IV, "The Development Toward the Ancient Church," is for Bultmann largely a story of decline.[251] He begins by tracing the evolution of church order wherein charismatic leaders are replaced by presbyters and bishops. According to Bultmann the eschatological community of faith is transformed into an institution of the world. Doctrine suffers essentially the same fate. In place of the eschatological proclamation he sees teaching turned into doctrine, concerned with the preservation of orthodox tradition. Bultmann believes the paradox of Jesus as both eschatological event and historical occurrence has been resolved. Luke, for example, transforms the salvation occurrence into a theology of salvation history, unfolding in the history of the world. Bultmann notes an increasing concern with right doctrine and the effort to define the kerygma over against heresy. In answer to the threat of Gnosticism the church responds (in Colossians and Ephesians) with cosmic Christology. Christ, according to Bultmann, is increasingly viewed as the one who brings salvation through sacrifice, and salvation is increasingly seen as escape from death and life in the otherworldly future. The dynamic of the indicative and imperative is eroded into legalism. "The more Christian faith degenerates into legalism, the more Christ's significance is reduced to that of being at work in the Church's sacrament. The less Christ is felt to be present in the proclaimed word, the more the Church becomes a sacramental institution of salvation."[252] In short, Christianity has abandoned the lofty peaks of kerygmatic theology and dynamic faith and moved to the barren plain of early catholic Christianity—a desert of dogmatic orthodoxy and ecclesiastical establishment.

Regarding Bultmann's work as a whole, the criticisms and critics are legion. In the context of this chapter Karl Barth's response should be mentioned. His monograph, *Rudolf Bultmann—An Attempt to Understand Him*, is seasoned with sarcasm.[253] According to Barth it is ironic that Bultmann, who talks so much about understanding, is so difficult to understand! Basically, Barth believes Bultmann has reduced theology to subjectivity: his idea of pre-understanding, adopted from existential philosophy, determines the results of his exegesis and theology. Barth says that "much as I am loath to charge Bultmann with heresy, I cannot deny that his demythologized New Testament looks suspiciously like docetism"—a statement that reveals that Barth has not really understood Bultmann.[254]

Also worth noting is the criticism of Schubert Ogden, a philosophical theologian who knows Bultmann better than most and is sympathetic with his work. According to Ogden, Bultmann's theological position is undermined by a fundamental structural inconsistency: on the one hand he says that authentic existence is open to all humans on the basis of existential understanding (a possibility in principle); on the other he insists that authentic existence is possible only through faith in Jesus (a possibility in fact).[255] In response, Bultmann insists that what Ogden calls an inconsistency is in truth the stumbling block of the NT: what is a possibility in principle is a possibility in fact only in the proclamation of the historical, crucified redeemer.

A host of other critics has attacked Bultmann at various points. Many have charged that his work is tainted by his philosophical presuppositions. For example, Bultmann's analysis of NT theology from the perspective of anthropology is not merely a methodology; it also determines his result: salvation is existential self-understanding. Bultmann's theology is also often criticized as reductionist at several points: Jesus is reduced to a bare "that"; the resurrection is reduced to the experience of faith; the kerygma is reduced in historical content and doctrine; eschatology is reduced to the present "now." Related is the criticism that Bultmann's preoccupation with human existence blinds him to larger concerns of theology, for example, the doctrine of creation; his focus on the individual misses the social and political aspects of theology. In regard to demythologizing, some believe Bultmann exchanges the riches of metaphorical language for the abstract truths of existentialism; others think his view of science is dated and dogmatic. More important for the history of research is the charge that Bultmann's criticism is overly skeptical: the documents are more reliable that Bultmann admits; there is continuity between Jesus and the early church and Paul. In particular, Bultmann's idea of the Gnostic redeemer myth is castigated as a scholarly fabrication built on late, flimsy sources. His complex theory concerning the sources and literary composition of the Fourth Gospel is said to be flawed and unconvincing.

In view of the variety and depth of the criticism, the question arises: How can Bultmann be hailed as the greatest NT scholar of the twentieth century? To the criticism above, of course, Bultmann and his friends have offered answers, however convincing or unconvincing they may be. Bultmann's greatness, however, is not in the details but in the overarching synthesis. Like Ferdinand Christian Baur in the nineteenth century, so Bultmann in the twentieth was able to gather major elements of the thought of his day into a comprehensive conception.[256] He joined philosophical existentialism, historical criticism, and dialectical theology into a mutually confirming synthesis.

Take, for example, Bultmann's understanding of Jesus. According to liberal historical criticism, the historical Jesus cannot be reconstructed. Indeed, historical criticism functions negatively to demolish this false basis of faith. At the same time, Pauline-Reformation-dialectical theology contends that a historical Jesus is not needed—that faith cannot rest on an object of human reconstruction and, moreover, existentialist philosophy declares that faith is not concerned with objectivity or with a Jesus *extra nos*, but with self-understanding, a Jesus *pro nobis*. Existentialism, however, does not provide the answer to authentic self-understanding; that can be provided only by the Word dialectical theology proclaims—the Word to which Jesus and the NT, according to historical criticism, bear witness. Moreover, what is significant about Bultmann's synthesis is that he incorporates major themes of mid-twentieth century thought. Historical criticism had become the dominant method of biblical research. Neo-orthodoxy prevailed in seminaries and pulpits. Existentialism flourished in literature and drama. Bultmann arranged these themes into a harmonious theological symphony for which Scripture was the score. Above all, Bultmann was concerned that this composition be heard and understood so that it could transform modern skeptics into people of faith. Although Bultmann is sometimes scorned as an enemy of biblical religion, he was indeed one of the twentieth century's most devoted apologists for the theology of the NT.

Summary

The new biblical theology did indeed bring something new to the history of NT research. Above all, it affirmed the importance of the Bible for theology and faith; it demanded a new way of reading Scripture. To be sure, it also renewed things that were old. Indeed, some of its critics viewed the new theology as a return to pre-Enlightenment biblicism. American liberals, in particular, saw the movement as a throwback to supernaturalism and dubbed the new theology "Neo-Orthodoxy" or "Neo-Calvinism." Of course, Barth's esteem of Calvin was apparent, and Bultmann himself claimed that his program of demythologizing was only a new way of expressing the doctrine of justification by faith. But Barth and Bultmann were not clones of the Reformers; much had happened in the meantime, including Kant and Kierkegaard—both of whom influenced twentieth-century biblical theology.

But had the gains of the past been thrown away? Had Johann Philipp Gabler's important distinction between dogmatic theology and biblical theology been abandoned?[257] And what of William Wrede's insistence that biblical theology was strictly a historical discipline? Had the hard-won victories over biblicism been surrendered? Barth, of course, was somewhat skeptical of historical criticism, but even he affirmed the method and spoke of the strange world of the Bible, implying the importance of historical distance. Bultmann, on the other hand, was devotee and master of the method, although he was never quite able to explain why so much effort should be devoted to historical critical research when it was of no importance for faith. In any event, the role of biblical criticism and questions of hermeneutics and methodology would continue to occupy scholars through the rest of the twentieth century.

The new biblical theology also raised questions about the importance of Jesus. For liberalism and the scholars reviewed in the previous chapter, Jesus—indeed, the historical Jesus—and his teaching were central. Both Barth and Bultmann affirmed the crucial importance of the historical Jesus, but for them Jesus was important as revelation, as "event." With the new biblical theology Jesus was swallowed up in Christology, and the center of the NT was found in Paul.

All these issues would continue to occupy scholars in the years to come. But the influence of Barth and Bultmann, especially the latter, would still be apparent in the scholars reviewed even in the last chapter of this history. Most important, recognition that the two most influential theologians of the century were biblical theologians is of the utmost significance. However, the question of historical objectivity continued to hover in the shadows. The biblical theology of Barth is Barth's theology; the biblical theology of Bultmann (the theology of Paul and John) is Bultmann's theology.

Notes

1. See *HNTR* 2: 144–51, 229–37.

2. Friedrich Gogarten, "Between the Times," in *The Beginnings of Dialectic Theology*, ed. James M. Robinson (Richmond: John Knox) 277–82; originally published in *Die Christliche Welt* 34 (1920): 374–78.

3. "Between the Times," 277.

4. Karl Barth, *How I Changed My Mind*, Introduction and Epilogue by John D. Godsey (Richmond: John Knox, 1966), 25.

5. Among the many works on Barth's life and thought see Eberhard Busch, *Karl Barth: His Life from Letters and Autobiographical Texts*, trans. John Bowden (Philadelphia: Fortress Press, 1976); Barth, *How I Changed*; Barth's "Autobiographical Sketches" in *Karl Barth–Rudolf Bultmann Letters 1922–1966*, ed. Bernd Jaspert, trans. Geoffrey W. Bromiley (Grand Rapids: Eerdmans, 1981), 150–58; Gary Dorrien, *The Barthian Revolt in Modern Theology: Theology Without Weapons* (Louisville: Westminster John Knox, 2000); J. C. O'Neill, *The Bible's Authority: A Portrait Gallery of Thinkers from Lessing to Bultmann* (Edinburgh: T & T Clark, 1991), 265–83; William Stacy Johnson, "Barth, Karl (1886–1968)," *Historical Handbook of Major Biblical Interpreters* (*HHMBI*) (Downers Grove: InterVarsity, 1998), 433–39; Garrett Green, "Introduction" to Karl Barth, *On Religion: The Revelation of God as the Sublimation of Religion*, trans. Garrett Green (London: T & T Clark, 2006), 1–29.

6. See Peter Matheson, ed., *The Third Reich and the Christian Churches* (Edinburgh: T & T Clark, 2000), 45–47.

7. Karl Barth, *Wolfgang Amadeus Mozart, 1756/1956* (Zürich: Theologischer Verlag, 1956); Eng. trans. by Clarence K. Pott, *Wolfgang Amadeus Mozart* (Grand Rapids: Eerdmans, 1986).

8. Barth, *How I Changed*, 71–72.

9. Quoted by Dorrien, *Barthian Revolt*, 121.

10. Barth presents summaries of his thought in his *Dogmatik in Grundriss* (Munich: Kaiser, 1947); Eng. trans.: *Dogmatics in Outline*, trans. G. T. Thomson (New York: Philosophical Library, 1949); and his *Einführung in die evangelische Theologie* (Zürich: Evangelischer Verlag, 1962); Eng. trans.: *Evangelical Theology: An Introduction*, trans. Grover Foley (New York: Holt, Rinehart and Winston, 1963).

11. See Dorrien, *Barthian Revolt*, 131, 154.

12. Karl Barth, *Fides quaerens intellectum: Anselms Beweis der Existenz Gottes im Zusammenhang seines theologischen Programms* (Zürich: Theologischer Verlag, 1931); Eng. trans.: *Anselm: Fides quaerens intellectum: Anselm's proof of the existence of God in the context of his theological scheme*, trans. Ian Robertson (London: SCM; Richmond: John Knox, 1960).

13. Barth, *How I Changed*, 43. Barth scholars debate Barth's theological development. For example, Richard E. Burnett, *Karl Barth's Theological Exegesis: The Hermeneutical Principals* [sic] *of the Römerbrief Period*, WUNT 2, 145 (Tübingen: Mohr Siebeck, 2001), argues that Barth made only one change: the shift away from liberalism, and that Barth remained a dialectical theologian for the rest of his career.

14. See Walter Lindemann, *Karl Barth und die kritische Schriftauslegung*, TF 54 (Hamburg-Bergstedt: Reich, 1973).

15. See "The Debate on the Critical Historical Method: Correspondence Between Adolf von Harnack and Karl Barth," in *The Beginnings of Dialectical Theology: Volume One*, ed. James M. Robinson, trans. Keith R. Crim and Louis De Grazia (Richmond: John Knox, 1968), 163–87.

16. Ibid., 166.

17. Ibid., 170.

18. Ibid., 174.

19. Ibid., 177.

20. Ibid., 186.

21. Ibid., 186. American liberals were unimpressed by Barth's *Romans*. See Donald W. Riddle, "Reassessing the Religious Importance of Paul," in *The Study of the Bible Today and Tomorrow*, ed. Harold R. Willoughby (Chicago: University of Chicago Press, 1947), 314–28; according to Riddle, "Further, neo-orthodoxy need have but slight, if any, effect in the study of Paul; Barth's commentary is sufficient illustration of the barrenness of that position, and this example is not likely to be followed" (p. 327).

22. Barth, *How I Changed*, 43.

23. Karl Barth, *The Humanity of God* (Richmond: John Knox, 1961).

24. Ibid., 37.

25. Ibid., 46.

26. Ibid., 65.

27. See Otto Weber, *Karl Barth's Church Dogmatics: An Introductory Report on Volumes I:1 to III:4*, trans. Arthur C. Cochrane (London: Lutterworth, 1953); John Webster, *Barth* (London: Continuum, 2000).

28. Barth, *How I Changed*, 14.

29. Karl Barth, *Church Dogmatics: The Doctrine of the Word of God* I/1, trans. Geoffrey W. Bromiley (Edinburgh: T & T Clark, 1975), 47–87.

30. Ibid., 95.

31. Ibid., 109.

32. Ibid., 119.

33. Ibid., 348.

34. Ibid., 406.

35. *Church Dogmatics: The Doctrine of the Word of God* I/2, trans. G. T. Thomson and Harold Knight (Edinburgh: T & T Clark, 1956), 1–202.

36. Ibid., 23.

37. Ibid., 77, 92. Barth, who elsewhere says "Antisemitism is a sin against the Holy Spirit" (Quoted by Busch, *Barth*, 290) does not escape anti-Judaism: "To this day the Synagogue repeats what it did when it crucified Christ, and at the same time exactly what Israel has always been doing" (*CD* I/2, 93).

38. *CD* I/2, 176.

39. Ibid., 191.

40. Ibid., 202.

41. *Church Dogmatics: The Doctrine of Reconciliation*, IV/1, ed. Geoffrey W. Bromiley and Thomas F. Torrance (Edinburgh: T & T Clark, 1956). In the foreword to this volume Barth says: "The present situation in theology and also the peculiar themes of this book mean that throughout I have found myself in an intensive, although for the most part quiet, debate with Rudolf Bultmann. His name is not mentioned often. But his subject is always present, even in those places where with his methods and results before me I have consciously ignored him" (p. ix). On Barth's Christology see Wolf Krötke, "Die Christologie Karl Barths als Beispiel für den Vollzug seiner Exegese," in *Karl Barths Schriftauslegung*, ed. Michael Trowitzsch (Tübingen: Mohr Siebeck, 1996), 1–21.

42. *CD* IV/1, 157. See David Ford, *Barth and God's Story: Biblical Narrative and the Theological Method of Karl Barth in the "Church Dogmatics"* (Frankfurt: Peter Lang, 1981), 33–46.

43. *CD* IV/1, 166.

44. Ibid., 254.

45. Ibid., 338. Also important for Barth's view of Jesus is Chapter 8 on "The Command of God" in *Church Dogmatics: The Doctrine of Reconciliation*, II/2, ed. Geoffrey W. Bromiley and Thomas F. Torrance (Edinburgh: T & T Clark, 1957). In this chapter Barth presents an extensive discussion in small print (pp. 686–70) of the Sermon on the Mount. It avoids questions of sources and literary composition and focuses on what Barth understands to be the theme of Matthew: the kingdom has come in the person of Jesus.

46. See Klaas Runia, *Karl Barth's Doctrine of Holy Scripture* (Grand Rapids: Eerdmans, 1962); Christina A. Baxter, "Barth—A Truly Biblical Theologian?" The Tyndale Historical Lecture 1985, *TynBul* 38 (1987): 3–27; Francis Watson, "The Bible," in *The Cambridge Companion to Karl Barth*, ed. John Webster (Cambridge: Cambridge University Press, 2000), 57–71; Geoffrey W. Bromiley, "The Authority of Scripture in Karl Barth," in *Hermeneutics, Authority, and Canon*, ed. Donald A. Carson and John D. Woodbridge (Grand Rapids: Baker, 1995), 271–94; Benoît Bourgine, *L'Herméneutique Théologique de Karl Barth*, BETL 171 (Leuven: Leuven University Press, 2003).

47. Karl Barth, *Das Wort Gottes und die Theologie* (Münich: Kaiser, 1924); Eng. trans.: *The Word of God and the Word of Man*, trans. Douglas Horton (New York: Harper & Brothers, 1957).

48. *Word of God*, 74.

49. *Church Dogmatics: The Doctrine of the Word of God*, I/2, ed. Geoffrey W. Bromiley and Thomas F. Torrance (Edinburgh: T & T Clark, 1956), 457–740. See Ford, *Barth and God's Story*; Thomas E. Provence, "The Sovereign Subject Matter: Hermeneutics in the Church Dogmatics," in *A Guide to Contemporary Hermeneutics: Major Trends in Biblical Interpretation*, ed. Donald K. McKim (Grand Rapids: Eerdmans, 1986), 241–62; Paul McGlasson, *Jesus and Judas: Biblical Exegesis in Barth*, AARAS 72 (Atlanta: Scholars, 1991).

50. *CD* I/2, 457.

51. Ibid., 466, 468. See Werner G. Jeanrond, "Karl Barth's Hermeneutics," in *Reckoning with Barth: Essays in Commemoration of the Centenary of Karl Barth's Birth*, ed. Nigel Biggar (London: Mowbray, 1988), 80–97; George Hunsinger, "Beyond Literalism and Expressivism: Karl Barth's Hermeneutical Realism," *MTh* 3 (1987): 209–23; repr. in George Hunsinger, *Disruptive Grace: Studies in the Theology of Karl Barth* (Grand Rapids: Eerdmans, 2000), 210–25; Georg Eichholz, "Der Ansatz Karl Barths in der Hermeneutik," in *Antwort: Karl Barth zum Siebzigsten Geburtstag am 10. Mai 1956* (Zollikon-Zürich: Evangelischer Verlag, 1956), 52–68.

52. *CD* I/2, 469.

53. Ibid., 470.

54. Ibid., 509.

55. Ibid., 536.

56. Ibid., 540.

57. See McGlasson, *Jesus and Judas*; James A. Wharton, "Karl Barth as Exegete and His Influence on Biblical Interpretation," *USQR* 28 (1972): 5–13; Bruce McCormack, "Historical Criticism and Dogmatic Interest in Karl Barth's Theological Exegesis of the New Testament," *LQ* 5 (1991): 211–25; repr. in *Biblical Hermeneutics in Historical Perspective: Studies in Honor of Karlfried Froehlich on His Sixtieth Birthday*, ed. Mark S. Burrows and Paul Rorem (Grand Rapids: Eerdmans, 1991), 332–38; David E. Demson, *Hans Frei and Karl Barth: Different Ways of Reading Scripture* (Grand Rapids: Eerdmans, 1997); Mary Kathleen Cunningham, *What is Theological Exegesis: Interpretation and Use of Scripture in Barth's Doctrine of Election* (Valley Forge, PA: Trinity Press International, 1995); Donald Wood, *Barth's Theology of Interpretation* (Aldershot: Ashgate, 2007).

58. *CD* I/2, 714.

59. Ibid., 723.

60. Ibid.

61. Karl Barth, *The Epistle to the Romans*, trans. from 6th German ed. by Edwyn C. Hoskyns (London: Oxford University Press, 1933), 1. On Barth's understanding and use of criticism see Walter Schmithals, "Zu Karl Barths Schriftauslegung: Die Problematik des Verhältnis von 'dogmatischer' und historischer Exegese," in *Karl Barths Schriftauslegung*, ed. Michael Trowitzsch (Tübingen: Mohr Siebeck, 1996), 23–52; Michael Trowitzsch, "'Nachkritische Schriftauslegung': Wiederaufnahme und Fortführung einer Fragestellung," ibid., 73–109. According to Schmithals, "whether one calls his method 'pre-critical' or 'post-critical' it is in any case, 'uncritical.'"

62. Barth, *How I Changed*, 69.

63. *CD* I/2, 728, 729.

64. Barth, *Epistle to the Romans*, 8.

65. *CD* I/2, 738.

66. *Epistle to the Romans*, 22.

67. Ibid., 11.

68. Ibid.

69. Ibid., 28.

70. Ibid., 46, 47.

71. Ibid., 49.

72. Ibid., 92.

73. Ibid., 96.

74. Ibid., 105.

75. Ibid., 112.

76. Actually, textual support for ἔχωμεν is better; see Bruce M. Metzger, *A Textual Commentary on the Greek New Testament* (London and New York: United Bible Societies, 1971), 511.

77. *Epistle to the Romans*, 171.

78. Ibid., 172. Years later Barth discussed Romans 5 in a monograph, *Christus und Adam* (Zürich: Evangelischer Verlag, 1952); Eng. trans.: *Christ and Adam: Man and Humanity in Romans 5*, trans. T. A. Smail (New York: Macmillan, 1968). In this work Barth stresses the parallel between Adam and Christ. "*Jesus Christ is the secret truth about the essential nature of man, and even sinful man is still essentially related to Him*" (pp. 107–8).

79. *Epistle to the Romans*, 195.

80. Ibid., 270.

81. Ibid., 276.

82. Ibid., 281.

83. Ibid., 422.

84. Reviews by Emil Brunner, Adolf Jülicher, Rudolf Bultmann, and Adolf Schlatter are reprinted in *Beginnings of Dialectical Theology*, 63–71, 72–81, 100–20, 121–25. Jülicher's conclusion is typical: "Much, perhaps even very much, may someday be learned from this book for the understanding of our age, but scarcely anything new for the understanding of the 'historical' Paul" (p. 81).

85. Karl Barth, *A Shorter Commentary on Romans* (Richmond: John Knox, 1959); original: *Kurze Erklärung des Römerbriefes* (Munich: Kaiser, 1941).

86. *Shorter Commentary on Romans*, 143.

87. *Die Auferstehung der Toten: Eine akademische Vorlesung über I. Kor. 15*, 4th ed. (Zollikon-Zürich: Evangelischer Verlag, 1953); Eng. trans.: *The Resurrection of the Dead*, trans. H. J. Stenning (New York: Fleming H. Revell, 1933; repr. New York: Arno, 1977).

88. *Resurrection of the Dead*, 5.

89. Ibid., 65–66.

90. Ibid., 105.

91. Ibid., 138.

92. Ibid., 154.

93. Ibid., 197.

94. Ibid., 211.

95. For example, Barth's stress on the unity of 1 Corinthians ignores the theory of some critics that the epistle is a composite of two or more letter fragments. Barth's criticism of scholars who find in 1 Corinthians a diverse list of topics does not acknowledge the evidence that the epistle responds to a number of questions sent to Paul by the Corinthians (see 7:1, 25; 8:1; 12:1; 16:1). Rudolf Bultmann, "Karl Barth, The Resurrection of the Dead," in *Faith and Understanding I*, ed. Robert W. Funk, trans. Louise Pettibone Smith (New York: Harper & Row, 1969), 66–94, contends that Barth does not adequately interpret the letter in its historical context. See Claudia Janssen, "Bodily Resurrection (1 Cor. 15)? The Discussion of the Resurrection in Karl Barth, Rudolf Bultmann, Dorothee Sölle and Contemporary Feminist Theology," *JSNT* 79 (2000): 61–78.

96. *Erklärung des Philipperbriefes* (Munich: Kaiser, 1927); Eng. trans.: *The Epistle to the Philippians*, trans. James W. Leitch (Richmond: John Knox, 1962); repr., *The Epistle to the Philippians: 40th Anniversary Edition* (Louisville: Westminster John Knox, 2002). See Bruce L. McCormack, "The Significance of Karl Barth's Theological Exegesis of Philippians," in Barth, *Philippians: 40th Anniversary Edition*, v–xxv; Francis B. Watson, "Barth's Philippians as Theological Exegesis," ibid., xxvi–li.

97. *Epistle to the Philippians*, 18.

98. Later (1935), in a letter to Bultmann concerning the latter's anticipated trip to receive an honorary degree at St. Andrews, Barth, with typical humor, wrote, "See to it that you adopt in good time the hypothesis of the Ephesian imprisonment, for your amiable colleague Duncan is very keen on this" (*Barth–Bultmann Letters*, 81).

99. *Epistle to the Philippians*, 32.

100. Ibid., 49. Ernst Lohmeyer's monograph, *Kyrios Jesus: eine Untersuchung zu Phil. 2:5-11*, SHAW (1927/28) 4 (Heidelberg: Carl Winter, 1928), which argues that this text is based on a pre-Pauline hymn, was published shortly after Barth's commentary; see *HNTR* 2: 463–64.

101. *Epistle to the Philippians*, 61.

102. Ibid., 65.

103. Ibid., 66.

104. Karl Barth, *Church Dogmatics: The Doctrine of Reconciliation*, ed. Geoffrey W. Bromiley and Thomas F. Torrance, (Edinburgh: T & T Clark, 1958), IV/2, 139.

105. Karl Barth, *Erklärung des Johannes Evangelium* (Zürich: Theologischer Verlag, 1976); Eng. trans.: *Witness to the Word: A Commentary on John 1: Lectures at Münster in 1925 and at Bonn in 1933*, ed. Walther Fürst, trans. Geoffrey W. Bromiley (Grand Rapids: Eerdmans, 1986). See Cunningham, *What is Theological Exegesis*, 50–67. Barth also presents exegesis of John 1:1-2 in his discussion of "The Election of God" (ch. 7) in §33, "The Election of Jesus Christ," *CD* II/2, 95–99.

106. *Witness to the Word*, 4–5.

107. Ibid., 86.

108. Ibid., 92.

109. *HNTR* 2: 280–86.

110. Konrad Hammann, *Rudolf Bultmann: Eine Biographie*, 2d ed. (Tübingen: Mohr Siebeck, 2009). See also William D. Dennison, *The Young Bultmann: Context for His Understanding of God* (New York: Peter Lang, 2008); Rudolf Bultmann, "Autobiographical Reflections," in *The Theology of Rudolf Bultmann*, ed. Charles W. Kegley (New York: Harper & Row, 1966), xix–xxv; David Fergusson, "Bultmann, Rudolf (*1884–1976*)," in *HHMBI*, 449–56; idem, *Bultmann* (Collegeville, MN: Liturgical, 1992); Roy A. Harrisville and Walter Sundberg, eds., *The Bible in Modern Culture: Baruch Spinoza to Brevard Childs*, 2d. ed. (Grand Rapids: Eerdmans, 2002), 217–48; John C. O'Neill, *The Bible's Authority: A Portrait Gallery of Thinkers from Lessing to Bultmann* (Edinburgh: T & T Clark, 1991), 284–309; Günther Bornkamm, "In Memoriam: Rudolf Bultmann," *NTS* 23 (1977): 235–42; Walter Schmithals, "Zu Rudolf Bultmanns 100. Geburtstag," *TRu* 51 (1986): 79–91; Hans Jonas, "Is Faith Still Possible? Memories of Rudolf Bultmann and Reflections on the Philosophical Aspects of His Work," *HTR* 75 (1982): 1–23; Erich Dinkler, "Rudolf Bultmann als Lehrer und Mensch," in *Im Zeichen des Kreuzes: Aufsätze von Erich Dinkler*, ed. Otto Merk and Michael Wolter (Berlin: de Gruyter, 1992), 421–32; Bernd Jaspert, ed., *Sachgemässe Exegese: Die Protokolle aus Rudolf Bultmanns Neutestamentliche Seminare 1921–1951*, MTS 43 (Marburg: N. G. Elwert, 1996).

111. "The Task of Theology in the Present Situation," in *Existence and Faith: Shorter Writings of Rudolf Bultmann*, trans. Schubert M. Ogden (New York: Meridian, 1960), 158.

112. Ibid., 165. On Bultmann's life and work during the Nazi period see Jack Forstman, *Christian Faith in Dark Times: Theological Conflicts in the Shadow of Hitler* (Louisville: Westminster John Knox, 1992), 222–42.

113. "Autobiographical Reflections," xxiv. See Hammann, *Bultmann*, 134–47.

114. "Autobiographical Reflections," xxiv.

115. *Karl Barth–Rudolf Bultmann: Briefwechsel, 1922–1966*, ed. Bernd Jaspert (Zürich: Theologischer Verlag, 1971); Eng. trans.: *Karl Barth–Rudolf Bultmann, Letters 1922–1966*, ed. Bernd Jaspert, trans. Geoffrey W. Bromiley (Grand Rapids: Eerdmans, 1981). A later German edition (1994) includes letters from 1911 to 1966.

116. *Barth–Bultmann Letters*, 109.

117. Ibid., 112.

118. Among the many works on the theology of Bultmann see André Malet, *The Thought of Rudolf Bultmann*, trans. Richard Strachan (Garden City, NY: Doubleday, 1971); Walter Schmithals, *Die Theologie Rudolf Bultmanns: Eine Einführung* (Tübingen: Mohr Siebeck, 1967); Eng. trans.: *An Introduction to the Theology of Rudolf Bultmann*, trans. John Bowden (Minneapolis: Augsburg, 1968); John Painter, *Theology as Hermeneutics: Rudolf Bultmann's Interpretation of the History of Jesus* (Sheffield: Almond, 1987); Gareth Jones, *Bultmann: Towards a Critical Theology* (Cambridge: Polity, 1991); Fergusson, *Bultmann*; Günther Bornkamm, "The Theology of Rudolf Bultmann," in *The Theology of Rudolf Bultmann*, ed. Charles W. Kegley (New York: Harper & Row, 1966), 3–20; Robert Morgan, "Introduction," in Rudolf Bultmann, *Theology of the New Testament* (Waco, TX: Baylor University Press, 2007), xi–xxxvii.

119. See *HNTR* 2: 280–86

120. "Autobiographical Reflections," xxiv.

121. "On the Question of Christology," in Rudolf Bultmann, *Faith and Understanding 1*, ed. Robert W. Funk, trans. Louise Pettibone Smith (New York: Harper & Row, 1966), 132.

122. "Rudolf Bultmann—An Attempt to Understand Him," in *Kerygma and Myth: a Theological Debate, 2*, ed. Hans-Werner Bartsch, trans. Reginald H. Fuller (London: SPCK, 1962), 123.

123. "Bultmann Replies to His Critics," in *Kerygma and Myth: A Theological Debate, 1*, ed. Hans-Werner Bartsch, trans. Reginald H. Fuller (London: SPCK, 1953; rev. ed. New York: Harper & Brothers, 1961), 210–11.

124. See Roger A. Johnson, *The Origins of Demythologizing: Philosophy and Historiography in the Theology of Rudolf Bultmann*, SHR 28 (Leiden: Brill, 1974), 38–86. For the influence of Herrmann see James M. Robinson, *Das Problem des Heiligen Geistes bei Wilhelm Herrmann* (Marburg/Lahn: Universitäts-Buchdruckerei, 1952), 79–92.

125. Quoted by Schmithals, *Theology of Bultmann*, 9.

126. See Bernd Jaspert, "Rudolf Bultmanns Wende von der liberalen zur dialektischen Theologie," in *Rudolf Bultmanns Werk und Wirkung*, ed. Bernd Jaspert (Darmstadt: Wissenschaftliche Buchgesellschaft, 1984), 25–43; Hartwig Thyen, "Rudolf Bultmann, Karl Barth und das Problem der 'Sachkritik,'" ibid., 44–52.

127. "The Significance of the Historical Jesus for the Theology of Paul," in *Faith and Understanding 1*, 241.

128. Rudolf Bultmann, "Liberal Theology and the Latest Theological Movement," in *Faith and Understanding 1*, 29. This essay was originally published as "Die liberale Theologie und die jüngste theologische Bewegung," *TBl* 3 (1924): 73–86.

129. "The Significance of 'Dialectical Theology' for the Scientific Study of the New Testament," in *Faith and Understanding 1*, 163; originally published as "Die Bedeutung der dialektischen Theologie für die neutestamentliche Wissenschaft," *TBl* 7 (1928): 57–67. See Rudolf Bultmann, "The Question of 'Dialectic' Theology: A Discussion with Erik Peterson," in *Beginnings of Dialectical Theology 1*, 257–74.

130. "Karl Barth's Epistle to the Romans in Its Second Edition," in *Beginnings of Dialectical Theology 1*, 104, 108.

131. "Karl Barth, The Resurrection of the Dead," in *Faith and Understanding 1*, 93.

132. Cited by Schubert M. Ogden, "The Debate on 'Demythologizing,'" *JBR* 27 (1959): 17–27, at 21.

133. "Humanism and Christianity," in Rudolf Bultmann, *Essays Philosophical and Theological*, trans. James C. G. Greig (New York: Macmillan, 1955), 153. See Schubert M. Ogden, "Introduction," in *Existence and Faith*, 9–21; Herbert C. Wolf, *Kierkegaard and Bultmann: The Quest of the Historical Jesus* (Minneapolis: Augsburg, 1965).

134. See Hammann, *Bultmann*, 192–206.

135. Quoted by Gareth Jones, *Bultmann*, 110. Painter (*Theology as Hermeneutics*, 13–43) argues that the influence of Heidegger on Bultmann has been exaggerated.

136. Bultmann did not write a systematic theology, but an overview of his thought can be found in his lectures (1926–1936) on introduction to theology or theological encyclopedia: *What Is Theology?* ed. Eberhard Jüngel and Klaus W. Müller, trans. Roy A. Harrisville (Minneapolis: Fortress Press, 1997).

137. "Question of Dialectical Theology," 273–74. See Eberhard Martin Pausch, *Wahrheit zwischen Erschlossenheit und Verantwortung: Die Rezeption und Transformation der Wahrheitskonzeption Martin Heideggers in der Theologie Rudolf Bultmanns* (Berlin: de Gruyter, 1995); John Macquarrie, *An Existentialist Theology: A Comparison of Heidegger and Bultmann* (New York: Harper & Row, 1965); Friedebert Hohmeier, *Das Schriftverständnis in der Theologie Rudolf Bultmanns*, AGThL 13 (Berlin: Lutherisches Verlagshaus, 1964), 64–79.

138. *The Presence of Eternity: History and Eschatology, Gifford Lectures 1955* (New York: Harper & Brothers, 1957; repr. New York: Harper, 1962), 151. See Johannes Körner, *Eschatology und Geschichte: Eine Untersuchung des Begriffes des Eschatologischen in der Theologie Rudolf Bultmanns*, TF 13 (Hamburg: Reich, 1957).

139. Rudolf Bultmann, *Der Begriff der Offenbarung im Neuen Testament* (Tübingen: Mohr Siebeck, 1929); Eng. trans.: "The Concept of Revelation in the New Testament," in *Existence and Faith*, 58–91. See also Rudolf Bultmann, "The Concept of the Word of God in the New Testament," in *Faith and Understanding 1*, 286–312; "What Does It Mean to Speak of God," ibid., 53–65; "How Des God Speak to Us Through the Bible?" in *Existence and Faith*, 166–70; "The Question of Natural Revelation," in *Essays*, 90–118.

140. "Concept of Revelation," 71.

141. Ibid., 85.

142. Ibid., 88.

143. Ibid., 90.

144. Rudolf Bultmann, *Jesus* (Berlin: Deutsche Bibliothek, 1926); Eng. trans.: *Jesus and the Word*, trans. Louise Pettibone Smith and Erminie Huntress Lantero (New York: Scribner's, 1934). See Walter Schmithals, "75 Jahre: Bultmanns Jesus-Buch," *ZTK* 98 (2001): 25–58; Ulrich H. J. Körter, *Jesus im 21. Jahrhundert: Bultmanns Jesusbuch und die heutige Jesusforschung* (Neukirchen-Vluyn: Neukirchener, 2002); Hammann, *Bultmann*, 179–92.

145. Bultmann denied that the book was influenced by Heidegger, though he was in conversation with him during the time of writing. He did acknowledge the influence of Kierkegaard and the importance of Wilhelm Herrmann in preparing the way for his acceptance of existentialist philosophy.

146. *Jesus and the Word*, 8.

147. See *HNTR* 2: 282–86.

148. Ibid., 2: 222–37.

149. *Jesus and the Word*, 52.

150. Ibid., 77.

151. Ibid., 94.

152. Ibid., 159.

153. Ibid., 178.

154. Ibid., 211.

155. Ibid., 217. Bultmann's view of Jesus remains essentially unchanged in his later works. He responds to the proponents of the "new quest" of the historical Jesus in his essay, *Das Verhältnis der urchristlichen Christusbotschaft zum historischen Jesus*, SHAW 1960 (Heidelberg: Carl Winter, 1962); Eng. trans.: "The Primitive Christian Kerygma and the Historical Jesus," in *The Historical Jesus and the Kerygmatic Christ: Essays on the New Quest of the Historical Jesus*, trans. and ed. Carl E. Braaten and Roy A. Harrisville (New York: Abingdon, 1964), 14–42. Here Bultmann maintains his position that a biography of Jesus cannot be written and that the historical Jesus cannot be the

object of faith. According to him there is a discontinuity between the preaching of Jesus and the Christ of the early Christian kerygma. "The Christ of the kerygma has, as it were, displaced the historical Jesus and authoritatively addresses the hearer—every hearer" ("Primitive Christian Kerygma," 30). The believer, in Bultmann's opinion, cannot go beyond the *Dass* (the "that"), the sheer fact of the revelation event. Charles Kingsley Barrett ("Jesus and the Word," in *Bultmanns Werk und Wirkung*, 81–91) contends that Bultmann does go beyond the mere "that" in his presentation of the teaching of Jesus and in his stress on the crucifixion, which involves a pre-history.

156. Rudolf Bultmann, *Glauben und Verstehen* (Tübingen: Mohr Siebeck, 1933), 245–67; Eng. trans.: "The Christology of the New Testament," in *Faith and Understanding 1*, 262–85. See Rudolf Bultmann, "On the Question of Christology," in *Faith and Understanding 1*, 116–44; James F. Kay, *Christus Praesens: A Reconsideration of Rudolf Bultmann's Christology* (Grand Rapids: Eerdmans, 1994).

157. "Christology of the NT," 278.

158. Ibid., 281.

159. Ibid., 284.

160. "Das christologische Bekenntnis des Ökumenischen Rates," *SThU* 21 (1951): 25–36; repr. In Rudolf Bultmann, *Glauben und Verstehen, Gesammelte Aufsätze* (Tübingen: Mohr Siebeck, 1952), 246–61; Eng. trans.: "The Christological Confession of the World Council of Churches," in *Essays*, 273–90.

161. "Christological Confession," 273.

162. Ibid., 287, 290.

163. *Beginnings of Dialectical Theology 1*, 236. The essay originally appeared in *Zwischen den Zeiten* 3 (1925): 334–57; repr. in *Anfänge der dialektischen Theologie*, ed. Jürgen Moltmann (Munich: Kaiser, 1963), 2: 47–72.

164. "Problem of Theological Exegesis," 239, 256.

165. "Das Problem der Hermeneutik," *ZTK* 47 (1950): 47–69; Eng. trans.: "The Problem of Hermeneutics," in Rudolf Bultmann, *New Testament and Mythology and Other Basic Writings*, ed. and trans. Schubert M. Ogden (Philadelphia: Fortress Press, 1984), 69–93.

166. "Problem of Hermeneutics, " 82.

167. Ibid., 86.

168. *Existence and Faith*, 290; the original essay, "Ist voraussetzungslose Exegese möglich?" appeared in *TZ* 13 (1957): 409–17.

169. See Hammann, *Bultmann*, 307–19. The lecture originally appeared as *Offenbarung und Heilsgeschehen*, BEvT 7 (Munich: A. Lempp, 1941); reprinted as "Neues Testament und Mythologie" in Hans-Werner Bartsch, ed., *Kerygma und Mythos 1*, 2d ed. (Hamburg-Volksdorf: Reich, 1951), 15–48. Two English translations have been published: "New Testament and Mythology," in *Kerygma and Myth: A Theological Debate*, ed. Hans-Werner Bartsch, trans. Reginald H. Fuller (London: SPCK, 1953), 1–44; "New Testament and Mythology: The Problem of Demythologizing the New Testament Proclamation," in Bultmann, *New Testament and Mythology*, 1–43. Citations below are from the latter English translation, by Schubert M. Ogden. The literature on demythologizing is enormous. A collection of important responses has been published in the series *Kerygma und Mythos*, ed. Hans-Werner Bartsch, 6 vols. (Hamburg: Reich, 1948–64); selections from vols. 1–5 have been published in English: *Kerygma and Myth*, ed. Bartsch, trans. Reginald H. Fuller, 2 vols. (London: SPCK, 1953, 1962). See also Roger A. Johnson, *The Origins of Demythologizing: Philosophy and Historiography in the Theology of Rudolf Bultmann*, SHR 28 (Leiden: Brill, 1974); Schubert M. Ogden, *Christ Without Myth: A Study Based on the Theology of Rudolf Bultmann* (New York: Harper & Row, 1961); Günther Bornkamm, "Die Theologie Bultmanns in der neueren Diskussion: Literaturbericht zum Problem der Entmythologisierung und Hermeneutik," *Geschichte und Glaube 1, Gesammelte Aufsätze* 3, BEvT 48 (Munich: Kaiser, 1968), 173–275; Theodor Lorenzmeier, *Exegese und Hermeneutik: Eine*

vergleichende Darstellung der Theologie Rudolf Bultmanns, Herbert Brauns und Gerhard Ebelings (Hamburg: Furche-Verlag, 1968); Hohmeier, *Schriftverständnis in der Theologie Rudolf Bultmanns*; René Marlé, *Bultmann et l'interprétation du Nouveau Testament*, Théologie 33 (Aubier: Montaigne, 1956); Bernd Jaspert, "Existenz—Mythos—Theologie: Fünzig Jahre nach Rudolf Bultmanns Entmythologisierungsprogramm," *NZSTRP* 34 (1992): 125–48; Bernd Jaspert, ed., *Bibel und Mythos: Fünfzig Jahre nach Rudolf Bultmanns Entmythologisierungsprogramm* (Göttingen: Vandenhoeck & Ruprecht, 1991); James D. G. Dunn, "Demythologizing—The Problem of Myth in the New Testament," in *New Testament Interpretation: Essays on Principles and Methods*, ed. I. Howard Marshall (Grand Rapids: Eerdmans, 1977), 285–307.

170. Rudolf Bultmann, *Jesus Christ and Mythology* (New York: Scribner's, 1958); German trans.: *Jesus Christus und die Mythologie: Das Neue Testament im Licht der Bibelkritik* (Gütersloh: Mohn, 1964).

171. *Jesus Christ and Mythology*, 18.

172. Ibid., 36.

173. Ibid., 53.

174. Ibid., 57.

175. Ibid., 68.

176. Ibid., 72.

177. Ibid., 82.

178. Ibid., 84.

179. "Zum Problem der Entmythologisierung," in *Kerygma und Mythos 2*, 179–208; Eng. trans.: "On the Problem of Demythologizing," *in New Testament and Mythology*, 95–130.

180. This theory of development in Bultmann's definition of myth is argued at length by Johnson, *Origins of Demythologizing*. Ogden, *Christ without Myth*, 24–31, contends that Bultmann's view of myth is clear and consistent, made up of three elements: objectification, supernatural causation, and dualistic understanding of history.

181. *New Testament and Mythology*, 42.

182. "Zum Problem der Entmythologisierung," in *Glauben und Verstehen 4*, 128–37; Eng. trans.: "On the Problem of Demythologizing," in *New Testament and Mythology*, 155–63, at 159.

183. Rudolf Bultmann, *Das Evangelium des Johannes*, KEK (Göttingen: Vandenhoeck & Ruprecht, 1941); Eng. trans.: *The Gospel of John: A Commentary*, trans. George R. Beasley-Murray, R. W. N. Hoare, and John K. Riches (Philadelphia: Westminster, 1971). See Hammann, *Bultmann*, 295–307; Walter Schmithals, *Johannesevangelium und Johannesbriefe: Forschungsgeschichte und Analyse*, BZNW 64 (Berlin: de Gruyter, 1992), 164–74; Jörg Frey, *Die johanneische Eschatologie, 1: Ihre Probleme im Spiegel der Forschung seit Reimarus*, WUNT 96 (Tübingen: Mohr Siebeck, 1997), 85–203; Tord Larsson, *God in the Fourth Gospel: A Hermeneutical Study of the History of Interpretations*, ConBNT 35 (Stockholm: Almqvist & Wiksell, 2001), 168–212.

184. See *HNTR* 2: 101–11, 223–29.

185. "Der religionsgeschichtliche Hintergrund des Prologs zum Johannes-Evangelium" (1923) in *Exegetica: Aufsätze zur Erforschung des Neuen Testaments*, ed. Erich Dinkler (Tübingen: Mohr Siebeck, 1967), 10–35; "Die Bedeutung der neuerschlossenen mandäischen und manichäischen Quellen für das Verständnis des Johannesevangeliums" (1925), *Exegetica*, 55–104 (on these essays see *HNTR* 2: 280–82); "Die Eschatologie des Johannesevangelium," *Zwischen den Zeiten* 6 (1928): 4–22; Eng. trans.: "The Eschatology of the Gospel of John," in *Faith and Understanding 1*, 165–83.

186. See D. Moody Smith, *The Composition and Order of the Fourth Gospel: Bultmann's Literary Theory* (New Haven: Yale University Press, 1965).

187. According to a story enjoyed by students at Marburg, John was dictating his Gospel when a gust of wind scattered pages all over the room. As the amanuensis scrambled to gather up the leaves and arrange them, the apostle declared, "Don't bother! There will come this fellow Bultmann; he'll put it all in order!"

188. *Gospel of John*, 361.

189. Ibid., 19.

190. Ibid., 25–26.

191. Ibid., 32.

192. Ibid., 44.

193. Ibid., 61.

194. Ibid., 63.

195. Ibid., 70.

196. Ibid., 81.

197. Ibid., 234.

198. Ibid., 404.

199. Ibid., 696.

200. Late in life Bultmann published a commentary on the Epistles of John: *Die drei Johannesbriefe*, KEK (Göttingen: Vandenhoeck & Ruprecht, 1967); Eng. trans.: *The Johannine Epistles: A Commentary on the Johannine Epistles*, trans. R. Philip O'Hara, Lane C. McGaughy, and Robert W. Funk; ed. Robert W. Funk, Hermeneia (Philadelphia: Fortress Press, 1973). See Schmithals, *Johannesevangelium und Johannesbriefe*, 196. In this commentary Bultmann argues that the author of 1 John is not the author of the Gospel but that he writes with a copy of the Fourth Gospel before him.

201. Erich Dinkler in "Editor's Foreword" to Bultmann, *The Second Letter to the Corinthians*, trans. Roy A. Harrisville (Minneapolis: Augsburg, 1985), 7. See Erich Grässer, "Der Schatz in irdenen Gefässen (2 Kor 4,7): Existentiale Interpretation im 2. Korintherbrief?" *ZTK* 97 (2000): 300–16.

202. "Author's Preface," *Second Letter*, 9.

203. Rudolf Bultmann, *Exegetische Probleme des zweiten Korintherbriefes* (Darmstadt: Wissenschaftliche Buchgesellschaft, 1963); originally published in Symbolae Biblicae Upsalienses 9, 1947.

204. Rudolf Bultmann, *Der zweite Brief an die Korinther*, ed. Erich Dinkler, KEK (Göttingen: Vandenhoeck & Ruprecht, 1976); Eng. trans. see n. 470 above.

205. *Second Letter*, 16.

206. Ibid., 153.

207. Ibid., 155.

208. Ibid., 156.

209. Ibid., 157.

210. Ibid., 159.

211. Ibid., 161.

212. Ibid., 167.

213. Rudolf Bultmann, *Theologie des Neuen Testaments*, 2d ed., NThG (Tübingen: Mohr Siebeck, 1954); Eng. trans.: *Theology of the New Testament*, trans. Kendrick Grobel, 2 vols. (New York: Scribner's, 1951, 1955; repr. 2 vols. in one paperback volume, Waco, TX: Baylor University Press, 2007); 9th [Ger.] ed. Otto Merk (Tübingen: Mohr Siebeck, 1984). See Dieter Georgi, "Rudolf Bultmann's *Theology of the New Testament* Revisited," in Edward C. Hobbs, ed., *Bultmann, Retrospect and Prospect: The Centenary Symposium at Wellesley*, HTS 35 (Philadelphia: Fortress Press, 1985), 75–87.

214. *Theology of the New Testament* 2: 238.

215. Ibid., 2: 251.

216. Ibid., 1: 3.

217. Ibid., 1: 3.

218. Ibid., 1: 21.

219. Ibid., 1: 89.

220. Ibid., 1: 124.

221. Ibid., 1: 109.

222. See Rudolf Bultmann, "Paulus," in *RGG*[3]4: 1019–45; Eng. trans.: "Paul" in *Existence and Faith*, 111–46; Werner Georg Kümmel, "Rudolf Bultmann als Paulusforscher," in *Bultmanns Werk und Wirkung*, 174–93.

223. *Theology of the New Testament*, 1: 187.

224. Ibid., 1: 191.

225. Ibid.

226. *Christ without Myth*, 148.

227. *Theology of the New Testament*, 1: 195–96.

228. Ibid., 1: 227.

229. Ibid., 1: 252.

230. Ibid., 1: 281. See E. P. Sanders, *Paul and Palestinian Judaism: A Comparison of Patterns of Religion* (Philadelphia: Fortress Press, 1977), 42–48.

231. *Theology of the New Testament*, 1: 293.

232. Ibid., 1: 300.

233. Ibid., 1: 302.

234. Ibid., 1: 303.

235. Ibid., 1: 307.

236. Ibid., 1: 316.

237. Ibid., 1: 332.

238. Ibid., 1: 352.

239. Ibid., 2: 21.

240. Ibid., 2: 38.

241. Ibid., 2: 41.

242. Ibid., 2:49.

243. Ibid., 2: 50.

244. Ibid., 2: 58.

245. Ibid., 2: 66.

246. Ibid., 2: 66.

247. Ibid., 2: 71.

248. Ibid. 2:78

249. Ibid. 2:81.

250. Ibid. 2:90.

251. In considering this history Bultmann does not limit himself to canonical literature but includes references to other early writings such as the apostolic fathers.

252. *Theology of the New Testament*, 2: 202.

253. *Rudolf Bultmann: ein Versuch ihn zu verstehen*, ThSt 34 (Zürich: Evangelischer Verlag, 1952); the English translation is published in *Kerygma and Myth 2*, 83–132.

254. *Kerygma and Myth 2*, 111.

255. Ogden, *Christ without Myth*, 95–126. Thomas C. Oden ("The Alleged Structural Inconsistency in Bultmann," *JR* 44 [1964]: 193–200) contends that Bultmann does not actually affirm the first of the two propositions.

256. See *HNTR* 1: 258–69.

257. See *HNTR* 1: 184–87.

3

The Bultmann School

During this troubled time of World War II and its aftermath, religion flourished. The World Council of Churches, which had been foreshadowed by various ecumenical conclaves, was officially constituted by an assembly in Amsterdam in 1948. In the next year the Kirchentag, a large gathering of lay Christians, began holding its annual meetings in Germany. After the war university enrollments exploded, and the number of theological students increased dramatically. In America churches were crowded and ministerial candidates, many supported by the GI Bill, flocked to seminaries and divinity schools. State-supported universities encouraged religious discussion by hosting "religious emphasis" weeks: programs in which visiting theologians offered lectures and small groups met in fraternity and sorority lounges to discuss Kierkegaard. Students who became seriously interested in theology, especially biblical studies, were convinced that their graduate study had to be crowned by a year Göttingen, Heidelberg, or Tübingen. Indeed, while Germany lost the military war, it won the theological battle: Germany was hailed as the triumphant citadel of NT research.[1] When the universities were reconstructed in the period of de-Nazification, professors who had not been identified with National Socialism were primary candidates for academic posts. Members of the Bultmann school, largely sympathetic with the Confessing Church, were appointed to important chairs in the leading universities.

THE BULTMANN SCHOOL IN GERMANY: KÄSEMANN AND BORNKAMM

Rudolf Bultmann did not intend to found a school. With typical modesty he simply hoped that his work might stimulate the ongoing discussion. Nevertheless, his students developed a distinct perspective that encompassed a large vista within the theological landscape.[2] The "Old Marburgers," Bultmann's pupils and friends, continued to meet throughout the century. Space will not permit discussion of the work of the many members of the school. Some of them (for example, Hans Conzelmann and Helmut Koester) will be treated in other contexts.[3] Erich Dinkler, one of Bultmann's most faithful followers, contributed to the German-American dialogue and influenced students during his tenure at Yale (1950–56). Heinrich Schlier, who converted to Catholicism, produced important work on the NT epistles.[4]

ERNST KÄSEMANN (1906–1998)

Käsemann was an enthusiastic theologian who was wary of enthusiasm. He thrived on combat. At 89 he confessed that he had "remained a revolutionary 'Partisan' my whole life long."[5] Earlier he had observed: "I have always in my life and in my work had fun, and, where it was possible, tried to overstep the boundaries, and scuffled with many opponents and—unfortunately!—with friends, when a gauntlet was thrown down before me. I have also paid the price for that, and received unhealed wounds."[6]

Ernst Käsemann was born in Dahlhausen near Bochum in Westphalia.[7] He began his theological studies at Bonn (1925), where he was influenced by Erik Peterson. Later he studied at Marburg with Bultmann and at Tübingen with Adolf Schlatter. From 1933 to 1942 Käsemann preached to a congregation of miners and steelworkers in Gelsenkirchen-Rotthausen. Members of the Gestapo were often in the gallery, since Käsemann had called the pro-Nazi Reichsbischof a traitor. In August of 1937 Käsemann preached a sermon on Isa 26:13 in which he declared that "Other lords rule over us beside you." We hear a false gospel, he said, which claims that "Germany is God's chosen people, the Führer is God's messenger to our day."[8] For this Käsemann was thrown into prison for four weeks; there he began his book on Hebrews. In 1942 he was drafted into the army and fought in France and Greece; he ended the war as an American prisoner. Käsemann taught at Mainz, Göttingen, and from 1959 to 1971 at Tübingen. His lectures drew large crowds and influenced a host of students including Peter Stuhlmacher and Americans like Leander Keck and J. Louis Martyn.[9]

Käsemann ardently supported social causes: women in the ministry, opposition to nuclear weapons, the Christian-Marxist dialogue. His daughter was assassinated as a revolutionary by the military junta in Argentina. Käsemann declared: "If the heart of the gospel, already contained in the first commandment, concretized in the New Testament, that Christ is for us the true Lord of the world, then it is not communicated without political judgment in preaching. . . . Who our Lord is and should be is the central question of existence."[10]

In a lecture to the Kirchentag in 1967, Käsemann announced:

> I see the whole of the New Testament as involving the cause of Christian freedom, and I have done my best to show that that cause is developed in much diversity. . . . Like God's faithfulness, the gospel is new every morning and has been heard in many tongues ever since Pentecost, although ecclesiastical convenience has tried to turn the Holy Spirit into a single gramophone record, and makes the human spirit nothing more than a loudspeaker.[11]

Clearly, Käsemann believed that Jesus was an activist who opposed the piety of his contemporaries.

> Christ's resurrection means Jesus' sovereignty, and such sovereignty becomes an earthly reality only in the realm of Christian freedom. . . . Jesus gives freedom. . . . He was free in that he came to serve, and he remains Lord by serving us. . . . Because Jesus' gift is Christian freedom and we live by that gift and grace of his, Christian freedom demands that we prove it on earth before it is perfected in heaven.[12]

Like that of many of his contemporaries, Käsemann's theology was influenced by Luther.[13] He stressed the Reformation understanding of justification by faith, the centrality of Christ, and the distinction between law and gospel. From F. C. Baur he inherited radical criticism, emphasis on history, and disdain for "early catholicism." Käsemann was influenced by Barth's dialectical theology and commitment to theological exegesis. He carried on a lover's quarrel with his teacher, Rudolf Bultmann.[14] He embraced demythologizing and the history of religion methodology, but criticized Bultmann's anthropology and individualism.

Käsemann's thought can be characterized as theology in combat. He fought on several dual fronts. Against enthusiasm, docetism, realized eschatology, and individualism he advocated concern with history, corporeality, apocalyptic eschatology, and community. Against legalism, nomism, and early catholicism he praised the Spirit, freedom, and variety. Against the theology of glory he championed the theology of the cross. Above all, Käsemann was a biblical theologian. He recognized a canon within the canon; the center of the canon was the Pauline epistles; the center of Paul's theology was the justification of the ungodly by God's action in Christ; the Christ is the Christ of the cross; the historical Jesus is crucial to Christology.

KÄSEMANN'S EARLY WRITINGS

According to David Way, Käsemann's publications can be divided into two periods: before 1950 and after 1960.[15] Indeed, Käsemann's thought does show development, even though many of his later ideas were implicit in his earlier works. In the early writings the influence of Bultmann is apparent, especially in the use of history of religion methodology. Käsemann's Marburg dissertation, *Leib und Leib Christi*, investigates the meaning of Paul's expression "body of Christ" by examining the understanding of "body" in Jewish, Greek, and Hellenistic sources.[16] He begins with an analysis of "body" and "flesh" in the OT and Judaism and then turns to Greek sources, where he finds anthropological dualism. He devotes over forty-five pages to the idea of the body in syncretism and Gnosticism. In this section he embraces the Gnostic myth of the redeemed redeemer as fabricated by R. A. Reitzenstein and Wilhelm Bousset.[17]

Turning to the NT, Käsemann investigates the use of "body of Christ" in the Deutero-Pauline letters, where he detects heavy Gnostic influence. In these epistles he discovers a realized eschatology whereby baptism already incorporates the believer into the heavenly body. In the genuine epistles Käsemann finds Gnostic anthropology in Paul's idea of Adam and Christ, and use of the redeemer myth in the hymn of Philippians 2. Paul, according to Käsemann, adopts a double eschatology in which the new eon is present but the future hope remains.

> The sacrament says that here and now a new history, a new divine order of salvation began, which is present as concrete and real in the church. 1 Cor. 15 holds, on the contrary, that this new order of salvation of the church is not realized, that it is not led in by the development of the kingdom of God, but that it stands or falls according to the grace of the Creator.[18]

To be in Christ is to be in the body of Christ—to be in the church, in the world. Käsemann returned to this theme over thirty years later.[19] In the later essay he does not stress the Gnostic background. "Generally speaking, it is possible to shed light on Paul's meaning even without detailed investigation into the history of religion."[20] Käsemann reinforces the historical and corporeal character of Paul's thought. "The exalted Christ really has an earthly body, and believers with their whole being are actually incorporated into it and have therefore to behave accordingly."[21]

Käsemann's book on the Epistle to the Hebrews, *The Wandering People of God*, was begun during his imprisonment in 1937 and first published in 1959.[22] In describing the book he writes: "By describing the church as the new people of God on its wandering through the wilderness, following the Pioneer and Perfecter of faith, I of course had in mind that radical Confessing church which resisted the tyranny in Germany, and which had to be summoned to patience so that it could continue its way through endless wastes."[23] He understands the wilderness wandering of the people of Israel as a type of life in Christ. According to Käsemann the people received the gospel in the form of a promise. "This means *that in a constitutive and fundamental way the divine revelation in Hebrews bears the character of promise and thus is purely eschatological in nature.*"[24] Käsemann believes the eschatology of the NT has two stages: the incarnation, death, and resurrection of Jesus and the fulfillment of these events at the end of time. In their wandering, the people, according to Käsemann, can respond to the gospel promise with either faith or apostasy.

Käsemann finds the background of the wandering motif in Gnosticism: the *Urmensch*-Redeemer is on the way to the heavenly goal, and the Gnostic believers follow. Similarly, he understands the title "Son" in relation to the *anthropos* of the Gnostic myth. "In other words, *in each of the passages dealt with, the doctrine of the εἰκών that creates the world has its continuation in the scheme of the God-man who humbles himself, and thus in the scheme of the Gnostic* Anthropos marked by the two foci of incarnation and death."[25] Yet, although the message of Christ in Hebrews borrows the mythical tradition to depict the redemptive event, the Christ of the kerygma is not myth, but revelation of God's grace in history. *"Here, then, Christ is the τέλος of the myth as he may elsewhere be described as τέλος of the law."*[26] Käsemann concludes that the NT message guards against two opposing dangers. *"Jesus' death and his heavenly activity are a mutual safeguard. That is, the death secures the high priestly office against being dissolved by the myth, and the high priestly office secures the death against the misinterpretation by way of a historically rigid dogmatism."*[27] In this book Käsemann reveals his commitment to history of religion research in the service of exegesis and biblical theology.

Käsemann produced essays on apostleship, ministry, and sacraments. First published in 1942, his monograph on the legitimacy of the apostle investigates 2 Corinthians 10–13.[28] According to Käsemann the opponents of Paul in these chapters are not Judaizers but pneumatics who have invaded the church from outside, claiming the support of the Jerusalem apostles. Käsemann believes they opposed Paul's apostleship as deficient because he had no relation to the historical Jesus. Paul argues that apostolic authority is not grounded in miracles or ecstatic experience but in weakness—in the power of the crucified Christ. In an essay on "Ministry and Community in the New Testament," Käsemann argues that Paul understands ministry as a charisma: as the eschatological gift to the church.[29] This charisma, in contrast to the enthusiasm of the pneumatics, comes to expression in service. "The Apostle's theory of order is not a static one, resting on offices, institutions, ranks and dignities; in his view, authority resides only within the concrete act of ministry as it occurs because it is only within this concrete act that the Kyrios announces his lordship and his presence."[30] Käsemann believes that in the post-apostolic church this dynamic understanding degenerates into early catholicism wherein the gospel is perverted into dogma, the church into institution, and the apostolic charisma into ordained office.[31]

KÄSEMANN AND CANON

As a biblical theologian, Käsemann was concerned with the canon of the NT.[32] He delivered a lecture at Göttingen in 1951 that raised the question, "Does the canon of the New Testament constitute the foundation of the unity of the church?"[33] After reviewing the variety and "irreconcilable theological contradictions" in the NT, he concludes that "the New Testament canon does not, as such, constitute the foundation of the unity of the Church. On the contrary, as such (that is, in its accessibility to the historian) it provides the basis for the multiplicity of the confessions."[34] The canon does not constitute the Word of God, and it is Word only "in so far as it is and becomes the Gospel." "But the question, 'What is the Gospel?' . . . cannot be settled by the historian according to the results of his investigations but only by the believer who is led by the Spirit and listens obediently to the Scripture."[35] Käsemann offers the same view in a lecture given at Göttingen two years later. "The Bible is neither the Word of God in an objective sense nor a doctrinal system, but the deposit left by the history and the preaching of primitive Christianity."[36] Some years later he edited a large volume on the NT as canon. This book presents essays on the canon by a variety of scholars of various theological persuasions, among them Werner G. Kümmel, Oscar Cullmann, Kurt Aland, and Willi Marxsen. In his summary Käsemann concludes that the NT canon is the book of the church, the result of a historical process. He acknowledges (with Catholics in mind) that the church is historically prior to the canon, but he contends that the canon is prior in content, as witness to the gospel. In his own contribution to the volume Käsemann reveals his understanding of the canon within the canon: the gospel of God's act of justification of the ungodly in Jesus Christ.

Therefore, the message of justification appears to me essentially as the qualifying and decisive criterion indeed of the New Testament. This can be true, since in historical critical perspective, the characteristic feature of Jesus, in distinction from his entire religious environment, was his association with sinners in the name of God, his crucifixion linked decisively with his breaking of the law, which also made possible the Gentile mission, and finally the early Christian proclamation was determined more or less as central from then on.[37]

According to Käsemann the canon within the canon is not primarily a selection of books from the larger collection, although his idea of justification as criterion implies a selection: the heart of the canon is the letters of Paul. Käsemann believes that Luke-Acts, the Deutero-Pauline letters, and the Pastoral Epistles display the decline into early catholicism.

Käsemann's freedom regarding the canon is evident in his understanding of the Gospel of John. "In the whole New Testament it is the Fourth Gospel which presents the greatest and most difficult riddles. Just as all that King Midas touched turned to gold, so almost everything which has any connection with this Gospel seems to become a problem."[38]

Käsemann acknowledged that when he touched the Fourth Gospel he stirred up a nest of hornets. His book, *The Testament of Jesus*, was originally presented as the Shaffer Lectures at Yale (1966).[39] His critics delight in his acknowledgment that "I shall be discussing a subject which, in the last analysis, I do not understand."[40] Käsemann believes the key to understanding the historical situation of the Gospel is to be found in the farewell discourses. In chapter 17 farewell is expressed in the form of a prayer, but according to Käsemann this prayer is—à la Gnosticism—secret instruction to the disciples. According to Käsemann the author replaces early Christian eschatology with docetic Christology. "From John we must learn that this is the question of the right christology, and we have to recognize that he was able to give an answer only in the form of a naïve docetism."[41] John depicts "Jesus as God walking on the face of the earth."[42] Käsemann concludes: "From the historical viewpoint, the Church committed an error when it declared the Gospel to be orthodox."[43] Nevertheless, Käsemann thinks this was a fortunate error, since it witnesses to the freedom and variety of biblical thought.

Important for Käsemann's view of Scripture is his distinction between letter and spirit.[44] In discussing this issue he affirms the Reformation antithesis between law and gospel. "We have now arrived at the first result of our investigation: what we call 'letter' is for Paul the Mosaic Torah in its written documentation, which is claimed by the Jews as saving privilege and which for Paul (as the essential portion and aspect of the Old Testament) is identical with scripture as a whole."[45] "Letter," according to Käsemann, also characterizes the legalistic method of interpretation used by Paul's Jewish opponents and by pietists and fundamentalists today. By way of contrast, Käsemann believes Paul to be the first in Christian history to develop a theological hermeneutic. This is illustrated by Paul's exegesis of Deut 30:11-13 in Rom 10:5-13. In his exegesis Paul interprets the text to mean that the law has been replaced by Christ, and Christ is proclaimed in the word of the gospel. Käsemann believes this is interpretation by the Spirit, and that Paul understands the Spirit christologically. He concludes:

> Those who hold the canon to be without error of any kind, perfectly evangelical, inspired in whole and parts alike, have a docetic understanding of it; this will necessarily lead them to a docetic understanding of Jesus; and then, like all Docetics, they will no longer comprehend the Cross, they will make faith into intellectual assent and the Church, which is admittedly now being restricted to the pious, into the flock of the blessed."[46]

THE QUEST OF THE HISTORICAL JESUS

Käsemann's paper presented to the meeting of the Old Marburgers in 1953 is usually hailed as the harbinger of the new quest of the historical Jesus.[47] At the outset Käsemann recounts reasons for the demise of the earlier quest: dialectical theology believed that the gospel was distorted when the Jesus of historical reconstruction was made the ground of faith; the form critics demonstrated that much of the tradition about Jesus was not historically reliable. The current return to the quest was encouraged, according to Käsemann, by the recognition that the Synoptic Gospels contain more reliable tradition than had been supposed, and that the kerygma included facts and presupposed a continuity with the historical tradition of Jesus. Moreover, he noted that theologians were concerned to maintain the historical reality of revelation. Käsemann, however, insists that the revived concern with the historical Jesus should recognize that the Gospels do not primarily chronicle facts; they proclaim the gospel. "Mere history is petrified history, whose historical significance cannot be brought to light simply by verifying the facts and handing them on. On the contrary, the passing on of the *bruta facta* can, as such, directly obstruct a proper understanding of it."[48]

Nevertheless, Käsemann says that revelation took place within the framework of history and in the life of the historical Jesus. The early Christians agreed "that the life history of Jesus was constitutive for faith, because the earthly and the exalted Lord are identical."[49] Failure to recognize this identity, he believes, opens the door to docetism. For all its skepticism, historical criticism does recognize some features of the tradition as historical, especially reports about the teachings of Jesus. Käsemann believes that in the authentic teachings Jesus made a claim about his own authority. "The only category which does justice to his claim . . . is that in which his disciples themselves placed him—namely, that of the Messiah."[50] Käsemann also thinks that Jesus made claims about the significance of his own behavior, which exceeded that of the prophets. "Above all, no prophet could be credited with the eschatological significance which Jesus obviously ascribed to his own actions."[51] Jesus, according to Käsemann, understood his mission eschatologically; he saw himself as the initiator of a new eon. He concludes:

> My own concern is to show that, out of the obscurity of the life story of Jesus, certain characteristic traits in his preaching stand out in relatively sharp relief, and that primitive Christianity united its own message with these. The heart of the problem lives here: the exalted Lord has almost entirely swallowed up the image of the earthly Lord and yet the community maintains the identity of the exalted Lord with the earthly. . . . The question of the historical Jesus is, in its legitimate form, the question of the continuity of the Gospel within the discontinuity of the times and within the variation of the kerygma.[52]

Käsemann took up the question again in response to Bultmann's reaction to the new quest.[53] Actually, Bultmann does not allot much space to Käsemann. He notes that Käsemann wants to go beyond the mere "that" (*dass*) of the historical Jesus and to demonstrate the material continuity between the historical Jesus and the kerygma. According to Bultmann, Käsemann fails to adequately develop an existential interpretation of Jesus, but describes "Jesus' uniqueness as a historical phenomenon."[54] Käsemann devotes most of his essay, "Blind Alleys in the 'Jesus of History' Controversy," to refutation of Bultmann.[55] According to Käsemann, Bultmann did not change his position in response to the new quest. He believes Bultmann affirms a radical historical and material discontinuity between Jesus and the kerygma. In contrast, Käsemann sees the relation as dialectical. "The Easter event is the bridge between Jesus and the whole of the later kerygma; it both divides and unites them."[56] He rejects Bultmann's attempt to reduce the historical Jesus to the *dass*—"a mathematical point."[57] Instead, Käsemann calls for more attention "to a more accurate evaluation of the relevance of the earthly Jesus for the kerygma."[58] He continues: "We can now put our problem in a nutshell: does the New Testament kerygma count the historical Jesus among the criteria of its own validity? We have to answer this question roundly in the affirmative."[59]

Käsemann believes his point is affirmed by the documents of the NT. The Gospels, he says, "are essentially *not* preaching but reporting."[60] Even the Fourth Gospel recognizes the relevance of the historical Jesus by presenting the Word in the form of a Gospel. Bultmann believes the continuity between Jesus and the kerygma is existential self-understanding; Käsemann believes the continuity is Christology, grounded in the historical Jesus.

> The question as to what is prior to faith in the sense that it supplies the criteria of faith can in the last resort only be answered christologically; and answered in such a way as to keep christology distinct from ecclesiology and anthropology and in no circumstances to substitute either for it. Christ alone is the Ground, the Lord and the Judge of faith, of the individual Christian as of the whole community.[61]

To Bultmann's famous observation that the proclaimer became the proclaimed, Käsemann responds that, from the perspective of the Gospel writers, the proclaimed became the proclaimer. According to Käsemann the historical Jesus provides protection from enthusiasm, docetism, and Bultmannian existentialism.

APOCALYPTIC AND THE RIGHTEOUSNESS OF GOD

Around 1960, Käsemann's thought took a decisive shift and he announced a surprising proposition: apocalyptic is the mother of Christian theology.[62] His lecture on 2 Peter in 1952 was a portent of things to come.[63] According to Käsemann the author of this document was answering the charge (of Gnostic opponents) that the Christian hope had already been fulfilled. However, in his attempt to explain the delay of the *parousia* the author of 2 Peter, according to Käsemann, robbed Christian eschatology of its true apocalyptic meaning. Käsemann's shift became explicit in his 1960 lecture on "The Beginnings of Christian Theology."[64] By means of analysis of the tradition behind Matthew he identifies a group of early Christian prophets who affirmed apocalyptic theology. In Käsemann's view this apocalyptic theology made historical thinking possible. "Since for apocalyptic the world has a definite beginning and a definite end, the course of history therefore takes a definite direction and is irrevocable, articulated into a series of epochs clearly distinguishable from each other."[65] From the apocalyptic perspective the kerygma was not only to be proclaimed; it was to be narrated. "The Gospel history, like the prophetic proclamation, is a fruit of the apocalyptic of the period after Easter."[66]

> The heart of primitive Christian apocalyptic, according to the Revelation and the Synoptists alike, is the accession to the throne of heaven by God and by his Christ as the eschatological Son of man—an event which can also be characterized as proof of the righteousness of God. It is this for which those referred to by the fourth beatitude have been hungering and thirsting—for the realization of the divine justice on and to our earth. But exactly the same thing seems to me to be happening in the Pauline doctrine of God's righteousness and our justification—which I therefore derive, so far as the history of religion is concerned, from apocalyptic.[67]

Käsemann's thesis is further advanced in his essay on "Primitive Christian Apocalyptic."[68] According to this essay Christian theology had its origins not in anthropology but in apocalyptic. Käsemann believes Paul opposed the realized eschatology of the Corinthian enthusiasts, and in Romans 6 argued that Christians already united with Christ would be resurrected in the future, affirming the "eschatological reservation."[69] Paul, according to Käsemann, does not speak of an end of history that has come to pass, even though he declares that the end-time has broken in. "No perspective could be more apocalyptic."[70]

By embracing apocalyptic Käsemann does not affirm the bizarre signs of the other world or the chronological speculation of Jewish apocalyptic literature. For him apocalyptic refers to an eschatology that is concerned with real events, with history, with community, with the end of history, with the whole cosmos. To be sure, Käsemann's shift involves a move from emphasis on Hellenistic-Gnostic sources to stress on the OT and Jewish backgrounds. Most of all, however, Käsemann is opposed to the existentialist eschatology of Rudolf Bultmann, to the individualism of Bultmannian anthropology.[71] Käsemann's apocalyptic eschatology includes not only the encounter with Christ in the decision of faith but also the future lordship of Christ over history and the cosmos.

The true theology of which apocalyptic is the mother is, according to Käsemann, Paul's doctrine of the righteousness of God.[72] This doctrine is emphasized throughout Käsemann's later work, but it is directly addressed in his 1961 lecture on the righteousness of God according to Paul.[73] "The Epistle to the Romans," says Käsemann, "subsumes the whole of the preaching and theology of Paul under the one head—the self-revealing righteousness of God. . . . Conversely, the central problem of Pauline theology is concentrated in this theme."[74] In regard to the grammatical issue concerning δικαιοσ'υνη θεοῦ, Käsemann believes the construction is both genitive of author ("the righteousness from God"; Phil 3:9) and subjective genitive ("his righteousness"; Rom 3:25).[75] According to Käsemann, Paul understands righteousness as both future and present. It is God's eschatological action in Jesus that establishes God's sovereignty over the world. "The apostle's present eschatology cannot be taken out of its context of future eschatology, any more than the gift of justification can be isolated from the context in which the righteousness of God is spoken of as a power which brings salvation to pass. Even when he became a Christian, Paul remained an apocalyptist."[76]

During his visit to America in the mid-1960s Käsemann lectured on "Justification and Salvation" in Romans.[77] This lecture reacted to Krister Stendahl's famous essay, "The Apostle Paul and the Introspective Conscience of the West," in which Stendahl contends that Paul has been misinterpreted by theologians from Augustine to Luther and Bultmann who understood Paul's doctrine of justification on the basis of an individualistic, introspective struggle with sin and guilt.[78] In response Käsemann argues that Paul's doctrine of justification is not primarily concerned with the individual but with the whole creation. "Paul's doctrine of justification means that under the sign of Christ, God becomes Cosmocrator, not merely the Lord of the believing individual or the god of a cult; it is not by chance that the doctrine has its roots in apocalyptic."[79]

Käsemann can also use the unbiblical term "Cosmocrator" to affirm Christ's lordship of the world.[80] Righteousness for Käsemann is not only the action of God that justifies the ungodly and triumphs over the world; it also results in a new ethical life. He insists that justification and sanctification cannot be separated. Christian ethics means life under the lordship of Christ; the Christian life is cruciform. According to Käsemann the consequence of justification is obedience—an obedience that responds to the freedom that righteousness conveys. This obedience is lived out in concrete act in the community, in the world following the example of Jesus Christ.

KÄSEMANN ON ROMANS

Käsemann's *Commentary on Romans* is his crowning achievement.[81] In the preface he recalls hearing Erik Peterson's lectures on Romans in 1925, an event that decided his theological life. "No literary document," he writes, "has been more important for me."[82] The commentary offers no critical introduction; an appendix argues that chapter 16 was originally a letter of recommendation for Phoebe, probably sent to Ephesus. Käsemann arranges his comments according to his understanding of the structure of the epistle: introduction, five main sections, and conclusion. Each main section is prefaced by an overview, and each subsection is introduced by Käsemann's translation of the text and a bibliography. The exegesis is in running paragraphs. There are no footnotes; references are presented in parentheses within the text. A few examples can illustrate the character of Käsemann's exegesis.

In the "Introduction" (1:1-17), the "Prescript" (1:1-7) follows the formal convention of Greek letter writing with three parts: superscription, adscription, greeting. Noting that the superscription is unusually long, Käsemann argues that the phrase δοῦλος Χριστοῦ echoes the OT honorific title of the people of God and expresses both election and submission. Käsemann believes Paul uses "Christ" as a proper name, and that he has coined the phrase "apostle of Christ." In regard to the term εὐαγγέλιον, Käsemann notes its use in inscriptions, the LXX, and the Qumran texts. He thinks the word expresses the good news about a definite event: the resurrection and lordship of Christ. The genitive construction, εὐαγγέλιον θεοῦ, according to Käsemann, indicates authorship; God is the author, Christ is the content of the gospel. Käsemann agrees with the growing consensus that detects a pre-Pauline liturgical formula in verses 3b-4. In contrast to Paul's view of the pre-existence and divine Sonship of Christ, the formula, in Käsemann's opinion, reflects an adoptionist Christology in which "Jesus receives the dignity of divine sonship only with his exaltation and enthronement."[83] Käsemann believes Paul corrects this formula by the use of the title Kyrios, the one that became dominant on Gentile soil. The omission of "in Rome" (v. 7) from some manuscripts indicates an early attempt to change the epistle into a general letter.

In regard to the subsection "Theme" (1:16-17), Käsemann comments on the meaning of "gospel." "It is God's declaration of salvation to the world, which is outside human control, which is independent even of the church and its ministers, and which constantly becomes a reality itself in proclamation in the power of the Spirit. It can thus be called δύναμις θεοῦ."[84]

The term σωτηρία "denotes deliverance in the final judgment."[85] "Faith," according to Käsemann, is not belief or trust but (à la Bultmann) decision:

receiving the gospel. He says that "faith is an appropriation of the eschatological public proclamation made to the whole world and to each individual. Each person is placed in a situation of personal responsibility."[86] The theme of Romans and the content of the gospel, according to Käsemann is "the righteousness of God."

> It speaks of the God who brings back the fallen world into the sphere of his legitimate claim . . . whether in promise or demand, in new creation or forgiveness, or in the making possible of our service, and . . . who sets us in the state of confident hope and . . . constant earthly change. With recourse to the Kyrios acclamation we may summarize the whole message of the epistle in the brief and paradoxical statement that the Son of God is as our Kyrios the one eschatological gift of God to us and that herein is revealed simultaneously both God's legitimate claim on us and also our salvation.[87]

In the first main section, "The Need for the Revelation of the Righteousness of God" (1:18–3:20), the first subsection deals with "The Revelation of God's Wrath on the Gentiles" (1:18-32). Käsemann, in the tradition of Barth, argues that Paul does not really advocate natural theology. He acknowledges that Paul uses popular Hellenistic expressions but argues that metaphysical concepts are alien to the apostle; natural theology is irreconcilable with Paul's eschatology and Christology.

Käsemann believes that the second main section, "The Righteousness of God as the Righteousness of Faith" (3:21–4:25), is the heart of the epistle.[88] The "Thesis" of the section is the subsection 3:21-26. In verse 22 Paul points out that the righteousness that is revealed is a righteousness of faith. Käsemann rejects the theory that πίστεως Ἰησοῦ Χριστοῦ is a subject genitive (the faith of Jesus Christ) and believes verse 26 also supports the objective genitive ("faith in Jesus"). Käsemann thinks that in verses 24-26 Paul is quoting the fragment of a hymn. The participle δικαιούμενοι (v. 24) means "being made righteous" and refers to "eschatologically transformed existence."[89]

Käsemann rejects the interpretation of ἀπολύτρωσις as reflecting the sacral manumission of slaves or as paying a ransom. He translates it "redemption" and stresses the eschatological, once-for-all event "in Christ." He does not believe that ἱλαστήριον means "cover of the ark" or the place of expiation; the Gentile Christians of Rome would not have understood such an allusion, and Christ cannot be at the same time the offering and the site of the offering. The meaning of the term, according to Käsemann, is "means of expiation." Also, Käsemann rejects the doctrine that Christ's sacrifice satisfies God's justice. Instead, "God himself makes this expiation and hence makes possible again the fellowship which had been disrupted."[90]

Using his characteristic terminology, Käsemann entitles the third main section (5:1–8:39) "The Righteousness of Faith as a Reality of Eschatological Freedom." The first subsection (5:1-21) is designated "Freedom from the Power of Death." As to the textual variant in verse 1, Käsemann prefers the reading ἔχομεν (indicative) to ἔχωμεν (subjunctive); Paul, he says, is speaking of the peace we have, not exhorting his audience to have peace. In discussing "The Dominion of the Last Adam" (5:12-21) Käsemann, reflecting his earlier interest in history of religion, believes that the background is to be found in the Gnostic idea of the primal man. "The intention of the apostle is to present the universality of the reign of Christ in antithesis to the world of Adam."[91] In addressing the notorious verse 12 ("sin came into the world through one man"), he rejects the traditional doctrine of original sin. He suggests translating the phrase ἐφ' ᾧ πάντες ἥμαρτον as "because all sinned"; the text emphasizes "responsible decision."[92] In discussing "Dead to Sin by Baptism" (6:1-11), Käsemann notes that baptism has its background in the Hellenistic cults and that early Christian enthusiasts celebrated it as a cult mystery in which they already experienced the resurrection. Paul counters this, according to Käsemann, with his stress on the cross, "actualized in the act of baptism."[93] Käsemann believes Paul maintains the "eschatological reservation." "We have yet to participate in the resurrection even though its power already rules us and sets us in the new walk."[94] The eschatological event of the cross, which is actualized in baptism, frees the Christian for ethical obedience.

In the subsection "The End of the Law in the Power of the Spirit" (7:1–8:39), Käsemann discusses chapters 7 and 8 as the climax of the larger section that began at 5:1. He believes that 7:7-13 describes pre-Christian existence from the Christian perspective; the text is not autobiographical. "As regards the I-statements this implies the use, stylistically, of a rhetorical figure with general significance."[95] In regard to the positive statements about the law (7:12-13), Käsemann writes: "Paul is no antinomian. The law in its truth does not belong with sin and death. It has been misused by the power of sin, which always perverts the good, and now effects the opposite of what was intended."[96] In exegeting 7:14-25 he notes the use of the present tense but argues that Paul is not referring to the Christian experience; he is describing the struggle of the old Adam in cosmic dimension. Käsemann thinks the chapter ends in answer to the cry of despair (v. 24) with the triumphant acclamation: "Thanks be to

God through Jesus Christ our Lord!" (v. 25a). (He thinks v. 25b is a non-Pauline interpolation).

In his general introduction to the exegesis of 8:1-39 ("Man in the Freedom of the Spirit"), Käsemann presents his understanding of Paul's doctrine of the Spirit:

> The Pauline doctrine of the Spirit is constitutively shaped by the fact that the apostle, so far as we can see, is the first to relate it indissolubly to christology. In the Spirit the risen Lord manifests his presence and lordship on earth. Conversely the absolute criterion of the divine Spirit is that he sets the community and its members in the discipleship of the Crucified, in the mutual service established thereby, and in the assault of grace on the world and the sphere of corporeality. The difference from enthusiasm is that the Spirit is to be tested in terms of christology, and christology is not set under the shadow of ecclesiology.[97]

Käsemann sees in the references to creation in 8:18-25 an apocalyptic and cosmic emphasis in opposition to enthusiasm and existentialist interpretation.

> If Marcion was forced by the inner logic of his theology to cut out vv. 18-22, he is followed today by an existentialism which individualizes salvation and thereby truncates Paul's message by describing freedom formally as openness to the future. . . . The truth in the existential interpretation is that it recognizes in pride and despair the powers which most deeply enslave mankind. Its theological reduction derives from a world view which no longer knows what to do with Pauline apocalyptic, allows anthropological historicity to conceal the world's history, obscures the antithesis of the aeons of 1:20ff. by natural theology and here through the assertion of mythology, and for this reason can no longer speak adequately of the dominion of Christ in its worldwide dimension.[98]

Obviously, shots fired at the ancient heretic ricocheted off Marcion and hit Rudolf Bultmann.

Käsemann believes the fourth main section, "The Righteousness of God and the Problem of Israel" (9:1–11:36), suffers excessive violence from misinterpretation. Much mistaken interpretation, in Käsemann's opinion, fails to see that the panoramic text presents the worldwide dimension of the righteousness of God, wherein the concept of the people of God is central.

According to Käsemann the argument develops in three stages: "the freedom of God, the guilt of Israel, and Israel's final redemption."[99] In regard to "Israel's Guilt and Fall" (9:30–10:21), he interprets τέλος (10:4) as depicting Christ not as the "goal," but as the "end" of the law. "The Mosaic Torah comes to an end with Christ because man now renounces his own right in order to grant God his right. . . . Even for Israel no other possibility of salvation exists."[100] Käsemann titles his exegesis of chapter 11 "The Mystery of Salvation History." On "Israel's Redemption" (11:25–32) he writes, "All that has gone before leads to the conclusion that Israel's obduracy leaves room for the conversion of the Gentiles. But the completion of the latter also carries with it Israel's salvation."[101] In regard to the "Deliverer from Zion" (11:26), Käsemann declares:

> Obviously the reference is neither to the historical Jesus . . . nor to the christological event as a whole . . . nor indeed to the parousia in Jerusalem . . . but to the return of the exalted Christ from the heavenly Jerusalem of Gal. 4:26. . . . Whereas Christianity is already living in the new covenant, Israel will begin to do so only at the parousia, and it will do it through the same Giver, Christ, and with the related gift . . . of the forgiveness of sins. Only the time, not the salvation, is different.[102]

The "all" of 11:32, according to Käsemann, refers to the whole world. Käsemann's apocalyptic and cosmic understanding of justification implies the paradox of the salvation of all the ungodly. "Hence salvation history in its universal breadth is linked to the doctrine of justification. . . . Paul is bold enough to view both each individual and world history from the standpoint of the doctrine of justification."[103]

Käsemann titles the last main section (12:1–15:13) "The Righteousness of God in Daily Christian Life." Because of his stress on ethics, this section is important for him. It begins with a general exhortation (12:1–13:14). Käsemann says that "Paul is the first to have considered exhortation theologically. . . . The apostle here draws the consequences of his message in the daily life of the community, and in this regard he emerges yet again as the theologian who now develops his theme under a final aspect."[104] In regard to the controversial 13:1-7 ("The Relation to Political Powers"), Käsemann cautions against the attempt to unearth some idea of natural order or political theory here. The text stands in the tradition of the Diaspora synagogue and supports order in opposition to the enthusiasts. "When all this added up, the result is that by God's will even the fallen world can point to manifestations and instruments of the order which God has set up, and that in this the Creator demonstrates his further dealings with it."[105]

Not since Karl Barth had dialectical theology produced a commentary on Romans. Although Bultmann gave major attention to Paul's theology in his monumental *Theology of the New Testament*, his major commentary is on the Gospel of John. With Käsemann, Romans is returned to the center. In the commentary he enlists text critical, linguistic, and historical research in the service of exegesis. The central concern, however, is theological interpretation. For Käsemann the theology of Romans is the right theology; Käsemann's exposition of the theology of Paul is the theology of Käsemann.

In sum, Ernst Käsemann is the most independent student in the Bultmann school. With his eye on some distant star, he set his own course. Indeed, the development of Käsemann's career expresses an increasing divergence from the route charted by his teacher. His early work employs the method of the history of religion school with special appreciation for Hellenistic and Gnostic backgrounds. His later work embraces Jewish apocalyptic, affirming as valid what Bultmann dismissed as myth. Although Käsemann continued to stress faith and existential decision, he resolutely moved away from the hermeneutic of existentialism. In place of the focus on anthropology he concentrates on Christology. In place of concern with the individual he stresses the importance of the community, its ministry and its sacraments. Rather than restricting eschatology to the "now" of faith, he embraces an apocalyptic that affirms both the reality of the historical present and the confident hope in the cosmic future. Although Käsemann agrees that God is known from the human perspective, theology for him is not anthropology, but doctrine of God as Creator and Christ as Cosmocrator. Although he acknowledges that one cannot write a biography of Jesus, he insists that the tradition of the words and deeds of Jesus is presupposed by the kerygma and that faith in Christ is grounded in the historical Jesus.

To be sure, Käsemann did not completely forsake Rudolf Bultmann. He continued his teacher's devotion to radical criticism. Like Bultmann, he believed the Reformation doctrine of justification to be absolutely central. Like Bultmann and much of the tradition of Lutheran biblical scholarship, Käsemann, in championing the gospel over law, tended to caricature Judaism. At the same time his attack on early catholicism betrays a latent aversion toward Rome. With Bultmann, Käsemann recognized the importance of the theology of Paul, but contrary to his teacher he saw in the Gospel of John a thinly veiled docetism—a view his critics consider an exaggeration. However, he surprises the critics even more by insisting that heresy within the canon is a beneficial witness to theological freedom. For his own part, Käsemann, on the one hand, battles every form of unhistorical docetism, and on the other he attacks the calcifying of history into early catholicism. He embraces a charisma expressed in ministry, sacrament, and ethics; he abhors a charisma expressed in self-asserting enthusiasm.

Perhaps a weakness in Käsemann's theology is his proclivity for combat. Much of his energy is devoted to refuting Rudolf Bultmann. Also, in abandoning existentialist hermeneutics Käsemann offers no clear hermeneutical basis for his work. While affirming dialectical theology's opposition to metaphysics, he does not articulate an ontological foundation for his own theology. In contrast to Bultmann's negative use of criticism to demonstrate that faith cannot be based on historical reconstruction, Käsemann employs criticism positively to delineate the central message of the NT and to confirm the continuity between the historical Jesus and the Christ of the kerygma. By critical analysis, working together with faith, Käsemann identifies the canon within the canon, and this canon is the Word of God. Indeed, he ignores the historical gap between the words of ancient Scripture and the hearing of faith today. In his commentary on Romans he shifts almost imperceptibly from "they" to "we," from the original hearers of Paul's letter to the modern readers of Käsemann's commentary. He assumes that the proclamation of Paul is the Word of God for ancient Romans and is also the Word of God for today. The question of the significance of historical distance and the task of translation would remain for other members of the Bultmann school.

GÜNTHER BORNKAMM (1905–1990)

In personality Bornkamm resembled Rudolf Bultmann: genial, modest, and unassuming.[106] During a year in Heidelberg (1971–72) I attended Bornkamm's lectures on NT theology. One morning as I was riding by streetcar to the university, Bornkamm boarded. He saw me and came to sit with me. "Did I usually take this route to class?" he asked. When I answered in the affirmative, he insisted that for the rest of the semester I must come to his house and ride with him. This sounded like a wonderful opportunity that I eagerly accepted. However, on the next class day, as I prepared to appear at Bornkamm's door, I was in a quandary as to when to arrive. The lecture was a 9 a.m. class, which meant it actually began at 9:15. I certainly did not want to be late, so I arrived before 8:45. Mrs. Bornkamm welcomed me, offered coffee and a place to sit; "Professor" was in his study. He remained in his study until 9 o'clock, or a minute or two after. He then rushed out; Mrs. Bornkamm helped him into his coat; he and I hurried to the vintage Audi parked out front; we jumped in; he revved up the car. We drove rapidly through "New Town," across the bridge, over the cobblestone streets to the lecture hall. After he parked, Bornkamm rushed to his office and I to the lecture hall, where he appeared to say, "Meine Damen und Herren . . ." at 9:15. This occurred every Monday, Wednesday, and Friday for the rest of the semester. The association with Bornkamm was rewarding, but what I learned above all was that this great teacher—in his last year of lecturing on a subject he had presented scores of times before—was still preparing for every lecture until the last minute.

Bornkamm was born in Görlitz in northeastern Germany, near the Polish border. He studied at Marburg, Tübingen, Berlin, and Breslau. While at Marburg he became associated with Bultmann and his students. Bornkamm began his teaching at Königsberg (1935), and in 1936 moved to Heidelberg, where after a semester he was forbidden to teach in a state-supported university because of his participation in the Confessing Church. He joined the faculty at the theological school at Bethel in 1937—a school closed by the Gestapo two years later. From 1940 to 1942 Bornkamm served as a pastor in Dortmund and Münster. He was drafted into the army in 1943 and fought on the eastern and western fronts. After the war he returned to Bethel, but in 1946 he moved to Göttingen. He was appointed to the faculty at Heidelberg in 1949, where he remained until retirement in 1972. Bornkamm was awarded honorary degrees from Glasgow and Oxford. He traveled and lectured widely, and was revered by his students. In 1977–78 he served as president of the SNTS.

Bornkamm was influenced by the revival of interest in Luther and the Reformation and by the dialectical theologians, especially Rudolf Bultmann. His assessment of Bultmann is presented in his essay, "The Theology of Rudolf Bultmann."[107] Bornkamm observes that Bultmann was influenced by two movements: historical criticism and dialectical theology. He supports Bultmann's concern with history but criticizes him at two points: his idea of pre-understanding, which is a presupposition that impedes the reception of biblical revelation, and his transformation of theology into anthropology and Christology into soteriology. Earlier Bornkamm had discussed Bultmann's program of demythologizing.[108] He agrees that demythologizing is necessary because modern humans cannot accept the worldview of the NT; myth must be interpreted in terms of its meaning for human existence. Bornkamm affirms Bultmann's belief that the doctrine of justification is the theological ground for demythologizing, but he is critical of Bultmann's reduction of the saving event to a brute fact. "Jesus Christ has become a mere saving fact and ceases to be a person. He himself has no longer any history; he himself is no longer really the One who speaks in his word. In other words, he is no longer the One who personally addresses me, who in speaking personally encounters me face to face."[109]

Along with this anticipation of his later work on Jesus, Bornkamm, like Käsemann, insists that eschatology is more than self-understanding, open to the future; it includes a new future and a new history.

BORNKAMM'S HISTORICAL-CRITICAL RESEARCH

Bornkamm's early work reveals the influence of Bultmann and his commitment to history of religion methodology. His Marburg dissertation, written under Bultmann, investigates the apocryphal Acts of Thomas in relation to the development of early Christian Gnosticism.[110] In this apocryphal document Bornkamm detects the use of myth and legend, in particular the myth of the Gnostic redeemer. He finds parallels in the Mandaean texts, the Odes of Solomon, *Pistis Sophia*, and the later documents of the Manicheans. According to Bornkamm, the Acts of Thomas represents a religious syncretism in which Gnosticism is presented in Christian garb. Bornkamm's concern with Gnosticism is seen in another early work on "The Heresy of Colossians."[111] Convinced that Colossians was not written by Paul, Bornkamm identifies the heresy refuted in the document as a variety of Jewish Gnosticism.

> The Colossian doctrine of the elements belongs to the ancient mythology and speculation of the Oriental Aeon-theology, which was widespread and active in Hellenistic syncretism. Its origins reach back to the Indo-Iranian cosmogony and its conception of a world-deity, whose gigantic body was composed of the elements of the universe. The cosmogonic myth of the body of the world-god and of the elements of his limbs occurs again in gnosis in the form of the myth of the primeval man, in which it receives a cosmic-soteriological meaning.[112]

In a later non-technical book Bornkamm presents an overview of his criticism of the NT.[113] His purpose is to provide "a clear and simple guide to the New Testament writings."[114] Special attention must be given to Jesus. "His priority . . . is . . . one of substance: every statement in the New Testament must be understood and evaluated with reference to him as its criterion."[115] In regard to the Synoptic Gospels, Bornkamm adopts the 2DH. He believes Mark was written in the east around 70. Matthew, according to Bornkamm, was composed in the 80s or 90s in the region of Palestine and Syria. The Gospel of Luke is the first of a two-volume work that intends to present a biography of Jesus and the history of the early church. Paul, according to Bornkamm, was the first to use the epistle as a form of Christian expression. Bornkamm accepts seven letters attributed to Paul as authentic; he rejects 2 Thessalonians, Ephesians, Colossians, and the Pastoral Epistles. Bornkamm believes all of the Catholic Epistles to be pseudonymous. He classifies Revelation as an apocalyptic book, dating probably from the reign of Domitian.[116] Bornkamm believes the Fourth Gospel was composed by an unknown author around 100. Sharing Bultmann's enthusiasm for this Gospel, Bornkamm writes that John has reflected upon the Christian message "more profoundly than any other writer, and has articulated it with a one-sidedness which, though sometimes monotonous, is truly magnificent."[117] He concludes: "Thus the New Testament is the 'charter' of Christian faith—and not just in the historian's sense of the word. The history of this faith will continue to be what it always was, the story of Jesus' passion—and the story of his resurrection."[118]

More representative of his critical skill are Bornkamm's essays on 2 Corinthians, Philippians, and Romans. The essay on the pre-history of 2 Corinthians was originally published in 1961 and was revised for publication in Bornkamm's collected works.[119] In regard to the opponents attacked in 2 Corinthians, Bornkamm agrees (with Dieter Georgi) that they are traveling "divine men" (like Apollonius of Tyana) who invaded the church after the writing of 1 Corinthians. Bornkamm attempts to reconstruct the fragments of the letter in relation to stages in Paul's battle with these "super apostles." According to his reconstruction Paul first wrote an apology for ministry that included 2 Cor 2:14—7:4 (except for 6:14—7:1, which he views as a non-Pauline interpolation). This apology, according to Bornkamm, was written after 1 Corinthians and before Paul's interim or "painful" visit to Corinth (implied in 2 Cor 2:1; 12:14; 13:1). After the interim visit Paul, in Bornkamm's opinion, wrote the "severe" letter of "many tears" (mentioned in 2 Cor 2:3-4), which consists of 2 Corinthians 10–13. After writing this letter Paul sent Titus to Corinth, and after meeting Titus in Macedonia and hearing his good report he wrote the letter of reconciliation (2 Cor 1:1—2:13; 7:5-16). Bornkamm argues that 2 Corinthians 8 presupposes the letter of reconciliation and is either the conclusion or an addition to that letter; chapter 9 is a separate letter written after chapter 8 to other churches in Achaia.

Of special interest is Bornkamm's rationale for the final order of the fragments as they appear in canonical 2 Corinthians. He believes the placing of chapters 10–13 at the end corresponds to the tendency of early Christian literature to put anathemas and warnings against heresy at the end of documents. Bornkamm believes the editor inserted the hymn of praise and apostolic apology (2:14–7:4) into the letter of reconciliation in order to depict Paul's journey from Troas to Macedonia as a triumphal resolution of the problem.

Bornkamm produced a similar analysis of Philippians.[120] Within this letter he finds evidence that Philippians, like 2 Corinthians, is a collection of fragments. For example, he notes the change of tone at 3:2 and the transition from the greeting of peace (4:9) to a section that ends with an expression of praise. On the basis of such evidence he identifies three separate letters: "A" (4:10-20) is a section of a letter that expresses thanks for the gift Epaphroditus had brought to Paul; "B" (1:1—3:1) is a letter that reports Paul's imprisonment and announces the return of Epaphroditus (4:21-23 is probably the ending of this letter); "C" (3:2-49) is a fragment of a polemic letter that warns against Jewish Christian Gnostics or gnosticizing Judaizers, written after Paul's release from prison. Bornkamm believes all three of these fragments were written from Ephesus. He thinks the editor put "A" last because of his pride in the special relation of the Philippian church to Paul.

Bornkamm also reflects on the notorious problem of the nature and purpose of Romans. He characterizes "The Letter to the Romans as Paul's Last Will and Testament."[121] In this essay he attends to T. W. Manson's article, "The Letter to the Romans—and Others."[122] Bornkamm agrees with Manson that the epistle deals with issues Paul had encountered in the east, and that Romans 16 was addressed to Ephesus. However, he thinks the original letter (Romans 1–15) was written to Rome; it was not a general letter to the Romans "and others." Bornkamm believes, nevertheless, that the epistle does not address the particular situation in Rome but presents a summary of Paul's major concerns: the apostolate to the Gentiles and the doctrine of justification by faith. These fundamental concerns prepare for the apostle's visit to Rome, but they are also composed in anticipation of serious trouble in Jerusalem. "This great document, which summarizes and develops the most important themes and thoughts of the Pauline message and theology and which elevates his theology above the moment of definite situations and conflicts into the sphere of the eternally and universally valid, this letter to the Romans is the last will and testament of the Apostle Paul."[123]

Bornkamm pioneered in the use of a method that later became known as "redaction criticism."[124] In distinction from form criticism, which analyzes the development of oral tradition, redaction criticism attends to the shaping of the tradition by the authors or editors of the written documents. Bornkamm's research applies this method primarily to the study of Matthew. In an essay originally published in 1948 he analyzes the account of the stilling of the storm in Matt 8:23-27.[125] He notes the distinctive features of Matthew's account in relation to his source (Mark 4:36-41). For example, Matthew puts the account in a different context: it follows two sayings about discipleship (Matt 8:19-22). This emphasis on discipleship is continued in the details of the text. Only in Matthew's account does Jesus enter the boat first and "his disciples follow him" (8:23). The cry for help, κύριε σῶσον, found only in Matthew (8:25), employs the confession of the "Lord" of the disciples. Jesus' accusation, "Why are you afraid, you of little faith," precedes the miracle (only in Matthew), and makes use of the distinctive Matthean term ὀλιγόπιστος (used once in Luke 12:28). Matthew does not limit the astonishment to the disciples (as in Mark and Luke), but broadens the audience to ἄνθρωποι who would hear the story in preaching. "The setting of the pericope is thus extended, its horizon is widened and from being a description of discipleship in which the disciples of Jesus experience trial and rescue, storm and security, it becomes a call to imitation and discipleship."[126]

In a longer essay on eschatology and church in Matthew, Bornkamm presents an overview of the evangelist's redactional activity.[127] As to the method, he says that

> . . . the Synoptic writers show—all three and each in his own special way—by their editing and construction, by their selection, inclusion and omission, and not least by what at first sight appears an insignificant, but on closer examination is seen to be a characteristic treatment of the traditional material, that they are by no means mere collectors and handers-on of the tradition, but are also interpreters of it.[128]

The first section of the essay deals with the union of eschatology and ecclesiology in the construction of the Matthean discourses. For example, the Sermon on the Mount includes requirements for admission to the community and presents eschatology by reference to judgment. Bornkamm views the discourse to the congregation (chapter 18) as a collection from various sources; it presents discipline for the church (18:15-18) and warns of the future judgment.[129] According to Bornkamm everything Matthew says about discipleship is related to his understanding of law and righteousness. "Matthew reaches his radical understanding of the law by regarding it in the light of the will of God made known in creation, but more still in the sense of the universal judgment, which all men, and particularly the disciples, have to face."[130] He notes the close connection between law and Christology in Matthew. Jesus is presented, according to Bornkamm, as a second Moses, interpreter of the law. He also finds a close connection between Christology and ecclesiology. "No other Gospel is so shaped by the thought of the Church as Matthew's."[131] In sum, Bornkamm has attempted "to show to what a high degree the first evangelist is an interpreter of the tradition which he collected and arranged. It should have become clear in the process that tradition and theological conception stand in a mutual relation to each other. Just as theology is placed at the service of tradition, the opposite is also true."[132]

NEW TESTAMENT EXEGESIS

Throughout his career Günther Bornkamm produced exegetical works on various books of the NT. In 1937, he published an exegetical study of 1 Corinthians 13[133] in which he explicates Paul's understanding of love and explains why love is greater than faith and hope. "If faith is based on what God has done and hope directs itself to what God will do, then love—from God, to God and thus simultaneously love toward the brother (cf. 1 John 4:7ff)—is the permanent presence of salvation, the 'bond of perfection' (Col. 3.14). As such it is the greatest."[134]

Bornkamm's exegetical work is often directed to problematic texts like 1 Cor 9:19-23, where Paul says that he has "become all things to all people."[135] Bornkamm acknowledges that Paul is sensitive to different historical situations, but he insists that the apostle is not advocating flexibility as a missionary strategy. "Paul intends the statements to characterize a practical stance of solidarity with various groups, rather than to describe several ways of adjusting his preaching in terms of content and language to various environments."[136] Instead, Bornkamm thinks Paul's missionary stance is grounded in the gospel of justification by faith—a doctrine he believes to be totally missing in Acts. The author of Acts, according to Bornkamm, fails to understand Paul's eschatological understanding of history and replaces justification with *Heilsgeschichte*, a succession of events whereby Paul turns from Jews to Gentiles.

Bornkamm also published exegetical essays on Romans and Philippians. In exegeting Romans 6 he understands Baptism as an eschatological event in which the believer is united with Christ.[137] The one who is baptized already walks in the new life, but resurrection, according to Bornkamm, is an event of the future. In discussing Romans 7 he raises the conventional questions: Is Paul speaking about his own experience? Is he describing the situation of humans under law or under grace?[138] Bornkamm answers that Paul is not speaking autobiographically; "I" here has a general meaning. He concludes:

"The exegesis has shown that the old dispute about whether man in Romans 7 is to be understood as man under the law or man under grace must be answered in the first sense."[139] In regard to Phil 2:6-11, Bornkamm rejects the interpretation that understands Christ as ethical example. Instead, he believes the hymn presents the incarnation and exaltation of the pre-existent Christ. Although he believes Paul makes use of the myth of the Gnostic redeemer, he finds that his emphasis on obedience unto death totally transforms the meaning. In the major issues of these texts Bornkamm agrees essentially with Käsemann.

Likewise, Bornkamm published exegetical studies in the Gospels. In an essay on the delay of the *parousia* he investigates two difficult texts.[140] Concerning Mark 9:1 ("Truly I tell you, there are some standing here who will not taste death until they see that the kingdom of God has come with power"), Bornkamm rejects efforts to avoid the problem of the text, for example, by C. H. Dodd's notion that the kingdom has already come.[141] Instead, he interprets Mark as implying delay of the *parousia*: though some will actually live to see the coming of the eschatological kingdom, others will not. In Matt 25:1-13 (the parable of the ten maidens) he argues that concern with the delay of the *parousia* is explicit. The wise maidens have prepared for the delay; the foolish have not. According to Bornkamm the parable represents the word of the exalted Lord who calls believers to be prepared. In the situation of delay the faithful can still trust in the coming salvation of Christ.

Bornkamm attacks Käsemann's position regarding the Fourth Gospel. In a paper presented to the Old Marburgers he rejects Käsemann's notion that the Gospel of John presents a "naive docetism."[142] Bornkamm believes Käsemann is blind to the anti-gnostic features of the Gospel. John, says Bornkamm, has not abandoned the theology of the cross but understood it paradoxically: the passion reveals the glory. He expresses the same idea in his essay on the paraclete in the Fourth Gospel. "Every mythological *theologia gloriae* is rejected and the community is held fast in John's distinctive *theologia crucis*; it means that in the cross of Christ itself his glory is revealed."[143]

THEOLOGICAL WRITINGS

As his critical and exegetical research indicates, Bornkamm was primarily a biblical theologian. In the NT he hears the word of God, spoken in the words of humans.[144]

> Wherever this word becomes audible, it can only speak of what God has done to us and the world, of the story of his grace and his judgment, culminating and summed up in the story of Jesus Christ.

> Therefore the gospel always has one and only one indispensable content for all time: Christ the crucified one, Christ the living one, Jesus Christ our Lord.[145]

This statement implies a canon within the canon—an idea Bornkamm develops vis-à-vis Roman Catholics in regard to the question of authority.

> The answer obviously cannot be given formally and have one and the same binding force in content for all scriptural expressions, but can only express the conviction, that within the canon of Scripture a substantial canon meets us, namely the proclamation of God's claim and God's grace, by which everything, even the Scripture itself, can be measured. From this perspective, the Protestant idea can be understood, that the message of Jesus Christ and his sending is better understood by no other early Christian witness than by Paul.[146]

Bornkamm's biblical theology gives special attention to the idea of confession.[147] His inaugural address at Königsberg dealt with "The Word of Jesus about Confession."[148] This address was delivered in the time of the Confessing Church under the shadow of National Socialism—a time when confession had serious political consequences. Bornkamm notes that Jesus' word about confession (recorded in Q), "Everyone . . . who shall confess Me before men, I will also confess him before my Father who is in heaven" (Matt 10:32, NASB), is found in different contexts (see Luke 12:8). Moreover, the corresponding saying about denial, "But whoever shall deny Me before men, I will also deny him before My Father who is in heaven" (Matt 10:33, NASB; Luke 12:9), is also found in the Markan tradition (Mark 8:38; Luke 9:26). The denial and confession formula is found in later texts as well (1 Tim 2:12; Rev 3:5). These observations, together with the use of "everyone who" (a phrase frequent in the Sermon on the Mount) in the Q saying, indicate to Bornkamm that the saying is independent and has the character of a rule. Bornkamm believes the confession (or denial) involves a decision early Christians had to make in the world: a public confession or denial of their relation to Jesus. The decision, according to Bornkamm, has its ultimate outcome in the eschatological judgment.

Bornkamm's concern with the NT idea of confession is developed in an essay on Hebrews, originally published in 1942.[149] He believes that holding to the confession is the fundamental theme of the document. "The ὁμολογία of the community must therefore be the basis of the letter, since it is at the same time the goal toward which the letter is ever anew directed."[150]According to Bornkamm this confession is the baptismal confession, and the content of the confession is Jesus the Son of God. The confession is the act of the individual, but the individual, in Bornkamm's view, is a member of the faithful community. He rejects Käsemann's notion that the presentation of Christ in Hebrews has its source in the myth of the Gnostic redeemer. Instead, the Christology of Hebrews, according to Bornkamm, is founded on the recognition of Jesus as the redeemer from sin—a concept that has its ground in the historical event of the cross. The once-for-all of the redeeming sacrifice of Christ corresponds to the unique event the believer has appropriated in the confession.

Turning to Paul, Bornkamm declares that the apostle's commitment to world mission is based on his confession of Jesus Christ as Lord.[151] According to Bornkamm this confession is totally different from the political confession of Caesar as Lord. Bornkamm believes the NT views the world and its political powers as dominated by sin, but the world of sinful humanity has come to an end in the cross. In the resurrection, he believes, the exalted Lord brings salvation; in Christ there is new creation. "The message of the Lordship of Jesus Christ is the gospel of justification, the word of reconciliation. As such, it is not a message that would have nurtured itself on the political myth of the emperor and the empire. It is at the same time the message of Jesus Christ as the end of the world and as the Lord of the world."[152]

Like the dialectical theologians, Bornkamm sounds the themes of the Reformation: law and gospel, judgment and justification, the righteousness of God. In 1934 he published a monograph on "Law and Creation in the New Testament."[153] In the introduction he observes that the question of the relationship between law and creation has become crucial in this time of the ascendancy of National Socialism because of its significance for problems of the relation of church and state. Bornkamm seeks to answer the question in terms of the NT. According to his reading of the Bible, the law presents the will of God, given by revelation; God's law created a people and called for obedience. Bornkamm, like many in the Reformation tradition, charges the Jews with formal obedience in contrast to Jesus' demand for absolute obedience. The NT, according to Bornkamm, understands creation to reveal the will of God but does not affirm natural law. When Paul says that Gentiles by nature φύσει do "what the law requires" (Rom 2:14) he is not referring to natural law but to the biblical law, which Gentiles perceive in God's actions in creation. Bornkamm believes Paul sees all humans under the wrath of God: Gentiles because they worship creation and Jews because they exploit the law for their own advantage. The message of the NT, according to Bornkamm, is that this situation is overcome by God's act of grace in the death and resurrection of Christ. In Christ both creation and law are fulfilled. The believer, according to Bornkamm, is the new creature who is called to obedience to the law of Christ. In the social and political realm, the believer, in his opinion, is not primarily obedient to the order of nature or the law of the people; the believer belongs to another fatherland; his or her citizenship is in heaven.

> Since the saving work of God in Christ is history and the church as the body of Christ is a cosmic power, the concrete reality of life in which the church finds itself has to be understood not under "nomos" or "ethos," but under the *kerygma*. In other words: the event of the *new* creation is not groundless, but is fulfilled *here*. Therefore the believer cannot run from his reality, but he must take his stand here and affirm himself in the situation in which he is called (1 Cor. 7:20).[154]

Bornkamm develops some of the same themes in his essay on "The Revelation of God's Wrath: Romans 1–3."[155] Beginning with 1:18, he argues that what is revealed in creation is an accusation: that humanity is disobedient and guilty. "Therefore, Rom. 1.18ff. is not an apologetic and pedagogical discussion, because *the intention of the Apostle is not to infer God's being from the world, but to uncover the being of the world from God's revelation; not to prove the revelation of God before the judgment of the world, but to unveil the judgment of God over the world revealed in the law.*"[156] He believes that in Rom 2:1 Paul turns to the Jews. He recognizes that they have received revelation in the law, but says they have perverted it into their own privilege; they, too, stand under the judgment of God, in need of the saving revelation of God's righteousness. This revelation, according to Bornkamm, is the eschatological event.

> The revelation of this saving "righteousness" of God is an eschatological event that is accomplished in the "Now" of salvation history. To this same hour is bound the revelation of his wrath from heaven over all the unrighteousness of men. Because he lets his "righteousness" be made known, all the "wickedness" of men also comes to light.[157]

This idea of judgment is taken up again by Bornkamm in a lecture presented at the end of World War II in which he observes that the recent catastrophe of Germany has been viewed as the judgment of God. This leads him to an investigation of the theological understanding of judgment. According to Bornkamm the judgment of God can be seen in history, but it must be understood in the light of revelation. From this perspective he believes Jesus Christ to be the supreme revelation of God in history: the eschatological action of God that is both judgment and righteousness. "Thus the question of the righteousness of God in history, the question of theodicy, is removed and resolved through the preaching here and now, since God has revealed his righteousness, no longer his righteousness in itself, no longer his righteousness against me, but the righteousness of God for me in Jesus Christ."[158]

Bornkamm had a special interest in a NT concept interpreters often avoid: the question of reward. He observes that it is an embarrassment to Protestant theology because of its abhorrence of the idea of reward for good works. Yet, as Bornkamm observes, Jesus and the NT frequently express the idea. In Judaism emphasis is placed on the punishment of the wicked and the reward of the righteous in heaven. Bornkamm believes Jesus has a different view: reward has to do with the coming and presence of God. *The treasure in heaven is the rule of God itself.*[159] According to Bornkamm the NT idea is not based on an obedience that seeks reward but on a spontaneous obedience that is unaware that it has done something for the Lord (Matt 25:31-46). He believes the parable of the workers in the vineyard (Matt 20:1-16) radically refutes the human idea of reward; God's grace is totally different from human expectation. The NT idea of reward, according to Bornkamm, is paradoxical: God acts in grace and humans react with obedience. "There is no more appropriate expression than the word of Phil 2:12f. for the unlimited power of God and the freedom of his grace, but at the same time for the limitation and lack of freedom of humanity before God, for the unconditional character of the divine demand, but at the same time for the conditional nature of humanity."[160]

TWO BEST-SELLERS: JESUS AND PAUL

Bornkamm's *Jesus of Nazareth* first appeared in 1956; it went through thirteen editions and was translated into ten languages; it sold over 120,000 copies.[161] The book is often hailed as the concrete realization of the new quest of the historical Jesus. Actually, Bornkamm addressed the question of the quest in publications written after the first edition of the book. In an essay on "The Significance of the Historical Jesus for Faith," originally published in 1961, he noted the failure of the old quest to recognize that the tradition about Jesus had been shaped by post-Easter faith and that the Gospels were not concerned with biography.[162] Nevertheless, he contends that we cannot be indifferent to the historical Jesus. The post-Easter church proclaimed God's action in Jesus and the early church had faith in Jesus. Faith cannot be separated from history and history is decisive for faith. "Nevertheless, faith remains constantly directed to a specific history, although not to one that offers proofs and supports which supposedly first make faith possible. . . . For faith everything depends upon the identity between Jesus and the Christ. . . . The center and content of faith, therefore, is that 'Jesus Christ is the same yesterday, today, and for ever' (Heb. 13:8)."

In another essay Bornkamm responds positively to Käsemann's proposal for a new quest.[163] He also argues that the Gospels, as distinct from the post-Easter kerygma, are concerned with the words and deeds of Jesus. "[T]hey bring the hearer back to the beginning and lead him into the encounter with Jesus as on the first day when he encountered his contemporaries with summons and promise, with call to repentance and saving act demanding an answer."[164]

Most of the editions of Bornkamm's book are reprints; the English translation (ET) was made from the third edition of 1956. However, the tenth German edition (1975) was revised and expanded. The revisions update the bibliography and respond to criticisms, notably the charge that Bornkamm had misrepresented first-century Judaism. The following review is based on the ET and expanded with reference to the German tenth edition. In the foreword to the first edition Bornkamm observes that publications on the life and teachings of Jesus, once numerous, have become rare. Some scholars have even supposed that historical criticism is not the way to investigate the subject. He responds: "Certainly faith cannot and should not be dependent on the change and uncertainty of historical research. . . . But no one should despise the help of historical research to illumine the truth with which each of us should be concerned."[165]

In the first chapter, "Faith and History in the Gospels," Bornkamm notes that the old quest, chronicled by Albert Schweitzer, has ended.[166] Nevertheless, he says that "it cannot be seriously maintained that the Gospels and their tradition do not allow enquiry after the historical Jesus. Not only do they allow, they demand this effort."[167] The post-Easter faith, according to Bornkamm, is concerned with the pre-Easter Jesus; "the primitive tradition of Jesus is brim full of history."[168]

Chapter 2, "Period and Environment," presents a review of the history of Judaism from the return from Babylonian captivity to the destruction of Jerusalem. In regard to religion, Bornkamm recounts the affirmation of the one Creator God who has revealed the will of God in the law. However, he believes that this religion in time degenerated into a scribal legalism. "The sole task of interpretation," he comments, "is to relate the Torah to the manifold situations of life in each particular period. Even the weirdest oddities of Jewish casuistry betray this understanding of the law."[169] These sentences remain in the tenth edition, although the section on "Groups and Movements" expands the discussion of the Pharisees and acknowledges that Matthew's hostility reflects the Jewish-Christian conflict in the time after Jesus. Nevertheless, Bornkamm continues to believe that the Pharisees represent a legalism "to which Jesus' message of the divine will stands in sharp contrast."[170]

In chapter 3, titled "Jesus of Nazareth," Bornkamm admits that a biography of Jesus cannot be written, but he claims that much can be known. We know that Jesus' childhood and adolescence were spent in Galilee, and we know the names of his father, mother, and brothers. We know that Jesus spoke Aramaic and that he was baptized by John. Bornkamm also believes that we know that Jesus conducted a prophetic ministry, heralding the coming of the kingdom of God. We know that he took his message to Jerusalem where he was crucified. Bornkamm asserts that Jesus cannot be fitted into any of the conventional categories of the time, such as rabbi or apocalyptic prophet. In contrast, Bornkamm believes he stressed the presence of God and claimed a direct authority from God. "To make the reality of God present: this is the essential mystery of Jesus. This making-present of the reality of God signifies the end of the world in which it takes place. This is why the scribes and Pharisees rebel, because they see Jesus' teaching as a revolutionary attack upon law and tradition."[171]

Chapter 4 on "The Dawn of the Kingdom" includes a section on "the Hour of Salvation." In the tenth edition Bornkamm adds material to illustrate the contrast between the eschatology of Jesus and that of the rabbis. Jesus, he thinks, is closer to apocalyptic Judaism, although Jesus is reticent to predict the time of the kingdom's coming; instead, he concentrates on the certainty of God's reign. According to Bornkamm, Jesus believes the kingdom is already dawning and understands himself as a sign of the kingdom. In regard to "the Hiddenness of God's Reign," Bornkamm believes Jesus speaks of the mystery of the kingdom—the kingdom that is already secretly at work. In view of the coming kingdom, Jesus calls for repentance. In contrast to John and the Jews, Jesus, in Bornkamm's opinion, understands the call to repentance as a call to joy. "God's future is God's call to the present, and the present is the time of decision in the light of God's future."[172]

In discussing Jesus' understanding of "The Will of God" (chapter 5), Bornkamm, in the tenth edition, revises his treatment of "Jesus and the Law" and "The New Righteousness." In the revision he recognizes that the later tradition, echoing the conflict between the church and Judaism, puts caustic words into the mouth of Jesus. Nevertheless, he continues to recount Jesus' attack on Jewish legalism. "He liberates the will of God from its petrifaction in tables of stone, and reaches for the heart of man which seeks seclusion and safety behind the stronghold of observance of the law. He detaches the law of God from the "traditions of men" and sets it free."[173]

By way of contrast, Jesus sums up the whole law in "The Commandment of Love"—a love that, grounded in the will of God, has no limitation. Jesus addresses God as "Father" (*Abba*), affirming, according to Bornkamm, the presence of God. Although faith involves the belief that Jesus can perform miracles, Bornkamm thinks Jesus did not want to be viewed as a miracle worker and opposed faith based on miracles. In regard to the idea of reward, Jesus, in contrast to the Jewish idea of retribution, understands reward in terms of God's grace. "Thus the idea of reward has received a completely new meaning. Detached from deeds of merit and the claims of man, it has become an expression of divine justice and grace, to which man is directed, now more than ever called to effort and faithfulness, and on which he must lean."[174]

Regarding "Discipleship" (chapter 6), Bornkamm observes that one becomes a disciple by the call of Jesus. The task of the disciple is to follow and join in the proclamation of the kingdom. Bornkamm believes "Jesus' Journey to Jerusalem" (chapter 7) was decisive. Jesus traveled to Jerusalem, according to Bornkamm, in order to take his message to the capital city. In Jerusalem, Jesus celebrated a last supper with his disciples, a meal that, in Bornkamm's opinion, was not a Passover observance. Bornkamm's account of the events in Gethsemane is revealing of his understanding of history.

> This story, too, should not be read simply as a historical record. The very fact that no human being witnessed Jesus' struggle is evidence of this. Yet this story, too, is a historical document in a higher sense: it presents Jesus, alone, at the fiercest point of his temptation, separated from his disciples, not as a "divine being," but in his complete humanity.[175]

In the tenth edition Bornkamm revises and expands his account of the trial of Jesus. In the revision he observes that the later tradition tended to exaggerate the responsibility of the Jewish authorities, although historically the action of Pilate was decisive for the crucifixion.

Bornkamm devotes chapter 8 to the controversial "Messianic Question." According to him Jesus did not make messianic claims or adopt messianic titles.

[A]though the historical Jesus spoke most definitely of the coming Son of man and judge of the world in the sense of the contemporary apocalyptic hope, and did so with the amazing certainty that the decisions made here with regard to his person and message would be confirmed at the last judgment, nevertheless he did not give himself the title Son of man. Also we can hardly assume that the earthly Jesus saw himself as destined to be the heavenly judge of the world.[176]

Nevertheless, Bornkamm is convinced that Jesus lived a "messianic" life and engaged in a mission that was messianic and more.

[T]he Messianic character of his being is contained *in* his words and deeds and *in* the unmediatedness of his historic appearance. No customary or current conception, no title or office which Jewish tradition and expectation held in readiness, serves to authenticate his mission, or exhausts the secret of his being. It is impossible to solve this mystery with the logic, of whatever type, of any preceding doctrinal system. We thus learn to understand that the secret of his being could only reveal itself to his disciples in his resurrection.[177]

Bornkamm takes up the question of the resurrection in his final chapter, "Jesus Christ." According to him the resurrection cannot be the object of historical inquiry; the historian can only deal with the rise of the Easter faith and the origin of the church. Bornkamm believes the resurrection narratives are not historical records but expressions of faith. Nevertheless, he thinks the risen Christ discloses the meaning of the Jesus of history. "It is the resurrected Christ, therefore, who first reveals the mystery of his history and his person, and above all the meaning of his suffering and death." He concludes:

By the events of Easter and the certainty of the resurrection of Jesus Christ from the dead, he who proclaimed the coming of the kingdom of God, as we have already said, became the one proclaimed, the one who called to faith became the content of the faith. Jesus' words and the gospel about Jesus Christ have become a unity.[178]

All in all, Günther Bornkamm's *Jesus of Nazareth* is a masterful accomplishment: thoughtful, readable, moving, and widely influential.[179] Of special significance is the relation of Bornkamm's work to Bultmann's *Jesus and the Word*.[180] The major difference is that Bultmann concentrates almost exclusively on the message of Jesus; Jesus is presented as "the bearer of the word." Bornkamm, while emphasizing the proclamation of the kingdom and Jesus' understanding of the will of God, gives more attention to the person and activity of Jesus, to the narrative. Also, Bornkamm affirms the continuity between the historical Jesus and the Christ of the post-Easter faith. A major criticism of Bornkamm's *Jesus* was launched by Leander E. Keck.[181] According to Keck, Bornkamm has confused historical criticism and faith. This is seen, for example, in his argument that Jesus did not use messianic titles but that his words and deeds witness to his messiahship. In making this argument Bornkamm, according to Keck, enlists criticism in the support of faith. Bornkamm responded to Keck in a *Nachwort* to his tenth edition.[182] He denies that he attempted to ground faith in historical facts confirmed by criticism. He insists that faith and history cannot be separated; we must seek history in the kerygma and the kerygma in history. According to Bornkamm the hermeneutical circle of faith and history cannot be avoided. An easy resolution of the Keck-Bornkamm debate is scarcely to be expected, but it indicates that the hermeneutical problem and its philosophical-theological basis demand further investigation.

Bornkamm's *Paulus* first appeared in 1969; it went through four editions (largely reprints), and was translated into English, Japanese, French, Italian, Spanish, and Norwegian.[183] In the introduction he deals with sources. He accepts seven epistles as authentic (Romans, 1 and 2 Corinthians, Galatians, Philippians, 1 Thessalonians, and Philemon). He believes Acts can be used as a secondary source. Part I reviews the "Life and Work" of apostle. Paul, according to Bornkamm, was a Diaspora Jew who joined the Pharisees and became devoted to the law; he persecuted the Christians because they did not keep the law. Bornkamm understands Paul's conversion as a prophetic call, not an ecstatic experience. In his encyclopedia article he writes: "the meaning of his conversion is concentrated on one point: it means his life-transforming recognition that God in the sending and sacrifice of Jesus as the Messiah and Son of God has brought an end to the Jewish way of salvation, and thereby at the same time has opened to all the saving way of faith."[184] Bornkamm believes that Paul began his mission in Arabia. After more than two years there he made a brief visit to Jerusalem and then continued his mission in Syria and Cilicia. He thinks the Apostolic Assembly (Gal 2:1-10; Acts 15:6-21) was held fifteen or sixteen years after Paul's conversion. The assembly, according to Bornkamm, acknowledged Paul's mission but did not fully consent to his gospel. The apostolic decree (Acts 15:23-29), in Bornkamm's view, was not enacted by the assembly when Paul was present. Bornkamm believes Paul's mission to Cyprus and southern Asia Minor (reported in Acts 13 and 14) took place after the assembly. The conflict between Paul and Peter in Antioch is important for Bornkamm because it illustrates Paul's uncompromising opposition to legalism.

In regard to the so-called second missionary journey, Bornkamm believes it proceeded through central Asia Minor where Paul founded the churches of (north) Galatia. During this journey Paul, in Bornkamm's opinion, came to the conviction that he should take his mission to the ends of the inhabited world. After crossing into Macedonia, Paul founded churches in Greece. Bornkamm believes the speech attributed to Paul in Athens to be a post-apostolic composition. During his stay in Corinth, Paul wrote 1 Thessalonians, which Bornkamm views as the first of the extant Pauline epistles.

Bornkamm rehearses his understanding of the composition of the Corinthian correspondence as presented in his earlier research. He believes Paul wrote Galatians from Ephesus; Philemon and part of Philippians were written from an Ephesian imprisonment. After leaving Ephesus and traveling through Macedonia, Paul visited Corinth prior to his final trip to Jerusalem. Although Bornkamm considers Paul's speech to the Ephesian elders (Acts 20:25-35) to be a later composition, he believes the Acts account of the event in Jerusalem, including Paul's participation in a Nazirite vow (Acts 21:23-26), is reliable. In regard to the exciting account of Paul's voyage and shipwreck, Bornkamm supposes the author of Acts used a written source that had no connection with Paul. He believes the author of Acts knew of the death of Paul in Rome but declined to report it because the report would have been counter to his purpose: to present the triumph of Christianity.

Part II on Paul's "Gospel and Theology" is longer than the first part.[185] Bornkamm begins by discussing the relation of Paul's gospel to the kerygma of the primitive church. With the preaching of the church a significant shift occurs. "The proclaimer has become the subject of proclamation, his life has assumed dimensions that it did not have on earth, and for Jesus' own words are substituted the word about Jesus, his death, resurrection, and second coming at the end of the world."[186] Although Paul knew and sometimes quoted the early tradition, "Paul expounds and develops the *Christian gospel as the gospel of justification by faith alone.* So far from this doctrine's being common property in the primitive church, it is a specifically Pauline creation."[187] Echoing Bultmann, Bornkamm interprets Paul as affirming that "every statement about God, Christ, Spirit, Law, judgment, and salvation is at the same time one about man in his world, the old lost man and the new one set free by God." He continues: "To lead man as confronted by God to self-understanding and thus to reflection on his situation and life in the world: this is the steadfast aim of the apostle's preaching and theology."[188]

As to the situation of humanity in the world, Bornkamm believes Paul views humans as lost, standing under the wrath of God. The law, which reveals the will of God, discloses human disobedience; it reveals humans as sinners. Bornkamm does not believe Paul affirmed the doctrine of original sin; sin is a responsible act of humans. Adam's sin is characteristic of humans who are in the world and under the power of Satan. The law, according to Bornkamm, cannot free humans because the law, as a means of salvation, had been destroyed. Christ is the end of the law (Rom 10:4). The saving event, says Bornkamm, is the righteousness of God. Righteousness, he thinks, is not a an attribute but an action of God.

> Grammatically, then, the genitive in "God's righteousness" is not subjective (if so, the transcendent God would be made utterly remote and inaccessible to man), but a genitive of origin. That is to say: God creates his righteousness for man, puts him in the right—man who apart from this verdict and act is lost, but now may have life in his sight.[189]

Righteousness is an action of God's grace, occurring the death of Christ. According to Bornkamm the response to this divine action is faith. "It signifies acceptance, in obedient trust and trustful obedience, of God's saving act as proclaimed in the gospel."[190] He rejects Käsemann's notion that righteousness to a gift to all humanity, the apocalyptic disclosure of the lordship of Christ over the cosmos. Instead, the saving event is directed to the individual. Bornkamm believes that Paul's doctrine of predestination does not mean determinism but affirms the idea of pure grace.

Bornkamm thinks Paul views the life of faith as a life of peace with God: a life of freedom from law, freedom from death. Faith works in love; love is not a precondition of salvation but a response to grace. According to Bornkamm, Paul's idea of life "in Christ" is not mysticism but "the full meaning of the new basic and all-comprehending reality into which believers are transferred once they have been delivered from the power of corruption."[191] Under the theme "Present Salvation," he discusses Paul's understanding of the word. The word is not information about the gospel; it is saving event. It is the word of the cross, which stands in opposition to the wisdom of the world yet paradoxically is the wisdom and power of God. The resurrection, according to Bornkamm, does not nullify the cross; it makes the cross operative as saving event, enacted in the proclamation. Bornkamm believes Paul understands his apostleship in relation to the gospel. He proclaimed the gospel with his life—a life of suffering for the gospel, not a display of martyrdom.

Bornkamm believes that the church arose in expression of the resurrection faith. He thinks Paul stressed the presence of the Spirit in the church. "Thus, for Paul God's Spirit is not the supernatural power that enables a man to transcend his earthly life and its limitations: instead, it is the power of God who shows himself mighty in lowliness and weakness."[192] In exercising discipline in his churches Paul draws from many sources—Scripture, words of the Lord, nature—but most of all from the gospel. "The most important source of Paul's directions, the basis of all else, is the church's *remembrance* of its origin, God's saving acts in Christ as proclaimed in the gospel."[193] Bornkamm believes Paul understands Baptism and the Lord's Supper as sacraments.[194] Baptism mediates the forgiveness of sins, bestows the Spirit, and incorporates believers into the eschatological community; the Supper makes present the reality of the saving death of Christ.[195] Bornkamm is convinced that Paul's description of the church as the "body of Christ" is more than a metaphor.

> [I]t is not something *like* a body, but—in a real sense—it *is* Christ's body. . . . Accordingly, it is not an organism in the strict sense of the word, but rather—though this, too, is open to misconception—an organ, a means and tool through which Christ himself organizes his lordship and gives it effect by the Spirit. The church is not just to become this: it *is* so already, in virtue of Christ's death and resurrection, released and endowed by him, all members without exception.[196]

Concerning eschatology and ethics, Bornkamm believes Paul views the coming of Christ as the turning point of the eons. In the time of faith—the time between the resurrection and the *parousia*—life is based on grace and oriented to God's action in Christ. Christian life, according to Bornkamm's reading of Paul, involves the indicative and the imperative: the new life in response to the grace of God. Christian life is characterized by love, grounded in God's love revealed in the cross of Christ. In describing the eschatological future Paul borrows imagery from Jewish apocalyptic. "However diverse all these statements in the Pauline letters about the future and whatever their application, they again reveal fixed basic motifs in the apostle's theology viewed as a whole: the sovereignty and final victory of God, who alone is to bring the work he began to completion."[197]

Bornkamm concludes with an important discussion of the relation of Paul to Jesus. In liberalism there was a tendency to detect a gulf between Jesus and the apostle, together with a plea to return to Jesus. Bornkamm acknowledges differences, but he affirms a fundamental unity.

> This makes clear that Paul's gospel of justification by faith alone matches Jesus' turning to the godless and the lost. In neither case is it a *concept* of God, the *idea* of the God who forgives, but the establishment and, in the full sense of the term, the bringing home to men of what is now happening and what the hour has proclaimed; the kingdom of God "in the midst of you" (Luke 17:20), "the fullness of time" (Gal. 4:4).[198]

Thus Bornkamm finds the continuity between Jesus and Paul to consist in the doctrine of justification by faith. Although Bultmann is inclined to acknowledge a discontinuity, much that is found in Bornkamm's *Paul* he had heard in Marburg. But what his teacher did not do—write a book on the life and work of Paul—Bornkamm did. And he did it with grace and clarity, making the thought of the master alive for the masses.

All in all, Günther Bornkamm is the complete NT scholar: competent historian, analytical critic, imaginative exegete, thoughtful theologian. After his earlier preoccupation with *Religionsgeschichte*, his later work shows mastery of all the critical and exegetical disciplines. His critical conclusions reflect the liberal consensus: the 2DH, non-apostolic authorship of John, authenticity of seven Pauline letters, inauthenticity of the Catholic epistles. Bornkamm pioneered in redaction criticism and contributed to advancing research on Matthew. He provided creative solutions to the problem of composition and redaction of the Pauline letters. His understanding of Jesus claimed a balance between history and faith. He was convinced that the history of Jesus was more than a bare fact and that the words and deeds of Jesus were important for faith. He insisted that faith could not rest on a Jesus reconstructed by historical research but that the historian, to understand the NT, had to share its faith. To be sure, Bornkamm had not explained fully how faith and history were interrelated; he did not provide a philosophy of history that could explain the relationship or develop a hermeneutic that could offer an adequate method. Nevertheless, Bornkamm enlisted criticism and exegesis in the service of theology. In some areas, notably the idea of confession and concept of reward, he made unique contributions to understanding the theology of the NT. Most of all, he was committed to the center of the NT message. Bornkamm embraced the theology of the NT as his own: a Christocentric theology, a theology of the cross.

BULTMANN IN AMERICA: JAMES M. ROBINSON (1924–)

When American graduate students returned from study in postwar Germany they brought with them the theology they had heard in Heidelberg and Tübingen. In pulpits and at lecterns they proclaimed the message of dialectical theology, and they found a largely receptive audience. Americans, too, were troubled by the crises of the time. They trembled at the threat of nuclear war and sought a faith that offered more than a well-stocked bomb shelter. Americans, of course, had not experienced the horrors of the war directly, and they tended to seek more moderate solutions. In theology they were attracted more to Emil Brunner than to Karl Barth, more to revelation and reason than to the God who was radically Other. Many rallied around the flag of Rudolf Bultmann and his followers. Bultmann embraced the Bible, and the Bible was dear to pious Americans. Yet he believed the Bible should be interpreted in harmony with science—a science that resonated with American empiricism and the Enlightenment tradition. Bultmann's stress on the proclamation and the call to decision echoed the American passion for religious revival. And, of course, Americans had been reading the existentialists, and though they were baffled by Heidegger they were excited by Gide and Faulkner. Bultmann's synthesis of biblical theology, historical criticism, and existentialist philosophy had a powerful appeal.[199]

Bultmann influenced a host of American NT scholars in various ways and to various degrees. Moreover, some of Bultmann's students and students of his students migrated to the USA and remained for the balance of their careers—scholars like Helmut Koester and Hans Dieter Betz. These and others will be discussed below in different connections. However, the scholar who intentionally promoted German-American theological dialogue was James M. Robinson. Robinson's contribution to the study of the Nag Hammadi texts (NHC) and to research regarding the Q document will be reserved for later treatment. In this chapter attention will be given to his early work, which dealt with the new quest of the historical Jesus and the new hermeneutic.

Born in Gettysburg, Pennsylvania, James M. Robinson was the son of William Childs Robinson, an orthodox Calvinist Presbyterian who taught for many years at Columbia Theological Seminary in Decatur, Georgia.[200] The younger Robinson was educated at Davidson College (AB, 1945) and Columbia Seminary (BD, 1946). He studied at Basel with Karl Barth. In 1950–51 Robinson spent a semester at Marburg, where he studied with Bultmann. Later he was to write: "By now I have come to recognize in demythologizing the only form in which I can believe, and, what is more significant, what makes believing important."[201] Robinson also studied at Zürich, Heidelberg, Strasbourg, and Paris. In 1953 he resumed studies he had begun earlier at Princeton Theological Seminary and completed a dissertation (ThD) under Otto Piper. From 1952 to 1958 Robinson taught at Candler School of Theology at Emory University. He moved to the Claremont School of Theology in 1958, where he was promoted to full professor in 1961. In 1964 he was named Arthur Lets, Jr. Professor of Religion in the Claremont Graduate University. From 1968 to 1999 he served as director of the Institute for Antiquity and Christianity at Claremont. He was named Emeritus Professor at Claremont in 1999. While serving as annual professor at the American School of Oriental Research in Jerusalem (1965–66) Robinson traveled to Cairo and became involved in the study of the NHC. He was later appointed permanent secretary of the International Committee for the Nag Hammadi Codices. For many years Robinson was a leader in the International Q Project sponsored by the Institute at Claremont and the SBL. He participated in various leadership posts in the Society and served as president 1980–81.

EARLY WORKS

Robinson's first major publication was his Basel dissertation on *The Problem of the Holy Spirit according to Wilhelm Herrmann*.[202] This research eminently prepared Robinson as an interpreter of Barth and Bultmann, since both had studied under Herrmann. In the dissertation Robinson observes that Herrmann was anxious to bring the thought of the Reformation into new expression. He opposed metaphysics, affirmed God's revelation in Jesus, and believed communion with God was accomplished through faith in the inner life of Jesus. For Herrmann, communion with God was the ground for ethics, and sanctification was more important than justification. According to Robinson, Herrmann increasingly moved from stress on the historical Jesus to concern with the Spirit of Jesus—a movement from the second person to the third person of the Trinity.

Especially interesting is Robinson's claim that the adverse trends in Herrmann's theology were continued by Rudolf Bultmann. Bultmann shared and expanded Herrmann's view of myth as expressing the meaning of the self-understanding of the ethical believer. Robinson thinks both Herrmann and Bultmann betrayed a subjectivity reflecting the influence of existentialist philosophy. In his conclusion Robinson suggests how Herrmann's thought should properly be continued. Most important, the revelation in "the historical

Christ" should again be emphasized; Herrmann had missed the scandal of the Word made flesh. In contrast to Herrmann's later thought, Robinson recommends a christocentric approach to Trinity that maintains both the divine and the human. It is obvious that Robinson at this time was critical of Bultmann and sympathetic with Barth.

A condensed version of Robinson's Princeton dissertation (1955) was published as *The Problem of History in Mark*.[203] Robinson's interest in the idea of history in the NT is seen in an earlier publication, "Jesus' Understanding of History."[204] In this essay Robinson contends that the parables of Jesus present an understanding of history; they address the situation of the hearer and call for a decision of faith in response to the eschatological rule of God. In the book on Mark, Robinson reviews the history of the interpretation of Mark. He points out that scholarship in the nineteenth century, celebrating the triumph of the 2DH, assumed that Mark was the earliest and most important source for the historical Jesus. Robinson's intent is to investigate Mark's understanding of history by analysis of the Markan text. "However it is only by defining Mark's understanding of history that a centre of interpretation can be located which does justice both to Mark's history of Jesus and to Mark's religious experience."[205]

In Mark's introduction (1:1-13) Robinson analyzes the accounts of John the Baptist and the temptation of Jesus. By narrating these events Mark, according to Robinson, intends to present "the inauguration of eschatological history."[206] Robinson believes that Mark presents the exorcisms as a dualistic cosmic struggle—between Jesus' action by the Spirit and the power of Satan.

> For Mark, history is not ultimately ambiguous or relativistic; rather it has two clear-cut and irreconcilable alternatives in it, which can at times be stated as simply as Son of God *versus* demon, Holy Spirit *versus* unclean spirit. . . . It is Jesus' function to enter this struggle on behalf of the true destiny of mankind and with his heavenly power to carry through to the victory, and to the life and communion it brings.[207]

Robinson turns to the accounts of Jesus' debates with opponents—what the form critics call *Streitgespräche* (acceding to Bultmann, "controversy dialogues"). In these debates, Robinson believes, truth is presented as the eschatological presence of the Son of Man in history. The acts of the Son of Man, according to Robinson's reading of Mark, confirm his teaching. The cosmic struggle reaches its apex in the passion narrative, which culminates is the triumph of the resurrection.

> This survey of the Markan material has made it clear that Mark sees the history of Jesus from an eschatological perspective. For Mark the driving force in history is the divine power of the end of time, operative already in the history of Jesus, propelling the whole course of history toward its ultimate destiny.[208]

According to Robinson, Mark interprets history from his own perspective within the life of the church after 30 CE. The whole course of history encompasses the time of the prophets, followed by the time of Jesus, and finally the time of the church. "Mark's understanding of history is rooted in the fact that Mark envisages the cosmic struggle as extending to all peoples and continuing to the culmination of history. Mark's understanding of history shares in the universality of the cosmic struggle itself."[209]

Although Mark presents Jesus as the heavenly Lord, Robinson does not believe that Mark's piety is dominated by a sense of the numinous. Instead, Mark has an eschatological understanding in which Jesus and the Spirit enter history and create history; Jesus' action created an eschatological community. Robinson concludes: "Mark's understanding of Christian existence consists in an understanding of history: the history of Jesus and the history of the Church."[210]

In 1958 Robinson presented a paper as part of a symposium on "The Meaning and Validation of Biblical Faith," at the annual meeting of the National Association of Biblical Instructors (now the AAR) at Union Theological Seminary in New York. Robinson's contribution was entitled, "New Testament Faith Today."[211] In his paper he contended that recent developments in theology (for example, Bultmann's review of Barth's *Romans*) call for a discussion of the meaning of the NT for faith and of the NT understanding of faith. He believes that the NT understands faith as the response to the eschatological event of salvation proclaimed in the kerygma. Faith in the eschatological event, he says, brings with it a new self-understanding. "In faith a new selfhood is affirmed, based upon the aeon to come which in the saving event has already broken in upon our world, providing a transcendent context of existence."[212]Robinson thinks this eschatological self-understanding of the believer corresponds to the self-understanding of Jesus. "Thus Christian selfhood is one with Jesus' selfhood."[213] According to Robinson, Christian existence involves thinking—a thinking that comes to expression in theology that expresses the meaning of existence in the language of today. Theology, says Robinson, is explication of the kerygma. "For the *kerygma* is the unveiling of the act of God in the actions of Jesus, as the power which rules the universe and as the reality of the believer's own existence. . . . As knowledge about my existence, the content of faith can be held to be true only by thus understanding my existence, i.e., only as the act of faith."[214] This paper makes it clear that Robinson has pitched his tent in Bultmann's camp and viewed the star that will guide his work in days to come.

THE NEW QUEST OF THE HISTORICAL JESUS

Robinson's most important early contribution to NT research is his book, *A New Quest of the Historical Jesus*.[215] The book grew out of a paper Robinson had presented at the Oxford Congress on the Four Gospels (1957) entitled "The Kerygma and the Quest of the Historical Jesus."[216] In this lecture he observes that German scholarship has been striving to renew the quest. He quotes Käsemann as saying: "Fuchs, G. Bornkamm, and I see ourselves compelled to restrict the assertion that Easter founded the Christian kerygma; we must inquire as to the meaning of the historical Jesus for faith."[217] According to Robinson the old quest was ended when it became apparent that the gospels do not present biography of Jesus.[218] However, he believes a new understanding of history makes possible an understanding of the selfhood of Jesus. "The decisive point with regard to the kerygma and history is not whether the kerygma preserves detailed historical memories about Jesus, but rather that the kerygma is decidedly an evaluation of the historical person."[219]

During the summer semester in 1959, Robinson used his *New Quest* as basis for his lectures as guest professor at the University of Göttingen. These lectures were expanded and published as *Kerygma und historischer Jesus*.[220] A second, revised and expanded edition of this German translation appeared in 1967. The following review presents a summary of the original work, with notice of additions made in the second German edition.

The introduction presents the historical background of the new quest. Robinson reviews "the Bultmann epoch in German Theology." Turning to "the Post-Bultmannian Quest of the Historical Jesus," he hails Käsemann's paper of 1954 as the point of new beginning. He notes Fuchs's stress on Jesus' conduct as the setting of his teaching. "Fuchs has carried through with regard to Jesus' action the same thesis which Käsemann presented with regard to his message: in the message and action of Jesus is implicit an eschatological understanding of his person, which becomes explicit in the *kerygma* of the primitive Church."[221]

Robinson also reviews Bornkamm's *Jesus of Nazareth*, noting Bornkamm's concern with narrative as well as teaching. Bornkamm affirms a continuity between the message of Jesus and the kerygma of the church. Robinson believes that Bultmann, in response to the new quest, has shifted his position. "Bultmann himself seems to have moved with the 'post-Bultmannian' move of his pupils with regard to the historical Jesus and the *kerygma*."[222] The German editions expand this introduction to include lengthy footnotes that enlarge the argument and respond to criticisms.

The first chapter of the *New Quest* discusses "The Impossibility and Illegitimacy of the Original Quest." In this chapter Robinson presents a definition of the historical Jesus: "What can be known of Jesus of Nazareth by means of the scientific methods of the historian."[223] The old quest tried to avoid the Christ of dogma and rediscover Jesus as he actually lived. But as Schweitzer shows, the quest reproduced the reflections of modern expectations and missed the Jesus of history. The old questers, according to Robinson, presupposed a positivistic historiography, but subsequent research demonstrated that the sources were not amenable to that sort of investigation. The sources were not factual reports but devotional and didactic literature designed to meet the needs of the early Christian community. Not only was the old quest impossible; Robinson is convinced it was illegitimate. The center of the gospel, he insists, was not the Jesus of historical reconstruction but the kerygma; the kerygma called for authentic faith, not for an inauthentic search for historical proof. "Now it became increasingly clear that 'the historical Jesus,' the scholarly reconstruction of Jesus' biography by means of objective historical method, was just such an attempt to build one's existence upon that which is under man's control and invariably at his disposal."[224]

In the next chapter Robinson presents "The Possibility of the New Quest." He is sure that attempts to resurrect the old quest—for example, C. H. Dodd's understanding of the kerygma as a collection of data—are doomed to failure.[225] However, Robinson is convinced that a new quest is possible on the basis of a new view of history and the self. This new view of history, according to Robinson, focuses on the encounter with persons and with the meaning of human existence. This new understanding of history is analogous to the proper understanding of the kerygma; the kerygma is also concerned with self-understanding, and "Jesus' understanding of his existence, his selfhood, and thus in the higher sense his life, is a possible subject of historical research."[226]

The next chapter of Robinson's book is devoted to "The Legitimacy of the New Quest." He argues that the new quest is legitimate and relevant because theology, like the new view of history and the kerygma, is concerned with human existence. "Man's quest for meaningful existence is his highest stimulus to scholarly enquiry; consequently a serious quest of the historical Jesus must have meaning in terms of man's quest for meaningful existence."[227] Whereas the old quest attempted to secure faith by historical research, the new quest confesses one's willingness to put his or her faith into question. Robinson believes the new quest is facilitated by demythologizing. This method, by looking through the objective mythical form of the message, exposes the existential meaning of the kerygma.

> From this position at which Bultmann has arrived it is only one step to the 'post-Bultmannian' recognition that the actual demythologizing which went on within the primitive Church was the 'historicizing' process taking place within the *kerygma* and leading to the writing of Gospels. . . . It is simply because Germany's leading exegetes have correctly understood the demythologized meaning of the New Testament *kerygma*, that they have looked through the *kerygma* not directly to a principle inherent in human nature, but rather to Jesus as the event in which transcendence becomes possible.[228]

Robinson not only believes the new quest is legitimate, he also insists it is necessary because of the new situation in which we find ourselves, and because of the nature of the kerygma itself. "It is this concern of the *kerygma* for the historicity of Jesus which necessitates the new quest."[229] Robinson concludes:

> Thus the *kerygma* is largely uninterested in historiography of the nineteenth-century kind, for the *kerygma* does not lie on the level of objectively verifiable fact. But it is decisively interested in historiography of the twentieth-century kind, for the *kerygma* consists in the meaning of a certain historical event and thus coincides with the goal of modern historiography.[230]

Thus all the pieces fit together—modern historiography, demythologizing exegesis, the existential understanding of the self, the meaning of the kerygma, Jesus's self-understanding—all shaped into a radiant mosaic reflecting the Jesus of history.

A final chapter in the original English edition deals with "The Procedure of the New Quest." The new quest, according to Robinson, continues to use the method of historical criticism; the method becomes illegitimate only when it fails to recognize its limitations. For example, the method must acknowledge that the sources of the Jesus tradition are not perfectly reliable as history. Nevertheless, says Robinson, "the material whose historicity has been established is sufficient in quality and quantity to make a historical encounter with Jesus possible."[231] Moreover, he believes the new quest can cut through some of the old clichés such as the contrast: "Jesus preached the kingdom; Paul preached Christ." According to the new quest there is more continuity than contrast: Jesus' call to decision implied a Christology, and the kerygma's call to faith presupposed the life and teaching of Jesus. The point of correlation and continuity is the self-understanding of Jesus and the self-understanding of faith. "If the existential decision originally called for by the *kerygma* corresponds to the existential decision called for by Jesus, then it is apparent that the *kerygma* continues Jesus' message; and if the decision called for by Jesus as well as by the *kerygma* was at the basis of his own selfhood, then it is apparent that his person corresponds to its christology."[232]

> Thus the deeper meaning of Jesus' message is: in accepting one's death there is life for others; in suffering, there is glory; in submitting to judgement, one finds grace; in accepting one's finitude resides the only transcendence. It is this existential meaning latent in Jesus' message which is constitutive of his selfhood, expresses itself in his action, and is finally codified in the Church's *kerygma*.[233]

Robinson believes that the new quest is effective because it combines modern historical method and faithful commitment to the kerygma. He says that "the selfhood of Jesus is equally available to us—apparently both *via* historical research and *via* the *kerygma*—as a possible understanding of our existence."[234]

In the second German edition Robinson expands the last chapter of the first edition into a new chapter and adds another. The new chapter, "Individual Problems of the New Research for the Historical Jesus," further explicates his idea of Jesus' understanding of existence. At his baptism Jesus, according to Robinson, abandoned his old understanding and embraced a new self-understanding. Robinson believes this new understanding corresponds to the understanding of existence in the early Christian kerygma. The old notion of a distinction between Jesus and Paul missed the eschatological: the act of God that both Jesus and Paul proclaim.[235] According to Robinson the preaching of Jesus demanded an existential decision, and this call to decision corresponds to Paul's call for faith.

Robinson's *New Quest* sparked a conflagration that swept over the theological landscape.[236] In an essay added to the 1983 edition of the *New Quest*, Robinson summarizes "The Recent Debate on the 'New Quest.' "[237] This essay was originally presented as a paper at the annual meeting of the National Association of Biblical Instructors in 1961 as part of a symposium on "The New Quest of the Historical Jesus." At the outset Robinson reproached American scholarship for its tardiness in recognizing the significance of the new quest. He pulled no punches: as a example of the moribund old quest he cited the recently published *The Prophet of Nazareth* (1961), whose author, Morton S. Enslin, was present as a participant in the Symposium. In contrast to American paralysis Robinson praised the activity of Europeans since the appearance of Käsemann's pioneering paper of 1954.[238] He illustrates this with reference to the 710-page symposium on *The Historical Jesus and the Kerygmatic Christ* edited by Ristow and Matthiae with contributions from a host of scholars.[239] Robinson gives special attention to Bultmann's response to the new quest in his essay, "The Primitive Christian Kerygma and the Historical Jesus."[240] In this essay Bultmann maintains that the preaching of Paul and message of John prove that the historical Jesus is not essential to the kerygma. Robinson criticizes Bultmann's claim that the kerygma does not go beyond the mere "*dass*" ("that") of the historical event:

> In the situation in which the synoptic authors found themselves, one could no longer maintain, as Paul could, the "*dass*," the historicalness of the worshipped Lord, merely by repeated assertion of the fact of his historicalness. In their situation—and ours—an emphasis upon the "*dass*," indispensable as it is for the kerygma and for Bultmann, could only be made in terms of the Jesus tradition and not by ignoring that tradition through an exclusive proclamation of the Easter gospel. In their situation, the synoptic writers could retain the "*dass*" only by maintaining the "*was*," that is, only by making corrective use of the Jesus tradition, by replacing the un–Christian understanding of existence, which had invaded the Jesus tradition, with a Christian understanding of existence.[241]

Robinson concludes that Bultmann's failure to recognize the importance of the historical Jesus for the kerygma has serious consequences. Thus the basic refutation of Bultmann's position on the relevance of the historical Jesus is that if carried to its ultimate consequence it would prove too much. It would bring to an end the scholarly study of the Bible and theological scholarship in general as they would have no function for the church.[242]

Among the most caustic critics of Robinson's version of the new quest are Van A. Harvey and Schubert M. Ogden in their essay, "How New is the 'New Quest of the Historical Jesus'?"[243] Much of this essay is concerned with the interpretation of Bultmann. Contra Robinson, Harvey and Ogden contend that Bultmann's position had not undergone a shift. As Ogden says in his contribution to the symposium of 1961, "Bultmann's present view on the problem of the historical Jesus is essentially the same as it has been for over three decades."[244] Harvey and Ogden also contend that Bultmann believes the historical encounter with Jesus provides a new understanding of human existence but not (contra Robinson) Jesus' understanding of his own existential self-hood; the latter is not accessible to historical investigation. These critics also address Robinson's claim that new historical method is appropriate for interpreting Jesus because it is concerned with the meaning of the self. This indicates to Harvey and Ogden that the new quest, like the old, attempts to ground faith in historical research. Moreover, the concern of the new quest with the existential selfhood of Jesus seems similar to the old quest's preoccupation with the inner life and personality of Jesus.[245] To Harvey and Ogden the new quest appears to rely on the same sort of data—chronology, relation of Jesus to John the Baptist, etc.—as the old. They conclude:

> The question remains, therefore, how new the new quest is in relation to the old quest of which Robinson is so critical. If the old quest was illegitimate because it rested on the unchristian search for security, the new quest apparently opens the door to an anxiety that historiography will disconfirm the kerygma and so can hardly be different in principle in its own motivation. Likewise, if the old quest was impossible because the sources do not yield the kind of chronological information necessary to write a life of Jesus, the new quest seems to presuppose the same kind of information and so, to that extent, to be equally impossible.[246]

To investigate the fine points of this dispute is beyond the scope of this survey. However, as regards the interpretation of Bultmann, his essay in response to the new quest does not seem to give much ground. As Harvey and Ogden have shown, the new quest is not all that new; it has certain similarities with the old: the use of historical method and the importance of historical data. Also Robinson's version of the quest, wherein the concern is with the self-understanding of Jesus, seems much like the old concern with the inner life of Jesus and the question of messianic consciousness, concerns that seem to elude both old and new historiography. Nevertheless, the new questers suppose they are doing something new, and to those who review the work of Schweitzer some differences seem to emerge. Perhaps instead of "the new quest," this quest should be known as the post-Bultmannian quest. What can be known about the historical Jesus after Bultmann by scholars who belong to the Bultmann school? Surely Jesus must be more than a bare historical "that." Surely there is continuity between Jesus and the early Christian proclamation of Jesus. Yet for his followers Bultmann is surely correct in his claim that faith cannot be based on fact or on the reconstruction of history by fallible criticism. In contrast to the historical positivism of the old quest, the new quest does assume a new view of history like that proposed in Bultmann's *Presence of Eternity*.[247] The Jesus of the new quest, as Bornkamm's book shows, is more modest than the biographies of the old quest. The new quest, too, is more aware of the historical distance, more cautious about creating a Jesus in a modern image. Nevertheless, the new questers, although viewing Jesus in his historical setting, seek a Jesus who is relevant for their own faith. The problem of the relation of faith and history remains a persistent concern of NT research.

As well as his work on the new quest, Robinson also made a significant contribution to the understanding of the "new hermeneutic."[248] This new approach to the ontology of interpretation had been promoted by Gerhard Ebeling and Ernst Fuchs. Inspired by the thought of the "later" Heidegger, these two theologians were concerned with the theology of language.[249] They believed that existence is linguistic and faith occurs in language. According to Fuchs, hermeneutical theology is faith's doctrine of language; it is concerned with the meaning of the word of God. The word of God speaks in history; it is speech event (*Sprachereignis*) or word event (*Wortereignis*). Fuchs believes that the speech event is the saving event, in which the historical Jesus is heard as word of address.[250]

Another important American contributor to the development of the new hermeneutic is Robert W. Funk. Throughout his career Funk made a variety of contributions to NT research including NT Greek grammar and leadership of the "Jesus Seminar"; these will be reviewed later in this volume.[251] The "early Funk" presents his hermeneutic in *Language, Hermeneutic, and Word of God: The Problem of Language in the New Testament and Contemporary Theology*.[252] In this book he presents an introduction to language and hermeneutic in relation to the biblical idea of the word of God. Funk observes that hermeneutic is engaged in "translation." Translation is necessary, he points out, because of the distance between the world of the Bible and the world of the interpreter. The ancient language of faith does not speak to the modern human being. In hermeneutic the language of faith must be translated into the language of non-faith so the non-believer can hear. Theology, according to the new hermeneutic, is not primarily language *about* God but language *from* God. God speaks in human words, and the word of God became flesh in Jesus Christ.

SUMMARY

The members of the Bultmann school are just that: pupils of Rudolf Bultmann. To be sure, they deviate from the teachings of the master—Ernst Käsemann more than Günther Bornkamm. According to Käsemann, Bultmann's existentialist anthropology should be replaced by a theocentric apocalyptic. For both Käsemann and Bornkamm more can be said about the narrative of the life of Jesus, adding significant content to the *dass* of the event of revelation and salvation. Bornkamm can stress the person of Jesus and write a Jesus book that looks a little like a biography. Both scholars emphasize the importance of the theology of the cross, but that is evident in Bultmann's essential scandal. Käsemann and Bornkamm agree with Bultmann on the use of historical critical method. Indeed, Käsemann can go beyond the master in radical criticism, for instance, with his detection of shades of Docetism in the Fourth Gospel. Bornkamm's use of redaction criticism represents a move beyond the historical criticism of Bultmann, though it may be implicit there. Käsemann and Bornkamm share the history of religion methodology with special attention to Gnosticism. They support Bultmann's affirmation of the heritage of Luther and the doctrine of justification by faith while refusing to construe it anthropologically or existentially.

James M. Robinson and the Americans play the role of communicators in the Bultmann school; they ring the bell to call new students. They are especially concerned with the existential understanding of the new quest and the new hermeneutic. Not all Americans welcomed the message. Besides the philosophical-theological critique of scholars like Harvey and Ogden, some older scholars were offended by the seeming arrogance of the "young Turks." Nevertheless, the Bultmannians provoked significant debate. Echoes of the Bultmann school would be heard again in the American biblical theology movement, in the later British biblical theologians, and in the American scholars in the last chapter of this book.

Notes

1. See William F. Albright, "The War in Europe and the Future of Biblical Studies," in *The Study of the Bible Today and Tomorrow*, ed. Harold R. Willoughby (Chicago: University of Chicago Press, 1947), 162–74.

2. See Raymond E. Brown and P. Joseph Cahill, *Biblical Tendencies Today: An Introduction to the Post-Bultmannians* (Washington: Corpus, 1969); James M. Robinson, "Basic Shifts in German Theology," *Int* 16 (1962): 76–97.

3. See pp. 324–38.

4. Reinhard von Bendemann, *Heinrich Schlier: Eine kritische Analyse seiner Interpretation paulinischer Theologie*, BEvT 115 (Gütersloh: Kaiser, 1995).

5. Quoted in Paul F. M. Zahl, "A Tribute to Ernst Käsemann and a Theological Testament," *AThR* 80 (1998): 382–94, at 386.

6. Ernst Käsemann, "Was ich als deutscher Theologe in fünzig Jahren verlernte," in idem, *Kirchliche Konflikte 1* (Göttingen: Vandenhoeck & Ruprecht, 1982), 233–44, at 244.

7. For Käsemann's biography see Ernst Käsemann, "The Freedom to Resist Idolatry," *Dialog* 38 (1999): 117–22; idem, "70 Jahre Theologie in meinem Leben," in *Dienst in Freiheit: Ernst Käsemann zum 100. Geburtstag*, ed. Jens Adam, Hans-Joachim Eckstein, Herrmann Lichtenberger (Neukirchen-Vluyn: Neukirchener, 2008), 91–104; idem, "A Theological Review," in Ernst Käsemann, *On Being a Disciple of the Crucified Nazarene: Unpublished Lectures and Sermons*, ed. Rudolf Landau, trans. Roy A. Harrisville (Grand Rapids: Eerdmans, 2010), xii–xxi; R. P. Martin, "Käsemann, Ernst (*1906–1998*)," *HHMBI*, 500–5; "Ernst Käsemann: Biblical Theology under the Cross," in Roy A. Harrisville and Walter Sundberg, *The Bible and Modern Culture: Baruch Spinoza to Brevard Childs*, 2d ed. (Grand Rapids: Eerdmans, 2002), 249–70; Käsemann, "Was ich als deutscher Theologe," 233–44; Robert S. Barbour, "Theologians of our Time: Ernst Käsemann and Günther Bornkamm," *ExpTim* 76 (1964–65): 379–83.

8. "One Lord Alone: A Sermon of Protest," *ExpTim* 110 (1999): 249–51.

9. See pp. 565–98.

10. "Was ich als deutscher Theologe," 244.

11. Ernst Käsemann, *Der Ruf der Freiheit*, 3d ed. (Tübingen: Mohr Siebeck, 1968); Eng. trans.: *Jesus Means Freedom*, trans. Frank Clarke (Philadelphia: Fortress Press, 1968), 9.

12. Ibid., 155.

13. For an overview of Käsemann's theology see David Way, *The Lordship of Christ: Ernst Käsemann's Interpretation of Paul's Theology*, OThM (Oxford: Clarendon, 1991); Paul Francis Matthew Zahl, *Die Rechtfertigungslehre Ernst Käsemanns*, SThK 13 (Stuttgart: Calwer, 1996); Roy A. Harrisville, "Crux sola nostra theologia: A Retrospective Review of the Work of Ernst Käsemann," *RelSRev* 11 (1985): 256–59; Pierre Gisel, *Vérité et histoire: La Théologie dans la modernité: Ernst Käsemann* (Paris: Beauchesne, 1977); "Ernst Käsemann: Biblical Theology under the Cross," in Harrisville and Sundberg, *Bible and Modern Culture*, 249–70; Robin Scroggs, "Ernst Käsemann: The Divine Agent Provocateur," *RelSRev* 11 (1985): 260–63; Jan Rohls, "Der Ruf der Freiheit: Ernst Käsemanns Theologie im Kontext der Zeit," in *Dienst in Freiheit*, 1–21.

14. See Ernst Käsemann, "New Testament Questions of Today," in *New Testament Questions of Today*, trans. W. J. Montague (Philadelphia: Fortress Press, 1969), 1–22.

15. Way, *The Lordship of Christ*. For bibliography of Käsemann's works see ibid., 293–99; Johannes Friedrich, Wolfgang Pöhlmann, and Peter Stuhlmacher, *Rechtfertigung: Festschrift für Ernst Käsemann* (Tübingen: Mohr Siebeck, 1976), 593–604.

16. Ernst Käsemann, *Leib und Leib Christi: Eine Untersuchung zur paulinischen Begrifflichkeit*, BHT 9 (Tübingen: Mohr Siebeck, 1933).

17. See *HNTR* 2: 140–41, 247–51.

18. *Leib und Leib Christi*, 183.

19. Ernst Käsemann, "Das theologische Problem des Motivs von Leibe Christi," *Paulinische Perspektiven* (Tübingen: Mohr Siebeck, 1969), 178–210; Eng. trans.: "The Theological Problem Presented by the Motif of the Body of Christ," *Perspectives on Paul*, trans. Margaret Kohl (Philadelphia: Fortress Press, 1971), 102–21.

20. Ibid., 103.

21. Ibid., 104.

22. Ernst Käsemann, *Das wandernde Gottesvolk: Eine Untersuchung zum Hebräerbrief*, 3d ed., FRLANT (Göttingen: Vandenhoeck & Ruprecht, 1959); Eng. trans.: *The Wandering People of God: An Investigation of the Letter to the Hebrews*, trans. Roy A. Harrisville and Irving L. Sandberg (Minneapolis: Augsburg, 1984).

23. Quoted in ibid., 13.

24. Ibid., 26.

25. Ibid., 107.

26. Ibid., 179.

27. Ibid., 237.

28. Ernst Käsemann, *Die Legitimität des Apostels: Eine Untersuchung zu II Korinther 10–13*, Libelli 33 (Darmstadt: Wissenschaftliche Buchgesellschaft, 1956).

29. Ernst Käsemann, "Amt und Gemeinde im Neuen Testament," in idem, *Exegetische Versuche und Besinnungen 1* (Göttingen: Vandenhoeck & Ruprecht, 1960), 109–34; Eng. trans.: "Ministry and Community in the New Testament," in Käsemann, *Essays on New Testament Themes*, SBT 41 (London: SCM, 1964; repr. Philadelphia: Fortress Press, 1982), 63–94.

30. Ibid., 83.

31. See Ernst Käsemann, "Paulus und Frühkatholizismus," in *Exegetische Versuche und Besinnungen 2*, 2d ed. (Göttingen: Vandenhoeck und Ruprecht, 1965), 239–51; Eng. trans.: "Paul and Early Catholicism," in Käsemann, *New Testament Questions of Today*, trans. W. J. Montague (Philadelphia: Fortress Press, 1969), 236–51; Hermann-Josef Schmitz, *Frühkatholizismus bei Adolf von Harnack, Rudolph Sohm und Ernst Käsemann* (Düsseldorf: Patmos, 1977), 145–201.

32. See Bernhard Ehler, *Die Herrschaft des Gekreuzigten: Ernst Käsemanns Frage nach der Mitte der Schrift*, BZNW 46 (Berlin: de Gruyter, 1986); see also Gisel, *Vérité et histoire*, 133–219.

33. "Begründet der neutestamentliche Kanon die Einheit der Kirche?" in *Exegetische Versuche und Besinnungen 1*, 214–23; Eng. trans.: "The Canon of the New Testament and the Unity of the Church," in *Essays on New Testament Themes*, 95–107.

34. Ibid., 100, 103.

35. Ibid., 106.

36. Ernst Käsemann, "Zum Thema der Nichtojektivierbarkeit," in *Exegetische Versuche und Besinnungen 1*, 224–36; Eng. trans.: "Is the Gospel Objective?" in *Essays on NT Themes*, 48–62, at 57–58.

37. Ernst Käsemann, ed., *Das Neue Testament als Kanon: Dokumentation und kritische Analyse zur gegenwärtigen Diskussion* (Göttingen: Vandenhoeck & Ruprecht, 1970), 368–69.

38. Käsemann, "New Testament Questions of Today," in *New Testament Questions of Today*, 16.

39. Ernst Käsemann, *Jesu letzter Wille nach Johannes 17* (Tübingen: Mohr Siebeck, 1966); Eng. trans.: *The Testament of Jesus: A Study of the Gospel of John in the Light of Chapter 17*, trans. Gerhard Krodel (Philadelphia: Fortress Press, 1968; 3d rev. German ed. Tübingen: Mohr Siebeck, 1971). Käsemann's lectures developed ideas he had suggested in his inaugural lecture at Göttingen: "Ketzer and Zeuge," *ZTK* 48 (1951): 292–311. For a critique of Käsemann's interpretation of Johannine eschatology see Jörg Frey, *Die johanneishe Eschatologie I: Ihre Problem im Spiegel der Forschung seit Reimarus*, WUNT 96 (Tübingen: Mohr Siebeck, 1997), 160–70.

40. *Testament of Jesus*, 1.

41. Ibid., 26. For criticism of Käsemann's view see A. K. M. Adam, "Docetism, Käsemann, and Christology," *SJT* 49 (1996): 391–410.

42. Ibid., 73.

43. Ibid., 76.

44. Ernst Käsemann, "Geist und Buchstabe," *Paulinische Perspektiven*, 237–85; Eng. trans.: "The Spirit and the Letter," *Perspectives on Paul*, 138–66; idem, "Zum gegenwärtigen Streit um die Schriftauslegung," *Exegetische Versuche und Besinnungen 2*, 268–90; Eng. trans.: "Thoughts on the Present Controversy about Scriptural Interpretation," *New Testament Questions of Today*, 260–85.

45. "The Spirit and the Letter," 143.

46. "Thoughts on the Present Controversy," 277.

47. The paper was first published in 1954 and reprinted as "Das Problem des historischen Jesus," *Exegetische Versuche und Besinnungen 1*, 187–214; Eng. trans.: "The Problem of the Historical Jesus," *Essays on New Testament Themes*, 15–47. See James M. Robinson, *A New Quest of the Historical Jesus and Other Essays* (Philadelphia: Fortress Press, 1983); Lewis M. Rogers, "The New Quest of the Historical Jesus—A Liberal Response," *IRev* 20 (1963): 3–10; Frederick Herzog, "Possibilities and Limits of the New Quest," *JR* 43 (1963): 218–33; Ehler, *Herrschaft des Gekreuzigten*, 167–217.

48. "Problem of the Historical Jesus," 24.

49. Ibid., 33–34.

50. Ibid., 38.

51. Ibid., 42.

52. Ibid., 46.

53. Rudolf Bultmann, *Das Verhältnis der urchristlichen Christusbotschaft zum historischen Jesus*, (see ch. 2, n. 155 above), 14–42.

54. Ibid., 35.

55. Ernst Käsemann, "Sachgassen im Streit um den historischen Jesus," *Exegetische Versuche und Besinnungen 2*, 31–67; Eng. trans.: "Blind Alleys in the 'Jesus of History' Controversy," *New Testament Questions of Today*, 23–65.

56. Ibid., 40.

57. Ibid., 43.

58. Ibid., 47.

59. Ibid., 48.

60. Ibid., 49.

61. Ibid., 60.

62. See Gisel, *Vérité et histoire*, 221–41.

63. Ernst Käsemann, "Eine Apologie der urchristlichen Eschatologie," in *Exegetische Versuche und Besinnungen 1*, 135–57; Eng. trans.: "An Apologia for Primitive Christian Eschatology," in *Essays on New Testament Themes*, 169–95.

64. Ernst Käsemann, "Die Anfänge christlicher Theologie," *Exegetische Versuche und Besinnungen 2*, 82–104; Eng. trans.: "The Beginnings of New Testament Theology," *New Testament Questions of Today*, 82–107.

65. "Beginnings of New Testament Theology," 96.

66. Ibid., 98.

67. Ibid., 105.

68. Ernst Käsemann, "Zum Thema der urchristlichen Theologie," *Exegetische Versuche und Besinnungen 2*, 105–31; Eng. trans.: "On the Subject of Primitive Christian Apocalyptic," *New Testament Questions of Today*, 108–37.

69. Ibid., 132.

70. Ibid., 133.

71. Käsemann's later writings increasingly oppose Bultmann's individualism and preoccupation with anthropology. See Käsemann, "Zur paulinischen Anthropologie," *Paulinische Perspektiven* (1969), 9–60; Eng. trans.: "On Paul's Anthropology," *Perspectives on Paul*, 1–31.

72. See Zahl, *Rechtfertigungslehre Ernst Käsemanns*.

73. "Gottesgerechtigkeit bei Paulus," *Exegetische Versuche und Besinnungen 2*, 181–93; Eng. trans.: "'The Righteousness of God' in Paul," *New Testament Questions of Today*, 168–82.

74. Ibid., 168.

75. Rudolf Bultmann, "ΔΙΚΑΙΟΣΥΝΗ ΘΕΟΥ," *JBL* 83 (1964): 12–16, argues that the genitive is *gen. auctoris* and that Käsemann has exaggerated Paul's understanding of righteousness as future (stressing the subjective genitive). Käsemann in "Justification and Salvation History in the Epistle to the Romans," *Perspectives on Paul*, p. 77, replies: "I have never maintained that the righteousness of God means exclusively or primarily a subjective genitive. . . . On the contrary, I have called the *genitivus auctoris*, i.e., the soteriological sense of the phrase, the dominating one."

76. "Righteousness of God," 181.

77. "Rechtfertigung und Heilsgeschichte im Römerbrief," in *Paulinische Perspektiven*, 108–39; Eng. trans.: "Justification and Salvation History in the Epistle to the Romans," *Perspectives on Paul*, 60–78.

78. In Krister Stendahl, *Paul Among Jews and Gentiles* (Philadelphia: Fortress Press, 1976), 78–96.

79. "Justification and Salvation," 75.

80. See Käsemann, "Kritische Analyse von Phil 2, 5–11," *ZTK* 47 (1950): 313–60; Eng. trans.: "A Critical Analysis of Philippians 2:5–11," *JTC* 5 (1968): 45–88; see Robert Morgan, "Incarnation, Myth, and Theology: Ernst Käsemann's Interpretation of Philippians 2:5–11," in *Where Christology Began: Essays on Philippians 2*, ed. Ralph P. Martin and Brian J. Dodd (Louisville: Westminster John Knox, 1998), 43–73.

81. Ernst Käsemann, *An die Römer*, HNT 8a (Tübingen: Mohr Siebeck, 1973); Eng. trans.: *Commentary on Romans*, trans. and ed. Geoffrey W. Bromiley (Grand Rapids: Eerdmans, 1980). The English translation is based on the 4th German edition of 1980, which is largely a reprint of the 3d revised edition of 1974.

82. *Romans*, vii.

83. Ibid., 12.

84. Ibid., 22.

85. Ibid.

86. Ibid., 23.

87. Ibid., 29.

88. See Walter Klaiber, "Gottes Gerechtigkeit und Gottes Herrschaft: Ernst Käsemann als Ausleger des Neuen Testaments," in *Dienst in Freiheit*, 59–82.

89. *Romans*, 96.

90. Ibid., 97.

91. Ibid., 157.

92. Ibid., 149.

93. Ibid., 168.

94. Ibid., 169.

95. Ibid., 193.

96. Ibid., 198.

97. Ibid., 213.

98. Ibid., 236.

99. Ibid., 260.

100. Ibid., 283.

101. Ibid., 313.

102. Ibid., 314.

103. Ibid., 317.

104. Ibid., 325.

105. Ibid., 356.

106. For an overview of Bornkamm's life and work see Robert Morgan, "Bornkamm, Günther (1905–1990)," *HHMBI*, 439–44; Barbour, "Theologians of our Time: Ernst Käsemann

and Günther Bonrkamm" (see n. 7 above); Dieter Lührmann and Georg Strecker, eds., *Kirche: Festschrift für Günther Bornkamm zum 75. Geburtstag* (Tübingen: Mohr Siebeck, 1980), iii–v; Gerd Theissen, "Theologie und Exegese in den neutestamentlichen Arbeiten von Günther Bornkamm," *EvT* 51 (1991): 308–32.

107. In *The Theology of Rudolf Bultmann*, ed. Charles W. Kegley (New York: Harper & Row, 1966), 3–20; German trans.: "Die Theologie Rudolf Bultmanns," in Bornkamm, *Geschichte und Glaube 1*, 156–72.

108. "Mythos und Evangelium: Zur Diskussion des Problems der Entmythologisierung der neutestamentlichen Verkündigung," in Günther Bornkamm and Walter Klaas, *Mythos und Evangelium: Zum Programm R. Bultmanns*, 3d ed., ThEH 26 (Munich: Kaiser, 1953), 3–29; Eng. trans.: "Myth and Gospel: A Discussion of the Problem of Demythologizing the New Testament Message," in *Kerygma and History: A Symposium on the Theology of Rudolf Bultmann*, trans. and ed. Carl E. Braaten and Roy A. Harrisville (New York: Abingdon, 1966), 172–96. See Günther Bornkamm, Rudolf Bultmann, and Friedrich Karl Schumann, *Die christliche Hoffnung und das Problem der Entmythologisierung* (Stuttgart: Evangelisches Verlagswerk, 1954), 9–20; this is a radio address in which Bornkamm presents a popular, largely sympathetic account of demythologizing.

109. "Myth and Gospel," 186. Bornkamm later presented a view of the entire discussion of demythologizing: "Die Theologie Rudolf Bultmanns in der neueren Diskussion: Zum Problem der Entmythologisierung und Hermeneutik," *TRu* 29 (1963): 33–141; repr.: "Die Theologie Bultmanns in der neueren Diskussion: Literaturbericht zum Problem der Entmythologisierung und Hermeneutik," *Geschichte und Glaube 1*, 173–275.

110. *Mythos und Legende in den apokryphen Thomas-Akten: Beiträge zur Geschichte der Gnosis und zur Vorgeschichte des Manichäismus*, FRLANT 49 (Göttingen: Vandenhoeck & Ruprecht, 1933).

111. "Die Häresie des Kolosserbriefes," *TLZ* 73 (1948): 11–20; repr. in *Das Ende des Gesetzes: Paulusstudien, Gesammelte Aufsätze 1*, BEvT 16 (Munich: Kaiser, 1958), 139–56; Eng. trans.: "The Heresy of Colossians," in *Conflict in Colossae: A Problem in the Interpretation of Early Christianity Illustrated by Selected Modern Studies*, ed. and trans. Fred O. Francis and Wayne A. Meeks, SBLSBS 4 (Missoula: Scholars, 1973), 123–45.

112. "Heresy of Colossians," 126.

113. *Bibel—Das Neue Testament: Eine Einführung in seine Schriften im Rahmen der Geschichte des Urchristentums* (Stuttgart: Kreuz, 1971); Eng. trans.: *The New Testament: A Guide to Its Writings*, trans. Reginald H. Fuller and Ilse Fuller (Philadelphia: Fortress Press, 1973).

114. Ibid., viii.

115. Ibid., 9.

116. In an early essay ("Die Komposition der apokalyptischen Visionen in der Offenbarung Johannis," *Studien zu Antike und Urchristentum, Gesammelte Aufsätze 2*, BEvT 28 [Munich: Kaiser, 1959], 204–22), Bornkamm argues that the key to interpreting the visions in Revelation is to distinguish between the opening of the seals (6:1–7:17) and the opening of the book; the book is not opened until the final, seventh seal is broken (8:1). He concludes that the content of the book (the central message of Revelation) is presented in 8:1–22:6.

117. *The New Testament: A Guide*, 142.

118. Ibid., 147.

119. "Die Vorgeschichte des sogenannten zweiten Korintherbriefes," *Geschichte und Glaube 2, Gesammelte Aufsätze 4*, BEvT 53 (Munich: Kaiser, 1971), 162–94. A short version appeared in English: "The History of the Origin of the So-Called Second Letter to the Corinthians," *NTS* 8 (1961–62): 258–64.

120. "Der Philipperbrief als paulinische Briefsammlung," *Geschichte und Glaube 2*, 195–205.

121. Originally published in *ABR* 11 (1963): 2–14; repr.: "The Letter to the Romans as Paul's Last Will and Testament," *in The Romans Debate*, revised and expanded edition, ed. by Karl P. Donfried (Peabody, MA: Hendrickson, 1991), 16–28; German trans.: "Der Römerbrief als Testament des Paulus," *Geschichte und Glaube 2*, 120–39; the German edition expands the original.

122. See p. 38.

123. "Letter to the Romans," 27–28.

124. See pp. 332–42 below.

125. "Die Sturmstillung im Matthäus-Evangelium," *WD* 1 (1948): 49–54; repr. in Günther Bornkamm, Gerhard Barth, and Heinz Joachim Held, *Überlieferung und Auslegung im Matthäusevangelium*, 4th ed., WMANT 1 (Neukirchen: Neukirchener, 1965), 48–53; Eng. trans.: "The Stilling of the Storm in Matthew," in *Tradition and Interpretation in Matthew*, trans. Percy Scott (Philadelphia: Westminster, 1963), 52–57.

126. "Stilling of the Storm," 56.

127. The essay "Enderwartung und Kirche im Matthäusevangelium" was first published in 1954 and was revised and expanded for publication in *Überlieferung und Auslegung im Matthäusevangelium*, 13–47; Eng. trans.: "End-Expectation and Church in Matthew," in *Tradition and Interpretation in Matthew*, 15–51.

128. *Tradition and Interpretation in Matthew*, 11.

129. Bornkamm presents a more detailed analysis of the redaction of this discourse in "The Authority to 'Bind' and 'Loose' in the Church in Matthew's Gospel: The Problem of Sources in Matthew's Gospel," in *Jesus and Man's Hope, Pittsburgh Perspective* 1 (Pittsburgh: Pittsburgh Theological Seminary, 1970), 37–50; German trans.: "Die Binde- und Lösegewalt in der Kirche des Matthäus," in *Geschichte und Glaube* 2, 37–50.

130. "End-Expectation and Church," 32.

131. Ibid., 38.

132. Ibid., 49. For another example of Bornkamm's research into Matthew's method and message see his "Der Auferstandene und der Irdische," in *Zeit und Geschichte: Dankesgabe an Rudolf Bultmann zum 80. Geburtstag*, ed. Erich Dinkler (Tübingen: Mohr Siebeck, 1964), 171–91; repr. in *Überlieferung und Auslegung im Matthäusevangelium*, 289–310; Eng. trans.: "The Risen Lord and the Earthly Jesus: Matthew 28:16-20," in *The Future of Our Religious Past: Essays in Honour of Rudolf Bultmann*, ed. James M. Robinson, trans. Charles E. Carlston and Robert P. Scharlemann (New York: Harper & Row, 1971), 203–29. Bornkamm's essays on Matthew have been collected and published in Günther Bornkamm, *Studien zum Matthäus-Evangelium*, ed. Werner Zager, WMANT 125 (Neukirchen-Vluyn: Neukirchener Verlag, 2009); as well as the works reviewed above, this volume includes four other essays on Matthew and also exegetical studies on Matthew that were preparatory for Bornkamm's projected commentary on the Gospel (HNT), which was never completed.

133. "Der köstlichere Weg: 1 Kor 13," reprinted with minor revisions in *Das Ende des Gesetzes*, 93–122; Eng. trans.: "The More Excellent Way: I Corinthians 13," in *Early Christian Experience*, trans. Paul L. Hammer (New York: Harper & Row, 1969), 180–93.

134. "More Excellent Way," 187.

135. "The Missionary Stance of Paul in I Corinthians 9 and in Acts," in *Studies in Luke-Acts: Essays presented in honor of Paul Schubert* (Nashville: Abingdon, 1966), 194–207; German trans.: "Das missionarische Verhalten des Paulus nach 1 Kor 9,1-23 und in der Apostelgeschichte," *Geschichte und Glaube* 2, 149–61.

136. "Missionary Stance," 202.

137. "Taufe und neues Leben bei Paulus," first published in 1939 (*Tbl* 18: 233–42), revised and published in *Das Ende Gesetzes*, 34–50; Eng. trans.: "Baptism and New Life in Paul: Romans 6," *Early Christian Experience*, 71–86.

138. "Der Mensch im Leibe des Todes. Exegetische Studie zu Römer 7," *WD* 2 (1950): 26–44; revised: "Sünde, Gesetz und Tod. Exegetische Studie zu Römer 7," *Das Ende des Gesetzes*, 51–69; Eng. trans.: "Sin, Law and Death: An Exegetical Study of Romans 7," *Early Christian Experience*, 87–104.

139. "Sin, Law and Death," 100.

140. "Die Verzögerung der Parusie: Exegetische Bemerkungen zu zwei synoptischen Texten," *Geschichte und Glaube 1*, 46–55.

141. See pp. 46–47.

142. "Zur Interpretation des Johannes-Evangelium: Eine Auseinandersetzung mit Ernst Käsemanns Schrift 'Jesu letzter Wille nach Johannes 17,'" *EvT* 28 (1968): 8–25; repr. in *Geschichte und Glaube 2*, 104–21; Eng. trans.: "Towards the Interpretation of John's Gospel: A Discussion of The Testament of Jesus," in *The Interpretation of John*, ed. John Ashton, 2d ed. (Edinburgh: T & T Clark, 1997), 97–119. See Jörg Frey, *Die johanneishe Eschatologie 1*, 180–85.

143. "Der Paraklet im Johannes-Evangelium," *Geschichte und Glaube 1*, 68–89, at 88.

144. "Gotteswort und Menschenwort im Neuen Testament," *Studien zu Antike und Urchristentum*, 223–36; Eng. trans.: "God's Word and Man's Word in the New Testament," *Early Christian Experience*, 1–14.

145. Ibid., 10.

146. "Die ökumenische Bedeutung der historisch-kritischen Bibelwissenschaft," *Geschichte und Glaube 2*, 11–20.

147. See Gerd Theissen, "Theologie und Exegese," 311–14.

148. "Das Wort Jesu vom Bekennen," *Geschichte und Glaube 1*, 25–36.

149. "Bekenntnis im Hebräer Brief," *TBl* 21 (1942): 56–66; repr. in *Studien zu Antike und Urchristentum*, 188–203.

150. Ibid., 189.

151. "Christus und die Welt in der urchristlichen Botschaft," *ZTK* 47 (1950): 212–26; repr. in *Das Ende des Gesetzes*, 157–72; Eng. trans.: "Christ and the World in the Early Christian Message," *Early Christian Experience*, 14–28.

152. Ibid., 22–23.

153. *Gesetz und Schöpfung im Neuen Testament* (Tübingen: Mohr Siebeck, 1934).

154. Ibid., 27.

155. "Die Offenbarung des Zornes Gottes (Rom 1–3)," *ZNW* 34 (1935); revised and expanded for publication in *Das Ende des Gesetzes*, 9–33; Eng. trans.: "The Revelation of God's Wrath: Romans 1–3," *Early Christian Experience*, 47–70.

156. Ibid., 59.

157. Ibid., 64.

158. "Das Gottesgericht in der Geschichte," in *Studien zu Antike und Urchristentum*, 47–68, at 67. For an explicit discussion of the his understanding of righteousness in relation to theodicy see Bornkamm, "Die Frage nach Gottes Gerechtigkeit (Rechtfertigung und Theodizee)," in *Das Ende des Gesetzes*, 196–210.

159. "Der Lohngedanke im Neuen Testament," *Studien zu Antike und Urchristentum*, 69–92, at 78.

160. Ibid., 92.

161. *Jesus von Nazareth*, 11th ed. (Stuttgart: Kohlhammer, 1977); Eng. trans.: *Jesus of Nazareth*, trans. Irene and Fraser McLuskey with James M. Robinson (New York: Harper & Brothers, 1960).

162. "Die Bedeutung des historischen Jesus für den Glauben," in *Die Frage nach dem historischen Jesus: Beiträge von Ferdinand Hahn, Wenzel Lohff und Günther Bornkamm* (Göttingen: Vandenhoeck & Ruprecht, 1962), 57–71; Eng. trans.: "The Significance of the Historical Jesus for Faith," in *What Can We Know About Jesus?: Essays on the New Quest by Ferdinand Hahn, Wenzel Lohff, Günther Bornkamm*, trans. Grover Foley (Edinburgh: Saint Andrew, 1969), 69–85.

163. "Glaube und Geschichte in den Evangelien," in *Der historische Jesus und der kerygmatische Christus: Beiträge zum Christusverständnis in Forschung und Verkündigung*, ed. Helmut Ristow and Karl Matthiae (Berlin: Evangelische Verlagsanstalt, 1960), 281–88.

164. "Geschichte und Glaube im Neuen Testament. Ein Beitrag zur Frage der 'historischen' Begründung theologischer Aussagen," *Geschichte und Glaube 1*, 9–24, at 24.

165. *Jesus of Nazareth*, 9.

166. See *HNTR* 2: 232–35.

167. *Jesus of Nazareth*, 22.

168. Ibid., 26.

169. Ibid., 37.

170. Ibid, 40.

171. Ibid., 62.

172. Ibid., 93.

173. Ibid., 105; see 10th ed., 92–93.

174. *Jesus of Nazareth*, 143.

175. Ibid., 162.

176. Ibid., 177.

177. Ibid., 178.

178. Ibid., 185, 188. The third German ed. and the Eng. trans. of *Jesus of Nazareth* include three appendices. The first (slightly revised in the tenth edition) deals with sources, affirming the 2DH and accepting the method and results of form criticism. The second reviews the history of interpretation of the Sermon on the Mount and recounts recurring efforts to blunt the ethical demands of Jesus. The third takes up the use of messianic titles—Son, Servant of God, Son of David, Son of Man—and argues that these were added by the later tradition. The tenth edition adds a fourth appendix on "the Twelve" and contends that the idea of the twelve apostles as an authoritative group arose in the post-Easter tradition.

179. See Theissen, "Theologie und Exegese," 319–25; Robert Morgan, "Günther Bornkamm in England," in *Kirche: Festschrift für Gunther Bornkamm*, 491–506. A short summary of his understanding of Jesus can be found in Bornkamm's article on "Jesus: The Christ and Christology," written for *The New Encyclopedia Britannica* (15 ed. [1974] 22: 336–46; the article is a masterpiece of concision, clarity, and depth without loss of detail.

180. See pp. 92–94.

181. "Bornkamm's Jesus of Nazareth Revisited," *JR* 49 (1969): 1–17. Similar is the criticism of Bultmann, *Das Verhältnis der urchristlichen Christusbotschaft zum historischen Jesus* (1962); Eng. trans.: "The Primitive Christian Kerygma and the Historical Jesus," (1964), 34–35. (See ch. 2, n. 155 above.)

182. See Dieter Lührmann, "Bornkamm's Response to Keck Revisited," in *The Future of Christology: Essays in Honor of Leander E. Keck*, ed. Abraham J. Malherbe and Wayne A. Meeks (Minneapolis: Fortress Press, 1993), 66–78. Keck's critique also opposes what he understands to be Bornkamm's caricature of Judaism. Bornkamm responds that revisions he has made to his 10th edition have modified his picture of the Jews. However, the specific references Keck cites remain unchanged in the revised edition.

183. Günther Bornkamm, *Paulus* (Stuttgart: Kohlhammer, 1969); Eng. trans.: *Paul*, trans. D. M. G. Stalker (New York: Harper & Row, 1971). A summary of Bornkamm's understanding of Paul is presented in his article, "Paulus, Apostel," *RGG*[3] 5: 166–90, another masterpiece of concision and clarity.

184. "Paulus," 171–72. See Günther Bornkamm, "The Revelation of Christ to Paul on the Damascus Road and Paul's Doctrine of Justification and Reconciliation: A Study in Galatians I," in *Reconciliation and Hope: New Testament Essays on Atonement and Eschatology presented to L. L. Morris on his 60th Birthday*, ed. Robert Banks (Grand Rapids: Eerdmans, 1974), 90–103.

185. On Bornkamm's understanding of Paul's theology, see Theissen, "Theologie und Exegese," 314–19. In regard to Paul's intellectual life Bornkamm argues that his opposition to the wisdom of the world does not represent irrationalism; instead, he finds evidence of reasoned arguments throughout the epistles; see "Glaube und Vernunft bei Paulus," *Studien zu Antike und Urchristentum*, 119–37; Eng. trans.: "Faith and Reason in Paul," *Early Christian Experience*, 29–46.

186. *Paul*, 110.

187. Ibid., 115.

188. Ibid., 118, 119.

189. Ibid., 138.

190. Ibid., 141.

191. Ibid., 155.

192. Ibid., 181.

193. Ibid., 185.

194. For Bornkamm's interpretation of Paul's understanding of worship, see his "Zum Verständnis des Gottesdienstes bei Paulus," *Das Ende des Gesetzes,* 113–32; Eng. trans.: "On the Understanding of Worship," *Early Christian Experience,* 161–79.

195. For Bornkamm's interpretation of Paul's understanding of the Lord's Supper, see his "Herrenmahl und Kirche be Paulus," *ZTK* 53 (1956): 312–49; repr. in *Studien zu Antike und Urchristentum,* 138–76; Eng. trans.: "Lord's Supper and Church in Paul," *Early Christian Experience,* 123–60.

196. Ibid., 194.

197. Ibid., 225.

198. Ibid., 237. These ideas are more fully discussed in Bornkamm's essay, "Paul's Christology," *Pittsburgh Perspective* 4 (1963): 11–24; see also the third appendix, "Christology and Justification," *Paul,* 248–49. The first two appendices deal with sources and critical problems in the Pauline letters that have been discussed above.

199. See William Baird, *The Quest of the Christ of Faith: Reflections on the Bultmann Era* (Waco, TX: Word, 1977).

200. For a review of Robinson's life and work see "Curriculum Vitae James M. Robinson," in *From Quest to Q: Festschrift James M. Robinson,* ed. Jón Ma. Asgeirsson, Kristin de Troyer, and Marvin W. Meyer, BETL 146 (Leuven: Leuven University Press, 2000), xiii–xxi; Stephen J. Patterson, "James M. Robinson: A Biography," in *Gnosticism and the Early Christian World: In Honor of James M. Robinson,* ed. James E. Goehring, Charles W. Hedrick, and Jack T. Sanders, with Hans Dieter Betz (Sonoma, CA: Polebridge, 1990), xxi–xxiv; Helmut Koester, "An Intellectual Biography of James M. Robinson," in *From Quest to Q,* xiii–xxi; John S. Kloppenborg, Helmut Koester, and Robert W. Funk, "Three Tributes to James M. Robinson," *For* 5 (1989): 4–6; James M. Robinson, "Lebenslauf," in *Das Problem des Heiligen Geistes bei Wilhelm Herrmann: Inaugural-Dissertation zur Erlangung der Doktorwürde der Theologischen Fakultät Basel* (Marburg/ Lahn: Universitäts-Buchdruckerei, 1952), 101.

201. Quoted in Patterson, "Robinson," xxii.

202. See n. 200 above. For Robinson's bibliography see "Bibliography of James M. Robinson," in *From Quest to Q,* xxv–xliv; "James M. Robinson: A Bibliography" prepared by Kathleen E. Corley, in *Gospel Origins & Christian Beginnings: In Honor of James M. Robinson,* ed. James E. Goehring, Charles W. Hedrick and Jack T. Sanders with Hans Dieter Betz (Sonoma, CA: Polebridge, 1990), xiii–xxvii.

203. James M. Robinson, *The Problem of History in Mark,* SBT 11 (London: SCM, 1957); chapters 2–5 of this edition were translated into German as *Das Geschichtsverständnis des Markus-Evangeliums,* trans. Karlfried Fröhlich, ATANT 30 (Zürich: Zwingli, 1956). The book was reprinted as Part II of *The Problem of History in Mark: And Other Marcan Studies* (Philadelphia: Fortress Press, 1982); Part I adds two late essays of Robinson, discussed later in this chapter. A short summary of the book is presented in Robinson's essay, "Mark's Understanding of History," *SJT* 9 (1956): 393–409.

204. James M. Robinson, "Jesus' Understanding of History," *JBR* 33 (1955): 17–25.

205. *Problem of History in Mark* (1957), 15; (1982), 63.

206. Ibid., 28 (76).

207. Ibid., 42 (90).

208. Ibid., 52 (100).

209. Ibid., 60 (108).

210. Ibid., 85 (133). A critical review of Robinson's book is presented by William H. Harter, "The Historical Method of Mark," *USQR* 20 (1964–65): 21–38; Harter accuses Robinson of lack of clarity in the analysis of Mark and dependence on (Bultmannian) theological presuppositions. For Robinson's response see James M. Robinson "The Problem of History in Mark, Reconsidered," *USQR* 20 (1964–65): 131–47. Robinson argues that Harter has largely misunderstood his book (and Mark) and tends to caricature Robinson's position. Robinson also observes that if he were to revise the book at this later date he would employ redaction criticism in relation to *Gattungsgeschichte*. How these methodological advances would contribute to the understanding of Mark is presented in one of the two essays that constitute Part I of the 1982 ed. of *The Problem of History in Mark*: "On the *Gattung* of Mark (and John)." The other essay, "Gnosticism and the New Testament," (revised repr. from *Gnosis: Festschrift für Hans Jonas*, ed. Barbara Aland [Göttingen: Vandenhoeck & Ruprecht, 1978], 125–43), argues that Mark's idea that Jesus spoke secrets in parables, and John's conviction that Jesus' teachings were not understood until after the resurrection, have their background in Gnosticism, where Jesus after the resurrection explains mysteries he had spoken before.

211. James M. Robinson, "The Meaning and Validation of Biblical Faith," *JBR* 27 (1959): 233–42.

212. Ibid., 235.

213. Ibid., 236.

214. Ibid., 239.

215. James M. Robinson, *A New Quest of the Historical Jesus*, SBT 25 (London: SCM, 1959); this book went through seven impressions and was reprinted in 1979 by Scholars Press. It was also reprinted in *A New Quest of the Historical Jesus: And Other Essays* (Philadelphia: Fortress Press, 1983), with the same pagination. This edition includes reprints of four additional essays.

216. James M. Robinson, "The Kerygma and the Question of the Historical Jesus," published as "The Quest of the Historical Jesus Today," *ThTo* 15 (1958–59): 183–97.

217. Ibid., 194.

218. Robinson's assessment of the old quest is presented in his "Albert Schweitzer's *Quest of the Historical Jesus* Today," originally published as an introduction to a new edition of Schweitzer's *The Quest of the Historical Jesus* (German ed. 1966; Eng. trans. 1968), revised and reprinted in Robinson's *A New Quest of the Historical Jesus: And Other Essays*, 172–95.

219. "The Quest of the Historical Jesus Today," 195. See James M. Robinson, "The Historical Jesus and the Church's Kerygma," *ReL* 26 (1956–57): 40–49.

220. James M. Robinson, *Kerygma und historischer Jesus* (Zürich: Zwingli, 1960).

221. *New Quest*, 15.

222. *New Quest*, 21.

223. Ibid., 26.

224. Ibid., 44. The 2d German ed., in discussing the meaning of the ambiguity of the phrase "the historical Jesus," adds a paragraph on the views of Fuchs and Ebeling but is otherwise little changed.

225. See pp. 47–50.

226. *New Quest*, 72. In the 2d German ed. Robinson adds seven pages to this chapter discussing his differences with Van Harvey and Schubert Ogden concerning the position of Bultmann in his *Jesus and the Word* and his response to the new quest, issues discussed later in this chapter.

227. *New Quest*, 75.

228. Ibid., 84–85.

229. Ibid., 88.

230. Ibid., 90. In the 2d German ed. footnotes are added and expanded, including a lengthy note in response to Ogden, *Christ without Myth*.

231. *New Quest*, 105.

232. Ibid., 112.

233. Ibid., 123.

234. Ibid., 125.

235. Robinson argues that the apparent difference in the eschatological views of Jesus and Paul—Jesus looked for the turn of the eons in the future whereas Paul believed the turn had already happened—has been exaggerated. According to Robinson, Jesus believed the kingdom was already breaking in, and Paul viewed the present as the eschatological time between the already and the not yet. Robinson believes this softening of the distinction between the eschatology of Jesus and that of Paul was acknowledged by Bultmann, who had, according to Robinson, shifted his position in responding to the new questers. In the course of the discussion Robinson attempts to refute the arguments of Van Harvey and Schubert Ogden, who contend that Bultmann had not changed his position. These issues are discussed later in this chapter.

236. For a general review and critique of the new quest see Frederick Herzog, "Possibilities and Limits of the New Quest," *JR* 43 (1963): 218–33.

237. James M. Robinson, "Recent Debate on the 'New Quest,'" *JBR* 30 (1962): 198–208; repr. in Robinson, *New Quest: And Other Essays*, 153–72. Besides this essay, this edition adds three others. Robinson's essay on Schweitzer has been noted above (n. 218). The added essay on "The Formal Structure of Jesus' Message" (ibid., 126–53; originally published in *Current Issues in New Testament Interpretation: Essays in Honor of Otto Piper*, ed. William Klassen and Graydon F. Snyder [New York: Harper & Row, 1962], 91–110, 273–84), further explicates Robinson's understanding of Jesus' view of existence as expressed in his eschatology. The added essay on "Jesus' Parables as God Happening" (pp. 196–210; originally published in *Jesus and the Historian: Written in Honor of Ernest Cadman Colwell*, ed. F. Thomas Trotter [Philadelphia: Westminster, 1968], 134–50), largely endorses Fuchs's understanding of the parables.

238. See pp. 136–37.

239. *Der historische Jesus und der kerygmatische Christus* (1960); see n. 686 above.

240. See ch. 2, n. 155 above.

241. *New Quest: And Other Essays*, 165–66.

242. Ibid., 171.

243. In *The Historical Jesus and the Kerygmatic Christ*, 197–242.

244. "Bultmann and the 'New Quest,'" *JBR* 30 (1962): 209–18, at 210.

245. This argument is more fully presented in Harvey's essay, "The Historical Jesus, the Kerygma, and Christian Faith," *ReL* 33 (1964): 430–50.

246. "How New is the 'New Quest of the Historical Jesus,'" *The Historical Jesus and the Kerygmatic Christ*, 197–242, at 242.

247. See at n. 405 above.

248. See Paul J. Achtemeier, *An Introduction to the New Hermeneutic* (Philadelphia: Westminster, 1969); Gerhard Ebeling, "Word of God and Hermeneutic," in *New Frontiers in Theology 2: The New Hermeneutic*, ed. James M. Robinson and John B. Cobb, Jr. (New York: Harper & Row, 1964), 78–110; Robert T. Osborn, "A New Hermeneutic?" *Int* 20 (1966): 400–11; Albert C. Moore, "Ernst Fuchs: A Poetic Approach to New Testament Hermeneutic," *ReL* 35 (1956–66): 106–21; Anthony C. Thiselton, "The New Hermeneutic," in *A Guide to Contemporary Hermeneutics: Major Trends in Biblical Interpretation*, ed. Donald McKim (Grand Rapids: Eerdmans, 1986), 78–107.

249. See James M. Robinson, "The German Discussion of the Later Heidegger," in *The Later Heidegger and Theology*, ed. James M. Robinson and John B. Cobb, Jr., NFT 1 (New York: Harper & Row, 1963), 3–76.

250. See Ernst Fuchs, *Hermeneutik*, 2d ed. (Bad Cannstatt: Müllerschön, 1958); idem, *Wagnis des Glaubens: Aufsätze und Vorträge*, ed. Eberhard Grötzinger (Neukirchen-Vluyn: Neukirchener, 1979).

251. See pp. 426–37.

252. Robert W. Funk, *Language, Hermeneutic, and Word of God: The Problem of Language in the New Testament and Contemporary Theology* (New York: Harper & Row, 1966).

PART II

The Revisiting of Critical Problems

4

New Discoveries, Archaeology, Textual Criticism

At the end of World War II science and technology, which had been forging swords and spears, turned to plowshares and pruning hooks. New methods for unearthing the past and harvesting knowledge were discovered. In 1947, W. F. Libby and his collaborators at the University of Chicago detected radiocarbon (or carbon-14) in nature. This discovery made possible the dating of organic material with considerable accuracy. When organic matter dies, its radiocarbon decays according to a fixed rate. Scientists, reducing the matter to pure carbon, are able to measure the remaining amount of radioactivity by recording the rays emitted from the carbon. For example, the carbon from a skeleton emitting 459 rays per hour is assessed to be 5,600 years old. In 1946 scientists at the University of Pennsylvania unveiled ENIAC (Electronic Numerical Integrator and Calculator). This "electronic brain," which was able to perform five thousand additions or subtractions per second, weighed thirty tons and occupied sixteen hundred square feet of floor space. This monster was the great-grandfather of the personal computer that sits on the desk of virtually every biblical scholar today. These little computers, crammed with microchips, are able to store and recover, arrange and analyze huge quantities of data at the touch of a key.

In mid-twentieth century two amazing manuscript discoveries provided NT research with a treasury of material that would occupy scholars for the rest of the century and beyond. In 1945 a few peasants in Egypt, digging for fertilizer, unearthed a jar containing the Nag Hammadi indices (NHC), and two years later a Bedouin shepherd in Palestine, searching for his sheep, threw a stone into a cave and heard it hit a jar containing texts of the Dead Sea Scrolls. While the news of the latter discovery made the front pages and continued to excite public interest, the former was hardly noticed. But some scholars believe the NHC may be of equal or possibly even greater significance for the study of the NT and the history of early Christianity.[1]

The Nag Hammadi Codices

Discovery and Publication

In 1947 Jean Doresse, a young French scholar, traveled to Egypt to study ancient Coptic monasteries.[2] While he was there Togo Mina, the director of the Coptic Museum in old Cairo, showed him a codex the museum had obtained from an antiquities dealer. Mina also took Doresse to the shop of Albert Eid, who had a copy of another Coptic codex containing *The Gospel of Truth*—a gnostic tractate known to Irenaeus. This codex was later brought to the United States and Europe in search of a buyer, and in 1952 was acquired by the Jung Institute in Zürich and named the "Jung Codex." During a later visit to Egypt, Doresse learned of other codices in the possession of another antiquities dealer, Phocion J. Tano.

In 1950 Doresse visited the area where the codices had been found in a jar buried in what he thought to be a cemetery, beneath the cliff of Jabal al-Tarif, near the ancient city of Chenoboskion, across the Nile from the town of Nag Hammadi, some seventy-five miles down river from Luxor. In 1966 James M. Robinson visited the site, and during subsequent visits in the 1970s in connection with geographical and archaeological surveys he reconstructed the oral tradition concerning the discovery of the texts.[3] According to Robinson's vivid account Mohammad Ali, a peasant farmer, accompanied by his brothers, unearthed and smashed the jar holding the codices and took them to his house. In time the codices were shown to the neighborhood priest and recognized as valuable by a school teacher. Eventually the texts were obtained by various antiquities dealers, and finally they were deposited in the Coptic Museum.

The Nag Hammadi collection contained thirteen codices, eleven of them in leather bindings or covers.[4] The codices consist of a total of some 1,200 papyrus pages containing more than fifty documents or tractates (some duplicates), forty of which were previously unknown. The texts, written in two principal dialects of Coptic, are the work of several scribes and are fourth-century translations of texts originally written in Greek.

Publication of the texts was delayed by scholarly rivalries and political interruptions.[5] Much of the success in making the texts available for research is the result of the tireless efforts of James Robinson. A facsimile edition has been published under the auspices of the Department of Antiquities of the Arab Republic of Egypt, in conjunction with UNESCO, by an international editorial board under the leadership of Robinson.[6] This edition includes ten volumes of photocopies of the pages from the thirteen codices, a volume on the cartonnage (the scraps of papyri used in construction of the bindings), and a volume of introduction to the whole edition by Robinson (1984). Critical editions of the tractates have been published in the series "The Coptic Gnostic Library, edited with English Translation, Introduction and Notes, published under the Auspices of The Institute for Antiquity and Christianity, 1975–1995." These volumes include critical introductions, transcriptions of the Coptic text (on the left page) and ET on the right (facing) page, and extensive notes. As the texts became available, English translations of a few of the individual tractates, some including critical introductions and notes, were published individually.[7] An ET of the whole collection appeared in 1977, edited by Robinson, revised and produced in paperback in 1990.[8] Work on German translations and editions was carried out by the Berliner Arbeitskreis für koptisch-gnostische Schriften under the direction of Hans-Martin Schenke, and a projected translation of the entire collection, *Nag Hammadi Deutsch,* was begun at the end of the century.[9] In 1974 a group of scholars at the University of Laval in Quebec, under the leadership of Jacques-É. Ménard, began work on a French edition (with introduction, Coptic text, French translation, and notes on each tractate) in a series: "Bibliothèque copte de Nag Hammadi," which began to appear in 1977.[10]

CONTENT, CLASSIFICATION, AND PROVENANCE

In the earlier period of research there was no uniform system for numbering the codices, naming the tractates, and citing the texts. These procedures have been standardized: codices are numbered by Roman numerals and individual tractates by Arabic numbers (in italics); references within the tractates are indicated by the page and line within each codex. For instance, *The Gospel of Truth* is identified as: NHC I, *3,* and the opening phrase of the document, "The gospel of truth is joy," is cited as NHC I, *3,* 16, 31, where I is the codex number, *3* is the tractate number, 16 is the page number (in Codex I), and 31 is the number of the line on page 16 of the codex. The content of the whole library is listed as follows:

- NHC I, *1 The Prayer of the Apostle Paul*; *2 The Apocryphon of James*; *3 The Gospel of Truth*; *4 The Treatise on Resurrection*; *5 The Tripartite Tractate.*

- NHC II, *1 The Apocryphon of John; 2 The Gospel of Thomas; 3 The Gospel of Philip; 4 The Hypostasis of the Archons; 5 On the Origin of the World; 6 The Exegesis of the Soul; 7 The Book of Thomas the Contender.*
- NHC III, *1 The Apocryphon of John; 2 The Gospel of the Egyptians; 3 Eugnostos the Blessed; 4 The Sophia of Jesus Christ; 5 The Dialogue of the Savior.*
- NHC IV, *1 The Apocryphon of John; 2 The Gospel of the Egyptians.*
- NHC V, *1 Eugnostos the Blessed; 2 The Apocalypse of Paul; 3 The First Apocalypse of James; 4 The Second Apocalypse of James; 5 The Apocalypse of Adam.*
- NHC VI, *1 The Acts of Peter and the Twelve Apostles; 2 The Thunder, Perfect Mind; 3 Authoritative Teaching; 4 The Concept of Our Great Power; 5 Plato, Republic 588b–589b; 6 The Discourse on the Eighth and Ninth; 7 The Prayer of Thanksgiving; 8 Asclepius 21-29.*
- NHC VII, *1 The Paraphrase of Shem; 2 The Second Treatise of the Great Seth; 3 The Apocalypse of Peter; 4 The Teachings of Silvanus; 5 The Three Steles of Seth.*
- NHC VIII, *1 Zostrianos, 2 The Letter of Peter to Philip.*
- NHC IX, *1 Melchizedek; 2 The Thought of Norea; 3 The Testimony of Truth.*
- NHC X, *1 Marsanes.*
- NHC XI, *1 The Interpretation of Knowledge; 2 A Valentinian Exposition; 3 Allogenes; 4 Hypsiphrone.*
- NHC XII, *1 The Sentences of Sextus; 2 The Gospel of Truth; 3 Fragments.*
- NHC XIII, *1 Trimorphic Protennoia; 2 On the Origin of the World.*

In some publications of the Library the tractates of the Berlin Codex (BG), which contains two texts found also in the NHC, are included:

- BG 8502, *1 The Gospel of Mary; 2 The Apocryphon of John; 3 The Sophia of Jesus Christ; 4 The Acts of Peter.*

Although the general public largely ignored the NHC, historians of religion and students of early Christianity engaged in massive, zealous programs of research. Scholarly congresses were held, beginning with the International Colloquium on the Origins of Gnosticism at Messina (1966), followed by conclaves at Stockholm (1969), Strasbourg (1974), Oxford (1975), Cairo (1976), New Haven (1978), Quebec (1978), Oxford (1979), Louvain (1980), Springfield, Missouri (1983), and Norman, Oklahoma (1984). A huge amount of research has been produced. Beginning in 1970, David M. Scholer published a bibliography on the NHC and related areas annually in *Novum Testamentum*. In 1971 and again in 1997 these bibliographies were collected and combined into separate volumes.[11] Starting with his first bibliography, Scholer numbered each entry; the last bibliography of the century (*NovT* 42 [2000]: 39–85) extended the list to 9,420 items. All of this makes it clear that the effort to summarize the research on the NHC in a short space is necessarily an oversimplification.

From the outset the Nag Hammadi material was characterized as "gnostic." Gnosticism has been a major concern of NT research since the days of F. C. Baur.[12] Many, especially British and American scholars, followed the lead of Adolf von Harnack, who viewed Gnosticism as the "acute Hellenization of Christianity," that is, as a Christian heresy that left essential Christianity untouched.[13] For the history of religion school, on the other hand, Gnosticism was a pre-Christian religious phenomenon that influenced the development of early Christianity.[14]As Christianity moved into the Gentile world it was shaped by gnostic ideas, and its Christology reflected the pre-Christian myth of the redeemer—a presupposition crucial for the theological reconstruction of Rudolf Bultmann and the Bultmann school.[15] Could the NHC—first-hand sources of the Gnostics themselves—help to adjudicate these differences?

Before the discovery of the NHC, sources for the knowledge of Gnosticism were limited.[16] Most of our information came from the heresiologists, fathers of the orthodox church who described and disputed the Christian gnostic heretics.[17] The main champions of orthodoxy were Irenaeus, Hippolytus, and Epiphanius. To this large body of polemic material a few primary sources were added by manuscript discoveries in the eighteenth and nineteenth centuries: Codex Brucianus (a fifth-century Coptic text, discovered in Egypt and purchased by James Bruce in 1769, which contained the *Book of Jehu*); Codex Askewianus (a fourth-century parchment codex, purchased by A. Askew in 1772, containing *Pistis Sophia*); and Codex Berolinensis 8502 (a fifth-century papyrus codex, purchased in Egypt in 1896, which contained *The Gospel of Mary*, *The Apocryphon of John*, *The Sophia of Jesus Christ*, and the *Acts of Peter*). The discovery of the NHC added a large number of primary sources.

Enriched with the new material, scholars investigated the origin and nature of Gnosticism. The conference at Messina recommended that the term "Gnosticism" be restricted to the developed systems of the second century, while the term "pre-gnostic" could be used for gnostic themes and motifs that appeared earlier and the term "proto-gnostic" for more developed forms of gnostic religion before the second century.[18] In some circles the classic work of Hans Jonas has dominated the understanding of Gnosticism.[19] Jonas, who studied with Bultmann and Heidegger, finds the meaning of Gnosticism in the understanding of human existence in the world. For Jonas, Gnosticism is the universal expression of the spirit of late antiquity. Although he added chapters to the revised editions of his books, Jonas asserted that his view of Gnosticism was not changed but confirmed by his reading of the NHC. A major analysis of the nature and history of Gnosticism has been written by Kurt Rudolph—a work in the tradition of the history of religion school that takes fully into account the material from Nag Hammadi.[20] A summary of the main features of Gnosticism, informed by recent research and responsive to the NHC, is provided by Birger A. Pearson:

1. The idea that salvation is by knowledge, especially knowledge of the origin and destiny of the self.
2. A theology that affirms a deity who is transcendent, incomprehensible.
3. A cosmology that views matter and the world as fundamentally evil.
4. A dualistic anthropology in which the body is the prison of the divine spark in humans.
5. An eschatology in which individuals and the elect are saved, but the world is dissolved.

Pearson also points out that Gnosticism has a social dimension (the devotees form communities), a ritual dimension (Gnostics observe religious ceremonies), and an ethical dimension (the devotees practice asceticism). In Gnosticism, women play a significant role.[21]

In the effort to assess their meaning and significance the NHC have been variously classified. Some scholars have ordered them according to the leather covers or bindings, or according to the different scribal hands of the copyists.[22] Of special interest is the classification according to literary genre:

1. Apocalypses: e.g., *The Apocalypse of Paul, The Apocryphon of John.*
2. Revelation dialogues: e.g., *The Dialogue of the Savior, The Discourse on the Eighth and Ninth.*
3. Revelation discourses: e.g., *The Thunder, Perfect Mind, The Second Treatise of the Great Seth.*
4. Gospels: e.g., *The Gospel of Thomas, The Gospel of Philip.*
5. Epistles: e.g., *The Letter of Peter to Philip.*
6. Acts: e.g., *The Acts of Peter and the Twelve Apostles.*
7. Doctrinal treatises: e.g., *The Tripartite Tractate, On the Origin of the World.*

8. Wisdom books: e.g., *The Teachings of Silvanus, The Sentences of Sextus.*

9. Homilies: e.g., *The Testimony of Truth, The Interpretation of Knowledge.*

10. Prayers or hymns: e.g., *The Prayer of the Apostle Paul, The Thought of Norea.*[23]

More important, and more difficult and controversial, is the classification according to religious ideology.[24]

1. GNOSTIC TEXTS

These can be further subclassified into texts of Sethian Gnosticism and texts of Valentinian Gnosticism. Sethian Gnosticism is known to the heresiologists.[25] It is a baptismal sect that derives its message from gnostic interpretation of Genesis 1–7. In the Sethian myth the transcendent deity is usually threefold: Father, Mother (sometimes called Barbelo), and Son. Sethian Gnosticism features Seth (and sometimes his sister Norea) as revealer(s) and redeemer(s). In Christian versions the pre-existent Christ is often identified with Seth. Within the NHC classified as Sethian, scholars distinguish non-Christian from Christian texts.[26] The texts judged to be non-Christian, although superficial Christian elements are detected in some, include *The Apocalypse of Adam, The Paraphrase of Shem, The Three Steles of Seth, Marsanes* (named for a gnostic prophet mentioned elsewhere in the NHC), and *Allogenes.* According to Giovanni Filoramo, "The Sethian myths . . . reveal soteric functions and entities that arise independently of any Christian influence and are embedded in the very logic of a system that has arisen and established itself outside Christianity."[27] However, *Melchizedek* is viewed as thoroughly Christian, as is *The Second Treatise of the Great Seth*, a tractate in which Simon of Cyrene is crucified in place of Christ. According to some scholars, a number of the NHC (*The Apocryphon of John, The Hypostasis of the Archons, The Gospel of the Egyptians, The Trimorphic Protennoia*) display the process of gnostic texts undergoing Christianization. *The Sophia of Jesus Christ* appears to be a Christianized version of *Eugnostos the Blessed*—a theory graphically presented in the ET, where the texts of the two documents are printed in parallel.[28]

As an example of Sethian Gnosticism, *The Apocryphon of John* is one of the most important texts in the Nag Hammadi collection: it appears in three versions (NHC II, *1*; III, *1*; and IV, *1*) and in the Berlin Codex (BG 8502, *2*).[29] The treatise claims to be a revelation to John, the son of Zebedee, from the Savior—although the ultimate source is the eternal Father-Mother-Son deity. From this perfect being emanate lights and aeons including Christ (the Autogenes, or self-generating one) and Sophia. The desire of Sophia brought forth the lion-faced serpent she called Yaltabaoth, the creator. He exclaimed: "I am God and there is no other beside me" (a frequent gnostic theme). He took power from the Mother and created the cosmos; the powers created Perfect Man and called him Adam. Man was placed in paradise where the serpent taught him the wickedness of lust and begetting. The chief archon seduced Eve and she produced Eloim and Yave. Adam recognized his own foreknowledge and produced the Son of Man, whom he called Seth. In the latter part of the tractate the Savior tells of his coming as the perfect Pronoia who entered the prison of the realms of darkness, raised up the believer, and ascended to perfect aeon.

Although this sampling does not do justice to the details and complexities of the myth, the themes of the treatise are evident: the utter transcendence of God, the evil of creation, the transcendent origin of humans, the disruption of the order and the imprisonment of the self, salvation by knowledge of the true origin and destiny of human individuals. The OT has an important, though distorted, place. The NT is scarcely noticed, and the Christian elements are superficial and secondary. The strange convolutions of the myth, the appearance of bizarre names (like Meniggesstroeth and Aesthesis-Ouch-Epi-Ptoe) are incomprehensible to the ordinary reader (ancient or modern), but the insiders who have heard the story many times and know the oral tradition understand their meaning.

Valentinian Gnosticism, a Christian Gnosticism that received much attention from Irenaeus, is represented by several texts of the NHC. Codex I (the Jung Codex) contains four texts judged to be Valentinian: *The Prayer of the Apostle Paul*, *The Gospel of Truth*, *The Treatise on the Resurrection*, and *The Tripartite Tractate*. Among these, *The Treatise on the Resurrection* presents Jesus the Savior who existed in the flesh but escaped the flesh at his resurrection; for the Gnostics the resurrection is present already. Valentinian Gnosticism is also evident in *The Apocryphon of James*, *The First Apocalypse of James*, *The Interpretation of Knowledge*, *On the Origin of the World*, and *The Thought of Norea*. In the Valentinian *Gospel of Philip*, Mary Magdalene plays a major role. In *The Exegesis of the Soul*, also considered Valentinian, the soul, which is feminine, falls into the world and is polluted by many lovers but is saved by being born again; this tractate makes use of both OT and NT texts. *A Valentinian Exposition* contains references to ritual practice: anointing, baptism, and eucharist.

In the complex Valentinian myth the transcendent Fore-Father projects himself and produces Mind (male) and Truth (female).[30] Further aeons emanate until thirty pairs, constituting the Pleroma, are produced. The female of the last pair is Sophia. A crisis is created when Sophia has a passion to know the Father; she fails, but her failure produces Limit, which separates Pleroma from the cosmos. The desire of Sophia is hypostasized as lower Sophia (Achamoth), who produces Demiurge, the creator of the material world. Demiurge creates the earthly human and breathes into it the psychic human; the *pneuma* is secretly implanted. Gnosis is brought down by Christ, who is united with Jesus at his baptism and departs before his passion. Salvation takes place when the pneumatic elements are gathered and united; the Pleroma becomes the bridal chamber of the marriage of Sophia and Jesus and the pre-temporal, eternal realm is restored.

Among the Valentinian treatises in the NHC, *The Gospel of Truth* is an important example. It appears twice in the collection (I, 3 and XII, 2); it may possibly be identified with the document of the same title known to Irenaeus, and if so is dated 140–180 CE.[31] The title is derived from the first line, which begins, "The gospel of truth is joy." However, the document is not a gospel in genre but a homily in three sections. The first describes the emergence of error and the work of Jesus Christ as revealer and teacher. Error did not come from the incomprehensible Father, but from ignorance. Jesus Christ enlightened those in darkness, who nailed him to a tree, but he stripped himself of perishable rags and put on imperishability. Those who receive his teaching are those who are called, who ascend to the higher realm. The second section presents the effects of the revelation: unity with the Father; the third describes the reintegration of all into the primal source. Those who are from above await the perfect one, the truth; they themselves are the truth, for "the Father is within them and they are in the Father, being perfect" (I, 3, 42, 26-28). In sum, *The Gospel of Truth* is a Christian document dependent on texts of the NT.

2. SAPIENTIAL, HERMETIC, AND PHILOSOPHICAL TEXTS

Christian wisdom literature is represented in the NHC by *The Teaching of Silvanus*, a document that admonishes the reader to walk in the way of wisdom taught by Christ. Christ is identified as the Logos who descended into the underworld to release the children of death. Also in this class is *The Sentences of Sextus*, a text that is extant in Greek manuscripts and ancient translations and promotes an ethic of asceticism.[32] Three texts of the NHC belong to Hermetic literature: *The Discourse on the Eighth and Ninth*, *The Prayer of Thanksgiving*, and *Asclepius*. This literature is a collection of second-century CE theosophical texts attributed to Hermes Trismegistus.[33] Philosophical texts are represented by a brief section from Book IX of Plato's *Republic*. None of these texts is essentially gnostic or Christian.

3. VARIOUS OTHER TEXTS

The NHC include texts that are related to traditional authorities in the church. James, the brother of Jesus and leader of the Jerusalem church, is represented by the *First* and *Second Apocalypse of James* and *The Apocryphon of James*. Paul is represented by *The Apocalypse of Paul* (which recounts his ascent through the fourth to the tenth heaven) and the fragmentary *Prayer of the Apostle Paul*. Peter is represented by the *Apocalypse of Peter* (in which the fleshly Jesus is crucified but the spiritual Jesus laughs), *The Letter of Peter to Philip* (which says that Jesus was crucified but was a stranger to suffering), and *The Acts of Peter and the Twelve Apostles* (which describes a trip of Peter and his friends to a city named "Habitation"). An apostle of lesser significance in the NT is promoted to a role of importance: Judas Thomas, the (twin) brother of Jesus who is represented by *The Book of Thomas the Contender* and *The Gospel of Thomas*. Texts that cannot readily be identified with a particular sect include *The Dialogue of the Savior*, in which the Savior engages in dialogue with Judas, Mary, and Matthew. Gnostic texts that have little or no Christian influence include *The Authoritative Teaching* and *The Thunder, Perfect Mind*. The tractate *The Testimony of Truth* attacks the disciples of Valentinus.

From the early days of Nag Hammadi research, scholars have been baffled by a perplexing question: How could texts of such astonishing variety be united in a single collection, indeed, crammed into single pottery jar?[34] Important data for answering the question has been derived from the cartonnage—scraps of papyri used in the production of the binding.[35] Some of these scraps are inscribed and include references to place names and fragments of a letter to the monastic leader Pachomius, as well as fragments from the Coptic text of Genesis. This evidence, along with inscriptions in the caves near the place of discovery, suggests that the production of the codices was connected with the Nag Hammadi area and with monastic life, perhaps with the neighboring Pachomian monastery at Pabau.[36] Torgny Säve-Söderbergh believes the codices were collected by heresiologists to assist in their search for heretical monks who harbored such documents. Others believe the collection was hidden by monks who had used the texts before receiving the letter from Bishop Athanasius of Alexandria, written in 367, requiring exclusive use of the orthodox canon of twenty-seven NT books. This scenario fits with the date (fourth century) and data of the production of the NHC. It is significant that among the collection of over fifty texts, many of them Christian and some of them dependent on NT sources, not a single book from the NT canon is included.

SIGNIFICANCE OF THE NAG HAMMADI CODICES

Research on the NHC is important for the understanding of Gnosticism.[37] Although much of the information offered by the heresiologists has been confirmed, several scholars have questioned the reliability of their accounts and noted the accelerating decline in the quality of reporting from Irenaeus through Epiphanius.[38] Two examples may be noted. For one, the heretic hunters accused the Gnostics of libertinism and attacked their ethics. The NHC provide no evidence for this. Instead, the people of the Nag Hammadi texts are largely devoted to asceticism. The heresiologists also charged their opponents with extensive use of perverted exegesis of biblical texts in support of their belief. Actually, the NHC seldom quote from NT documents in order to use them as proof texts. Martin Krause has argued that the Christian Gnostics of the NHC are not essentially polemic but adaptive and syncretistic, borrowing canonical texts and orthodox practices in order to win converts.[39]

The NHC have provided additional data regarding the hotly debated issue of the background of Gnosticism. Many scholars believe the texts confirm the view of the history of religion school that Gnosticism has its roots in the religious syncretism of the Hellenistic age, fed by streams that flow from Greece, Iran, and Egypt.[40] A major result of research on the NHC is the increasing recognition of Judaism as a major source of gnostic thought.[41] This is supported by the extensive use of Genesis, especially in Sethian Gnosticism, along with parallels in the Dead Sea Scrolls and Jewish apocalyptic literature. At first sight the idea seems to be confounded by the fact that many of the NHC are anti-Jewish, distorting the biblical record, degrading the creator God, and attacking Jewish rituals. The advocates of Jewish background, however, find the sources of Gnosticism in heterodox Judaism—a Judaism that has been disillusioned by the strictures of orthodoxy and the fall of Jerusalem. Gilles Quispel writes, "We may say then that almost all the elements which made Gnosticism, but not a consistent system, were there already in the Diaspora before Philo and the rise of early Christianity."[42] Although some scholars like Van Unnik and Hans Joachim Schoeps question the theory of Jewish origins, the presence of Jewish (and anti-Jewish) elements in many of the NHC is significant.[43]

As regards Christianity, the view that Gnosticism originated as a Christian heresy has been virtually abandoned. George W. MacRae observes, "For a growing number of scholars now clearly in the majority, such evidence . . . regarding certain Nag Hammadi tractates enables us to rule out one of the oldest and most enduring options, namely that Gnosticism is to be seen as heretical offshoot from Christianity."[44] British scholar Robert McLachlan Wilson, unsympathetic with the history of religion school and reluctant to acknowledge pre-Christian Gnosticism, affirms in his presidential address to the SNTS that Gnosticism "grew and developed alongside nascent Christianity"; he continues: "This means that the origins of the gnostic movement must be placed somewhere in the first century, in the period of the New Testament itself."[45] On the other hand, opponents of pre-Christian Gnosticism point out that no text from the Nag Hammadi collection can be certainly dated earlier than the beginnings of Christianity. Edwin M. Yamauchi, who has amassed a collection of scholarly judgments against the pre-Christian origin of Gnosticism, has added a chapter to his earlier book that reconsiders the question in relation to the Nag Hammadi material. He concludes: "In the last two decades the existence of a non-Christian Gnosticism has been amply demonstrated, but the existence of a pre-Christian Gnosticism in the first century or before—that is, a fully developed Gnostic system early enough to have influenced the New Testament writers—remains in doubt."[46]

As to the gnostic redeemer, the hypothesis of a fully developed, universally recognized pre-Christian myth of the redeemed redeemer as conceived by Reitzenstein and adopted by Bultmann has been exposed as a scholarly fabrication.[47] However, just as the NHC have provided evidence for a non-Christian Gnosticism, so they have offered data in support of a non-Christian redeemer. Rudolph writes:

> The idea of the "redeemed redeemer" is therefore indeed a logical and characteristic formulation of the gnostic redeemer conception, which unites redeemer and redeemed very closely together, but it is only one variation of this. There is no uniform gnostic "redeemer myth," such as theologians in particular have imagined. The Nag Hammadi texts have shown us what breadth of variation we must assume in the redeemer conceptions of Gnosis.[48]

Indeed, the NHC present, even within the same tractate, a variety of revealers and redeemers, avatars and saviors, with a variety of titles (like Christ, Logos, Son) and strange names (like Barbelo and Derdekeas). In some texts (e.g., *The Gospel of Truth*) Jesus Christ seems to be the primary revealer and redeemer, while in others (e.g., *The Apocalypse of Adam*) Seth is the redeemer or

Illuminator; in the *Gospel of the Egyptians*, Seth is converted and puts on Jesus. Actually, most of the gnostic texts in the Nag Hammadi library, even the Christian and Christianized tractates, do not need a redeemer who comes into history to enact atonement or expiation or redemption or reconciliation; they only need illumination—knowledge that reveals to humans their true origin and destiny.

The NHC have contributed to the understanding of early Christianity. According to some scholars these texts confirm Walter Bauer's thesis, expounded in *Orthodoxy and Heresy*, that heresy preceded orthodoxy in the history of the early church.[49] In fact, the terms "orthodoxy" and "heresy" are anomalous in earliest Christianity, and what the NHC display is variety. This collection of disparate texts is a microcosm of the larger Christian movement, a particular example of the variety and pluralism that characterized early Christianity. A feature of that variety is the role of women affirmed in some of the NHC.[50] Sophia, the divine Mother, Barbelo, and Norea are major actors in the gnostic myths. In the Berlin Codex of *The Gospel of Mary* special revelation is given to Mary Magdalene. When Peter challenges her authority, Levi defends her and claims that Jesus loved her more than the other disciples. In *The Gospel of Philip*, Mary is described as a special companion of Jesus whom he kissed—an idea apparently without physical sexual implication since the text affirms asceticism and opposes sexual intercourse.[51] In *The Dialogue of the Savior*, Mary is depicted as "a woman who understood completely" (NHC III, 5, 139, 12). The texts display variety in this matter, too: Peter, in *The Gospel of Thomas*, denounces Mary because "women are not worthy of life," but Jesus promises that she will be made male, "for every woman who will make herself male will enter the kingdom of heaven" (Logion 114). Some texts view the separation of humanity into male and female as a cosmic evil (*The Gospel of Philip*) and others affirm the superiority of androgyny (*The Apocryphon of John*, *Trimorphic Protennoia*, *Eugnostos the Blessed*).

The discovery of the NHC has contributed to the debate about the relation of Gnosticism and the NT.[52] Space permits only a few examples. In 1 Cor 2:6–3:4 Paul speaks of the hidden *sophia* of God that was not known to the *archons* of this *aeon*, and uses the anthropological terms σαρκικός, ψυχικός, and πνευματικός; he refers to the "unspiritual" (psychic) person who does not receive the spirit, and he contrasts the "spiritual people" with the "people of the flesh." A similar threefold anthropology is found in *The Tripartite Tractate*. *The Concept of the Great Powers* describes three aeons: the aeon of the flesh, the psychic aeon, and the final aeon of purity and the kingdom. In 1 Cor 4:8 Paul reprimands opponents who claim to posses the benefits of the eschaton already, and those who say there is no resurrection (1 Corinthians 15) may be rejecting a futuristic eschatology. The idea of a present resurrection is affirmed in *The Treatise on the Resurrection*, which reads, "already you have the resurrection" and should "consider yourselves as risen" (NHC I, 4, 49, 15-24). In the Pastoral Epistles the author attacks Hymenaeus and Philetus "who have swerved from the truth by claiming that the resurrection has already taken place" (2 Tim 2:17-18). Timothy is admonished to instruct people "not to teach any different doctrine, and not to occupy themselves with myths and endless genealogies that promote speculation" (1 Tim 1:3-4).

The Johannine literature offers a treasury for those seeking parallels: the pre-existent Logos, the only Son who reveals the unseen Father; the dualism of light and darkness; the denigration of the world.[53] "You are from below, I am from above," says Jesus, "you are from this world, I am not of this world" (John 8:23). The use of the formula "I am" to introduce sayings in the Fourth Gospel has parallels in *The Apocryphon of John*; *The Thunder, Perfect Mind*; *Trimorphic Protennoia*; *The Gospel of Thomas*; and *On the Origin of the World*. Scholars have noted parallels between the prologue of the Gospel of John and *Trimorphic Protennoia*, some even suggesting that the author of the former knew and used some version of the latter.[54] It is more likely that the parallels result from the independent use of common ideas and expressions. Indeed, if the thesis is correct that Gnosticism and early Christianity arose and developed during the same period, virtually all the parallels can be explained in this way. Rather than arguing that the NT is dependent on pre-Christian Gnosticism, it may be better to assume that the writers of the NT and the early (pre-gnostic or proto-gnostic) thinkers drew from a common conceptual and linguistic reservoir that was deep and wide in the Hellenistic world.

NAG HAMMADI AND THE JESUS TRADITION: THE GOSPEL OF THOMAS

About half of the NHC contain references to Jesus Christ. These references have been thoroughly investigated by Majella Franzmann, who analyzes the material under major headings: the origin of Jesus, Jesus as revealer, and the activity of Jesus. She finds great variety. "No single portrait of Jesus emerges from the study, nor any type of composite Christology."[55]

Most important for the study of the Jesus tradition is *The Gospel of Thomas*.[56] "It alone," says James Robinson, "would make the Nag Hammadi library a very important discovery, probably doing more as a single text to advance our understanding of the historical Jesus and of the transmission of his teaching than all the Dead Sea Scrolls put together."[57] The Coptic translation in the Nag Hammadi Library is dated in the fourth century.[58] However, fragments of the Greek text have been found among the Oxyrhynchus papyri and dated around 200 CE. Scholars have variously dated the original composition all the way from 50 CE to the end of the second century. The place of writing was probably Syria, or possibly (in an early version) Palestine. The document claims to be "the secret sayings which the living Jesus spoke and which Didymos Judas Thomas wrote down" (NHC II, *2*, 32, 10-11). "Didymos" means "twin" in Greek, and "Thomas" means "twin" in Aramaic. In Mark 6:3 (Matt 13:55) Judas is identified as one of the brothers of Jesus, and in John 11:16; 20:24; and 21:2, Thomas is called "the Twin." *The Book of Thomas the Contender* claims to be "the secret words that the savior spoke to Judas Thomas" (NHC II, 7, 138, 1-2) whom the savior addresses as "my twin" (138, 6-7).

The Gospel of Thomas is a collection of 114 sayings (*logia*) of Jesus, mainly wisdom sayings. About half of them have parallels in the Synoptic Gospels, but the other half appear to be "gnostic." For example, Logion 7 reads, "Blessed is the lion which becomes man when consumed by man; and cursed is the man whom the lion consumes, and the lion becomes man." When the disciples ask when Jesus will be revealed, he replies, "When you disrobe without being ashamed" (Log. 37). The Son of Man is lacking in *Thomas*, and the kingdom is already present "inside of you and it is outside of you" (Log. 3). After Jesus has taken Thomas aside and told him three things, the disciples ask what Jesus said, only to be warned, "If I tell you one of the things which he told me, you will pick up stones and throw them at me; a fire will come out of the stones and burn you up" (Log. 13). Women (Mary, Salome) are participants in the dialogue, and the true disciples are the "elect" (Log. 49) who "came from the light" (Log. 50) and "renounce the world" (Log. 110).

Although it is recognized that much of this teaching is relatively late, some scholars have contended that the *Gospel of Thomas* also preserves a tradition of the sayings of Jesus that is independent and primitive. Stephen J. Patterson (a student of James Robinson) argues that material in *Thomas* can be proved to be independent by the same methods that show Matthew and Luke to be dependent on Mark and the Gospel of John to be independent of the Synoptics.[59] The arguments have to do with content and sequence. In regard to content, Patterson contends that, even in the case of close parallels, Thomas is independent. For example, Logion 54 reads, "Jesus said, 'Blessed are the poor, for yours is the kingdom of heaven.' " This saying is usually thought to have its source in Q, which Luke 6:20 presents: "Blessed are you who are poor, for yours is the kingdom of God," and Matt 5:3: "Blessed are the poor in spirit, for theirs is the kingdom of heaven." Patterson says that the phrase "kingdom of heaven" (agreeing with Matthew) is typical of *Thomas* and of Jewish usage, while the phrase "in spirit" is a Matthean addition. Although Luke seems to be close to the primitive form Patterson finds in *Thomas*, the latter provides no indication that the saying is from a sermon, but instead presents it as an independent saying that later tradition incorporated into a sermon. In regard to sequence, Patterson prints a table of four columns (*Thomas*, Matthew, Mark, Luke) that indicates that only five sequences in *Thomas* have parallel sequences in the Synoptics. The order of Thomas, according to Patterson, is constructed by the linking of catchwords and is totally independent of the order of Mark, Matthew, and Luke.

The argument for independent tradition gained ground when Joachim Jeremias entered the fray.[60] Jeremias, who spent much of his career battling Bultmann and the history of religion school, argues that some of the parables in the *Gospel of Thomas* are presented in more original form than in the Synoptics, notably the Mustard Seed (Log. 20), and the Leaven (Log. 96). Jeremias also observes that the Parable of the Sower (Log. 9) and the Parable of the Great Supper (Log. 64) in *Thomas* lack the allegorical additions these parables have suffered in Mark and Matthew. However, many scholars remain unconvinced. One could argue, for example, that *Thomas* is dependent on the Synoptics without using them in the way Matthew and Luke use Mark, and that the author of *Thomas* may have supposed that presenting parables without interpretation enhanced their mysterious meaning. Christopher M. Tuckett argues, in regard to the whole Nag Hammadi collection, that "there appears to be no evidence for the use of pre-synoptic sources by the authors of the texts studied," although he acknowledges that *Thomas* might be an exception.[61] Two scholars, Haenchen and Gärtner, have published studies on the theology of the *Gospel of Thomas*, and both believe that *Thomas* is dependent on the Synoptics.[62] The investigation of the question is complicated by the evidence that the document has undergone revision and redaction, so that isolating the original from its sources and redaction is difficult.[63]

Convinced that *Thomas* preserves independent, primitive tradition, Helmut Koester, James Robinson, and their students have advanced a bold proposal in regard to the Jesus tradition. According to Koester, *The Gospel of Thomas* represents a genre of early Christian writing Papias described as "*logia*."[64] Koester believes that *Thomas*, which includes kingdom sayings but lacks apocalyptic sayings, is more primitive than Q, which contains apocalyptic and Son of man sayings. Robinson, who identifies this primitive genre of the *logia* as the *Logoi Sophon* (the sayings of the wise), traces a trajectory of this genre that begins with the Jewish wisdom literature and runs through early collections of the sayings of Jesus (as seen in *Thomas* and Q) to the secret sayings of Gnosticism.[65] In his presidential address to the SBL (1981), Robinson refines his thesis.[66] The earliest sayings tradition (as seen in *Thomas*) moved into Q, where the trajectory bifurcated: one trajectory moved through the pre-Easter sayings of the canonical gospels to the Apostles' Creed; the other moved beyond Q through Gnosticism to the secret post-Easter sayings of the risen Christ.

Stephen Patterson takes up this reconstruction of early Christian history and applies it to the historical Jesus.[67] He thinks the *Gospel of Thomas* provides data for a new (third) quest. Following Koester and Robinson, Patterson believes the sayings collection used by the author of *Thomas* to be older than Q, which, he thinks, has two stages: an earlier one that is in essential agreement with the earliest tradition in *Thomas*, and a later one that adds apocalyptic material. According to Patterson the earlier tradition is the authentic tradition of Jesus. In this view Jesus was not an apocalyptic prophet as Schweitzer supposed, but a wandering teacher of wisdom. This thesis indicates how the discovery of the NHC has given new impetus to the investigation of Q and the reconsideration of the historical Jesus, issues to be discussed in subsequent chapters. For the history of NT research a new trajectory has appeared on the horizon: one that begins with Wrede, moves through the history of religion school, through Bultmann and his followers, through James Robinson and Helmut Koester to their students at Claremont and Harvard, and finally to the Jesus seminar.[68]

In general the discovery of the NHC provided the NT scholar with a vast amount of source material for the study of the historical setting of the NT. The material, in the main, presented information on the Hellenistic background and the variety of early Christianity. Gnosticism, which had been known primarily through hostile secondary sources, could now be examined according to its primary texts. The newly discovered texts did not solve the questions of pre-Christian Gnosticism and the use of extra-canonical tradition for the study of Jesus, but they provided firsthand sources for study of the issues.

The Dead Sea Scrolls

Discovery and Research

Like the discovery of the Nag Hammadi texts, that of the Dead Sea Scrolls (DSS) took on legendary dimensions.[69] In 1947, according to the standard story, a group of young Bedouin herdsmen were tending their flocks in the rocky terrain west of the Dead Sea. One of them, nicknamed "the Wolf," tossed a stone into a cave and heard a strange sound (rock hitting pottery?). He climbed into the cave to find pottery jars containing parchment scrolls wrapped in linen. He and his companions took the manuscripts to a dealer in Bethlehem who sold four of them to the Metropolitan of the Syrian Church in Jerusalem and three to Prof. E. L. Sukenik of Hebrew University. The latter collection included the *Thanksgiving Hymns*, the *War Scroll*, and an incomplete scroll of *Isaiah*. Early in 1948 the scrolls obtained by the Metropolitan were taken to the American School of Oriental Research in Jerusalem, where they were photographed by a young graduate student, John Trevor. These texts included a virtually complete scroll of *Isaiah*, the *Commentary on Habakkuk*, the *Manual of Discipline* (or the *Community Rule*), and the *Genesis Apocryphon*. In 1954 the Metropolitan placed an advertisement in the *Wall Street Journal*, offering these scrolls for sale. Through an intermediary, Yigael Yadin (military hero, statesman, and archaeologist) purchased them for $250,000. Thus all seven of the Scrolls were in Israeli hands, and eventually they were placed in the imposing Shrine of the Book in Jerusalem.

In the meantime, discovery and research advanced. In 1949 the cave of the original discovery (now called Cave 1) was located and excavated by G. L. Harding (director of antiquities for Jordan) and Roland de Vaux (director of the École Biblique). The Bedouin, with an eye for treasure, continued to find caves with scrolls, and de Vaux and scholars from the ASOR explored over 200 caves in the area. By 1956 a total of eleven caves containing scrolls had been searched and numbered according to the order of their discovery. Most impressive was Cave 4, found by Bedouin, containing some 15,000 fragments of over 500 texts. The scrolls from all the caves totaled over 800, some of them duplicates, composed mainly in Hebrew and Aramaic, written mainly on parchment, and a few in Greek, inscribed on papyrus. All manuscripts were scrolls; none were codices. Besides the finds near Qumran, fragments of scrolls were discovered at Masada and other sites in the region.

In 1951 de Vaux began excavations at Khirbet ("ruin") Qumran that were continued for five seasons.[70] According to de Vaux, occupation of the site began around the middle of the second century BCE and continued until 68

CE. De Vaux identified levels of occupation these were later revised by Jodi Magness, who believes the community did not settle in Qumran until about 100 bce. The excavations uncovered a large assembly room or dining hall and a system of water supply, including cisterns and pools used for ritual baths. Most important, remains of a unique type of pottery were found, identical with the pottery jars containing the scrolls and thus linking the Qumran ruins with the caves. Although some scholars concluded that the site was originally a country villa or a fortress, the vast majority believe it was the habitation of a religious community.[71]

A majority of scholars think the community consisted of members of a Jewish sect, the Essenes.[72] These sectarians are known through the writings of Josephus and Philo. According to Pliny the Elder (23–79 CE), a settlement of Essenes was situated on the northwest shore of the Dead Sea. Data from the Scrolls confirm this identification. A growing consensus of scholars believes the sectarians of Qumran constituted a fraction of a larger group living throughout Palestine.[73]Josephus estimated the total of Essenes to be about four thousand, and the buildings of Qumran could accommodate no more than two hundred at a time. In any event, the inhabitants of Qumran viewed themselves as the true people of God, summoned into the wilderness to prepare the way of the Lord (Isa 40:3; 1QS 8:14).[74]

Most scholars believe the Qumran community originated during the Maccabean period.[75] At that time a group of pious Jews arose in opposition to the Hasmonean government that had combined king and high priest in a single figure, constituting a priesthood that did not belong to the Zadokite-Levitical line. The leader of these malcontents, the "Teacher of Righteousness," was opposed by the "Wicked Priest." Although the Teacher cannot be certainly identified, the Priest is usually thought to be Jonathan Maccabaeus, who was appointed high priest by the occupying Seleucids (152–142 BCE), or his brother Simon (142–134 BCE). The Teacher was driven into exile, where he died, and eventually his followers settled at Qumran, sometime before or around 100 BCE. They occupied the site until 68 CE, when Qumran was captured by the Romans. This history is confirmed by the dating of the Scrolls. According to paleography and carbon-14 testing (refined by the method of accelerator mass spectrometry), the Scrolls were written or copied during the last two centuries BCE and the first century CE.[76]

The story of research on the Scrolls reads like a mystery novel.[77] The material from Cave 1 was published within a relatively short time. In 1953 an editorial committee of seven scholars, under the leadership of Father de Vaux, was appointed by officials of the Jordanian government. With the discovery of Cave 4 and its 15,000 fragments the task of editing became formidable. Publication was painfully slow during the 1960s, and tensions developed within the editorial team. After the war of 1967 the Palestinian Archaeological Museum, where the work was going on, came under the control of Israel and was renamed the Rockefeller Museum. The Israelis continued the authorization of the same small group of editors. In 1971 de Vaux died and was replaced by Pierre Benoit, the new director of the École Biblique. Benoit resigned the editorship in 1984 and was replaced by John Strugnell of Harvard. A few scholars were added to the team, but the allegation was circulated that the editorial committee was deliberately monopolizing the study of the Scrolls. Hershel Shanks, editor of the popular *Biblical Archaeological Review*, launched a vigorous campaign to make the texts available to the entire scholarly community. In 1990 Strugnell, in an interview with the Israeli press, made a disparaging remark about Judaism and was abruptly dismissed from the editorial team. The Israel Antiquities Authority replaced him with Emanuel Tov of Hebrew University, and the editorial committee was enlarged to more than fifty members.

The end of the "monopoly" was accomplished by two surprising events. In 1991 Ben Zion Wacholder of Hebrew Union College in Cincinnati, together with his graduate student Martin Abegg, published *A Preliminary Edition of the Unpublished Dead Sea Scrolls*.[78] Wacholder and Abegg, with the help of a computer, had reconstructed the texts of Cave 4 by using a little-known concordance that had been made years earlier under the auspices of the editorial committee. Shortly thereafter the director of the Huntington Library in San Marino, California, announced that photographic copies of the Scrolls the library possessed (hitherto unknown to the public) would be made available to all qualified scholars. Later in the same year Robert H. Eisenman and James M. Robinson published a two-volume *Facsimile Edition of the Dead Sea Scrolls* consisting of photographic copies that had been obtained from the archives of the Rockefeller Museum.

In the meantime, the allegation of monopoly provided fertile soil for the flourishing of conspiracy theories. For example, Michael Baigent and Richard Leigh, already famous for their sensational *Holy Blood, Holy Grail*, published the best-selling *The Dead Sea Scrolls Deception,* in which they argued that the Scrolls had been suppressed by the Vatican in order hide historical data that would be damaging to the orthodox faith.[79] Extravagant claims about the Scrolls reached their nadir with Barbara E. Thiering's *Jesus and the Riddle of the Dead Sea Scrolls*.[80] According to Thiering the "Teacher of Righteousness" was John the Baptist and the "Wicked Priest" was Jesus, who married Mary Magdalene, survived crucifixion, produced offspring, and lived to old age in Rome.[81]

With the universal availability of the Scrolls, conspiracy theories were largely laid to rest. The long-delayed standard critical edition of the texts, which had begun to appear in 1955, was completed under Tov's leadership in 2002—a series of thirty-nine volumes with the series title, "Discoveries in the Judaean Desert."[82] These volumes contain critical introductions, facsimile (photographic) copes of the texts, transcriptions and translations, notes and comments, and concordance or index of the words in the texts. A facsimile edition was published on microfiche and on CD-ROM, and texts with grammatical tags were made available for use with computers.[83] Excellent translations of the Scrolls became readily available.[84]

CONTENT OF THE DEAD SEA SCROLLS

The Scrolls can be classified in two main ways: by the caves in which they were discovered or by the content of the Scrolls.[85] According to the second method, which will be followed here, the Scrolls can be divided into two main classes: biblical and non-biblical. References to particular scrolls are made according to a system that has become virtually standard. Individual texts are identified according to the number of the cave in which they were discovered and the abbreviated title and/or number assigned to the scroll. For example, the *Temple Scroll*, found in Cave 11, is identified as 11QT or 11Q19-21.[86]

Some 220 scrolls containing biblical texts have been found at Qumran. Virtually all the books that were eventually included in the Hebrew canon are represented, although there is no separate manuscript of Esther. At the same time, the Qumran collection includes other books—usually classified as apocryphal or pseudepigraphical—that the Qumran community apparently viewed as Scripture. The biblical scrolls are of special significance for the study of the Hebrew Bible, particularly for the understanding of the canon and text. In regard to canon, the DSS indicate that there was not a fixed collection of authoritative books in the period of the Qumran writings.[87] Most scholars now recognize that the standardization of the canon did not occur until after the destruction of Jerusalem, and that the notion of an official conciliar action establishing the canon (the so-called Council of Jamnia) is a fiction. The discussion of canon is complicated by the fact that different religious communities define the canon differently. The Jewish canon includes the same thirty-nine books accepted by most Protestants, although it names and arranges them differently, resulting in a collection of twenty-four books ordered in three sections: law (Torah), prophets (Nebiim), and writings (Kethubim), abbreviated as "Tanakh." The Roman Catholic Bible includes other books that are contained in the Greek translation (the Septuagint) but not in the Hebrew Bible; these are designated as the Apocrypha.

Within the DSS there are references to "books of the law," "books of the prophets," and "sacred writings." The standard English translation of the biblical texts from Qumran includes all the books of the Hebrew Bible (except Esther and Nehemiah) and arranges them in three sections: Torah, Prophets, and Other Books.[88] However, the section on Torah includes Jubilees, and the section on the Prophets includes 1 Enoch, both books usually classified as Pseudepigrapha. The section on Other Books includes Ben Sirah (Sirach), the Epistle of Jeremiah, and Tobit, all books that belong to the Apocrypha. Within the Qumran collection the number of copies of individual books indicates the popularity and importance of individual writings: Psalms (36 copies), Deuteronomy (30 copies), Isaiah (21 copies) Genesis (20 copies); over seventy of the biblical scrolls are from the Pentateuch. At the same time, apocryphal and pseudepigraphic books exist in multiple copies: Jubilees (15 copies), 1 Enoch (12 copies), Tobit 5 (copies)—data that imply that these book were recognized as Scripture.[89] The Scrolls also provide explicit recognition of biblical authority. The *Damascus Document*, for example, refers to what "God said by Isaiah the prophet" (CD 4:13). The great *Psalms Scroll* claims that David wrote a total of 4,050 psalms, and "All these he composed through prophecy given him by the Most High" (11Q5 27:11).

For the biblical text, the DSS are of utmost importance.[90] Before the discovery of the Scrolls, the text of the OT was the Masoretic Text (MT), produced by the Masoretes—guardians of the tradition (*masorah*)—who in the Middle Ages standardized the text and added the vowel points. The oldest manuscripts of this text are the Aleppo Codex (ca. 925 CE) and the Leningrad Codex (1008 or 1009 CE). Textual critics also made use of the Greek translation of the Hebrew Bible (the Septuagint [LXX]) which had been made from the third to the first century BCE; the oldest manuscripts of this version date from the third and fourth centuries CE.[91] For the first five books of the Bible textual critics also use the Samaritan Pentateuch, a text that was finalized before the Christian era and is represented by manuscripts no earlier than the twelfth century CE.

The Scrolls provide scholars of the OT with manuscripts that are a thousand years older than the manuscripts of the MT. For instance, the great *Isaiah Scroll* from Cave 1 is dated around 125 BCE. The Scrolls, nevertheless, provided evidence that the MT represents a very old and reliable tradition. To be sure, the biblical texts from Qumran offer a multitude of variants, some involving whole verses, some of only one or two words, and many consisting of such minor matters as variations in spelling. The Scrolls also indicate that the text of the OT was transmitted in a variety of textual traditions, since some of the Qumran texts have affinity with the LXX and some with the Samaritan Pentateuch. The texts from Qumran have already made an impact on English translations.[92] For example, the great *Psalms Scroll* (11QPs) includes the sentence, "God is faithful in his words, and gracious in all his deeds"—words not found in older translations, but included in the NRSV.

The non-biblical scrolls constitute about three-fourths of the total collection. They can be arranged according to content. Of special interest to NT research are texts concerned with the interpretation of Scripture. Some of these explicate the law of Moses, for example, a fragmentary text called the *Reworked Pentateuch* (4Q158; 4Q364-65). Other scrolls engage in a type of narrative interpretation that retells or rewrites the biblical account. *Jubilees*, a favorite at Qumran, retells the narrative of Genesis and part of Exodus. In its account of the sacrifice of Isaac, the evil angels of Mastemah believe that Isaac will be destroyed and Abraham will prove to be unfaithful (4Q225). In the *Genesis Apocryphon* (1QapGen = 1Q20), the leading characters, like Noah, recount their stories in the first person singular. The DSS include commentaries (or *pesherim*) on Genesis, Isaiah, Hosea, Micah, Nahum, Habakkuk, Zephaniah, Malachi, and Psalms. The longest of these, the *Commentary on Habakkuk* (1QpHab), is of interest because of the use of Hab 2:4 in the NT (Rom 1:17; Gal 3:11; Heb 10:38). In exegeting the words "the righteous live by their faith" (NRSV), the Commentary says, "Interpreted, this concerns all those who observe the Law in the House of Judah, whom God will deliver from the House of Judgement because of their suffering and because of their faith in the Teacher of Righteousness" (1QpHab 8:1-3 [Vermes]). The Scrolls also include Targums (Aramaic translations) of Job (two copies) and Leviticus. In general the exegetes of Qumran believe the prophecies of Scripture refer to the present as the eschatological time; they are convinced that the Teacher of Righteous was an inspired interpreter.

Besides the exegetical works, the Scrolls also contain legal texts. Texts concerned with the conduct of sacrifice and ritual include the *Temple Scroll* (11QT = 11Q19-21). This Scroll, the longest in the Qumran collection (over 25 feet), presents instruction for the eschatological rebuilding of the temple and the restoration of the festivals and sacrifices. The plan for the temple is idealized, depicting a structure of grandiose proportions that would have filled the entire Herodian city of Jerusalem. Of special interest is the text *Some Works of the Law* (4QMMT = 4Q394-99), also known as the *Halakhic Letter*. Several scholars believe this to be a letter from the leadership of Qumran to the Jerusalem authorities, demanding the correction of errors in regard to sacrifices and ritual practiced in the temple in Jerusalem. The Scrolls also include texts that contain rules for the life and order of the Qumran community. The *Damascus Document* (CD), discovered in the Geniza (storeroom) of the synagogue in old Cairo in 1896, is represented by ten fragments from Qumran. This document deals with such matters as rules for the admission and dismissal of members of the community, criteria for the disqualification of priests, requirements for the ritual of the renewal of the covenant, and laws about purity and observance of the Sabbath. The *Rule of the Community* (1QS), also called the *Manual of Discipline*, covers some of the same subjects as CD. It also describes the function of the officials of the community (the priests and Levites) and the role of the inner council and a leader called "the Instructor" (משכיל). Attention is also given to the conduct of the community meals. The *War Scroll* (1QM) depicts the final battle between the faithful, the "sons of light," and the "sons of darkness." The battle is presented in vivid detail, with descriptions of trumpets, banners, and complex military tactics.

The caves at Qumran contained a variety of other texts. Some of these can be classified as calendars, liturgies, and prayers. The Qumranites were preoccupied with the schedules for celebrating festivals and ordering the duties of the priests. To this end they produced about twenty texts that present calendars, with special fidelity to the solar calendar. Of interest is the *Songs of the Sabbath Sacrifice* (4Q400-407; 11Q17) also called the *Angelic Liturgy*, a document that views the earthly priesthood as corresponding to the heavenly hierarchy and worship. Among the poetic texts are the *Thanksgiving Hymns* (1QHa) or *Hodayot*, which repeats the phrase "I give thanks to You, O Lord." The Scrolls include Psalms that are not included in the canon. In Psalm 151, David speaks autobiographically: "They [my brothers] were tall of stature with beautiful hair, yet the Lord did not choose them. He sent and took me from behind the flock, and anointed me with holy oil, as prince of his people, and a ruler among the sons of his Covenant" (11Q5 28:10-11 = 11QPs[a] [Vermes]). Among scrolls that can be classified as wisdom texts is the *Wiles of the Wicked Woman* (4Q184), also called the *Seductress*, an allegorical warning about false teaching. Eschatological texts include the *New Jerusalem* (1Q32; 4Q554-55), which measures the streets and buildings of the eschatological city. Qumran also included various documentary texts that preserve receipts, records, contracts, and letters. The mysterious *Copper Scroll* (3Q15) refers to over sixty locations where treasures were supposed to have been hidden—a total quantity of gold and silver estimated at about one hundred tons. Not a single ounce has been found.

THE RELIGIOUS IDEAS OF THE QUMRAN COMMUNITY

Although they offer variety, the DSS echo some common theological themes. In relation to Judaism the Scrolls show that the idea of a "normative" Judaism in the Qumran era is untenable.[93] Judaism exhibited variety and vitality. The Essenes at Qumran, according to recent research, were not a tiny, isolated sect but were related to major movements within Judaism. The references in the Scrolls to "those who look for smooth things" (or the "flattery-seekers") and the "builders of the wall" probably depict the Pharisees. The Qumranites show some affinity with the Sadducees, although they criticize a group called "Manasseh"—socially prominent people like the Sadducees.

The idea of God is central to Qumranian theology,[94] according to which there is One God, Creator and ruler of history. God is the God of grace, present with his faithful people. God, according to the Scrolls, made covenant with his people and revealed to them his will. The revelation of God is particularly disclosed in the law of Moses, and the Teacher of Righteousness is the inspired interpreter of Torah. Although God had chosen Israel in the past, the Qumranites believed the majority of the Jews and their leaders had apostatized and corrupted the Jerusalem temple. But in the eschatological time God had acted to call the faithful, the elect people of God. As people of the new covenant, the Qumranites annually celebrated the renewal of the covenant. Although the temple in Jerusalem had been corrupted, the community of Qumran remained dedicated to spiritual ritual, substituting prayers for animal sacrifices and requiring ritual ablutions before their common meals. The people of Qumran stressed dietary laws and strict observance of the Sabbath.

The Scrolls give much attention to eschatology.[95] The Qumran sect can be described as an apocalyptic movement. The members copied and preserved apocalyptic documents like Jubilees, Enoch, and Daniel, and they composed works like the *New Jerusalem* (5Q15; 11Q18) and the *War Scroll* (1QM). Also, the sectarian writings, for instance the *Damascus Document* (CD), discuss such matters as the judgment and eternal life. In contrast to most Jewish groups of the time, the people of Qumran advocated a realized eschatology; they believed the blessings of the eschatological age were already present and the last judgment and final victory were at hand. Although the messiah is not mentioned frequently in the Scrolls, the Qumran community apparently expected two: a royal messiah (descendant of David) and a priestly messiah (the messiah of Aaron).[96] The royal messiah would lead the "sons of light" to victory in the eschatological battle, restore the Davidic dynasty, and establish the rule of righteousness and peace. The priestly messiah would replace the spurious priesthood of the Hasmoneans with true priests in the line of Aaron, Levi, and Zadok. The people of Qumran also seem to have expected another eschatological figure: the prophet of the end time.[97] The Qumranites envisaged a resurrection of the soul (נפש) to eternal life with the angels or to torture in the netherworld.

THE DEAD SEA SCROLLS AND THE NEW TESTAMENT

Earlier theories asserting a close relationship between the Scrolls and the literature and personnel of the NT have been discredited by research, especially since the complete collection became accessible.[98] There is no mention of the Essenes or Qumran in the NT, and no reference to the NT or early Christians has been ascertained in the DSS.[99] Essenism and Christianity are two independent movements that developed within and, in the case of Christianity, beyond Judaism. Many of the supposed parallels belong to beliefs that are common to the Jewish background. The Scrolls provide a large quantity of primary source material from the Judaism of the time of Jesus and the beginnings of the church.

The early Christians and the sectarians of Qumran shared a common Scripture. The NT refers to "the law and the prophets" (Matt 7:12; Luke 16:16; Rom 3:21), and Luke 24:44 mentions "the law of Moses, the prophets and the psalms," terminology that has parallels in the Scrolls. On the basis of usage the writers of the NT appear to assume a canon within the canon that contained the books most popular at Qumran: Genesis, Deuteronomy, Isaiah, and Psalms. The NT, mostly written at a later time, gives almost no attention to the non-canonical books except for a quotation from *1 Enoch* (Jude 14). Both groups use the same introductory formulae for presenting quotations: "it is written"; "God said." The Scrolls, like the NT (notably in Hebrews) use chains of quotations from the Hebrew Scriptures. Both groups believe that biblical prophecy is being fulfilled in the present, and both can use the same texts in this way, though with differences. For example, the NT hails John the Baptist as the fulfillment of Isa 40:3, "the voice of one crying in the wilderness" (Matt 3:3; Mark 1:3; Luke 3:4; John 1:23); the Scrolls, on the other hand, understand Isaiah to say (as in the NRSV) "In the wilderness prepare the way of the Lord" (1QS 8:13-14), predicting the call for the faithful to locate at Qumran.

Early assessment of the Dead Sea Scrolls conjectured a relation with John the Baptist.[100] According to the account in Luke, John belonged to a priestly lineage and was a child of elderly parents. Perhaps, after the death of Zechariah and Elizabeth, John was adopted by the sectarians and reared at Qumran. From Qumran, continues the conjecture, he learned baptism, and in their neighborhood he carried out his mission. Like the people of Qumran, John practiced asceticism and announced an apocalyptic message. The differences, however, are greater. The ablutions at Qumran were performed for ritual purity and repeated daily; John's baptism was once-and-for-all. Qumran received members into an exclusive community; John's message was open to all. In sum, John and the Qumranites belonged to the same region and religious milieu; there is no compelling evidence that they had direct contact.

There has been even more speculation about the relation of the teachings of Jesus to the Dead Sea Scrolls.[101] Like the Qumran sectarians, Jesus embraced a theology based on Scripture that acknowledged God as Creator, revealed in Torah, who made covenant with the people. Jesus and Qumran shared the same view of the cosmos, populated with angels and demons. Both called for humility before God and stressed the mercy and forgiveness of God. One of the Qumran texts, the *Beatitudes* (4Q525), has parallels in Jesus' teachings in Matt 5:3-12. Although Jesus and the people of Qumran believed that the present was the time of eschatological fulfillment, Jesus' understanding of his central message—the kingdom of God—was different. He declared that the kingdom was breaking into history, while Qumran viewed the kingdom as present in heaven and only after the eschatological battle to be realized on earth. Jesus and the Qumranites recognized the authority of Scripture but interpreted the Torah differently. The Qumranites, in contrast to Jesus, believed the law demanded ritual purity and strict observance of the Sabbath. For example, Qumran said, "No one should help an animal give birth on the Sabbath; and if it falls into a well or a pit, he may not lift it out on the Sabbath" (CD 11:13-14). Jesus said, "Suppose one of you has only one sheep and it falls into a pit on the sabbath; will you not lay hold of it and lift it out?" (Matt 12:11). In regard to Jesus' citation of the law, "You shall love your neighbor and hate your enemy" (Matt 5:43), no command to hate your enemy can be found in the OT. However, in the *Community Rule* the sectarians of Qumran are taught "to love all the Children of Light," and "to hate all the Children of Darkness" (1QS 1:9-10). Jesus, in contrast, commanded "Love your enemies" (Matt 5:44).

No direct contacts between Jesus and Qumran are attested. Attempts to identify Jesus with the Teacher of Righteousness fail. Jesus and the Teacher were two different figures, living in different centuries. In contrast to the sectarians at Qumran, Jesus eschewed asceticism and associated with sinners. As to the identity of Jesus, there is a striking parallel between his response to the inquirers from John the Baptist and a reference to the work of the messiah in

Qumran's *Messianic Apocalypse*. According to Matt 11:4-5, Jesus responds: "Go and tell John what you hear and see: the blind receive their sight, the lame walk, the lepers are cleansed, the deaf hear, the dead are raised, and the poor have good news brought to them" (see Luke 7:22). The *Messianic Apocalypse* describes the messiah as "He who liberates the captives, restores sight to the blind. . . . For He will heal the wounded, revive the dead and bring good news to the poor" (4Q521 2:8-12 [Vermes]). Both texts are dependent on Isa 61:1, but that text makes no reference to the raising of the dead, a phrase that appears in both the Qumran and the Gospel (Q) accounts. This passage from Isaiah is also Jesus' text for his inaugural sermon at Nazareth (Luke 4:18-19).

The Scrolls offer some significant parallels with titles used for Jesus in the NT. The Aramaic title מרא ("the Lord"), which is frequently applied to Jesus in the NT, is used for YHWH in the Scrolls. This indicates that the term was used as religious title in pre-Christian Judaism and could have been applied to Jesus in the Palestinian, Aramaic-speaking church. In the *Aramaic Apocalypse* there is reference to a king of the future, possibly the messiah, who is called "the Son of God" and "the son of the Most High" (4Q246 2:1)—the latter title applied to Jesus, the child promised in the Annunciation (Luke 1:32).[102] Apart from this possible reference, no use of the title "Son of God" for the messiah has been found in pre-Christian Judaism. The use of these titles in the Qumran texts suggests that interpreters do not have to move into the Hellenistic world, as the scholars of the history of religion school and Bultmann supposed, in order to find the confession of Jesus as Son of God and Lord.[103] The title "Son of Man," so frequently used for Jesus in the NT, does not appear as a title in the Scrolls. The phrase usually has the meaning "someone" or "a human being." The twelve manuscripts of 1 Enoch found in Cave 4 do not include the "Book of Parables" (chs. 37–71), the section that depicts the apocalyptic Son of Man.

As a sect of Judaism (Acts 24:5; 28:22), the early church displays features parallel to those of the Qumran community.[104] Both groups identify themselves as followers of "the way." Both view themselves as the true people of God, the people of the new covenant, the Israel of God. The Qumranites describe themselves as the twelve tribes and the author of the letter of James addresses "the twelve tribes of the Dispersion" (1:1); the disciples of Jesus will "sit on twelve thrones, judging the twelve tribes of Israel" (Matt 19:28; Luke 22:30). Some of the Essenes may have converted to Christianity, but efforts to identify the Hellenists of Acts 6:1 or the priests of Acts 6:7 as people from Qumran are mere conjecture. After a period of probation, new members of the Qumran sect were required to consign their possessions to the community. Some scholars detect a parallel in Acts 4:32: "no one claimed private ownership of any possessions, but everything they owned was held in common." However, as the subsequent text makes clear, the practice entailed a voluntary contribution, not a universal requirement. Moreover, community of property, an idyllic feature of the infant church, was only temporary. The people of Qumran observed common meals twice daily and prepared for these with ritual washings. The meals, however, were not sacramental in the sense of the Lord's Supper as practiced in the Pauline churches. The primitive Christian custom of breaking bread "day by day . . . at home" (Acts 2:46) is closer to Qumran practice. Like the early Christians, the Qumranites view their common meals as anticipation of the messianic banquet. In regard to the behavior of individuals within the sect, the prescription that one should discipline another prior to taking the matter, with witnesses, to the whole community (Matt 18:15-17) has a parallel in the *Community Rule* (1QS 5:23-6:1). Among the officials of the Qumran community is the Overseer or Guardian (מבקר) who plays a role similar to the bishop (ἐπίσκοπος) of the post-apostolic church, but the model for the latter is more likely the steward of Greco-Roman society. Nevertheless, many Dead Sea Scrolls scholars conclude that the early church was closer to Qumran than to any other Jewish group.

Parallels between the Scrolls and the Pauline epistles have been observed.[105] These two collections of documents share terminology: flesh, spirit, truth. Paul's frequent phrase "works of the law" occurs over ten times in the ET of the Qumran texts. Whereas Qumran encourages the works of the law, Paul declares that "we know that a person is justified not by works of the law" (Gal 2:16). Nevertheless, Paul's basic theme of "the righteousness of God" (Rom 1:17; 3:21-22) is anticipated in the Scrolls (1QS 10:23,25; 11:12).[106] The belief that humans are saved by God's righteousness, mercy, and lovingkindness is expressed in the Community Rule:

> Surely justification is of God; by His power is the way made perfect. All that shall be, He foreknows, all that is, His plans establish; apart from Him is nothing done. As for me, if I stumble, God's lovingkindness forever shall save me. If through sin of the flesh I fall, my justification will be by the righteousness of God which endures for all time.[107]

The identification of the community as the temple of God is expressed in the Qumran texts and in 1 Corinthians (3:16-17; 6:19). Paul, alluding to Deut 21:23, refers to crucifixion as hanging on a tree, and the *Commentary on Nahum* (4Q169), alluding to the same text, mentions the Lion of Wrath who used to hang people alive—a probable reference to Alexander Jannaeus (103–76 BCE), who ordered the crucifixion of eight hundred Jews. The Qumran texts affirm the new covenant (fulfilling the prophecy of Jer 31:31), but for Qumran the new covenant is the renewal of the old; for Paul it is a radically new covenant, ratified by the blood of Christ (1 Cor 11:25).

In relation to the Scrolls, 2 Cor 6:14–7:1 is a text of special interest.[108] Scholars for years have considered these verses to be an interpolation since they appear to interrupt Paul's argument and to contain a number of non-Pauline terms and concepts. However, the text seems quite at home in Qumran. It presents the typical Qumranian dualism of light and darkness, and it contrasts Christ and Beliar. Belial (alternate spelling of the same name) is found nowhere else in the NT, but over one hundred times in the Dead Sea Scrolls. Seven words not found elsewhere in the NT appear in 2 Cor 6:14–7:1. The text affirms that "we are the temple of the living God" and that this temple has nothing to do with idols. The text contends that believers share nothing with unbelievers—ideas similar to Qumran's call for separation and purity. Consequently, some scholars believe the text was written by a Christian who had been influenced by the kind of Jewish thought found at Qumran. Another baffling text, 1 Cor 11:10, declares that "a woman ought to have a sign of authority [a veil] on her head because of the angels." Does this presume the Qumranian belief that angels were present during the assemblies of the community at worship?[109] Some interpreters detect evidence of Essene ideas in the opponents addressed in Colossians and Ephesians. Ephesians, in particular, has been a fruitful field for gleaning parallels.[110] For example, "mystery," a favorite term in the Scrolls, is used six times in this epistle. Qumran and the author of Ephesians also share the idea of the unity of the community with the angels of heaven. According to the author, God "made us alive together with Christ . . . and raised us up with him and seated us with him in the heavenly places in Christ Jesus" (Eph 2:5-6). These parallels do not prove that Paul and his followers were directly influenced by Qumran; they do suggest that many of Paul's ideas have their background in Palestinian Judaism: that Paul may be more a debtor to Jews than to Greeks.

The appearance of parallels in the Johannine literature came as a surprise, since the Fourth Gospel had been characterized for years as the gospel of the Hellenists.[111] John and Qumran share the dualism of light and darkness, truth and falsehood. They both affirm a determinism that does not deny human responsibility. Like the Teacher of Righteousness, Jesus is a revealer of God and an inspired interpreter of Scripture. John's view of Jesus as the pre-existent Logos, however, is far removed from Qumran's understanding of the Teacher.

The attempt to resolve the conflict between John's chronology of the Last Supper and that of the Synoptics by supposing that John followed the Qumran calendar is unconvincing. On the other hand, 1 John offers a number of parallels with the Scrolls: for example, the contrast between the "spirit of truth" and the "spirit of error," a contrast explicated, for instance, in the *Treatise on the Two Spirits* (1QS 3:13–4:6), a text that apparently had been incorporated into the *Community Rule*. Parallels of this sort have convinced several scholars that the Qumran documents are closer to John than to the Mandaean texts, Philo, and the Hermetic literature, lending support to the argument for a Palestinian background of Johannine thought.

Jesus is presented in the letter to the Hebrews as priest and king, important actors in Qumran's eschatological drama.[112] Hebrews presents Jesus as high priest after the order of Melchizedek (5:6, 10; 6:20; 7:11, 15, 17), and the story of this mysterious figure, based on Gen 14:18-20, is related in chapter 7. One of the Qumran texts, *Melchizedek* (11Q13), presents him as an exalted being (identified with the archangel Michael or even with God) who will save the faithful in the eschatological judgment. The story of Melchizedek is also related in the *Genesis Apocryphon* (1Q20:22) and he is mentioned in other texts from Qumran.

The book of Revelation, the major example of apocalyptic writing in the NT, shares the eschatological outlook of Qumran.[113] Both Revelation and the *War Scroll* (1QM) depict the bloody final battle between the forces of God and the powers of evil. The description of the eschatological Jerusalem in Revelation (21:9–22:9) has parallels with Qumran's *New Jerusalem,* preserved in six fragments, found in five different caves. Both texts describe the gates of the city and record its measurements in accounts inspired by Ezekiel 40–48. In Revelation the New Jerusalem has no temple, but in the *Temple Scroll* the temple is enormous.

All in all, the Dead Sea Scrolls are of great significance for NT research. The earliest expectations, of course, have been disappointed. Study of the Scrolls has shown that a direct relation between Qumran and the NT cannot be confirmed. The major importance of the Qumran texts is the information they offer about Judaism in the period before and during the advent of Christianity. The Scrolls provide the student of Judaism with an enormous quantity of primary source material heretofore unknown or unavailable. This material shows that Judaism was a complex phenomenon, fostering a variety of sects and religious expressions. Christianity had its origin within this multifaceted milieu. The early Christians shared with the people of Qumran the conviction that Scripture was being fulfilled in the present, that the end was at hand, that they were the elect people of God. Both groups affirmed the importance of community, but how different the communities were: one seeking to restore the covenant by separation and asceticism, the other by inclusion and mission. Students of early Christianity recognized a new importance for Jewish backgrounds; the Jewishness of Paul and John was affirmed. However, in the larger sense the old dichotomies of Judaism and Hellenism, Palestinian Judaism and Hellenistic Judaism were eroding. Since the time of Alexander a tidal wave had swept from Greece across the Middle East, leaving a syncretism of cultural and religious ideas in its wake. This is apparent when the Scrolls are set beside the NHC. As the Qumran material has been used to confirm Jewish backgrounds, the NHC have been employed to affirm the Hellenistic. Still, parallels are apparent. Recent research in Nag Hammadi has noted the Jewish element in Gnosticism, and Qumran scholars have observed common features: dualism, determinism, election. The Dead Sea Scrolls indicate that the rising tide of syncretism had reached even to the isolated caves of Qumran.

ARCHAEOLOGY AND THE NEW TESTAMENT

The discoveries of the Nag Hammadi texts and the Dead Sea Scrolls were exciting chapters in the larger story of NT archaeology. A division of biblical archaeology, the archaeology of the NT is concerned with the "recovery, classification, and description of the material remains of antiquity."[114] For much of its history, biblical archaeology focused on the OT and the history of Israel. But in the second half of the twentieth century some archaeologists turned to the NT and the history of early Christianity. New Testament archaeology and biblical archaeology employ the methods used by archaeologists in general.[115] They engage primarily in excavation, an activity that requires a succession of steps.[116] Archaeologists begin with a survey that involves selecting the site, exploring the surface, and determining the scope of the project. Next, they formulate a proposal, ascertaining the goal and feasibility of the endeavor. Then a staff is assembled, consisting of experts in a plethora of disciplines including geology, architecture, ceramics, numismatics, and photography. Archaeologists also must secure approval of the project from the government, local officials, and landowners of the site. They have to secure financial and often institutional support and recruit workers. The actual excavating, or field work, usually follows the "Wheeler-Kenyon" method developed by Mortimer Wheeler and Kathleen Kenyon, sometimes called the "Wheeler Box-Grid" method. It establishes grids that are excavated in squares between balks on which stratification is recorded.[117] Careful records must be kept of the content of each stratum; pottery, coins, and inscriptions are important for dating. The results of this investigation are analyzed and interpreted. The project is complete when the results and the supporting data are published.

In the second half of the twentieth century archaeologists employed a multitude of new methods.[118] These include underwater archaeology, aerial and infrared photography, paleozoology, and paleobotany, including such sophisticated procedures as palynological analysis.[119] Carbon-14 dating has been refined by the method of accelerator mass spectrometry, which requires a smaller amount of organic material and is more accurate. The use of computers has virtually transformed archaeology. Computers are used to store, catalogue, retrieve, and compare data; they provide the means to image a three-dimensional reconstruction of a site.

Archaeology is related to history, and for purposes of archaeological analysis history is classified chronologically according to periods. For the NT these periods are usually identified as:

- Hellenistic Period (332–63 BCE)
- Early Roman Period (63 BCE–135 CE)
- Middle Roman Period (135 BCE–217 CE)
- Late Roman Period (217 CE–324 CE)

Some scholars designate the Early Roman as 63 BCE–70 CE and the Middle Roman as 70 CE–180 CE, and some refer to the Herodian Period (37 BCE–70 CE).

Throughout its history, biblical archaeology has developed according to different perspectives. Much of the older archaeology was devoted to apologetics—archaeology enlisted in defense of the historicity of the biblical narrative.[120] This approach countered the skepticism that had dominated the Tübingen school and captivated the devotees of the history of religion method. In recent times a more sophisticated version of this approach has appeared, informed by sensitivity to presuppositions and using advanced methods of research. This version, for example, supports the accuracy of topographical and historical details recorded in the Fourth Gospel.[121] Moving beyond the earlier apologetic perspective, much archaeology has been dominated by a descriptive approach: the attempt to use archaeological data to depict the sites and illuminate the biblical record.

NT ARCHAEOLOGY AS SURVEY OF SITES

A host of books adopting the descriptive approach has been published.[122] A few examples of their content can be provided by making a geographical tour of some of the major sites. In southern Palestine scholars survey Bethlehem.[123]

Here the major monument is the Church of the Nativity, built over the grotto where Jesus is supposed to have been born. The church was built in the fourth century under the direction of Constantine and rebuilt in the sixth century by Justinian; beneath the floor of the present church a mosaic floor that may go back to the earlier building is visible. Five kilometers southwest of Bethlehem lies the Herodium. Built by Herod the Great as his burial place between 22 and 15 BCE), this cone-shaped mound included a synagogue. Masada, a fortress rebuilt by Herod, has been found on the cliffs above the western shore of the Dead Sea. Excavated in 1963–65 by Yigael Yadin, Masada also contained a first-century synagogue. North of the Dead Sea is Jericho, site of Herod's winter palace, which included three palaces and a bath.

Major attention is directed at Jerusalem, which is crowded with traditional sites.[124] The primary monument, of course, is the Temple. Herod began rebuilding this shrine in 20 BCE, and the huge aslar stones of the supporting wall (the "wailing wall") are visible. On the west side, the arch identified by Edward Robinson (1838) led to a stairway that descended to the street in the Tyropaeon Valley.[125] Farther north, the arch discovered by Charles Wilson (1864) supported a bridge that crossed the Valley to the upper city. Excavations south of the Temple have uncovered a broad stairway that led to gates and ramps providing entrance to the higher Temple platform. North of the Temple area is the Church of St. Anne, and nearby is the excavation of the Pool of Beth-zatha (John 5:2), which has unearthed a double pool with porticoes.

Archaeologists have expended much effort in the attempt to identify the location of the death and burial of Jesus.[126] A vast majority agree that the Church of the Holy Sepulchre marks the place. At the time of Jesus this spot was outside the city wall. Kokim-type graves (horizontal recesses or niches in the rock) have been found in the area. In regard to the route over which Jesus carried the cross (Via Dolorosa), a majority believe the trial of Jesus took place at Herod's palace (on the western side of the city), so that the route ran west to east, opposite the direction of the traditional way. In regard to the method of crucifixion, information has been supplied by the discovery in 1968 at Giv'at ha Mivtar, north of the old city, of an ossuary with the skeleton of a man who had been crucified. A single nail goes through the heel bones, with the legs turned sideways and knees flexed.

In northern Palestine attention has been given to sites related to the life of Jesus and the early church.[127] At Nazareth, the modern Church of the Annunciation enshrines the Grotto of the Annunciation, the traditional location of the house of Mary.[128] Adjacent to this cave, the ruins of a third-century church were found, including a rock-hewn baptistry. At Capernaum two major monuments have been explored.[129] The imposing synagogue, made of white limestone and adorned with Corinthian columns, was probably built in the fourth or fifth century, though an earlier structure has been detected beneath it. A stone's throw to the south, the remains of a fifth-century octagonal church have been found. This church was built on the ruins of an earlier house-church that had been rebuilt from a first-century house, possibly the house of Peter. In the ruins of the second- or third-century synagogue at Chorazim a stone seat was discovered (1962) that may have been the chair of the leader of the synagogue: "Moses' seat" (Matt 23:2). In 1986 the remains of a fishing boat were found in the shallow waters of the Lake of Galilee near Magdal, dated by Carbon-14 from 120 BCE to 40 CE. Much work has been done at Caesarea Maritima.[130] The city was built into an important seaport by Herod the Great. The harbor was established by the construction of a circular breakwater, which has been explored by underwater archaeologists. Among the main monuments is Herod's palace or praetorium (Acts 23:35), which became the residence of the Roman governors. Excitement was created by the discovery of an inscription that has been reconstructed and translated to read: "Pontius Pilate the prefect of Judea has dedicated to the people of Caesarea a temple in honor of Tiberius."[131]

Moving westward, the scholars have surveyed sites in Syria, Asia Minor, and Rome.[132] Antioch on the Orontes enjoyed extensive building during the Roman period and was noted for its grandeur.[133] The city was laid out in a grid and boasted a wide, colonnaded street with sidewalks and all the accoutrements of a Roman metropolis. At Daphne, the western suburb, magnificent floor mosaics have been uncovered.[134] At Seleucia Pieria, the seaport, a canal was cut through the rock in the time of Vespasian and Titus, who are commemorated by an inscription. On the hillside east of Antioch a grotto called the Church of St. Peter contains fragments of floor mosaics that are dated in the fourth or fifth century.

Extensive excavation and reconstruction has been accomplished at Ephesus.[135] Most of the remains that are visible today—for instance, the splendid Library of Celsus—were constructed after the time of Paul. The theater (Acts 19:29) was built in the second century BCE and enlarged by Claudius at about the time Paul was there. Toward the end of the century a temple was erected in honor of Domitian. This monument to the power of the imperial cult is important for interpreting Revelation.

In Corinth, remains related to the mission of Paul are visible.[136] Destroyed by the Romans in 146 BCE, Corinth was rebuilt as a colony by Julius Caesar in 44 BCE—an action confirmed by the Senate and supported by Augustus. A Greek inscription found near the major street leading into the huge forum has been reconstructed to read "Synagogue of the Hebrews." An inscription has also been found near the forum that identifies a shop as a *macellum*—the Latin equivalent of μάκελλον ("meat market"), like those mentioned in 1 Cor 10:25. The *bema*, where Paul appeared before the recently appointed governor Gallio (Acts 18:12-17), is usually identified as the large platform located in the middle of the forum, but this has been contested.[137] The date of Gallio's governorship in Corinth (51 CE) has been established by an inscription discovered at Delphi. Of special interest is another inscription located near the theater, which reads: ERASTVS.PRO.AED/S.P. STRAVIT. This has been translated: "In return for his aedileship [position of a city official] Erastus laid [the pavement] at his own expense." This Erastus is possibly the person mentioned in Rom 16:23.

Many of the major monuments in Rome, like the Coliseum, were erected after the time of Paul.[138] The nearby Arch of Titus, which was built in 81 CE, commemorates the Roman victory at Jerusalem in 70. The Mamertine Prison, the traditional place of the incarceration of Peter and Paul, consists of two chambers hollowed out beneath the Capitoline Hill. The lower chamber dates from 300 BCE and the upper from 100 BCE. There is evidence that this place was used as a prison as early as the first or second century BCE, and early Christians may have been imprisoned there. The deaths of both Peter and Paul, according to tradition, took place in Rome during the persecution under Nero (64–65 CE). Excavations beneath St. Peter's basilica at the Vatican have uncovered an ancient shrine dating from about 160 CE that has been claimed as the tomb of Peter. On the Ostian Way, a little over a mile outside the gate in the area of several ancient tombs, Constantine built a church ("St. Paul's Outside the Walls") over an altar with an inscription commemorating the martyrdom of Paul. In the catacombs under the Church of St. Sebastian on the Appian Way a room has been found with third-century graffiti honoring Peter and Paul, inspiring the theory that the bodies of these apostles were temporarily entombed in this place.

THE NEW ARCHAEOLOGY

Descriptive archaeology cast light on texts and provided helpful guidebooks for visitors to the biblical sites. Then, in the second half of the twentieth century, a new archaeology emerged. Instead of following the steps of Jesus and tracing the journeys of Paul, the new archaeology focuses on daily life in Galilee and the social structures of Hellenistic culture. This new science, sometimes called "processural" or "cognitive-processural" archaeology, is concerned less with monuments and more with people and communities with their political, social, cultural, and religious lives.

For NT archaeology the new approach has been applied in Galilee.[139] Pioneering work was done by American archaeologists Eric M. and Carol L. Meyers, James F. Strange, and a number of Israeli scholars. In their intent to investigate the cultural and ideological aspects of Galilean society these scholars employed an interdisciplinary method correlating archaeological and literary evidence. Although surveys and excavations were undertaken at a number of sites, the work at Sepphoris offers a key example.[140] In 1976 work was begun by E. Meyers and Strange. In 1983 Strange organized a new team, and Eric Meyers, Ehud Netzer, and Carol L. Meyers established a joint expedition that engaged in five campaigns. The excavations of these scholars provide data related to the history of Galilee. Herod Antipas rebuilt Sepphoris early in the first century. In that period the city remained loyal to Judaism, as the presence of ritual baths (*miqvot*) indicates.[141] But from the second to the fourth centuries Sepphoris became increasingly Hellenized. At the beginning of the first Jewish revolt (66–70 CE) the city welcomed the army of Vespasian, and coins minted in 68 honored this Roman general and called Sepphoris the "City of Peace."[142] Strange excavated a villa he believed to have been built in the late first century, although its mosaic floor is dated around 300—an example of an overlay of Hellenistic-Roman culture on an essentially Jewish city.[143]

A major issue addressed by these archaeologists is the question of the relation of larger towns like Sepphoris to the surrounding villages and rural areas.[144] The majority of scholars believe the relationship was largely reciprocal. They find evidence for an extensive road system in the first century, prior to the major building of Roman roads under Hadrian. These roads facilitated commerce between the villages and the larger towns. Galilee was rural, and its economy was primarily agricultural. The villages supplied food and labor for the cities and towns, and the rural farmworkers traded in the town markets. Most of the farms were small, although there were large landowners who employed rural people as day-laborers (Matt 20:1). Pottery manufactured in villages like Kefar Hanania was found extensively in the cities and towns. In regard to the ideology of the Galilean peasants, most scholars believe the village and rural people were primarily concerned with safety and security. In response to the increasing urbanization seen in cities like Sepphoris—with increased taxation, rent collection, and absentee landlords—the rural Galileans tended to conform and to increase their self-reliance.[145] Studies of households have argued that women were not confined to the house but participated in the production and marketing of goods.[146] The discovery of weights that were attached to vertical threads (warp) on the loom indicates a method of weaving that was used by women.[147]

Another important issue has to do with the extent of Roman influence in Galilee.[148] The increasing presence of Rome contributed to the growing urbanization of Galilean cities. This was already evident in the time of Herod the Great, as dramatically portrayed in building of Caesarea Maritima, which included at temple dedicated to Augustus. The advancing Romanization is also attested by coins, which in the second and third centuries increasingly presented the images of the emperors.[149] However, in the first century Roman influence was confined mainly to the cities. During the revolts of 66–70 CE and 132–135 CE opposition to Roman power was intense, but it was concentrated principally in Jerusalem.[150]

The question of the religious situation in Galilee in the first century has provoked considerable debate.[151] Three main views have been advanced:

> 1. The people of Galilee are thought to have been descended from the remnant who remained after the invasion by the Assyrians in the eighth century BCE; these people preserved the old Israelite prophetic tradition, which was in conflict with Jerusalem and the Temple.[152]
>
> 2. The people of first-century Galilee were seen as primarily Gentile; after the deportation of Israelites in the eighth century Galilee was depopulated but was gradually resettled by non-Jewish immigrants like the Itureans and the Greeks—a view supported by the slogan "Galilee of the Gentiles" (1 Macc 5:15; Matt 4:15).
>
> 3. The people of Galilee were essentially Jewish; although the region had been sparsely populated for some time, Galilee was annexed and colonized by the Hasmoneans. Aristobulus (104–103 BCE) conquered Galilee, forced the conversion of Gentiles to Judaism, and promoted the migration of Jews to Galilee.

A majority of archaeologists affirm the third view. Although external signs of paganism are evident, the underlying, fundamental religion of the Galileans was Jewish. Even in the most urban cities like Sepphoris, evidence of the prevailing Judaism is seen in the presence of ritual baths (*miqvot*), stone vessels that were used according to Jewish practices of purification, and an absence of pig bones. Galileans who could afford it continued to pay the Temple tax and make pilgrimage to Jerusalem.

Related to the discussion of the Jewishness of Galilee and the degree of Hellenization are issues related to the development of the synagogue and questions of language and literacy. In regard to the synagogue, scholars agree that this institution flourished in the Diaspora and expanded in Galilee after 70 CE.[153] Scholars also note that the synagogue functioned as an institution of community life and worship as early as the Hellenistic period, often meeting in houses or public buildings. Although some scholars contend that synagogue buildings were not constructed in Palestine until the third century, archaeologists have uncovered the remains of buildings they identify as synagogues and date in the first century.[154] In regard to language, it is widely agreed that Aramaic was the main spoken language in Galilee in the first century. There is some archaeological evidence that even villagers could read and write Aramaic.[155] Although Greek was the language of the elites and the administration in cities like Sepphoris and Tiberias, Greek inscriptions are rare in first-century Galilee and most of the names found in Galilean inscriptions are Semitic.[156]

The issue of religious background is crucial for understanding the history of Jesus.[157] The majority of archaeologists tend to stress the Jewishness of Jesus in the setting of Jewish Galilee. They note that he grew up in Nazareth, a small agricultural village. Capernaum, which was a center of his ministry, was a relatively small town without signs of Roman planning and construction. There is no record that Jesus ever visited Sepphoris or Tiberias. He did journey to the regions of Tyre and Sidon, but even in his travels outside Galilee he only went to the "villages of Caesarea" (Mark 8:27) and the "region of the Decapolis" (Mark 7:31). The message of Jesus, according to most scholars, had social implications. He exorcised persons and cured lepers, making it possible for them to return to society. Jesus opposed the luxury of the urban elites and identified with the rural peasants. His apocalyptic message challenged the political structures of the time, and his message of the kingdom affirmed the universality of God's care. The extreme views—on the one hand, that Jesus was a social revolutionary, or on the other that he was a wandering Hellenistic Cynic teacher of wisdom—are rejected by most archaeologists.[158] Some of the new archaeologists have investigated the question of the social perspective of the Gospel sources. For example, Jonathan Reed observes that agricultural images pervade Q, but the perspective is the city or town, suggesting that the Q community may have had been located at Sepphoris, Tiberias, or Capernaum.[159] In regard to Mark, Cilliers Breytenbach argues that the attempt to relate Jesus to an urban setting is not supported by Mark; instead, Mark locates the Jesus narrative in villages and small towns and in the fields of rural peasants.[160]

The opposing view is eloquently articulated by Richard Batey,[161] who takes up the position, already expressed by Shirley Jackson Case in 1927, that Jesus probably labored in the rebuilding of Sepphoris.[162] As Batey observes, this city was only five kilometers from Nazareth, and Jesus, as carpenter or artisan, may have been employed in Antipas's extensive building project. Evidence that Jesus had at least visited Sepphoris is seen in his use of the term ὑποκριτής—a word associated with the ancient theater and used some seventeen times in the Synoptic Gospels. Batey thinks Jesus learned this word by attending the Sepphoris theater.[163] Batey also points out that Jesus criticized those who wore soft robes and lived in palaces (Matt 11:8; Luke 7:25), reminiscent of the behavior of Antipas, who built palaces in Sepphoris and Tiberias. According to Batey, Jesus spoke Greek, and his words about banking and earning interest (Luke 19:23) indicate that he was familiar with urban financial transactions. Scholars of various persuasions have speculated as to why there is no record that Jesus visited Sepphoris (and Tiberias). Was it because he avoided centers where the officers of Antipas dominated (Luke 13:31-32), or that he opposed the culture and luxury of the urban elite?

An unusual collaboration between a historical-critical scholar and a NT archaeologist is reported in *Excavating Jesus*, by John Dominic Crossan and Jonathan L. Reed.[164] These scholars review important archaeological discoveries like the Pilate inscription at Caesarea and the fishing boat in the Sea of Galilee and their importance for understanding the historical Jesus. They point out that as there are archaeological layers of strata at a site like Nazareth, so also are there exegetical layers of sources and tradition in the story of Jesus; at the earliest layer is the historical Jesus—a "Jewish peasant" according to Crossan and Reed.[165] Archaeological and literary evidence, they believe, displays a Jesus in contrast to his social, economic, and political setting. Cities like Caesarea Maritima and Sepphoris constitute a commercial kingdom; Jesus commands loyalty to a covenant kingdom. An elaborate dining room for the powerful and the elite was discovered at the palace of Herod in Masada; Jesus, in contrast, ate with the poor and sinners. Some Jews engaged in violent resistance to Roman power; Jesus, according to Crossan and Reed, exemplified a radical nonviolent resistance. "Wherever you locate Jesus on that continuum of covenantal to eschatological to apocalyptic resistance, the Kingdom of God is a force for nonviolent resistance to the normalcy of both social oppression by class and colonial oppression by Rome."[166]

Beyond Galilee, examples of the new archaeology can be seen in the study of sites in Asia Minor, Greece, and Rome.[167] Important research has been done at Antioch. Glanville Downey traces the history of the Christian community there from its beginning to the fourth century. In a description of Antioch as the "Fair Crown of the Orient" he views the cultural life of the populace by interpreting the floor mosaics, some of which were found in relatively modest dwellings. Wayne A. Meeks and Robert L. Wilken report the results of a working group of the SBL and the AAR on "The Social World of Early Christianity."[168] The purpose of the project was to investigate sources for the study of early Christianity in the setting of urban culture. Meeks and Wilken note the importance of Antioch for the Christian mission among Gentiles. These scholars believe the dispute between Paul and Peter (and Barnabas: Gal 2:11–14) resulted in separate congregations of Jewish and Gentile Christians. The break between Christians and Jews in Antioch probably occurred, according to Meeks and Wilken, during the Jewish revolt of 66–70 CE.

Magnus Zetterholm takes up the question: How did Christianity in Antioch, which began as a movement within Judaism, develop into a different, even an anti-Jewish religion by the time of Ignatius (ca. 110)?[169] Zetterholm attempts to answer this question by social-scientific as well as ideological analysis. In regard to religion, Zetterholm notes that Antioch honored the major deities, observed the important pagan festivals, and supported the imperial cult. He speculates that there may have been twenty to thirty Jewish synagogues in Antioch in the first century CE, each with as many as five hundred members. As Jews migrated from Palestine to Antioch, Zetterholm believes they responded to their new situation in three main ways: total assimilation (rejecting Judaism and adopting a secular style of life), total opposition (strictly observing the Torah), or accepting various mediating alternatives (for example, joining the Jewish followers of Jesus who associated with Gentiles). These various responses, according to Zetterholm, contributed to the formation of distinctive synagogues. Zetterholm believes the division between Jewish followers of Jesus and Gentile Christians was encouraged by social and political developments. For example, when Vespasian imposed a tax on Jews, Jesus-believing Gentiles found it advantageous to separate from Judaism. These Gentile Christians, according to Zetterholm, became increasingly anti-Jewish, embracing the anti-Jewish ideology already present in Hellenistic society. Much more is known about the social, economic, political, and religious life of Antioch in the fourth century because of the information provided by some 1,500 extant letters of the rhetorician Libanius.[170]

In regard to Ephesus, papers presented at a symposium held at Harvard Divinity School in 1994 were published as *Ephesos: Metropolis of Asia*.[171] This volume includes a paper on "Urban Development and Social Change in Imperial Ephesus" by L. Michael White.[172] White observes that the growth of the city in the Roman period, inaugurated under the Julio-Claudian emperors and expanded under Domitian, was facilitated by its harbor and large market. According to White, Ephesus had a population of 100,000 at the beginning of the first century—a number that doubled by the beginning of the second. This increase of population was the result of the arrival of some 2,500 immigrants a year, consisting of foreigners from various ethnic groups. The growth of population was accompanied by the construction of monumental buildings during the reign of Domitian and still more under Trajan and Hadrian. White observes that it was during the time of Domitian that Ephesus replaced Pergamon as the "temple warden" (neokoros) of the imperial cult (Acts 19:35). This designation is discussed in "The Cult of the Roman Emperors in Ephesus: Temple Wardens, City Titles, and the Interpretation of the Revelation of John," by Steven Friesen in the same volume.[173] Friesen notes that a coin dated 65/66 CE already applies the term neokoros to Ephesus, but it was at the dedication of the Temple of the Sebastoi (89/90 CE) that other Asian cities recognized Ephesus as the "temple warden" of the province. This evidence of the power of the imperial cult in the city is important for interpreting the Apocalypse. "The Book of Revelation," writes Friesen, "must be understood in its local setting as part of a clash of religious ideologies, for it represents an assault on fundamental issues of social organization in late first-century Asia. The text was seditious not because it attacked the emperor, but because it indicted the emerging social order in Asia as a blasphemous force that deceived all people and spilled the blood of the saints."[174]

Archaeological research has informed the understanding of the socio-economic life of Corinth. The commercial activity of Corinth has been investigated by C. K. Williams II.[175] Williams observes that the colony established in the mid-first century BCE included many ex-slaves—freedmen who served as commercial agents for their former Roman masters. Corinth, according to Williams, exported bronze ware, wool, woven goods, olive oil, and honey; the city imported agricultural products and building materials from various parts of the empire. Some of the many shops in and around the forum, according to Williams, were offices of bankers; Corinth was noted as a financial center. Markets have been found in various parts of the city, some with large storage facilities.

The importance of archaeology for understanding the life and worship of the Corinthian church has been demonstrated by Jerome Murphy-O'Connor.[176] In discussing "House Churches and the Eucharist," he describes the remains of a first-century house to illustrate the character of the meeting places of Corinthian Christians.[177] This house could barely accommodate a congregation of forty to fifty people, and the triclinium, where the Lord's Supper would have been celebrated, could not have held the whole assembly. Discussing "Temple Banquets and the Body," Murphy-O'Connor provides archaeological data for illuminating the practice of "eating in a temple" (1 Cor 8:10).[178] The excavation of the Temple of Asclepius uncovered the remains of three dining rooms where meals, both sacred and social, could be consumed. Murphy-O'Connor also speculates about the place where Paul (with Aquila and Pricilla, Acts 18:2-8) plied his trade—perhaps in one of the shops of the north market that could have accommodated a house church of ten to fifteen people (Rom 16:5; 1 Cor 16:19).[179]

The use of archaeology to illuminate a particular Pauline text is illustrated by John R. Lanci.[180] In regard to 1 Cor 3:16-17, Lanci argues that the imagery of the temple should be interpreted from the perspective of the Corinthian readers. He notes that Corinth as a commercial center attracted people of various social and ethnic groups from all over the empire. This variety, he thinks, was also evident in the membership of the church and contributed to conflicts within the congregation. According to Lanci the entire argument of 1 Corinthians is directed against these internal dissensions. In developing the argument Paul uses imagery drawn from the city's thriving construction industry, in particular the building of temples. "Writing to a group of people residing in a Roman city that was thriving economically and experiencing extensive recent building and renovation," says Lanci, "Paul employs the language of building construction as he attempts to win over the Corinthians to his way of thinking concerning the importance of unity. The community, he suggests, should understand itself as a building project [temple], with Christ as its foundation; the community's leaders are co-workers with God in the construction."[181]

An impressive array of studies incorporating archaeological data and literary evidence in the service of socio-political and cultural-religious understanding has focused on Philippi. In 1993 a "Symposium on Paul and Philippi" was held at nearby Kavala.[182] A contribution by Chaido Koukouli-Chrysantaki presents the history of Philippi and a description of its character in the time of Paul.[183] In the first century BCE the city was constituted as a Roman colony and populated by a large number of veterans and a mixture of Thracians, Romans, and Greeks. Information about the administration of the city is recorded on inscriptions; the officials included *duoviri* who are called στρατηγοί in Acts (16:22, 35, 38). The city displayed a variety of cults and religious associations. Although an inscription confirms the presence of a synagogue in the third century, Jews in Paul's day worshiped at a place of prayer (προσευχή; Acts 16:13) outside the walls. Charalambos Bakirtzis, in a paper on "Paul and Philippi: The Archaeological Evidence," concentrates on the area east of the forum, south of the Via Egnatia, where the Octagon church has been excavated. Under this building a mosaic has been found that marks a church from the early fourth century dedicated to Paul. Near this church is the tomb of a martyr, possibly the burial place of Paul. Allen Dwight Callahan argues that evidence that Paul was martyred in Philippi is supported by an inscription that reads: "The burial place of Paul, elder of the church of the Philippians."[184] Although one would expect the title "apostle," Paul never refers to himself as ἀπόστολος in the letter to the Philippians.

An important study of city of Philippi as the setting for Paul's ministry was prepared by Lukas Bormann.[185] Bormann notes the importance of colonies in Roman expansion to the east. Philippi was founded as a Roman colony by Antony (42 BCE) and refounded by Augustus in 31 BCE. According to Bormann the refounding was celebrated in a ritual act that venerated the victory of Augustus and advanced the power of the imperial cult. Two temples in Philippi were dedicated to the imperial cult, and participation in the cult required swearing an oath to Caesar. The account of Paul's mission to the city reports the accusation that he and his associates advocated customs unlawful for Romans to observe (Acts 16:21). Bormann thinks this indicates that Paul represented opposition to Roman power, an attitude that had popular support in the east. In his opinion the letter to the Philippians is a composite of three letters; 4:10-20, which belongs to the earliest letter, is the key to understanding the relationship between Paul and the church. The paradigm that best represents this relationship, according to Bormann, is the patronage or clientele relationship, parallel to the role of Augustus as patron of the city. Thus Bormann sees the relation of Paul to the Philippian church as a relationship of patron to emancipated clientele—a relationship that requires loyalty and allows the Philippians to share in the suffering that Paul (and the church) endures in conflict with the authorities of Philippi and the power of Rome.

Peter Pilhofer's work on Philippi is a model of archaeological research in the service of socio-cultural understanding as context for the interpretation of NT texts.[186] His work makes use of the vast treasury of inscriptions discovered at Philippi.[187] Pilhofer notes that the city was relatively small in Paul's day, with a population of only five or ten thousand. The economy of Philippi was primarily agricultural with some industry related to the gold and silver miners of the region. The populace included Thracians, the original settlers, and the Roman colonists who became the dominant group, augmented by Greeks who migrated to the city. Pilhofer believes the Philippians participated in a variety of cults and religions of which three were the most important: the cults of the Thracian Rider (or Horseman), Dionysus, and Silvanus. Paul, according to Pilhofer, was conscious of Philippi as a Roman city. This is seen in his use of political terms like πολιτεύεσθε ("live as a citizen," Phil 1:27), a word used only here in the Pauline letters. Paul also declares that "our citizenship is in heaven" (3:20) using the term πολίτευμα which is not found elsewhere in the NT. Pilhofer thinks Paul's reference to "bishops and deacons" (Phil 1:1), which has no parallel in the authentic letters, indicates a distinctive organization in Philippi, typical of the concern of the Roman colony with rank and hierarchical titles. He believes the account in Acts of Paul mission displays such accuracy of detail that Luke, the author, must have been himself an inhabitant of Philippi.[188]

Two studies of Philippi consider the archaeological and textual data from a feminist perspective. Lilian Portefaix investigates the way first-century Philippian women viewed Christianity in the context of their socio-cultural and religions background.[189] In regard to religion, she thinks the most important deity was Diana, who was assimilated to the Greek huntress, Artemis. The Egyptian goddess Isis was also worshiped at a temple found on the acropolis; Isis was revered for providing special help and healing to women. Portefaix believes that women who joined the church were conscious of living in a celestial colony in conflict with the colony of Rome. They viewed Euodia and Syntyche as leading women, struggling along with Paul in the conflict alluded to in the letter (Phil 4:2-3). They were accustomed to religious struggle, according to Portefaix, because of their familiarity with the rock carvings on the acropolis hill depicting Diana as armed with bow and lance; they resonated with Paul's idea of joy in suffering (Phil 2:17-18) because they remembered the myth of Isis, who wept over the demise of Osiris but rejoiced at his revival. Valerie A. Abrahamsen gives much attention to the rock carvings at Philippi.[190] She says that of the total of some two hundred of these stone reliefs, 138 represent females and 90 of these depict Diana. This leads Abrahamsen to stress the prominence of women in the cult of Diana and to affirm the leadership of women in the Philippian church.

An excellent study of the daily life of urban Christians in first- and second-century Rome is presented by Peter Lampe. In his research Lampe employs primarily literary, but also epigraphical and archaeological sources. "My approach," he writes, "involves abolishing the false alternative between interpreting texts either on the basis of theology and history of tradition, one the one hand, or on the basis of sociological categories, on the other. Each approach should be connected with the other."[191] Lampe begins by tracing the history of the Roman church from its beginnings to its separation from the synagogue. He believes the edict of Claudius (probably to be dated at 49) addressed the conflict between Jews and Jewish Christians; those who were expelled, like Aquila and Priscilla, were Christians. By the time of the persecution under Nero (64–65) the Roman officials, according to Lampe, could distinguish Christians from Jews. Lampe takes up the question: In what quarters of the city did Christians dwell? Using such data as Christian burials, he concludes that the main concentrations of Christians were in the Trastevere and outside the Capena Gate on both sides of the Appian Way. These were densely populated areas inhabited by lower-class persons, common laborers, and slaves. Lampe believes that documents from the late first century and the second century (*1 Clement, Shepherd of Hermas,* Justin) indicate social stratification among Christians: widows and orphans, rich and poor. Although he thinks that the majority of Christians before the third century were poor, Lampe observes an increasing number of upper-class, educated, and affluent members. He detects diversity and theological variety within the church, evidenced by the presence of Marcionites, Valentinians, and Montanists. Lampe believes orthodoxy triumphed because of its simplicity and its concern for the needy; the diversity resulted, in part, from the large number of immigrant members.

Graydon Snyder analyzes non-literary remains in order to understand the life and faith of Christians before Constantine, mainly in Rome.[192] He begins with an interpretation of such symbols as the lamb, the boat, the fish, and the cross. According to Snyder the lamb did not symbolize sacrifice or suffering, but represented kinship and community. Snyder also claims that the cross as symbol of the passion is not found before Constantine. Turning to pictorial representations, Snyder describes frescoes and mosaics. These media depict scenes from the Bible, and express such motifs as deliverance from danger (the youths in the fiery furnace), the importance of community (Noah in the ark), and paradise (Adam and Eve in the garden). As for buildings, Snyder notes that the earliest Christians worshiped in houses, some of which were reconstructed to accommodate worship. The title (*tituli*) churches of Rome were buildings that became churches and were designated by the name of the owner or patron, for example, *titulus Clementis*; Snyder believes nine of these churches were associated with pre-Constantinian places of worship. He notes that the church at Dura Europus in Syria included a room that had been converted into a baptistry in the third century. According to Snyder these material remains reflect the development of such theological concepts as Christology. Prior to 180 Jesus was depicted as a wandering wonder-worker; by 200 he was portrayed as a youth who performed marvelous deeds; in the fourth century he was transformed into a royal figure, bearded and majestic. In summary, Snyder believes the conflict of church and state has been overemphasized; instead, he sees Christianity as an urban movement that assimilated the surrounding culture but at the same time maintained its distinctive character—a movement of "small-group caring and hospitality" that "infused people with a vision of cross-cultural universality."[193]

In sum, archaeological research has contributed—and will continue to contribute—to the understanding of the NT. New discoveries will be made. Most of the ancient sites have only been partially excavated, and many have never been subjected to the archaeologist's spade. New methods, invented by advancing technology, will be employed. On the other hand, the older apologetic and descriptive approaches have proved valuable in providing a historical realism to the biblical narrative. Students of the NT, guided by reliable archaeological texts, visiting the ancient sites in person or in perception, have been moved to a more vivid understanding of the setting of the biblical message—an understanding of context, crucial for exegesis. The new archaeology is in its infancy. It is not clear about its presuppositions and its use of social-scientific models. Little wonder that scholars scrutinize the same data from Galilee and reach different conclusions. Little wonder that Jesus is dressed in the robe of a Cynic philosopher by some and garbed as a Jewish peasant by others. A method that is concerned with people, their socio-cultural and religious lives, their ideological beliefs and aspirations, cannot be expected to provide clear, objective results. Little wonder that its practitioners run the risk of subjectivity, for the human *subject* is the *object* of their research. Yet much has been accomplished, providing a sharper image of Christians worshiping in a house in urban Corinth or confessing their faith in the shadow of the temple of Domitian in Ephesus.

TEXTUAL CRITICISM

Some observers have supposed that textual criticism is the most objective of the subdisciplines of NT research. After all, it makes use of hard data that can be empirically observed and statistically evaluated. Textual criticism, however, has been defined as

> the science and art of assessing the transmission of the New Testament text by (1) evaluating its variations, alterations, and distortions, and then attempting its restoration—its earliest recoverable forms—and (2) seeking to place the variants within the history and culture of the early church, both to determine the age, meaning, and likely motivation of variants and also to extract from them some knowledge of the development and character of early Christian theology, ecclesiology, and culture.[194]

The previous contributions of scholars in this field have been reviewed in earlier volumes of this *History*: John Mill and Richard Bentley, J. A. Bengel, J. J. Wettstein, J. J. Griesbach, Karl Lachmann, Constantin von Tischendorf, and J. M. A. Scholz in Volume 1; Brooke Foss Westcott and F. J. A. Hort, Bernhard Weiss, B. H. Streeter, Silva and Kirsopp Lake, Marie-Joseph Lagrange, Hermann von Soden, J. Rendel Harris, and Frederic G. Kenyon in Volume 2.[195] This host of scholars has been succeeded in the twentieth century by a company of notable textual critics; a few of them merit biographical notes.

American scholars have made important contributions. Ernest Cadman Colwell (1901–74), noted for his charismatic personality, was born in Pennsylvania.[196] Educated at Emory University and the University of Chicago (PhD 1930), Colwell had an outstanding career as an academic administrator. He served as Dean of the Divinity School at Chicago, and from 1945 to 1951 as the President of the University. In 1951 he moved to Emory, where he was Vice President and Dean of the Faculties. From 1957 to 1968 he was President of the newly reconstituted School of Theology at Claremont, California. Colwell was named President of the SBL in 1947.

Like Colwell, Bruce M. Metzger (1914–2007) was also born in Pennsylvania.[197] He studied at Princeton Theological Seminary and Princeton University (PhD 1942). Metzger began as a teaching fellow at the Seminary in 1938, moved through the ranks, and was appointed George L. Collard Professor of New Testament Language and Literature in 1964. He served as president of both the SBL and the SNTS. Among his many students were the important textual critics Michael W. Holmes and Bart D. Ehrman.

Eldon Jay Epp was born in Minnesota in 1930 and educated at Wheaton College, Fuller Theological Seminary, and Harvard (PhD 1961).[198] From 1966 to 1968 he served as a fellow at the Claremont Graduate School and consultant to the International Greek New Testament Project. At Claremont he was associated with Colwell, whom he came to admire as mentor and model. Epp taught at the University of Southern California and Case Western Reserve University, where he was Harkness Professor of Biblical Literature and Dean of Humanities; after retirement (1998) he was named Visiting Professor of New Testament at Harvard Divinity School. He served as President of the SBL (2003). Important textual critics who studied with Epp include Gordon D. Fee and Larry W. Hurtado.

Europe continued to produce important textual critics. In Germany the leader was Kurt Aland (1915–94). He was born and educated at Berlin and taught in East Berlin and at the University of Halle. In 1958 he escaped from the German Democratic Republic, and the next year he was appointed Professor of

New Testament and Textual Criticism at the University of Münster, where he founded the *Institut für Neutestamentliche Textforschung*; after retirement in 1983 he was succeeded as director by his wife Barbara Aland.

Among the British a principal textual critic was a Canadian, George D. Kilpatrick (1910–89).[199] Born in British Columbia, Kilpatrick studied at University College, London, and Oriel College, Oxford. He taught at University College, Nottingham, and at Oxford where, in 1949, he was appointed Dean Ireland's Professor of the Holy Scripture at Queen's College, Oxford. His leading disciple was James K. Elliott of the University of Leeds. In France, Christian-Bernard Amphoux established at Montpellier the *Centre de documentation sur les manuscrits de la Bible* in 1984; in 1988 the name was changed to *Centre Jean Duplacy pour l'étude des manuscrits de la Bible* in honor of Amphoux's teacher. Amphoux, like Duplacy before him, taught in the *Faculté de théologie catholique* at Lyons.

INTRODUCTIONS TO TEXTUAL CRITICISM

NT textual critics have published valuable surveys of the whole field.[200] Typically these surveys recount the collecting and canonizing of the NT documents. They depict the habits of scribes, the materials and methods of writing, and the production of scrolls and codices.[201] A major feature of these introductions is a review of the material of text criticism. The introductions list and describe the known Greek manuscripts, including papyri, uncial (or majuscule) manuscripts, minuscules, and lectionaries. The Alands, for example, list all the known papyri (at the time of publication, 96), all the known uncials, the most significant minuscules, and the most important Greek Fathers.[202] These lists testify to the enormous quantity of material that is the subject of the text-critical task: some 5,700 manuscripts and a host of quotations from the patristic writers.[203] No other ancient document even approaches the NT in the wealth of textual witnesses. Fewer than seven hundred manuscripts of Homer's *Iliad* exist, and the tragedies of Euripides are preserved in a little more than thirty texts. As well as this mountain of Greek manuscripts, the textual critic must assess the significance of early translations of the NT. For the Latin Vulgate alone there are more than 8,000 manuscripts. Besides the Old Latin and the Vulgate, early translations were made into Syriac, Coptic, Armenian, Georgian, Ethiopic, and other lesser-known languages. This material is analyzed in a masterful book by Bruce Metzger.[204]

The standard introductions also include a review of the history of the transmission of the text. They note the identification of early text-types.

Westcott and Hort employed a genealogical method whereby they attempted to trace the relationship of manuscripts to their ancestors and to groupings of texts. They believed the extant manuscripts could be classified in relation to four major text-types: Syrian (or Byzantine), Western, Alexandrian, and Neutral. The introductions note problems with these groupings and introduce the ongoing debate about text-types. They also survey the history of the printed editions of the NT from the text of Erasmus (1516) to the modern editions of Nestle-Aland and the United Bible Society.

The introductions devote much attention to the methods of textual criticism.[205] In the evaluation of readings and variants, textual criticism assesses two major kinds of evidence: external and internal. External evidence has to do with the age and quality of the individual manuscripts. The geographical distribution of the textual witnesses is taken into account, and manuscripts are evaluated according to their relation to text-types or groupings. Internal evidence has to do with transcriptional and intrinsic probability. Transcriptional probability is concerned with variants that result from scribal habits—some unintentional, some intentional. Various principles for this assessment have been derived, for example, that the shorter reading and the more difficult reading are preferred. Intrinsic probability is concerned with readings that relate to the vocabulary, style, and ideology or theology of the original author. A basic principle in the evaluation of evidence is widely affirmed: the reading that best explains the origin of all the other variants is preferred.

THE HISTORY OF TEXTUAL CRITICISM IN THE TWENTIETH CENTURY

In a series of essays, Eldon Epp lamented the meager accomplishments of the discipline. Thus in "The Twentieth Century Interlude in New Testament Textual Criticism," a lecture presented to the SBL in 1973, Epp contends that little has been accomplished in textual criticism since Westcott and Hort.[206] As evidence he cites the lack of progress in popular editions, in moving toward a theory and history of the earliest text, in producing major critical editions and apparatuses, and in methods of evaluating readings. "In short," concludes Epp, "New Testament textual criticism is an area seriously affected by decreasing attention, diminishing graduate opportunities, and dwindling personnel."[207]

Kurt Aland was offended. Although Epp may have been partially correct in his assessment of the American scene, Aland believed his pessimistic view overlooked the fruitful activity in Europe, notably at the Institute in Münster.[208] In an earlier essay Aland had lauded the achievements of the Institute in collecting, copying, and collating texts.[209] By 1967, the well-staffed and well-funded Institute had photographed and microfilmed 4,410 manuscripts, a repository that made available four-fifths of the known texts of the NT. Also, the scholars of the Institute had collated some one thousand minuscules, demonstrating that 10 percent of these were virtually useless for the reconstruction of the earliest text.

Epp was undeterred. In a paper presented to the Textual Criticism section of the SBL in 1979 he described "A Continuing Interlude in New Testament Textual Criticism."[210] In the face of Aland's evidence, Epp wrote that "all of these exemplary advances in our accumulated materials, in the tools of research, and in our control of the data have not yet resulted, it seems to me, in decisive progress in certain critical areas of New Testament textual criticism, namely in the textual character of the critical editions of the twentieth century; in the theory and history of the earliest New Testament text; and in the evaluation of readings."[211] Two years earlier Epp had presented a paper to the same audience entitled "New Testament Textual Criticism in America: Requiem for a Discipline."[212] Epp acknowledged that America had produced some text-critical giants such as Colwell and Metzger, and that centers of textual criticism had been established at Chicago, Emory, Duke, and Claremont. But in the meantime leaders had retired or died, and centers of research and graduate study had dissipated or disappeared.

At the end of the century Larry W. Hurtado, Epp's former student, painted a brighter picture.[213] Hurtado noted the appearance of significant publications: the series "The New Testament in the Greek Fathers," published by the SBL, has produced seven volumes; a monograph series, "Histoire du text biblique," edited by Christian-Bernard Amphoux and Bernard Outtier, published its initial volume in 1996; the International Greek New Testament Project published its two-volume critical apparatus of Luke (1984, 1987) and its first volume on John; an innovative periodical, *TC: A Journal of Text Criticism* has appeared online. Although the saints have retired or gone to their reward, a number of younger textual critics such as Bart Ehrman and Michael Holmes have arisen. The fledgling graduate student could study textual criticism with David Parker at Birmingham or Bart Ehrman at the University of North Carolina. Moreover, textual criticism has moved beyond the narrow quest for the original text to the larger question of the meaning of text-critical research for the understanding of the life and thought of the church.[214]

DEVELOPMENTS AND DEBATES IN THE SECOND HALF OF THE TWENTIETH CENTURY

In the area of new developments, textual criticism has been enriched by the discovery of additional papyri.[215] Westcott and Hort made no mention of the papyri, and Tischendorf knew only five. During the twentieth century the number of known papyrus manuscripts of the NT has multiplied: from fourteen in 1909, to forty-eight in 1933, to one hundred sixteen in the 27th edition of the Nestle-Aland text. Among these manuscripts more than thirty can be dated in the third or early fourth century. The major discovery of the second half of the century was the Bodmer Papyri.[216] These texts were purchased in the 1950s and 1960s from a Cairo antiquities dealer by Martin Bodmer, founder of the Bodmer Library of World Literature in Cologny, near Geneva. These papyri were thought to have been found around 1952 by an Egyptian peasant near the town of Dishna, not far from Nag Hammadi. The collection contains Greek biblical writings (including John, 1 and 2 Peter, Jude, Luke, Acts, and James), Greek Christian writings (for example, the correspondence of Paul with the Corinthians), Coptic biblical and Christian writings (including John, Matthew, Romans, and 2 Corinthians), and literary writings (including works of Homer and Thucydides). Most of these texts date from the third or fourth centuries and may have belonged to the library of a Pachomian monastery. Most important for NT textual criticism are: P^{66} (Bodmer II), dated around 200, which contains most of the Gospel of John and has affinity with the Alexandrian text; P^{72} (Bodmer VII-VIII), dated in the third or fourth century, which contains 1 and 2 Peter and Jude and has affinity with Codex Vaticanus (B); and P^{75} (Bodmer XIV-XV), dated to the third century, which contains sections of Luke and John and largely agrees with Vaticanus.

During the century, methods for evaluating textual material were devised and refined. Epp, in 1974, presented a paper to the Textual Criticism Seminar of the SBL entitled, "Toward the Clarification of the Term 'Textual Variant.'"[217] The older view had understood variants as readings that differed from some standard text, for example, the *Textus Receptus*. Instead, Epp, following the lead of Colwell, called for the identification of the "variation-unit"—a section or length of text wherein there are variant readings.[218] Epp says that "a variation-unit is that segment of text where our Greek manuscripts present at least two variant forms and where, after insignificant readings have been excluded, each form has the support of at least two manuscripts."[219] Earlier, Colwell had insisted on evaluating readings and groupings of manuscripts by a quantitative method.[220] Colwell wrote that "the quantitative definition of a text-type is a group of manuscripts that agree more than 70 per cent of the time and is separated by a gap of about 10 percent from its neighbors."[221]

Methods for collating a large number of manuscripts were devised. Two of Colwell's students, Paul McReynolds and Frederik Wisse, developed the

"Claremont Profile Method."[222] In working on the International Greek New Testament Project, scholars were faced with the task of collating a huge number of minuscule manuscripts. The leaders of the Project had assumed that some three hundred minuscules would be advisable for inclusion in the proposed critical apparatus of Luke. To select the proper three hundred from a total of over 2,500 texts seemed virtually impossible within the limits of time and labor. McReynolds and Wisse identified a series of test-readings, that is, variants (from the *Textus Receptus*) that had the support of a two-thirds majority of the members of an identifiable group of manuscripts. They found sixty-one variants in chapter 1 of Luke that qualified as test-readings. Using the 163 manuscripts in the Project's file that had already been collated, McReynolds and Wisse were able to tabulate agreements and disagreements that could be plotted in a configuration (or profile) of readings characteristic of a group; in the process they identified fourteen groups, each with a distinctive profile. To provide a larger basis for testing, the same procedure was followed for Luke 10 (which contained 64 test-readings) and 20 (78 test-readings). Using these chapters and the test-readings, made it possible to examine a manuscript and determine its group identity within a couple of hours. Wisse, perhaps a bit optimistic, says that "an experienced person can profile a MS within half an hour."[223] After manuscripts had been classified according to groups (scholars working in the Project classified over 1,300 texts), the importance of individual manuscripts and groups of manuscripts for inclusion in a critical apparatus could be assessed.

According to Bart Ehrman the Claremont Profile Method leads to incomplete and inaccurate classifications; it uses sample passages to determine the textual affinities of a whole manuscript.[224] The weakness of the method seemed obvious when reviewers noted that both Codex Bezae (a major representative of the Western text) and Codex Vaticanus (a major representative of the Alexandrian text) were included in Wisse's "Group B." As an alternative Ehrman proposed the "Comprehensive Profile Method." This method "considers a full range of readings, those found widely or universally within a group (irrespective of their occurrence elsewhere) and those found exclusively or principally among members of one group but not of another."[225] Although this method provides more information about the individual texts and their relation to textual groupings, it does not serve the purpose of the Claremont method: to make possible the collating of a large number of manuscripts in a relatively short time.

In contrast to these profile methods, the Institute in Münster, under the leadership of Kurt Aland, developed a method of collating manuscripts by "test-passages" (*Teststellen*).[226] This method, which was developed in the study of the text of the Catholic Epistles, involves the selection of test-passages (for example, Jas 1:12) that are decisive for identifying textual groupings and relationships. By investigating the test-passages one can readily identify manuscripts that belong to the majority (or Byzantine) text. These are manuscripts that agree with the majority text in 60 to 70 percent (or more) of the test-passages. Manuscripts that show less than 60 percent agreement with the majority text represent the ancient text and should be considered in the construction of a major critical edition.

David C. Parker compares the Münster method and the Claremont method.[227] He notes that the aims of the two differ: Münster is concerned to distinguish manuscripts that represent Byzantine text from other, more important forms of the text. Claremont intends to classify manuscripts into subgroupings. In working on Luke, Claremont makes use of test-readings in three chapters; Münster uses test-passages from the entire gospel: a total of fifty-four *Teststellen*. Parker concludes that the Münster method does confirm the identification of some of the Claremont groupings but it reveals more about the history of the transmission of the text than the Claremont method.

In the larger debate about methods of textual criticism, three basic approaches are promoted.[228] First, the "historical documentary" method stresses the importance of the history of the transmission of the text. The older application of this "genealogical method," whereby it was assumed that the critic could trace the family tree of a text, fitting the manuscripts into *stemma* with direct connection to the trunk and a tap-root, was overconfident.[229] More realistic is Epp's procedure of locating manuscripts on a trajectory of textual transmission. Second, the "rigorous (or thoroughgoing) eclectic" method, advanced by George D. Kilpatrick and his student, James Keith Elliott, stresses internal evidence.[230] These scholars believe the characteristics of the author and the habits of the scribe are more important than the "cult" of the "best manuscripts." Third, the "reasoned (or moderate) eclectic" method is practiced by the majority of contemporary textual critics.[231] "On this third procedure when faced with any variation-unit, we would choose the variant reading that appears to be in the earliest chronological group *and* that also makes the best sense when the internal criteria are applied."[232]

Considerable debate was been generated over the question of the history of the transmission of the text, and the problem of grouping of texts or identification of text-types.[233] Westcott and Hort's confidence in the Neutral text evaporated, and the so-called "Caesarean" text was increasingly recognized as a mixture of Alexandrian and Western readings.[234] The problem of identifying early recensions of the text was complicated by the discovery of additional papyri. The evidence that P^{75} was much the same as Codex Vaticanus (B) led to the conclusion that the B-text did not represent a fourth-century recension. Although many critics argued that distinct text-types did not exist prior to 200, Epp contends that early clusters of manuscripts can be identified: an early B-text with roots in the second century (witnessed by P^{75} and B) and an early D-text (represented by D, the Old Latin, and the Old Syriac). The antiquity and importance of the Western text has been affirmed by Duplacy and Amphoux.[235] Amphoux believes Codex Bezae represents a text that was composed in Smyrna about 120, and that an exemplar of this text appeared in Lyons around 170.

Kurt and Barbara Aland have largely abandoned the traditional identification of text-types. Instead, they group manuscripts into categories according to their assessment of manuscript quality. Category I consists of manuscripts that have a high proportion of "early" readings, including all texts up to the beginning of the fourth century (for example, P^{75} and P^{45}, B, a). Category II consists of manuscripts with a considerable proportion of early readings, but with some alien (Byzantine) influences, including manuscripts identified as Egyptian or late Alexandrian (for example, L [019], and θ [038]). Category III consists of manuscripts with a small portion of early readings, but with considerable Byzantine influence (for example, W [032]). Category IV consists of manuscripts of the Western text, and Category V is made up of manuscripts of the predominantly Byzantine text. These categories indicate, in descending order, the relative importance of the various manuscripts for the reconstruction of the original text. As Ehrman points out, this system of classification involves a circular argument: those texts that are closest to the original are found in the first category, but the criterion for inclusion in the first category is closeness to the original.

Two conservative alternatives to the main line of textual criticism have been proposed, and they are diametrically opposed to each other. The attempt to reestablish the primacy of the majority text has been promoted by the Majority Text Society, founded in 1988, which swelled to a membership of over 160 scholars from seventeen countries within two years.[236] According to this view God has preserved the authentic text, the one that has been available to the church through the centuries; this text was maliciously corrupted by unbelievers and heretics. Zane C. Hodges and Arthur L. Farstad have published a critical edition of the Greek NT according to this theory. In their introduction they affirm their basic premise: "Any reading overwhelmingly attested by the manuscript tradition is more likely to be original than its rival(s)."[237] The theory is refuted by Daniel Wallace and Gordon Fee.[238] Fee points out that the earliest texts show variety and fluidity, that the early versions and patristic quotations do not support the majority text, that there is no evidence that a Byzantine-type text existed before the fourth century, and that the majority text did not become the majority until the ninth century.[239] The contrasting conservative view is expressed by Philip Wesley Comfort.[240] Comfort believes the early papyri, which he dates earlier than most textual critics, antedate the major uncials. He thinks the best-quality papyri were produced by Christian scribes who faithfully copied the Scriptures. Modern editions, according to Comfort, have failed to make adequate use of these earliest sources. In fact, Comfort's assessment of the papyri is questionable, and modern editions make abundant use of papyri.[241]

Textual criticism has been facilitated by new and advancing technologies. Photography has made it possible to collect and make accessible virtually all known manuscripts. Also, new photographic techniques have facilitated the reading of damaged and previously unreadable texts. Readings that were earlier thought to be scribal corrections have been shown by photographic analysis to be offsets from the facing page of the manuscript.[242] The major advance, of course, has been in the use of computers—a technology still in its infancy, but destined to revolutionize the whole discipline.[243] Using computers, the Institute at Münster produced an exhaustive concordance of the Greek NT.[244] Procedures and software are being developed for scanning and reproducing manuscripts in electronic form.[245] Computers have been used in the identification and reconstruction of fragments of manuscripts.[246] The increasing availability of electronic texts has transformed the task of collating manuscripts, quantitative analysis of texts, and preserving the results. Software is making available a host of text-critical databases that individual scholars can have at their fingertips, for example, the critical apparatuses of Tischendorf, Nestle-Aland, and the Center for New Testament Textual Studies (New Orleans). All of this is but a small glimpse of things yet to be seen.

RESULTS OF TEXTUAL CRITICISM: THE PUBLICATION OF EDITIONS OF THE NEW TESTAMENT

Since Westcott and Hort's *The New Testament in the Original Greek* (1882), several editions have been published, including texts by Alexander Souter (1910, 2d ed. 1947), H. J. Vogels (1920, 4th ed. 1955), Augustin Merk (1933, 10th ed. 1984), J. M. Bover (1943, 6th ed. 1981), and Randolph V. G. Tasker (1964).[247] A new edition of the widely-used text of the British and Foreign Bible Society, edited by G. D. Kilpatrick, was published in 1958. Two manual or popular editions, the Nestle-Aland text and the text of the United Bible Societies, have increasingly claimed the field.

The Nestle-Aland text had its beginning in 1898 when the Württemberg Bible Society published the first edition of the text by Eberhard Nestle.[248] This was a composite text based on those of Tischendorf, Westcott and Hort, and Richard F. Weymouth (2d ed. 1892); after 1901 Weymouth's text was replaced by that of Bernhard Weiss. Erwin Nestle, who succeeded his father, edited the 13th edition in 1927, including in it a textual apparatus with attestations from several major manuscripts. In 1952 Kurt Aland was appointed associate editor; he reviewed and expanded the apparatus for inclusion in the 25th edition of 1963. In 1979 the Nestle-Aland *Novum Testamentum Graece* (26th edition) adopted the same text that had been published by the United Bible Societies in 1975, although with a decidedly different critical apparatus. The apparatus was revised and expanded for the twenty-seventh edition (1993), citing the evidence of over two hundred manuscripts in support of the text and the variants. All the papyri and major majuscules are consistently cited. The apparatus is equipped with signs and abbreviations that identify and support the text and the variants, a system that concentrates a vast amount of data in a relatively short space.[249] In the outer margins of the text are notes indicating NT parallels and OT quotations. The inner margins include the Eusebian canons, the system developed by Eusebius for locating Gospel parallels. The appendices contain a list of the Greek and Latin codices cited in the apparatus, a list of minor variants (presented in parentheses in the apparatus), a list of textual differences from this edition found in other major editions, and a list of quotations and allusions to the OT, Apocrypha, and non-Christian writings—a cornucopia of text-critical information. "A hundred years after Westcott-Hort," boasts Aland, "the goal of an edition of the NT 'in the original Greek' appears to have been reached."[250]

As well as the text of the NT, the Institute at Münster, under the leadership of Kurt Aland, has published a Gospel synopsis.[251] The first edition appeared in 1963 and, in contrast to other synopses, included the entire text of the Gospel of John. The fourth edition (1967) included additional uncial manuscripts in the apparatus, and the ninth edition of 1976 replaced the text with the text of the twenty-sixth edition of Nestle-Aland. The fourteenth edition (1994) added readings from recently discovered papyri, and the fifteenth edition (1996) added an appendix that included the Gospel of Thomas in Coptic, with German and English translations.

The first edition of the United Bible Societies' text appeared in 1966.[252] It was the work of a committee appointed in 1955 by the American Bible Society, the National Bible Society of Scotland, and the Württemberg Bible Society to prepare an edition of the text for use by translators. Later the Netherlands Bible Society and the British and Foreign Bible Society joined the project. In this edition the critical apparatus was restricted to readings significant for translators and for establishing the text. The relative certainty of the readings adopted was indicated by letter (A through D) in the apparatus. For these readings and the variants a full citing of the evidence was presented. Compared with Nestle-Aland, the UBS text generally cites a smaller number of variants but provides more evidence for each. The edition also included a second apparatus that presented differences of punctuation of the text according to major editions and translations. The original committee included Kurt Aland, Matthew Black, Bruce M. Metzger, Allen Wikgren, and for the early stages of the work, Arthur Vööbus.

The text of the first edition was based on Westcott and Hort and made use of other editions, critical apparatuses, and study of the manuscripts. The third edition (1975) made a thorough revision. Carlo Maria Martini—the only Roman Catholic member, named a cardinal in 1979—had joined the editorial committee and Kurt Aland provided material he had been collecting for a revision of Nestle-Aland. As a result, the text of the third edition of the UBS, *The Greek New Testament*, was adopted as the text of the twenty-sixth edition of the Nestle-Aland *Novum Testamentum Graece*. During preparation for the fourth edition of the UBS text, Black and Wikgen were replaced by Barbara Aland and Johannes Karavidopoulos. This edition (1992) made major revisions in the critical apparatus, with the result that an almost complete account of the manuscript evidence through the ninth century was included. The punctuation apparatus was replaced with a segmentation apparatus that notes only major and minor divisions (clauses and paragraphs) that are important for translation and interpretation. Cross references, including quotations from biblical and non-biblical documents, allusions, and literary parallels are given at the bottom of the page. The volume ends with indices of the quotations, allusions and verbal parallels, and a list of the principal manuscripts cited in the apparatus.

In 1970 a *Textual Commentary* on the UBS text, written by Bruce Metzger, was published.[253] This commentary presents the reasoning that led the committee to adopt the readings presented in the text and to the assigning of letter "grades" in the evaluation of readings. Metzger discusses 1,440 sets of variants that are cited in the apparatus and some six hundred more he believes deserve discussion. The second edition of the commentary (1993) discusses 284 additional variants that had been added to the fourth edition of the text.

The end of the century saw the publication of early installments of two major text-critical projects: the critical apparatuses of the International Greek

New Testament Project (IGNTP) and the *Editio Critica Maior* of the Münster Institute. The roots of the IGNTP go back to 1926, when a British committee was formed to produce an edition of the Greek NT with full critical apparatus.[254] In 1935 an extensive apparatus of Mark was published, edited by Stanley C. E. Legg, and a companion volume on Matthew in 1940. Both volumes were severely criticized. In 1948 a conference held at the University of Chicago discussed the preparing of a critical apparatus and endorsed cooperation between British and American scholars. Later that year the SBL approved the project and appointed a committee with Colwell as chairman. In 1952 the American committee met with a British committee, chaired by Robert Henry Lightfoot, and the decision was made to work on the Gospel of Luke. In 1951 Colwell moved to Emory and in 1958 to Claremont, taking with him the files of the IGNTP. In 1965 a specimen of the proposed apparatus (covering Luke 20:1-6) was circulated among some forty scholars.[255] Colwell was succeeded by Metzger as chair of the American committee, and J. Neville Birdsall became executive editor of the British committee, succeeded by James K. Elliott in 1978. After years of unfulfilled promises, volume 1 (on Luke 1–12) was finally published in 1984, followed by the second volume in 1987.[256] These publications conformed to the principles on which the edition was based: to present the textual evidence (not to construct a text); to use the *Textus Receptus* as the collating base; and to present evidence from a large number of Greek manuscripts, derived from new collations.

After the publication of the volumes on Luke the reorganized British committee, with Elliott as secretary, wrote to Metzger to see if the Americans were interested in continuing the project with work on the Gospel of John.[257] In 1988 the Textual Criticism Section of the SBL elected a new American committee with Gordon D. Fee as chairman and Michael W. Holmes as editor. In the same year an International Steering Committee was formed, including Elliott, Fee, C. D. Osburn, and David C. Parker. In 1995 the project published a critical apparatus that included data from all the known papyri of John.[258] This superb volume has three main sections: a transcriptions of twenty-one of the twenty-three papyrus texts of John (the longer texts, P^{66} and P^{75}, are not included); the extensive critical apparatus (almost 300 pages); and photographs of all the known papyri of John (except P^{66} and P^{75}, for which only sample pages are included).

The *Editio Critica Maior* had its origins in a discussion at the meeting of the SNTS in 1967.[259] An editorial committee was established, consisting of Kurt Aland, Jean Duplacy, and Bonifatius Fischer. However, the work was not restricted to individuals but also incorporated the research of text-critical institutes, including the Institut für neutestamentliche Textforschung (Münster); Vetus-Latina-Institut (Beuron); Centre d'Analyse et de Documentation Patristiques (Strasbourg), and Centre Jean Duplacy pour l'étude des manuscrits de la Bible (Montpellier). The intention of this project, in contrast to the IGNTP, was not only to construct an extensive critical apparatus but to reconstruct the text on the basis of research into an enormous amount of textual evidence. This evidence included all known papyri and uncials, carefully selected witnesses of the minuscules and lectionaries, and extensive evidence from the three most important versions (Latin, Coptic, and Syriac) and some evidence from other versions, and quotations from all the Greek Fathers up to the time of John of Damascus (ninth and tenth century). By the end of the twentieth century the first installments of this massive project began to appear.[260] David Parker observes that this edition is worthy of the appellation "the new Tischendorf."[261] He also notes that the new text of James is very close to that of the twenty-seventh edition of Nestle-Aland, in fact, differing in only two places (Jas 1:22 and 2:3).

TEXTUAL CRITICISM AND THE SOCIO-CULTURAL AND THEOLOGICAL DEVELOPMENT OF EARLY CHRISTIANITY

In the second half of the twentieth century an exciting new movement emerged within textual criticism. This movement flies in the face of the confident assertion of F. J. A. Hort that "even among the numerous unquestionably spurious readings of the New Testament there are no signs of deliberate falsification of the text for dogmatic purposes."[262] In contrast to Hort, recent research has detected changes not only for dogmatic purposes but also for other cultural and ideological reasons. As Eldon J. Epp observes, "Textual criticism . . . is, on its cutting edge, primarily art, primarily a humanistic discipline that reveals to us, not a lifeless text, but an exciting, dynamic world of people and ideas in action."[263] The pioneering work in this new direction was Epp's *The Theological Tendency of Codex Bezae Cantabrigiensis in Acts*, a revision of his Harvard dissertation of 1961.[264] Epp's aim is to investigate the variants in this text in order to probe its underlying inclinations, specifically its anti-Judaic tendencies. Epp investigate these tendencies in terms of three topics. First, "the Jews and Jesus": here Epp detects variants in which the D-text tends to diminish the idea that the Jews, in crucifying Jesus, acted in ignorance. As Epp points out, the idea that the Jews acted in ignorance is peculiar to Luke, but in Luke 23:34 Codex Bezae omits "Father, forgive them, for they do not know what they are doing." Second, "the Jews, Gentiles and Christianity": here Epp argues that the D-text stresses Christian universalism in contrast to the narrowness of the Jews. For example, in the D-text of the apostolic decree (Acts 15:20, 29; 21:25) the requirements are changed from Jewish ritual rules to a universal moral admonition. Third, "the Jews and the Apostles": here Epp finds evidence that the D-text magnifies the work of the apostles and sharpens the Jewish opposition to them.[265]

In his later work Epp continued to advance this perspective. His presidential address to the SBL (2003) investigates the papyri from Oxyrhynchus in order to throw light on the life and faith of early Christians in Egypt. Among this collection of texts, which included almost half of the 116 known papyri of the NT, there is evidence indicating that early Christian women were literate and may have been leaders in the church. In an earlier essay Epp had explored anti-feminist tendencies in the text of Rom 16:7, later expanded into his book, *Junia: The First Woman Apostle*.[266] In discussing Romans 16, Epp points out that Paul sends greetings to seventeen men and eight women, but of those commended as contributing most to the church, seven are women, five are men. In 16:7, "Greet Andronicus and Junia," the best reading is Ιουνιαν (rated "A" by the UBS editors) rather than Ιουλιαν. The form Ιουνιαν can be either feminine Ἰουνίαν (from Ἰουνία, -ας, ἡ, "Junia"), or it can be masculine: either Ἰουνιᾶν (from Ἰουνιᾶς, -ας, ὁ, "Junias") or Ἰουνίαν (from Ἰουνίας, -α, ὁ, "Junias"). These two alleged masculine forms are imagined to be short forms of Ἰουνιανός (Junianos), that is, the Latin name *Iunianus*. Epp argues that "Junia" (feminine) is the original: Junia was a common Roman name, and the name was translated as feminine in all the ancient versions. Neither of the alleged masculine forms of the name "Junias" has ever been found in ancient literature. Some interpreters who have accepted the feminine form as original have interpreted the text to mean that Junia was "well known among the apostles," but Epp argues that the text should be translated "outstanding among the apostles." Convincing support is provided by Chrysostom, who says, "How great the wisdom of this woman that she was even deemed worthy of the apostle's title."[267]

The role of theological influence on the development of the text is documented by Bart Ehrman. In his provocative *The Orthodox Corruption of Scripture*, Ehrman contends that "scribes occasionally altered the words of their sacred texts to make them more patently orthodox and to prevent their misuse by Christians who espoused aberrant views."[268] In general accord with Walter Bauer, Ehrman believes the primitive church displayed doctrinal variety; what emerged as orthodoxy in the fourth century was merely one of the earlier competing views.[269] Those who were moving toward the orthodox consensus can be described as the proto-orthodox. Ehrman explicates their influence on the scribes who copied the texts of the NT under four headings. First, "Anti-Adoptionist Corruptions of Scripture": under this topic Ehrman traces the development of the notion that Jesus was adopted as Son of God. To counter this view the proto-orthodox stressed the uniqueness and supernatural birth of Jesus. Ehrman believes the original text of Luke 3:22 read "you are my Son, today I have begotten you." This reading is supported by external evidence (D and the Old Latin); the alternative, "with you I am well pleased," is probably a harmonization with Mark 1:11. Second, "Anti-Separationist Corruptions of Scripture": here Ehrman notes the belief of the Gnostics that Jesus had two distinct natures, human and divine; they said the body of Jesus was crucified, but the true, spiritual Christ escaped. Ehrman thinks the original text of Heb 2:9 read χωρὶς θεοῦ (apart from God), which the Gnostics interpreted to mean that Jesus tasted death "apart from" or separated from God. Under the influence of the proto-orthodox, the text, according to Ehrman, was revised to read χάριτι θεοῦ: "by the grace of God [he might taste death]." Third, "Anti-Docetic Corruptions": under this heading Ehrman argues that the text of Luke 22:43-44, which presents the anguish of Jesus in the garden, was added to the original text in order to confound the docetic idea that Christ did not suffer. Fourth, "Anti-Patripassianist Corruptions": here Ehrman reviews the idea of the Modalists that God had only one nature, so that Christ's suffering meant that God suffered. An example of the proto-orthodox corruption to counter this view is seen in John 14:9; to the words, "whoever has seen me has see me has seen the Father," P[75] and some other manuscripts add καί, resulting in the translation "whoever has seen me has seen the Father also." Ehrman concludes, "I . . . take my overarching thesis to be established: proto-orthodox scribes of the second and third centuries occasionally modified their texts of Scripture in order to make them coincide more closely with the christological views embraced by the party that would seal its victory at Nicea and Chalcedon."[270]

The most innovative of the new textual critics is David Parker. In his *The Living Text of the Gospels*, Parker writes, "The book has been written with the growing conviction that, once the present approach has been adopted, much else in our understanding of the Gospels requires revision."[271] He believes that a good deal of the effort of text criticism, in particular the quest for the original text, has been misguided. The whole notion of an "original text" he believes to be an illusion. There is no original text; the text is a process. The balance of the book provides examples in support of this thesis. For example, in discussing the texts of the accounts of the Lord's Prayer (Matt 6:9-13; Luke 11:2-4) Parker notes that there are six different forms of the Prayer, all of them used in the early church. Although two forms may be more original (Matthew without the doxology and the short text of Luke), all of the forms contribute to our understanding of the tradition. Parker points out that in this liturgical text, where we would have expected uniformity, instead there is variety.

In regard to the sayings of Jesus about divorce Parker notes a similar variety. For the account in Mark 10:2-13 he finds seven different versions, and for Matt 5:27-32, five. He notes that in all the versions of Mark the woman is presented as divorcing the husband—an action impossible in Judaism, so that the text cannot represent the words of Jesus. Thus Mark, according to Parker, adapts the teachings of Jesus to new circumstances wherein women did have the right to divorce. "The main result of this survey is to show that the recovery of a single original saying of Jesus is impossible."[272] For Parker this means that "the concept of a Gospel that is fixed in shape, authoritative, and final as a piece of literature has to be abandoned."[273]

In his penultimate chapter Parker traces the shifting shape of the forms of the text from the free and fluid text of the second century to the codex, to printed edition, to the electronic text. He concludes: "The reconstruction which has emerged from the present study is that the text and with it the traditions remained fluid for centuries, and that the work of the evangelists did not end when they laid down their pens."[274] As to the illusive traditional goal, "we find the original text in the variations."[275]

In sum, textual criticism, despite delays and disappointments, has accomplished much in the twentieth century. New interest in the field, the enlistment of younger scholars, the establishment of centers and institutes: all have contributed to important results. The popular editions—the Nestle-Aland and United Bible Society texts—provide highly reliable texts supported by extensive, carefully collected and evaluated data, formatted with signs and devices that facilitate their use. The larger text-critical projects—the critical apparatuses of the International Greek New Testament Project and the text of the *Editio Critica Maior*—offer the first installment of dividends still to come. These projects present an enormous amount of well-documented data for the reconstruction of the text and for understanding the history of its transmission. The fact that the Nestle-Aland-UBS text is close to Westcott and Hort, and that the *Editio Critica Maior* is close to the Nestle-Aland-UBS text, does not prove that progress has not been made; these texts provide a mountain of evidence that the earlier work, now vastly amplified, has been on track.

As to method, the "reasoned-eclectic" approach, despite continuing debate, has largely prevailed. The importance of both external and internal evidence is confirmed by their effective use in the production of the popular and major editions. Computers and new technology have contributed and will continue dramatically to facilitate the collection, collation, quantitative analysis, and preservation of the documents and data. The debate about the history of the transmission of the text and the identification of text-types or textual groupings has not been put to rest. Most agree that some kind of groupings emerged in the early life of the text, and that Alexandrian and "Western" texts can be identified. Is it possible that new manuscripts, buried in a corner of Egypt or hidden in a distant monastery, may come to light and illuminate this continuing problem? The new approach of analyzing the development of the text in relation to the socio-cultural and ideological life of the church is in its infancy; much more can and will be done. The view that the text from its beginning has been living and changing will provoke ongoing discussion. Many will cling to the hope that the original text can be restored, and some will claim that the new editions have virtually done that very thing. Others will acknowledge that the quest for the original is an illusion, perhaps a mistake. For them the text is not an ancient object to be venerated but witness to the living Word that transcends the objective.

SUMMARY

As the sections of this chapter demonstrate, the NT scholar has been provided a huge amount of source material with which to work. Also, the chapter has shown that the task of NT research is a "many-splendored thing." To comprehend the Nag Hammadi texts one must know Coptic; the study of archaeology demands numerous disciplines; the science of textual criticism requires expertise in papyrology and palaeograhy. No individual can master all of these skills. The scholar becomes increasingly dependent on the work of others and recognizes the importance of cooperative work (exemplified in the scholarly societies described in Chapter 8). What all the sections of this chapter demonstrate, however, is a common social concern: the Scrolls lead us into the life of a particular Jewish sect; the new archaeology is concerned with the daily life of ordinary people; textual criticism has become aware of political forces functioning in the shaping of the text.

The source material provided by the Nag Hammadi texts offers extensive information on the Hellenistic setting of the NT. The Dead Sea Scrolls, on the other hand, provide a treasury of material for the study of Judaism. In the course of the century Hellenism and the legacy of the history of religion would not be forgotten (e.g., by Hans Dieter Betz), but major attention would be directed toward Judaism.

Notes

1. This view, expressed by scholars who stress Hellenistic-Gnostic backgrounds and affirm the importance of the Gospel of Thomas as a source of independent Jesus tradition, has turned out to be an exaggeration.

2. Jean Doresse, *The Secret Books of the Egyptian Gnostics: An Introduction to the Gnostic Coptic Manuscripts Discovered at Chenoboskion*, trans. Philip Mairet (New York: Viking, 1960); John Dart, *The Jesus of Heresy and History: The Discovery and Meaning of the Nag Hammadi Gnostic Library* (San Francisco: Harper & Row, 1988); James M. Robinson, "The Discovery of the Nag Hammadi Codices," *BA* 42 (1979):206–24.

3. See James M. Robinson, "Introduction," *BA* 42 (1979): 201–4. On the archaeological research see Bastiaan Van Elderen, "The Nag Hammadi Excavation," *BA* 42 (1979): 225–31.

4. See Robinson, "Introduction," 201–4; Martin Krause, "Die Texte von Nag Hammadi," in *Gnosis: Festschrift für Hans Jonas*, ed. Barbara Aland (Göttingen: Vandenhoeck & Ruprecht, 1978), 216–43; Birger A. Pearson, "Nag Hammadi Codices," *ABD* 4: 984–93.

5. See James M. Robinson, *Nag Hammadi: The First Fifty Years*, OPIAC 34 (Claremont, CA: Claremont Graduate School, 1995). This address, originally presented at the Annual Meeting of the SBL in 1995, is also published in *The Nag Hammadi Library After Fifty Years: Proceedings of the 1995 SBL*, ed. John D. Turner and Anne McGuire, NHMS 44 (Leiden: Brill, 1997), 3–33; see also James M. Robinson, "Getting the Nag Hammadi Library into English," *BA* 42 (1979): 239–48.

6. *The Facsimile Edition of the Nag Hammadi Codices* (Leiden: Brill, 1982–84). See James M. Robinson, "The Construction of the Nag Hammadi Codices," in *Essays on the Nag Hammadi Texts: In Honour of Pahor Labib*, ed. Martin Krause, NHS 6 (Leiden: Brill, 1975), 170–90.

7. See, e.g., *The Gospel According to Thomas*, Trans. Antoine Guillaumont, et al. (Leiden: Brill; New York: Harper & Brothers, 1959); *The Gospel of Truth: A Valentinian Meditation on the Gospel*, trans. with commentary by Kendrick Grobel (New York: Abingdon, 1960); *The Gospel of Philip*, trans. with commentary by Robert McLachlan Wilson (New York: Harper & Row, 1962).

8. James M. Robinson, et al., *The Nag Hammadi Library in English*, translated and introduced by members of the Coptic Gnostic Library Project of the Institute for Antiquity and Christianity, Claremont, California, 3d ed. (San Francisco: Harper, 1990; Leiden: Brill, 1996).

9. *Nag Hammadi Deutsch*, ed. Hans-Martin Schenke, Hans-Gebhard Bethge, and Ursula Ulrike Kaiser (Berlin: de Gruyter, 2001–).

10. See Jacques-É. Ménard, "La bibliothèque copte de Nag Hammadi," in *Nag Hammadi and Gnosis: Papers read at the First International Congress of Coptology (Cairo, December 1976)*, ed. R. McL. Wilson, NHS 14 (Leiden: Brill, 1978), 108–12.

11. David M. Scholer, *Nag Hammadi Bibliography 1948–1969*, NHS 1 (Leiden: Brill, 1971); idem., *Nag Hammadi Bibliography 1970–1994*, NHMS 32 (Leiden: Brill, 1997).

12. See *HNTR* 1: 258–69.

13. See *HNTR* 2: 122–35.

14. See *HNTR* 2: 238–53.

15. See pp. 87–175 above.

16. See Giovanni Filoramo, *A History of Gnosticism*, trans. Anthony Alcock (Oxford: Basil Blackwell, 1990), 1–19; Kurt Rudolph, *Die Gnosis: Wesen und Geschichte einer spätantiken Religion*, 2d ed. (Göttingen: Vandenhoeck & Ruprecht, 1980), Eng. trans.: *Gnosis: The Nature and History of Gnosticism*, trans. Robert McLachlan Wilson (San Francisco: Harper & Row, 1983), 9–52.

17. See Gérard Vallée, *A Study in Anti-Gnostic Polemics: Irenaeus, Hippolytus, and Epiphanius*, Studies in Christianity and Judaism 1 (Waterloo, ON: Wilfrid Laurier University Press, 1981).

18. Ugo Bianchi, ed., *The Origins of Gnosticism: Colloquium of Messina, 13–18 April 1966*, Studies in the History of Religions 12 (Leiden: Brill, 1967), xxvi–xxix. On the difficulty of defining Gnosticism see Karen L. King, *What is Gnosticism?* (Cambridge, MA: Harvard University Press, 2003), 5–19. See also Walter Beltz, "Wie gnostisch sind die Gnostiker (Gewesen)?" in *For the*

Children, Perfect Instruction: Studies in Honor of Hans-Martin Schenke on the Occasion of the Berliner Arbeitskreis für koptisch-gnostische Schriften's Thirtieth Year, ed. Hans-Gebhard Bethge, Stephen Emmel, Karen L. King, and Imke Schletterer, NHMS 54 (Leiden: Brill, 2002), 231–45; Michael Allen Williams, *Rethinking "Gnosticism": An Argument for Dismantling a Dubious Category* (Princeton: Princeton University Press, 1996).

19. Hans Jonas, *Gnosis und spätantiker Geist, Erster Teil: Die mythologische Gnosis: Mit einer Einleitung zur Geschichte und Methodologie der Forschung*, 3d ed., FRLANT 33 (Göttingen: Vandenhoeck & Ruprecht, 1964). A popular version of Jonas's view is presented in his *The Gnostic Religion: The Message of the Alien God and the Beginnings of Christianity*, 2d ed. (Boston: Beacon, 1963). For Jonas's contribution to the Messina meeting see his "Delimitation of the Gnostic Phenomenon—Typological and Historical," in *Origins of Gnosticism*, 90–108.

20. Rudolph, *Gnosis*.

21. Birger A. Pearson, *Gnosticism, Judaism, and Egyptian Christianity*, SAC (Minneapolis: Fortress Press, 1990), 7–9. See Rudolph, *Gnosis*, 53–272. King, *What is Gnosticism*, 191–217, argues that the variety evident in the NHC proves that the effort to present a taxonomy of Gnosticism (including such features as dualism, docetism, asceticism, etc.) is misguided.

22. See Williams, *Rethinking "Gnosticism,"* 241–47; Robinson, "Introduction," *Facsimile Edition*, 71–86; idem, "The Construction of the Nag Hammadi Codices," in *Essays on the Nag Hammadi Texts*, 170–90; Martin Krause, "Zur Bedeutung des gnostisch-hermetischen Handschriftenfundes von Nag Hammadi," ibid., 65–89.

23. See Pearson, "Nag Hammadi Codices," 988–89.

24. See ibid., 989–91; Krause, "Zur Bedeutung des gnostisch-hermetischen Handschriftenfundes," 65–89; idem, "Texte von Nag Hammadi," 238–43; idem, "Der Stand der Veröffentlichung der Nag Hammadi-Texte," in *Origins of Gnosticism: Colloquim of Messina*, 66–88; King, *What is Gnosticism*, 154–68; Doresse, *Secret Books*, 146–309.

25. See John D. Turner, "Sethian Gnosticism: A Literary History," in *Nag Hammadi, Gnosticism, & Early Christianity*, ed. Charles W. Hedrick and Robert Hodgson, Jr. (Peabody, MA: Hendrickson, 1986), 55–86; Michel Tardieu, "Les Livres mis sous le nom de Seth et les Séthiens de l'hérésiologie," in *Gnosis and Gnosticism: Papers read at the Seventh International Conference on Patristic Studies (Oxford, September 8th–13th 1975)*, ed. Martin Krause, NHS 8 (Leiden: Brill, 1977), 204–10; Dart, *Jesus of Heresy*, 75–83.

26. See John D. Turner, "Sethian Gnosticism: A Literary History," in *Nag Hammadi, Gnosticism, & Early Christianity*, 55–86; Michel Tardieu, "Les Livres mis sous le nom de Seth et les Séthiens de l'hérésiologie," in *Gnosis and Gnosticism*, 204–10; Dart, *Jesus of Heresy*, 75–83.

27. *History of Gnosticism*, 116.

28. *Nag Hammadi Library*, 222–43.

29. See the introduction (by Frederik Wisse) and translated text in *Nag Hammadi Library*, 104–23; for more detailed introduction, Coptic text, translation, and notes, see *The Apocryphon of John: Synopsis of Nag Hammadi Codices II,1, III,1, and IV,1 with BG 8502,2*, ed. Michael Waldstein and Frederik Wisse, NHMS 33 (Leiden: Brill, 1995).

30. See Jonas, *Gnostic Religion*, 179–205; Dart, *Jesus of Heresy*, 102–8.

31. See Introduction and English translation by Harold Attridge and George W. MacRae in *Nag Hammadi Library*, 38–51; for more detailed introduction, Coptic text, and notes, see *Nag Hammadi Codex I (The Jung Codex)*, ed. Harold Attridge, 2 vols., NHS 22, 23 (Leiden: Brill, 1985), 1: 55–146, 2: 39–135.

32. See Henry Chadwick, *The Sentences of Sextus: A Contribution to the History of Early Christian Ethics*, Texts and Studies 5 (Cambridge: Cambridge University Press, 1959).

33. The standard edition is *Corpus Hermeticum*, 4 vols., ed. Arthur Darby Nock and André Jean Festugière, Collections des universités de France (Paris: "Les Belles Lettres," 1945, 1954).

34. For various theories see Krause, "Texte von Nag Hammadi," 238–43; Filoramo, *History of Gnosticism*, 18–19; Williams, *Rethinking "Gnosticism,"* 241–47.

35. See Robinson, ed., *Facsimile Edition: Cartonnage*, vi–xxiii; idem, *Nag Hammadi Library in English*, 16–17.

36. For the caves and the monastery see Dart, *Jesus of Heresy*, 15–24, and Van Elderen, "Nag Hammadi Excavation," 225–31.

37. Berliner Arbeitskreis für koptisch-gnostische Schriften, "Die Bedeutung der Texte von Nag Hammadi für die moderne Gnosisforschung," in *Gnosis und Neues Testament: Studien aus Religionswissenschaft und Theologie*, ed. Karl-Wolfgang Tröger (Berlin: Evangelische Verlagsanstalt, 1973), 13–17.

38. See Edwin M. Yamauchi, *Pre-Christian Gnosticism: A Survey of the Proposed Evidence*, 2nd ed. (Grand Rapids: Eerdmans, 1983), 200–201.

39. "Christlich-gnostische Texte als Quellen für die Auseinandersetzung von Gnosis und Christentum," in *Gnosis and Gnosticism: Papers Read at the Eighth International Conference on Patristic Studies (Oxford, September 3rd–8th 1979)*, ed. Martin Krause, NHS 17 (Leiden: Brill, 1981), 46–65.

40. See Rudolph, *Gnosis*, 275–94; Geo Widengren, "Les Origines du Gnosticisme et l'histoire des religions," in *Origins of Gnosticism: Colloquium of Messina*, 28–60; Alexander Böhlig, "Die griechische Schule und die Bibliothek von Nag Hammadi," in *Les Textes de Nag Hammadi: Colloque du Centre d'Histoire des Religions (Strasbourg, 23–25 octobre 1974)*, ed. Jacques-É. Ménard, NHS 7 (Leiden: Brill, 1975), 41–44; Ugo Bianchi, "Le Gnosticisme: Concept, Terminologie, Origines, Délimitation," in *Gnosis: Festschrift für Hans Jonas*, 51–64; idem, "Le Problème des origines du Gnosticisme," in *Origins of Gnosticism: Colloquium of Messina*, 1–27.

41. See Birger A. Pearson, "Jewish Elements in Gnosticism and the Development of Gnostic Self-Definition," in *Gnosticism, Judaism, and Egyptian Christianity*, SAC (Minneapolis: Fortress Press, 1990), 124–35; Alexander Böhlig, "Der jüdische und judenchristliche Hintergrund in gnostischen Texten von Hag Hammadi," in *Origins of Gnosticism: Colloquium of Messina*, 109–40; Pheme Perkins, *Gnosticism and the New Testament* (Minneapolis: Fortress Press, 1993), 9–28; Petr Pokorny, "Der soziale Hintergrund der Gnosis," in *Gnosis und Neues Testament*, ed. Tröger, 77–87; Maddalena Scopello, "Un rituel idéal d'intronisation dans trois textes gnostiques de Nag Hammadi," in *Nag Hammadi and Gnosis: Papers Read at the First International Congress of Coptology (Cairo, December 1976)*, ed. Robert M. Wilson (Leiden: Brill, 1978), 91–95.

42. "Judaism, Judaic Christianity and Gnosis," in *The New Testament and Gnosis: Essays in honour of Robert McL. Wilson*, ed. A. H. B. Logan and A. J. M. Wedderburn (Edinburgh: T & T Clark, 1983), 63.

43. Willem Cornelius van Unnik, "Gnosis und Judentum," in *Gnosis: Festschrift für Hans Jonas*), 65–86; Hans Joachim Schoeps, "Judenchristentum und Gnosis," in *Origins of Gnosticism: Colloquium of Messina*, 528–37. Robert M. Grant ("Les Êtres intermédiaires dans le judaïsme tardif," ibid., 141–57) acknowledges that there are elements of Judaism in Gnosticism, but that Gnosticism is not derived from normative Judaism; in an earlier work, *Gnosticism and Early Christianity* (New York: Columbia University Press, 1959), Grant found the background of Gnosticism in the failure of Jewish apocalyptic.

44. "Nag Hammadi and the New Testament," in *Gnosis: Festschrift für Hans Jonas*, 149; see Doresse, *Secret Books*, 110; Robinson, *Nag Hammadi Library*, 10; Perkins, *Gnosticism*, 29.

45. "Nag Hammadi and the New Testament," *NTS* 28 (1982): 291, 292.

46. *Pre-Christian Gnosticism*, 245; see also Yamauchi's essay, "Pre-Christian Gnosticism, the New Testament and Nag Hammadi in Recent Debate," in *Gnosticism in the Early Church*, ed. David M. Scholer, SEC 5 (New York: Garland, 1993), 26–31.

47. Carsten Colpe, *Die religionsgeschichtliche Schule: Darstellung und Kritik ihres Bildes vom gnostischen Erlösermythus*, FRLANT 78 (Göttingen: Vandenhoeck & Ruprecht, 1961).

48. *Gnosis*, 131. See Filoramo, *History of Gnosticism*, 101–27; Dart, *Jesus of Heresy*, 84–89; Berliner Arbeitskreis, "Bedeutung der Texte von Nag Hammadi," 13–75; Perkins, *Gnosticism*, 93–108.

49. *Rechtgläubigkeit und Ketzerei im ältesten Christentum*, 2d ed. Georg Strecker (Tübingen: Mohr Siebeck, 1964), Eng. trans.: *Orthodoxy and Heresy in Earliest Christianity*, ed. Robert A. Kraft and Gerhard Krodel (Philadelphia: Fortress Press, 1971); see *HNTR* 2: 452–54. For scholars who believe the NHC confirm Bauer's thesis, see King, *What is Gnosticism?* 110–15; Helmut Koester, "Gnomai Diaphoroi: The Origin and Nature of Diversification in the History of Early Christianity," in *Trajectories through Early Christianity*, ed. James M. Robinson and Helmut Koester (Philadelphia: Fortress Press, 1971), 114–19; idem, *Ancient Christian Gospels: Their History and Development* (Philadelphia: Trinity Press International, 1990), xxix–xxxii. For scholars who reject Bauer's view see, e.g., Yamauchi, *Pre-Christian Gnosticism*, 210.

50. See Perkins, *Gnosticism*, 164–76.

51. Some of the texts display a dual understanding of sexual activity: although physical sexual intercourse is opposed, sexual imagery can be used positively, for example, spiritual marriage and entering the bridal chamber can signify oneness with the pleroma or entering the heavenly unity. See Jean-Pierre Mahé, "Les Sens des symboles sexuels dans quelques textes hermétiques et gnostiques," in *Textes de Nag Hammadi: Colloque du Centre d'Histoire des Religions*, 123–45.

52. See Walter Schmithals, "Die gnostischen Elemente als hermeneutisches Problem," in *Gnosis und Neues Testament*, ed. Tröger, 359–81; James M. Robinson, "Gnosticism and the New Testament," in *Gnosis: Festschrift für Hans Jonas*, 125–43; Robert McL. Wilson, "Gnosis, Gnosticism and the New Testament," in *Origins of Gnosticism: Colloquium of Messina*, 511–27; George W. MacRae, "Nag Hammadi and the New Testament," in *Gnosis: Festschrift für Hans Jonas*, 144–57; Perkins, *Gnosticism*, 53–142; Birger A. Pearson, "Philo, Gnosis and the New Testament," in *New Testament and Gnosis: Essays in honour of Robert McL. Wilson*, 73–89 (also published in Pearson, *Gnosticism, Judaism, and Egyptian Christianity*, 165–82).

53. George W. MacRae, "Gnosticism and the Church of John's Gospel," in *Nag Hammadi, Gnosticism, & Early Christianity*, 89–96.

54. See Robert McL. Wilson, "The *Trimorphic Protennoia*," in *Gnosis and Gnosticism: Papers read at the Seventh International Conference (Oxford)*, 50–54; Perkins, *Gnosticism*, 114–17. The theory that a NT author knows and uses a version of a NH tractate is seldom made and difficult to sustain. Instead, most scholars assume that the Christian or Christianized texts of the NHC know some of the canonical books of the NT; see Andrew K. Helmbold, *The Nag Hammadi Gnostic Texts and the Bible* (Grand Rapids: Baker, 1967).

55. Majella Franzmann, *Jesus in the Nag Hammadi Writings* (Edinburgh: T & T Clark, 1996), 207.

56. See Elaine Pagels, *Beyond Belief: The Secret Gospel of Thomas* (New York: Random House, 2003); Dart, *Jesus of Heresy*, 138–52; Jean-Marie Sevrin, "L'Interprétation de l'Évangile selon Thomas: Entre tradition et rédaction," *in Nag Hammadi Library after Fifty Years: Proceedings of the 1995 SBL Commemoration*, 347–60; Jacques-É. Ménard, *L'Évangile selon Thomas*, NHS 5 (Leiden: Brill, 1975).

57. "Introduction," *BA* 42 (1979): 201–2.

58. For critical introduction see Helmut Koester in "Tractate 2: The Gospel According to Thomas," in *Nag Hammadi Codex II, 2-7: Together with XIII, 2, Brit. Lib. Or. 4926(1), and P. Oxy. 1, 654, 655*, ed. Bentley Layton, vol. 1, NHS 20 (Leiden: Brill, 1989), 37–45; Beate Blatz, "The Coptic Gospel of Thomas," in *New Testament Apocrypha*, rev. ed. Wilhelm Schneemelcher, trans. Robert McL. Wilson (Louisville: Westminster John Knox, 1991) 1: 110–14; *Nag Hammadi Library*, 124–26.

59. *The Gospel of Thomas and Jesus*, FF (Sonoma, CA: Polebridge, 1993). Throughout his book Patterson makes frequent reference to Wolfgang Schrage, *Das Verhältnis des Thomas-Evangeliums zur synoptischen Tradition und zu den koptischen Evangelienübersetzungen: Zugleich ein Beitrag zur gnostischen Synoptikerdeutung*, BZNW 29 (Berlin: Töpelmann, 1964), who argues from dependence of Thomas on the Synoptics. More recently the argument for independence has been

advanced by Thomas Zöckler, *Jesu Lehren im Thomasevangelium*, NHMS 47 (Leiden: Brill, 1999).

60. Joahim Jeremias, *Die Gleichnisse Jesu*, 6th ed. (Göttingen: Vandenhoeck & Ruprecht, 1962), Eng. trans.: *The Parables of Jesus*, rev. ed. (New York: Scribner's, 1963).

61. Christopher M. Tuckett, *Nag Hammadi and The Gospel Tradition: Synoptic Tradition in the Nag Hammadi Library*, Studies of the New Testament and Its World, ed. John Riches (Edinburgh: T & T Clark, 1986), 149.

62. Ernst Haenchen, *Die Botschaft des Thomas-Evangeliums* (Berlin: Töpelmann, 1961); Bertil Gärtner, *The Theology of the Gospel according to Thomas*, trans. Eric J. Sharpe (New York: Harper & Brothers, 1961).

63. See Dart, *Jesus of Heresy*, 162–75; Hans-Martin Schenke, *On the Compositional History of the Gospel of Thomas*, OPIAC 40 (Claremont: Claremont Graduate School. 1998), 1–28; Margaretha Lelyveld, *Les Logia de la vie dans l'Évangile selon Thomas: A la recherche d'une tradition et d'une rédaction*, NHS 34 (Leiden: Brill, 1987).

64. Helmut Koester, "Gnomai Diaphoroi," in *Trajectories*, 114–57 (originally published in *HTR* 58 [1965]: 279–318); idem, "One Jesus and Four Primitive Gospels," in *Trajectories*, 158–204; idem, *Ancient Christian Gospels*, 75–171.

65. James M. Robinson, "Logoi Sophon: On the Gattung of Q," in *Trajectories*, 71–113 (originally published in *Zeit und Geschichte: Dankesgabe an Rudolf Bultmann zum 80. Geburtstag*, ed. Erich Dinkler [Tübingen: Mohr Siebeck, 1964], 77–96).

66. "Jesus: From Easter to Valentinus (or to the Apostles' Creed)," *JBL* 101 (1982): 5–37. See James M. Robinson, "On Bridging the Gulf from Q to the Gospel of Thomas (or Vice Versa)," in *Nag Hammadi, Gnosticism, & Early Christianity*, 127–75.

67. *The Gospel of Thomas and Jesus*, 217–41.

68. See HNTR 2:144–51, 238–51; see pp. 426–37 below.

69. The bibliography of the Scrolls is huge. Two excellent introductory surveys are notable: James VanderKam and Peter Flint, *The Meaning of the Dead Sea Scrolls: Their Significance for Understanding the Bible, Judaism, Jesus, and Christianity* (San Francisco: HarperCollins, 2002 [HarperCollins Paperback Edition, 2004]); Philip R. Davies, George J. Brooke, and Phillip R. Callaway, *The Complete World of the Dead Sea Scrolls* (London: Thames & Hudson, 2002). Also useful is Geza Vermes, *An Introduction to the Complete Dead Sea Scrolls* (Minneapolis: Fortress Press, 1999). A detailed and comprehensive critical introduction, including introduction to the discovery of and research on the texts, classification of the Scrolls into various categories, concordances and indices, etc., is presented by Emanuel Tov, ed., *The Texts of the Judaean Desert: Indices and an Introduction*, Discoveries in the Judaean Desert 39 (Oxford: Clarendon, 2002). For extensive bibliographies on the Scrolls, see Joseph A. Fitzmyer, *The Dead Sea Scrolls: Major Publications and Tools for Study*, rev. ed. (Atlanta: Scholars, 1990); Florentino García Martínez and Donald W. Parry, *A Bibliography of the Finds in the Desert of Judah 1970–1995* (Leiden: Brill, 1996); Avital Pinnick, *The Orion Center Bibliography of the Dead Sea Scrolls (1995–2000)*, STDJ 41 (Leiden: Brill, 2001). Periodicals dedicated to the study of the scrolls include *Revue de Qumrán* (Paris: Letouzey et Ané, 1958–); *The Dead Sea Discoveries: A Journal of Current Research on the Scrolls and Related Literature* (Leiden: Brill, 1994–); *The Qumran Chronicle* (Cracow, 1990–).

70. For the archaeology of Qumran see Jodi Magness, *The Archaeology of Qumran and the Dead Sea Scrolls*, SDSSRL (Grand Rapids: Eerdmans, 2002); Vanderkam and Flint, *Meaning of the Dead Sea Scrolls*, 34–54; Davies, Brooke, and Callaway, *Complete World of the Dead Sea Scrolls*, 168–91.

71. See Norman Golb, *Who Wrote the Dead Sea Scrolls? The Search for the Secret of Qumran* (New York: Scribner, 1995). Golb argues that the site was a fortress and that the Scrolls had no relation to the site; they were brought from libraries in Jerusalem and hidden in these caves during the time of the revolt against Rome (66 CE). Although the De Vaux-Magness interpretation of the site has prevailed with most Scroll scholars, there is no unanimity among archaeologists: See Katharina Galor, Jean-Baptiste Humbert, and Jürgen Zangenberg, eds., *Qumran, The Site of the*

Dead Sea Scrolls: Archaeological Interpretations and Debates: Proceedings of a Conference Held at Brown University, November 17–19, 2002, STDJ 57 (Leiden: Brill, 2006); a chapter by Yitzhak Magen and Yuval Peleg, "Back to Qumran: Ten Years of Excavation, 1993–2004" (pp. 55–113) argues that the site was originally a fortress but from 63 BCE to 31 BCE was a center for producing pottery.

72. Besides the sources cited above, see Joseph A. Fitzmyer, *The Dead Sea Scrolls and Christian Origins*, SDSSRL (Grand Rapids: Eerdmans, 2000), 249–60. The question of the nature, history, and identity of the sectarians at Qumran is thoroughly investigated by John J. Collins, *Beyond the Qumran Community: The Sectarian Movement of the Dead Sea Scrolls* (Grand Rapids: Eerdmans, 2010).

73. Some scholars find evidence for an Essene community in Jerusalem; see Bargil Pixner, "Mount Zion, Jesus, and Archaeology," in *Jesus and Archaeology*, ed. James H. Charlesworth (Grand Rapids: Eerdmans, 2006), 309–22.

74. A number of scholars believe the Qumranites were a splinter group or conservative faction of the Essenes. Hartmut Stegemann (*The Library of Qumran: On the Essenes, Qumran, John the Baptist, and Jesus* [Grand Rapids: Eerdmans, 1998], 139–210) argues that the settlement at Qumran was established by a group of Essenes for the purpose of producing texts.

75. As well as the general sources cited above, see Geza Vermes, *The Complete Dead Sea Scrolls in English*, rev. ed. (London: Penguin, 2004), 49–66; idem, *Introduction to the Complete Dead Sea Scrolls*, 127–44.

76. For a summary of this research and an account of technological procedures that have been employed in the analysis of the Scrolls, see VanderKam and Flint, *Meaning of the Dead Sea Scrolls*, 20–33; 55–84.

77. For the history of research see VanderKam and Flint, *Meaning of the Dead Sea Scrolls*, 381–403; George J. Brooke and Lawrence H. Schiffman, "The Past: On the History of Dead Sea Scrolls Research," in *The Dead Sea Scrolls at Fifty: Proceedings of the 1997 SBL Qumran Section Meetings*, ed. Robert A. Kugler and Eileen M. Schuller, SBLEJL 15 (Atlanta: Scholars, 1999), 9–20; Emanuel Tov, "The Publication of the Texts from the Judean Desert: Past, Present, and Future," ibid., 21–27; Adam S. van der Woude, "Fifty Years of Qumran Research," in *The Dead Sea Scrolls after Fifty Years: A Comprehensive Assessment*, ed. Peter W. Flint and James C. VanderKam (Leiden: Brill, 1998) 1: 1–45.

78. Ben Z. Wacholder and Martin Abegg, *A Preliminary Edition of the Unpublished Dead Sea Scrolls* (Washington, DC: Biblical Archaeological Society, 1991).

79. Robert H. Eisenman and James M. Robinson, eds., *Facsimile Edition of the Dead Sea Scrolls*, 2 vols. (New York: Summit, 1991). Baigent and Leigh's earlier *Holy Blood, Holy Grail* (New York: Delacorte, 1982) provided much of the research used by Dan Brown in the popular novel, *The Da Vinci Code* (New York: Doubleday, 2003). The conspiracy theory was also encouraged by Robert H. Eisenman and Michael Wise, eds., *The Dead Sea Scrolls Uncovered: The Complete Translation and Interpretation of 50 Key Documents Withheld for Over 35 Years* (Shaftesbury, Dorset: Element, 1992).

80. Barbara E. Thiering, *Jesus and the Riddle of the Dead Sea Scrolls: Unlocking the Secrets of His Life Story* (San Francisco: HarperSanFrancisco, 1992).

81. For a survey and refutation of theories of this sort see Otto Betz and Rainer Riesner, *Jesus, Qumran and the Vatican: Clarifications* (New York: Crossroad, 1994).

82. Emmanuel Tov, editor in chief *Discoveries in the Judaean Desert*, 39 vols. (Oxford: Clarendon, 1955–2002).

83. Timothy H. Lim and Philip S. Alexander, eds., *The Dead Sea Scrolls: Electronic Reference Library*, vol. 1 (Oxford: Oxford University Press, 1997); Noel B. Reynolds, Donald W. Parry, and E. Jan Wilson for Foundation for Ancient Research and Mormon Studies, *The Dead Sea Scrolls Database (Non-Biblical Texts): The Dead Scrolls: Electronic Reference Library*, vol. 2 (Leiden: Brill, 1999); Martin G. Abegg Jr., ed., *Qumran Sectarian Manuscripts: Qumran Texts with Grammatical Tags* (Altamonte Springs, FL: Oak Tree Software, 2001); Oak Tree has also produced a very useful

"Index of Qumran Manuscripts" that lists the major Qumran texts according to the cave where they were discovered, lists related texts, presents descriptions, language, and date of each text, and contains bibliography.

84. For English translations of the biblical Scrolls see Martin Abegg Jr., Peter Flint, and Eugene Ulrich, eds., *The Dead Sea Scrolls Bible: The Oldest Known Bible, Translated for the First Time into English* (San Francisco: HarperCollins, 1999). For English translations of the non-biblical Scrolls see Geza Vermes, *The Complete Dead Sea Scrolls in English*, rev. ed. (London: Penguin, 2004); Michael O. Wise, Martin Abegg Jr., and Edward Cook, *The Dead Sea Scrolls: A New Translation* (San Francisco: HarperSanFrancisco, 1996); Florentino García Martínez, T*he Dead Sea Scrolls Translated: The Qumran Texts in English*, 2d ed. trans. Wilfred G. E. Watson (Leiden: Brill, 1996); idem and Eibert J. C. Tigchelaar, eds., *The Dead Sea Scrolls: Study Edition*, 2 vols. (Leiden: Brill, 1997, 1998).

85. The first method is used by Davies, Brooke, and Callaway, *Complete World of the Dead Sea Scrolls*, 82–165, and by Martínez and Tigchelaar, *Dead Sea Scrolls: Study Edition*. This method is complicated by the fact that copies of some of the texts have been found in more than one cave. The second is followed by VanderKam and Flint, *Meaning of the Dead Sea Scrolls*, 20938; Vermes, *Complete Dead Sea Scrolls in English*; García Martínez, *Dead Sea Scrolls Translated*.

86. The system for referring to individual scrolls has other refinements. A letter "p" indicates that the scroll is a *pesher* (or commentary) text. Thus, "1QpHab" refers to the *Habakkuk Commentary* found in Cave 1. The letters "ar" indicate that the scroll is written in Aramaic. Thus, "6QApo ar" refers to the *Aramaic Apocalypse* from Cave 6. The letters "pap" before the cave number indicate that the text in written on papyrus. Thus, "pap6Q16" (or "papBen") refers to *Benedictions* written on papyrus and found in Cave 6. Citations within an individual text are indicated by the number of the column and the number of the line. Thus, "11QT 2:5" refers to the fifth line in the second column of the *Temple Scroll*. Different editions and translations employ this system with minor variations; for example, some editions indicate the column number by Roman numerals.

87. See VanderKam and Flint, *Meaning of the Dead Sea Scrolls*, 154–81; James A. Sanders, "The Scrolls and the Canonical Process," in *Dead Sea Scrolls after Fifty Years* 2: 1–23; Shemaryahu Talmon, "The Crystallization of the 'Canon of Hebrew Scriptures' in the Light of Biblical Scrolls from Qumran," in *The Bible as Book: The Hebrew Bible and the Judaean Desert Discoveries*, ed. Edward D. Herbert and Emanuel Tov (London: British Library, 2002), 5–20; Armin Lange, "The Status of the Biblical Texts in the Qumran Corpus and the Canonical Process," ibid., 21–30; Devorah Dimant, "The Scrolls and the Study of Judaism," in *Dead Sea Scrolls at Fifty*, 43–59.

88. Abbeg, Flint, and Ulrich, *Dead Sea Scrolls Bible*.

89. See Peter Flint, "'Apocrypha,' Other Previously Known Writings, and 'Pseudepigrapha' in the Dead Sea Scrolls," *Dead Sea Scrolls after Fifty Years* 2: 24–66; Vermes, *Introduction to the Complete Dead Sea Scrolls*, 63–90.

90. See VanderKam and Flint, *Meaning of the Dead Sea Scrolls*, 87–153; Vermes, *Introduction to the Complete Dead Sea Scrolls*, 170–91; Eugene Ulrich, "The Dead Sea Scrolls and the Biblical Text," in *Dead Sea Scrolls after Fifty Years* 1: 79–100; idem, "The Scrolls and the Study of the Hebrew Bible," in *Dead Sea Scrolls at Fifty*, 31–41; Arie van der Kooij, "The Textual Criticism of the Hebrew Bible Before and After the Qumran Discoveries," in *The Bible as Book*, 167–77.

91. See Leonard J. Greenspoon, "The Dead Sea Scrolls and the Greek Bible," in *Dead Sea Scrolls after Fifty Years* 1: 101–27.

92. See Stephen C. Daley, "Textual Influence of the Qumran Scrolls on English Bible Versions," *The Bible as Book*, 253–87.

93. See VanderKam and Flint, *Meaning of the Dead Sea Scrolls*, 275–92; Davies, Brooke, and Callaway, *Complete World of the Dead Sea Scrolls*, 194–99; Dimant, "Scrolls and the Study of Judaism," 43–59.

94. See VanderKam and Flint, *Meaning of the Dead Sea Scrolls*, 255–74; Vermes, *Complete Dead Sea Scrolls in English*, 67–90; Stegemann, *Library of Qumran*, 201–10.

95. John J. Collins, *Apocalypticism in the Dead Sea Scrolls*, Literature of the Dead Sea Scrolls (London: Routledge, 1997); idem, "Apocalypticism and Literary Genre in the Dead Sea Scrolls," in *The Dead Sea Scrolls after Fifty Years*, 2: 403–30.

96. See John J. Collins, *The Scepter and the Star: Messianism in Light of the Dead Sea Scrolls*, 2d ed. (Grand Rapids: Eerdmans, 2010); idem, "The Nature of Messianism in the Light of the Dead Sea Scrolls," in *Dead Sea Scrolls in Their Historical Context*, 199–217; Michael A. Knibb, "Eschatology and Messianism in the Dead Sea Scrolls," in *The Dead Sea Scrolls after Fifty Years*, 2: 379–402; Fitzmyer, *Dead Sea Scrolls and Christian Origins*, 73–109; Florentino García Martínez, "Two Messianic Figures in the Qumran Texts," in *Current Research and Technological Developments on the Dead Sea Scrolls: Conference on the Texts from the Judean Desert, Jerusalem, 30 April 1995*, ed. Donald W. Parry and Stephen D. Ricks, STDJ (Leiden, Brill, 1996), 14–40; Craig A. Evans, "The Messiah in the Dead Sea Scrolls," in *Israel's Messiah in the Bible and the Dead Sea Scrolls*, ed. Richard S. Hess and M. Daniel Carroll R. (Grand Rapids: Baker Academic, 2003), 85–101; A. S. van der Woude, "Le Maître de justice et les deux Messies de la Communauté de Qumrân," in *La Secte de Qumrân et les origines du Christianisme*, ed. J. P. M. van der Ploeg, et al. (Paris: Desclée De Brouwer, 1959), 121–34.

97. The meaning of the crucial text concerning the two messiahs and the eschatological prophet (1QS 9:10-11) is debated. Some scholars believe the prophet is to be identified with the Messiah of Aaron.

98. The bibliography on the DSS and the NT is extensive; among the more important works see George J. Brooke, *The Dead Sea Scrolls and the New Testament* (Minneapolis: Fortress Press, 2005); idem, "The Scrolls and the Study of the New Testament," in *Dead Sea Scrolls at Fifty*, 61–78; Neil S. Fujita, *A Crack in the Jar: What Ancient Jewish Documents Tell Us About the New Testament* (New York: Paulist Press, 1986); VanderKam and Flint, *Meaning of the Dead Sea Scrolls*, 311–20; Vermes, *Introduction to the Complete Dead Sea Scrolls*, 182–91; idem, *Complete Dead Sea Scrolls in English*, 21–23; Fitzmyer, *Dead Sea Scrolls and Christian Origins*; Jerome Murphy-O'Connor, "Qumran and the New Testament," in *The New Testament and Its Modern Interpreters*, ed. Eldon Jay Epp and George W. MacRae, SBLBMI 3 (Atlanta: Scholars, 1989), 55–71; Pierre Benoit, "Qumran and the New Testament," in *Paul and the Dead Sea Scrolls*, ed. Jerome Murphy O'Connor and James H. Charlesworth (New York: Crossroad, 1990), 1–30; Herbert Braun, *Qumran und das Neue Testament*, 2 vols. (Tübingen: Mohr Siebeck, 1966); Lucien Cerfaux, "Influence de Qumrân sur le Nouveau Testament," in *La Secte de Qumrân*, 233–44; Krister Stendahl and James H. Charlesworth, eds., *The Scrolls and the New Testament* (New York: Crossroad, 1992; first published 1957); John J. Collins and Craig A. Evans, eds. *Christian Beginnings and the Dead Sea Scrolls*, ASBT (Grand Rapids: Baker Academic, 2006).

99. The claim of José O'Callaghan that Cave 7 contained fragments from the NT rests on meager evidence and has been rejected by a host of scholars; see José O'Callaghan and Carlo María Martini, *New Testament Papyri in Qumrân Cave 7?* Trans. William L. Holladay, JBLSup 91 (Philadelphia: Society of Biblical Literature, 1972), including O'Callaghan's "New Testament Papyri in Qumrân Cave 7?" 1–14, and Carsten P. Thiede, "7Q: eine Rückkehr zu den neutestamentlichen Papyrusfragmenten in der siebten Höhle von Qumran," *Biblica* 65 (1984): 538–59.

100. On the relation of John the Baptist to the Scrolls see Stegemann, *Library of Qumran*, 211–27; Braun, *Qumran und das Neue Testament*, 2: 1-19.

101. VanderKam and Flint, *Meaning of the Dead Sea Scrolls*, 330–45; Brooke, *Dead Sea Scrolls and the NT*, 19–26; Braun, *Qumran und das Neue Testament*, 2: 54–74; 85–118; Stegemann, *Library of Qumran*, 228–57; Craig A. Evans, "Jesus and the Dead Sea Scrolls," in *The Dead Sea Scrolls after Fifty Years*, 2: 573–98; James H. Charlesworth, "The Dead Sea Scrolls and the

Historical Jesus," in *Jesus and the Dead Sea Scrolls*, ed. idem, ABRL (New York: Doubleday, 1992), 1–74.

102. The figure in the Aramaic Apocalypse is variously identified as an earthly king, an angel, the anti-Christ, or a collective being.

103. See *HNTR* 2: 238–53; pp. 87–116 above.

104. See Richard Bauckham, "The Early Jerusalem Church, Qumran, and the Essenes," in *The Dead Sea Scrolls as Background to Postbiblical Judaism and Early Christianity: Papers from an International Conference at St. Andrews in 2001*, ed. James R. Davila, STDJ 46 (Leiden: Brill, 2003), 63–89; Stegemann, *Library of Qumran*, 258–64; Braun, *Qumran und das NT*, 2: 144–65; Otto Betz, "Le Ministère cultuel dans la secte de Qumrân et das le Christianisme primitif," in *Secte de Qumrân*, 163–202; Joseph Schmitt, "L'Organisation de l'église primitive et Qumrân," ibid., 217–31.

105. See Timothy H. Lim, "Studying the Qumran Scrolls and Paul in Their Historical Context," in *The Dead Sea Scrolls as Background to Postbiblical Judaism*, 135–56; Joseph A. Fitzmyer, "Paul and the Dead Sea Scrolls," in *The Dead Sea Scrolls after Fifty Years*, 2: 599–621; James H. Charlesworth, "Foreword," in *Paul and the Dead Sea Scrolls*, ix–xvi; Braun, *Qumran und das NT*, 2: 165–80.

106. See Walter Grundmann, "The Teacher of Righteousness of Qumran and the Question of Justification by Faith in the Theology of the Apostle Paul," in *Paul and the Dead Sea Scrolls*, 85–114.

107. 1QS 11:10-12.

108. See Joachim Gnilka, "2 Cor 6:14–7:1 in the Light of the Qumran Texts and the Testaments of the Twelve Patriarchs," in *Paul and the Dead Sea Scrolls*, 48–68.

109. See Joseph A. Fitzmyer, "Paul and the Dead Sea Scrolls," in *The Dead Sea Scrolls after Fifty Years*, 2: 599–621.

110. See Karl Georg Kuhn, "The Epistle to the Ephesians in the Light of the Qumran Texts," in *Paul and the Dead Sea Scrolls*, 115–31; Franz Mussner, "Contributions Made by Qumran to the Understanding of the Epistle to the Ephesians," ibid., 159–78.

111. See James L. Price, "Light from Qumran upon Some Aspects of Johannine Theology," in *John and the Dead Sea Scrolls*, ed. James H. Charlesworth (New York: Crossroad, 1990), 9–37; Gilles Quispel, "Qumran, John and Jewish Christianity," ibid., 137–55; Braun, *Qumran und das Neue Testament*, 2: 118–44.

112. See ibid., 2: 181–84.

113. See VanderKam and Flint, *Meaning of the Dead Sea Scrolls*, 362–78; David Aune, "Qumran and the Book of Revelation," in *The Dead Sea Scrolls after Fifty Years*, 2: 622–48.

114. Leslie J. Hoppe, *What Are They Saying About Biblical Archaeology?* (New York: Paulist Press, 1984), 8. For surveys and history of NT archaeology see E. M. Blaiklock, *The Archaeology of the New Testament* (Grand Rapids: Zondervan, 1970); Merrill F. Unger, *Archaeology and the New Testament* (Grand Rapids: Zondervan, 1962).

115. See Colin Renfrew and Paul Bahn, *Archaeology: Theories, Methods and Practice*, 3rd ed. (London: Thames and Hudson, 2000).

116. See Hoppe, *Biblical Archaeology*, 13–33; John McRay, "The Bible and Archaeology," in *Discovering the Bible: Archaeologists Look at Scripture*, ed. Tim Dowley (Grand Rapids: Eerdmans, 1986), 7–26; John R. Bartlett, "What Has Archaeology To Do with the Bible—or Vice Versa?" in *Archaeology and Biblical Interpretation*, ed. John R. Bartlett (London: Routledge, 1997), 1–19; John S. Holladay, Jr., "Method and Theory in Syro-Palestinian Archaeology," in *Near Eastern Archaeology: A Reader*, ed. Suzanne Richard (Winona Lake: Eisenbrauns, 2003), 3347.

117. Some archaeologists prefer the "Open Area" method that excavates larger areas, not using balks but making vertical cuts into the strata. In deep excavations the vertical cuts or trenches are sometimes made in large steps. In all these procedures the primary concern is with the analysis of stratification. See Renfrew and Bahn, *Archaeology*, 107–10.

118. See McRay, "Bible and Archaeology," 7–26; Renfrew and Bahn, *Archaeology*, 117–70; Hoppe, *Biblical Archaeology*; Thomas E. Levy, ed., *New Approaches in Anthropological Archaeology* (London: Leicester University Press, 1998); Edward B. Banning, "Computer Applications in Archaeology," in *Near Eastern Archaeology: A Reader*, ed. Suzanne Richard (Winona Lake: Eisenbrauns, 2003), 225–30; J. E. Doran, *Mathematics and Computers in Archaeology* (Cambridge, MA: Harvard University Press, 1975).

119. See Thomas R. W. Longstaff and Tristram C. Hussey, "Palynology and Cultural Process: An Exercise in the New Archaeology," in *Archaeology and the Galilee: Texts and Contexts in the Graeco-Roman and Byzantine Periods*, ed. Douglas R. Edwards and C. Thomas McCollough, SFSHJ 143 (Atlanta: Scholars, 1987), 151–62; Renfrew and Bahn, *Archaeology*, 38–43, 471–73, 483–96.

120. See Blaiklock, *Archaeology*; Unger, *Archaeology*; James L. Kelso, *An Archaeologist Looks at the Gospels* (Waco, TX: Word, 1969).

121. See Urban C. von Wahlde, "Archaeology and John's Gospel," in *Jesus and Archaeology*, ed. James H. Charlesworth (Grand Rapids: Eerdmans 2006). 523–86; Paul N. Anderson, "Aspects of Historicity in the Gospel of John: Implications of Jesus and Archaeology," ibid., 587–618.

122. See Jack Finegan, *The Archaeology of the New Testament: The Life of Jesus and the Beginning of the Early Church*, rev. ed. (Princeton: Princeton University Press, 1992); idem, *The Archaeology of the New Testament: The Mediterranean World of the Early Christian Apostles* (Boulder, CO: Westview, 1981); Roland K. Harrison, *Archaeology of the New Testament* (New York: Association, 1964); John McRay, *Archaeology and the New Testament* (Grand Rapids: Baker Academic, 1991); Hans Bardtke, *Bibel, Spaten und Geschichte* (Göttingen: Vandenhoeck & Ruprecht, 1967); LaMoine F. DeVries, *Cities of the Biblical World* (Peabody, MA: Hendrickson, 1997).

123. See Finegan, *Archaeology: Jesus*, 22–42; DeVries, *Cities*, 249–54, Blaiklock, *Archaeology of the New Testament*, 25–32; Bardtke, *Bibel*, 274–77.

124. See Finegan, *Archaeology: Jesus*, 183–287; W. Harold Mare, *The Archaeology of the Jerusalem Area* (Grand Rapids: Baker, 1987); John Wilkinson, *Jerusalem as Jesus Knew It* (London: Thames and Hudson, 1978); Bardtke, *Bibel*, 250–74; DeVries, *Cities*, 288–98.

125. *HNTR* 2:28-31.

126. As well as the sources cited in nn. 114 and 116 above, see also John Wilson, "Archaeology and the New Testament," in *Discovering the Bible*, ed. Dowley, 128–40.

127. See Finegan, *Archaeology: Jesus*, 76–116; Unger, *Archaeology and the New Testament*, 118–46; Wilson, "Archaeology and the New Testament," 67–140.

128. See Finegan, *Archaeology: Jesus*, 43–65; Bardtke, *Bibel*, 277–78.

129. See Finegan, *Archaeology: Jesus*, 97–111; Hoppe, *Biblical Archaeology*, 58–78; DeVries, *Cities*, 269–75; Cilliers Breytenbach, "Mark and Galilee: The Text World and Historical World," in *Galilee through the Centuries: Confluence of Cultures*, ed. Eric M. Meyers, DJS 1 (Winona Lake: Eisenbrauns, 1999), 75–85.

130. See Finegan, *Archaeology: Jesus*, 128–44; idem, *Archaeology: Mediterranean*, 184–91; DeVries, *Cities*, 255–68; Bardtke, *Bibel*, 312–25. For the history of the ancient city see Lee I. Levine, *Caesarea Under Roman Rule*, SJLA 7 (Leiden: Brill, 1975). For recent archaeological work see Kenneth G. Holum, Robert L. Hohlfelder, Robert J. Bull, and Avner Raban, *King Herod's Dream: Caesarea on the Sea* (New York: Norton, 1988); Lee I. Levine and Ehud Netzer, *Excavations at Caesarea Maritima: 1975, 1976, 1979—Final Report*, Qedem: Monographs of the Institute of Archaeology, the Hebrew University of Jerusalem 21 (Jerusalem: Hamakor, 1986).

131. See Craig A. Evans, "Excavating Caiaphas, Pilate, and Simon of Cyrene: Assessing the Literary and Archaeological Evidence," in *Jesus and Archaeology*, 323–40.

132. See Finegan, *Archaeology: Mediterranean*; Edwin M. Yamauchi, *The Archaeology of New Testament Cities in Western Asia Minor* (Grand Rapids: Baker, 1980); Winfried Elliger, *Paulus in Griechenland: Philippi, Thessaloniki, Athen, Korinth*, StBS 92/93 (Stuttgart: Katholisches Bibelwerk,

1978); Blaiklock, *Archaeology and the New Testament*, 99–178; DeVries, *Cities*, 333–36; Unger, *Archaeology and the New Testament*, 181–323.

133. See Finegan, *Archaeology: Mediterranean*, 63–71; DeVries, *Cities*, 345–50; Unger, *Archaeology and the New Testament*, 170–80. For the major report of the archaeological research see George W. Elderkin and Richard Stillwell, eds., *Antioch-on-the-Orontes*, Publications of the Committee for the Excavation of Antioch and Its Vicinity, 3 vols. (Princeton: Princeton University Press, 1934–41); for a summary of the history and archaeological results see Glanville Downey, *Ancient Antioch* (Princeton: Princeton University Press, 1963).

134. See Doro Levi, *Antioch Mosaic Pavements*, 2 vols. (Princeton: Princeton University Press, 1947); Downey, *Ancient Antioch*, 200–16.

135. See Finegan, *Archaeology: Mediterranean*, 155–70; Unger, *Archaeology and the New Testament*, 248–63; DeVries, *Cities*, 372–79; Yamauchi, *Archaeology of New Testament Cities*, 79–114. For an account of the history and results of the excavations (especially the work of the Austrian Archaeological Institute), see Wilhelm Alzinger, *Die Stadt des siebenten Weltwunders: Die Wiederentdeckung von Ephesus* (Vienna: Wollzeilen, 1962); for a survey of major finds from the Roman and early Christian period see Franz Miltner, *Ephesos: Stadt der Artemis und des Johannes* (Vienna: Franz Deuticke, 1958).

136. See Jerome Murphy–O'Connor, *St. Paul's Corinth: Texts and Archaeology*, 3rd ed. (Collegeville, MN: Liturgical Press, 2002); Henry S. Robinson, *The Urban Development of Ancient Corinth* (Athens: American School of Classical Studies, 1965); James Wiseman, *The Land of the Ancient Corinthians*, Studies in Mediterranean Archaeology 50 (Göteborg: Paul Aström, 1978); Finegan, *Archaeology: Mediterranean*, 142–52; Elliger, *Paulus in Griechenland*, 200–51; Bardtke, *Bibel*, 324–25. Major archaeological work at Corinth has been undertaken since 1896 by the American School of Classical Studies at Athens. Reports of the excavations are published in a series of volumes, *Corinth: Results of Excavations by the American School of Classical Studies at Athens* (published by Harvard University Press and the American School of Classical Studies). A one-volume summary of the results, Charles K. Williams II and Nancy Bookidis, eds., *Corinth: Centenary, 1896–1996* (Princeton: American School of Classical Studies at Athens, 2003), is vol. 20 in the series. See also Timothy E. Gregory, ed., *The Corinthia in the Roman Period*, JRASup 8 (Ann Arbor, MI: Cushing-Malloy, 1993).

137. See Erich Dinkler, "Das Bema zu Korinth: Archäologische, lexikographische, und ikonographische Bemerkungen zu Apostelgeschichte 18,12-17," in *Signum Crucis: Aufsätze zum Neuen Testament und zur Christlichen Archäologie* (Tübingen: Mohr [Siebeck], 1967), 118–33.

138. See Finegan, *Archaeology: Mediterranean*, 22–36; 217–34; DeVries, *Cities*, 380–85; Bardtke, *Bibel*, 325–29; Unger, *Archaeology and the New Testament*, 297–323.

139. See Douglas R. Edwards and C. Thomas McCollough, "Archaeology and the Galilee: An Introduction," in *Archaeology and the Galilee*, 1–6; Sean Freyne, *Galilee and Gospel: Collected Essays*, WUNT 125 (Tübingen: Mohr Siebeck, 2000); idem, "Galilee and Judea: The Social World of Jesus," in *The Face of New Testament Studies: A Survey of Recent Research*, ed. Scot McKnight and Grant R. Osborne (Grand Rapids: Baker Academic, 2004), 21–35; Carsten Claussen and Jörg Frey, eds., *Jesus und die Archäologie Galiläas*, Biblisch–Theologische Studien 87 (Neukirchen-Vluyn: Neukirchener Verlag, 2008).

140. See Eric M. Meyers, "Sepphoris in Light of New Archaeological Evidence and Recent Research," in *The Galilee in Late Antiquity*, ed. Lee I. Levine (New York: Jewish Theological Seminary of America, 1992), 321–38; Jonathan L. Reed, *Archaeology and the Galilean Jesus: A Re-examination of the Evidence* (Harrisburg, PA: Trinity Press International, 2000), 100–38.

141. The identification of the pools has been contested; see Hanan Eshel, "A Note on 'Miqvaot' at Sepphoris," in *Archaeology and the Galilee*, 131–33.

142. 1Eric M. Meyers, "Sepphoris on the Eve of the Great Revolt (67–68 C.E.): Archaeology and Josephus," in *Galilee through the Centuries*, 109–22.

143. See James F. Strange, "Six Campaigns at Sepphoris: The University of South Florida Excavations, 1983–1989," in *Galilee in Late Antiquity*, 339–55.

144. See James F. Strange, "First Century Galilee from Archaeology and from the Texts," in *Archaeology and the Galilee*, 39–48; Douglas Edwards, "The Socio–Economic and Cultural Ethos of the Lower Galilee in the First Century: Implications for the Nascent Jesus Movement," in *Galilee in Late Antiquity*, 53–73; Freyne, *Galilee, Jesus and the Gospels: Literary Approaches and Historical Investigations* (Philadelphia: Fortress Press, 1988); Peter Richardson, "Khirbet Qana (and Other Villages) as Context for Jesus," in *Jesus and Archaeology*, 120–44.

145. Some scholars believe the relation of cities to villages was not reciprocal but confrontational. Richard A. Horsley, *Archaeology, History, and Society in Galilee: The Social Context of Jesus and the Rabbis* (Valley Forge, PA: Trinity Press International, 1996), 66–130, argues that Galilee in the first century had not a market economy but a tributary economy: people paid tribute to the Temple and taxes to the Herods. The villagers and rural people opposed the urban elite and resisted Roman oppression. Hayim Lapin, *Economy, Geography, and Provincial History in Later Roman Palestine*, Texts and Studies in Ancient Judaism 85 (Tübingen: Mohr Siebeck, 2001) contends that the market economy that developed in the later period had its beginnings in the first century.

146. See Cynthia M. Baker, "Imagined Households," in *Religion and Society in Roman Palestine: Old Questions, New Approaches*, ed. Douglas R. Edwards (New York: Routledge, 2004), 113–28; Marianne Sawicki, "Spatial Management of Gender and Labor in Greco–Roman Galilee," in *Archaeology and the Galilee*, 7–28; Miriam Peskowitz, "Gender, Difference, and Everyday Life: The Case of Weaving and Its Tools," in *Religion and Society in Roman Palestine*, ed. Edwards, 129–45.

147. Miriam Peskowitz, "Gender, Difference, and Everyday Life: The Case of Weaving and Its Tools," in *Religion and Society in Roman Palestine*, 129–45.

148. See James D. Anderson, "The Impact of Rome on the Periphery: The Case of Palestina—Roman Period (63 BCE–324 CE)," in *The Archaeology of Society in the Holy Land*, ed. Thomas E. Levy, New Approaches in Anthropological Archaeology (London: Leicester University Press, 1998), 446–68; Reed, *Archaeology and the Galilean Jesus*, 62–99.

149. See Mark A. Chancey, "City Coins and Roman Power in Palestine: From Pompey to the Great Revolt," in *Religion and Society in Roman Palestine*, 103–12.

150. See Uriel Rappaport, "How Anti–Roman Was the Galilee?" in *Galilee in Late Antiquity*, 95–102

151. See Reed, *Archaeology and the Galilean Jesus*; Mark A. Chancey, *The Myth of a Gentile Galilee*, SNTSMS 118 (Cambridge: Cambridge University Press, 2002); Mordechai Aiam, "First Century Jewish Galilee: An Archaeological Perspective," in *Religion and Society in Roman Palestine*, 7–27; Sean Freyne, "Town and Country Once More: The Case of Roman Galilee," in *Archaeology and the Galilee*, 49–56; idem, *Jesus, a Jewish Galilean: A New Reading of the Jesus Story* (London: T & T Clark, 2004).

152. See Richard A. Horsley, *Archaeology, History, and Society in Galilee*, 15–42. This view is countered by Reed, *Archaeology and the Galilean Jesus*, 223–61.

153. See Lee I. Levine, "The First Century Synagogue: Critical Reassessments and Assessments of the Critical," in *Religion and Society in Roman Palestine*, 70–102; Gideon Foerster, "The Ancient Synagogues in the Galilee," in *Galilee in Late Antiquity*, 289–319; Steven Fine, "Synagogues in the Land of Israel," in *Near Eastern Archaeology: A Reader*, 455–64; James D. G. Dunn, "Did Jesus Attend the Synagogue?" in *Jesus and Archaeology*, 206–22.

154. See John S. Kloppenborg, "The Theodotos Synagogue Inscription and the Problem of First–Century Synagogue Buildings," in *Jesus and Archaeology*, 236–82; Zvi 'Uri Ma'oz, "Golan Synagogues," in *Near Eastern Archaeology: A Reader*, 265–72.

155. Esther Eshel and Douglas R. Edwards, "Language and Writing in Early Roman Galilee: Social Location of a Potter's Abecedary from Khirbet Qana," in *Religion and Society in Roman Palestine*, 49–55.

156. Mark A. Chancey, *Greco-Roman Culture and the Galilee of Jesus*, SNTSMS 134 (Cambridge: Cambridge University Press, 2005), 122–65.

157. See James H. Charlesworth, "Jesus Research and Archaeology: A New Perspective," in *Jesus and Archaeology*, 11–63; Reed, *Archaeology and the Galilean Jesus*; Freyne, *Jesus and the Gospels*, 219–68; idem, "Archaeology and the Historical Jesus," in *Galilee and Gospel*, 160–82; idem, *Jesus, a Jewish Galilean*; idem, "Archaeology and the Historical Jesus," in *Jesus and Archaeology*, 64–83; Eric M. Meyers, "Jesus and His Galilean Context," in *Archaeology and the Galilee*, 57–66; J. Andrew Overman, "Jesus of Galilee and the Historical Peasant," in *Archaeology and the Galilee*, 67–73.

158. Richard Horsley, "Jesus and Galilee: The Contingencies of a Renewal Movement," in *Galilee through the Centuries*, 57–74, opposes the idea that Jesus was a Cynic wisdom teacher wandering in a Hellenized Galilee, but he sees Jesus as the leader of a movement of renewal and resistance to Roman domination—a movement of peasants and lower-class rural people that was anti–urban. Eric Meyers, "Jesus and His Galilean Context," 57–66, also rejects the notion that Cynic philosophy was at home in Galilee, but he opposes the idea of conflict between village and city in first-century Galilee. See also Chancey, *Greco-Roman Culture and the Galilee of Jesus*, SNTSMS 134 (Cambridge: Cambridge University Press, 2005), 24–70. In regard to the view of Jesus as wandering Hellenistic wisdom teacher, see pp. 429–31 below.

159. *Archaeology and the Galilean Jesus*, 170–96. For twentieth-century research on the Q document, see pp. 355–58 below.

160. "Mark and Galilee: The Text World and Historical World," in *Galilee through the Centuries*, 75–85.

161. Richard A. Batey, *Jesus and the Forgotten City: New Light on Sepphoris and the Urban World of Jesus* (Grand Rapids: Baker, 1991).

162. *HNTR* 2: 322.

163. Some archaeologists believe the theater at Sepphoris was not built until the end of the first century or later. Batey defends the earlier date in a more recent publication, "Did Antipas Build the Sepphoris Theater?" in *Jesus and Archaeology*, 111–19.

164. John Dominic Crossan and Jonathan L. Reed, *Excavating Jesus: Beneath the Stones, Behind the Texts*, rev. ed. (San Francisco: Harper, 2001).

165. Ibid., 52.

166. Ibid., 220.

167. Downey, *Ancient Antioch*, 120–216.

168. *Jews and Christians in Antioch in the First Four Centuries of the Common Era*, SBLSBS 13 (Missoula: Scholars, 1978).

169. Magnus Zetterholm, *The Formation of Christianity in Antioch: A Social–Scientific Approach to the Separation between Judaism and Christianity* (London: Routledge, 2003).

170. See John H. W. G. Liebeschuetz, *Antioch: City and Imperial Administration in the Later Roman Empire* (Oxford: Clarendon, 1972).

171. *Ephesos: Metropolis of Asia: An Interdisciplinary Approach to Its Archaeology, Religion, and Culture*, ed. Helmut Koester, HTS 41 (Valley Forge, PA: Trinity Press International, 1995). For additional research on Ephesus see Jerome Murphy–O'Connor, *St. Paul's Ephesus: Texts and Archaeology* (Collegeville, MN: Liturgical Press, 2008); Paul R. Trebilco, *The Early Christians in Ephesus from Paul to Ignatius*, WUNT 166 (Tübingen: Mohr Siebeck, 2004).

172. Ibid., 27–79.

173. Ibid., 229–50.

174. Ibid., 250.

175. "Roman Corinth as a Commercial Center," in *The Corinthia in the Roman Period*, 31–46.

176. Jerome Murphy-O'Connor, *St. Paul's Corinth: Texts and Archaeology,* 3rd ed. (Collegeville, MN: Liturgical, 2002).

177. Ibid., 178–85.

178. Ibid., 186–91.

179. Ibid., 192–98.

180. *A New Temple for Corinth: Rhetorical and Archaeological Approaches to Pauline Imagery* (New York: Peter Lang, 1997).

181. Ibid., 134.

182. The papers from the symposium are collected in Charalambos Bakirtzis and Helmut Koester, eds., *Philippi at the Time of Paul and after His Death* (Harrisburg, PA: Trinity Press International, 1998).

183. Ibid., 5–35.

184. "Dead Paul: The Apostle as Martyr in Philippi," ibid., 67–84.

185. Lukas Bormann, *Philippi: Stadt und Christengemeinde zur Zeit des Paulus*, NovTSup 78 (Leiden: Brill, 1995).

186. Peter Pilhofer, *Philippi I: Die erste christliche Gemeinde Europas*, WUNT 87 (Tübingen: Mohr Siebeck, 1995).

187. Pilhofer's second volume of over 800 pages, *Philippi II: Katalog der Inschriften von Philippi*, WUNT 119 (Tübingen: Mohr Siebeck, 2000), presents transcriptions, translations, and critical notes on virtually all the inscriptions found at Philippi and the surrounding area.

188. Similar research has been done for Thessalonica. See Laura Nasrallah, Charalambos Bakirtzis, and Steven J. Friesen, eds., *From Roman to Early Christian Thessalonikē: Studies in Religion and Archaeology*, HTS 64 (Cambridge, MA: Harvard University Press, 2010).

189. *Sisters Rejoice: Paul's Letter to the Philippians and Luke-Acts as Received by First-Century Philippian Women*, ConBNT 20 (Stockholm: Almqvist & Wiksell, 1988).

190. *Women and Worship at Philippi: Diana/Artemis and Other Cults in the Early Christian Era* (Portland, ME: Astarte Shell, 1995).

191. *Die stadtrömischen Christen in den ersten beiden Jahrhunderten: Untersuchungen zur Sozialgeschichte*, WUNT 2d ser. 18 (Tübingen: Mohr Siebeck, 1987); Eng trans: *From Paul to Valentinus: Christians at Rome in the First Two Centuries*, trans. Michael Steinhauser, ed. Marshall D. Johnson (Minneapolis: Fortress Press, 2003), 411.

192. *Ante Pacem: Archaeological Evidence of Church Life Before Constantine* (Macon, GA: Mercer University Press, 1985).

193. Ibid., 169.

194. *Eldon Jay Epp, Perspectives on New Testament Textual Criticism: Collected Essays, 1962–2004* (Leiden: Brill, 2004), xxxv, 468–69.

195. *HNTR* 1: 25–29, 72–74, 103–7, 141–43, 321–22, 323–28, 331–32; *HNTR* 2: 62–65, 109–11, 338, 407–9, 292, 398–401, 402–6, 410–11.

196. See F. Thomas Trotter, *Jesus and the Historian: Written in Honor of Ernest Cadman Colwell* (Philadelphia: Westminster, 1968), 11–19.

197. Bruce Manning Metzger, *Reminiscences of an Octogenarian* (Peabody, MA: Hendrickson, 1997).

198. See "Introduction: A Half-Century Adventure with New Testament Textual Criticism," in Eldon Jay Epp, *Perspectives on New Testament Textual Criticism: Collected Essays, 1962–2004* (Leiden: Brill, 2004), xxvii–xl; "Introduction to the 'Presidential Address,'" by D. L. Petersen, ibid., 741–42.

199. See "Biographical Notes and Bibliography," in *Studies in New Testament Language and Text: Essays in Honour of George D. Kilpatrick*, ed. James Keith Elliott (Leiden: Brill, 1976), 1–13.

200. Among the standard works: Kurt Aland and Barbara Aland, *The Text of the New Testament: An Introduction to the Critical Editions and to the Theory and Practice of Modern Textual Criticism*, trans. Erroll F. Rhodes, 2d. rev. and enl. ed. (Grand Rapids: Eerdmans, 1989); Bruce M.

Metzger and Bart D. Ehrman, *The Text of the New Testament: Its Transmission, Corruption, and Restoration*, 4th ed. (New York: Oxford University Press, 2005); Leon Vaganay, *An Introduction to New Testament Textual Criticism*, 2d rev. ed. Christian-Bernard Amphoux, trans. Jenny Heimerdinger (Cambridge: Cambridge University Press, 1991). An older standard work that is still useful is Heinrich Joseph Vogels, *Handbuch der Kritik des Neuen Testaments*, 2d ed. (Bonn: Peter Hanstein, 1955). For an engaging introduction to the discipline, see Robert F. Hull, Jr., *The Story of the New Testament Text: Movers, Motives, Materials, Methods, and Models*, SBLRBS 58 (Atlanta: SBL, 2010).

201. This is especially well done by Meztger and Ehrman, *Text of the New Testament*, 3–51. See also Bruce M. Metzger, *Manuscripts of the Greek Bible: An Introduction to Greek Palaeography* (New York: Oxford University Press, 1981).

202. *Text of the New Testament*, 72–184.

203. For an extensive list and description of the Greek texts see Kurt Aland, *Kurzgefasste Liste der griechischen Handschriften des Neuen Testaments*, 2d rev. ed., ANTF 1 (Berlin: de Gruyter, 1994). For a complete list of papyri known at the time of publication see idem, *Repertorium der griechischen christlichen Papyri I: Biblische Papyri: Altes Testament, Neues Testament, Varia, Apokryphen*, PTS 8 (Berlin: de Gruyter, 1976).

204. Bruce M. Metzger, *The Early Versions of the New Testament: Their Origin, Transmission, and Limitations* (Oxford: Clarendon, 1977).

205. See Vaganay, *Introduction*, 52–88; Epp, "Textual Criticism (NT)," *ABD* 6: 431–33; Heinrich Zimmermann, *Neutestamentliche Methodenlehre: Darstellung der historisch-kritischen Methode* (Stuttgart: Katholisches Bibelwerk, 1967), 37–53; Jean Duplacy, *Où en est la critique textuelle du Nouveau Testament?* (Paris: Gabalda, 1959), 26–39.

206. Reprinted in Epp, *Perspectives*, 59–100.

207. Ibid., 98.

208. Kurt Aland, "The Twentieth-Century Interlude in New Testament Textual Criticism," in *Text and Interpretation: Studies in the New Testament Presented to Matthew Black*, ed. Ernest Best and Robert McL. Wilson (Cambridge: Cambridge University Press, 1979), 1–14.

209. "Die gegenwärtige Stand der Arbeit an den Handschriften wie am Text des griechischen Neuen Testaments und das Institut für neutestamentliche Textforschung in Münster (Westf.)," in Kurt Aland, *Studien zur Überlieferung des Neuen Testaments und Seines Textes*, ANTF 2 (Berlin: de Gruyter, 1967), 202–14.

210. Reprinted in Epp, *Perspectives*, 185–209.

211. Ibid., 189.

212. Reprinted in Epp, *Perspectives*, 175–84.

213. "Beyond the Interlude? Developments and Directions in New Testament Textual Criticism," in *Studies in the Early Text of the Gospels and Acts: The Papers of the First Birmingham Colloquium on the Textual Criticism of the New Testament*, ed. David G. K. Taylor, SBLTCS (Atlanta: SBL, 1999), 26–48.

214. In a note attached to the reprint of his 1973 essay Epp acknowledges the increased activity in the field but tends to stand by his earlier views: *Perspectives*, 98–100.

215. See Kurt Aland, "The Significance of the Papyri for Progress in New Testament Research," in *The Bible in Modern Scholarship: Papers Read at the 100th Meeting of the SBL, December 28–30, 1964*, ed J. Philip Hyatt (Nashville: Abingdon, 1965), 325–46; Eldon Jay Epp, "The New Testament Papyrus Manuscripts in Historical Perspective," in idem, *Perspectives*, 311–43.

216. See Philip Wesley Comfort, *The Quest for the Original Text of the New Testament* (Grand Rapids: Baker, 1992), 85–99; Zimmermann, *Neutestamentliche Methodenlehre*, 78–82.

217. Reprinted in Epp, *Perspectives*, 101–24. See Gordon D. Fee, "On the Types, Classification, and Presentation of Textual Variation," in Eldon Jay Epp and Gordon D. Fee, *Studies in the Theory and Method of New Testament Textual Criticism*, SD 45 (Grand Rapids: Eerdmans, 1993), 62–79.

218. Ernest C. Colwell (with Ernest W. Tune), "Method in Classifying and Evaluating Variant Readings," in Ernest C. Colwell, *Studies in Methodology in Textual Criticism of the New Testament*, NTTS 9 (Grand Rapids: Eerdmans, 1969), 95–105.

219. Epp, "Towards the Clarification," 157.

220. Ernest C. Colwell (with Ernest W. Tune), "Method of Establishing Quantitative Relationships between Text-Types of New Testament Manuscripts," in Colwell, *Studies in Methodology*, 56–62. See Thomas C. Geer Jr., "Analyzing and Categorizing New Testament Greek Manuscripts: Colwell Revisited," in *The Text of the New Testament in Contemporary Research: Essays on the Status Quaestionis, A Volume in Honor of Bruce M. Metzger*, SD 46, ed. Bart D. Ehrman and Michael W. Holmes (Grand Rapids: Eerdmans, 1995), 253–67; Bart D. Ehrman, "Methodological Developments in the Analysis and Classification of New Testament Documentary Evidence," in Bart D. Ehrman, *Studies in the Textual Criticism of the New Testament*, NTTS 33 (Leiden: Brill, 2006), 9–32.

221. Colwell, "Method of Establishing," 59.

222. Eldon J. Epp, "The Claremont Profile Method for Grouping New Testament Minuscule Manuscripts," in Epp, *Perspectives*, 41–57; Frederik Wisse, *The Profile Method for the Classification of Manuscript Evidence as Applied to the Continuous Greek Text of the Gospel of Luke*, SD 44 (Grand Rapids: Eerdmans, 1982).

223. Ibid., 120.

224. Bart D. Ehrman, "The Use of Group Profiles for the Classification of New Testament Documentary Evidence," in idem, *Studies in the Textual Criticism of the New Testament*, 33–56.

225. Metzger and Ehrman, *Text of the New Testament*, 239.

226. Kurt and Barbara Aland, *Text of the New Testament*, 317–32; Metzger and Ehrman, *Text of the New Testament*, 237–38.

227. David C. Parker, "A Comparison Between the *Text und Textwert* and the Claremont Profile Method Analyses of Manuscripts in the Gospel of Luke," *NTS* 49 (2003): 108–38.

228. See Epp, "Toward the Clarification"; Fee, "On the Types, Classification, and Presentation."

229. See Ernest C. Colwell, "Genealogical Method: Its Achievements and Its Limitations," in idem, *Studies in Methodology*, 63–83; Colwell advocates a revised genealogical method, stressing the importance of the history of textual transmission; see his "Hort Redivivus: A Plea and a Program," ibid., 148–71.

230. See James K. Elliott, "The Case for Thoroughgoing Eclecticism," in *Rethinking New Testament Textual Criticism*, ed. David Alan Black (Grand Rapids: Baker Academic, 2002), 201–24. For criticism of this method and support of "reasoned" eclecticism see Gordon D. Fee, "Rigorous or Reasoned Eclecticism—Which," in Epp and Fee, *Studies in the Theory and Method*, 124–40.

231. See Michael W. Holmes, "The Case for Reasoned Eclecticism, in *Rethinking New Testament Textual Criticism*, 77–100.

232. Epp, "Textual Criticism," in *New Testament and Its Modern Interpreters*, 96.

233. See Metzger and Ehrman, *Text of the New Testament*, 272–80; Vaganay, *Introduction*, 89–128, 168–71); Epp, "Textual Criticism," *New Testament and Its Modern Interpreters*, 97–106; Jacobus H. Petzer, "The History of the New Testament Text: Its Reconstruction, Significance and Use in New Testament Textual Criticism," in *New Testament Textual Criticism, Exegesis and Church History: A Discussion of Methods*, ed. Barbara Aland and Joël Delobel (Kampen: Kok Pharos, 1994), 11–36.

234. See Bruce M. Metzger, "The Caesarean Text of the Gospels," in Bruce M. Metzger, *Chapters in the History of New Testament Textual Criticism*, NTTS 4 (Grand Rapids: Eerdmans, 1963), 42–72.

235. Jean Duplacy, *Où en est la critique textuelle*, 89–91; Christian-Bernard Amphoux, "Le Texte," in *Codex Bezae: Studies from the Lunel Colloquium, June 1994*, ed. David C. Parker and

Christian-Bernard Amphoux, NTTS 22 (Leiden: Brill, 1996), 337–54. See also Marie-Émile Boismard, "Le Codex de Bèze et le texte Occidental des Actes," in ibid., 257–70.

236. See Wilbur N. Pickering, *The Identity of the New Testament Text*, 3rd ed. (Eugene, OR: Wipf and Stock, 2003); Maurice A. Robinson, "The Case for Byzantine Priority," in *Rethinking New Testament Textual Criticism*, 125–39; Daniel B. Wallace, "The Majority Text Theory: History, Methods, and Critique," in *Text of the New Testament in Contemporary Research*, ed. Ehrman and Holmes, 297–320.

237. *The Greek New Testament According to the Majority Text* (Nashville: Nelson, 1982), xi.

238. Wallace, "Majority Text Theory," 307–15; Gordon D. Fee, "The Majority Text and the Original Text of the New Testament," in Epp and Fee, *Studies in the Theory and Method*, 183–208.

239. Related to the theory of the majority text is the view of Harry A. Sturz, *The Byzantine Text-Type and New Testament Textual Criticism* (Nashville: Nelson, 1984). Sturz does not contend that the Byzantine text is primary but that it was early and independent, probably emerging in Antioch as early as the third century.

240. Philip W. Comfort, *The Quest for the Original Text of the New Testament* (Grand Rapids: Baker, 1992).

241. See Kurt Aland, "The Significance of the Papyri"; idem, "Der neue 'Standard-Text' in seinem Verhältnis zu den frühen Papyri und Majuskeln," in *New Testament Textual Criticism*, ed. Epp and Fee, 257–75.

242. James R. Royse, "Corrections in the Freer Gospels Codex," in *The Freer Biblical Manuscripts: Fresh Studies of an American Treasure Trove*, ed. Larry W. Hurtado, SBLTCS 6 (Atlanta: SBL, 2006), 185–226.

243. See Robert A. Kraft, "The Use of Computers in New Testament Textual Criticism," in *Text of the New Testament in Contemporary Research*, 268–82; Metzger and Ehrman, *Text of the New Testament*, 240–46.

244. Institut für neutestamentliche Textforschung und vom Rechenzentrum der Universität Münster, eds., *Computer-Konkordanz zum Novum Testamentum Graece, von Nestle-Aland, 26. Auflage und zum Greek New Testament, 3rd Edition* (Berlin: de Gruyter, 1980).

245. Timothy J. Finney, "Manuscript Markup," in *Freer Biblical Manuscripts*, 263–87.

246. Kurt Aland, "Über die Möglichkeit der Identifikation kleiner Fragmente neutestamentlicher Handschriften mit Hilfe des Computers," in *Studies in New Testament Language and Text*, ed. Elliott, 14–38.

247. See Kurt Aland, "Der heutige Text des griechischen Neuen Testaments: Ein kritischer Bericht über seine modernen Ausgaben," in *Studien zur Überlieferung des Neuen Testaments*, 58–80; Metzger and Ehrman, *Text of the New Testament*, 189–94; Kurt and Barbara Aland, *Text of the New Testament*, 20–47: Epp, "Textual Criticism," in *New Testament and Its Modern Interpreters*, 84–97; Epp, "Issues in New Testament Textual Criticism, in *Rethinking New Testament Textual Criticism*, 44–51.

248. See "Introduction" (German 1–43; English 44–83) in, Barbara and Kurt Aland, Johannes Karavidopoulos, Carlo M. Martini, Bruce M. Metzger, eds, *Novum Testamentum Graece* (Nestle-Aland), 27th rev. ed. (Stuttgart: Deutsche Bibelgesellschaft, 1993; 2d corrected printing 2000; 4th printing, 2004); Barbara Aland and Beate Köster, "Preface" to *100 Jahre Novum Testamentum Graece, 1898–1998: Jubiläumsausgabe* (Stuttgart: Deutsche Bibelgesellschaft, 1998), v–xx; Kurt and Barbara Aland, *Text of the New Testament*, 232–60; Kurt Aland, "Der heutige Text."

249. Instruction in reading a critical apparatus (in this and other editions) is provided by J. Harold Greenlee, *Introduction to New Testament Textual Criticism*, rev. ed. (Peabody, MA: Hendrickson, 1995), 92–111.

250. "Der neue 'Standard-Text,'" 274.

251. Kurt Aland, ed., *Synopsis Quattuor Evangeliorum*, 15th rev. ed.; 3d corrected and expanded printing (with Papyri 101–111) (Stuttgart: Deutsche Bibelgesellschaft, 2001). See Kurt

and Barbara Aland, *Text of the New Testament,* 260–67; here the Alands discuss this synopsis and other major synopses: Huck-Greeven (1981), the synopsis edited by Bernard Orchard (1983), the synopsis edited by Marie-Émile Boismard and Arnaud Lamouille (1986), and the synopsis of Reuben J. Swanson (1984).

252. Barbara Aland, Kurt Aland, et al., eds., *The Greek New Testament,* 4th ed., 10th printing (2005). See Metzger, *Reminiscences,* 67–75; Kurt and Barbara Aland, *Text of the New Testament,* 224–32.

253. *A Textual Commentary on The Greek New Testament: A Companion Volume to the United Bible Societies' Greek New Testament,* 4th rev. ed. (Stuttgart: Deutsche Bibelgesellschaft, 1994; 6th printing 2005).

254. See Eldon Jay Epp, "The International Greek New Testament Project: Motivation and History," in Epp, *Perspectives,* 437–59; James K. Elliott, "The International Project to Establish a Critical Apparatus to Luke's Gospel," *NTS* 29 (1983): 531–38.

255. The specimen was sharply criticized by Kurt Aland, "Bemerkungen zu Probeseiten einer grossen kritischen Ausgabe des Neuen Testaments," *NTS* 12 (1966): 176–85.

256. American and British Committees of the International Greek NT Project, eds., *The New Testament in Greek: The Gospel according to St. Luke: Part One: Chapters 1–12; Part Two: Chapters 14–24* (Oxford: Clarendon, 1984, 1987).

257. David C. Parker, "The International Greek New Testament Project: the Gospel of John," *NTS* 36 (1990): 157–60.

258. *The New Testament in Greek IV: The Gospel according to St. John, Volume One, The Papyri,* ed. W. J. Elliott and David C. Parker, NTTS 20 (Leiden: Brill, 1995).

259. David C. Parker, "The Development of the Critical Text of the Epistle of James: From Lachmann to The *Editio Critica Maior,*" in *New Testament Textual Criticism and Exegesis: Festschrift J. Delobel,* ed. Adelbert Denaux, BETL 161 (Leuven: Leuven University Press, 2002), 317–30; Kurt Aland, "Novi Testamenti Graeci editio maior critica: Der gegenwärtige Stand der Arbeit an einer neuen grossen kritischen Ausgabe des Neuen Testamentes," *NTS* 16 (1969–70): 163–77; Vaganay, *Introduction to New Testament Textual Criticism,* 164–66.

260. Institute for New Testament Textual Research, ed., *Novum Testamentum Graecum Editio Critica Maior: 4 Catholic Letters,* ed. Barbara Aland, Kurt Aland, Gerd Mink, and Klaus Wachtel, *Part 1: Text; Installment 1: James* (Stuttgart: Deutsche Bibelgesellschaft, 1997).

261. Parker, "Development of the Critical Text," 317–30.

262. Brooke Foss Westcott and Fenton John Anthony Hort, *The New Testament in the Original Greek: Introduction and Appendix* (New York: Harper & Brothers, 1882), 2: 282.

263. Eldon J. Epp, "Introduction," in idem, *Perspectives,* xl. See idem, "Issues in NT Textual Criticism," in *Rethinking New Testament Textual Criticism,* 52–70; Metzger and Ehrman, *Text of the New Testament,* 280–99.

264. Eldon J. Epp, *The Theological Tendency of Codex Bezae Cantabrigiensis in Acts,* SNTSMS 3 (Cambridge: Cambridge University Press, 1966).

265. In looking back on this work from a later perspective Epp notes that most reviewers acknowledged that he had demonstrated an anti-Judaic bias in Codex Bezae; see "Anti-Judaic Tendencies in the D-Text of Acts: Forty Years of Conversations," in idem, *Perspectives,* 699–739.

266. Eldon J. Epp, *Junia: The First Woman Apostle* (Minneapolis: Fortress Press, 2005); the essay "Text-Critical, Exegetical, and Socio-Cultural Factors Affecting the Junia/Junias Variation in Romans 16,7," is in *New Testament Textual Criticism,* ed. Adelbert Denaux, 227–91.

267. Quoted in *Junia,* 290.

268. Bart D. Ehrman, *The Orthodox Corruption of Scripture: The Effect of Early Christological Controversies on the Text of the New Testament* (New York: Oxford University Press, 1993), xi. A summary of Ehrman's approach is presented in his essay, "The Text as Window: New Testament Manuscripts and the Social History of Early Christianity," in *Text of the New Testament in Contemporary Research,* ed. Ehrman and Holmes, 361–79. See also Ehrman, "Text and

Transmission: The Historical Significance of the 'Altered' Text," in idem, *Studies in the Textual Criticism of the New Testament*, 325–42. A popular account of Ehrman's view is presented in his bestseller: *Misquoting Jesus: The Story Behind Who Changed the Bible and Why* (San Francisco: Harper, 2005).

269. See *HNTR* 2: 452–54.

270. *Orthodox Corruption*, 275. In his essay, "Text as Window," and in his *Misquoting Jesus*, Ehrman notes textual changes that reflect other aspects of the social history of early Christianity, including tendencies to anti-Judaism and the suppression of women.

271. David C. Parker, *The Living Text of the Gospels* (Cambridge: Cambridge University Press, 1997), xi.

272. Ibid., 92.

273. Ibid., 93.

274. Ibid., 205.

275. Ibid., 207. Besides Epp, Ehrman, and Parker, other scholars have noted the significance of new perspectives in textual criticism for understanding the meaning of the NT documents; see, e. g., Joël Delobel, "Textual Criticism and Exegesis: Siamese Twins?" in *New Testament Textual Criticism, Exegesis, and Early Church History*, 98–117; Barbara Aland, "Welche Rolle spielen Textkritik und Textgeschichte für das Verständnis des Neuen Testaments? Frühe Leserperspektiven," *NTS* 52 (2006): 303–18. That this kind of research will continue and flourish in the future is evidenced, for example, by a book published early in the twenty-first century: Wayne C. Kannaday, *Apologetic Discourse and the Scribal Tradition: Evidence of the Influence of Apologetical Interests in the Text of the Canonical Gospels*, SBLTCS 5 (Atlanta: SBL, 2004).

5

Historical Backgrounds: Judaism

World War II was the theater in which the "Greatest Generation" gave its stellar performance. The war, however, had its darker features, among them the deliberate targeting of civilians by both sides. The nadir was reached with the Holocaust. In this horrendous endeavor the German National Socialists exterminated six million Jews. The mastermind of the program was Adolf Hitler, who came to office in 1933 and soon attained absolute power. In 1935 the "Nuremberg Laws," designed to protect German "blood" and its purity, were enacted. These laws deprived Jews of their civil and political rights. The Nazis moved relentlessly toward their "final solution": the extermination of all the Jews in the German empire. Jews were herded into boxcars like cattle and transported to the gas chambers of detention camps at notorious sites like Auschwitz and Buchenwald. Most of this took place with the knowledge and tacit consent of many Christians. Even the "Confessing Church," which opposed the pro-Nazi "German Christians," was largely silent in face of the anti-Judaism of the Hitler regime.[1] Most of the European nations and the United States had been unwilling to accept Jewish refugees during the 1930s.

The Holocaust provoked NT scholars to a reassessment of Judaism.[2] A new review of history, for example, revealed the rise of anti-Semitism in the ancient and medieval world, and especially in the Reformation. Scholars who formerly investigated Judaism from a Christian perspective, viewing the religion of the Jews as the dark backdrop for the more important drama of Christianity, now turned to the study of Judaism in its own right. Some advocated a "new perspective" for understanding the epistles of Paul.[3]

INTRODUCTIONS, TEXTS, AND TRANSLATIONS

The scholars who engaged in the renewed study of Judaism were provided with a rich treasury of resources.[4] In the area of introduction to Judaism the standard work for American students had been Pfeiffer's *History of New Testament Times*.[5] This useful work included a history of Judaism from 200 BCE to 100 CE, and an introduction to the Apocrypha. In the late twentieth century an exemplary introduction, *Jewish Literature Between the Bible and the Mishnah*, was published by George W. E. Nickelsburg.[6] This introduction focuses on the Jewish sources: the literature of the "intertestamental" period, including all of the Apocrypha, most of the Pseudepigrapha, and selections from the Dead Sea Scrolls. The material is presented in chronological order. Each chapter begins with a historical survey; the discussion within the chapters of each individual document includes historical-critical introduction, summary of content, review of religious ideas, and bibliography.

Although primarily a scholar of Judaism, Nickelsburg was also sensitive to its significance for the understanding of early Christianity. His *Ancient Judaism and Christian Origins: Diversity, Continuity, and Transformation* was written for non-specialists.[7] The book is concerned with two questions: "How have the discovery of the Dead Sea Scrolls and revolutions in methodology of biblical scholarship in the past two generations changed our perceptions of Judaism in the Greco-Roman period, and how do—or should—these developments lead us to rethink the origins of Christianity?"[8] The body of the book presents the results of recent research in Judaism, ordered according to major topics: Torah and religious life, God's activity on behalf of humanity, agents of God's activity, and eschatology. The conclusion recognizes the diversity of both early Judaism and early Christianity and notes the importance of eschatology for both. Also important for the study of early Christianity is Nickelsburg's *Resurrection, Immortality, and Eternal Life in Intertestamental Judaism*.[9] This book, based on his dissertation, presents a history of the theology of Judaism in regard to important features of eschatology. Nickelsburg argues (*contra* Oscar Cullmann) that the Jewish sources do not affirm a single idea of bodily resurrection but express variety, including the idea of bodiless existence after death.[10]

Nickelsburg has made a significant contribution to the study of the sources of Judaism by editing studies on Jewish texts, including the *Testament of Moses* and the *Testament of Joseph*.[11] With Michael E. Stone he published a collection of Jewish texts (in English translation) that illuminates the life and thought of early Judaism.[12] A major work for the study of Judaism is Nickelsburg's monumental commentary on *1 Enoch*. This first volume of a two-volume work is concerned with *1 Enoch* 1–36 and 81–108; the commentary on the Parables of Enoch (*1 Enoch* 37–81) is presented in second volume.[13] The comprehensive introduction (125 pages) thoroughly investigates all of the significant historical-critical issues. The commentary proper (pp. 129–560) presents the critical text in English translation with extensive notes on the text and translation, and concludes with a bibliography of over ten pages. This book, the abundant harvest of thirty years of labor, is a crowning achievement of a career of distinguished scholarship.

In the first half of the twentieth century the standard collection of Jewish texts was R. H. Charles, *The Apocrypha and Pseudepigrapha of the Old Testament*.[14] In 1972 James H. Charlesworth was invited by Doubleday to prepare a new edition of these documents in order to replace Charles's second volume (on the *Pseudepigrapha*), which contained only seventeen documents. The result was *The Old Testament Pseudepigrapha*, edited by Charlesworth.[15] In Charlesworth's two-volume work, which contains fifty-two documents, the material is organized according to literary types: Apocalyptic, Testaments, Expansions of the OT and Legends, Wisdom and Philosophical Literature. Within these categories the documents are presented in chronological order. Each document was assigned to an editor—a total of fifty-one scholars for the entire work. Each contributor followed a format: a synopsis of the central ideas, the original language, date, provenance, historical importance, theological importance, relation to canonical books, relation to apocryphal books, and cultural importance of the document. The text of each document is presented in English translation with notes and a bibliography. Charlesworth has prefaced the entire collection with a useful introduction for the general reader.

Collections of the documents of the Pseudepigrapha have been published in other languages, including Danish, Italian, Spanish, French and Hungarian. Of special interest to students of the history of NT research are the editions in German.[16] Corresponding to the work of Charles is the two-volume *Die Apokryphen und Pseudepigraphen des Alten Testaments*, edited by Emil Kautzsch.[17] Volume I includes the books of the Apocrypha, with a historical-critical introduction to each document and the text (in German) with notes. Volume II on the Pseudepigrapha consists of 528 pages and includes introduction and translation of thirteen documents. In 1958 a new German edition was proposed and launched under the editorship of Werner G. Kümmel.[18] The result is a publication of six volumes within which the documents are arranged according to literary type: Historical and Legendary Narratives, Instruction in Narrative Form, Instruction in Didactic Form, Poetic Texts, Apocalypses, and a supplementary volume with additional texts and bibliography. The collection includes fifty-two documents from both Apocrypha and Pseudepigrapha (which are not segregated into separate sections). For each document a historical-critical introduction, bibliography, German translation, and extensive notes are provided. The editorship was assumed by Hermann Lichtenberger in 1987.

JUDAISM AS THE CONTEXT OF EARLY CHRISTIANITY: JOACHIM JEREMIAS AND MATTHEW BLACK

JOACHIM JEREMIAS (1900–1979)

LIFE AND EARLY WORK

The conventional view that focuses on Judaism through the lens of early Christianity was refined by Joachim Jeremias.[19] Born in Dresden, Jeremias was the son of a Lutheran pastor. From age 10 to 15 he lived in Jerusalem, where his father served as leader of the German Christian congregation. Jeremias was educated at Leipzig, where he studied under Gustaf Dalman. He began teaching at the theological seminary of the Brüdergemeinde in Herrnhut and was appointed instructor at Leipzig in 1925. In 1928 he became associate professor in Berlin and director of the Institutum Judaicum. Jeremias served as professor at Greifswald from 1929 to 1934, and from 1935 to 1968 at the University of Göttingen. He was awarded honorary degrees from Oxford, St. Andrews, and Uppsala. He wrote more that 250 articles (including 28 for Kittel's famous *Theological Dictionary*) and over thirty books. Jeremias was noted for his prowess as a teacher and for his authentic Christian piety. J. Louis Martyn, who was studying in Göttingen in 1957–58, recalls his amazement at seeing Jeremias stride to the blackboard, open his Greek NT to Mark, and begin to transcribe the text into Aramaic.[20]

Jeremias's interest in the study of Judaism emerged early in his career. He edited the two volumes of excurses for the Strack-Billerbeck *Kommentar zum Neuen Testament aus Talmud und Midrasch*.[21] His archaeological, geographical, and historical research were already evident in his Leipzig qualifying dissertation (Habilitationsschrift) entitled *Golgotha*.[22] In this work Jeremias addressed the question of the location of Golgotha and the tomb of Jesus. After reviewing the evidence from the NT, archaeology, topography, and history, he concluded: "The history of the tradition about Golgotha and the Holy Sepulcher shows that their sites are rightly to be sought in the present Church of the Holy Sepulcher."[23] Jeremias proceeded with a fascinating account of the legendary traditions about Golgotha: that the skull of Adam was buried there; that Golgotha is the center of the earth; that it is the place of the sacrifice of Isaac. He also investigated the use of "rock" as symbol in the NT, observing that the Jewish shrine of Golgotha has been replaced by the Christian tradition about the place of crucifixion.

Jeremias also engaged in archaeological observation and field archaeology. Of special interest is his eyewitness account, with photographs, of a celebration of the Passover by Samaritans in 1931.[24] Jeremias believed that the modern Samaritan observance reflects some of the features of the pre-Deuteronomic ritual of the Passover.

Jeremias also visited and collected data about forty-six ancient tombs in Palestine and neighboring regions. On the basis of this information he reflected on the meaning of tomb-building in the folk religion of the time of Jesus.[25] He presents a more detailed investigation of a particular site in his *Die Wiederentdeckung von Bethesda: Johannes 5,2.*[26] This monograph presents a history and interpretation of the archaeological research on the pool depicted in John 5:2. On the basis of his analysis of the textual data, Jeremias argues that the translation should be "Sheep Pool" (rather than "Sheep Gate") and that the name of the pool is "Bethesda." The location of the Pool, according to Jeremias, is the site near the Church of St. Anne where extensive excavation has been undertaken. He concludes: "The find with which we have dealt has a special significance in that it presents new and imposing evidence for the reliability of our Gospel tradition in general, but in particular for the validity of local references concerning Jerusalem in the Fourth Gospel."[27] Similarly, in another monograph Jeremias argues that the Dead Sea Scrolls provide evidence that the Gospel of John is not Hellenistic but Jewish, and that there is a broad gap between the Essenes and Jesus.[28]

Jeremias published a widely-used history of Jerusalem in the first century.[29] This book deals with the economic conditions of Jerusalem under Roman rule and the economic and social status of the people of Jerusalem in the time of Jesus. Jeremias believes the Jerusalem Jews were much concerned with maintaining "racial" purity:

> Up to the present, it has not been sufficiently recognized that from a social point of view the whole community of Judaism at the time of Jesus was dominated by the fundamental idea of the maintenance of racial purity. . . . [T]he entire population 'itself, in the theory and practice of religious legislation at the time of Jesus, was classified according to purity of descent. Only Israelites of legitimate ancestry formed the pure Israel.[30]

Other examples of Jeremias's historical research can be seen in his monographs on infant baptism. In 1938 he produced a work contending that the church practiced infant baptism, a practice that had its background in Jewish proselyte baptism, virtually from the beginning. He expanded his argument in *Infant Baptism in the First Four Centuries* and maintained his position in debate with Kurt Aland in the 1960s.[31]

MAJOR WORKS

Jeremias published two major works: a book on the Lord's Supper and one on the Parables. The book on the Supper, entitled in English *The Eucharistic Words of Jesus*, was first published in 1935, expanded in a second edition, and further expanded in a third.[32] Jeremias begins with the question: was the Last Supper a Passover meal? The Synoptic Gospels agree that the Supper observed the Passover, but John 18:28 implies that it took place twenty-four hours before the official time of observance. Jeremias rejects the possibility that the Last Supper was some other type of Jewish meal. He also answers arguments contending that events are recorded that could not have occurred on the day of the Passover. Jeremias concludes that the Lord's Supper was a Passover meal.

Jeremias investigates the meaning of the eucharistic words of Jesus within the framework of the Jewish Passover. The meal had four features: (1) the preliminary course (which included a word of dedication over the first cup), (2) the Passover liturgy (which involved the recounting of the Passover story, the singing of the first part of the Passover hymn, and the drinking of the second cup), (3) the main meal (which included grace over the unleavened bread, eating of the meal, and grace over the third cup), and (4) the conclusion (which involved the singing of the second part of the Passover hymn and grace over the fourth cup). According to Jeremias's analysis of the Last Supper, Jesus pronounced the word concerning the bread in connection with the grace over the main meal, and after the eating of the meal pronounced the word over the cup. In other words, the main events of the Last Supper correspond to the third element of the Passover observance.

Jeremias believes the account of the Supper, especially the words of institution, represent independent, early tradition. This tradition is preserved in 1 Cor 11:23, a text written, according to Jeremias, before Mark and recounting a pre-Pauline tradition. In investigating the tradition Jeremias concludes that the earliest written accounts are 1 Cor 11:23-25 and Mark 14:22-25. He detects Semitisms in the text that prove the primitive character of the Markan account. He believes both 1 Corinthians and Mark are dependent on the earliest form of the tradition, which was transmitted in Aramaic or Hebrew. Paul's assertion that he "received" the words "from the Lord" indicate, according to Jeremias, that the tradition goes back to Jesus himself. As to the meaning of the eucharistic words, Jeremias stresses the importance of the meal as anticipating the eschatological consummation. He also believes that in the words of institution Jesus speaks of himself as sacrifice, as the eschatological Passover lamb. "This is therefore what Jesus said at the Last Supper about the meaning of his death: his death is the vicarious death of the suffering servant, which atones for the sins of the 'many,' the peoples of the world, which ushers in the beginning of the final salvation and which effects the new covenant with God."[33]

Jeremias's book on the *Parables*, a book of 118 pages, first appeared in 1947. He expanded the work in subsequent editions until is morphed into a work of 242 pages; the English version is based on this sixth edition.[34] Jeremias, going beyond the work of Jülicher and Dodd, takes up the questions: "What did Jesus intend to say at this particular moment? What must have been the effect of his word upon his hearers?"[35] The first part of the book deals with the developing tradition of the parables. During their transmission the parables were transformed: translated into Greek, placed in different settings, embellished with details, influenced by the church. Major transformations have had a detrimental effect on the parables, especially changing them into allegories. Jeremias also observes the role of the redactor of the gospel texts, including placing the parable into different contexts, adding introductions and conclusions, and consequently changing the meaning; but he views none of these obstacles as insurmountable. "Our task is a return to the actual living voice of Jesus. How great the gain if we succeed in rediscovering here and there behind the veil the features of the Son of Man!"[36]

The balance of the book is dedicated to explicating the message of the parables. According to Jeremias the main themes are the announcement of the day of salvation (the present is the eschatological time, for the Savior is here); the declaration of God's mercy for sinners (vindication of Jesus' proclamation of good news to the outcasts); announcement of the imminent catastrophe (judgment and warning); the call to discipleship (encouraging the hearers to labor in the harvest and share the suffering Jesus faced). Jeremias believes that Jesus not only spoke parables but performed parabolic actions like "cleansing" the temple. "The Messianic Age has arrived. That means that the symbolic actions are kerygmatic actions; they show that Jesus not only proclaimed the message of the parables, but that he lived it and embodied it in his person."[37] Jeremias concludes:

In attempting to recover the original significance of the parables, one thing above all becomes evident: it is that all the parables of Jesus compel his hearers to come to a decision about his person and mission. For they are all full of "the secret of the Kingdom of God" (Mark 4.11), that is to say, the recognition of "an eschatology that is in the process of realization."[38]

Besides his two major books, Jeremias published notable exegetical works. These include a short monograph on the Sermon on the Mount.[39] He believes the Sermon is a composition by the author of Matthew, who collected and arranged individual sayings of Jesus. "What we find in the Matthean composition . . . is not simply the ethic of late Judaism, but a refined, humanized, radicalized, simplified, concentrated Judaism that finds its fulfilment in the confession of Jesus."[40] Jeremias also published a short commentary on the Pastoral Epistles for a popular German series.[41] In the introduction he concludes that the situation reflected in these documents must reflect events after Paul's release from a first Roman imprisonment. Jeremias believes Paul to have been the author; the differences from the main Pauline letters can be explained by different situations and the use of a different amanuensis.

JESUS AND NEW TESTAMENT THEOLOGY

Jeremias published a number of works dedicated to the study of NT theology. He is especially concerned with Christology, and fundamental to Jeremias's Christology is his understanding of the historical Jesus.[42] Jeremias rejects the view of Bultmann that dismisses the historical Jesus in favor of the kerygma of the church. Jeremias believed "we are in danger of surrendering the affirmation 'the Word became flesh' and of dissolving 'salvation history,' God's activity in the man Jesus of Nazareth and in his message; we are in danger of Docetism, where Christ becomes an idea; we are in danger of putting the proclamation of the apostle Paul in the place of the good tidings of Jesus."[43] According to Jeremias, the kerygma is based on Jesus; it is the interpretation of the historical event. "According to the witness of the New Testament, there is no other revelation of God but the incarnate Word. The preaching of the early church, on the other hand, is the divinely inspired witness to the revelation, but the church's preaching is not itself the revelation."[44]

For Jeremias, Jesus' use of the Aramaic term *abba* (אבא) in address to God is the key to understanding the significance of Jesus for Christology.[45] He investigates Jesus' usage in relation to the idea of God as Father in the OT and Judaism, concluding that "there is as yet no evidence in the literature of ancient

Palestinian Judaism that 'my Father' is used as a personal address to God."[46] In the Gospels, on the other hand, "Father" is used as a title for God over 170 times. In the Gospel texts "Father" is used in three ways: ὁ πατήρ (without personal pronoun), "your Father," and "my Father." Jeremias argues that all three expressions represent authentic words of Jesus. "Jesus bases his authority on the fact that God has revealed himself to him like a father to his son. 'My Father' is thus a word of revelation. It represents the central statement of Jesus' mission."[47]

According to Jeremias the Aramaic word Jesus uses in his prayers is *abba*, a term used by children in speaking to their father. Jeremias finds not a single use of the term in the literature of Jewish prayers, but he asserts that Jesus, with the sole exception of Mark 15:34 (Matt 27:46), always addressed God by this term. In investigating the Lord's Prayer he contends that Jesus taught his disciples to pray in the same way, addressing God as *abba*.[48] Jeremias, in an appendix to the *Prayers of Jesus*, presents the characteristics of what he calls the *ipsissima vox Jesu* (the very voice of Jesus). Jeremias is too careful a historian to claim that he can detect the exact words (*ipsissima verba*) of Jesus, but he believes that in Jesus' use of *abba* and ἀμήν (in expressions like Ἀμὴν λέγω ὑμῖν σοι ["truly I tell you"]) we hear the authentic voice—we experience the presence of Jesus himself.

Another example of Jeremias's enlistment of linguistics in the service of theology is seen in his article on παῖς θεοῦ for Kittel's *Theological Dictionary of the New Testament*.[49] Jeremias notes that the phrase can be used in two ways: as "child of God" or "servant of God." In the LXX it translates עבד יהוה and is used in the plural for the righteous people ("servants of God") and in the singular for important instruments of God like Moses. According to Jeremias the phrase "Servant of God" is also used for the Messiah. The phrase appears frequently in Second Isaiah, where it was understood in a collective sense, but also in the singular as referring to the prophet himself or to the Messiah. Jeremias believes *1 Enoch* describes the "Son of Man" in features borrowed from Second Isaiah. He notes that in the NT the phrase is used five times to refer to Jesus; he believes that this was a title used for Jesus in Palestinian Christianity. Jeremias acknowledges that quotations from Second Isaiah that refer to Jesus as Servant of God are rare, but he detects several allusions. He believes that Jesus thought of himself as the Servant of Second Isaiah. "Because He goes to His death innocently, voluntarily, patiently, and in accordance with the will of God (Is. 53), His dying has unlimited atoning power. The life which He pours out is life from God and with God."[50]

These ideas about *abba* and the Servant are incorporated in Jeremias's *The Central Message of the New Testament*.[51] The substance of this book was originally presented in lectures given at various theological schools in America in 1963, and it has been translated into French, Japanese, Spanish, and Italian.[52] Chapter 1, "Abba," is a condensed version of material found in "Abba" and *Prayers of Jesus*, described above. Chapter 2 on "The Sacrificial Death" investigates the doctrine of atonement as found in Hebrews, 1 Peter, and the Pauline letters. Paul, according to Jeremias, affirms the idea of substitutionary atonement. In regard to the words of Jesus predicting his own death, Jeremias argues that these were not *vaticinia ex eventu*; Jesus expected and interpreted his death. In regard to "Justification by Faith" (ch. 3), he acknowledges that the doctrine is not found in all of Paul's epistles, but insists that it is central to the apostle's theology:

> To sum up: it remains true that justification is forgiveness, nothing but forgiveness. But justification is forgiveness in the fullest sense. It is not only a mere covering up of the past. Rather, it is an antedonation of the full salvation; it is the new creation by God's Spirit; it is Christ taking possession of the life already now, already here.[53]

Chapter 4, "The Revealing Word," is an exposition of the Prologue of the Gospel of John. Jeremias notes that the use of "Logos" as a title for Jesus is unique in the NT, but argues that its source is to be found in Hellenistic Judaism (the LXX, Wisdom of Solomon), not in Gnosticism.[54]

Late in his career Jeremias began publishing a major work, *New Testament Theology*.[55] He was able to finish only the first part on "the proclamation of Jesus," but this constitutes a volume of over three hundred pages and is, for all practical purposes, a summary of Jeremias's work and thought. In regard to the authenticity of the sayings of Jesus, Jeremias questions the criterion of dissimilarity because it overlooks the continuity of Jesus with Judaism. More reliable, according to Jeremias, are the evidence of Jesus' use of Aramaic and the distinctive features of Jesus' teaching. Ironically, Jeremias affirms a sort of dissimilarity in his claim that Jesus' speech—his parables, his use of ἀμήν] and *abba*—lacks contemporary analogies.[56]

In regard to the mission of Jesus, Jeremias observes that all the accounts of the baptism agree that the Spirit descended—a clear sign of prophetic inspiration. According to Jeremias the Jews of Jesus' time believed that the Spirit had become silent. Jesus' address to God as *abba* proves, according to Jeremias, that Jesus was conscious of his authorization by divine revelation. Jeremias believes that Jesus viewed himself as the messenger of God who understood his message as the proclamation of an eschatological event. Although he acknowledges that the developing tradition enlarged Jesus' miraculous activity, Jeremias believes that Jesus cast out demons and healed the sick—activity demonstrating that Satan was being defeated. The central feature of the preaching of Jesus is the proclamation of the kingdom, the announcement that the day of salvation was dawning. This message was directed to the poor and translated into action with Jesus' practice of dining with publicans and sinners. This message and action demonstrated that God was infinitely gracious, the expression of the love of God. According to Jeremias, "nothing comparable is to be found in contemporary Judaism."[57]

Jeremias characterizes the time of Jesus' activity as the "Period of Grace." The message had two sides: the proclamation of salvation and the announcement of judgment. The present was a time of woe, a time to repent. During this period Jesus gathered the community of salvation in which the people were called to a life of discipleship, becoming like children, obeying the rule of love. By way of contrast, Jeremias perceives Pharisaic Judaism as a *religion of achievement.*[58] He finds evidence of Jesus' own testimony to his mission. "In short, he designated his preaching and his actions as the eschatological saving event. An awareness of mission of this kind can no longer be kept in the prophetic sphere. Rather, all these statements mean that Jesus believed himself to be the bringer of salvation."[59]

Crucial to Jeremias's Christology is his understanding of "Son of Man." He notes that, except for Acts 7:56, this phrase is used exclusively by Jesus himself. This usage, according to Jeremias, belongs to the earliest tradition and goes back to Jesus himself. Jeremias believes that Jesus understood the "Son of Man" in the context of *1 Enoch* (where the title refers to a person) and 4 Ezra (where the attributes of the Servant of Second Isaiah are transferred to the Son of Man). He acknowledges that Jesus always refers to the Son of Man in the third person, apparently distinguishing himself from the Son of Man. But Jeremias believes that Jesus, in speaking this way, distinguishes between his present and his future: "he is not yet the Son of man, but he will be exalted to be the Son of man."[60]

Jeremias believes that Jesus' predictions of his resurrection belong to early, authentic tradition. Jesus, he thinks, expected his own suffering and death and understood his death in the light of Isaiah 53 as a death of atonement. Jeremias also believes that Jesus predicted his own resurrection; the references to after "three days" (Mark 8:31; 9:31) belong to the pre-Easter tradition. He does not appear to sense that prescience of the resurrection tends to blunt the impact of the crucifixion.[61] As to the resurrection accounts, Jeremias recognizes the puzzling disparity of the texts and believes they reflect the developing tradition, which involves elaboration of details and apologetic purpose. For the early Christians, according to Jeremias, the resurrection of Jesus is the eschatological event that heralds the future enthronement of Christ: the dawn of the *parousia*.

Looking back over the work of Joachim Jeremias we see a scholar of great erudition with command of a mass of primary and secondary sources and mastery of linguistic and exegetical detail. According to Martin Hengel, Jeremias is "the most significant New Testament scholar of the last generation in Germany."[62] In the German context Jeremias represents the antithesis to Rudolf Bultmann and his school.[63] The distinctive feature of Jeremias's work is his detection of the *ipsissima vox Jesu*, in particular his claim that Jesus always addressed God with the term *abba* is the key to unlocking the self-understanding of the historical Jesus. According to this understanding, Jesus saw himself as standing in unique relationship to God as God's eschatological messenger, as the messiah. Jeremias, in filling in this portrait, believed that Jesus viewed himself as a combination of the Servant of Isaiah and the Son of Man of Jewish apocalyptic. The resulting Christology, in Jeremias's opinion, is the foundation of the Christian faith and the heart of Christian theology—a theology that affirms the doctrine of atonement and the centrality of justification by faith.

To be sure, Jeremias is not without his critics. Attention, for example, has been given to his analysis of the Aramaic word *abba*. Scholars have demonstrated that this term did not originate with the babbling of infants.[64] Nevertheless, Jeremias's claim that the term was never (or hardly ever) used in Jewish prayers seems to have been sustained.[65] More serious is the observation that Jeremias continues to view Judaism from a pre-Holocaust perspective, as the somber background against which Christianity is depicted.[66] The result is a presentation of Judaism from the standpoint of Christian confession rather than an understanding of Judaism in its own right.

MATTHEW BLACK (1908–1994)

Black was born in Scotland and educated at the Universities of Glasgow and Bonn.[67] He taught at Glasgow, Manchester, Aberdeen, Leeds, and Edinburgh. Most of his career was spent at the University of St. Andrews, where he served as Professor of Divinity and Biblical Criticism and Principal of St. Mary's College. Black was the first editor (from 1954–57) of *New Testament Studies*, the periodical of the SNTS.

Black's overview of Judaism is presented in his article, "The Development of Judaism in the Greek and Roman Periods," in *Peake's Commentary on the*

Bible.[68] This article provides a summary of the history of Judaism from Alexander to the Bar Cochba revolt and a survey of the development of the religious ideas of Judaism. Black discusses the importance of eschatology and the replacement of apocalyptic with rabbinic Judaism. "It was succeeded by the perpetuation in the Judaism of the rabbis (the descendants of the Pharisees), of the religion of the Book, the legalism and exclusive nationalism, which have gone to the making of what is called 'normative' Judaism."[69]

Black made important contributions to the study of Jewish texts. He published *The Book of Enoch or I Enoch*,[70] which was earlier than and less extensive than Nickelsburg's work. Of interest to NT scholars is Black's discussion of the "Parables of Enoch" in which he rejects J. T. Milik's argument that this part of *1 Enoch* was not composed until 250 CE; Black believes the "Parables" were written earlier than the Gospels. Previously Black had collaborated with Milik on a study of the Aramaic fragments of *Enoch* found in Cave 4 at Qumran.[71] Still earlier he had published a critical edition of the Greek text of *Enoch*.[72] Black also published research on early Christian liturgical texts written in Syriac.[73] All these works attest to Black's mastery of Semitic linguistics.

Black's affirmation of the importance of Jewish texts for understanding early Christianity is seen in his work on the Dead Sea Scrolls: *The Scrolls and Christian Origins*.[74] In this book he accepts the scholars' consensus that the Scrolls were produced by the Essenes living at Qumran. He believes that the link between the Essenes and the Jerusalem church is to be found in the "Hebrews" of Acts 6:1. As to religious ideas, Black believes the sectarians of Qumran advocated legalistic perfection and embraced apocalyptic beliefs, including the recognition of three messianic figures: the messiah of Israel, the high-priestly messiah, and the prophet like Moses.

Black's most important contribution to NT research is his *An Aramaic Approach to the Gospels and Acts*.[75] Since Jesus spoke Aramaic, there must be an Aramaic tradition behind the texts of the Gospels. "The 'Aramaic problem' of the Gospels is to determine, by internal evidence, to what extent the Greek Gospels are written in or embody 'translation Greek' or how much Aramaic influence can be detected in them."[76] The sources available to reconstruct the Aramaic of Jesus include Christian Palestinian Syriac, the Palestinian Targum of the Pentateuch, and texts and fragments from Qumran.[77] Black also notes the importance of textual criticism; he detects Semitisms in the Western text (Codex D).[78] Important for investigating Aramaic influence are the linguistic features of syntax, grammar, and vocabulary. Also important is the Semitic poetic form.

Jesus did not commit anything to writing but by His use of poetic form and language He ensured that His sayings would not be forgotten. The impression they make in Aramaic is of carefully premeditated and studied deliverances; we have to do with prophetic utterance of the style and grandeur of Isaiah, cast in a medium which can express in appropriate and modulated sound the underlying beauty of the sentiment or the passion out of which the thought arose—soft and gentle in the kindly sayings, as in the promise to the heavy-laden, inexorable and hard in the sayings about Offences, strongly guttural and mockingly sibilant where hypocrites and 'the rest of men' are contrasted with the Christian disciples.[79]

Black employs this sort of data in an effort to identify Greek documents as translations of written Aramaic sources. In investigating Q he concludes that a case for an Aramaic original cannot be proved. Black also takes up the attempt to identify underlying Aramaic texts on the basis of "mistranslations." The major weakness with this method, he says, is that it rests largely on conjecture. Black believes that the presence of Semitic influence is found most frequently in the words of Jesus, and that an Aramaic sayings-source lies behind the Synoptic Gospels. "Whether that source was written or oral, it is not possible from the evidence to decide."[80] In conclusion, Black writes: "The consequence is that, in the transmission of the Teaching of Jesus, the end-product in Greek is often less the mind of Jesus than the ideas and interpretation of the Greek Evangelists."[81]

In sum, Matthew Black made important contributions to NT research. His discussion of the Aramaic backgrounds is a classic work of continuing importance. In the main, however, Black reflects the view of Judaism that was conventional before the "new perspective." He views Judaism from the perspective of Christian conviction. This is particularly evident in his article on the "Pharisees" in the *Interpreter's Dictionary of the Bible* (1962).

Pharisaism is the immediate ancestor of rabbinical (or normative) Judaism, the arid and sterile religion of the Jews after the fall of Jerusalem, and finally, the Bar Cocheba debacle (A.D. 135). . . . It is a sterile religion of codified tradition, regulating every part of life by a halachah, observing strict *apartheid*, and already as entrenched in its own conservatism as that of the Sadducees.[82]

This view is confirmed in Black's commentary on *Romans*.

The key to an understanding of Paul's essential thesis is his conviction of the total bankruptcy of contemporary Pharisaic "scholasticism," which seemed to base the whole range of active right relationships within the Covenant ("righteousness") on the meticulous observation of *torah* as expounded and expanded in the "tradition of the elders." This was "legalistic righteousness," a form of ethics based entirely on a code, external and "written," losing sight entirely of the gracious personal will of a holy and good God, of which it was originally intended to be the divine vehicle of expression.[83]

As these quotations indicate, "anti-Judaism" is not limited to German Lutherans.

The New Perspective

THE DAWN OF THE NEW PERSPECTIVE: W. D. DAVIES (1911–2001)

Born in a village in South Wales, Davies was educated at the University of Wales, Memorial College (Wales), and Cambridge, where he studied with C. H. Dodd (with whom he shared a common Welsh heritage).[84] Davies was appointed professor of New Testament at Yorkshire United College in 1946, and four years later moved to America, where he taught successively at Duke, Princeton University, Union Theological Seminary (New York), and Texas Christian University. In rehearsing his own development in biblical studies, Davies recalls his realization that the dominant Hellenistic approach had to be abandoned. "It became even clearer that the ark of the New Testament floated on Jewish waters."[85] This led to a new understanding of Paul. Davies came to the conviction that "many aspects of Paulinism previously labeled Hellenistic were better understood as Pharisaic."[86] In reflecting on the history of NT research Davies was disturbed by the tendency to see Christianity over against Judaism. He concluded "that Judaism and Christianity need not be in opposition; that Christianity is not an anti-Judaic phenomenon, but itself, in its origin, a particular form of Messianic Judaism; that both Judaism and Christianity belong to the same family, so that the tension that inevitably exists between them need not develop into an antithesis."[87]

Davies's overview of the NT can be seen in his *Invitation to the New Testament: A Guide to Its Main Witnesses*, a book based on lectures presented on educational television in 1963.[88] In the introduction Davies affirms the importance of the study of Judaism for understanding the NT. Regarding the Synoptic Problem, Davies accepts the 2DH and is sympathetic to B. H.

Streeter's four-source theory.[89] The Gospels, he says, present the message of the kingdom of God, with Jesus as the messianic agent of the kingdom. On Paul, Davies accepts the seven major letters plus 2 Thessalonians, and believes Colossians and Ephesians may be Pauline. Davies thinks the Gospel of John was written between 90 and 100. "[W]hile the author of the Fourth Gospel is unlikely to have been an apostle, he did draw upon early sources which contained the apostolic testimony."[90] Davies concludes: "Like the Synoptics and Paul, and all the New Testament writers, the Fourth Gospel points us to one figure, Jesus, as the revelation of the glory of God."[91]

PAUL AND JUDAISM

Davies's most important book is *Paul and Rabbinic Judaism: Some Rabbinic Elements in Pauline Theology*.[92] The fourth edition is prefaced with a paper on "Paul and Judaism since Schweitzer," which Davies had originally presented to the SBL in 1964.[93] In this paper Davies traces a shift in understanding the background of Paul from an overemphasis on Hellenism to a recognition of the greater importance of Judaism. In the preface to the first edition (1947), Davies sets forth his purpose: "The work is . . . an attempt to set certain pivotal aspects of Paul's life and thought against the background of the contemporary Rabbinic Judaism, so as to reveal how, despite his Apostleship to the Gentiles, he remained, as far as was possible, a Hebrew of the Hebrews, and baptized his Rabbinic heritage into Christ."[94]

In the extensive preface to the fourth edition (1980) Davies reviews research on Paul and Judaism since 1948. Citing the work of Martin Hengel, he advocates the elimination of the sharp line of distinction between Hellenism and Judaism.[95] Davies also believes that the old dichotomy between law and gospel in the understanding of Paul should be abolished. "The centre of his theology lay not in justification by faith as opposed to works, important as that was, but in participation in the life, death, and resurrection of Jesus the Christ. Christ crucified . . . was his point of departure."[96] As to the practice of viewing Judaism as a foil for understanding early Christianity, Davies praises the work of E. P. Sanders. Davies differs from Sanders, however, and argues that Sanders's distinction between Paul's Judaism and his Christianity is overdrawn; Davies believes there is more continuity.

In his introduction to *Paul and Rabbinic Judaism*, Davies records his intent "to prove that Paul belonged to the main stream of first-century Judaism, and that elements in his thought, which are often labelled as Hellenistic, might well be derived from Judaism."[97] Davies goes on to say that "we shall endeavor to show that in the central points of his interpretation of the Christian dispensation

Paul is grounded in an essentially Rabbinic world of thought, that the Apostle was, in short, a Rabbi become Christian and was therefore primarily governed both in life and thought by Pharisaic concepts, which he had baptized 'unto Christ'."[98]

The subsequent chapters present Davies's understanding of the major Pauline concepts. In regard to "The Old Enemy: the Flesh and Sin," Davies agues that these ideas do not reflect Hellenistic dualism but an anthropology found in the OT and in harmony with rabbinic thought. In regard to "The Old and the New Humanity: the First and the Second Adam," Davies believes this concept is grounded in the Jewish idea of two ages. As to "the Old and the New Israel," Davies observes a tension in Judaism between nationalism and universalism; Paul proclaimed a new universalism in Christ but continued to be concerned with the salvation of Israel. In regard to "The Old and the New Man," Davies says that Paul affirmed a personal relation to Christ but did not borrow this idea from Hellenistic mysticism; Paul's ethical teaching reflects the practice of a Jewish rabbi. Very important for Davies's understanding is his chapter on "The Old and the New Torah: Christ the Wisdom of God." In this chapter Davies contends that Paul identifies Christ and Torah. He writes: "[N]ot only did the words of Jesus form a Torah for Paul, but so also did the person of Jesus. In a real sense conformity to Christ, His teaching and His life, has taken the place for Paul of conformity to the Jewish Torah. Jesus Himself—in word and deed or fact is a New Torah."[99] The background of Paul's Christology, according to Davies, is found in the OT idea of personified Wisdom; Davies believes Paul combined the ideas of Christ as Wisdom and Christ as Torah, producing a Christology with cosmic dimensions.

In regard to "The Old and the New Obedience," Davies rejects the notion that Christianity is a religion of the Spirit and Judaism a religion of works.

> In the light of this, even if we could accurately characterize Rabbinic Judaism as entirely a religion of works we must deprecate the approach to our problem which exaggerates the antithesis between Pauline Christianity as a religion of Faith and the Spirit and Rabbinic Judaism as a religion of obedience and the Torah, and which has elevated the doctrine of Justification by Faith to the primary place in Paul's thought. In some contexts justification is merely one metaphor among many others employed by Paul to describe his deliverance through Christ, and we are not justified in petrifying a metaphor into a dogma. Moreover, in those contexts where the idea of Justification by Faith is central, we find that this is so only because of certain

polemical necessities. It is only in those Epistles, namely, Galatians and Romans, where Paul is consciously presenting the claims of his Gospel over against those of Judaism that Justification by Faith is emphasized.[100]

Under this same rubric Davies investigates Paul's understanding of the death of Christ; Paul viewed that death as sacrifice, but like the rabbis he did not stress blood and sacrifice. In regard to the resurrection, Davies notes that the rabbis expected resurrection at the coming of the messiah; for Paul the resurrection of Christ is the dawn of the new age. Davies concludes: "The source of Pauline Christianity lies in the fact of Christ, but in wrestling to interpret the full meaning and implications of that fact Paul constantly drew upon concepts derived from Rabbinic Judaism; it was these that formed the warp and woof if not the material of his thought."[101] This understanding of the Jewish background does not, in Davies's opinion, erode the distinctiveness of Paul's Christianity. "While, therefore, our study has led us to the recognition of Paul's debt to Rabbinic Judaism, it has also led us to that challenge which Pauline Christianity, and indeed all forms of essential Christianity, must issue to Judaism no less than to other religions: What think ye of Christ."[102] A shorter, more recent presentation of Paul and Judaism is found in Davies's essay, "Paul: From the Jewish Point of View."[103] The major lines from the larger work are maintained, and some attention is given to the apostle's biography—his birth in Tarsus, his call to Gentile mission.

THE GOSPEL OF MATTHEW AND THE LAND OF ISRAEL

W. D. Davies made a significant contribution to the study of the Gospel of Matthew.[104] In this area the primary work is his masterful book, *The Setting of the Sermon on the Mount*.[105] Davies goes beyond studies that view the Sermon as a mere collection of individual sayings to a consideration of the whole Sermon in the context of the Gospel of Matthew. At the outset he investigates the thesis that the author of Matthew understands the Christian dispensation in terms of the New Exodus. He finds this motif in the distinctive Matthean material of the Gospel of Matthew.

> The case would seem to be that, while the category of a New Moses and a New Sinai is present in v–vii, as elsewhere in Matthew, the strictly Mosaic traits in the figure of the Matthaean Christ, both there and in other parts of the Gospel, have been taken up into a deeper and higher context. He is not Moses come as Messiah, if

we may so put it, so much as Messiah, Son of Man, Emmanuel, who has absorbed the Mosaic function. The Sermon on the Mount is therefore ambiguous: suggestive of the Law of the New Moses, it is also the authoritative word of the Lord, the Messiah: it is the Messianic Torah.[106]

Davies proceeds to consider the setting of the Sermon within the purview of Jewish messianic expectation.[107] Here he notes the importance of the Exodus motif for the OT and Judaism. In the OT, Jeremiah predicts a new covenant whereby the Torah will be written on the heart, and Second Isaiah presents the Servant of YHWH as the teacher of Torah. In the Apocrypha and Pseudepigrapha Davies finds the hope for the true understanding of Torah in the messianic age. The rabbinic sources, according to Davies, stress the idea that the Torah is perfect and unchangeable, yet the rabbis did expect Elijah to return and give the true interpretation. "One thing is clear: even if the concept of a new Torah in the Messianic Age had not become explicit in Judaism before Christ (which is not at all sure), his figure was a catalyst which gave life to what was inchoate: with him came also a νόμος χριστοῦ."[108] As to the Judaism of the time of Matthew, Davies notes that both the Essenes and the early Christians claimed to be the eschatological community. Davies discusses the relationship of the Matthean community to rabbinic religion as formalized by the Council of Jamnia and believes the Sermon on the Mount may be understood as the Christian answer to Jamnia.[109]

Turning to the setting of the Sermon in the early church, Davies refutes the argument that Matthew was written in opposition to Paul. Paul speaks of the "law of Christ," and according to Davies, Paul understands Christ as the New Torah. After considering other NT evidence, Davies writes: "In sum, there is no reason to believe that Matthew's presentation of the teaching of Jesus as the Law of the Messiah would have been alien even to the Gentile Churches."[110] In regard to the setting in the ministry of Jesus, Davies notes that "Matthew drew around the figure of Jesus the mantle of a lawgiver. . . . There remains to ask the question whether in thus rabbinizing Jesus . . . Matthew has decked his Lord in an alien garb which falsifies the 'Jesus of history.'"[111] In response, Davies points out that the historical Jesus did teach like a rabbi. Although Matthew fosters moralism, Davies believes the author remains true to the Jesus of history. On the larger question of authenticity of the teachings of Jesus as preserved in the Gospels, Davies concludes that "the actual words of Jesus had a fair chance of survival. . . . That there was a wholesale creation of sayings by the primitive communities, which were foisted on to the earthly Jesus, we should not assume.

Far more likely is it that the Church inherited and preserved sayings of Jesus which floated in the tradition, modified them for its own purposes, and then again ascribed them to Jesus in a new form."[112]

Davies is credited with the publication of a massive, three-volume commentary on the Gospel of Matthew,[113] in which all three volumes list him as the lead author. Although Davies was the inspiration, architect, and supervisor of this monumental project, most of the actual research and writing (virtually all in volumes 2 and 3) was done by Dale Allison. Allison became a student of Davies at Duke in 1977 and worked with him on the Gospel of Matthew for almost two decades. He served as Davies's research assistant during the time when Davies was at Texas Christian University (1981–85). Allison knew the mind and method of Davies and incorporated them into this comprehensive commentary on Matthew.

Davies made a unique contribution to NT research with his *The Gospel and the Land*.[114] This book has two main parts. In the first, Davies deals with the understanding of the land in Israelite religion and in Judaism. He finds that in the first part of the OT emphasis is place on the promise of the land. "Of all the promises made to the patriarchs it was that of the land that was most prominent and decisive. It is the linking together of the promise to the patriarchs *with* the fulfilment of it in the settlement that gives to the Hexateuch its distinctive theological character."[115]

With the prophets, the exile from the land was understood as judgment, but they also expressed hope for the restoration of Israel to the land. Davies believes that the concern for the land continued in the Apocrypha, Pseudepigrapha, and the Dead Scrolls. He says that the rabbis maintained that "Jewish sanctity is only fully possible in the land."[116] Davies rejects the theories that Israel embraced a nomadic idea, or that Judaism tended to spiritualize or understand the land as mere symbol. Instead, the land is "accorded its full terrestrial or physical and historical actuality."[117] Davies concludes: "Among many Jews the certainty of the ultimately indissoluble connection between Israel and the land was living and widespread in the world within which Christianity emerged."[118]

In the second part of the work Davies turns to the meaning of the land in the NT. He believes that Jesus was not concerned with the religious or theological significance of the land. As to Paul, Davies finds no explicit references to the land, but he notes the apostle's recognition of the importance of Jerusalem and the temple.

> For a long time Paul apparently felt no incongruity [in] retaining his apocalyptic geography, centered in Jerusalem, even though, since he was "in Christ," it had become otiose. Theologically he had no longer any need of it: his geographical identity was subordinated to that of being "in Christ," in whom was neither Jew nor Greek.[119]

The authors of Mark and Matthew, according to Davies, in locating the ministry of Jesus in Galilee ran counter to the Jewish conviction that Jerusalem would be the place of the advent of the messiah. Davies notes that the author of Luke-Acts viewed Jerusalem as the center of Christian beginnings but emphasized the imperative of moving beyond the land of Israel. "The New Testament finds holy space wherever Christ is or has been: it personalizes 'holy space' in Christ, who, as a figure of History, is rooted in the land; he cleansed the Temple and died in Jerusalem, and lends his glory to these and to the places where he was, but, as Living Lord, he is also free to move wherever he wills."[120]

In sum, Davies was a scholar of immense learning and thoughtful reflection. He handled the sources with care and did not force the material into a mold to support his own position. He criticized the conventional assessment of Judaism, but without rancor. He demonstrated that a scholar can investigate Judaism objectively and in its own right without abandoning one's own Christian convictions. He wrote with clarity, even elegance.

THE NEW PERSPECTIVE: E. P. SANDERS (1937–)

A student of W. D. Davies, like the zealous Paul in relation to tolerant Gamaliel, Sanders does not share his teacher's spirit of moderation.[121] Sanders is a militant foe of every vestige of anti-Judaism. Born in Grand Prairie, Texas, to a family of low economic status, Sanders was educated at Texas Wesleyan College (1955–59), which, as he said, was "the only college I could afford."[122] After graduation he moved to Perkins School of Theology (at Southern Methodist University), where he was befriended by William R. Farmer. Sanders graduated from Perkins in1962, and with the help of Farmer and others received funds to support study in Oxford, Göttingen, and Jerusalem, where he was instructed in both modern Hebrew and rabbinics. In 1963 he entered Union Theological Seminary, where he decided that his career would be devoted to the investigation of Judaism. At Union, Sanders studied with W. D. Davies and also walked across the street for courses at Jewish Theological Seminary. He completed his doctoral dissertation in 1966; it was concerned with the transmission of tradition and had implications for the Synoptic Problem, to which he had been introduced by Farmer.

Sanders began teaching at McMaster University in Canada in 1966. In 1968 he won a fellowship that allowed him to study for a year in Jerusalem with Mordechai Kamrat, an expert in rabbinic Judaism. When he returned to McMaster, Sanders continued to concentrate on the study of Judaism and also began to investigate the epistles of Paul. This came to fruition in his *Paul and Palestinian Judaism* (1977). In the period from 1975 to 1984 Sanders concentrated on the study of Jesus, an effort culminating in his *Jesus and Judaism* (1985). In 1984 he was named Dean Ireland's Professor of Exegesis at Oxford and Fellow of Queens College, a singular honor. During his time at Oxford, Sanders further investigated Jewish sources, leading to *Judaism: Practice and Belief, 63 B.C.E.–66 C.E.* (1992). Sanders joined the faculty of Duke University in 1990; he retired in 2005.[123]

SANDERS ON JUDAISM

Sanders's most influential book is *Paul and Palestinian Judaism* (1977), but his overview of Judaism is presented in later publications. In *Judaism: Practice and Belief,* his intent is to present the theology of Judaism within the context of religious practice.[124] After a sketch of the history of Judaism in the Roman period, Sanders concentrates on religious practice: what he calls "common Judaism." The religion of Judaism, according to Sanders, was centered in the temple, where the primary ritual was the offering of sacrifices. The common people participated in the worship of the temple and its annual festivals. Basic to the religious life of the people, according to Sanders, was observance of the law of God. The law was concerned with purity, and ordinary people kept the rules of purity. The law, continues Sanders, stressed love of neighbor, charity, and honesty. The Jews shared a common theology that stressed the worship of the One God who was creator of all and ruler of history; Sanders characterizes this religion as "covenantal nomism," a religion that stressed election and covenant and obedience to the Law. Sanders points out that early Judaism was a religion of grace; the grace of God preceded the requirement of obedience.

During the Roman period, parties developed within Judaism. The Sadducees were the aristocrats and included the high priest; they did not believe in the resurrection, but stressed morality and public responsibility. The Essenes (known through the Dead Sea Scrolls) understood their community as replacement for the temple. The Pharisees were active in the Herodian period and were popular with the people; they stressed purity and precise interpretation of the law; they were not exclusive, and they affirmed election and grace. Sanders believes the Pharisees have been unfairly maligned as self-righteous legalists who controlled almost everything in Judea. According to

Sanders "they loved God, they thought he had blessed them, and they thought that he *wanted* them to get everything just right. I do not doubt that some of them were priggish."[125] Sanders's portrait of the common people is illuminating: "They worked at their jobs, they believed the Bible, they carried out the small routines and celebrations of the religion: they prayed every day, thanked God for his blessings, and on the sabbath went to the synagogue, asked teachers questions, and listened respectfully."[126]

Sanders's view of Judaism is further explicated in *Jewish Law from Jesus to the Mishnah*.[127] In this book he investigates Judaism in relation to Jesus as presented in the Synoptic accounts—texts that present Jesus in relation to Jewish practice. In regard to the observance of the Sabbath, Sanders writes: "I conclude, then, that the synoptic Jesus behaved on the sabbath in a way which fell inside the range of current debate about it, and well inside the range of permitted behaviour."[128] The saying attributed to Jesus that "whatever goes into a person from outside cannot defile" (Mark 7:18) would have been, according to Sanders, a direct rejection of dietary laws, but Sanders believes it not to be authentic. He insists that the Jewish sources do not support the supposition that Pharisees always washed before ordinary meals. In regard to tithing, Sanders notes that the Pharisaic practice of tithing trivial things reflects their concern to bring all aspects of life under the law. This practice, Sanders maintains, does not mean that the Pharisees were unconcerned with justice, mercy, and faith. Summarizing the practice of Jesus, Sanders writes: "The synoptic Jesus was a law-abiding Jew. . . . He attended the synagogue, he did not eat pork, he did not work on the sabbath in any obvious way. He accepted the sacrificial system both as atoning (Matt. 5.23f.) and purifying (Mark 1.40-44)."[129]

Sanders takes up the question: Did the Pharisees observe oral law? He notes that they did accept tradition that had the support of antiquity, but they did not view tradition as equal with Moses. "The Pharisees intentionally went beyond the letter of the law, and they seem to have considered themselves to be doing so voluntarily, rather than because they 'knew' more laws than did others and thought that obedience to these further laws was strictly required."[130] In regard to the religious practice of Jews in the Diaspora, Sanders argues that the assumption that the Pharisees ran everything in Palestine and that their authority extended into the Diaspora is mistaken. "Yet Diaspora practice, where we can test it, seems not to have been dependent on rules from Jerusalem—much less on rules originating from the Pharisees there."[131]

PAUL AND PALESTINIAN JUDAISM

E. P. Sanders's most influential book, the Magna Carta of the new perspective on Paul, is *Paul and Palestinian Judaism*.[132] Sanders says that this project emerged as he immersed himself in the study of rabbinic literature. He became convinced that a host of NT scholars had misrepresented the religion of the rabbis. As to method, Sanders intends to compare an entire religion with another entire religion according to "patterns of religion." His method focuses on how a person "gets in" and "stays in" a religion and how the practice of a particular religion is understood by its adherents.

The first part of the book (about 400 pages) is devoted to the study of the history, theology, and religious practice of Judaism during the period of the origin of Christianity. At the outset Sanders traces the development of the distorted view whereby rabbinic Judaism is depicted as a legalistic religion devoted to works-righteousness. He notes the wide influence of Ferdinand Weber, whose path was followed by such notables as R. H. Charles and Wilhelm Bousset, who promoted the idea that Judaism viewed God as remote and inaccessible.[133] Major support was given to this approach by the massive *Kommentar zum Neuen Testament aus Talmud und Midrasch* by Strack and Billerbeck.[134] Sanders intends to demolish this approach "by showing that the Weber/Bousset/Billerbeck view, as it applies to Tannaitic literature, is based on a massive perversion and misunderstanding of the material."[135]

In contrast to this distorted view, Sanders presents a summary of his own understanding of rabbinic Judaism:

> There does appear to be in Rabbinic Judaism a coherent and all-pervasive view of what constitutes the essence of Jewish religion and of how that religion "works," and we shall occasionally, for the sake of convenience, call this view "soteriology." The all-pervasive view can be summarized in the phrase "covenantal nomism." Briefly put, covenantal nomism is the view that one's place in God's plan is established on the basis of the covenant and that the covenant requires as the proper response of man his obedience to its commandments, while providing means of atonement for transgression.[136]

Sanders proceeds to present the major elements in the Jewish pattern of religion—the pattern that represents "covenantal nomism."[137] Of fundamental importance is the idea of election. "We may begin by noting several passages in which a Rabbi explicitly states that entrance into the covenant was prior to the fulfilment of commandments; in other words, that the covenant was not earned, but that obedience to the commandments is the consequence of the prior election of Israel by God."[138] Sanders points out that the rabbis believed that election was totally gratuitous and that the gift of the covenant was the fruit of God's love. The rabbis did expect obedience to the commands of God; they believed that God rewarded obedience and punished transgression, but Sanders finds evidence that they warned against obeying the commandments in order to receive a reward. Moreover, "the Rabbis state that God's mercy predominates over his justice when the two conflict, just as they thought that God's reward is always greater than his punishment."[139]

Since the rabbis believed in the resurrection, they discussed reward and punishment in the world to come. Again, the rabbis stressed the justice and mercy of God. They did not believe that obedience had to be perfect.

> Although obedience is required, no number of good deeds can earn salvation if a man acts in such a way as to remove himself from the covenant. Obedience and the intention to obey are required if one is to remain in the covenant and share in its promises, but they do not earn God's mercy.[140]

In short, membership in the covenant assured salvation. For sins committed by those within the covenant, including the ordinary people, God has provided a means of atonement. "The intent and effort to be obedient constitute the *condition for remaining in the covenant*, but they do not *earn* it.[141]

Sanders proceeds to extensive study of the Dead Sea Scrolls and the Apocrypha and Pseudepigrapha. He points out that the Essenes were much concerned with election and covenant. This is true also of most of the books of the Apocrypha and Pseudepigrapha. A notable exception is 4 Ezra, where Sanders discovers that the author promoted a religion of self-righteousness and legalistic perfectionism. Apart from this exception, the Judaism of 200 BCE to 200 CE reflects a common pattern:

> The "pattern" or "structure" of covenantal nomism is this: (1) God has chosen Israel and (2) given the law. The law implies both (3) God's promise to maintain the election and (4) the requirement to obey. (5) God rewards obedience and punishes transgression. (6) The law provides for means of atonement, and atonement results in (7) maintenance or re-establishment of the covenantal relationship. (8) All those who are maintained in the covenant by obedience, atonement and God's mercy belong to the group which will be

saved. An important interpretation of the first and last points is that election and ultimately salvation are considered to be by God's mercy rather than human achievement.[142]

The second part of the book is devoted to Paul, a section of a little more than a hundred pages; the book might better have been entitled *Palestinian Judaism and Paul*. As to sources, Sanders accepts seven epistles as genuine and rejects the use of Acts. He believes that Paul is not a systematic theologian but he is a coherent thinker.[143] According to Sanders, two major convictions govern Paul's life: that Jesus is Lord through whom salvation is provided for all who believe; that Paul was called to be the apostle to the Gentiles. To discover the pattern of Paul's religion, Sanders believes, attention must be focused on soteriology. Paul expected that salvation would be realized in the near future and believed that Christians had been given the Spirit as a guarantee. According to Sanders, Paul emphasized the idea of participation and unity: there is one body and one Spirit. He used various terms to describe the transfer of persons into Christ: participation in the death of Christ, freedom from sin, new creation, reconciliation, and justification.

In regard to the law and the human plight, Sanders insists "that, for Paul, the conviction of a universal solution preceded the conviction of a universal plight."[144] Since God has provided universal salvation, all persons must need salvation, and since salvation is only in Christ, all other ways, including the law, must be wrong. "Faith represents man's entire response to the salvation offered in Jesus Christ, *apart from law*; and *the argument for faith is really an argument against the law*."[145] Sanders thinks that in Paul's soteriological expressions participative categories are more important than juristic categories; "the goal of religion is 'to be found in Christ' and to attain, by suffering and dying with him, the resurrection."[146] Like Davies (and contra Jeremias), Sanders rejects the idea that justification is the center of Paul's thought. He also rejects Bultmann's belief that anthropology is the center and Davies's theory that the coming of the Messiah has replaced the law.[147] In sum, Sanders believes that Paul affirms salvation by grace and judgment by works. "On both these points—punishment for transgression and reward for obedience as required by God's justice, but *not* as constituting soteriology, and correct behaviour as the condition of remaining 'in'—Paul is in perfect agreement with what we found in Jewish literature."[148]

Despite these agreements, Sanders concludes that Paul's religion cannot be designated "covenantal nomism."

> Thus in all these essential points—the meaning of "righteousness," the role of repentance, the nature of sin, the nature of the saved "group" and, most important, the necessity of transferring from the damned to the saved—Paul's thought can be sharply distinguished from anything to be found in Palestinian Judaism. . . . Further, the difference is not located in a supposed antithesis of grace and works . . . but in the total type of religion.[149]

Paul's opposition to the law, according to Sanders, is grounded in his exclusivist soteriology: his conviction that one can be saved only by faith in Christ. "In short, this is what Paul finds wrong in Judaism: it is not Christianity."[150]

Sanders further explicated his position in *Paul, the Law, and the Jewish People*.[151] This book includes two essays. In the first, Sanders presents Paul's understanding of the law. According to Sanders, Paul does not consider the law to be a requirement for salvation. Salvation is through faith in Christ; Paul advocates a soteriology different from that of Judaism. As to the purpose of the law, Paul, according to Sanders, believes that God gave the law in order to condemn all people and prepare for salvation by faith. Although he rejects the law as a way to salvation, Paul, according to Sanders, advocates obedience to the law—a law that has been reduced in regard to such matters as circumcision, days and seasons, and dietary restrictions. In conclusion, Sanders rejects the notion that Paul opposes the law because it is impossible to keep or because keeping the law leads to self-righteousness; he opposes it simply because it does not provide the way to salvation.

> God has appointed Christ for the salvation of the world, for the salvation of all without distinction. God always intended this—he proclaimed it in advance to Abraham—and his will is uniform and stated in Holy Writ. That salvation is being accomplished now, in the last days, with himself, Paul, unworthy though he is, as the apostle whose task is to bring in the Gentiles.[152]

In the second essay Sanders considers Paul's understanding of the Jewish people. Paul considered Christians to be the true Israel—a new people, neither Jew nor Greek. Sanders believes that Paul continued to grapple with a problem he could not resolve: God would keep his promise to Israel, but salvation was granted only by faith in Christ. In conclusion, Sanders observes that Paul departed from Judaism at two important points: he rejected the traditional Jewish doctrine of election; he insisted that faith in Christ was necessary for entrance into the people of God.[153]

JESUS AND JUDAISM

Less known, but even more provocative, is Sanders's *Jesus and Judaism*.[154] "It is the purpose of the present work to take up two related questions with regard to Jesus: his intention and his relationship to his contemporaries."[155] Sanders is also concerned with the question: Why was Jesus executed? In regard to method, Sanders contends that the attempt to understand Jesus primarily from his teaching has failed. He prefers to focus on the "facts" about Jesus. To understand the facts (the actions of Jesus), Sanders believes one must begin with an investigation of Jesus' intention. According to Sanders, Jesus' primary intention is to herald the restoration of Israel. The point of departure for understanding this intention, says Sanders, is Jesus' action in "cleansing" the temple. Sanders believes this event was a dramatic act that symbolized the destruction and restoration of the temple. "Thus we conclude that Jesus publicly predicted or threatened the destruction of the temple, that the statement was shaped by his expectation of the arrival of the eschaton, that he probably also expected a new temple to be given by God from heaven, and that he made a demonstration which prophetically symbolized the coming event."[156] Sanders presents the evidence that Jewish texts also expected the eschatological temple, but he observes that Jesus did not promote the traditional way to restoration. "What is surprising is that, while looking for the restoration of Israel, he did not follow the majority and urge the traditional means towards that end: repentance and a return to observance of the law."[157]

In regard to Jesus' proclamation, Sanders believes Jesus understood the kingdom of God as an eschatological reality. According to Sanders the kingdom refers to the future, but the power of God is working in the present.

> Just as we cannot yet say precisely what Jesus thought would happen in the future, so also we cannot say just what he thought was taking place in the present. Our study of sayings confirms general points—Jesus looked for a future event and saw his own work as important—but does not precisely define them.[158]

Sanders rejects the notion that the miracles identify Jesus as a particular religious type, for example, a "divine man"; Jesus probably saw the miracles as evidence of his status as a spokesman for God. Sanders agrees that Jesus called sinners and associated with them, and these sinners were truly wicked: traitors like the tax collectors, not ordinary people who might be ritually impure. Judaism provided atonement and a way for sinners to repent, but Sanders argues that Jesus offered the kingdom to sinners without first requiring repentance.

Sanders proposes two main causes for Jesus' execution: his attack on the temple and his acceptance of sinners. Jesus' view that the wicked had a place in the kingdom was contrary to the law, as was his implicit rejection of the command to honor one's father and mother (Matt 8:21-22; Luke 9:59-60). Regarding the meaning of the crucifixion, "We should begin our study with two firm facts before us: Jesus was executed by the Romans as would-be 'king of the Jews,' and his disciples subsequently formed a messianic movement which was not based on the hope of military victory."[159] Sanders believes that evidence for the charge that Jesus entertained royal expectations is found in his entry into Jerusalem, which Sanders understands as a historical event that symbolized the coming kingdom and Jesus' role in it. The opposition to Jesus, according to Sanders, was led not by the Pharisees but by the Jewish aristocracy and temple leaders. In sum, Sanders believes we can know the basic facts about Jesus: it is certain that he proclaimed the coming kingdom of God as eschatological miracle; it is probable that he believed the kingdom would have leaders and that his disciples thought of him as king, and it is conceivable that Jesus identified himself with the cosmic Son of Man. What cannot be supported by the evidence, according to Sanders, is the notion that Jesus was an exceptional Jew who alone believed in love, mercy, grace, and forgiveness, and that for such views he was executed.

Toward the end of the book Sanders provides insight into to his own methodology. "I have been engaged for some years in the effort to free history and exegesis from the control of theology; that is, from being obligated to come to certain conclusions which are pre-determined by theological commitment."[160] He continues:

> I am a liberal, modern, secularized Protestant, brought up in a church dominated by low christology and the social gospel. I am proud of the things that that religious tradition stands for. I am not bold enough, however, to suppose that Jesus came to establish it, or that he died for the sake of its principles.[161]

Thus Sanders affirms an objectivity that is colored by polemic. His book may be seen as a new Schweitzer: a picture of Jesus set in distant Judaism, alien to the modern world, devoid of relevance.[162] Sanders's result, however, may be even more potent since it avoids the sort of fanciful reconstruction of Jesus that debilitated Schweitzer's entire project.

In a later book, *The Historical Figure of Jesus*, Sanders presents a survey of Jesus' life and work.[163] "The aim of this book is to lay out, as clearly as possible, what we can know, using the standard methods of historical research, and to distinguish this from inferences, labelling them clearly as such."[164] According to Sanders, Jesus must be seen in his political and religious setting. Jesus called disciples and was supported by a larger group, including women. In regard to the miracles, Sanders believes Jesus should be viewed from the perspective of his own contemporaries; they probably saw the miracles, especially the exorcisms, as signs of the beginning of God's triumph over evil. The main message of Jesus was the coming of the kingdom, which, according to Sanders, Jesus expected in the near future. Sanders believes that the message of Jesus involved a reversal of values; it called for ethical perfectionism but was compassionate toward human frailty. In answer to the question why one who affirmed God's love would be executed, Sanders repeats the answers from the previous book: Jesus' attack on the temple and his action that led people to hail him as king. Sanders believes that Jesus regarded himself as owning the authority to speak and act on behalf of God. "Jesus was a *charismatic and autonomous prophet*; that is, his authority (in his own view and that of his followers) was not mediated by any human organization, not even by scripture."[165] At the Last Supper, according to Sanders, Jesus anticipated the coming of the kingdom, and on the cross he expected the kingdom would arrive immediately, but after a few hours he cried out that he had been forsaken. Sanders concludes that much can be known about the historical Jesus, but historical reconstruction is never certain. "Perhaps most important, we know how much he inspired his followers, who sometimes themselves did not understand him, but who were so loyal to him that they changed history."[166]

Sanders's work on the historical Jesus was informed by his research on the Synoptic Problem. At Perkins he had studied with William R. Farmer, the champion of the Griesbach hypothesis,[167] and at Union he wrote a dissertation on the Synoptic Problem (directed by Davies).[168] The purpose of the dissertation was to investigate criteria by which developing tradition can be assessed. Sanders's method was to trace the development of tradition in post-canonical literature (including the Apostolic Fathers and early Christian apocryphal texts) in order to discern criteria for investigating the pre-canonical, synoptic tradition. His assessment was made on the basis of three categories: length (was the tendency toward greater length or toward abbreviation?), detail (was the tendency toward detail or toward simplicity?), Semitism (was the tendency toward use of Semitisms or toward "better" Greek?). Sanders concluded that, in regard to length, the evidence argued against the priority of Mark and against the 2DH. In the category of details, some of the evidence supports Markan priority, some the priority of Matthew. In regard to the use of Semitisms, Sanders contends that the residue of Semitic syntax and grammar does not prove that a tradition is earlier. He concludes: "*The evidence does not seem to warrant the degree of certainty with which many scholars hold the two-document hypothesis.*"[169]

Many years later Sanders (with Margaret Davies) published *Studying the Synoptic Gospels*.[170] The authors survey the various theories on the Synoptic Problem and conclude that there is no totally satisfactory solution. They believe that Matthew used Mark and other sources, and Luke used Mark and Matthew and other sources; there was cross-copying among the Gospels. They believe the form-critical method is useful in seeking information about Jesus. They also note the usefulness of redaction criticism for understanding each Gospel as a whole. They believe historical information about Jesus can be recovered and that some of the criteria (dissimilarity, multiple attestation) are useful; they especially favor tradition that is "against the grain" and material that is "common to friend and foe." The result of these methods is a picture of a Jesus who expected the kingdom as a cosmic event or a new social order or both. His mission was to all Israel, including sinners; he advocated love of neighbor and enemy; he believed the new order demanded new ethical standards.

The work of E. P. Sanders generated a storm of controversy,[171] most of it centered around Sanders's "new perspective on Paul."[172] Some scholars called for a more nuanced treatment of the issues and many suggested that there were several "new perspectives." Major opposition came from scholars who considered the doctrine of justification by faith to be central to Paul and basic to the Christian gospel. Actually, the opposition to Sanders was directed more to his interpretation of Paul than to his understanding of Judaism. In regard to the latter a large number of scholars agreed with Sanders's rejection of the older view that evaluated Judaism from the perspective of Christianity and caricatured it as a religion of legalism and self-righteousness. Of course, some scholars acknowledged that covenantal nomism could have been distorted at times and by individuals. The NT appears to oppose legalism, but this does not prevent fundamentalists from reading it in another way. In the main, Sanders's positive assessment of Judaism has been accepted; what he achieved was a "new perspective" on Judaism.

Since he is the next major figure to be treated in this *History*, Martin Hengel can be cited as an example of sharp criticism of Sanders.[173] Hengel argues that Sanders has minimized the role of the Pharisees in opposition to Jesus. He also believes Sanders does not give adequate attention to Jesus' messianic claim. Hengel charges Sanders with "radical historical skepticism" and says that Sanders caricatures the position of his opponents in order to "make it look ridiculous."[174] No doubt much of Hengel's attack is in reaction to Sanders's criticism of Hengel's teacher, Joachim Jeremias. It is also true that Hengel was a staunch supporter of the centrality of justification by faith; he did not share the new perspective. "Sanders' concern is apologetic and is directed against the anti-Judaism which he thinks is traditional in New Testament scholarship, not least in Germany."[175] Actually, much of the difference between Sanders and Hengel is rooted in their presuppositions, their basic points of view. Sanders believes the trouble with many NT scholars is their preoccupation with theology. Hengel, on the other hand, believed that NT interpreters must be dedicated to the pursuit of truth.[176] Careful examination of these commitments may suggest that Sanders is more of a theologian than he supposes, while Hengel is less.

A REVIVAL OF THE OLD PERSPECTIVE: MARTIN HENGEL (1926–2009)

Hengel was born in Reutlingen in Baden Württemberg.[177] As a school boy of seventeen he was drafted into the German Army in 1943 and served on the Western Front. Hengel studied at Heidelberg and at Tübingen under Otto Michel. He completed his Promotion (doctorate) at Tübingen in 1959 and, interrupted by work in his family's textile business, his Habilitation (also at Tübingen) in 1966. Hengel taught at Erlangen (1968–1972) and then at Tübingen from 1972 until his retirement in 1992. In Tübingen, Hengel served as director of the Institute for Ancient Judaism and Hellenistic Religion. He was elected president of the SNTS in 1993. Hengel received honorary degrees from several universities including Uppsala, Cambridge, and Durham. He produced a mountain of publications, including major works in retirement.[178]

Hengel is devoted to the use of the historical critical method, which he characterizes as "philological-historical." "There is only one appropriate exegesis, namely that which does justice to the text (and its contexts)."[179] Hengel is critical of much of contemporary scholarship.

> Unfortunately, theologians today increasingly lack historical knowledge and an interest in history, and above all are too ignorant of the legacy of the past, whether of the Old Testament and Judaism, or of Graeco-Roman antiquity. Since the so-called "scholars" are gradually failing us here, it is doubly important for us as Christians

to try to acquire a deeper historical understanding of what took place more than 1900 years ago; without such historical understanding our theological thinking, too, will all too easily become barren.[180]

In his presidential address to the SNTS, Hengel eschews the new methods in favor of the old. "The decisive point of departure remains—in spite of reader response and deconstructionism—*the early Christian author . . .* what he meant, and in the perspective of those addressed, hearer and reader, what he intended."[181] Hengel is skeptical of skepticism.

> The destructive scepticism, a particular feature of the modern world, which works in a predominantly analytical way, often ultimately ends up, not by furthering real historical understanding but by making it impossible. It is striking here that in particular those authors who apply radical criticism to early Christian narrators . . . often invent facts of their own which have no basis whatever in the sources and indeed go directly against them. Despite the anxiety of fundamentalists we cannot and should not refrain from the consistent application of historical methods. . . . A few months ago my American publisher asked me, "Why are you so conservative?" At that time I simply replied, "Why not?" Perhaps I should have added: these distinctions between "conservative" and "liberal" or even "progressive" . . . are ultimately meaningless. We are concerned only with the *truth*, theological and historical. The truth is our sole obligation; we have to seek and to present it, and in the end it will prevail against all our conjectures, all our desires to be right, our imaginative constructions and our anxiety.[182]

HENGEL ON JUDAISM

Hengel began his research on Judaism early; his qualifying dissertation (Habilitationsschrift) at Tübingen was on the Zealots.[183] The purpose of the dissertation was to investigate the nature and development of the Zealot movement from the time of Herod to the Jewish War. Hengel's thesis is "that the 'Zealots' formed a relatively exclusive and unified movement with its own distinctive religious views, and that they had a crucial influence on the history of Palestinian Judaism in the decisive period between 6 and 70 A.D."[184] After a discussion of the sources (Josephus, contemporary Jewish writings, Christian texts), Hengel investigates the various names by which the freedom movement was identified: "robbers," "Sicarii" (users of daggers), and οἱ ζηλωταί (the

Zealots)—the term Josephus uses to designate the freedom party within Judaism at the time of Jesus.

According to Hengel the pioneering figure in the emergence of the freedom movement was "Judas the Galilean" (Acts 5:37), who led a revolt in reaction to the census enacted by Quirinius in 6/7 CE. Judas believed the census would result in slavery to Rome. Hengel thinks Judas's movement was entirely religious. It was inspired by the OT idea of zeal for God and was fueled by the eschatological hope. The Zealots, according to Hengel, believed the eschatological message called for militant action; they affirmed the sole rule of God and embraced the idea of martyrdom. Evidence of the activity of the movement in the time of Jesus can be seen in Simon, "who was called the Zealot," one of the Twelve (Luke 6:15). Zealots increasingly resisted the action of Roman governors in 40s, and with the appointment of Gessius Florus in 64 the country erupted in chaos. In the beginning of the revolt against Rome the Zealots had the support of most of the inhabitants of Jerusalem. But the movement came increasingly under the control of the radicals, the Sicarii, and the Zealots divided into factions. With the fall of Jerusalem in 70, the movement of the Zealots crumbled. Hengel believes the activity of the Zealots illustrates the eschatological ferment of the time. He thinks Jesus was handed over to the Romans as an alleged Zealot, a messianic pretender.

Hengel's magnum opus is his *Judaism and Hellenism*.[185] His intent is to illuminate the social, religious, and historical background of early Christianity. Hengel is particularly concerned to overcome the distinction between Judaism and Hellenism that dominated earlier scholarship. He begins with a survey of Hellenism as a political and economic force. Hellenism reached Palestine with the conquest of Alexander and increased its influence during the time of conflict between the Ptolemies and the Seleucids; it attained a high point with the invasion of Jerusalem by Antiochus IV (169 BCE). However, according to Hengel, Hellenism affected only the urban centers.

> Interest in Hellenistic civilization, however, *remained predominantly limited to the well-to-do aristocracy of Jerusalem.* Intensive economic exploitation and social unconcernedness of the new masters and their imitators, who were concerned purely with economics, only served to exacerbate the situation of the lower strata of the population. It prepared the ground for apocalyptic speculation and later revolts, which had increasingly strong social elements, right down to the time of the Bar Kochba rebellion.[186]

Most important, according to Hengel, was the influence of Hellenism as a cultural force. The Greek language, he says, was widely used in Jerusalem, and Greek education is attested by the establishment of a gymnasium in Jerusalem in 176 BCE; Hellenistic literature and philosophy were introduced. "From about the middle of the third century BC *all Judaism* must really be designated '*Hellenistic Judaism*' in the strict sense."[187]

Hengel turns to the conflict between the older Judaism (which he continues to call "Palestinian Judaism") and Hellenism. He points out that Hellenization was opposed by apocalyptic writers like Daniel. "The picture of history in apocalyptic is above all a fruit of the Jewish struggle for spiritual and religious self-determination against the invasion of Jerusalem by the Hellenistic spirit."[188] The Hasidim, the forerunners of the Essenes, who appeared in the second century BCE, also opposed Hellenization. In the struggle against Hellenizing, the Jews affirmed the centrality of the temple and the primacy of the law. Hengel believes that the Jewish reaction led to a strident nationalism and a strict understanding of Torah. He sees evidence of this in the opposition to the Jesus movement.

> Here is the profound tragedy of the reaction of Judaism to the primitive Christian movement which developed from its midst. Jesus of Nazareth, Stephen, Paul came to grief among their own people because the Jews were no longer in a position to bring about a creative, self-critical transformation of the piety of the law with its strongly national and political colouring.[189]

Within this religious context Christianity had its origin. "Christianity is to be seen as an eschatological and revolutionary movement within Judaism itself."[190] The depth and breadth, the mastery of material, the attention to detail of Hengel's research are abundantly evident in the second volume of *Judaism and Hellenism*, which consists of over two hundred pages of notes and a bibliography of fifty pages.

Hengel continued his work on Judaism and Hellenism in later publications. His book on *Jews, Greeks, and Barbarians* summarizes the earlier work, clarifies some issues, and updates the research (for instance, the archaeological evidence).[191] In this book Hengel points out that "Hellenism" refers to more that a historical period; "it is to be understood as the designation of an apparently clearly defined culture which because of its aggressive character also sought to take over ancient Judaism."[192] Hengel also notes the complexities of the subject.

Thus when analysing the concept of "Hellenization," we have to distinguish between very different components. These would include: first, close professional contacts; secondly, the physical mixing of populations; thirdly, the adoption of Greek language and culture by orientals; and fourthly, the complete assimilation of "orientalized" Greeks and "Hellenized" orientals.[193]

In *The "Hellenization" of Judaea in the First Century after Christ*, Hengel presents a short version of what he had originally planned as the sequel to *Judaism and Hellenism*.[194] Here he turns to the effects of Hellenism (Greek lifestyle, economy, technology, education, philosophy, and religion) on Palestine in the first century. Hengel finds evidence of Hellenizing in the building of cities in Galilee like Sepphoris and Tiberias. In regard to political and social aspects of Hellenization, Hengel notes the Jewish desire to emulate Hellenistic rulers and to get along with Rome. He observes that Christianity may be understood as influenced by both Jewish and Hellenistic ideas, yet he believes the whole development of Christianity could have taken place within Judaism. Despite the force of Hellenistic influence, Hengel recognizes that most of the writers of the NT were Jewish Christians, unschooled in Greek writing and culture. "We may assume that those men who bore the new message from Jewish Palestine to Syria and Asia Minor and indeed to Rome came neither from the illiterate proletariat nor from the aristocracy but from the creative middle class, which nowadays is so readily dismissed as 'petty-bourgeois,' a social milieu from which Jesus and Paul probably came."[195]

In various essays Hengel treated subtopics within the larger framework of Judaism and Hellenism. In "Jerusalem als jüdische und hellenistische Stadt," he traces the efforts to transform the Holy City into a Hellenistic center.[196] Hengel finds evidence of Hellenization in the use of the Greek language and in the building program of Herod. A test-case for Hengel's theory that Hellenism had penetrated Judaism is presented in "Qumran und der Hellenismus."[197] Although the Essenes, with their retreat into the wilderness, would appear to be the epitome of anti-Hellenistic Judaism, Hengel finds evidence of Hellenistic influence among them. The water system at Qumran displays technical knowledge, and the *War Scroll* shows familiarity with Hellenistic military tactics. The Essenes' stress on the two spirits ("sons of light" and "sons of darkness") reflects Hellenistic dualism, and they affirmed immortality of the soul rather than resurrection of the body. Hengel's "'Schriftauslegung' und 'Schriftwerdung' in der Zeit des Zweiten Tempels" highlights the Jewish concern with the interpretation of Scripture in the Hellenistic period.[198]

Hengel notes the formalizing of the canon of the Pentateuch and the Prophets in the first century CE, an action that shows that Judaism had become a religion of the book. According to Hengel the Jews believed the prophetic line ended with Ezra, with the result that the scribe was honored as interpreter; in order to be taken as authoritative, writings had to claim authorship by an ancient prophet like Daniel.

HENGEL ON JESUS AND CHRISTOLOGY

Hengel's stress on the importance of Judaism as background to early Christianity is expressed in "Early Christianity as a Jewish-Messianic Movement."[199] In this essay he contends that the entire background of Christianity is to be found exclusively in Judaism; if pagan influences can be detected, they have been filtered through Judaism. Hengel understands the early Christians as a sect of Judaism; the dispute between the followers of Jesus and the Jews was an inner-family quarrel. Christology, which is the heart of the Christian message, is grounded, according to Hengel, in the Jewish idea of the messiah; it is not a syncretism of Jewish and Greek concepts. Hengel rejects the idea that the NT expresses anti-Judaism and insists that it is a reliable source for understanding first-century Judaism.

Important for Hengel's understanding of Christianity is his monograph, *Nachfolge und Charisma*.[200] In the preface to the English edition of 1996 Hengel notes impediments to the study of the historical Jesus, including the continuing skepticism of the Bultmann school and recent fanciful work by Americans. "Today a special danger seems to arise from the pseudo-critical ignorance expressing itself in a flood of 'modern' and 'fashionable' books on Jesus."[201] Hengel believes that understanding the historical Jesus can be facilitated by investigating his call to discipleship. To the excuse "first let me go bury the dead," Jesus responds, "let the dead bury their own dead" (Matt 8:21-22). Hengel believes this text reveals the radical nature of the call, since Jesus' response constitutes an attack on the Fourth Commandment. Hengel observes that "this hardness on Jesus' part as to the unconditional nature of following him . . . is to be explained only on the basis of his unique authority as the proclaimer of the *imminent Kingdom of God*."[202] Comparing this with other calls—for example, Elijah's call of Elisha—Hengel stresses "the charismatic and eschatological distinctiveness" of the call of Jesus.[203] This distinctive character of Jesus' call, according to Hengel, indicates that Jesus fits none of the contemporary categories: rabbi, scribe, wisdom teacher; "Jesus stood outside any discoverable uniform teaching tradition of Judaism."[204]

Hengel's understanding of the historical Jesus is advanced in *The Four Gospels and the One Gospel of Jesus Christ*.[205] In regard to the Gospels, Hengel argues that Mark was earliest, written in Rome and recording the reminiscences of Peter.[206] Hengel questions the existence of Q as a single document but finds the theory of a *logia* source to be plausible. He believes Matthew was dependent on Mark and Luke and probably on collections of *logia*. In the developing history of the church, the view emerged that there is one gospel but four apostolic witnesses. Hengel believes the Christians at Rome replaced the tabernacle in the Jewish synagogue with a cupboard in the place of worship that contained the four canonical Gospels in codex form. The narrative of the Gospels had its ultimate source in the reports of eyewitnesses, and the early Christians and the Gospel writers, according to Hengel, were conservative in preserving the tradition. "Despite all the sometimes considerable differences and tensions, these authors all point back to the one centre: the person of Christ, the foundation stone, the Son of God incarnate of John 1.14 and the salvation brought about by him."[207]

The historical Jesus is the basis for Christology, a topic of major important for Hengel. His book on the Son of God and the origin of Christology is based on his inaugural lecture at Tübingen in 1973.[208] The book grapples with the problem of the discrepancy between the shameful death of Jesus and the confession of him as pre-existent divine figure within only two decades. Hengel investigates the attempt to solve the problem by the history of religion school. He finds their theories—that the origin of the divine Son was to be found in the mystery cults or in the gnostic redeemer—to be hopelessly mistaken. According to Hengel the background of the idea of the Son of God is to be found in ancient Judaism, where pre-existence is attributed to Wisdom, the mediator of creation.[209] In this context Hengel traces the rise of early Christology as witnessed by such texts as Rom 1:3-4, a pre-Pauline tradition that confesses the messiahship of Jesus (son of David) and the divine sonship of Jesus. Hengel believes this primitive confession to be confirmed by history: Jesus' unique relation to God is expressed in his use of *Abba* and proved by his execution as a messianic pretender. "Thus the problem of 'pre-existence' necessarily grew out of the combination of Jewish ideas of history, time and creation with the certainty that God had disclosed himself fully in his Messiah Jesus of Nazareth."[210]

Hengel's understanding of Christology is developed in essays published in his *Studies in Early Christology*.[211] The first of these, "Jesus, The Messiah of Israel," was originally presented in lectures at the University of Cardiff in 1991.[212] In this essay Hengel raises the question: Does the title "Christ" (the

Anointed, the Messiah) have any connection with the historical person of Jesus? He rejects the idea that the title was first applied to Jesus after the resurrection and argues that its usage has its origin in the messianic claim of Jesus himself. The most compelling evidence, according to Hengel, is the fact that Jesus was executed as a messianic pretender, as King of the Jews. Hengel acknowledges that Jesus did not use this title for himself but observes that he did not reject its use by others. "In my judgement," says Hengel, "the messianic secret in the Second Gospel stems *in nuce* from the—eschatological—secret of Jesus himself, and his conduct. In other words, the messianic 'mystery' originates in the 'mystery' of Jesus."[213] In regard to the Son of Man, a title exclusively used by Jesus, Hengel believes it to be a messianic title. "The earthly and suffering Son of Man are a cipher with which Jesus, in certain situations, expresses both his authority as 'eschatological proclaimer of salvation' (indeed, we may say as *'Messias designatus'*), and his humility and tribulation, which ultimately lead him to suffering and death."[214] This essay offers Hengel the platform to expound on the frailties of contemporary scholarship.

> Orthodox-fundamental biblicism has its counterpart in critical biblicism. Both are naïve and in danger of doing violence to historical reality—the one, because of its ahistorical biblical literalism, and the other, because it selects and interprets in accordance with its modern world-view, and theological interests. Against the view, since Wrede, of the unmessianic Jesus, it must be admitted that Jesus conducted himself with 'messianic' authority, and was executed as a messianic pretender. Only thus are the development of post-Easter christology, the account of his Passion, and his efficacy historically comprehensible.

Crucial to Hengel's Christology is the doctrine of the atonement. In his book on that subject he investigates the question: How was the death of Jesus understood as atoning sacrifice so early?[215] At the outset Hengel points out that the idea of death as atoning sacrifice is not unknown in the Greco-Roman world, but he argues that the Christian idea is distinctive. According to Hengel's reading of the Christian view atonement was universal, the action of God that had eschatological significance. Hengel searches for the origin of the soteriological understanding of the death of Jesus and finds the first written evidence in 1 Cor 15:3, a text that preserves pre-Pauline tradition. Hengel believes the idea of atonement is also present in the pre-Markan tradition of the passion narrative and that it has its origin in Jesus himself. Hengel finds evidence for this in the earliest tradition of the Lord's Supper. At the Supper, Jesus, according to Hengel, interprets his own impending death as universal, atoning sacrifice.

HENGEL ON PAUL, ACTS, AND JOHN

In regard to Paul, Hengel presents interesting research on the lesser-known periods of the apostle's life. His book, *The Pre-Christian Paul*, examines Paul's life in Judaism.[216] Hengel believes Paul was born in Tarsus, but in his adolescence moved to Jerusalem where he was educated in a Greek-speaking Pharisaic school. Although the nature of Pharisaic thought in this period cannot be ascertained, Hengel believes parallels can be found in rabbinic literature. For this he finds Billerbeck's *Kommentar* helpful. About Billerbeck, Hengel says that "his work is still unsurpassed. . . . He contributed more towards a positive understanding of early Judaism in the sphere of theology than any New Testament scholar of his time and indeed down to the present day."[217] Hengel thinks it probable that Paul had personally witnessed the crucifixion of Jesus.

As a Pharisee, Paul persecuted the Christians in Jerusalem, who were divided into two groups: Hebrews (Aramaic speaking) and Hellenists (Greek-speaking); Paul, according to Hengel, attacked the latter. Hengel believes Paul accepted a commission from the synagogues of Jerusalem to pursue and persecute the Hellenistic Christians who had fled to Damascus. On the way to Damascus, Paul had a vision of the risen Christ.

> The Jewish teacher becomes the missionary to the Gentiles; the "zeal for the law" is replaced by the proclamation of the gospel without the law; justification of the righteous on the basis of their "works of the law" is replaced by justification of the "godless" through faith alone; the free will is replaced by the faith which is given by grace alone as the creation of the word; and hatred of the crucified and accursed pseudo-messiah is replaced by a theology of the cross which grounds the salvation of all men and women in the representative accursed death of the messiah on the cross.[218]

Despite this radical change, Paul, in Hengel's opinion, still stood in the shadow of Judaism.

> Despite this rigorous reversal of all previous values and ideals (Phil. 3.7-11), Pauline theology—and therefore also Christian theology—remains very closely bound up with Jewish theology. Its

individual elements and thought-structure derive almost exclusively from Judaism. This revolutionary change becomes visible precisely in the fact that its previous theological views remain present even in their critical reversal as a negative foil, and help to determine the location of the new position. Paul first learned his theological thinking in no other place than at a Jewish house of learning, and before he proclaimed Christ to the Gentiles, he had interpreted the law in the synagogue—very probably in Jerusalem itself—to Jews of the Diaspora.[219]

Continuing his research on Paul, Hengel turns to the life of the apostle from his conversion to his ministry in Antioch.[220] He describes Paul's conversion experience as "a real, objective seeing of a supernatural reality in divine splendor of light."[221] Paul, according to Hengel, was baptized by the Christian community of Damascus, from whom he received Christian tradition. Hengel believes that Paul did not immediately return to Jerusalem because he had been called to preach; he began his mission in Nabatea where he preached to "God-fearers" in the synagogues. After two years he returned to Damascus and then visited Jerusalem. Hengel believes the account in Acts 9:26 displays inconsistencies; he prefers Paul's own account (Gal 1:18-20), which indicates that the important feature of the trip was a visit with Peter. After the short stay in Jerusalem, Paul moves his mission to Tarsus and Cilicia and neighboring regions including Syria. Although Acts does not report Paul's mission to Gentiles until his visit to Antioch of Pisidia (13:46), Hengel believes Paul had been preaching to Gentiles already in Damascus and Nabatea. In Antioch of Syria and the surrounding region, Paul, according to Hengel, worked with Barnabas for eight or nine years. Hengel rejects the theory that Paul's theology was influenced by Hellenistic ideas during the Antioch period.

> [A]ll the elements of Pauline theology, in so far as they have not been shaped by the apostle himself—and their proportion should not be over-estimated—come from the abundantly rich Jewish tradition of his time. In so far as they are of Greek or "oriental" origin, they are mediated by Judaism (which was many-sided). Basically speaking, this is also true of the whole of earliest Christianity.[222]

Hengel believes that Paul's thought did not undergo major changes and was largely formulated by the time of his Antioch mission. "'Justification of the godless by grace alone' is not an insight from the apostle's late period, but shaped his proclamation from his earliest period as the cause of his theology of the cross."[223]

Hengel notes the importance of eschatology in Paul's theology, especially his interest in apocalyptic.[224] He observes that liberalism scorned apocalyptic and Bultmann demythologized it. In contrast, Hengel argues that apocalyptic was crucial for Judaism, Jesus, and the NT. He writes that "the whole of Christianity (just as for Paul), on the basis of its Christology which rests on the eschatological revelation of God, its self-understanding as the eschatological people of the end-time redeemer, and its intensive hope must be designated as 'apocalyptic.'"[225] The background of Paul's apocalyptic thought is found, according to Hengel, in the synoptic tradition, which has its source in Jesus himself.

Hengel further explicates apocalyptic eschatology in his discussion of Paul's understanding of the burial and bodily resurrection of Jesus.[226] Important for this issue is the formulation of the early kerygma found 1 Cor 15:3-5; the phrase καὶ ὅτι ἐτάφη ("and that he was buried") indicates to Hengel that the body was important and the tomb was empty. The background of this kerygmatic expression is to be found, according to him, in Jewish apocalyptic: a view of life after death that affirmed bodily resurrection. Hengel believes Paul's idea of bodily resurrection had its origin in the earliest tradition, and that it is crucial for the Christian faith.

Late in his career Hengel published a provocative monograph on Peter, "the underestimated apostle."[227] The crucial text, Matt 16:17-19, does not originate with Jesus but, according to Hengel, was added by Matthew at the time of writing his gospel (ca. 90–100). This points to the importance of Peter in the post-apostolic age. However, Hengel believes the nicknaming of Simon as the Rock does go back to the historical Jesus and proves the importance of Peter in the early tradition. Peter was the first witness to the resurrection; he was the leader of the earliest church in Jerusalem. Hengel also accepts the tradition that Mark was the interpreter of Peter and wrote his Gospel in Rome a few years after Peter's martyrdom. As to the conflict between Peter and Paul in Antioch, Hengel notes that the story is told by Paul, with Peter's side unfairly neglected. "*The deep divide that was signified by the dramatic, public, drawn-out dispute between Peter and Paul is something we cannot portray deeply enough.*"[228] Hengel attempts to fill in the unknown years between Peter's disappearance after the conflict with Paul (Gal 2:11-14) and his martyrdom at Rome. Hengel detects evidence of Peter's important role as organizer and leader of extensive mission and as theological thinker. He believes it possible that some reconciliation between Peter and Paul occurred; they were both executed under the Neronian persecution. Hengel concludes: "Peter was still a theologically powerful thinker, an impressive proclaimer, and a competent organizer; otherwise, he would not have played such a unique role within the circle of Jesus' disciples, in Jerusalem and later as missionary to both Jews and Gentiles, and he would not have been able to achieve a unique position and be held in such high regard."[229]

Hengel did important research on the Acts of the Apostles. In his essay on early Christian historical writing he investigates Christian texts in the context of historical writings of antiquity.[230] In regard to Acts, Hengel acknowledges that his own view is unfashionable: that it was written by Luke, the traveling companion of Paul. He considers Luke to be the first theological historian of Christianity; "as a Christian 'historian' he sets out to report the events of the past that provided the foundation for the faith."[231] Although Acts is not wholly accurate (for instance, the account of Paul's first visit to Jerusalem and the point of the beginning of Paul's preaching to Gentiles), Luke is generally reliable.[232]

Hengel gives special attention to one of the decisive events in early Christian history: the expulsion of the Hellenists from the Jerusalem church.[233] He identifies the "Hellenists" of Acts 6:1 as Greek-speaking Jewish Christians of Jerusalem. He believes their point of view is expressed in the speech of Stephen: they were critical of the temple and they transformed the gospel into a universal message. Hengel believes the source of this message is to be found in Jesus himself.

> Precisely through the activity of the early Greek-speaking community, more of the proclamation of Jesus is present in the synoptic gospels than basically anti-historical modern hyper-criticism is willing to concede. Twenty years after Stephen, the earliest Christian kerygma shone out in all its glory in Paul's "mission theology." We owe the real bridge between Jesus and Paul to those almost unknown Jewish-Christian "Hellenists" of the group around Stephen and the first Greek-speaking community in Jerusalem which they founded; this was the first to translate the Jesus tradition into Greek and at the same time prepared the way for Paul's preaching of freedom by its criticism of the ritual law and the cult. Only this community can be called the "pre-Pauline Hellenistic community" in the full sense of the word.[234]

Hengel made a distinctive contribution to the study of the Fourth Gospel as well. His book on the "Johannine Question" presents his solution to the problem of the origin and authorship of the Fourth Gospel.[235] Hengel believes the ultimate source of the Gospel of John is the eyewitness tradition of John the Elder. This little-know figure, according to Hengel, was born in Jerusalem around 15 CE, a member of the priestly hierarchy; he had contact with Jesus, witnessed his death, and belonged to the early Jerusalem church; his language was Semitic and he understood the concept of pre-existence from the Jewish idea of Wisdom. Hengel thinks the Elder moved to Ephesus around 60, founded a school, and lived until about 100 CE. The Elder, according to Hengel, wrote the Gospel over a period of time, using Mark and Luke and his own reminiscences. The author, says Hengel, could not have been a Galilean fisherman. Hengel thinks the Gospel was published after the death of the Elder and edited by his followers. These editors, according to Hengel, identified the author as "the beloved disciple"; the Elder had considered John the son of Zebedee to be the ideal disciple. In time the "beloved disciple" was identified as the apostle and author of the Gospel, and by 200 he was hailed as "the theologian." The Elder was much concerned with theology, a concern that sometimes changed his own recollections. Consequently Hengel cautions against the notion that the Fourth Gospel is an objective witness to the historical Jesus. He says that "in most parts the Gospel really is important and ingenious, 'inspired' christological 'poetry' and not real 'history.'"[236] Hengel's caution is more fully expressed in the expanded German edition: "Whoever still intends to adhere to the authorship of the Zebedean cannot thereby 'save' the historical reliability of the Fourth Gospel, which was the most disputed problem of the earlier generations of Johannine research; this question is—to a great extent—decided in the negative, which however does not exclude individual historically valuable traditions, on occasion, against Mark.[237]

Martin Hengel is one of the great NT scholars of the twentieth century. A master of all the skills of research and exegesis, and equipped with boundless energy for scholarly work, Hengel was above all an eminent historian. His argument that Judaism had been penetrated by Hellenistic influence has been praised by many NT scholars. The notion of a sharp distinction between Palestinian Judaism and Greco-Roman Hellenism has become problematic. To be sure, some critics have found Hengel's claim that Palestine was permeated by Hellenism to be exaggerated, and some believe that distinctions between the Jews of the Holy Land and Jews of the Diaspora can still be detected.[238] Also exaggerated is Hengel's claim that Hellenistic influence on early Christianity comes exclusively through Judaism. This claim appears to revert to the old Judaism/Hellenism dichotomy and seems to suppose that Christians living in the amalgamated culture of Greco-Roman cities like Corinth lived in a vacuum.

Actually, Hengel appears to be ambivalent about both Judaism and Hellenism. He insists that Judaism is the true background of Christianity, the fund of terminology, the intellectual framework for the development of Christian thought. Yet he argues that Christianity is distinct from the Judaism that, in reaction to Hellenism, had become nationalistic and unbending. With this emphasis Hengel appears to continue the old perspective: to interpret Judaism from the Christian point of view. "I have suggested here," says John Collins, "that at some points Hengel has not entirely shed the negative view of Judaism which has been endemic in Christian biblical scholarship."[239] Indeed, Hengel seems reluctant to acknowledge the presence of "anti-Judaism" in either the history of NT research or in the NT itself. However, he is not insensitive to the issue; he says: "We should be thankful if we as scholars know more today . . . than past generations, and thankful if our understanding of Judaism has changed in many respects owing to the terrible historical experiences in Germany in particular."[240] In regard to Hellenism, Hengel focuses favorably on cultural matters such as the use of the Greek language and education, but his picture of Hellenism gives little attention to Greek-oriental syncretism, to the mysteries and cults so prominent in places like Ephesus and Philippi. This aspect of Hellenism seems to be abhorrent to Hengel as a paganism from which distinctive Christianity remained unsullied.

Hengel's critique of skepticism and fanciful exegesis has considerable merit, even though he sometimes indulges in the latter himself (e.g., the notion that Paul witnessed the crucifixion; the reconstruction of the career of John the Elder). Some NT scholars approach the texts with a hypercriticism that exceeds the objectivity that solid historical method warrants. Conservative scholars have embraced Hengel's support of more traditional solutions to critical problems, for example, his view that Acts was written by Luke, the travel companion of Paul. Similarly, the belief that almost every worthy feature of Christianity has its origin in the historical Jesus is a comfort to those disturbed by the excesses of form and tradition criticism. But, although the assignment of all creativity to the post–Easter church is mistaken, the majority of scholars are correct in recognizing the magnitude of the resurrection experience in molding the ongoing life and faith of the early Christians. Conservatives should take caution, too, about exaggerating Hengel's orthodoxy. He explicitly condemns biblicism and fundamentalism. In particular, he recognizes Acts as a tendency document and finds it historically unreliable at more than one point. Similarly, Hengel rejects of the Fourth Gospel as a major source for the reconstruction of the historical Jesus. For all the variations in detail, Hengel is above all a champion of the historical-critical method.

Summary

In regard to the history of NT research, this chapter shows a prevailing problem in historical criticism: scholars using the method do not produce the same results. Experts who have devoted the major efforts of their careers to studying the Jewish material do not agree on what the sources mean; indeed, they sometimes come to conclusions that are diametrically opposed. This is due in part to the presuppositions with which the scholars approach the material, despite the claim of most of them that they function as "objective" historians. Personal perspectives, too, play a role, but surely we should agree that non-Christians ought to be able to understand Christian documents, and similarly that non-Jews ought be able to understand Jewish sources. Nevertheless, Hengel, for example, seems oblivious to the presence of anti-Judaism in the NT itself and among NT scholars, despite the evidence Davies and Sanders provide. Indeed, the views of Jeremias, Black, and Hengel imply a lingering of the older view of Judaism as a foil for Christianity.

Very important is the ongoing debate about Palestinian and Hellenistic or Diaspora Judaism. Although Hengel intends to erase the distinction, his actual practice suggests that it still remains. His oft-repeated theory that the thought of Paul and the other early Christians can be explained exclusively on the basis of Jewish backgrounds seems not only to revive the old distinction but also to assume a pejorative assessment of Hellenism—a sort of scholarly docetism. In regard to Paul, the question of his relation to Judaism remains in controversy. For Davies and Sanders he has much in common with rabbinic Judaism. Hengel sees the center of Paul's theology as justification by faith, whereas Davies and Sanders believe that to be peripheral. There is dispute as to how Paul viewed the law. There is considerable agreement, however, with the recognition that Paul's religious experience, his conversion, is crucial for his theological understanding. The ancient notion that Paul was the second founder of Christianity has claimed little support, although the evidence for continuity may be somewhat overdrawn, for example, by Hengel.

In regard to Jesus, the differences multiply. For Jeremias and Hengel, Jesus was conscious of his messianic role, as were his disciples; the exalted titles have their source in Jesus himself. Most of the scholars insist that Jesus must be understood in his Jewish context but differ as to what that means. Jeremias and Hengel, who eschew the criterion of dissimilarity, affirm a kind of dissimilarity of their own by advancing the superiority of Jesus to Judaism. There is considerable agreement about the importance of eschatology for understanding Jesus' proclamation of the kingdom of God. As to the political implications of the kingdom, there is dispute: most of the scholars acknowledge some political understanding (or misunderstanding) as evidenced by the Roman responsibility for the crucifixion. Virtually all the scholars of Judaism acknowledge the significance of Jesus for delineating the issues. Most of the scholars recognize the Christian identification of Jesus as Messiah, and above all as a divine figure, to be the defining difference between Jews and Christians.

All in all, the study of Judaism has advanced in the twentieth century. Most important, a vast wealth of primary sources—notably the Dead Sea Scrolls—has become available. The debate about Judaism as context for NT research has flourished with significant contributions. The discussion will continue, of course, but an important principle has prevailed: Judaism will be studied in its own right.

Notes

1. Robert P. Ericksen and Susannah Heschel, eds., *Betrayal: German Churches and the Holocaust* (Minneapolis: Fortress Press, 1999); Franklin H. Littell and Hubert G. Locke, eds., *The German Church Struggle and the Holocaust* (Detroit: Wayne State University Press, 1974). Susannah Heschel (*The Aryan Jesus: Christian Theologians and the Bible in Nazi Germany* [Princeton: Princeton University Press, 2008], 4–8, 112–13, 160–61, 286) presents evidence that the Confessing Church held anti-Jewish and even anti-Semitic views.

2. See Tod Linafelt, "Holocaust, Biblical Interpretation and The," *DBI* 1: 514–15; idem, ed., *A Shadow of Glory: Reading the New Testament after the Holocaust* (New York: Routledge, 2002).

3. The phrase "new perspective" on Paul was coined by James D. G. Dunn; see pp. 518–23 below.

4. George W. E. Nickelsburg, with Robert A. Kraft, "Introduction: The Modern Study of Judaism," in *Early Judaism and Its Modern Interpreters*, ed. Robert A. Kraft and George W. E. Nickelsburg, SBLBMI 2 (Atlanta: Scholars, 1986), 1–30; John G. Gager, "Judaism as Seen by Outsiders," in ibid., 99–116.

5. Robert H. Pfeiffer, *History of New Testament Times: With an Introduction to the Apocrypha* (New York: Harper & Brothers, 1949).

6. *Jewish Literature Between the Bible and the Mishnah: A Historical and Literary Introduction* (Philadelphia: Fortress Press, 1981; repr., 2005).

7. George W. E. Nickelsburg, *Ancient Judaism and Christian Origins: Diversity, Continuity, and Transformation* (Minneapolis: Fortress Press, 2003).

8. Ibid., xv.

9. George W. E. Nickelsburg, *Resurrection, Immortality, and Eternal Life in Intertestamental Judaism* HTS 56 (Cambridge, MA: Harvard University Press, 2006).

10. See pp. 455 below.

11. George W. E. Nickelsburg, ed., *Studies on the Testament of Moses*, SBLSCS 4 (Atlanta: SBL, 1973); *Studies on the Testament of Joseph*, SBLSCS 5 (Missoula: Scholars Press, 1975).

12. George W. E. Nickelsburg and Michael E. Stone, *Early Judaism: Text and Documents on Faith and Piety*, 2d ed. (Minneapolis: Fortress Press, 2009).

13. George W. E. Nickelsburg, *1 Enoch: A Commentary on the Book of 1 Enoch, Chapters 1–36; 81–108*, ed. Klaus Baltzer, Hermeneia (Minneapolis: Fortress Press, 2001). Nickelsburg's second volume, *1 Enoch 2: A Critical Commentary on the Book of 1 Enoch, Chapters 37–82*, written

in conjunction with James C. VanderKam, appeared ten years later, also in Hermeneia (Minneapolis: Fortress Press, 2011).

14. Robert Henry Charles, *The Apocrypha and Pseudepigrapha of the Old Testament in English*, 2 vols. (Oxford: Clarendon, 1913); see *HNTR* 2: 205–6.

15. James H. Charlesworth, ed., *The Old Testament Pseudepigrapha* (Garden City, NY: Doubleday, 1983, 1985).

16. See Hermann Lichtenberger, "Einführung," in Hermann Lichtenberger and Gerbern S. Oegema, eds., *Jüdische Schriften in ihrem antik-jüdischen und urchristlichen Kontext*, JSHRZ 1 (Güterloh: Gütersloher Verlagshaus, 2002), 1–8; James H. Charlesworth, "The JSHRZ and the OTP: A Celebration," in ibid., 11–34).

17. 6 vols. (Gütersloh: Mohn, 1973-2003).

18. Jüdische Schriften aus hellenistic-römischer Zeit, 6 vols. (Gütersloh: Mohn, 1973-2003).

19. On Jeremias's life and work see K. C. Hanson, "Foreword," in Joachim Jeremias, *Jesus and the Message of the New Testament* (Minneapolis: Fortress Press, 2002), xi–xiii; L. D. Vander Broek, "Jeremias, Joachim (1900–1979)," *DMBI*, 560–65; Matthew Black, "Theologians of Our Time: II. Joachim Jeremias," *ExpTim* 74 (1962–63): 115-19.

20. J. Louis Martyn, *Theological Issues in the Letters of Paul* (Nashville: Abingdon, 1997), 210.

21. Herman L. Strack and Paul Billerbeck, eds., *Kommentar zum Neuen Testament aus Talmud und Midrasch*, 6 vols. (Munich: Beck, 1922–28); see *HNTR* 2: 419–22.

22. Joachim Jeremias, *Golgotha*, ΆΓΓΕΛΟΣ: Archiv für neutestamentliche Zeitgeschichte und Kulturkunde Beiheft 1 (Leipzig: Pfeiffer, 1926).

23. Ibid., 33.

24. *Die Passahfeier der Samaritaner und ihre Bedeutung für das Verständnis der alttestamentlichen Passahüberlieferung*, BZAW 59 (Giessen: Töpelmann, 1932).

25. *Heiligengräber in Jesu Umwelt (Mt. 23,29; Lk. 11,47): Eine Untersuchung zur Volksreligion der Zeit Jesu* (Göttingen: Vandenhoeck & Ruprecht, 1958).

26. *Die Wiederentdeckung von Bethesda: Johannes 5,2*, FRLANT 41 (Göttingen: Vandenhoeck & Ruprecht, 1949); ET: *The Rediscovery of Bethesda: John 5:2*, NTAM 1 (Louisville: Southern Baptist Theological Seminary, 1966).

27. *Rediscovery of Bethesda*, 38.

28. Joachim Jeremias, *Die theologische Bedeutung der Funde am Toten Meer* (Göttingen: Vandenhoeck & Ruprecht, 1962).

29. *Jerusalem zur Zeit Jesu: Eine kulturgeschichtliche Untersuchung zur neutestamentlichen Zeitgeschichte*, 3d ed. (Göttingen: Vandenhoeck & Ruprecht, 1962); ET: *Jerusalem in the Time of Jesus: An Investigation into Economic and Social Conditions in the New Testament Period*, trans. F. H. and C. H. Cave (Philadelphia: Fortress Press, 1969).

30. *Jerusalem in the Time of Jesus*, 270.

31. The earlier work: *Hat die Urkirche die Kindertaufe geübt?* 2d rev. ed. (Göttingen: Vandenhoeck & Ruprecht, 1949); the expansion: *Die Kindertaufe in den ersten vier Jahrhunderten* (Göttingen: Vandenhoeck & Ruprecht, 1958); ET: *Infant Baptism in the First Four Centuries*, trans. David Cairns (Philadelphia: Westminster, 1960). Kurt Aland countered with *Die Säuglingstaufe im Neuen Testament und in der Alten Kirche: Eine Antwort an Joachim Jeremias* (Munich: Kaiser, 1961); Aland argued that there was no evidence of an actual incidence of infant baptism before 200. Jeremias responded with *Nochmals: Die Anfänge der Kindertaufe: Eine Replik auf Kurt Alands Schrift* (Munich; Kaiser, 1962); ET: *The Origins of Infant Baptism: a Further Study in Reply to Kurt Aland*, STH 1 (Naperville, IL: Alec R. Allenson, 1963).

32. *Die Abendmahlsworte Jesu*, 3d ed. (Göttingen: Vandenhoeck & Ruprecht, 1960); ET: *The Eucharistic Words of Jesus*, trans. Norman Perrin (London: SCM, 1966).

33. *Eucharistic Words*, 231.

34. Joachim Jeremias, *Die Gleichnisse Jesu*, 8th ed. (Göttingen: Vandenhoeck & Ruprecht, 1970); ET: *The Parables of Jesus*, rev. ed., trans. S. H. Hooke (New York: Scribner's, 1963). A later

version written for a general audience was *Rediscovering the Parables* (New York: Scribner's, 1966). See Norman Perrin, *Jesus and the Language of the Kingdom: Symbol and Metaphor in New Testament Interpretation* (Philadelphia: Fortress Press, 1976), 91–107. The 7th and 8th editions are essentially reprints. The 6th and following editions include a discussion of the Gospel of Thomas.

35. *Parables*, 22; for Jülicher and Dodd see *HNTR* 2: 158–59, and pp. 46–47 above.

36. *Parables*, 114.

37. Ibid., 228–29.

38. Ibid., 230. In a footnote Jeremias refers to Dodd's "realized eschatology"; Jeremias believes the expression "an eschatology that is in the process of realization" (suggested by Ernst Haenchen) is better, and says Dodd has agreed.

39. *Die Bergpredigt* (Stuttgart: Calwer, 1959); repr. in Jeremias, *Abba: Studien zur neutestamentlichen Theologie und Zeitgeschichte* (Göttingen: Vandenhoeck & Ruprecht, 1966), 171–89; ET: *The Sermon on the Mount*, trans. Norman Perrin (Philadelphia: Fortress Press, 1963). The English translation was reprinted in Jeremias, *Jesus and the Message of the New Testament*, 18–38.

40. *Sermon on the Mount*, 6.

41. Jeremias, *Die Briefe an Timotheus und Titus*, NTD 9, 6th rev. ed. (Göttingen: Vandenhoeck & Ruprecht, 1953).

42. Joachim Jeremias, *Das Problem des historischen Jesus* (Stuttgart: Calwer, 1960); ET: *The Problem of the Historical Jesus*, trans. Norman Perrin (Philadelphia: Fortress Press, 1964). Reprinted in *Jesus and the Message of the New Testament*, ed. K. C. Hanson, (Minneapolis: Fortress Press, 2002), 1–17; reprint of German ed. "Der gegenwärtige Stand der Debatte um das Problem des historischen Jesus," in *Der historische Jesus und der kerygmatische Christus*, ed. Helmut Ristow and Karl Mattiae (Berlin: Evangelische Verlagsanstalt, 1960), 12–25.

43. *Problem of the Historical Jesus*, 11.

44. Ibid., 23.

45. See Joachim Jeremias, "Abba," in idem, *Abba: Studien zur neutestamentlichen Theologie und Zeitgeschichte* (Göttingen: Vandenhoeck & Ruprecht, 1966); ET: *The Prayers of Jesus* (Philadelphia: Fortress Press, 1978), 9–81; "Das Vater-Unser im Lichte der neueren Forschung," *Abba*, 152–71; ET: "The Lord's Prayer in Recent Research," *Prayers*, 82–107.

46. *Prayers*, 29.

47. Ibid., 53.

48. *Prayers*, 82–107. This material was originally published as a monograph: *Vater-Unser im Licht der neueren Forschung* (Stuttgart: Calwer, 1962); ET: *The Lord's Prayer*, trans. John Reumann (Philadelphia: Fortress Press, 1964); repr. in *Jesus and the Message of the New Testament*, 39–62.

49. *TDNT* 5: 677–717; also published as a separate monograph: Walther Zimmerli and Joachim Jeremias, *The Servant of God*, SBT 20 (London: SCM, 1957; rev. ed. 1965).

50. *TDNT* 5:717.

51. *The Central Message of the New Testament* (New York: Scribner's, 1965); repr. in *Jesus and Message of the New Testament*, 63110.

52. Parts of the book were translated into German and published under various titles: Ch. 1: *Die Botschaft Jesu vom Vater* (Stuttgart: Calwer, 1968); Ch. 4: *Der Prolog des Johannesevangeliums* (Johannes 1,1-18), Calwer Hefte 88 (Stuttgart: Calwer, 1967). The substance of chapter 2 is presented in *Der Opfertod Jesu Christi* (Stuttgart: Calwer, 1963).

53. *Central Message*, 66.

54. Jeremias published another theological work, *Jesu Verheissung für die Völker*, Franz Delitzsch-Vorlesungen 1953 (Stuttgart: Kohlhammer, 1959); ET: *Jesus' Promise to the Nations*, trans. S. H. Hooke (Philadelphia: Fortress Press, 1982). This book takes up the question: since Jesus did not engage in a Gentile mission, why should his followers undertake a worldwide mission? Jeremias answers that the issue should be interpreted eschatologically: Jesus promised the Gentiles a

share in the kingdom and identified himself with the Servant of Second Isaiah, who was a light to the Gentiles.

55. *Neutestamentliche Theologie: Erster Teil: Die Verkündigung Jesu* (Gütersloh: Mohn, 1970; ET: *New Testament Theology*, vol. 1, trans. John Bowden (New York: Scribner's, 1971).

56. In an appendix on the Synoptic Problem, Jeremias affirms the priority of Mark but believes the 2DH to be an oversimplification: the existence of Q is questionable.

57. *New Testament Theology*, 121.

58. Ibid., 215.

59. Ibid., 250.

60. Ibid., 278.

61. As an irreverent critic might say, "Anybody can put up with a bad weekend!"

62. Martin Hengel, *The Atonement: The Origins of the Doctrine in the New Testament*, trans. John Bowden (Philadelphia: Fortress Press, 1981), xii.

63. See pp. 87–175 above.

64. See James Barr, "'Abba Isn't 'Daddy,'" *JTS* 39 (1988): 28–47; Geza Vermes, *Jesus and the World of Judaism* (Philadelphia: Fortress Press, 1984), 41–42.

65. See Joseph A. Fitzmyer, "Abba and Jesus' Relation to God," in *À Cause de l'évangile: Études sur le Synoptiques et les Actes: Offertes au P. Jacques Dupont à l'occasion de son 70e anniversaire* (Paris: Cerf, 1985), 15–38.

66. A major critic of Jeremias in this regard is E. P. Sanders. Sanders's criticism has been judged as extreme; see Ben F. Meyer, "A Caricature of Joachim Jeremias and His Scholarly Work," *JBL* 110 (1991): 451–62; Sanders responded with his typical vigor: "Defending the Indefensible," *JBL* 110 (1991): 463–77.

67. For the life and work of Matthew Black see David Garland, "Black, Matthew (1908–1994)," *DMBI*, 197–201; "A Curriculum Vitae of Matthew Black," in *Neotestamentica et Semitica: Studies in Honour of Matthew Black*, ed. E. Earle Ellis and Max Wilcox (Edinburgh: T & T Clark, 1969), vii–viii; Craig A. Evans, "Introduction: An Aramaic Approach Thirty Years Later," in the reprint of Black's *An Aramaic Approach to the Gospels and Acts*, 3d ed. (Peabody, MA: Hendrickson, 1998), v–xxv.

68. *Peake's Commentary on the Bible*, ed. Matthew Black and H. H. Rowley (London: Nelson, 1962), 693–98.

69. "Development of Judaism," 698.

70. *The Book of Enoch or I Enoch: A New English Edition: With Commentary and Textual Notes*, SVTP (Leiden: Brill, 1985).

71. J. T. Milik, *The Books of Enoch: Aramaic Fragments of Qumran Cave 4* (Oxford: Clarendon, 1976).

72. *Apocalypsis Henochi Graece*, PVTG 3 (Leiden: Brill, 1970).

73. *Rituale Melchitarum: A Christian Palestinian Euchologion*, ed. and trans. Matthew Black (Stuttgart: Kohlhammer, 1938); *A Christian Palestinian Syriac Horologion*, TS (Cambridge: Cambridge University Press, 1954).

74. Black, *The Scrolls and Christian Origins* (New York: Scribner's, 1961).

75. Matthew Black, *An Aramaic Approach to the Gospels and Acts*, 3d ed. (Oxford: Clarendon, 1967; repr., Peabody, MA: Hendrickson, 1998); German translation: *Die Muttersprache Jesu: das Aramäisch der Evangelien und der Apostelgeschichte* (Stuttgart: Kohlhamer, 1982).

76. *Aramaic Approach*, 16.

77. At the time of Black's 3d ed. (1967) only a limited amount of Aramaic material was available; this was before the major publication of the Qumran texts.

78. Black's competence as a text critic is confirmed by his work on the editorial committee of the first three editions of the United Bible Society *Greek New Testament* (see pp. 241–42 above).

79. *Aramaic Approach*, 185.

80. Ibid., 271.

81. Ibid., 275.

82. Matthew Black, "Pharisees," *IDB* 3: 781.

83. Matthew Black, *Romans*, NCB (LondonGreenwood, SC: Attic, 1973), 47–48.

84. For the life and work of Davies see D. R. A. Hare, "Davies, W(illiam) D(avid) (b. 1911)," *DMBI*, 350–54; Dale C. Allison, Jr., "Davies, W. D. (1911–)," in *DBI*, 253; W. D. Davies, "My Odyssey in New Testament Interpretation," *BRev* 5, no. 3 (June 1989): 10–18 (repr. in W. D. Davies, *Christian Engagements with Judaism* [Harrisburg, PA: Trinity Press International, 1999], 1–12); Gustaf Aulén, *Jesus in Contemporary Research*, trans. Ingalill H. Hjelm (Philadelphia: Fortress Press, 1976), 32–42.

85. "My Odyssey," 14.

86. Ibid.

87. Ibid., 18. Davies's own Christocentric theology is evident in his preaching: W. D. Davies, *The New Creation: University Sermons* (Philadelphia: Fortress Press, 1971).

88. *Invitation to the New Testament: A Guide to Its Main Witnesses* (Garden City, NY: Doubleday, 1966).

89. *HNTR* 2: 265–66.

90. *Invitation to the New Testament*, 381.

91. Ibid., 518.

92. *Paul and Rabbinic Judaism: Some Rabbinic Elements in Pauline Theology*, 4th ed. (Philadelphia: Fortress Press, 1980). See Hare, "Davies," 351–53; Stephen Neill and N. T. Wright, *The Interpretation of the New Testament 1861–1986*, 2d ed. (Oxford: Oxford University Press, 1988), 412–15, at 412: "one of the few epoch-making books in modern Pauline studies."

93. W. D. Davies, "Paul and Judaism since Shweitzer," originally published in *The Bible in Modern Scholarship,* ed. J. Philip Hyatt (Nashville: Abingdon, 1965), 178–86.

94. *Paul and Rabbinic Judaism*, xvii.

95. See pp. 284–93 below.

96. *Paul and Rabbinic Judaism*, xxvii.

97. *Paul and Rabbinic Judaism*, 1.

98. Ibid., 16.

99. Ibid., 148.

100. Ibid., 221–22.

101. Ibid., 323.

102. Ibid., 324.

103. In W. D. Davies and Louis Finkelstein, eds., *The Cambridge History of Judaism*, 4 vols. (Cambridge: Cambridge University Press, 1984–2006), vol. 3, *The Early Roman Period*, ed. William Horbury, W. D. Davies, and John Sturdy (Cambridge: Cambridge University Press, 1999), 678–730.

104. See Hare, "Davies," 353–54.

105. W. D. Davies, *The Setting of the Sermon on the Mount* (Cambridge: Cambridge University Press, 1964); a short popular version of this book is W. D. Davies, *The Sermon on the Mount* (Cambridge: Cambridge University Press, 1966).

106. *Setting of the Sermon*, 93.

107. This section is based on Davies's *Torah in the Messianic Age and/or the Age to Come*, SBLMS 7 (Philadelphia: SBL, 1952).

108. *Setting of the Sermon*, 189.

109. In recent research the reconstruction of the "Council of Jamnia" and its role in canonizing Scripture has been questioned. See Burton L. Visotzky, "Jamnia, Council of," *NIDB* 3: 197–98.

110. *Setting of the Sermon*, 414.

111. Ibid., 415.

112. Ibid., 418.

113. W. D. Davies and Dale C. Allison, *A Critical and Exegetical Commentary on the Gospel According to Saint Matthew*, 3 vols., ICC (Edinburgh: T & T Clark, 1988–97).

114. *The Gospel and the Land: Early Christianity and Jewish Territorial Doctrine* (Berkeley: University of California Press, 1974). Davies presents a short view of this subject in *The Territorial Dimension of Judaism* (Berkeley: University of California Press, 1982); this shorter monograph deals with the land only from the Jewish perspective; it also gives attention to the significance of the concept for twentieth-century history.

115. *Gospel and the Land*, 24.

116. Ibid., 60.

117. Ibid., 157.

118. Ibid.

119. Ibid., 220.

120. Ibid. 367.

121. For the life and thought of Sanders, see D. Moody Smith, "Professor Sanders at Duke," in *Redefining First-Century Jewish and Christian Identities: Essays in Honor of Ed Parish Sanders*, ed. Fabian E. Udoh, with Susannah Heschel, Mark Chancey, and Gregory Tatum (Notre Dame, IN: University of Notre Dame Press, 2008), 3–10; E. P. Sanders, "Comparing Judaism and Christianity: An Academic Autobiography," ibid., 11– 41.

122. "Comparing Judaism," 12.

123. For bibliography (through 2008), see "Bibliography of the Works by E. P. Sanders," in *Redefining First-Century Jewish and Christian Identities*, 391–96.

124. *Judaism: Practice and Belief, 63 B.C.E.–66 C.E.* (London: SCM, 1992; Philadelphia: Trinity Press International, 1992; repr. Valley Forge, PA: Trinity Press International, 1994; repr. Eugene, OR: Wipf & Stock, 2004; repr. London: SCM, 2005).

125. Ibid., 494.

126. Ibid.

127. *Jewish Law from Jesus to the Mishnah: Five Studies* (London: SCM; Philadelphia: Trinity Press International, 1990).

128. Ibid., 23.

129. Ibid., 90.

130. Ibid., 125.

131. Ibid., 257.

132. *Paul and Palestinian Judaism: A Comparison of Patterns of Religion* (Philadelphia: Fortress Press, 1977; repr. 1989); German translation: *Paulus und das palästinische Judentum: ein Vergleich zweier Religionsstrukturen* (Göttingen: Vandenhoeck & Ruprecht, 1985).

133. See *HNTR* 2: 424, 204–9, 243–51.

134. See *HNTR* 2: 419–22.

135. *Paul and Palestinian Judaism*, 59.

136. Ibid., 75.

137. In a later essay ("Common Judaism Explored," in *Common Judaism: Explorations in Second-Temple Judaism*, ed. Wayne O. McCready and Adele Reinhartz [Minneapolis: Fortress Press, 2008], 11–23) Sanders clarifies the distinction between "common Judaism," which he describes in *Judaism: Practice and Belief* (see above) and "covenantal nomism." "Covenantal nomism" basically has to do with theology; "common Judaism" has to do with the religious practices of the ordinary people. "Thus, I regard 'covenantal nomism' (the election part of the law) as part of 'common Judaism'" (p. 21).

138. *Paul and Palestinian Judaism*, 85.

139. Ibid., 123.

140. Ibid., 146–47.

141. Ibid., 180.

142. Ibid., 422.

143. In a later essay, "Did Paul's Theology Develop?" in *The Word Leaps the Gap: Essays on Scripture and Theology in Honor of Richard B. Hays*, ed. J. Ross Wagner, C. Kavin Rowe, and A. Katherine Grieb (Grand Rapids: Eerdmans, 2008), 325–50, Sanders further clarifies his conviction that Paul, although not a systematic theologian, was a coherent thinker. Also in this essay Sanders, in contrast to the view expressed in *Paul and Palestinian Judaism*, argues that Paul's thought (e.g., in regard to eschatology) has developed. "Thus, I see growth and development all around" (p. 349).

144. *Paul and Palestinian Judaism*, 474.

145. Ibid., 491.

146. Ibid., 506.

147. See pp. 98, 108–11, 282 above.

148. *Paul and Palestinian Judaism*, 518.

149. Ibid., 548.

150. Ibid., 552.

151. E. P. Sanders, *Paul, the Law, and the Jewish People* (Philadelphia: Fortress Press, 1983).

152. Ibid., 162.

153. Sanders also published a survey of the life and thought of Paul, written for the general reader: *Paul* (Oxford: Oxford University Press, 1991), reissued a decade later as *Paul: A Very Short Introduction* (Oxford: Oxford University Press, 2001).

154. E. P. Sanders, *Jesus and Judaism* (Philadelphia: Fortress Press, 1985).

155. *Jesus and Judaism*, 1.

156. Ibid., 75.

157. Ibid., 119.

158. Ibid., 154.

159. Ibid., 294.

160. Ibid., 333–34.

161. Ibid., 334.

162. See *HNTR* 2: 299–335.

163. E. P. Sanders, *The Historical Figure of Jesus* (London: Penguin, 1993).

164. Ibid., 5.

165. Ibid., 238.

166. Ibid., 281. In an essay, "Jesus in Historical Context," (*ThTo* 50 [1993]: 429–48) Sanders discusses (and largely opposes) recent attempts to present Jesus as a champion of the repressed people of Palestine, or to view Galilee as largely Hellenized and Jesus as an un-Jewish wandering teacher.

167. See pp. 343–49 below.

168. E. P. Sanders, *The Tendencies of the Synoptic Problem*, SNTSMS 9 (Cambridge: Cambridge University Press, 1969).

169. Ibid., 278.

170. E. P. Sanders and Margaret Davies, *Studying the Synoptic Gospels* (London: SCM; Philadelphia: Trinity Press International, 1989). The section that discusses redaction criticism, structuralism, and rhetorical criticism (Part IV) was written by Davies; Sanders wrote the rest (Parts I–III).

171. An extensive criticism of Sanders's work is presented by Jacob Neusner, *Judaic Law from Jesus to the Mishnah: A Systematic Reply to Professor E. P. Sanders*, SFSHJ 84 (Atlanta: Scholars, 1993). Although he is sympathetic to Sanders's idea of "covenantal nomism" and appreciative of Sanders's attack on anti-Judaism, Neusner opposes Sanders at many points, including his understanding of "Judaism," the Mishnah, purity, and the Pharisees.

172. For a survey of the discussion and the issues see James D. G. Dunn, "The New Perspective on Paul: Whence, What, Whither?" in *The New Perspective on Paul: Collected Essays*, WUNT (Tübingen: Mohr Siebeck, 2005), 1–88. For an extensive discussion of the issues and of the work of Sanders in historical perspective see Stephen Westerholm, *Perspectives Old and New on Paul: The "Lutheran" Paul and His Critics* (Grand Rapids: Eerdmans, 2004).

173. See Martin Hengel and Roland Deines, "E. P. Sanders' 'Common Judaism,' Jesus, and the Pharisees: Review article of *Jewish Law from Jesus to the Mishnah* and *Judaism: Practice and Belief* by E. P. Sanders," *JTS* 46 (1995): 1–70.

174. Ibid., 16, 68.

175. Ibid., 18.

176. In his essay, "Eine junge theologische Disziplin," in *Neutestamentliche Wissenschaft: Autobiographische Essays aus der Evangelischen Theologie*, ed. Eva-Marie Becker (Tübingen and Basel: Francke, 2003), 28, Hengel notes that in Sanders's *Paul and Palestinian Judaism* there are three references in the index to "Truth, ultimate"; all three refer to blank pages. Hengel considers this to be "ein schlechter Scherz" ("a bad joke").

177. For Hengel's life and work see ibid., 18–29; T. C. Penner, "Hengel, Martin (1926–)," *DBI* 1: 493–94; Petr Pkorný, "Hengel, Martin (1926–)," *DBCI*, 156–57; Roland Deines, "Martin Hengel: A Life in the Service of Christology," *TynBul* 58 (2007): 25–42.

178. For bibliographies see *Geschichte—Tradition—Reflexion: Festschrift für Martin Hengel zum 70. Geburtstag*, vol. 3, *Frühes Christentum*, ed. Hermann Lichtenberger (Tübingen: Mohr Siebeck, 1996), 695–722; Martin Hengel, *Judaica, Hellenistica et Christiana: Kleine Schriften II*, ed. Jörge Frey and Dorothea Betz, WUNT 109 (Tübingen: Mohr Siebeck, 1999), 391–97; Martin Hengel, *Paulus und Jakobus: Kleine Schriften III*, WUNT 141 (Tübingen: Mohr Siebeck, 2002), 583–87.

179. Hengel, "Eine junge theologische Disziplin," 21.

180. Martin Hengel, *Acts and the History of Earliest Christianity* (Philadelphia: Fortress Press, 1980), viii.

181. "Aufgaben der neutestamentlichen Wissenschaft," *NTS* 40 (1944): 351.

182. Martin Hengel, *Between Jesus and Paul: Studies in the Earliest History of Christianity*, trans. John Bowden (Philadelphia: Fortress Press, 1983), xiv–xv.

183. *Die Zeloten: Untersuchungen zur Jüdischen Freiheitsbewegung in der Zeit von Herodes I. bis 70 n. Chr.*, 2d ed., AGSU 1 (Leiden: Brill, 1976); ET: *The Zealots: Investigations into the Jewish Freedom Movement in the Period from Herod I until 70 A.D.*, trans. David Smith (Edinburgh: T & T Clark, 1989).

184. *Zealots*, 5.

185. Martin Hengel, *Judentum und Hellenismus: Studien zu ihrer Begegnung unter besonderer Berücksichtigung Palästinas bis zur Mitte des 2 Jh. v. Chr.*, 2 vols., 2d ed. WUNT 10 (Tübingen: Mohr [Paul Siebeck], 1973); ET: *Judaism and Hellenism: Studies in their Encounter in Palestine during the Early Hellenistic Period*, trans. John Bowden, 2 vols. (Philadelphia: Fortress Press, 1974).

186. *Judaism and Hellenism*, 56.

187. Ibid., 104.

188. Ibid., 198.

189. Ibid., 309.

190. Ibid., 314.

191. *Juden, Griechen und Barbaren: Aspekte der Hellenisierung des Judentums in vorchristlicher Zeit*, SBS 76 (Stuttgart: Katholisches Bibelwerk, 1976); ET: *Jews, Greeks and Barbarians: Aspects of the Hellenization of Judaism in the pre-Christian Period*, trans. John Bowden (Philadelphia: Fortress Press, 1980); this monograph is based on two articles ("The Political and Social History of Palestine from Alexander to Antiochus III (333–187 B.C.E.)," and "The Interpretation of Judaism and Hellenism in the pre-Maccabean Period") in *The Cambridge History of Judaism*, ed. W. D. Davies and Louis Finkelstein (Cambridge: Cambridge University Press, 1989), 2: 35–78; 3: 167–88).

192. *Jews, Greeks, and Barbarians*, 52.

193. Ibid., 60.

194. *The "Hellenization" of Judaea in the First Century after Christ*, written in collaboration with Christoph Markschies, trans. John Bowden (London: SCM; Philadelphia: Trinity Press International, 1989).

195. Ibid., 56.

196. In *Judaica, Hellenistica et Christiana: Kleine Schriften II*, with Jörg Frey and Dorothea Betz, WUNT 109 (Tübingen: Mohr Siebeck, 1999), 115–56.

197. In *Judaica et Hellenistica: Kleine Scriften I*, with Roland Deines, Jörg Frey, Christoph Markschies, and Anna Maria Schwemer, WUNT 90 (Tübingen: Mohr Siebeck, 1996), 258–94.

198. In *Schriftauslegung in antiken Judentum und im Urchristentum*, ed. Martin Hengel and Hermut Löhr, WUNT 73 (Tübingen: Mohr Siebeck, 1994), 1–71.

199. "Das früheste Christentum als eine jüdische messianische und unversalistische Bewegung," in *Judaica, Hellenistica et Christiana*, 200–18; ET: "Early Christianity as a Jewish-Messianic Movement," in *Conflicts and Challenges in Early Christianity*, ed. Donald A. Hagner (Harrisburg, PA: Trinity Press International, 1999), 1–41.

200. Martin Hengel, *Nachfolge und Charisma: Eine exegetisch-religionsgeschichtliche Studie zu Mt 8.21f und Jesu Ruf in die Nachfolge*, BZNW 34 (Berlin: de Gruyter, 1968); ET: *The Charismatic Leader and His Followers*, trans. James C. G. Greig, ed. John Riches (Edinburgh: T & T Clark, 1996).

201. *Charismatic Leader*, x.

202. Ibid., 15.

203. Ibid., 38, 63–64.

204. Ibid., 49.

205. *The Four Gospels and the One Gospel of Jesus Christ: An Investigation of the Collection and Origin of the Canonical Gospels*, trans. John Bowden (Harrisburg, PA: Trinity Press International, 2000); this book is based on lectures Hengel gave in various venues in the United States in 1998; German ed.: *Die vier Evangelien und das eine Evangelium von Jesus Christus*, WUNT 224 (Tübingen: Mohr Siebeck, 2008).

206. Hengel believes the importance of Peter is often slighted. See Martin Hengel, *Der unterschätzte Petrus: Zwei Studien* (Tübingen: Mohr Siebeck, 2006).

207. *Charismatic Leader*, 165.

208. *Der Sohn Gottes: Die Entstehung der Christologie und die jüdisch-hellenistische Religionsgeschichte* (Tübingen: Mohr Siebeck, 1975); ET: *The Son of God: The Origin of Christology and the History of Jewish-Hellenistic Religion*, trans. John Bowden (Philadelphia: Fortress Press, 1976); a 2d German ed. of 1977 slightly expands the 1st ed.

209. Hengel's understanding of Wisdom as the important background for NT Christology is more fully developed in "Jesus as Messianic Teacher of Wisdom and the Beginnings of Christology," in idem, *Studies in Early Christology* (Edinburgh: T & T Clark, 1995), 73–117. This essay is based on a lecture given at a colloquium in Strasbourg (1976) and published in *Sagesse et Religion: Colloque de Strasbourg* (Paris: Presses universitaires de France, 1979), 146–88; German ed. in *Der messianische Anspruch Jesu und die Anfänge der Christologie*, WUNT 138 (Tübingen: Mohr Siebeck, 2001), 81–133.

210. *Son of God*, 72.

211. See n. 484 above.

212. *Studies in Early Christology*, 1–72; German ed.: "Jesus der Messias Israels," in Hengel, *Der messianische Anspruch Jesu und die Anfänge der Christologie*, WUNT 138 (Tübingen: Mohr Siebeck, 2001), 1–80.

213. "Jesus, The Messiah of Israel," 59.

214. Ibid., 61.

215. *The Atonement: The Origins of the Doctrine in the New Testament*, trans. John Bowden (Philadelphia: Fortress Press, 1981). This book is based on Hengel's T. W. Manson Memorial Lecture, Manchester University, 1979; the lecture was expanded (by revision and the adding of notes) for this English version; a more extensive version has been published in German: "Die stellvertretende Sühnetod Jesu: Ein Beitrag zur Enstehung des urchristliche Kerygmas," IKZ 9 (1980): 1–25, 135–47.

216. "Der vorchristliche Paulus," in *Paulus und das antike Judentum*, ed. Martin Hengel and Ulrich Heckel, WUNT 58 (Tübingen: Mohr Siebeck, 1991), 177–291; ET: Martin Hengel, in collaboration with Roland Deines, *The Pre-Christian Paul*, trans. John Bowden (London: SCM; Philadelphia: Trinity Press International, 1991).

217. *Pre-Christian Paul*, 47. As noted above, advocates of the "new perspective," especially E. P. Sanders, are highly critical of Billerbeck's work.

218. *Pre-Christian Paul*, 86.

219. Ibid.

220. Martin Hengel and Anna Maria Schwemer, *Paulus zwischen Damaskus und Antiochien: Die unbekannten Jahre des Apostels*, WUNT 108 (Tübingen: Mohr Siebeck, 1998); ET: *Paul Between Damascus and Antioch: The Unknown Years* (Louisville: Westminster John Knox, 1997); in this work Hengel is the lead writer and director of the project; he acknowledges the assistance (and writing of some sections) by Schwemer.

221. Ibid., 39.

222. Ibid., 282–83.

223. Ibid., 313.

224. See "Paulus und die frühchristliche Apokalyptik," in *Paulus und Jakobus*, 302–417.

225. Ibid., 397.

226. "Das Begräbnis Jesu bei Paulus und die leibliche Auferstehung aus dem Grabe," in *Studien zur Christologie: Kleine Schriften* IV, ed. Claus-Jürgen Thornton, WUNT 201 (Tübingen: Mohr Siebeck, 2006), 386–450; this essay was originally published in *Auferstehung—Resurrection: The Fourth Durham-Tübingen Research Symposium: Resurrection, Transfiguration and Exaltation in the Old Testament, Ancient Judaism and Early Christianity (Tübingen, 1999)*, WUNT 125 (Tübingen: Mohr Siebeck, 2001), 119–84.

227. *Der unterschätze Petrus: Zwei Studien* (Tübingen: Mohr Siebeck, 2006); ET: *Saint Peter: The Underestimated Apostle*, trans Thomas H. Trapp (Grand Rapids: Eerdmans, 2010).

228. Ibid., 63.

229. Ibid., 101.

230. *Zur urchristlichen Geschichtsschreibung* (Stuttgart: Calwer, 1979); ET: *Acts and the History of Earliest Christianity* (Philadelphia: Fortress Press, 1980).

231. Ibid., 67.

232. Hengel, for example, confirms Luke's knowledge of Palestinian geography; see Martin Hengel, "Luke the Historian and the Geography of Palestine in the Acts of the Apostles," in idem, *Between Jesus and Paul*, 97–128. Hengel also had an interest in the social history of early Christianity; see Martin Hengel, *Eigentum und Reichtum in der frühen Kirche: Aspekte einer frühchristlichen Sozialgeschichte* (Stuttgart: Calwer, 1973); ET: *Property and Riches in the Early Church: Aspects of the Social History of Early Christianity*, trans. John Bowden (Philadelphia: Fortress Press, 1974).

233. See "Between Jesus and Paul: The 'Hellenists,' the 'Seven' and Stephen (Acts 6.1-15; 7.54-8:3)," in *Between Jesus and Paul*, 1–29.

234. Ibid., 29.

235. Martin Hengel, *The Johannine Question* (London: SCM; Philadelphia: Trinity Press International, 1989); this book is based on Hengel's Stone Lectures at Princeton Theological Seminary in 1987; an expanded version in German is, *Die johanneische Frage: Ein Lösungsversuch* (Tübingen: Mohr Siebeck, 1993).

236. *The Johannine Question*, 131.

237. *Die johanneische Frage*, 320.

238. See Louis H. Feldman, "Hengel's Judaism and Hellenism in Retrospect," *JBL* 96 (1977): 371–82; John J. Collins, "Judaism as *Praeparatio Evangelica* in the Work of Martin Hengel," *RelSRev* 15 (1989): 226–28.

239. Collins, "Judaism as Praeparatio Evangelica," 228.

240. Hengel, "E. P. Sanders' 'Common Judaism,'" 69.

6

Developments in Historical Criticism

The culture of the second half of the twentieth century was marked by diversity and conflict. World War II left Germany, the center of biblical study, split in two. The chasm between east and west broadened into the "cold war," and soon into hot wars in Korea and Vietnam. The conflicts on the world scene were mirrored in America. In 1954 the United States Supreme Court ruled that racial segregation in the public schools was unconstitutional. This provoked race riots and outbreaks of violence by the Ku Klux Klan and other reactionary groups. Martin Luther King led a massive movement for racial equality but paid for his efforts with his life. These conflicts did not leave religion untouched. Attacks were launched against the World Council and National Council of Churches, charging that the leaders were tainted with liberalism, soft on communism. The Moral Majority, led by fundamentalist Jerry Falwell, entered the political arena in support of conservative causes. Mainline churches declined; conservative mega-churches mushroomed. The feminist movement and the advocates of gay rights were attacked from the right.

These competing forces also impacted the community of biblical scholarship. The liberal domination of the academy was challenged by the rise of evangelical scholars. These conservatives enrolled in major graduate schools like Harvard and graduated to teach in expanding theological schools: Fuller, Trinity Evangelical, Gordon Conwell, Dallas—all dedicated to excellence in scholarship. Many of the evangelicals joined the guild—the Society of Biblical Literature (SBL)—but also founded their own, the Evangelical Theological Society (ETS). These scholars produced important publications with the major publishing houses. To be sure, many scholars from both sides reached across the barriers to embrace common goals and affirm mutual respect. But, on a host of critical and exegetical issues, polarizing and polemics flourished. Battles also raged within the stereotyped groups. Scholars who shared commitment to the historical critical method differed sharply over their results. These conflicts are especially apparent in regard to critical issues of introduction, gospel research, and the Synoptic Problem.

THE SCIENCE OF INTRODUCTION: KÜMMEL AND KOESTER

"Introduction" is the discipline most characteristic of the Enlightenment.[1] It attends to the famous "W" questions: Who wrote, When, Where, to Whom? A host of introductions of all shapes and forms has been published, from textbooks for undergraduates to advanced reference works for scholars. Attention will be given here to two representative examples by two important scholars: the introductions of Werner G. Kümmel and Helmut Koester.

WERNER GEORG KÜMMEL (1905–1995)

LIFE AND PAULINE RESEARCH

Kümmel was born in Heidelberg, the son of a professor of medicine.[2] He was educated at Heidelberg, Berlin, and Marburg. At Marburg he served as assistant lecturer 1930–32. To escape the Nazi threat he moved to Zürich, where he was appointed associate professor (1932) and promoted to full professor in 1946. After the war Kümmel taught for a time at Mainz, but in 1952 he succeeded Rudolf Bultmann at Marburg, where he remained until his retirement in 1973. He was a coeditor and frequent contributor to *Theologische Rundschau* (1957–83).[3] Kümmel was also instigator and editor of the series "Jüdische Schriften aus hellenistisch-römischer Zeit."[4] He was elected president of SNTS and received an honorary degree from Glasgow.

Kümmel was devoted to objective critical research. In spring semester 1963, I attended his seminar on baptism and the Lord's Supper. The class was relatively large, and Kümmel did most of the talking, giving a seated lecture. His method focused exclusively on the texts. After a student had translated the text, Kümmel would analyze the exegetical details and then summarize its significance for the topics. In the summary he would review the various ways in which the text had been (or could be) interpreted—sometimes as many as five. He then he would proceed through the list to adjudicate the possibilities. "The first cannot be correct, because . . ." (often he gave more than one reason) and similarly through the rest of the list. Often he would conclude: "Between four and five, no decision is possible. We shall go on to the next text."

Kümmel made an auspicious debut to his scholarly career. At age twenty-three he completed his dissertation (written under Martin Dibelius at Heidelberg), *Römer 7 und die Bekehrung des Paulus*, a monograph that remained a definitive work on the subject throughout the twentieth century.[5] Impetus for this project was generated in Bultmann's seminar on the anthropology of Paul at Marburg, which Kümmel attended in 1925–26. As Kümmel observed, interpretation of Romans 7 is plagued by two controversial questions: Does this chapter describe the pre-Christian or post-Christian experience? Is Paul speaking autobiographically when he uses the first person pronoun? Kümmel insists that these questions must be answered by rigorous exegetical research. Within the context of Romans 6 to 8, Rom 7:7-24, according to Kümmel, is an apology for the law. In regard to "I," which Paul introduces in v. 7 and repeats throughout the section, he argues that the use is not autobiographical. Paul's language, according to Kümmel, is rhetorical; "I" refers to the unredeemed human being. "Since it is correct that we in Rom. 7 have a description of the non-Christian from the Christian standpoint, so the possibility of viewing Rom. 7 as a presentation of the inner development of Paul is excluded."[6] Kümmel advances his case by an investigation of Paul's conversion, an experience that must be interpreted by critical exegesis of the crucial texts: Gal 1:12-17; 1 Cor 15:8; 9:1; Phil 3:7. Kümmel concludes that nothing in these texts supports the notion that Paul had been engaged in life-rending ethical or religious struggle, a conclusion that supports his conviction that Romans 7 is not autobiographical.

Throughout his career Kümmel continued his interest in Paul. For instance, he published an essay on Paul's eschatology—an important concern of Kümmel—in which he argues that Schweitzer's notion of "Christ-mysticism" is mistaken.[7] According to Kümmel, Paul's eschatological thought is grounded in Judaism; it stresses the historical: the Christian lives in the time between God's saving action in history and its consummation in the future. He also completed the popular edition of *Paul* that Dibelius left unfinished at his death in 1947,[8] and he published a revision of Hans Lietzmann's commentary on 1 and 2 Corinthians for the series Handbuch zum Neuen Testament (HNT).[9]

INTRODUCTION

Kümmel's *Einleitung* remained the standard work on introduction in Germany for several years.[10] Its first edition was published in 1963 as the twelfth edition of the venerable Feine-Behm *Einleitung*.[11] The first edition that listed Kümmel as the author was the 17th (Kümmel's 6th), a totally rewritten work that rightly bore the author's name. In the introduction, Kümmel defines the discipline.

> Accordingly the science of introduction is a strictly historical discipline which, by illuminating the historical circumstances of the origin of the individual writings, provides for exegesis the necessary

presuppositions for understanding the writings in their historical uniqueness. Through the study of the development and preservation of the collection, it furnishes a sure historical foundation for the question of the doctrinal content of the New Testament.[12]

Kümmel believes an introduction ought to arrange the NT books chronologically, but because the dates of writing are problematic, he adopts canonical order. Part One deals with the formation of the NT documents. Kümmel begins with the narrative books: the Synoptic Gospels and Acts. After an extensive discussion of the Synoptic Problem (some forty pages, prefaced by four pages of bibliography), Kümmel opts for the 2DH.[13] In regard to Mark, he argues that the author's major concern is theology; the "messianic secret" presents the hidden dignity of the Son of God. Kümmel rejects the tradition that Mark preserves the reminiscences of Peter and the theory that John Mark is the author. In regard to Matthew, Kümmel writes, "There is really no foundation for the notion that Mt tries to portray Jesus as the 'New Moses.' "[14] The author, according to Kümmel, uses Jewish-Christian tradition as ammunition against non-believing Jews. Matthew was written, Kümmel believes, from some place in Syria (probably Antioch) around 80–100 CE. Luke was written, according to Kümmel, by a Gentile Christian writing for Gentiles, probably between 70 and 90. Kümmel thinks Acts had an apologetic purpose: to prove that early Christians always enjoyed cordial relations with Rome. As to the "we sections," he rejects the theory that they represent the account of a travel companion of Paul; more likely they indicate the author's use of a source, perhaps a diary.

Kümmel presents five pages of bibliography about the Fourth Gospel. He believes the author—who certainly was not John the son of Zebedee—used both Mark and Luke; borrowing the language of Gnosticism, the author affirms the historical Jesus as the true revelation of God.

Turning to the NT Epistles, Kümmel discusses the letters of Paul. He thinks the apostle wrote 2 Thessalonians, and he believes both 1 Corinthians and 2 Corinthians represent unified, not composite, documents. At Corinth, according to Kümmel, Paul is fighting on one front only, against a gnostic perversion of the gospel. Kümmel believes Galatians was written to the original ethnic Galatians (he thus adopts the "north Galatian" hypothesis). The opponents are Jewish Christians who preach circumcision and observance of the law. Romans, according to Kümmel, was written to summarize Paul's gospel, but also with an eye toward anticipated conflict with Jews in Jerusalem; Romans 16 was part of the original letter. As to Philippians, Kümmel believes it was probably written from a Caesarean imprisonment, or possibly from

Ephesus; it is a unity, not a composite. Kümmel accepts Colossians as authentic, written in opposition to a religious syncretism that was influenced by Judaism. Neither Ephesians nor the Pastorals, in his judgment, were written by Paul.

As to Hebrews and the Catholic Epistles, Kümmel notes that the former—which was not written by Paul—is not a letter but a discourse or sermon. The Epistle of James was written, according to Kümmel, by an unknown Jewish Christian around the turn of the century. The rest of the Catholic Epistles—1 and 2 Peter, Jude, and the Johannine letters—are, in Kümmel's opinion, pseudonymous. Revelation does not bear some of the typical features of apocalyptic literature: it is not pseudonymous and it is not concerned with the distant past. According to Kümmel it addresses the suffering church of the author's own time, probably the reign of Domitian.

Parts Two and Three of Kümmel's *Introduction* discuss the formation of the canon and textual criticism of the NT. In regard to the canon, Kümmel notes that the Scripture of the earliest Christians was the OT. He sees the beginnings of the formation of a canon in Justin's "memoirs of the apostles" and Marcion's canon of ten letters of Paul and the Gospel of Luke. By the end of the second century the basic content of the canon was crystallized: four Gospels and Acts, and thirteen Epistles of Paul. The canon was closed in the East in the fourth century and in the West by the beginning of the fifth. Kümmel concludes that the closing of the canon was necessary, in spite of his suspicion that ancient judgments about apostolicity were flawed. "The factual delimitation and the actual openness of the limits of the canon correspond to the historicity of the revelation of God in Jesus Christ."[15] In regard to the text, Kümmel traces the history of research and notes the work of the International Greek Project and the work on the *Editio Critica Maior* at the Institute in Münster.[16] He believes the modern critical texts. even the student editions like Nestle/Aland, are very close to the original.

All in all, Kümmel's *Introduction* is a monumental work; it displays mastery of an enormous number of secondary sources, attention to detail, clear arguments, and avoiding premature conclusions where the evidence is insufficient. Although Kümmel tends to be conservative on issues of literary unity, his judgment on most issues reflects the "liberal" consensus of modern historical criticism at mid-twentieth century.

HISTORY OF RESEARCH

Closely related to the science of introduction is Kümmel's work on the history of NT research.[17] His book does not intend to cover the entire history, "but limits itself deliberately to the delineation of the lines of inquiry and the methods which have proved to be of permanent significance or to anticipate future developments."[18] In other words, it is an appraisal of research from the Enlightenment to the twentieth century, and one that heralds the triumph of the historical critical method. The book, roughly organized in chronological order, is problem-oriented, concerned with critical issues. A distinctive feature is Kümmel's presentation of extensive quotations from the primary sources.

After brief discussions of the pre-history and the rise of early textual criticism Kümmel takes up "The Beginnings of the Major Discipline of NT Research" (Part III). He honors the pioneers: "Scientific study of the New Testament is indebted to two men, Johann Salomo Semler and Johann David Michaelis for the first evidences of a consciously historical approach to the New Testament as a historical entity distinct from the Old Testament."[19] In regard to literary problems, Kümmel reviews the work of Griesbach, Lessing, Herder, Schleiermacher, and Bretschneider, who rejected the authenticity of the Gospel of John. In discussing research into the history of early Christianity, Kümmel attends to the contribution of Reimarus and the rationalism of Paulus. He believes Gabler's distinction between historical biblical theology and dogmatic theology to be of major importance. He praises rigorous exegesis as the proper foundation of NT research, noting, for example, the commentary series of H. A. W. Meyer (KEK), which was dedicated to the historico-grammatical investigation of the text.

In the next major part Kümmel hails the victory of the "Consistently Historical Approach." Although he disagrees with him on a host of issues, he praises F. C. Baur:

> Baur recognized two problems to whose clarification New Testament research continues to devote itself: the arrangement of the New Testament writings in a total historical perspective, and the understanding of the sequence and of the historical development of the New Testament world of ideas. And more than that, Baur recognized the fundamental significance of the historical understanding of the person and proclamation of Jesus and the importance for the historical evaluation of the New Testament writings of the question concerning the object in view ("tendency") of every single book. Since Baur's time, scientific work on the New Testament has been possible only when the fundamental methodological principles he indicated have been followed and his overall historical view has been superseded or improved.[20]

Baur and his student D. F. Strauss had adopted the Griesbach hypothesis concerning the Synoptic Problem, a hypothesis Kümmel believes was overcome by the work of Christian Gottlob Wilke, Christian Hermann Weisse, and H.-J. Holtzmann. Similarly, Baur's Hegelian reconstruction of early Christianity was corrected by scholars like J. B. Lightfoot and Adolf von Harnack. Also in the latter part of the nineteenth century, contributions were made to the understanding of various individual questions, for example, Jülicher's work on the parables. Kümmel is less sanguine about attempts to derail the consistently historical view by scholars like Adolf Schlatter and the skeptical Franz Overbeck.

Kümmel's final sections deal with the "History-of-Religions School" and the "Historical-Theological View of the NT." In regard to the former he notes the pioneering work of C. F. G. Heinrici, Edwin Hatch, and Adolf Deissmann, and the theory of "consistent eschatology" by Johannes Weiss and Albert Schweitzer. The main figures in the history of religion school are discussed: Wilhelm Bousset, Wilhelm Heitmüller, and Richard Reitzenstein.[21] Kümmel sympathizes with the method—the concern to probe the religious-historical setting—but not with many of the conclusions of the school. He also notes the radical criticism of William Wrede and Alfred Loisy and the conservative reaction by scholars like Paul Feine. In the post-World War I period, Kümmel reviews the form-critical work of Dibelius and Bultmann and the new history-of-religion stress on Jewish backgrounds by Paul Billerbeck. A distinctive theological emphasis emerged in Barth's *Epistle to the Romans*, but Kümmel concludes that biblical theology must be built on solid historical exegesis.

In a related work Kümmel focused on twentieth-century research,[22] heir to a legacy from the nineteenth century that included the recognition of the separation between OT and NT research and the necessity of understanding NT documents in their historical and religious setting. Kümmel believed that major achievements of the nineteenth century were advanced and confirmed in the twentieth: the triumph of the 2DH (despite opposition from Scandinavian scholars and William R. Farmer), the move from form to redaction criticism, and the investigation of sources and background of the Gospel of John (for example, in the Qumran texts). He concludes: "New Testament research in the 20th century has in no way reached unanimous results in important areas, and great as the advances in New Testament scholarship have been, one can speak of acknowledged results only to a limited degree, so that there still remains in New Testament research very much to clarify and to do."[23]

TEACHINGS OF JESUS AND THEOLOGY OF THE NEW TESTAMENT

Kümmel's other research includes a major work on the preaching of Jesus, *Promise and Fulfilment*.[24] In the first chapter he investigates texts indicating that Jesus believed the coming of the kingdom of God to be imminent, yet still future. Although he acknowledges that Jesus used apocalyptic language, Kümmel insists that Jesus' message is not essentially apocalyptic. Turning to texts suggesting that the kingdom is present, Kümmel says that "it is quite firmly established that the eschatological consummation, the Kingdom of God, has already become a present reality in the ministry of Jesus."[25] The presence of the kingdom, according to Kümmel, is restricted to Jesus and his ministry; the coming of the kingdom remains future. Jesus was mistaken about the time of the future coming, but the important factor for Kümmel is the meaning of his message: "the inseparable union of hope and present experience demonstrate the fact that the true meaning of Jesus' eschatological message is to be found in its reference to God's action in Jesus himself, that the essential content of Jesus' preaching about the Kingdom of God is the news of the divine authority of Jesus, who has appeared on earth and is awaited in the last days as the one who effects the divine purpose of mercy."[26] In a closely related monograph Kümmel argues that Jesus identified himself with the coming Son of Man and understood his present activity as the manifestation of that identity. "The statements of Jesus about the present and coming "Man" fit fully into the total proclamation of Jesus."[27] Kümmel repeats this conclusion in his contribution to the "new quest" of the historical Jesus.

> Indeed, the answer to the question about the historical Jesus allows us to recognize a man who interprets his acts and mission as the present realization of the future eschatological action of God over against the world, and ascribes to himself the decisive role in the end time of God's salvation history. This claim of Jesus, which according to the faith of the early church, God has confirmed through the cross and resurrection, explains the eschatological, salvation historical meaning of the person of Jesus in early Christianity.[28]

Kümmel also devoted attention to the theology of the NT. In an early work he investigated the NT understanding of "man."[29] Later in his career Kümmel published his understanding of NT theology according to the three major witnesses: Jesus, Paul, and John.[30] In regard to the proclamation of Jesus, Kümmel argues (contra Bultmann) that the message of Jesus is an essential aspect of NT theology. The central feature of the message, according to

Kümmel, is the kingdom of God: the rule of God already present in Jesus' own life and deeds, to be realized in the imminent future. Kümmel thinks that Jesus did not claim to be messiah but that he did identify himself with the coming Son of Man, already active in his ministry. Turning to Paul, Kümmel believes the experience of conversion involved the recognition of Christ as the revelation of God's eschatological action. In regard to the human situation, Paul affirms the universality of sin and declares that salvation comes by faith in Jesus Christ. The gift of salvation involves the task of the Christian; the indicative of new life entails the imperative of obedience. As to the Fourth Gospel, Kümmel believes it witnesses not to the historical Jesus but to the Christ of faith. Christ is the pre-existent Logos, the Son sent from the Father, the lamb of God who takes away the sin world. Salvation is received by faith, but faith involves keeping the commandments, above all the new commandment of love. "[T]he three major witnesses of the theology of the New Testament are in agreement in the twofold message, that God has caused his salvation promised for the end of the world to begin in Jesus Christ, and that in this Christ event God has encountered us and intends to encounter us as the Father who seeks to rescue us from imprisonment in the world and to make us free for active love."[31]

HELMUT KOESTER (1926–)

LIFE AND EARLY WORK

Born in Hamburg, Helmut Koester was the son of an architect.[32] He served in the German armed forces during World War II and was taken prisoner by the Americans in 1945. From 1945 to 1950 he studied under Bultmann at Marburg, and during the academic years 1947/1948 he was invited weekly to lunch at the professor's home, an occasion that "provided the opportunity to experience personally the unerring human integrity, humility, and piety of my beloved teacher."[33] In 1954 Koester finished his doctoral dissertation at Marburg and became research assistant to Günther Bornkamm at Heidelberg. In 1956 he completed his qualifying dissertation (*Habilitations-schrift*) and was appointed instructor. In 1958 Koester began teaching at Harvard Divinity School where, in 1963, he was named John H. Morison Professor of NT Studies and, in 1968, Winn Professor of Ecclesiastical History; he continued to hold both chairs until his retirement in 1991. In 1972 Koester received a grant from the American Council of Learned Societies for archeological study in Greece and Turkey, and in the following years he offered seminars on location for doctoral students. Looking back over his career, Koester wrote that "it has been a long way from the time when I was an enthusiastic student of Bultmann with the firm belief that demythologizing was the most important issue of New Testament scholarship to a stage in life where bringing archaeologists and students of early Christianity together would occupy much of my time and seemed to me the most worthwhile thing I could contribute."[34] He added, "I have never given up my first love: biblical exegesis and theology."[35]

Koester's Marburg dissertation on the Synoptic tradition in the Apostolic Fathers set the course for much of his later work.[36] In investigating this tradition, Koester discovers that most of the writings of the Apostolic Fathers do not indicate the use of written texts but give evidence of knowledge of the pre-Synoptic tradition. Koester concludes that the Synoptics stand in the midst of the transmission of tradition, neither at the beginning nor at the end. The Apostolic Fathers, he believes, stand beside the Synoptics and reflect parallel, not later development. Even where there is evidence that the Gospels are known, they do not appear, according to Koester, to command a special authority.

INTRODUCTION

Whereas Kümmel's *Introduction* was widely used as a text in German universities and American seminaries, Koester's two-volume contribution is a resource for the advanced scholar.[37] He presents the early Christian documents in the context of the history of early Christianity. "My primary concern is to present the history of the early Christian churches, since it seems to me that the student of the New Testament must learn from the outset to understand the writings of the earliest period within their proper historical context."[38] As well as the books of the NT, Koester provides critical introductions to over sixty other documents. "These non-canonical books are witnesses to early Christian history no less valuable than the New Testament."[39]

The first volume presents the "history, culture, and religion of the Hellenistic age." After a survey of the history of the Hellenistic age, Koester offers chapters on economics and society, education and literature, and philosophy and religion. In regard to the "new religions" of the Hellenistic period, he writes: "What mattered was the appropriation of power and the securing of protection of higher authorities in the adversities of life and for the passage of the soul into a better world after death—ideas that also were widely accepted by Christianity."[40] Koester also presents a history of Israel in the Hellenistic age, noting the Hellenistic influence on Judaism. "As a development of cultural history," writes Koester, "Hellenization affected all Israelites, whether they were Jews or Samaritans, Essenes or Pharisees, living in the diaspora or in Palestine. But in the dispersion, the effects of Hellenization were more profound."[41] Koester also traces the rise of Rome as a world power and its impact on Palestine. He notes the development of religions in the Roman period, with attention to the rise of the imperial cult. In regard to Gnosticism, Koester writes, "Gnosticism thus cannot be derived from anything but the experience of the world as a foreign place and of the liberating message of the divine call through which humans were able to recognize themselves and their true being."[42]

Koester's second volume deals with the "history and literature of early Christianity." "This book endeavors to introduce the student of the New Testament to all of these writings in the context of a reconstruction of the expansion and growth of the Christian communities from their beginnings to the middle of the second century ce."[43] In the first chapter of this volume Koester investigates the sources of early Christianity. He describes the formation of early Christian writings and the development of the canon. In the latter, an important role was played by a heretic. "The impelling force for the formation of the canon, that is, for the singling out of a limited number of traditional writings of Christian authors as authoritative Holy Scripture, came from a radical theologian of the first half of the 2nd century, who came from the tradition of the Pauline churches: Marcion."[44] In this chapter Koester also explicates critical methods including textual, form, and source criticism. "As gospels are not free creations of their authors but compilations of sources and oral traditions, also the epistles must not be envisioned as products of the free-ranging minds of creative theological thinkers but as elaboration of various and diverse traditional materials that were current in Israel, the Hellenistic-Roman world, and specifically in early Christian communities."[45]

The next chapter surveys the history of early Christianity from John the Baptist to the emergence of the church. Koester believes that Jesus was born and raised in Nazareth. He associated for a time with John the Baptist but withdrew to conduct his own mission. According to Koester, Jesus announced the imminent coming of the kingdom of God, which was already present in his words and deeds. His proclamation demanded an ethical response: "the command to love also one's enemies calls for a move into a new realm that lies beyond the boundaries of Israel's traditional ethics."[46] Jesus, according to Koester, did not fully fit any of the typical religious categories of his time: prophet, magician, wisdom teacher, or exorcist. After the execution of Jesus by the Romans, his followers believed he was alive. This resulted in the founding of a community that shared a common meal, anticipating the messianic banquet. Within the Jerusalem church a group of Greek-speaking Jewish Christians advocated a mission to the Gentiles; they established a church in Antioch that, according to Koester, became a center of Greek-speaking, Gentile Christianity.

Turning to Paul, Koester describes his life and ministry up to the Apostolic Council. Paul was a Pharisee, a diaspora Jew, who had a vision that constituted a call to Gentile mission. Paul's view of the law was established in his conflict with Peter at Antioch. "Henceforth Paul insisted that the constitution of the church 'in Christ' abolished all traditional religious, social, and cultural particularities and every claim based upon such privileges (Gal 3:26-28)."[47] Koester believes that 1 Thessalonians was Paul's first letter, written around 50. Much of Paul's writing was composed in Ephesus. Galatians was addressed, according to Koester, to north Galatian churches that had been invaded by wandering Jewish Christian missionaries who insisted that Gentile Christians observe circumcision and Jewish ritual regulations. Koester thinks 1 Corinthians was aimed at a single group of opponents: wisdom teachers, spiritual enthusiasts who embraced realized eschatology. The troublemakers of 2 Corinthians, according to Koester, were a different group: false apostles who assumed the posture of the divine man. Koester believes Paul wrote Philippians (a composite of three letters) and Philemon from an Ephesian imprisonment. The Epistle to the Romans, according to Paul, is a letter of recommendation of himself, summarizing his gospel. After his final trip to Jerusalem and imprisonment in Caesarea and Rome, little is known about Paul. He may have been martyred in Philippi.

Following the model of Walter Bauer, Koester surveys the history and literature of early Christianity according to geographical regions.[48] Koester believes sayings of Jesus were collected and translated into Greek, beginning in Palestine and Syria, forming Q at around 50 CE. He thinks the Synoptic Apocalypse and a collection of parables were also composed in this period. Early tradition presented Jesus as a teacher of wisdom, and a collection of sayings was made around 50; Koester believes this is attested by the *Gospel of Thomas* and the *Dialogue of the Savior* (NHC). Tradition also developed, according to Koester, about the life and order of the church, as seen in the letter of James and the *Didache*, which contains earlier tradition. Koester also traces the development from the resurrection kerygma to the gospel of the church. Traditions of the authority of Peter are reflected in the *Gospel of Peter* and the *Kerygma of Peter*. Mark, according to Koester, was probably written about 70–80 in Syria, and the Gospel of Matthew, using both Mark and Q, appeared in Syria toward the end of the century. Koester thinks the Johannine tradition also emerged in Syria and is reflected in the Nag Hammadi texts (NHC). Syria is also, in Koester's view, the seat of the development of Jewish Christianity, a movement that produced the *Gospel of the Nazoreans* and the

Gospel of the Ebionites. Koester thinks Syria was the country of origin of Christian Gnosticism.

Moving on to Egypt, Koester sees evidence there of Syrian Christianity in second-century fragments of the Fourth Gospel. Early Christian Gnosticism is witnessed by the NHC. "As Jewish Gnostic speculations were the predecessors of Christian Gnosis in Syria, pagan Gnostic mythology and philosophy preceded its Christian offspring in Egypt and even developed further without direct borrowings from Christianity."[49] Koester expresses his assumption about the burial of the NHC:

> [T]he monks of Pachomius, founder of cenobite Christian monasticism, read and copied Gnostic writings for their own religious edification. Thanks to this Christian monastic activity, the writings of the Nag Hammadi Library have been preserved: members of the Pachomian monastery hid these precious books in order to protect them from the officially sanctioned heresy hunters. Thus orthodoxy and heresy continued to exist side by side in Egypt for centuries.[50]

Turning to Asia, Macedonia, Greece, and Rome, Koester notes the revival of apocalypticism in pseudonymous 2 Thessalonians and the use of apocalyptic weapons in the battle with the Gnostics by the author of the letter of Jude. He observes that the *Shepherd of Hermas* combines apocalyptic thought and church order. In this region Pauline theology was transformed, according to Koester, into ecclesiastical doctrine as seen in Colossians and Ephesians. Koester notes that the authority of both Peter and Paul was recognized: 1 Peter, which purports to be from Peter, actually reflects the teachings of Paul, and the Pastoral Epistles (written 120–160) promote church order in the name of Paul. In this region, especially Rome, Christianity encountered the social world. Koester sees this in Luke-Acts, the work of a Gentile Christian writing to Gentiles in about 100. The idea of miracle-working apostles confronting the world is carried on in the *Acts of Peter* and the *Acts of Paul.* In time the apologists appear, eager to prove by philosophical argument that Christianity is the true religion.

Koester's research on critical introduction is more narrowly focused in his book, *Ancient Christian Gospels.*[51] "My study of the gospel traditions in the Apostolic Fathers had brought me to the conclusion that gospel materials that were not dependent upon the canonical writings might indeed have survived well into the second century."[52] This observation led to his conviction that apocryphal as well as canonical gospels should be used in the study of early

Christianity. In regard to the term "gospel," Koester notes that it was not used for documents until the mid-second century. When it is applied to documents the term is used for a variety of genres, confounding the notion that canonical and apocryphal gospels represent two distinctly different genres.

> On the basis of these observations one must establish a criterion by which it can be determined whether any extant writing from the early period of Christianity belongs to the corpus of gospel literature. This corpus should include all those writings which are constituted by the transmission, use, and interpretation of materials and traditions from and about Jesus of Nazareth.[53]

Koester proceeds to investigate early collections of the sayings of Jesus. Paul reflects knowledge of the teachings of Jesus, and in 1 Corinthians he disputes with Christians who claim to possess wisdom. Koester believes this implies a collection of wisdom sayings known to Paul and his opponents. A major witness to early collections of sayings of Jesus, according to Koester, is found in the *Gospel of Thomas*, a later document that embodies early tradition. *Thomas* includes parables that are also found in Q but, according to Koester, *Thomas* reflects a stratum of tradition earlier than Q. As to Q, Koester believes it underwent at least one redaction in which apocalyptic material was added; the earlier Q, he thinks, was a collection of wisdom sayings of Jesus. "Therefore, the entire development of Q, from the first collection of the sayings of Jesus and their assembly into sapiential discourses to the apocalyptic redaction and, finally, the pre-Matthean redaction, must be dated within the first three decades after the death of Jesus."[54]

Koester detects a tradition that evolves from early dialogues of Jesus into the narratives of the Gospel of John. The *Dialogue of the Savior* (NHC) has parallels in the *Gospel of Thomas* and in the Fourth Gospel. Koester believes Mark used an early collection of miracle stories that presented Jesus as a Divine Man. In the *Gospel of Peter*, Koester finds evidence of an earlier passion narrative.

> The *Gospel of Peter*, as a whole, is not dependent upon any of the canonical gospels. It is a composition which is analogous to the Gospels of Mark and John. All three writings, independently of each other, use an older passion narrative which is based upon an exegetical tradition that was still alive when these gospels were composed and to which the Gospel of Matthew also had access.[55]

The Gospel of John makes use of a *semeia* or sign source that presented Jesus as Divine Man; the author also used dialogue sources that have parallels in the documents of Nag Hammadi. The composition of John, according to Koester, took place over a period of time; the result was a biography of Sophia who comes as the Logos: a polemic against Gnosticism.

Taking up the Synoptics, Koester believes the author of Mark used a collection of parables and a collection of miracle stories. "All arrangements of the sources and traditional materials serve the theological intention of the author to present, in the form of a written document, the 'messianic secret' of Jesus that God's revelation in history is not fulfilled in the demonstration of divine greatness, but in the humiliation of the divine human being in his death on the cross."[56] Koester thinks that stories about the birth and childhood of Jesus circulated prior to their use in Matthew and Luke and represent a tradition that was developed in other documents like the *Proto-Gospel of James* and the *Infancy Gospel of Thomas*. The author of Matthew, using Mark, Q and other sources, composed a gospel that highlights the discourses of Jesus. A summary of Koester's book is presented in his preface:

> This book . . . includes extensive treatments of all those writings from which one might, in my judgment, learn more about the earliest stages of the history and development of gospel literature—a history that must have begun with smaller written collections of materials about Jesus and eventually resulted in the composition of a number of gospel writings, including so-called apocryphal gospels as well as the Gospels of the New Testament canon. . . . This historical development culminated in the only partially successful attempt to create the one gospel for the church, that is Tatian's Diatessaron.[57]

ARCHAEOLOGY AND THEOLOGY

For Koester, archaeology is another tool in the kit of the history of religion—a way to understand early Christian documents in their social-historical setting. Along with his students and colleagues, Koester investigated sites in Asia Minor and Greece that are important for interpreting the NT. The results have been collected in a series of publications Koester edited. In *Ephesos: Metropolis of Asia*, he published papers that were read at a "Symposium Ephesos" held at Harvard Divinity School in 1994. Participants included archaeologists from the Austrian excavations and American scholars: archaeologists, classicists, and scholars of the history of religion and the NT. Koester writes: "If students of the New Testament wish to benefit from archaeological scholarship, they must become better acquainted with nonliterary materials unearthed by others, and thus must participate in the process of interpretation."[58] A companion volume on Pergamon includes papers from a similar symposium held at Harvard in 1996. In his introduction Koester affirms his commitment to the "new archaeology":

> Biblical archaeology can no longer be limited to the paths of Jesus of Nazareth, nor should it seek to trace the footsteps of Paul in Asia Minor and Greece, or unearth the remains of the seven churches of the Book of Revelation. Rather, interdisciplinary discussions of scholars from various fields will create a better understanding of the Greco-Roman world, the world in which the New Testament was written, and in which both early Christianity and diaspora Judaism flourished.[59]

To a collection of essays on Philippi, Koester contributed "Paul and Philippi: The Evidence from Early Christian Literature."[60] In this essay he observes that excavations at the Octagonal Church in Philippi may have located the place of Paul's martyrdom.

Koester's critical and tradition-historical research has implications for theology. This can be seen in his essay, "The Structure and Criteria of Early Christian Beliefs."[61] At the outset he rejects the notion that Christianity began with a unified faith that later eroded into heresies. Instead, he believes Christianity began with a historical person to whom faith and doctrine variously responded; there was diversity from the beginning. He thinks the most primitive belief identified Jesus as the Lord of the future. The application of the titles Lord and Son of Man, according to Koester, interrupted continuity with the preaching of Jesus. This christological development advanced as the church moved into the Hellenistic world. There, says Koester, Jesus was viewed as a Divine Man and the acts of Jesus became the object of faith. "The power of the miracle and the documentation of divine presence in the miraculous events is indeed a symbol that tends to separate Christian faith completely from the criterion of a historical revelation in Jesus and that replaces historical and communal responsibility of Christian faith with personal piety and religious edification."[62] Koester also notes a theological tradition that recognized Jesus as the envoy of Wisdom, in time identified Jesus as Wisdom, and eventually hailed Jesus as the preexistent Logos. The resurrection of Jesus was also stressed in the early development of doctrine; the creed of the resurrection, according to Koester, was the only confession that took the human life and suffering of Jesus seriously.

> Yet in this creed Jesus' humanity remained the criterion of a gospel that called all those who suffer and die, who are poor and deprived, who neither have social or political identity nor possess accepted moral and religious virtues. It calls them regardless of class, creed, or sex: "Neither Jew nor Greek, neither slave nor free, neither male nor female."[63]

In conclusion Koester notes that the ideologies from which the early creed arose are not our presuppositions. If Christianity has anything to say today, it must be based on the fact that with Jesus, God has come into the life of humankind in a unique way.

REDACTION CRITICISM: CONZELMANN AND MARXSEN

In the era of World War I, Gospel studies were dominated by form criticism; in the post–World War II era attention shifted to redaction criticism.[64] Redaction criticism "is concerned with studying the theological motivation of an author as this is revealed in the collection, arrangement, editing, and modification of traditional material, and in the composition of new material or the creation of new forms within the traditions of early Christianity."[65] Actually, redaction criticism, or *Redaktionsgeschichte*, is nothing new. Wrede, for example, viewed Mark as a composition that presented a theology.[66] The redaction criticism discussed in this chapter, however, has a different historical context: it functions in the wake of form criticism. In relation to form criticism, redaction criticism presupposes a third *Sitz im Leben*: the first is the setting of the life of Jesus, the second is the setting of the community that shaped the oral tradition, and the third is the situation of the Gospel writers themselves. The work of Günther Bornkamm in redaction criticism has been reviewed in Chapter 3. In this chapter attention will be given to Hans Conzelmann and to Willi Marxsen, who coined the term "redaction criticism."

HANS CONZELMANN (1915–1989)

Conzelmann was born in Thailfingen, Württemberg, to parents of modest means.[67] From 1934 to 1938 he studied at Tübingen and at Marburg, where he fell under the spell of Rudolf Bultmann. Returning to Tübingen, he joined the Church Theological Society, a group in Württemberg that corresponded to the Confessing Church. Conzelmann was drafted into the army and served on the Russian front; later in France he was wounded and his leg amputated. After the war he completed his doctorate at Tübingen and his *Habilitation* in

Heidelberg under Bornkamm. Conzelmann taught at Heidelberg and Zürich, and in 1960 he was called to the faculty at Göttingen. He suffered a heart attack in 1975, but continued to teach for two more years. Conzelmann was described as a professor "whose work was not merely a matter of command of the materials, but one who placed his whole person on the line for his theological convictions."[68]

REDACTION CRITICISM AND JESUS

Conzelmann launched his scholarly career with a dissertation (*Habilitationsschrift*) that utilized redaction criticism: *Die Mitte der Zeit*.[69] Beyond form criticism, Conzelmann is concerned with the whole composition as expressing the message of the author of Luke-Acts. "What distinguishes him is not that he thinks in the categories of promise and fulfilment, for this he has in common with others, but the way in which he builds up from these categories a picture of the course of saving history, and the way in which he employs the traditional material for this purpose."[70]

Conzelmann begins with an investigation of the geographical elements in the composition of Luke's Gospel. He observes that Luke presents the ministry of Jesus in three stages. The first is the ministry in Galilee, a period in which the devil, who had departed after the temptation, is absent. Luke, according to Conzelmann, views the mountain as place of revelation and the lake as the abyss. The second stage is the journey to Jerusalem, a creation of Luke, who adds material so as to make this stage as long as the other two. The third stage is the time in Jerusalem, a time when Satan is again present (Luke 22:3), a time of trial. In presenting the trial of Jesus, Luke minimizes the role of Pilate, who delivers Jesus to the Jews for execution. Luke also locates the resurrection appearances in or around Jerusalem.

Conzelmann then turns to Luke's eschatology. He believes Luke avoids the idea of the imminence of the kingdom, stressing its nature rather than its timing. Events that belong to the end, like the destruction of Jerusalem, Luke presents as historical happenings.

> The main motif in the recasting to which Luke subjects his source proves to be the delay of the Parousia, which leads to a comprehensive consideration of the nature and course of the Last Things. . . . The delay has to be explained, and this is done by means of the idea of God's plan which underlies the whole structure of Luke's account.[71]

The divine plan, according to Conzelmann's reading of Luke, is God's redemptive history—a history with three stages: the period of Israel, the period of Jesus, and the period of the church. At the center of redemptive history is Jesus Christ. Luke's major titles are "Lord" and "Christ," but he assumes subordination and has no idea of preexistence. Although Jesus must suffer and die, Luke does not, according to Conzelmann, understand the death of Jesus as a sacrifice that provides forgiveness for sins. The period of Jesus ends with his ascension. "In conclusion, therefore, we may say that the Lord is now in Heaven, whilst on earth there lives the community of the Church, equipped with the Spirit, provided with the message which is communicated by the witnesses, and with the abiding blessings of the sacrament."[72]

The third stage is the period of the church. "In the Church we stand in a mediated relationship to the saving events—mediated by the whole course of redemptive history—and at the same time in an immediate relationship to them, created by the Spirit, in whom we can invoke God and the name of Christ; in other words, the Spirit dwells in the Church, and is imparted through its means of grace and its office-bearers."[73] The church has a universal task, filled with the Spirit, moved to mission. The church proclaims the message of God for salvation; its life in the "way"—the ethical life, participating in God's saving history.

The result of Conzelmann's redaction criticism for understanding Jesus is expressed in his article, "Jesus Christus," in the third edition of *Religion in Geschichte und Gegenwart*.[74] In regard to sources, Conzelmann points out that Mark's framework is not a historical record but a witness to faith. Thus the perspective of redaction criticism must be maintained in reconstruction of the life and teaching of Jesus. Conzelmann, discussing the historical background, notes that the activity of Jesus took place within Palestinian Judaism, that he spoke Aramaic, and that his teaching reflects no interest in economic or political relationships. Concerning the birth and heritage of Jesus, Conzelmann believes the location of the birth in Bethlehem and the idea of Davidic descent represent theology rather than history. Jesus' ministry was prepared by his baptism by John the Baptist. As he began his own mission, Jesus gathered a group of twelve disciples, representative of the people of God.

Conzelmann investigates the self-consciousness of Jesus in terms of titles. He notes that "Christ" (Messiah) is seldom used (not at all in Q), and that texts that apply the title to Jesus, for example the confession of Peter, are not historical. "Son of Man" is a title used exclusively by Jesus, but Conzelmann believes the application of the title to Jesus is a post-Easter phenomenon. Conzelmann points out that the title "Servant of God" is not found in the oldest stratum of tradition, and he rejects the popular theory that Jesus understood himself as the Servant of Second Isaiah. "Son of God" was not used as a messianic title in first-century Judaism, and Conzelmann does not believe Jesus viewed himself as Son in any unique sense. In any event, Conzelmann concludes that Jesus did not use titles directly.

> And Jesus does not represent his own relationship to the coming of the kingdom directly as he himself shows with the messianic title. Rather he does so in the indirectness which characterizes his entire ministry—hence through his preaching and his miracles, through his call to repentance, his interpretation of the command of God, through the disclosure of God's immediacy [*Unmittelbarkeit*] for sinners and the poor. His "Christology" then is an indirect one.[75]

Conzelmann gives major attention (some thirty pages) to the teachings of Jesus.

> The primary element is the absoluteness of the promise of salvation [*Heilszusage*]. It takes shape in the presentation of God as Father, i.e., in the recovery of immediacy to him through the proclamation of forgiveness. Precisely from this follows the radical understanding of the demand of God which—in its unconditional nature—carries with it its fulfillment, and the understanding of the present time as the last hour, which opens up access to the kingdom of God.[76]

According to Conzelmann, Jesus did not oppose the cult or piety of Judaism; he opposed Jewish hypocrisy. "It is immediately obvious that this preaching had to lead to a fundamental conflict with *all* the trends within Judaism."[77] Conzelmann believes that Jesus offered no new doctrine of God, but stressed the absolute will of God, summed up in the command of love. Jesus proclaimed the imminent coming of the kingdom of God, looking to the future, but seeing signs in the present.

> If the signs are already here and effect salvation . . . then one cannot any more ask "when?" because the kingdom is no longer represented in a picture. The salvation of the kingdom becomes existentially intelligible to me in the present moment. I understand that on the basis of this present salvation I now can only still repent. And futurity is now no longer "not yet," but is a positive qualification of this final time, the ground of hope, and the condition for the present experience of salvation.[78]

This statement, of course, is reminiscent of Conzelmann's teacher, Rudolf Bultmann.

Conzelmann believes the Passion narrative was the earliest fixed form of the Synoptic tradition, formed from the perspective of the Easter faith. Some of the content, he thinks, was historical, based on eyewitness accounts. Of certain historicity is the execution of Jesus by the Romans; Pilate pronounced the death sentence and ordered the crucifixion.

In a final section Conzelmann discusses the question of the relation of the historical Jesus and faith. He notes that some interpreters have argued that faith is the result of historical research and others have insisted that historical reconstruction is not binding for faith. Both of these arguments, in Conzelmann's view, rest on an objectifying conception of faith—to see faith as an object that can be verified or not verified by historical research. The decisive issue, says Conzelmann, is the transition from Jesus' ministry to the gathering of his followers under the impact of the appearances of the Risen One and faith in him as messiah and Son of God. Thus Conzelmann sees the line of continuity in the resurrection, but historical research cannot establish its facticity.

> This assertion implies that theology can postulate no historical facts [*Tatsachen*] and does not need to do so, since it lives by proclamation. On the other hand, it implies that the church cannot altogether interpret historical research disinterestedly by constricting itself to a witness of faith. Otherwise the result is the fatal consequence that this witness becomes the object of faith, and faith would then mean accepting a historical fact as true on the basis of someone else's faith. Faith would then have become a matter of human resolve [*Entschluss*] and thus a "work." . . . Precisely in view of the witness to the resurrection, we must maintain that the object of faith appears only to faith itself. Revelation is not "facts laid out before a person"; it emerges—today—in the word.[79]

THEOLOGY OF THE NEW TESTAMENT AND EXEGESIS

Redaction critics are concerned with the theology of the final documents, and Conzelmann has exercised this concern for the whole NT. His *Outline of the Theology of the New Testament* is designed as a textbook for students.[80] He begins with an investigation of the kerygma of the primitive community and the Hellenistic community. The earliest church, he notes, was divided with the emergence of the Hellenists who engaged in Gentile mission.[81] The members of the church viewed themselves as the people of the end time, the true Israel. Their worship included preaching, prayers, Scripture reading and the observance of the Lord's Supper. Conzelmann believes the central feature of the message was the person and work of Christ. The members of the early community expressed their understanding of Christ, Conzelmann thinks, by the use of titles: Messiah and Son of God.

Conzelmann turns to the Synoptic kerygma. Here emphasis is put on Jesus' proclamation of the coming of the kingdom of God. "The contradiction between the 'present' and the future sayings," writes Conzelmann, "is only an apparent one. The two have the same significance for human existence: man's attitude of the moment toward the coming kingdom."[82] Jesus' announcement of the kingdom included the command of God. "In its absoluteness," says Conzelmann, "the commandment of love thus does away with casuistry. The individual ethical regulations are not intended to regulate individual instances, but to disclose the immediacy of acting in the moment."[83] As to his understanding of himself, Jesus, according to Conzelmann, did not use the titles Son of God, Messiah, or Son of Man for himself.

The longest section of the book is Conzelmann's explication of the theology of Paul. In essence, according to Conzelmann, Paul's theology is response to God's action in Christ. "Theology is the understanding of this event."[84] Conzelmann believes the idea of faith is crucial for Paul's thought; faith is response to the word of God; it includes knowledge, trust, and obedience. Apart from faith the human person in the world, according to Conzelmann's reading of Paul, is trapped in the fatal, universal power of sin. Salvation comes only by the action of God in Christ, the preexistent one, sent by God. In regard to Paul's phrase δικαιοσύνη θεοῦ, Conzelmann acknowledges that the genitive may be subjective, but he believes the emphasis is on the righteousness *from* God.

> Paul's theme is not "God's righteousness" (that is the Jewish version of the problem), but God's righteousness as the righteousness of faith. It remains God's "alien" righteousness, to be experienced in the word, by being spoken. In hearing, we recognized ourselves as really being made righteous, and are freed for "newness of life."[85]

Conzelmann notes that Paul believes response to God's saving action creates the community, the church. Life in he community, according to Conzelmann's understanding of Paul, is a life of freedom: freedom from the flesh for life in the spirit.

The last two sections of Conzelmann's *Outline* deal with developments after Paul and with the Johannine writings. Conzelmann takes a dim view of the former. He believes the church degenerated into an institution and theology descended into dogma. The eschatological vitality of Paul was stifled by the delay of the parousia. Salvation was increasingly seen as otherworldly, and this descended into either apocalypticism or Gnosticism. In regard to the Fourth Gospel, Conzelmann sees the major concern of the author as Christology. This author takes up the term Logos, which has its background in Jewish Wisdom and Hellenistic Gnosticism, to present Christ as the preexistent one who can be confessed as Lord and God. According to Conzelmann, the Gospel of John, before its ecclesiastical editing, presented salvation as present, expecting no *parousia*, no future resurrection.

Conzelmann's reconstruction of NT theology rests on rigorous exegetical work, the kind of research demonstrated in his commentaries. Early in his career he edited and expanded Dibelius's commentary on the Pastoral Epistles for the Handbuch zum Neuen Testament (HNT) series, and that volume was adopted into the Hermeneia commentaries.[86] Later Conzelmann wrote a commentary on Acts for the HNT; this, too, became the representative volume in Hermeneia.[87] The English version is much more "user friendly" than the original; the notes, for example, are printed separately at the bottom of the page, not crammed into the comments. This commentary displays Conzelmann's philological research and concern with history background, expressed tersely and concisely.

For the venerable Meyer series (KEK), Conzelmann produced a commentary on 1 Corinthians that also was adopted by Hermeneia.[88] In the introduction he discusses and dismisses partition theories. He also objects to the notion that 1 Corinthians is weak theologically; instead, he believes this epistle expresses profound thought in terms of applied theology. Of interest is Conzelmann's demolition of the popular fable that Corinth was a center of sacred prostitution.[89] He does not believe it possible to identify Paul's opponents precisely, but they represent a single group who can be described as "proto-Gnostics." In the commentary proper Conzelmann divides the text into three main sections with clearly identified subsections. For each pericope the text is presented in translation and followed by comments, verse by verse. Conzelmann also wrote short commentaries on Ephesians and Colossians for the series Das Neue Testament Deutsch (NTD).[90] His concern for the practice of exegesis is demonstrated in his workbook (written with Andreas Lindemann) on exegetical method.[91]

WILLI MARXSEN (1919–1993)

Born in Kiel, Marxsen served in the German armed forces during World War II.[92] After the war he studied theology in Kiel (1945–48), and served as a pastor in Lübeck from 1948 to 1953. Marxsen competed his education at Kiel in 1954 with a qualifying dissertation (*Habilitationsschrift*) on the redaction criticism of Mark. Marxsen taught for a time at the theological school in Bethel, and from 1961 to retirement in 1984 he was professor at the University of Münster.

REDACTION CRITICISM AND INTRODUCTION

Marxsen's dissertation, *Der Evangelist Markus*, set the stage for his future work.[93] In selecting Mark as the text for redaction-critical analysis, Marxsen faced a challenge. Whereas redaction criticism of Matthew and Luke could analyze the editorial work of the authors in relation to their use of Mark and Q, Mark's redaction had to be investigated without extant written sources. Marxsen explains his method: "First we shall go back behind Mark and separate tradition from redaction, then by way of construction, illumine and explain his composition."[94] Marxsen pursues his project in four major studies.

First he analyzes Mark's redaction of the tradition about John the Baptist. Marxsen believes that Mark's statements about John are primarily christological: the author presents John as forerunner; the fate of John anticipates the fate of Jesus. "Mark's achievement lies not only in collecting pieces from his sources and combining them by adding material of his own, but in connecting them from a topical viewpoint."[95]

Marxsen's second study investigates Mark's geographical outline. Mark locates the ministry of Jesus in Galilee, and for the author, according to Marxsen, Galilee has a special significance. In Mark 14:28, Jesus is reported as saying, "But after I am raised up, I will go before you to Galilee." This same motif is repeated by the young man at the empty tomb: "he is going ahead to you to Galilee; there you will see him" (16:7). Marxsen says that "this redactional note cannot deal with an appearance of the Risen Lord awaited in Galilee; in Mark's context this passage can only refer to the expected Parousia."[96] He concludes: "Galilee is not primarily of historical but rather of theological significance as the locale of the imminent Parousia."[97]

Marxsen's third redaction-critical study has to do with the use of the term εὐαγγέλιον (gospel). Mark introduced this term into the Synoptic tradition, and Marxsen thinks Mark's usage presupposes Paul's understanding of the gospel. For Mark, says Marxsen, Jesus is both the subject and the object of the gospel. "The material as a whole becomes a gospel which Christ, the Risen Lord, proclaims *and* which proclaims Christ, the Risen Lord."[98]

The final study investigates Mark 13. Marxsen thinks this chapter is a composition by Mark, using an earlier, apocalyptic source to which he adds material. Mark and his community, according to Marxsen, live in a time of persecution; they believe the *parousia* is near. Marxsen thinks Mark transforms apocalyptic into eschatology; he eliminates the many apocalyptic acts and focuses on one: the end that has already begun. Marxsen concludes: "This, then defines Mark's 'place.' As a thoroughly unique theologian, he occupies a position between Paul and the anonymous tradition on the one hand, and the later evangelists on the other."[99] Mark's intention, according to Marxsen, is to announce that now is the time of the imminent *parousia*.

Marxsen gave an overview of the NT in his *Introduction*,[100] in which he intends to bridge the gap between the science of introduction and the larger field of theology. He orders the material chronologically. In regard to the Pauline epistles Marxsen denies the authenticity of 2 Thessalonians, adopts the north Galatian hypothesis, and views Philippians as a composite of three letters, the second of which was probably written from Ephesus. In the fourth edition Marxsen says that the possibility that 1 Corinthians is a composite of two letters—a view he had dismissed in the earlier editions—has to be taken seriously. He believes 2 Corinthians is a composite of five letters. Romans, according to Marxsen, is directed to Rome, but with an eye to Paul's imminent visit to Jerusalem.

Turning to the Synoptics and Acts, Marxsen embraces the 2DH. He believes the tradition from Papias to be historically worthless. He thinks Mark was written in or near Galilee around 70 CE. The author of Matthew, according to Marxsen, presents Christology: "Jesus is the Teacher of the Church; and he is this because he is the Messiah, the King of Israel, who has proved himself as such by the fulfillment of Old Testament prophecies."[101] Luke, according to Marxsen, has abandoned the idea of the imminent parousia; the author does not perceive the death of Jesus as the means of salvation. Marxsen contends that "Acts cannot have been written by a companion of Paul."[102]

Concerning the pseudo-Pauline letters, Marxsen insists that each document should be understood in its own particular situation. These pseudonymous letters include Colossians, Ephesians, the Pastorals, and 2 Thessalonians. Marxsen thinks Hebrews is a homily written by an unknown author, possibly from Rome. He does not believe any of the Catholic Epistles were written by the authors to whom they are ascribed. In regard to the Johannine literature, Marxsen believes the author of the Fourth Gospel used a passion-resurrection account and a book of signs as a sources. He thinks the

Gospel underwent an ecclesiastical redaction that added the idea of a futuristic eschatology. The author of Revelation adopted the apocalyptic genre; Marxsen thinks he is a Jewish Christian, writing in the time of Domitian. In sum, Marxsen's *Introduction* is somewhat to the left of Kümmel's; it is out of balance, with over one hundred pages dedicated to Paul and only fifty-five to the Synoptics and Acts.

THEOLOGY

As noted about Conzelmann, redaction critics are wedded to theology; Marxsen is no exception. Indeed, the work of Marxsen has even caught the attention of systematic theologians.[103] According to Marxsen, "responsible theology is the handmaid of faith. A handmaid does not perform the work herself—that is the function of her master. But she clears everything out of the way which might hinder her master and holds everything in readiness, as far as possible, so that he can do his work."[104]

Marxsen published a variety of works that deal directly with theology; basic is his essay "Der Exeget als Theologe,"[105] in which he affirms the importance of exegesis for theology and the importance of theology for exegesis. The exegesis of Scripture, he observes, confronts the problem of canon. Marxsen objects to the idea that the exegete is restricted to the canon imposed by the authority of the church. The norm for the earliest tradition was Jesus Christ, says Marxsen, and that norm is expressed in the earliest stratum of tradition.

Marxsen's view of Scripture is developed in his monograph, *Das Neue Testament als Buch der Kirche*.[106] Here again he attacks the idea that the canon is the norm. "The norm of the church, therefore, is not the New Testament but the *apostolic testimony* which is found in the New Testament but is not identical with it."[107] "The norm for the Christian church and its preaching, however, must always remain Jesus."[108] For Marxsen, Jesus as norm is found in the earliest tradition, the one that goes back to Jesus himself. This tradition Marxsen calls the "Jesus kerygma," which preceded the "Christ kerygma" that arose after Easter and makes Christ the object of reflection.[109] The Jesus of the Jesus-kerygma is the person of Jesus, acting and preaching. Marxsen believes this early tradition is continued in the Christian proclamation. "Understood correctly, preaching is not the announcement that there is an eschatological event, but preaching is itself such an event because it is the continuation of the accomplishment of Jesus."[110] "The truth of faith becomes a truth of faith for me as I meet God through Jesus, and am able to describe the event anew in my own words without being bound to any creedal formula of the past."[111]

Crucial for Marxsen's theology is his controversial understanding of the resurrection. His major book on the resurrection of Jesus is based on lectures presented at the University of Münster in 1967–68[112] in response to the furor created by Marxsen's earlier pamphlet on the resurrection.[113] The lectures intend to explicate the meaning of the widely-accepted statement: "Jesus is risen." Marxsen begins with the texts. After noting the various contradictory features of the accounts in Mark, Matthew, Luke, and John, he writes, "The conclusion is inescapable: a synchronizing harmony of the different accounts proves to be impossible."[114] Marxsen proceeds to analyze the pre-Gospel tradition recounted in 1 Cor 15:3-7. This tradition preserves the recognition of the first appearance to Peter, and Marxsen believes the other appearances depend on Peter's witness. Paul claims for himself the same kind of experience, but the proof that he has seen the Lord is the community, "my work in the Lord" (1 Cor 9:1). In 1 Corinthians 15, according to Marxsen, Paul is not proving the resurrection but affirming its result: the faith of the Corinthians. Marxsen asks, "[C]an one deduce the resurrection of Jesus as a *factual event* from the existence of faith? The answer is an unequivocal no. . . . But faith can give certainty about the truth of the preaching of the resurrection."[115] Marxsen believes the resurrection must be seen as a miracle.

> I hope that it is now clear why I said earlier that the miracle belongs to today. For the miracle is the birth of faith. But since it is a miracle, it eludes my description. And that is the reason why I said about the resurrection that it eludes our grasp. For "Jesus is risen" simply means: today the crucified Jesus is calling us to believe.[116]

Thus Marxsen's view rests on his understanding of faith, and the language of faith is not creedal language but experiential language—language that confesses the recognition that Jesus' activity on God's behalf continues after his death.[117]

Willi Marxsen wrote important monographs on Christology.[118] His view is expressed succinctly in his article, "Christology of the New Testament,"[119] in which he presents Christology in terms of the development of the Christian kerygma. He finds the earliest (and most authentic) Christology in the Jesus kerygma—the implicit Christology of those who knew and accepted Jesus as saving event. After Easter, Christology became explicit, according to Marxsen, in the Christ kerygma. He traces the development of the Christ kerygma in Paul, especially in his use of titles. When he confesses Jesus as "Lord," Paul hails Jesus as mediator of the relation to God, and with "Son of God" Paul affirms the special relation of Jesus to God. However, according to Marxsen,

Paul does not speculate on the nature of Christ but speaks functionally about Christ as action of God. The final stage of development is the Jesus Christ kerygma. Here the attention has shifted from function to the one who performs the function; functional Christology is replaced by doctrine. Jesus is expected as the apocalyptic Son of Man; he is understood as Son of God in terms of his supernatural birth. The Jesus Christ kerygma, according to Marxsen, is expressed in the Gospel of John, which stresses preexistence and incarnation as doctrine.

Late in his career Marxsen published a major work on NT ethics.[120] At the outset he contends that ethics is an essential aspect of theology, though one often neglected by NT theologians. Marxsen begins with an investigation of the ethical teachings of Jesus. He believes that the earliest witnesses viewed Jesus as "an inside-out turner"—one in whom God was acting. According to Marxsen, ethics was a feature of the earliest, pre-Easter Christology. "The Christian Christology," says Marxsen, "is that Christology in which eschatological existence is experienced and lived. *Christian ethics* is the actualization of this risky activity."[121] Turning to Paul, Marxsen asserts that his theology was grounded in the Damascus experience, which engendered a new theology and a new ethic. "In the Christian Paul's ethic people must *let themselves be changed*, so they can bear fruit."[122] The Pauline ethic, according to Marxsen, involves the indicative and the imperative—the gift and the task. "Since there are no unambiguous concrete imperatives in Pauline ethics, but Christianity has to be practiced concretely in the flesh, each decision is always a risk."[123] Authentic Christian ethics, according to Marxsen, is an expression of worship. "The criterion of a Christian ethics that is authentically Christian remains: Is the worship *of God* taking place in the concrete secular deed?"[124]

Marxsen turns to post-Pauline development, which he considers to be fallacious. Matthew, according to Marxsen, represents a false development; he stresses the imperative but misses the indicative. He levels the same charge at 2 Thessalonians, the Pastoral Epistles, and the letter of James. These documents are crammed with imperatives, but the authors do not ground their ethics in Christology. By way of contrast, Marxsen believes the author of 1 Peter, who tells the readers who they really are, calls for Christian existence founded on Christology. Similarly, the Gospel of John has only one imperative, the command of love, and that command is grounded in the author's Christology. "Hence the quest for John's ethic," says Marxsen, "proves to be a quest for his Christology. Insofar we can say that ethics and Christology are identical for John."[125] Marxsen concludes with a plea for the restoration of the unity between Christology and ethics. "The sending of the church into the world."

according to Marxsen, "has only one single purpose: to communicate the indicative to humankind again and again. . . . For the indicative is precisely what makes possible an action that can be called authentically 'Christian.'"[126]

In sum, the work of Conzelmann and Marxsen has established redaction criticism as a viable and essential method. Their focus on the final composition of the Gospels is crucial for understanding the literature of the NT and for the reconstruction of the history and theology of the early church. Both scholars have shown, too, how redaction criticism has implications for the study of the historical Jesus. Both have also affirmed, from the perspective of historical critics and exegetes, the importance of NT theology. Conzelmann and Marxsen display considerable agreement regarding critical and theological detail. They both understand eschatology existentially—an influence of Rudolf Bultmann that subsequent research has found to be questionable. Similarly, both Conzelmann and Marxsen echo dialectical theology's Christocentrism and theology of the word. In the same tradition, they affirm a non-objective understanding of faith—faith as risk, not verifiable by historical research. Both scholars affirm the authority of revelation in Christ, but Marxsen's focus on the Jesus kerygma of the earliest tradition as normative is unique. He believes that this norm of the earliest witness of faith in Jesus avoids the false objectifying of later christological doctrine. However, despite his own objections, Marxsen's understanding of this witness depends on the objectivity of historical research and reconstruction.

THE SYNOPTIC PROBLEM: CHALLENGES TO THE CONSENSUS

Once hailed as the "assured results" of nineteenth-century criticism, the dominant Two-Document hypothesis (2DH) for solving the Synoptic Problem has come under attack in the twentieth. The attack has been launched primarily by two movements: the revival of the Griesbach hypothesis by William R. Farmer and his associates, and the proposal to dispense with Q articulated by Michael Goulder.

THE REVIVAL OF THE GRIESBACH HYPOTHESIS: WILLIAM R. FARMER (1921–2000)

William R. Farmer was born in Needles, California.[127] He studied at Occidental College and Cambridge, and earned his ThD at Union Theological Seminary, New York (1952) under John Knox.[128] Farmer taught at Emory, DePauw, and Drew universities. In 1959 he joined the faculty of Perkins School of Theology at Southern Methodist University, where he remained until retirement in 1991. Farmer was devoted to ecumenicity. In 1990 he joined a Roman Catholic church in Dallas, hoping to retain his status as an ordained minister of the United Methodist Church. However, the Judicial Council of the UMC ruled that by joining the Catholic Church, Farmer had in effect withdrawn membership from the Methodist Church and surrendered his ministerial orders.[129]

While teaching at Drew, Farmer offered a graduate seminar on the Synoptic Problem. In the course of conducting the seminar he came to the conviction that the 2DH should be abandoned. In its place he promoted a revival of the Griesbach hypothesis, soon renamed the "Two-Gospel Hypothesis" (2GH). Farmer's major work on the Synoptic Problem was published in 1964.[130] He begins with a history of the research on the problem. In the eighteenth century Griesbach's hypothesis—the view that Mark used Matthew and Luke—was dominant. A variety of views appeared in the nineteenth century; especially influential was Karl Lachmann's belief that Mark best preserved the order of a primitive gospel, and C. H. Weisse's view that Matthew and Luke used two sources: Mark and the *logia* of Matthew.[131] The Griesbach hypothesis was adopted by F. C. Baur and the Tübingen school, but support for the 2DH gained momentum with the endorsement of H. J. Holtzmann.[132] Farmer devotes considerable space to the triumph of the 2DH in England, especially in the work of B. H. Streeter.[133] Farmer concludes that the 2DH "exhibited features which commended itself to men who were disposed to place their trust in the capacity of science to foster the development of human progress."[134]

In chapter 6, Farmer presents his own understanding of the Synoptic Problem. "It is historically probable that Mark was written after Matthew and Luke and was dependent upon both."[135] Farmer proceeds to support this conclusion in sixteen steps or theses. Among the most important are the following: (1) "The similarity between Matthew, Mark, and Luke is such as to justify the assertion that they stand in some kind of literary relationship to one another." (6) "The phenomena of agreement and disagreement in the respective order and content of material in each of the Synoptic Gospels constitute a category of literary phenomena which is more readily explicable on a hypothesis which places Mark third with Matthew and Luke before him than on any alternative hypothesis." (7) "The Minor Agreements of Matthew and Luke against Mark constitute a second category of literary phenomena which is more readily explicable on a hypothesis where Mark is regarded as third with Matthew and Luke before him than on any alternative hypothesis." (9) "It possible to understand the redactional process through which Mark went, on the hypothesis that he composed his Gospel based primarily on Matthew and

Luke." (16) "A historico-critical analysis of the Synoptic tradition, utilizing both literary-historical and form-critical canons of criticism, supports a hypothesis which recognizes that Matthew is in many respects secondary to the life situation of Jesus, and the primitive Palestinian Christian community, but that this Gospel was nonetheless copied by Luke, and that Mark was secondary to both Matthew and Luke, and frequently combined their respective texts."[136] In the ensuing debate, two of these theses—(7) on the minor agreements and (9) on the redactional process—received major attention.

In the next chapter Farmer addresses the redactional process. He proceeds though Mark, assembling data he believes will prove that Mark is editing material from Matthew and Luke. For example, in the account of the cleansing of the temple Farmer believes that Mark's insertion of the cursing of the fig tree (Mark 11:12-14) is redactional; Matthew and Luke agree against Mark that the cleansing of the temple took place on the same day as the entry to Jerusalem. In regard to the apocalyptic discourse, Farmer argues that Mark 13 is dependent on Matthew 24; the Matthean account reflects Palestinian Jewish motifs, for instance, reference to the Sabbath, while Mark (13:9, 23) adds the admonition to watch (βλέπετε), a typical Markan motif. Farmer concludes that the writer of Mark intended to present a new Gospel, based on harmonizing Matthew and Luke in the service of unity. "Mark could have been viewed as a remarkably successful form of the Gospel, by practical-minded church authorities who were more concerned with finding the common ground on which all Christians could stand together than in defending or perpetuating the special interest of any particular group, including their own."[137]

Another example of Farmer's argument from redaction is his *The Last Twelve Verses of Mark*.[138] In this monograph Farmer contends that 16:9-20 (the so-called "longer ending" of Mark) is the original ending. He begins with the external evidence, where he finds twenty patristic sources that indicate knowledge of this ending. "In fact, external evidence from the second century for Mk. 16:9-20 is stronger than for most other parts of that Gospel."[139] In regard to the textual evidence, Farmer notes that the Alexandrian text omits this ending but the Western text includes it—evidence of early support for inclusion. Farmer turns to internal evidence, proceeding through the section verse by verse, finding evidence for what he believes to be the use of Markan terms and expressions. Farmer concludes: "Mk. 16:9-20 represents redactional use of older material by the evangelist and belonged to the autograph."[140] Very few Markan scholars have been convinced.

One of the basic complaints of the advocates of the 2GH is that the standard synopses, for example, Aland's *Synopsis Quattor Evangeliorum*, are arranged on the presumption of the 2DH. An attempt to answer this complaint is made by J. B. Orchard, who edited synopses in both Greek and English.[141] Orchard orders the parallel columns according to the Griesbach hypothesis: Matthew—Luke—Mark—John. In time, however, the devotees of the 2GH found Orchard's synopsis inadequate.[142] Farmer made an important contribution to this issue with the publication of his *Synopticon*.[143] This book presents the complete text of each of the Gospels in canonical order, with indication of the verbatim and significant agreements by color code. The result is a highly useful tool for study of the Synoptic problem, regardless of the various hypotheses.

Farmer's book *The Gospel of Jesus* has a polemic purpose: to attack the results of the 2DH that have created what Farmer views as a distorted portrait of Jesus.[144] The main villains in the plot are the members of the Koester-Robinson school who accept the priority of Mark and view Q as the most important source for understanding Jesus. Farmer also believes the adoption of the 2DH had drastic political consequences in Germany.

> A "critically correct" civil religion, pushed by university-trained German-Christian theologians like Emanuel Hirsch, gloried in the idea of Markan priority with its understanding of Christian theology based on the Two-Source Hypothesis, while Christians who witnessed unto blood and resisted unto death the Nazi horrors that led to the Holocaust drew spiritual support from a reading of the Gospels that called them to be saints and martyrs of the church (an understanding of Christ called for by any hypothesis that recognized the primary character of the Matthean text).[145]

Farmer had apparently forgotten that many scholars who accepted the 2DH, for instance, the members of the Bultmann school, were identified with the anti-Hitler Confessing Church.

Farmer proceeds to explicate and defend the 2GH. He notes that the priority of Matthew was supported by Augustine and the 2GH was defended in the eighteenth century by Henry Owen. Farmer presents major arguments in support. In regard to order, he says that Mark usually follows the order of Matthew and Luke; when they disagree, Mark follows sometimes one, sometimes the other.[146] Minor agreements between Matthew and Luke against Mark contradict the theory that they are independently using Mark as a source. According to Farmer's reconstruction Mark, probably writing from Rome, unites Matthew and Luke, combining the apostolic tradition of Matthew with the Greek-oriented message of Luke. Farmer presents evidence from the texts that he believes supports the 2GH. For example, he thinks the agreement between Matthew and Luke is so exact in some texts (for example, the account of the healing of the centurion's slave [Matt 8:5-13; Luke 7:1-10]) that it cannot be adequately explained by their independent use of hypothetical Q.

Farmer takes up the question of what difference the adoption of the 2DH makes for worship, theology, and ethics. For instance, he notes that the phrase "for the forgiveness of sins" (Matt 26:28), lacking in Mark, is depreciated as a later addition, thereby casting doubt on "the universal faith and practice of Christians in their worship at the table of the Lord."[147] But if the results were so detrimental, how did the theory of Markan priority arise and flourish? Farmer replies that it rests on mistaken assumptions like the notion that the earliest Gospel is shortest but, much more ominous, the triumph of the 2DH was facilitated, he thinks, by social and political forces. In the *Kulturkampf* of the 1870s—the struggle between Bismarck and Pius IX—the primacy of Peter was a critical feature of the debate. "Markan primacy offered support for discounting the claims for a papal authority, which rested on the Peter passage in Matthew that was absent in Mark."[148] And what is to explain the current fascination with Q? Farmer blames it on the "Claremont-Harvard Connection" in which "Professors Robinson and Koester have worked together in using the idea of Q to achieve their stated purpose of dismantling the categories of New Testament scholarship to reshape our understanding of Christian origins."[149] Farmer quotes Robinson: "The saving significance of Jesus, according to Q, does not consist in Jesus having died for our sins."[150] Farmer concludes, sarcastically, that the 2DH has been useful in supporting mistaken beliefs. He adds, however, "It should be pointed out that many scholars adhere to the Two-Source Hypothesis who have no sympathy with any of the pragmatic benefits listed here."[151] He might also have added that a large number of scholars in Britain and America who supported the 2DH were in no way captive to the German policies of the 1870s or the 1930s.

In an earlier book, *Jesus and the Gospel*, Farmer traces the lines of development of the tradition from Jesus to Eusebius and Constantine.[152] In the course of his discussion of Matthew he fires another broadside at the 2DH.

It is the human capacity for credulity that helps explain why, in spite of the fact that no hypothesis has been more thoroughly falsified over a period of many years in learned books, in articles in scholarly journals, and in scientific monographs published by university presses, the two-document hypothesis continues as the generally accepted solution to the synoptic problem. In any case, this hypothesis appears to be incapable of being falsified because of its infinite capacity for modification.[153]

In the first part of this work Farmer discusses the origin and development of the gospel tradition. He emphasizes the continuity between Jesus and Paul. In discussing the move from the gospel tradition to gospel genre he presents his understanding of the chronology of the Gospels: Matthew in the early 70s, Luke-Acts in the later 70s, Mark in the early 80s, and John in the late 80s. In a final section he discusses the development of the canon.[154] He notes the importance of persecution in the formation of the canon and emphasizes the intriguing concept of the "martyr's canon." Thus Farmer says that "the New Testament books which are not in dispute in the church after Irenaeus are almost without exception books which had special meaning for certain known churches that had experienced persecution."[155]

Other scholars, including students and associates of Farmer, have made significant contributions to the discussion of the Synoptic Problem. One of the most important is David L. Dungan, who studied at Harvard (ThD 1967) and spent most of his career as professor at the University of Tennessee. In his article, "The Two-Gospel Hypothesis," written for the *Anchor Bible Dictionary*, Dungan presents a concise account of the history and character of the revival of Griesbach hypothesis.[156] As to methodological presuppositions, Dungan articulates a basic conviction of the advocates of the 2GH: "A source hypothesis which limits the number of hypothetical sources needed to explain the perceived literary phenomena (cf. "Occam's Razor") is preferable to one which invents numerous imaginary 'lost sources,' multiple 'lost earlier versions' of the Gospels, hypothetical 'lost recensions' of Q, etc., to explain the literary data."[157] In support of the 2GH, Dungan emphasizes the argument from order that Farmer had articulated. In regard to the external evidence, Dungan believes the 2GH preserves the continuity in the development of early Christian tradition: Matthew represents the teaching of the apostles; Luke revised Matthew along more universal lines; Mark combined Matthew (the tradition of Peter) and Luke (the tradition of Paul). As to theological consequences, Dungan notes the difference between the Two-Document and the Two-Gospel Hypotheses: the former assumes the Enlightenment notion of a gulf between Jesus and Paul; the latter affirms a continuity from 2 Isaiah through Jesus to Paul and the early church to the great church. Dungan also provides an excellent bibliography on the Synoptic Problem.[158]

Dungan's major contribution is his lengthy book (over 500 pages) on the history of the Synoptic Problem.[159] Dungan's work has some distinctive features: he deals with the entire history (beginning in the first century); he considers all four components of the problem (composition, canon, text, and hermeneutics); he investigates the cultural, political, economic, and technical presuppositions. The book is ordered in three parts. The first deals with the period from the first to the fifth centuries, that is, the patristic evidence, including the data from Papias, Justin Martyr, Marcion, Origen, Eusebius, and Augustine. The second part focuses on the emergence of the modern historical-critical method. Here Dungan surveys the view of the Reformers, the problems of text and canon, and the discussion of the Synoptic Problem (with attention to Griesbach and Holtzmann). In regard to "extra-scientific factors," Dungan charges that the 2DH was promoted by menacing social and cultural forces such as an anti-Judaism prevalent in German universities in the late nineteenth and early twentieth centuries. "With the Two Source Hypothesis in hand, that is, a historical scenario that locates the beginning of the Christian faith in the un-Jewish, pro-Pauline Gospel of Mark, accompanied by a theoretical Sayings Source having a conveniently non-Jewish message, German biblical scholars could *decanonize* the very Jewish Gospel of Matthew *and split* the New Testament from the Old in biblical theology."[160]

The third part of Dungan's book reviews trends in the postmodern period—the Synoptic Problem in late-twentieth-century research. In this part he begins with the conviction that his account of the previous history has devastated the claim that historical critical method is neutral; instead, he has disclosed "its belligerent ideological mission."[161] Dungan believes that the historical critical method helped to prepare the way for National Socialism in Germany. The method also, according to Dungan, has damaging effects on the understanding of the canon, text, composition, and interpretation of the Gospels.

Support for the 2GH has been promoted by the International Institute for the Renewal of Gospel Studies. Since the 1970s the Institute has been instrumental in sponsoring research, conferences, and publications. The "research team," sponsored and supported by the Institute, has produced significant publications. For example, a volume addresses the issue of Luke's use of Matthew.[162] In the introduction the authors, members of the research team, investigate the origin of what they view as the mistaken belief that Luke had no knowledge of Matthew. The balance of the book proceeds through the text of Luke, presenting arguments in support of the thesis that Luke used Matthew. Another book by the research team deals with the question of Mark's use of

Matthew and Luke.[163] In the introduction the authors note problems with the 2DH and describe alternative proposals. The balance of the book proceeds through the text of Mark, collecting data in support of the theory that Mark uses Matthew and Luke. In their introduction the authors cite the work of E. P. Sanders and Margaret Davies, which lists four hypotheses that provide possible solutions to the Synoptic Problem: the Two Source Hypothesis, the Griesbach Hypothesis, Michael Goulder's rejection of Q, and the multiple-source theory of Marie-Émile Boismard.[164] The supporters of the 2GH are grateful for the independent judgment that their solution is possible (which seems modest, compared with the claims of Farmer and Dungan), and they also rejoice that Sanders and Davies believe Luke knew Matthew.

DISPENSING WITH Q: MICHAEL GOULDER

EARLIER WORK

The movement to dispense with Q was inspired by Austin Farrer. Under Farrer's leadership a series of "Q Parties" was held at Oxford beginning in 1954.[165] The parties took place three times each term and were attended by some two dozen Oxford biblical scholars. The members soon divided along party lines: supporters of the 2DH and opponents of the existence of Q. During the debate both sides scored points, but no clear winner was acclaimed. The major document emerging from the parties was Farrer's "On Dispensing with Q."[166] Farrer's basic argument: "The Q hypothesis is not, of itself, a probable hypothesis. It is simply the sole alternative to the supposition that St. Luke had read St. Matthew (or *vice versa*). It needs no refutation except the demonstration that its alternative is possible. It hangs on a single thread; cut that, and it falls by its own weight."[167]

Farrer argues that there is no evidence that early Christians composed a document that was anything like Q. He also contends that arguments against Luke's use of Mark are unconvincing. He concludes:

> St. Matthew will be seen to be an amplified version of St. Mark, based on a decade of habitual preaching, and incorporating oral material, but presupposing no other literary source beside St. Mark himself. St. Luke, in turn, will be found to presuppose St. Matthew and St. Mark, and St. John to presuppose the other three.[168]

MICHAEL GOULDER (1927–2010)

Goulder studied at Eaton and Trinity College, Cambridge.[169] While in Hong Kong on business he was ordained deacon and priest of the Anglican Church. Goulder returned to England and studied at Trinity College, Oxford, where he fell under the spell of Farrer, "my tutor and mentor."[170] Back again in Hong Kong (1962), Goulder served for a time as principal of a small Anglican college. In 1991 he was appointed professor of biblical studies at Birmingham University. Prior to this he had resigned his clerical orders and declared himself an atheist.

Goulder's first major work on the Synoptic Problem was his *Midrash and Lection in Matthew*.[171] The basic thesis is that Matthew was a Christian scribe who used only Mark as a source. The first part of the book deals with the material in Matthew. Goulder describes his approach:

> I shall take it for granted that Matthew had Mark in front of him, and shall ask at each point whether we can provide an adequate account of any new material on the hypothesis that Matthew had very little non-Marcan tradition, written or oral. Or, to put it in other words, I shall consider the grounds for thinking that Matthew was writing a midrashic expansion of Mark: that the new teaching is his teaching, that the new poetry is his poetry, that the new parables are his parables.[172]

Goulder believes that "Matthew's greatest theological achievement is his reconciliation of the radical position of Mark with the continued validity of the full Torah."[173] Matthew, according to Goulder, adopted the midrashic method that probed meaning and reconciled older with newer expressions; Matthew writes a midrashic expansion of Mark especially in the area of teachings. He writes poetry and uses distinctive imagery; he is, according to Goulder, a Greek-speaking Jew with a Semitic mind. "Matthew is not merely a scribe, but a Christian scribe; and the rabbi to whom he owes far and away the most is Paul."[174]

Goulder summarizes his view of the composition of Matthew:

> The theory that I wish to propose is a lectionary theory: that is, that the Gospel was developed liturgically, and that it was intended to be used liturgically; and that its order is liturgically significant, in that it follows the lections of the Jewish Year. Matthew, I believe, wrote his Gospel to be read in church round the year; he took the Jewish Festal

Year, and the pattern of lections prescribed therefore, as his base. . . .
A Gospel is not a literary *genre* at all, the study of Matthew reveals: it
is a liturgical *genre*. A Gospel is a lectionary book, a series of 'Gospels'
used in worship week by week in *lectio continua*.[175]

In the second part of the book Goulder proceeds through Matthew, noting
how sections of the Gospel relate to the Jewish festivals. For example, Goulder
believes the Sermon on the Mount was composed to be read during Pentecost;
Matthew 24–26 is to be read during Passover. Goulder concludes:

> I have accepted the common conclusion that Matthew was
> overwriting Mark. I have found no considerable passage in the
> Gospel which seemed to require a written or an oral source, and
> I have suggested reasons for thinking it to be unlikely that there
> were many non-Marcan traditions in Matthew's ambit in the 70s. .
> . . The more closely a passage corresponds to the liturgical structure
> of the Gospel and the Matthaean manner, in so far as they can be
> established, the more heavily does the burden of proof rest upon
> those who claim underlying non-Marcan traditions.[176]

Goulder develops his lectionary theory in a later book, *The Evangelists'
Calendar*.[177] In this work he contends that all the Synoptic Gospels were written
to be read in church. As the first-century synagogue followed a cycle of
readings from the law, so the early church, according to Goulder, followed a
cycle of reading from the Gospels. Goulder explicates his theory in relation to
Luke, Matthew, and Mark, and concludes:

> I have now, I hope, given sufficient reasons for believing two theses
> to be plausible: first, that Luke wrote his Gospel as a cycle of liturgical
> gospels, to be used round the year in fulfilment of the Old Testament
> lections; and second, that in the first century the Torah cycle in use
> in the Western Diaspora of Judaism and Christianity was an annual
> cycle beginning on the first sabbath in Nisan.[178]

Although Goulder's lectionary theory has been rejected by most scholars, he
reaffirmed it at a symposium on his NT scholarship held at Johns Hopkins
University in 2000. In his contribution, Goulder says, "This brings us to my
hypothesis: Matthew wrote the Gospel to be read out in church in short units
of some sixteen verses each Saturday night; the whole was designed to give

readings for a complete year, beginning after Easter and ending at the next Easter."[179]

Goulder published a major two-volume work on Luke.[180] The first section is devoted to the argument against the 2DH, which Goulder characterizes as "the house built on sand." Goulder notes that the 2DH assumes the existence of several bodies of lost tradition. He also argues that the minor agreements between Matthew and Luke against Mark support the idea that Luke used Matthew.[181] Goulder believes the only feature of the 2DH that is valid is the recognition of the priority of Mark. According to Goulder's reconstruction Mark wrote around 70, and some of his tradition goes back to the life of Jesus; Matthew wrote around 80—an expansion of Mark written for Jewish Christians. Luke, written around 90 for a Gentile church, combined Mark and Matthew; John, writing around 100, used all three of the Synoptics. The distinctive feature of this reconstruction is Goulder's belief that material usually identified as Q and the theoretical special Matthean material (M) are actually the composition of Matthew. Similarly, Goulder believes the so-called special material of Luke (L) was composed by Luke.

Goulder proceeds to discuss Q. He writes, "The most damage has been caused by . . . the Q hypothesis, which has been the grandfather of all synoptic errors."[182] Goulder recounts the history of the Q hypothesis from Credner to Holtzmann; he believes the hypothesis was based on a misunderstanding of the report attributed to Papias about the *logia* of Matthew. Goulder also challenges current arguments in support of Q, for instance, the theory that Luke would not have omitted material found in Matthew. Goulder also argues that the *Gospel of Thomas* does not represent the genre of a document like Q. In regard to recent efforts to discern a distinctive theology in Q, Goulder insists that the so-called Q material displays the same theology as Matthew.

Goulder turns to the special material of Luke. At the outset he writes, "I do not wish to suggest that Luke had *no* tradition other than that in Mark and Matthew; but I do suggest that if this alternative line is pursued, it will often yield a highly plausible account of the L matter."[183] In pursuit of the alternative, Goulder investigates the style of Luke. This section of his work is thoroughly analyzed by Mark Goodacre.[184] Goodacre believes Goulder argues that the so-called L material reflects the distinctive and characteristic style of Luke, supporting Goulder's case for identifying the special material of Luke as the creation of Luke. As to the relation of Luke to Paul, Goulder believes Luke was a traveling companion of the apostle. The balance of volume 1 and all of volume 2 presents Goulder's commentary on Luke. Throughout the commentary he develops an exegesis that supports the theory that Luke was using two sources: Mark and Matthew. In regard to the account of the Emmaus pilgrims, for example, Goulder believes Luke developed the story in relation to Mark: the young man at the tomb says Jesus "is going ahead of you to Galilee" (16:7); Goulder thinks Luke created the story to depict disciples seeing Jesus on the way to Galilee.

Critics have reacted to Goulder's work. Many, including Goodacre, have questioned his lectionary hypothesis.[185] They argue that lectionaries are not the work of individual authors; rather, they evolve over time in communities. Also, the existence of early Christian lectionaries is not confirmed by evidence regarding the worship of the early church. As to Goulder's basic solution to the Synoptic Problem, the advocates of the 2DH, of course, do not agree. For instance, John S. Kloppenborg Verbin insists that Goulder has not demolished the 2DH; the problem of the minor agreements can be explained, and not all of Goulder's examples of Lukan style are convincing.[186] However, Kloppenborg does recognize Goulder as the most important scholar, next to Farmer, for keeping the Synoptic Problem alive as an important issue in NT research. Goulder's program was taken up and expanded by a gifted British scholar, Mark Goodacre, who migrated to the faculty of Duke University in 2005.[187]

Some attention should be given to a lesser-known proposal for the solution of the Synoptic Problem—the work of Marie-Émile Boismard and his French colleagues, sometimes designated the "Multiple Source Hypothesis."[188] Boismard, who has no use for Occam's razor, writes, "The synoptic problem is complex; it can be solved only by a complex solution."[189] In essence, Boismard proposes several lost sources and a complex theory of redaction. He presented his understanding of the sources of Mark in a monograph published in 1994.[190] However, the overview of his proposal is most clearly seen in the introduction to the second volume of his synopsis (written with Pierre Benoit).[191] Boismard detects three levels of tradition: primitive sources, intermediary redactions, and final redactions. In regard to the primitive sources, Boismard posits four early documents: A (a Jewish-Christian document of Palestinian origin); B (a revision of A, designed for use by Gentile Christians); C (an independent ancient source, probably originating in Palestine); and Q (similar to the Q of the 2DH, but possibly not a single document). In regard to the intermediary redactions, Boismard detects three: Matthew-Intermediary (which uses A and Q); Mark-Intermediary (which used A, B, and C); and Proto-Luke (which uses B, C, and Q). As to the final redactions, Boismard believes Matthew used Matthew-Intermediary and Mark-Intermediary; Mark used Matthew Intermediary, Mark-Intermediary, and Q; Luke used Mark-Intermediary and Proto-Luke; John used B and C, and the final redaction of John used John and the final redaction of Matthew. Boismard appears uncharacteristically simple in his conclusion that the final redactor of Matthew and the final redactor of Mark are one and the same, and similarly, the redactor of Proto-Luke and the final redactor of Luke were probably the same individual.

Despite the vigor of the advocates of alternative hypotheses, the 2DH has survived and prevailed. In 2008 a Conference on the Synoptic Problem was convened at Oxford, commemorating the Oxford seminar of a century earlier. The results of the recent Conference were published in 2011, one hundred years after the publication of *Studies in the Synoptic Problem*.[192] The 2008 Oxford Conference, attended by a large number of scholars from Europe and North America, published essays representing virtually all the major hypotheses. In an overview, Christopher M. Tuckett says that "the most widely held theory probably remains some form of the 2HD."[193] Tuckett concludes that though the general results do not differ widely from the those of the earlier Oxford seminar, the recent challenges to the majority have sharpened the issues and exposed the provisional nature of all hypotheses. The 2DH may be the most plausible, but it is not the only possible, and indeed, not the final solution to the Synoptic Problem.

Two scholars whose work in support of the 2DH is exemplary deserve recognition. Christopher Tuckett has been mentioned.[194] Born and educated in England (Cambridge), Tuckett taught at Manchester, where he held the Rylands Chair of Biblical Criticism and Exegesis before moving to Oxford in 1996. Tuckett's PhD thesis (Lancaster) was on *The Revival of the Griesbach Hypothesis*.[195] For the Synoptic Problem his most important book is *Q and the History of Early Christianity*.[196] Frans Neirynck, the dean of Synoptic research, was born in Wingene, Belgium and educated at the Catholic University of Leuven.[197] From 1960 to 1992 he served on the theological faculty at Leuven. He was elected president of the SNTS in 1989. Neirynck's major works on the Synoptic Problem include *The Minor Agreements of Matthew and Luke against Mark*,[198] *Duality in Mark*,[199] and *Evangelica*—three large volumes of collected essays.[200]

In regard to the major issues, the 2DH rests on two premises: the priority of Mark and the existence of and independent use of Q by Matthew and Luke.[201] Mark contains some 660 verses, over 80% of which are reproduced in Matthew, some 60% in Luke. Mark is shorter than either of the other Synoptics. Although some have claimed that Mark intentionally shortened or epitomized Matthew and Luke, in many pericopes Mark is actually longer. Why, ask the advocates of priority of Mark, would Mark omit the birth narratives or the Lord's Prayer? It is more likely that Matthew and Luke expanded Mark. As regards language and style, Mark writes an unliterary Greek in infelicitous style with unrefined vocabulary and many redundancies. Matthew and Luke, working independently, tend to improve Mark's language and style. Mark confronts the reader with "harder" readings that call for mollification; for example, in Nazareth, according to Mark 6:5-5, Jesus could do "no" mighty deeds, but in Matthew's revision (13:58) Jesus did not do "many" mighty deeds there. In regard to theology, Mark (like Paul) uses the title "Lord" almost exclusively for the exalted Christ, but with Matthew and Luke this title is frequently applied to the historical Jesus, as is typical in later usage.

As to the existence and use of Q, the advocates of the 2DH observe that some 230 verses of Matthew and Luke are parallel in non-Markan passages.[202] Against the view that these parallels are to be explained by independent use of a hypothetical document, the advocates of the Farrer-Goulder Hypothesis (reviewed above) point to the problem of the "minor agreements" of Matthew and Luke against Mark. The defenders of the 2DH offer several explanations: independent redaction of Mark by Matthew and Luke, the influence of oral tradition, the belief that Matthew and Luke used different editions of Mark (Ur-Markus or Deutero-Marcus).[203] In any case it is obvious that Matthew and Luke did not use the 27th edition of the Nestle-Aland *Novum Testamentum Graece.*

Those who would dispense with Q must answer why Luke omitted material like the flight into Egypt, and above all they must explain why (and how) Luke so drastically rearranged the teaching material from the discourses of Matthew. In support of Q and its use, the advocates of the 2DH observe that after the narrative of the Temptation, Matthew and Luke never agree in placing Q material in the same Markan context—evidence of independent use of the same document. Also in support of Q, sometimes the common material appears in the earlier or more original form in Matthew, sometimes in Luke. The genre of a gospel that is largely a collection of teachings has been confirmed by the discovery of the *Gospel of Thomas.*[204]

Research on Q

The polarization of NT research is apparent in the research on the hypothetical Q. While scholars like Farmer, Goulder, and Goodacre argue vigorously that Q never existed, another coterie of scholars claims not only to have reconstructed Q but to have detected stages of Q redaction, and have attempted to described the nature and theology of the community that produced Q.

INTRODUCTION AND TEXTS

Q, according to its defenders, includes all the material of the "double tradition," that is, the non-Markan material common to Matthew and Luke.[205] In citing Q, scholars refer to chapter and verse according to Luke, who is understood to reproduce Q more faithfully that Matthew. Q, according to most experts, begins at Luke 3:7-9 and ends at Luke 22:28-30. It contains material from Luke chapters 4, 6, 7, 8–19, although the exact verses are not entirely certain. Q mainly contains teaching material, although it also includes narrative: the preaching of John the Baptist, the temptation, the healing of the centurion's servant; it does not contain the passion narrative. Most scholars agree that Q was written in Greek and that it represents a single source. The provenance is usually said to be Palestine, or Galilee, or the Galilee-Syrian border region. Q is usually identified as a document of Jewish Christianity, dated (in its final form) slightly before or after 70.

The text of Q is available in various editions. For the study of Q, John Kloppenborg's *Q Parallels* is useful, especially for the English reader.[206] The book consists of the text of Q according to the Matthew/Luke parallels in Greek, with English translation. Agreements between Matthew and Luke are indicated by underlining. This synopsis also presents parallels from other sources including Mark, the Septuagint, the Apostolic Fathers, the *Gospel of Thomas* (in Coptic), and other NT documents. It also includes critical notes, a concordance of Greek words, and bibliography. The *Critical Edition* of Q is a huge volume that assembles comprehensive research on the Q document. The introduction, by James M. Robinson, presents an extensive account of the history of Q research, which extends from the *logia* of Papias to the recent work of Kloppenborg. The Greek text is presented in eight columns, across facing pages: (1) any Markan parallel to Matthew, (2) any Matthean doublet, (3) Matthean text derived from Q, (4) the critical text of Q, (5) Lukan text derived from Q, (6) any Lukan doublet, (7) any Markan parallel to Luke; (8) any parallel from the *Gospel of Thomas* (in Coptic). Below the columns a critical apparatus indicates variant readings suggested by the major editors; below the critical apparatus are critical notes; below the critical notes are text-critical notes; below the text-critical notes is the text of Q in Greek and in English, German, and French translation; and below the text of Q are parallels from the *Gospel of Thomas*. The presentation of the critical text is over 550 pages. A concordance, which is essentially the same as Kloppenborg's in *Q Parallels*, is included.

An abbreviated and simplified version of the critical text[207] presents the text of the *Critical Edition* on the left and the English translation on the right facing page. Also included is Robinson's introduction to the *Critical Edition* and that edition's history. The project was begun at the Institute for Antiquity and Christianity at Claremont in 1983. Q consultations were held at the annual meetings of the SBL in 1983 and 1984. These consultations developed into the Q Seminar of the SBL (1985–89), which became the International Q Project in 1989. A German branch of the Project was established at the University of Bamberg in 1992. The International Project also began a series of studies of individual texts of Q, beginning in 1994, published by Peeters: *Documenta Q: Reconstructions of Q Through Two Centuries of Gospel Research Excerpted, Sorted, and Evaluated.*

WORK OF JOHN S. KLOPPENBORG

Research on Q has been extensive.[208] The work of John Kloppenborg, a recognized leader in Q research, provides a notable example.[209] Kloppenborg was educated at St. Michael's College, University of Toronto (PhD 1984), where he later has served as Professor in the Department and Centre for the Study of Religion.

Kloppenborg published two major works on Q. The purpose of the earlier book, *The Formation of Q*, is "to trace the literary evolution of Q as a document of primitive Christianity and then to view that development within the context of antique literary genres."[210] At the outset Kloppenborg summarizes the character of Q: it is a document written in Greek; a substantial portion of it is included in Matthew and Luke; the order is better preserved in Luke. Q, according to Kloppenborg, is not a random collection. Instead, he believes the material has been organized into topical clusters. Kloppenborg detects clusters of material around two themes: the announcement of judgment and the teaching of wisdom. He thinks that the latter, sapiential sayings belong to the earliest stratum of Q, to which the judgment oracles were later added. Kloppenborg also thinks the narrative material has been added. He concludes that the genre of the original Q is "instruction," and with the addition of narrative it is evolving into proto-biography.

Kloppenborg's larger work, *Excavating Q*, reflects an archaeological imagery.[211] In this book he is concerned about two issues: how to talk about Q, and why Q matters. The first part of the book deals with the text of Q and the history of Q research. The reconstruction of the text assumes the validity of the 2DH for the solution of the Synoptic Problem. In an irenic spirit Kloppenborg reviews other views, including the Griesbach Hypothesis and the Farrer-Goulder Hypothesis. He believes the case for the 2DH is strongest, but insists that "*[h]ypotheses are all that we have and all we will ever have.*"[212] As to the character and reconstruction of Q, Kloppenborg reaffirms the conclusion of his earlier book. He observes that Q contains sixty-eight pericopes. In regard to methodology, Kloppenborg notes that analysis of Q uses the methods of redaction criticism such as detecting repetitive elements and recurring motifs. Working backward from the final form of Q, Kloppenborg discovers three stages in its development: an early stage of hortatory instruction, a stage adding oracles of judgment, and a final stage that added material about the law.

Kloppenborg turns to the Q community and the theology of Q. He believes the people of the formative stage (Q^1) were village or town scribes who were concerned with instruction; the people of the main redaction (Q^2) were people who lived in towns with markets and who emphasize judgment; the people of Q^3 were concerned with the law and the temple. In regard to the original scribes (Q^1), Kloppenborg writes:

> [T]he Sayings Gospel and the scribes who framed it proposed a model of local cooperation based on strategies of tension reduction, debt release, and forgiveness, and appealing to an image of God as generous patron and parent who could be depended upon for sustenance. These scribes also resisted any efforts to impose a southern, hierocratically-defined vision of Israel in which human affairs are centered on a central sanctuary and its priestly officers. This is not opposition to the Temple; but it is also not an endorsement of the hierocratic worldview of either the priestly aristocracy or the Pharisees, both of whom come in for serious criticism. Q is thus engaged in a struggle on two fronts: in support of town and village culture against the encroachments of the cities, and in support of local forms of Israelite religion in the face of pressures from the hierocratic worldview of Judaea.[213]

In discussing the theology of Q, Kloppenborg notes the ideological and theological features of Q research. F. C. Baur, for example, adopted the Griesbach theory, which supported his reconstruction of early Christian history, and Holtzmann believed the priority of Mark advanced his liberal view of Jesus. More recently, notes Kloppenborg, studies in Q (and the *Gospel of Thomas*) have provided the basis for Robinson's identification of an early genre, "the sayings of the sages," and encouraged the identification of Jesus as a sage. Kloppenborg believes that "Q's silence concerning a salvific interpretation of

Jesus' fate makes it difficult or impossible to conclude that the historical Jesus considered his own death vicarious," and that "Q displays no signs of applying *resurrection* language to Jesus."[214] The theological center of Q, according to Kloppenborg, is not Christology but the understanding of the kingdom. Also, since the earliest stratum of Q is sapiential, Kloppenborg believes that apocalyptic does not belong to the earliest Jesus tradition. Since the earliest tradition is sapiential, he thinks it possible that Jesus and his earliest followers were Cynics.

All in all, Kloppenborg has constructed a masterful work, built on a mountain of research in the primary and secondary sources. He writes clearly and attends to detail. He argues his case in an irenic spirit. However, in regard to his theological reconstruction critics may wish he had more faithfully followed his own methodological principle: "It is a fundamental error . . . to allow considerations of nonliterary utility or advantage to influence the solutions to a literary problem."[215] Those who have not been initiated into the mysteries of Q may be wary of what appears to be overinterpretation. A lost document that is hypothesized on the basis two independent uses of it, about which there is debate as to its exact content and scope, and is then subjected to an analysis that can predicate three stages of development related to three different social groups and adhering to three different theologies seems top-heavy. As Kloppenborg himself admits, other Q specialists, using the same data, arrive at different conclusions.[216]

In sum, research on Q in the twentieth century has advanced far beyond earlier work. The detailed analysis of Q has provided additional support for the 2DH, although the opponents suppose that the excesses of Q research illustrate the hazards of the whole Q hypothesis. The theories about Q have perhaps contributed more than any other feature of recent criticism to the polarization of NT research. On the other hand, research in Q has encouraged the study of pre-Gospel tradition and has provided data in the quest for the historical Jesus. Redaction criticism, with its stress on the theology of the evangelists, has reduced the importance of the final form of the Gospels for the reconstruction of the historical Jesus, which instead must rely on the study of the earliest tradition. Redaction criticism, in turn, has provided a methodology for investigating Q and other early tradition. For scholars suspicious of the whole historical critical enterprise, the debate about Q illustrates the triumph of elitism in biblical research.

SUMMARY

The research reviewed in this chapter makes it abundantly clear that historical criticism continues to function with vigor: older questions have been reconsidered, ancient arguments have been resurrected and revised, new issues have been addressed, and creative hypotheses from new perspectives have emerged. As to the science of introduction, issues that arose in the Enlightenment continue to be debated—questions of authorship, date, provenance, and recipients. Both Kümmel and Koester are committed to the historical critical method. Kümmel is a shade more conservative, for example, in regard to authorship and the unity of NT documents. Koester more than Kümmel stresses Hellenist backgrounds. In the discussion, a new perspective has emerged, namely that of social and cultural research. Already emphasized in the "new archaeology" discussed in Chapter 4, this approach has influenced virtually all aspects of NT research.

Redaction criticism, although practiced under other names in the nineteenth century, has developed as an important method. The attention to the final composition—the stress on the particular point of view of the individual authors—has contributed to the understanding of the history, sociology, and theology of the NT. Marxsen's research on the Jesus-kerygma uses the methods of redaction criticism to detect the earliest layer of tradition, just as Kloppenborg employs similar analysis to discover the earliest stratum of Q. The results are very different: Marxsen uncovers an eschatological motif; Kloppenborg detects a non-apocalyptic, sapiential theme. Methodologically, the differences are substantial: Marxsen's approach is essentially, almost exclusively, theological. Kloppenborg's method is socio-cultural. Marxsen seems to view the early church as a community of university-trained theologians, while Kloppenborg sees them as inhabitants of Palestinian villages whose faith was shaped in the context of their socio-economic setting.

The major result of the challenges to the consensus concerning the Synoptic Problem is the energetic reinvestigation of the issues. Before the challenges, many scholars were content simply to repeat the time-worn solutions found in the standard textbooks. The challenges have forced Synoptic scholars to restudy the issues with direct attention to the Greek texts, to sharpen their colored pencils and trace the agreements and variations verse by verse. The majority still adhere to the 2DH, but their reasons for doing so are better informed because of rigorous attention to the data from the texts.

Various issues discussed in this chapter have implications for the study of the historical Jesus. Here again, conflict is apparent. This is seen in the analysis of sources. Koester (and James M. Robinson) make extensive use of non-canonical sources and hypothetical reconstruction of literary genres. The result is a portrait of Jesus as a wisdom teacher, possibly a Cynic—an idea supported by Kloppenborg's research on Q. As discussion of the historical Jesus in subsequent chapters will show, many scholars support a Jesus whose message of the kingdom has its meaning in an eschatological context. Of special interest is Marxsen's view of the Jesus-kerygma as primary and authoritative. Whereas most interpreters believe the Christian message has its origin in the resurrection faith, Marxsen goes back to an earlier source: a message that has its origin in the historical Jesus himself. The message can only be understood by faith, but it can only be recovered by historical research. The relation of faith and history, and the relation of criticism and faith, are methodological-theological issues that will continue to confound the history of NT research throughout the century.

Notes

1. See Donald Guthrie, "Questions of Introduction," in *New Testament Interpretation: Essays on Principles and Methods*, ed. I. Howard Marshall (Grand Rapids: Eerdmans, 1977), 105–16; Jürgen Roloff, "Neutestamentliche Einleitungswissenschaft: Tendenzen und Entwicklungen," *TRu* 55 (1990): 385–423.

2. For biography and summary of Kümmel's work see Otto Merk, "Kümmel, Werner Georg (1905–1995)," *DMBI*, 625–27; idem, "Kümmel, Werner Georg (1905–95)," in *DBI* 2: 40–41; idem, "Werner Georg Kümmel 1905–1995: Ein Neutestamentler im 20. Jahrhundert," in *History and Exegesis: New Testament Essays in Honor of Dr. E. Earle Ellis for His 80th Birthday*, ed. Sang-Won (Aaron) Son (New York: T & T Clark, 2006), 355–71. For bibliographies of Kümmel's work see Erich Grässer, Otto Merk, and Adolf Fritz, eds., Werner Georg Kümmel, *Heilsgeschehen und Geschichte: Gesammelte Aufsätze 1933–1964*, MTS 3 (Marburg: Elwert, 1965), "Bibliographie 1929–64," 471–82; Erich Grässer and Otto Merk, eds., Werner Georg Kümmel, *Heilsgeschehen und Geschichte: Gesammelte Aufsätze 1965–1977*, MTS 16 (Marburg: Elwert, 1987), "Bibliographie 1965–1978," 261–66.

3. For an example of Kümmel's contributions see Werner Georg Kümmel, *Vierzig Jahre Jesusforschung (1950–1990)*, ed. Helmut Merklein, 2d ed. (Weinheim: Beltz Athenäum, 1994); this is a collection of Kümmel's reviews of Jesus-research in a volume of some 700 pages.

4. See pp. 267 above.

5. Werner Georg Kümmel, *Römer 7 und die Bekehrung des Paulus*, UNT 17 (Leipzig: Hinrichs, 1929; repr. Lexington: ATLA, 1965). See Otto Merk, "Werner Georg Kümmel als Paulusforscher: Einige Aspekte," in *Paulus, Apostel Jesu Christi: Festschrift für Günter Klein zum 70. Geburtstag*, ed. Michael Trowitzsch (Tübingen: Mohr Siebeck, 1998), 245–56.

6. *Römer 7*, 138.

7. "Die Bedeutung der Enderwartung für die Lehre des Paulus," in *Heilsgeschehen* 1 (1965), 36–47.

8. Martin Dibelius and Werner Georg Kümmel, *Paulus* (Berlin: de Gruyter, 1951); ET: *Paul* (Philadelphia: Westminster, 1953).

9. Hans Lietzmann, *An die Korinther I/II*, HNT 9, ergänzt von Werner Georg Kümmel, 5th ed. (Tübingen: Mohr Siebeck, 1969). Besides his practice of exegesis Kümmel published an

introduction to exegetical method: "Die neutestamentliche Exegese," in Gottfried Adam, Otto Kaiser, and Werner G. Kümmel, *Einführung in die exegetischen Methoden*, Studium Theologie 1 (Munich: Kaiser, 1975), 61–95; ET: Otto Kaiser and Werner G. Kümmel, *Exegetical Method: A Student's Handbook*, trans. E. V. N. Goetschius and M. J. O'Connell (New York: Seabury, 1981).

10. Werner Georg Kümmel, *Einleitung in das Neue Testament*, 21st ed. (Heidelberg: Quelle und Meyer, 1983); ET: *Introduction to the New Testament*, rev. ed., trans. Howard Clark Key (Nashville: Abingdon, 1975). Kümmel's *Einleitung* has largely been replaced in Germany by Udo Schnelle, *Einleitung in das Neue Testament*, 7th ed. (Göttingen: Vandenhoeck & Ruprecht, 2011; 1st ed. 1994); ET: *The History and Theology of the New Testament Writings*, trans. M. Eugene Boring (Minneapolis: Fortress Press, 1998).

11. Paul Feine and Johannes Behm, *Einleitung in das Neue Testament*, 12th ed. W. G. Kümmel (Heidelberg: Quelle und Meyer, 1963); the 14th ed. (Kümmel's 3d) was translated into English: *Introduction to the New Testament*, trans. A. J. Mattill, Jr. (Nashville: Abingdon, 1966).

12. *Introduction* (rev. ed. 1975), 28.

13. For an analysis of Kümmel's research in the Synoptic problem, and especially on Q, see Otto Merk, "Die synoptische Redenquelle im Werk von Werner Georg Kümmel: Eine Bestandsaufnahme," in *Von Jesus zum Christus: Christologische Studien: Festgabe für Paul Hoffmann zum 65. Geburtstag*, ed. Rudolf Hoppe and Ulrich Busse, BZNW 93 (Berlin: de Gruyter, 1998), 191–200.

14. *Introduction*, 106.

15. Ibid., 510.

16. See pp. 242–43 above.

17. Werner Georg Kümmel, *Das Neue Testament: Geschichte der Erforschung seiner Probleme*, 2d ed., Orbis academicus 3/3 (Freiburg: Alber, 1970); ET: *The New Testament: The History of the Investigation of Its Problems*, trans. S. McLean Gilmore and Howard C. Kee (Nashville: Abingdon, 1972).

18. Ibid., 7.

19. Ibid., 62.

20. Ibid., 142–43.

21. In this volume the terminology "history of religion" school is preferred. The "s" in *religionsgeschichtliche* indicates a genitive singular, not a plural.

22. Werner Georg Kümmel, *Das Neue Testament im 20. Jahrhundert: Ein Forschungsbericht*, SBS 50 (Stuttgart: Katholisches Bibelwerk, 1970).

23. Ibid., 146.

24. *Verheißung und Erfüllung: Untersuchungen zur eschatologischen Verkündigung Jesu*, 3d ed., ATANT 6 (Zürich: Zwingli, 1956); ET: *Promise and Fulfilment: The Eschatological Message of Jesus*, 2d ed. trans. Dorothea M. Barton, SBT 23 (London: SCM, 1961); see Erich Grässer, "*Verheißung und Erfüllung*: Werner Georg Kümmels Verständnis der Eschatologie Jesu," in *Glaube und Eschatologie: Festschrift für Werner Georg Kümmel zum 80. Geburtstag*, ed. Erich Grässer and Otto Merk (Tübingen: Mohr [Paul Siebeck], 1985), 33–49.

25. *Promise and Fulfilment*, 114.

26. Ibid., 155.

27. Werner Georg Kümmel, *Jesus der Menschensohn?* (Wiesbaden: Franz Steiner, 1984), 181. Also important for Kümmel's understanding of early Christian eschatology is his essay, "Futurische und präsentische Eschatologie im ältesten Urchristentum," in *Heilsgeschehen und Geschichte* 1 (1965), 351–63.

28. "Das Problem des geschichtlichen Jesus in der gegenwärtigen Forschungslage," in *Der historische Jesus und der kerygmatische Christus: Beiträge zum Christusverständnis in Forschung und Verkündigung*, ed. Helmut Ristow and Karl Matthiae (Berlin: Evangelische Verlagsanstalt, 1960), 39–53, at 53.

29. Werner Georg Kümmel, *Das Bild des Menschen im Neuen Testament* (Zürich: Zwingli, 1948); repr.: *Römer 7 und Das Bild des Menschen im Neuen Testament: Zwei Studien* (Munich: Kaiser, 1974); ET: *Man in the New Testament*, trans. John J. Vincent, rev. ed. (Philadelphia: Westminster, 1963).

30. *Die Theologie des Neuen Testaments nach seinen Hauptzeugen: Jesus, Paulus, Johannes*, 2d ed. (Göttingen: Vandenhoeck & Ruprecht, 1972); ET: *The Theology of the New Testament: According to its Major Witnesses: Jesus—Paul—John*, trans. John E. Steely (Nashville: Abingdon, 1973).

31. *Theology of the New Testament*, 332. See also Werner Georg Kümmel, "Das Problem der 'Mitte des Neuen Testaments,'" in *Heilsgeschehen und Geschichte* 2 (1987), 62–74.

32. See "Curriculum Vitae of Helmut Koester," in *The Future of Early Christianity*, ed. Birger A. Pearson (Minneapolis: Fortress Press, 1991), xi–xii; Helmut Koester, "Epilogue: Current Issues in New Testament Scholarship," ibid., 467–76; Helmut Koester, "Insights from a Career of Interpretation," in *Paul and His World: Interpreting the New Testament in Its Context* (Minneapolis: Fortress Press, 2007), 279–90. For bibliography see David M. Scholer, "Biography of Helmut Koester," *Future of Early Christianity*, 477–87; "Publications of Helmut Koester, 1991–2007," in Helmut Koester, *From Jesus to the Gospels: Interpreting the New Testament in Its Context* (Minneapolis: Fortress Press, 2007), 293–99.

33. "Insights from a Career," 280.

34. Ibid., 289.

35. Ibid., 290.

36. *Synoptische Überlieferung bei den apostolischen Vätern*, TU 65 (Berlin: Akademie-Verlag, 1957).

37. Helmut Koester, *Introduction to the New Testament*, vol. 1: *History, Culture, and Religion of the Hellenistic Age*; vol. 2: *History and Literature of Early Christianity*, 2d ed. (New York: de Gruyter, 1995, 2000).

38. Ibid., 1: xxiii.

39. Ibid.

40. Ibid., 1: 196.

41. Ibid., 1: 214.

42. Ibid., 1: 367.

43. Ibid., 2: xxxix.

44. Ibid., 2: 8.

45. Ibid., 2: 68.

46. Ibid., 2: 88.

47. Ibid., 2: 114.

48. See *HNTR* 2: 451–55.

49. *Introduction*, 2: 231.

50. Ibid., 2: 245.

51. Helmut Koester, *Ancient Christian Gospels: Their History and Development* (Philadelphia: Trinity Press International, 1990).

52. Ibid., xxix.

53. Ibid., 46.

54. Ibid., 170.

55. Ibid., 240.

56. Ibid., 291.

57. Ibid., xxxi.

58. Helmut Koester, ed., *Ephesos: Metropolis of Asia: An Interdisciplinary Approach to Its Archaeology, Religion, and Culture*, HTS 41 (Valley Forge, PA: Trinity Press International, 1995), xviii.

59. Helmut Koester, ed., *Pergamon: Citadel of the Gods: Archaeological Record, Literary Description, and Religious Development*, HTS 46 (Harrisburg, PA: Trinity Press International, 1998), xx.

60. Charalambos Bakirtzis and Helmut Koester, eds., *Philippi at the Time of Paul and After His Death* (Harrisburg, PA: Trinity Press International, 1998), 49–65.

61. Helmut Koester, "The Structure and Criteria of Early Christian Beliefs," in James M. Robinson and Helmut Koester, *Trajectories through Early Christianity* (Philadelphia: Fortress Press, 1971), 205–31. Sees also idem, "The Theological Aspects of Early Christian Heresy," in *Paul and His World*, 238–50.

62. "Structure and Criteria," 219.

63. Ibid., 228.

64. See Norman Perrin, *What Is Redaction Criticism?* (Philadelphia: Fortress Press, 1969); Robert H. Stein, *Gospels and Tradition: Studies on Redaction Criticism of the Synoptic Gospels* (Grand Rapids: Baker, 1991); John R. Donahue, "Redaction Criticism, New Testament," *DBI* 1: 376–79; Stephen S. Smalley, "Redaction Criticism," in *New Testament Interpretation: Essays on Principles and Methods*, ed. I. Howard Marshall (Grand Rapids: Eerdmans, 1977), 181–95.

65. Perrin, *Redaction Criticism*, 1.

66. See *HNTR* 2: 147–49.

67. See Charles H. Talbert, "Conzelmann, Hans Georg (1915–1989)," *DMBI*, 324–28; Dietz Lange, "In Memoriam Hans Conzelmann," in Hans Conzelmann, *Heiden, Juden, Christen: Auseinandersetzungen in der Literatur der hellenistisch-römische Zeit* (Tübingen: Mohr Siebeck, 1981); ET: *Gentiles, Jews, Christians: Polemics and Apologetics in the Greco-Roman Era*, trans. M. Eugene Boring (Minneapolis: Fortress Press, 1992), xiii–xvii; Eduard Lohse, "Theology as Exegesis: Hans Conzelmann," ibid., xix–xxxiii. For bibliography see *Jesus Christus in Historie und Theologie: Neutestamentliche Festschrift für Hans Conzelmann zum 60. Geburtstag*, ed. Georg Strecker (Tübingen: Mohr [Paul Siebeck], 1975), 549–57.

68. Lange, "In Memoriam," xv.

69. Hans Conzelmann, *Die Mitte der Zeit: Studien zur Theologie des Lukas*, 3d ed., BHT 17 (Tübingen: Mohr [Paul Siebeck], 1960); ET: *The Theology of Luke*, trans. Geoffrey Buswell (New York: Harper & Brothers, 1960).

70. *Theology of Luke*, 13.

71. Ibid., 131–32.

72. Ibid., 206.

73. Ibid., 208.

74. *RGG*[3] 3: 619–53; ET: Hans Conzelmann, *Jesus: The Classic Article from RGG Expanded and Updated*, trans. J. Raymond Lord, ed. John Reumann (Philadelphia: Fortress Press, 1973); see Hans Conzelmann, "Jesus von Nazareth und der Glaube an den Auferstandenen," in *Der historische Jesus und der kerygmatische Christus*, 188–99.

75. *The Classic Article*, 46.

76. Ibid., 51.

77. Ibid., 54. Late in his career Conzelmann published a major contribution to the Jewish-Christian dialogue in his: *Heiden, Juden, Christen* (ET *Gentiles, Jews, Christians*, 1992). In this book Conzelmann insists that the dialogue becomes superfluous if Christians keep quiet about their faith in the saving action of God in Christ. He believes that all people are confronted by the word of God. "They are confronted by this Word not as Jews or Gentiles, Greeks or barbarians, but simply as human beings, i.e., as sinners who must renounce all boasting before God, including boasting that they are Christians, since the renunciation of all such boasting is inherent in faith. All are justified before God in exactly the same way, by faith alone, which Paul in Rom 3:30 bases on the confession that God is *one*."

78. Ibid., 76.

79. Ibid., 94–95.

80. Hans Conzelmann, *Grundriss der Theologie des Neuen Testaments*, 2d ed. (Munich: Kaiser, 1968); ET: *An Outline of the Theology of the New Testament*, trans. John Bowden (New York: Harper & Row, 1969).

81. Conzelmann's understanding of the early church is more fully explicated in his book, *Geschichte des Urchristentums*, GNT 5 (Göttingen: Vandenhoeck & Ruprecht, 1969); ET: *History of Primitive Christianity*, trans. John E. Steely (Nashville: Abingdon, 1973).

82. *Outline of Theology*, 114.

83. Ibid., 121.

84. Ibid., 165.

85. Ibid., 220.

86. Martin Dibelius, *Die Pastoralbriefe,* ed. Hans Conzelmann, 3d ed., HNT 13 (Tübingen: Mohr Siebeck, 1955); ET: *The Pastoral Epistles*, trans. Philip Buttolph and Adela Yarbro, Hermeneia (Philadelphia: Fortress Press, 1966).

87. Hans Conzelmann, *Die Apostelgeschichte*, HNT 7 (Tübingen: Mohr Siebeck, 1963); ET: *Acts of the Apostles: A Commentary on the Acts of the Apostles*, trans. James Limburg, A. Thomas Kraabel, and Donald H. Juel, Hermeneia (Philadelphia: Fortress Press, 1987).

88. Hans Conzelmann, *Der erste Brief an die Korinther*, KEK 5/11 (Göttingen: Vandenhoeck & Ruprecht, 1969); ET: *1 Corinthians: A Commentary on the First Epistle to the Corinthians*, trans. James W. Leitch, Hermeneia (Philadelphia: Fortress Press, 1975).

89. Conzelmann's case is more fully made in his monograph, *Korinth und die Mädchen der Aphrodite: Zur Religionsgeschichte der Stadt Korinth*, NAWG (1967) 8 (Göttingen: Vandenhoeck & Ruprecht, 1967); repr. in Hans Conzelmann, *Theologie als Schriftauslegung: Aufsätze zum Neuen Testament*, BEvT 65 (Munich: Kaiser, 1974), 152–66.

90. Hans Conzelmann, *Die kleineren Briefe des Apostels Paulus*, NTD 8 (Göttingen: Vandenhoeck & Ruprecht, 1970).

91. Hans Conzelmann and Andreas Lindemann, *Arbeitsbuch zum Neuen Testament*, 8th ed. (Tübingen: Mohr Siebeck, 1985); ET: *Interpreting the New Testament: An Introduction to the Principles and Methods of New Testament Exegesis*, trans. Siegfried S. Schatzmann (Peabody, MA: Hendrickson, 1988).

92. See P. E. Devenish, "Marxsen, Willi (1919–1993)," *DMBI*, 711–16; "Curriculum vitae," in Dietrich-Alex Koch, Gerhard Sellin, and Andreas Lindemann, eds., *Jesu Rede von Gott und ihre Nachgeschichte im frühen Christentum: Beiträge zur Verkündigung Jesu und zum Kerygma der Kirche: Festschrift für Willi Marxsen zum 70. Geburtstag* (Gütersloh: Mohn, 1989), 458. For bibliography see Devenish, "Marxsen," 714–16; "Bibliographie Willi Marxsen 1929–1989," in *Jesu Rede von Gott*, 459–72.

93. Willi Marxsen, *Der Evangelist Markus: Studien zur Redaktionsgechichte des Evangeliums*, 2d ed., FRLANT 67 (Göttingen: Vandenhoeck & Ruprecht, 1959); ET: *Mark the Evangelist: Studies on the Redaction History of the Gospel*, trans. James Boyce, Donald Juel, and William Poehlmann with Roy A. Harrisville (Nashville: Abingdon, 1969).

94. *Mark the Evangelist*, 28.

95. Ibid., 52.

96. Ibid., 85.

97. Ibid., 92.

98. Ibid., 149.

99. Ibid., 216.

100. Willi Marxsen, *Einleitung in das Neue Testament: Eine Einführung in ihre Probleme*, 4th rev. ed. (Gütersloh: Mohn, 1978); ET (of the 3d ed.): *Introduction to the New Testament: An Approach to its Problems*, trans. Geoffrey Buswell (Philadelphia: Fortress Press, 1974).

101. *Einleitung*, 154.

102. Ibid., 172.

103. See Schubert M. Ogden, "Fundamentum Fidei: Kritische Überlegungen zu Willi Marxsens Beitrag zur Systematischen Theologie," in *Jesu Rede von Gott*, 11–27. Ogden reviews Marxsen's contribution to systematic theology, namely, his understanding of faith as personal trust (in contrast to orthodoxy) and his view of theology as servant of faith.

104. *The Resurrection of Jesus of Nazareth,* trans. Margaret Kohl (Philadelphia: Fortress Press, 1970), 10.

105. In *Der Exeget als Theologe: Vorträge zum Neuen Testament* (Gütersloh: Mohn, 1968), 104–14.

106. Willi Marxsen, *Das Neue Testament als Buch der Kirche* (Gütersloh: Mohn, 1966); ET: *The New Testament as the Church's Book,* trans. James E. Mignard (Philadelphia: Fortress Press, 1972).

107. *The New Testament as the Church's Book,* 29.

108. Ibid., 63.

109. See Philip E. Devenish, "Introduction: The Jesus-Kerygma and Christian Theology," in Willi Marxsen, *Jesus and the Church: The Beginnings of Christianity,* Selected, Translated, and Introduced by Philip E. Devenish (Philadelphia: Trinity Press International, 1992), xi–xxxiii.

110. *The New Testament as the Church's Book,* 123.

111. Ibid., 149.

112. Willi Marxsen, *Die Auferstehung Jesu von Nazareth* (Gütersloh: Mohn, 1968); ET: *The Resurrection of Jesus of Nazareth* (see n. 104 above). See also Willi Marxsen, *Jesus and Easter: Did God Raise the Historical Jesus from the Dead?* trans. Victor Paul Furnish (Nashville: Abingdon, 1990).

113. *Die Auferstehung Jesu als historisches und als theologisches Problem* (Gürtersloh: Mohn, 1964); ET: "The Resurrection of Jesus as a Historical and Theological Problem," in *The Significance of the Message of the Resurrection for Faith in Jesus Christ,* ed. C. F. D. Moule, SBT 8 (Naperville, IL: Alec R. Allenson, 1968), 15–50.

114. *Resurrection of Jesus of Nazareth,* 74.

115. Ibid., 110.

116. Ibid., 128.

117. See Philip E. Devenish, "The So-Called Resurrection of Jesus and the Explicit Christian Faith: Wittgenstein's Philosophy and Marxsen's Exegesis as Linguistic Therapy," *JAAR* 51 (1983): 171–90.

118. Willi Marxsen, *Anfangsprobleme der Christologie,* 2nd ed. (Gütersloh: Mohn, 1964); ET: *The Beginnings of Christology: A Study in Its Problems,* trans. Paul J. Achtemeier (Philadelphia: Fortress Press, 1969); idem, *Das Abendmahl als christologisches Problem* (Gütersloh: Mohn, 1963); ET: *The Lord's Supper as a Christological Problem,* trans. Lorenz Nieting (Philadelphia: Fortress Press, 1970).

119. Willi Marxsen, "Christology of the New Testament," *IDBSup,* 146–56.

120. *"Christliche" und christliche Ethik im Neuen Testament* (Gütersloh: Mohn, 1989); ET: *New Testament Foundations for Christian Ethics,* trans. O. C. Dean Jr. (Minneapolis: Fortress Press, 1993).

121. *New Testament Foundations,* 86.

122. Ibid., 167.

123. Ibid., 219.

124. Ibid., 227.

125. Ibid., 290.

126. Ibid. 311.

127. See D. B. Peabody, "Farmer, William Reuben (1921–)," in *DBI* 1: 385–86; idem, "Farmer, William Reuben (1921–2000)," in *DMBI,* 432–38.

128. Farmer's dissertation, *Maccabees, Zealots, and Josephus: An Inquiry into Jewish Nationalism in the Greco-Roman Period* (New York: Columbia University Press, 1956; repr. Westport, CT: Greenwood, 1973), stresses the importance of historical backgrounds for understanding the NT.

129. Farmer promoted ecumenical research. This is evident in his book, written with Roman Catholic scholar Roch Kereszty, *Peter and Paul in the Church of Rome: The Ecumenical Potential of a Forgotten Perspective* (New York: Paulist, 1990). Farmer also led a movement to produce an international and ecumenical commentary on the Bible. The result is a huge volume

that includes over 300 pages of general articles, about 900 pages of commentary on the OT, and some 650 pages on the NT: William R. Farmer, ed., *The International Bible Commentary: A Catholic and Ecumenical Commentary for the Twenty-First Century* (Collegeville, MN: Liturgical, 1998).

130. William R. Farmer, *The Synoptic Problem: A Critical Analysis* (New York: Macmillan, 1964; repr. Dillsboro, NC: Western North Carolina, 1976).

131. See *HNTR* 1: 305–8.

132. Ibid., 2: 116.

133. Ibid., 2: 265–66.

134. *Synoptic Problem*, 179.

135. Ibid., 202.

136. Ibid., 202–27.

137. Ibid., 281.

138. William R. Farmer, *The Last Twelve Verses of Mark* (Cambridge: Cambridge University Press, 1974).

139. Ibid., 31.

140. Ibid., 107.

141. John Bernard Orchard, ed., *A Synopsis of the Four Gospels in Greek* (Macon, GA: Mercer University Press, 1983); idem, *A Synopsis of the Four Gospels in a New Translation* (Macon, GA: Mercer University Press, 1982).

142. See Allan J. McNicol, ed., with David L. Dungan and David B. Peabody, *Beyond the Q Impasse: Luke's Use of Matthew: A Demonstration by the Research Team of the International Institute for Gospel Studies* (Valley Forge, PA: Trinity Press International, 1996), 13 n. 2.

143. William R. Farmer, *Synopticon: The Verbal Agreement Between the Greek Texts of Matthew, Mark and Luke Contextually Exhibited* (Cambridge: Cambridge University Press, 1969).

144. William R. Farmer, *The Gospel of Jesus: The Pastoral Relevance of the Synoptic Problem* (Louisville: Westminster John Knox, 1994).

145. Ibid., 8.

146. The argument from order is also used by the supporters of the 2DH; they observe that Matthew and Luke follow the order of Mark, and when either diverges from Mark's order they seldom agree with each other. The two ways of arguing from the same data simply show that Mark is the "middle term" between Matthew and Luke.

147. *Gospel of Jesus*, 63.

148. Ibid., 156.

149. Ibid., 163.

150. Ibid., 170; the original quotation is from James Robinson, "The Sayings of Jesus: Q," *Drew Gateway* 54 (1983), 26–38, at 32.

151. *Gospel of Jesus*, 200.

152. William R. Farmer, *Jesus and the Gospel: Tradition, Scripture, and Canon* (Philadelphia: Fortress Press, 1982).

153. Ibid., 10.

154. The substance of this section is presented in William R. Farmer and Denis M. Farkasfalvy, *The Formation of the New Testament Canon: An Ecumenical Approach*, Theological Inquiries (New York: Paulist, 1983), 7–95.

155. *Jesus and the Gospel*, 214–15.

156. David L. Dungan, "The Two-Gospel Hypothesis," *ABD* 6: 671–79.

157. Ibid., 673.

158. See also Thomas R. W. Longstaff and Page A. Thomas, *The Synoptic Problem: A Bibliography, 1716–1988* (Macon, GA: Mercer University Press, 1988).

159. David Laird Dungan, *A History of the Synoptic Problem: The Canon, the Text, the Composition, and the Interpretation of the Gospels*, ABRL (New York: Doubleday, 1999). The history of the problem is important for the supporters of the 2GH; they believe the triumph of the 2DH

results in large part from mistakes that were made in the history of research. See, for example, Hans-Herbert Stoldt, *History and Criticism of the Marcan Hypothesis*, trans. Donald L. Niewyk (Macon, GA: Mercer University Press, 1970).

160. *History of the Synoptic Problem*, 339.

161. Ibid., 346.

162. Allan J. McNicol, ed., with David L. Dungan and David Peabody, *Beyond the Q Impasse—Luke's Use of Matthew: A Demonstration by the Research Team of the International Institute for Gospels Studies* (Valley Forge, PA: Trinity Press International, 1996).

163. David B. Peabody, ed., with Lamar Cope and Allan J. McNicol, *One Gospel from Two: Mark's Use of Matthew and Luke: A Demonstration by the Research Team of the International Institute for Renewal of Gospel Studies* (Harrisburg, PA: Trinity Press International, 2002).

164. E. P. Sanders and Margaret Davies, *Studying the Synoptic Gospels* (Philadelphia: Trinity Press International, 1989). The work of Goulder and Boismard is reviewed below in this chapter.

165. See Hollis W. Huston, "The 'Q Parties' at Oxford, *JBR* 25 (1957): 123–28.

166. Austin M. Farrer, "On Dispensing with Q," in *Studies in the Gospels: Essays in Memory of R. H. Lightfoot* (Oxford: Basil Blackwell, 1957), 55–86; repr. in *The Two-Source Hypothesis: A Critical Appraisal*, ed. Arthur J. Bellinzoni, Jr. (Macon, GA: Mercer University Press, 1985), 321–56.

167. "Dispensing with Q," 62 (repr. 330).

168. Ibid., 85 (355).

169. See Dennis Nineham, "Foreword: Michael Goulder—An Appreciation," in *Crossing the Boundaries: Essays in Biblical Interpretation in Honour of Michael D. Goulder*, ed. Stanley Porter, Paul Joyce, and David Orton (Leiden: Brill, 1994), xi–xv. For bibliography see Stanley E. Porter, "Bibliography of Michael D. Goulder" (1957–1994), *Crossing the Boundaries*, 379–81; Mark S. Goodacre, *Goulder and the Gospels: An Examination of a New Paradigm*, JSNTSup 133 (Sheffield: Sheffield Academic, 1996), 370–75.

170. Michael D. Goulder, *Midrash and Lection in Matthew*, The Speaker's Lectures in Biblical Studies (SLBS), 1969–71 (London: SPCK, 1974), xv.

171. Ibid.

172. Ibid., 4.

173. Ibid., 19.

174. Ibid., 153.

175. Ibid., 172.

176. Ibid., 474.

177. Michael D. Goulder, *The Evangelists' Calendar: A Lectionary Explanation of the Development of Scripture*, SLBS, 1972 (London: SPCK, 1978).

178. Ibid., 73.

179. "Matthew's Gospel Round the Year," in *The Gospels According to Michael Goulder: A North American Response*, ed. Christopher A. Rollston (Harrisburg, PA: Trinity Press International, 2002), 1–11.

180. *Luke: A New Paradigm*, 2 vols., JSNTSup 20 (Sheffield: Sheffield Academic, 1989). An analysis and critique of this work is presented by Goodacre, *Goulder and the Gospels*.

181. For an extensive investigation of Goulder's argument from minor agreements see Goodacre, *Goulder and the Gospels*, 89–130.

182. *Luke* 1: 27. See Michael D. Goulder, "On Putting Q to the Test," *NTS* 24 (1978): 218–40.

183. Ibid., 1: 75–76.

184. *Goulder and the Gospels*, 13–58.

185. See, for example, Bruce Chilton, "Festivals and Lectionaries: Correspondence and Distinctions," in *Crossing the Boundaries*, 12–28; Goodacre, *Goulder and the Gospels*, 294–369.

186. John S. Kloppenborg Verbin, "Goulder and the New Paradigm: A Critical Appreciation of Michael Goulder on the Synoptic Problem," *Gospels According to Michael Goulder,* 29–60.

187. After his dissertation, *Goulder and the Gospels* (noted above), Goodacre's most important books are: *The Synoptic Problem: A Way Through the Maze* (London: Sheffield Academic Press, 2001); and *The Case Against Q: Studies in Markan Priority and the Synoptic Problem* (Harrisburg, PA: Trinity Press International, 2002).

188. Marie-Émile Boismard, "Theorie des niveaux multiples," in *The Interrelations of the Gospels,* ed. David L. Dungan, BETL 95 (Leuven: Leuven University Press, 1990), 231–43.

189. Ibid., 232.

190. Marie-Émile Boismard, *L'Évangile de Marc: sa préhistoire,* EBib 26 (Paris: Gabalda, 1994).

191. Pierre Benoît and Marie-Émile Boismard, *Synopse des Quatre Évangiles en Français,* vol. 2: *Commentaire,* by Marie-Émile Boismard (Paris: Cerf, 1972).

192. *Studies in the Synoptic Problem: By Members of the University of Oxford,* ed. William Sanday (Oxford: Clarendon, 1911); see *HNTR* 2: 261–66.

193. Christopher M. Tuckett, "The Current State of the Synoptic Problem," in *New Studies in the Synoptic Problem: Oxford Conference, April 2008: Essays in Honour of Christopher M. Tuckett,* ed. Paul Foster, Andrew F. Gregory, John S. Kloppenborg, and Jozef Verheyden, BETL 239 (Leuven: Peeters, 2011), 12.

194. See David R. Catchpole, "Christopher M. Tuckett: An Appreciation," in *New Studies in the Synoptic Problem,* xiii–xviii.

195. Christopher M. Tuckett, *The Revival of the Griesbach Hypothesis: An Analysis and Appraisal* (Cambridge: Cambridge University Press, 1983).

196. Christopher M. Tuckett, *Q and the History of Early Christianity: Studies on Q* (Edinburgh: T & T Clark; Peabody, MA: Hendrickson, 1996). For complete bibliography see *New Studies in the Synoptic Problem,* xix–xxv.

197. See "Preface" (vii–viii) and "Curriculum F. Neirynck" (49–50) in *The Four Gospels 1992: Festschrift Frans Neirynck,* vol. 1, ed. Frans Van Segbroeck, Christopher M. Tuckett, Gilbert Van Belle, and Jozef Verheyden (Leuven: Leuven University Press, 1992); Joël Delobel, "Professor F. Neirynck: 1960–1992," in *The Synoptic Gospels: Source Criticism and the New Literary Criticism,* ed. Camille Focant, BETL 110 (Leuven: Leuven University Press, 1993), xv–xx.

198. Frans Neirynck, *The Minor Agreements of Matthew and Luke against Mark with a Cumulative List,* BETL 37 (Leuven: Leuven University Press, 1974).

199. Frans Neirynck, *Duality in Mark: Contributions to the Study of Markan Redaction,* rev. ed. BETL 31 (Leuven: Leuven University Press, 1988).

200. Frans Neirynck, *Evangelica,* 3 vols., BETL 60, 99, 159 (Leuven: Leuven University Press, 1982, 1991, 2001).

201. For an overview of the issues from the 2DH perspective see Franz Neirynck, "The Synoptic Problem," in *NJBC,* 587–95.

202. For recent support of the existence and character of Q see Delbert Burkett, *Rethinking the Gospel Sources,* vol. 2: *The Unity and Plurality of Q,* Early Christianity and Its Literature (Atlanta: SBL, 2009).

203. The issue is thoroughly discussed by M. Eugene Boring, "The 'Minor Agreements' and Their Bearing on the Synoptic Problem," in *New Studies in the Synoptic Problem,* 227–51. Boring concludes: "Within this larger picture, the Minor Agreements will play a *minor* role" (p. 251).

204. See pp. 201–3 above.

205. For introduction to and survey of Q research see John S. Kloppenborg, "Q (The Sayings Gospel)," in *DBI* 2: 343–45; idem, *Q, The Earliest Gospel: An Introduction to the Original Stories and Sayings of Jesus* (Louisville: Westminster John Knox, 2008); Christopher M. Tuckett, "Q (Gospel Source)," in *ABD* 5: 567–72; Andreas Lindemann, "Die Logienquelle Q: Fragen an

eine gut begründete Hypothese," in idem, ed., *The Sayings Source Q and the Historical Jesus*, BETL 158 (Leuven: Leuven University Press, 2001), 3–26; Siegfried Schulz, *Q: Die Spruchquelle der Evangelisten* (Zürich: Theologischer Verlag, 1972).

206. John S. Kloppenborg, *Q Parallels: Synopsis, Critical Notes, and Concordance*, Foundations & Facets (FF) (Sonoma, CA: Polebridge, 1988). For other editions see Wolfgang Schenk, *Synopse zur Redenquelle der Evangelien* (Dusseldorf: Patmos, 1981); Athanasius Polag, *Fragmenta Q: Textheft zur Logienquelle* (Neukirchen-Vluyn: Neukirchener Verlag, 1979); ET: Ivan Havener, *Q: The Sayings of Jesus* (Wilmington, DE: Michael Glazier, 1987), 111–61.

207. James M. Robinson, Paul Hoffmann, and John S. Kloppenborg, eds., *The Sayings Gospel of Q in Greek and English with Parallels from the Gospels of Mark and Thomas*, Biblical Exegesis and Theology 30 (Leuven: Peeters, 2001). This abbreviated version is also available in an edition without the Greek text: James M. Robinson, ed., *The Sayings of Jesus: The Sayings Gospel Q in English* (Minneapolis: Fortress Press, 2001).

208. For introductions and general works see Dieter Lührmann, *Die Redaktion der Logienquelle*, WMANT 33 (Neukirchen-Vluyn: Neukirchener Verlag, 1969); Migaku Satō, *Q und Prophetie: Studien zur Gattungs- und Traditionsgeschichte der Quelle Q*, WUNT 29 (Tübingen: Mohr Siebeck, 1988); Arland D. Jacobson, *The First Gospel: An Introduction to Q*, FF (Sonoma, CA: Polebridge, 1992); Harry T. Fleddermann, *Q: A Reconstruction and Commentary*, Biblical Tools and Studies 1 (Leuven: Peeters, 2005). For collected papers from conferences and symposia see Ronald A. Piper, ed., *The Gospel Behind the Gospels: Current Studies on Q*, NovTSup 75 (Leiden: Brill, 1995); Andreas Lindemann, ed., *The Sayings Source Q and the Historical Jesus*, BETL 158 (Leuven: Leuven University Press, 2001).

209. Besides his two major works, reviewed above, see, John S. Kloppenborg, ed., *The Shape of Q: Signal Essays on the Sayings Gospel* (Minneapolis: Fortress Press, 1994); idem, *Conflict and Invention: Literary, Rhetorical, and Social Studies on the Sayings Gospel Q* (Valley Forge, PA: Trinity Press International, 1995); idem, with John W. Marshall, *Apocalypticism, Anti-Semitism and the Historical Jesus: Subtexts in Criticism*, JSHJSup, JSNTSup 275 (London: T & T Clark, 2005).

210. John S. Kloppenborg, *The Formation of Q: Trajectories in Ancient Wisdom Collections*, SAC (Philadelphia: Fortress Press, 1987), xv.

211. John S. Kloppenborg Verbin, *Excavating Q: The History and Setting of the Sayings Gospel* (Edinburgh: T & T Clark, 2000).

212. Ibid., 54.

213. Ibid., 261. Kloppenborg's concern with social, cultural, and economic backgrounds is demonstrated in a later major work: John S. Kloppenborg, *The Tenants in the Vineyard: Ideology, Economics, and Agrarian Conflict in Jewish Palestine*, WUNT 196 (Tübingen: Mohr Siebeck, 2006).

214. *Excavating Q*, 362, 378.

215. Ibid., 268.

216. For example, Migaku Satō, *Q und Prophetie*, construes Q as a different genre from that proposed by Kloppenborg; see *Excavating Q*, 136–43. See also Birger A. Pearson, "A Q Community in Galilee," *NTS* 50 (2004): 476–94.

7

Confessional Research: Roman Catholic Scholarship

In the history of NT research in the twentieth century nothing has been more dramatic than the rapid advance of Roman Catholic biblical studies.[1] The church that excommunicated Alfred Loisy in 1908[2] has increasingly affirmed the methods and results of historical criticism.[3] This affirmation is marked by a series of papal encyclicals and the remarkable ecumenical council, Vatican II. The situation at the beginning of the century was shaped by the encyclical *Providentissimus Deus* (1893) of Leo XIII. Although Leo affirmed the inspiration and inerrancy of Scripture, he permitted the study of the Bible in the original languages and the cautious use of historical method. In 1920, Benedict XV published *Spiritus Paraclitus*, which acknowledged that the truth of Scripture was confined to the religious elements of the text. The authorship of Scripture, according to Benedict, was divine and human, with the human writer as instrument of God. Pius XII's *Divino Afflante Spiritu* (1943) is usually hailed as the Magna Carta of Catholic biblical studies. This encyclical gave more credit to the human author, acknowledging the role of the writer's own faculties and powers. Pius encouraged the study of archaeology, biblical languages, text criticism, and hermeneutics. Attention was to be given to the ancient "modes of writing," different from the kinds of speech used today. The Bible should be interpreted in the context of the ancient literature of the East.

Vatican II represents a giant step in the advance of Catholic research.[4] In 1959, Pope John XXIII astounded the hierarchy with the announcement of his intention to summon an ecumenical council, dedicated to the modernizing of the church. The council began in October of 1962, held four lengthy sessions, and finally finished its work in November, 1965. John died in the course of the council (1963), but was succeeded by Paul VI, who supported its continuation. The drama of the opening event is hard to exaggerate: some 2,700 bishops assembled under the splendor of the vault of St. Peter's, clad in their vivid vestments, speaking a host of languages but united in the common Latin of the ancient church. The council produced sixteen major documents, of which the most important were four "constitutions." For the study of the Bible the crucial document is the Constitution on Divine Revelation, adopted during the last session (1965) by a vote of 2,344 to 6.[5] This constitution was published as *Dei Verbum*. The most striking feature of the document was the conclusion that revelation did not have two separate sources, Scripture and tradition, but one: revelation is the Word of God, expressed in the person and work of Jesus Christ; Scripture and tradition witness together in presenting the Word. In regard to hermeneutics, the human author was recognized as the true author whose work should be interpreted by historical critical methods. "For the words of God, expressed in human language, have been made like human discourse, just as of old the Word of the eternal Father, when he took to Himself the weak flesh of humanity, became like other men."[6] In the final section the constitution reads: "This sacred Synod encourages the sons of the Church who are biblical scholars to continue energetically with the work they have so well begun, with a constant renewal of vigor and with loyalty to the mind of the Church."[7]

Biblical scholarship flourished in the wake of the council, but attacks from disgruntled critics continued. Much of this was dispelled with the publication of "The Interpretation of the Bible in the Church" by the Pontifical Biblical Commission in 1993.[8] This document has four main parts: methods and approaches, hermeneutical questions, characteristics of Catholic interpretation, and the interpretation of the Bible in the church. The document asserts that historical critical method is indispensable, since the Bible witnesses to revelation in history. At the same time the document acknowledges limitations of the method, including the questionable presuppositions of some exegetes and an overemphasis on the literal meaning to the neglect of the deeper, spiritual understanding of the text.

A European Example: Rudolf Schnackenburg (1914–2002)

There are a host of worthy candidates who might serve as examples of European Roman Catholic scholarship—Pierre Benoît, Lucien Cerfaux, Stanislas Lyonnet, Otto Kuss, François-Marie Braun, and others—but time and space allow for only one. Born in Kattowitz, Upper Silesia, Rudolf Schnackenburg was educated at Breslau and Munich, where he completed his *Habilitation* in 1947.[9] He was ordained to the priesthood and in 1955 began teaching at Bamberg. From 1957 until retirement in 1982 he was professor of New Testament at Würzburg. Like an academic magnet, Schnackenburg drew students from around world, adopting a personal interest in their various topics of research. Schnackenburg lived a simple life, dominated by his scholarly research; on a typical day he worked from 5:30 AM to 11:00 PM. He was a man of the church and served on the Pontifical Biblical Commission. His scholarship was honored by his election as President of the SNTS.

Schnackenburg produced an abundance of critical, exegetical, and theological work.[10] Basic to his NT research is his understanding of revelation.[11] Schnackenburg observes that the belief that the Bible is a book of revelation raises the question of the biblical understanding of revelation. He finds a key in Heb 1:1-2, where the writer describes several aspects of revelation: it is spoken by God; it has been given in various ways; it has been given through prophets, and finally in the Son. The last point affirms Schnackenburg's conviction that revelation is given in history. Also crucial for the understanding of revelation, according to Schnackenburg, is the biblical understanding of faith. Paul (in 2 Cor 4:3-4 and 1 Cor 1:18-25) says that revelation is hidden from some but open to others: those who respond in faith. Schnackenburg defines faith as a personal response of complete dependence on God. Schnackenburg believes revelation is given in tradition as well as in Scripture. He notes that revelation was transmitted in tradition before the writing of Scripture, and that revelation continues after the writing in the interpretation of Scripture.

This concern with tradition is typical of Roman Catholic scholarship, which displays a distinctive exegetical practice.[12] Schnackenburg notes that the encyclical *Divino Afflante Spiritu* (1943) affirmed the use of historical critical method. However, some practitioners of the method, according to him, have overemphasized the literal meaning of Scripture at the expense of the deeper spiritual meaning, the *sensus plenior*. Schnackenburg did not believe that commitment to tradition hinders the use of historical critical research. He agreed with Bultmann that exegesis without presuppositions is not possible; the Catholic exegete presupposes the faith and tradition of the church.

THE GOSPEL OF JOHN AND OTHER EXEGETICAL WORKS

Schnackenburg's major contribution to NT research is his massive multivolume commentary on the Gospel of John.[13] "I should like the commentary to make its contribution to the present state of studies," writes Schnackenburg, "without abandoning Catholic tradition or the scientific method used by New Testament scholars of all confessions."[14] He begins with an exhaustive (over 200 page) introduction concerning the historical-critical issues. He acknowledges that the author is primarily concerned with theology, but this does not mean that he provides no historical information. To be sure, the Fourth Gospel differs from the Synoptics, for instance in the presentation of long discourses that "cannot and do not intend to be historical reporting or a word for word record."[15] Schnackenburg does not believe that the author used the Synoptics, but does think he knew early tradition. "All this suggests that behind John there is an older tradition, going back to 'synoptic' or 'pre-synoptic' times, with many contacts with the synoptic tradition, but still an independent one."[16] In regard to the composition, Schnackenburg believes chapters 1–20 constitute a unity, but chapter 21 is a later addition.

In regard to the debated question of authorship, Schnackenburg begins with a theological affirmation. "From the theological point of view, therefore, the question of authorship really comes down to the 'apostolic authority' behind the Scriptures which were then recognized and proclaimed by the Church as inspired and canonical."[17] As to the identity of the actual writer, Schnackenburg recognizes the weight of the late-second-century tradition in support of John, the son of Zebedee. He also believes that the elusive "beloved disciple" of the Fourth Gospel is this same John, and offers a hypothesis: the primary source of the tradition was John, but the evangelist was a disciple of John who eventually put the tradition in writing, using sources, probably including a "signs source"; a final redaction, incorporating chapter 21, was the work of a later member of the Johannine school. Schnackenburg believes that the language and style imply a Diaspora Jew who wrote a simple Greek colored by Semitic influence. He locates the religious background of the Fourth Gospel in the OT and Judaism with only incidental contacts with Gnosticism.

The main concern of the evangelist, according to Schnackenburg, is Christology from the perspective of realized eschatology. "In John, however, the strongest motive is the Christology, which shows the glory of the Logos still dwelling in the earthly Jesus, and the power of the exalted and glorified Lord already present in his word and work of salvation. In John, Christ is really the 'eschatological present.'"[18]

As to the history of interpretation, Schnackenburg notes the extensive use of the Fourth Gospel by the gnostics in the second century. Among the orthodox the first clear dependence on John is seen in Justin and Tatian. Origen interpreted the Gospel allegorically, and a high point of theological exegesis is reached by Augustine. In the Enlightenment the authenticity of John was questioned. In recent times the commentary by Bultmann has been influential—an influence Schnackenburg largely resists.[19]

The commentary proper orders the material into two main sections: "Jesus Reveals Himself to the World" (chaps. 1–12); "Jesus in the Circle of His Own: Passion and Resurrection" (chaps. 13–20, plus the addition of chap. 21). The first section constitutes Volumes 1 and 2; the second is, Volume 3. The fourth volume (only in the German edition) includes expanded exegesis and additional excursuses.[20] Each pericope is preceded by an introduction, followed by the text in translation (including the Greek text in the first volume of the English edition), followed by verse-by-verse exposition. Space allows only a few examples.

Schnackenburg devotes sixty pages to the interpretation of the prologue (1:1-18). He believes the evangelist took up a hymn or poem and adapted it to his introduction. This poem, according to Schnackenburg, was composed by a Christian Hellenist. As adapted by the evangelist, the poem has three parts: the pre-existent being of the Logos, the coming of the Logos, and the incarnation of the Logos. Schnackenburg believes that in 1:1 the evangelist depicts the Logos without a body and stresses his divine nature. The climax of the poem is v. 14, which affirms the event of incarnation as historical happening. "The ἐγένετο announces a change in the mode of the being of the Logos: hitherto he was in glory with his Father (cf. 17:5, 24), now he takes on the lowliness of human, earthly existence; formerly he was 'with God' (1:1b), now he pitches his tent among men, and in human form in the full reality of the σάρξ, to attain once more the glory of his heavenly mode of being after his return to the Father (17:5)."[21]

John 2:1-11 presents "The Beginning of the Signs: The Miracle at the Marriage-Feast in Cana." At first glance the account looks like a simple miracle story, but hints of a deeper meaning are scattered through the text: the enigmatic words about the "hour," the great quantity of wine, the revelation of "glory," and the response of the disciples. Schnackenburg does not believe the notice of "the third day" has symbolic meaning, nor does he find eucharistic symbolism in the text. The central meaning of the sign, according to Schnackenburg, is the self-revelation of Jesus as the Messiah; the wine represents the eschatological gift the Messiah brings. In a section in smaller print Schnackenburg notes alleged parallels in the myth of Dionysus, but he believes they have no significance for the interpretation of the Cana miracle.

Schnackenburg's comments on "The Raising of Lazarus" (11:1-54) are found in Volume 2. He believes the account is based on a miracle story from the "signs source" and oral tradition the evangelist has shaped in order to present his theology, to point ahead to the resurrection of Jesus and the revelation of God's glory. Schnackenburg believes the Synoptics do not include this miracle because they do not know it; the miracle belongs to the Jerusalem tradition, which did not make its way into the Galilean tradition used by the Synoptics. The theological climax of the story, according to Schnackenburg, is found in the conversation of Jesus with Martha, expressed in the declaration "I am the resurrection and the life" (11:25).

> The powerful "I am" saying stands immovable at the beginning; only through Jesus is this life released and given to believers; he is not just the revealer, but also the giver of this indestructible life. But he is not the life-giver in his role as raiser of the dead on the "last day," but as the giver of salvation in the present, in whom we must believe here and now.

The interpretation of the climactic story of the conversion of Thomas (20:24-29) is found in Volume 3. Schnackenburg believes this account was composed by the evangelist in order to encourage the faith of the members of the community who are unable to "see" the risen Christ. Before his conversion Thomas represents the weakness of the faith of the pre-Easter disciples; his conversion points to a faith that goes beyond seeing. Schnackenburg does not believe that Thomas actually touched Jesus, since only "seeing" is mentioned in the account. He concludes that "the Thomas pericope can be understood entirely in the light of the main objective of the evangelist, to lead his readers to a deepened faith in Christ."[22] In regard to John 21, Schnackenburg writes, "The entire added chapter has been written from a pronouncedly 'ecclesiastical' point of view, from the viewpoint of the Church at the time when it was compiled."[23]

Volumes 1 to 3 include eighteen excursuses. An example is "The Son of Man in the Fourth Gospel."[24] At the outset Schnackenburg observes that the use of the title in the Fourth Gospel provides no material for the investigation of the question whether the historical Jesus applied it to himself. In John the title is used thirteen times, primarily to present Jesus as the figure who has come from heaven and ascends there again; he is the Messiah, the giver of life and the judge. "We must conclude that it was not through the synoptic tradition that the fourth evangelist arrived at his affirmations relating to the presence of the Son of Man, but by his own processes of theological reflection on the data."[25] Schnackenburg does not believe that John's usage reflects the image of the Primordial Man or the myth of the gnostic redeemer.

Schnackenburg also published commentaries on other NT books. He carries on his Johannine research in a sizeable commentary on the Epistles of John.[26] In the introduction he notes that 1 John is not a letter in the proper sense. He believes it was addressed to readers who were in danger of apostasy, the target of opponents who promoted a docetic Christology influenced by gnostic thought. Schnackenburg notes similarities with the Fourth Gospel but concludes that the authors are not the same.

Schnackenburg produced a two-volume commentary on Mark, addressed to the non-expert, concerned with the spiritual meaning of the text.[27] More attention is given to critical details in his commentary on Matthew.[28] Schnackenburg believes the author used Mark, the sayings source (Q), and oral tradition. Matthew, he thinks, was addressed to a Christian community in a city, probably Antioch. Schnackenburg rejects the traditional authorship by Matthew (Levi), and argues that the Gospel was written by a second-generation Hellenistic Jewish Christian after the destruction of Jerusalem, probably around 85 or 90. This author, according to Schnackenburg, is concerned with Christology and the history of salvation; he affirms the importance of the community, which he calls the "church." An example of Schnackenburg's exegesis is seen in his discussion of Matt 16:18-19. In response to Peter's confession, Jesus designates Peter as the "rock" on which the church is built. "The foundation of the church, in this image, is not Peter's faith, or Jesus' messianic dignity, but the person of Peter himself."[29]

Schnackenburg ventured into the epistles with his commentary on Ephesians, a contribution to the highly regarded ecumenical series, Evangelisch-katholischer Kommentar zum Neuen Testament (EKKNT), for which he, along with Eduard Schweizer, was the founding coeditor.[30] In the introduction Schnackenburg takes up the debated question of the literary form of Ephesians, and concludes that it is "a theologically-based, pastorally-oriented letter."[31] He notes the shift in Catholic scholarship away from Pauline authorship; he believes Ephesians was written in the post-apostolic age, around 90. He thinks the author used Colossians, and transformed the central concern from Christology to ecclesiology. The commentary includes an important excursus, "The Church in the Epistle to the Ephesians." "In the whole of the NT literature," writes Schnackenburg, "there is nowhere an ecclesiology which is so extensively structured or which is revealed so effectively as that in the Epistle to the Ephesians."[32] Schnackenburg discusses the various symbols of the church in Ephesians, for example, the image of Christ as the head of the body—a symbol that depicts the church as universal and cosmic.

NT Ethics and Jesus

Next to his commentary on John, Schnackenburg's two-volume work on NT ethics is his most important publication. It was originally written in 1954, and an English translation was made on the basis of the second edition of 1962.[33] Schnackenburg's extensively revised third edition is only available in German (and in Spanish translation).[34] The first volume deals with ethics "From Jesus to the Early Church." According to Schnackenburg the point of departure is the proclamation of the coming kingdom of God and its basic demands. The announcement of the kingdom includes an ethical imperative: the hearer is called to respond to God's mercy with acts of mercy; the eschatological rule of God demands acts of love in the present. Schnackenburg notes that Jesus calls persons to be his disciples, to accept the radical demands of the kingdom, to leave home and family, to take up the cross. The antitheses of the Sermon on the Mount, according to Schnackenburg, indicate that the commands of Jesus exceed those of the OT.

As to social issues, for example the relation to the state, Schnackenburg states that Jesus did not promote revolution; he believed the state had authority in its own sphere, but the duty to God was greater than obligation to the state. In the economic arena Jesus did not promote social reform but criticized the rich and identified with the poor. Schnackenburg notes that women played important roles in support of the ministry of Jesus.

Turning to the ethics of the early church, Schnackenburg believes the expectation of the *parousia* provided a motive for ethical obedience. The ethical teaching of the church stressed the imitation of Jesus: readiness to accept suffering and the life of selfless service. The center of the ethical demand is the command of love. "Agape is the distinctive mark of the Christian religion."[35] The early Christians, according to Schnackenburg, grappled with the problem of life in the world. The church had its setting in a pagan society and called for distinctive ethical behavior. Schnackenburg finds Paul's advice in Romans 13 to be surprising, but a counterview is offered by Revelation, advocating resistance to the demonic power of the state.

Schnackenburg's second volume on ethics explicates the ethical teaching of the early Christian preachers. He notes that Paul's ethic is grounded in his theology. Paul assumed the unsaved situation of humanity: Jews and Greeks under the power of sin. The turning point, according to Schnackenburg, is the action of God in Christ, which offers redemption and reconciliation by God's grace, received by faith. This action of justification calls for ethical obedience; the imperative is grounded in the indicative of the new situation. The ethical imperative, according to Schnackenburg's reading of Paul, reaches its high point in the law of Christ—the law of love that fulfills the whole law.

Schnackenburg believes a distinctive feature of Paul's ethic is his idea of "conscience." This idea, borrowed from popular philosophy, indicates that humans have a sense of judgment and responsibility. For the Christian, conscience is illuminated by faith, and faith calls for the response of love. Paul carried his mission into the pagan world and his message called people to turn from idols to serve the true God (1 Thess 1:9); Paul urged believers not to be conformed to the world (Rom 12:2).

> In everything, not only the intimate life and practice of the apostle is apparent, but also a conscious effort to come into contact with the former pagans and to move them to new life in Christ. The apostle to the Gentiles wants, with human affection, to draw them to himself and win them for his gospel without abandoning its truth and ethical demand.[36]

After a chapter on Colossians and Ephesians, Schnackenburg proceeds to the ethical teaching of the Gospels. His concern is with the individual evangelists, and consequently he employs redaction criticism. In regard to Mark, Schnackenburg writes: "In a word: It is a call to following Jesus, and indeed, in the community of faith which knows itself obligated to the person of Jesus, to his example, to his way."[37] Matthew insists that no part of the Law can fall away, but he understands the Law as fulfilled in the command of love. For Matthew the church is important, and the ethical life of believers is lived out in the community of faith. Luke recognizes the delay of the *parousia* but, as Schnackenburg points out, he instructs the believers to remain faithful in the meantime. "Summing up, one can say: Luke is the 'social' evangelist who takes up the message of Jesus for the poor, needy, sick, and oppressed, and sustains it in his communities."[38] For John the call of God comes through the Son of God who has been sent into the world. Jesus, the revelation of God, is "the way, the truth, and the life" (14:6). According to Schnackenburg, John believes the command of love is the new commandment—new because it is embodied in the love of Jesus. In a chapter on the ethical teachings of the letter of James, Schnackenburg contends that there is no real conflict between James and Paul. For James, works emerge as a sign of faith, a concept not antithetical to the ethics of Paul. A single chapter reviews Schnackenburg's understanding of the ethics of the remaining NT documents: 1 Peter, Hebrews, Jude, 2 Peter, and Revelation.

A concluding chapter views NT ethics within the horizon of today. Schnackenburg says that some observers suppose that the ethical instruction of the NT is irrelevant: it addresses a different situation and it does not deal with today's issues. Schnackenburg, however, believes the NT ethic has continuing significance: it understands humanity from the perspective of faith; it understands the world as creation of God; it understands the community, the church, as the locus of Christian living. According to Schnackenburg the NT is concerned with the salvation of all human beings; it calls the church to service in the larger social community.

Along with his commentaries and his work on ethics, Schnackenburg devoted much attention to the life and teaching of Jesus. His most important contribution in this area is his book, *The Person of Jesus in the Mirror of the Four Evangelists.*[39] In this book he presents Jesus according to the faith of the evangelists.

> My book, which has grown out of long years of research and reflection, is intended to be a stimulus to renewed consideration of the basic questions. It seeks to be of service to believing Christians who today have been made insecure by scientific research and critical discussion, so that they may hold fast to faith in the person of Jesus Christ as the bringer of salvation and Savior of the world.[40]

In the introduction Schnackenburg acknowledges that much can be known about the historical Jesus, but he insists that this sort of knowledge is not adequate for faith. Faith can be informed, according to him, by reflection on the view of Jesus presented by the christologies of the individual evangelists.

Schnackenburg believes the Christology of Mark is disclosed in the use of titles. "Son of God" is a title indicating the nearness of Jesus to God but, according to Schnackenburg, it does not refer to Jesus' divine nature.

> Ultimately his [Mark's] Christology is oriented toward the "Son of God," who at the same time reveals and conceals himself in the ministry of Jesus, and toward the "Son of Man" who goes his way through suffering and death to the resurrection and will one day prove to be the one coming in power and glory. The full confession is possible only in death (15:39) or after the resurrection (9:9).[41]

The high point of the Gospel of Matthew, according to Schnackenburg, is the confession at Caesarea Philippi (16:13-20). Here Jesus is presented as Messiah and Son of God. Matthew also used "Son of Man" in referring, according to Schnackenburg, to the future, apocalyptic role of Jesus. Matthew views Jesus as fulfiller of OT prophecy and as a moral teacher like Moses. Luke, according to Schnackenburg, presents Jesus as Savior, Messiah, and Lord: the proclaimer of good news to the poor, to sinners and to Gentiles. "From the standpoint of the Lukan picture of Christ, the prospect of the Parousia also gains importance: the resurrected Lord exalted to God will one day come, in spite of his noticeable delay in the age of the church, in order to bring to final fulfillment the work of salvation begun by him."[42] Regarding the Fourth Gospel, Schnackenburg writes: "One must regard the Gospel of John as a Gospel writing that combines history and kerygma, historical reporting and believing interpretation. What is special is the christological view, which concentrates everything into one question: Who is the one speaking here and doing signs?"[43] The distinctive feature of John's Christology, according to Schnackenburg, is his presentation of Jesus as the pre-existent, incarnate Logos.

In a final chapter Schnackenburg acknowledges that the four Gospels present Jesus in four forms but argues that they are united in their testimony to Christ. "Jesus Christ is the one sent by God who testifies to God's otherness, his redemptive will, and his unchangeable devotion to humankind; he is the Savior of the world."[44] Besides this major work, Schnackenburg published a number of books about Jesus written for the non-specialist, written to encourage faith.[45]

Related to his research on Jesus is Schnackenburg's book on the kingdom of God, a work that employs historical critical work in the service of biblical theology.[46] After a discussion of the OT and Jewish background he gives primary attention to the kingdom of God in the preaching of Jesus. Jesus announced the imminence of the eschatological rule of God but also believed the kingdom was present in his own deeds.

> Jesus did claim to be the Messias. This claim was sufficiently concealed to avoid misunderstanding, but it was evident enough for those who could understand. He claimed to be the Messias with a purely religious mission that was revealed in his preaching and salvific actions, and at the core of this was the near approach of the reign of God.x[47]

Jesus also emphasized the future kingdom and expressed his relation to it by the title "Son of Man."

> This "Son of Man" is no other that Jesus himself. For the present, in the form of humiliation and to a certain degree in concealment, he is fulfilling his Messianic tasks on earth. But then he will manifest himself to all the world as possessed of kingly dignity and divine power to establish in God's name . . . God's perfect, universal cosmic reign.[48]

In the last part of the book Schnackenburg discusses the understanding of the kingdom in early Christian teaching. Paul, according to Schnackenburg, used "kingdom" to refer exclusively to the future rule of God but viewed Christ as the present ruler over the church.

> One and the same body of Christ that died on the cross and rose to the transfigured life is built up in a new manner in the Church by Christ, the head. It is in a real sense the "body of Christ," the concrete body on earth of Christ, its head in heaven, truly "his" body, belonging to him as the physical body belonged to Jesus on earth and the glorified body of the Risen Christ, indeed "the" body of Christ, which is no second body in addition to the individual body of the transfigured Lord but is "mystically identified" with it.[49]

Schnackenburg published several other works directly concerned with the theology of the NT. A book on the current state of the discipline, originally published in French, affirms both the possibility and legitimacy of NT theology.[50] In this book he reviews the major representatives: the history of religion school, the advocates of salvation history, and the devotees of existentialist theology. He then turns to the main sections of the NT: the kerygma of the early church, the theology of the Gospels, the theology of Paul, and the theology of John. This discussion is carried further in lectures Schnackenburg presented at the University of Notre Dame in 1965.[51] Collections of various essays and lectures on theological themes have also been published.[52] Schnackenburg also wrote monographs on theological topics: on Paul's understanding of baptism, on the NT concept of the church, and on the meaning of faith in the NT.[53]

In sum, Rudolf Schnackenburg demonstrates the dramatic advance of Roman Catholic NT research. He affirms the use of historical-critical method. He accepts the priority of Mark and adopts the 2DH. In his use of critical method and in his exegetical practice his concern is primarily with the theological understanding of the NT texts. Theological interpretation, according to Schnackenburg, is undergirded by serious reflection on the meaning of revelation and the nature of inspiration. Central to his theological concerns is the life and teaching of Jesus and the understanding of Christology. In this area his conclusions tend to be conservative; for example, he believes that the historical Jesus used the title "Son of Man" as a self-designation.

The work of Rudolf Schnackenburg reflects some particular Roman Catholic concerns. He stresses the importance of tradition for both the period before writing and for the later interpretation of Scripture. He insists that the honoring of tradition does not restrict the use of historical method, but in some areas tensions are evident. In observing the limits of the historical method Schnackenburg detects an inordinate concern with the literal meaning of texts, which misses the deeper meaning (*sensus plenior*) that God intends. Although this fuller meaning is thought to be visible from the perspective of faith, its relation to the literal meaning will remain a concern for subsequent Catholic exegetes. Schnackenburg has special interest in texts that present the importance of the church—texts like Matt 16:13-20 that affirm the primacy of Peter. He recognizes that interpretation without presuppositions is impossible. Although some of his presuppositions may seem arbitrary, this Catholic exegete does not hide, or pretend not to have, presuppositions—a commendable attitude.

American Examples: Brown and Meier

Raymond E. Brown (1928–1998)

A perceptive reviewer has remarked, "The era ushered in by *Divino Afflante Spiritu* became the wind beneath the wings of Fr. Raymond Brown."[54] Brown was born in New York City, but moved with his parents to Florida in 1944.[55] He studied at St. Charles College in Maryland (1945–46), and held several degrees from various colleges and universities including the Catholic University of America (MA 1949), St. Mary's Seminary in Baltimore (STD 1955), Johns Hopkins (PhD 1958). Brown was ordained to the priesthood in 1953 and became a member of the Society of St. Sulpice in 1955. He taught at St. Charles College and St. Mary's Seminary before accepting a joint appointment at Woodstock College and Union Theological Seminary in New York. When Woodstock closed in 1974, Brown accepted a fulltime position at Union, where he remained until retirement in 1990.

Brown's scholarship has been widely recognized. He was the first person to serve as president of all three major scholarly societies: the SBL, the Catholic Biblical Association (CBA), and the SNTS. Brown attended Vatican II as advisor to the archbishop of St. Augustine, Florida. He was appointed twice to the Pontifical Biblical Commission (1972–1978; 1996 to his death). Brown participated in the Catholic-Lutheran Dialogue (1965–73). He was awarded more than thirty honorary degrees. About him, Joseph Fitzmyer wrote, "Brown's absolute dedication to the study of the written Word of God will never be forgotten."[56] In spite of this dedication Brown was bitterly attacked by conservative Catholics. After retirement he lived and worked at St. Patrick's Seminary in Menlo Park, California, until a heart attack claimed his life in 1998.

"The singular achievements of this remarkable person are unparalleled by any Catholic biblical scholar in the twentieth century."[57]

In view of the extent of Brown's publications (over twenty-five major works and more the fifteen smaller books), attention must be limited to his works that are most important for NT research.[58]

EARLY WORK AND HERMENEUTICS

Brown's dissertation at St. Mary's was *The* Sensus Plenior *of Sacred Scripture*.[59] In this work he investigates a hermeneutic that goes all the way back to the patristic writers: the view that Scripture has more than one, literal, meaning.

> *The* sensus plenior *is that additional, deeper meaning, intended by God but not clearly intended by the human author, which is seen to exist in the words of a biblical text (or group of texts, or even a whole book) when they are studied in the light of further revelation or development in the understanding of revelation."*[60]

Brown answers objections, for example, the charge that the *sensus plenior* goes beyond the meaning of Scripture. He replies that God is the ultimate author of Scripture, including revelation that the human writer does not fully comprehend. However, Brown insists that the fuller sense cannot contradict the literal. He says that "God must have willed that the fuller sense be contained in the literal sense. . . . Thus one is not permitted to indiscriminately use the *sensus plenior* to hang new doctrine upon."[61]

HISTORICAL-CRITICAL RESEARCH

Brown's historical-critical work is exemplified by his *An Introduction to the New Testament*.[62] In the foreword he says that the book is not written for scholars. However, the casual reader who picks up this eight-hundred-page tome will not find it easy going. Actually Brown seems to assume the use of the book as a text. He supplies summary material in tables and boxes, and at the end of chapters a section on "Issues and Problems for Reflection," and relevant bibliographies. He begins with a presentation on preliminaries. In discussing the way to read the NT, Brown surveys various methods, notably the historical-critical approach. He also notes special problems raised by varying views of revelation and inspiration. In contrast to those who find revelation in every word of Scripture, Brown sympathizes with those who accept inspiration but "do not think that God's role as an author removed human limitations."[63] The reader of Scripture, according to Brown, is not only concerned with what the NT books meant, but also with what they mean. This section on preliminaries also includes a discussion of the text of the NT and a review of its political, social, religious and philosophical backgrounds.

Part Two of Brown's *Introduction* deals with the Gospels. In regard to the Synoptic problem, he adopts the 2DH. Brown says that "*the existence of Q (without many of the added hypotheses) remains the best way of explaining the agreements between Matt and Luke in material they did not borrow from Mark.*"[64] He summarizes the content and message of Mark. Concerning the critical problems, Brown notes the tradition of Papias concerning Mark and Peter in Rome and concludes that "ancient traditions often have elements of truth in a garbled form."[65] Brown dates Mark in the late 60s or early 70s. Matthew, according to Brown, used Mark and Q as major sources; Matthew's unique material is from other written and oral tradition. Regarding the author, Brown says that "it is best to accept the common position that *canonical Matt was originally written in Greek by a noneyewitness whose name is unknown to us and who depended on sources like Mark and Q.*"[66] In regard to Luke, Brown observes that over one-third of the material is peculiar to that Gospel. Brown also includes his discussion of Acts in this section. "Therefore, whatever history Acts preserves," says Brown, "is put to the service of theology and pastoral preaching."[67] He concludes that it is not impossible for Acts to have been written by a traveling companion of Paul, and that there is no reason why that person should have been anyone else than Luke. Brown concludes this section with his introduction to the Fourth Gospel, a topic that can be better treated in connection with his extensive research on the Johannine literature.

Part III of Brown's *Introduction* turns to the Pauline letters. An introductory section deals with general issues in Paul's life and thought. For the study of these issues, says Brown, the Pauline letters are the primary source, supplemented by a cautious use of Acts. Brown recounts Paul's life as persecutor, his conversion, his missionary activity, his imprisonment and trip to Rome. As to theology, Brown detects questions that defy easy answers. Brown, in appreciation of Paul, depicts him in the setting of the grandeur of ancient Ephesus. "Yet here was a Jew with a knapsack on his back who hoped to challenge all that in the name of a crucified criminal before whom, he proclaimed, every knee in heaven, on earth, and under the earth had to bend."[68]

Brown proceeds to investigate the letters according to the majority understanding of their chronological order. The earliest is 1 Thessalonians, written about 50–51 from Corinth. Galatians, probably written from Ephesus around 54 or 55, counters the claim of Judaizers (probably from Jerusalem) who are requiring the circumcision of Gentile converts in Galatia. Brown favors the North Galatian hypothesis. In regard to Philippians, he believes it to be a unity (not a composite letter) written from an Ephesian imprisonment. Philemon was also written from this imprisonment. Before his move to Ephesus, Paul had worked in Corinth (abut 50/51–52). From Ephesus, according to Brown, Paul wrote "Letter A" to the Corinthians—a letter that has been lost. Later Paul wrote 1 Corinthians ("Letter B")—a unity that responds to opponents, whom Brown believes to have been people claiming a superior knowledge that led to libertinism. When Paul learned that this letter did not accomplish its purpose he made a quick trip to Corinth and back, the so-called "painful visit." The visit, according to Brown, made the situation even worse, so that Paul responded with the letter of "many tears" (2 Cor 2:4)— "Letter C"; Brown believes this letter was lost. Paul left Ephesus, finally met Titus in Macedonia, and wrote "Letter D" (2 Corinthians). Brown considers 2 Corinthians to be a unity; the opponents addressed in 2 Cor 10–13, he believes, have recently arrived. Romans was written from Corinth in about 57/58. In this letter Paul, according to Brown, is preparing himself for his upcoming encounter with Jewish Christians in Jerusalem and clarifying his gospel for the Christians at Rome to enlist their support of his mission to the west.

Next Brown presents chapters on the pseudonymous or Deutero-pauline letters. He insists that pseudonymous documents were not fraudulent but were written in the name of an apostle with the sense of the authority of that apostle. As to 2 Thessalonians, Brown is himself unsure about the author, but with the majority he classifies it among the pseudonymous. Brown is also uncertain about the authorship of Colossians, but he believes the argument from theology against authenticity to be weighty. Brown notes that some 80 percent of modern scholars do not accept Ephesians as authentic. "*A plausible theory, then, would be that on the basis of the undisputed Pauline letters and especially Col (which had been composed in the school earlier) someone in the Ephesian school of Paul's disciples produced Eph as an encouraging portrayal of aspects of Pauline thought.*"[69] Brown believes that all three of the Pastoral Epistles were written by the same author, who probably was not Paul. Brown says that "*about 80 to 90 percent of modern scholars would agree that the Pastorals were written after Paul's lifetime, and of those the majority would accept the period between 80 and 100 as the most plausible context for the composition.*"[70]

The final part of Brown's *Introduction* deals with other NT writings. He believes that Hebrews is a written sermon with an epistolary ending. The author was probably "a Jewish Christian with a good Hellenistic education and some knowledge of Greek philosophical categories."[71] In regard to 1 Peter,

Brown notes strong arguments against authenticity, but remains uncertain; if authentic it would have been written from Rome, 60–63, if pseudonymous, 70–90. Brown believes the high quality of the Greek argues against the authenticity of James. The authorship of Jude remains uncertain, but 2 Peter, according to Brown, is clearly pseudonymous. Brown sees Revelation in the context of apocalyptic literature. It was written, he thinks, by an otherwise unknown person named "John"—an individual not to be identified with the Johannine school that produced the Fourth Gospel. Brown dates Revelation during the reign of Domitian.

Brown's *Introduction* includes two useful appendices: "The Historical Jesus" and "Jewish and Christian Writings Pertinent to the NT." All in all, Brown's book is a monumental accomplishment, carefully investigating virtually every critical issue from a moderate perspective. A special feature of Brown's *Introduction* is the attention he gives to the message and theology of the NT documents.

EXEGETICAL WORK

Raymond Brown's exegetical work is illustrated by his commentaries on the Johannine Literature and his massive studies of the birth and death of the Messiah. In the foreword to his *The Community of the Beloved Disciple*, Brown recalls his first seminar paper at Johns Hopkins on the Johannine Gospel and Epistles: "Little did I realize then that I was beginning a quarter-century love affair with the most adventuresome body of literature in the New Testament."[72] Brown's two-volume commentary on the Fourth Gospel was published in 1966 and 1970. At the time of his death he was working on a revised edition. The introduction was virtually complete and has been published, providing the reader with Brown's final view.[73]

The new *Introduction* begins with an overview of Johannine studies. Brown notes the problems surrounding the question of the Gospel's composition: differences of style, breaks and inconsistencies, material out of place. Brown's own view about the development of the tradition and composition of the Gospel involves three stages. In the first, a disciple (who became known as the Beloved Disciple) witnessed the ministry of Jesus; he was not one of the Twelve (as Brown had suggested in the first edition of his commentary) but an unnamed disciple. In the second stage, which lasted for some decades, Jesus was proclaimed in the community; the Beloved Disciple played a major role; this was a period of oral tradition, but some writing may have been undertaken toward the end of this stage. The third stage had two aspects: (a) the writing of the bulk of the Gospel by the Evangelist—not the Beloved Disciple, but a member of the community of the Beloved Disciple; (b) the work of the Redactor (not the Evangelist) who added the prologue (1:1-18) and the epilogue (21:1-25).[74]

Brown does not believe John is dependent on the Synoptic Gospels. "John drew on an independent tradition about Jesus, similar to traditions that underlie the Synoptics."[75] All the evangelists were theologians, but John, according to Brown, was the theologian *par excellence*. "[A]lthough I think that the Fourth Gospel reflects historical memories of Jesus, the greater extent of the theological reshaping of those memories makes Johannine material harder to use in the quest for the historical Jesus than most Synoptic material."[76] Brown investigates influences on the religious thought of the Fourth Gospel. He rejects the notion that Gnosticism played a significant role. The Hellenistic influence on the Fourth Gospel, according to Brown, is largely by way of Hellenistic Judaism. John was also influenced by traditional Judaism, seen, for example, in the use of OT themes. Brown acknowledges that the Fourth Gospel engages in apologetics, especially against the "Jews" who refused to believe in Jesus. John's polemic against the "Jews" has its meaning in the context of readers of the Gospel who had been expelled from the synagogue. "Regarding the Bible as sacred does not mean that everything described therein is laudable."[77] Brown also believes that the Fourth Gospel included apologetics against Christians of inadequate faith. The main purpose of the Gospel, however, was to encourage believing Christians. "Thus John's primary purpose of deepening the faith of believers has a secondary goal of thereby bringing others to make an act of faith."[78]

Regarding the author, date, and place, Brown argues that the Evangelist, the principal writer, was a member of the Johannine community. The Redactor, another member of the community, added material and produced the final edition. As to the place of composition, Brown writes: ". . . in my judgment the Ephesus region fits the internal evidence of John best of all the proposals, and is the only site that has ancient attestation."[79] He thinks the probable date of composition and redaction was 90–110.

Theological issues Brown discusses include ecclesiology, sacramentalism, and eschatology. In regard to the last, he thinks John presents both a realized and a future eschatology. Brown gives attention to Christology, but he insists that "Johannine Christology never replaces theology."[80] According to Brown, the Wisdom motifs from the OT and Jewish literature provide the background for understanding John's Christology. He writes that "the Wisdom Literature offers better parallels for the Johannine picture of Jesus than do the later Gnostic,

Mandaean, or Hermetic passages sometimes suggested."[81] John, according to Brown, stresses the historical, incarnate Wisdom.

The massive shape of Brown's commentary on the Fourth Gospel means that only a few samples of his exegetical work can be presented. The format is that of the Anchor Bible: first an English translation is printed, and this is followed by notes (attending to words and phrases, verse by verse), general comments and detailed comments.

Brown titles the prologue (1:18) "The Introductory Hymn." A few examples of his notes are illustrative. In v. 1 he discusses the phrase *was God*. He objects to the use of "divine" and affirms the translation, "the Word was God." In v. 11 Brown offers a note on *To his own*. Since the neuter is used, Brown takes the phrase to mean "to his own home," that is, the promised land or Jerusalem. The phrase *his own people* (in the same verse) is masculine and means the people of Israel. In v. 14 the Greek term translated *only Son* means "of a single kind"; Brown says there is little justification for the translation "only begotten." In his general comment, Brown discusses the relation of the Prologue to the rest of the Gospel. He believes it was an independent poem, composed in Johannine circles and added to the Gospel. In the detailed comments he discusses the content of the hymn as ordered into four strophes. The first discusses the Word with God and stresses what the Word does. The second presents the role of the Word in creation. The third describes the Word in the world; Brown believes these verses (10-12) already assume the action of the Incarnate One. The fourth strophe presents the community's share in the Word become flesh. In becoming flesh, says Brown, the Word has not ceased to be God.

Following the Prologue, the next main section of the Fourth Gospel is "The Book of Signs." Brown's exegesis of this section begins with "The First Sign in Cana of Galilee—Changing the Water to Wine" (2:1-11). His notes consider, among others, the following terms and phrases. In v. 14, *woman* is an expression Brown believes does not express rebuke or lack of affection, although it is a peculiar usage for a son addressing his mother. He thinks the *six stone water jars* (v. 6) represent the levitical laws of ritual impurity. In his comments (there is no distinction here between general and detailed), Brown observes that of the seven signs in the Fourth Gospel only this one has no parallel in the Synoptics. The background of the story, he insists, is not to be found in the Dionysus festival but in the miraculous gifts of oil by Elijah and Elisha (1 Kgs 17:8-16; 2 Kgs 4:1-7). Brown believes that beneath the sign there is a basic narrative that reflects the customs of the time: the wine supply was dependent on the gifts of the guests; the mother's suggestion may imply that Jesus and his poor disciples have not provided the gift. Brown reflects on theological motifs hidden in the account. For example, the wedding reflects the symbolism of the messianic days, apparent in the word of the headwaiter (NRSV: "steward"): "Everyone serves the good wine first, and then the inferior wine after the guests have become drunk. But you have kept the good wine until now" (John 2:10).

The last and greatest sign is presented in 11:1-44, "Jesus Gives Men Life—the Story of Lazarus." In the notes Brown discusses the phrase *fallen asleep* (v. 12). Although this expression is widely used in Hebrew and Greek as a euphemism for death, the disciples misunderstand and take the remark literally. The reference to *four days* in v. 17 indicates, according to Brown, that Lazarus was truly dead; the rabbis held the opinion that after death the soul hovered around the corpse for three days. The phrase in v. 33, *shuddered, moved with the deepest emotions* (NRSV: "he was greatly disturbed in spirit and deeply moved") has been a persistent problem for exegetes. The word Brown translates "shuddered" usually means to express anger, but it is not clear where Jesus' anger was directed. In his general comments Brown rejects the view that this narrative is a fictional composition. "From the contents of the Johannine account, then, there is no conclusive reason for assuming that the skeleton of the story does not stem from early tradition about Jesus."[82] The distinctive feature of the Johannine account, according to Brown, is the view that the raising of Lazarus was the cause of the death of Jesus (11:45-53). In the detailed comments Brown investigates various sections of the narrative. Verses 17-27 present Martha greeting Jesus. She makes exalted statements about Jesus as Lord, but she does not really understand. She displays knowledge of the Jewish doctrine of the resurrection, but Johannine eschatology stresses the conquest of death by the present reality of Christ. In discussing Mary's meeting with Jesus (vv. 28-33) Brown suggests that the anger Jesus expresses is directed at Satan, the ruler of the realm of death. The prayer Jesus offers at the tomb (11:41-42) expresses a typical Johannine theme: Jesus does nothing on his own; he does only the will of the Father. Brown makes a final comment on this last sign: "What is crucial is that Jesus has given (physical) life as a sign of his power to give eternal life on this earth (realized eschatology) and as a promise that on the last day he will raise the dead (final eschatology)."[83]

Raymond Brown also wrote an extensive (over 700-page) commentary on the Johannine Epistles.[84] The introduction alone is almost 150 pages. In this section Brown discusses problems of authorship. He believes all three Epistles were written by the same author, who was not the writer of the Fourth Gospel. As to the order of writing, Brown thinks the Epistles were written in the canonical order (1, 2, and 3 John) and all three were written later than the

Gospel of John. He offers a theory of the composition of this literature, more fully explained in his *The Community of the Beloved Disciple*, described below. The date of 1 John, Brown thinks, is around 100. The author writes in a community that has house churches within and nearby, probably Ephesus.

The Prologue to 1 John (1:1-4) provides a sample of Brown's exegesis. In the main he follows the same format and method as in his commentary on the Fourth Gospel. His notes on this section are extensive. For v. 1, *from the beginning,* he finds several possible backgrounds, for example, the usage in Gen 1:1 or the incarnation as beginning. Brown concludes that a reference to the beginning of the ministry of Jesus is most likely. In his comments he observes that this prologue echoes that of the Gospel of John. Brown says that "the Prologue sets the tone for I John in terms of a polemically exclusive claim, namely, that the proclamation about Jesus made by the author represents the authentic Gospel stemming from a true witness to Jesus, and those who refuse to accept it have communion with neither Father nor Son."[85] The "we" of the prologue, Brown believes, represents the Johannine school, loyal to the Beloved Disciple.[86]

Related to Brown's commentaries and important for his understanding of the Johannine literature is his book, *The Community of the Beloved Disciple*,[87] in which he traces the phases of development of the Johannine community. The first includes the time before the writing of the Fourth Gospel. In this phase the original group, made up of Jews who had accepted Jesus as the Messiah, was formed under the leadership of the Beloved Disciple. The group developed a high Christology, but they were joined by a second group that held an even higher Christology. Brown believes this latter group included converts from the Samaritans and had affinity with the Hellenists of Acts 6. Phase Two is the time of the writing of the Gospel. Brown believes it possible to identify seven groups in this period: (1) the nonbelievers (these include those designated as "the world"); (2) the "Jews"; (3) adherents of John the Baptist; (4) crypto-Christians (Christian Jews remaining in the synagogue); (5) Jewish Christians of inadequate faith; (6) Christians of the apostolic faith (like Peter, loyal to Jesus but different from the Johannine group, followers of the Beloved Disciple); (7) the Johannine Community (the group of the Beloved Disciple and the Presbyter of the Johannine letters). Phase three is the time when the Epistles were written—the period of Johannine internal struggles. Brown believes all three letters were written (ca. 100) by the Elder, who had become the leader of the Johannine School. In this period, according to Brown, a schism occurred. A group of secessionists went out of the Johannine community. Brown says that "the secessionists believed that the *human existence of Jesus, while real, was not salvifically significant.*[88] They also believed, according to Brown, that ethical behavior was not important for salvation and that realized eschatology supported their claim to a special position. Phase Four is the time of Johannine dissolution: the Johannine group merged into what Brown calls the "Great Church"; the secessionists merged into Gnosticism.[89]

Brown's monumental exegetical achievement is seen in his two massive works on the birth and death of the messiah. In the foreword to *The Birth of the Messiah* he states his purpose: "I am primarily interested in the role these infancy narratives had in the early Christian understanding of Jesus. . . . It is the central contention of this volume that the infancy narratives are worthy vehicles of the Gospel message; indeed, each is the essential Gospel story in miniature."[90]

Brown expresses his sensitivity in interpreting the tradition about Mary. "As a Roman Catholic myself," he says, "I share their faith and their devotion; but it is my firm contention that one should not attempt to read Marian sensibilities and issues back into the New Testament. . . . I see no reason why a Catholic's understanding of what Matthew and Luke meant in their infancy narratives should be different from a Protestant's."[91]

In his introduction, Brown observes that the infancy narratives are concerned to answer a christological question: How is Jesus understood as Son of God in relation to his birth? Brown notes that the accounts in Matthew and Luke agree at several points, but there are major differences. He concludes that "it is unlikely that either account is completely historical."[92] Brown begins with an investigation of the Matthean Infancy Narrative. He supports "the thesis that Matthew composed the infancy narrative as an integral part of his Gospel plan."[93] In presenting his exegesis Brown follows the format of his other commentaries: Translation, Notes, Comment.

In regard to the genealogy (1:1–17), Brown's note on Matt 1:5 deals with the phrase *Salmon was the father of Boaz by Rahab*; Brown points out that Rahab lived at the time of the conquest, two centuries before Boaz. Regarding 1:16, *Jacob was the father of Joseph, the husband of Mary; of her was begotten Jesus, called the Christ*, Brown reviews textual variants including the reading of the Sinaitic Syriac: *Jacob was the father of Joseph, and Joseph, to whom the virgin Mary was betrothed, was the father of Jesus, called Christ*. In his commentary Brown says that Matthew's purpose was to present Jesus as Son of David, son of Abraham. Brown wonders why four women were included in the genealogy: Tamar, Rahab, Ruth, and (Bathsheba) the wife of Uriah. He believes their inclusion has two features: there is something unusual about their relation to their partners, and they play an important role in God's plan. Brown compares Matthew's genealogy with that of Luke. He notes that in the sections where the two overlap, Luke has fifty-six names whereas Matthew has only forty-one. Both genealogies cannot be historically correct. Brown says that "Matthew's intention [is] to show that Jesus is the Davidic Messiah, and Luke's intention [is] to show that Jesus is the Son of God."[94] "There is not the slightest indication in the accounts of the ministry of Jesus," writes Brown, "that his family was of ancestral nobility or royalty."[95]

The most important section of Matthew's birth narrative is 1:18–25 on "The Conception of Jesus." Brown's note on v. 18 deals with *betrothed*. He points out that betrothal involved two stages: the exchange of consent before witnesses; the taking of the bride to the groom's family home. In the narrative in Matthew, Mary and Joseph are between the two stages. In his comment Brown says that Matthew is concerned with who Jesus is: he is son of David, but more important, he is conceived as Son of God. Brown insists that the begetting of Jesus was not sexual but represents the agency of God's creative power. In regard to the quotation of Isa 7:14 in v. 23, the use of the term *alma* ("young woman") in the Hebrew text does not predict the virgin birth of a future messiah but a child from David's line, to be born in Isaiah's time. The LXX, which uses the term *parthenos* ("virgin"), refers to a woman who is now a virgin but will in the future conceive. Nothing in the Hebrew or Greek, says Brown, is concerned with the manner of conception. Brown points out that virginal conception is found in both Matthew and Luke; he believes it belongs to the pre-Gospel tradition.

Other features of Brown's exegesis of the Matthean birth narrative can be viewed in summary. He believes the magi from the east symbolize Gentiles who receive the message the Jewish leaders reject. Matthew's account is supported by Scripture: the importance of Bethlehem is reflected in Mic 5:2, the trip to Egypt fulfills Hos 11:1, and the slaughter of infants recalls Pharaoh's execution of male infants. Brown points out that a flight to Egypt is not mentioned in the accounts of the ministry of Jesus and that it contradicts Luke's narrative of Mary and Joseph's return to Nazareth. He concludes:

> The dramatis personae may be exotically costumed as Eastern potentates and as a Jewish king and priests, and for that reason they are not easily forgotten. But beneath the robes one can recognize the believers of Matthew's time and their opponents. And, indeed, a perceptive reader may even recognize some of the drama of the Christian proclamation and its fate in all times.[96]

Turning to the Lukan Infancy Narrative, Brown deals with a longer text. Material about the annunciation and birth of John the Baptist will not be not reviewed here. The most important section of Luke's account considers "The Annunciation and Birth of Jesus" (1:26-38). In his comment on this section Brown devotes over ten pages to "virginal conception."[97] He argues against the theory that the virginal conception was added to an earlier account. He discusses the logic of Mary's question, "How can this be?" (1:34). Brown believes the question makes good sense, since the following verse answers it: it explains how the child was to be conceived. Luke's meaning, according to Brown, is that Jesus is Son of God by means of his virginal conception. Brown argues that conception by the Holy Spirit is not sexual but a reflection of creation, which was accompanied by the overshadowing of the Spirit (Gen 1:2).

Other features of Luke's account can be reviewed in summary fashion. In regard to the canticles that decorate Luke's narrative, Brown believes they were pre-Christian, composed by the Jewish Christian *anawim* (the "Poor Ones") and inserted into Luke's narrative. The account of the birth and naming of Jesus (2:1-21) includes the census, which Brown regards as unhistorical; there was no worldwide census under Augustus, and the census under Quirinius took place ten years after the death of Herod. The annunciation to the shepherds in the region of Bethlehem, Brown believes, is reminiscent of the city of David, the shepherd king. Brown points out that the announcement of the angel of the Lord presents the child in kerygmatic terms: Savior, Messiah, Lord. Regarding the account of the boy Jesus in the temple (2:41-52), Brown's note on v. 50, *they did not understand*, reviews various attempts to explain why the parents, who had witnessed miracles, did not understand. Brown solves the problem by taking the text literally: Mary and Joseph did not understand what Jesus meant when he said: "Did you not know that I must be in my Father's house?" The question, according to Brown, goes beyond the temple to an emphasis on Jesus' vocation. Mary, though she did not fully understand, "treasured all these things in her heart."

Brown's *Birth of the Messiah* contains nine appendices. Two examples can illustrate these additions. In regard to the "Birth at Bethlehem," Brown asks if it is historical. Although both Matthew and Luke agree, Brown notes problems. There is no mention of Bethlehem in the later account of the life of Jesus in the Gospels, and there is considerable evidence that Nazareth was his home town. Brown's appendix on the "Virginal Conception" updates the research of his earlier book, *The Virginal Conception and Bodily Resurrection of Jesus*.[98] In the earlier book he expressed considerable skepticism. "In short, the presence of the virginal conception in the infancy narratives of two Gospels carries no absolute guarantee of historicity."[99] Also in the earlier book Brown rejects the belief that the sinlessness of divine sonship depends on supernatural conception. Brown says that "it is difficult to argue that in order to be free from original sin Jesus had to be conceived of a virgin."[100] In the appendix to the *Birth of the Messiah*, Brown has moved to the right. He does acknowledge that the main concern of Matthew and Luke was not history but theology. However, Brown does not believe that the silence of the rest of the NT or the view that the virginal conception compromises the humanity of Jesus are major impediments to the doctrine. He concludes: "I think that it is easier to explain the NT evidence by positing historical basis than by positing pure theological creation."[101] The virginal conception is "an extraordinary action of God's creative power."[102]

Brown's *Death of the Messiah* is even more formidable—interpreting texts from all four Gospels, presented in two hefty volumes with a total of 1,313 pages.[103] "In sum," says Brown, "from every point of view the passion is the central narrative in the Christian story."[104] He also says in the preface that the research and writing took ten years and that "the time consumed has been the most enriching of my life."[105] In his introduction Brown points out that his purpose is "to explain in detail what the evangelists intended and conveyed to their audiences by their narratives of the passion and death of Jesus."[106] The introduction also discusses the role of history, noting that the evangelists were not eyewitnesses but heirs of a tradition. In regard to the role of theology, Brown observes that each evangelist had his own perspective.

In this commentary Brown presents the material as a drama. He treats the material from all four Gospels in parallel, prefacing each major section with a bibliography. In the format of the exegetical sections Brown first presents his own translation (intentionally literal), followed by comments (discussion of what the evangelists intended to say), and analysis (questions of historicity, composition, sources; some sections do not include the analysis). The sort of material included in the notes of Brown's earlier commentaries is found in the abundant footnotes.

In Act I, "Jesus Prays and Is Arrested in Gethsemane," Scene One is entitled "Jesus Goes to the Site and Prays There." The "Prayer in Gethsemane" (Part Two) is presented in Mark 14:35-36; Matt 26:39; Luke 22:41-42. On the use of *abba* (only in Mark), Brown agrees with scholars who find no evidence for the use of this term as address to God in pre-Christian or first-century Judaism. He points out that Jesus did not say "Abba, ho Pater," that is, he did not address God as Father in two languages. Since the exact phrase is used in Gal 4:6 and Rom 8:15, Brown believes the Pauline usage reflects a Hellenistic Christian prayer formula.

Act II presents "Jesus before the Jewish Authorities." In an introduction to this section Brown deals with the background of the Jewish trial. This introduction includes a discussion of "A Sanhedrin's Competence to Condemn to Death and Execute." Brown concludes that Jews had the right in some religious cases, but in others they handed the person over to Rome. In this same introduction Brown includes a discussion of "Responsibility and/or Guilt for the Death of Jesus"—an issue that leads him into a discussion of anti-Judaism in the passion narrative. Mark depicts the Jewish leaders handing Jesus over to Pilate, who yields to the crowd, but Brown detects no emphatic anti-Judaism. Matthew (27:25), on the other hand, presents the Jewish people and their descendants as guilty; Pilate washes his hands. Luke reduces the opposition of the Jews, noting that some of the crowd followed and supported Jesus. Throughout the Gospel of John, the "Jews" are depicted as opposing Jesus, but this reflects a later time when the Johannine community had been expelled from the synagogue. Brown believes the issue should be discussed in terms of "responsibility," not "guilt." He also points out that it was a violent time. Those who opposed Jesus supposed they were doing God's will; the dispute was Jews against Jews, not Jews against a Christian Jesus.

Scene One of Act II includes two sections on the proceedings of the Sanhedrin. The second considers "Questions about the Messiah, the Son of God" (Mark 14:60-61; Matt 26:62-63; Luke 22:67-70a). In Brown's comments he indicates that the main issue of the texts is the question by the high priest, "Are you the Messiah, the Son of the Blessed One?" Brown believes that Mark's use of the surrogate, "Son of the Blessed," indicates the Jewish context of the question. Matthew changes the expression to "Son of God." In the analysis section Brown states the crucial question as: Was Jesus called Messiah before his resurrection, and if so, by whom? He reviews various theories and concludes that it is likely that Jesus' opponents believed he or his followers claimed that he was Messiah. Brown also believes it is very likely that during his lifetime some of Jesus' followers thought or confessed him to be Messiah. Jesus was ambivalent, according to Brown, because he had his own understanding of the Messiah's role and because he believed the role of the Messiah was in God's hands. In regard to the title "Son of God," Brown concludes: ". . . there is reason in the Gospels, read perceptively, to think that unlike 'the Messiah,' the title 'the Son of God' was *not* applied to Jesus in his lifetime by his followers or, *a fortiori*, by himself."[107]

Act III deals with the most decisive part of the proceedings: "Jesus before Pilate, the Roman Governor." Part One of the Roman trial is the "Initial Questioning by Pilate" (Mark 15:2-5; Matt 27:11-14; Luke 23:2-5; John

18:28b-38a). As to historicity, Brown's comment observes that the evangelists are not presenting legal reports or eyewitness accounts but, he believes, they do give accounts that preserve a historical kernel: Pilate sentenced Jesus on the charge of being king of the Jews. Brown thinks that the question, "are you the king of the Jews?" and the answer: "You say so" are the earliest elements of the tradition. Brown notes that Luke adds, "He stirs up the people by teaching throughout all Judea, from Galilee where he began even to this place"—words that provide the reason for sending Jesus to Herod. John's account expands even more, with episodes that occur inside and out of the Praetorium. John also notes that the Jews did not enter in order to avoid impurity that would have prevented them from observing the Passover, implying, according to Brown, that the Last Supper was not a Passover meal. In his appearance before Pilate, Jesus insists (three times in John 18:36) that his kingdom is not of this world.

In Act IV, Scene One, "Jesus is Crucified and Dies." Part Three presents "Last Events, Death" (Mark 15:33-37; Matt 27:44-50; Luke 23:44-46; John 19:28-30). Brown's comment discusses the darkness at the sixth hour. He thinks the evangelists probably understood this literally, although the apocalyptic Day of the Lord is described as a day of darkness. In regard to Jesus' death cry, "My God, my God, why have you forsaken me?" (Mark 15:34), Brown argues at length for the literal interpretation of the text: Jesus really felt forsaken. Brown also points out that this is the only place in the Gospels where Jesus is described as praying to "God." Brown believes this quotation from Ps 22:1 represents the oldest tradition of the last words of Jesus—a tradition Brown accepts as historically true.

HISTORICAL AND THEOLOGICAL RESEARCH

A select sample of Brown's other works includes his historical studies. His book, *The Churches the Apostles Left Behind,* presents witnesses to the apostolic tradition in the post-apostolic period.[108] The "Pauline heritage in the Pastorals," according to Brown, is concerned with church structure and the pastoral qualities of the officials. Brown believes that the "Pauline heritage in Colossians /Ephesians" responds to doctrinal dangers and promotes a high Christology and ecclesiology. The "Pauline heritage in Luke–Acts," according to Brown, stresses the work of the Spirit in the life of the community. In the "Petrine heritage in 1 Peter" he notes how the Israelite idea of the people of God is taken up and applied to the church of Gentile Christians. Brown discusses the "Heritage of the Beloved Disciple in the Fourth Gospel," namely, a community of people personally attached to Jesus. Ecclesiology in this Gospel, according to Brown, is swallowed up in Christology. Concerning the "Heritage of the

Beloved Disciple in the Epistles of John," Brown notes the appearance of schism. The "Heritage of Jewish/Gentile Christianity in Matthew" affirms, Brown believes, a high respect for authority. He concludes: "Taken collectively, however, these emphases constitute a remarkable lesson about early idealism in regard to Christian community life."[109]

Brown's *An Introduction to New Testament Christology* provides an example of his theological research.[110] The book is concerned with the Christology of Jesus and that of the NT. In the introductory section he points out that Christology is concerned with the nature of Jesus and the role he played in the divine plan. Brown discusses various approaches to the problem and advocates a scholarly, moderate conservatism. Regarding Jesus' Christology, Brown counsel's caution: the accounts presuppose the resurrection; on the one hand, attitudes should be avoided that reject the supernatural at the outset, and on the other, views that compromise the humanity of Jesus should be rejected. As to the knowledge of Jesus, some texts, Brown believes, show that he shared the limits of human knowledge while others suggest that he possessed extraordinary knowledge, for example, foreknowledge. "In summary," says Brown, "it is difficult to decide about Jesus' foreknowledge of his passion, crucifixion, and resurrection. Modern criticism would cast serious doubt on a detailed foreknowledge."[111] In regard to his proclamation of the kingdom of God, Jesus viewed himself as playing a unique role. "Jesus is the eschatological figure through whom God's final salvation breaks through, but his relationship to the one whom Israel calls God is so uniquely close that his followers had to find titles different from the designation that had been used for previous actors in God's plan."[112] In regard to messiahship Brown concludes: "Finally, I would judge it *probable that Jesus never clearly or enthusiastically accepted the title in the sense in which both followers and opponents proposed it for him.*"[113] Jesus, according to Brown, did refer to God as Father and himself as Son, implying a unique relationship.

Brown turns to the christologies of the NT writers. He finds christologies expressed in terms of the resurrection and second coming: Jesus will return as Son of Man, risen and exalted. Other early Christians express christologies in terms of Jesus' public ministry. In these Brown detects a tension between the exalted messiah and the lowly servant. Finally, Brown investigates christologies that focus on the pre-ministry, for example, "conception Christology" and "pre-existence Christology." Brown concludes that the Christology expressed in the Nicene Creed is faithful to the direction of the christologies of the NT. "How impoverished would be our understanding of the revelation in Christ had the earlier ways of speaking about the identity of Jesus been erased in favor of the Nicene formulation!"[114]

In sum, Raymond E. Brown was a NT scholar of exceptional ability. In the quantity and quality of his work he was certainly one of the best of the second half of the twentieth century. Brown was master of all the skills of the discipline: linguistic, grammatical, historical—all in the service of theological understanding. He was the master of a huge quantity of secondary sources, and his own writing is marked by clarity and grace. Brown was not a great innovator; he was heir and conveyor of the critical tradition. In the history of NT research, few have done it better.

JOHN P. MEIER (1942–)

Some scholars are noted for producing one particular book. This is true of John Meier. But what a book!—a work of four giant volumes crammed with meticulous detail, carefully argued, loaded with hundreds of pages of notes. John Meier's *A Marginal Jew* is one of the most important books on the historical Jesus in the history of NT research.

Meier was educated at St. Joseph's Seminary, Dunwoodie, Yonkers, New York (BA 1964), the Gregorian University in Rome (STL 1968), and the Biblical Institute in Rome (Doctorate in Sacred Scripture, 1976); the last two degrees were awarded *summa cum laude*. Meier has held professorships at St. Joseph's Seminary and The Catholic University of America, and is currently Professor of New Testament in the Department of Theology at the University of Notre Dame. He has lectured widely across the country.

EARLY WORK: MATTHEW

Early in his career Meier made an important contribution to research on Matthew that provided a foundation of his monumental work on the historical Jesus. Meier's *Law and History in Matthew's Gospel* is essentially his doctoral dissertation, written in Rome, 1974–75. "The purpose of this thesis is to investigate the meaning of the programmatic statement on the Law in Mt 5:17-20 in the light of the antitheses that follow (5:21-48) and in the larger context of Mt's theology of salvation-history, eschatology and Christology."[115] Meier adopts the 2DH and believes the Gospel of Matthew was written in Greek, toward the end of the first century, possibly in Antioch. In contrast to most scholars who view the author of Matthew as Jewish Christian, Meier writes: "We are inclined to think that it is more probable that the final redactor of Mt was a Gentile Christian."[116] Meier gives attention to the relation of Matthew's community, a church in transition, to the church's Jewish tradition.

"Here, then, more than anywhere else, we can appreciate Mt's theology of salvation-history as a hermeneutical key, the key he uses to preserve yet reinterpret strict Jewish-Christian tradition for his changing community."[117]

Meier believes the staring point for investigating Matthew's history of salvation is to be found, on the one hand, in texts like 10:5-6 that command the disciples to "go nowhere among the Gentiles" and, on the other, in Matt 28:16-20, which commands the disciples to "go . . . and make disciples of all nations." Meier writes: "The great turning point in the schema is the death-resurrection seen as apocalyptic event, the definitive breaking in of the new aeon."[118] Meier proceeds to an analysis of tradition and redaction in Matt 5:17-20. He presents a careful study of each verse and comes to the conclusion that "Mt has done a masterful job of welding together disparate Jewish-Christian material to create a unit that speaks his own mind, makes a rich and profound statement on the Law, addresses the pastoral needs of his church, and introduces the all-important antitheses."[119] Meier takes up the question whether the antitheses (5:31-48) nullify the interpretation he has given to the preceding section and concludes:

> Jesus stated in 5:17-20 that he had an eschatological mission with regard to the Law and the prophets. Despite what is to follow in the antitheses, Jesus warns his disciples not to imagine that his mission involves total destruction of Law and prophets. Rather, his mission is a positive one: to give both Law and prophets their prophetic eschatological fulfillment, a "fulfillment" that "spills over" the top of the old vessel, a completion that transcends the letter (Mt 5:17).[120]

Related to his work on Matthew, Meier later coauthored with Raymond Brown a book on *Antioch and Rome*.[121] Meier wrote the section on Antioch. He describes the history of the Antioch church in three periods. The first generation (40–70) is depicted in Galatians 2 and Acts 11–15. In this period the members of the church took a new name, "Christian." The period also saw disputes among Peter, Paul, and James. The main source for the second generation (70–100) is the Gospel of Matthew, which Meier believes was written in Antioch, about 80 to 90. In this period the church was facing struggles within and opposition from outside. Matthew solved the problem, as Meier had argued in his dissertation, by a theology of salvation history—a theology of the past, present, and future triumph. The third generation was after 100. In that period Ignatius supported a rigid hierarchy, while the *Didache* promoted a more primitive structure. Meier believes the leadership in the early second century struggled to reach a middle position. He concludes that the church at Antioch made an important contribution to the ongoing life of the Christian community.

THE HISTORICAL JESUS

The first volume of Meier's *A Marginal Jew* has the subtitle *The Roots of the Problem and the Person*.[122] In the introduction Meier makes clear what he means by the "historical Jesus": "a scientific construct, a theoretical abstraction that does not and cannot coincide with the full reality of Jesus of Nazareth as he actually lived and worked in Palestine during the 1st century of our era."[123] This sort of study demands rigorous objectivity. "In what follows I will try my best to bracket what I hold by faith and examine only what can be shown to be certain or probable by historical research and logical argumentation."[124] As to the title, *A Marginal Jew*, Meier points out that Jesus was on the margin in many ways: his teaching came into conflict with the main religious teachings of the day and he was executed as a criminal.

Volume One, as the subtitle suggests, is divided into two parts: "The Roots of the Problem," and "The Roots of the Person." In the first part Meier attends to the problems of sources and method. The main source is the four Gospels of the NT. In studying this material Meier identifies three main sources: Mark, Q, and John (which, according to Meier, contains, historical tradition). Turning to the sources outside the NT, Meier notes the paucity of material. "This simply reminds us that Jesus was a marginal Jew leading a marginal movement in a marginal province of a vast Roman Empire."[125] Meier makes a meticulous analysis of the data in Josephus and concludes that the longer reference to Jesus in *Jewish War* is a Christian interpolation and a shorter one in *Jewish Antiquities* is probably authentic. Meier also reviews pagan writers, including Tacitus and Suetonius, and investigates the *agrapha*, which, he believes, contribute almost nothing to the picture of Jesus. Meier is equally skeptical of the apocryphal gospels and documents like the so-called "Secret Gospel of Mark." Concerning the Nag Hammadi texts (NHC), Meier believes they represent second-century compositions that are dependent on the Synoptic Gospels. "Since I think that the Synoptic-like sayings of the *Gospel of Thomas* are in fact dependent on the Synoptic Gospels and that the other sayings stem from 2nd-century Christian gnosticism, the *Gospel of Thomas* will not be used in our quest as an independent source for the historical Jesus."[126] Meier concludes that the search for the historical Jesus is almost wholly dependent on the canonical Gospels, with a few references in the later NT and a small amount of material from Josephus.

Meier believes that the crucial aspect of method in the search for the historical Jesus is the delineation of the criteria of authenticity. He identifies five primary criteria: (1) the criterion of embarrassment (or contradiction), that is, material that was embarrassing or that created difficulty for the church: for instance, the baptism of Jesus by John; (2) the criterion of discontinuity (or dissimilarity), that is, words or deeds of Jesus that cannot be derived either from Judaism or the early church: for example, Jesus' teaching about divorce;[127] (3) the criterion of multiple attestation, that is, material that is found in more than one independent source (Mark, Q, M, or L) or in more than one literary genre (e.g., parable, aphorism, miracle story): for instance, the words of Jesus over the bread and wine at the Last Supper; (4) the criterion of coherence (or consistency or conformity), that is, material that correlates with the database achieved by applying the previous criteria; (5) the criterion of rejection and execution, that is, information about Jesus that is consistent with the historical fact that he met a violent death at the hands of Jewish and Roman officials.

In view of the complexity involved in the quest for the historical Jesus, Meier asks: why bother? He offers four reasons. The quest shows that Christ cannot be reduced to a cipher or symbol; he was a particular person. It also opposes docetism and affirms the humanity of Jesus. The quest also shows the error of domesticating Jesus. Finally, it indicates that Jesus cannot be coopted to serve our programs.

Part Two of the first volume of *A Marginal Jew* probes the "Roots of the Person." Meier investigates the beginnings. The name Jesus is a shortened form of Joshua, which means "YHWH helps," or "May YHWH help." In regard to the birth and lineage of Jesus, Meier notes that the information is found only in two places in the NT and that the accounts are not entirely consistent and are shaped by theological concerns. "A major theological point made by the Infancy Narratives thus becomes clear; what Jesus Christ was fully revealed to be at the resurrection (Son of David, Son of God by the power of the Holy Spirit) he really was from his conception onward."[128] Concerning the place of Jesus' birth, Meier concedes that Matthew and Luke agree on Bethlehem; however, he concludes that this is not a historical fact but a theological affirmation. The virginal conception is mentioned only in Matt 1:18-25 and Luke 1:26-38. Like Brown, Meier contends that virginal conception does not suggest sexual union but the action of the Holy Spirit. As to historicity, Meier says: "Taken by itself, historical-critical research simply does not have the sources and tools available to reach a final decision on the historicity of the virginal conception as narrated by Matthew and Luke."[129] He concludes that during the reign of Herod the Great, around 7–4 BCE, a Jew named Jesus was born, most likely in Nazareth, who during his lifetime was recognized as descendent of David.

Meier turns to an investigation of the interim between the birth of Jesus and the beginning of his public ministry, a period of thirty-two years that are virtually unknown and unknowable. Meier believes Jesus' main language was Aramaic, and that he probably had some knowledge of Hebrew. On the basis of the accounts of Jesus' debates with Scribes and Pharisees, Meier surmises that Jesus could read and interpret Scripture. Jesus, according to Meier, was a woodworker, and as such was situated at the lower end of the middle class. In regard to the immediate family of Jesus, Meier thinks that Joseph probably died before the beginning of Jesus' ministry. Mary, whom Meier estimates to have been about fourteen when Jesus was born, bore at least six other children and lived into the early days of the church.[130] There is no evidence that Jesus was married, and some Jewish leaders, like the prophets, chose celibacy. Meier believes the text "there are eunuchs who have made themselves eunuchs for the sake of the kingdom of heaven" (Matt 19:12) has its setting in the celibate life of Jesus. After carefully analyzing all the data concerning chronology, Meier concludes that Jesus was born about 7 or 6 BCE; he was baptized and began his ministry in 28 (at about the age 33 or 34); he carried out his ministry, which lasted two years and a few months, in Galilee and Jerusalem; he celebrated a farewell meal (not a Passover) with his disciples on Thursday, April 6, and was crucified on Friday, April 7, when he was about 36 years old.

Meier, who cannot resist the lure of alliteration, subtitles his second volume *Mentor, Message, and Miracles*.[131] Part I of this volume deals with John the Baptist whom Meier labels (inappropriately) "Mentor." First Meier discusses "John without Jesus: The Baptist in His Own Rite." The historical existence of the Baptist is confirmed by Josephus, but the infancy stories about John are even more problematic than those about Jesus. Meier believes a few features may be gleaned from the account in Luke: John was the son of a priest who later rejected his filial duty to become an anti-establishment prophet. Meier investigates a first block of material from Q (Matt 3:7-12; Luke 3:7-9, 15-18). In the first part of this material John is presented as "an eschatological prophet tinged with some apocalyptic motifs."[132] In the second he is described as expecting the "stronger one" yet to come. Mark 1:1-8 depicts John in the wilderness proclaiming baptism as a sign of repentance. Meier believes this rite should be understood in relation to the eschatological drama. According to him, "Jesus' being baptized by John is one of the most historically certain events ascertainable by any reconstruction of the historical Jesus."[133] Meier believes this to have been a decisive turning point in the career of Jesus—his decision to dedicate his life to mission. Jesus accepted John's eschatological message and remained, for a time, in John's circle. Meier calls John and Jesus the "eschatological 'odd couple.' "[134]

Meier then turns to Jesus' view of John. Here a second block of material from Q contains three units. According to the first (Matt 11:2-6//Luke 7:19-23), John sends his disciples to Jesus to ask if he is the one to come. Jesus does not answer, but calls attention to events that, according to Meier, reveal that the day of the Lord has started to come. In the second unit (Matt 11:7-11//Luke 7:24-28) Jesus depicts John as prophet and more. The third (Matt 11:16-19//Luke 7:31-35) includes the parable of the children playing in the marketplace. According to Meier the parable depicts John and Jesus: John demands repentance and judgment; Jesus presents the joyous life of the kingdom.

In his conclusion of this first part of volume 2, Meier affirms the significance of John's eschatology for Jesus and the importance of John for understanding Jesus. He says that "almost every topic that remains to be treated in this work on the historical Jesus is somehow touched on in Jesus' sayings about the Baptist."[135] At this point Meier adds an excursus on Q. He accepts the existence of Q but rejects complex theories. Meier believes all Gospel exegetes should begin each morning by reciting a mantra: "Q is a hypothetical document whose exact extension, wording, originating community, strata, and stages of redaction cannot be known."[136]

Part II of Volume 2 is entitled "Message." Here Meier investigates the meaning of the "kingdom of God." In the introduction he observes that the authenticity of the kingdom sayings is confirmed by the criterion of dissimilarity: the phrase "kingdom of God" is rarely used in Judaism and in the NT outside of the Gospels. Meier points out that "kingdom" here means "rule" or "reign"; it does not refer to territory, and eschatology is an important component. In the OT the phrase is rarely used, but God's kingship of Israel is frequently mentioned. The prophets envisaged the restoration of the kingdom, and Daniel depicted the future coming of the kingdom of God. Meier says that "by the time of Jesus, the symbol of God's kingship/kingdom has acquired many facets and dimensions. Eternal, present, and future expressions of God's rule can sit side by side within the same work."[137] Meier proceeds to investigate uses in the OT pseudepigrapha and in the Dead Sea Scrolls. He concludes that reference to the kingdom is absent from some, mentioned in some, and given significant attention in some, but it is not a dominating theme.

Following on from this, Meier discusses Jesus' understanding of the kingdom. Basically, he believes it means "God coming in power to rule." Meier contends that the idea of the kingdom is central to the proclamation of Jesus, but not to contemporary Jewish writings. He reviews sayings of Jesus that refer to the future coming of the kingdom. These include the word from the Lord's Prayer, "Your kingdom come" (Matt 6:10//Luke 11:2). This petition, according to Meier, refers to the eschatological coming of God as king. "In short, when Jesus prays that God's kingdom come, he is simply expressing in a more abstract phrase the eschatological hope of the latter part of the OT and the pseudepigrapha that God would come on the last day to save and restore his people Israel."[138] Meier believes Jesus' saying at the Last Supper about drinking wine in the kingdom of God (Mark 14:25) is authentic and refers to his death and the future coming of the kingdom. According to Meier, Jesus did not give a deadline for the time of the coming; Meier believes the texts (Matt 10:23; Mark 9:1; 13:30) that give a time limit are a creation of the church. In sum, Meier contends that Jesus proclaimed an eschatological coming of the rule of God in the imminent future but did not give a timetable. "Any reconstruction of the historical Jesus that does not do full justice to this eschatological future must be dismissed as hopelessly inadequate."[139]

Meier turns to sayings of Jesus that indicate that the kingdom is already present. He attends to the three main sayings: first, Luke 11:20 (Matt 12:28), "but if it is by the finger of God that I cast out the demons, then the kingdom of God has come to you." Meier believes Luke has the more original form of this Q saying and that the verb means "has come" or "has arrived." "Jesus does present his exorcisms as proof that the kingdom of God that he proclaims for the future is in some sense already present."[140] The second major text is Luke 17:20-21: "the kingdom of God is in the midst of you." The third is Mark 1:15, "the kingdom of God has come near." Meier believes this is an authentic saying but does not think it can be used to support realized eschatology.

Besides these three main texts, Meier also reviews sayings about the presence of salvation, for example, the beatitude that expresses blessings on those who now see what the prophets had longed to see (Matt 13:16-17//Luke 10:23-24), a Q saying Meier accepts as authentic. In conclusion, Meier thinks Jesus believed that the kingdom was in some sense present, seen especially in the actions of Jesus, particularly his exorcisms. "The most significant *sayings* of Jesus about the kingdom's presence contain references to significant *actions* of Jesus that communicate or symbolize this presence."[141]

The understanding of the kingdom in relation to the actions of Jesus leads Meier into the third main part of volume 2: "Miracles." At the outset he discusses the question of miracles and the modern mind. A miracle, by Meier's definition, is an unusual event that has no reasonable explanation or cause; it is the result of an act of God. "Hence it is my contention that a positive judgment that a miracle has taken place is always a philosophical or theological judgment. Of its nature it goes beyond any judgment that a historian operating precisely as a historian can make."[142] Consequently, he concludes that the questions of the historical interpreter must be kept modest. For example: are the reports about the miracles inventions of the church, or do they go back to the time of Jesus? Did Jesus perform startling actions that his contemporaries and followers believed to be miracles? What did the supposed miracles mean to Jesus, his disciples, and other observers in the context of his ministry?

Meier turns to miracles and ancient minds. When one looks at the world of Jesus one sees that miracles were a feature of the landscape. Nevertheless, Meier argues that many of the alleged parallels to the miracles of Jesus are different and late. Some observers, for example, have confused miracles with magic. The Gospel miracles involve a personal relationship, make use of intelligible words, and show a relation to the kingdom. In magic, the action involves a manipulation of supernatural forces, makes use of ritual recipes, and is related to no larger purpose. Jesus' actions are never described in the NT in terms of magic, and the charge that Jesus was a magician is not made until the time of Justin. Meier presents a lengthy excursus on "Parallels to the Gospel Miracles."[143] The excursus investigates alleged parallels with such ancient figures as Apollonius of Tyana, Ḥoni the Circle-Drawer, and Ḥanina ben Dosa. Meier also discusses miracles attributed to humans in the Dead Sea Scrolls and in Josephus, and miracles attributed to Vespasian. He reviews problems related to the terminology of the "Divine Man" (*theos anēr*) and "aretology." In none of these examples does he find genuine parallels to the miracles of Jesus.

Meier takes up the global question of the historicity of Jesus' miracles. He deals with the basic question: Did Jesus perform acts that were considered miracles by himself or by his audience? Meier answers in terms of the major criteria. Most important is the criterion of multiple attestation; all the sources—Mark, Q, M, L, John, and Josephus—witness to the miracles. Miracles are also confirmed by the criterion of coherence: miracle accounts cut across the sources and form critical categories to create a consistent whole. The criterion of discontinuity comes into play when one views the total pattern of the behavior of Jesus. "Still more to the point: the overall configuration, pattern, or *Gestalt* of Jesus as popular preacher and teller of parables, *plus* authoritative interpreter of the Law and teacher of morality, *plus* proclaimer and realizer of the eschatological kingdom of God, *plus* miracle-worker actualizing his own proclamation has no adequate parallel in either the pagan or the Jewish literature of the time."[144] The criterion of embarrassment is seen in the charge that Jesus performed miracles by Beelzebul. The criterion of rejection and execution is seen in the fact that there is no evidence that miracles were a cause of the crucifixion.

Meier proceeds to an investigation of various types of miracles attributed to Jesus. In regard to exorcisms, he discusses seven examples and concludes that some of them were historical. The case of the possessed boy (Mark 9:14-29) may, according to Meier, represent epilepsy. In regard to healings, Meier discusses cases of paralysis, blindness, and so-called "leprosy." For many of these the criterion of multiple attestation comes into effect, and in the case where Jesus spits in the eyes of the blind man, and the cure requires a second attempt (Mark 8:22-26), the criterion of embarrassment is obvious. About blind Bartimaeus (Mark 10:46-52), the only recipient of a healing in the Synoptics identified by name, Meier says that "the Bartimaeus story is one of the strongest candidates for the report of a specific miracle going back to the historical Jesus."[145] In short, the various criteria support the belief that Jesus performed healings.

Meier then turns to the raising of the dead. Stories of this phenomenon are affirmed by multiple attestation, but the question for the historian is: do the reported events go back to the life of Jesus? The Markan tradition preserves the account of the raising of the daughter of Jairus (Mark 5:21-43). Meier detects evidence of early tradition in the use of Aramaic, and notes that Jairus is the only named petitioner for a miracle in the Gospels. He concludes that "the Jairus story does reflect and stem from some event in Jesus' public ministry."[146] In regard to the raising of the son of the widow of Nain (Luke 7:11-17), Meier says that "I incline (with some hesitation) to the view that the story goes back to some incident involving Jesus at Nain during his public ministry."[147] The Johannine tradition presents the startling account of the raising of Lazarus (John 11:1-45). Meier attempts to reconstruct the earliest form of the tradition: the message sent to Jesus and his remaining where he was for two days; a short dialogue with the disciples, and Jesus goes to the tomb of Lazarus; a short dialogue with Mary, and Jesus calls Lazarus, who comes forth. Meier believes the earliest version goes back to tradition prior to the writing of the Gospel and reflects an incident in the life of Jesus. He contends that the story was not a creation of the evangelist but "the question of what actually happened cannot be resolved by us today."[148]

Finally, there is a treatment of the so-called nature miracles. Among the most familiar examples are walking on the water (Mark 6:45-52; Matt 14:22-27; John 6:16-21) and stilling the storm (Mark 4:35-41). Meier believes both of these stories were creations of the early church. Concerning the changing of water to wine (John 2:1-11), Meier finds the account filled to the brim with theological motifs; he believes it to be a creation of John or the Johannine school. As to the feeding of the multitude, Meier points out that it is the only miracle reported in all four Gospels, and is even mentioned twice, with variations, in Mark and Matthew. Meier believes this miracle has its roots in history.

> In my opinion, the criteria of both multiple attestation and coherence make it likely that, amid the various celebrations of table fellowship Jesus hosted during his ministry, there was one especially memorable one: memorable because of the unusual number of participants, memorable also because, unlike many meals held in towns and villages, this one was held by the Sea of Galilee.[149]

"In sum," says Meier of the miracles as a whole,

> the statement that Jesus acted as and was viewed as an exorcist and healer during his public ministry has as much historical corroboration as almost any other statement we can make about the Jesus of history. . . . His miracles-working activity not only supported but also dramatized and actuated his eschatological message, and it may have contributed to some degree to the alarm felt by the authorities who finally brought about his death.[150]

Volume 3 carries the subtitle *Companions and Competitors*.[151] In the introduction Meier declares that Jesus must be understood in relation to others. Part I considers "Jesus the Jew and His Jewish Followers." Meier begins with the multitude, pointing out that all the sources—Mark, Q, M, L, and Josephus—report that Jesus attracted large crowds. He then narrows the circle and discusses the relation of Jesus to his closer followers. He notes that the "Twelve" meet the criteria of multiple attestation and discontinuity: the term is never used by the early church for self-designation, and never by Paul. "In sum, Mark, John, Paul, probably L and probably Q give multiple attestation from independent sources that the Twelve existed as an identifiable group during the public ministry."[152] The Twelve were symbolic of the re-gathering of the Twelve Tribes of Israel in the eschatological time. As to the identity of the Twelve, Meier points out that the various lists contain names of persons about whom almost nothing is known.

Meier turns to the three disciples who constitute an "inner circle." James is never mentioned without John, his brother. He was martyred under Herod

Agrippa (Acts 12:1-2), and James is always mentioned first. In regard to John, five persons have been collapsed into this individual: the son of Zebedee, the Beloved Disciple, the author of the Fourth Gospel, the author of three Johannine Epistles, and the seer of Revelation. Peter is always named first in the references to the inner circle and in the listing of the Twelve. He was a Jewish fisherman to whom Jesus gave the nickname Cephas. Meier believes a case can be made for the historicity of Matt 16:17-29 and Peter's confession, but he accepts the argument that the text is post-Easter. As to the account in Mark (8:31), he writes: "While Mark may not have created the three predictions of Jesus' passion, death, and resurrection out of whole cloth, in their present form they are most likely the product of early Christian preaching and catechesis."[153] Meier, however, accept the historicity of Peter's denial, noting its support by multiple attestation and the criterion of embarrassment.

Next Meier considers the relation of Jesus to competing groups, beginning with the Pharisees. Using the major sources—the NT, Josephus, and rabbinic literature (applied with caution)—he presents a minimalist sketch of the Pharisees. They were, he believes, a religious and political group of devout Jews concerned with the study and practice of the Law; they accepted the tradition of the elders and believed in the resurrection. As to the relation of Jesus to the Pharisees, Meier notes that the polemical material from Matthew and John reflects the post-resurrection conflict between Judaism and Christianity. Mark depicts Jesus in conflict with the Pharisees over marriage and divorce. The Markan Jesus also pronounced "woes" on the Pharisees. Meier believes some of this to be historical; he also points out that Jesus' conflict with the Pharisees was not a major factor in his execution.

As to the Sadducees, Meier presents "a few clear lines in a fuzzy portrait."[154] They were not, according to Meier, a large group, but they included members of the aristocracy with connections to the high priests. The Sadducees rejected the traditions of the elders, honored the Pentateuch, and did not believe in the resurrection or apocalyptic theology. According to Mark 12:18-27, Jesus disputed with them about the resurrection; this is the only reference to the Sadducees in Mark's Gospel. Jesus' argument rests on Exod 3:6, where God says, "I am the God of Abraham, the God of Isaac, and the God of Jacob," a text that implies a continuing and present relationship: God is the God "of the living." Meier argues from discontinuity (there is no other use of Exod 3:6 for the resurrection) and coherence (citing other texts where Jesus speaks of resurrection) that "the debate with the Sadducees over the resurrection in Mark 12:18-27 does reflect an actual incident in the ministry of the historical Jesus that took place, naturally enough, in Jerusalem."[155]

Finally, Meier presents the relationship of Jesus to other groups. About the Essenes he writes: "'What does the NT directly say about Jesus' relation to or interaction with the Essenes and/or Qumran?' the answer must be brutally brief: nothing."[156] There were, of course, points of contact, for instance, a concern with eschatology. Meier concludes that this comparison shows that Jesus and his followers were one group among various religious expressions of the time: eschatological groups with distinct lifestyles in conflict with the Jewish establishment. He also discusses the Samaritans, whom he considers a marginal group straddling Jewish and Gentiles worlds. Meier cautions against considering the "scribes" as representing a party somehow related to the Pharisees; instead, the term simply denotes persons engaged in the profession of writing. Meier believes the Herodians, probably officials of Herod Antipas, to be of no significance for the historical Jesus. The Zealots, in Meier's opinion, were not important until the time of the Jewish revolt.

At the end of the volume Meier incorporates the new data into the expanding picture of Jesus. From the beginning he had been on the margin of the Jewish establishment. Whereas other religious leaders were educated, Jesus did not have the benefit of formal study. Jesus emerges as an Elijah-like prophet who selected the Twelve to represent the restoration of the people. He disputed with competitors like the Pharisees and Sadducees.

Volume 4 of *A Marginal Jew* may be the most important.[157] This volume bears the subtitle *Law and Love*. In the introduction Meier affirms what for him is basic: the historical Jesus is the halakic Jesus, that is, Jesus must be understood in terms of his relation to the Law. At the outset Meier acknowledges the difficulties in dealing with Jesus and the Law. He says he is convinced that "although I may not be right in my position, every other book or article on the historical Jesus and the Law has been to a great degree wrong."[158] Meier notes various difficulties in regard to the issue. In the main these relate to the failure to distinguish Christology or faith in Jesus from the quest of the historical Jesus. He emphasizes the distinction "between Christian moral theology and ethics on the one hand and Jesus' teachings about the Jewish Law on the other."[159] Meier also believes confusion has resulted from a misunderstanding of the meaning of the Law. In particular, there has been an attempt to draw a distinction between the "ritual" and the "moral" law.

Meier explores the issue by taking up specific examples of Jesus' teaching about the law. He begins with divorce and considers the sayings in chronological order. In 1 Cor 7:10-11, Paul presents a saying of the Lord against divorce that he, Paul, will alter in his own teaching. Meier proceeds to the Q tradition (Matt 5:32//Luke 16:18), which he reconstructs as follows:

1a) Everyone who divorces his wife and marries another
  1b) causes her to be involved in adultery,
  2a) and whoever marries a divorced woman
  2b) commits adultery.

He comments: "I might note here that this succinct and balanced rhetorical bombshell, which explodes all traditional views of divorce in the Jewish Scriptures and Palestinian Judaism, would not be unworthy of the masterful wordsmith named Jesus. Hence it is not surprising that many commentators consider this Q version to be the most primitive form of the divorce saying in the NT."[160] Meier contends that the historicity of Jesus' opposition to divorce is confirmed by the criteria of authenticity. "The most important single conclusion of our investigation is that the criteria of multiple attestation, of discontinuity and embarrassment, and of coherence all argue for the historicity of Jesus' prohibition of divorce."[161]

Next, Meier discusses Jesus' teaching about oaths. He notes that in the history of Judaism the first step toward the regulation of oaths was not taken until the Mishnah. In reviewing the NT, Meier notes the parallel between Matt 5:34-37 and Jas 5:12. He believes the earliest forms show parallelism.

Matthew 5	James 5
34b: Do not swear [at all]	12b: Do not swear
34c: either by heaven	12c: either by heaven
35a: or the earth	12d: or by the earth
	12e [or by any other oath]
37a: But your speech must be "yes yes, no no."	12f: But your yes must be a yes and [your] no [must be] a no.

Meier believes the simple form represented by both texts, goes back to the historical Jesus. He writes: "I conclude that the prohibition of oaths can take its place alongside the prohibition of divorce as a second example of the historical Jesus' revocation of individual institutions and/or commandments of the Mosaic Law."[162]

Meier turns to the observance of the Sabbath. The OT pseudepigrapha and Qumran texts provide examples of many prohibitions. As to Jesus' relation to the Sabbath, Meier discusses actions of Jesus that might have seemed to violate the Sabbath. Some miracles, he notes, provoked no dispute. Meier believes that the miracles that did cause disputes are not historical. He concludes that "in all four Gospels, we have not a single narrative of a Sabbath dispute occasioned by a healing that probably goes back to the historical Jesus."[163] Meier believes the story about the plucking of grain on the Sabbath (Mark 2:23-28) is a composition of the early (pre-70) Jewish church. In regard to the two sayings attached, he thinks that "the Sabbath was made for man" (v. 27; RSV) probably goes back to the historical Jesus, while "the Son of man is lord even of the sabbath" (v. 28) does not. Meier concludes that, although supported by multiple attestation, the reports concerning Jesus and the Sabbath are largely a product of the early Christian-Jewish conflict.

Meier also investigates Jesus' relation to purity laws. In the discussion of ritual purity in Mark 7:1-23 he finds most of the saying attributed to Jesus to be inauthentic. Only the word about "Corban" in vv. 9-13 has any claim to historicity, on the criterion of dissimilarity. "In short, Jesus' studied indifference to ritual impurity must be seen within the larger framework of his claim to be the charismatic prophet of the end time."[164]

Meier then widens his focus to include a consideration of the "Love Commandments of Jesus." He begins by an analysis of the double command of love in Mark 12:28-34. According to this text Jesus quotes two passages commanding love: Deut 6:5 (love of God) and Lev 19:18 (love of neighbor). Meier acknowledges that Mark develops this tradition for his own purposes, but he believes the tradition originates with Jesus. He also calls attention to Mark's inclusion of the reaction of a scribe (vv. 32-34). "We have here the very rare case of an early Christian tradition willing to portray positively a Jewish teacher who agrees with and praises Jesus, but who does not follow Jesus as a disciple (at least within the story)."[165] Meier argues for the authenticity of the double command mainly on the basis of dissimilarity: this combination of the two texts is not found elsewhere in the OT, the Qumran texts, the OT pseudepigrapha, Philo, Josephus, or the early rabbis; the double command of love is not found elsewhere in the NT. Meier also reviews the command to love enemies found in the Q tradition (Matt 5:44; Luke 6:27, 35). Again arguing from dissimilarity, Meier notes that the command of love of enemies is not included in the texts that do not have the double commandment or in the Greco-Roman philosophers. "Our argument that this command goes back to Jesus thus rests on discontinuity."[166]

The conclusion to Volume 4 is extensive. Meier calls attention to positive insights that have taken shape. Most important is his insistence on seeing Jesus as a Jew in his Jewish setting; Jesus is a halakic Jew. "Whatever the errors of Volume Four of *A Marginal Jew*, and no doubt they are many, this volume at least rejects a major academic failure of Jesus research: mouthing respect for Jesus' Jewishness while avoiding like the plague the beating heart of that Jewishness: the Torah in all its complexity."[167] Meier believes that the investigator of the historical Jesus must take seriously the result of Jesus' engagement with Torah, for example, his prohibition of divorce and his emphasis on love. Meier cautions against efforts to find a unifying principle or system, for example, the double command of love. In contrast to a studied synthesis, Jesus' moral pronouncements, according to Meier, are *ad hoc*—the pronouncements of a charismatic leader like the expected Elijah. There is, according to Meier, a fusion of Law and eschatology in the message of Jesus, but Jesus does not explicitly ground his legal pronouncements in the presence or imminence of the coming of the kingdom. Meier ends with a promise: "Having wrestled with and gained some insight into the enigma of Jesus' teaching on Torah, we must turn our attention in the next volume of *A Marginal Jew* to the three outstanding enigmas: the riddle-speech of Jesus' parables, the riddle-speech of his self-designations, and the final riddle of his death."[168]

What can one say in looking back over the work of John P. Meier? At first sight the reviewer is overwhelmed by the magnitude of his research. The four hefty volumes contain a total of 2,792 pages, and a fifth is yet to come! Meier's work is comprehensive, treating all the major and relevant minor issues. The magnitude of his work is also apparent in his extensive notes; the notes on Chapter 36 (vol. 4) on "The Love Commandments of Jesus" extend to seventy pages. These notes testify to Meier's mastery of an enormous number of secondary sources and his command of languages, both ancient and modern. Within the major text Meier displays mastery of the methods of historical criticism: text criticism, knowledge of the historical setting, tradition criticism, form and redaction criticism, and theological sensitivity. Meier makes a good case for his designation of Jesus as *A Marginal Jew*. This title notes that Jesus lived and taught on the margin, but most of all, that Jesus must to be understood as a Jew in his Jewish setting.

Despite its length and depth, Meier's book on Jesus is a joy to read. He writes clearly and with occasional humor. Where does Meier stand, one may ask, in the various quests of the historical Jesus? He certainly does not belong to the "new quest" or the "third quest," and he is diametrically opposed to recent studies of Jesus that view him against the Hellenistic background as wandering Stoic or Cynic teacher. Is it too much to say that Meier supports the revival of the old quest?—certainly not the quest Schweitzer chronicled, whereby the resulting Jesus is a reflection of the scholar. No, Meier's Jesus is a marginal Jew, accommodated to no ancient or modern portrait. What resonates with the old quest is Meier's unswerving devotion to the historical critical method.

What is new is that he does it well—better than most of his predecessors and contemporaries.

Summary

The three scholars reviewed in this chapter illustrate the increasing vitality of Roman Catholic biblical research; they represent only a sample of a larger group.[169] These scholars demonstrate that historical critical work can be accomplished from the perspective of a faith commitment. They employ the methods of lower and higher criticism. Although they reflect the traditional Roman Catholic concern with the Gospel of Matthew, they accept the priority of Mark. They continue their loyalty to tradition, but this allows a degree of freedom in the interpretation of Scripture. The "liberal" critic may be suspicious of the *sensus plenior*, but the search for the deeper meaning of the text is not unfamiliar to the devotees of the new hermeneutic. Although the Catholics tend to be conservative in criticism and exegesis, their results—in contrast to excessive skepticism (e.g., the Jesus Seminar, discussed in the next chapter)—may be all the more convincing. Their critical and exegetical work is consistently directed to the theological meaning of the text. Their boundless energy, their dedication of time, and the magnitude of their productivity represent a model to be emulated.

Notes

1. See Kenneth Scott Latourette, *Christianity in a Revolutionary Age: A History of Christianity in the Nineteenth and Twentieth Centuries*, vol. 4: *The Twentieth Century in Europe: The Roman Catholic, Protestant, and Eastern Churches* (Grand Rapids: Zondervan, 1969); Timothy G. McCarthy, *The Catholic Tradition: the Church in the Twentieth Century*, 2d ed. (Chicago: Loyola, 1998).

2. See *HNTR* 2: 163–72.

3. See Joseph G. Prior, *The Historical Critical Method in Catholic Exegesis*, TGST 50 (Rome: Gregorian University Press, 1999); Robert Bruce Robinson, *Roman Catholic Exegesis Since Divino Afflante Spiritu: Hermeneutical Implications*, SBLDS 111 (Atlanta: Scholars, 1988); Patricia M. McDonald, "Biblical Scholarship: When Tradition Met Method," in *The Catholic Church in the Twentieth Century: Renewing and Reimaging the City of God*, ed. John Deedy (Collegeville, MN: Liturgical, 2000), 113–30.

4. See Giuseppe Alberigo, *A Brief History of Vatican II*, trans. Matthew Sherry (Maryknoll, NY: Orbis, 2006); Robert Murray, "Vatican II and the Bible," *DRev* 121, no. 422 (2003): 14–25; McCarthy, *Catholic Tradition*, 57–74; Gerald P. Fogarty, *American Catholic Biblical Scholarship: A History from the Early Republic to Vatican II*, SBLCPS (San Francisco: Harper & Row, 1989), 334–50; Carolyn Osiek, "Catholic or catholic? Biblical Scholarship at the Center," *JBL* 125 (2006): 5–22.

5. See Walter M. Abbott, *The Documents of Vatican II: All Sixteen Official Texts Promulgated by the Ecumenical Council, 1963–1965* (New York: Herder and Herder, 1966), 111–36; Ronald D. Witherup, *Scripture: Dei Verbum* (New York: Paulist, 2006).

6. Abbott, *Documents*, 121.

7. Ibid., 124.

8. Prior, *Historical Critical Method*, 229–63; Peter S. Williamson, *Catholic Principles for Interpreting Scripture: A Study of the Pontifical Biblical Commission's* The Interpretation of the Bible in the Church (Rome: Pontifical Biblical Institute, 2001); Pontifical Biblical Commission, *The Interpretation of the Bible in the Church: Address of His Holiness Pope John Paul II and Document of the Pontifical Biblical Commission* (Rome: Libreria Editrice Vaticana, 1993).

9. See Helmut Merklein, *Neues Testament und Ethik: Für Rudolf Schnackenburg* (Freiburg: Herder, 1989), 7–9; Karlheinz Müller, "Anstelle eines Nachrufs: Ungeordnete Anmerkungen zu einem wichtigen Lehrer," *BZ* 47 (2003): 161–66; Gerhard Dautzenberg, "Schnackenburg, Rudolf," *RGG*[4] 7: 942.

10. For bibliography (1937–88) see Merklein, *Neues Testament und Ethik*, 590–97.

11. Rudolf Schnackenburg, "Zum Offenbarungsgedanken in der Bibel," in idem, *Schriften zum Neuen Testament: Exegese in Fortschritt und Wandel* (Munich: Kösel, 1971), 34–56.

12. Rudolf Schnackenburg, "Der Weg der Katholischen Exegese," in ibid., 15–33.

13. Rudolf Schnackenburg, *Das Johannesevangelium*, 4 vols., HTKNT (Freiburg: Herder, 1965–75); ET: *The Gospel According to St. John*, 3 vols., HTKNT (New York: Herder and Herder, 1968; Seabury, 1980; Crossroad, 1982).

14. *Gospel According to St. John*, 1: 3.

15. Ibid., 1: 23.

16. Ibid., 1: 38.

17. Ibid., 1: 77.

18. Ibid., 1: 160.

19. See pp. 98–104 above. The fourth volume of Schnackenburg's commentary (*Ergänzende Auslegungen und Exkurse*, 1984) provides a summary of research on the Fourth Gospel since 1955.

20. *Das Johannesevangelium: IV Teil: Ergänzende Auslegungen und Exkurse*, HTKNT (Freiburg: Herder, 1984).

21. *Gospel According to St. John*, 1: 267.

22. Ibid., 3 :335.

23. Ibid., 3: 344.

24. Ibid., 1: 529–42.

25. Ibid., 1: 537.

26. *Die Johannesbriefe*, HTKNT (Freiburg: Herder, 1975); ET: *The Johannine Epistles,* trans. Reginald and Ilse Fuller (New York: Crossroad, 1992).

27. Rudolf Schnackenburg, *Das Evangelium nach Markus*, 2 vols. (Düsseldorf: Patmos, 1966, 1970); ET: *The Gospel According to St. Mark*, 2 vols., NTSR (New York: Herder and Herder, 1971).

28. Rudolf Schnackenburg, *Das Mattäusevangelium*, 2 vols. (Würzburg: Echter, 1985, 1987); ET: *The Gospel of Matthew*, trans. Robert R. Barr (Grand Rapids: Eerdmans, 2002).

29. *Gospel of Matthew*, 159.

30. Rudolf Schnackenburg, *Der Brief an die Epheser*, EKKNT (Cologne: Benziger, 1982); ET: *Ephesians: A Commentary*, trans. Helen Heron (Edinburgh: T & T Clark, 1991).

31. *Ephesians*, 23.

32. Ibid., 293.

33. Rudolf Schnackenburg, *The Moral Teaching of the New Testament*, trans. J. Holland-Smith and W. J. O'Hara (New York: Seabury, 1973).

34. Rudolf Schnackenburg, *Die sittliche Botschaft des Neuen Testaments*, HTKNTSup 1, 2 (Freiburg: Herder, 1986); *El mensaje moral del Nuevo Testamento*, 2 vols. (Barcelona: Herder, 1989, 1991).

35. *Sittliche Botschaft des Neuen Testaments*, 1: 214.

36. Ibid., 2: 71.

37. Ibid., 2: 112.

38. Ibid., 2: 147.

39. Rudolf Schnackenburg, *Die Person Jesu Christi im Spiegel der vier Evangelien*, HTKNTSup 4 (Freiburg: Herder, 1993); ET: *Jesus in the Gospels: A Biblical Christology*, trans. O. C. Dean, Jr. (Louisville: Westminster John Knox, 1995).

40. *Jesus in the Gospels*, x.

41. Ibid., 73.

42. Ibid., 181.

43. Ibid., 229.

44. Ibid., 316.

45. Rudolf Schnackenburg, *Die Geburt Christi ohne Mythos und Legende* (Mainz: Matthias-Grünewald, 1926); *Wer war Jesus von Nazareth* (Düsseldorf: Patmos, 1970); *Freundschaft mit Jesus* (Freiburg: Herder, 1995); ET: *The Friend We Have in Jesus*, trans. Mark A. Christian (Louisville: Westminster John Knox, 1997); *Deutet die Zeichen der Zeit: Meditationen zum Advent* (Freiburg: Herder, 1976); ET: *Christ, Present and Coming* (Philadelphia: Fortress Press, 1978); *Alles kann, wer glaubt: Bergpredigt und Vaterunser in der Absicht Jesu* (Freiburg: Herder, 1992); ET: *All Things are Possible to Believers: Reflections on the Lord's Prayer and the Sermon on the Mount*, trans. James S. Currie (Louisville: Westminster John Knox, 1995).

46. Rudolf Schnackenburg, *Gottes Herrschaft und Reich: Eine biblisch-theologische Studie* (Freiburg: Herder, 1959); ET: *God's Rule and Kingdom*, trans. John Murray (New York: Herder and Herder, 1963).

47. *God's Rule*, 119.

48. Ibid., 177.

49. Ibid., 304–5.

50. *La Théologie du Nouveau Testament: État de la question*, StudNeot (Bruges: Desclée de Brouwer, 1961); ET: *New Testament Theology Today*, trans. David Askew (New York: Herder and Herder, 1963); German trans.: *Neutestamentliche Theologie: Der Stand der Forschung* (Munich: Kösel, 1963).

51. Rudolf Schnackenburg, *Present and Future: Modern Aspects of New Testament Theology* (Notre Dame, IN: University of Notre Dame Press, 1966).

52. Rudolf Schnackenburg, *Christliche Existenz nach dem Neuen Testament: Abhandlungen und Vorträge*, 2 vols. (Munich: Kösel, 1967, 1968); ET: *Christian Existence in the New Testament*, 2 vols. (Notre Dame, IN: University of Notre Dame Press, 1968, 1969).

53. *Das Heilsgeschehen bei der Taufe nach dem Apostel Paulus: Eine Studie zur paulinischen Theologie*, MThS (Munich: Zink, 1950); ET: *Baptism in the Thought of St. Paul: A Study in Pauline Theology*, trans. G. R. Beasley-Murray (New York: Herder and Herder, 1964); *Die Kirche im Neuen Testament: Ihre Wirklichkeit und theologische Deutung: Ihre Wesen und Geheimnis* (Freiburg: Herder, 1961); ET: *The Church in the New Testament* (London: Burns and Oates, 1974); *Glaubensimpulse aus dem Neuen Testament* (Düsseldorf: Patmos, 1973); ET: *Belief in the New Testament*, trans. Jeremy Moiser (New York: Paulist, 1974).

54. Terrence T. Prendergast, "The Church's Great Challenge: Proclaiming God's Word in the New Millennium," in *Life in Abundance: Studies of John's Gospel in Tribute to Raymond E. Brown*, ed. John R. Donahue (Collegeville, MN: Liturgical Press, 2005), 3.

55. For biography see, Marion L. Soards, "Brown, Raymond E. (1928–1998)," *DMBI*, 227–34; idem, "Brown, Raymond E. (1928–1998)," *HHMBI*, 562–70; Ronald D. Witherup, "Foreword," in *Raymond E. Brown, An Introduction to the Gospel of John*, ed. Francis J. Moloney,

ABRL (New York: Doubleday, 2003), xi–xvi; idem, "Biography of Raymond E. Brown," in *Life in Abundance*, 254–58; Joseph A. Fitzmyer, "Raymond E. Brown, S.S.: In Memoriam," *USQR* 52 (1998): 1–18, repr. in Joseph A. Fitzmyer, *The Interpretation of Scripture: In Defense of the Historical-Critical Method* (New York: Paulist, 2008), 101–14).

56. "In Memoriam," 18.

57. Witherup, "Biography," 254.

58. For bibliography of Brown's works see "A Bibliography of the Publications of Raymond E. Brown," prepared by Michael L. Barré, in *Life in Abundance*, 259–89.

59. Raymond E. Brown, *The* Sensus Plenior *of Sacred Scripture* (Baltimore: St. Mary's University, 1955).

60. Ibid., 92.

61. Ibid., 145-46. Kevin Duffy, "The Ecclesial Hermeneutic of Raymond E. Brown," *HeyJ* 39 (1998): 37–56, contends that Brown's work was divided into two periods: (1) a time of stress on the *sensus plenior* that ended in 1968; (2) a more piecemeal approach that largely ignores the *sensus plenior* (after 1970). But later in the article Duffy acknowledges that Brown does employ a two-stage hermeneutic, even though he emphasizes the literal. This two-stage approach is also confirmed by Brown's article "Hermeneutics," *NJBC*, 1146–65.

62. Raymond E. Brown, *An Introduction to the New Testament*, ABRL (New York: Doubleday, 1997).

63. *Introduction*, 30.

64. Ibid., 122.

65. Ibid., 161.

66. Ibid., 210–11.

67. Ibid., 322.

68. Ibid., 448.

69. Ibid., 630.

70. Ibid., 668.

71. Ibid., 695.

72. Raymond E. Brown, *The Community of the Beloved Disciple* (New York: Paulist, 1979), 5.

73. Raymond E. Brown, *An Introduction to the Gospel of John*, ed. Francis J. Moloney, ABRL (New York: Doubleday, 2003); see also Francis J. Moloney, "Raymond Brown's New Introduction to the Gospel of John," *CBQ* 65 (2003): 1–21.

74. In the first edition of the commentary Brown proposed five stages, but since the first two stages are incorporated into the new first stage, and the third stage in the new *Introduction* has two aspects, the overall difference in not significant.

75. *Introduction to the Gospel of John*, 104.

76. Ibid., 107.

77. Ibid., 168.

78. Ibid., 183.

79. Ibid., 206.

80. Ibid., 249.

81. Ibid., 263.

82. Raymond E. Brown, *The Gospel According to John*, 2 vols., AB (Garden City, NY: Doubleday, 1966, 1970) 1: 429.

83. Ibid., 1: 437. On Brown's work on the Fourth Gospel see Francis J. Moloney, "The Gospel of John: The Legacy of Raymond E. Brown and Beyond," in *Life in Abundance*, 19–39.

84. Raymond E. Brown, *The Epistles of John*, AB 30 (Garden City, NY: Doubleday, 1982).

85. Ibid., 175.

86. Brown published a short version of his Johannine commentaries for non-specialists: *The Gospels and Epistles of John: A Concise Commentary* (Collegeville, MN: Liturgical, 1988).

87. Raymond E. Brown, *The Community of the Beloved Disciple* (New York: Paulist, 1979).

88. Ibid., 113.

89. For more examples of Brown's research on the Johannine literature, see several essays in Raymond E. Brown, *New Testament Essays* (Milwaukee: Bruce, 1965).

90. Raymond E. Brown, *The Birth of the Messiah: A Commentary on the Infancy Narratives in the Gospels of Matthew and Luke*, new updated ed., ABRL (New York: Doubleday, 1993), 7.

91. Ibid., 8.

92. Ibid. 36.

93. Ibid., 50.

94. Ibid., 85.

95. Ibid., 88.

96. Ibid., 232.

97. Brown clearly distinguishes "virginal conception" from "virgin birth." The birth of Jesus is normal; the unique aspect of the origin of Jesus is his conception.

98. Raymond E. Brown, *The Virginal Conception and Bodily Resurrection of Jesus* (New York: Paulist, 1973).

99. Ibid., 32.

100. Ibid., 41.

101. *Birth of the Messiah*, 527–28.

102. Ibid., 531.

103. Raymond E. Brown, *The Death of the Messiah: From Gethsemane to the Grave: A Commentary on the Passion Narratives in the Four Gospels*, 2 vols., ABRL (New York: Doubleday, 1994).

104. Ibid., 1: vii.

105. Ibid., 1: viii.

106. Ibid., 1: 4.

107. Ibid., 1: 482.

108. Raymond E. Brown, *The Churches the Apostles Left Behind* (New York: Paulist, 1984).

109. Ibid., 147. Also among Brown's historical works is *Antioch and Rome: New Testament Cradles of Catholic Christianity* (New York: Paulist, 1983), written with John P. Meier. Brown wrote the section on Rome, which traces the history of Christianity in Rome from its beginnings through its second and third generation until the early second century.

110. Raymond E. Brown, *An Introduction to New Testament Christology* (New York: Paulist, 1994). This book discusses issues considered in Brown's earlier work, *Jesus God and Man: Modern Biblical Reflections,* Impact Books (Milwaukee: Bruce, 1967).

111. *New Testament Christology*, 49.

112. bid., 70.

113. Ibid., 79.

114. Ibid., 149.

115. John P. Meier, *Law and History in Matthew's Gospel: A Redactional Study of Mt. 5:17-48*, AnBib 71 (Rome: Biblical Institute Press, 1976), 1.

116. Ibid., 20.

117. Ibid., 23.

118. Ibid., 40.

119. Ibid., 124.

120. Ibid., 160. Meier later published a book on Matthew for the general reader: *Matthew*, NT Message (Wilmington, DE: Michael Glazier, 1980).

121. Raymond E. Brown and John P. Meier, *Antioch and Rome: New Testament Cradles of Christianity* (New York: Paulist, 1982).

122. John P. Meier, *A Marginal Jew: Rethinking the Historical Jesus*, vol. 1: *The Roots of the Problem and the Person*, ABRL (New York: Doubleday, 1991).

123. Ibid., 1.

124. Ibid., 6.

125. Ibid., 56.

126. Ibid., 139.

127. Meier points to the weakness of this criterion: "To paint a portrait of Jesus completely divorced from or opposed to 1st-century Judaism and Christianity is simply to place him outside of history" (ibid., 173).

128. *A Marginal Jew 1*, 213.

129. Ibid., 222.

130. Meier observes that the doctrine of the perpetual virginity did not originate until the second century. He points out that it was accepted by both Luther and Calvin. Meier rejects the view that those designated as brothers and sisters of Jesus were his cousins. He believes that texts like Mark 3:31-35 make better sense if the brothers and sisters were blood relations.

131. John P. Meier, *A Marginal Jew: Rethinking the Historical Jesus*, vol. 2: *Mentor, Message, and Miracles*, ABRL (New York: Doubleday, 1994).

132. Ibid., 31.

133. Ibid., 129.

134. Ibid., 127.

135. Ibid., 176.

136. Ibid., 178.

137. Ibid., 252.

138. Ibid., 299.

139. Ibid., 350.

140. Ibid., 423.

141. Ibid., 451.

142. Ibid., 514.

143. Ibid., 576–601.

144. Ibid., 624.

145. Ibid., 690.

146. Ibid., 787.

147. Ibid., 798.

148. Ibid., 831.

149. Ibid., 966.

150. Ibid., 970.

151. John P. Meier, *A Marginal Jew: Rethinking the Historical Jesus*, vol. 3: *Companions and Competitors*, ABRL (New York: Doubleday, 2001).

152. Ibid., 141.

153. Ibid., 236.

154. Ibid., 391.

155. Ibid., 443.

156. Ibid., 489.

157. John P. Meier, *A Marginal Jew: Rethinking the Historical Jesus*, vol. 4, *Law and Love*, AYBRL (New Haven: Yale University Press, 2009).

158. Ibid., 2.

159. Ibid., 7.

160. Ibid., 108.

161. Ibid., 124.

162. Ibid., 205.

163. Ibid., 259.

164. Ibid., 415.

165. Ibid., 498.

166. Ibid., 550.

167. Ibid., 648.

168. Ibid., 658.

169. Among the Europeans, a significant example is Pierre Benoît (1906–1978). Benoît was director of the École Biblique in Jerusalem (1965–72). He made important contributions (noted above) to the study of the Dead Sea Scrolls. Several of his essays were published in collections, the most important of which are: *Jesus and the Gospel* (2 vols., trans. Benet Weatherhead [New York: Herder and Herder, 1973, 1974]), and *Passion et résurrection du Seigneur* (Paris: Cerf, 1966; ET: *The Passion and Resurrection of Jesus Christ*, trans. Benet Weatherhead [New York: Herder and Herder, 1969]). Among the Americans, an important example is Joseph A. Fitzmyer (1920–). Fitzmyer spent the last years of his teaching career at The Catholic University of America. He made significant contributions (noted above) to the study of the Dead Sea Scrolls and the Aramaic background of the NT (*A Wandering Aramean: Collected Aramaic Essays,* SBLMS 25 [Missoula, MT: Scholars, 1979]). Fitzmyer is a major contributor to the Anchor Bible commentary series: *Luke* (two vols.), *Acts*, *Romans*, *1 Corinthians*, and *Philemon*.

8

The Development of Scholarly Societies

The twentieth century witnessed the advance of cooperative research. The arrival of the space age was heralded by Neil Armstrong's prophetic words: "one small step for [a] man; one giant leap for mankind." The small step, however, had been prepared by years of scientific and technological labor. This involved a host of experts, working at the vast Space Center in Houston and the launch site at Cape Canaveral in Florida. Rockets were developed, complicated systems of communication and navigation were devised. The flight to the moon was preceded by earlier, more modest ventures in space. It was a time of group research—the era of the "think-tank."

New Testament research displayed a parallel kind of cooperative study, seen especially in the development of scholarly societies. The Society of Biblical Literature (SBL) has been around for a long time, but in the second half of the twentieth century it flourished in new forms and promoted new projects. The Catholic Biblical Association of America (CBA), with relatively late and inauspicious beginnings, became in the course of the century a vital organization. The Studiorum Novi Testamenti Societas (SNTS) is younger, largely maintaining its original shape but not without change and expansion. And what is one to say of the Jesus Seminar?—bold, brash, feeding radical research to the hungry media. All of this constitutes a complex, fascinating story.

The Society of Biblical Literature

The SBL, according to its website, is "the oldest and largest international scholarly membership organization in the field of biblical studies."[1] The society was born in 1880 in the New York study of Philip Schaff, where a small group of scholars gathered to consider the formation of an organization for the study of the Bible. Among those present was Charles A. Briggs, later to be charged with heresy by the Presbyterian Church.[2] The first meeting of the Society, attended by eighteen scholars, was held in June of the same year. They adopted the name "Society of Biblical Literature and Exegesis," which was shortened in 1962. The Society continued to expand in size, with 45 members in 1881 and 592 in 1940. The years from 1940 to 1967 saw extensive growth; in 1956 alone some 500 new members were added. The 100th meeting in 1964 (semi-annual meetings were held through 1896) was attended by 891 out of a total membership of 2,185.[3] Regional societies were formed, beginning in 1936, and by 1946 there were three: Midwest, Canadian, and Pacific; by 1977 the number had swelled to thirteen. In 1948 a committee on structure presented a proposal that was adopted: the scheduling of one meeting every four years outside of New York.

Massive restructuring of the Society took place in 1968, largely under the leadership of Robert W. Funk, who served as executive secretary from 1968 to 1974. A new constitution and bylaws were adopted at the meeting in Toronto in 1969. The major feature of this constitution was a restructuring of the annual meeting. Instead of three main sections (Plenary, OT, and NT), the program would consist of sections (scholars concentrating on a major area of research), groups (working sessions of scholars exploring new areas of research), seminars (a limited number of scholars engaged in research on a clearly focused topic), consultations (individuals exploring areas of interest that might lead to the formation of a section, group, or seminar), and plenary sessions (the presidential address and other special programs). By this time the annual meeting could not be accommodated by seminaries or educational institutions and had to be moved to cities with large hotels and spacious convention centers.

The 1970s were marked by trouble and possible scandal at the level of leadership. Funk resigned as executive secretary and cut his ties with the Society. He had been dismissed as editor of Scholars Press under bizarre circumstances, including a charge of misusing funds, and through a devious procedure whereby he was locked out of his own office.[4] Apparently Funk felt that the leadership of the Society did not adequately support him, although in time the Council of the SBL took action to reimburse Funk for his financial losses and clear his name of unsubstantiated charges. The post of Secretary was given to the highly respected George W. MacRae (1975–76), who was succeeded by Paul Achtemeier (1977–80), a solid scholar and judicious leader. Kent Harold Richards served as secretary from 1981 to 1986, when he was succeeded by David Lull (1987–95), the first full-time Executive Secretary. Richards resumed the post in 1996 and continued until 2010. A competent OT scholar, with a doctorate from Claremont and post-doctoral study at Heidelberg, Richards presided over the remarkable advances of the Society at the end of the century. The SBL became a highly efficient organization with a staff of twenty, assets of over $3,300,000, and total membership of over 8,500. Richards was the chief architect of the international meetings that began in 1983 and continued into the twenty-first century. These meetings were mainly held in Europe, but some have taken place in Cape Town, Jerusalem, and Melbourne.

Major activities of the Society are publication and the annual meetings. The flagship publication of the SBL is the *Journal of Biblical Literature* (*JBL*), begun in 1881. As Gail R. O'Day pointed out in her essay on "Editorial Reflections," written for the commemoration of the 125th anniversary of the *Journal*, the task of the editor is "to maintain the quality of *JBL* as the premier English-language refereed journal in biblical studies."[5] The SBL Monograph Series (SBLMS) first appeared in 1945. The innovative periodical *Semeia* was begun in 1974. Scholars Press, founded in 1974, was a joint venture of the SBL and the American Academy of Religion (AAR). To accommodate the increasing number of book reviews, the press published *Critical Review of Books in Religion* (1988–97), succeeded in 1998 by *Review of Biblical Literature*. In cooperation with Harper and Row the Society provided editors and authors for the publication of a Bible dictionary and a one-volume commentary.[6]

The annual meeting has evolved into a spectacular event. Some have dubbed it a "three ring circus," but it is more like a Cecil B. DeMille movie with a cast of hundreds. The meeting in the year 2000, with a program book of 360 pages that included the meetings of the AAR and 145 pages of publishers' advertisements, featured fifty-eight sections, eighteen groups, seven seminars, twelve consultations, and six pages listing additional meetings. A major aspect of the program has been the presidential address. One observer noted: "In most years, the audience for the presidential address is larger than the audience for any other scholarly address devoted to the Bible anywhere in the world."[7] The list of the presidents of the Society, OT and NT scholars in alternating years, reads like a who's who of biblical scholars. The addresses have marked significant developments, current issues, and portents of the future.[8]

The thousands who attend the current meetings could scarcely imagine the shape of the annual meeting of December 1950. As was customary (three out of every four years), the meeting was held at Union Theological Seminary in New York. Attendees stayed in rooms at the seminary, vacated by students who had gone home for the holidays. Inexpensive meals were provided by the seminary refectory. The meeting began with a business session that elected 140 persons to membership. Rudolf Bultmann and Anton Fridrichsen were elected honorary members. After the business session the presidential address was delivered by R. H. Pfeiffer, followed by a short discussion. The hallowed custom that presidential addresses were non-discussable emerged some time later. The pattern of the main meetings involved united sessions (OT and NT scholars) in the morning (with about 200 in attendance) and separate OT and NT sections in the afternoon; the meeting lasted two days. The final evening session was held in conjunction with the American Schools of Oriental Research (ASOR) and the National Association of Biblical Instructors (which became the AAR in 1964); the program, as customary, included an illustrated archaeological report, "The Winter Palace of Herod the Great at Jericho." The novice whose abstract had been approved, and who had the courage to read a paper before the leading scholars of the country, approached the lectern, as I remember, in fear and trembling.

Nevertheless, apart from the lingering nostalgia, even the aging scholar can welcome new things. The Society is no longer the exclusive club of the eastern elite. Anyone who can afford the dues and the expensive hotels can attend. The multiplying of groups and the delineation of varying interests has stimulated a host of scholars and engendered a multitude of new ideas. The Society has become increasingly sensitive to social and ethnic issues, with sections on African, Asian, Latino/a, and feminist hermeneutics. Platforms are provided for the unknowns who some day may perform wonders. The book displays, with their special bargains, have become a treasure trove for the aspiring scholar. The prospective teacher can arrange interviews with potential employers. Recent PhDs can seek out conferences with editors who might be interested in their dissertations. Old friendships are renewed, new ones are made, and scholarship moves onward—if not always upward.

The Catholic Biblical Association

The moving force behind the formation of the Catholic Biblical Association of America (CBA) was Bishop Edwin O'Hara, chair of the Episcopal Committee of the Confraternity of Christian Doctrine.[9] O'Hara, who was concerned to improve the quality of the translation of the NT used by Catholics, called a meeting of Scripture professors in Washington, DC, in January 1936. During the meeting, which gave major attention to the translation of the NT, Romain Butin proposed the establishment of a permanent association of Catholic biblical scholars (or, as Catholics like to say, "Scripture scholars"). Those in attendance supported the proposal and agreed to meet again in connection with the annual meeting of the Confraternity of Christian Doctrine (the branch of the Catholic church that directs Christian education). All priests engaged in teaching Scripture were invited to the organizing convention, which met in

New York in October 1936. About fifty attended this meeting and voted to establish the Catholic Biblical Association of America. The purpose of the Association was twofold: to provide the Confraternity with a body of scholars qualified to work on biblical problems, and to provide Scripture scholars opportunity to become better acquainted and thereby encourage biblical research. This meeting drafted a constitution and bylaws that were adopted at the first general meeting in St. Louis in October of 1937. Some one hundred scholars had joined the Association and were designated "charter members." At the meeting the following year in Hartford the *Catholic Biblical Quarterly* (*CBQ*), which first appeared in 1939, was launched. The first editor, Wendell S. Reilly, wrote, "Ours will be the only Catholic review devoted exclusively to the Bible in the English speaking world."[10]

The early work of the CBA reflected the conservatism of the Catholic scholarship of the time. The first issue of the *Quarterly* included an article on the Synoptic problem by Charles Callan. According to Callan an early catechesis, known to Peter, evolved into an Aramaic version of Matthew; Mark was based on the testimony of Peter and Aramaic Matthew. The Greek version of Matthew, according to Callan, was based on Aramaic Matthew and Mark; Luke was dependent on Mark, Paul, and the Virgin Mary. The third general meeting of the Association, held in Toronto (1940), voted to publish a commentary designed to accompany the new English translation, a revision of the Challoner–Rheims version, which was based on the Vulgate. The resulting *Commentary on the New Testament* appeared in 1942.[11] In the *Commentary* an article on "Literary Relations of the First Three Gospels" supported the canonical order of the gospels but believed Matthew wrote in Hebrew; the order of the Greek gospels may have been Mark, Matthew, and Luke (which was dependent on Matthew).

The 1940s saw the rapid advance of the CBA. In 1942, Roger O'Callaghan entered Johns Hopkins to study with W. F. Albright—the first of a succession of Catholic students that included Raymond E. Brown and Joseph A. Fitzmyer. In 1944 the Association, meeting in South Bend, Indiana, invited Albright to deliver a lecture and accept honorary membership. Later, in a letter, he praised the CBA:

> What I liked particularly was the fresh enthusiasm and interest, which were most stimulating by comparison with the rather bored attitude characteristic of most members of the Society of Biblical Literature. Nor do I blame them, in view of the waste of time involved in listening to the numerous papers which expose half-

baked theories and wild hypotheses of various kinds. Such papers are not likely to be presented at meetings of the Catholic Biblical Association.[12]

In 1947, Sister Kathryn Sullivan was elected to membership, which had previously been restricted to priests. In 1958 she was elected vice president, and should (according to custom) have been elevated to the presidency "had they dared at the time to elect a woman as president."[13] The general meeting of 1948 heard a report on the progress of a new translation from the Greek text, which was published in 1954 as the Kleist-Lilly New Testament.[14]

In the 1950s the CBA and the *CBQ* displayed a new boldness. This move was championed by Edward Siegman, who served as editor of the *Quarterly* from 1951 to 1958. Papers and articles were presented by younger scholars who had attended secular institutions like Johns Hopkins. David Stanley published essays on form criticism, and at the 1953 meeting he presented a paper that concluded that the hymn of Phil 2:5-11 was pre-Pauline. The presidential address in 1959 (by Brendan McGrath) contended that scholars could find truth in places outside conventional Catholic circles, for example, in the work of Rudolf Bultmann.

Before Vatican II the CBA had come under attack, especially by *American Ecclesiastical Review* and a few conservative members of the faculty of Catholic University. The CBA, which had been on the defensive, was exonerated by the council, and after that Catholic biblical scholarship flourished. Two major projects of the CBA were completed. *The Jerome Biblical Commentary*, edited by Raymond E. Brown, Joseph A. Fitzmyer, and Roland E. Murphy, appeared in 1968, with NT books arranged in chronological order (Mark before Matthew and Luke).[15] *The New American Bible*, a fresh translation from the original languages, was published in 1970.[16] In 1971, Pope Paul VI changed the composition of the Pontifical Biblical Commission, made up of scholars from around the world, to include CBA members David Stanley, Raymond E. Brown, and Joseph A. Fitzmyer. CBA members were recognized in the larger arena: Brown and Fitzmyer as presidents of the SBL, and Brown as the first American Catholic elected to the presidency of the SNTS. By 1996, membership in the CBA had grown to 1,280. Women became increasingly active, with eleven attending the meeting in 1963. Pheme Perkins, a married Catholic laywoman, was named president in 1986, a year before the SBL elected a woman to its presidency.

The organization of the CBA is outlined in its constitution and bylaws.[17] Originally adopted in 1937, the constitution was amended in 1962 to provide for the admission of non-Catholics. Protestant and Jewish scholars were now welcomed. The purpose of the Association is "to devote itself to the scientific study of the Bible and to such branches of learning as are connected with it, in conformity with the spirit and the instructions of the Catholic Church, which the Association acknowledges to be the only divinely appointed custodian and authoritative interpreter of the Holy Scriptures." The purpose is further "to promote a better mutual acquaintance among the Catholic biblical scholars of America and to provide them with encouragement and support in their special fields of study." Active members must have a Licentiate in Scripture from the Biblical Institute in Rome or the equivalent (a doctorate from a good biblical studies program) and a record of scholarly publications.

The major activities of the CBA, like those of the SBL, are publications and annual meetings. The *CBQ*, which earlier had addressed a broad readership, increasingly focused on scholarly issues. The CBQ Monograph Series (CBQMS) was begun in 1971, and by 1996 listed forty-five items. In 1943 the *CBQ* began publishing a section on "Survey of Periodicals," which evolved in 1956 into a separate publication, *New Testament Abstracts*. By 1987 the pattern of the annual general meeting had become standard.[18] The presidential address was given on the opening evening. On the next three days the mornings began with meetings of task forces and continuing seminars. The balance of the morning sessions featured two papers (OT and NT) in simultaneous sessions. During the first afternoon, four sessions were held in which research reports were presented. The program of the second afternoon, a general session, featured a panel discussion. General sessions were held on the second and third evenings, each featuring a major paper. Eucharist or service of the Word was observed every noon. This pattern, with little variation, prevailed until the end of the century.[19] The charter members of 1937 would have been surprised, however, to hear, at the end of the century, a presidential address delivered by Charles H. Talbert, a Southern Baptist.

Thus the CBA, launched by a small number of Catholic priests who were interested in Bible translation, has become a sophisticated ecumenical company of scholars dedicated to the advancement of critical research. Although the method of scientific historical criticism has largely triumphed, the CBA did not accede to a methodological orthodoxy. At the 1997 meeting of a discussion was instigated that questioned the validity of the so-called "advance."[20] This ongoing discussion witnesses to the maturity the CBA has achieved. The freedom to pursue critical issues is practiced in a context of faith, as seen in the continuing attention to worship at the annual meetings.

Studiorum Novi Testamenti Societas

The SNTS is distinguished from the SBL and the CBA by its primary focus on NT research.[21] The Society was the brain child of Prof. Johannes de Zwaan of Leiden. At the Faith and Order Conference at Edinburgh in 1937, de Zwaan arranged for a meeting of NT scholars in an Edinburgh restaurant. Those attending were enthusiastic about the idea of forming an international society of scholars for the study of the NT. C. S. Duncan of St. Andrews wrote a letter to several scholars, enlisting their interest. In response to a number of encouraging replies, a meeting of nineteen scholars was held at Carey Hall, Selly Oak, Birmingham in September 1938. J. M. Creed of Cambridge was elected conference chairman, and papers were read by T. W. Manson, W. F. Howard, and de Zwaan.[22] During the fourth session of the meeting, C. H. Dodd proposed "that we do form ourselves into a New Testament Society having for its object the furtherance of our New Testament studies."[23] The proposal was unanimously adopted, and a provisional committee was appointed to draft a constitution and invite other scholars to the first general meeting. This committee met on the last day of the Carey Hall meeting and adopted the Latin name in order to highlight the international character of the Society.[24] The provisional committee met again in London in December of 1938 and made plans to hold the first general meeting in Birmingham in September of the following year. By June of 1939 the Society had seventy members, including twenty-five from the Continent. The program was set and printed, but the meeting was cancelled, one of the first casualties of World War II.

After the War the British members of the provisional committee met in April of 1946. The committee decided to issue further invitations and arrange for the first general meeting to by held in Oxford the following year. That meeting took place at Christ Church, Oxford, in March of 1947. Thirty-eight members attended. The presidential address was delivered by de Zwaan and papers were read by Anton Fridrichsen, William Manson, and A. E. J. Rawlinson. From these small beginnings the SNTS has grown into an organization of some one thousand members representing about forty countries, mostly from Europe and North America, but also South Africa, South America, the Middle East, Asia, and Australia. Presidents have included the leading scholars of the twentieth century, among them individuals whose lives and works are featured in this *History*: C. H. Dodd, T. W. Manson, Vincent Taylor, Joachim Jeremias, Rudolf Bultmann, Werner G. Kümmel, Ernst Käsemann, Günther Bornkamm, W. D. Davies, Martin Hengel, F. F. Bruce, Raymond E. Brown, C. K. Barrett, and Hans-Dieter Betz.

The shape of the Society is sketched in its constitution.[25] As prescribed by the constitution, membership requires written nomination by two members of the Society, review by committee, and election at a general meeting. Emphasis is placed on scholarly promise and a record of publication. A major activity of the Society is publication. Beginning in 1950 a *Bulletin* was published, including papers read at meetings from 1950 through 1952. The major publication of SNTS is the journal *New Testament Studies* (*NTS*).[26] At the planning meeting in Birmingham in 1938 de Zwaan had already expressed the hope for an international journal for the study of the NT. The formal decision to launch the journal was made at the Cambridge meeting of 1953. The first issue appeared in 1954 with Matthew Black as editor. Black wrote that *New Testament Studies* would serve the goal of promoting international research in the NT

> by bringing together the results of the labours of scholars of different nations and traditions; by making known valuable and important work which is all too often carried out in unadvertised ways or to be found only in inaccessible publications; by reporting on different undertakings and research projects in various countries; by encouraging constructive criticism across political and confessional frontiers, and, in general, by offering articles, studies and reviews by the main authorities in their subjects, whatever their country of origin.[27]

The NTS Monograph Series (SNTSMS) was begun in 1965, and since then more than one hundred monographs have been published.

A major activity of SNTS is the annual general meeting. During the first years of the Society these meetings were usually held in Great Britain, although the sixth convened on the Continent at Bern (1952). The tenth general meeting, held in Bangor, North Wales, was attended by fifty-one members, sixteen wives, and eight guests.[28] This meeting is noted for its election of a record number of new members, including an impressive list of Americans, among them Henry J. Cadbury, Ernest C. Colwell, Floyd V. Filson, John Knox, Paul S. Minear, Paul Schubert, Allen Wikgren, and Amos N. Wilder.

The 50th General Meeting in Prague in 1995, attended by about four hundred members, spouses, and guests, exemplifies the form and content of the customary program.[29] The first evening included a business session. On the following morning, prayers were conducted by a member, followed by the presidential address. The early afternoon was devoted to the first sessions of eighteen seminar groups, each with two leaders; seminars continue for a minimum of three and maximum of five years. The seminars in 1995 considered such topics as "The Dead Sea Scrolls and the New Testament" and "The Historical Jesus." In the remainder of the afternoon two short papers and one main paper were presented. The evening featured a reception at Charles University. The second full day began again with prayers, followed by another (second) main paper. In late morning the second sessions of the seminar groups began. The afternoon included a visit to the National Gallery, and the evening featured a concert in the National Museum. The third full day began again with prayers, followed by a third main paper. This was followed by the third sessions of the seminar groups. In the afternoon six short papers were presented in simultaneous sessions, and later in the afternoon the fourth main paper was presented. A final business meeting included reports from the editors of *NTS* and NTSMS; forty-four new members were elected. On the three following days several members enjoyed excursions.

Although meetings are usually held in Europe, the Society has met a few times in the United States. Notable was participation in the International Congress of Learned Societies in the Field of Religion in 1972. The SNTS met first at Claremont and then moved to the larger meeting in Los Angeles. I remember the amazement of C. F. D. Moule at the operation of an American luxury hotel: the balmy Southern California climate was sealed out by closed windows, the room kept cool by air-conditioning, and comfortable sleep assisted by an electric blanket!

In sum, the SNTS is the primary international association for the study of the NT. It promotes the highest quality of research and confers on its members a degree of scholarly prestige.

Robert W. Funk (1926–2005) and the Jesus Seminar

Life and Work

One of the most controversial figures of twentieth-century NT research is Robert Funk, founder and soul of the Jesus Seminar. Funk's early work, when he was a star pupil in the Bultmann school, has been noted in Chapter 3. I first became acquainted with Bob Funk at annual meetings of the SBL when a small group of Disciples of Christ scholars would go out for conversation and refreshments after evening sessions. I remember him as a bright, congenial scholar, articulate and skilled in debate. One evening he mentioned that he was thinking of translating the Blass-Debrunner grammar and asked if I thought it was a good idea. I later quipped that that was the last time Bob *asked* me anything! During the years I served as editor of the SBL Dissertation Series, Bob was executive secretary of the Society. I found him to be a superb editorial advisor, providing helpful recommendations regarding difficult decisions. Although Funk could be charming and even charismatic, he could also be caustic. At a discussion following a complex sermon he delivered at the chapel in Brite Divinity School a student observed that he appreciated Dr. Funk's exegesis, but couldn't understand it. Bob replied, "Frankly, I don't give a damn!"

Robert W. Funk was born in Evansville, Indiana, and educated at Johnson Bible College, Butler University (AB, BD, MA) and Vanderbilt (PhD, 1953).[30] He was honored as a Guggenheim Fellow and a Senior Fulbright Scholar. Funk taught at Texas Christian University (1953–56), Harvard Divinity School (1956–57), Emory University (1958–59), Drew University (1959–66), Vanderbilt University (1966–69), and the University of Montana (1969–86). His work in leadership of the SBL has been reviewed earlier in this chapter. Lane McGaughy is correct when he writes that Funk "was instrumental in transforming the Society of Biblical Literature from a small circle of scholars from the eastern region of the United States into a large inclusive, international learned society during his tenures as executive secretary (1968–73) and president (1974–75)."[31] After his break with the SBL, Funk founded Polebrige Press (1981), the Jesus Seminar (1985), and Westar Institute (1986). He traces his theological migration in the early pages of his *Honest to Jesus.* As a youth he was persuaded by his minister to attend a Bible college in Tennessee, and he became a teenage evangelist. Dissatisfied with this role, he transferred to Butler University and enrolled in the classics department. After teaching in church-related universities and seminaries, Funk sought intellectual freedom at the University of Montana. In time, he decided to abandon the academic world. He moved to California in 1986, and with a group of like-minded intellectuals founded the Westar Institute, which, he wrote, "was formed to bring the best in high scholarship—the best we can enlist—to bear on the religious issues that matter in our time, and to do so within earshot of literate readers."[32]

Much of Funk's early research was dedicated to the study of Greek grammar.[33] He was prepared for this by his work in classics at Butler and his dissertation at Vanderbilt, written under the direction of Kendrick Grobel, on "The Syntax of the Greek Article: Its Importance for the Critical Pauline Problems." Funk made a major contribution with his translation of the Blass/Debrunner grammar, which had become standard in Germany.[34] In the process of working on the translation, which one competent reviewer said was better than the original, Funk came to the view that the language of the NT should be treated as a dynamic idiom of its own, not a mere corruption of the Attic dialect. Funk also believed that the study of NT Greek should be informed by the methods of modern linguistics.

These views were incorporated in Funk's *A Beginning-Intermediate Grammar of Hellenistic Greek*.[35] The emphasis of this grammar is on the structure of the language rather than the traditional stress on learning paradigms by rote memory. Later, in the preface to his *The Poetics of Biblical Narrative*, Funk wrote:

> This work, like my *Hellenistic Greek Grammar*, is based on an absolutely fresh compilation of textual data. The Greek grammar went unrecognized for what it was, viz., a new compilation of syntactical data, based on 3,000 actual sentences taken from extant Hellenistic texts. In addition, the Greek grammar was organized around new categories, some borrowed from modern linguistics, others invented at the behest of the recalcitrant data.[36]

Volume I is essentially an introduction to Greek grammar. In an opening section Funk discusses the character of the sentence, reflecting his understanding of "descriptive grammar." According to this kind of grammar, words and other elements of grammar are classified not according to traditional "parts of speech" but by morphological considerations. Part I of the *Grammar* presents the "Sight and Sound of Greek" (where Funk deals with the alphabet, pronunciation, breathing, syllables, etc.). Part II is concerned with the nominal and verbal systems. Volume II presents syntax, and Volume III is a collection of useful appendices and paradigms. All in all, this work shows a mastery of the material and an advanced understanding of linguistics—much that is beyond the beginner, but helpful to the advanced student.

Another example of Robert Funk's critical research is seen in his two-volume *New Gospel Parallels*.[37] Volume 1, as the subtitle indicates, includes the Synoptic Gospels. The preface notes Funk's concern to develop a synopsis that is useful for the study of the gospels as narrative. He points out that the gospel narratives have both vertical (paradigmatic) and horizontal (syntagmatic) dimensions. In the history of criticism, synopses have highlighted the paradigmatic, showing the vertical relation of accounts in a way useful for the study of the synoptic problem or redaction criticism. Harmonies, on the other hand, stress the horizontal, smoothing out the differences and presenting the material in sequence. "The combination of paradigmatic and syntagmatic research in their new forms," writes Funk, "will open up new horizons in understanding the gospel narratives. The *New Gospel Parallels* is designed to make such study possible."[38]

Primary features of the new synopsis are: each gospel is presented in turn as the primary text; the narrative sequence of the texts is preserved; each gospel is divided into segments according to principles derived from recent studies of narrative. These features are apparent in the arrangement of the page. Each page is divided into three vertical columns and horizontally into three more columns. The primary text (in RSV translation) is printed in bold type in the upper left column, with textual variants noted below. The parallels are presented in columns two through six, in canonical order followed by the *Gospel of Thomas* and other (apocryphal) gospel sources. Verbal parallels are indicated by bold type. Volume 2, *John and the Other Gospels,* presents the primary text (and parallels) in the sequence: Gospel of John, *Gospel of Thomas*, Sayings Gospels, Passion Gospels, and Fragments. The two volumes total about 900 pages and include pictures, graphs and maps. This is one of the most useful English synopses ever published—unfortunately, now out of print.[39]

Funk's concern with narrative is also seen in his *The Poetics of Biblical Narrative*.[40] During a sabbatical year in Canada he spent time with Henry A. Gleason, Jr. at the Linguistics Centre of the University of Toronto. This provided Funk with insights that informed his way of reading NT texts. In this complicated book Funk begins with a discussion of "Poetics and the Narrative Text." Narrative, he says, refers to the discourse or story (what is told) and the performance (act of narrating). Narrative consists of three elements: the focusing process (introduction), a train of events (nucleus), and a defocusing process (conclusion). A chapter on "Showing and Telling" discusses different kinds of narrative. "Showing" refers to a narrative in which the narrator, functioning like a camera, transports the reader to the scene of the events. "Telling" refers to the "unfocused scene" in which the narrator tells the reader what the reader cannot see. Two chapters late in the book illustrate the procedures of narrative analysis, using popular stories and biblical parallels. Regarding "Narrative Introductions," Funk shows that features of the introduction to the novel *Shane* are parallel to the elements of the introduction of the Gospel of Mark. In discussing "Passion Narratives," Funk finds parallels in the chapter "Death," in *Uncle Tom's Cabin* and the passion narrative of Mark. Funk's final chapter explores the significance of the study of narrative for NT research. "Biblical scholarship," he writes, "is perhaps at a major crossroads in its modern development as regards the nature of biblical narratives. It has been difficult to decide whether biblical narratives are about real or fictive events."[41] To literary critics who focus exclusively on the text, Funk replies, "It is patent nonsense, in historical narration, to claim that there is no relation between the historical events to which the text refers and the narrative text. But it is equally nonsensical to claim that the relationship is univocal."[42] This book is an example of Funk's broad learning and creative imagination.

Related to Funk's concern with narrative is his work on the parables, already apparent in *Language, Hermeneutic, and Word of God*.[43] His later research is published in *Parables and Presence: Forms of the New Testament Tradition*.[44] As the subtitle indicates, this book is concerned with NT tradition. Thus, beyond the sections on the parables, it includes two chapters on "The Apostolic Presence" as reflected in Paul and John the Elder (of 2 and 3 John), chapters that present Funk's view that their epistles make Paul (or John) "present" for their readers. Funk believes the parables to be decisive for understanding the historical Jesus.

> Jesus was a poet. It would then not be incorrect to say that Jesus, as maker of parables, invites his hearers, by means of his tales or riddles, to pass over from the attenuated world of jaded senses to some fabulous yonder he sees before him. He calls this fabulous beyond the Kingdom of God, and he wonders why others about him cannot see what is so evident to him. He admonishes them: you cannot point to the Kingdom there or here, as though it were an object among other objects; rather, the Kingdom is in your midst, if you would but look. The poet and the parabler produce language of promise.[45]

In regard to the "Narrative Parables" (e.g., the Good Samaritan), Funk observes that they are carefully constructed with a parsimonious use of everyday words, an economy of characters, and conciseness of plot. He claims that "the narrative parable tradition took shape in Greek, whether at the hands of Jesus or someone else, at some point proximate to the threshold of the Christian tradition."[46] In discussing "The Temporal Horizon of the Kingdom," Funk affirms the criterion of dissimilarity: "The difference in expectation between Jesus and the early church, on the one hand, and contemporary Judaism, on the other, is spectacular."[47] Moreover, in discontinuity with the early church, Jesus stressed the presence of the kingdom. "The mercy of God," says Funk, "does not wait upon some future—near or remote—but is already 'there' for those who care to quit the immense solidity of the mundane world and step through the looking glass of the parable. The kingdom is 'there' as certainly as Jesus goes in to eat with sinners."[48]

Much of Funk's later writing is directed to the historical Jesus. Most important is *Honest to Jesus: Jesus for a New Millennium.*[49] The book is a manifesto—a declaration of faith of one who has moved from teenage evangelist to propagator of secularism. The book is addressed to seekers: people starved for the truth, including clergy, lay leaders, scholars, journalists, and others who welcome an open, honest investigation. Part I, "Return to Nazareth," presents Funk's conviction that "the aim of the quest of the historical Jesus is to set Jesus free, to liberate him from prevailing captivities."[50] Funk proceeds to trace the decline of Christianity "From Nazareth to Nicea," or "How the Iconoclast became the Icon." "The quest of the historical Jesus is a way of restoring interest in the iconoclastic dimension."[51] Funk depicts an array of barriers that block the way of the quest: people's ignorance, popular images of Jesus, the fundamentalist view of Scripture, the silence and elitism of the scholars. The renewal of the quest will, in Funk's opinion, require a strong dose of skepticism. "*As historians we are obliged not to take anybody's word for anything; we must attempt to verify every scrap of information we decide to use in our reconstructions.*"[52] Funk proceeds to review the history of the old quest as chronicled by Schweitzer and the new quest advanced by the disciples of Bultmann.[53] "The third questers, like Raymond E. Brown and John P. Meier in the United States," Funk charges, "take critical scholarship about as far as it can go without impinging on the fundamentals of the creed or challenging the hegemony of the ecclesiastical bureaucracy. In their hand, orthodoxy is safe, but critical scholarship is at risk."[54] Instead of the "third quest," Funk proposes the "renewed quest," one reflecting a shift in biblical scholarship that occurred around 1975, characterized as "secularism."

Part II, "The Gospel of Jesus," begins with "The Search for the Rhetorical Jesus." Funk declares that "the earliest sources portray Jesus as a teacher of wisdom, a sage."[55] According to him, the theme of Jesus' teaching is the kingdom of God: "God's domain," the sphere in which God's dominion is immediate and absolute. Jesus, Funk believes, understood the kingdom as bringing an end to the old order. "His deviation and promiscuity were a part of the kingdom of God, which he claimed his Father had authorized him to announce. He practiced what he preached. As a consequence, he ignored, or transgressed, or violated purity regulations and taboos."[56]

Funk believes that for Jesus the kingdom is present, but elusive. "Strictly speaking, of course, arrival in the kingdom is not even possible. Arrival is by departure only. Entrance into God's domain is the same thing as exodus. . . . It is forsaking mother and father, wife and children, in order to acquire true relatives. For it no map is available. It is truly an immense journey."[57]

Part III investigates "the Jesus of the Gospels," not Funk's historical Jesus. In discussing the death of Jesus, Funk challenges the historian to acknowledge the role of myth-making. He declares that "the time has come for Christian scholars to discriminate what is mythical from what is historical in the interests of their own integrity and in the interest of a reduction in Christian arrogance, a trait notably lacking in the historical Jesus."[58] According to the bare facts, Jesus was executed in Jerusalem under the jurisdiction of Pontius Pilate. The myths and legends that shape the story reflect the imagination of the early believers. Funk believes a major shift developed in the tradition when Jesus the teacher was replaced by the teaching about Jesus.

> The mythical Christ gradually replaced the Galilean sage as the gospels grew. Jesus' fantasy of the kingdom was embedded in a larger picture that had Jesus himself as the center of attention. Jesus' vision of the kingdom became his followers' vision of him. Having given Jesus the leading role in the story, they then wrote a part for themselves into the drama. The result was the disenchantment of God's kingdom.[59]

Funk believes the idea of the resurrection had its origin in later Judaism, reflected in Qumran, the Pharisees, and the Jesus movement. The idea, in Funk's opinion, is not really consistent with the teachings of Jesus. Funk believes that the picture of Jesus as icon developed backward: from the resurrection to the baptism to the supernatural birth to the preexistent divine being.

In the Epilogue, Funk heralds Jesus for a new age; the Christian era has ended; a new age has dawned. He summarizes his understanding of the quest for this Jesus in twenty-one theses. The second, for example, reads: "*The renewed quest prompts us to revamp our understanding of the origins of the Christian faith itself.*"[60] Between theses four and five he inserts a section on "Breaking the Easter Barrier." Here he decries the neo-orthodoxy he once embraced. Neo-orthodoxy, Funk says, "was the last dying gasp of creedal Christianity."[61] According to thesis nine, "*We need to cast Jesus in a new drama, assign him a role in a story with a different plot,*" and according to the twenty-first thesis we should "*Declare the New Testament a highly uneven and biased record of various early attempts to invent Christianity.*"[62] Having assumed the mantle of the reforming Luther, Funk concludes by lampooning it: "These are the twenty-one theses. If I had a church, I would scotch tape them to the door."[63]

THE JESUS SEMINAR

The last phase of Robert Funk's career was devoted to the work of the Jesus Seminar. Funk was the founder, and according to one caustic critic the "ringmaster-entrepreneur" of the Seminar.[64] The Jesus Seminar was founded in Berkeley, California, in March 1985. In his opening remarks, with a touch of drama, Funk declared: "We are about to embark on a momentous enterprise. We are going to inquire simply, rigorously after the voice of Jesus, after what he really said."[65] "The religious establishment," Funk continued, "has not allowed the intelligence of high scholarship to pass through pastors and priests to a hungry laity, and the radio and TV counterparts of educated clergy have traded in platitudes and pieties and played on the ignorance of the uninformed. A rude and rancorous awakening lies ahead."[66]

The activity of the Seminar is divided into two periods. From 1985 to 1991, work concentrated on the sayings of Jesus; from 1991 to 1996, attention was directed to the acts of Jesus. The Seminar met twice a year. The work of the first period is summarized in *The Five Gospels*.[67] In this book the text of the gospels is presented according to the "Scholars Version," a translation fostered by the Seminar and characterized by striking colloquialisms, the language of the marketplace.[68]

The introduction to *The Five Gospels* observes that the work of the Seminar is built on seven pillars of scholarly wisdom, including the distinction between the historical Jesus and the Christ of faith, the recognition that the Synoptic Gospels are closer to the historical Jesus than the Gospel of John, and the acceptance of the priority of Mark and the existence of Q. Less widely accepted, but basic to the work of the Seminar, are pillars that assume liberation from the eschatological Jesus and the conviction that the burden of proof has shifted from what is not historical to what is. A long and complex section reviews the "rules of written evidence." In contrast to the usual criteria (delineated, for example, by John Meier),[69] Funk and the leaders of the Seminar present a lengthy list of rules. These are grouped according to major categories: "clustering and contexting" (the evangelists' arranging and relocating of sayings), "revision and commentary" (the evangelists' revising and editing of sayings), "false attribution" (words from common lore, Scripture, or the evangelists themselves, attributed to Jesus), "difficult sayings" (hard sayings that are softened, reflecting the struggle of the early Christian community in its own setting), "Christianizing Jesus" (sayings that express Christian apologetic and betray knowledge of events that transpired after the death of Jesus). A careful reading of these rules (and their application in the later text) indicates major use of the criterion of dissimilarity or discontinuity, especially discontinuity between Jesus and the early Christian community.

A similarly long section of the introduction to *The Five Gospels* delineates the "rules of oral evidence." The most basic rules include the recognition that only sayings that can be traced to the early period (30–50 ce) can be authentic, that sayings attested in two or more different sources are older than the sources in which they are embedded, that tradition presented in sources that are relatively late may preserve early, authentic material. These rules, of course, reflect the criterion of multiple attestation. As with the rules of written evidence, the rules of oral evidence are expanded under major categories: "orality and memory" (oral memory best retains sayings that are short and provocative: aphorisms and parables), "the story teller's license" (the evangelists imagined what Jesus said on various occasions, summed up his message, and predicted the outcome), "distinctive discourse" (Jesus' authentic sayings cut against the social and religious grain; they use concrete language; they surprise and shock), "the laconic sage" (the Jesus who does not make pronouncement about himself or claim to be Messiah). Many of these rules appear to be presuppositions that determine the results in advance.

The introduction proceeds to describe "the Jesus Seminar at work."[70] The Seminar began with the scholars who participated in the first meeting of 1985. Funk had invited thirty scholars, and twenty-two attended. Membership was open to anyone with a PhD, or equivalent, in biblical studies. Over the years the total number who participated in at least one meeting or joined as corresponding members may have reached four hundred. A typical meeting was attended by thirty or forty scholars ranging from "heavyweights" like Funk, John Dominic Crossan, and Marcus Borg to untested scholars fresh from their doctoral programs. The first step was the collection of more than 1,500 versions of approximately 500 sayings. In view of this vast amount of material, the Seminar faced two fundamental issues: how to reach decisions about authenticity (they decided to vote); how to report the results (they decided to publish a variation of the "red-letter version"). The Fellows of the Seminar voted by dropping colored beads into boxes, a procedure that replaced simple up-or-down votes with a system of qualifications. A red bead represented something Jesus undoubtedly said; a pink bead indicated that Jesus probably said something like this; a gray bead indicated that Jesus did not say this, but the ideas expressed are close to his; a black bead represented something Jesus did not say. The results of the votes were assessed according to "weighted averages." The colors were assigned numerical value: red = 3, pink = 2, gray = 1, black = 0. Each value was multiplied by the number of votes in each category and the sum divided by the total number of votes. The results were converted into percentages. Before each meeting, papers concerning the texts to be considered were circulated among the members, and before the votes the issues were discussed and debated. The final results: 18 percent of the sayings were rated as authentic (red or pink) and 82 percent as inauthentic (gray or black).

The Five Gospels presents in detail the results of the Seminar's deliberations. The text totals almost five hundred pages. It includes, in order, Mark, Matthew, Luke, John, and the *Gospel of Thomas*. The inclusion of *Thomas*, resulting in five gospels, reflects the Seminar's concern to break the imperialism of the canon and their conviction that *Thomas* contains very early tradition of the teachings of Jesus. As well as presenting the text in the Scholars Version according to the color scheme of the voting, *The Five Gospels* includes commentary, usually following each pericope, primarily explaining the judgments of the Seminar. The margin includes the title of the pericope, the chapter and verse of the primary text, the location of parallels, and the identification of sources. At various points in the text, boxes that include items of special interest to the editors are included. For example, a two-page box on "God's Imperial Rule: Present or Future?" is inserted between the texts of Matthew 4 and 5.

A few examples can illustrate the character of this work. The only saying in Mark to be printed in red is 12:17: "Pay the emperor what belongs to the emperor and God what belongs to God." The comment notes that this saying has parallels in Matthew, Luke, *Thomas*, and the Egerton Gospel, indicating that the saying circulated independently. "Everything about this anecdote commends its authenticity."[71] Readers may be surprised to find that the dying words of Jesus, "Eloi, Eloi, lema sabachthani" (Mark 15:34), are printed in black. Most commentators accept these words as authentic according to the criteria of multiple attestation, embarrassment, and the use of Aramaic.[72] The Seminar, however, believes the words demonstrate "how free the individual evangelists were in putting words of scripture on Jesus' lips."[73] In Matthew's Sermon on the Mount five verses, or parts of verses, are printed in red, notably three words from Matt 5:44: "Love your enemies." According to the comment, "the admonition 'love your enemies' is somewhere close to the heart of the teachings of Jesus to the extent that we can recover them from the tradition. . . . The injunction to love enemies is a memorable aphorism because it cuts against the social grain and constitutes a paradox: those who love their enemies have no enemies."[74] In the text of the Gospel of Luke, the parable of the Good Samaritan (10:30-35) is printed in red even though it has no parallels. The Seminar liked the Samaritan because he "stepped across a social and religious boundary."[75]

Regardless of the great value the Seminar placed on the *Gospel of Thomas*, only three of the 114 sayings are printed in red, and these have their sources in Q; of the several pink sayings in *Thomas* only two are not found in the Synoptics. Notable is the parable of the Mustard Seed (*GThom* 20:1-4; 2b-3, printed in red); the margin indicates *Thomas*, Q, and Mark as sources. "The Fellows judged the version in Thomas to be the closest to the original," says the comment. "The three synoptic versions have been accommodated to a greater or lesser degree to the apocalyptic tree theme and so were designated pink."[76]

The second main phase of the Jesus Seminar's work is recounted in *The Acts of Jesus*, edited by Funk and the Jesus Seminar.[77] In this phase the Fellows of the Seminar examined 387 reports of 176 events. Parallel to their work on the sayings, they voted, using colored beads: red (indicating a high level of confidence that the event actually happened), pink (indicating the view that the event probably took place), gray (indicating belief that the event was possible, but without adequate evidence), black (indicating the conviction that the event was largely or entirely fictive). The weighted evidence was assessed according to the same method used for the sayings, with the result that ten of the 176 events were rated red and nineteen pink—a total of 16 percent. Among the red-rated events are the Beelzebul controversy (Luke 11:15-17), the core event of the baptism of Jesus (Mark 1:9-11), and Jesus dining with sinners (Mark 2:15-17; Matt 9:10-11).

After this summary of the results, the introduction to *The Acts of Jesus* presents a critical introduction to the study of the gospels. This introduction discusses oral components of the gospels, understood according to the categories of form criticism. The Seminar adopts the 2DH and believes Mark created the basic outline of the gospel story. The editors think the tradition developed in layers.

> At the bottom—in the earliest stratum—Jesus talks about the kingdom of God. . . . At the next level, members of the early Jesus movement tell stories about the disciples talking about Jesus talking about God's domain. At the last stage of the written gospels, the evangelists represent their own communities reflecting on their appropriation of what the disciples had said about Jesus, who himself talked about God's kingdom in parables and aphorisms. Close observations regarding the layering of the tradition lie at the base of most critical assessments of the historical reliability of each gospel segment.[78]

For their criteria for determining historical judgments Funk and the Seminar rely on a version of multiple attestation: if a story appears in two or more independent early sources it is probably to be considered authentic. Criteria drawn from form criticism are adopted for evaluating oral tradition. The editors stress the distinction between "showing" (enactment) and "telling" (recounting); the former, they believe, is more likely to preserve the historical. Funk and the Seminar list other tests for historicity, many of which appear to be presuppositions of the Seminar or results of their earlier work, for example, the portrait of Jesus as an itinerant sage, a social deviant who does not speak of himself or claim to be messiah.

As to order, *The Acts of Jesus* presents first the narrative material from Q, followed by Mark, Matthew, Luke, and the *Gospel of Peter*. The material from each gospel is presented in pericopes, with title, chapter, and verses of the account, location of parallels and sources indicated in the margin. Following the text is a section of commentary, primarily explaining the decisions of the Seminar. At various points boxed sections ("cameo essays") that deal with particular issues, for instance, "John the Baptist and the Qumran Community," are added. The text of the Gospel of John has a few gray passages: for instance, a part of the account of the Temple incident (2:13–16a). It also prints one verse in pink (19:1) and three words of a verse in red (19:16), but no complete event in red or pink. Separate sections in the latter part of the book discuss the "Empty Tomb, Appearances and Ascension" and the "Birth and Infancy Stories." The end material includes a brief section, "What Do We Really Know about Jesus?" According to the editors, "The short answer is that we don't know a great deal."[79] Nevertheless, a small summary is possible:

> We are quite confident that a person Jesus of Nazareth once existed. . . . We are confident that he began as a disciple of John the Baptist, that he quit John at some point and returned to Galilee where he launched his own career as an itinerant sage. We believe he spoke about God's domain or God's imperial rule in parables and short, pithy sayings and attracted a substantial following. There is little doubt that he was also a charismatic healer and exorcist and that he was eventually put to death by Romans around the year 30 C.E.[80]

Criticisms of the Jesus Seminar are many and varied.[81] A vehement attack has been launched be a group of well-trained and respected evangelical scholars.[82] This group charges the Seminar with excessive skepticism, but for its own part advocates the total reliability of the gospel accounts. Another broadside is fired by Luke Timothy Johnson.[83] He has in his sights not only on Funk and the Fellows of the Seminar but mainline Jesus scholars like John P. Meier. Actually, Johnson opposes the whole enterprise of the quest of the historical Jesus. He acknowledges that historical research can collect data, but he believes it does not offer the information that can connect the dots and produce a reliable historical biography.[84] Among the views of the various critics are that: the Seminar claims to represent a consensus of critical scholars (Blomberg, Johnson); the methodology of the Seminar is flawed (Pearson); the Seminar claims too much for the *Gospel of Thomas* (Blomberg, Pearson); the Seminar's portrait of Jesus obscures his Jewishness (Blomberg, Pearson).[85] Most important, the Seminar has rejected the eschatological element in the life and teaching of Jesus. Pearson charges that this decision was made *a priori*, and it is evident that the most powerful members of the Seminar (Funk, Crossan, and Borg) had come to this conclusion prior to the deliberations of the Seminar. In regard to this point several critics have pointed out that the view of the kingdom as already fully present does little for the poor and hungry, whose condition remains unchanged.

From the perspective of the history of research, Funk and the Seminar's "renewed" quest appears to be essentially a revival of the old quest. Like some modern-day Rip Van Winkle, the Fellows seem to have fallen asleep in the seventeenth century only to awaken in the twentieth and discover that the Enlightenment had taken place. Their view is reminiscent of Reimarus.[86] His belief that the intentions of Jesus and of the early Christians were totally at odds anticipates Funk's account of how the iconoclast became an icon. But how did it happen so fast? How did the true historical Jesus change into the Christ of the early Christians? According to tradition reported by Paul in the 50s—a tradition probably going back to Paul's meeting with Peter, three years after his conversion—the risen Christ had appeared to a number of disciples. The notion that the Seminar was pioneering the publication of the results of critical scholarship fails to remember that the English deists were lampooning the miracles and the resurrection in highly popular, widely distributed pamphlets in the eighteenth century.[87] It is ironic that in its passion to broadcast the results of criticism to the public the Seminar seems to have won more opponents to historical criticism than converts.

Summary

The formation and growth of scholarly societies is a major feature of NT research in the twentieth century. The societies have promoted cooperative work and intellectual stimulation among NT scholars. They have provided venues for the presentation of new ideas and methods, and instruments for their dissemination and publication. Scholars have become not merely names in a bibliography but living persons, engaged in face-to-face discussion. The SBL, with roots in the nineteenth century, is the oldest but also the largest and most diverse. Although it has encouraged cooperation, the vast number of individual sections, groups, seminars, and consultations has tended to promote specialization. Scholars attending the annual meeting often gravitate to the particular program units of their special interests, attended by scholars of similar presuppositions and views.

The CBA, *contra* the Jesus Seminar, has demonstrated that a scholarly society can remain faithful to an ecclesiastical institution without compromising rigorous scholarship, working with members who do not share the same religious tradition. The notion that the Christian (or religious) era has come to an end and that secularism has triumphed ignores the continuing growth of Christianity and Islam, especially in the burgeoning Third World. Indeed, throughout its relatively short history the CBA has "advanced" in historical critical scholarship beyond the achievements of the other societies—from small concerns with translating the Vulgate to the magisterial works of Brown and Meier.

The SNTS is distinctive in its concentration on NT research. It also emphasizes the international scene, although the SBL and CBA also share this larger perspective. Of all the societies discussed in this chapter, the SNTS is most restrictive in membership. This has resulted not in an elitism but in a stress on quality of scholarly work. This Society reminds the scholarly community of the great heritage of European, especially German, scholarship. While the center of gravity may have shifted to America (with larger numbers of Europeans attending the annual meetings of the SBL), young American scholars should not neglect the history of research, the rigors of European study of critical details, and the importance of the mastery of European languages for the investigation of the NT.

Little more needs to be said in critique of the Jesus Seminar. It does not represent a consensus, but a minority of scholars captive to a particular point of view. The center of NT research has not shifted from seminaries and church-related colleges and universities to secular institutions as Funk and the Seminar predicted. However, it is a mistake to dismiss the work of the Seminar and Robert Funk with a casual gesture. One of the ironies of the Seminar is its concern to communicate with the laity when much of its work (for example, critical introductions to the Gospels) is highly technical. Scholars who do not share its view can learn much from this material. Also, some of the claims of the Seminar, perhaps exaggerated, contain considerable truth. It is true that criticism taught in the seminaries is not communicated to people in the pews. Whatever one may conclude about Robert Funk, much of his work is profound, creative, and bordering on genius. At the very least, Funk and the Jesus Seminar can confront the more traditional scholar with the need to give a reason for the hope within.

One of the great benefits of the societies is the fact that a scholar can belong to more than one, even all. Some do, with profit. Others do not have time. There are many societies, but one spirit: the concern to pursue historical research in the service of a better understanding of the NT.

Notes

1. On the nature and history of the Society see Kent Harold Richards, "Societies, Scholarly," in *Dictionary for Theological Interpretation of the Bible*, ed. Kevin J. Vanhoozer (London: SPCK, 2005), 757; Ernest W. Saunders, *Searching the Scriptures: A History of the SBL, 1880–1980*, SBLBSNA 8 (Chico, CA: Scholars, 1982).

2. For Schaff, see *HNTR* 2: 43–52; for Briggs, ibid., 289–93.

3. See J. Philip Hyatt, ed., *The Bible in Modern Scholarship: Papers Read at the 100th Meeting of the Society of Biblical Literature, December 28–30, 1964* (Nashville: Abingdon, 1965).

4. See James M. Robinson, "Afterword," in Birger A. Pearson, *The Gospel According to the Jesus Seminar*, OPIAC 35 (Claremont, CA: Institute for Antiquity and Christianity, 1996), 44–48; "Statement Regarding Robert Funk," *Bulletin of the Council on the Study of Religion* 12 (Dec. 1981): 143.

5. "Journal of Biblical Literature: 125th Anniversary: Commemorative Essays," *JBL* 125 (2006): 153–65, at 153.

6. *Harper's Bible Dictionary* (1985), revised as *HarperCollins Bible Dictionary*, ed. Paul J. Achtemeier (San Francisco: HarperSanFrancisco, 1996); *Harper's Bible Commentary* (1988), revised as *HarperCollins Bible Commentary*, ed. James L. Mays (San Francisco: HarperSanFrancisco, 2000).

7. Patrick Gray, "Presidential Addresses of the SBL: A Quasquicentennial Review," "Journal of Biblical Literature: 125th Anniversary: Commemorative Essays," *JBL* 125 (2006): 167–177, at 167.

8. See Harold W. Attridge and James C. VanderKam, eds., *Presidential Voices: The SBL in the Twentieth Century*, SBLBSNA 22 (Atlanta: SBL, 2006).

9. For the history of the CBA see Gerald P. Fogarty, *American Catholic Biblical Scholarship: A History From the Early Republic to Vatican II*, SBLCPS (San Francisco: Harper & Row, 1989); Francis S. Rossiter, "Forty Years Less One: An Historical Sketch of the C.B.A. (1936–1975)," *CBQ* 66 (2004) *Supplement*, 1–13; Joseph Jensen, "Y2K Plus 4," ibid., 14–16; Carolyn Osiek, "Catholic or catholic: Biblical Scholarship at the Center," in *Presidential Voices*, 325–42.

10. Quoted by Rossiter, "Forty Years Less One," 4.

11. *A Commentary on the New Testament Prepared by the CBA under the Patronage of the Episcopal Committee of the Confraternity of Christian Doctrine* (Washington, DC: Catholic Biblical Association, 1942).

12. Quoted by Fogarty, *American Catholic Biblical Scholarship*, 241–42. Albright did what he could to enliven the meetings of the SBL. I remember a session some time in the 1950s when he, with commanding presence and in booming voice, totally dismantled the paper of another prominent scholar with whom he ardently disagreed.

13. Carolyn Osiek, "Catholic or catholic," 332. Professor Osiek was herself elected to the presidency of the CBA some years later.

14. *The New Testament: Rendered from the Original Greek with Explanatory Notes* (Milwaukee: Bruce, 1954).

15. *The Jerome Biblical Commentary*, ed. Raymond E. Brown, Joseph A. Fitzmyer, and Roland E. Murphy (Englewood Cliffs, NJ: Prentice-Hall, 1968). This was succeeded by *The New Jerome Biblical Commentary*, with the same editors (Englewood Cliffs, NJ Prentice-Hall, 1990).

16. *The New American Bible: Translated from the Original Language with Critical Use of All the Ancient Sources, by Members of the Catholic Biblical Association of America* (New York: P. J. Kenedy, 1970). The NT section was revised and republished: *The New American Bible: Revised New Testament Authorized by the Board of Trustees of the Confraternity of Christian Doctrine and Approved by the Administrative Committee/Board of the National Conference of Catholic Bishops, and the United States Catholic Conference* (Grand Rapids: Eerdmans, 1988). The complete NAB, with a revised OT, was published in 2010.

17. *CBQ* 66 *Supplement* (2004): 17–26.

18. "Report of the Fiftieth General Meeting of the Catholic Biblical Association of America," *CBQ* 49 (1987): 626–32.

19. See "Report of the Sixty-third International Meeting of the Catholic Biblical Association of America, *CBQ* 62 (2000): 701–8.

20. See Osiek, "Catholic or catholic," 335–38. The paper that "caused a stir" at the meeting was read by Luke Timothy Johnson, "What's Catholic about Catholic Biblical Scholarship," later published in Luke Timothy Johnson and William S. Kurz, *The Future of Catholic Biblical Scholarship: A Constructive Conversation* (Grand Rapids: Eerdmans, 2002), 3–34. Johnson was answered at the next meeting by one of the scarred veterans of the earlier battles, Roland E. Murphy: "What is Catholic about Catholic Biblical Scholarship—Revisited," *BTB* 28 (1998): 112–19.

21. For the history of the SNTS see G. H. Boobyer, "Studiorum Novi Testamenti Societas," *NTS* 1 (1954–55): 66–70; "SNTS, its Origins, and Robin McL. Wilson's Contribution to the Society: An Address given by former Secretary, Dr William R. Telford, on the occasion of the 90th Birthday Celebrations for Prof. Robin McL. Wilson, held at the School of Divinity, St Mary's College, University of St Andrews (Saturday, February 18, 2006)," www.surfgroepen.nl/sites/SNTS/default.aspx >SNTS Documents >History of SNTS.

22. For the life and work of T. W. Manson, see pp. 33–40 above.

23. Quoted by Boobyer, "Studiorum," 67.

24. At the meeting in Norwich in 1959 it was suggested that the name should be reviewed by some expert Latinists.

25. "Constitution" (as Approved at the General Meeting, September 1949), *NTS* 1 (1954–55): 70–71.

26. See Matthew Black, "Foreword," *NTS* 1 (1954–55): 1–4; C. K. Barrett, "*New Testament Studies*: 1954–2004," *NTS* 50 (2004): 1–4.

27. Black, "Foreword," 1–2.

28. "Studiorum Novi Testamenti Societas: The Tenth General Meeting," *NTS* 2 (1956): 215–26.

29. See "Studiorum Novi Testamenti Societas: The Fiftieth General Meeting, 31 July–3 August 1995," *NTS* 42 (1996): 295–320.

30. For summaries of the life and work of Funk, see Robert W. Funk, *Honest to Jesus: Jesus for a New Millennium* (San Francisco: HarperSanFrancisco, 1966), 1–14; Lane C. McGaughy,

"Funk, Robert W. (1926–2005)," *DMBI*, 446–51; idem, "Funk, Robert W. (1926–)," *DBI* 1: 423–24; Andrew D. Scrimgeour, *Just Call Me Bob: The Wit and Wisdom of Robert W. Funk* (Santa Rosa, CA: Polebridge, 2007).

31. *DBI* 1: 423.

32. *Honest to Jesus*, 6.

33. See McGaughy, *DBI* 1: 423.

34. Friedrich Blass and Albert Debrunner, *A Greek Grammar of the New Testament and Other Early Christian Literature. A Translation and Revision of the nineteenth German edition incorporating supplementary notes of A. Debrunner*, by Robert W. Funk (Chicago: University of Chicago Press, 1991).

35. Robert W. Funk, *A Beginning-Intermediate Grammar of Hellenistic Greek*, 3 vols. 2d ed., SBS 2 (Missoula, MT: SBL, 1973).

36. Robert W. Funk, *The Poetics of Biblical Narrative*, FF (Sonoma, CA: Polebridge, 1988), viii.

37. Robert W. Funk, *New Gospel Parallels*, 2 vols. FF (Philadelphia: Fortress Press, 1985).

38. *New Gospel Parallels*, vol. 1, *The Synoptic Gospels*, xiii.

39. A decade later, in the context of the work of the Jesus Seminar, Funk produced another synopsis: Robert W. Funk, ed., *New Gospel Parallels, Vol. 1, 2: Mark*, 3d ed. (Santa Rosa, CA: Polebridge, 1995). The original plan was to publish two parts: (1) The Synoptics; (2) John, Thomas and the other Gospels. Only vol. 2 of Part I (Mark) was published. The volume includes some significant introductory material concerning the study of the gospels. This new synopsis incorporates the texts in the "Scholars Version" (discussed below) and does not present the narrative feature of the texts as well as the earlier synopsis.

40. See n. 422 above.

41. *Poetics*, 296.

42. Ibid.

43. See pp. 174 above.

44. Robert W. Funk, *Parables and Presence: Forms of the New Testament Tradition* (Philadelphia: Fortress Press, 1982). For a collection of shorter writings on the parables see Robert W. Funk, *Funk on Parables: Collected Essays*, ed. Bernard Brandon Scott (Santa Rosa, CA: Polebridge, 2006).

45. *Parables and Presence*, 17.

46. Ibid., 28.

47. Ibid., 70.

48. Ibid., 74.

49. Robert W. Funk, *Honest to Jesus: Jesus for a New Millennium* (San Francisco: HarperSanFrancisco, 1966).

50. Ibid., 21.

51. Ibid., 45.

52. Ibid., 58.

53. See pp. 136–37, 156–60 above.

54. *Honest to Jesus*, 65.

55. Ibid., 143.

56. Ibid., 204.

57. Ibid., 216.

58. Ibid., 219.

59. Ibid., 254.

60. Ibid., 301.

61. Ibid., 304.

62. Ibid., 306, 314.

63. Ibid., 314. Much less polemical and more imaginative is Funk's *Jesus as Precursor*, SBLSSup 2 (Philadelphia: Fortress Press, 1975). The distinctive feature of this book is Funk's

comparison of gospel material with the works of modern literary figures: Kafka, Samuel Beckett, Henry Miller, Carlos Castaneda, and others. In the epilogue he draws implications for understanding theology. "Theology must forsake the cloistered precincts of the church, where nothing real is being addressed, in favor of a radical openness to mundane experience" (p. 156). In a final twist of humor Funk writes, "All teachers and students of theology should learn to fly-fish, wander in the wilderness, and bake bread" (p. 159). Funk's *A Credible Jesus: Fragments of a Vision* (Santa Rosa, CA: Polebridge, 2002) repeats his conviction that the quest of the historical Jesus must focus on his rhetoric. "Jesus is remembered as a sage whose dominant forms of public speech included the aphorism, the parable, and the dialogue" (p. 6). The balance of the book deals with themes of the teaching of Jesus, including the kingdom, the trust ethic, celebration, love of enemies. Funk believes Jesus advocated a reversal: "the unkingdom of the unGod" (p. 133). The cross is not, according to Funk, and instrument of sacrificial atonement. "Absolute, uncompromising integrity is the true meaning of the cross" (p. 145).

64. Luke Timothy Johnson, *The Real Jesus: The Misguided Quest for the Historical Jesus and the Truth of the Traditional Gospels* (San Francisco: HarperSanFrancisco, 1996), 6. The activities of the Seminar have been reported in the Westar Institute's journal, *Forum*. See also Robert J. Miller, *The Jesus Seminar and its Critics* (Santa Rosa, CA: Polebridge, 1999); Marcus J. Borg, *Jesus in Contemporary Scholarship* (Harrisburg, PA: Trinity Press International, 1994); The Jesus Seminar; Robert W. Funk, et al., *The Once and Future Jesus* (Santa Rosa, CA: Polebridge, 2000).

65. Robert W. Funk, "The Issue of Jesus," in *Jesus Reconsidered: Scholarship in the Public Eye*, ed. Bernard Brandon Scott, JSemG (Santa Rosa, CA: Polebridge, 2007), 5.

66. Ibid., 6.

67. Robert W. Funk, Roy W. Hoover, and the Jesus Seminar, *The Five Gospels: The Search for the Authentic Words of Jesus: New Translation and Commentary* (San Francisco: HarperSanFrancisco, 1993).

68. The Scholars Version is published as *The Complete Gospels: Annotated Scholars Version*, ed. Robert J. Miller (Sonoma, CA: Polebridge, 1992). Subsequent editions added gospel material; a 4th edition appeared in 2010. For a criticism of the translation see Birger A. Pearson, *The Gospel According to the Jesus Seminar*, OPIAC 35 (Claremont, CA: Institute for Antiquity and Christianity, 1996), 29–34.

69. See p. 399 above.

70. See also Miller, *Jesus Seminar*, 1–60; Borg, *Jesus in Contemporary Scholarship*, 160–81; Roy W. Hoover, "The Work of the Jesus Seminar: Honesty, Collaboration, Accessibility: A Defense of the Seminar and to Its Critics," in *Jesus Reconsidered*, 13–24; Bernard Brandon Scott, "How Did We Get Here? Looking Back at Twenty Years of the Jesus Seminar," ibid., 47–64.

71. *Five Gospels*, 102.

72. See, for example, Raymond E. Brown, *The Death of the Messiah* (New York: Doubleday, 1993), 2: 1085–88.

73. *Five Gospels*, 126.

74. Ibid., 147.

75. Ibid., 324.

76. Ibid., 485. An earlier publication, Robert W. Funk, Bernard Brandon Scott, and James R. Butts, *The Parables of Jesus: Red Letter Edition*, JSemS (Sonoma, CA: Polebridge, 1988), presents the decisions of the Seminar in regard to the parables. Here, too, high value is placed on the *Gospel of Thomas*, which, according to the editors, embodies tradition as early as 50–60 CE. "There is no pattern of relationships between Thomas and the Synoptics that would require Thomas' dependence on them" (p. 11). The bulk of the book presents the parables in the order of the Seminar's ranking. Thirty-three parables are included: five red, sixteen pink, six gray, six black. The five red parables are: Leaven, Good Samaritan, Dishonest Steward, Vineyard Laborers, and Mustard Seed. Each parable is printed (according to the Seminar's color code) on a page with parallels. The text is RSV and the sources are noted. The end material includes various tables, a brief history of parable interpretation, and a list of the Fellows of the Seminar, including William

Baird, who never attended a meeting and never cast a vote. The Seminar also published *The Gospel of Mark: Red Letter Edition*, ed. Robert W. Funk with Mahlon H. Smith (Sonoma, CA: Polebridge, 1991).

77. Robert W. Funk and the Jesus Seminar, eds., *The Acts of Jesus: The Search for the Authentic Deeds of Jesus* (San Francisco: HarperSanFrancisco, 1998).

78. *Acts of Jesus*, 24.

79. Ibid., 527.

80. Ibid. A summary of the Seminar's work in the form of a reconstructed gospel with Prologue, 21 Chapters, and Epilogue is presented in Robert W. Funk and the Jesus Seminar, *The Gospel of Jesus: According to the Jesus Seminar* (Santa Rosa, CA: Polebrige, 1999).

81. For a summary see Miller, *Jesus Seminar*, 61–146; Pearson, *The Gospel According to the Jesus Seminar*.

82. Michael J. Wilkins and J. P. Moreland, eds., *Jesus Under Fire* (Grand Rapids: Zondervan, 1995). The more direct and detailed critique of the Seminar in this collection is Craig L. Blomberg's "Where Do We Start Studying Jesus?" (pp. 17–50).

83. *The Real Jesus*.

84. Johnson's position would seem to preclude the production of any biography (or interpretive history). His view is reminiscent of Martin Kähler, *Der sogenannte historische Jesus und der geschichtliche, biblische Christus* (1896; ET: *The So-Called Historical Jesus and the Historic, Biblical Christ* [Philadelphia: Fortress Press, 1964]), a work not mentioned in Johnson's book. It is also ironic that Johnson, who criticizes the Seminar for it passion for publicity, uses the same publisher who published many of the works of the Seminar. His title, *The Real Jesus*, seems to suggest the same sort of sensationalism he criticizes in the work of the Seminar.

85. Pearson, *Gospel According to the Jesus Seminar*: "The Jesus of the Jesus Seminar is a non-Jewish Jesus. To put it metaphorically, the Seminar has performed a forcible epispasm on the historical Jesus, a surgical procedure removing the marks of his circumcision" (p. 42).

86. See *HNTR* 1: 170–73.

87. Ibid., 1: 31–57.

PART III

Theological and Synthesizing Movements

9

Theological and Hermeneutical Developments

The new biblical theology that was planted by Barth and flourished with Bultmann continued in the post–World War II period. The culture of the era reflected troubled times. The dissonant chords of Shostakovich's Seventh Symphony echoed the bombs of the siege of Leningrad. Operas had been tragic before, but few had reached the despair expressed in Alban Berg's atonal "Wozzek." Sigmund Freud traced the source of violence to the depths of the human psyche. T. S. Eliot envisaged people wandering in a desolate "Waste Land," and Jean-Paul Sartre viewed humans as trapped in a meaningless existence from which there was "No Exit." For Albert Camus the human person was "The Stranger," living a pointless life in an irrational world. Samuel Beckett, proponent of the theater of the absurd, dramatized the futility of "Waiting for Godot," who never showed up.

Could the Bible or a biblically oriented theology offer any hope in this time of trouble? Many thought so, and young students hurried off to theological schools in search of answers. Most were attracted to institutions dominated by a variety of what was known as "neo-orthodoxy." The citadel of this sort of biblical theology was Union Theological Seminary in New York, where the major voices were those of Paul Tillich and Reinhold Niebuhr. At Yale Divinity School, long a center of liberal Christianity, the most prominent theologian was H. Richard Niebuhr, famous for his castigation of liberalism for believing that "a God without wrath brought men without sin into a kingdom without judgment through the ministrations of a Christ without a Cross."[1]

The kind of biblical theology that had wide appeal, notably in America, focused on the "history of salvation." This view stressed the importance of revelation and God's redemptive action in the "event" of Jesus Christ. American biblical theologians, for example G. Ernest Wright and Floyd V. Filson, liked to speak of "the mighty acts of God." Although they had trouble pointing to contemporary examples, they found many in the OT and NT. Important for the shaping and disseminating of salvation-history theology was Oscar Cullmann, who commuted between Basel and Paris and attracted students from all over the world. America, however, produced biblical theologians of distinctive character: John Knox and Paul Minear. Representative of the growing importance of evangelical scholars is F. F. Bruce.

Salvation History: Oscar Cullmann (1902–1999)

Life and Early Work

Born in Strasbourg, Cullmann was nurtured in the liberalism of a Protestant home and church.[2] From 1920 to 1924 he studied at the University of Strasbourg, where he heard Albert Schweitzer's lectures on the history of life-of-Jesus research. Cullmann also studied in Paris under such luminaries as Alfred Loisy and Maurice Goguel.[3] He served on the faculty at Strasbourg from 1930 to 1939, teaching NT and history of the early church. In 1938 Cullmann was appointed professor of New Testament and Early Church History at the University of Basel, where he remained until his retirement in 1972. The breadth of his influence is attested in his Festscrift, *Oikonomia*, a collection of essays by thirty-six scholars, all former students from Europe, the United States, and South America. Cullmann was committed to ecumenicity; he had friends in the Catholic hierarchy and attended Vatican II as an observer.[4]

Cullmann was troubled by drooping eyelids. When he spoke with someone he tilted back his head, giving the impression of talking down his nose. Actually, Cullmann enjoyed conversation with students. When he conversed with a group of us at Yale, sometime around 1950, he had already visited other institutions in the United States. At one of these he had been speaking, as often, about the Clementine literature. The students there taught him to sing "My Darling Clementine," which he did with humor, displaying the engaging personality that made him an effective teacher.

Cullmann's theological development saw his early commitment to liberalism eclipsed by his reading of Karl Barth.[5] In time, however, Cullmann questioned Barth's preoccupation with theological exegesis and affirmed the necessity of scientific, philological-historical research. Later he came to recognize the importance of eschatology and salvation history, and he forged a hermeneutics that integrated historical critical method and theological interpretation. Theodore Martin Dorman writes:

Specifically, we contend that from the outset of his career Cullmann has sought to define the relationship between revelation and history in a way that avoids the narrow historicism of Liberalism's "historical Jesus" on the one hand, and Dialectical Theology's renunciation of historically-based revelation on the other. Cullmann has thus sought to articulate a hermeneutics that accurately reflects the positive relationship he sees between revelation and history.[6]

Cullmann's commitment to historical criticism is reflected in his essay, "The Necessity and Function of Higher Criticism."[7] An overview of his critical work can also be seen in his introduction to the New Testament, written for the general reader.[8] In this short book Cullmann accepts the Two-Document solution to the Synoptic problem and rejects the Pauline authorship of the Pastorals, but, displaying a conservative tendency, accepts the authenticity of 2 Thessalonians, Ephesians, and 1 Peter. A late example of Cullmann's research can be seen in his work on the Fourth Gospel.[9] He believed that this Gospel was a product of the "Johannine Circle," but that the primary author was "the beloved disciple," an anonymous follower of Jesus.

Cullmann was a prodigious scholar who produced an abundance of publications.[10] His dissertation, an exercise in *Religionsgeschichte*, was concerned with the Pseudo-Clementine writings.[11] After a critical analysis of the literature he concludes that the texts indicate the existence of an early Jewish-Christian Gnosticism. This means, for example, that the historian need not look to Hellenistic sources to find the background of the thought of the Gospel of John, a view Cullmann believed to be confirmed by his later study of the Dead Sea Scrolls.[12]

HISTORY OF SALVATION

Cullmann's first major work on the history of salvation is his *Christ and Time*,[13] which had been anticipated by his earlier *Königsherrschaft Christi und Kirche im Neuen Testament*.[14] In this monograph Cullmann focuses on eschatology. He argues that the rule of Christ began with his exaltation to the right hand of God. With this event Christ rules over the world, but his rule is not yet complete; it awaits Christ's return. The latter expectation is discussed in Cullmann's lecture, "Die Hoffnung der Kirche auf die Wiederkunft Christi nach dem Neuen Testament."[15] Here Cullman focuses on future eschatology and argues that the return of Christ is essential to the Christian hope. He affirms the centrality of Christ in salvation history and uses for the first time the term *Heilsgeschichte*.[16]

Christ and Time was first published in 1946.[17] In this book Cullmann responds to the question: "In what does the *specifically Christian element* of the New Testament consist?"[18] He begins by presenting his understanding of the NT terminology for "time." The distinctive terms, says Cullmann, are καιρός (which designates a point in time) and αἰών (which means "age," and refers to duration of time); the καιροί of past, present, and future constitute the redemptive time-line.

> The terminology of the New Testament teaches us that, according to the primitive Christian conception, time in its unending extension as well as in its individual periods and moments is given by God and ruled by him. Therefore all his action is so inevitably bound up with time that time is not felt to be a problem. It is rather the natural presupposition of all that God causes to occur.[19]

Cullmann proceeds to contrast the biblical linear concept of time with the cyclical understanding he detects in Hellenism. For the Greeks, according to Cullmann, the goal is to escape time. Christianity, in contrast, sees the sequence of events as redemptive history.

> An event of the past, the death and resurrection of Christ, is regarded as the decisive mid-point of the entire line of revelation, and in this way the connection of the future with what has previously happened is no longer left vague and undefined; rather now for the first time, on the basis of the fixed orientation to *that mid-point in time*, the line can be clearly drawn from the beginning on, in its unbroken continuity.[20]

For Christianity, according to Cullmann, the decisive eschatological event has occurred but the end has not yet happened. At this point Cullmann introduces his favorite imagery: the decisive battle (D-day) has been won, but the complete victory (V-day) is still future. "*The hope of the final victory is so much the more vivid because of the unshakably firm conviction that the battle that decides the victory has already taken place.*"[21] According to Cullmann, Christ, the mid-point, is the key to understanding the whole line of salvation history: the time before creation, the creation, the election of Israel, the founding of the church, and the future consummation. "The Pre-existent One, the One who yesterday was crucified, he who today exercises hidden lordship, he who returns at the turn of the ages—they are all one; it is the same Christ, but in the execution of his functions in *the successive stages of time in the redemptive history.*"[22] Cullmann also depicts the time-line spatially: at creation, all nature is included; with the call of Israel the line in narrowed; it is further narrowed to one in Christ; with the founding of the church the line is broadened; and with the consummation all the cosmos is again encompassed.

Cullmann believes the present is to be understood in terms of its location on the time line. In the present, the new age has already begun in the life and worship of the church. "The missionary proclamation of the Church, its preaching of the gospel, gives to the period between Christ's resurrection and Parousia its meaning for redemptive history; and it has this meaning through its connection with Christ's present Lordship."[23] Cullmann also notes the role of the individual in the history of salvation: justification is the application of the redemptive process to the individual and the connecting link is faith.

> Thus the individual man stands related to the past phase of redemption in a twofold way. On the one side it is precisely for him, the sinner, that this entire process has occurred, and there is salvation for him only if he believes that this past concerns him in a quite personal way. On the other side, he as one foreordained to this faith and thereby to redemption, is chosen from the beginning to become an active fellow bearer of the redemptive process, and in view of this role he belongs in the past phase of redemptive history; *it is his own past.*[24]

In 1962 Cullmann published a third edition of *Christus und die Zeit.*[25] This edition includes minor revisions throughout but adds an introductory chapter that responds to some of his critics. This chapter is reproduced in the English translation of 1962 (pp. xvii–xxxi). In response to Bultmann's criticism that Christ is not the middle but the end of history and his charge that future eschatology is myth, Cullmann replies that redemptive history is linear and future eschatology has temporal and historical significance.[26] Cullmann also insists that his view of Christ as the mid-point is not intended to stress quantity of time (time divided into two halves), but the decisive incision into time. He notes that most of the criticisms are directed against his linear view of time.

> I am interested in this concept merely because it provides the New Testament *background* to that which is important to me: the present-future tension. I am as much interested in the redemptive-historical moving from plurality to the unique, "the middle," and *vice versa*, as

I am in the way all periods are orientated from the middle, i.e., the events of the first decades of the Christian era. These . . . points of interest, and not linear time as such, constitute the concern of my book.[27]

Cullmann's theology of salvation history is fully developed in his *Heil als Geschichte*.[28] This book, sensitive to the critics and more nuanced than *Christ and Time*, is probably Cullmann's magnum opus, although far too much space is allotted to battling Bultmann and his school.[29] In the prolegomenon Cullmann repeats his conviction that salvation history is the essence of the Christian message. He says that "*Christian faith, like Jewish faith, was distinguished from all other religions of the time by this salvation-historical orientation.*"[30] In the scholarly debate about eschatology, Cullmann sides with Kümmel: the kingdom is both present and future.[31] He acknowledges, with Bultmann, that exegesis without presuppositions is impossible, but he thinks too much has been made of "pre-understanding," and he has no sympathy for existentialist (or virtually any other philosophically-based) hermeneutics. "The *scholarly* requirement to find out first of all by means of the philological, historical method what the text has to say to us that is new and perhaps completely foreign, thus coincides with the *theological* requirement to listen to the Word of Scripture as to a revelation completely new to us and to let ourselves be given *new questions* by that Word."[32]

Cullmann turns to the genesis of the concept of salvation history. He believes the source is to be found in the recognition of the life of Jesus as the fulfillment of the Hebrew Scriptures. "Finally, we note that in the genesis of New Testament salvation history, all events, the past, the present, and the ones expected in the future, are summed up in one event as their high-point and mid-point: the crucifixion of Christ and the subsequent resurrection."[33] He acknowledges that the Bible describes such events as creation and the consummation in mythological language but argues that the biblical writers demythologize these events by historicizing them. He believes, therefore, that salvation history occurs in history. Salvation history is different from ordinary history, according to Cullmann, because it includes revelation and the unfolding of God's redemptive plan; salvation history is prophetic history. "The material relationship between salvation history and history, theologically speaking, is that salvation history in essence rests upon election, on reduction to a very narrow line, and that this line continues on for the salvation of all mankind, leading ultimately to a funneling of all history into this line, in other words, a merging of secular history with salvation history."[34] A key feature of salvation history, according to Cullmann, is the eschatological tension between the present and the future. "The *new element* in the New Testament," he writes, "is not eschatology, but what I call the *tension* between the decisive 'already fulfilled' and the 'not yet completed,' between present and future. The whole theology of the New Testament, including Jesus' preaching is qualified by this tension."[35]

The balance of *Salvation in History* explicates the doctrine of salvation in the NT from Jesus to the end of the apostolic age. In regard to the Gospels, Cullmann, wary of the criterion of dissimilarity, accepts a large number of the sayings attributed to Jesus as authentic. He admits that some texts indicate that Jesus expected the end to come very soon, but he argues that the time element is secondary.

> We conclude that in Jesus' preaching the present which extends beyond his death is *already the end*. But this does not in any way justify asserting that Jesus is the end of all salvation history. *The end time is, on the contrary understood as belonging completely to salvation history, since each of its periods, short as they may be, has it own significance and is distinguished from others.*[36]

Cullmann believes Paul saw himself as playing a decisive role in the history of salvation. His mission to the Gentiles was, according to Cullmann, a prerequisite of the future consummation. The Gospel of John, which had been de-eschatologized by Bultmann, is rehabilitated by Cullmann. John stressed the incarnate Christ as the center. "In this life the *whole history of salvation*, past and future, is *summed up vertically*, and yet this life is *incorporated into a horizontal line*."[37] Although Cullmann agrees that the Fourth Gospel emphasized an eschatology realized in Christ, he contends that the author also affirms a futuristic eschatology. Cullmann thinks the course of salvation continues beyond the NT to the final consummation. However, he believes that the period from the time of the apostolic eyewitness to the time of the formation of the canon constitutes a special segment of salvation history. "The canon represents the end of the process of revelation and interpretation."[38] Cullmann concludes that the message of salvation history is crucial to contemporary theological reflection. "The task of the preacher and exegete is to interpret the past and future of salvation history *in relation to its present development in our time. Thus, all our theological work belongs to the development of salvation history.*"[39]

CHRISTOLOGY

Cullmann's other major works reflect his continuing concern with salvation history. Most important is his book on NT Christology.[40] In the introduction Cullmann, like other scholars reviewed in this chapter, notes that post-biblical Christology is (mistakenly) preoccupied with the person and nature of Christ. "The New Testament hardly ever speaks of the person of Christ without at the same time speaking of his work."[41] The bulk of Cullmann's book is an investigation of christological titles, arranged according to his view of the history of salvation.

Cullmann begins with titles that refer to the earthly work of Jesus. In regard to the title "prophet" he cites texts indicating "that during his lifetime a part of the people considered Jesus to be the Prophet expected at the end time."[42] Cullmann agrees that this title explains the preaching of Jesus and his eschatological vocation, but says that it fails to affirm his preexistence and role in the future. Cullmann turns to the "Suffering Servant of God" ('ebed YHWH). Although he acknowledges that this was not a messianic title in the Judaism of the NT period, Cullmann believes early Christianity interpreted the Servant (of Second Isaiah) as the messiah whose major task was vicarious suffering and sacrificial death. "We conclude that the concept 'Jesus the ebed Yahweh' has its origin with Jesus himself, just as does the concept 'Jesus the Son of Man.' "[43] In regard to the "High Priest," he believes this title represented an ideal figure in Judaism, as seen in the speculation about Melchizedek. When Jesus quotes from Psalm 110 (Mark 12:35-37), Cullmann supposes that Jesus refers to himself, identifying himself with the order of Melchizedek (Ps 110:4).

Next, Cullmann investigates titles that refer to the future work of Jesus. "Messiah" (Christ) is the most important title for Christianity. Cullmann notes that the term basically means "anointed" and refers in the OT primarily to the king. According to Cullmann, Jesus acknowledges the title but is reticent to use it, being wary of political implications. Cullmann believes that Jesus preferred the title "Son of Man." Although the term in Aramaic may simply mean "man," he thinks Jesus used it in the context of Jewish expectation about the eschatological Heavenly Man. He also believes that Jesus combined this title with the Servant of YHWH. "We conclude that . . . Jesus used the title Son of Man to express his consciousness of having to fulfill the work of the Heavenly Man in two ways: (1) In the glory at the end of time—a thought familiar to the expectation of the Son of Man in certain Jewish circles; (2) in the humiliation of the incarnation among sinful men—a thought foreign to all earlier conceptions of the Son of Man."[44] Cullmann believes that the Hellenists of Acts 6:1 embraced a Son of Man Christology, and that the idea is also reflected in the Second Adam of Rom 5:14.

Among titles used for the present work of Jesus, Cullmann considers "Lord" to be most important. The Romans hailed Caesar as *Kyrios*, and Hellenistic Judaism (in the LXX) used the term to translate the Aramaic *Adonai*, the substitute for the name of God. This title was not applied to Jesus, according to Cullmann, until after Christ's resurrection and exaltation.

> There is no reason at all, then, for contesting the fact that the very earliest community called Jesus "the Lord." He was considered the invisible Lord who rules his Church and appears in worship among the brothers "where two or three are gathered in his name"—although at the same time he sits at the right hand of God and rules the whole world.[45]

The use of *Kyrios* for God in the LXX (the early church's Bible) implies, according to Cullmann, that the early Christians affirmed the deity of Christ. "The New Testament unquestionably presupposes the deity of Christ, but it does so in connection with the faith in the lordship he exercises since his exaltation; that is, primarily in connection with his work rather than with his being."[46]

Cullmann wades into even deeper water when he discusses titles that refer to the preexistence of Jesus. Although the term *Logos* is widely used in Hellenism, Cullmann believes the more important background is to be found in two features of Judaism: the OT idea of the Word of God and the later concept of the personified Logos-Wisdom. Although the Logos is used (in the NT) as a christological title only in the Johannine literature, Cullmann believes "this title expresses very forcefully an important aspect of New Testament Christology—the unity in historical revelation of the incarnate and the pre-existent Jesus."[47] He goes on to say that "the Logos is God himself in so far as God speaks and reveals himself. The Logos is God in his revelation."[48] Also important is the designation of Jesus as "Son of God." Cullmann traces the origin of the use of this title back to Jesus himself. After the resurrection Christians confessed Jesus as the Son of God. Cullmann also believes early Christians designated Jesus as "God." This is implied, he thinks, by the use of *Kyrios* and "Son of God." However, he warns against construing this title metaphysically and insists that we can speak of the deity of Christ only from the standpoint of salvation history. He concludes: "Therefore all Christology is *Heilsgeschichte* and all *Heilsgeschichte* is Christology."[49]

PETER

Related to his theology of salvation is Cullmann's book on Peter, a work also significant for the ecumenical discussion.[50] He begins with an investigation of the historical evidence about Peter the disciple. His original name was Symeon (Hebrew) or Simon (Greek). He was called *Kepha*, which means "Rock" (*petros*), a nickname given him by Jesus at the time of his confession of Jesus as Messiah (Matt 16:18). Peter became the spokesman for the disciples, named first in all the lists. As apostle, Peter became the leader of the early church in Jerusalem. According to Acts he supervised the mission to Samaria and engaged in mission to the Palestinian coast. He was later imprisoned in Jerusalem, and after his release he was succeeded by James. Peter participated in the Jerusalem Council, an event that, according to Cullmann, is reported in both Acts 15 and Galatians 2. Cullmann believes that Peter had been commissioned to apostleship by the historical Jesus—a commission confirmed by a resurrection appearance (1 Cor 15:5). According to Cullmann an account of this appearance may have been recorded in the "lost" ending of Mark. In regard to Peter's theology, he notes the use of *pais theou* (Greek for *'ebed YHWH*) in speeches attributed to Peter in Acts 3 and 4.

In regard to Peter as martyr, Cullmann recognizes the paucity of sources. He supposes that the author of Acts knew of but for some unknown reason did not mention the deaths of Peter and Paul. Cullmann detects a hint of martyrdom in 1 Pet 5:1 and believes "Babylon" (1 Pet 5:13) connects Peter with Rome. In a complex (and not entirely convincing) argument he contends that 1 Clement 5 implies the martyrdom of Peter in Rome; he also believes this martyrdom is hinted in the letter of Ignatius to Rome. More solid support for the martyrdom of Peter in Rome is supplied by Irenaeus and Tertullian. Cullmann reviews the reports of excavations, especially those made under St. Peter's; his second edition updates the bibliography and adds extensive notes, but the conclusion is the same as in the first edition,

> The archaeological investigations do not permit us to answer in either a negative or an affirmative way the question as to the stay of Peter in Rome. The grave of Peter cannot be identified. The real proofs for the martyrdom of Peter in Rome must still be derived from the indirect literary witnesses, and from them we have reached the conclusion that probably Peter actually was in Rome and suffered execution under Nero. The excavations speak in favour of the report that the *execution of Peter took place in the Vatican district*.[51]

In concluding his historical investigation, Cullmann writes:

> we must say that during the life time of Peter he held a pre-eminent position among the disciples; that after Christ's death he presided over the church at Jerusalem in the first years; that he then became the leader of the Jewish Christian mission; that in this capacity, at a time which cannot be more closely determined but probably occurred at the end of his life, he came to Rome and there, after a very short work, died as a martyr under Nero."[52]

Cullmann turns to the exegetical and theological questions about Peter. The crucial exegetical question is the meaning of Matt 16:17-19. Cullmann believes the original framework of the account was provided by Mark, and that the author of Matthew inserted these verses. Nevertheless, he thinks that the naming of Simon as Peter took place prior to the resurrection and probably had its historical setting in Luke 22:31-34. Cullmann imagines that Matt 16:17-19 originally belonged to the passion narrative and had its setting at the Lord's Supper. Moreover, Cullmann believes the text is genuine, preserving an authentic saying of Jesus. The argument that Jesus would not have used the term "church," according to Cullmann, fails to recognize that the word *ekklēsia* is frequent in the LXX in reference to the people of God. Cullmann argues that Jesus, who expected the future coming of the kingdom, could also speak of the founding of the church in the present. As to the details of the text, Cullmann insists that the Aramaic word *Kepha* used for Peter is the same word used for the foundation. Thus he agrees with his Catholic friends that Peter is the foundation of the church, but he argues that this role as founder and keeper of the keys (the administrator of the house) is not passed on to Peter's successors. Peter has a unique apostolic function at the beginning, not in the ongoing life of the church.

Cullmann proceeds to discuss the doctrinal question of the application of Matt 16:17-19 to the later church. He argues that the saying was addressed to Jesus' own time and should not be applied to the later periods of the church's life. The church, he insists, is built on the apostles and the prophets (Eph 2:20; Rev 21:14). To be an apostle one had to be an eyewitness of the resurrection and, according to Cullmann, the role of the eyewitness is unique and cannot be transmitted to successors. Thus Cullmann affirms the priority of the apostolic witness in Scripture over the ongoing tradition of the church; the foundation of the church occurred once; "it was laid, that is, at the beginning, at the midpoint of the times, in the time of revelation, when Christ lived on earth, died, and rose."[53] He concludes: "The history of Primitive Christianity gives no warrant of any kind for the assumption that Peter came to Rome to transfer the primacy to that place."[54]

Cullmann published shorter works related to his doctrine of salvation history. Among these is the popular *Immortality of the Soul or Resurrection of the Dead?*[55] He states his thesis at the outset: "The concept of death and resurrection is anchored in the Christ-event . . . and hence is incompatible with the Greek belief in immortality; because it is based in *Heilsgeschichte* it is offensive to modern thought."[56] Cullmann argues (largely on the basis of 2 Cor 5:1-5) that at death the Christian sleeps in an intermediate state, awaiting participation in the final resurrection.

In *The State in the New Testament*, Cullmann explores the problem of the Christian living in the time between the victory of Christ and the ultimate triumph of Christianity over the worldly powers.[57] Jesus, too, faced political problems in his encounter with the Zealots, a group of revolutionaries whose movement Jesus rejected.[58] Cullmann calls attention to the fact that Jesus was executed by the Roman state. This implies, according to him, that Jesus was recognized by some of his contemporaries as Messiah, performing a political role. Cullmann argues that Jesus' "condemnation would be incomprehensible if Jesus had not in fact regarded himself as the Son of Man who came to establish the Kingdom of God in the world. To me this is the strongest evidence of what we call Jesus' self-consciousness."[59] Cullmann believes the trial Jesus faced in Gethsemane was the temptation to be a political messiah.

Cullmann produced a shelf of short books on early Christian life and worship. An early example is his monograph on early Christian confessions.[60] Here he addresses the question: why did the early Christians need another formula besides Scripture to summarize their faith? Before the writing of the NT they needed a summary of their faith in oral form. According to Cullmann, "the ancient Church regarded the *proclamation of Christ as the essential element in all confessions.*"[61]

Cullmann also published a book on early Christian worship.[62] In the first part he describes the basic characteristics of the early Christian worship service. The components of the service included preaching, prayer, and the breaking of bread. Cullmann says that "*the first eucharistic feasts of the community look back to the Easter meal*, in which the Messianic Meal promised by Jesus at the Last Supper was already partly anticipated."[63] In the second part of the book

Cullmann argues (*contra* Bultmann) that the message of the Fourth Gospel is saturated with sacramental imagery.[64] For example, he believes the wedding at Cana (John 2:1-11) symbolizes the Eucharist and anticipates the messianic meal; the conversation with Nicodemus (3:1-21) presents the sacrament of baptism as new birth; the blow of the lance (19:34) produces blood and water, symbols of both sacraments.[65]

Cullmann addresses the sacraments in two interesting books. In regard to baptism, he argues that this practice is based on the death and resurrection of Christ.[66] Cullmann relates baptism to salvation history. "The temporal centre of all history, the death and resurrection of Christ, is also the centre of the history of baptism."[67] He defends infant baptism, arguing that baptism requires no prior faith and that there is no evidence in early Christianity for the baptism of adult children of Christians. He concludes that "both adult and infant Baptism are to be regarded as equally biblical."[68]

In regard to the Lord's Supper, Cullmann believes that there were two early forms of the Eucharist: one that stressed the death of Christ and one that expressed the joy of celebration.[69] He believes the latter form has its origin in the meals at which the risen Christ appeared. Paul, according to Cullmann, stressed the relation of the Supper to the last meal of Christ with the disciples and the union of the disciples with the death of Christ. In time the two types of Eucharist were united, but Cullmann believes that (unfortunately) the joyous celebration was pushed into the background and increasing emphasis was placed on the importance of the elements of bread and wine for the remission of sins.

In the main, the work of Oscar Cullmann has been well received, especially among Americans who sympathize with salvation-history theology and by evangelicals who resonate with his doctrine of Scripture and tendency toward "conservative" criticism.[70] Among his critics, Jean Frisque charges that Cullmann ignores the transcendental element and fails to consider ontology and the nature of Christ.[71] Cullmann's view of history, according to Frisque, is reductionist—a positivism of history. Karl-Heinz Schlaudraff contends that Cullmann does not give adequate attention to soteriology, in particular to the doctrine of justification.[72] He also accuses Cullmann of reducing the message of the Bible to a particular view of salvation history, thereby forcing it into a straitjacket. Theodore M. Dorman, who generally agrees with Cullmann, detects an inconsistency: Cullmann says that revelation includes both event and interpretation but then allows that distortions have crept into the biblical record.[73] When one views Cullmann from a perspective beyond the horizon of salvation history his stress on history appears to give too little attention to history's nature and meaning. Despite the aversion of the history-of-salvation theologians to philosophy, every view of history rests on a philosophy of history, on an ontology. Cullmann reduces history to a sequence of objective events, but what is an event? What does it mean to speak of the "Christ event?"

BIBLICAL THEOLOGY IN AMERICA: KNOX AND MINEAR

JOHN KNOX (1900–1999)

Born in Frankfort, Kentucky, Knox was the son of a Southern Methodist minister.[74] At a young age he entered Randolph-Macon College, where he resisted the historical-critical study of the Bible. After graduation from Randolph-Macon (1919) he was assigned a six-church circuit; in storied Methodist style he made the rounds on horseback. Knox served for a time as the pastor of a parish in Bethesda, Maryland (1928–29). In 1929 he began his work at Fisk University in Nashville; about this experience he wrote: "I look back upon my five years as Minister of the Chapel at Fisk University as the most significant period of my career."[75]

At Candler School of Theology, Emory University (BD 1925) Knox came to accept the critical approach. He began study at the University of Chicago in 1927 and competed his PhD in 1935; he was influenced by the critical work of Edgar J. Goodspeed and the sociological method of Shirley Jackson Case.[76] Knox served as associate professor of New Testament at Hartford Theological Foundation (1938–39), and from 1939 to 1943 he was associate professor of Homiletics at the University of Chicago; he was promoted to professor of Homiletics and New Testament at Chicago in 1942.

In 1943 Knox was named Baldwin Professor of Sacred Literature at Union Theological Seminary in New York, where he remained until his retirement in 1966. Knox spent his final years of teaching at The Episcopal Seminary of the Southwest in Austin, Texas (1966–72). He was revered by his students and respected by colleagues as one who combined sincere piety with profound scholarship. Knox was a devoted churchman. First ordained to the Methodist ministry, he was confirmed in the Episcopal Church in 1959 and ordained to its priesthood in 1962.

I remember being in awe of John Knox at meetings of the SBL at Union. He was a tall, commanding figure, totally without pretense. When a young member presented a paper that opposed Knox's chronology of Paul, he responded in abject humility, commending the other scholar for his research and acknowledging deficiencies in his own.

PHILEMON, CANON, AND CHRONOLOGY

Knox's early work was primarily directed toward historical criticism.[77] His first important publication is his book on *Philemon*, based on his Chicago dissertation, first published in 1935 and later revised.[78] Essential to his thesis is his view of the relation of Philemon to Colossians, which, according to Knox's theory, has to be authentic. Knox supposes that the letter to Philemon is actually "the letter from Laodicea" (Col 4:16). In contrast to the usual reading, Knox believes Archippus, not Philemon, to be the owner of the slave Onesimus. Knox surmises that the epistle is addressed to Philemon (who lived in Laodicea) because he is the supervisor of the churches of the region, in a position of authority over Archippus and the church that meets in his house. The rest of the story reads like a novel: Onesimus is freed; he becomes a fellow-worker of Paul and eventually bishop of Ephesus, the collector of the Pauline letters, and the author of the cover letter, Ephesians.

Knox's critical imagination is also displayed in his *Marcion and the New Testament*.[79] In this book Knox argues that Marcion, with his collection of ten Pauline letters and a Gospel, was the first to establish a canon of NT Scripture. "Marcion is primarily responsible for the idea of the New Testament."[80] Knox believes the orthodox canon was developed in reaction to Marcion. Marcion's canon consisted of the "Apostle" and the "Gospel." According to Knox, Marcion's "Apostle," which included ten letters, represents the original collection of the Pauline epistles. Marcion's "Gospel" is recognized as bearing some relation to Luke. The traditional view is that Marcion abridged the Gospel of Luke. Knox argues, to the contrary, that Marcion used a primitive gospel (which he shortened) that was later expanded by the author of canonical Luke. In reaction to Marcion's ten letters of Paul, the orthodox church added to the canon the Pastoral Epistles and the writings of other apostles. In response to Marcion's single Gospel, the church added three others; Knox finds no evidence for the existence of a fourfold gospel before mid-second century, the time of Marcion. The plot thickens when Knox discusses the relation of Luke-Acts to Marcion's "Apostle-Gospel." According to Knox there is no evidence of the existence of Luke and Acts (in their present form) before the middle of the second century. He concludes that Luke-Acts was written in response to Marcion's canon.

> I regard Luke-Acts as being under one of its aspects an early apologetic response to Marcionism. The "Gospel and Apostle" of "Luke" follow the "Gospel and Apostle" of Marcion, as they also anticipate the "Gospel and Apostle" of the official canon. The author

of Luke–Acts sought to reclaim both a Gospel and Paul from the Marcionites.[81]

Knox's unconventional criticism is also reflected in his *Chapters in a Life of Paul*.[82] This book has two sections: an investigation of Pauline chronology (Parts 1 and 2), and an exposition of Paul's thought (Part 3). At this point the section on Paul's chronology will be reviewed; Part 3 will be discussed later in relation to Knox's theological work. *Chapters in a Life of Paul* was originally published in 1950. The revision expands and refines the first edition but also includes an introduction (by Douglas R. A. Hare) that reviews the work of various scholars in response to Knox's original proposal. The major feature of Knox's work is his attempt to reconstruct the chronology of Paul (almost) exclusively from the data of the epistles.

Knox begins with an assessment of the sources. He insists that the primary sources for reconstructing the chronology are the nine epistles of Paul that Knox accepts as authentic: Romans, 1 and 2 Corinthians, Galatians, Philippians, Colossians, 1 and 2 Thessalonians, and Philemon. Knox observes that chronological data is provided by Acts, but he finds much of it unreliable. Although most scholars recognize the epistles as the primary source, there is a tendency, Knox believes, to harmonize the sources in a way that overvalues Acts.

Knox proceeds to reconstruct the career of Paul according to the data provided by the epistles: Paul was converted in Damascus (Gal 1:15-17); he spent three years in Syria and Arabia (Gal 1:17-18); after these three years he made his first visit (since his conversion) to Jerusalem. Paul's second visit to Jerusalem was fourteen years later, at the time of the Jerusalem conference (Gal 2:1-10). According to Knox, Paul, during this fourteen-year period, engaged in mission in Galatia, Asia, Macedonia, and Greece. In the period immediately after the conference (probably three or four years) Paul was busy collecting the offering he had pledged at the conference (Gal 2:10; 1 Cor 16:1-4; 2 Cor 8, 9). Paul made a final trip to Jerusalem with the collection (1 Cor 16:3-4; Rom 15:25-32). Basic to Knox's chronology is his insistence that Paul made three trips, and only three, after his conversion (despite the data from Acts, which implies five). On the basis of this chronology Knox offers some tentative dates in Paul's career: conversion (34 ce), first Jerusalem visit (37), arrival in Macedonia (40), arrival in Corinth (43), arrival in Ephesus (46), second Jerusalem visit (51), last visit to Corinth (54), final Jerusalem visit (54 or 55).[83]

EXEGESIS, THEOLOGY, AND CHRISTOLOGY

Knox produced no major critical commentaries, but he contributed the section on "Introduction and Exegesis" of Romans in the *Interpreter's Bible*.[84] The *IB* was itself a remarkable venture in publication. It reflected the broad interest in biblical studies at the time, and it encouraged use of the RSV (the NT section had been completed in 1946, the whole Bible in 1952), the first major revision of the English Bible since the 1901 ASV. Published over a period of years (1951–57), the *IB* consisted of twelve volumes (six for each testament). The text (KJV and RSV in parallel columns) was printed at the top of the page; a band in the middle of the page was devoted to exegesis, with a two-column section on exposition at the bottom. Knox served on the editorial board and contributed, besides his work on Romans, the "Introduction and Exegesis" on Philemon.

Knox expressed high praise for the Epistle to the Romans. "It is thus the principal source book for the study of Paul's gospel, and in consequence it is unquestionably the most important theological book ever written."[85] Among the questions of critical introduction, Knox attends to the debated problem of the purpose of the letter. He notes that Paul's projected visit to Rome and his plan to travel to Spain constitute the occasion of the letter, but he does not believe Paul's primary purpose was to enlist support for his mission to the west. The purpose, according to Knox, should be understood in light of two situations: Paul's own (he now has the opportunity to summarize his gospel for a church he has never visited), and that at Rome (Paul is concerned to correct misunderstandings about him that may be abroad in the church). Most of all, Paul is eager to proclaim the gospel.

Knox also discusses the knotty problem of the text. He observes that "Rome" is missing from some MSS at 1:7 and 1:15. However, Knox believes "Rome" was in the original text and was probably omitted by a scribe who knew another form of the letter, or perhaps when Romans was placed first in the collection of the Pauline epistles. In regard to the doxology (16:25-27), Knox agrees with the majority that it is not genuine. He also notes that in the manuscripts this text appears variously at the end of chapters 14, 15, and 16. Knox investigates problems in chapter 16: the polemic paragraph (vv. 17-20), which does not fit the situation of the letter, and the list of names not connected to Rome. Knox, however, rejects the once-popular hypothesis that chapter 16 was addressed to Ephesus. He concludes that the original letter consisted of 1 to 15; a version of the letter ending at 14 (probably shortened by Marcion) also circulated; Romans 16 is a pseudonymous composition later added, along with the doxology, to the original letter. Knox, in accord with his chronology, dates Romans earlier than most scholars, to 53 CE.

His exegesis proceeds verse by verse, with some attention to details (e.g., analysis of Greek terms). His commentary, in contrast to most examples of the genre, is eminently readable. A few examples can illustrate the character of his exegetical work.

Within the larger section, "Address and Salutation" (1:1-7), Knox's discussion of 1:3-4 includes a review of early Christian Christology. He believes that the phrase "designated Son of God . . . by his resurrection" reflects an early adoptionist view. However, Knox thinks the term ὁρισθέντος, "designated" (NRSV: "declared") indicates that the resurrection designated what was true already: that Jesus Christ was the incarnate Son of God.

The crucial section of the epistle Knox designates as "The Saving Act: Justification by Faith" (3:21—4:25). Within this section, 3:21-30 is titled "Justification Defined," as being a text that presents the justifying action of God. In vv. 21-22, Knox observes, the justifying act of God is said to be received by "faith in Jesus Christ." He notes that some exegetes interpret the genitive, "faith of Jesus Christ" (KJV), as subjective: "Jesus Christ's own faithfulness." Knox comments, "Almost certainly, however, the RSV translators are correct in understanding the genitive to be objective and rendering it as they do: 'the faith of Jesus Christ' is our 'faith in Jesus Christ.'"[86] Knox considers vv. 24b-26 to be one of the most important but at the same time most difficult texts in the epistle. He rejects the translation of the debated term ἱλαστήριον as "mercy seat," and argues that the meaning cannot be "propitiation," since it is God who "put forward" Christ as expiation. However, Knox insists that Paul is not using mere metaphor. "A price must be paid; a penalty must be suffered; a sacrifice must be offered"[87]—a view with which Knox himself has little sympathy.

Within the larger section "The New Life into Which This Justifying Act Admits the Believer" (5:1—8:39), Knox recognizes 7:14-25 to be one of the most controversial texts in Romans. He addresses two hotly debated questions: (1) is the passage autobiographical? and (2) does it refer to life before or after faith? Knox answers the first in the affirmative: "In using the first personal pronoun Paul is not trying merely to give vivid expression to what is imaginary or hypothetical."[88] In regard to the second he concludes: "We shall assume that Paul in this passage is not merely remembering an earlier situation, but is also speaking naturally and sincerely out of his present experience."[89] Although this, and his other exegetical conclusions, are debatable, Knox has provided a thoughtful commentary for the clergy and laity for whom the IB was designed.[90]

In the late 1940s or early 1950s Knox's major interest shifted from critical research to theological reflection.[91] The transition can be traced in his Criticism *and Faith.*[92] The decisive question is raised in the Foreword: "What bearing does the historical method of studying the Bible have upon Christian faith?"[93] In answer, Knox argues that the apprehension that criticism is a threat to faith is "utterly groundless"; "biblical historical criticism not only has no strangle-hold on Christian faith, but does not have it in its power to destroy one jot or one tittle of the gospel."[94] The importance, even the necessity, of historical criticism is grounded in the nature of Christianity as a historical religion. "Christianity, then, is by definition a religion for which history is of supreme concern; an historical event is indeed the very source and centre of it."[95] Knox continues: "This event was remembered as centring in the life, death, and resurrection of Jesus, and was interpreted by the community as nothing less that God's decisive act for the salvation of mankind."[96] The balance of the book elaborates a fundamental theme of Knox's theology: the truth of Christian revelation belongs to the essential experience of the Christian community, to our very being as Christians. Thus the historian, although he or she may offer important details and provide defense against docetism, can neither confirm nor refute the fundamental truth of the Christian faith.

Later in his career Knox published a book on the nature of faith entitled *Limits of Unbelief.*[97] In this book he affirms the necessity of faith. "Being a Christian means, among other things, believing something—or, better said perhaps, *seeing* with one's *mind*, *thinking* about, the world and human life in certain characteristic ways."[98] As to the content of belief, faith in Christ and the church are fundamental. "Christology and ecclesiology belong indissolubly together. The Church's doctrine of Christ is its way of stating its understanding of itself."[99] The revelation through Christ, known in the community of faith, is revelation of God, the Father of Jesus Christ. According to Knox, essential to the life of the community is hope in the life everlasting.[100] To live in the community, says Knox, is to live by the law of Christ: to accept ethical obligation.

Important for Knox's theology is his understanding of the language of faith, depicted in his book *Myth and Truth.*[101] Here Knox contends that myth is necessary for the expression of Christian truth. "When we say, then, that a Christian myth is indispensable, we are saying that something of decisive importance in the inner being and nature of the Church cannot be expressed or explained or even definitively referred to except in terms of it. Such a myth is thus an irreplaceable symbol."[102] Knox differentiates between myth and legend. Legends, he says, purport to be historical but are not (historically) true; myths present, in symbolic form, the truth of revelatory history. The birth narratives, according to Knox, are legend; the resurrection is myth (although some of the resurrection narratives are legends).

Knox's understanding of the theology of Paul is presented in Part 3, "The Man in Christ," in *Chapters in a Life of Paul*. According to Knox, the crucial theological themes for Paul are Jesus as Lord, the new creation (the community), and the gift of the Spirit. He proceeds to discuss Paul's idea of "life in Christ." "To be 'in Christ' was to be an organic part of the new creation, of which the risen Christ was the supreme manifestation and the effective symbol; it was, indeed, to belong to the eschatological kingdom of God that had already appeared within history as the church."[103] Knox is critical of what he considers Paul's failure to emphasize forgiveness, a concept Paul describes by two terms: justification and reconciliation. Knox exclaims that "it must be said that the division that Paul made in the meaning of forgiveness was one of the most tragically fateful developments in the whole history of Christian theology and, therefore, in the intellectual history of the west."[104] Knox argues that repentance is necessary, and that it is possible only on the basis of forgiveness. Instead, Paul, according to Knox, stresses the death of Christ as acquitting the guilty and overstates the doctrine of justification.[105] Knox also charges that Paul's lack of emphasis on forgiveness undercuts the ethical imperative; forgiveness, properly understood, acknowledges the reality of sin and the necessity of obedience. Paul, according to Knox, harbors an incipient antinomianism.[106]

Knox's major theological contribution is in Christology. The development of his position can be traced in the trilogy, *Jesus: Lord and Christ*.[107] The first of the three books, *The Man Christ Jesus*, focuses on the life and teaching of Jesus but is sensitive to theological dimensions.[108] Knox affirms the importance of the historical Jesus even though a biography is not possible. For him two important features in the life of Jesus stand out: he was a Jew; he was an individual of exceptional stature, "a figure of heroic dimensions."[109] Concerning the teachings of Jesus, Knox stresses ethics. "In no other source, Jewish or non-Jewish, do we find religion interpreted so exclusively and so richly in ethical terms."[110] Knox, like the salvation history theologians, emphasizes God's action in Christ. "The center of this event was the character and career of the man Christ Jesus. In him God had acted to redeem those who would receive him, and in the community which had been formed about him, and of which he was still the living center, that redemption was offered to all mankind."[111]

The second book of the trilogy explores the meaning of Jesus for the Christian community.[112] This book is divided into three parts: He Was Remembered; Jesus Was Still Known; He Was Interpreted. In the first part

Knox affirms the importance of historical criticism for the study of the historical Jesus.[113] The Jesus of history is remembered as the one who proclaimed the kingdom of God—according to Knox, God's eternal sovereignty, which is present and to be complete in the age to come. Most of all, Jesus is remembered as the crucified one. "The cross became the central symbol of the church's faith only because it had first been the actual center around which the whole remembered meaning of the life of Jesus had been gathered."[114] In discussing "Jesus Was Still Known," Knox sounds a theme that dominates much of his succeeding work: Jesus is known as Savior and Lord in the life of the church. "It was in Jesus as *known in the church,* both before his death and afterwards, that the fresh activity of God among men, which we call the revelation in Christ, first occurred."[115] In Part III ("He Was Interpreted") Knox traces the development of Christology from belief in the resurrection to the confession of Christ in the creeds. "Reflection upon the resurrection led to the idea of pre-existence, and reflection upon pre-existence led to the gradual supernaturalizing of Jesus' whole career."[116] Although he laments this development, Knox recognizes the necessity of christological formulations. "The reason the basic and common christological terms will always prove to be both indispensable and irreplaceable is that they stand, as mythological terms invariably do, not primarily for abstract ideas, but for concrete realities known within the experience of the community."[117]

The third work of the trilogy, *On the Meaning of Christ*, deals directly with Christology.[118] "Christology," says Knox, "is the most important area of Christian theology and, in virtue of that very fact, the most dangerous."[119] Knox begins with an investigation of the "fact of revelation." "Revelation is not a conception of God; it is God himself acting within certain communal events and becoming known there in the concrete way in which we know one another. In other words, revelation is *revelation*: it is not information or indoctrination."[120]

Knox argues that revelation must be understood primarily as event. As to the content of the event, he writes: "I should say that this central event must be thought of as including . . . the personality, life and teaching of Jesus, the response of loyalty he awakened, his death, his resurrection, the coming of the Spirit, the faith with which the Spirit was received, the creation of the community."[121] The NT, according to Knox, asked what God was doing in the event of Christ, a question often neglected in the developing christological quest. "The Christological question, which was originally a question about the eschatological and soteriological significance of an event, has become a question about the metaphysical nature of a person."[122] Crucial to Knox's Christology is his conviction that the church belongs to the event. "The church came into existence, not *after* the event, but *along with* the event, and is really inseparable from it at every stage, just as the event is inseparable from the church."[123]

A little over a decade after the writing of the last book of the trilogy, Knox published *The Death of Christ: The Cross in New Testament History and Faith*.[124] In analyzing the NT accounts of the crucifixion he notes three tendencies: to elaborate the bare accounts, to play down the part played by the Romans and exaggerate the role of the Jews, and to discount the political significance of the execution of Jesus. Knox wrestles with the question of Jesus' own understanding of his death. Responding to a popular theory, he asks whether Jesus understood himself as a synthesis of the Suffering Servant and the Son of Man. According to Knox this synthesis had its origin in the post-resurrection church, and he concludes that "Jesus did not think in terms of a personal Messiah, a David or Moses or Elijah redivivus."[125] Concerning the Son of Man, Knox acknowledges that some of Jesus' sayings about this apocalyptic figure are authentic, but he does not believe Jesus identified himself with the Son of Man of Daniel or Enoch. "A sane person, not to say a good person, just could not think of himself in such a way."[126] Knox concludes that "Jesus did not regard himself as the Servant-Messiah."[127] "His 'self-consciousness' was predominantly the consciousness of being called to bear witness in deed and word to the kingdom of God—what it was and how near it was."[128] Jesus, according to Knox, saw himself as prophet.

Concerning the "divinity of Christ," Knox writes:

> The "divinity" was not half of his nature or a second nature, but was that purpose and activity of God which made the event which happened around him, but also in him and through him, the saving event it was. The divinity of Jesus was the deed of God. The uniqueness of Jesus was the absolute uniqueness of what God did in him.[129]

Crucial to Knox's Christology is his understanding of "the cross in the church." "It must be recognized, first, that the death of Jesus was the actual center of the event to which the Church looked back in memory and in which lay the beginning of its own life."[130] In recounting the crucifixion, the church, according to Knox, used mythological language that was not entirely consistent: the death of Christ as victory; the death of Christ as sacrifice and atonement.

And so there came into being—almost as a part of the event itself—the story of God's sending his own Son into the world to meet our enemies, sin and death, of his struggle with them, of his victory over them. This story is not only true; it is indispensable and irreplaceable.[131]

Knox believes the cross to be the supreme symbol of the Christian way of life—the way of love.

Knox's last major publication on Christology is *The Humanity and Divinity of Christ*.[132] He discloses his purpose in the introduction. "I wish to suggest and defend a way of understanding the *structure* of the New Testament christology as a whole, a way of seeing the *pattern* of its development."[133] Knox traces the development of three ancient patterns in Christology: first, adoptionism, followed by kenotic Christology (which explained how the preexistent being could assume human nature), and finally, full-blown incarnationalism. Knox thinks this development posed a threat to early Christian belief in the humanity of Christ. He detects in Paul "a reservation, or misgiving, as to the full genuineness of the humanity of Jesus."[134] Knox sees this reservation in Paul's view that Christ came "in the likeness of sinful flesh" (Rom 8:3) and in the evidence that the writer of Hebrews cannot conceive of Jesus as a sinner. Although the humanity of Christ was increasingly at risk, Knox notes that the early church never succumbed to docetism.

The rest of the book deals with the question: "how are *we* to think of Jesus' humanity and of its place within the total meaning of Christ?"[135] In answer, Knox stresses the idea that the humanity and divinity of Christ belong to the memory of the church where Jesus Christ is known as Lord; the preexistence of Christ, insists Knox, cannot be known in that way. Flirting with heresy, Knox puts in a good word for adoptionist Christology. "I believe it can be said not only that the most primitive christology—what we have been calling 'adoptionism'—is the minimally essential christology but also that in its basic structure it was, and might conceivably have continued to be, an entirely adequate christology."[136] Repeating a recurring theme of this chapter, Knox believes Christological problems appeared under the shadow of Hellenism, where attention was diverted from event to person. For Knox the humanity of Christ is absolutely essential and cannot be compromised; "the humanity is both more sure and more important than the pre-existence."[137] Knox asserts that "it is simply incredible that a divine person should have become a human person—that is, if he was also to continue to be, in his essential identity, the same person."[138] Nevertheless, Knox believes we can speak of preexistence as myth or story. "When we join the congregation in confessing the pre-existence, we are asserting, as we are bound by our own existence as Christians to do, that God, the Father Almighty, Maker of the heavens and the earth, was back of, present in, and acting through the whole event of which the human life of Jesus was the centre."[139] Thus, while defending Christ's humanity, we must also affirm his divinity. "For this divinity consists in the central and integral involvement of Jesus' human life in God's supremely redemptive action and the pervasive presence of God's supremely redemptive action in his human life."[140]

The idea of the church, the Christian community, has been presupposed in virtually all that has been said about Knox's theology. However, the doctrine of the church is discussed explicitly in two of his major works. *The Early Church and the Coming Great Church* addresses the question of the normative nature of the NT church.[141] Knox begins with the observation, "There has never been a time when the church could be truly said to be united."[142] Nevertheless, he discovers a basic unity within the diversity, one especially apparent in the Lord's Supper and the common life in the Spirit. This unity, according to Knox, is grounded in the event of Christ. Participating in this event, the church has a common faith. "The common faith of the church—even though it is expressed in terms of belief about the person—rests always, and only, upon the common memory of the event and the common experience of the Spirit."[143] In its developing history, rudiments of church order appeared: the practice of baptism, the observance of the Lord's Supper, worship on the Lord's Day.

Knox observes the emergence of a growing unity of the church at the end of the first century: so-called "early Catholicism." In contrast to some scholars, he views this development as positive. He says that "early Catholicism cannot be thought of as a mere distortion of primitive Christianity owing to the inevitable loss of some of its original inspiration or to the operation of temporary environmental pressures . . . but that it was the outworking of tendencies implicit from the beginning."[144] Knox believes that the early church has authority because of its unique relation to the event of Christ. However, he insists that the early church is normative for life and faith, not for ecclesiastical form. Knox contends that none of the major forms—episcopal, presbyterial, or congregational—can claim to have dominated the apostolic age. "But there must be a comprehensive and fundamental structure in which all participate. One Spirit implies one body."[145] Knox believes study of the early church makes an important contribution to ecumenicity. "The coming great church." says Knox, "will be apostolic as well as Catholic, and Catholic as well as apostolic. Only by seeking to be both can the church learn the true meaning of being either, and thus become what it truly is, holy and one."[146]

The Church and the Reality of Christ explicates Knox's understanding of the relation of ecclesiology and Christology.[147] He begins with a discussion of the church and the event of Christ. "The historical Event to which all distinctively Christian faith returns is not an event antedating the Church, or in any sense or degree prior to it, but is the coming into existence of the Church itself."[148] According to Knox, the resurrection of Christ belongs to the essential being of the church. "The Church affirms the Resurrection because its own existence as the community of memory and the Spirit is the essential and continuing meaning of the Resurrection."[149] Also basic to the existence of the church is faith in the Incarnation. "The conviction that the God of all nature and history and of the heaven beyond, in an action without parallel, entered into man's life with mighty power in a particular historical happening is one of the most intimate convictions of the Church."[150] Knox seems to take Paul's metaphor literally, "The Church is not merely *like* a body; it is *in fact* the body of Christ."[151] Although Knox often affirms the importance of the event of Christ, here he subsumes the event to the church; "unless the Church had come to be, the Event would not have occurred at all."[152] He continues: "To deny the actual existence of the Church would be to deny more than the possibility of our *knowing* God's act in Christ; it would be to deny the very existence of the act itself."[153] As Cushman observes, to say that Knox holds a high doctrine of the church is an understatement.[154]

In sum, Knox is a scholar who combines critical insight and theological sensitivity. His critical views are imaginative and distinctive, if not entirely convincing. At the very least they have stimulated the rethinking of traditional views. Many who do not accept the details of Knox's reconstruction of Pauline chronology agree that the Jerusalem conference occurred relatively late in Paul's career. Most will agree, too, that the letters of Paul, rather than Acts, should be recognized as the primary sources for reconstructing the chronology of Paul. Similarly, Knox has called attention to the importance of Marcion for the development of the canon, though he tends to overstate it. Knox's weakness in the area of criticism is his propensity to build hypothesis upon hypothesis, leading to the increasing improbability of his conclusions. For instance, to support his theory about Philemon, Knox must assume the authenticity of Colossians, the identification of the Epistle to Philemon as the "letter to Laodicea," and the Onesimus of this epistle as the bishop of Ephesus and the author of Ephesians.

The central feature of Knox's theological thought is his doctrine of the church. Indeed, the whole theological enterprise, especially Christology, seems to be swallowed up in Knox's ecclesiology. He argues that the truths of the

Christian faith are unassailable because they belong to the very essence of the community. To deny these truths would be to deny the believer's very existence, which the believer cannot do. But isn't this a subjective argument that members of any other faith community could employ? For Knox the event of Christ and the event of the church are one and the same. But doesn't the homogenizing of these events erode the importance of the historical (human) Jesus and the necessity of historical criticism, which Knox also affirms?

Distinctive features of Knox's biblical theology are his suspicion of the Pauline doctrine of justification (which he probably misunderstands) and his criticism of the development of Christology that tends to compromise the humanity of Jesus (where he may have a point). However, in the regard to the latter, Knox believes the failure of the tradition can be forgiven since the language of the church is myth, and under the rubric of myth even metaphysical speculation has meaning. But if this is true, why must we accept the metaphor of the body as "in fact the body of Christ"?

PAUL SEVIER MINEAR (1906–2007)

Minear was born in Mt. Pleasant, Iowa, and reared in a Methodist parsonage.[155] He attended Iowa Wesleyan (AB 1927) and Garret Biblical Institute (BD 1930), at the time a stronghold of liberalism. After earning an MA at Northwestern University (1930), Minear continued graduate study at Yale, where he received his PhD in 1932. Minear began teaching at the Hawaii School of Religion (1933–34). From 1934 to 1944 he served on the faculty of Garrett, which at the time faced financial strictures and paid low salaries. In 1944 Minear was appointed Norris Professor of New Testament at Andover Newton Theological School. He moved to Yale Divinity School in 1956, and in 1958 he was named Winkley Professor of Biblical Theology—a chair he occupied until retirement in 1971. Minear was a magnetic teacher who inspired a multitude of ministers and scholars, notably Leander E. Keck and J. Louis Martyn.[156]

Minear was a devoted churchman, ordained to the Methodist ministry in 1938, and in 1944 to the ministry of the Congregational Christian Church (now the United Church of Christ). Committed to ecumenism, Minear was a member of the Faith and Order Commission of the World Council of Churches and served as its chairman from 1963 to 1967. From 1969 to 1970 he was involved in the establishment of the Ecumenical Institute for Advanced Study at Tantur (near Jerusalem) and served as it first vice rector. Minear was a member (1960–89) of the translation committee of the NRSV. He was elected to the presidency of SNTS (1964–65), and received honorary degrees from Iowa Wesleyan, Aberdeen, Notre Dame, and Utrecht.

I became acquainted with Paul Minear when he was a visiting professor at Yale Divinity School in 1950. I enrolled in his course on Revelation and was awed by his exegetical skill and theological insight. Our friendship deepened when Minear served as visiting professor at Brite Divinity School during my tenure there. In 1999 I was spending Thanksgiving in Connecticut and made arrangements to interview Minear at his home in Guilford. When I called to confirm the appointment he asked if it would be all right to invite Lee Keck and Lou Martyn to join us. I was delighted, and the resulting tape recording is a treasure, with comments by Minear and two of his most able students on a variety of issues. The most memorable moment of the conversation was Minear's account of a "conversion" experience during his latter years at Garrett. He recalled that he was a "psychological wreck," losing interest in scholarly research and in teaching conventional criticism. He took a leave from Garrett, moved to Maine, and spent his time fishing, hiking, and reading nothing—except the Bible. The result was a revitalized vision of his calling as scholar and teacher, and most of all, a new view of Scripture. This view came to expression in his remarkable book, *Eyes of Faith*.

HISTORICAL-CRITICAL RESEARCH

Prior to this transformation Minear was engaged in critical research.[157] Based on his Yale dissertation, his first major book, *And Great Shall Be Your Reward,* is an investigation, as the subtitle indicates, of the origins of Christian views of salvation.[158] This work displays commitment to historical criticism and use of the history of religion method. Minear begins by tracing the development of the idea of rewards in Judaism. He finds that Hebrew religion in the early period stressed the salvation of the nation, but increasingly it focused on the individual. Minear believes that the reward of the righteous individual, who experienced suffering, was salvaged by the apocalyptic hope of resurrection.

Turning to Hellenistic sources, Minear thinks the Hellenists viewed salvation as escape from the world, ignoring ethical and social demands. In contrast, Jesus shared the Jewish tradition of the prophets and apocalyptic; he believed justice would be restored with the coming of the kingdom. Minear declares that Jesus' message of the kingdom called for an ethical response. "But his promises of rewards and punishment remain consistently oriented toward the future judgment and coming age."[159] With Paul, Christianity moved into the Hellenistic arena, which was not congenial to apocalyptic. Minear believes that the apostle, in this setting, modified Jewish eschatology: he spiritualized the kingdom and viewed it as a present reality. Minear thinks Paul also modified the Hellenistic idea of mystical regeneration: he believed conversion was related to past historical events (the life, death, and resurrection of Christ) and to future historical events (the return and triumph of Christ). Although this book shows an uncritical dedication to criticism and affirms the liberalism that Minear came to regret, it anticipates his later work: sensitivity to theological issues and recognition of the importance of apocalyptic.

In his later work Minear did not abandon historical critical research. This is abundantly evident, for example, in *The Obedience of Faith: The Purposes of Paul in the Epistle to the Romans*.[160] Minear believes the purpose of Romans can be found in the situation of the Roman church, described in Rom 14:1—16:27. In this passage he uncovers evidence of five different Christian groups in Rome: (1) the "weak in faith" (Jewish converts and some Gentiles who intend to keep the law) who condemn the "strong in faith"; (2) the "strong in faith" (converts who believe they are free of Jewish rules) who despise the "weak in faith"; (3) the "doubters" (those who are uncertain, who do not act from faith); (4) the "weak in faith" who do *not* condemn the "strong" (they observe the law but do not demand that the "strong" do as they do); (5) the "strong in faith" who do *not* despise the "weak" (they are free but do not compel others to practice such freedom). Minear thinks Paul is urging the Romans to move to the fourth and fifth positions, that is, to accept those with whom they disagree. In the rest of the book Minear proceeds through the earlier chapters of Romans, detecting evidence of the existence of the five groups and Paul's specific instructions to each.[161]

THE EYES OF FAITH: HERMENEUTICS AND EXEGESIS

The dramatic shift in Minear's work is epitomized in *Eyes of Faith*, first published in 1946.[162] In the introduction he indicates that he is, as the subtitle indicates, primarily concerned with the biblical point of view, the unique perspective of the Bible. In the first part Minear focuses on "the angle of vision." He declares that the biblical vision reflects the reality and action of God. Minear declares that the God of the Bible is the God who speaks and chooses humans. This choosing is the meaning of "foreknowledge," which is not, according to Minear, a dogma but an action of grace, perceived by faith. God's election, God's call, demands decision.

> To sum up the ubiquitous aspects of the biblical ethic: When God visits and chooses the human being, God communicates a demand for decision. The human person apprehends his or her responsibility in terms of ultimate seriousness. One must respond in immediate, absolute obedience.[163]

Despite the call of God, humans seek other lovers. Minear declares that the story of human rebellion is recounted in biblical myth: the appearance of the devil and the story of the kingdom of Satan. "No interpretation of the Bible is adequate that does not do justice to the intrinsic experiential realities which were expressed in such terms as sin, idolatry, death, and Satan."[164] Like Cullmann, but with different results, Minear presumes that the Bible has a unique understanding of time. According to Minear, biblical time is not a matter of the calendar, not quantitative; the meaning of time is wholly determined by God's purpose and will. Within biblical time, according to Minear, humans seek an egocentric salvation, but their efforts are in vane. As a result, humans are destined for the supreme punishment: death and alienation from God; but they can also glimpse the supreme reward: life in the presence of God and the promise of redemption.

In the second part of *Eyes of Faith*, Minear illumines "the focus of vision." He believes the object of vision is obscure because God conceals God's word. Thus, for him, a major feature of the revelatory act is the hiddenness of God. Minear believes God is hidden because of the situation of the hearers: human beings in their blindness; but God is also hidden because of the situation of the speaker: the God who is the hidden God. God's speech is not ordinary or univocal. "Revelatory events, therefore, are always ambiguous and paradoxical. They reveal what is hidden, and hide what is revealed."[165]

In the third part of the book Minear reflects on "the horizons of vision." The primary horizon is delineated by history—a history the viewer forgets and remembers. Minear charges that humans forget the history of God's action in the past, but the prophets call them to remembrance. He finds this view affirmed in the NT.

> Here is no objective historical record, but witness to that historical act whereby God re-creates human history from within. The disclosure of God's purpose in Christ is a single Word that incorporates the whole of genuine history, past, present, and future.[166]

Minear believes that eschatology is indigenous to the biblical viewpoint but alien to modern thought. Biblical eschatology assumes a unique vision of the future.

> It is clear, then, that a true vision of the future discloses the situation that obtains between human beings and God. It is in an act of decision that the human being gains her or his knowledge of the

future, and conversely, it is through God's self-disclosure of the bent of divine purpose that God confronts the human being with the necessity of decision.[167]

Minear believes the limits of the prophetic view, which is directed primarily to history, are transcended in apocalyptic, which is directed primarily beyond history.

> With reference to the process of revelation, "beyond history" connotes the source and ground of present existential reality, pointing to the divine will as it is mediated through a word. . . . As such, that which is "beyond history" actually constitutes the only genuine history, while that which is "within history" actually constitutes a pseudo history to which men are enslaved. In other words, to say that the Kingdom of God lies "beyond history" is equivalent to saying that a particular age of rebellion lies within the span of God's overarching purpose.[168]

Minear concludes *Eyes of Faith* by highlighting the "re-vision of vision." He believes the re-vision is inspired by the coming of Christ. "The rebirth of the Christian is a re-enactment of the sign of the resurrection of Jesus as Messiah."[169] The cross stands in judgment on sin but also provides the way of resurrection and victory. From the perspective of the revised vision, the Christian sees new horizons. Minear assumes that the Christian experiences a revision in memory: the past is seen in the light of the cross. The Christian also experiences a revision of hope: the future is seen as determined by the return of the Messiah. "Insofar as the Christian shares in the life of the risen Lord, he participates already in the power of the general resurrection; he enters the gateway into eternal life."[170] Minear closes with an epilogue entitled, "To See or Not to See." He says that the view of the prophets and apostles assumes the perspective of faith. "Their authority is a God who communicates his purposes and his demands in what he says and does. And since, to them, he is the only true Lord of history, the history which he creates and guides is the only true history. And the only standpoint wherein man apprehends that history is the standpoint of faith."[171] At the end, Minear confronts the reader with an existential question: Where shall I stand?[172]

Minear's hermeneutical perspective is reflected in his exegetical writings. Apart from his major work on the Apocalypse (which will be reviewed below in connection with his work on eschatology), Minear published a few commentaries written for the general reader. For The Layman's Bible

Commentary (LBC) he produced the volume on Mark.[173] On matters of critical introduction he follows the tradition: the Gospel was written in Rome during the time of the Jewish War by John Mark. Mark's purpose was to record the teaching of the apostles, with special attention to the passion narrative. Mark understood his gospel as the good news about Jesus Christ who proclaimed the good news of the kingdom of God. An example of Minear's exegesis is seen in his interpretation of Mark 13, a text that appeals to his passion for apocalyptic. The main concern of Jesus, according to Minear's reading of the text, is to prepare the disciples for the trials they will face. Jesus warns that they must not be encouraged by false hopes; the evil powers must be dethroned before the triumph of the Son of Man. In regard to the controversial ending of the Gospel, Minear contends that Mark intended to conclude at v. 8: "fear and trembling" is the typical biblical description of the behavior of humans in response to the power of God.[174]

The Gospel of John provides the perfect venue for Minear's distinctive heremeneutical–exegetical approach.[175] He believes we should understand this Gospel as a conversation between the author and his readers who share participation in the Christian community. Minear supposes that the Gospel has four sources: Jesus, the Paraclete, the disciples (represented by the Beloved Disciple), and the narrator. The primary purpose of the author is to address the problems the community faces, notably the threat of their adversaries who, from the eschatological perspective, are the children of the devil, the ruler of this world. In contrast to most critics, Minear dates the Fourth Gospel relatively early: before the Jewish War while the temple was still standing. He claims that a major feature of the Gospel is the message of the victorious martyr. This message is seen in the lifting up of the Son of Man, an event that is predicted three times (3:14; 8:28; 12:34) and fulfilled in the lifting up of Christ on the cross. Minear finds this event crammed with symbolic meaning. According to John's account the soldiers did not break the legs of Jesus, but one of them pierced his side so that blood and water poured out (19:31-37). In the notice that the legs were not broken Minear sees an allusion to the Passover lamb. In mention of the water from Jesus' wound he finds the fulfillment of the prediction, "out of the believer's heart shall flow rivers of living water" (7:38). The reference to "blood" Minear sees as reminiscent of the command of Jess to drink his blood (6:53-56). In a unique exegetical move, Minear supposes that the one who witnessed the piercing of Jesus (19:35) was the soldier who committed the deed. "Belief in the soldier's testimony embraced two major components: confidence that the pollution of the world's sins had receive cleansing in the blood and water, and confidence that among those who had lifted up the Son of man there were at least some who had been drawn to him by his love for them."[176]

THEOLOGY AND ESCHATOLOGY

Minear's major theological work is *The Kingdom and the Power*.[177] Leander Keck has written: "I have long regarded *The Kingdom and the Power* as the most original presentation of New Testament Theology produced in North America."[178] In the preface Minear declares that his purpose is to present and explicate the NT theology of history. He begins (Part I) with rumination on the imagery of the Apocalypse: "Behold the Lamb." The writer, prisoner on the isle of Patmos, has a vision of the scroll that is sealed. Within the scroll are inscribed all the secrets of history that the human mind, according to Minear, cannot decipher. But he observes that the seer has a second vision: the lamb who had been slain, who can open the scroll. The lamb is Jesus Christ, to whom the NT bears witness.

> As far as possible he [the interpreter] will enter into the perspectives of the New Testament witnesses, seeking to grasp the inner and outer dimensions of their experience, as seen from within. Not content simply to hear *what* they said, he will listen for what lies behind the words, that is, what had happened to them to make them want to say what they said. He will consider himself a member of the apostles' own community and occasionally speak in the first person plural, even at the risk of alienating the reader who insists on preserving a fancied objectivity.[179]

In the second part of *The Kingdom and the Power* Minear investigates the "eternal purpose," disclosed in the sayings of Christ. First he explicates the saying, "I am . . . the beginning" (Rev 22:13). The one who speaks, says Minear, is the crucified one who is the exalted Lord. In the time before the cross, Jesus proclaimed the kingdom. "God's Kingdom is already at work, powerfully turning and overturning men's lives."[180] In the time after the cross, says Minear, the world was judged, but in the death of Christ, sin, death and the world were defeated. In the resurrection, God glorified Jesus—a miracle in which God had won a victory. After God's triumph, according to Minear, the disciples were reborn. Before faith came, they forsook and disobeyed Christ and viewed the historical event from the perspective of the old age. After faith came, their shame was transformed to glory; the victory of Christ brought release from the slaveries of the world. "Thus was all history transfigured to the eyes of the disciple, although all history remained the same to the eyes of the world."[181] From the perspective of the world the old age continues, the time of the kingdom of Satan. With the coming of the Messiah a new day dawns. Jesus subjected himself to the power of the earthly rulers, but God vindicated him by the resurrection. Minear believes this action created a new race: the disciples who follow the way of Christ.

Minear next reflects on the saying, "I am . . . the end" (Rev 22:13). In the end, the promise of salvation will be fulfilled. Minear declares that God is the sole source of salvation, and the promise is perceived only by faith. The believer follows the example of Jesus, becoming like him in his death, as demonstrated in daily decisions. In oneness with Jesus the believer has already received salvation, but the consummation is future. "The one victory and advent has taken place; the other victory and advent are awaited at the end of his course. . . . From another standpoint, there are not two victories but one, the victory of Jesus Christ, to which triumph every act of faith belongs."[182] Minear continues: "The final event is underway, and this event communicates a mysterious solidarity between Jesus' victory, the victory of the individual disciple, and the victory of the Church."[183]

Part III is entitled, "Thine is the Kingdom and the Power." In this section Minear explores the mystery of the kingdom. Basic to the mystery is the biblical view of history—a view seen only by the eyes of faith. This view sees in history the action of God, and the key to unlocking the mystery of biblical history is "the work of Jesus Christ in reconciling the world to God."[184] According to Minear's reading of the NT, the kingdom is the kingdom of God, inseparable from God's power and glory; it is in continual warfare with Satan; it is entered by the new birth in the Spirit; it is realized only through fellowship in the community; it is the kingdom of God's love. "The act of perfect love is the perfect fulfillment of all history, uniting in final glory the work of the individual disciple, the work of the church, the work of Jesus of Nazareth, and the work of God."[185] The kingdom seems strange, because it presents a radical challenge to the old, conventional view of history and the world. Although he understands it as a mystery, Minear believes the kingdom to be relevant—relevant for the heart, the mind, the world and existence as a whole. The message of the kingdom, Minear concludes, brings peace of mind to the individual and peace to the nations to the world.[186]

Throughout his career Minear had a special affinity for eschatology. In 1954 he wrote: "A far-reaching revolution is under way, spurred on by a world-wide revival of Biblical theology, and spearheaded by a new respect for Biblical eschatology."[187] However, in contrast to many theologians who, while embracing eschatology, eschew apocalyptic, Minear declares that apocalyptic eschatology is exactly what biblical interpretation requires. He deals directly with the subject in *New Testament Apocalyptic*.[188] He defines the term: "the word apocalyptic designates the disclosure through human agents of God's presence and activity, which otherwise would remain hidden from his people."[189] Minear observes that apocalyptic writers (like John of Revelation) viewed themselves as prophets and claimed to possess the Spirit. He observes that this claim raises a hermeneutical question: How can the gap between the charismatic speaker and the non-charismatic interpreter by bridged? Minear is convinced that the first step is to take seriously the prophets' own awareness of their vocation. At the same time, the interpreter must believe in the God of the prophets as the God who calls and gives specific tasks to particular individuals. Minear also insists that the community that hears the prophet must possess the gift of understanding. This implies that the interpreter must be aware of the dynamics of worship in which listening to the Spirit takes place.

Minear gives special attention to the prophetic vision of the end. Whereas many interpreters draw a distinction between prophets who deal with history and apocalyptic visionaries who are preoccupied with a future cosmic catastrophe, Minear venerates the biblical apocalyptic prophets, who include not only John of Patmos but also Jesus of Nazareth. The vision of the end, which makes use of apocalyptic imagery, includes the consummation of God's purposes, revealing the goodness and power of God and the defeat of God's enemies. These observations lead Minear to propose guidelines for the interpretation of apocalyptic literature: the interpreter must be sensitive to the symbolic, poetic, and mythical character of the prophecy, must avoid assessing the prophetic vision my modern measurements of time, and must recognize that the apocalyptic view of coming events is related to the present. In the remainder of the book Minear illustrates the application of his methodological principles to the exegesis of several biblical texts.

Minear's major contribution to the study of NT apocalyptic is his *I Saw a New Earth*.[190] In the introduction he announces his purpose: "My chief desire is that each reader will find the Book of Revelation fully absorbing and that this companion volume will both enhance his excitement and guide it toward constructive ends."[191] The book is arranged in three parts: his interpretation of the larger blocks of consecutive visions, review and analysis of issues debated by exegetes, and a new translation of Revelation with notes. Only the first two parts will be considered here.

The first part, "The Visions," is essentially a commentary that follows the format: translation of the text, literary analysis, issues for reflection and discussion, and references for further study. The first main vision of Revelation discloses the speaker (1:12-20). According to literary analysis, Minear notes that the speaker is described as a Christ-figure. "Few verses could make clearer the intention of John in the entire book: to proclaim how the lordship of Christ over every situation had made transparent for the prophet the entire enigma of human existence."[192] In presenting issues for reflection and discussion, Minear insists that the reader should avoid precise identification of particular symbols. The intent of this text, he says, is to show that "Jesus is one with God in wisdom, power, steadfastness and penetrating vision."[193] For further study he lists christological pictures and titles used in Revelation and recommends items for additional reading.

The next major vision is "The Lamb as Victor" (Rev 4:1—8:1). This larger vision provides the setting for the vision of the heavenly throne room in chapters 4 and 5. Minear notes that "this vision serves to prepare for all the later visions."[194] In presenting literary analysis, Minear raises two questions: Where in the text is the center of gravity? Answer: in the hymns addressed to God and to the Lamb. What kind of action is going on? Answer: the action of the Lamb, particularly his death, and the action of the participants in worship. For this text Minear offers no issues for reflection and discussion, but for further study he notes references for the use of Revelation in visual art.

In the penultimate section of this part of his book Minear presents an interpretation of "The New Creation" (21:1—22:7). In his literary analysis he observes that the final visions of Revelation include elements from the earlier visions. For reflection and discussion Minear delineates two issues. First, the concept of "the death of death" indicates that John is concerned with the struggle of the "christic" forces with the "antichristic." The antichristic forces, according to Minear, include Babylon, the beast, and his false prophet, the Devil himself. Revelation declares that God defeats every hostile force. According to Minear the millennium symbolizes the penultimate victory of Christ, prior to the ultimate triumph of God. He opposes attempts to construe the millennium according to specific events or chronology. The second issue for reflection is the coming of Christ. Minear charges that many interpreters are confused about the author's understanding of time, supposing it is concerned with the temporal or chronological. "The most important thing that will happen," says Minear, "is the coming of Christ in fulfilment of his promise. Christ's coming thus becomes the effective future horizon for every decision of believer and congregation."

Part II of *I Saw a New Earth* identifies and discusses issues involved in the interpretation of Revelation. Minear first considers the significance of suffering. He argues that the early Christians saw suffering as intrinsic to the redemptive purpose of God, revealed in the crucifixion of Christ. This is why Minear refuses to identify Rome as the ultimate adversary; that adversary is Satan. Minear discusses the conflict between the King of kings and the kings of the earth and rejects the interpretation of kings of the earth as the Roman rulers. "For us to *equate* Babylon with Rome would be literalism and historicism of the worst sort."[195] He continues: "He [John] would have betrayed the redemptive power of the cross by too hasty an identification of God's enemies with specific men or institutions."[196] In the death and resurrection of the sea-beast (Rev 13:1-3) Minear detects no reference to Nero *redivivus*. Similarly, he does not believe that 666 refers to Nero (or any other emperor); rather, it is a parody on the perfect number 7. In discussing the meaning of "heaven" and "earth" Minear warns against interpretations that attempt to distinguish sharply between the historical and the timeless. John is concerned with the ultimate that transcends space and time. In the final chapter of this part of the book Minear discusses "Comparable Patterns of Thought in Luke's Gospel." Here he notes that Luke also stresses the gift of prophecy and the messiah's struggle with Satan.[197]

THE CHURCH

Like John Knox, Paul Minear devoted considerable attention to the doctrine of the church. In *Horizons of Christian Community* his purpose is to present the understanding of the church in the NT.[198] Since the church is grounded in the action of God and the life of the risen Lord, Minear believes its existence is permeated with mystery. He says that the life of the church involves doxophany (the appearance of the glory of God) and doxology (the worship of God's glory). In this vein he approaches a definition: the church is the body of glory wherein the fullness of God is pleased to dwell. Minear observes that the NT adopts the language of myth and sees the church as the army of God, engaged in cosmic warfare with Satan. This mythical language shows that the struggles of the church have ultimate significance. The NT also depicts the church as the city in which God dwells. In explicating this imagery, Minear employs typology. He understands biblical typology to be concerned with the invisible but real connections between two communities. The seer John has a vision of the new Jerusalem; the church has solidarity with this heavenly city.

Minear turns to a discussion of the time of the church and insists that the church's time is eschatological. From this perspective the time of the church is a time of battle with Satan. "Against the mythological background of cosmic struggle, then, the New Testament witnesses to the present time of the church's life as a time of salvation, in which the gift of heavenly life precipitates an earthly struggle wherein God first protects and then abandons his messengers, and thus enables them to share fully in the victory of his Messiah."[199] Important for the idea of the church is the NT understanding of the relation of the church to the work of Christ. Minear believes the church is a supernatural entity that incorporates heavenly and earthly activities. Thus it embodies a movement from beyond to the here and now, one mediated by the death and resurrection of Christ. "In witnessing to the revelation of God in the cross and the resurrection, it witnesses to the coming epiphany of Jesus Christ with all who belong to him."[200] The church, Minear concludes, has solidarity with Christ and with the world. In oneness with Christ it has a final, eschatological freedom.

Minear's major work on the church is his *Images of the Church in the New Testament.*[201] This book is not a systematic doctrine of the nature of the church; it focuses instead on the images of the church presented in the NT. Typically for Minear, the image does not symbolize some other meaning; "the image *is* the meaning."[202] Looking over Minear's book as a whole, the reader is astounded by the plethora of images he finds in the NT—a total of ninety-six. However, he admits that many of these are secondary, and presents a chapter in which thirty-two minor images are surveyed. These include, for example, "the boat," "the olive tree," "the bride of Christ." The subsequent chapters present Minear's interpretation of the main NT images, grouped into major categories.

The first of these, "the people of God," includes a sub-grouping of political and national images: "Israel," "the chosen race," "the holy nation," "the twelve tribes," "the patriarchs." Minear believes these images affirm the unity of the community and its oneness with the God of the fathers. Images of "the elect" and "the remnant" reflect the continuity of God's call. He also includes in this group metaphors drawn from the pastoral economy (the flock, the lambs) and images from the cultic traditions: "Jerusalem" (the eschatological city), "sacrifice" (imagery related to the passion of Christ).

Minear presents another group of images under the rubric of "the new creation." These depict the church in its universal, cosmic setting. Among them is "the last Adam," a figure that reflects the new humanity created by the death and resurrection of Christ. Minear incorporates several images of this group into the larger image of "the kingdom of God." Typically, he sees God's kingdom opposed by the kingdom of Satan. He also finds kingdom imagery reflected in related eschatological images: "the new heaven and the new earth," "the Son of Man," "the glory" of Christ and God. Closely related to this group is another that Minear labels "the fellowship of faith." Some of the items included do not seem to constitute images in the sense usually used in the book, for example, "followers," "friends," "servants."

Minear believes the image of "the body of Christ" to be most important. He thinks that this image, primarily used by Paul, has more than a single meaning. To belong to the body of Christ is to share the redemption Christ has accomplished. To partake of the body and blood of Christ in the covenantal meal is to participate in the death of Christ. Although there is one body, the believers are individual members with different gifts, all united in the gift of love.

In a significant chapter Minear discusses the interrelation of the images. "If all the images, thought together, provide a richer tapestry than any image, thought alone, then each image becomes richer in content when seen in the context of others."[203] All the images, according to Minear, represent a single reality: the divine mystery of the church. He illustrates the interrelation of the images by highlighting the combination of the all-important image of the "body of Christ" with the images of "the people of God," "the new creation," and "the fellowship of faith." "If we would comprehend the same reality, we should make full use of the body image, but we should supplement it with many other images, and we should perceive the whole mystery of God's purpose in Christ before using either the term 'body' or the term 'church.'"[204]

In summary, it can be said that Minear displayed a certain uniqueness within the community of NT scholars. The reader of his work is easily baffled by the density and apparent lack of clarity in his writings. This, of course, is not unintentional: he was convinced that the message of the NT is complex, crowded with ambiguity and paradox. Nevertheless, he was committed to historical criticism—though with reservations. In particular he was critical of a pseudo-objectivity and an erudite overconfidence. Minear, with Barth, rejected the famous Enlightenment premise that the Bible should be understood like any other book. Indeed, Minear believed the interpretation of the Bible demands the adoption of a radically different perspective—that of the Bible itself. The language of the Bible, he declared, is not ordinary speech, but is symbolic, mythical. According to Minear the meaning is not beyond the myth (Bultmann) but is in the myth itself. The language of myth shows the Bible speaks of the ultimate, the cosmic.

Minear, like other biblical theologians of his time, stressed the crucial significance of revelation, especially the act of God in the "event" of Christ. Decisive for Minear's theology is his preoccupation with eschatology. Even more, he did not shrink from, but embraced apocalyptic. Apocalyptic eschatology, in Miner's view, is not focused on some distant, illusive future but on the present, disclosed in its cosmic dimensions. For Minear, ethics and church do not represent the application of theology; they belong to the essence of theology itself. God's revelation includes the ethical demand. God's action in Christ creates the community in which the message of the Bible is heard, obeyed, and embodied. Not everything in Minear's work is convincing, but the breadth of his imagination and depth of his commitment are worthy of praise.

A Conservative Alternative: F. F. Bruce

F. F. Bruce (1910–1990)

The twentieth century saw the advance of evangelical scholars.[205] A stellar representative of this group is the studious Scotsman, Frederick Fyvie Bruce.[206] He was born in Elgin, Scotland, and educated at the Elgin Academy; he began the study of Greek at thirteen. Bruce attended the University of Aberdeen (MA 1932) and Cambridge (1932–34 BA, MA). He started to pursue a PhD at the University of Vienna but accepted a teaching position at Edinburgh instead. From 1938 to 1947 he was a lecturer at Leeds University. In 1947 Bruce was called to develop a new department of Biblical History and Literature at Sheffield University. He served as head of the department from 1947 to 1959 and as professor from 1955 to 1959. In 1959 he was called to the prestigious John Rylands Chair of Biblical Criticism and Exegesis at the University of Manchester. Bruce's scholarship was confirmed by his election as president of both the Society for Old Testament and the SNTS. He was editor of *Palestine Exploration Quarterly* (1957–71), although he did not visit the Holy Land until 1969. Bruce lectured widely in the United States, Canada, Australia, New Zealand, and Europe. His students described him as "a saintly scholar, a man whose life is being moulded by what he so thoroughly studies and so capably teaches."[207]

As to his basic point of view, Bruce was devoted to Scripture as the written word of God. He never owned a car and had no interest in learning to drive; he was comfortably at home in the biblical world. In his autobiography, Bruce wrote:

> I should not find the career of a Bible teacher so satisfying as I do if I were not persuaded that the Bible is God's word written. The fact that I am so persuaded means that I must not come to the Bible with my own preconceptions of what the Bible, as God's word written, can or cannot say. It is important to determine, by the canons of grammatical, textual, historical and literary study, what it actually does say. Occasionally, when I have expounded the meaning of some biblical passage in a particular way, I have been asked, "But how does that square with inspiration?" But inspiration is not a concept of which I have a clear understanding before I come to study the text,

so that I know in advance what limits are placed on the meaning of the text by requirements of inspiration. On the contrary, it is by the patient study of the text that I come to understand better not only what the text itself means, but also what is involved in biblical inspiration. My doctrine of Scripture is based on my study of Scripture, not *vice versa*.[208]

Bruce was a conservative, but no fundamentalist. He was master of the skills of historical criticism. "The Christian acceptance of the Bible as God's word written," he wrote, "does not in the least inhibit the unfettered study of its contents and setting; on the contrary, it acts as an incentive to their most detailed and comprehensive investigation."[209] Bruce was anxious, too, not to impose his views on others. He writes:

I have held and expressed over the years a fair number of minority views—not to say unpopular views—in many fields. But I have never thought it my duty to press my views on others; if they differ from me they could be right. Only, I claim for myself the liberty which I gladly allow them, to hold and express the views which I believe to be justified by the evidence.[210]

APOLOGETICS AND THEOLOGY

Much of Bruce's work was devoted to apologetics. This is evident in his first book, *The New Testament Documents: Are They Reliable?* originally written in 1943.[211] The answer is Yes; the character of Jesus, central to our faith, is known only through these trustworthy records. Bruce proceeds to discuss the dates and attestation of the NT documents. He tends to date them early, for example, he believes that Colossians and Ephesians were written (by Paul) around 60, and the Pastoral Epistles, also authentic, were composed around 63 to 64. Bruce points out that the manuscripts of the NT are vastly more numerous than the records of other ancient persons and events. Turning to the canon, he says: "The historic Christian belief is that the Holy Spirit, who controlled the writing of the individual books, also controlled their selection and collection, thus continuing to fulfill the Lord's promise that He would guide His disciples into all the truth."[212] In regard to the miracles Bruce writes: "If we reject from the start the idea of a supernatural Jesus, then we shall reject His miracles, too; if, on the other hand, we accept the Gospel picture of Him, the miracles will cease to be an insuperable stumbling-block."[213] After reviewing the evidence of archaeology and early Jewish and Gentile writings, he concludes: "The historicity of Christ is as axiomatic for an unbiased historian as the historicity of Julius Caesar."[214]

Bruce, like the other scholars reviewed in this chapter, was a biblical theologian. In his book, *The New Testament Development of Old Testament Themes,* he summarizes biblical theology in one breathtaking sentence:

> In Jesus the promise is confirmed, the covenant is renewed, the prophecies are fulfilled, the law is vindicated, salvation is brought near, sacred history has reached its climax, the perfect sacrifice has been offered and accepted, the great priest over the household of God has taken his seat at God's right hand, the Prophet like Moses has been raised up, the Son of David reigns, the kingdom of God has been inaugurated, the Son of Man has received dominion from the Ancient of Days, the Servant of the Lord, having been smitten to death for his people's transgression and borne the sin of many, has accomplished the divine purpose, has seen light after the travail of his soul and is now exalted and extolled and made very high.[215]

Bruce believes the theme of the "Servant Messiah" to be of crucial importance. In the Book of Consolation (Isaiah 40–55) the function of the Servant was to bring light to the Gentiles. Bruce believes Jesus combined this figure with the Son of Man and applied the combination to himself. He was the suffering Servant, the Son of Man who gave his life a "ransom for many" (Mark 10:45).[216]

Bruce's NT theology is mainly concerned with Christology. This is seen in his small, non-technical work, *Jesus: Past, Present, and Future.*[217] Jesus' primary purpose, says Bruce, was to do his Father's will, to follow the way of the cross. At his trial Jesus, according to Bruce, acknowledged his role as Messiah and Son of Man. In discussing "Christ our righteousness," Bruce notes that the contemporaries of Jesus considered the idea of a crucified Christ to be a contradiction in terms. But whereas they quoted Deuteronomy 21:23, "anyone hung on a tree is under God's curse," Paul combined this text with another from Deuteronomy: "Cursed be anyone who does not uphold the words of this law by observing them" (27:26.). Paul declares, "Christ redeemed us from the curse of the law by becoming a curse for us" (Gal 3:13). Bruce proceeds to present the NT view of Christ according to other pictures: the conqueror, the high priest, the lamb. Of special interest is his discussion of what Christ did before the incarnation: he was creator; he accompanied the people of God in the wilderness. Similarly, Bruce envisions the future work of Christ: he will raise the dead and preside at the future judgment.[218]

HISTORICAL RESEARCH

Bruce is at his best when he is writing history. This is especially seen in his *New Testament History*.[219] The early chapters deal with the historical background to the NT story. In this setting John the Baptist heralds the Christian era; Bruce believes John recognized Jesus as the Coming One. Three chapters are devoted to the life and teaching of Jesus. After his baptism by John, Jesus came into Galilee proclaiming the Kingdom of God: the rule of God, already present, Bruce believes, in Jesus' actions. The Jewish leaders delivered Jesus to Pilate, accusing him of sedition, the charge for which he was executed.

Turning to the primitive church, Bruce observes that the disciples proclaimed the risen Christ as Messiah. Within the Jerusalem community a distinctive group was identified as "Hellenists." These members, in Bruce's opinion, were Greek-speaking Jewish Christians. Their leader was Stephen, who made a speech before the Jewish Council, attacking the Temple. This resulted in the stoning of Stephen and a persecution of the church that drove the Hellenists into mission and left the Jerusalem church in the hands of the Hebrews, the Aramaic-speaking Jewish Christians.

Bruce devotes a chapter to the early life of Paul that tends to harmonize the accounts in Acts and in the Pauline letters. Paul was born in Tarsus, a Roman citizen. In contrast to his tolerant teacher, Gamaliel, Paul became a bitter opponent of the Christians. He engaged in a mission of persecution that led him to Damascus, but on the way he was confronted by a vision of Christ, an event Bruce understands to be both a conversion and a call. After his conversion Paul made a trip to Arabia (Nabataea) where, Bruce believes, he engaged in preaching.

Bruce's discussion of early Gentile Christianity focuses on Antioch. There the gospel had been preached to Gentiles, and the disciples were called Christians. This church was led by Barnabas, who secured the assistance of Paul. When a famine struck Judea, the Antioch church sent Paul and Barnabas with relief funds (Acts 11:30). At this time, according to Bruce's reconstruction, the Jerusalem conference described in Gal 2:1-10 was held. This, he believes, was a private meeting between Paul and the Jerusalem leaders that resulted in their acceptance of Paul's Gentile mission. Upon returning to Antioch, Paul and Barnabas were sent on a mission to (south) Galatia. After this mission, the Jerusalem Council was held (Acts 15:6-29). This gathering, according to Bruce, was primarily concerned with the social association of Jewish and Gentile Christians. Its result was the formulation of the "Apostolic Decree," a letter sent to the Gentile churches, requiring their members to observe Jewish food laws.

The remainder of the book is devoted to Paul's missions in Macedonia and Achaia, his ministry in Asia (Ephesus), and his final trip to Jerusalem, all fully explicated in Bruce's major book on Paul, reviewed below. In the final chapters Bruce recounts the last days of the Temple and the church in Jerusalem. The head of the church was James, the brother of Jesus. Opposition to him by the high priest led to his execution, probably by stoning. Rumblings in Judea against Rome led to the outbreak of revolt, which was crushed by the Romans. Bruce concludes:

> By the end of the first century A.D. Christianity was well established in the Roman world. From its birthplace in Judaea it had spread west along the northern shore of the Mediterranean as far as Gaul, if not as far as Spain; it had spread along the North African coast to Cyrenaica, if it had not already reached the Roman province of Africa. Two hundred years were to elapse before the Roman state accepted the presence of the church; before that time intermittent attempts were made to repress and, if possible, extirpate Christianity, but the historian, looking back on the situation with all the advantages of hindsight can see that by A.D. 100 Christianity had come to stay, that its abolition was no longer practicable.[220]

The story of the development of the canon is carefully traced in Bruce's book, *The Canon of Scripture*.[221] Part III of this work is dedicated to the canon of the NT. Bruce, like Knox, recognizes the importance of Marcion. In response to Marcion's truncated canon (ten letters of Paul and an edited version of Luke), the orthodox church produced the Muratorian Canon, which Bruce dates at the end of the second century. About this same time Irenaeus made a case for four Gospels, no more and no less. In Alexandria, Origen distinguished between the undisputed (4 Gospels, Acts, 13 Epistles of Paul, 1 John, and Revelation) and the disputed books (2 Peter, 2 and 3 John, James and Jude). Bruce also recounts the opinions of Eusebius and of Athanasius, who accepted a twenty-seven-book canon, identical with ours except for order. Particularly helpful is Bruce's review of the books contained and their order in the major uncial manuscripts: Sinaiticus, Vaticanus, and Alexandrinus. The twenty-seven-book canon was approved by councils in the east and west and became standard in the Middle Ages. The question of canonicity was raised again during the Reformation, but the standard canon was accepted by the Council of Trent, the Thirty-Nine Articles, and the Westminster Confession. In the last section of the book Bruce attends to the important question of the criteria of canonicity.

He notes the importance of apostolic authority, a criterion that has to do both with antiquity and orthodoxy. Regarding authorship, Bruce concludes: "It is doubtful if any book would have found a place in the canon if it had been *known* to be pseudonymous."[222]

As a historian, Bruce was concerned with the historical setting of early Christianity. This is demonstrated in his research on the Dead Sea Scrolls. His first publication was a short monograph, *The Teacher of Righteousness in the Qumran Texts.*[223] Bruce points out that the identity of the Teacher remains unknown. The Teacher's chief opponent was the "Wicked Priest," probably to be identified with Alexander Jannaeus, who ruled as king and priest from 103 BCE to 76 BCE. In 1959 Bruce published *Biblical Exegesis in the Qumran Texts.*[224] The commentaries among the Scrolls use a method of exegesis designated as *pesher*, so the texts are called *pesherim*. This type of interpretation followed three principles: God had revealed his purpose to the Teacher of Righteousness; all the words in the texts refer to the end; the end is at hand. Bruce points out that the texts were "atomized," that is, each phase was forced to fit the new eschatological situation regardless of its original context. "Biblical prophecies of varying date and reference are reinterpreted so as to apply to the end-time introduced by the ministry of the Teacher of Righteousness, and not least to the career of the Teacher himself."[225]

Bruce's *Second Thoughts on the Dead Sea Scrolls* can serve as a useful introduction.[226] In this book he recounts the first discoveries in Cave 1 and the later finds in a total of eleven caves. Bruce notes that there are three issues in dating: the time of the original writing, the time of copying, and the time when the manuscripts were placed in the caves. He affirms the important information provided about the OT text. There is no evidence, for example, that Isaiah ever existed as two or more separate books. "The new evidence confirms what we had already good reason to believe— that the Jewish scribes of the early Christian centuries copied and recopied the text of the Hebrew Bible with the utmost fidelity."[227] In this later book Bruce is inclined to identify the "Wicked Priest" as Jonathan, the brother of Judas Maccabeus. Bruce reviews the evidence from Pliny, Philo, and Josephus and writes that "a reasonable conclusion is that the Qumran community was one Essene group, diverging in several particulars from other Essene groups."[228] Efforts to relate Jesus or even John the Baptist to the community are largely illusory.

EXEGESIS

Bruce was a biblical commentator as well as a historian. He published works in various series. For the New International Greek Testament Commentary

(NIGTC) he produced a commentary on the Greek text of Galatians. For the New International Commentary on the New Testament (NICNT; a series for which Bruce served for a time as editor), he wrote commentaries on Hebrews, Acts, and (in a single volume) Colossians, Philemon, and Ephesians. For the New International Bible Commentary: New Testament Series (NIBC) he wrote a commentary on Philippians. For the Tyndale New Testament Commentaries (TNTC), he contributed a commentary on Romans. For the New Century Bible (NCB) Bruce wrote a commentary on 1 and 2 Corinthians. For the Word Biblical Commentary (WBC) he produced a commentary on 1 and 2 Thessalonians. His little book, *Paul and His Converts*, as its subtitle shows, is a commentary on 1 and 2 Thessalonians and 1 and 2 Corinthians (Bible Guides 17). Bruce also published independent commentaries on Ephesians, the Gospel of John, and Acts that belonged to no series.[229] From this lengthy list only a few samples can be investigated.

Bruce's commentary on the Greek text of Acts is regarded as one of his best.[230] He begins with an Introduction of ninety-six pages. In regard to authorship, Bruce defends the tradition. The author is a companion of Paul, the obvious implication of the "we-sections." Bruce identifies him as Luke, the "beloved physician" of Col 4:14. In response to Cadbury's argument about medical language, Bruce writes: "The presence of medical language in Luke-Acts cannot by itself prove anything about authorship, but if it could be rendered probable on other grounds that the author was Luke the physician, then the more striking instances of medical terminology might properly be used to illustrate, and perhaps even to support this conclusion."[231] Concerning date, Bruce concludes that Acts was written in the late 70s or early 80s. He characterizes Luke as the first Christian apologist, who defends Christianity against Judaism and paganism and portrays Christians as law-abiding citizens. Nevertheless, Bruce believes Luke deserves high marks as a historian. In regard to sources, Bruce believes that with the exception of the "we-sections" (probably Luke's own travel diary), the identification of sources is difficult.

Despite his tendency to harmonize, Bruce does acknowledge differences between Luke's portrait of Paul and Paul's picture of himself. According to Acts, "He is always sure of himself; he always triumphs. But the Paul of the letters does not triumph; he is 'led in triumph' by Christ."[232] For Luke, Paul is a self-confident hero, but "Paul was no hero in his own eyes. In his letters, he is often the victim of conflicting emotions."[233] Nevertheless, Bruce believes that "The Paul whose portrait Luke paints is the real Paul."[234]

In regard to theology, "Luke is a biblical theologian: he sees the worldwide expansion of the gospel as the fulfillment of God's self-revelation progressively imparted in earlier days through mighty work and prophetic word, as recorded in the Hebrew scriptures."[235] Bruce believes that Luke was a literary artist, writing a Greek that is closer to classical than most of the rest of the NT. In regard to the text of Acts, Bruce thinks that the longer readings of the "Western" text are usually secondary. The introduction concludes with a useful collection of chronological and genealogical tables.

The Text and Commentary are presented in pages 97–543. The text is presented in Greek and the comments are made verse by verse. These notes deal with terms and phrases in the text and give careful attention to technical details: text, grammar, historical references, cross references, and secondary sources. Time and space allow only a few examples of Bruce's exegesis.

In interpreting "The Appointing of the Seven" (6:1-6), Bruce says that the word Ἑλληνιστής occurs here for the first time in Greek literature. Bruce also notes that the designation of the apostles as οἱ δώδεκα is used only here in Acts. The waiting on tables, Bruce says, may refer to meals or to financial matters. As the activity of Stephen and Philip shows, the Seven were not restricted to these matters. The laying on of hands confers the authority of the apostles. Bruce sees the Seven and the apostles in harmony. To the critical eye, on the contrary, Stephen's speech and execution represent a radical departure from the behavior described in Acts 2:46.

Bruce's interpretation of Acts 20:7-12, "Paul at Troas," is intriguing. He points out that the name of the young man who fell from the third floor, Eutychus, means "Fortunate"—an understatement, we may add. Bruce's fanciful description is vivid: "The hot, oily atmosphere caused by the crowd and the torches made it difficult for a youth who may have put in a hard day's work to keep awake, despite the priceless opportunity of learning truth from apostolic lips."[236] When the text says that Eutychus was "picked up dead," Bruce believes the author is speaking in his professional role. "Luke no doubt means that he was 'clinically' dead."[237] As to the description in v. 10, where the reader is told that Paul "threw himself on the young man and put his arms around him" (NIV), Bruce asks, "Is a form of artificial respiration implied?"[238] But why, asks the wary reader, did Paul not defer to Dr. Luke?

Bruce's commentary on the Greek text of Galatians is also important.[239] In the introduction he gives considerable attention to the identification of the churches to which the Epistle is addressed. He summarizes the two major theories: the north Galatian hypothesis holds that the letter was written to churches in the north, the region of the original location of the Galatians; the south Galatian hypothesis believes the letter was written to churches of the southern region that had been incorporated into the imperial province of

Galatia in 25 BCE: the churches of Antioch of Pisidia, Iconium, Lystra, and Derbe. "The fact that so many competent scholars can be cited in support of either position," says Bruce, "suggests that the evidence for neither is absolutely conclusive. But the weight of the evidence, it seems to me, favors the South Galatian view."[240] According to Bruce, Paul had received word that troublemakers had invaded the Galatian churches, compelling the Gentile converts to adopt circumcision. By requiring circumcision they claimed to proclaim the whole gospel, not the truncated gospel of Paul. According to Paul, theirs was no gospel at all. The dating of Galatians depends on the adoption of either the north or the south hypothesis. Bruce, choosing the latter, believes Galatians was the earliest of Paul's letters, written on the eve of the Jerusalem Council (Acts 15).

Bruce believes the first main section of the letter is autobiographical. In discussing 1:15-17 he points out that Paul's call to apostleship is reminiscent of the prophets (Jer 1:5). When Paul says that God revealed his son ἐν ἐμοί, he is probably stressing the inwardness of the experience. However, that experience, Bruce supposes, was objective—the same sort of experience as that of Peter and the others (1 Cor 15:5-8). Paul says that after this experience he did not go to Jerusalem to those who were apostles before him. Bruce believes that the phrase πρὸ ἐμοῦ (before me) is temporal; it does not denote status.

Bruce thinks, contra the majority, that Gal 2:1-10 recounts a conference in Jerusalem that occurred before the Jerusalem Council of Acts 15. This earlier meeting, according to Bruce, occurred at the time when Paul and Barnabas brought famine relief to Jerusalem as recorded in Acts 11:30. Bruce does not believe Paul's participation in this meeting indicated that he was submitting to the authority of the Jerusalem leaders. "But the approval of those leaders made his task less difficult and (as here) could serve his apologetic purpose."[241] He acknowledges that Paul's account does express some disparagement of the leaders when he says "what they actually were makes no difference to me; God shows no partiality" (v. 6). Here Paul, according to Bruce, was not questioning the leaders, but countering the appeal to them his opponents made.

Galatians 2:11-14 deals with "Conflict in Antioch." Bruce believes this event took place after the Jerusalem conference of Galatians 2 but before the Jerusalem Council of Acts 15. According to Bruce, the Apostolic Decree adopted at the Council was formulated to deal with the kind of issue that had arisen in Antioch. When people came from James, Peter, who had been eating with Gentile converts, withdrew from table fellowship with them. Paul believed this action to be inconsistent with the truth of the gospel.

Immediately following this rebuke of Peter, Paul presents the theme of the letter: "Both Jews and Gentiles are justified by faith" (2:15-21). In v. 16 Paul says that no one is justified by "works of the law," a phrase, as Bruce points out, repeated three times in the verse. According to Bruce the word ωθῆναι means to be put in the right, set right with God, pardoned and accepted by God. The genitive phrase διὰ πίστεως 'Ιησοῦ Χριστοῦ can be translated as subjective (Christ's faith or Christ's faithfulness) or objective (faith in Christ). Bruce favors the objective meaning, noting that the next sentence speaks of believing in Christ. By showing Jews to be sinners, Paul asks: Does this mean that Christ is a servant of sin? Certainly not. The law-free gospel revealed them to be sinners, but the law increased sin. The believer, however, has died to the law, crucified with Christ. "Having died with Christ in his death," concludes Bruce, "the believer now lives with Christ in his life—i.e. his resurrection life. In fact, this new life in Christ is nothing less than the risen Christ living his life in the believer. The risen Christ is the operative power in the new order, as sin was in the old."[242]

THE LIFE AND THOUGHT OF PAUL

Bruce's crowning achievement is his *Paul: Apostle of the Heart Set Free*.[243] His devotion to the apostle is declared at the outset:

> For half a century and more I have been a student and teacher of ancient literature, and to no other writer of antiquity have I devoted so much time and attention as to Paul. Nor can I think of any other writer, ancient or modern, whose study is so richly rewarding as his.[244]

In general, the book is a review of the life, letters, and thought of Paul of Tarsus. The structure follows the outline of Acts and repeats much of the material found in Bruce's *New Testament History* and commentaries. Consequently, the following review treats topics, especially literary and theological, that have not been explicated already. About Paul's conversion Bruce writes: "No single event, apart from the Christ-event itself has proved so determinant for the course of Christian history as the conversion and commissioning of Paul."[245] In regard to Paul's visit to Jerusalem after his conversion, Bruce affirms the account in Acts wherein Barnabas "brought Paul and leaders of the Jerusalem church together. Although Paul says nothing of this, it is antecedently probable that someone acted as mediator."[246] Paul's own account says that he saw only Cephas and James. From them, Bruce believes Paul received such tradition as that recorded in 1 Cor 15:5-7. But how, he asks, could Paul claim that he did not receive his gospel from "a human source" (Gal 1:15) if he received it from Cephas and James? Bruce replies:

> We may say then, in general, that those aspects in Paul's ministry which were distinctively his belong to the gospel as revelation, while those elements which he shared with others . . . belong to the gospel as tradition, and in the first instance, to the information he received in Jerusalem when he went up there to make inquiry of Peter in the third year after his conversion.[247]

Bruce devotes a chapter to "Paul and the Historical Jesus." He believes Paul was familiar with the main features of the life and teaching of Jesus. In his conversion experience Paul had an experience of the "exalted Christ." Bruce describes Paul as a man of vision and action.

> Many others were engaged in Gentile evangelization, but none with the overall strategic planning conceived in Paul's mind and so largely executed by his dynamic energy. This energy was the fruit of his conviction that he was a figure of eschatological significance, a key agent in the progress of salvation history, a chosen instrument in the Lord's hands to bring Gentiles into the obedience of faith as a necessary preparation for the ultimate salvation of all Israel and the consummation of God's redeeming purpose for the world.[248]

Paul's missionary strategy, according to Bruce, was to begin in the synagogues, because there he could evangelize the Gentile "God fearers."

In connection with his discussion of Galatians, Bruce explicates the central Pauline doctrine. "Justification by faith, so vigorously asserted in the letter to the Galatians, was implicit in his conversion, but now it became in his hands a fighting doctrine—not only a principle for which to contend but a weapon with which to contend."[249] In Romans this doctrine is discussed in relation to the law. In regard to the oft-debated Rom 10:4, Bruce believes that Paul viewed Christ as both the goal and the end of the law. Dividing Romans 7 into two sections, he writes that in 7:7-13 Paul is speaking of humanity in general whereas in 7:10-25 he is speaking autobiographically. Christ, according to Bruce, liberates the believer from the law, but the believer follows the law of Christ. He urges interpreters to let Paul be Paul. "And when we do that, we shall recognize in him the supreme libertarian, the great herald of Christian freedom, insisting that man in Christ has reached his spiritual majority and must no longer be confined to the leading-strings of infancy but enjoy the birthright of the freeborn sons of God."[250]

Bruce believes that Paul wrote both letters to the Thessalonians shortly after his mission there. He thinks the Corinthian correspondence consists of five letters: (A) a letter that has been lost; (B) 1 Corinthians; (C) a stern letter (that has not survived); (D) 2 Corinthians 1–9; (E) 2 Corinthians 10–13. In connection with the Corinthian correspondence, Bruce discusses Paul's understanding of baptism and the Lord's Supper. For Paul the gift of the Spirit is related to baptism. Paul preserves the earliest tradition of the Supper. His enigmatic remark about "discerning the body" (1 Cor 11:29), according to Bruce, means that the readers should not mistreat other members of the Christian community. After a description of Paul's stormy mission in Ephesus, Bruce discusses the apostle's view of the life to come. On the basis of his experience of the risen Christ, Paul believed Christians would be raised with a transformed body. Bruce interprets 2 Cor 5:1-10 to mean that the believer receives the resurrection body at death.

Turning his back on Macedonia and Achaia, Paul directs the goal of his mission to the west. But first he must take the offering, for which he has so long labored, to the Jerusalem church. On the eve of his final trip to the holy city he writes his Epistle to the Romans, a document Bruce views as a summary of Paul's gospel. The central theme is the righteousness of God, given by grace, received by faith. This message, Bruce believes, meets a universal need, offering freedom from sin, law, and death.

The next chapters, again following Acts, present Paul's last trip to Jerusalem, his imprisonment in Caesarea, and his shipwreck on the way to Rome. In regard to Paul's gathering sticks for the fire at Malta, Bruce quips, "Paul knows (unlike many theologians) that a fire will not continue to burn unless it is fed with fuel."[251] In connection with Paul's imprisonment in Rome (a two-year house arrest), Bruce discusses letters he believes were written there. He agrees with John Knox that Philemon would not have been preserved if it had not been concerned with an important person: Onesimus, who became Bishop of Ephesus.[252] Also from the Roman imprisonment, according to Bruce, were Colossians and Ephesians. Colossians presents a doctrine of the cosmic Christ. Ephesians, in Bruce's opinion, represents the "Quintessence of Paulinism." This epistle praises the divine mystery, the plan hidden for ages in God.

An interesting penultimate chapter deals with the last days of Paul according to history and tradition. Bruce supposes that Paul was released from the Roman imprisonment of Acts 28, arrested again, and executed during the Neronian persecution, around 65. Bruce rehearses the tradition of Paul's execution and burial on the Ostian Way and the less credible tradition of his grave at St. Sebastian's on the Appian Way. A final chapter presents Bruce's reflections on Paul's personality—a man who was zealous, impetuous, and strong in face of adversity. Bruce concludes:

> Campaigner for spiritual liberty that he was, he gave one thing precedence even over liberty, that one thing was love. But spiritual liberty is not really diminished by love; both together are imparted by the Spirit, and to serve in love is perfect freedom. In this, as in so many other respects, Paul has remained unsurpassed in his insight into the mind of Christ.[253]

All in all, it is an excellent book—solidly researched, lucidly written, sympathetic with its subject.

In sum, F. F. Bruce made a significant contribution to the history of NT research. He demonstrated mastery of the major aspects of the method, especially linguistic and historical insight. Bruce was steeped in the study of the classics and the atmosphere of the ancient world. To be sure, he may have had a tendency to harmonize, and sometimes he gives the impression that he believes Acts to be the primary source for reconstructing the life of Paul. Nevertheless, when Bruce took a position he did so in full cognizance of the contrary view, and he was always able to give a reason for the conclusion he adopted. He was tolerant of those with whom he disagrees, and he enjoyed the admiration of most who disagreed with him. In general, Bruce affirms the viability of the historical method. Just as Roman Catholics can continue their confessional stance and use the critical method, so Bruce demonstrates that Protestant evangelicals can embrace historical criticism and maintain their faith.

Summary

If conflict characterizes developments in historical criticism (chap. 6), that is even more evident in this chapter on theological and hermeneutical developments! The spectrum runs all the way from Knox on the left to Bruce on the right. However, judging from the personalities involved, one might suppose that these two would have been the most tolerant. At the same time, the commitment of Cullmann and Minear to ecumenicity indicates that both would respect the opinions of scholars of other confessions and persuasions. All four of the scholars are united in one concern: the importance of Scripture for the life and thought of the church.

Among the issues involved in the research treated in this chapter is the question of biblical authority. Bruce has a high doctrine of biblical authority, whereas Knox feels free to criticize Paul. All four scholars stress the centrality of Christ and tend to affirm the concept of Christ as event. They also tend to be suspicious of christologies that appropriate philosophical presuppositions and expositions. Stress, they believe, should be on the action of God in Christ, not on the person and nature of Christ; Knox is anxious that the humanity of Christ not be compromised. In regard to hermeneutics, Cullmann and Bruce tend to emphasize the literal, while Knox, and even more so Minear, embrace the mythical and symbolic. Bruce and Cullmann take a straightforward, literal view of history, whereas Minear and Knox express sophisticated notions of history's nature and meaning. All are alert to the importance of eschatology, but with Minear apocalyptic moves to the very core of God's activity, a view diametrically opposed to Cullmann's timeline of salvation history. There is no easy resolution to these disagreements—nor, for the historian, should there be. In any case, most of the issues reviewed here will continue to occupy NT research for the balance of this book.

Notes

1. H. Richard Niebuhr, *The Kingdom of God in America* (New York: Harper & Row, 1959), 193.

2. For a biography and overview of Cullmann's work, see Oscar Cullmann, "Autobiographische Skizze (1960)," in *Vorträge und Aufsätze, 1925–1962*, ed. Karlfried Fröhlich (Tübingen: Mohr Siebeck, 1966), 683–87; D. P. Moessner, "Cullmann, Oscar (1902–)," in *DBI* 1: 234–35; Theodore Martin Dorman, "Cullmann, Oscar (1902–1999)," in *DMBI*, 333–38; James D. G. Dunn, "Cullmann, Oscar (1902–1999)," in *DBCI*, 62–63; Karlfried Fröhlich, "Die Mitte des Neuen Testaments: Oscar Cullmanns Beitrag zur Theologie der Gegenwart," in *Oikonomia: Heilsgeschichte als Thema der Theologie: Oscar Cullmann zum 65. Geburtstag gewidmet,* ed. Felix Christ (Hamburg-Bergstedt: Reich, 1967), 203–19; Karl-Heinz Schlaudraff, *"Heil als Geschichte"? Die Frage nach dem heilsgeschichtlichen Denken, dargestellt anhand der Konzeption Oscar Cullmanns,* BGBE 29 (Tübingen: Mohr Siebeck, 1988), 3–5; Hans-Georg Hermesmann, *Zeit und Heil: Oscar Cullmanns Theologie der Heilsgeschichte,* Konfesssionskundliche und kontroverstheologische Studien 43 (Paderborn: Bonifatius, 1979), 17–29; Robert W. Yarbrough, *The Salvation Historical Fallacy? Reassessing the History of New Testament Theology* (Leiden: Deo, 2004), 213–60.

3. See *HNTR* 2: 163–72, 442–51.

4. See Karlfried Froehlich, ed., *Testimonia oecumenica: in honorem Oscar Cullmann octogenarii, dei XXV Februarii A. D. MCMLXXXII* (Tübingen: Vogler, 1982), a collection of letters from a large number of ecumenical leaders praising Cullmann for his contribution. Among Cullmann's publications on ecumenism see, for example, *Einheit durch Vielfalt: Grundlegung und Beitrag zur Diskussion über die Möglichkeiten ihrer Verwirklichung* (Tübingen: Mohr Siebeck, 1986); ET: *Unity Through Diversity: Its Foundation, and a Contribution to the Discussion concerning the Possibilities of Its Actualization,* trans. M. Eugene Boring (Philadelphia: Fortress, 1988).

5. See Theodore Martin Dorman, *The Hermeneutics of Oscar Cullmann* (San Francisco: Mellen Research University Press, 1991); Fröhlich, "Mitte des Neuen Testaments"; Schlaudraff, *"Heil als Geschichte?"* 9–49; Jean Frisque, *Oscar Cullmann: Une théologie de l'histoire du salut*, Cahiers de l'actualité religieuse 11 (Tournai: Casterman, 1960); Hermesmann, *Zeit und Heil*.

6. Dorman, *Hermeneutics of Oscar Cullmann*, 2.

7. In his *The Early Church: Studies in Early Christian History and Theology*, ed. A. J. B. Higgins (Philadelphia: Westminster, 1956), 3–16; Originally published in *Student World* 42/2 (1949); repr.: "Notwendigkeit und Aufgabe der philologisch-historischen Bibelauslegung," *Vorträge und Aufsätze*, 110–24.

8. *Le Nouveau Testament*, Que sais-je? (Paris: Presses Universitaires de France, 1966); ET: *The New Testament: An Introduction for the General Reader*, trans. Dennis Pardee (Philadelphia: Westminster, 1968).

9. *Der johanneische Kreis: Sein Platz im Spätjudentum, in der Jüngerschaft Jesu und im Urchristenheit* (Tübingen: Mohr Siebeck, 1975); ET: *The Johannine Circle*, trans. John Bowden (Philadelphia: Westminster, 1976).

10. For bibliographies of Cullmann see Heinrich Baltensweiler and Bo Reicke, eds., *Neues Testament und Geschichte: Historisches Geschehen und Deutung im Neuen Testament: Oscar Cullmann zum 70. Geburtstag* (Zürich: Theologischer Verlag, 1972), 329–44; Frisque, *Cullmann*, 262–76. For the major collection of Cullmann's shorter writings see Oscar Cullmann, *Vorträge und Aufsätze, 1925–1962*; of special interest to the English reader is *The Early Church*; for the French reader *Études de théologie biblique*, Bibliothèque théologique (Neuchâtel: Delachaux et Niestlé, 1968); *Des sources de l'Evangile à la formation de la théologies chrétienne* (Neuchâtel: Delachaux et Niestlé, 1969).

11. *Le Problème littéraire et historique du roman Pseudo-Clémentin: Étude sur le rapport entre le Gnosticisme et le Judéo-Christianisme* (Paris: Alcan, 1930).

12. Oscar Cullmann, "Die Neuentdeckten Qumrantexte und das Judenchristentum der Pseudoklementinen," *Neutestamentliche Studien für Rudolf Bultmann zu seinem 70. Geburtstag am 20. August 1955*, ed. Walther Eltester (Berlin: Töpelmann, 1957), 35–51; repr. in *Vorträge und Aufsätze*, 241–59.

13. *Christus und die Zeit: Die urchristliche Zeit- und Geschichtsauffassung*, 1st ed. (Zollikon-Zürich: Evangelischer Verlag, 1946); ET: *Christ and Time: The Primitive Christian Conception of Time and History*, rev. ed. trans. Floyd V. Filson (London: SCM, 1962).

14. Oscar Cullmann, *Königsherrschaft Christi und Kirche im Neuen Testament*, ThSt 10 (Zollikon-Zürich: Evangelischer Verlag, 1941); ET: "The Kingship of Christ and the Church in the New Testament," *Early Church*, 105–37.

15. In *Vorträge und Aufsätze*, 378–402; ET: "The Return of Christ: The New Testament Hope," *Early Church*, 141–62.

16. According to Dorman, *Hermeneutics of Oscar Cullmann*, 50.

17. For discussion of this book see ibid., 78–100; Schlaudraff, *"Heil als Geschichte?"* 50–97; Yarbrough, *Salvation Historical Fallacy?*

18. *Christ and Time*, xii.

19. Ibid., 49–50.

20. Ibid., 59.

21. Ibid., 87.

22. Ibid., 109.

23. Ibid., 157.

24. Ibid., 221.

25. Oscar Cullmann, *Christus und die Zeit*, 3rd rev. ed. (Zürich: EVZ Verlag, 1962).

26. Bultmann's "Heilsgeschichte und Geschichte: zu Oscar Cullmann, *Christus und die Zeit*" (1948), is reprinted in his *Exegetica* (1967), 356–68.

27. *Christ and Time*, xxv. In an addendum to the 3rd. ed. Cullmann responds to the criticism of James Barr (*The Semantics of Biblical Language* [Oxford: Oxford University Press, 1961]; *Biblical*

Words for Time [London: SCM, 1962]) in regard to Cullmann's understanding of biblical terms; he acknowledges truth in Barr's lexicography but contends that his own view is grounded in biblical exegesis, quite apart from linguistic details.

28. Oscar Cullmann, *Heil als Geschichte: Heilsgeschichtliche Existenz im Neuen Testament* (Tübingen: Mohr Siebeck, 1965); ET: *Salvation in History*, trans. Sidney G. Sowers (London: SCM, 1967).

29. See Schlaudraff, *"Heil als Geschichte?"* 97–180.

30. *Salvation in History*, 25.

31. See pp. 323–24 above.

32. *Salvation in History*, 71.

33. Ibid., 86.

34. Ibid., 166.

35. Ibid., 172.

36. Ibid., 230.

37. Ibid., 271.

38. Ibid., 296.

39. Ibid. 326.

40. *Die Christologie des Neuen Testaments* (Tübingen: Mohr Siebeck, 1957); ET: *The Christology of the New Testament*, trans. Shirley C. Guthrie and Charles A. M. Hall (Philadelphia: Westminster, 1959). See Dorman, *Hermeneutics of Oscar Cullmann*, 101–24.

41. *Christology of the New Testament*, 3.

42. Ibid., 35.

43. Ibid., 80.

44. Ibid., 164.

45. Ibid., 208.

46. Ibid., 235.

47. Ibid., 258.

48. Ibid., 265.

49. Ibid., 328.

50. *Petrus: Jünger, Apostel, Märtyrer: Das historische und das theologische Petrusproblem* (Zürich: Zwingli, 1952); ET: *Peter: Disciple, Apostle, Martyr: A Historical and Theological Study*, trans. Floyd V. Filson (Philadelphia: Westminster, 1953). In 1960 Cullmann published a 2d ed. of his German work; it was translated into English as *Peter* (Philadelphia: Westminster, 1962), repr.: *Peter: Disciple, Apostle, Martyr* (Waco, TX: Baylor University Press, 2011); the reprint edition includes an "Introduction" (pp. 11–16) by Helen K. Bond that reviews Cullmann's book from an early-twenty-first-century perspective.

51. *Peter*, 2d ed., 156.

52. Ibid., 157.

53. Ibid., 225.

54. Ibid., 236.

55. Oscar Cullmann, *Immortality of the Soul or Resurrection of the Dead? The Witness of the New Testament* (New York: Macmillan, 1958); French trans.: *Immortalité de l'âme, ou resurrection des morts? Le témoignage du Nouveau Testament* (Neuchâtel: Delachaux & Niestlé, 1959).

56. *Immortality of the Soul*, 15.

57. Oscar Cullmann, *The State in the New Testament* (New York: Scribner's, 1956).

58. See Cullmann's *Jesus and the Revolutionaries*, trans. Gareth Putnam (New York: Harper & Row, 1970).

59. *State in the New Testament*, 25–26.

60. Oscar Cullmann, *Les Premièrs confessions de foi chrétiennes* (Paris: Presses Universitaires de France, 1943); German trans.: *Die ersten christlichen Glaubensbekenntnisse* (Zollikon-Zürich:

Evangelischer Verlag, 1943); ET: *The Earliest Christian Confessions*, trans. J. K. S. Reid (London: Lutterworth, 1949).

61. *Earliest Christian Confessions*, 41.

62. Oscar Cullmann, *Urchristentum und Gottesdienst* (Zürich: Zwingli, 1950); ET: *Early Christian Worship*, trans. A. Stewart Todd and James B. Torrance, SBT 10 (London: SCM, 1953).

63. *Early Christian Worship*, 15.

64. Much of this material is also presented in *Les Sacrements dans l'évangile johannique: La Vie de Jésus et le cult de l'église primitive*, EHPR 42 (Paris: Presses Universitaires de France, 1951).

65. Related to Cullmann's concern with worship is his *Das Gebet im Neuen Testament* (Tübingen: Mohr Siebeck, 1944); ET: *Prayer in the New Testament*, trans. John Bowden (Minneapolis: Fortress Press, 1944).

66. Oscar Cullmann, *Die Tauflehre des Neuen Testaments: Erwachsenen- und Kindertaufe* (Zürich: Zwingli, 1948); French ed.: *Le Baptême des enfants et la doctrine biblique du baptême* (Neuchâtel: Delachaux & Niestlé, 1948); ET: *Baptism in the New Testament*, trans. J. K. S. Reid, SBT 1 (London: SCM, 1950).

67. *Baptism in the New Testament*, 22.

68. Ibid., 70.

69. "The Meaning of the Lord's Supper in Primitive Christianity," in Oscar Cullmann, *Essays on the Lord's Supper*, ESW 1 (Richmond, VA: John Knox, 1958).

70. Yarbrough, *Salvation Historical Fallacy?* (pp. 231–60) presents an extensive review of the criticisms of Cullmann, especially the major criticism of Bultmann. Yarbrough carefully delineates and assesses the issues. In the setting of the history of research he traces a line from Baur to Wrede to Bultmann, and sees Cullmann in the tradition of the salvation-history theologians, J. C. K. von Hofmann and Adolf Schlatter.

71. Frisque, *Cullmann*, 206–59.

72. Schlaudraff, *"Heil als Geschichte?"* 181–256.

73. Dorman, *Hermeneutics of Oscar Cullmann*, 151–71.

74. For biographical information see John Knox, *Never Far from Home: The Story of My Life* (Waco, TX: Word, 1975); "John Knox: *Cursus Vitae*," in *Christian History and Interpretation: Studies Presented to John Knox,* ed. William R. Farmer, C. F. D. Moule, and Richard R. Niebuhr (Cambridge: Cambridge University Press, 1967), xxi–xxii; John C. Bennett, "John Knox at Union," in ibid., xiii–xix; Lyle D. Vander Broek, "Knox, John (1900–1990)," *DMBI*, 618–22; William R. Farmer, "Knox, John (1900–1990)," *DBI* 2: 34–35. Late in his career Knox wrote *A Glory in it All: Reflections after Eighty* (Waco, TX: Word, 1985), a collection of short essays expressing his views on a variety of issues.

75. *Never Far from Home*, 96.

76. See *HNTR* 2: 317–30.

77. For bibliography see "Bibliography of the Work of John Knox" [1929–1967] in *Christian History and Interpretation*, xxiii–xxxii; Vander Broek, *DMBI*, 621–22.

78. *Philemon Among the Letters of Paul: A New View of Its Place and Importance*, rev. ed. (New York and Nashville: Abingdon, 1959).

79. John Knox, *Marcion and the New Testament* (Chicago: University of Chicago Press, 1942).

80. Ibid., 31.

81. Ibid., 139.

82. John Knox, *Chapters in a Life of Paul*, rev. ed. (Macon, GA: Mercer University Press, 1987).

83. Knox's final word on this subject is "On the Pauline Chronology: Buck-Taylor-Hurd Revisited," in *The Conversation Continues: Studies in Paul and John, In Honor of J. Louis Martyn*, ed. Robert T. Fortna and Beverly R. Gaventa (Nashville: Abingdon, 1990), 258–74. In this essay Knox gives considerable attention to the chronological order of the epistles. On the larger question he

essentially reaffirms the chronology he presented in the first edition of *Chapters in a Life of Paul*.

84. John Knox, "The Epistle to the Romans: Introduction and Exegesis," *IB* 9: 355–668.

85. Ibid., 9: 355.

86. Ibid., 9: 429.

87. Ibid., 9: 433.

88. Ibid., 9: 499.

89. Ibid., 9: 500.

90. Knox also published a short book that presents an exposition of the themes of the central chapters of Romans: *Life In Christ Jesus: Reflections on Romans 5–8* (Greenwich, CT: Seabury, 1961). In addition to his work on Romans, Knox published a short study on the later writings of the NT, written for the beginner: *The Fourth Gospel and the Later Epistles* (New York: Abingdon, 1945). This book combines the features of an introduction and commentary. On critical issues Knox largely affirms the ("liberal") scholarly consensus: the Fourth Gospel was not written by John the son of Zebedee; Hebrews was written to Rome before 95; neither 1 nor 2 Peter is authentic.

91. On Knox's theology see Norman Pittenger, "Some Implications, Philosophical and Theological, in John Knox's Writing," in *Christian History and Interpretation*, 3–16; Daniel Day Williams, "John Knox's Conception of History," in ibid., 17–34.

92. John Knox, *Criticism and Faith* (London: Hodder and Stoughton, 1953).

93. Ibid., 7.

94. Ibid., 21.

95. Ibid., 24.

96. Ibid., 29.

97. John Knox, *Limits of Unbelief* (New York: Seabury, 1970).

98. Ibid., 14.

99. Ibid., 67.

100. This theme is discussed in Knox's short book, *Christ and the Hope of Glory* (New York: Abingdon, 1960).

101. John Knox, *Myth and Truth: An Essay on the Language of Faith* (Charlottesville: University Press of Virginia, 1964).

102. Ibid., 42.

103. *Chapters in a Life of Paul*, 117.

104. Ibid., 122.

105. Knox repeats this point in his book, *The Ethic of Jesus in the Teaching of the Church: Its Authority and Its Relevance* (New York: Abingdon, 1961), 79: "But the truth of the matter is that justification is not the most apt way of representing the meaning of God's act in Christ in its bearing upon our plight as guilty sinners. Forgiveness is the more appropriate term."

106. See Paul Schubert, "Paul and the New Testament Ethic in the Thought of John Knox," in *Christian History and Interpretation*, 363–88. Schubert, with great appreciation for Knox, refutes the charge of antinomianism and offers a more convincing alternative to Knox's view of Paul's understanding of justification. Schubert's essay also presents an insightful summary of Knox's theology.

107. John Knox, *Jesus: Lord and Christ. A Trilogy Comprising: The Man Christ Jesus, Christ the Lord, On the Meaning of Christ* (New York: Harper & Brothers, 1958). See Robert E. Cushman, "Christology of Ecclesiology? A Critical examination of the Christology of John Knox," *ReL* 27 (1958): 515–26.

108. *Jesus: Lord and Christ. The Man Christ Jesus*. The original was published in 1941 (New York: Willett, Clark, and Co.).

109. Ibid., 10.

110. Ibid., 13. Knox develops his understanding of the ethical teachings in *Ethic of Jesus*. In this book he faces the problem of the impossibility of the ethical demands. The answer, he believes, must assess the demands in the context of God's grace.

111. *Jesus, Lord and Christ: The Man Christ Jesus*, 57.

112. *Christ the Lord: The Meaning of Jesus in the Early Church* (Chicago: Willett, Clark & Co., 1945).

113. Without using the terms, Knox adopts a version of the criterion of dissimilarity (or embarrassment). Such details as the baptism of Jesus at the hand of John the Baptist—details that were contrary to the interests of the early church—are historically reliable. However, Knox (appropriately) qualifies this criterion. "The fact that an item sustains a later belief or serves a later need does not mean *ipso facto* that it cannot be regarded as belonging to the earliest tradition. Only when it *also* fails to conform to the original situation as our most primitive sources give it to us is an item to be rejected" (*Christ the Lord*, 80). The last sentence implies a version of the criterion of multiple attestation.

114. *Jesus, Lord and Christ: Christ the Lord*, 116.

115. Ibid., 131.

116. Ibid., 147.

117. Ibid., 188.

118. *On the Meaning of Christ*. Originally published in 1947 (New York: Scribner's).

119. *Jesus: Lord and Christ. On the Meaning of Christ*, 194.

120. Ibid., 202.

121. Ibid., 217.

122. Ibid., 233.

123. Ibid., 264.

124. John Knox, *The Death of Christ: The Cross in New Testament History and Faith* (New York: Abingdon, 1958).

125. Ibid., 85.

126. Ibid., 65.

127. Ibid., 106.

128. Ibid., 112.

129. Ibid., 123.

130. Ibid., 131.

131. Ibid., 154.

132. John Knox, *The Humanity and Divinity of Christ: A Study of Pattern in Christology* (Cambridge: Cambridge University Press, 1967).

133. Ibid., x.

134. Ibid., 33.

135. Ibid., 54.

136. Ibid., 56.

137. Ibid., 74.

138. Ibid., 98.

139. Ibid., 107–8.

140. Ibid., 113. Knox's argument is not entirely clear or convincing. He wants to protect the humanity of Christ but still affirm his divinity. His method is to use his favorite ploy: the conviction that the church is an autonomous entity, grounded in the essential, unassailable experience of faith. But in doing so he subsumes the humanity of Christ under the (subjective) reality of the church. In response to this maneuver, Cushman ("Christology or Ecclesiology," 526) accuses Knox of "methodological docetism."

141. John Knox, *The Early Church and the Coming Great Church* (New York: Abingdon, 1955).

142. Ibid., 12.

143. Ibid., 74.

144. Ibid., 129.

145. Ibid., 136.

146. Ibid., 155.

147. John Knox, *The Church and the Reality of Christ* (New York: Harper & Row, 1962).

148. Ibid., 22.

149. Ibid., 77.

150. Ibid., 78.

151. Ibid., 83.

152. Ibid., 124.

153. Ibid., 129.

154. "Christology or Ecclesiology," 526. Knox was not only concerned with the doctrine of the church, he was also committed to the practical life and ministry of the church; see, for example, his *The Integrity of Preaching* (New York: Abingdon, 1957).

155. For biography see William Baird, "Minear, Paul Sevier (1906–2007)," *DMBI*, 742–45; Leander Keck, "Foreword," in Paul S. Minear, *Images of the Church in the New Testament*, New Testament Library (Louisville: Westminster John Knox, 2004), xiii–xxvii; J. Louis Martyn, "Foreword," in Paul S. Minear, *The Bible and the Historian: Breaking the Silence About God in Biblical Studies* (Nashville: Abingdon, 2002), 11–16; "Prologue: Stages in the Study," in Paul Sevier Minear, *Christians and the New Creation: Genesis Motifs in the New Testament* (Louisville: Westminster John Knox, 1994), ix–xvi.

156. See pp. 565–98 below.

157. For bibliography of Minear's publications see Minear, *Christians and the New Creation,* 131–38; Baird, *DMBI*, 744–45. For overviews of Minear's work see C. Freeman Sleeper, "Some American Contributions to New Testament Interpretation," *Int* 20 (1966): 322–29; Steven J. Kraftchick, "Facing Janus: Reviewing the Biblical Theology Movement," in *Biblical Theology: Problems and Perspectives: In Honor of J. Christiaan Beker*, ed. Steven J. Kraftchick, Charles D. Myers, Jr., and Ben C. Ollenburger (Nashville: Abingdon, 1995), 54–77.

158. Paul S. Minear, *And Great Shall Be Your Reward: The Origins of Christian Views of Salvation*, YSR 12 (New Haven: Yale University Press, 1941).

159. Ibid., 51.

160. Paul S. Minear, *The Obedience of Faith: The Purposes of Paul in the Epistle to the Romans*, SBT, 2d Series 19 (Naperville, IL: Alec R. Allenson, 1971).

161. This work tends toward "hyper-criticism," assuming precise knowledge of the Roman situation by Paul and practicing overly precise exegesis. Most scholars have not been convinced; see, for example, Robert J. Karris, "Romans 14:1–15:13 and the Occasion of Romans," in *The Romans Debate*, ed. Karl P. Donfried, rev. ed. (Peabody, MA: Hendrickson, 1991), 65–84. However, in attempting to interpret Romans on the basis of the situation of the church Minear anticipated the later sociological approach; see Francis Watson, *Paul, Judaism and the Gentiles: Beyond the New Perspective*, rev. ed. (Grand Rapids: Eerdmans, 2007), 164, 175–82.

162. Paul S. Minear, *Eyes of Faith: A Study in the Biblical Point of View*, rev. ed. (St. Louis: Bethany, 1966). The revised edition includes minor changes and corrections, revised and updated footnotes, but the text remains largely unchanged.

163. Ibid., 81. The concern with ethical obedience runs through virtually all of Minear's writings. His understanding of the ethics of Jesus is developed in *The Commands of Christ* (Nashville: Abingdon, 1972).

164. *Eyes of Faith*, 111.

165. Ibid., 186.

166. Ibid., 264–65.

167. Ibid., 282.

168. Ibid., 311.

169. Ibid., 318.

170. Ibid., 346.

171. Ibid., 353.

172. A few years later Minear made another contribution to the discussion of hermeneutics: *The Interpreter and the Birth Narratives*, SymBU 13 (Uppsala: Wretmans Boktryckeri, 1950). In this monograph he discusses the perspective, presuppositions, and intent of the historian. He insists that

the biblical historian should go beyond the *Sitz im Leben* (the context of the stories in the life of the church) to the *Sitz im Glauben* (the meaning of the stories for faith) and to the *Sitz im Loben* (the role of the stories in Christian worship). Late in his career Minear published *The Bible and the Historian: Breaking the Silence About God in Biblical Studies* (Nashville: Abingdon, 2002). This is largely a collection and adaptation of essays written over an extensive period of time. The essays echo the major themes of Minear's hermeneutics: the necessity of both historical criticism and the perspective of faith, the importance of revelation for understanding biblical history, the significance of eschatology for biblical revelation, the centrality of Christ for understanding the biblical message.

173. Paul S. Minear, *The Gospel According to Mark*, LBC 17 (Atlanta: John Knox, 1962); by 1974 this volume had undergone a seventh printing.

174. In the introduction to his *Matthew: The Teacher's Gospel* (New York: Pilgrim, 1982), Minear follows scholarly conventions: the author was not the apostle Matthew but a Jewish Christian of northern Palestine or Syria; the date was between 70 and 100; the author used Mark and Q as sources. In regard to Peter's confession (Matt 16:16-17), Minear agrees that the source was Mark and that the additions (16:18-19) were made by the Matthean editor, probably influenced by the tradition of post-Easter appearances to Peter. Late in life Minear published *The Good News According to Matthew: A Training Manual for Prophets* (St. Louis: Chalice, 2000). In this book he views the five discourses of Jesus as training lectures for the Twelve and their successors.

175. Paul S. Minear, *John: The Martyr's Gospel* (New York: Pilgrim, 1984).

176. Ibid., 80. Minear's exegetical endeavors are enhanced by his aesthetic sensitivity. His writings are enriched by citations from literature and descriptions from the visual arts. This sensitivity is also seen in his historical novel, *The Choice: A Story of Christian Faith* (Philadelphia: Westminster, 1948). Minear had deep appreciation for music, demonstrated in *Death Set to Music: Masterworks by Bach, Brahms, Penderecki, Bernstein* (Atlanta: John Knox, 1987). In this book he investigates musical compositions inspired by NT texts on the suffering and death of Jesus.

177. Paul S. Minear, *The Kingdom and the Power: An Exposition of the New Testament Gospel* (Philadelphia: Westminster, 1950; repr. 2004).

178. Leander Keck, "Foreword," *Images of the Church in the New Testament, New Testament Library* (Louisville: Westminster John Knox, 2004), xxi.

179. *Kingdom and Power*, 45.

180. Ibid., 60.

181. Ibid., 79.

182. Ibid., 147.

183. Ibid., 159.

184. Ibid., 218.

185. Ibid., 230.

186. Minear made a unique contribution to the study of NT theology in his *The God of the Gospels: A Theological Workbook* (Atlanta: John Knox, 1988). This book provides practical ways of studying texts from the Gospels that refer to the reality and activity of God.

187. Paul S. Minear, *Christian Hope and the Second Coming* (Philadelphia: Westminster, 1954), 88.

188. Paul S. Minear, *New Testament Apocalyptic* (Nashville: Abingdon, 1981).

189. Ibid., 15.

190. Paul S. Minear, *I Saw a New Earth: An Introduction to the Visions of the Apocalypse* (Washington, DC: Corpus, 1968). For review and critique see Myles M. Bourke, "Foreword," *I Saw a New Earth*, vii–xiv.

191. Ibid., xxvi.

192. Ibid., 30.

193. Ibid., 31.

194. Ibid., 67.

195. Ibid., 246.

196. Ibid.

197. See Minear's *To Heal and to Reveal: The Prophetic Vocation According to Luke* (New York: Seabury, 1976). Minear made another significant contribution to the study of eschatology in his *Christian Hope and the Second Coming*, a response to the theme of the Second Assembly of the World Council of Churches: "Jesus Christ, the Hope of the World." Here Minear's unique understanding of biblical eschatology is evident, above all, in the relevance of eschatology for the life of the church. This approach is also apparent in his shorter work, *To Die and to Live: Christ's Resurrection and Christian Vocation* (New York: Seabury, 1977).

198. Paul S. Minear, *Horizons of Christian Community* (St. Louis: Bethany, 1959).

199. Ibid., 95.

200. Ibid., 123.

201. Paul S. Minear, *Images of the Church in the New Testament* (Philadelphia: Westminster, 1960).

202. Ibid., 17.

203. Ibid., 222.

204. Ibid., 249.

205. Such outstanding scholars as George E. Ladd and Leon L. Morris readily come to mind, both of whom are reviewed in substantial articles in *DMBI* (628–33; 751–55). Others worthy of notice include I. Howard Marshal, E. Earle Ellis, and Ralph P. Martin. See G. R. Osborne, "Evangelical Biblical Interpretation," *DBI* 1: 357–61.

206. For biographical information see W. Ward Gasque, "Bruce, F(rederick) F(yvie)," *DMBI*, 237–42; J. J. Scott, Jr., "Bruce, Frederick Fyvie (1910–90)," *DBI*, 1: 143; F. F. Bruce, *In Retrospect: Remembrance of Things Past* (Grand Rapids: Eerdmans, 1980); "Curriculum Vitae," in *Pauline Studies: Essays Presented to Professor F. F. Bruce on His 70th Birthday*, ed. Donald A. Hagner and Murray J. Harris (Exeter, Devon: Paternoster, 1980), xxxvii–xxxviii. For bibliographies of Bruce's work see "Select Bibliography, 1933–1969," in W. Ward Gasque and Ralph P. Martin, eds., *Apostolic History and the Gospel: Biblical and Historical Essays presented to F. F. Bruce on his 60th Birthday* (Grand Rapids: Eerdmans, 1970), 21–34; "Select Bibliography, 1970–1979." in *Pauline Studies*, xxii–xxxvi.

207. Quoted in *Pauline Studies*, xxi.

208. *In Retrospect*, 311.

209. Ibid., 144.

210. Ibid., 172. A collection of Bruce's views on a variety of topics can be found in his *Answers to Questions* (Exeter, UK: Paternoster, 1972). Beginning in 1952 he wrote a page in *The Harvester* (monthly), answering questions sent by readers. Over the years he answered some 1,800 queries. The selection in this volume is organized in two parts: Answers to Biblical Texts; Answers on Various Subjects.

211. F. F. Bruce, *The New Testament Documents: Are They Reliable?* (London: InterVarsity, 1961).

212. Ibid., 21.

213. Ibid., 62.

214. Ibid., 119. In the same genre is Bruce's book *The Defence of the Gospel in the New Testament* (Grand Rapids: Eerdmans, 1959). Here he sees early Christianity in conflict with contemporary forces: Judaism, paganism, and pseudo-Christianity. He concludes: "Christianity will not come to terms with other religions, nor will it relax its exclusive claims so as to countenance or accommodate them. It presents itself, as it did in the first century, as God's final word to man; it proclaims Christ, as it did in the first century, to be the one Mediator between God and man" (p. 88).

215. F. F. Bruce, *New Testament Development of Old Testament Themes* (Grand Rapids: Eerdmans, 1968), 21.

216. A similar small book by Bruce is *The Time is Fulfilled: Five Aspects of the Fulfilment of the Old Testament in the New* (Grand Rapids: Eerdmans, 1978). Other books by Bruce on the OT: *The Hittites and the Old Testament* (London: Tyndale, 1947); *Israel and the Nations: From the Exodus to the Fall of the Second Temple* (Grand Rapids: Eerdmans, 1963).

217. F. F. Bruce, *Jesus: Past, Present, and Future: The Work of Christ* (Downers Grove, IL: InterVarsity, 1979).

218. Another small book summarizes Bruce's understanding of NT thought: *The Message of the New Testament* (Grand Rapids: Eerdmans, 1972; paperback, 1994).

219. F. F. Bruce, *New Testament History*, NLTh (London: Nelson, 1969).

220. *New Testament History*, 394. Bruce also wrote a popular church history, *The Spreading Flame: The Rise and Progress of Christianity from its First Beginnings to the Conversion of the English* (London: Paternoster, 1958). Part I deals with "The Dawn of Christianity" and covers the period from the first beginnings until the fall of Jerusalem. Part II traces the progress of Christianity to the accession of Constantine in 313. A book on the history of the leaders of the early church is Bruce's *Men and Movements in the Primitive Church: Studies in Early Non-Pauline Christianity* (Exeter, UK: Paternoster, 1979. This was later reprinted as *Peter, Stephen, James, and John: Studies in Early Non-Pauline Christianity* (Grand Rapids: Eerdmans, 1980). The book gives attention to the role of the brothers of Jesus, the development of Christianity in Alexandria, and the Johannine circle in Ephesus. Related to his historical works is Bruce's well-documented work on tradition: *Tradition Old and New* (Grand Rapids: Zondervan, 1970).

221. F. F. Bruce, *The Canon of Scripture* (Downers Grove, IL: InterVarsity, 1988).

222. Ibid., 261.

223. F. F. Bruce, *The Teacher of Righteousness in the Qumran Texts* (London: Tyndale, 1957).

224. F. F. Bruce, *Biblical Exegesis in the Qumran Texts* (Grand Rapids: Eerdmans, 1959).

225. Ibid., 16.

226. F. F. Bruce, *Second Thoughts on the Dead Sea Scrolls* (Grand Rapids: Eerdmans, 1966). Original publication 1956; 2d ed 1961; paperback 1964.

227. Ibid., 61.

228. Ibid., 135.

229. F. F. Bruce, *The Epistle to the Ephesians: A Verse by Verse Exposition* (London: Pickering & Inglis, 1961); *The Gospel of John: Introduction, Exposition and Notes* (Grand Rapids: Eerdmans, 1983); *The Acts of the Apostles: The Greek Text with Introduction and Commentary*, 3d ed. (Grand Rapids: Eerdmans, 1990; first ed. 1951).

230. Bruce, *Acts of the Apostles*.

231. Ibid., 7. For Cadbury's argument see pp. 25 above.

232. Ibid., 52.

233. Ibid.

234. Ibid., 59.

235. Ibid., 63–64.

236. Ibid., 426.

237. Ibid.

238. Ibid.

239. F. F. Bruce, *The Epistle to the Galatians: A Commentary on the Greek Text*, NIGTC (Grand Rapids: Eerdmans, 1982).

240. Ibid., 18.

241. Ibid., 109.

242. Ibid., 144. Among Bruce's other commentaries, his *The Epistle to the Hebrews*, NICNT, rev. ed. (Grand Rapids: Eerdmans, 1990) is of interest. It is longer than most of the contributions to this series (almost 400 pp.). Bruce's notes deal with Greek terms and phrases, making the work virtually a commentary on the Greek text. Also of interest is his commentary on the Fourth Gospel: *The Gospel of John* (see n. 227 above). About the author Bruce writes: "The eyewitness

testimony discerned in the Gospel is mainly that of the beloved disciple, and therefore of the apostle John (if his identity with the beloved disciple can be established). But if it was a disciple of his who wrote down (or wrote up) the Gospel on his behalf, he also may have been an eyewitness of some of the incidents recorded" (p. 5).

243. F. F. Bruce, *Paul: Apostle of the Heart Set Free* (Grand Rapids: Eerdmans, 1977; paper 2000). It is unfortunate that when the attractively bound paperback edition was published it included old, unappealing black and white photographs. The book would have been improved by the incorporation of some of the excellent photos from Bruce's book, *Jesus and Paul: Places They Knew* (Nashville: Nelson, 1981).

244. *Paul*, 15.

245. Ibid., 75.

246. Ibid., 83.

247. Ibid., 88.

248. Ibid., 146.

249. Ibid., 188. In his commentary on Galatians (pp. 50–51) Bruce discusses the role of the doctrine of justification by faith in the dating of Galatians. Since he is convinced that this doctrine was implicit in Paul's conversion and implicit or explicit in virtually all of the letters, Bruce rejects the effort of some scholars to date Galatians, for example, in relation to Romans.

250. *Paul*, 202.

251. Ibid., 373.

252. Bruce, however, does not accept all of Knox's views about Philemon.

253. *Paul*, 474.

10

Critical, Exegetical, and Theological Accomplishments: Europe

The latter half of the twentieth century saw the beginning of a new era: the age of electronic communications. This age is exemplified by the development of the Internet: a system of global communications connecting people from all over the world. By means of a relatively inexpensive personal computer persons from remote places can enjoy the benefits of worldwide communication. By 2011 it has been estimated that some 2.095 billion persons, about 30.2 percent of the world's population, were connected by the Internet. This new method made older means of communication—telephone, telegraph, newspapers, and (alas) books—increasingly obsolete. The new method was so popular that persons working in the same building would email their colleagues rather than walk a few feet down the hall.

This new technology has been a boon for NT research. The catalogs of libraries from all over the world are available for perusal. Through WorldCat virtually all books in print can be located in libraries across the world, and borrowed by interlibrary loan. Individual scholars can communicate across land and sea by e-mail. For instance, when working on this chapter I lacked biographical information about James D. G. Dunn. I simply sent an email to Professor Dunn. His answer, with attached curriculum vitae, arrived the same day.

As a setting for this chapter, the information revolution reminds us that excellent scholarship can be found outside of the acclaimed academic centers like Oxford and Cambridge. Of course, readers of Volume 2 of this *History* will not be surprised to discover superb NT research in Durham. That had been the seat of two of the greatest scholars of an earlier generation: J. B. Lightfoot and B. F. Westcott.[1] This notice of important scholarship in peripheral places also points to a seriously neglected locus of NT research: scholarship in Scandinavia.

NT Interpretation in England: Barrett and Dunn

C. K. Barrett (1917–2011)

Life and Early Work

Charles Kingsley Barrett was born in Salford, Lancashire, England, the son of a Methodist minister.[2] Educated at Pembroke College and Wesley House at Cambridge, he was awarded a BD in 1947 and a DD in 1956. Barrett was ordained to the Methodist ministry and served for a time as minister of the Methodist Church in Darlington. He spent most of his academic career in the shadow of the great Norman cathedral at Durham. He was named lecturer in theology in 1945 and was promoted to professor of Divinity at the university in 1958. Barrett's reputation as a teacher attracted students from across Europe and from America. He was elected president of the SNTS in 1973. Many would agree with John Painter: "C. K. Barrett is the outstanding British New Testament scholar of the second half of the twentieth century."[3]

In 1943 a manuscript was circulated among a group of scholars who saw it as a sign of great things to come. The manuscript, the work of a scholar still in his twenties, was published a few years later under the title *The Holy Spirit and the Gospel Tradition*—a work that remains one of Barrett's most important books.[4] Part One deals with Jesus and the Spirit. Here Barrett begins with the conception of Jesus by the Spirit. Barrett is more concerned with the theological significance than with the search for pagan parallels. "The part played by the Holy Spirit in the birth narratives is thus seen to be the fulfilment of God's promised redemption in a new act of creation, comparable with that of Gen. 1."[5] Barrett believes that Jesus' submission to the rite of baptism shows his affirmation of John's eschatological outlook. "The work of the Spirit is to call into being part of the New Creation of the Messianic days, namely, to inaugurate the ministry of the Messiah, and this Messianic conception underlies the whole intention and significance of the narrative, and stands in closely interlocking unity with the conception of the Spirit involved."[6] Barrett also discusses the conflict of Jesus with the evil spirits seen in the exorcisms and the role of the Spirit in the miracles of Jesus. The miracles, according to Barrett, are signs of the coming kingdom, yet Jesus refused to perform signs. "It is in this paradox, of the fullness of God's power and its inevitable concealment, that we shall find the clue to the problems connected with the doctrine of the Spirit in the Synoptic Gospels."[7]

Part Two deals with the Spirit and the church. In this section Barrett rejects the idea that Jesus predicted the existence of a community endowed with the Spirit. "We have found no sayings of Jesus which unmistakably pointed to such a gift of the Spirit, and the passages which come nearest to doing so are demonstrably late, and reflect the events which took place after the crucifixion."[8] Barrett notes that the Gospels say little about the church, but instead emphasize the eschatological kingdom of God. Indeed, Jesus' view of the future left little room for the church. "We may suppose, then, that Jesus foretold his suffering and death, and that these would be followed by a divine act of vindication, in which he did not differentiate between a resurrection and a parousia."[9]

THE GOSPEL OF JOHN

C. K. Barrett made an important contribution to the study of the Johannine literature. His commentary on the Gospel of John first appeared in 1955 and a second, revised edition was published in 1978.[10] The commentary features a long introduction (over 140 pages). As to the Gospel's main characteristics and purpose, Barrett believes the author was a man with two convictions. "The conviction is, first, that the actual history of Jesus of Nazareth is of paramount significance because in it the eternal God confronted men, enabling faith and offering to faith the gift of eternal life; and, secondly, that the mere historical data of the life of Jesus are trivial, apart from the faith God-given, that he is the Word become flesh."[11] Barrett is skeptical of source theories and notions about displacement and redaction. In regard to the non-Christian background, he reviews material from the OT and Judaism. He recognizes the significance of the Dead Sea Scrolls but displays his usual reticence. "Now that the excitement of the first discoveries is past it is possible to see that Qumran has not revolutionized the study of the New Testament—certainly it has not revolutionized the study of John."[12]

In regard to the Christian background, Barrett believes the author knew Mark and possibly Luke. John, according to Barrett, is not primarily interested in the historical details but in theological interpretation of the tradition.

> He sought to draw out, using in part the form and style of narrative, the true meaning of the life and death of one whom he believed to be the Son of God. It is for this interpretation, not for accurate historical data, that we must look in the Fourth Gospel.[13]

In regard to the theology of the Fourth Gospel, Barrett discusses eschatology and Christology. He believes the miracles to be an expression of John's Christology. John, according to Barrett, is not a systematic theologian but a person of faith who expresses a profound theological understanding of the Gospel. "The story of Jesus requires that, just as God must be understood in terms of Jesus, so the humanity of Jesus, and with that the humanity of the race, must be seen and understood in terms of God. For God and for man the future lies only in the unity of the two, a unity to which the figure of Jesus points."[14]

In regard to traditional questions—date, place, and authorship—Barrett offers an imaginative reconstruction.

> John the apostle migrated from Palestine and lived in Ephesus, where, true to character as a Son of Thunder, he composed apocalyptic works. These, together with his advancing years, the death of other apostles, and predictions such as Mark 9.1, not unnaturally gave rise to the common belief that he would survive to the *parousia*. A man of commanding influence, he gathered about him a number of pupils. In course of time he died; his death fanned the apocalyptic hopes of some, scandalized others, and induced a few to ponder deeply over the meaning of Christian eschatology. One pupil of the apostle incorporated his written works in the canonical Apocalypse; this was at a date about the close of the life of Domitian—c. A.D 96. Another pupil was responsible for the epistle (probably 1 John came from one writer, 2 and 3 John from another). Yet another, a bolder thinker, and one more widely read both in Judaism and Hellenism, produced John 1–20.[15]

Reconstructions of this sort—with a disciple who moves to Ephesus and forms a community that produced the Johannine literature—are common. The distinctive feature of Barrett's construct is that this disciple, one of the Sons of Thunder (that is, John) is an apocalyptic teacher. The writer of the Gospel, the "bolder thinker," produced what Barrett accepts as an apostolic book: a document that presents both history and interpretation.

The rest of Barrett's book consists of commentary and notes: over 400 pages of critical analysis of the text. Barrett orders the material into forty-two sections. In each, he presents an overview of the whole section. This is followed by notes on every verse. The notes include textual, linguistic, grammatical, and historical detail; no stone is left unturned.

A few examples, taken out of context, can provide only a hint of the breadth and depth of Barrett's research. In regard to the prologue, Barrett's overall commentary notes that John has set his Gospel in a theological framework. Barrett points out that Logos is used as a christological title only in the prologue. These general comments are followed by twenty pages of notes. On v. 1, discussing Logos, Barrett investigates the various backgrounds: Greek usage, Gnosticism, OT, Jewish wisdom, and Philo. He emphasizes the Christian background, that is, the tradition in which the "Word" was the "Gospel." For Barrett the most important feature is not the background but the distinctive way John has developed the concept of the Logos.

Barrett's interpretation of the sign at Cana is important for his understanding of the miracle stories of John. He believes that this is the first of Jesus' miracles. The action of Jesus in turning the water from the jars for the Jewish rites of purification into a huge amount of fine wine is symbolic. "Jesus as the fulfiller of Judaism, as the bearer of supernatural power, becomes henceforth an object of faith to his disciples."[16] Barrett mixes historical and symbolic-theological interpretation: he says that Cana may be one of three possible locations, but "the third day" is a reference to the resurrection. Similarly, Barrett believes "my hour" refers to the crucifixion. "The hour had not come for manifesting the glory; yet, as indeed in all the signs, a partial and preliminary manifestation was granted that the disciples might believe."[17]

In regard to the raising of Lazarus, Barrett notes that this is the most striking miracle in the Fourth Gospel. The meaning of the story, according to Barrett, is that "Jesus in his obedience to and dependence upon the Father has the authority to give life to whom he will."[18] Barrett discusses the historical value of the story without reaching a definite conclusion. He rejects the approach that assumes *a priori* that miracles are impossible. However, he recognizes that the failure of Mark to recount this miracle constitutes a serious problem for its historicity. In his note on 11:24, where Martha says "I know that he will rise again in the resurrection on the last day," Barrett observes, "Martha's statement of faith is thus orthodox Pharisaism."[19] On the problem of the anger of Jesus recorded 11:33 and 11:38, he says: "It is clearly the presence and grief of Mary and the Jews which form the occasion of the anger of Jesus, but it is far from clear why the sight of lamentation should have moved him to anger. . . . We must consider more seriously the suggestion that it was the *unbelief* of the Jews and Mary that provoked the indignation of Jesus."[20]

PAUL

Barrett also made important contributions to the study of Paul. An overview of the apostle's theology is presented in *Paul: An Introduction to His Thought*.[21] Barrett begins with a survey of Paul's career. He believes the primary sources are the seven undisputed letters of Paul, but also thinks that Acts provides additional information. The Damascus Road experience, according to Barrett, is both call and conversion. Barrett believes a way into the study of Paul's theology can be found in the apostle's controversies. "As a preacher he was despised, as a pastor he was flouted, and as a theologian he was constantly engaged in controversy with those who bitterly disagreed with him."[22] Barrett reviews the controversies at Galatia, Corinth, Philippi. In all these venues he tends to discover Judaizers as Paul's opponents. In any case, controversy seems to be a feature of Paul's vocation. "It was however because he was a theologian . . . that he was obliged to fight; in turn, the fighting made him the kind of theologian that he was, and gave his letters the combative air that most of them have."[23] In these controversies Paul's argument is Christocentric. "*Solus Christus*, Christ alone, is the primary motto of Paul's theology, and most of the errors against which he fights can be regarded as in some form or other qualifications of that *solus*."[24]

Barrett presents a lengthy chapter discussing Paul's primary theological themes: law and covenant, grace and righteousness, Christ crucified, the Church, the Holy Spirit and ethics. The Christocentric note is sounded again at the conclusion.

> *Solus Christus* is the substance of Paul's theology, and justification by faith is its cutting edge. The theological task that Paul has left to his successors is, first, the refinement of Christology in terms of developing philosophical and psychological concepts of being and personality, and, secondly, the application of the principle of justification by faith to all the apparatus of Christendom—church order, church dogmatics, liturgy, ethics—and all those individual lives of which the church is made up.[25]

Barrett also wrote commentaries on Romans and the Corinthian correspondence for the Harper's (or Black's) New Testament Commentaries (HNTC, BNTC). Barrett's *Romans* begins with a short introduction: thirteen pages.[26] He believes the epistle was written from Corinth, where Paul spent three months prior to his trip to Jerusalem, probably in 55. Barrett discusses the complex problem of the ending of Romans and concludes that the original letter consisted of 1:1—16:23; later the letter circulated in shorter editions. In regard to theology, Barrett believes that Paul's thought had been revolutionized by his conviction that Jesus had been raised from the dead. The result was a new eschatology: the Messiah had come and the first fruits were available for faith. Paul also recognized that Jesus had been condemned by the law. This meant that the law was no longer mediator between God and humans; Christ was mediator.

The material is divided into forty-two sections. Each section is introduced by a translation, followed by running commentary on the text in which quotations from the text are presented in bold type. The character of Barrett's exegesis may be illustrated by a few examples. He titles 1:16-17 "The Gospel." He believes these verses constitute the text for the epistle and provide an introduction to Paul's thought. Although he is writing to a church where his credentials might be questioned, Paul says he is not ashamed. In the gospel, God's power works for salvation. In the gospel, God's righteousness is revealed—the first mention of the theme of the epistle. This theme, the "righteousness of God," becomes the title of the section exegeting 3:21-31. According to Barrett this phrase means both that God is righteous and that God is also the justifier. All humans need the gift of righteousness because they have fallen short of the glory of God, the glory Adam had at creation. The righteousness of which Paul speaks is, according to Barrett, a new, non-legal righteousness. This righteousness is received by faith—faith in Jesus, the means of reconciliation. "So far, then, we see God moved by love to perform an act of grace by means of which it becomes possible for him to manifest his righteousness in justification."[27]

A little over a decade later, Barrett published a commentary on 1 Corinthians for the same series.[28] Here he has written a longer introduction: over twenty-six pages. In the introduction Barrett follows the convention of describing the city of Corinth and its history. Barrett believes 1 Corinthians was a unity, not a composite, written from Ephesus in early 54 or late 53. He notes that this epistle presents developments in Paul's theology, notably in Christology and anthropology. For the modern reader 1 Corinthians provides information about the structure and institutions of the early church. The commentary on 1 Cor 1:10-17 deals with "The Corinthian Groups." Although there are divisions, Barrett notes that Paul assumes that all would come together for the reading of the letter. Barrett assumes the traditional view: the groups are related to the leaders who have worked in the church. This leads him to conclude that Peter had worked in Corinth and that the faction of Cephas represents Jewish Christianity. Barrett offers no solution to the problem of those who claim to belong to Christ, but concludes that the text as it stands in the best MSS suggests the existence of a fourth group. The section on 1 Cor 11:2-16 focuses on "Men and Women." In this section Paul presents a hierarchy: God, Christ, man, woman. Verse 5 says that "any woman who prays or prophesies with her head unveiled disgraces her head." Barrett observes that this verse proves that women did speak in church, despite 14:34-35. He believes Paul is instructing women to wear the veil, for two reasons: woman is the glory of man, and "her veil represents the new authority given to the woman under the new dispensation to do things which formerly had not been permitted her."[29]

A few years later, Barrett published a commentary on 2 Corinthians.[30] In this commentary the introduction totals fifty pages. The space is needed for Barrett's complicated discussion of the special problems of 2 Corinthians. He notes various theories that treat the epistle as composite. His own view strives for simplification: 2 Corinthians is composed of two letters, 2 Corinthians 1–9 and 2 Corinthians 10–13, written in that order. Barrett identifies the opponents as Judaizers.[31] In a section on theology Barrett notes the importance of Christ crucified and risen for Paul's understanding of eschatological existence; the believer lives in the time between the resurrection and the *parousia*, the time of already, but not yet. The discussion of 5:11-21 is entitled "The Treasure: The Ambassador's Message of Reconciliation and New Creation Arising out of the Death of Christ." With good reason Barrett contends that "this is one of the most pregnant, difficult, and important in the whole of the Pauline literature."[32] In v. 16, the phrase "according to the flesh" should be understood as adverbial; Paul is describing how one knows, not the nature of Christ who is known. The reference to new creation in v. 17 is another instance of Paul's belief in eschatological existence. "Christian existence means that by faith one lives in the midst of the old creation in terms of the new creation that God has brought about through Jesus."[33]

Readers who expect these "middle-level" commentaries of the Harper (Black) series to be simple are in for a surprise. Barrett rarely simplifies, and these commentaries are no exception. Although the comments are on the English translation, Greek terms often appear in the exegesis, and comments in German (without translation) are sprinkled through the commentaries. Besides these commentaries on Romans and the Corinthian correspondence, Barrett published a book on Galatians that is topical rather than exegetical.[34]

An important work on Paul's theology is *From First Adam to Last: A Study in Pauline Theology*.[35] The book is essentially an investigation of Paul's anthropology through a study of the representative figures in Paul's thought. Barrett begins with Adam. Adam sinned and the result was death. According to Barrett's reading of Paul, everything that can be said about Adam can be said about humankind as a whole. Turning to Abraham, Barrett writes that Paul sees him as believer, as model for the person of faith. Moses is important for the giving of the law, but for Paul the glory of the law was superseded by the glory of Christ. Barrett believes that Paul views all the previous figures in relation to Christ. Christ was a man like Adam, but he was the obedient man. He was the seed of Abraham. He was the interpreter of the law who understood it as the law of love. Barrett discusses "The Man to Come" as the risen Christ who will appear at the *parousia*. He will bring the new creation of the individual (justification), the new creation of the church, and the new creation of the world. The conclusion is vintage Barrett. "The Pauline conception is delicately balanced," he says, "and impossible to express in simple and rigid terms. Its delicacy stands out most clearly when it is compared with the heavy-handed attempts of later Christian generations to hammer Paul's theology into dogmatics."[36]

THE ACTS OF THE APOSTLES

Barrett's magnum opus is his massive, two-volume commentary on Acts in the International Critical Commentary series.[37] Scholars who are accustomed to seeing on their shelves the dull green binding of the venerable ICC will rejoice to view the bright red cover of Barrett's 2004 paperback edition. Once inside, however, they will be confronted by pages in small print and a labyrinth of critical and exegetical detail. A distinctive feature of Barrett's work is his location of the main introduction at the beginning of the second volume. His theory is that introductory matters are best considered after the reader has already wrestled with some of the text. A short introduction in Volume One deals with the text, the author, the sources, the plan and content of Acts 1–14. Each section begins with a translation of the text, followed by bibliography, commentary, and notes.

A couple of examples can illustrate Barrett's exegesis. In his five-page commentary on "Peter's Pentecost Sermon" (2:14-40) he notes that Acts views the first preaching of the Gospel as attached to the Pentecost event. At 2:22 Peter turns to christological interpretation. Jesus had been killed by his own people, but God had set right this wrong by raising him from the dead. In general, Peter's speech, according to Barrett, does not display a developed theology or ascribe positive significance to the death of Jesus. Barrett's notes extend from pages 133 to 157. As an example, Barrett observes that 2:14, where the text refers to "the eleven," seems to ignore the Matthias tradition. Barrett's note on v. 22 points to the identification of Jesus as a "man." Luke, according to Barrett, never abandons the humanity of Jesus and tends to embrace a low Christology. "Luke's Christology cannot by any means be described as advanced or developed; it does not include the notion of the incarnation of a pre-existent divine being."[38]

In regard to "Saul's Conversion" (9:1-19a), Barrett presents the main points of the three Acts accounts (9:3-19; 22:6-16; 26:12-18) in parallel columns. He finds the agreements to be greater than the discrepancies. Barrett believes the background to the experience is found in Isa 6:1-13 and Jer 1:4-10. "What happened to Paul was not the resolution of an inward conflict in an unhappy, divided, and unsatisfied man; it was the appearance of Christ to a self-satisfied and self-righteous man, an appearance that had the immediate effect both of providing a new basis for his personal life and of initiating the Gentile mission."[39] However, Barrett believes that major questions remain. How and when was the substance of the Gospel communicated to Paul? Why is there no reference to Ananias in the Pauline letters? Typical of Barrett's penchant for detail is his three-page note on 9:2. He investigates the question of the authority of the high priest over provincial synagogues. He provides information about the city of Damascus. He notes the use of "the Way" in the Dead Sea Scrolls. In regard to Paul's arrest and bringing to a place of trial, Barrett cites Aristophanes.

The introduction at the beginning of Volume 2 considers the conventional questions. Barrett discusses the two main text-types, Old Uncial (represented by B and Sinaiticus) and Western; he believes the former provides the more reliable text. In regard to sources, Barrett gives considerable attention to the famous "we-sections." He notes three main views: "we" is a reference to the author of the whole work; "we" represents a source used by the author; "we" is a fiction. Barrett acknowledges that it is difficult to conclude that the whole book was written by a companion of Paul, so he understands the we-sections as a source. Why the author left "we" in the text is a problem with no easy solution. As to Acts as a historical document, Barrett characterizes it as "popular history." "That means that it is biographical, focusing on a few outstanding characters, episodic in style, highly coloured with wonderful and exciting incidents, and not given to philosophizing about the nature and meaning of history or about the theological content of the message."[40] Barrett believes the council of chapter 15 is the central event of the whole document and the important point for understanding the author's view of early Christian history. In regard to the author, Barrett notes Cadbury's disproof of the argument from medical language. He says, perhaps with tongue in cheek, "Luke's use of technical vocabulary suggests, if anything, that he was not a doctor but a sailor."[41]

Turning to the theology of Acts, Barrett notes the importance of eschatology. The author recognizes the interval between resurrection and *parousia*, and views the gift of the Spirit as the first step in the fulfillment of the of the eschatological hope. "There is in Acts no profound Christological thought, yet it is clear that Jesus Christ of Nazareth is the person who initiated and will conclude the whole story and directs the whole course of it."[42] Barrett also discusses the theology of Acts in relation to church, ministry, baptism and the Christian meal, the Jews, the Law, the Gentile mission. In the end, Luke is a well-informed historian. He celebrates the victory of the Hellenists—the center party. In composing the Gospel and Acts he gave the church its first New Testament.

Barrett discusses "The Council in Jerusalem" (15:6-29). He investigates various theories about sources and believes that Luke may have found the Apostolic Decree (15:20, 29) in use in the churches. The council concluded that Gentile converts need not be circumcised but did need to follow the ritual food laws of the decree. Barrett's notes on this subsection are over twenty pages long. On v. 7, he observes how Peter functions as instigator of the Gentile mission. "The verse affirms the absolute priority if not the primacy of Peter in the Gentile mission."[43] In v. 11, Barrett views Peter's support of salvation by grace to be superficial Pauline language. Verse 13 presents James as the leader of the church. Verses 19 and 20 present the decision of James that Gentile converts must abide by the four abstentions: food that has been sacrificed to idols, fornication, what is strangled, and blood. Barrett notes that the Western text has added a negative version of the Golden Rule, thus turning the decree into an ethical admonition. The decision of the apostles and elders is confirmed by the Holy Spirit. The provisions of the decree are repeated, with slight variations, in the letter of v. 29.

JESUS AND TRADITION

Important for understanding Barrett's thought is his book, *Jesus and the Gospel Tradition,* lectures given at Yale in 1967.[44] He begins with a discussion of "the Tradition." Paul points to the importance of the tradition in 1 Corinthians 15. The Gospels, according to Barrett, present us with a paradoxical understanding: they preserve the tradition that Jesus was Messiah and Son of God, though Jesus claimed neither. "Thus the historical tradition was obliged to go beyond history, precisely because it was historical. This fact," says Barrett, "constitutes the problem of the historical Jesus; at the same time it contains the only solution of the problem that we are likely to find."[45]

Barrett turns next to "Christ Crucified." He believes that Jesus predicted his own death and interpreted it. However, the tradition about the meaning of the death of Christ continued to develop.

> It is perhaps not unnatural that before the passion, the notion of the suffering with the Son of man should be unclearly and variably expressed, and connected mainly with the apocalyptic vindication of the suffering group; and that afterwards, as the Church looked back upon the cross in which one died alone for all, it should make the comment, Christ died for our sins, and in our place.[46]

The concluding chapter is a discussion of "Christ to come." Barrett believes that the basis for this is the idea of the Son of man. Early tradition understood Jesus as foreseeing his death in relation to the purposes of God; this would be followed by resurrection and ultimately by his vindication as the Son of man. "The great achievement of those who transmitted and edited the gospel tradition was so to reconstruct the eschatological framework of the teaching of Jesus as to make room for the continuing existence of a community between the resurrection and the coming Son of man."[47]

All in all, Barrett may not be one of the most exciting NT scholars in the history of research, but he is certainly one of the most competent. He was master of all the elements of the discipline: textual criticism, linguistic and grammatical analysis, historical backgrounds, patristic usage, and theological application. Barrett remained throughout his career devoted to the church and its ministry, a commitment that motivates and refines his work.[48] He avoided fads and easy answers. He was convinced that NT research is important for life and faith today.

JAMES D. G. DUNN (1936–)

A notable NT scholar has written, "Professor James Dunn is the most prolific New Testament scholar of his generation."[49] The son of Scottish parents, Dunn was born in Birmingham, UK.[50] He was educated at the University of Glasgow, where he earned an MA in Economics and Statistics (1961), education that would later serve him well in his role as treasurer of SNTS. Dunn was awarded the BD with distinction from Glasgow's Trinity College. He studied at Cambridge under the tutelage of C. F. D. Moule and was granted the PhD in 1968. After completion of his doctorate Dunn moved to Edinburgh, where he served as chaplain to the overseas students at the University. He served on the faculty at the University of Nottingham from 1970 to 1982. In 1982 Dunn was appointed Professor of Divinity at the University of Durham (succeeding C. K. Barrett), and in 1990 was named Lightfoot Professor of Divinity at Durham, a chair honoring the memory of J. B. Lightfoot, Dunn's academic hero. Over his years of teaching Dunn supervised more than thirty PhD students, several becoming significant scholars in their own right; all of the contributors to the Festschrift, *Jesus and Paul*, were his students.

Throughout much of its life Dunn was an active member of the seminar on the theology of Paul of the SBL. At the meeting of 1991 he participated in the famous debate with Richard Hays on the disputed phrase *pistis Iesou Christou,* arguing that the genitive is objective: "faith in Jesus Christ." N. T. Wright recalls that at the end of the vigorous argument some members of the audience called for a vote. The jovial Leander Keck, who was in the chair, replied, "Nope, this ain't the Jesus Seminar."[51]

The magnitude of Dunn's research—his long list of publications, some in mammoth proportions—defies succinct summary.[52] Of interest is Dunn's own assessment of his work.

> One of my besetting sins as a scholar (but perhaps it's a strength!) is the desire to see the large picture, to gain (so far as possible) comprehensive overview. . . . It's not that I am unwilling to engage in the fine detailed work necessary in the analysis of particular texts. Far from it. But all the time I want to step back and see how my findings cohere with the rest of our information (not just the New Testament, but the New Testament writings within their historical contexts). Like a painter of a large canvas, I need to step back time and again to check how the fine detail of particular parts blends into the whole.[53]

Actually, Dunn's work moves forward in a trajectory that set its course early, then shifted direction, and finally resumed its progress toward its ultimate target.

EARLY WORK

Dunn's first major publication is *Baptism and the Holy Spirit.*[54] Based on his Cambridge dissertation, this book responds to the claim of Pentecostals that the baptism of the Spirit is a second, higher experience after the original experience of conversion. Dunn investigates the records of Jesus' baptism, the accounts concerning the gift of the Spirit in Acts, and the understanding of the Spirit in Paul and the rest of the NT. His conclusion regarding Paul is representative:

"Our study has shown: that Paul knows of only one reception of the Spirit, not two; that concepts of anointing, sealing, outpouring, gift, etc., all refer to that one coming of the Spirit; that this coming of the Spirit is the very heart and essence of the conversion-initiation."[55]

Dunn's second major book, *Jesus and the Spirit*, evolves naturally out of the first.[56] He begins with an investigation of the religious experience of Jesus. Fundamental, according to Dunn, is Jesus' experience of God—an experience of sonship. Dunn believes this experience is evident in Jesus' address to God in prayer as "Abba." He proceeds to discuss Jesus' experience of God in relation to the Spirit. According to Dunn, Jesus viewed himself as heir of prophetic expectations. "*Jesus believed himself to be the one in whom Isa. 61.1. found fulfilment; his sense of being inspired was such that he could believe himself to be the end-time prophet of Isa. 61.1*; he had been anointed with the Spirit of the Lord."[57]

Turning to the religious experience of the earliest Christian communities, Dunn observes an important shift: Jesus becomes the object of religious experience. The fundamental feature of this religious experience is the conviction of the early Christians that the risen Christ had appeared to them. An important event in the post-resurrection communities was the gift of the Spirit on Pentecost. Dunn believes the account in Acts to be largely historical, although he supposes the event was an outburst of glossolalia rather than a miracle of linguistics. Turning to Paul and the Pauline churches, he discusses the religious experience of the individual communities as the "body of Christ," Paul's term for the charismatic community. "*Each church becomes Christ's body through charisma.*"[58] Dunn concludes with a glance toward the second generation, seeing the vision fade. It almost disappears with the Pastoral Epistles. "*Spirit and charisma have become in effect subordinate to office, to ritual, to tradition*—early-Catholicism indeed!"[59]

After tracing the varieties of religious experience, Dunn took up another issue in his *Unity and Diversity in the New Testament*,[60] originally published in 1977. The second edition updates the bibliography, adds notes, and makes a few minor changes in the text. In 2006, a third edition was published, including a foreword that reviews Dunn's recent thinking on the major issues of the book; the final chapter is revised, and an appendix, "Unity and Diversity in the Church: A New Perspective," is added. The introduction states the purpose: "Our basic question thus becomes: *Was there a unifying strand in earliest Christianity which identifies it as Christianity?*"[61] In the first part Dunn deals with unity in diversity. He begins with a discussion of the kerygma or kerygmata. The kerygma of Jesus, according to Dunn, included the proclamation of the kingdom, the call for repentance and faith, and the offer of forgiveness. He detects a core kerygma in Acts: the proclamation of the resurrection of Jesus, the call to repentance and faith in Jesus, and the promise of salvation and the gift of the Spirit. Paul, according to Dunn, had a clear definition of the gospel but recognized a variety of forms—a variety attested in the rest of the NT. Dunn says that "*within the NT itself we have not simply diverse kerygmata, but in fact kerygmata which appear to be incompatible.*"[62] Dunn proceeds to investigate early Christian confessional formulae: Jesus is the Messiah; Jesus is the Son of God; Jesus is Lord. All these confessions witness to what Dunn believes to be the fundamental unifying feature of the NT: the oneness of the earthly Jesus and the exalted Christ. He concludes: "In short, *the identity of historical Jesus with kerygmatic Christ is the one basis and bond of unity which holds together the manifold diversity of first-century Christianity.*"[63]

In the second part of the book Dunn reverses the topic and writes about diversity in unity. He pursues the issue by investigating four main types of early Christianity, beginning with Jewish Christianity, where he finds abundant evidence of diversity. In regard to Hellenistic Christianity, Dunn recalls that the first split in the church resulted from the conflict between the Hellenists and the Hebrews in Jerusalem (Acts 6). However, the real threat within Hellenistic Christianity is to be seen in gnostic tendencies. "*Gnosticism was able to present its message in a sustained way as teaching of Jesus only by separating the risen Christ from the earthly Jesus and by abandoning the attempt to show a continuity between the Jesus of the Jesus-tradition and the heavenly Christ of their faith.*"[64] Dunn identifies a third type as "apocalyptic Christianity." According to him, "*Christianity began as an eschatological sect within Judaism, a sect which in its apocalypticism was in substantial continuity with the messages both of John the Baptist and of Jesus.*"[65] Within this type, according to Dunn, unity could be maintained by confessing the oneness of "*the man of Nazareth and the coming Christ.*"[66]

Finally, Dunn investigates "early Catholicism." This movement within Christianity is distinguished by the fading of the eschatological hope, the increasing emergence of institutionalism, and the crystallization of the faith into fixed forms. Dunn finds evidence for this development in the Pastoral Epistles, 2 Peter, and Jude. "Perhaps then the tragedy of early catholicism was its failure to realize that the biggest heresy of all is the insistence that there is only one ecclesiastical obedience, only one orthodoxy."[67] He concludes with a discussion of the authority of the NT. The canon, he argues, witnesses to both diversity and unity.

The point is, of course, that only when we recognize the full *diversity of function* of the canon as well as the full diversity of the NT material can the NT canon *as a whole* remain viable. Or, more concisely, only when we recognize the unity in diversity and the diversity in unity of the NT and the ways they interact can the NT continue to function as canon.[68]

Dunn's recognition of the unity of the NT in Christ led to his next major work: *Christology in the Making*,[69] first published in 1980. The second edition, a reprint, is prefaced with a Foreword in which Dunn responds to the critics of the earlier edition, notably to the charge that he had not given adequate attention to the Hellenistic backgrounds. In the introduction he articulates the thematic question: "*How did the doctrine of the incarnation originate?*"[70] He purports to answer the question by "a *historical investigation into how and in what terms the doctrine of the incarnation came to expression.*"[71] Following a well-worn path, he pursues the answer by an investigation of NT titles. He begins with "Son of God" and notes the wide usage and varied meaning of the title in the ancient world. "*Certainly 'son of God' as applied to Jesus would not necessarily have carried in and of itself the connotation of deity.*"[72] In regard to Jesus' understanding of the title, Dunn denies that Jesus thought himself to be the unique, preexistent Son of God. He does believe, however, that Jesus' sense of sonship implies a "*high christology.*"[73] In the earliest Christian writings, the letters of Paul, Dunn notes the evidence of a pre-Pauline tradition (Rom 1:3-4) in which "*the resurrection of Jesus was regarded as of central significance in determining his divine sonship.*"[74] Dunn observes that Paul refers to the sending of the Son (Gal 4:4; Rom 8:3), but finds in this expression no clear affirmation of preexistence. According to Dunn, Hebrews "*seems to be the first of the NT writings to have embraced the specific thought of a pre-existent divine sonship.*"[75] The high point is reached, however, in the Fourth Gospel:

> In short, *for the first time in earliest Christianity we encounter in the Johannine writings the understanding of Jesus' divine sonship in terms of the personal pre-existence of a divine being who was sent into the world and whose ascension was simply the continuation of an intimate relationship with the Father which neither incarnation nor crucifixion interrupted or disturbed.*[76]

Next Dunn tackles the notorious problem of the Son of Man. He reviews the evidence from Daniel 7 and the *Similitudes of Enoch* and concludes that "*we have thus far found no evidence of a Son of Man concept in pre-Christian Judaism.*"[77] As to the Christian understanding, Dunn believes the first identification of the Son of Man of Dan 7:13 is to be found in earliest Christianity, perhaps with Jesus himself. Very important for Dunn's view of NT Christology is the title "the last Adam." Dunn, employing questionable exegesis, detects Adam Christology in Phil 2:6-11.

> The Christ of Phil. 2.6-11 therefore is the man who undid Adam's wrong; confronted with the same choice, he rejected Adam's sin, but nevertheless freely followed Adam's course as fallen man to the bitter end of death; wherefore God bestowed on him the status not simply that Adam lost, but the status which Adam was intended to come to, God's final prototype, the last Adam.[78]

At any rate, Dunn finds no evidence in this text or in 2 Cor 8:9 for a doctrine of preexistence.

Also very important for Dunn is the concept of the Wisdom of God. Although he believes the idea of pre-existent Wisdom to have influenced early Christian Christology, Dunn finds "*it is very unlikely that pre-Christian Judaism ever understood Wisdom as a divine being in any sense independent of Yahweh.*"[79] According to Dunn, Paul's Wisdom Christology affirms that "*Christ fully embodies the creative and saving activity of God,*" but this does not imply belief in the preexistence of Christ.[80] Closely related to the Wisdom of God is the title "Word of God." As Dunn points out, this title takes on dramatic meaning with the author of the Fourth Gospel. Dunn says that "*the author of John 1.1-16 was the first to take the step which no Hellenistic-Jewish author had taken before him, the first to identify the word of God as a particular person; and so far as our evidence is concerned the Fourth Evangelist was the first Christian writer to conceive clearly of the personal pre-existence of the Logos-Son and to present it as a fundamental part of his message.*"[81] He concludes that apart from the Johannine literature no NT writing affirms the preexistence of Christ. However, with the development of Wisdom in the later Pauline letters (notably Colossians) we see "*the womb from which incarnational christology emerged.*"[82] "'Incarnation' means initially that *God's* love and power had been experienced in fullest measure in, through and as this man Jesus, that Christ had been experienced as God's self-expression, the Christ-event as the effective re-creative power of God."[83]

THE NEW PERSPECTIVE

The change in the course of the trajectory of Dunn's writings was caused by his adoption of the "new perspective on Paul," a phrase he himself coined. His original view of the new perspective is expressed in his Manson Memorial Lecture at the University of Manchester in 1982, but a fuller account of his mature understanding is presented in his essay, "The New Perspective: whence, what and whither?"[84] Dunn had lectured on Romans during his early days at Nottingham, and at the time he assumed the traditional Lutheran/Reformation picture of Paul as the foe of a literalistic, self-righteous Judaism. Reading E. P. Sanders's revolutionary *Paul and Palestinian Judaism* brought about Dunn's conversion.[85] He abandoned his former view of Paul and embraced Judaism, in Sanders's terms, as a religion of "covenant nomism." But while he applauded Sanders's correction of the old caricature of Judaism, Dunn found Sanders's assessment of Paul to be flawed. According to Dunn, Sanders did not properly identify what Paul was battling against. Dunn found his solution in Paul's attack on the "works of the law" (Gal 2:16; 3:2, 5). According to Dunn this phrase did not refer, as the in the traditional view, to Jewish egocentric striving for salvation by works, but served a social function: the "works of the law" were boundary markers to identity the distinctive and separate character of the true people of God. The "works of the law," according to Dunn, reinforced Israel's exclusive claim on God—the claim to the primary status of Israel. In contrast to this Jewish view, *"Pauline scholarship simply must not diminish the importance for Paul of the gospel as the power of God in breaking down barriers (not least of the law) between Jew and Gentile."*[86] Dunn's final comment focuses on his view of Paul's doctrine of salvation.

> The significance Paul saw in Jesus Christ remains the primary difference between his gospel for all and the understanding of salvation in the scriptures and traditions of Israel. The eschatological significance of Christ put the old covenant into the past tense and signalled the opening of God's grace to *all* who *believe*, the fulfilment of God's purposes through Israel to the world.[87]

Dunn's first major publication to show the impact of the new perspective is his two-volume commentary on Romans.[88] In the introduction he discusses the recipients of the letter. Dunn believes the majority of the Christians in Rome were Gentile, and that Paul had considerable information about the situation there. As to the purpose of the epistle, he surmises that Paul writes for three reasons: a missionary purpose (he is seeking support for his mission to the West);

an apologetic purpose (Paul wants the Romans to understand his message); a pastoral purpose (Paul is promoting unity among believers). On the question of the original composition of the letter, Dunn believes that chapter 16 belongs to the original. In a final section of the introduction Dunn, advocating the new perspective, insists that Romans must be interpreted in the context of Paul's view of the law and "covenant nomism."

In view of the magnitude of Dunn's *Romans* (over 900 pages), only a few examples of his exegesis can be offered. In presenting the material, Dunn follows the format of the Word Biblical Commentary (WBC): Notes, Translation, Form and Structure, Comment, and Explanation. In the Explanation sections Dunn presents a running commentary on the text; he understands the section on Comment to be notes on the Explanation.

Within the first section of the epistle (1:1-17), Dunn interprets "Introductory Statement and Greetings" (1:1-7). Under Notes he deals with text critical issues, for example, the omission ἐν Ῥώμῃ from some manuscripts. Following the notes, Dunn presents his translation of the text. In regard to Form and Structure, he observes that Paul follows the conventional epistolary opening but expands the introduction of himself. Under Comment, Dunn notes that in this greeting, in contrast to most of his epistles, Paul mentions no associates. In the Explanation he observes that Paul identifies himself in relation to the gospel and defines the gospel in relation to Christ. Christ, in turn, is presented according to a pre-Pauline creedal formula that designates Jesus Christ as Son of God by his resurrection; Dunn sees here evidence of the developing of early Christology.

Later in this introductory part of the epistle Dunn investigates the "Summary Statement of the Letter's Theme" (1:16-17). His translation renders the quotation from Habakkuk: "He who is righteous by faith shall live." Under Notes, Dunn observes that πρῶτον is omitted in some witnesses, perhaps the result of Marcion's opposition to Jewish priority. In the Comment section Dunn discusses the phrase δικαιοσύνη θεοῦ. Reflecting the new perspective, he understands this phrase to refer to God's covenant faithfulness. Dunn's Explanation affirms "the gospel" as the theme of the letter. "It not merely contains somewhere in it the secret of or bears witness to the power of God through other channels, but *is itself* the power of God to salvation."[89]

In the main section of the epistle, "God's Saving Faith" (Rom 3:21—5:21), Dunn interprets 3:21-26 ("The Decisive Demonstration of God's Righteousness in the Death of Jesus"). Under Form and Structure he affirms the centrality of this text, confirmed by the reappearance of the theme (1:16-17), seen in the terms "righteousness" and "faith." Dunn summarizes the meaning of the text:

"Christ's death, a sacrifice for sin provided by God in accordance with the law, is God's means of extending his righteousness to all who believe (including those outside the law)."[90] In his Comment, Dunn investigates the controversial phrase διὰ πίστεως 'Ιησοῦ Χριστοῦ (3:22). He argues at some length and with considerable vigor that the genitive is objective. "What Paul says is that God's righteousness comes to expression *through* faith in Christ."[91] In regard to the phrase ὃν προέθετο ὁ θεὸς ἱλαστήριον (v. 25), Dunn notes that ἱλαστήριον is used in the LXX with the meaning "mercy seat," but also in Jewish literature to mean "means of expiation." Dunn recommends avoiding an either/or and adopting "means of atonement" in order to preserve the ambiguity. He says that "it can hardly be doubted that Paul (and the pre-Pauline tradition) was thinking of Jesus' death as a sacrifice . . . a judgment that is confirmed by the reference to Jesus' blood."[92] Dunn provides an extensive Explanation of this text. He notes the decisive shift in perspective signaled by the use of "now" (v. 21): the now of eschatological salvation, the new state of affairs resulting from God's act in Christ. In v. 22 he highlights Paul's turn from the faithfulness of God to human faith in Christ. In antithesis to works of the law, this faith depicts "*a relationship which is not dependent on specific ritual acts, but is direct and immediate, a relying on the risen Christ rather than a resting on the law.*"[93] Dunn understands the double qualifier, "grace as a gift" (v. 24), to prove that the redemptive action depends "entirely from start to finish on God's gracious power."[94]

Dunn's exegesis of Romans 7 goes against the stream of most interpreters who follow the course of the monumental monograph of W. G. Kümmel.[95] In his Comment on 7:7-25, Dunn notes that the first use of ἐγώ in Romans is in v. 9. In his Exposition concerning 7:7-13 Dunn finds allusions to the fall of Adam; the "I" in these verses represents Adam. However, in 7:14-25 Paul, according to Dunn, is speaking autobiographically and depicting his own Christian experience.

> The existential anguish of v. 15 must therefore express or at least include Paul's experience as one who has already been accepted by and through Christ and already received the Spirit. . . . It is not Paul the pious Pharisee who speaks here, but Paul the humble believer; and whoever else he speaks of, he certainly speaks of himself.[96]

Dunn does not see Romans 9–11 ("The Righteousness of God—From God's Faithfulness: The Outworking of the Gospel in Relation to Israel") as an excursus or an appendix but as a major exposition of Paul's understanding of the church's continuity with Israel. Paul's argument reaches a climax in 11:25-32

("The Final Mystery Revealed"). In his Comment, Dunn raises the crucial question: Whom does Paul include in the "all Israel" who will be saved? "There is now a strong consensus that πᾶς Ἰσραήλ must mean Israel as a whole, as a people whose corporate identity and wholeness would not be lost even if in the event there were some (or indeed many) individual exceptions."[97] This does not mean, Dunn insists, a remnant or "spiritual" Israel. In his Explanation, Dunn observes that Paul believes that the fall of Israel has a purpose within the mystery of history's outcome. The blindness of Israel was only temporary, awaiting the fullness of the Gentiles. "Certainly there will be a full measure of the Gentiles, the full number intended by God, but how many that would be Paul does not say—all, many, or only some; he is content simply to specify all that God will call."[98] As to Paul's assertion that "all Israel shall be saved" (11:26), Dunn says, "Whatever is happening to Israel now, Paul has been given the divinely revealed assurance that all will come out right for Israel in the end, that God's faithfulness to his first love will be demonstrated for all to see."[99] This indicates, according to Dunn, that the Jews will abandon their rejection of Jesus as Messiah and accept the gospel. In 11:29 ("for irrevocable are the gifts and call of God") Dunn sees Paul's ultimate expression of the faithfulness of God. "But now at last he states in clear and unambiguous terms what is obviously one of the basic postulates of his faith as both Jew and Christian, reaffirmed no doubt by the mystery revealed to him—that God is faithful to the covenant relationship he first established with Abraham and his seed."[100]

Dunn's continuing reflection on the new perspective led him to publish a remarkable book, *The Partings of the Ways*.[101] As the subtitle suggests, this book takes up the question of when and how Christianity separated from Judaism. Originally presented as lectures at the Gregorian Pontifical University in Rome, the book was first published in 1991; the second edition is a reprint with new preface and added appendix. Dunn investigates the split between Christianity and Judaism on the basis of what he calls the "four pillars" of Judaism: monotheism, election, Torah, and Temple.

Dunn begins with the Temple. Jesus, Dunn points out, is presented in the Gospels as a loyal Jew who participated in the worship of the Temple. Dunn interprets the "cleansing" of the Temple as a prophetic, eschatological act that provoked the lethal hostility of the hierarchy. He writes that *the most probable historical reconstruction of the death of Jesus is that on the Jewish side the principal movers were the high-priestly faction.*[102] According to Dunn the decisive break with the Temple was provoked by the Hellenists of the Jerusalem church (Acts 6). Stephen, the spokesman of the Hellenists, presented a lengthy speech in which he launched a frontal attack on the Temple, a house "made with humans hands" (Acts 7:48). Dunn observes that "*the Stephen episode marks the beginning of a clear parting of the ways*, between Christian and Jew."[103] With Paul, the break with the Temple has become complete. "In sum, so far as Paul was concerned, *the whole conception of sacred space, cultic sacrifice, priestly ministry and the question of who may enter and engage in their eschatological equivalents had been wholly transformed.*"[104]

Next, Dunn considers the pillars election (covenant) and Torah. Dunn believes that Jesus challenged the boundaries drawn by the Pharisees. However, he observes, "*There is no parting of the ways evident here, on either Torah or covenant.*"[105] Dunn views Paul vis-à-vis Judaism in the light of "covenant nomism." According to Dunn, Paul agreed with the Jewish view of the covenant: that God had given the covenant by grace and that the law included the rules for life within it. Paul's conversion, however, commissioned him to go to the Gentiles. Therefore, according to Dunn, Paul's dispute with Second Temple Judaism was the claim that the "works of the law" were intended to demonstrate Israel's distinctiveness, its separation from "Gentile sinners." Dunn says that "we can indeed say that it was Paul who effectively undermined this third pillar [Torah] of second Temple Judaism."[106] Nevertheless, despite the harsh words of Matthew and John about the Jews, Dunn concludes that "*the issues of Torah and election need not have proved sufficient in themselves to cause the final split between Christianity and rabbinical Judaism.*"[107]

Dunn turns to the most basic pillar of Judaism: the absolute commitment to monotheism. In regard to Jesus, Dunn sees him as "*at heart a devout Jew whose basic springs and expressions of piety were Jewish through and through.*"[108] Dunn considers the titles of Jesus he reviewed in his *Making of Christology* and finds nothing in their meaning that conflicts with the Jewish affirmation of the oneness of God. He does admit: "*The Jesus of the Fourth Gospel would have put a severe strain on Jewish monotheism.*"[109] Dunn also recognizes the problem created by the confession of Jesus as Lord—a confession complicated by the fact that *Kyrios* is the translation of the name of God in the LXX. However, Dunn concludes, "*To call Jesus 'Lord', therefore, was evidently not understood in earliest Christianity as identifying him with God.*"[110]

A final chapter summarizes the partings of the ways. As to the time of the final split, Dunn believes it occurred in the period between the two Jewish wars (70 and 132). In this period rabbinic Judaism took the form of orthodox, normative Judaism. Christianity became increasingly Gentile as Jewish Christianity separated and died out. Dunn says that "*by the end of the second Jewish revolt, Christian and Jew were clearly distinct and separate.*"[111] In reflecting on the ongoing history, Dunn acknowledges the claim of Christians to be the true people of God—a claim that encouraged a blatant anti-Judaism. Dunn believes a way to begin repairing the damage is to acknowledge "*the enduring Jewish character of Christianity.*"[112] "My thesis restated is that Israel cannot understand itself, cannot be Israel, unless the Christian recognizes that the Jew is also Israel and the Jew acknowledges that without the Christian Israel's destiny is incomplete."[113]

THEOLOGY OF PAUL

Dunn's work on Judaism and his exegetical research on the Pauline letter culminates in his magnum opus, *The Theology of Paul the Apostle.*[114] At the outset Dunn makes a decision concerning the way to order his analysis of Paul's thought: the use of Romans as template.[115] He begins with a prolegomenon to a theology of Paul that states his method and goal.

> So my endeavour in the following pages is, first of all, to get inside the skin of Paul, to see through his eyes, to think his thoughts from inside as it were, and to do so in such a way as to help others to appreciate his insight and subtlety and concerns for themselves. At the same time I wish to theologize with Paul, to engage in mutually critical dialogue with him, as one would hope a maturing student would engage critically with the thought of his or her teacher.[116]

As a point of departure Dunn investigates Paul's understanding of God and humankind. God, according to Dunn, is the foundation of Paul's theology—the one God who is creator of the cosmos and final judge. Dunn investigates Paul's understanding of humanity according to his use of anthropological terms, concluding that humans function at different levels: as embodied, we are social; as fleshly, we are vulnerable; as rational, we can soar to intellectual heights. Turning to the dark side of humanity, Dunn investigates the indictment of humankind in Rom 1:18—3:20: humans seen as sinners, enemies of God. According to Dunn, Paul develops this portrait of the human plight in parallel to Adam and his fall (Genesis 2–3). Like Adam, humanity was created for relationship with God, but humans revolted against the creator and lost their share of divine majesty; instead of sharing life, humanity is dominated by death. Dunn believes that Paul views sin as a personified power. Death, for Paul, is not a natural outcome of life; it is punishment for sin. Dunn discusses Paul's understanding of the law in relation to sin and death. The law is the measure of God's requirements; it functions in identifying sin. The law has a special relation with Israel, to protect and discipline, but, as Dunn points out, Israel failed to recognize the role of the law as temporary and misconstrued the possession of the law as evidence of a privileged relation to God.

Paul finds the answer to the human plight in the gospel of Jesus Christ. Paul believed his gospel was based on the scriptures, which, as Dunn points out, he exegeted according to a Christocentric hermeneutic. Paul claimed that his gospel was given by revelation, an *apocalypse* (Gal 1:12), an eschatological turning point. "The point to be emphasized in conclusion, however, is that Paul's gospel, the divine response to the divine indictment, was centred wholly on Jesus Christ."[117] This centrality of Jesus Christ leads Dunn into a discussion of Paul's understanding of Jesus. He points out that Paul had received tradition about Jesus and could assume with his readers common knowledge about the man from Nazareth. "It can be demonstrated with a fair degree of probability, then, that Paul both knew and cared about the ministry of Jesus prior to his passion and death."[118]

Although Paul had information about the life and teaching of Jesus, his primary concern, as Dunn observes, is the crucified Christ. As to Paul's theology of atoning sacrifice, Dunn does not believe it should be described as "substitution." "But Paul's teaching," says Dunn, "is not that Christ dies 'in the place of' others so that they escape death (as the logic of 'substitution' implies). It is rather that Christ's sharing their death makes it possible for them to share his death."[119] Dunn notes that Paul uses other metaphors to describe the saving work of Christ, including "redemption" and "reconciliation." As in his *Making of Christology*, Dunn finds no evidence in the Pauline letters to support the doctrine of the preexistence of Christ. He notes Paul's emphasis on the resurrection. However, he does not believe that Paul gave major attention to the imminent return of Christ, and he thinks the "delay of the parousia" made no impact whatsoever on the theology of Paul.

According to Dunn, Paul believed salvation had two stages: a beginning and a process. The primary feature of the beginning is God's action of grace. In the history of Pauline interpretation, emphasis has been placed on the doctrine of justification by faith. As Dunn had argued in his earlier writings, this doctrine must be understood from the new perspective on Paul. From this perspective it is clear that Paul's quarrel with the Jews is not about their effort to attain salvation by works but about their understanding of the "works of the law" as boundary markers to maintain their covenant distinctiveness and separation from the Gentiles. Indeed, Dunn implies that Paul understood "covenant nomism" better than the Jews; he knew that Abraham had been justified by faith and the covenant promised inclusion of the Gentiles.

> This, then, is what Paul meant by justification by faith, by faith alone. It was a profound conception of the relation between God and humankind—a relation of utter dependence, of unconditional trust. . . . That was why Paul was so fiercely hostile to the qualification which he saw confronting him all the time in any attempt to insist on works of the law as a necessary accompaniment of or addition to faith. . . . Justification was by faith alone.[120]

As well as justification, Dunn believes Paul viewed salvation as participation in Christ—the so-called "Christ mysticism." This neglected concept is expressed, according to Dunn, in the Pauline phrases "in Christ" and "with Christ." Closely related is Paul's understanding of the gift of the Spirit, which functions in human life providing freedom, ethical guidance, and hope.

Turning to Paul's understanding of the process of salvation, Dunn emphasizes the eschatological tension. Paul believed the new age had arrived with the coming of Christ, but it was not yet complete. Reminiscent of Cullmann, Dunn thinks that Paul viewed Christ as the midpoint in time and saw the *parousia* as the end.[121] Thus the present is the time of tension between the "already" and the "not yet." Dunn finds this eschatological tension in the divided "I" of Romans 7 and in the conflict of the flesh and the Spirit; the Spirit is the present pledge of the Spirit's triumph in the future. In concluding this chapter Dunn notes the importance of the Spirit in both stages of salvation: the Spirit functions in the beginning and in the eschatological tension of the salvation process.

After a discussion of the problem of Israel, ground he had plowed in his commentary on Romans 9–11, Dunn takes up Paul's doctrine of the church. Paul explicates this doctrine by the metaphor of the "body of Christ," which highlights the corporate character of the Christian communities. Dunn points out that these are religious communities without cult: no temple, no priests, no sacrifices. Paul describes these churches as charismatic communities—communities in which the gifts of the Spirit are active. Dunn observes that the central element of worship in the Pauline churches is the Lord's Supper. Paul's understanding of the Lord's Supper, according to Dunn, is wholly christological: the Supper is the sharing of the body of Christ; the Supper is observed at the table of the Lord. The Lord's Supper remembers the death and resurrection of Christ and anticipates his coming; it is the bridge across the eschatological tension.

The final chapter of Dunn's *Theology of Paul* is dedicated to ethics. As to the motivating principles, Dunn notes the importance of the indicative (the new situation resulting from the event of Christ) and the imperative (the response of the believer in Christ). The believer responds to the "law of Christ," the law of love. As to the practice of ethics, Dunn observes that the life of the believer is lived out in a social context. In Corinth the Christians lived between two worlds: the external world of Hellenistic society and the inner world of the Christian community. In this dual context Christians face problems about sexual conduct, slavery, and food that has been offered to idols. Dunn points out that in this situation Paul does not advocate asceticism but stresses opposition to idolatry and devotion to the Lord.

Dunn adds an epilogue he titles "postlegomena to a theology of Paul." According to Dunn, Paul viewed his new faith as a fulfillment of the old. Christ, for Paul, is the fulcrum point in Paul's theological development: Christ as the revelation of God, Christ as the eschatological event.

> The centrality of Christ, as showing what God is like, as defining God's Spirit, as the channel of Israel's blessing for the nations, as demonstrating what obedience to Torah means, as the light which illumines Israel's scriptures, as embodying the paradigm of creation and consummation, his death and resurrection as the midpoint of time, as the magnet of faith, as the focus of all sacramental significance, as determining the personal and corporate identity of Christians, as the image to which the salvation process conforms, is simply inescapable in the theology of Paul the apostle.[122]

HISTORY OF EARLY CHRISTIANITY

Late in his career Dunn launched a project of phenomenal dimensions: a three-volume history of early Christianity from the beginning until 150, entitled *Christianity in the Making*. By the end of the first decade of the twenty-first century the first two volumes had been published. The sheer bulk of these books defies the possibility of an adequate review within limited space. However, since much of Dunn's work focused on Paul and the early church, some attention must be given to the first volume: *Jesus Remembered*.[123] In the first part of this hefty tome (over 900 pages) Dunn is concerned with the quest of the historical Jesus.[124] He notes two movements in the Enlightenment view of Jesus: the flight from dogma and the flight from history. In the former he traces the rejection of revelation from Reimarus to the Jesus Seminar. As to the flight from history, Dunn argues that the "objective" application of historical criticism led to relativizing and skepticism. With Rudolf Bultmann the quest for the historical Jesus was seen as both impossible and unimportant. However, the pupils of Bultmann, notably Ernst Käsemann, detected historical elements in the kerygma and proposed a new (second) quest.[125] Dunn thinks a third quest is possible, this time inspired by the work of E. P. Sanders, who stressed the Jewishness of Jesus, a quest in which Dunn is ready to enlist.

Dunn's chapter, "History, Hermeneutics and Faith," explores the methodology of the third quest. The quest is necessary, he says, because of the importance of the historical figure of Jesus. The study of history, according to Dunn, can offer the perspective of historical distance and provide probability, not certainty. In place of the illusion of objectivity Dunn calls for a "critical realism" that opposes historical positivism and recognizes the importance of meaning. Dunn's method focuses on the text in its historical context. He believes the recent allegiance to the "autonomy" of the text to be an illusion. "The meaning intended by means of and through the text is still a legitimate and viable goal for the NT exegete and interpreter."[126] Dunn favors a hermeneutic that recognizes the role of faith. Interpretation, he believes, should be a dialogue that includes listening to the text, being sensitive to both the objective and subjective meaning. Recognition of the role of faith in interpretation prompts Dunn to the historical question: When did a faith perspective first influence the Jesus tradition? The answer, according to Dunn, is that faith was present from the beginning: a truth form criticism missed. The key issue in the quest for the historical Jesus is the hermeneutical tension between faith and history.

The second part of Dunn's *Jesus Remembered* traces the path from the Gospels back to Jesus. Dunn accepts the Two-Document Hypothesis with minor qualifications. He recognizes the priority of Mark and thinks both Matthew and Luke had distinctive material of their own as well as oral tradition. As to the *Gospel of Thomas*, Dunn does not believe it preserves tradition independent of and older than the Synoptics. He is impressed with recent studies that find the genre of the Gospels in ancient biographies. Dunn is also impressed with studies of the oral tradition, notably the work of Birger Gerhardsson (reviewed in the next section). As a result, he believes some of the variants visible in the Synoptic parallels are better explained by the analysis of oral tradition than by traditional literary source criticism. Like Gerhardsson, Dunn thinks the tradition goes back to the original encounter of the disciples with Jesus. In his quest for the historical Jesus, Dunn does not resort to the conventional list of criteria. Instead, he advocates beginning with the big picture. "The criterion is this: any feature which is *characteristic within the Jesus tradition and relatively distinctive of the Jesus tradition* is most likely to go back to

Jesus."[127] "In short, there is a 'historical Jesus,' or better, a historic Jesus, who is the legitimate and possible goal of further questing."[128]

In Part III, Dunn investigates the "Mission of Jesus." The mission begins, according to him, with John the Baptist. Dunn hesitates to identify Jesus as a disciple of John, but he acknowledges that Jesus was for a time associated with the Baptist. Jesus' baptism by John, which according to Dunn is better understood as an anointing with the Spirit, marks the beginning of the ministry of Jesus. The major feature of this ministry was the proclamation of the kingdom of God. Dunn believes the investigation of the meaning of the kingdom must begin with the recognition of the present/future tension preserved in the tradition. The understanding of the kingdom as future is expressed in sayings that announce that the kingdom has drawn near and in the parables of crisis that call for vigilance. On the other hand, Dunn calls attention to evidence indicating that the kingdom is already present. This is seen, for example, in Jesus' claim that exorcisms demonstrate that the kingdom has come. Dunn interprets the parables of growth as pointing to the end of the development: the harvest has already happened. In sum, Dunn finds the understanding of the kingdom as both future and present to be firmly rooted in the tradition. He rejects the theory that the earliest stratum of Q and the *Gospel of Thomas* provide an early, reliable tradition of a non-eschatological Jesus. Instead, the historian has to admit that Jesus expected imminent events that did not happen. Dunn says that the early Christian could accept failed prophecy without deserting the core faith expressed in the prophecy—faith in God as King and Father.

Dunn turns to the question: "For whom did Jesus intend his message?" He believes the message was addressed first and foremost to Israel. It was a call to return to trust in God. Dunn observes that the call was also directed to sinners. Here again he hears the language of Jewish factionalism: "sinners," like toll-collectors, were those who, according to the "righteous," had put themselves outside the covenant people. Those who heard and accepted the message with repentance and faith became disciples of Jesus. The disciples, according to Dunn, were accepted as children of the Father. Dunn believes that Jesus taught the disciples to address God in prayer as he himself did, as "Abba." He also notes that discipleship involved suffering, taking up a cross. In the life of the disciples, love is the fundamental motivation. This life comes to expression in a new family, an open fellowship without boundaries that separated insiders from outsiders. Jesus affirmed "the character of kingdom life, lived already here and now in anticipation of God's ordering of society when his will is done on earth as it is in heaven."[129]

With Part IV the plot thickens: Dunn takes up the murky question of Jesus' self-understanding. He begins with the easier question: How did others see Jesus? Most obvious is the answer that he was recognized as Messiah. Dunn rejects the view that this recognition did not occur until after the resurrection, and he detects evidence to the contrary. However, for the larger question this evidence is counterproductive: Dunn finds abundant evidence that royal messiahship was a role Jesus resolutely rejected. He does believe that some of Jesus' contemporaries hailed him as a prophet and a doer of extraordinary deeds. No one doubts that Jesus was recognized as a teacher, but astonishing is the authority with which he taught. Dunn points out that Jesus' expression, "I say to you," is stronger than the prophetic assertion, "Thus says the Lord." In summing up the significance of these various designations of Jesus, Dunn sees two lasting impressions:

> One is that Jesus' mission seems to have broken through all the most obvious categories by which his mission could be evaluated; he evidently did not fit into any of the pigeon-holes by which observers might have wished to label him. The other is the tantalising possibility that Jesus deliberately claimed a degree of distinctiveness for his mission, for all its thoroughly Jewish character, which left both hearers and disciples struggling for words to express the significance of what they were seeing and hearing—and remembering.[130]

Dunn moves to the more difficult question: "How did Jesus see his own role?" As in his *Christology*, he pursues the question according to the conventional titles. The crucial title, of course, is "Son of Man," and Dunn devotes almost forty pages to it. He rehearses the two basic approaches to the question: the philological (various understandings of the Aramaic phrase with generic meaning) and the apocalyptic (reference to Son of Man in Dan 7:13-14). Turning to the evidence, Dunn is impressed by that fact that virtually every allusion to the Son of Man in the NT is put into the mouth of Jesus. Dunn says that the phrase "*was remembered as a speech usage distinctive of Jesus because that is precisely what it was.*"[131] As to the philological approach, Dunn finds occasions where Jesus uses the Aramaic phrase with the meaning "I" or "humankind." He also finds evidence for the influence of Daniel and references to the Son of Man who would come on the clouds. As to the apocalyptic being of the *Similitudes of Enoch*, Dunn believes this figure does not appear until late in the first century. He hypothesizes that Jesus' reference to Dan 7:13 does not indicate identification with an apocalyptic figure but is an allusion to the Son of Man as symbol of the suffering role of the faithful of Israel. In concluding what he has to say about Jesus' self-understanding, Dunn says that Jesus laid no claim to any particular title and rejected some that others tried to impose on him. Dunn thinks the closest expression is the non-titular use of "son of man" as an anticipation of Jesus' suffering and hope of vindication.

The last part of *Jesus Remembered* deals with the climax of the mission of Jesus. This part addresses two final features: the crucifixion and the resurrection. In regard to the crucifixion, Dunn notes the role of Pilate and the Romans as decisive. He thinks the best attested word from the cross is "My God, my God, why have you forsaken me?" As to the question of why Jesus was executed, Dunn thinks that Jesus' action in "cleansing" the temple and his disregard of cultic regulations provoked the hostility of the high-priestly families and the Temple authorities, the officials most responsible for handing Jesus over to the Romans. Also important is the question whether Jesus anticipated his own death, and if so, how he understood it. Dunn finds sufficient evidence that Jesus did anticipate his death, but he rejects the theory that Jesus saw himself as the Suffering Servant of Second Isaiah. More likely, Jesus viewed himself as an heir of the tradition of the righteous sufferers, and recognized that he would have to endure the woes of the eschatological tribulation. Dunn is convinced that Jesus would not have understood his execution to be a sign of the failure of God's purpose. The vindication Jesus expected was "*to share in the general and final resurrection of the dead.*"[132]

In investigating the resurrection, Dunn begins with the tradition of the empty tomb. He concludes that this tradition is early, reliable, and independent of the tradition of the resurrection appearances. As to the latter, he examines the various accounts and finds a common core: the witnesses saw Jesus and they received a commission. "*What we should recognize as beyond reasonable doubt is that the first believers experienced 'resurrection appearances' and that those experiences are enshrined, as with the earlier impact made by Jesus' teaching and actions, in the traditions which have come down to us.*"[133] Dunn is dismissive of any interpretation that smacks of subjectivity. He concludes that the tradition requires us to recognize that something had happened to Jesus, not that something had happened to the disciples. Nevertheless, Dunn designates the resurrection as metaphor, as interpretation of the data. "In short, resurrection of Jesus is not so much a historical fact as a foundational fact, or meta-fact, the interpretative insight into reality which enables discernment of the relative importance and unimportance of all other facts."[134]

A final chapter reflects on the title of the book, *Jesus Remembered*. Dunn understands the book to reflect "a new perspective on the Jesus tradition."[135] According to this view, "*The primary formative force in shaping the Jesus tradition was the impact made by Jesus during his mission on the first disciples*, the impact which drew them into discipleship."[136] Two features of the new perspective should be highlighted: the recognition of the importance of oral tradition for assessing the sources and the emphasis on seeing Jesus in his Jewish context. According to Dunn, the impact of the Jesus tradition can still be felt today. "In short, *through the Jesus tradition the would-be disciple still hears and encounters Jesus* as he talked and debated, shared table-fellowship and healed. . . . Through that tradition it is still possible for anyone to encounter the Jesus from whom Christianity stems, the remembered Jesus."[137]

Looking back over the work of James Dunn, the viewer stands in awe. The sheer magnitude of the work, built on exegetical detail and informed by a mastery of a mountain of secondary sources, staggers the imagination. Dunn's writings are marked by thoughtful order and clarity of style. Above all, Dunn is a biblical theologian; his work is characterized by a devotion to the text. He has a high view of biblical authority, and some of his critical judgments tend to be conservative. Nevertheless, Dunn's view of the unity of the NT message does not compromise his recognition of the New Testament's diversity. Dunn's theology is Christocentric, and he embraces a high Christology. However, he seems reluctant to acknowledge that some texts (notably in the Pauline letters) imply the preexistence of Christ. Nevertheless, sensitive to theological distinctions, Dunn affirms the doctrine of the incarnation.

A distinctive feature of Dunn's NT research is his emphasis on Jewish backgrounds. His critics are correct, however, in noting his inadequate attention to the Hellenistic setting. In regard to Judaism, Dunn's view is dominated by the new perspective. While he is certainly correct in preferring this view to the traditional caricature of Judaism, he may have gone too far. He sees Paul as more knowledgeable about "covenant nomism" than the Jews, and he finds a continuity between Paul and Israel that can hardly explain Paul's conflict with the Jews. There must have been more than a quarrel about boundary markers to result in five sentences of forty lashes (2 Cor 11:24). Despite the Christocentric character of his own theology, Dunn does not sufficiently stress Paul's major difference from his fellow-Jews: Paul had accepted Jesus as the Messiah.

New Testament Research in Scandinavia: Birger Gerhardsson

The twentieth century witnessed the research of some outstanding Scandinavian scholars. The pioneer of historical-critical research in Scandinavia in that time was Anton Fridrichsen. After study in his native Norway, Fridrichsen did additional academic work in Germany and completed a doctorate at Strasbourg. He spent most of his career as a professor at Uppsala. Among Fridrichsen's important works are his *The Apostle and His Message*[138] and *The Problem of Miracle in Primitive Christianity*.[139] Fridrichsen was a demanding teacher who numbered among his students such luminaries as Bo Reicke, Harald Riesenfeld, and Krister Stendahl (who became a professor and, later, Dean at Harvard Divinity School). Another important Scandinavian NT scholar was Nils Dahl; educated at Oslo, where he taught for a time, Dahl was a professor at Yale from 1965 to 1980. Birger Gerhardsson, therefore, serves as representative of a larger group. Moreover, he deserves attention in his own right: Gerhardsson has a distinctive view of the history of early Christianity that has enjoyed a revival early in the twenty-first century.

Birger Gerhardsson (1926–)

Birger Gerhardsson was educated at the University of Uppsala, where he studied with Harald Riesenfeld.[140] From 1965 to 1992 Gerhardsson served as professor of exegetical theology as the University of Lund. He was honored by election to the presidency of the SNTS (1990). According to a notable British scholar, "Birger Gerhardsson is well known throughout the international New Testament scholarly world as a scholar of highest repute."[141]

The Transmission of Tradition

Gerhardsson is recognized primarily for his major work, *Memory and Manuscript*.[142] Based on his Uppsala dissertation of 1956, the book was first published in 1961. It was reprinted in 1998 with a new preface by the author and a foreword by Jacob Neusner. In the new preface Gerhardsson recalls his original purpose in writing: previous research had not provided a clear picture of the origin and transmission of early Christian tradition. Gerhardsson believed, and still does, that in the time of Jesus the only coherent methods for handling tradition were to be found in Pharisaic-rabbinic Judaism. This conviction provided the key to Gerhardsson's analysis of early Christian tradition. Neusner's foreword confesses a conversion: he regrets his review of the first edition (following the lead of Morton Smith) in which he attacked Gerhardsson's use of later sources in the exposition of first-century tradition.

In the foreword Neusner praises Gerhardsson for discovering a model of how tradition was formed: one that was explicit in later rabbinic literature, but relevant for the time of Jesus.

In the introduction to the original book Gerhardsson asserts that the prevailing theory of the origin and development of tradition (form criticism) has not provided an adequate understanding of early Christian tradition. "It seems therefore highly necessary to determine what was the technical procedure followed when the early Church *transmitted*, both gospel material and other material."[143] In the first and largest part of the book Gerhardsson discusses, oral and written tradition in rabbinic Judaism. He begins by investigating written and oral Torah. It is important, he contends, to differentiate between the two. "The distinction is therefore this: the one part of Torah is in principle Scripture, Scripture which is read, whilst the other is oral tradition, tradition which is repeated."[144] In his research Gerhardsson concentrates on the Tannaitic and Amoraic periods. "Our task is to attempt to give a concrete picture of how, *from a purely technical point of view*, the sacred Torah was transmitted during these centuries."[145]

Gerhardsson begins with a discussion of the transmission of written Torah. Great care, he says, was taken for the preservation of the text. The Torah was copied by experts who were skilled in writing and knowledge of Scripture. "Thus the centuries of care lavished on the sacred text by learned copyists and Scripture teachers has spread, and become an overall effort, approved of by all Rabbis, to give all Israel copies, correct in the most minute detail, of those sacred Scriptures in which not even the smallest point was without importance."[146] Gerhardsson notes the importance of schools where boys were taught Torah by experts. The students, he says, learned by memorizing. Gerhardsson also recognizes the importance of public worship (where Scripture was read and interpreted) for the preservation of the text.

Gerhardsson turns to the transmission of oral Torah, an issue of greater importance for his purposes. He investigates the way the oral Torah was transmitted in rabbinic Judaism. Gerhardsson refers to oral Torah as "text," that is, as a fixed form. "The balance of probability is that the basic material in the oral Torah was transmitted and learned in a fixed form as early as during the last century of the Temple."[147] Oral as well as written Torah was studied in the schools, and again the method was memorization. The teacher taught by repetition of the text (according to a convention, four times) and the pupils repeated until they learned by heart.

Gerhardsson proceeds to discuss the theory and practice of the transmission of tradition. Emphasis was placed on preservation of the authentic words.

"The pupil is thus in duty bound to maintain his teacher's exact words."[148] The material to be learned was condensed and put into concise expression. Mnemonic techniques—catch-words and word associations—were employed. Pupils used notebooks or scrolls to assist their memories. Oral tradition included sayings tradition (the sayings of the older teachers) and narrative tradition (the stories about teachers). "*There is no distinct boundary between these deliberate pedagogical measures and the teacher's way of life as a whole.*"[149]

The second part of *Memory and Manuscript* investigates the "Delivery of the Gospel Tradition in Early Christianity." Here Gerhardsson applies the results of his research on Judaism to the study of early Christian tradition. At the outset he underlines the importance of the evidence from Luke. According to Gerhardsson, Luke is concerned with Torah, what Luke calls "the word of the Lord." This word in closely connected to Jerusalem, the center of the world, the messianic city. Also concerned with the "word of the Lord" are the apostles, whose main task is to witness to their teacher, Jesus. The early Christians viewed Christ as the fulfillment of Scripture; their interpretation of Scripture Gerhardsson characterizes as a "Christ-midrash."[150]

> The connection between the tradition of Christ and the Holy Scriptures was thus according to Luke not merely an idea or a concept but a reality that determined the entire method of the early church when presenting the Logos. And the apostles were considered to be the bearers both of the tradition of Christ and of the correct interpretation of the Scriptures.[151]

Gerhardsson sees the division of labor between the Twelve and the Seven (Acts 6:1-6) as fortuitous: "The college of Apostles is therefore freed from even the important diaconal work in order to be able entirely to devote themselves to prayer and the service of the Word."[152] The service of the word, according to Gerhardsson, included teaching. He sees in the Jerusalem Council (Acts 15) an early Christian "General Session" and finds parallels in the general sessions at Qumran and in the ancient Sanhedrin. Gerhardsson claims that "what Luke is here describing is the way in which *an important doctrinal question is referred to the Church's highest doctrinal authority* in Jerusalem."[153]

Gerhardsson detects important information about early Christian tradition in the life and letters of Paul. Although Paul claimed that his gospel was given to him by revelation, he recognized the importance of the Jerusalem apostles. The conference in Jerusalem (Galatians 2), according to Gerhardsson, resulted in two apostolates and two gospels: one to the uncircumcised (the apostolate of Paul) and one to the circumcised (the apostolate of Peter). Although Paul claimed independence, he recognized the centrality of Jerusalem. He acknowledged that his preaching began in Jerusalem (Rom 15:19), and his effort to collect and deliver the offering acknowledged the precedence of the Jerusalem church. Paul explicitly refers to "traditions of my fathers" (Gal 1:14; RSV) in depicting his former life in Judaism.

According to Gerhardsson, Paul had acquired the rabbinic method of learning and transmitting tradition at the feet of Gamaliel. In describing his receiving and handing on of tradition after his conversion, Paul uses the technical terms παραλαμβάνειν and παραδίδοναι. These terms are used for the traditions of the resurrection (1 Cor 15:3) and of the Lord's Supper (1 Cor 11:23). Gerhardsson believes the fundamental element of the Christian tradition is the gospel. "The only reasonable conclusion in this case is therefore that what we have here is a logos fixed by the college of Apostles in Jerusalem."[154] Paul received this tradition, according to Gerhardsson, during his visit with Cephas, three years after his conversion (Gal 1:18). Paul also knew and transmitted the tradition of Jesus. In 1 Cor 7:10 he applies the word of the Lord to the practical life of the community and at the same time distinguishes his own teaching from the Lord's command. Gerhardsson asserts that "Paul is here reproducing a tradition which he believed to have been derived from Jesus via the college of Apostles."[155]

A final chapter of *Memory and Manuscript* deals with the origin and transmission of the gospel tradition. According to Gerhardsson the source of the tradition is Jesus. Jesus was a teacher who taught and interpreted Scripture in the synagogues. Gerhardsson supposes that his teaching methods were similar to those used by the Jewish teachers of his time. "He must have made his disciples learn certain sayings off by heart; if he taught he must have required his disciples to memorize."[156] This teaching of Jesus was transmitted by the Twelve, not as individuals but as a *collegium*. Gerhardsson, contra Acts 4:13, objects to the characterization of the apostles as "unlearned and ignorant men" (KJV). Their function, according to Gerhardsson, was to present the "word of the Lord" as an eyewitness account, confirmed by Scripture. They remembered the teachings of Jesus and his actions. In contrast to the rabbis, the disciples believed there was only one teacher (Matt 23:10). The traditions of Jesus were gathered into blocks or, to use Gerhardsson's term, "tractates." These can be identified in the Gospels; for example, Mark 4 is a parable tractate. Gerhardsson stresses his conviction that the tradition was passed on orally. The teachings, he thinks, were taught by continual repetition and learned by memorization. He concludes: "They [the Evangelists] worked on the basis of a fixed, distinct tradition from, and about, Jesus—a tradition which was partly memorized and partly written down in notebooks and private scrolls, but invariably isolated from the teachings of other doctrinal authorities."[157]

Three years after the original publication of *Memory and Manuscript,* Gerhardsson published *Tradition and Transmission in Early Christianity.*[158] In this shorter work he attempts to clarify issues raised by the earlier book and answer criticisms directed against it. He begins by addressing a basic objection of his critics: Gerhardsson had used later rabbinic sources to represent the method of teaching in the time of Jesus. In response, Gerhardsson argues that the pedagogical principles used by the rabbis had a continuity that goes back to OT times, and he claims that the instruction by repetition and memorization is attested prior to Aqiba (ca. 50 CE–135 CE). Gerhardsson also contends that the Pharisees were the predominant group in Judaism in the first century and used teaching methods that were in widespread use in Judaism and the larger world. "We conclude that for an observer *these men were noteworthy less as members of a particular party than as representatives of a professional teaching class.*"[159]

Turning to the tradition and teaching methods of early Christianity, Gerhardsson observes that Jesus and early Christianity operated in a sphere where Pharisaic teachers had wide influence. He believes (in accord with Acts 22:3) that Paul had been trained in a Pharisaic school and certainly would not have forgotten what he learned. "When all is said and done there remains the incontestable historical fact that Jesus and the early Church had a great deal in common with their milieu, including Pharisaism-Rabbinism."[160] Although he interprets early Christian tradition within the context of rabbinic tradition, Gerhardsson affirms its distinctiveness. He insists that the Christ-tradition was on a higher plane than the oral Torah of the rabbis: Jesus was the Messiah, the only teacher. This higher tradition, according to Gerhardsson, was altered very little. "The evidence suggests that memories of Jesus were so clear, and the traditions with which they were connected so firmly based that there can have been relatively little scope for alteration."[161]

Gerhardsson provides further clarification of his understanding of early Christian tradition in three lectures, all collected into a single volume entitled *The Reliability of the Gospel Tradition.*[162] In 1976 he gave lectures in Germany under the title *Die Anfänge der Evangelientradition,*[163] and an English translation, *The Origins of the Gospel Tradition,* appeared in 1979.[164] The English translation is reprinted in *The Reliability of the Gospel Tradition* (pp. 1–58). In the introduction Gerhardsson states his concern "to work out the historical truth about Jesus of Nazareth."[165] He charges that form criticism's attempt to understand oral tradition was not "sufficiently *historical.*"[166] Gerhardsson begins his own investigation with a review of the Jewish understanding of tradition. For Judaism the norm was Torah, which encompassed all revelation and instruction. Torah, according to Gerhardsson, functioned in three forms: verbal tradition (words or texts imprinted on the mind), practical tradition (normative conduct presented by verbal instruction and example), and institutional tradition (embodied in the temple and taught in the synagogue). To learn Torah, one had to go to a teacher; students learned by listening and observing. Gerhardsson acknowledges that the written evidence for these pedagogical methods dates from the years following the Jewish War, "but in essential aspects these methods are clearly ancient."[167] The most important feature of the method was memorizing; the texts and sayings were learned by heart. The teacher spoke clearly and concisely and used didactic devices, for example, alliteration and parallelism. The method involved repetition: the teacher repeated the teaching many times and the students were drilled until they learned the texts by heart.

Gerhardsson, as in his earlier work, finds parallels in the NT. He says that "in Paul's time early Christianity is conscious of the fact that it has *a tradition* of its own—including many traditions—which the church leaders hand on to the congregations, which the congregations receive, and which they are to guard and live by."[168] Again, he presents evidence of Paul's concern with the Jesus tradition. Gerhardsson contends that tradition like that recounted in 1 Cor 11:23-25 was communicated orally and learned by heart. Since the early Christians revered only one teacher, one ultimate source of tradition, they believed the Jesus tradition was of utmost importance. "If one thinks about this, it becomes extremely difficult to imagine that there ever was a time when Jesus' followers were not interested in preserving his teachings and committing his deeds to memory."[169] Gerhardsson vigorously rejects the notion that tradition about Jesus did not arise until after the resurrection. He is convinced that the tradition was preserved by select persons, the collegium of the apostles, eyewitnesses of the tradition.

Gerhardsson presumes that Jesus mirrored the teaching methods of the rabbis. His teachings "consist of brief, laconic, well-rounded texts, or pointed statements with a clear profile, rich in content and artistic in form."[170] Jesus taught in parables or *meshalim*. "If Jesus created meshalim during his public ministry, it is reasonable to assume that his disciples preserved these texts right from the beginning."[171] After reviewing the evidence, Gerhardsson concludes, "It thus seems historically very probable that the Jesus traditions in the Gospels have been preserved for us by persons reliable and well-informed."[172] In regard to variations in the Synoptic parallels, Gerhardsson rejects the view that they prove that the tradition was not memorized. To him, the kinds of variations—additions, omissions, transpositions, minor alterations—indicate that they rest on a fixed text. "My position is that one must proceed on the belief that the synoptic material in principle comes from the earthly Jesus and the disciples who followed him during his ministry, but that one must also do full justice to the fact that this memory material has been marked by insights and interpretations gradually arrived at by the early Christian teachers."[173]

In 1982 Gerhardsson presented a paper at a symposium in Tübingen on "The Gospel and the Gospels," entitled "Der Weg der Evangelientradition."[174] This paper was revised and published in English translation in *The Reliability of the Gospel Tradition*.[175] In it, Gerhardsson begins with a basic presupposition: "In short, we make the following statement of fact: in the New Testament the concrete Jesus tradition is treated as an *independent entity*."[176] By this Gerhardsson means that the Jesus tradition is isolated in special "texts" that preserve a unique tradition, one that is concerned exclusively with Jesus. Gerhardsson believes this tradition was isolated from the beginning and not, as the form critics supposed, filtered out of general tradition and shaped by the later *Sitze-im-Leben*. This precise tradition was needed, according to Gerhardsson, for worship services, catechetical instruction, and regular study of the words and deeds of Jesus.

Gerhardsson delineates two forms of the Jesus tradition: the sayings tradition and the narrative tradition. In regard to the former, he believes the sayings were transmitted in fixed form. As to the narrative tradition, Gerhardsson observes that it is one step removed: it is formulated by someone who saw or heard about what had happened. Nevertheless, he believes this kind of tradition was also handed down in memorized form. He is ardently opposed to the notion of the form critics that tradition was shaped (even created) by the life situations of the community. According to Gerhardsson, Christian tradition had its origin in Jesus. He also attacks the view of the form critics that the tradition was transmitted by anonymous persons. According to Gerhardsson, Christian tradition was handed down by important leaders, selected and trained for the task: Peter and the apostles. He concludes "that early Christianity took its starting point in something handed down, and, in the final analysis, something historical. Briefly expressed: *it only gave an interpretation where there was something to be interpreted*."[177]

The last of the trilogy of lectures was a paper presented at a symposium on the Gospels held in Jerusalem in 1984. Gerhardsson's lecture was published as a separate monograph, *The Gospel Tradition*, and reprinted in *The Reliability of the Gospel Tradition*.[178] In this chapter Gerhardsson focuses on the Gospel tradition within Christian tradition. His method applies phenomenological insights about the ways humans function and uses insights from the historical setting of early Christianity. In regard to the latter, he investigates early Christian tradition in relation to its Jewish mother tradition. In this investigation Gerhardsson draws a distinction between inner and outer tradition. Inner tradition he describes as animated and living; it inspires. Outer tradition, according to Gerhardsson, refers to the forms in which tradition is expressed: verbal, behavioral, institutional, and material. In Christianity's Jewish mother tradition, inner tradition is rich and multifarious: remembering the true God, reciting the Shema. Outer tradition in Judaism takes four forms: verbal (the words of Torah), behavioral (life in Torah), institutional (social structures and hierarchy), and material (temple, synagogue, scrolls).

Gerhardsson finds a parallel in early Christianity and proceeds to discuss the Christian understanding of inner and outer tradition. Regarding inner tradition, he believes Jesus created a new tradition in the bosom of the mother tradition. Christianity was "a new tradition with an eruptive center of inner tradition which expresses itself in words and behavior."[179] Gerhardsson reviews Christian outer tradition in reverse order, beginning with the least important form—material tradition. He believes the early Christians related to the Jewish material tradition (temple, synagogue) with freedom. The early Christians venerated the OT Scriptures, but Christian writings were not regarded as holy Scripture until later. In regard to institutional tradition, Gerhardsson notes that Jesus gathered around himself a primary group from which emerged an embryonic organization with the Twelve as leaders. As to the behavioral tradition, Jesus showed little interest in halakic minutiae, but he embraced the central mother tradition and stressed the first and greatest commandment.

Gerhardsson gives major attention to verbal tradition, the central element of early Christian tradition. He believes this kind of tradition—one first reported by eyewitnesses and handed on by faithful traditionists—is depicted in the Lukan prologue. Gerhardsson discusses the origin and character of the Christian tradition. This tradition begins, he believes, when Jesus teaches and gains adherents. Jesus teaches in parables and *logoi*, forms of speech Gerhardsson designates as "texts." These "texts," he thinks, were transmitted and memorized in much the same way as teaching and learning were practiced in Judaism. Although Jesus wrote nothing, the Gospels, according to Gerhardsson, were composed by the late 60s. He rejects the notion that each of the later gospels (particularly Luke and John) was written to replace the earlier. He seems to suppose that a fourfold gospel was envisaged early. "The written gospel of the church is a polyphonic gospel—or tetraphonic gospel."[180] Gerhardsson concludes:

> Jesus and the early Christians presented their own, new, specific message—from the eruptive center of their inner tradition—in oral forms first of all, and did so in a cultural setting where writings were never far away. This means that the transition to a stage where the oral gospel had basically become one of many books was not a superficial, technical triviality. Granted this significant change did not occur immediately when the Gospels were written (the oral tradition and the oral activity of other forms continued), something started which would have important consequences. One hundred years later the written gospels had attained the stature of holy scripture and of primary sources for the Christian message.[181]

Although Gerhardsson had investigated gospel tradition in the last lecture reviewed above, he had given little attention to actual texts. This lacuna is filled to considerable degree by his essay, "Illuminating the Kingdom: Narrative Meshalim in the Synoptic Gospels."[182] This essay, too, had originally been presented as a paper at another symposium, this time on oral tradition, with a session in Dublin and a second in Italy in 1990. Gerhardsson's paper was read at this second session. In the introduction he notes that Jesus taught in parables, what the Jews called "*meshalim*." The parable or *mashal* was a short, carefully crafted "text" of two kinds: aphoristic and narrative. In this paper Gerhardsson is concerned with the latter. His overview of the material finds fifty-five narrative *meshalim* in the Synoptic Gospels. "Our central question is how these 55 texts have been transmitted in the period between Jesus and the evangelists."[183]

Gerhardsson's analysis of this material begins with some general observations. As to the location of the *meshalim*, they are incorporated into the composition of the story of Jesus and set in the context of Jesus' teaching. Regarding the external details, Gerhardsson observes that the *meshalim* are usually short. He identifies two basic types: the similitude (comparison with a universal phenomenon) and the parable (presentation of an individual case). The purpose of the *meshalim*, according to Gerhardsson, is to illuminate the teaching, to make the lesson concrete, to lead the listener to understand and agree. He points out that, in general, the message of Jesus' parables is the kingdom of God; they are not about Jesus. In comparing the parallel accounts of the same parable in the Synoptics, Gerhardsson notes variations; this indicates that the evangelists felt free to change wordings.

Gerhardsson turns to the transmission of the *meshalim*. He draws conclusions from the textual material preserved in the Gospels. Gerhardsson believes that this was material that was taken over: the evangelists passed on what they had received. The traditionists who transmitted the *meshalim* were, at the beginning, disciples of Jesus, and later, early Christian teachers. He grapples with the problem of the variability of the parables, observing that it is "very difficult to decide if a narrative mashal has been created by Jesus himself or by a disciple," but he concludes that "the secondary meshalim are few."[184] "The main impression our material gives us is that the teachers of the early Church have, despite their didactic freedom, treated our narrative meshalim as texts, texts susceptible of a certain reformulation but yet fixed in form."[185] Gerhardsson also supposes that conclusions can be drawn concerning Jesus' method of teaching. "Although not a word is said about it, this ought to mean that, according to the evangelists, Jesus had implanted the text of the mashal in the minds of its listeners; he has not just narrated it but also repeated it. Shall we guess that he narrated it four times?"[186]

Gerhardsson believes that when the Gospels were eventually written and canonized they lost their vital linguistic character. "The Synoptic narrative meshalim," he says, "became teaching *material* rather than teaching *tools*. They no longer had the simple purpose of illuminating and making concrete one specific point in the message about the Kingdom."[187]

MIDRASH, MIRACLES, AND ETHICS

Related to his work on early Christian tradition is Gerhardsson's *The Testing of God's Son (Matt 4:1-11 & Par)*.[188] In this intriguing monograph he is again concerned with Jewish/Christian parallels. However, here he does not focus on the history of tradition, but on the composition of midrash—on the parallel between Jewish midrash and Matthew's account of the temptation of Jesus. In the introduction he outlines the purpose of his study: to trace the origin and development of the temptation narrative and to explicate its meaning. Gerhardsson believes the two versions of the narrative, Matthew-Luke and Mark, are two versions of one tradition. He supposes (without providing much evidence) that Mark is the abbreviation of the longer and older tradition found in Matthew (not Luke).

Gerhardsson's point of departure is his conviction that the temptation narrative is *haggadic midrash*. The tempter bases his arguments on Scripture and Jesus answers with quotations from Deuteronomy 6–8. This text, according to Gerhardsson's exegesis, relates how God had allowed his "son" (Israel) to wander in the desert for forty years so that he might be tested. The temptation account is "a narrative whose every detail bears the stamp of the late-Jewish (and early Christian) scribal tradition."[189] It is an example of an early "Christian midrash."

Gerhardsson proceeds to investigate the temptation narrative (Matt 4:1-11) in relation to Deuteronomy 6–8. At the outset Jesus, the Son of God, is led into the wilderness by the Spirit of God. Gerhardsson observes that, in the Judaism of the time, negative actions of God were often attributed to Satan. Thus the temptation of Jesus, like the testing of Israel, is actually a testing by God. After forty days of fasting (a motif with OT parallels), Jesus is hungry (the first temptation). This recalls the account of the wilderness wandering (Deut 8:2-6), when the people did not trust YHWH to provide food. Gerhardsson sees in this a lack of faith and the divided or hardened heart. Whereas Israel failed the test, Jesus resists the temptation and, quoting Deut 8:3, expresses his trust in "every word that comes from the mouth of God."

Gerhardsson believes the issue of the second temptation is divine protection. During the wilderness wanderings YHWH protected Israel from snakes and scorpions (Deut 8:15). Gerhardsson detects this motif throughout the OT and notes that in the exodus Yhwh bore Israel on "eagles' wings" (Exod 19:4). He points out that the temple was the place of protection *par excellence*. This is expressed in Psalm 91, the very text Satan quotes—a text that, according to Gerhardsson, the rabbis associated with the wilderness wandering. He insists that πτερύγιον, the word usually translated "pinnacle," means "wing," and symbolizes the protective function of the temple. Satan's temptation, according to Gerhardsson, admonishes Jesus to endanger himself by testing God's promise of protection. Jesus replies by quoting Deut 6:16, "Do not put the Lord your God to the test."

In reaction to the third temptation, Jesus cites Deut 6:13, evidence that convinces Gerhardsson that the themes of Deuteronomy are still in view. He imagines that the transport of Jesus to a high mountain recalls Moses on Mount Nebo. From that high point Moses viewed the promised land—a vision that, Gerhardsson says, the rabbis understood to include the whole world. Gerhardsson also calls attention to the references to the high places that were scenes of pagan worship and idolatry. The temptation, therefore, is to seek for worldly riches (mammon) and to succumb to idolatry (the worship of Satan), a temptation Jesus soundly rejects.

In summary, Gerhardsson asks if the link between the temptation narrative and Deuteronomy 6–8 has a fundamental theme. He finds the answer in the love command of the Shema (Deut 6:5). Echoing the method of the rabbis, the narrator of the temptation account interprets the threefold command of love. In the first temptation Jesus resists the temptation of the divided heart: he loves with the whole heart. In the second he resists the temptation to protect his life: he loves with the whole soul. In the third he resists mammon: he loves with his whole might (property). Gerhardsson concludes that the narrator was an early Christian scribe with knowledge of the Scriptures and familiarity with the exegetical tactics of the Pharisees. He is convinced that "the creator of the temptation narrative must have been highly educated in the Jewish (pharisaic) learning of his time. One result of our study is the conviction that *the young Christian church numbered among its ranks more that one learned ex-pharisee of the stature of Paul.*"[190] In contrast to Gerhardsson's earlier work, this book appears to call attention to the creativity of the early church, not to memorized tradition from Jesus.

Gerhardsson published two other books, not primarily concerned with tradition, that are worthy of review. His *The Mighty Acts of Jesus According to Matthew* is an analysis of the miracle narratives in the first Gospel.[191] In the first part of the book he investigates the Matthean accounts of the "therapeutic activity" of Jesus. Gerhardsson's analysis attends to such matters as the persons, the places, and the diseases mentioned in Matthew's summaries. In overview, he notes that attention is focused on Jesus as the one who performs the healings; the disciples rarely appear. Gerhardsson proceeds to review the individual pericopes in which the healing miracles of Jesus are presented. He lists a total of fourteen examples in Matthew and offers some generalizations. The descriptions of the diseases include both general accounts and specific diagnoses. As to the persons, Gerhardsson notes a variety, but observes that Jesus is always the leading actor. The principal themes include the power of Jesus and the faith of those seeking help.

Gerhardsson turns to the "non-therapeutic miracles," which are, in his view, improperly designated "nature miracles." He finds six clear examples in Matthew of this type of mighty deed. The *personae* are Jesus and, in the main, the disciples. As to the meaning of these miracles, Gerhardsson writes: "It seems to me that Matthew has seen these miraculous events as revelations, clarifying mysteries of the Reign for the disciples."[192] Gerhardsson analyzes each of the pericopes. For example, in regard to the stilling of the storm he finds two features of the narrative to be significant: the plea of the disciples for help and their confession at the conclusion. This miracle, like all the others of this type, reveals the power of Jesus and reflects the christological interests of the narrators.

Gerhardsson draws some illuminating comparisons between the two types of miracle: The therapeutic respond to a request; the non-therapeutic are instigated by Jesus. The therapeutic are public; the non-therapeutic are faith experiences of the church. The non-therapeutic are more difficult to accept as historical and more likely to be seen as symbolic. After a discussion of the miracle texts that reflect resistance and controversy, Gerhardsson concludes, "It is obvious that the driving force behind Matthew's interpretation and presentation of Jesus' mighty acts is the endeavour to reach a positive understanding of the mysteries around Jesus and his *exousia* and the desire to teach the community about them—and not apologetic intentions."[193]

In sum, Birger Gerhardsson's major contribution to NT research is his innovative appraisal of early Christian tradition, an area in which his approach has enjoyed a revival.[194] However, Gerhardsson appears to have begun with a view of how rabbinic tradition was transmitted and then imposed that view on the NT texts. The question, of course, is whether Gerhardsson's approach provides a better method for understanding the history of Jesus and early Christianity than the model offered by form criticism.[195] Gerhardsson argues that form criticism attributes too much to the *Sitz-im-Leben* for the creation and shaping of tradition, and it attributes too little to the role of special persons in the transmission of the tradition. One can certainly agree that much tradition goes back to Jesus, but surely not all. One can recognize the role of leaders like Peter, but some members of the Twelve are virtually "anonymous," and what of the five hundred faceless witnesses of the resurrection? Do the Twelve really constitute an official "collegium," in view of the evidence that the Seven broke with them and became the leaders of the more significant mission? There can be no doubt that the eyewitnesses remembered what Jesus said and did, but is it realistic to suppose that Jesus repeated the words of institution four times? There is the suggestion, notably in Mark, that the disciples didn't even "get" it, let alone memorize it.

For all of his insightful analysis of early Christian tradition and his commendable command of the Jewish sources, Gerhardsson's main weakness may be his failure to take the eschatological setting of early Christianity with adequate seriousness. One might quip that Jesus didn't have time to repeat his message again and again. The sort of tradition the rabbis transmitted was for the long haul—for an extended earthly history. Jesus, it seems, thought that one should not worry about tomorrow.

SUMMARY

Little needs to be said beyond the summaries that have been offered in this chapter in regard to the work of each of the scholars. Barrett and Dunn develop their research along the well-established lines of historical criticism.

They demonstrate skill in all the major elements of the critical method: text criticism, linguistic analysis, knowledge of the context, theological sensitivity. With Dunn the observer is struck with the magnitude of his work, the tireless energy and discipline, the mastery of secondary sources. In this regard he is reminiscent of Brown and Meier. With Gerhardsson the reviewer recognizes that, even after a couple of centuries, new and imaginative hypotheses are possible. On common ground, all three of these scholars tend toward conservative conclusions—certainly when compared with the radical criticism of Bultmann, the Bultmann school (especially the Americans), and above all, the Jesus Seminar. Barrett and Dunn have a high view of biblical authority, and with Gerhardsson a new method is devised to promote the reliability of the gospel tradition. Related to this conservatism—and typical of conservative trends in the history of research—is the stress on Jewish rather than Hellenistic backgrounds. For Dunn, Paul is a champion of "covenant nomism," and for Gerhardsson, Jesus, the disciples, and Paul appear in the garb of the rabbis. That these views would not remain unchallenged will be apparent in the following chapter.

Notes

1. *HNTR* 2: 66–84.

2. For biographical information see John Painter, "Barrett, C(harles) K(ingsley) (1917–)," *DMBI*, 155–61; K. H. Kuhn, "Introduction," in *Paul and Paulinism: Essays in Honour of C. K. Barrett*, ed. Morna D. Hooker and S. G. Wilson (London: SPCK, 1982), 1–3; John Reumann, "Introduction," in C. K. Barrett, *Biblical Problems and Biblical Preaching* (Philadelphia: Fortress Press, 1964), vii–xii. A select bibliography is included in Painter's article and the complete bibliography through 1980 is listed in *Paul and Paulinism*, 373–81.

3. *DMBI*, 155.

4. C. K. Barrett, *The Holy Spirit and the Gospel Tradition* (London: SPCK, 1947, repr. 1954).

5. Ibid., 24.

6. Ibid., 45.

7. Ibid., 93.

8. Ibid. 135.

9. Ibid., 155.

10. C. K. Barrett, *The Gospel According to John: An Introduction with Commentary and Notes on the Greek Text*, 2d ed. (Philadelphia: Westminster, 1978).

11. Ibid., 5.

12. Ibid., 34.

13. Ibid., 54.

14. Ibid., 99.

15. Ibid., 133.

16. Ibid., 189.

17. Ibid., 193.

18. Ibid., 388.

19. Ibid., 395.

20. Ibid., 398. Barrett also published *The Gospel of John and Judaism*, trans. D. Moody Smith (London: SPCK, 1975). In this book Barrett contends that the Fourth Gospel was influenced by both Jewish and Hellenistic backgrounds. As to the former he says: "The fact is that this gospel contains Judaism, non-Judaism and anti-Judaism" (p. 71).

21. C. K. Barrett, *Paul: An Introduction to His Thought* (Louisville: Westminster John Knox, 1994).

22. Ibid., 22.

23. Ibid., 44.

24. Ibid.

25. Ibid., 174–75.

26. C. K. Barrett, *A Commentary on the Epistle to the Romans*, HNTC (New York: Harper, 1957).

27. Ibid., 76. Barrett also produced a work for the general reader, *Reading Through Romans* (Philadelphia: Fortress Press, 1977).

28. C. K. Barrett, *A Commentary on the First Epistle to the Corinthians*, HNTC (New York: Harper, 1968).

29. Ibid., 255.

30. C. K. Barrett, *A Commentary on the Second Epistle to the Corinthians*, HNTC (New York: Harper, 1973).

31. See Barrett's "Paul's Opponents in 2 Corinthians," in *Essays on Paul* (Philadelphia: Westminster, 1982), 60–86. For a more recent collection of Barrett's essays see *On Paul: Aspects of His Life, Work and Influence in the Early Church* (London: T & T Clark, 2003).

32. *Second Epistle to the Corinthians*, 163.

33. Ibid., 175.

34. C. K. Barrett, *Freedom and Obligation: A Study of Galatians* (Philadelphia: Westminster, 1985). Two chapters discuss the theology of freedom; two discuss the ethics of obligation.

35. C. K. Barrett, *From First Adam to Last: A Study in Pauline Theology* (New York: Scribner's, 1962).

36. Ibid., 118. One of Barrett's most useful publications is *New Testament Background: Selected Documents*, rev. ed. (San Francisco: Harper and Row, 1989). The book is a collection of primary sources that illustrate the world of religion and thought into which Christianity was born.

37. C. K. Barrett, *A Critical and Exegetical Commentary on The Acts of the Apostles*, 2 vols., ICC 30 (London: T & T Clark, 2004). Readers who find this commentary difficult to use will welcome Barrett's *The Acts of the Apostles: A Shorter Commentary* (London: T & T Clark, 2002). This volume, which totals 434 pages (as against 1,272 in the two-volume ed.), eliminates references to Greek and other technical details from the notes. Instead, the phrases from the text, in English, are printed in bold type. For the overall understanding of Barrett's interpretation, little is lost by this shorter edition. He also published a small book, *Luke the Historian in Recent Study* (London: Epworth, 1961).

38. *Critical and Exegetical Commentary on The Acts*, 141.

39. Ibid., 443.

40. *Critical and Exegetical Commentary on The Acts* 2: xxxv.

41. Ibid., xlv.

42. Ibid., lxxxvii.

43. Ibid., 715.

44. C. K. Barrett, *Jesus and the Gospel Tradition* (London: SPCK, 1967).

45. Ibid., 34.

46. Ibid., 67.

47. Ibid., 100.

48. On Barrett's concern with church and ministry, see his *Church, Ministry, and Sacraments in the New Testament* (Grand Rapids: Eerdmans, 1985). Also important for Barrett's understanding

of ministry and church is his book, *The Signs of an Apostle* (London: Epworth, 19970). Collections of Barrett's shorter works can be found in his *New Testament Essays* (London: SPCK, 1972) and *Jesus and the Word: And Other Essays*, PMS (Allison Park, PA: Pickwick, 1995).

49. Graham Stanton, "Profile: James Dunn," *EpRev* 27 (2000): 28–37, at 29.

50. For biography see Stanton, "Profile," 28–37; R. Barry Matlock, "Dunn, James Douglas Grant (1939–)," *DBCI*, 76–77; James Dunn, "Personal Introduction," in James D. G. Dunn, *Jesus, Paul, and the Gospels* (Grand Rapids: Eerdmans, 2011), xii–xvii; Richard B. Hays, "Foreword," in *Jesus and Paul: Global Perspectives in Honor of James D. G. Dunn for his 70th Birthday*, ed. B. J. Oropeza, Charles K. Robertson, and Douglas C. Mohrmann (London: T & T Clark, 2009), xi–xvi; "Foreword by N. T. Wright," ibid., xv–xix; "Editors' Preface," ibid., xxi–xxiv.

51. Wright, "Foreword," *Jesus and Paul*, xviii.

52. The summary of Dunn's work presented in this book is restricted to his major books. A collection of his important essays is found in his *The Christ and the Spirit*: vol. 1, *Christology*; vol. 2, *Pneumatology* (Grand Rapids: Eerdmans, 1998). Dunn's *The Living Word*, 2nd ed. (Minneapolis: Fortress Press, 2009; 1st ed. 1988) is a collection of lectures from various venues directed to the interpretation and authority of the NT. An example of Dunn's concern to communicate the NT message to the general reader is seen in his *Jesus' Call to Discipleship* (Cambridge: Cambridge University Press, 1992). For a bibliography of Dunn's research see "List of Publications by James D. G. Dunn," in *The Holy Spirit and Christian Origins: Essays in Honor of James D. G. Dunn*, ed. Graham N. Stanton, Bruce W. Longenecker, and Stephen C. Barton (Grand Rapids: Eerdmans, 2004), 360–75; this includes publications from 1970 through 2003, an incomplete list since Dunn's works continued to flow from the presses beyond the first decade of the twenty-first century.

53. James D. G. Dunn, *The Partings of the Ways: Between Christianity and Judaism and their Significance for the Character of Christianity*, 2nd ed. (London: SCM, 2006), xxxi.

54. James D. G. Dunn, *Baptism and the Holy Spirit: A Re-examination of the New Testament Teaching on the Gift of the Spirit in Relation to Pentecostalism Today*, STB, 2nd ser. 15 (London: SCM, 1970).

55. Ibid., 170.

56. James D. G. Dunn, *Jesus and the Spirit: A Study of the Religious and Charismatic Experience of Jesus and the First Christians as Reflected in the New Testament* (Philadelphia: Westminster, 1975).

57. Ibid., 61.

58. Ibid., 298.

59. Ibid., 349.

60. James D. G. Dunn, *Unity and Diversity in the New Testament. An Inquiry into the Character of Earliest Christianity*, 3rd. ed. (London: SCM, 2006).

61. Ibid., 6.

62. Ibid., 27.

63. Ibid., 247.

64. Ibid., 312.

65. Ibid.,354.

66. Ibid.,367.

67. Ibid.,400.

68. Ibid., 433.

69. James D. G. Dunn, *Christology in the Making: A New Testament Inquiry into the Origins of the Doctrine of the Incarnation*, 2nd ed. (Grand Rapids: Eerdmans, 1989).

70. Ibid., 5.

71. Ibid., 10.

72. Ibid., 22.

73. Ibid., 32.

74. Ibid., 35.

75. Ibid., 55.

76. Ibid., 59.

77. Ibid., 81.

78. Ibid., 119.

79. Ibid., 176.

80. Ibid., 212.

81. Ibid., 249.

82. Ibid., 256.

83. Ibid., 262.

84. The original lecture is reprinted in Dunn's *The New Perspective on Paul*, rev. ed. (Grand Rapids: Eerdmans, 2008), 99–120, and the later essay appears for the first time in the same volume, pp. 1–97. The 2008 edition of *The New Perspective*, although billed as "revised," appears to be only a paperback reprint of the original: *The New Perspective on Paul: Collected Essays*, WUNT 185 (Tübingen: Mohr Siebeck, 2005). The "new perspective" on Paul released a flood of publications. See the overview in Kent L. Yinger, *The New Perspective on Paul: An Introduction* (Eugene, OR: Cascade, 2011). Some of the insights of the new perspective were anticipated by Krister Stendahl in his famous essay, "The Apostle Paul and the Introspective Conscience of the West," in *Paul Among Jews and Gentiles* (Philadelphia: Fortress, 1976), 78–96. Dunn's view is criticized by Francis Watson (*Paul, Judaism, and the Gentiles: Beyond the New Perspective*, rev. ed. [Grand Rapids: Eerdmans, 2007], 2–21), and even more sharply by R. Barry Matlock ("Sins of the Flesh and Suspicious Minds: Dunn's New Theology of Paul," *JSNT* 72 [1998]: 67– 90).

85. See pp. 286–89 above.

86. *New Perspective*, 32.

87. Ibid., 97. For some readers, Dunn's idea of Pauline openness vs. Jewish exclusivism may not represent a great advance over the traditional view; see Matlock, "Sins of the Flesh," 72–86.

88. James D. G. Dunn, *Romans 1–8*, WBC 38A; *Romans 9–16*, WBC 38B (Dallas: Word, 1988).

89. *Romans 1–8*, 47.

90. Ibid., 164.

91. Ibid., 167.

92. Ibid., 171.

93. Ibid., 178.

94. Ibid., 179.

95. See pp. 318–19 above.

96. *Romans 1–8*, 407.

97. *Romans 9–16*, 681.

98. Ibid., 691.

99. Ibid., 691.

100. Ibid., 694. Five years after his *Romans*, Dunn published *The Epistle to the Galatians*, BNTC (Peabody, MA: Hendrickson, 1993). He adopts the "south Galatian hypothesis." He sees in Galatians a rerun of the battles fought in Jerusalem (2:1-10) and Antioch (2:11-14). In the same year Dunn published *The Theology of Paul's Letter to the Galatians* (Cambridge: Cambridge University Press, 1993), a short book that presents in systematic form the exegetical results of the commentary. Dunn also published an important commentary on the Greek texts of Colossians and Philemon (*The Epistles to the Colossians and Philemon*, NIGTC [Grand Rapids: Eerdmans, 1996]). In discussing the theology of Paul, Dunn frequently cites material from Colossians. Thus his conclusion in the introduction is somewhat surprising: "I have to confirm the strong likelihood that the letter comes from a hand other than Paul's" (p. 35). Dunn also published a commentary on Acts: *The Acts of the Apostles* (Valley Forge, PA: Trinity Press International, 1996) that tends to harmonize material from Acts with the data from the Pauline epistles. Dunn also published a short commentary on 1 Corinthians: *1 Corinthians* (London: T & T Clark, 2003), originally published in 1995 by Sheffield Academic Press.

101. James D. G. Dunn, *The Partings of the Ways: Between Christianity and Judaism and their Significance for the Character of Christianity*, 2nd ed. (London: SCM, 2006). This book should not be confused with *Jews and Christians: The Parting of the Ways, A.D. 70–135*, ed. James D. G. Dunn, WUNT 66 (Tübingen: J. C. B. Mohr [Paul Siebeck], 1992); paperback reprint Eerdmans, 1999. The latter is a collection of papers presented at the Second Durham–Tübingen Research Symposium on Earliest Christianity and Judaism, held at Durham in September 1989. The book reviewed above was anticipated by a collection of earlier essays, *Jesus, Paul, and the Law: Studies in Mark and Galatians* (Louisville: Westminster John Knox, 1990). Since much of Dunn's work has concentrated on Paul, the two essays on Mark are of special interest.

102. *Partings*, 70.

103. Ibid., 94.

104. Ibid., 114.

105. Ibid., 153.

106. Ibid., 183.

107. Ibid., 214.

108. Ibid., 218.

109. Ibid., 232.

110. Ibid., 251. An important contribution to the discussion of this issue is Dunn's *Did the First Christians Worship Jesus? The New Testament Evidence* (Louisville: Westminster John Knox, 2010). Here he observes that Jesus is the one through whom worshipers come to God, but insists that veneration of Jesus was not a denial of monotheism. He concludes, "No, by and large, the first Christians did not worship Jesus as such" (p. 150).

111. *Partings*, 318.

112. Ibid., 337.

113. Ibid., 364.

114. James D. G. Dunn, *The Theology of Paul the Apostle* (Grand Rapids: Eerdmans, 1998). Dunn's interest and competence in biblical theology is demonstrated in James D. G. Dunn and James P. Mackey, *New Testament Theology in Dialogue* (London: SPCK, 1987), a dialogue between Dunn (from the perspective of NT theology) and Mackey (from the perspective of systematic theology), taking up the issues of Christology and ministry as test cases.

115. For problems resulting from this preliminary decision see Leander E. Keck, "James D. G. Dunn's *The Theology of Paul the Apostle*," *SJT* 53 (2000): 380–89.

116. *Theology of Paul*, 24–25.

117. Ibid., 181.

118. Ibid., 206.

119. Ibid., 223.

120. Ibid., 379.

121. See pp. 447–49 above.

122. *Theology of Paul*, 729.

123. James D. G. Dunn, *Christianity in the Making*, vol. 1: *Jesus Remembered* (Grand Rapids: Eerdmans, 2003). Dunn had written much about Jesus in his earlier works, but nothing so direct and extensive. Earlier short works on Jesus include his *The Evidence for Jesus* (Philadelphia: Westminster, 1985), a book that argues that "Christianity has nothing to fear from scholarship!" (p. 103).

124. For a succinct rehearsal of this issue see Dunn's essay, "Remembering Jesus: How the Quest of the Historical Jesus Lost Its Way," in *The Historical Jesus: Five Views*, ed. James K. Beilby and Paul Rhodes Eddy (Downers Grove, IL: IVP Academic, 2009), 199–225.

125. See pp. 136–37 above.

126. *Remembering Jesus*, 122.

127. Ibid., 333.

128. Ibid., 335.

129. Ibid., 610.

130. Ibid., 704.

131. Ibid., 738.

132. Ibid., 822.

133. Ibid., 861–62.

134. Ibid., 878.

135. See Dunn's *A New Perspective on Jesus: What the Quest for the Historical Jesus Missed*, ASBT (Grand Rapids: Baker, 2005).

136. *Jesus Remembered*, 882.

137. Ibid., 893.

138. Anton Fridrichsen, *The Apostle and His Message* (Uppsala: Lundequist, 1947).

139. Anton Fridrichsen, *The Problem of Miracle in Primitive Christianity*, trans. Roy A. Harrisville and John S. Hanson (Minneapolis: Augsburg, 1972).

140. For overviews of Gerhardsson's life and work see Werner H. Kelber, "The Work of Birger Gerhardsson in Perspective," in *Jesus and Memory: Traditions in Oral and Scribal Perspective*, ed. Werner H. Kelber and Samuel Byrskog (Waco, TX: Baylor University Press, 2009), 173–206; Samuel Byrskog, "Introduction," in ibid., 1–20; Ben F. Meyer, "Some Consequences of Birger Gerhardsson's Account of the Origins of the Gospel Tradition," in *Jesus and the Oral Gospel*, ed. Henry Wansbrough, JSNTSup 64 (Sheffield: JSOT Press, 1991), 424–40; Peter H. Davids, "The Gospels and Jewish Tradition: Twenty Years After Gerhardsson," in *Gospel Perspectives: Studies of History and Tradition in the Four Gospels*, vol. 1, ed. R. T. France and David Wenham (Sheffield: JSOT Press, 1980), 75–99.

141. Christopher Tuckett, "Form Criticism," in *Jesus and Memory*, 21.

142. Birger Gerhardsson, *Memory and Manuscript: Oral Tradition and Written Transmission in Rabbinic Judaism and Early Christianity*, trans. Eric J. Sharpe (Grand Rapids: Eerdmans, 1998; first ed. ASNU 22 [Lund: Gleerup, 1961]).

143. Ibid., 14–15.

144. Ibid., 29.

145. Ibid., 30.

146. Ibid., 55.

147. Ibid., 111.

148. Ibid., 133.

149. Ibid., 186.

150. Ibid., 227.

151. Ibid., 234.

152. Ibid., 241.

153. Ibid., 251.

154. Ibid., 297.

155. Ibid., 321.

156. Ibid., 328.

157. Ibid., 335.

158. Birger Gerhardsson, *Tradition and Transmission in Early Christianity*, trans. Eric J. Sharpe, ConBNT 20 (Lund: Gleerup, 1964); this monograph is included as an appendix in the reprint of *Memory and Manuscript* (1998).

159. *Tradition and Transmission*, 21.

160. Ibid., 35.

161. Ibid., 43.

162. Birger Gerhardsson, *The Reliability of the Gospel Tradition* (Peabody, MA: Hendrickson, 2001).

163. Birger Gerhardsson, *Die Anfänge der Evangelientradition*, Glauben und Denken 919 (Wuppertal: Brockhaus, 1977).

164. Birger Gerhardsson, *The Origins of the Gospel Tradition* (Philadelphia: Fortress Press, 1979).

165. *Reliability*, 1.

166. Ibid., 2.

167. Ibid., 9.

168. Ibid., 16.

169. Ibid., 29.

170. Ibid., 42.

171. Ibid., 45.

172. Ibid., 50.

173. Ibid., 57.

174. The papers from the symposium were published: Peter Stuhlmacher, ed., *Das Evangelium und die Evangelien: Vorträge vom Tübinger Symposium 1982*, WUNT 28 (Tübingen: Mohr, 1983); ET: *The Gospel and the Gospels* (Grand Rapids: Eerdmans, 1991).

175. "The Path of Gospel Tradition," *Reliability*, 59–87.

176. Ibid., 62.

177. Ibid., 87.

178. *Reliability*, 89–143.

179. Ibid., 103.

180. Ibid., 141.

181. Ibid., 143.

182. In *Jesus and the Oral Gospel*, ed. Henry Wansbrough, JSNTSup 64 (Sheffield: JSOT Press, 1991), 266–309.

183. "Illuminating the Kingdom," 269.

184. Ibid., 297.

185. Ibid., 298–99.

186. Ibid., 303.

187. Ibid., 309.

188. Birger Gerhardsson, *The Testing of God's Son (Matt 4:1-11 & Par). An Analysis of an Early Christian Midrash*, trans. John Toy, ConBNT 2:1 (Lund: Gleerup, 1966). The work was designed to include eleven chapters, but only four have been published; this material was published in connection with Gerhardsson's application for the chair in exegetical theology at Lund in 1963.

189. Ibid., 11.

190. Ibid., 80. Gerhardsson's concern with the Shema is further developed in his *The Shema in the New Testament: Deut 6:4-5* (Lund: Novapress, 1996); this is a collection of seventeen of Gerhardsson's articles published earlier in various venues.

191. Birger Gerhardsson, *The Mighty Acts of Jesus According to Matthew*, Scripta Minora Regiae Societatis Humaniorum Litterarum Lundensis (Lund: Gleerup, 1979). Gerhardsson understood this research to be spadework for a commentary on Matthew, a project that apparently was never completed.

192. *Mighty Acts*, 54.

193. Ibid., 79–80. Besides his work on early Christian tradition, Gerhardsson also published *The Ethos of the Bible*, trans. Stephen Westerholm (Philadelphia: Fortress Press, 1981). In this short book Gerhardsson finds the center of NT ethics in the command of love.

194. This is seen in the re-issuing of *Memory and Manuscript*. Also of note is the book, *Traditions in Oral and Scribal Perspective*, edited by Werner Kelber and Samuel Byrskog. Kelber, himself an expert on orality, praises Gerhardsson's emphasis on oral tradition. Although he is grateful for Kelber's kind words, Gerhardsson rejects Kelber's fundamental position. "The society where Jesus appeared . . . was no preliterary society" (*Reality of the Gospel Tradition*, 115). See also (earlier in this chapter) Dunn's commendation of Gerhardsson's work. However, Dunn does not agree that the gospel tradition depicts Jesus as teaching by repetition or that early Christian tradition had the fixity Gerhardsson assumes.

195. For a vigorous affirmative answer see Ben F. Meyer, "Some Consequences of Birger Gerhardsson's Account of the Origins of the Gospel Tradition," in *Jesus and the Oral Gospel*, 424–40.

11

Critical, Exegetical, and Theological Accomplishments: North America

The American ascendancy in the political and cultural arena is reflected in biblical studies. Germany is no longer the center of NT research. European scholars have joined the Society of Biblical Literature and cross the sea to participate in the annual meetings. American graduate students no longer assume that at least a year of study at Göttingen, Heidelberg, or Tübingen is necessary. Graduate schools in America—notably at Harvard, Yale, and Chicago (and Princeton Theological Seminary and Duke and others) with fine faculties and superb libraries—have made notable advances, often assisted by scholars imported from Germany, Great Britain, and Scandinavia. This shift from east to west is not necessarily salutary. American students, by and large, are not rigorously trained in the classical languages; some do not study Greek until seminary, and that restricted to Koinē. Also, by missing the opportunity to study abroad, many do not gain competence in the European languages so essential for the understanding of the history and current state of the discipline. Anyone who supposes that NT research has withered in Germany need only peruse the catalogues from Mohr Siebeck and Vandenhoeck & Ruprecht.

The arrangement of material in this chapter follows the order of the historical development of NT research in America. The work was accomplished primarily (not exclusively) in academic centers, in the order: Harvard, Yale, and Chicago. The scholars reviewed, then, are associated in some way, as professors or students, with these universities. It is important to note that two of the scholars reviewed are Germans who migrated to America, and that the other three all studied in Germany.

Harvard: Schüssler Fiorenza

Elisabeth Schüssler Fiorenza (1938–)

Life and Early Work

Elisabeth Schüssler Fiorenza is unique in this volume.[1] She attacks the historical critical method; she reflects the variety of new methods that emerged in the last half of the century; she represents feminist biblical criticism, an approach that has become increasingly important. Elisabeth Schüssler was born into a Catholic family in a village of a German section of Romania. Since Romania had sided with Russia, her family fled to Hungary, later to Austria, and finally settled in central Germany.[2] She remembers the privations of war: begging for food, witnessing the devastation of Würzburg. After graduating from the classical gymnasium—exceptional for a girl from the working class—Schüssler entered the University of Würzburg (1958); she was the first woman to enroll in the course in theological studies there. She graduated summa cum laude with the licentiate in theology in 1963.[3] Schüssler began doctoral studies at Würzburg under Rudolf Schnackenburg, who refused to award her a scholarship because "as a woman you have no future in theology."[4] Nevertheless, she was granted a research assistantship at the University of Münster, and Schnackenburg continued as her dissertation advisor. Since she had no chance for a theological teaching position in Germany, Schüssler Fiorenza moved with her husband Francis Fiorenza to the US (1970), where she was appointed to the faculty at Notre Dame, eventually was granted tenure (1975), and was promoted to full professor in 1980. At Notre Dame her avowal of a feminist theology of liberation was not adequately appreciated, so she moved to the Episcopal Divinity School in Cambridge (1984) and later to Harvard (1988). About her experience at Harvard, Schüssler Fiorenza has reflected, "Ironically, of all the faculty here, besides Harvey Cox, I am probably best known around the world, yet I have very much been relegated to the sidelines by the politics of the school."[5] Nevertheless, at Harvard Divinity School Schüssler Fiorenza was named Krister Stendahl Professor of Divinity. She served as visiting professor at, among other places, Union Theological Seminary (New York), the University of Tübingen, and the University of Heidelberg. She was the first woman to be elected president of the SBL. At age 65 she characterized her role in America as that of a "resident alien," a "migrant worker."[6]

Before the development of her distinctive feminist hermeneutic, Schüssler Fiorenza's work exemplifies her training and skill in historical-critical NT research.[7] But even there, hints of things to come were already evident. In her thesis for the licentiate Schüssler Fiorenza investigated the role of women in the pastoral work of the church and engaged in exegesis from her own perspective. Also, her doctoral dissertation demonstrates a concern with the implicit democracy of the concept of the priesthood of believers. At the same time, the dissertation offers a brilliant display of historical-critical analysis of texts from the book of Revelation.

The dissertation, *Priester für Gott*, begins with a review of research on the problem of the understanding of the priesthood in the NT.[8] The main section of the dissertation is devoted to the interpretation of the concept of the priesthood of the redeemed as presented in the Apocalypse. In the first part of this section Schüssler Fiorenza investigates the texts of Rev 1:6; 5:10; and 20:6 and their background in the OT. She begins with a text-critical analysis of these texts and their relation to Exod 19:6. She proceeds to a discussion of the ideas of the priestly kingdom and the eschatological people of God in Exod 19:4-6 and Isa 61:6. In the second part of the main section she investigates the idea of the priesthood and the royal rule (*Königsherrschaft*) of the redeemed in the present. Here she presents a form-critical and tradition-historical analysis of Rev 1:4-8 and an investigation of the author's redactional reworking of the traditional baptismal confession. In the third part Schüssler Fiorenza investigates the priesthood and rule of the redeemed in the eschatological future. This involves the messianic rule of the priests of God as seen in Rev 20:4-6 and the eschatological reign of the servants of God and their eschatological worship of God (Rev 22:3-5).

The dissertation concludes with a summary of the results. According to Schüssler Fiorenza's research, the author of Revelation has reworked the early Christian tradition concerning the royal priesthood. This reworking, she believes, is shaped by the cultic and lordship ideas of the author's own time. The author warns against an enthusiastic misunderstanding that salvation is already realized, and admonishes the Christians of Asia Minor to worship God and the Lord Jesus Christ in face of the imperial cult and pagan syncretism. According to Schüssler Fiorenza, the author, by reworking the tradition of the baptismal confession, views the redeemed as already appointed priests who will function in the eschatological future. Schüssler Fiorenza anticipates later themes of her work when she says that "the author of Rev in his argument seeks to present more strongly the ruling-political rather than the priestly-cultic element."[9]

IN MEMORY OF HER

Schüssler Fiorenza's most important work is *In Memory of Her*, first published in 1983 and eventually translated into at least ten languages.[10] The title is inspired by the story of the woman who anointed Jesus. Although her name has been forgotten, "what she has done will be told in remembrance of her" (Mark 14:9). In the introduction Schüssler Fiorenza sets forth her purpose. "The explorations of this book have two goals: they attempt to reconstruct early Christian history as women's history not only to restore women's stories to early Christian history but also to reclaim this history as the history of women and men."[11] Schüssler Fiorenza also stresses the importance of methodological issues. She calls for a paradigm shift in biblical interpretation from the androcentric, male-dominated reading to a feminist perspective that can reclaim the role of women in the history of early Christianity.

The first part of the book is devoted to the explication of this methodological shift. Schüssler Fiorenza proposes a critical feminist hermeneutics. She begins with an analysis of current models: the doctrinal, the positivist historical, the dialogical-hermeneutical, and liberation hermeneutics. She points out that already in the nineteenth century Elizabeth Cady Stanton had recognized biblical interpretation as a political act.[12] Schüssler Fiorenza also reviews varieties of feminist hermeneutics she finds inadequate, for example, those who follow a neo-orthodox model (Letty Russell, Rosemary Radford Ruether, and Phyllis Trible). This model, according to Schüssler Fiorenza, fails to confront the religious-political legitimization of patriarchal oppressions and tends to use the feminist perspective to rehabilitate the authority of the Bible. Instead, Schüssler Fiorenza calls for a hermeneutics that recognizes that the Bible itself is androcentric—a hermeneutics that counters the oppression of women and recognizes the socio-political context of biblical study. "A feminist critical hermeneutics must therefore move from androcentric texts to their social-historical contexts."[13]

In response to this demand, Schüssler Fiorenza promotes her own methodology. "If the locus of revelation is not the androcentric text but the life and ministry of Jesus and the movement of women and men called forth by him, then we must develop critical-historical methods for feminist readings of the biblical texts."[14] These methods must be sensitive to the "silence" of the texts—the silence about woman that has been perpetuated by androcentric translations and interpretations. "A theoretical model for the reconstruction of women's early Christian history, therefore, must do justice to the fact that early Christian women, *as women*, were part of a submerged group, and *as Christians* they were part of an emergent group that was not yet recognized by the dominant patriarchal society and culture."[15]

In the second part of *In Memory of Her*, Schüssler Fiorenza turns to the NT texts and interprets early Christian history as "the History of Discipleship of Equals." This history begins with the Jesus movement, which Schüssler Fiorenza identifies as a renewal movement within Judaism. All Jewish people, according to Schüssler Fiorenza, were concerned with the reign of God and the hope of liberation from Rome. Within this setting, Jesus had a vision of the *basileia* as the praxis of inclusive wholeness. Schüssler Fiorenza believes that Jesus stressed the idea of the kingdom as present, celebrated at the festive table to which all (including women) were invited. The *basileia* came to tax collectors, sinners, and prostitutes, that is, women of low social status. Schüssler Fiorenza characterizes the God of Jesus as the Divine Sophia, the God of goodness and unlimited grace. "To sum up, the Palestinian Jesus movement understands the ministry and mission of Jesus as the prophet and child of Sophia sent to announce that God is the God of the poor and heavy laden, of the outcasts and those who suffer injustice."[16]

Like the woman looking eagerly for the lost coin, Schüssler Fiorenza searches the androcentric texts for signs of liberation from patriarchal structures. She sees in the mention of "mother" and "sisters" in Mark 3:31-35 the implication that women were followers of Jesus. She hears in Matt 23:9 ("call no one your father on earth") a rejection of patriarchal power. "Thus liberation from patriarchal structures is not only explicitly articulated by Jesus but is in fact at the heart of the proclamation of the *basileia* of God."[17] Schüssler Fiorenza extols the importance of women as witnesses to the empty tomb and the resurrection of Jesus.

Turning to the early Christian missionary movement, Schüssler Fiorenza believes the importance of women can be detected in the Pauline epistles. Paul refers to women as his coworkers. Phoebe is a *diakonos* (Rom 16:1) and Junia is recognized as an apostle (Rom 16:7).

> The Pauline literature and Acts still allow us to recognize that women were among the most prominent missionaries and leaders in the early Christian movement. They were apostles and ministers like Paul, and some were his co-workers. They were teachers, preachers, and competitors in the race for the gospel. They founded house churches and, as prominent patrons, used their influence for other missionaries and Christians.[18]

Schüssler Fiorenza believes that the importance of women is also seen in the theological self-understanding of the early Christian movement. She thinks the early Christians identified the risen Lord with the Sophia of God, and she sees Wisdom Christology reflected in the pre-Pauline hymn of Phil 2:6-11. The understanding of the Spirit, according to Schüssler Fiorenza, presumes a sense of equality among the members of the new community. "They are all equal, because they all share in the Spirit, God's power; they are all called elect and holy because they are adopted by God, all without exception: Jews, pagans, women, men, slaves, free poor, rich, those with high status and those who are 'nothing' in the eyes of the world."[19] It is no surprise that Schüssler Fiorenza values the baptismal confession quoted in Gal 3:28. "It proclaims that in the Christian community all distinctions of religion, race, class, nationality, and gender are insignificant."[20] However, Paul, according to Schüssler Fiorenza, compromises the confession and its meaning. On the one hand he affirms the equality and freedom of women, but on the other he advocates their subordination. He uses the imagery of "father" to confirm his authority (1 Cor 4:15) and insists that wives should be silent in the churches (1 Cor 14:34).In the third part of the book Schüssler Fiorenza investigates post-Pauline texts, with attention to the household codes. In Colossians the ethic of the Greco-Roman patriarchal household code is adopted. In 1 Peter the household code deals primarily with the subordination of slaves and wives. In Ephesians the code is understood in relation to the household of God. The subordination of wives to husbands is defended on the analogy of the relation of Christ and the church. Schüssler Fiorenza concludes that "Ephesians christologically cements the inferior position of the wife in the marriage relationship."[21] Although the post-Pauline literature displays the increasing patriarchalization of the church and the genderization of its ministry, Schüssler Fiorenza sees glimmers of light in the Gospels of Mark and John. She notes that in John the male disciples flee from the crucifixion while the women follow Jesus to the cross. Similarly, the Fourth Gospel accents the role of women: the mother of Jesus, the woman of Samaria, and Mary Magdalene (first witness of the resurrection). "While—for apologetic reasons—the post-Pauline and post-Petrine writers seek to limit women's leadership roles in the Christian community to roles which are culturally and religiously acceptable, the evangelists called Mark and John highlight the alternative character of the Christian community, and therefore accord women apostolic and ministerial leadership."[22]

In the epilogue Schüssler Fiorenza issues a summons to action: "A feminist Christian spirituality, therefore, calls us to gather together as the *ekklēsia of women* who, in the angry power of the Spirit, are sent forth to feed, heal, and liberate our own people who are women."[23]

JESUS

Next to *In Memory of Her*, Schüssler Fiorenza's *Jesus: Miriam's Child, Sophia's Prophet* is most important for the history of NT research.[24] As in the earlier book, the first part is preoccupied with hermeneutics and methodology, issues that have been more fully explicated in the meantime in Schüssler Fiorenza's works on hermeneutics (reviewed below). She writes, "I seek to employ a critical feminist hermeneutics in order to explore the theoretical frameworks of various discourses about Jesus the Christ, and I do so from the social location of a biblical scholar who works from within the critical interpretive discourses of a critical feminist theology of liberation."[25] In the current situation of "malestream" economic and political domination Schüssler Fiorenza declares that feminist liberation theology must move to the center of academy and religion. "The image I want to suggest is that of the feminist theologian as troublemaker, as resident alien, who constantly seeks to destabilize the centers, both the value-free, ostensibly neutral research ethos of the academy and the dogmatic authoritarian stance of patriarchal religion."[26] In this book she is particularly concerned to dismantle to the "kryriarchal" domination of orthodox Christology. "In short, the form and shape of feminist christological inquiry has been conditioned not only by its biblical-dogmatic location but also by its rhetorical-theological location within the preconstructed modern frame of the sex/gender system."[27] Schüssler Fiorenza proceeds to investigate various efforts by feminist theologians to grapple with the problem of the maleness of Jesus. One of the strategies is to argue that the humanity of Jesus, not his maleness, is primary. Other feminists propose a shift from the concept of Jesus as heroic individual to the view of Jesus in relationship to others, providing a relational Christology. However, Schüssler Fiorenza believes these efforts assume and perpetuate the sex/gender system.

In the second part of the book Schüssler Fiorenza investigates various approaches to the interpretation of Jesus. She identifies three major methods: the doctrinal-historical (a method that employs historical criticism but fails to assess the social-cultural structure), the liberal psychological-anthropological (a method that uses historical imagination to enrich spiritual Christianity but also assumes the kyriarchal, sex/gender system), and the social-rhetorical (a method that is concerned with the linguistic and symbolic worlds of the biblical texts but also adopts a kyriocentric framework). Schüssler Fiorenza also reviews the quests of the historical Jesus. In the old quest (chronicled by Schweitzer),

Jesus was envisioned as the liberal, male hero. In the kerygmatic quest (Kähler and Bultmann) a Christ of faith was found who had little interest in feminist concerns. In the "new quest" (identified by James Robinson) excessive use of the criterion of dissimilarity led to an anti-Jewish Jesus. In the "newest quest" (e.g., the Jesus Seminar), the scientific objective method of malestream biblical studies was exclusively embraced with no sensitivity to the socio-political-cultural context.

In reaction, Schüssler Fiorenza asserts that: "a critical feminist theology of liberation has to challenge the notion that Christian identity must remain contingent upon scientific reconstructions of the historical Jesus as founding father, feminist hero, or divine man, since such kyriocentric scientific reconstructions reproduce not only androcentrism but also anti-Judaism in Christian historical-theological terms."[28] Positively, Schüssler Fiorenza reaffirms her argument in *In Memory of Her*: the Jesus movement should be recognized as a Jewish emancipatory movement of wo/men.

> Since this process of kyriarchal reinterpretation of the gospel has produced the reconstructed, by now "common sense" frame of meaning that marginalizes women and vilifies Jews, it is necessary to dislodge our readings from such a preconstructed frame of reference and to reconfigure the Christian testament discourses about Jesus not as "scientific" but as rhetorical. The reconstruction of the Jesus movement as an emancipatory *basileia* movement, I suggest, provides such a different historical frame of reference.[29]

In this reconstruction Schüssler Fiorenza focuses on the execution of Jesus and the theology of the cross. Like the maleness of Jesus, the idea of Jesus' death as atonement or as necessary for salvation is troublesome for feminists. Various feminist theologians respond in various ways, running all the way from the charge that the doctrine of atonement promotes suffering (e.g., child abuse) to the belief that the crucified Jesus shares in the suffering of oppressed women. Schüssler Fiorenza believes these solutions continue to imply the support of the sex/gender system of domination. She says that "to willingly suffer violence always serves kyriarchal interests, even when such suffering is understood as redemptive."[30] In her view, the Sophia-God of Jesus does not need atonement or require sacrifices. "A theology that is silent about the sociopolitical causes of Jesus' execution and stylizes him as the paradigmatic sacrificial victim whose death was either willed by God or was necessary to propitiate God continues the kyriarchal cycle of violence and victimization instead of empowering believers to resist and transform it."[31] Schüssler Fiorenza calls for a reinterpretation of the theology of the cross in terms of a different politics of meaning. She points out that Jesus was executed as "King of the Jews," that is, as a political criminal; Jesus was executed by the Roman imperial, kyriarchal system.In the third part of her Jesus book Schüssler Fiorenza sounds a favorite theme: the importance of the concept of Wisdom for feminist Christology. She begins this exposition with a review of the development of Wisdom theology in Judaism. Schüssler Fiorenza believes that after the exile the concept of Wisdom replaced the role of the king. According to Schüssler Fiorenza's reading of Jewish theology, God is present in Israel as a female personification of Divine Wisdom. Turning to early Christian sources, Schüssler Fiorenza thinks that the earliest tradition embedded in the Q document presents Jesus as the prophet of Sophia. She also detects the witness to Sophia in the pre-Markan tradition. This is especially seen in the story of the baptism, where Jesus is depicted as empowered with the Spirit as messenger of Sophia. As in *In Memory of Her*, Schüssler Fiorenza sees the Sophia-Christ in the pre-Pauline hymn of Phil 2:6-11; like Isis, the Sophia-Christ is praised as ruler over the cosmic powers. She also finds reference to Sophia in Matt 11:19—Sophia vindicated by her deeds. The Gospel of John, according to Schüssler Fiorenza, implies a theology of Wisdom incarnate but subsumes this concept to the idea of Father/Son, resulting in anti-Judaism and kyriarchal domination. She concludes: "Feminist theology must rearticulate the symbols, images, and names of Divine Sophia in the context of our own experiences and theological struggles in such a way that the ossified and absolutized masculine language about G*d and Christ is radically questioned and undermined and the Western cultural sex/gender system is radically deconstructed."[32]

The final chapter of *Jesus: Miriam's Child, Sophia's Prophet* investigates mariology—a concept important in Schüssler Fiorenza's own Roman Catholic tradition. Her intent is to deconstruct Mary, the mother of Jesus. She believes that malestream mariology was developed by the early church fathers in support of the kyriachal system and the subordination of women. In post-Vatican II Roman Catholic biblical scholarship the excesses of the Marian cult have been eliminated, while the subordination of women has been continued. With her typical sensitivity to symbolic expression, Schüssler Fiorenza reflects on the story of Mary's visit to Elizabeth (Luke 1:39-56): "Rather it is the young pregnant woman, living in occupied territory and struggling against victimization and for survival and dignity. It is she who holds out the offer of untold possibilities for a different christology and theology."[33] The final sentence in Schüssler Fiorenza's captivating drama reads, "Jesus, Miriam's child and Sophia's prophet, goes ahead of us on the open-road to Galilee signifying the beginnings of the still-to-be-realized *basileia* discipleship of equals."[34]

Schüssler Fiorenza later published another book on Jesus that focuses on the methods of historical Jesus research: *Jesus and the Politics of Interpretation*.[35] "In short, in this book I seek to inquire into the rhetoricity and politics of Historical-Jesus interpretation as a rhetorical process of meaning making."[36] In the introduction she delineates two dominant types of research on the historical Jesus: conservative biblicist reconstruction, and historical-critical reconstruction. In regard to the latter, Schüssler Fiorenza renders a devastating indictment: "Thus Historical-Jesus research as a scientific discourse shares in the dualistic rhetoric of the discourses of prejudice, racism, sexism, heterosexism, elitism, ethnocentrism, and other discourses of domination."[37] As an alternative she again proposes a paradigm shift. "Historical-Jesus research, I argue throughout, must engage in a progressive emancipatory politics of interpretation that ceases to maintain scientific discourses of domination."[38]

After the introduction Schüssler Fiorenza again reviews the quests of the historical Jesus and charges that they uniformly fail to acknowledge the socio-political location of the discussion. She writes that feminist research on the historical Jesus—notably her own—has largely been ignored by the academy. Schüssler Fiorenza also assails the split between the historical-critical and the theological investigation of Jesus. She finds evidence of this split in the work of such heavyweights as John Dominic Crossan and John Meier. In contrast, "[A] feminist reconstruction must adopt both a sociopolitical frame of conflict and struggle and a theological-inclusive frame of radical equality and well-being as its reconstructive framework of interpretation."[39]

Schüssler Fiorenza proceeds to investigate the social-scientific quest for the historical Jesus. Although she believes this approach makes advances over the historical-critical method, it, too, is dominated by elite white males and presupposes the sex/gender dualism. In Schüssler Fiorenza's view most methods of historical Jesus research are plagued by anti-Judaism and antifeminism. She believes the remedy is to be found in her own particular formulation of a feminist hermeneutic. "In short, only an emancipatory feminist model of historical and theological reconstruction can do justice both to our common struggles for transforming religious kyriarchy and to our particular historical struggles and religious identity formations that are different."[40] This model assumes that the Jesus movement can only be understood as a first-century Jewish movement, one that views itself as a prophetic movement of Divine Sophia-Wisdom.

HERMENEUTICS

As well as these major books, Schüssler Fiorenza has published works that can be classified under the general rubric of hermeneutics. Her views are expounded in three books: *Bread Not Stone*; *But She Said*; and *Rhetoric and Ethic*.[41] Since much of the content of these books is repetitious, this review will order the material according to common themes.

In explicating her hermeneutics Schüssler Fiorenza creates an idiosyncratic terminology. Most of the terms are listed and defined in the preface of *Rhetoric and Ethic*. The term "ekklēsia" is the Greek word for "assembly" or "church"; in Schüssler Fiorenza's usage it designates the radical equality of the religious community and democratic society. Schüssler Fiorenza uses the designation "Christian Testament" (CT) rather than "New Testament" (NT) to avoid any taint of Christian supersessionism. Similar to Jewish practice, Schüssler Fiorenza employs the spelling "G*d" (in earlier publications "G-d") in order to acknowledge the inadequacy of language to speak of the divine; in later works she reflects this concern in terms like "the*logy." The term "kyriarchal/kyrocentric" is derived from the Greek word for "lord"; Schüssler Fiorenza uses this term to depict the patriarchal and hierarchal structures of domination and oppression; the same concept is conveyed by the adjective "androcentric." The words "wo/man" and "wo/men" are used to avoid an essentialist view that defines woman exclusively by gender; "wo/men" is inclusive and is often used as the equivalent of "people." Not listed in this preface, but used elsewhere, is the term "phallocentrism," a term that emphasizes the sexual aspect of male domination.[42] Used throughout Schüssler Fiorenza's publications is the word "malestream," a word that characterizes the mainstream of political-cultural-religious domination as male.

Schüssler Fiorenza heralds a militant hermeneutic—a call to battle. The object of her attack is the all-pervasive, systemic domination that rules culture, politics, society, and religion. This system of oppression she characterizes as patriarchal or kyriarchal. The system was already present in the Greek ideal of "democracy," which Schüssler Fiorenza views "as a complex pyramidal political structure of dominance and subordination, stratified by gender, race, class, religious and cultural taxonomies and other historical formations of domination."[43] Schüssler Fiorenza sees the same structure of domination mirrored in modern capitalistic patriarchy, a system that confirms white, Euro-American supremacy.

As a biblical scholar Schüssler Fiorenza is especially alarmed by the kyriarchal system dominant in the Bible and in biblical studies. The Bible, she points out, is written in androcentric language and promotes systems of suppression. The canon of Scripture was formalized by the male-dominated, politically-motivated orthodox church. Biblical scholars follow the malestream methods of biblical interpretation, and in this Schüssler Fiorenza finds the devotees of the "scientific" positivist paradigm no better than the advocates of the doctrinal-fundamentalist approach.[44] The system of oppression reaches its nadir in antifeminism. Schüssler Fiorenza finds this explicit or implicit in all aspects of the patriarchal and kyriarchal systems. According to her, antifeminism is more fundamental than colonialism and the oppression opposed by liberation theology; all oppressed people include women, and women, she believes, are paradigmatic for the whole concept of oppression.

Against this massive system of domination Schüssler Fiorenza calls for a counterattack: a hermeneutics of feminist liberation. "In short, a critical model of feminist interpretation for liberation seeks to articulate a rhetorical practice that can *displace* objectivist and depoliticized academic practices of biblical interpretation—practices which at present seem to be gaining ground in biblical women's studies."[45] Schüssler Fiorenza subdivides feminist hermeneutics into various types.[46] Most important is the hermeneutics of *suspicion*. According to this approach interpretation must be alert to the androcentric language of the Bible and wary of the malestream methods of biblical interpretation. A hermeneutics of *remembrance* recalls the role of women in the Jesus movement and in the early church. "A feminist hermeneutics of remembrance proposes theoretical models for historical reconstructions that place women in the center of biblical community and theology."[47] A hermeneutics of *evaluation* and *proclamation* affirms the importance of women as interpreters of Scripture and participants in ministry. Schüssler Fiorenza insists that "ministry should be understood as 'equality from below,' as a democratic practice of solidarity with all those who struggle for survival, self-love, and justice."[48] A hermeneutics of *imagination* indicates that the text should be approached with openness to new, wider meanings.

Schüssler Fiorenza investigates methods of biblical criticism and interpretation in the light of the various types of hermeneutics. She detects a crisis in biblical scholarship. She proposes that the dominant model of objective, value-neutral research is no longer viable; it is not really objective and its demise is heralded by a variety of new methods; it creates a chasm between what the text meant and what it means. Above all, Schüssler Fiorenza charges that the old method fails to recognize the socio-political location of biblical research. Although the "scientific" positivistic paradigm claims objectivity, its focus on the "facts" makes it, like the doctrinal-fundamentalist, literalistic. The (post-) modern cultural paradigm has spawned a host of new methods and recognizes a wide range of social worlds. In place of these, Schüssler Fiorenza promotes the rhetorical emancipatory method. "The transformation of biblical studies into such a theo-ethics of interpretation calls for a rhetorical method of analysis that is able to articulate the power of relations and radical democratic visions of well-being inscribed in biblical texts."[49]

The main sources to which this method is to be applied are found in the Bible, especially the CT, and in the Jewish wisdom literature. Using the historical critical method she claims to abhor, Schüssler Fiorenza gives careful attention to the early stratum of Q, the pre-Markan tradition, and the pre-Pauline tradition. Following the course launched in the Reformation, she views the succeeding historical tradition as decline, flowing into the malestream of biblical interpretation. In *But She Said*, Schüssler Fiorenza addresses the problem of biblical authority.[50] She contends that authority is not located in the canon of Scripture, the historical Jesus, or the earliest Christian witness. Instead, authority has its locus in the ekklēsia of women inspired by the Sophia-Spirit. "A critical feminist hermeneutics that articulates itself within the logic of democracy must be grounded in a spirituality of vision and imagination."[51]

Two other books illustrate the application of Schüssler Fiorenza's feminist hermeneutics to particular topics. In *The Power of the Word: Scripture and the Rhetoric of Empire* she explores the relationship of her feminist hermeneutics of liberation to the recent interest of biblical research in empire (seen, for example, in the work of Neil Elliott and Warren Carter).[52] This approach, of course, fits hand in glove with Schüssler Fiorenza's idea of kyriarchy. In the main she argues that these studies are not sufficiently radical. They continue to work with the antiquated paradigm of positivistic historical criticism, and they fail to adopt the feminist hermeneutic that exposes the kryriarchal function of the Scriptures themselves. Schüssler Fiorenza concludes, "The arguments of . . . [this] whole book are framed toward nurturing scholars, preachers, and Christian readers who are able to identify the rhetoric of empire inscribed in scripture and to make the connections between the rhetoric of scripture and contemporary global struggles for justice and well-being."[53] In *Democratizing Biblical Studies: Toward an Emancipatory Educational Space* Schüssler Fiorenza explicates the implication of her hermeneutic for programs of education in biblical studies.[54] She calls for a radical democratic pedagogy for the study of the Bible.

The application of Schüssler Fiorenza's hermeneutics is demonstrated in her exegetical and critical work. An example is provided by her research on the Apocalypse: *The Book of Revelation: Justice and Judgment*, originally published in 1985.[55] In the original Prologue she writes, "I propose to look for the integrating center, that is, the distinct historical–social–religious experience and resulting theological perspective that have generated the particular form-content figuration (*Gestalt*) of Rev."[56] In the introduction Schüssler Fiorenza reviews earlier research on the book of Revelation. She concludes that the document is a Christian prophetic-apocalyptic work, written in Asia Minor at the end of the first century. More important, according to Schüssler Fiorenza, is the literary-functional interpretation. This approach recognizes the poetic character of the language and the document's preoccupation with the problem of power. Thus, she says, Revelation must be read politically.

In Part 1, Schüssler Fiorenza investigates "Theological Perspectives and Frameworks." She surmises that Revelation does not present a sequence of events, but rather pieces of a mosaic to describe the imminent eschatological event. The present suffering of the community is understood in relation to the future of the coming kingdom. Schüssler Fiorenza does not believe the author holds a spiritual or individualistic view of redemption. "Instead, he conceives of redemption and salvation in political terms and in socio-economic categories."[57] Although salvation is present, it is not fully realized; the community lives now under the domination of the Roman empire.

In Part 2, Schüssler Fiorenza discusses "Revelation in the Context of Early Christianity in Asia Minor." She believes that the author was the leader of a prophetic-apocalyptic school, and that he was opposed a gnostic-libertine faction within the church. "In conclusion," she writes, "I have attempted to argue that Rev. must be understood as a literary product of early Christian prophecy. As such it must be situated within the theological context of Asia Minor which was greatly determined by Pauline and post-Pauline theology."[58]

In Part 3, Schüssler Fiorenza investigates the "Literary Vision and Composition of the Apocalypse." She reviews various theories about the sources, genre, and literary form of the document. She concludes that Revelation has the frame of a early Christian apostolic letter to which the author has added visions, images, and symbols; the result is a "prophetic-apostolic letter."[59] Schüssler Fiorenza contends that the language of Revelation is not only mythopoeic but also rhetorical and political. The author calls for radical resistance to Satanic power, the power of Rome.

In the Epilogue, Schüssler Fiorenza critiques the reading of Revelation according to a dualism of gender, seen, for instance, in the contrast between the bad woman (Babylon) and the good woman (Jerusalem). "I have tried to show, therefore, that a reading of Revelation in terms of a dualistic gender framework inscribes or reinscribes the Western sex/gender system, whereas a rhetorical-political reading is able to underscore the sociopolitical-religious power of Roman imperialism that affects wo/men differently."[60]

In the history of NT research, Elisabeth Schüssler Fiorenza is without parallel. She is an evangelist of a distinctive hermeneutics, a particular methodology, and an uncommon theology. She presents her views in vivid, dramatic prose. Schüssler Fiorenza calls for a rhetoric of power and she herself writes powerful rhetoric. As a biblical scholar she is vitally concerned with what the Bible means—a meaning directed to the social and political problems of today's world. In all of this Schüssler Fiorenza displays keen intellect and command of a broad spectrum of research in the historical and social sciences.

Fundamentally, Schüssler Fiorenza advocates an approach to biblical studies that is grounded in the experience of the interpreter. While this appears vulnerable to the charge of subjectivism, Schüssler Fiorenza embraces subjectivity and intentionally puts the interpreter in the center. Moreover, hers is not an arbitrary, egoistic subjectivism but one based on a larger, broadly conceived worldview. Surely liberation, freedom, and democracy are universal values, shared with the majority of humanity.

Much of the substance of Schüssler Fiorenza's work is negative: an attack on the dominant socio-cultural-political structures, which she so graphically depicts as kyriarchy. Nevertheless, Schüssler Fiorenza, as Ng points out, is an "insider-outsider."[61] As a professor at Harvard, the recipient of honorary degrees, the publisher of "best-sellers," a star on the lecture circuit, Schüssler Fiorenza belongs to and is supported by the "kyriarchal" system. While this may provide her with a firsthand perspective, it does not protect her from the fallout from her own charges.

Schüssler Fiorenza has a mixed view of the Bible. On the one hand she decries its androcentric language and its affirmation of patriarchy. On the other she detects, beneath the debris of suppression, treasures of inspiration, glimpses of the role and importance of women in the early Christian movement. Schüssler Fiorenza claims that the authority of the Bible is not located in the canon but in the experience of the feminist interpreter. But why this book? Surely a feminist hermeneutic of liberation can be readily found in a variety of less oppressive sources. The observer is tempted to conclude that Schüssler Fiorenza puts more stock in the biblical tradition than her rhetoric appears to warrant.

Most important for the history of NT research is Schüssler Fiorenza's critique of the historical critical method. Her argument is given considerable force by her own command of historical criticism. She is not an untutored critic from the outside but a master of the method. The most telling feature of her criticism is her attack on the pretended objectivity of some critics—a pretense that many recent historical critics have renounced. However, despite Schüssler Fiorenza's attack on the critical method, she continues to use it, tacitly acknowledging that it still has an important role to play in the interpretation of Scripture. The dramatic change in biblical methodology she has championed through the years has not come to pass. "Although this paradigm shift has been underway for quite some time and has brought ferment and upheaval . . . to the once stable field of biblical and religious studies, it has not been able to unseat the positivist scientific, supposedly disinterested, ethos of the discipline."[62]

The scene in biblical studies, of course, has changed since Elisabeth Schüssler Fiorenza was denied a stipend and when, without hope of a position in Germany, she had to flee to America. In the meantime women have been appointed to positions of prominence in academia. One thinks of Adela Yarbro Collins (Yale), Beverly Roberts Gaventa (Princeton Seminary), Margaret M. Mitchell (Chicago), Judith Lieu (Cambridge), Barbara Aland (Münster), Oda Wischmeyer (Erlangen)—all doing research according to the methods of historical criticism, though with insights from the feminist perspective.[63] Has Schüssler Fiorenza's vision of liberation and freedom become reality? No, that will have to await a future eschatology she tends to ignore. Her vision with its imperfections, nonetheless, has pointed the way to an open road ahead—a space where a renewed and relevant biblical research can flourish.

YALE: MARTYN, KECK, AND FURNISH

J. LOUIS MARTYN (1925–)

Born in Dallas, Texas, Martyn was reared a Southern Baptist.[64] He was educated at Texas A&M, a university noted for football and the military corps, not for theologians. After graduating (BS 1946), Martyn followed his girlfriend to Andover Newton Theological School (BD 1953). At Andover Newton he met two individuals who were decisive for his career: Professor Paul Minear and fellow student Leander Keck. Minear sent them to Yale (MA 1956; PhD 1957).[65] There they worked side by side under the tutelage of Paul Schubert and submitted their completed dissertations on exactly the same day. After graduation from Yale, Martyn received a Fulbright Fellowship to the University of Göttingen (1957–58), where he studied with Joachim Jeremias and Ernst Käsemann. Later (1963–64) he was awarded a Guggenheim Fellowship that supported a leave in Tübingen, where he carried on the conversation with Käsemann.

Martyn began his teaching career at Wellesley College (1958–59). He soon moved to Union Theological Seminary in New York, where he advanced from assistant to associate professor (1959–67) to Edward Robinson Professor of Biblical Theology (1967–87). His role as colleague and teacher was praised by faculty and students. The distinguished Raymond E. Brown, who came to Union in 1971, observed how Martyn's decisions were determined by the Bible. "No one who has dealt with Lou Martyn long can doubt that he is a man who lives by what he teaches."[66] Beverly Gaventa, a student, later to become an important NT scholar in her own right, was inspired by Martyn's scholarly focus. "His attention was unabashedly riveted to the text—to every letter and each nuance."[67]

THE GOSPEL OF JOHN

Lou Martyn is recognized primarily for his work on John and Paul, essentially encapsulated in four major books. He is known not for the quantity of his work but for its quality. His research on John is presented in *History and Theology in the Fourth Gospel*.[68] According to most scholars, research on the Fourth Gospel during the twentieth century can be characterized as "before Bultmann" and "after Bultmann." John Ashton, an important Johannine scholar, wrote of Martyn's book that "for all its brevity it is probably the most important single work on the Gospel since Bultmann's commentary."[69] First published in 1968, Martyn's book was revised and published again in 1979. The third edition of 2003 is a paperback reprint of the second: proof of the ongoing significance of Martyn's work.

In the introduction Martyn calls attention to the problem of the historical setting. "Our first task, however, is to say something as specific as possible about the actual circumstances in which John wrote his Gospel."[70] Fond of imagery drawn from the theater, Martyn begins Part I with a depiction of "A Synagogue-Church Drama: Erecting a Wall of Separation." He plunges immediately into the text with a careful analysis of the story of the blind beggar who receives his sight (John 9). Martyn detects the transposition to dramatic form in v. 4: it is "we" who do the works of him who sent "me." Thus, there are two levels of witness: the event of Jesus ("me") and the later witness of the church ("we"). Martyn presents the narratives of the chapter in a series of scenes. These scenes, according to Martyn, reveal that the Fourth Gospel presents a drama on two levels: the level of the time of Jesus (the *einmalig* time), and the level of the time of John and his church. A decisive element in the drama at the second level is the expulsion of persons from the synagogue. Martyn points out that that the decision to put people out had previously had been made. When, asks Martyn, had that been done? He observes that the term ἀποσυνάγωγος is found exclusively in the Fourth Gospel; it is a distinctive Johannine term, used three times, that relates to a particular action.

> At some time prior to John's writing an authoritative body within Judaism reached a formal decision regarding messianic faith in Jesus. Henceforth whoever confessed such faith was to be separated from the synagogue. Many Jews, even rulers, did in fact believe, but they managed somehow to conceal their faith lest they be excluded from the company of their brethren.[71]

Martyn explores various possibilities as to when and how this was done, and concludes that the formal decision and action were related to the Jewish benediction against heretics. During the time he was head of the Jamnia Academy (ca. 80–ca. 115 CE), Rabban Gamaliel requested a reformulation of the twelfth of the Eighteen Benedictions: the Benediction Against Heretics (*Birkath ha Minim*). This, says Martyn, is the decision that has already been made (9:22); the "Pharisees" are the messengers who deliver the newly formulated Benediction to the members of the Gerousia, who enforce it (12:42); this is the instrument by which they will put members of John's community out of the synagogues.

Part II continues the exposition of the drama, "After the Wall is Erected." The stage is set for the conflict between John's church and the neighboring Jewish community: Christian missionaries arrive, proclaiming that Jesus was the messiah. The authorities of the Jewish community view this with alarm and officials come from Jamnia with the reworded Benediction Against Heretics in hand. The resulting expulsion from the synagogue narrowed the stream of converts to the Christian movement but did not end it. More drastic action was needed; the heretics had to be destroyed—a second-level drama parallel to the first (the execution of Jesus).

Martyn turns to the unfolding drama as enacted in John 5 and 7. Again a traditional miracle story, the healing of a crippled man, has been expanded. John 5:1-18 includes a series of dramatic scenes. Martyn notes the action of the drama is set in the *einmalig* frame of the life of Jesus, as indicated in the charge that Jesus healed on the Sabbath (v. 16). In this drama the Jewish Christian (speaking through Jesus) does not lead the healed man to confession (as in

9:35-38) but warns that something worse might happen to him (5:14). Thus threat of expulsion is not enough; something more dire is threatened.

Martyn points out that in John 7 a controversy erupts in Jerusalem in regard to Jesus, who is threatened with arrest for being a deceiver. Martyn sees this drama unfolding on the second level. The idea of the arrest of Jesus is based on the Synoptic tradition (Mark 12:12), but John revises the tradition. In the Synoptics Jesus' popularity with the crowd is the reason for the failure to arrest him; in John the popularity with the crowd is the reason for the arrest—a clear sign of the second level of the drama. Martyn also sees evidence of the two-level drama in the identification and action of the authorities. In chapter 7 they are described as "chief priests" and "Pharisees" (vv. 32, 45). The chief priests belong to the first level drama, the *einmalig* of Jesus. The Pharisees, on the other hand, represent the authorities of Jamnia in the second level.

In Part III, Martyn investigates the "Major Theological Terms of the Conversation." In the Fourth Gospel the "Jews" have much to say about Moses: God spoke to Moses; we are disciples of Moses; Moses gave the Law; the common people (*am ha'arets*) do not know the Law. In Jewish expectation a key concept is the coming of a prophet like Moses (Deut 18:15, 18), the Mosaic Prophet-Messiah who would perform signs. According to Martyn's reconstruction there was within the Jewish community of John's city the hope for a Mosaic prophet. In the latter part of the first century some Jewish Christians arrived and persuaded some of the members of the synagogue that Jesus was the Prophet-Messiah like Moses. This success provoked official resistance from the Jamnia loyalists. John believed that the theology of the Jewish Christian group was not adequate for the situation. In developing his own theology, John, according to Martyn, could either enter the exegetical arena and try to convince the common folk by exegesis or he could take a totally different tack. John chose the latter, and developed a Christology of polarity: "Just as (καθώς) Moses lifted up the serpent . . . so (οὕτως) must the Son of man be lifted up" (3:14). John acknowledges that Jesus is a prophet and the Messiah (4:19, 25-26) but denies that the Moses/Messiah typology has dogmatic force. In 7:15 the Jews assert that Jesus has never studied; Jesus declares that the issue is not a matter of midrash but of dualism of decision: anyone who decides to do the will of God will know whether Jesus' teaching is from God.

Martyn points out that, in major texts where he speaks of the Mosaic Prophet-Messiah, John moves to the affirmation of Jesus as the Son of Man. For instance, in the dialogue with Nicodemus (3:1-21) attention is drawn to Jesus' signs; the text also declares, "And just as Moses lifted up the serpent in the wilderness, so must the Son of Man be lifted up" (3:14). Martyn believes that the source for John's identification of Jesus as Mosaic Prophet-Messiah is the miracle tradition. However, John transforms this *einmalig* tradition into the two-level drama of Jesus as the Son of Man. Martyn observes that John did not invent the framework of the two-level drama but found it in apocalyptic: the dual drama of heavenly/earthly, future/present. John, however, reconstructs the framework: both stages are on earth, and the stages are past and present. But the plot thickens: the Son of Man is an actor right out of the apocalyptic drama. According to John, Jesus is to be identified with this apocalyptic figure. Nowhere else in the gospel tradition, except in John 9:35, does Jesus request someone to confess him as Son of Man. As Son of Man, Jesus plays the major role in both levels of the drama. In his conversation with Nicodemus, Jesus says that no one *has* ascended, as if that might have happened in the past (3:13), but in 14:12 Jesus says that he will ascend to the Father in the future.

Martyn finds the resolution of this paradox in John's figure of the Paraclete. John's account depicts the essential task of the Paraclete: to bring the disciples to remembrance of what Jesus said, to bear witness to Jesus, to glorify Jesus, and to continue Jesus' "suit with the world." "The Paraclete," says Martyn, "makes Jesus present on earth as the Son of Man who binds together heaven and earth (1:51). Therefore the Son of Man cannot be located exclusively either in heaven or on earth."[72] In face of the departure of Jesus, says Martyn, the theologian can either promise a place in heaven or speak of a mystical presence. Jesus appears to do both: he goes to prepare rooms (14:2) and he promises his continual presence. But John, according to Martyn, has modified the picture: instead of "rooms" he speaks of a room—not in heaven but on earth. This is accomplished by the Paraclete. "*It is, therefore, precisely the Paraclete who creates the two-level drama.*"[73] Martyn concludes:

> The two-level drama makes clear that the Word's dwelling among us and our beholding his glory are not events which transpired in the past. They do not constitute an ideal period when the kingdom of God was on earth, a period to which one looks back with the knowledge that it has now drawn to a close with Jesus' ascension to heaven as the Son of Man. These events to which John bears witness transpire on both the *einmalig* and the contemporary levels of the drama, or they do not transpire at all. In John's view, their transpiring on both levels of the drama is, to a large extent, the good news itself.[74]

The second edition of *History and Theology in the Fourth Gospel* includes a final chapter, "Glimpses into the History of the Johannine Community: From Its Origin through the Period of Its Life in Which the Fourth Gospel Was Composed."[75] This is not the typical historical reconstruction with speculation about the Beloved Disciple and the growth of a community in Ephesus (or elsewhere), but a history reconstructed exclusively from the Gospel itself. To facilitate this reconstruction Martyn views the Gospel of John as an archaeological site with different strata of tradition. In the early period (from before 70 to the 80s) Martyn detects a messianic group within the community of the synagogue. In time, the message of this group came to include pieces of the Jesus tradition: elements of the passion-resurrection and miracles seen as signs. Later the preachers of this messianic group produced a rudimentary document, similar to the Signs Source (identified by Bultmann, Robert Fortna, and others). Their missionary activity had considerable success; they had a simple understanding of faith. The members of the group observed the Torah and had little sense of alienation from the synagogue; they were Christian Jews.

In the middle period Martyn sees the emergence of a part of this messianic group as a separate community that had experienced two traumas: expulsion from the synagogue and the threat of execution. According to Martyn the leaders of this group developed a dualistic theology according to the above/below pattern. They believed the Messiah was the Sophia-Logos through whom God created the world, but in view of their earthly traumas they came to perceive the Messiah as one who came into his world as a stranger from above. They developed a theological geography in which they, like their Christ, were "not of the world."

In the late period, when the Gospel of John was being written, the Jewish Christians were moving toward firm social and theological configurations. In the course of this development the Jewish Christians of John's community reached the decision that they were disciples of Jesus, not Moses (9:28). They came to reject the view of some Jews who believed in Jesus (8:31) but tried to hold a dual alliance to the synagogue and to the Christ of the new community; the possibility of remaining a secret disciple no longer existed. Thus, Martyn concludes, this community was sharply differentiated from the parent synagogue and it was clearly differentiated from Christian Jews who remained in the synagogue.[76]

PAUL

Along with his seminal contribution to the study of the Gospel of John, Martyn is recognized for his work on Paul. Here his major contribution is his monumental commentary on Galatians, one of the great commentaries of the twentieth century.[77] He begins with an introduction, written in his usual lively style. Again drawing imagery from the theater, Martyn depicts Galatians as a drama. The *dramatis personae* include three main actors: the messenger (who brought and read the letter from Paul), the catechetical instructors (who had been trained by Paul), and the Teachers and their followers (traveling evangelists who have introduced a different gospel to Galatia). Martyn proceeds to recount the birth and early life of the Galatian churches. They received the gospel when, on the way to the cities of the Aegean region, Paul stopped off because of an illness.

At this point Martyn tackles the notorious question: Where were the Galatian churches located? On the basis of Paul's address to his hearers as "Galatians" (3:1), which he reads as an ethnic designation, Martyn concludes that the recipients of the letter were descendants of the original Celts of the north. The membership of these churches, according to Martyn, was exclusively Gentile. Indeed, he believes there is no evidence for Jewish communities in the northern, Celtic kingdom in the mid–first century. As to date, Martyn concludes that the Galatian churches were founded shortly after Paul's break with Barnabas and the churches of Jerusalem and Antioch, which occurred around 48–49 CE. After Paul's departure, the Teachers, a group of Jewish Christian evangelists, invaded Galatia. This group, which Martyn does not label as "opponents" or "Judaizers," made two claims: they were in some way connected with the Jerusalem church; they centered their message on the covenantal Sinaitic Law. The bad news about these Teachers and their inroads on the Galatian churches was carried to Paul while he was working in Macedonia or Achaia.

The Epistle to the Galatians is Paul's response. The date of the letter Martyn calculates according to the order of the Pauline letters, seen in their relationship to the offering Paul had agreed at the Jerusalem conference to collect. This means that Galatians should be dated after 1 Thessalonians and earlier than the Corinthian correspondence. As to the structure of the epistle, Martyn rejects the theory that Galatians is ordered according to the model of classical rhetoric (à la Betz). Instead, he characterizes it as a "situational sermon." "Rhetorically, the body of the letter is a sermon centered on factual and thus indicative answers to two questions, 'What time is it?' and 'In what cosmos do we actually live?'"[78] Martyn proceeds to present his understanding of the structure, based on his analysis of the content of the epistle. To summarize his result in oversimplified form, Martyn identifies the Prescript (1:1-5) followed by the Theme (1:6-9). The balance of the letter he designates as "Theses and Supporting Arguments"

(1:10—6:10). Within this main body of the letter Martyn identifies two major exegetical arguments: 3:6—4:7 and 4:21—5:1. The last part of the letter includes a section on "Pastoral Guidance" (5:13—6:10). The epistle concludes with an "Autobiographical Subscript" (6:11-18).

In the Introduction, Martyn also reviews the history of the interpretation of Galatians. The earliest interpreters, the Teachers, rejected Paul's view of Jerusalem, the Law, and the Israel of God; Martyn thinks they probably won the day. Especially interesting is Martyn's view of Paul's interpretation of his own letter. Paul wrote to the Romans, probably concerned about how his letter to the Galatians might have influenced the acceptance of the offering by the Jerusalem church. As a result, Paul, in Romans, presented a nuanced view of the Law and a theology that affirmed the election of Israel. Martyn's history of interpretation also recounts the opposition to Paul in second-century Jewish Christianity and Marcion's misguided appropriation of Paulinism. Luther embraced Galatians as his favorite epistle but misshaped it into a weapon to support his anti-Judaism. In the current scene some Jewish scholars misread Galatians as attacking Judaism. To interpret the epistle properly, Martyn writes, "it becomes doubly important . . . for the modern interpreter to take a seat in one of the Galatian congregations, in order—as far as possible—to listen to the letter with Galatian ears."[79]

The bulk of the commentary, "Translation, Notes, and Comments," is presented on pages 81 to 577. The material is divided into short sections according to the arrangement of the letter. Each section includes Martyn's translation, an analysis of the Literary Structure, and a Synopsis, Notes, and Comments. The Notes deal with every important term and phrase of the text, verse by verse. The result is a literary-historical-critical analysis of the Epistle to the Galatians. The Comments are presented throughout the sections of the commentary, numbered from 1 to 52. These Comments, incorporating the results of the critical work in the Notes, function as brief exegetical essays on the major historical and theological issues in the epistle. In overview, two features dominate Martyn's commentary: the role of the Teachers as key to the analysis of the historical situation and exegetical investigation, and the importance of apocalyptic for the polemical theology of Paul. The breadth and depth of this magisterial work defies any attempt at an adequate review within limited space. At best, a few examples can be offered in illustration.

We may take some examples of features of the section beginning with the "Prescript" (1:1-5). In Martyn's translation(v. 1) he includes a phrase explaining the meaning of "apostle": "that is to say a person who has been sent on a mission." Regarding literary structure and synopsis, Martyn observes that Paul usually follows the conventional epistolary form: author, addressee, greeting. In Galatians 1, Paul transforms the greeting into a prayer of blessing (vv. 3-4) and doxology (v. 5). The Notes (ten pages on this section) comment on the term *apostle*, pointing out that it is a verbal adjective referring to the effect of the action denoted by the verb *apostellō*. Martyn notes various uses in the early church according to which a person is given a task by God and sent to carry out the task. Martyn also observes that the person who was sent carried not only the message but also the authority of the sender. Martyn's note on v. 4, "*who gave up his very life for our sins*," puts the phrase in quotation marks to indicate that Paul is recalling an early Christian hymn or confession.

Within the section "Prescript," Martyn includes four Comments. Comment 3, "Apocalyptic Theology in Galatians," is one of the most important in the entire commentary.[80] This Comment is sparked by Paul's reference to *the present evil age* in v. 4. Martyn observes that the reference to the present age implies the existence of another age, thereby displaying the framework of the apocalyptic concept of two ages. He proceeds through the epistle, noting and exegeting texts—a total of ten—in which apocalyptic thought is expressed or implied. Crucial, for example, is Paul's declaration of *God's apocalyptic revelation in Jesus Christ* (1:12). Martyn sees in this verse the genesis of Paul's "christological apocalyptic."[81] According to Martyn the typical lexicographical translation of *apokaluptō* as "to reveal" (something that is hidden) is not adequate for Paul's usage. "The genesis of Paul's apocalyptic—as seen in Galatians—lies in the apostle's certainty that God has *invaded* the present evil age by sending Christ and his Spirit into it."[82] This invasion has provoked an apocalyptic warfare, a battle between the flesh and the spirit. *Indeed, these two powers constitute a pair of opposites at war with one another* (5:17). In the thick of the battle stands the cross of Christ; "the cross is the foundation of Paul's apocalyptic theology."[83] As Martyn points out, Paul does not understand the crucifixion as an isolated event of the past but as paradigm for the life of all Christians. Paul can say *I have been crucified with Christ* (2:19), and that *those who belong to Christ Jesus have crucified the Flesh, together with its passions and desires* (5:24). In summarizing the result of his review of these texts Martyn observes that Paul makes no reference in Galatians to the future coming of Christ. He points out that Paul's apocalyptic in Galatians stresses Christ's advent in the past and the present war against the powers of evil. Christ's advent is already the victory, but that victory can only be seen in the bifocal vision of apocalyptic.

It is this apocalyptic vision, then, that has given Paul his perception of the nature of the human plight. God has invaded the world in order to bring it under his liberating control. From that deed of God a conclusion is to be drawn, and the conclusion is decidedly apocalyptic: God would not have to carry out an invasion in order merely to forgive erring human beings. The root trouble lies deeper than human guilt and is more sinister. The whole of humanity—indeed, the whole of creation (3:22)—is, in fact, enslaved under the power of the present evil age.[84]

In the section "The Letter's Theme"(1:6-9) Martyn includes another Comment that is decisive for his exegesis of the epistle: Comment 6: "The Teachers."[85] Martyn begins with data from Galatians, citing texts (e.g., 1:6-9; 3:1-2) in which the Teachers are clearly in view, along with numerous allusions to them and their work. He proceeds to describe them and their message in detail. In sum, the Teachers are outsiders who have invaded the Galatian churches: Christian-Jewish evangelists who declare that the Law is good news for all people, including Gentiles. Acceptance of the Law, they claim, requires circumcision as a requirement for Gentiles to receive salvation. The Teachers view Christ as the savior who will complete the ministry of Moses, but in truth their Christ is secondary to the law. They see themselves as the true descendants of Abraham, the true Israel. They hail Jerusalem as their mother, probably posing as representatives of the Jerusalem church. Responding to the Gentile style of life, the Teachers promise that keeping the Law is the antidote for falling prey to the desires of the flesh.

In the section "Paul and the Jerusalem Apostles" (1:17-24) Martyn presents Comment 17: "Chronology and Geography: Paul's Labors Prior to the Meeting in the Jerusalem Church."[86]In regard to chronology, Martyn notes three uses of the adverb "then": "then" after three years I went to Jerusalem (1:18); "then" I went to Syria and Cilicia (1:21); "then" after fourteen years I went again to Jerusalem (2:1). Martyn believes that all these "thens" refer back to the time of Paul's call, not to the immediate previous event. Martyn also notes that within this chronological narrative Paul makes no mention of the Antioch church or of the founding of the Galatian churches. As Martyn points out, Paul must have journeyed to Antioch after his visit with Peter but he avoids mentioning these matters because of his subsequent painful break with the Antioch church. Regarding the founding of the Galatian churches, Martyn marshals weighty evidence in support of his conclusion that this was not accomplished until after Paul's break with Barnabas; the Galatian churches were not (e.g., contra Dunn) daughter churches of Antioch.[87]

Also important for the understanding of Galatians is Paul's account of "A Conference Involving Two Churches" (2:1-10). Two of the extensive Notes deserve attention. In regard to the phrase *lest it should somehow turn out that in my work I was running or had run in vain* (2:2), Martyn argues that Paul is in no way putting his call in question but is worried that the Jerusalem leaders would fail to see God's work in his mission to the Gentiles. Martyn identifies *the false brothers* with the "circumcision faction" within the Jerusalem church (2:12). In regard to Paul's claim that *those leaders did not add anything to my gospel*, Martyn says that "Paul denies that the leaders of the Jerusalem church gave him instruction of any kind."[88]

In this section Martyn includes Comment 18: "The Conference Held in Jerusalem by the Churches of Jerusalem and Antioch Narrated as a Two-Level Drama."[89] He notes the use of "we" and "they" in the narrative, indicating two negotiating parties: "they" represent the church of Jerusalem, "we" the church in Antioch. Using one of his favorite metaphors, Martyn envisages two levels of action: the first (historical) level is the conference at Jerusalem; the second level is the situation of the Galatian churches. The common theme of both dramatic levels is the truth of the gospel. Martyn believes that Paul's account is shaped by the question, "What was God doing in Jerusalem that is revealing as to what God is now doing in Galatia?"[90]

The section "An Incident in the Antioch Church" (2:11-14) is fraught with exegetical problems. In investigating the literary structure and writing the synopsis Martyn addresses the debated question of where Paul's address to Peter comes to an end. He perceives that this difficulty is intentional: Paul deliberately moves from the historical level of address to Peter to the second level of address to the Teachers of Galatia. In his Notes Martyn explicates the implication of the expression *Cephas ate regularly with Gentile members of the Antioch church* (v. 12). He believes this implies that the meals of the Antioch church, including the Eucharist, were held without observance of Jewish food laws. The *messengers from James*, says Martyn, represent an official delegation from the leader of the Jerusalem church. Under pressure from the Jerusalem delegation and the hypocritical example of Peter, the Gentile members of the Antioch church concede and agree to participate in common meals prepared according to Jewish regulations. What Peter is doing, according to Paul, is compelling Gentile Christians *to live in a Jewish manner* (v. 14).

In Comment 26 in this section, "Peter in Antioch and Infidelity to the Truth of the Gospel," Martyn points out that the bone of contention between Paul and the Jerusalem leaders has shifted from circumcision to common meals.[91] Martyn believes the shift is the result of changed leadership in the Jerusalem church and the concern of James about Peter's leadership of the Jewish mission (2:7-8). For Paul the issue is the truth of the gospel, something about which he would not compromise. "To compel the Gentile members to observe even a part of the Law was to imply that the Law, rather than Christ's atoning death, was God's appointed means of salvation for the whole of humanity."[92]

The section, "Making Right What Is Wrong" (2:15-21) is important for Martyn's view of the theology of Galatians. In his Notes he wrestles with the difficult problem of translating *dikaioō*; he (like Keck) chooses "to rectify," a verb that describes God's action of making right what has gone wrong. Martyn notes how important this concept is in Philippians and Romans and contends that it was formulated here in Paul's struggle with the Teachers. He observes that the antinomy *observance of the law / faith of Christ* is repeated three times in this text. He argues that the phrase *pistis Christou Iēsou* should be translated "faith of (not faith in) Jesus Christ."

All this is brought into focus in Comment 28: "God's Making Things Right by the Faith of Christ."[93] Martyn believes that Paul and the Teachers share the Jewish-Christian tradition about rectification: rectification is an action that sets right what has gone wrong; what has gone wrong is transgression against God's covenant; what has made things right is God's forgiveness accomplished by God's sacrificial action in Christ; God's rectifying forgiveness is confessed without explicit reference to faith. Martyn believes, however, that the Teachers have given this shared tradition their special spin: they contend that when Gentiles enter the people of God they acknowledge the authority of the Law; Gentiles transfer from pagan existence into God's Law-observant people. Martyn believes that Paul interprets the shared tradition in the light of developments in Galatia. He now hears the tradition in a new context, one in which God is creating churches apart from observance of the Law. Paul notes that although the tradition is largely silent about the Law, it is eloquent about Christ. This, says Martyn, alerts Paul to a new antinomy: observance of the Law / faith of Christ. This emphasis on the faith of Christ is, according to Martyn, crucial for Paul's whole theology: the radical contrast between the action of humans and the apocalyptic act of God in the faithful Christ.

The section "Descent from Faithful Abraham" (3:6-9) introduces the first of Paul's extensive exegetical arguments (3:6—4:7). The main issues of the first section are explored in Comment 33: "The Teachers' Sermon on Descent from Abraham and Paul's Modulation of That Theme into Descent from God."[94]Martyn begins with his reconstruction of the sermon of the Teachers. They announce to the Galatian Gentile Christians: As children of Ishmael, you can become children of Abraham by accepting the Law, submitting to circumcision, and following the prescriptions of the Law. Paul, according to Martyn, modulates the theme of Abrahamic descent into descent from God.

Paul agrees that they become children of Abraham but contends that this relationship is accomplished through identity with Abraham's *singular* seed (3:16), that is, through Christ. As a result, the descent from Abraham becomes secondary to the vastly more important descent from God; they become children of God through baptism into Christ (3:26-28).

Paul's exegetical dexterity is further displayed in the section, "The Law's Curse and the End of That Curse" (3:10-14). In the Notes Martyn investigates v. 10, which includes a quotation from Deut 27:26: *For those whose identity is derived from observance of the Law are under the power of a curse, because it stands written, "Cursed is everyone who is not steadfast in observing all of the things written in the book of the Law, so as to do them."* Martyn reviews various efforts to interpret this text and rejects, in particular, the popular notion that Paul is arguing that those who claim to observe the Law are under a curse because observing *all* that is in the Law is impossible. Martyn believes that Paul interprets the Deuteronomy text in the light of his gospel: law does not have the power to bless; its business is to curse, and its curse falls both on those who are observant and on those who are not. In the development of his argument Paul cites another text: *for it stands written, "Cursed is everyone who is hanged on a tree."* This text (Deut 21:23) ordered that the corpse of a criminal who had been hanged on a tree should not be left overnight. Paul quotes only part of the verse in order to make it refer to the crucifixion. Martyn points out that Paul uses ἐπικατάρατος for "cursed"—the same word he used in quoting Deut 27:26, so that there is a link between the crucified Christ and the curse that the Law pronounced on all human beings.

Martyn unravels these complications in Comment 34: "The Blessing of God, the Cursing of the Law, and the Cross."[95] The Teachers, according to Martyn, present the blessing and the curse in the framework of the ancient doctrine of the two ways. The Galatians are confronted with a choice between the way of obedience to the Law and receiving the blessing, or the way of nonobservance of the Law and suffering the curse. Paul, according to Martyn, understands the blessing and the curse in a radically different way. Paul believes that God blesses, while the Law curses. Although God's blessing antedated the Law's curse, the blessing is waiting in the wings. The promissory blessing met the curse of the Law for the first time in the Crucified One, so that the one cursed was Christ. But this apparent defeat, says Martyn, expressed the paradox of power in weakness. "It is indeed typical of Paul's theology that the true meaning of things emerges only in the light of God's act in Christ."[96] In contrast with the Teachers, Paul believes the curse not to be exclusively on the nonbelievers but on all humanity; Christ's act was liberation for all.

Another notable section of chapter 3 is "Baptism Into Christ Who Is Neither Jew Nor Gentile" (3:26-29). Regarding the Literary Structure and Synopsis, Martyn observes that Paul is quoting and interpreting an early liturgical tradition used in baptism. In the Notes he discusses the phrase *you were baptized into Christ, you put on Christ as though he were your clothing* (v. 27). Martyn assumes that the baptismal liturgy involved removal of clothing, signifying separation from the old existence. He believes that Paul uses the clothing imagery to depict the equipping of the baptizand for apocalyptic warfare. In this section he includes Comment 40: "Not Jew and Gentile, but One in Christ."[97] In this Comment he points out that Paul's interpretation of the baptismal formula is not concerned with the individual but with the corporate entity of the church. Paul's main interest is in the dichotomy, Jew and Greek, and the unity of the people of God in the new creation.

> Thus this corporate people is determined to no degree at all by the religious and ethnic factors that characterized the old creation (5:6; 6:15). This people is determined solely by incorporation into the Christ in whom those factors have no real existence.[98]

Paul presents his second exegetical argument in the section "Two Gentile Missions" (4:21—5:1), which includes Comment 45: "The Covenant of Hagar and Sarah: Two Covenants and Two Gentile Missions."[99] Paul is interpreting the stories of Genesis 16–21. In his exegesis Paul distinguishes two begettings: Ishmael was begotten by the power of the flesh; Isaac was begotten by the power of the Spirit. Martyn believes Paul sees parallels to these two begettings in the contemporary scene: the begetting of Isaac represents the original birth of the Galatian churches; the begetting of Ishmael represents the birth of slavery initiated by the Teachers. Martyn also detects in Paul's exegesis the identification of two covenants. According to the Genesis account there was only one covenant, and as sign of the covenant Abraham circumcised every male of his household, including Ishmael. However, as Martyn points out, God established his covenant not with Ishmael but with Isaac. Thus there are two covenants: the covenant of Hagar and the covenant of Sarah. "In short, Paul identifies the two women as two covenants, in order to speak of two missions."[100]

The main discussion of ethics in Galatians is found in 5:13-24, "Pastoral Guidance"; the major themes are explicated in Comment 48: "The Law and Daily Life in the Church of God."[101] Martyn observes that in view of his negative presentation of the Law, Paul's positive understanding of the Law in relation to the life of the church is astonishing. In two verses in Galatians 5, Paul refers to the "whole law." In 5:3 he speaks of the Sinaitic Law that is linked to the works of the Law—the Law that pronounces a curse on humanity. Martyn believes that in 5:14 Paul hears a voice of the Law that is different from the Sinaitic Law. Paul, in this verse, says that the Law is brought to completion in one "sentence" (*logos*). This indicates to Martyn that Paul does not see the Law as a collection of commands, but as singular. "Whereas Paul refers in 5:3 to the voice of the Sinaitic Law that curses and enslaves (3:10, 13, 19; 4:3-5, 21a, 24-25), he speaks in 5:14 of the voice of the original, pre-Sinaitic law that articulates God's own mind (3:8; 4:21b)."[102] Thus Martyn detects in Paul's understanding of the Law two voices: the cursing Law and the promising Law. He also discovers a relation between these two voices and Christ; the Law did something to Christ and Christ did something to the Law. As to what the Law did to Christ, he was born into the state of enslavement under the power of the Law; as he hung on the cross, the Law pronounced a curse on him. As to what Christ did to the Law, he silenced the cursing voice of the Law and echoed the Law's original voice: the imperative that provides guidance for the everyday life of the church. The imperative, says Martyn, is expressed in Lev 19:18—love your neighbor—which is not a command but a sentence, a word from the pre-Sinaitic Law.

> To recapitulate, then, in Galatians the promise of Gen 12:3 (Gal 3:8) and the imperative of Lev 19:18 (Gal 5:14) constitute the voice of the original Law of God. As accents of that voice, this promise and this imperative have waited, so to speak, for the time when Christ would decisively differentiate them from the accents of the cursing voice of the Sinaitic Law. And when Christ carried out that differentiation he brought the Law to completion, restoring the promissory and guiding accents of the Law to their original singularity, indeed to their original unity.[103]

Paul's ethic is further explicated in the next Comment, 49: "The Galatians' Role in the Spirit's War of Liberation," one of the longest in the commentary.[104] In providing guidance for the church's daily life, Paul, according to Martyn, could have reverted to the Law or drawn various commandments from the law of love. Martyn believes he does neither. Instead, Paul makes four major moves. First, he focuses on the Spirit instead of the Law. This, according to Martyn, is contrary to the instruction of the Teachers, who promise that if the Galatians keep the Law they will not fall prey to the desires of the flesh. Second, Paul depicts the Spirit and the flesh as combatants in a war. Martyn notes that Gal 5:13-24 is the first place in the epistle where Paul presents the flesh as actor, a force that can only be overcome by the Spirit. Third, Paul provides a description of the war. According to Martyn the war is an apocalyptic battle, the result an invasion: God has sent the Spirit into the territory of the flesh. The Galatians are not observers but participants in the war, soldiers in the Spirit's army, equipped by the Spirit itself. Finally, Paul announces an imperative, according to Martyn's translation: *Lead your daily life guided by the Spirit.*

Other examples of Martyn's work on Paul can be found in a collection of his essays, *Theological Issues in the Letters of Paul.*[105] Important for his understanding of Judaism is the essay, "Galatians, An Anti-Judaic Book?"[106] At the outset he notes that recent studies by Jewish scholars have served to advance the understanding of Paul. However, Martyn believes that some texts in Galatians have been misread as anti-Jewish. To the contrary, he argues that Paul does not present an antithesis to Judaism but an antithesis between God's apocalyptic act and religion as a human enterprise. He explicates this antithesis according to four themes. First, Paul's references to "Jews": when Paul uses the term *Ioudaios* ("Jew") in Galatians he is referring to Christian Jews, not to Jews. The conflicts of Galatians are within the church. Second, the opposition among religions: the polarity between apocalypse and religion brings to an end all forms of opposition among religions (Gal 3:28). "With the advent of Christ, then, the antinomy between apocalypse and religion has been enacted by God once for all."[107] This antinomy militates against the emergence of religion within the church; Christianity is not a new religion set over against the old, Judaism. Third, turning to religion after the apocalypse of Christ, Martyn declares that the observance of the Law by Gentiles is nothing other than religion. Fourth, the horizon of Galatians: the epistle is concerned about two conflicting Gentile missions; no Jews are addressed in Galatians and no Jews are spoken about in the letter.

Also important is Martyn's essay, "Epistemology at the Turn of the Ages: 2 Corinthians 5:16-17."[108] He begins by answering three initial exegetical questions. First, what is the meaning of "from now on" and "no longer" in 2 Cor 5:16? Answer: these phrases refer to the turn of the ages, accomplished by the death/resurrection of Christ, an event of apocalyptic, cosmic dimensions. Second, what is the role of v. 16 in context? Answer: the verse is not a digression or insertion but the explicit expression of the epistemological concern that is related to Paul's eschatology from 2 Cor 2:14 onward. Third, how is *kata sarka* to be understood? Is it adjectival, modifying "Christ," or is it adverbial, modifying the verb "know"? Answer: the phrase is adverbial, indicating two ways of knowing, that is, before and after the apocalyptic event. Martyn believes these answers give rise to two further questions: What does Paul mean by the old way of knowing; what is the meaning of the new way of knowing for Paul's epistemology? As to the old way of knowing, Martyn believes Paul is referring to knowing "according to the flesh." Martyn proceeds to investigate how 2 Cor 5:16 would have been heard by the "enthusiasts" within the Corinthian church. He then asks how 2 Cor 5:16 would have been understood by the "the pseudo-apostles" who had invaded the Corinthian church (2 Cor 11:13). Martyn believes that this group claimed to have experienced a vision of God that literally changed their faces. Turning to the Paul's intention in 2 Cor 5:16, Martyn believes the apostle is announcing a wake-up call to the enthusiasts, since they, dazzled by the faces of the pseudo-apostles, are still knowing according to the flesh. For his own part, however, Paul does not say that the true way of knowing is by the Spirit. Instead, according to Martyn, Paul insists that the true way of knowing is knowing at the juncture of the two ages—knowing according to the cross. Paul's epistemology is christological. "That is to say, together with the community that is being formed in him, *Christ* defines the difference between the two ways of knowing, doing that precisely in his cross."[109]

Martyn's essay, "The Abrahamic Covenant, Christ, and the Church," includes a section in which he identifies theological motifs that are *wrongly* attributed to Paul.[110] Among these is "covenantal nomism," the motif popular with the advocates of the "new perspective."[111] According to Martyn, Paul strongly stresses the divorce between the covenant and the law. Another motif wrongly attributed to Paul, and repeatedly rejected throughout Martyn's work, is the theology of redemptive history or *Heilsgeschichte*. According to Martyn, Paul does not conceive the idea of the seed of Abraham extending from generation to generation; instead, Paul's idea of redemption is not linear but punctiliar. This essay also discusses Paul's idea of God's non-ethnic election of ancient Israel. In this discussion Martyn asks: Does Paul, in Galatians, deny God's election of Israel and rescind that denial in Romans? He observes that in Galatians Paul uses the term *kaleō* exclusively for the call of Christians. As to the concept of "promise," Paul, according to Martyn, believes that the promise to Abraham remained un-embodied until the advent of Christ. In Romans 9–11, however, Paul emphasizes the election of Israel. Consequently, Martyn concludes that Paul did rescind his earlier implied denial of the election of Israel. He believes this shift is to be explained in terms of the different setting. In Romans, Paul reflects on the massive rejection of the gospel by the Jewish people and the charge that he is responsible for it; he has come to recognize the great significance of the Jewish Christians. In Galatians, Paul is engaged in a battle in regard to the Gentile mission. In this context Paul is reacting to the claim of the Teachers that Gentiles are moving into the ethnically distinctive people of God. Martyn concludes: Paul contends that neither the promise to Abraham nor the Sinaitic Law was an act of ethnic election.

Martyn's essay, "John and Paul on the Subject of Gospel and Scripture," is one of the most important in the collection for understanding his method and thought.[112] The essay is based on a lecture presented at the meeting of the SBL in 1990 in the series, "How My Mind Has Changed." Martyn begins by recalling his sojourn in Göttingen (1957–58), where Walter Bauer was still alive in retirement. This contact called to mind Bauer's advice that to understand a document the interpreter first had to ask how the original readers (or hearers) understood it. This method of reading as listening, according to Martyn, was also informed by F. C. Baur's conviction that one had to hear the text within the context of the strains and stresses of early Christian theology. Martyn proceeds to illustrate this approach by listening to John and Paul. According to Martyn, many of John's references to Scripture are spoken in a polemical voice. Within John's audience are some whom Martyn characterizes as "simple exegetes." They believe that whenever God acts, he does so in relation to Scripture; they see a trajectory from Scripture to the figure of the Messiah. John, according to Martyn, has a different view; he finds radical disjunctions in the landscape of the gospel that are evident in the relation between Scripture and Christ (John 5:39-40). John rejects the notion that a linear sacred history flows out of Scripture into the gospel. For John, says Martyn, the Logos is the only exegete of the Father; nothing other can provide a criterion against which God can be measured, not even Scripture.

Martyn turns to the understanding of gospel and Scripture in Paul. In listening to Paul's description of the gospel in 1 Cor 1:17-24, the Corinthians might suppose it suggests a two-step dance: the apostle serves up the gospel, and the human hearer assesses the message. According to Paul, however, the gospel is God's advent. Those who are being redeemed, says Martyn, discover that the event of the gospel changes the foundations of their existence. Paul's hermeneutic does not proceed from Scripture to gospel but from the foolish gospel of the cross to the previously misunderstood Scripture. "But one finds this testifying voice—the voice of God in scripture—only because one already hears God's voice in the gospel, that is to say in the story of the cross, the story, therefore, that brings its own criteria of perception, the story, therefore, that brings its own criteria of exegesis."[113]

In view of the quality of J. Louis Martyn's research, criticism seems presumptuous, almost irreverent. His intense focus on two main areas—John and Paul—has resulted in superb contributions to both. His vivid depiction of John as a two-level drama reflects Martyn's creative imagination. To be sure, questions have been raised about his use and dating of the Benediction Against Heretics, but quite apart from that, Martyn's bifocal vision has provided a compelling hermeneutic for the Fourth Gospel: John's twofold concern with the historical tradition and his proclamation of the present Christ. Martyn provides a fundamental explanation of the reason why John did not write a treatise on Christology, but instead proclaimed a christological gospel.

As to Martyn's magisterial commentary on Galatians, the extensive research, the exegetical rigor, and the perceptive reconstruction—all in lively, eloquent style—constitute a remarkable accomplishment. He may be faulted, and rightly so, for his decision to view the Pauline corpus through the lens of Galatians. He presents the polemical, indeed, the angry Paul. Nevertheless, Martyn's sorties into the Corinthian correspondence and Romans provide adequate evidence for the apocalyptic Paul in those epistles as well. Martyn is probably right that Paul first formulated his apocalyptic theology in his battle with the Galatian Teachers, but surely that perspective was already visible in the "apocalypse of Jesus Christ" (Gal 1:12). And surely Martyn has provided the key for unlocking the mystery of Galatians, that most difficult of the Pauline letters: the battle with the invading Teachers. At the same time, Martyn's understanding of this battle provides compelling answers to the charge of anti-Judaism.

Martyn is a biblical theologian, indeed, an apocalyptic Johannine-Pauline theologian. It is of utmost importance to grasp how he understands apocalyptic: not as failed prophecy, not as calculated determinism, not as futuristic escapism, but as declaration of the action of God in history, calling for enlistment in a battle of cosmic dimensions. As to the support of this conviction—the exegetical detail, the complexity of argument—is this "too good"? Could the Galatians have understood Martyn's complex explanation? Regardless of the response, one thing is certain: Martyn offers no easy answers for questions that are profoundly difficult. What is significant for the history of NT research, above all, is Martyn's relentless attention to he text. His is a biblical theology grounded in solid historical-critical research.

LEANDER E. KECK (1928–)

Leander Keck was born in Washburn, North Dakota.[114] He was reared in a family of German Baptists who in winter rode to a small church on the windswept prairie in a horse-drawn sleigh. During the Depression the Kecks moved to western Washington, where young Lee did farm work and lumbering. He attended Linfield College in Oregon (BA 1949), where he majored in sociology and religion, preached, managed a choir, and worked in the wheat harvest. As a student, he met Nels Ferré, who influenced him to attend Andover Newton Theological School in distant Massachusetts. At Andover, Keck began his lifelong friendship with J. Louis Martyn and came under the spell of Paul S. Minear, who urged him to pursue graduate study at Yale. There he studied with Erich Dinkler (of the Bultmann school) and the perceptive Paul Schubert. Before completing his dissertation, Keck received a grant for study at Kiel and Göttingen. He returned to Yale and received his PhD in 1957.

Keck began his teaching career at Wellesley College in 1957 and moved to Vanderbilt Divinity School, where he advanced from assistant professor to professor of New Testament (1959–72). In 1972 he was named professor of New Testament at Candler School of Theology and Chairman of the Division of Religion in the Graduate School of Emery University. In 1979 he moved to Yale Divinity School, where he served as Dean for ten years and continued as Winkley Professor of Biblical Theology—a chair once occupied by Paul Minear—until his retirement in 1997. As teacher, Keck inspired a coterie of excellent scholars, among them Charles H. Talbert and M. Eugene Boring. As Brevard Childs observed, "Lee Keck has long established his reputation as an eminent New Testament scholar, a brilliant teacher and lecturer, and a wise theological educator."[115]

Leander Keck's early works were addressed to the general reader, but they provide an overview of his understanding of the NT.[116] In *Taking the Bible Seriously* he writes: "This essay asserts that there is a way of reading the Bible which opens the door to vital faith without shutting the door to critical thought."[117] Keck says that *"the Bible functions as Scripture as it is brought to bear on the actual faith and life of the readers."*[118] Within the Bible there is a norm by which all else is evaluated. "Jesus as the Christ is the gauge by which every disclosure of God's will is measured."[119] A work that provides an overview of Keck's understanding of early Christian history is his *The New Testament Experience of Faith.*[120] Keck unfolds the story of the church by means of a guided tour through cities where early Christianity flourished: Jerusalem, Antioch, Corinth, Ephesus, and Rome.[121]

PAUL

Keck produced works of major significance on Paul and Jesus. First published in 1979, *Paul and His Letters* is widely viewed as a classic.[122] The first part of the book is devoted to "The Quest for the Historical Paul." Keck notes that Paul is a problem in the NT (where there are different Pauls), in early Christianity (where Paul is a controversial figure), and in critical scholarship (where the question of Paul's historical-religious background is debated). Turning to the theology of Paul as reflected in his letters, Keck notes that we do not have all his letters, and those that survive have been edited. Moreover, Paul's letters were addressed to particular situations not fully known to the modern interpreter. The letters have their setting in Paul's career; they are letters of a Pharisee, called by God to mission to the Gentiles. "In short, the personal background of each letter is the career of Paul up to the moment of dictation."[123]

In the next part Keck investigates "The Gospel Paul Preached." Paul's gospel is the message about Christ, a message that presents the crucifixion and resurrection as God's action for salvation from sin. Keck argues that Paul does not have extensive knowledge of the details of this pivotal event: "This means that for Paul what matters is the event as a whole, not individual segments of it, whether incidents or sayings. What is important for Paul is what God did through the event (cross/resurrection), not what Jesus himself had said or done in God's name."[124]

As to the shape of the event, Keck traces three main contours: preexistence, incarnation, and post-existence. Paul, Keck points out, emphasizes the salvific response to the Christ-event. "Paul's statements about God and Christ were always worked out vis-à-vis their significance for the human condition. . . . Christology implies soteriology . . . and vice versa."[125] Paul's message calls for the response of faith, understood as trust, baptism into Christ, and life and worship in the new community.

Keck turns to what he calls "the deeper logic of Paul's gospel." Here he identifies three major motifs: first, the sovereign freedom of God. This involves the intentionality and achievement of God. According to Keck, Paul saw God as acting with a will, moving history toward a future. As to God's achievement, Keck says that "what is commonly regarded as Paul's doctrine of election and predestination is really his exposition of God's sovereign freedom to achieve the divine purpose ultimately (Romans 9–11)."[126] He continues: "The sovereign freedom of God is just that—God's innate capacity to achieve his ends without coercion."[127] In this context a question arises: Does the newness of the gospel conflict with the constancy of God? This leads Keck into a discussion of Paul's understanding of the Law. Paul affirms that the Law was given by God, but it was temporary. "The newness of the gospel, then, does not reflect a U-turn in God's intent but a new time. Now the era of the law is superseded because God's intent has been realized, inasmuch as Christ marks the time when God's promise is kept."[128]

The second major motif in the logic of Paul's gospel is his understanding of creation and new creation. Paul, Keck points out, accepted the idea that the cosmos revealed the Creator, but he believed that this knowledge shows that God-forsaking humans are without excuse. Paul also accepted the apocalyptic idea of two ages. The new aeon will involve the redemption of creation and the new creation of the redeemed. The third major motif is Paul's understanding of proclamation and anticipation. Paul, according to Keck, believes that the Christian is freed from the old participation (from sin) into a new participation in a new structure. Anticipation, says Keck, is the eschatological horizon of participation; participation in the Christ event means participation in the eschatological event. The Christian, according to Keck's view of Paul, lives in the "already" and the "not yet"—an eschatological tension that is decisive for Paul's ethics.

The final part of *Paul and His Letters* investigates "What Paul Fought For." Fundamental to Paul's battles is his conviction concerning the adequacy of trust/faith. This conviction is the foundation of his argument in Galatians. In conflict with the false teachers there, Paul insists that there is no additional requirement. "In other words, Paul spread the gospel and founded churches on the assumption that trust/faith, followed by baptism and the receipt of the Spirit, was the response that was wholly appropriate and fully adequate for salvation and participation in the body of Christ."[129] Keck proceeds to argue that Paul's stress on the adequacy of trust does not mean that the believer is without obligation. Indeed, faith's freedom involves the obligation of love. Because of his eschatological perspective—his view of the imminence of the *parousia*—Paul has been charged with a "conservative ethic"; he counsels his readers to stay in the state in which they were called (1 Cor 7:2). This charge fails to recognize the eschatological horizon: God will change the present order. "Actually, then, by depriving the status quo of its divine sanction, of its inherent goodness or rightness and permanence, Paul opened the way for Christians to change the world once they ceased to rely on God's impending act to do so."[130]

Paul also weighs in on battles about Spirit and flesh. At Corinth the Christians were threatened by a Gnosticism that saw salvation as escape from the body. Although Paul sees the flesh as the sphere of the power of the old age, he understands "body" as the self—a self that may be raised as a "spiritual body."

> In short, because Spirit is the power-sphere of the new age, flesh is the power-sphere of the old age. The struggle between the Spirit and the flesh is not a battle between higher and lower nature, between bodily drives and our minds or spirits. Rather, the struggle is between the power of the eschatological future and the power of the empirical present.[131]

The bodies of Christians are a part of the body of Christ; their bodies are the shrine of the Spirit. Thus, Keck points out, life in the body means a life of ethical responsibility.

Paul also does battle in support of the moral integrity of God in God's dealing with the human situation. Keck identifies Paul's God as the rectifier of the ungodly. In view of problems related to the terms "justify" and "make righteous," Keck, like Martyn, recommends the verb "rectify." The rectifying action of God in Christ is necessary, according to Keck's reading of Paul, because of the failure of the law. "For Paul, law fails, not because there is something inherently wrong with it (were that the case, the answer would be to get rid of the law) but because it is frustrated by another reality, sin."[132] The rectifying God is the God who keeps faith: a God whose will completes what God began.

> The gospel for which Paul fought so strenuously and passionately is centered in the God who liberated humanity from bondage to sin, death, and the law by sending the Son to be born under the law (Gal. 4:4), to be identified with sin (2 Cor. 5:21) and subject to death (Rom. 6:9). For those who believe this, the Christ-event strips away illusions about who God is and who they are.[133]

The appendix to the second edition, "Paul's Theology in Historical Criticism," is important for providing additional information about Keck's view of Pauline theology. The first section deals with five turning points in the history of Pauline interpretation: the work of F. C. Baur, the influence of the history of religion school, the discovery of the apocalyptic factor, the contribution of Bultmann, and the disintegrating of the Bultmannian synthesis. Against this historical background Keck depicts two persistent issues: first, the problem of accounting for Paul's thought historically; second, the problem of understanding Paul's thought as theology. Keck notes efforts to find coherence in theology as anthropocentric (Baur, Bultmann) or as theocentric (Käsemann); Käsemann (and J. C. Beker) also recognize the integrating role of apocalyptic. In "Instead of a Conclusion," Keck offers some general observations: the acknowledgment that Paul's thought must be derived from his seven uncontested letters, the need for historical-critical scholars to be sufficiently self-critical about historiography, and attention to the problem of understanding Paul's use of tradition. Keck insists that Paul's thought should not be viewed as a disembodied set of ideas.

> Rather, he and his thought were deeply rooted in a particular time and place, and he addressed readers who were also at home in a culture in many ways different from our own, yet one that faced certain issues endemic to the human condition. It is part of the genius of the historical-critical method that it has the capacity to make this concrete, even if in a limited way, and that it can be self-correcting as well. The newer literary/structuralist and sociological/anthropological approaches are supplementing it, but they will never replace it. Nor should they, for it is the historical-critical method that keeps us in touch with the unrepeatable reality of the past, and so reminds us of our own contingency as well as Paul's.[134]

Keck's major contribution to Pauline research is his masterful commentary on Romans.[135] In the preface he speaks of the audacity of Paul.

> In the effort to convey Paul's audacity, I have reached for that dimension of the God-reality that his assertions assume—namely, God's otherness, expressed as God's freedom, the unstated theme of Romans. Paul's audacity in writing Romans, then, reflects his effort to grasp the audacity of God. The commentary reflects my effort to grasp the audacity of Paul.[136]

The commentary is dedicated to Paul Minear, whose course on Romans at Andover Newton inspired Keck for his continuing fascination with the epistle. In the introduction Keck offers an overview of the "phenomenon of Romans." He believes Romans is a discourse presented in the form of a letter. In investigating the epistolary frame, Keck notes problems with chapter 16. He believes the letter originally included this chapter and that the various shorter texts indicate the attempt to turn Romans into a general letter. As to the historical context, Keck finds the widely accepted hypothesis to be plausible: Jewish Christians were expelled from Rome by Claudius but later returned; in the meantime Gentiles had become the majority in the church. Keck believes that Romans was written from Cenchreae around 57 CE, at a pivotal point in Paul's career when he turned from the east to the west (to Spain). Paul, says

Keck, could not count on support for his western mission as long as the Roman Christians were squabbling over dietary observations. However, Keck sees these quarrels as mere symptoms of a more serious malady: the negative attitude of Gentile Christians toward Jews. In the epistle Paul explains the meaning of the gospel in a way that emphasized God's dealing with the human condition. Thus, surmises Keck, Paul writes his "theology of mission."

Of major significance in this Introduction is Keck's summary of Paul's theology in Romans. "If one is to engage Romans, one must engage in its theology, for every line in it is affected by Paul's theological thinking."[137] In his theology Paul is not concerned to clarify concepts but to explicate the import of the Christ event for the human plight. As to Keck's intention, he says: "The basic task of this commentary . . . is not to make Paul's theology credible, but to expose that theology's own distinct intelligibility, so that the reader can engage the apostle's thought and so decide whether, and to what extent, Paul was right."[138] The center of Paul's theology, according to Keck, is the pivotal event of the death and resurrection of Christ. Keck sees this event in the light of Jewish apocalyptic eschatology: the resurrection dramatically changed the present, but it did not fully bring in the New Age. "Paul's whole theology is marked by the tension between 'the already' and 'the not yet.'"[139] "Above all, what is noteworthy about Paul's theology in Romans is the way the pivotal significance of Jesus' death and resurrection emphasizes the character of God. The theology of Romans is theocentric because it is christomorphic."[140]

In regard to Paul's use of the OT in Romans, Keck remarks that "Paul appears as the first biblical theologian in the early church. He not only reads his Bible in the light of Christ, but also reads the Christ-event in the light of his Bible."[141]

After the introduction, Keck presents the commentary (pp. 39–385). The material is organized according to the structure of the epistle. Keck identifies six main sections: "The Messenger and the Message" (1:1-15), "The Message for the Human Plight" (1:16—8:39), "The Freedom of God's Sovereignty" (9:1—11:36), "Daybreak Ethos" (12:1—15:13), "The Messenger: Between Past and Future" (15:14-33), and "Concluding Concerns" (16:1-27). Each of these main sections is divided into subsections, and some of the subsections are further divided into sub-subsections. The comments on sections, each section introduced by an overview and concluded with a summary, are presented as running interpretation of the text. Greek terms are transliterated and references to the work of other scholars are put in parentheses. A few selections may provide examples of Keck's exegetical accomplishment.

Within the first main section, "The Messenger and the Message" (1:1-15), Keck presents an analysis of the "Salutation" (1:1-7). He notes that Paul modifies the conventional epistolary form by inserting an expression of Christology. This expression is joined to Paul's presentation of himself as Christ's slave, called by God to be an apostle, set apart for the gospel. Keck presents an explication of *euaggelion*, noting the background in the LXX and the importance of texts like Isa 40:9. In vv. 2-4 Paul outlines the content of the "gospel of God." The gospel was promised beforehand and God keeps the promise; the gospel, according to Keck, is the means by which God's fidelity to God's promise is made known. Since it is the gospel concerning God's Son, what Paul says in v. 3 is significant for Christology. Here Paul recalls a tradition that had been formulated, Keck believes, in Jewish Christian circles. The traditional confession includes two parallel expressions: descended from David; declared Son of God. Keck thinks this reference to the Son implies preexistence. He believes the qualifying phrases, "according to the flesh" and "according to the spirit of holiness," do not refer to "natures" of Christ but to sequences in the status of the Son. Thus the statement asserts that the Son having occurred from the stock of David, was designated or appointed to a higher status, Son of God with power—power greater than that enjoyed as a historical figure. Now he is "Jesus Christ our Lord." Keck concludes:

> This remarkable christological statement expresses the identity and significance of the Son by concentrating on his becoming a historical figure and on his being given (by God) a new trans-historical status by the resurrection. . . . Here, what matters for Christ's identity is his Sonship *before* he became "Son of David" and his *present* Sonship with power because (or since) he was resurrected.[142]

The first subsection of the large section "The Message for the Human Plight" (1:16—8:39) is entitled "The Gospel Stated" (1:16-17). In the opening overview Keck notes that these verses express the theme of the larger section. Paul says (v. 16) that the gospel "is the power of God for salvation," echoing words from 1 Cor 1:18-25, but here in Romans he adds "to the Jew first." Keck says that Paul's term "faith" means "active trust." In v. 17 Paul asserts that the gospel is saving power because of what is revealed in it: God's rectifying rightness. "Taken together, verses 16-17 announce that the gospel is God's power to save because it is the means by which God saves, disclosing God's true character, rectitude/righteousness."[143] To support his claim, Paul cites Hab 2:4, a quotation that bristles with problems. Keck points out that Paul's translation does not agree with either the LXX or the Hebrew. According to Keck, Paul understood the text as a messianic promise, fulfilled in Jesus Christ. He is the promised "righteous one" who will live by faithfulness—a conviction to be explicated in 3:21-31 and 5:12-21.The central argument of this large section on the "Message for the Human Plight" is "God's Rectifying Rectitude Apart from the Law" (3:21-31), a sub-subsection of the subsection "The Impartiality of God's Rectifying Rectitude (3:21—5:11). In regard to this text Keck notes the possibility that Paul is using a fragment of early Christian tradition. Crucial for him is the translation of *dia pisteōs Iēsou Christou* (v. 22a) as "through the faithfulness of Jesus Christ." In other words, in contrast to many interpreters Keck insists that Paul is not speaking of faith "in Jesus Christ," but about the "faithfulness of Jesus Christ": his fidelity, his obedience to God. According to Keck, the translation "faith in Christ" would claim that God's rectitude is made manifest in *our* believing.

Paul also says that God's righteousness is manifest through "the redemption that is in Christ Jesus," a metaphor for the freeing of slaves. But what, asks Keck, is the basis for saying the redemption in Christ is a manifestation of God's rectitude? The answer is provided by v. 25, "whom God put forward as *hilastērion*." Keck rehearses the various meanings assigned to this term, including "Mercy Seat" (of the Ark of the Covenant), and the timeworn debate about "propitiation" vs. "expiation." He concludes that a simple answer is not forthcoming, though he finds "propitiation" anomalous, since Paul says it is *God* who put forward the *hilastērion*. The reason is that the *hilastērion* is a demonstration of God's rectitude: God's passing over of previously committed sins. Paul expresses this by the term *anochē* (v. 26), which describes God's "restraint." But, asks Keck, does not God's failure to punish show God's lack of rectitude? That would be true, he answers, if rectitude were according to the Law. But the rectitude of God is revealed through Christ and is totally different from the rectitude of the Law. Keck concludes: "In short, God is never more true to God's Godhood as the radically Other than when God rectifies the person who lives by Jesus' faithfulness."[144]

Later in this major section (1:16—8:39) is a controversial text that Keck titles "The Role of the Law in the Reign of Sin" (7:7-25), a sub-subsection of the subsection "Liberation from Bondage" (5:12—8:39). According to Keck, the basic questions of the text are: Why does one obey the evil powers, and why does the Law turn out to be a power from which one must be liberated? In the course of discussing these questions Keck tackles the notorious problem of the meaning of the repeated use the first person singular. He concludes the use of "I" is rhetorical, not autographical. He says that "the allusions to Genesis suggest that the 'I' portrays the Adamic self (not simply Adam himself), whose plight has become clear in Christ."[145]

Keck believes that in vv. 7-12 Paul is describing the Law as the unwilling accomplice of sin. When Paul says "if it had not been for the law, I would not have known sin" (v. 7), someone might suppose he is suggesting that the "law is sin." Paul replies, "By no means!" Instead, his argument will show the opposite: that the Law is holy (v. 12). Why, asks Keck, does Paul cite the tenth commandment of the Decalogue, "You shall not covet," to illustrate how knowledge of sin comes through the law? Because, answers Keck, the command not to covet (or desire) is the only one among the ten that forbids an inner disposition prior to action. In v. 10, where Paul says that "the very commandment that promised life proved to be death to me," Keck sees an allusion to Gen 3:4, where the serpent says, "you will not die"—an illustration of how sin deceived Eve into supposing that God would not inflict punishment. "In short, sin uses the law to deceive by creating the illusion the one can get away with disobedience."[146] The culprit is not the Law, which is "holy and just and good" (v. 12), but sin, which uses the Law and makes it, according to Keck, the unwilling accomplice of sin's destructive work.

Beginning in 7:13, Paul, according to Keck, reflects on the conflicted self. The perverse power of sin uses the Law to bring death; vv. 14-25 explain how this comes about. Keck believes v. 14 depicts the disparity between the character of the Law and the character of the self: the Law is spiritual, but I am *sarkinos*—the fleshliness that manifests itself in desire (or covetousness). The result is to be sold under sin. Keck believes this result has implications for the ancient argument as to whether Paul, in this section of Romans, is describing the pre-Christian or the post-Christian experience. "This explanation ["sold under sin"] is the chief reason Paul is not talking about Christian existence."[147] Keck points out that v. 15 begins to explain how being fleshly is manifest in what one does or does not achieve. The disparity between intention (will) and actual deed is described in vv. 15-20, and the disparity between the inner self and the outer self is depicted in vv. 21-24. "For Paul, the problem is neither ignorance of the good nor lack of will to do it, but the inability to do the willed good that is known through the law."[148] In the disparity between what is willed and what is done, Paul, according to Keck, believes the real doer is sin, which is resident in the self. Paul says that "nothing good dwells within me" (v. 18); what does dwell within him is sin (v. 20). In exegeting vv. 22-23 Keck takes up the debated question of how *nomos* is used in these verses. He admits that there is no easy answer, but he thinks that Paul refers to two fundamental laws in conflict: "the law of God" (= "the law of my mind") and the law in my members (=

"the law of sin," that is, the commanding power of sin). This crippling conflict elicits Paul's impassioned outburst "Wretched man that I am! Who will rescue me from this body of death?" (v. 24).

In summarizing Paul's argument in 7:7-25, Keck calls attention to what Paul does *not* say. He does not try to define the essence of sin, the self, or the Law; he makes no mention of Satan. Instead, Keck says that Paul depicts the human plight by showing the power of sin to enslave, the Law's lack of power to prevent its misuse by sin, and the incapacity of the self to realize what it wills. "Here, no qualifying considerations or extenuating circumstances are allowed to mitigate the dilemma in which the self is caught, blur what caused it, or imply a spurious solution from it. The self cannot extricate itself; it can only be rescued."[149]

In the third main section of Romans, "The Freedom of God's Sovereignty" (9:1—11:36) Keck identifies a subsection, "God's Freedom as Fidelity" (11:1-32); within this subsection is a sub-subsection, "The Mystery of God's Way with All" (11:25-32). In v. 25 Paul says that he wants the Roman Christians to understand a mystery, that is, that the destined future is now disclosed. Keck believes the mystery includes four interconnected elements. First, a temporary hardening has come upon Israel until a full number of Gentiles has come in. Keck believes that what the Gentiles come into is the people of God; he says that the meaning of "full number" is not clear. Second, Paul says that this hardening has come on "part of Israel," an expression that assumes a distinction between Christian Jews and the rest who are hardened. Third, Paul's assertion that "all Israel will be saved" has been qualified in 9:6 ("For not all Israelites truly belong to Israel"). Nevertheless, Keck says that "it is likely that here Paul does envision ethnic Israel as a whole (not every Israelite) as destined for salvation."[150] Fourth, Paul describes the manner in which Israel will be saved—a manner that is in accord with Scripture (Isa 59:20-21). However, Keck points out that Paul's translation follows neither the Hebrew nor the LXX; in distinction from both, Paul says that the Deliverer will come *from* Zion. Keck notes that interpreters are divided as to the identity of the Deliverer: for some, the Deliverer is Christ, an interpretation that would look to salvation in the *parousia*; for others, the Deliverer is God, an interpretation supported by the OT idea of Zion as God's dwelling place. Keck believes the latter interpretation is preferable, but he does not believe Paul can envisage salvation apart from the Christ event.

In v. 29 Paul says that the "gifts and call (election) of God are irrevocable." Keck believes this statement proves how God's self-consistency is squared with the refusal of the gospel by the majority of Jews. According to the previous verses the unbelieving Jews can be viewed from two perspectives: from the gospel perspective they are enemies of God for your sake; from the perspective of election they are beloved by God for the sake of the patriarchs (who received the promises). But how, asks Keck, can the same people be both God's enemies and God's beloved? The answer is provided in v. 32: "For God has imprisoned all in disobedience so that he may be merciful to all." Paul's point, according to Keck, is that God's impartial justice treats Gentiles and Jews in the same way. "The identical way in which God responds to the disobedience of both Gentile and Jew disallows the much-discussed claim that Paul envisions the salvation of Israel apart from Christ."[151] "Further," Keck continues, "had Paul thought that all Israel would be saved apart from Christ, he would have implied that for Israel, Jesus is not the promised Messiah after all."[152]

This third main section of the epistle concludes with the celebration of "God's Awesome Ways" (11:33-36). In overview, Keck observes that this text "expresses his [Paul's] keen sense that in disclosing the mystery of God's dealings with Israel and the Gentiles he has glimpsed the magnitude of God's awesome otherness."[153] In a poetic benediction, Paul heralds the transcendent mystery of God and God's action. "In a way, the whole passage is the stone against which theology stumbles when it claims too much, when it forgets that the Reality called 'God' is a mystery, when it neglects the task of showing why it is a mystery—one too deep to be fathomed but which must be acknowledged gratefully."[154]

JESUS

Even more important than his research on Paul, I believe, is Keck's work on Jesus. His two major books, *A Future for the Historical Jesus* and *Who is Jesus?* are informed by his command of the history of research, seen in his editorial work on the Lives of Jesus Series and in his own contribution to the series, his edition of David Friedrich Strauss, *The Christ of Faith and the Jesus of History.*[155]

Keck's *A Future for the Historical Jesus* is essentially an analysis of the history and methodology of the quest for the historical Jesus and a reflection on the related theological assumptions and implications.[156] He begins with a discussion of "Jesus in the hands of determined critics." He launches this discussion with the question: Who is the "historical Jesus?" Keck proceeds to sharpen the question. "Is the historian's Jesus, the Jesus reconstructed by critical methods, centrally significant for Christian faith and thought, or is such a Jesus irrelevant or even inimical to it?"[157] The historian's Jesus, says Keck, is the Jesus reconstructed on the basis of a historical investigation of the sources. He recognizes the problems and presuppositions involved in the reconstruction, but concludes that the attempt is worth the effort. "While we cannot know Jesus

634 | History of New Testament Research

as completely as we once may have thought, we can know important things solidly. . . . This modest result is sufficient to tell us what Jesus was like and ample enough to work with fruitfully in theology."[158]

Keck emphasizes the theological importance of the quest for the historical Jesus. The Jesus known by historical method is essential to preaching; the historical understanding of Jesus is essential to Christology; the historicity of Jesus reflects the historicity of faith and theology as a whole. Keck contends that "the historical Jesus (the historian's Jesus) does have a role in Christian faith."[159] He elaborates this point by tracing contours in the history of the debate with examples from Bultmann, Jeremias, and Ebeling, none of whom provides an adequate solution. According to Keck the term "faith" is open to misunderstanding, and it better to describe the relation to Jesus as "trust." But how does the historical Jesus relate to trust? Trust involves confidence in the historian's work, trust in witnesses who recommend Jesus as trustworthy, and one's own "reading" of Jesus' trustworthiness. "One does not trust a proclamation or entrust himself to it; trust is directed toward a person and the function of the kerygma is to make it possible for trust in Jesus to commence."[160]

Keck turns to the relation of the historical Jesus to the gospel. Fundamental is the question: What is Gospel? In answer, Keck appeals to three basic distinctions: between the formal structure of the gospel and a material statement of it; between preaching a theology of grace and communicating a grace-full event; between the gospel and propaganda, between theology and ideology. The significance of these distinctions can be summarized in the larger question:

> How shall we speak of Jesus so that the formal character of the gospel can be expressed materially in a way that reaches the hearer as good news for his sake and not the church's propaganda? Specifically, how shall one articulate the good news so that the historical Jesus comes through in a way that the hearer may trust him for his salvation?[161]

Keck continues his explication of the nature of the gospel by exploring the understanding of the gospel in the early church. In the Jewish setting the appeal to Scripture was central and Jesus was presented as the messiah. In the Hellenistic milieu Christ was depicted according to the drama of the descent of the heavenly redeemer. "In this way, the material content of the gospel was changed precisely in order to maintain the formal character—good news of God's decisive act for mankind."[162] This implies that we cannot adopt a particular formulation of the gospel, but we can restate it in ways that do not surrender its essential character. "The historical Jesus helps to keep the church honest through the constant pressure of having to do with a real human, historical figure."[163] The recognition of the problematic shape of the historical Jesus is, according to Keck, an extension of the "scandal of the cross." But a more fundamental question arises: Why Jesus? Keck answers: because the centrality of Jesus is constitutive for historical Christianity.

Keck turns to the question of the relation of the historical Jesus and salvation. The question, he believes, needs rehabilitation. The need is apparent in the widespread notion that the problem of humanity is unrealized potential: salvation is self-fulfillment. A reformulation of the question must acknowledge that the problem is the self, the human situation at its deepest level. Since salvation is by trust, distrust is at the root of the problem. Keck proceeds to review various views of salvation through Jesus. In preparing for the exposition of his own view, he writes: "No aspect of Jesus saves us, but the whole life touches our life as a whole."[164] For Keck, salvation is realized by trust in Jesus. He argues that we can know Jesus by historical study and reconstruction of the traditions about him. "Accordingly, one trusts a figure in the past when he trusts his integrity and the validity of what he stood for."[165] To trust in Jesus is to trust God and to come into right relation with God. Keck also believes that trusting in Jesus produces a community of trust; those who trust in Jesus trust in others who trust in him.

Keck turns to the crucial question of the relation of the historical Jesus to the character of God. He says that "in starting with the historical Jesus to reflect on God, we are beginning at the point which for Christians has always been pivotal and where contemporary persons can more readily commence."[166] In discussing "the God of Jesus," Keck notes the importance of revelation. "Only when we perceive God through the prism of the event of Jesus can we justly speak of God's revealing himself in Jesus."[167] He cautions against the tendency to appropriate Jesus' conceptions of God (as if he were a rational theologian) or to emphasize Jesus' self-understanding (as if we had access to his inner life). Attention to Jesus' understanding of God also reminds us of the Jewishness of Jesus; he was a Jew who trusted God. Jesus proclaimed the kingdom of God; he believed that God was the sovereign Creator. According to Keck, Jesus understood the kingdom as an act of God, an event of judgment and grace. Jesus believed that the kingdom had come but was not completely present. "The fact that the Jesus-event was constituted by this expectation of the impending One and that this expectation was not fulfilled as expected is not a surd to be negated but a condition to be grasped affirmatively: the impending God retains his freedom even vis-à-vis Jesus."[168]

Keck believes the death of Jesus presents a crisis for our understanding of God. Jesus anticipated his own death and expected to be vindicated, but God did not intervene. "The only God who is trustworthy is the One who does not interfere to protect the pious but who is present in the thick of darkness, perhaps even as the thick darkness."[169] Keck asks: What is the meaning of the resurrection for the problem of God? He answers that it "can only mean that God had not repudiated him but vindicated him."[170] Keck points out that it is Jesus, and no one else, whom God raised. In Jewish theology God was expected to vindicate the faithful, but with Jesus the final resurrection was present proleptically. This view, according to Keck, assumes an apocalyptic theology, a recognition of the decisive act of God. "Resurrection, therefore, is grounded in the freedom and power of God to create afresh, out of death, as he originally created absolutely, *ex nihilo*."[171] Keck says that the one who trusts in Jesus does not vindicate himself or demand God to vindicate him. "Instead, on the basis of Jesus he ventures to entrust himself and his vindication to God, and is prepared to receive it where Jesus did—beyond death."[172]

Finally, Keck says that Jesus was "the parable of God." "Jesus concentrated on parabolic speech because he himself was a parabolic event of the kingdom of God."[173] Like the parable, Jesus points beyond himself to God and calls for relying on God. "Since his kingdom is present now only as prolepsis and as parable, we live by parable. That is, we trust the historical Jesus."[174] In the Epilogue, Keck reiterates the major point of the book. He insists "that thorough criticism of the Gospels does provide us with sufficient data about Jesus that the contour of his life as a whole can come into view, and that this can be the core of Christian preaching and the dominant datum with which theology works."[175]

Leander Keck's own contribution to the quest of the historical Jesus is his remarkable book, *Who is Jesus?*[176] In describing the book, Keck writes: "The result is something of a hybrid, neither history nor Christology proper but rather theological reflection on history—on those aspects of the Jesus of history that are central to his continuing significance."[177] He begins by discussing the Jesus of the past. He limits his discussion to what can be investigated historically, thus excluding the birth narratives, the miracle stories, and the accounts of the resurrection. "The goal, in short, was a chastened but accurate portrayal of the Jesus who once was, set in the context of the society that once was."[178] Keck notes the weight that past research has placed on the criterion of dissimilarity (negative criticism). However, he believes that the Enlightenment legacy of negative criticism has overemphasized Jesus' differences from Judaism and early Christianity. At the same time, he thinks it important to recognize that there is a difference between the historical Jesus and the Jesus presented in the Gospels.

Turning to the particularity of Jesus, Keck emphasizes the historical fact that Jesus was a Jew and proceeds to investigate what kind of a Jew Jesus was and was not. He points out that Jesus addressed Jews as part of his mission. Jesus called twelve followers, a number symbolic of Israel. He believed that when God's kingdom would be actualized, God's people would be Israel. As to Jesus' view of the Gentiles, Keck observes that he did not go to Gentile cities or to Gentiles. "In short, it is altogether likely that Jesus had not one good thing to say about Gentiles as a group."[179] Nevertheless, Keck insists that Gentiles had a stake in the Jewishness of Jesus. "It is precisely Jesus' concentration of his mission on Israel that grounds his permanent significance for Gentiles."[180] The promise of God to Abraham, says Keck, comes to Gentiles through Jesus. Jesus is the link for Gentiles to Israel's Scripture.

Keck next focuses on the role of Jesus as teacher. At the center of the teachings of Jesus is proclamation of the kingdom of God. Keck describes the kingdom as God's "rectifying power." The kingdom is the coming reign of God, but it has not yet fully come. Keck takes up the question of the kingdom as present or future. He notes that the saying that the kingdom is present (Luke 17:20-21) is immediately followed by a saying that speaks of the apocalyptic future (Luke 17:22). According to Keck's emphasis, Jesus brought a new situation—the situation of the relation to God, the time of salvation. When a person lives in the new situation, Jesus' teaching of the sovereignty—the actualizing of the rule of God—is coming into view. Keck describes the kingdom as God's "rectifying impingement." The kingdom is coming soon, but "God's kingdom changes things before it actually arrives. When it impinges on the present, rectification begins."[181] "Living now by the future is what makes it truly eschatological."[182]

Keck moves from the discussion of the kingdom of God to the God of the kingdom. Although Jesus proclaims the kingdom of God, he rarely uses the image of "king." More frequently Jesus employs the imagery of the father. Like a father, God give good gifts to God's children. Jesus calls the disciples to imitate the goodness of God the father, not God the king. According to Keck, Jesus does not make public claims to be the son of God. However, he notes that "the gospel traditions can portray Jesus acting as God's son, one whose life and work are so determined by God that he replicates on earth his Father in heaven."[183] He is the obedient son; he represented the coming of the kingdom by what he said and did.

Echoing his subtitle, Keck elaborates the meaning of the gospels' understanding of Jesus in the "perfect tense." By this he means that the writers of the gospels presented Jesus in terms of his ongoing significance for their communities. Mark, in chapter 13, added material relevant to his own time (the revolt against Rome) but reflected earlier teachings of Jesus. A stumbling-block of the early Christians was the failure of the promise of the future (Mark 9:1). Keck acknowledges that Jesus did expect God to act soon, but he argues that the delay did not destroy the rectifying power of the kingdom. "In short, the real question is not whether Jesus was right or wrong about the time of the kingdom but whether he was right or wrong about the God he imaged as king and father."[184]

Keck explores the significance of the death of Jesus for the revelation of the living God: what he calls "the fractured prism." According to Keck, the prediction of the passion indicates that Jesus anticipated his suffering and death. Jesus went to Jerusalem by his own decision. "He went to do what he had always done: embody what he knew was coming. In the temple he took the risk of symbolizing it."[185] Keck believes the resurrection reveals the living God whom Jesus trusted. "In short, if God validated and vindicated precisely the Jesus who was executed on Golgotha, then he remains the fractured prism through which one sees into that mysterious Reality called 'God.'"[186] In this context Keck affirms the often-neglected idea of the holiness—the radical otherness—of God. The death-resurrection of Jesus, according to Keck, shows two sides of God's holiness: the negative side (the silence of God in response to the cry of Jesus) and the positive side (the crucifixion as expression of God's love). "God's radical otherness is neither remoteness nor indifference but the ground of holy love that loves the unlovable into a rectitude that enables the rectified recipient to love the other, be it neighbor or enemy."[187]

Keck explicates his concept of "the Golgotha hermeneutic." By this he refers to the conviction that Jesus' death and resurrection were according to Scripture. The gospel narrators present the Golgotha event in two ways: the historical explanation of what happened and the recognition of divine necessity. "Thereby the narrator's intelligible historical story is really the visible actualization of what God had purposed and intimated in scripture."[188] "For Christians, Jesus is not the messiah despite Golgotha but because of it, since after Easter it was Golgotha that redefined *messiah*."[189] Indeed, from Keck's perspective the traditional view of "messianism," with its expectation of the exercise of God's political power, was crucified. Keck believes that to follow Jesus is to appropriate Golgotha. Jesus called his followers to take up a cross, to lose life to find it. "In short, seen as a paradigm, Jesus' cross symbolizes a way of life marked by love free of self-regard and the need for approbation for doing good."[190]

Keck turns to a discussion of the ethics of Jesus, "the authorizing judge." Jesus' stance toward the moral life was one of uncompromising absoluteness; the kingdom "requires total resolve and unhesitating commitment."[191] In regard to the ethics of Jesus, Keck points out that Jesus does not analyze but addresses; he does not present principles or offer a system. Instead, Jesus addresses particular situations; he focuses on the deed. Jesus is prophet, not sage. Keck suggests a shift from concern with the "ethics of Jesus" to the person of Jesus. Jesus' moral teachings are related to his person. "In short, it is Jesus' life, captivated by the kingdom, that endows his teaching with moral power."[192] Jesus, the historical figure, is the shaper of the moral life. The gospels "do narrate the story of Jesus' mission and execution, thereby anchoring the sayings of Jesus in the portrayal of his life and character."[193]

Keck observes that the gospels present Jesus as the judge who authorizes. This can be seen, for example, in his explicit commands. Keck stresses the importance of internalizing the external authorizer by "persistent appropriation of Jesus into the moral life so that he becomes the internal compass and criterion of the doer and the deed."[194] "Finally, in authorizing the moral life Jesus evokes a commitment to what he was committed to himself—the kingdom of God and the rectifying import of its impingement."[195] In regard to Jesus as judge, Keck emphasizes the function of the internalized authorizer. "This judge makes the doer judge oneself."[196] Keck also stresses the accountability of the authorized self. Although accountability is often related to the future judgment, the concern here is with the accountable self in the present. Nevertheless, says Keck, the trans-historical has relevance: the future judge is none other than Jesus; this symbolizes the ultimate significance of the moral life. Mention of the future, however, raises the question of reward. Keck says that "the whole theme of reward is transposed into another key: because Jesus was vindicated beyond death, they [those whose lives are on the line] carry their crosses in confident hope that they, and what they may have to die for, too will be vindicated as he was— on the yonder side of history and by the One whose holiness unites goodness and power."[197]

A final section of Keck's book deals with "power of the perfect tense." He notes common expressions: "for Jesus' sake" (a phrase that can be "because of" or "for the benefit of"); "on account of Jesus" (a phrase that means to act in a way that finds its warrant in who Jesus was); "for the good of Jesus" (a phrase that describes the work of those who do good for Jesus, for the gospel, and for the kingdom). Keck concludes:

Nonetheless, those who respond positively to Jesus voluntarily suffer for the sake of the kingdom, whether "on account of" it, in order to grasp it and be changed by it, or to advance it. . . . Such persons usually do not talk of their own suffering but talk of others' for whose sake they are ready to accept what may befall them. Such voluntarily accepted suffering has two names: one is love, the other is Jesus—in perfect tense.[198]

Scholars familiar with the stellar work of Leander Keck have expectantly awaited his projected book on NT christology. He presented lectures on the subject in his Shaffer Lectures at Yale (1980), but these have not appeared in print. However, hints of what Keck would do in his culminating work can be heard in his programmatic essay, "Toward a Renewal of New Testament Christology," originally a paper presented at the General Meeting of the SNTS in 1985.[199] The burden of Keck's paper is his conviction that much of what has been written recently under the title of Christology is actually the history of christological material, as is seen especially in the preoccupation with titles. What is needed is a thoroughly and intentionally *theological* approach that concentrates on the NT texts.

In sum, the work of Leander Keck has made a significant contribution to the history of NT research. Skilled in all the disciplines of historical criticism, he also has the gift of communicating in a lucid, lively style. To be sure, his style functions at two levels: that of the general reader and that of the scholar. His Romans commentary, for example, sets its sights above the intended audience of the Abingdon commentaries and is a challenge to the seasoned scholar. His books on Jesus are densely written, with a careful analysis of complex issues.

Above all, Keck is a biblical theologian. For most biblical scholars, required by the discipline to master the skills of linguistic, literary, and historical criticism, there has not been sufficient time to master the methods and insights of theology. Most are primarily historians, not theologians. Keck is an exception. He is well-read in the field, and even more, gifted with a theological sensitivity and penetrating theological mind. Of course, some may suppose that the thought of the NT cannot be that complex—that biblical theologians like Keck have imposed a theology on the NT. But any scholar who has wrestled with Romans is forced to recognize the depth of Paul's thought. Many of the original readers would have been unable to understand Keck's comments, but some of them sensed that Romans was important enough to save and circulate. In any case, Keck's understanding of the theology of Romans is based on solid historical-critical exegesis.

VICTOR PAUL FURNISH (1931–)

Born in Chicago, Furnish is the son of a Methodist minister.[200] He did his undergraduate study at Cornell College (Iowa), where he majored in philosophy and graduated Phi Beta Kappa (AB 1952). In 1955 he received the BD from Garrett-Evangelical Theological Seminary with "highest distinction." At Yale, where he received MA (1957) and PhD (1960) degrees, Furnish was influenced by Dinkler and Schubert. "My interest in Pauline theology," he wrote, "was first kindled by Professor Paul Schubert at Yale, and under his guidance my doctoral dissertation—a first tentative venture into the subject of Pauline ethics—was conceived and completed."[201] Furnish did postdoctoral study in Jerusalem and in Tübingen (1964), and, with the support of the Alexander von Humboldt Foundation, in Bonn (1965–66), Munich (1972–73), and Münster (1987).

Furnish began his teaching career at Perkins School of Theology, Southern Methodist University, where he advanced through the ranks from Instructor (1959–60) to University Distinguished Professor of New Testament (1983–2000). Although beckoned to prestigious positions, Furnish remained in the place of his original academic appointment, primarily teaching ministerial candidates. "His teaching style," former students observed, "is a lesson in both helping and prodding students to develop capacities for interpreting the New Testament. His patient persistence with the less disciplined among his students and his challenge and encouragement to the more energetic are exemplary."[202] Furnish's contribution to the NT scholarly guild has been large. He has served as president of the SBL (1993) and editor of the *JBL* (1983–88). He has also been general editor and chair of the editorial board of the Abingdon New Testament Commentaries (1988–2011).

ETHICS

Furnish's major works are in the field of NT ethics. His *Theology and Ethics in Paul* is hailed as a classic.[203] One perceptive observer has said that "it constitutes one of the most comprehensive and judicious assessments of Pauline ethics in the century."[204] Like Keck's research, Furnish's work is solidly grounded in a comprehensive knowledge of the history of the discipline.[205] The book was first published in 1968 and had its 6th printing in 1988; the edition of 2009 is essentially a reprint.[206] In the original preface Furnish sets forth his purpose: "The thesis which finally emerges from this investigation is that the apostle's ethical concerns are not secondary but radically integral to his basic theological convictions."[207]

Furnish begins with an investigation of the sources of Paul's ethical teaching. First, he notes the influence of the OT and Judaism. He observes that Paul's ethical instruction quotes frequently from Scripture. Furnish also detects a relationship to material from the Apocrypha and Pseudepigrapha but finds little evidence of literary dependency. Turning to the Hellenistic sources, Furnish notes the use of philosophical terms and of the diatribe style, but he concludes that the influence flows primarily through the syncretistic culture of the day. Next, Furnish takes up the difficult question of the influence of the teachings of Jesus on Paul's ethic. While he recognizes that Paul can quote sayings of the Lord, references to the teachings of Jesus are relatively sparse. Furnish concludes his chapter on sources with the observation that it is a mistake to place a one-sided emphasis on Paul's Jewishness over against his "Hellenism" or vice versa; Paul is neither an ethical philosopher nor a rabbinic sage. "He writes always as an apostle, as a man in Christ."[208]

Furnish next investigates Paul exhortations. In shaping these, Paul makes use of traditional material. His use of this material reflects his concern to be concrete and relevant. "He wishes to make it clear that the new life in Christ is not some vague experience of detachment from the world, but manifests itself in multiple and concrete engagements in and with the world."[209] Paul is also concerned to be inclusive and persuasive. Furnish points out that Paul does not merely select traditional material but assimilates it into new contexts. For example, Paul defines the Law "solely in relation to the Christ-event."[210] He makes use of traditional vice lists and lists of virtues and includes them in the context of the argument of his letters. Furnish observes that Paul uses a variety of modes of exhortation: questions, indicatives and imperatives, hortatory and autobiographical narratives. In regard to the understanding of *kerygma* and *didache,* Furnish rejects C. H. Dodd's familiar distinction.[211] Paul's exhortations involve both proclamation and moral instruction. "It is inaccurate to say," writes Furnish, "either that his concern is primarily theological and secondarily ethical, or the reverse, that it is primarily practical, secondarily theoretical. His concern is, in a word, *evangelical*: to preach the gospel."[212]

Furnish devotes a chapter to the themes of Paul's preaching. "Just as his ethical teaching has significant theological dimensions, so do the major themes of his preaching have significant ethical dimensions."[213] These themes, according to Furnish, are rooted in "the apostle's eschatological perspective."[214] Consequently a major theme, reflecting the Jewish image of two ages, is "this age and the age to come." In analyzing this theme Furnish depicts the powers of this age (the present evil era) and the transcendent power of God that will destroy the evil forces in the future. God's action in the death and resurrection of Christ brings salvation and "the new creation." Yet, although total triumph of God will be in the future, God's power is already at work. "Thus, Paul sees the 'eschatological' power of God as already operative and says that the man 'in Christ' *is* a 'new creation.' "[215] Paul expresses this, says Furnish, with the metaphors of the "first fruits" of salvation and the "guarantee" of hope. With the coming of the Spirit the presence of God's love becomes operative in the lives of believers. "The Spirit, then, is the *presentation*—construed literally, the 'making-present'—of that which belongs to another 'age' and which, in spite of its 'presentation,' continues to belong to that age."[216] The coming age is an apocalyptic motif, but Paul breaks the categories of apocalyptic by declaring that the eschatological power of God has broken into the present.

Another major theme for Paul is summed up in his understanding of the Law, sin, and righteousness. In discussing this theme, Furnish notes the intertwining of eschatological and anthropological categories; humanity is the focal center of the battle between the forces of evil and the power of God. Through the flesh, says Paul, sin gains entry into the human person.

> Sin, therefore, is given a very radical meaning in Paul's thought. It is not just life's perversion, but ultimately its negation. For him sin means hostility to God's purposes and rebellion against his rule, an *alienation* from God so serious and (from man's side) so irremediable that only the concept of "death" is finally appropriate to describe it.[217]

Even more alarming, in the context of Paul's upbringing, is his conviction that the Law is the agent of sin. Sin entered humanity through Adam, but it is not tabulated where there is no law (Rom 5:12ff.); the law brings knowledge of sin (Rom 7:7ff.); the law was added to provoke transgression (Gal 3:19ff.). According to Paul, the remedy for this fatal human situation is the righteousness of God and God's action of justification. Furnish defines Paul's concept of the righteousness of God as God's covenant faithfulness and truth. The righteousness of God is seen preeminently in Christ's death and resurrection. For Paul, the righteousness of God "stands at the very center of his gospel."[218] To describe God's action of justification, Furnish—to avoid problems in translating the Greek verb—uses the word "rightwised" (the term adopted from Old English by Kendrick Grobel in his translation of Bultmann's *Theology of the New Testament*). To be "rightwised" means to be restored to the proper relation with God; it means to receive a verdict of acquittal in the eschatological judgment. Paul emphasizes God's initiative and justification as an action of

God's grace, another major theme. The event of God's grace is enacted in the death and resurrection of Christ. "Paul's christology, like his pneumatology and doctrine of righteousness (justification), has a thoroughly eschatological orientation. . . . Jesus' 'historical' activities are seen to have meaning and effect because they manifest the power of the age to come already operative in the present."[219] As Furnish says, "It is clear beyond question that Christ's death and resurrection represent the decisive element in the Pauline gospel."[220] The believer participates in the death and resurrection of Christ; he or she is united with the death of Christ and will be raised in the future. "But primarily the lordship of Christ is seen as already operative, and his death and resurrection are seen to constitute the eschatological event."[221] "In Christ, supremely in his death and resurrection, God's sovereign love is at work making new the lives of those who 'believe' in him and 'give' themselves to him."[222]

Furnish proceeds to discuss Paul's concepts of faith, love, and obedience—concepts that constitute another Pauline theme. Reminiscent of Bultmann, Furnish affirms Paul's understanding of faith as obedience. The obedience of faith means belonging radically to Christ; "the object of the Christian's obedience is Christ himself."[223] In regard to the will of God, Furnish observes that Paul seldom speaks of God's will as any specific act or pattern of conduct. Instead, the apostle affirms the total claim that God lays upon the believer. Paul can speak of the "law of faith" in contrast to the written code. "The believer, because his whole life is given to God for obedience, is freed *from* the law's works and *for* the law's fulfillment in a new sense."[224] Moreover, the law the believer is commanded to obey is the law of love. To obey that command is to participate in the community of the people of God, the household of faith.

Following this eloquent review of Pauline theology, Furnish proceeds to an investigation of the character of the Pauline ethic, beginning with an analysis of the theological structure of Paul's ethic. Furnish contends that Paul did not have a system of ethics but that he was concerned with the conduct of Christians in relation to the central themes of his preaching. In regard to studying Paul's ethic, Furnish writes: "It is the study, first of all, of the theological convictions which underlie Paul's concrete exhortations and instructions, and, secondly, of the way those convictions shape his responses to practical questions of conduct."[225] Paul's ethic, according to Furnish, has three main motifs. First, the ethic is *theological*. "The Pauline ethic is first of all radically theological because it presupposes that man's whole life and being is dependent upon the sovereign, creative, and redemptive power of God."[226] Second, Paul's ethic is *eschatological*. "The Pauline eschatology is not just one motif among numerous others, but helps to provide the fundamental perspective within which everything else is viewed."[227] For Paul, eschatology is not exclusively directed to the future since it sees the power of the transcendent God already active in the present. Crucial to Paul's ethic and his eschatology is the dialectic of the indicative and the imperative. Third, Paul's ethic is *christological*. According to Paul, the believer is united with the death and resurrection of Christ, although the resurrection of the believer will be in the future. "But the resurrection power of God in Christ is already operative in the believer's present life."[228]

Furnish proceeds to explicate the meaning of the indicative and the imperative for Paul's theology and ethics. He rejects the notion that the imperative is based on the indicative; instead, the two belong inseparably together. "God's *claim* is regarded by the apostle as a constitutive part of God's *gift*. The Pauline concept of grace is *inclusive* of the Pauline concept of obedience. . . . The Pauline imperative is not just the result of the indicative but fully integral to it."[229]

Related to the imperative is the problem of ethical action. In investigating this problem Furnish notes the difficulty of discerning the will of God. Paul believes that God's will must be perceived in the setting of the community, and that its fundamental meaning is found in the command of love.

> It is, therefore, the Pauline concept of love which supplies the key to the apostle's thinking about the discernment of the divine will in the various "normal crises" of daily conduct. God's redemptive activity in Christ is an expression of his love, and Christ's own act of obedience unto death for the sake of others is commended as exemplary for all who belong to Christ. To "imitate Christ" means to give one's self in love for others as he gave himself.[230]

The application of the love command calls for discernment. "What is to be done must be discerned and decided in the individual case but always with reference to God's gift of love as it has been met in Christ and God's demand of love as it is repeatedly met in the neighbor."[231] These concluding remarks from *Theology and Ethics* flow easily into a discussion of Furnish's next major book on ethics, *The Love Command in the New Testament*.[232] In the introduction, he presents the purpose of the book. "It focuses on the love *ethic*, the love *command*, what the New Testament teaches and otherwise reflects about earliest Christianity's view of loving one's brother, one's neighbor, or one's enemy."[233] Furnish begins with a review of the commandments to love in the teachings of Jesus. The "double command" (love of God and love of neighbor) is recorded in Mark 12:28-34. The Matthean redactor adds a point: "On these two commandments hang all the law and the prophets" (22:40). In Luke (10:25-37) the double command is joined to the parable of the Good Samaritan. The parable, Furnish observes, is a dramatic presentation of what the love command means. "Thus, the parable teaches that what counts is not just knowledge of the law . . . but an obedience to the law of love, so complete that where love is operative all the artificial barriers of race, nation, and religion are broken down."[234]

A distinctive feature of Jesus' teaching, observes Furnish, is the command to love one's enemies. Matthew presents this teaching as the sixth of the antitheses in the Sermon on the Mount (5:43-48), a text that culminates in the command to be perfect like God. For Luke, the command to love one's enemies is the first direct command in his Sermon on the Plain (6:27-36). Looking back over the teachings of Jesus, Furnish concludes that the double commandment of love was probably formulated by Jesus. But, more than this, "It is Jesus' commandment to love the enemy which most of all sets his ethic apart from other 'love ethics' of antiquity, and which best shows what kind of love is commanded by him."[235]

Furnish proceeds to investigate how the command of love is understood by the gospel writers. He notes that it plays no significant role in Mark but is very important for the author of Matthew. The unique depiction of the final judgment (Matt 25:31-46) declares that those who will inherit the kingdom have done deeds of love. Furnish observes that Luke-Acts also emphasizes the love command—seen, for example, in narratives that feature acts of charity.

Furnish moves to the function of the love command in the rest of the NT. For Paul, a distinctive idea is faith working in love. In regard to the great commandment, Furnish notes that Paul cites only Lev 19:18. Paul says that the whole law is summed up in *one* command, "Love your neighbor as yourself" (Rom 13:9; Gal 5:14). "Paul emphasizes the importance of love as the guiding power of the church's life and the means by which one's freedom in Christ is authentically realized."[236] Love has a prominent place in the Fourth Gospel. The farewell discourses (chaps. 13–17) begin and end with an emphasis on love. The scene begins with the narrative of the footwashing (13:1-20), an enacted parable that presents the mission of love. The chapter ends with the announcement of a new commandment (13:34-35): to love one another. "Thus, the newness of the command to love one another consists in the christological-eschatological context in which it is given. The one who commands such love is the bringer of the new age which makes love possible and meaningful, so the command is that his followers should love *as he has loved them* (vs. 34)."[237]

The emphasis on love is continued in the Johannine epistles. "[T]he author of I John, like the Fourth Evangelist, regards God's love as the basic fact of man's existence."[238] Indeed, the writer of 1 John goes beyond the Fourth Gospel in seeing love as the characteristic of the divine being: God is love.

After a review of the role of the love command in the remaining documents, Furnish summarizes the results of his research. First, the love commandment is a *command* to love, that is, a command to be obeyed. Second, the love commandment is the command of the sovereign Lord; it is closely related to eschatology and calls for radical obedience. Third, the love commandment created a community that is the embodiment of love. Finally, the command of love is also a call to repentance and an offer of forgiveness.[239]

Furnish's third book on NT ethics, *The Moral Teaching of Paul: Selected Issues*, is aimed at the general reader.[240] The purpose of the book is to consider "how Paul's approach to moral issues specific to his day may inform and guide us in thinking through the moral issues that are specific to our times and places."[241] Furnish begins with a discussion of Paul's teaching about sex, marriage, and divorce—issues primarily addressed in 1 Corinthians. Furnish believes that Paul advocates mutuality in marriage but prefers celibacy for practical reasons. In regard to divorce, Paul recalls the word of the Lord that prohibits it, but acknowledges that instances of divorce will occur. On the question of separation from a nonbelieving spouse, Paul has no word from the Lord but expresses his opinion that the marriage can be maintained.

Furnish turns his attention to homosexuality, an issue that has claimed much of his time and effort.[242] Basic to Furnish's approach is his observation that the modern concept of "homosexuality" is not found in the Bible. He acknowledges, of course, that there are texts in the OT and NT that refer to same-sex activity. The most direct in the OT is the Levitical Rule (Lev 18:22; 20:13), a part of the Holiness Codes that explicitly opposes same-sex intercourse. In the NT, 1 Cor 6:9-10 uses two terms that describe homoerotic behavior. Romans 1:24-27 is the only text in the Bible that refers to same-sex relations between women. In context, Paul presents this activity as evidence that humanity stands under divine condemnation. Paul's denunciation of homoerotic behavior, says Furnish, has no distinctive Christian roots. In any event, Paul knows nothing of what the modern biological, social, and behavioral sciences have taught us about sexual orientation.

Turning to the role of women in the church, Furnish attends primarily to texts in 1 Corinthians. He believes that 14:34-35 (where women are consigned to silence) is a later, non-Pauline interpolation. Paul's positive view is expressed in Gal 3:28 (a baptismal confession) and supersedes the old distinction between male and female. Furnish notes the complexities of 1 Cor 11:2-16, where Paul does not approve the practice of women praying or prophesying in the church with uncovered heads. Paul, according to Furnish, says that the head covering shows their authority, but what this means and how the angels are involved remain a mystery. The importance of the role of women in Paul's churches is evidenced by names of individual women who had positions of leadership in the churches, including a deacon and an apostle.

A final chapter deals with the church in the world. At the outset Furnish affirms the fact that the church is planted in the world; it does not flee from the world. Nevertheless, Christians live in the world as though not living in it (1 Cor 7:29). "It is now their belonging to Christ that defines both who they are and, no less, what it means to 'remain with God,' whatever the circumstances of their lives and however long this age endures."[243] Most important is Paul's insistence that Christians be responsible citizens, subject to the governing authorities, paying their taxes. But, above all, they owe no one anything except to obey the command of love (Rom 13.8). However, beyond their life in the world the Christians are already citizens of the heavenly commonwealth. "In short, while the apostle addressed believers as already citizens of a heavenly commonwealth and summoned them to discern and do the will of God, he also counseled them to take seriously their responsibilities as members of society."[244]

EXEGESIS

Along with his classic, *Theology and Ethics in Paul*, Furnish's masterful commentary on 2 Corinthians may be his most important work.[245] It is without peer in the second half of the twentieth century and will remain the "standard work" for years to come. He begins with an extensive critical introduction.[246] The first section reviews the history of Corinth, its political and commercial importance, its civic and cultural life. Furnish offers a vivid description of the city and its archaeological remains. Special attention is given to the religious life of Corinth: the deities and cults, the imperial cult, the presence of Judaism. Next, Furnish recounts the beginning of Christianity in Corinth, the fruit of Paul's mission.

In the introduction, Furnish gives careful attention to the literary composition of 2 Corinthians. He observers that before the writing of 2 Corinthians, Paul had sent two letters to Corinth: Letter A (mentioned in 1 Cor 5:9) and Letter B (1 Corinthians). As Furnish points out, it is widely held that 2 Corinthians is a composite of letter fragments. He reviews some of the proposed reconstructions, notably Bornkamm's popular thesis that 2

Corinthians is a composite of parts of five or possibly six letter fragments. Furnish finds none of these reconstructions convincing, and opts instead for the "two-letter hypothesis"—a popular theory that identifies chapters 1–9 and chapters 10–13 as separate letters. However, in contrast to many who view 10–13 as earlier (and identify them as part of the "tearful letter" mentioned in 2:4, 9; 7:8, 12), Furnish argues that 10–13 (Letter E) were written after 1–9 (Letter D). His major argument is that 10–13 do not fit the description of the letter provided in 1–9: Letter E (10–13) was not written in tears, but in anger; the major topic of the "tearful letter" was the brother who had wronged Paul (2 Cor 2:3-11; 7:8-12), a topic not noticed in 10–13. Furnish believes the "tearful letter" (Letter C) has been lost.

On the basis of this hypothesis, Furnish proceeds to present an introduction of Letter D (2 Corinthians 1–9). This letter was written, according to Furnish, shortly after Paul had received news about Corinth from Titus at their meeting in Macedonia (2:13; 7:6-7), probably in 55 CE. The purpose of the letter was to show Paul's concern for the Corinthians (despite the severity of the "tearful letter"), to clarify his apostolic commission, and to strengthen their commitment to the gospel and encourage their cooperation with Titus on behalf of the contribution for Jerusalem.

Furnish next provides an introduction to Letter E (2 Corinthians 10–13). Paul's purpose is primarily to respond to the claims of rival apostles who have invaded Corinth, attacking Paul's apostleship. Furnish believes this letter was written from Macedonia, probably in 56, prior to his final visit to Corinth and his departure to Jerusalem with the offering. The crucial question of critical introduction is the identification of the opponents, variously characterized as "false apostles," "super-apostles," and "ministers of Satan." Furnish reviews various theories about their identity and concludes that they have come to Corinth from outside; they have a Jewish background, but they are not "Judaizers"; they are Hellenistic Jewish Christian missionaries.

The commentary proper (Translation, Notes, and Commentary) is almost five hundred pages in length. The material is ordered according to the structure of the two letters, with main sections, subsections, and in some places sub-subsections. The format largely follows the pattern of the Anchor Bible series. Each section and subsection includes Translation (by Furnish), Notes (verse-by-verse analysis of terms and phrases), Comment: General(an overview of the following section); Comment: Detailed (running commentary on the issues of the section or subsection). In accord with other commentaries of the series, Greek terms are presented in transliteration, a bane to Greeks and a questionable blessing to the barbarians. A few examples can provide merely a glimpse of the treasures in this excellent commentary.

In the first main section (Letter Opening, 1:1-11), the second subsection analyzes the "Blessing," 1:3-11. The Comment: Detailed takes up the question: Why, in contrast to most of his epistles, does Paul substitute a blessing in place of the usual thanksgiving? Furnish (following Paul Schubert) believes that the change is the result of the particular epistolary situation. Paul is overwhelmed by his experience of deliverance from some affliction he had recently suffered in Asia. Furnish supposes this affliction was the hypothetical imprisonment of Paul in Ephesus.

In the Letter Body (1:12—9:15) the second subsection presents Paul's understanding of apostolic service, the heart of the epistle. The first sub-subsection provides an introduction (2:14—3:6) to the discussion. A few selections can offer examples of Furnish's meticulous Notes. In regard to 2:14, he investigates the phrase he translates as *who puts us on display (as if we were prisoners in a triumphal procession)*. Furnish observes that the crucial issue of the verse is the meaning of *thriambeuein*. Is this an allusion to the triumphal procession celebrated in Rome after military victories? Furnish presents several interpretations. Among these are speculations about the role Paul might have seen himself playing: "in triumphal progress" (assuming that Paul is identified with the victorious general), "to lead someone captive" (supposing that Paul was a captive in the procession), and interpretations that insist that the triumphal procession is nowhere in view. Furnish puts mention of the procession in parentheses, indicating a plausible but not certain reference to the procession.

In the Comment: General, Furnish deals with several topics, indicated by italics. In 2:16b—3:6, Paul discusses the *Question of Adequacy*. Furnish notes the change of style at v. 16b from praise to dialogue. Here Paul raises the question of the awesome responsibilities of apostleship. When he asks, *who is sufficient?* Paul is not, according to Furnish, implying the answer, "I am." Instead, the apostle is stressing the futility of claiming to be adequate; one's adequacy comes solely from God. In v. 17, Paul provides the justification for raising the question of adequacy. There are some who peddle an adulterated gospel for their own profit. Furnish observes that this is the first indication in the Corinthian correspondence that Paul is aware of the presence of rival claimants to apostolic office.

Concerning *Letters of Recommendation*, Paul, according to Furnish, insists that he (and his associates) need none, but implies, at the same time, that his rivals have come bearing such credentials. The notice of these letters leads Paul to develop the imagery of the letter to explicate the character of his ministry.

The only letter Paul needs is the Corinthians themselves—a letter written on Paul's heart. When he says that this is a letter of Christ, Furnish does not believe that Paul shifts his image from the letter of recommendation to the "heavenly letter" (also attested in the ancient sources), but that he continues his explication of the letter of recommendation as a letter from Christ. This letter is written by the Spirit, inscribed on our hearts—an allusion to Jer 38(31):31ff. The reference *tables of stone*, as Furnish notes, is reminiscent of Moses receiving the law at Sinai. In 3:4-6, Paul expresses his *Apostolic Confidence*. His is a confidence that comes from God, who has made him a competent minister of a new covenant—again recalling the word from Jeremiah. The mention of the Spirit in the context of the stone tablets leads Paul to reflect on the contrast between letter and Spirit. "In Paul's view, however, what is written kills because it enslaves one to the presumption that righteousness inheres in one's doing of the law, when it is actually the case that true righteousness comes only as a gift from God."[247]

The second sub-subsection of this subsection (2:14—5:19) Furnish entitles "The Ministry of the New Covenant" (3:7—4:6) A few examples from the extensive Notes can be illustrative. The mention of *Moses's face* (3:7) indicates that Paul is recalling the story of Exod 34:29-35, where the face of Moses, as he descended from Sinai bearing the tablets of the covenant, shone with a divine splendor. In v. 7, Paul says that that splendor was *being annulled*, and in v. 11 he indicates that the whole ministry of the old covenant *was being annulled*. Furnish notes that in these verses (8, 9, 11) Paul uses the rabbinic argument "from the lesser to the greater." In v. 13, Paul refers to the *veil* that was put over the face of Moses and the *end* of what was being annulled. Furnish's note on "the Lord" (v. 17) is distinctive. He puts the words in quotation marks to indicate that Paul is referring to the same *Lord* mentioned in the preceding verse, that is, to God.

In the Comment: Detailed, Furnish begins with a discussion of the *Surpassing Splendor* (3:7-11). The theme of this text is "splendor" (*doxa*), a term used at least once in every verse. In the text Paul presents his comments on Exod 34:29-30. He refers to the tables of stone as the ministry of death, and recalls his words from 3:6: "the letter kills." Furnish says that the idea that the splendor on the face of Moses was being annulled has no support in Exodus 34; some rabbis imagined that the radiance continued forever. Developing his argument from the lesser to the greater, Paul declares that if the ministry of death came with splendor, the ministry of the Spirit will be accompanied by even greater splendor. Regarding v. 9, Furnish points out that Paul uses the same method of argument with different terms: the ministry of condemnation and the ministry of righteousness. Although Paul does not use the language of justification extensively in the Corinthian correspondence, Furnish observes that the concept is integral to Paul's idea of apostleship and the gospel. He hears the rising crescendo of Paul's argument: the Law is temporary; the splendor of the ministry of the new covenant outshines the splendor of the ministry of Moses; and finally, the whole ministry of Moses is being annulled.

Paul turns to *The Boldness of the True Apostles* (3:12-13). Furnish (continuing in the Comment: Detailed) observes that Paul develops the theme by contrasting apostolic boldness with the timidity of Moses, who veiled his face, aware that the splendor of his ministry was destined for destruction. Furnish does not believe that Paul suspected Moses of deception but that Moses intended to spare the Israelites the agony of witnessing the end of the splendor. Regarding 3:14-15 (*Unveiling Israel*), Furnish detects a shift in argument from attention to Moses to attention to the people of Israel. Paul wants to make the point that Israelites are responsible for their unbelief. Furnish notes that Paul accomplishes the shift by use of the metaphor of the veil; the veil is on their hearts (minds) when Moses is read; they fail to acknowledge that the whole ministry of Moses has been annulled.

In regard to *The Removal of the Veil*, 3:16-18, Furnish's continuing detailed Comment observes that Paul turns from unbelieving Israel to *anyone* (v. 16). He is probably thinking about the situation of the Corinthians and their conversion. Furnish argues, primarily from the context, that the use of "Lord" here refers to God. He thinks this interpretation is supported by the mention of the Spirit. The last verse in this text (3:18) is expressed in confessional style. The subject is *we all*, meaning all believers. Furnish notes that they are described by two phrases: *with unveiled face*, and *beholding as in a mirror*. These expressions contrast the believers with Israelites who are veiled. As Furnish observes, the believers behold the glory of God and are transformed by it.

In *Further Remarks on Apostolic Boldness* (4:1-6), Paul declares that those who engage in apostolic ministry are recipients of God's mercy, that is, ministry is a gift of God. Furnish believes that v. 2 implies that serious charges have been made against Paul. The charge has been made that Paul's gospel, not the covenant of Moses, has been veiled. Paul replies that if the gospel is veiled, it is veiled to the unbelievers. They have been blinded by Satan, *the god of this world*—a statement in which Paul betrays the influence of Jewish apocalypticism. The paragraph ends on a climactic note: Christ, the content of Paul's gospel, is the image of God. "The gospel is introduced as the fundamental re-presentative agency for the splendor of God. That splendor is present as Christ is proclaimed the crucified and resurrected one through the gospel."[248] Paul declares that the apostolic preachers do not proclaim themselves, but—echoing the early Christian confession—*Jesus Christ as Lord*. According to Furnish, the reference to *the face of Jesus Christ* is not a recollection of Paul's own conversion but is to be understood as a dramatic contrast to the blindness of the unbelievers.

The next sub-subsection of the subsection, "Comments on Apostolic Service" (2:14—5:19), is entitled "The Ministry and Mortality" (4:7—5:10). In exegeting this sub-subsection Furnish offers a distinctive interpretation of the hotly debated pericope 5:1-10. Most exegetes view these verses as taking up a new theme: death and the interim between the burial of the earthly body and the resurrection of the spiritual body. Furnish, however, understands these verses as carrying on the discussion of 4:16; he believes that *our earthly, tent-like house* (5:1) refers to our *outer nature*. As to the destruction of the earthly tent (5:1), Furnish thinks Paul is probably referring to death. However, his real concern, according to Furnish, is about suffering and mortality and not about what happens to the body. Furnish reviews various interpretations of the words *a building from God, a house not made with hands, eternal in the heavens*. Whereas most interpreters understand this text anthropologically, referring to the new body that will be given to the believer, Furnish favors a reading according to Jewish and early Christian apocalyptic: the building from God is the temple of the new Jerusalem "which awaits the righteous as their proper destiny."[249] In regard to *The Sighing of the Spirit* (5:2-5), Furnish interprets the phrase as depicting the suffering preliminary to the future glory (Rom 8:18-25). In 5:2, Paul shifts from the metaphor of the dwelling to the clothing metaphor. Furnish rejects the popular interpretation that sees the clothing metaphor as a reference to putting on the spiritual body (1 Cor 15:53-54). He argues that the longing of 2 Cor 5:2 is for more than a spiritual body: it is the longing for "the fulfillment of salvation."[250]

The final sub-subsection of the subsection on "Apostolic Service" is titled "The Ministry of Reconciliation" (5:11-19). In the Comment: Detailed, Furnish investigates the major themes. His exposition of "A New Creation" (5:16-17) is noteworthy. He points out that Paul's statement in v. 16a provides a further explication for the confessional statement in v. 14b (*one has died for all*). As a result, *from now on we regard no one according to worldly standards*. According to Furnish, the "we" is the believing community, and the "now" is the eschatological "now" of God's saving action in the death of Christ (vv. 14-15). Furnish rehearses the arguments about whether *kata sarka* is adjectival (referring to Christ) or adverbial (modifying *we have regarded*). His translation shows that he supports the adverbial: *if indeed we have regarded Christ according to worldly standards, now we no longer regard him in that way.* Furnish notes that v. 17 emphasizes in a more comprehensive way the radical newness of the eschatological existence. Those who are in Christ have not only abandoned worldly standards, they have become part of a totally new creation. Furnish believes this is one of the most significant texts in which Paul uses the expression *in Christ*. "To be *in Christ*, and thus a participant in the *new creation*, means to be claimed by the rule of love instituted in the cross, and to be liberated from the powers of this present age."[251]

The final theme in Furnish's Comment is "Reconciliation" (5:18-19). Here Paul concludes his discourse on apostleship with a description of the ministry of reconciliation. Various scholars (e.g., Käsemann) have argued that Paul is using an earlier formula or hymn. Furnish believes the traditional material includes only v. 19ab. According to him, the tradition affirms three convictions: *God* was reconciling the world; Christ was the agent of reconciliation; reconciliation means not charging trespasses against trespassers. Furnish notes that the theme of reconciliation is developed in Judaism, but there, for example in 2 Maccabees, God is the object of reconciliation. For Paul it is *God* who is reconciling the world to himself. Paul also adds the concepts of the *ministry of reconciliation* and the *word of reconciliation*. Furnish insists that the ministry of reconciliation is a constituent part of the reconciliation event. He also believes that the ministry is given to the whole Christian community, not just the apostles. The *word of reconciliation* is the word of the cross.

Time and space allow only one example of Furnish's exegesis of Letter E (2 Corinthians 10–13). In the Letter Body, the second subsection is characterized as "A Fool's Speech" (11:1—12:13). Within this section, the second sub-subsection includes "The Speech Proper" (11:21b—12:10). In Furnish's detailed Comment on this material he discusses the topic On *"Visions and Revelations,"* 12:1-10. The Comment begins with an exposition of *A Journey to Paradise* (12:1-4). Paul presents the account of this journey under the necessity of boasting, even though nothing is to be gained by it. Furnish believes Paul is responding to the claim of his competitors that he lacks apostolic credentials such as ecstatic experience. Thus, says Furnish, Paul's account is a "sort of parody" on the practice of his rivals. He believes Paul's use of the third person is typical of someone who, in such ecstatic experiences, senses a kind of self-transcendence. But even more, Paul wants to distance himself from any notion that the experience would warrant any claim to apostolic credentials.

Furnish believes the notice *fourteen years ago* reflects ancient accounts of visions in which mention of the time of the event lends realism to the story.

Assuming with Furnish that Letter E was written in 56, Paul's dating would put the vision in 42, shortly after his escape from Damascus. Furnish insists that the journey to paradise has no relation whatsoever to Paul's "conversion" experience. Actually, Paul provides little detail about the journey. He says, reflecting Jewish cosmology, that he was caught up to the third heaven. He also says that *he heard things that must not be divulged*. As Furnish observes, Paul says nothing about seeing anything, but instead focuses on the word-character of the event. Paul's ignorance as to whether his experience was *in the body or out the body* is not an allusion to some Gnostic experience but, as Furnish argues, evidence that the difference is of no moment to Paul.

In the theme *A Further Comment About Boasting* (12:5-10) Paul continues his argument that he will boast only of his weakness. He says that to keep him from being too elated about his experiences of revelation, God has given him *a thorn in the flesh*. Paul also designates this thorn as an *angel from Satan*: as Furnish says, Satan understood as the agent of God's purposes. Furnish summarizes the three main interpretations of the thorn: (1) it was some sort of spiritual torment; (2) it was some kind of physical malady; (3) it refers to persecution. Furnish concludes that (2) is most likely. Paul says that he appealed for relief from this affliction *three times*, indicating how intent he was in seeking relief. Paul proceeds to present the *Lord's response*. Paul's appeal remains unanswered, but he receives instead a word from the exalted Christ, declaring the truth that in weakness God's powerful grace is at work. "This is why weakness is the hallmark of his apostleship, because he has been commissioned to the service of the gospel through the grace of this Christ—a grace whose power is made present in the cross."[252]

Some years after the publication of *II Corinthians*, Furnish contributed the volume on the Thessalonian correspondence in the Abingdon New Testament Commentaries, the series for which he was the general editor.[253] He begins with a short, informative introduction to 1 Thessalonians. The occasion of the letter, he points out, is the report that Timothy has brought from Thessalonica. Furnish believes the purpose of the epistle is to commend the congregation for their faith and love, to motivate them to continuing fidelity to the gospel, and to send them further instruction. In discussing the historical occasion and context, he recounts the history of the city and Paul's mission there (arriving in 49 and staying several months). He notes that the converts faced opposition from Gentile residents of the city. According to Furnish this epistle was written shortly after Paul's departure, early in his Corinthian mission (50 CE). As to the theological and ethical orientation of the letter, Furnish notes that it includes no quotations from the OT. The major theological emphasis is on faith as acceptance of God's election as a manifestation of God's love.

The commentary on 1 Thessalonians (pp. 37–126) is ordered according to Furnish's understanding of the structure of the letter. In format (largely following the pattern of the ANTC series), the main sections are introduced with an overview and concluded with a summary. The comments are presented in running paragraphs; abundant references to secondary sources are given in parentheses. Furnish's comments on 4:13-18 provide a small sample. These verses are considered in the second major section, entitled "Pastoral Instruction and Encouragement" (4:1–5:24). In a subsection on "Matters of Special Concern" (4:1—5:11) Furnish explicates Paul's instruction concerning *Those Who Have Fallen Asleep* (4:13-18). In his comment on v. 13 he notes that "falling asleep" is a common euphemism for death in Paul's day. Those who do not have hope, according to Furnish, are unbelievers, whether Jewish or pagan. In vv. 15-17 Paul describes the return of the Lord, an event he apparently expects to happen soon. Furnish delineates three features of Paul's description: the Lord will descend from heaven; the believers who have died will be resurrected; those resurrected and those who are still alive will be taken up together to meet the Lord. The description is decorated with apocalyptic military symbols: the shout of command, the sound of God's trumpet. Furnish points out that the motif of being caught up (the famous "rapture") is found in Jewish texts. He notes a distinctive Pauline feature: the meeting of the Lord "in the air," that is, in the space just above the earth. Paul does not explain what happens after the meeting: do those who are caught up return to the earth or ascend to heaven? Paul has only one concern: those who meet the Lord will remain with the Lord forever. In the concluding summary Furnish says of Paul, "What he offers here is not a comprehensive depiction of the end-time events, but pastoral instruction and assurance on one particular issue that was troubling his congregation."[254]

THEOLOGY

Victor Furnish's exegetical work is always directed toward a purpose: to set forth the theological meaning of the text. Like Martyn and Keck, Furnish is a biblical theologian. This is demonstrated in his essay, "Paul the Theologian."[255] After a review of the work of several representative scholars on the theology of Paul, Furnish raises the question: Was Paul a theologian? He answers that Paul was not a systematic theologian. However, when Christian theology is defined "as critical reflection on the beliefs and rites of the Christian tradition and on the social structures within which these beliefs and rites are continued," then Paul is a theologian.[256] If Paul was a theologian, Furnish asks, what is required to understand his theology? He provides a lengthy list of requirements, but basically he argues that Paul's theology is to be found by historical-critical and exegetical study of each authentic Pauline letter. Special attention should be given to passages in which Paul is intentionally explicating theological conceptions and passages in which he uses kerygmatic formulations, references to Scripture, summaries of teaching and preaching. Once the epistles have been rigorously investigated individually, theological conceptions or arguments that emerge in more than one letter should be noted and compared. The theological interpreter must be wary, however, of rushing to an easy synthesis. "No 'synthesis' of Pauline theology, if by that one means the construction of a comprehensive theology in the scholastic sense, can adequately represent his thought. . . . Rather, what these sources yield are comments about the meaning of the gospel as the apostle wishes that to be discerned by particular readers and acted on in their particular circumstances."[257]

Important for Furnish as a biblical theologian is his book, *The Theology of the First Letter to the Corinthians*.[258] Although the epistle is much concerned with pastoral problems, Furnish believes these to be symptomatic of underlying misunderstandings of Paul's gospel. Consequently, the gospel, according to Furnish, is the primary subject of Paul's theological reflection and exposition. Furnish analyzes the theology of 1 Corinthians according to the theological themes in the main sections of the epistle. In chapters 1–4 the themes are "knowing God" and "belonging to Christ." According to Paul, the wisdom of God—contrary to the wisdom of the world—is of a totally different order, the wisdom of the cross. In this foolish wisdom God's saving power is at work. Through this wisdom humans come to know God, resulting in a new relationship. The believers belong to Christ and they belong to God. Furnish turns to the meaning of "belonging to Christ in an unbelieving society." How, he asks, can believers be the church in pagan Corinth—the problem addressed in 1 Cor 5:1—11:1. For Paul, the primary principle is holding to the center, embracing the gospel; when this is faithfully done, the identity of the community is maintained. In dealing with the world the believers should recognize that the visible world is passing away. Moving on, Furnish explicates the meaning of belonging to Christ in the believing community (the concern of 11:1—14:40). Central to the life of the community is the observance of the Lord's Supper. Paul understands this celebration as proclamation. His command to discern the body, according to Furnish, means to recognize that "the bread of the Lord's supper is both 'Christ's body' given for others and that the 'many' for whom Christ died are 'one body' in him."[259]

First Corinthians 15, as Furnish notes, is a chapter in which doctrinal instruction is primary. He titles his discussion, "Hoping in God, the 'all in all.' " Paul's intent in the chapter is to argue that denial of the resurrection of the dead contradicts the truth of the gospel. In his presentation of the resurrection Paul makes use of Jewish apocalyptic imagery. He cites the resurrection of Christ (confirmed by witnesses) as proof of the resurrection. Christ is *the first fruits* and those who belong to Christ will be raised. At the end of the chapter Paul announces God's final victory: Christ will overcome the evil powers and hand the kingdom over to God. In a final chapter, Furnish summarizes the significance of 1 Corinthians for theology. The center of that theology is Christology. "Yet nowhere in the New Testament is the image of the resurrected-crucified Christ so finely drawn as in 1 Corinthians."[260]

In sum, Victor Paul Furnish is a skilled interpreter who practices exegesis in the service of theology. He is master of the methods of historical criticism and his work is informed by a comprehensive command of the secondary sources. In making exegetical decisions, Furnish does not rush to judgment; if the evidence is not adequate, he refuses to draw conclusions. He eschews overstatement. Although Furnish is viewed, and views himself, as a Pauline scholar, his competence extends to the canon and beyond.

Furnish's research is centered in the theological ethic of Paul. He insists on the mutual interdependence of theology and ethics. Although he honors (even embraces) the theology of Paul, he does not impose a theology on Paul's letters or construe Paul's doctrine as dogmatics. Furnish correctly observes that Paul's ethic is set in an eschatological context, that the central feature of his ethic is the indicative and the imperative. Central to Paul's theological ethic is his Christology—faith in Christ that, more than a doctrine, is a way of life. This way of life is shaped in response to the command of love.

Given Furnish's irenic spirit and the cogency of his arguments, it is difficult to sound a negative note. An extensive review and critique of his work is presented by Michael Cullinan, but his criticisms are largely based on Roman Catholic doctrine rather than on exegesis of the Pauline texts.[261] More germane is the criticism of Richard Hays, who in general applauds Furnish's work. Negatively, Hays believes that Furnish has not adequately appreciated the "new perspective" on Paul. There is some substance in this criticism, even though the "new perspective" is no longer "new." Although Furnish reflects nothing of the old caricature of Judaism, and although he avoids capitulation to the new perspective (à la Dunn), his work could be enhanced by more attention to Paul's understanding of the Law in the mode of Martyn and Keck.

Hays also believes that Furnish does not adequately swear allegiance to a Pauline theological principle dear to him (i.e., Hays): the understanding of faith as the "faithfulness of Jesus Christ." Whereas both Martyn and Keck have been converted to this interpretation of πίστις Ἰησοῦ Χριστοῦ, not all scholars agree (e.g., Dunn). As Furnish's work indicates, the idea of Christ as the object of faith is appropriate in the context of Paul's understanding of theology and ethics. To be sure, not every exegete will agree completely with Furnish's interpretations, but all will acknowledge that his conclusions are supported by careful argument and grounded in a profound understanding of NT theology.

CHICAGO: HANS DIETER BETZ

HANS DIETER BETZ (1931–)

Born in Lemgo, Germany, Betz began theological study at the *Theologische Hochschule* in Bethel (1951).[262] In 1953 he moved to University of Mainz, where he studied with Herbert Braun (usually viewed as a member of the left wing of the Bultmann school). Recipient of a grant from the World Council of Churches, Betz studied at Cambridge with J. Y. Campbell and C. F. D. Moule (1955–56). He returned to Mainz to complete his doctoral dissertation, accepted in 1957. From 1961 to 1963 Betz served as pastor of a church in the lower Rhine region. In response to an invitation as visiting professor at the Graduate School and School of Theology at Claremont, Betz, along with his wife and three young children, arrived in America in 1963, where he remained for the rest of his career. At Claremont, Betz was soon appointed Professor of New Testament and Early Christian Literature. In 1978 he was invited to the faculty of the Divinity School and the Department of New Testament and Early Christian Literature at the University of Chicago.[263] At Chicago, Betz participated in interdisciplinary scholarship, for example, co-teaching with professors in the classics department. In 1990 he was named Shailer Mathews Professor of New Testament. He retired in 1999.[264] As a teacher Betz was renowned for his Friday morning seminar, reading texts ranging from Romans to the Hermetica, attended by students from throughout the university. Ministerial students cherished his course, "From Exegesis to Sermon."

Betz has been active in the SBL and the SNTS, having served as president of both. He has been guest professor across the world: at Uppsala, Zürich,

Oxford, and Jerusalem, to mention only a few. Betz is one of the four major editors of the fourth edition of the venerable multi-volume *Religion in Geschichte und Gegenwart*, now even more widely recognized in view of the English translation, *Religion Past and Present*.

> What perhaps most distinguishes Hans Dieter Betz's scholarship is its combination of amazing range with consistency of vision. Defying the traditional boundaries of the academy, Betz has made significant contributions in the fields of New Testament, classics, church history, theology, and history of religions. . . . Betz is the consummate humanist, schooling himself and others in the art of ancient learning.[265]

EARLY WORK AND THE HISTORY OF RELIGION

As a young man Betz had aspired to be an artist, an aspiration reflected in "his extraordinary creativity as a scholar."[266] However, quite apart from the artistic details, the reviewer is overwhelmed by the sheer magnitude of his work. The publications reviewed here are only the first fruits of an abundant harvest.[267] Betz's early work reflects his concern with Hellenistic backgrounds and his ongoing contribution to the tradition of the history of religion school. His doctoral dissertation, *Lukian von Samosata und das Neue Testament; religionsgeschichtliche und paränetische Parallelen*, is essentially a collection of materials from the writings of Lucian that have parallels in the NT, especially references to the so-called "divine man."[268]

Betz's Habilitationsschrift, *Nachfolge und Nachahmung Jesu Christi im Neuen Testament*, enlists history of religion methodology in the service of theology.[269] In essence this work demonstrates that the motif of imitation of Christ, crucial for Paul, is distinctly different from the concept of following Jesus, predominant in the Gospels. In regard to the continuity between the historical Jesus and the Christ of the community, Betz notes the importance of the idea of following Jesus. In the earliest tradition, according to Betz, the idea of following is scarce. Later, independent sayings on self-denial and fulfilling the commands of Jesus are collected (e.g., Mark 10:21). According to Betz, the idea of following Jesus developed in stages in the life of the early community. In Mark, discipleship is understood as the call of the Exalted One. For Matthew, church and discipleship are one. For John, the tradition of following Jesus is understood in relation to the existence of the believer: following means participation in the drama of redemption.

In the longest section of the book (some ninety pages), Betz moves to the history of religion material, where he investigates the history and structure of the concept of *mimesis*. This concept, according to Betz, has its origin in Greek cults, especially that of Dionysus. Betz believes the concept then spreads to other cults: the Eleusinian, the cult of Isis and Osiris. Features of the *mimesis* motif are reflected in myths, ritual dramas, and cultic meals. Betz explores the larger question of the meaning of the *mimesis* motif in the study of the history of religions. In the myths of ancient religions, earthly religious expression is seen as the reflection of an *Urbild* or *Urform* of higher existence. Betz also investigates the interpretation of the imitation concept in ancient philosophy, where it is significant for both Plato and Aristotle.

In the final section Betz applies the results of his history of religion research to the theology of Paul. He begins with a linguistic analysis, pointing out that the Gospels use the term ἀκολουθεῖν for following the historical Jesus and the Exalted One. Paul does not use this terminology. Instead, he expresses the idea of "imitation" (usually expressed by the noun μιμηταί, "imitators") of the risen Christ—a concept, according to Betz, influenced by the Hellenistic cultic background. Betz proceeds to exegete the major texts: 1 Thess 1:6; 2:14; Phil 3:17; 1 Cor 4:16; 11:1. He concludes: "The call to mimesis is in no way oriented to the ethical or moral example of the historical Jesus or to a pre-existent Christ-figure or of Paul, but to the Christ-myth itself."[270]

COMMENTARIES

Hans Dieter Betz's major contribution to the history of NT research is expressed in his three remarkable commentaries—on Galatians, 2 Corinthians 8–9, and the Sermon on the Mount. Although they belong to a celebrated series (Hermeneia), the commentaries display unique features, especially in the use of history of religion materials, the concern with genre and classical rhetoric, and the interrelation of historical critical issues and exegetical research.

Betz's commentary on Galatians begins with a historical-critical introduction.[271] Although no question about Pauline authorship has been raised, the identification of the addressees is hotly debated. Betz reviews the issues in the time-worn debate between the north Galatian (territorial) hypothesis and the south Galatian (province) hypothesis. He favors the former. More important, according to Betz, is the question of the identification of the opponents. Betz believes they had come to Galatia after Paul founded the churches there. He says that "the opponents of Paul were Jewish-Christian missionaries rivaling Paul."[272] Betz notes the difficult problem of dating the epistle. Before its composition the Jerusalem conference had been held, a bitter conflict had erupted in Antioch, and Paul's collection for the church in Jerusalem had been launched. Betz is wary of attempts to date Galatians in relation to data provided by Acts. The only thing that can be claimed as certain is that Galatians was written before Romans. Betz believes a date of around 50–55 is a reasonable guess. He is equally hesitant about designating the place of writing; any of the popular locations—Ephesus, Macedonia, or Corinth—is possible, as are others.

Most important and distinctive is Betz's theory of the literary composition of the letter. Following the principles of ancient rhetoric, he classifies Galatians as an "apologetic letter," a genre that arose as early as the fourth century BCE. On the basis of this classification Betz construes the structure of the epistle according to categories of classical rhetoric: *exordium* (1:6-11), *narratio* (1:12—2:14), *propositio* (2:15-21), *probatio* (3:1—4:31), and *exortatio* (5:1—6:10). These sections are set within the conventional epistolary framework: prescript (1:1-5) and postscript (6:11-18). According to Betz the apologetic letter presumes the situation of a law court: the addressees are the jury, Paul is the defendant, the opponents are the prosecutors. The purpose of the letter is to persuade, with scant concern for establishing the truth.

Betz turns to the theological argument of Galatians. In Galatia, Christianity is confronted by a crisis: a questioning of the gospel by its own converts. "Hence it [Galatians] presents the first systematic apology of Christianity, not to outsiders, but to Christians themselves."[273] After Paul had departed, the Galatians had difficulty in coping with a question: How could spiritual people deal with the problems of the flesh? The invading opponents provided a solution: embrace the Torah and practice circumcision. Paul defends himself and his gospel, says Betz, by a defense that employs the rhetoric of his time. Betz delineates the major arguments Paul uses, including the argument from experience, proof from Scripture, and, most important, the argument from freedom.

The body of the commentary (pp. 37–325) orders the material according to Betz's rhetorical outline of the epistle. The format follows the pattern of the Hermeneia series: Translation (by Betz), Analysis (overview of the section), Interpretation (running commentary, proceeding verse by verse). The extensive footnotes occupy, on the average, about half the page, with cross references, text-critical notes, and extensive references to secondary sources. Excursuses are introduced at appropriate places in the interpretation of the text. A few examples can provide a small sample of Betz's virtuoso exegetical performance.

In regard to the *narratio* (1:12—2:14), the analysis observes that the ancient rhetoricians believed this element should be brief, clear, and plausible; the purpose of *narratio* is to state the facts. Betz notes that this *narratio* has three subjects: Paul's life from birth (1:13-24), the apostolic council (2:1-10), and the episode at Antioch (2:11-14). The Interpretation presents a detailed exegesis. In 1:12 Paul responds to the accusation that his gospel was "according to man" (1:11). He contends that it was received δι' ἀποκαλύψεως Ἰησοῦ Χριστοῦ. Betz interprets the genitive as objective: the revelation revealed Christ.

At this point Betz inserts an Excursus: "Conversion, Revelation, and Tradition,"[274] in which he insists that Paul's revelatory experience should not be understood as a conversion. Instead, it was a call to ministry to the Gentiles, patterned after the call of Jeremiah. Betz sees no contradiction between this text and 1 Cor 15:1-11, where Paul says that he received the gospel by tradition: there Paul refers to his receiving of the kerygma; here he speaks of receiving a commission to Gentile mission.

In v. 13 Paul begins the *narratio* proper, which is intended to support his claim in v. 12. He starts with a description of his pre-Christian life. He was not merely a Jew but a zealous observer of the Jewish way of life. Paul's transformation, he claims (v. 15), was totally the action of God. His vocation involved two stages: he was set apart from his mother's womb; he was called through God's grace. In regard to v. 16, Betz says it is not clear why Paul uses the title "his Son." Also, Paul's use of the phrase ἐν ἐμοί could simply be a dative ("to me"), or Paul may understand "in me" to reflect a visionary experience. Betz thinks the two views complement each other. "This would mean that Paul's experience was ecstatic in nature, and that in the course of his ecstasy he had a vision (whether external or internal or both—"I do not know, God knows" [cf. 2 Cor 12:2, 3])."[275] The purpose of the vision is Paul's commission to preach the gospel among the Gentiles. Betz notes that the object of the verb εὐαγγελίζωμαι ("that I might preach the gospel") is masculine ("him") where we might have expected neuter ("it," i.e., the gospel). This shows, Betz observes, that Paul identifies Christ and the gospel. In vv. 16c-17 Paul tells what he did *not* do: he did not confer with humans and he did not go to Jerusalem. This is to answer the charge of his opponents that his gospel was "from men" (v. 11) or that his apostleship was derived from the Jerusalem authorities.

After the account of his Jerusalem visit Paul recounts the Jerusalem conference (2:1-10). Betz presents an Excursus on "The Conference at Jerusalem" that addresses the major problems.[276] As to the reasons for the conference, he notes the problem created by increasing numbers of Gentiles joining the church. Concerned conservative Jewish Christians came to

Antioch—a center of Gentile Christianity—and demanded circumcision of the Gentile men (Acts 15:1). In response, a delegation was sent from Antioch to Jerusalem to discuss the issue. The negotiations were carried out by three groups: the delegation from Antioch (headed by Paul and Barnabas), the leaders of the Jerusalem church (James, Cephas, and John), and the conservative Jewish Christians (the "false brothers"). The final agreement, Betz points out, affirmed the Antioch position and rejected the view of the conservatives. However, the agreement involved a compromise: there were to be two missions and two gospels; the leaders of the Gentile mission pledged to collect an offering for the poor Christians of Jerusalem.

In the Interpretation Betz comments on 2:1-10, the second part of the *narratio*. The phrase "after fourteen years" (2:1) he understands as referring back to Paul's first visit to Jerusalem after his call (1:18). As Betz points out, the conference includes two events: one a presentation "to them," and another presentation to the reputed leaders. Paul makes it clear that the issue of controversy is his gospel—a gospel that did not require circumcision of Gentile converts. Betz insists that the phrase "that perhaps I may be running or might have run in vain" does not mean that Paul was seeking approval of his gospel from the Jerusalem authorities. Instead, it reflects the present concern of the Galatians, who have been warned by the opponents that without circumcision and Torah they (the Galatians) were running in vain. Paul presents as evidence the case of Titus (v. 3), who demonstrates that Paul was "running well" (5:7).

Paul's description of the proceedings of the conference (2:4-10) is convoluted, including an anacoluthon in v. 4. However, Betz believes the basic meaning is clear. In v. 4 Paul employs the language of political demagoguery to describe the "false brothers" who had been "secretly smuggled in" to spy out our "freedom"—the very tactics the opponents are employing in Galatia. Verses 6-10 constitute a single sentence that presents the Jerusalem authorities in analogy to the opponents in Galatia. The Jerusalem leaders were hailed as "men of eminence," but Paul, in a parenthesis, presents his own evaluation of them: what "they were" makes no difference to him; "God shows no partiality"—an idiom widely used in the OT.

Verses 6d-10 present the outcome of the conference. Paul asserts that the Jerusalem leaders did not add anything, that is, they did not require Gentile converts to submit to the requirements of Torah and circumcision. However, as Betz points out, Paul's argument is precarious since he wants to avoid the impression that he acknowledged the higher authority of the Jerusalem leaders. Paul implies that he did not recognize them, but that they recognized him. Betz believes the statement in parentheses (v. 8)—"for he who worked through Peter making him an apostle to the circumcised also worked through me in sending me to the Gentiles"—may be an actual quotation from the agreement formulated at the conference. The statement affirms the equality of both missions: God worked through both. Verse 9 confirms that the Jerusalem leaders, now named (James, Cephas, and John) and designated "pillars," recognized the "grace" (a Pauline term) that had been given Paul. The agreement was confirmed by an official act: "the right hand of fellowship," sign of an agreement between equal partners. Betz believes the description of the two missions—"to the Gentiles" and "to the circumcised"—does not represent a territorial but an ethnic division. In v. 10 Paul reports a third result of the conference: "that we should remember the poor." He says they (the Jerusalem leaders) asked "only" one thing. His use of "only," Betz says, indicates Paul's effort to gloss over the inconsistency: he claimed that the leaders added nothing, but now he acknowledges that they did add something. But since Paul says that he was eager to comply, he easily dismisses his concession as immaterial. Actually, as Betz points out, the argument contributed to Paul's case with the Galatians: they knew of the offering and had actually participated in it, making them also participants in Paul's argument.

The third part of the section Betz has designated *narratio* (2:11–14) is crammed with exegetical problems. Before his interpretation of these verses Betz inserts an Excursus on "The Conflict at Antioch."[277] Paul's account of this event, according to Betz, brings the history of Paul's narration into contact with the present situation in Galatia. It indicates that the good relations between Paul and the Jerusalem authorities that had been established at the conference had deteriorated. "It appears that the break between Paul and the other Jewish missionaries . . . was irreparable."[278]

In the Interpretation Betz observes that, in keeping with the prescriptions of *narratio*, Paul recounts the facts. Cephas came to Antioch (v. 11) for reasons that are not explained. Apparently it had become customary there for Jewish and Gentile members of the church to share common meals including, perhaps, the Lord's Supper. In v. 12 Paul describes the behavior of Cephas: before the arrival of the "men from James," Cephas participated in table fellowship with the Gentile Christians; after they came, he withdrew; he was afraid of the "men of the circumcision." Betz says Paul's terminology is military ("withdraw") and cultic ("separate"). The men who came, probably with the backing of James, assumed they were supporting the Jerusalem agreement. They believed that Cephas, as leader of the mission to the circumcised, should exemplify the Jewish way of life. Cephas apparently recognized the logic of their argument and withdrew.

In sum, Cephas may have concluded that, given the theological presuppositions of the Jewish Christians he was expected to represent, his table fellowship was indefensible. In Paul's terms Cephas "feared" the "political" consequences of losing his position of power. Peter chose the position of power and denied his theological convictions.[279]

In v. 14 Paul describes his bold accusation: "If you, though a Jew, live like a Gentile and not like a Jew, how can you compel the Gentiles to live like Jews?" Betz supposes that this confrontation occurred in something like a plenary assembly of the Antioch church. Paul's charge is that Cephas is caught in a situation of self-contradiction. Although he was a Jew, his behavior in Antioch showed that he had abandoned Jewish ritual customs (lived "like a Gentile and not like a Jew"). In withdrawing table fellowship from the Gentiles he was, in effect, compelling Gentiles to observe Jewish restrictions ("to live like Jews").

Ironically, therefore, by attempting to preserve the integrity of the Jewish Christians as Jews, Cephas destroys the integrity of the Gentile Christians as believers in Christ. Instead of welcoming them as converts to Christianity, he wants to make them into converts of Judaism. This contradicts the principles of the doctrine of justification by faith, which had been the basis of the faith thus far.[280]

This conclusion of the *narratio* leads into the *propositio* (2:15-21), a section Betz divides into four main parts. First, Paul sets forth the point of agreement: the doctrine of justification by faith (2:15-16). In v. 16, he presents his understanding of this foundational doctrine. As Betz points out, Paul sees the distinction between Christian and Jew as a difference in theological conviction. Jews believe that humans will be justified in the eschatological judgment by observing the ordinances of Torah. Paul argues instead that justification is by faith in Christ. Betz contends that the phrase ἡμεῖς εἰς Χριστὸν Ἰησοῦν ἐπιστεύσαμεν interprets the genitive of the previous phrase (πίστεως Ἰησοῦ Χριστοῦ). "This interpretation rules out the often-proposed but false idea that the genitive refers to the faith which Jesus himself had."[281] Next, Paul presents a point of disagreement: the consequences for Gentile Christians (2:17-18). Betz attempts to unravel the complexities of Paul's argument. Paul begins by identifying a false argument (that of the opponents). The first part of v. 17 is true ("we are seeking to be justified in Christ"); the second part is false ("we are found to be sinners"). Betz believes that the question, "Is Christ then a servant of sin?" reflects the implicit charge of the opponents, one that is obviously false.

Next, Paul sets forth the exposition of the *propositio* (2:18-20). Betz believes that Paul develops the exposition by means of four theses. These are expressed in the first person singular, indicating that Paul is prototype and example for all. (1) "Through the Torah I died to the Torah in order that I might live for God." This means that the role of Torah has come to an end. (2) "I have been crucified together with Christ." (3) "It is no longer I who live, but Christ lives in me." Betz points out that to be crucified with Christ implies not only death to the Law, but death to the "I." (4) "What I now live in the flesh I live by faith in the Son of God, who loved me and gave himself for me." Betz says that Paul further defines faith by a statement that combines a christological title ("Son of God") with a christological formula of two expressions: "loved me" and "gave himself up for me," showing that Christ's death was an act of love and self-sacrifice on behalf of the Christian.

Finally, Paul presents the refutation (2:21). In this verse he denies the charge that he is nullifying the grace of God. Betz believes this may be a charge of the opponents, supposing that redemption (the grace of God) requires participation in the Torah covenant. In any case, the charge is false: justification does not come through (the works of) the Law. Betz believes Paul has turned the charge into an accusation: it is Cephas and the Galatian opponents who have rejected the grace of God.

The next main section of the letter Betz labels "*probatio*" (3:1—4:31). In this section he arranges the material according to a series of arguments. The sixth (4:21-31) can serve as a final example of Betz's commentary. In the Interpretation he observes that the whole section is doctrinal in character. The opening question (v. 21) displays the use of diatribe style. In ironic tone Paul addresses the Galatians who are about to submit to Torah. The second part of Paul's question implies that if they would really listen to the Law they would become aware of the absurdity of their intentions. To make his point, Paul turns to Scripture. Although he uses an introductory formula ("it is written"), he does not actually quote but, as Betz observes, presents a tradition that summarizes Gen 16:15; 21:2-3, 9. In v. 23 Paul advances the argument by contrasting the two sons of Abraham: one is born "according to the flesh," the other "according to the promise." In v. 24 he moves beyond the allegory of the two sons to another "allegory," this time actually using the term. According to this allegory, the two mothers represent two diametrically opposed covenants. The covenant represented by Hagar is that of Sinai, and Hagar's children are destined to slavery, that is, slavery under the Law. In v. 25 Paul's allegory is further expanded: Hagar corresponds to "the present Jerusalem," but the free woman corresponds to "the Jerusalem above." As Betz observes, the image of the heavenly Jerusalem is common in both Jewish and Christian apocalyptic. Paul concludes the allegory (v. 27) by quoting Isa 54:1, a text important for Jewish eschatology. Paul interprets the text as referring to Sarah ("the barren one"), who will become the mother of many, that is, the Christians whose mother is the "heavenly Jerusalem."

In v. 28 Paul presents the consequences of the proof from Scripture: "but you, my brothers, are children of promise, like Isaac." He uses second person plural to address the Gentile Christians of Galatia. In v. 29 Betz indicates that Paul employs typology: "as it was then . . . so it is now." The typology contrasts the child born "according to the flesh" and the child born "according to the Spirit." In v. 30 Paul quotes another proof from scripture (Gen 21:10: "Cast out this slave woman with her son"). Betz believes that Paul understands this text to mean that Jews are totally excluded from the promise, a view Paul was to revise when he wrote Romans 11. Verse 31 concludes the whole argument of 3:1—4:30. Paul uses first person plural, Betz observes, so as to include himself among the Gentile Christians, children of the "free woman."

Betz's second contribution to the Hermeneia series is a commentary on 2 Corinthians 8 and 9.[282] This work was, in fact, preceded by another historical-critical work on 2 Corinthians: *Der Apostel Paulus und die sokratische Tradition.*[283] In essence this earlier book maintains that 2 Corinthians 10–13 is an "apology" in which Paul employs arguments reminiscent of the Socratic tradition. Betz begins with an investigation of the place of this section of 2 Corinthians within the Pauline letter corpus. He rehearses the history of research on the problem and agrees with scholars who identify 2 Corinthians 10–13 as a separate letter. He proceeds to discuss the "form-critical problem" of the letter. The *Sitz im Leben*, according to Betz, is a "trial" in the Corinthian community where the charge is made that Paul is not a legitimate apostle. Following the Socratic tradition, Paul adopts the method of the true philosophers in arguing against the sophists. He lists the charges made by the opponents against him (10:10): his letters are strong; his appearance is weak; his speech in contemptible. Betz observes that similar charges were made against Socrates by the Sophists. In 12:12 Paul refers to the "signs of the apostle," a phrase coined by his opponents. The opponents, according to Betz, claim that they can perform such signs: wonders and mighty works. In response, Paul contends that he too can boast of such signs, but the examples he gives—parodies of a heavenly journey (12:2-4) and an oracle of "healing" (12:7-10)—actually prove Paul's weakness. This weakness, however, is related to Paul's basic christological argument. Paul's weakness reflects the crucifixion of Christ, the weakness in which the power of God is at work. Looking back over the "apology," Betz concludes that Paul argues on two levels: he employs the tradition of Socratic humanism; he affirms a christological theology. According to Betz these two approaches find a unity in the deepest experience of humanism and theology: the power of divine agape.

In the preface to his commentary on 2 Corinthians 8 and 9, Betz notes the significance of these chapters. "Here the great theologian that he was reveals himself to be involved with the toughest parts of church leadership: the raising of money for the needy; the establishing of voluntary cooperation among very different people, despite distances and fragile communication; the reconciliation between churches in different lands and cultures; and last but not least, the preservation of the church as a Christian institution."[284] An introductory chapter rehearses the investigation of these chapters in the history of NT scholarship. In this historical account Betz reviews a variety of partition theories running all the way from J. S. Semler to Dieter Georgi. Betz reserves his own conclusion to the end of the commentary; his intention is to answer the question on the basis of thorough exegesis of the two chapters. He treats each chapter as a separate letter and considers each according to the categories of classical rhetoric. Space allows only a short survey of Betz's detailed exegesis.

In regard to 2 Corinthians 8, Betz designates vv. 1–5 as an "advisory section" in which Paul commends the collection for the church in Jerusalem. In the *exordium* (8:1–5) he reminds the Corinthians of the generosity of the Macedonian churches. In 8:6, the *narratio*, Paul tells the Corinthians that Titus, who earlier had begun work on the collection, was coming to bring that work to completion. The *propositio* (8:7–8) typically sets forth agreements: in this case, the virtues of the Corinthians—faithfulness, eloquence, and knowledge. Paul also expresses his hope that they will excel in generosity in regard to the collection. In this matter Paul will not issue a command, although he does say that the collection will be a test of the genuineness of their love. The *probatio* (2 Cor 8:9–15) sets forth a series of proofs. The first (v. 9) is doctrinal: the Jerusalem offering presents an opportunity to respond to the example of Christ. The second proof (vv. 10–12) is an argument from expediency: it is expedient to complete what has been begun. Betz notes that in v. 11 Paul uses the word "willingness," a business term. The third proof (vv. 13–15) is from equality: the abundance of the Corinthians can balance the poverty of Jerusalem.

Betz describes 8:16–23 as the "legal section," one in which Paul moves from argument to official business. The significance of this section is the authorization of envoys (Titus and the two brothers) to serve in the completion of the collection. Betz observes that technical terms associated with official procedures of this sort are used. According to Betz's reconstruction, Titus is the leader of the delegation, one of the brothers was chosen by the churches, and the second brother was selected by Paul. The letter (2 Corinthians 8) was carried to Corinth by these envoys. Verse 24 (the *peroratio*) presents the final appeal that summarizes the letter. Paul urges the Corinthians to give proof of their love and provide the occasion for Paul to boast about them.

Betz next presents his commentary on 2 Corinthians 9. In investigating the *exordium* (9:1-2) he notes that the major critical issue is the question: Is Paul beginning a new letter or is he merely moving to a new section of the same letter? Betz argues in support of the former. When Paul says (v. 2) that he has been boasting to Macedonia that Achaia has been ready for a year, Betz says that he is referring to the churches of Achaia, not to Corinth.[285] In the *narratio* (9:3-5a) Paul justifies the sending of the two brothers. His use of the epistolary aorist in v. 3 (ἔπεμψα), on the analogy of his use of συνεπέμψαμεν in 8:18, 22, suggests to Betz that Paul wrote two letters at about the same time: 2 Corinthians 8 to Corinth, 2 Corinthians 9 to Achaia. In the *propositio* (9:5bc) Paul implies that the Achaians should take responsibility for completing the collection, including encouraging the participation of the Corinthians. The *probatio* (9:6-14), in which Betz finds evidence of Paul's use of "agrarian theology," consists of a series of arguments that support the importance of giving generously. According to Betz, Paul's purpose is to persuade the Achaians that their help is necessary for completing the collection. The letter concludes with the *peroratio*, which includes a prayer that sets in motion, according to Betz, a service of thanksgiving in the Achaian churches.

After the commentaries on the two letters Betz presents a chapter summarizing his understanding of their literary genre and function. He concludes that the letter of Chapter 8 is a type of official epistle: a letter of recommendation meant to accompany royal envoys. "[I]t is an official letter sent by an individual writing with an official capacity to a corporate body, the church at Corinth, along with the officially appointed envoys."[286] The letter of Chapter 9, according to Betz, is an advisory letter of deliberative rhetoric. This is a letter sent to the Christians of Achaia, urging them to provide an example for the Corinthians in the successful completion of the offering.

Betz's final chapter deals with the relation of the two letters to the rest of the Corinthian correspondence. First Corinthians 16:1-4 indicates that the collection had already begun in Corinth. Between the time of 1 Corinthians and the writing of 2 Corinthians 8 and 2 Corinthians 9, a crisis and its resolution have occurred. Betz believes the climax of the crisis is reflected in 2 Corinthians 10–13 (an apologetic letter). Before 2 Corinthians 10–13, according to Betz, an earlier apologetic letter (2 Cor 2:14–6:13 + 7:2-4) had been written, responding to charges against the legitimacy of Paul's apostleship that were already evident in 1 Corinthians. The resolution of the conflict is seen in the "letter of reconciliation" (2 Cor 1:1–2:13 + 7:5-16 + 13:11-13). This letter, according to Betz, immediately precedes the two letters of 2 Corinthians 8 and 2 Corinthians 9. Thus the observer can conclude that Betz construes 2 Corinthians as a composite of five letter fragments: the first apologetic letter (2:14—6:13 + 7:2-4), the second apologetic letter (10:1—13:10), the letter of reconciliation (1:1—2:13 + 7:5-16 + 13:11-13), an official letter sent to Corinth (2 Corinthians 8), and a advisory letter sent to Achaia (2 Corinthians 9).

Hans Dieter Betz's *magnum opus* is his massive commentary on the Sermon on the Mount, a pyrotechnic display of erudition.[287] In his introduction he presents a review of the history of research on the Sermon on the Mount (SM) and the Sermon on the Plain (SP) from the ancient church to the twentieth century. Historical critical work on the Sermon began with the Enlightenment. In the nineteenth century, J. G. Eichhorn believed Matthew and Luke used a common source. Betz is particularly interested in the work of C. F. Georg Heinrici, who believed the SM and the SP were two separate redactional products of pre-Synoptic origin. He observes that in the course of historical critical work on the two sermons, scholars increasingly favored Q as the underlying source. After reviewing various options, Betz concludes that the SM and the SP were formulated independently and later incorporated into Q. To explain the differences between SM and SP, Betz says that "the conclusion is most likely that Matthew as well as Luke found the SM and the SP, respectively, in their recension of Q (Q^{Matt} and Q^{Luke})."[288]

Next Betz takes up the question of the literary compositions. He believes both the SM and the SP are the work of pre-Synoptic authors or redactors, not the compositions of Matthew and Luke. To present the structure of the composition Betz offers a very detailed (nine-page) conspectus of the SM. The Sermon has four main sections: exordium (Matt 5:3-16), the main part (Matt 5:17—7:12), the eschatological warnings (Matt 7:13-23), and peroration (Matt 7:24-27). Betz also presents a conspectus of the SP (three pages) and orders the material in three parts: exordium (Luke 6:20b-26), rules for the conduct of disciples (Luke 6:27-45), and peroration (Luke 6:46-49). In overview, Betz observes that the two sermons display great similarity and great difference. "The evidence leads me to conclude that the SM and the SP represent two separate and textually independent elaborations of a common pattern of composition."[289] The differences are the result of different elaborations of similar material, designed for different audiences: the SM for hearers who are culturally Jewish, the SP for an audience that is culturally Greek. "These observations lead me to conclude that one must explain the compositions of the SM and the SP, their similarities and their differences, by their literary genre and function, rather than by source criticism as understood in the terms of Harnack."[290]

In regard to the literary genre, Betz contends that each sermon should be classified as an *epitome*, comparable to the *Encheiridion* of Epictetus, which follows the prototype of the *Kyriai Doxai* of Epicurus. As to the literary function of the sermons, Betz believes both served as instruction for disciples. He thinks they were originally conceived as oral texts. Both sermons, Betz points out, repeat the idea of "doing"; they are intended to maintain what in Hellenistic-philosophical terms is called ἀσκεῖν ("training") and μελετᾶν ("practicing")." "My hypothesis is, therefore, that the two *epitomai* of the SM and the SP were created by the early Jesus movement, one (the SM) to instruct converts from Judaism, the other (the SP) to instruct those coming from the Greek background."[291]

Betz's commentary on the SM is some 480 pages in length. A few examples from two of the most important sections—the beatitudes and the antitheses—can provide small samples. Betz begins his investigation of the beatitudes (5:3-12) with an introduction. As to the basic meaning of the beatitudes (or macarisms), he says that they represent a literary genre that has parallels in Greek literature. The beatitudes in the SM are declarative in nature; they express the eschatological judgment of God; they are concerned with morality and ethical action. In his interpretation Betz takes up the beatitudes one by one. In regard to the first (v. 3), he says the blessing of the "poor" is an ancient topos that assumes the human condition to be one of poverty and misery. He contends that the phrase "in spirit" does not represent a spiritualizing or softening of Jesus' original radicalism, but instead indicates an intellectual insight into the human condition. The use of the phrase "kingdom of the heavens" reflects a worldview of multiple heavens and affirms that the realm of God is beyond earth and sky and is already present.

Betz notes that the second beatitude (v. 4) praises those who mourn. Since poverty is the human condition, grief is the expected response. Betz notes, however, that the beatitude is "unconditionally affirmative"; mourning is praised. The reason for this assessment is expressed in v. 4b: "they shall find consolation"—an idea confirmed by Scripture (Isa 61:2). Betz believes the promise of consolation is an eschatological prediction: God will provide consolation in his eternal reign of justice. In regard to the third beatitude (v. 5), Betz suggests that "meek" is a variation on "poor in spirit." He notes that meekness was valued in Jewish piety and is a synonym for humility—a virtue, according to the Greeks. The second part of the beatitude (v. 5b) is an adaptation of Ps. 36:11 (LXX) and constitutes an eschatological promise: in the new age God will hand over the earth to the faithful. Betz believes the fourth beatitude (v. 6) is important for the theology of the SM. This beatitude assumes that the human condition is unrighteousness. Those who hunger and thirst for righteousness are seeking a way out of the world of injustice. Betz believes the SM understands "righteousness" in the Jewish sense: God represents righteousness and the kingdom of the heavens is the realm of God's righteousness. The hunger for righteousness will not be satisfied until the eschatological future, a metaphor anticipating the eschatological banquet.

"Blessed are the merciful," the fifth beatitude (v. 7), reflects a well-known doctrine of Jewish religion. Betz observes that Greek literature also affirms the value of mercy. The consequence of the blessing (v. 7b) is again to be understood eschatologically. Betz believes the future passive (ἐλεηθήσονται) indicates that at the last judgment God will show mercy to those who have done deeds of mercy in their lives. According to the sixth beatitude (v. 8), the "pure in heart" are blessed. In the history of religion, as Betz observes, stress is put on ritual purity. He believes the concept of purity of heart intensifies the internal aspect. The promise of seeing God implies an experience of vision—rare in the OT and NT, but common in apocalyptic. Betz believes the SM assumes that those who enter into the kingdom (7:21-23) will see God. The seventh beatitude (v. 9) presents peacemaking as a virtue. The SM sees God as the principal peacemaker and the disciples as God's agents in making peace. As a consequence they shall be called "sons of God," the promise of honorific titles in the eschatological future.

Betz observes that the eighth beatitude (v. 10) stands as the end of the beatitudes formulated in the third person, and that the second line (v. 10b) repeats the second line of the first beatitude (v. 3b), creating an *inclusio*. The theme of righteousness reaches a climax in the eighth beatitude. Betz believes the use of the perfect participle (οἱ δεδιωγμένοι) indicates that persecution has occurred in the past and continues in the present. This beatitude sums up the beatitudes of 5:3-10: the sequence of virtues in vv. 3a-9a is combined with the sequence of eschatological promises (vv. 4b-9b) and "is held together by the theme of the kingdom of the heavens, in which righteousness reigns and will ultimately prevail."[292]

The exegesis of the antitheses can provide additional examples of Betz's exegetical research.[293] The examples will be drawn from the first, second, and fourth antitheses, that is, those that are usually considered "original" or "authentic." In his introduction to the antitheses Betz raises questions. What kind of argument do the antitheses present? He answers that antithesis is a rhetorical device that states an argument: a scriptural interpretation is refuted as false; the false interpretation is countered by the interpretation of Jesus. Do the antitheses imply a "higher christology"? Betz's basic answer is "no"; the SM is not concerned with messianism. The main intent of the sermon is to present Jesus as the righteous man who teaches with authority. In regard to the controversial question of sources, Betz concludes that "the set of six antitheses are the creation of the redactor of the SM and are thus pre-Matthean."[294]

The first antithesis in concerned with murder (Matt 5:21-26). In the Interpretation section Betz explicates the details of the antithesis. He believes it addresses the listeners in terms of their present situation; they are recipients of previous interpretation, the tradition given "to the men of old." The SM rejects the interpretation and the claim that it represents authoritative tradition. The alleged tradition is presented in two statements: a quotation from the Decalogue ("you shall not kill") and an interpretation of the command in the form of casuistic law (everyone who kills will be "answerable to the court"). In v. 22 Jesus is presented as contradicting the casuistic law by offering an alternative: "every one who is angry with his brother shall be answerable to the court." According to Betz, the SM presents Jesus as changing casuistic criminal law into moral rule. Jesus supports his interpretation by two illustrations. First (v. 22c) he says, "Everyone who says to his brother 'empty-head' shall be answerable to the high court." Betz interprets this as a parodistic exaggeration that ridicules the notion that moral offense is subject to court action. The second illustration (v. 22d) is even more absurd: "Everyone who says (to him) 'fool' shall be guilty (enough) for the Gehenna of fire."

These illustrations are supported by two narratives. The first (vv. 23-24) depicts an episode in ritual offering, illustrating a cultic-ethical conflict. The altar, Betz believes, is the altar of burnt offering in the Jerusalem temple. At the moment of offering the gift, the one making the offering ("you") remembers that "your brother has something against you." Betz thinks this recalls the command of Lev 19:18 ("love your neighbor"); the gift at the altar, he believes, is an expression of love toward God. "Going ahead with the sacrifice without reconciling oneself with the brother would in effect separate love of God and love of brother."[295] The solution is to leave the gift at the altar and go and be reconciled to your brother. Betz calls attention to the wording "go first." "It establishes a religious priority: reconciliation must precede the sacrifice."[296] The second illustrative narrative depicts two people on the way to obtain a decision regarding a dispute between them. They are advised to settle out of court. Betz says this advice is not merely prudence but is related to the text; the term εὐνοεῖν ("to be well disposed") indicates that the underlying issue is anger, the subject of the whole antithesis. Jesus' teaching calls for control over anger and changing it into friendship so that there will be no need to go to court. The conclusion of the argument of the antithesis, according to Betz, is that the root cause of murder is anger, the opposite of brotherly love. The message of the SM is that one should come to grips with anger by reconciliation and the restoration of brotherly love.

The second antithesis (Matt 5:27-30) deals with the prohibition of adultery in the Decalogue (Exod 20:14). In v. 28, the SM presents the adequate interpretation: a redefinition of adultery. "Everyone who looks at a woman with lust" has committed adultery. Betz notes the role of the eye in erotic love: to look arouses desire. The movement is from outside to inside: from the eye to the desire of the heart. Betz says the terminology indicates that the woman is married. The SM presents a shift from the physical violation of a taboo to a decision of the heart prior to the physical act. The demonstration of the validity of the interpretation (v. 29) employs two examples, one concerning the eye, the other the hand. The example of the eye presents a hypothetical situation whereby a physiological problem presents a moral example: trouble with the eye causes adultery. The cure seems absurd, but, as Betz observes, the choice is the lesser of two evils. Losing the eye is bad, but it is better than losing the whole body. The second example (v. 30) is parallel to the first. Again self-mutilation is better than loss of the whole body. As in the earlier example, the choice is put into an eschatological context: the whole body could be thrown into Gehenna. Betz sums up the SM's understanding of Jesus' interpretation. Adultery leads to the disruption of family relations; it begins with a man's look at another man's wife with desire. Prevention must begin with gaining control of the erotic process that moves from heart to eye to physical act. "Considering the overall framework of the antitheses, the point should be clear: avoidance of adultery is a special application of the love-command, 'Love your neighbor as yourself.'"[297]

Betz observes that the fourth antithesis (Matt 5:33-37), like the first, presents the full expression of the chain of tradition ("you have heard that it was said") and includes the source of the tradition, "the men of old." Verse 33 also includes the quotation "you shall not swear an oath falsely." But, as Betz asks, what is the text to which the SM refers? He notes various suggestions, including the idea that the quotation is from Exod 20:16 ("you shall not bear false witness against your neighbor"). Betz also observes that prohibition of perjury is found in Hellenistic Judaism, especially in the wisdom literature. He believes the form of the expression suggests a religious vow; the issue is not only perjury but oaths sworn before God, constituting a debt to God. The use of ἀποδίδωμι ("giving back"), according to Betz, means making good on a religious vow. The correct interpretation is given in v. 34, "do not swear at all," but how this relates to keeping vows (v. 33c) is not clear. In any case, vv. 34–37 present four examples of things by which one should not swear. Betz notes the progression: from heaven to earth to the center of the earth (Jerusalem) to one's head. Swearing by heaven ("the throne of God"), according to Betz, means overstepping human limitations. The second example, "nor by the earth, for it is his footstool" (Isa 66:1) is forbidden for the same reason; the earth is not under human control but is the realm of God. Betz thinks the reference to Jerusalem may suggest that the provenance of the SM may be the early Christian community in that city. The fourth and final example is swearing by one's head. Betz says that the idea that one cannot make one's hair white or black is proverbial; ancient medicine and cosmetic art had developed methods of dying hair. The conclusion is expressed in v. 37: "Let your word be 'Yes, Yes' or 'No, No'; anything more than this comes from the evil one." This command, according to Betz, transcends the issue of oathtaking and makes a statement about the nature and use of language. The view of the SM is radical, prohibiting anything beyond ordinary language. "Yes, Yes" and "No, No" is not an oath, but intensified affirmation and denial.

In view of the breadth and depth of the work of Hans Dieter Betz, any attempt at critique is presumptuous. Above all, one is impressed, indeed overwhelmed, by his mastery of the material of the history of religions. Betz's emphasis, to be sure, is on the classical and Hellenistic sources. However, he displays extensive knowledge of the Jewish sources as well. Nevertheless, one gets the impression that Betz is more at home in Athens than in Jerusalem. Also in regard to his history of research there is ongoing debate concerning the "divine man." While Betz affirms the importance of the idea, others have argued that the whole concept is a scholarly construct. Yet, whether or not one agrees with Betz, everyone will have to acknowledge that he has collected source material essential for the discussion.

In regard to Betz's commentaries, some reviewers have objected to his use of classical rhetoric and his identification of the genre of the texts. For instance, in the Galatians commentary objections have been raised to his identification of the epistle as an "apologetic letter." Is it really valid to view the setting as a courtroom scene in which Paul is the defendant? Is it not equally possible to see the Galatians or the opponents as defendants and Paul as the prosecutor? But what these questions seem to suggest is that imposing rhetorical or genre patterns on the epistles is not without problems.

Despite these objections, Betz's work proves that the study of classical rhetoric and literary genres is essential to NT research. His reconstruction in the commentary on 2 Corinthians 8 and 9 is imaginative. Here, it seems to me, his use of genre criticism is especially insightful. His detection of technical business terms in 2 Corinthians 8 is compelling, and his argument for two separate letters is impressive. However, his ingenious theory that the two letters have different recipients, Corinth and Achaia, is less than convincing. Also, Betz does not provide an adequate explanation for the redactional ordering of the five letter fragments into canonical 2 Corinthians.

As to the magisterial commentary on the Sermon on the Mount, questions have been raised concerning Betz's source theory. Most scholars continue to suppose that the source of both the SM and the SP is to be found in Q, and that the sermons as we have them are the independent redactional work of the authors of Matthew and Luke. However, this criticism, like the criticisms of the two other commentaries, is minor in comparison with the vast contribution of Betz's exegetical research. His work is marked by careful analysis, attention to textual and linguistic detail, theological sensitivity, and mastery of an immense number of secondary sources. Betz belongs to the venerable tradition of German scholarship, grounded in the mastery of the classical languages and skilled in the methods of historical and literary research. Let us hope he is not the last!

Summary

All that can be said in summary of the work of Elisabeth Schüssler Fiorenza has been said at the end of the review of her work. As a unique scholar who opposes historical critical method, she should not be compared with others who adopt it, nor would she want to be.Each of the other scholars reviewed in this chapter has some distinguishing feature: Martyn's affirmation of apocalyptic, Keck's perception of theology, Furnish's emphasis on ethics, Betz's commitment to history of religion research. To be sure, the distinguishing features are not exclusive. All four scholars recognize the importance of eschatology. All attend to ethics and all are NT theologians. All are concerned with the historical setting, but Betz gives more attention to the Hellenistic context. Martyn and Keck emphasize OT and Jewish backgrounds, but neither has adopted the "new perspective." Furnish properly avoids an *either* Jewish *or* Hellenistic context.

The four scholars differ in their assessment of the same sources. Betz analyzes Galatians according to rubrics of classical rhetoric; Martyn rejects this approach. Furnish views 2 Corinthians as a composite of two letters; Betz identifies five. All recognize the importance of Paul but view him from different perspectives: Martyn through the lens of Galatians, Keck through Romans, Furnish through the Corinthian correspondence, and Betz from the history of religion perspective.

The Yale scholars emphasize the "Christ-event," an expression that reflects the continuing influence of the new biblical theology (Barth and Bultmann) on the entire history of NT theology in the twentieth century. One wonders whether this terminology does justice to the understanding of Jesus as a person, an emphasis found in Keck's early work and implicit in Furnish. Related is the ongoing, unresolved debate about faith "in Christ" or the "faithfulness of Christ." Another feature that belongs to the legacy of Bultmann is the tendency to identify one's own theology with the theologians of the NT. The theology of Martyn, Keck, and Furnish is the theology of their understanding of the theology of Paul.

On one point all four scholars are in total agreement: the importance, indeed, the necessity of the historical-critical method for NT research. These scholars demonstrate beyond question that historical criticism is alive and well at the beginning of the twenty-first century. The continuing value of the method is brilliantly illustrated by the excellence of research these exceptional scholars have produced. They also agree on the crucial importance of the theological understanding of the text, an understanding toward which their critical and exegetical endeavors are directed.

Notes

1. Also significant as a representative of NT research at Harvard in the latter half of the twentieth century is Helmut Koester, whose significant scholarship has been reviewed earlier in this volume; see pp. 324–30 above.

2. For biographical information see Fernando R. Segovia, "Looking Back, Looking Around, Looking Ahead: An Interview with Elisabeth Schüssler Fiorenza," in *Toward a New Heaven and a New Earth: Essays in Honor of Elisabeth Schüssler Fiorenza* (Maryknoll, NY: Orbis, 2003), 1–30; Mitzi L. Minor, "Schüssler Fiorenza, Elisabeth (b. 1938)," *DMBI*, 895–99; idem, "Schüssler Fiorenza, Elisabeth (b. 1938)," *HHMBI*, 606–610; Elisabeth Schüssler Fiorenza, "Neutestamentliche Wissenschaft als kritisch-emanzipatorische Wissenschaft," in *Neutestamentliche Wissenschaft: Autobiographische Essays aus der Evangelischen Theologie*, ed. Eve-Marie Becker (Tübingen: Francke, 2003), 347–60; Shelly Matthews, Cynthia Briggs Kittredge, and Melanie Johnson-DeBaufre, eds., "Introduction," in *Walk in the Ways of Wisdom: Essays in Honor of Elisabeth Schüssler Fiorenza* (Harrisburg, PA: Trinity Press International, 2003), 1–14.

3. Her thesis was published as *Der vergessene Partner: Grundlagen, Tatsachen und Möglichkeiten der beruflichen Mitarbeit der Frau in der Heilssorge der Kirche* (Düsseldorf: Patmos, 1964); sections in English translation are presented in "The Forgotten Partner: The Professional Ministry of Women in the Church," in Elisabeth Schüssler Fiorenza, *Discipleship of Equals: A Critical Feminist Ekklēsia of Liberation* (New York: Crossroad, 1993), 16–22.

4. Quoted in "Looking Back," 7.

5. Ibid., 22.

6. Ibid., 22.

7. A detailed analysis and critique of Schüssler Fiorenza's work is presented by Esther Yue L. Ng, *Reconstructing Christian Origins? The Feminist Theology of Elisabeth Schüssler Fiorenza: An Evaluation* (Carlisle, UK: Paternoster, 2002), based on a PhD dissertation written at the University of Aberdeen. Although Ng has given diligent attention to the works of Schüssler Fiorenza and offers some apt criticisms, her work is impeded by her own presuppositions; she rejects Schüssler Fiorenza's position at the outset. Ng assumes a view of biblical authority that restricts criticism and supports the very system of domination Schüssler Fiorenza opposes. A much shorter but more faithful summary is provided by Minor, "Schüssler Fiorenza," 895–99. For bibliographies of Schüssler Fiorenza's work see "Bibliography of the Writings of Elisabeth Schüssler Fiorenza," in *Walk in the Ways of Wisdom*, 371–85, and *JFSR* 25 (2009): 221–40.

8. Elisabeth Schüssler Fiorenza, *Priester für Gott: Studien zum Herrschafts- und Priestermotiv in der Apocalypse*, NTAbh 7 (Münster: Aschendorff, 1972).

9. *Priester für Gott*, 418.

10. Elisabeth Schüssler Fiorenza, *In Memory of Her: A Feminist Reconstruction of Christian Origins* (New York: Crossroad, 1992).

11. Ibid., xiv.

12. See *HNTR* 2: 335–37.

13. *In Memory of Her*, 29.

14. Ibid., 41.

15. Ibid., 84.

16. Ibid., 135.

17. Ibid, 151.

18. Ibid., 183.

19. Ibid., 199.

20. Ibid., 231.

21. Ibid., 270.

22. Ibid., 334.

23. Ibid., 346.

24. Elisabeth Schüssler Fiorenza, *Jesus: Miriam's Child, Sophia's Prophet: Critical Issues in Feminist Christology* (New York: Continuum, 1995).

25. Ibid., 4.

26. Ibid., 10.

27. Ibid., 43.

28. Ibid., 88.

29. Ibid., 96.

30. Ibid., 102.

31. Ibid., 106.

32. Ibid., 162.

33. Ibid. 187.

34. Ibid, 190.

35. Elisabeth Schüssler Fiorenza, *Jesus and the Politics of Interpretation* (New York: Continiuum, 2000).

36. Ibid., ix–xi.

37. Ibid., 20.

38. Ibid., 29.

39. Ibid., 73.

40. Ibid., 164.

41. Elisabeth Schüssler Fiorenza, *Bread Not Stone: The Challenge of Feminist Biblical Interpretation* (Boston: Beacon, 1984); eadem, *But She Said: Feminist Practices of Biblical Interpretation*

(Boston: Beacon, 1992); eadem, *Rhetoric and Ethic: The Politics of Biblical Studies* (Minneapolis: Fortress Press, 1999). A more recent work is eadem, *Transforming Vision: Explorations in Feminist Theology* (Minneapolis: Fortress Press, 2011).

42. *Rhetoric and Ethic*, 163–65.

43. *But She Said*, 115.

44. See *Rhetoric and Ethic*, 39–42.

45. *But She Said*, 40.

46. See *Bread Not Stone*, 15–22; *But She Said*, 57–76.

47. *Bread Not Stone*, 20.

48. *But She Said*, 73.

49. *Rhetoric and Ethic*, 55.

50. *But She Said*, 134–63.

51. Ibid., 157.

52. Elisabeth Schüssler Fiorenza, *The Power of the Word: Scripture and the Rhetoric of Empire* (Minneapolis: Fortress Press, 2007).

53. Ibid., 33.

54. Elisabeth Schüssler Fiorenza, *Democratizing Biblical Studies: Toward and Emancipatory Educational Space* (Louisville: Westminster John Knox, 2009).

55. Elisabeth Schüssler Fiorenza, *The Book of Revelation: Justice and Judgment*, 2d ed. (Minneapolis: Fortress Press, 1998). Schüssler Fiorenza also published a commentary on Revelation, written for the laity: *Invitation to the Book of Revelation* (Garden City, NY: Doubleday, 1981). Earlier she had published a simple introduction to Revelation: *The Apocalypse* (Chicago: Franciscan Herald Press, 1976).

56. *Book of Revelation*, 2.

57. Ibid., 68.

58. Ibid., 151.

59. Ibid., 175.

60. Ibid., 226.

61. *Reconstructing Christian Origins?*, 9.

62. *Rhetoric and Ethic*, 33.

63. See, for example, Gaventa's *Mary: Glimpses of the Mother of Jesus* (Columbia: University of South Carolina Press, 1995), and *Our Mother Saint Paul* (Louisville: Westminster John Knox, 2007).

64. For biographical information see "Martyn, James Louis," *DAR* 4: 279; Raymond E. Brown, "A Personal Word," in *Apocalyptic and the New Testament: Essays in Honor of J. Louis Martyn*, ed. Joel Marcus and Marion L. Soards, JSNTSup 24 (Sheffield: Sheffield Academic Press, 1989), 9–12; Beverly Roberts Gaventa, "Attentive to the Text," *Christian Century*, 122 no. 4 (22 Feb. 2005): 23–25.

65. Prominent among other scholars associated with Yale is Wayne A. Meeks. Educated at Yale (PhD 1965) and Woolsey Professor there (1984–99), Meeks pioneered in the study of the social setting of early Christianity; his *The First Urban Christians: The Social World of the Apostle Paul* (2nd ed. New Haven: Yale University Press, 2003) is a classic. Another important Yale PhD is D. Moody Smith, who spent most of his teaching career at Duke and made major contributions to the study of the Johannine literature.

66. "A Personal Word," 11.

67. "Attentive to the Text," 24.

68. J. Louis Martyn, *History and Theology in the Fourth Gospel*, 3rd ed. (Louisville: Westminster John Knox, 2003).

69. John Ashton, *Understanding the Fourth Gospel* (Oxford: Oxford University Press, 1991), 107. See also D. Moody Smith, "The Contribution of J. Louis Martyn to the Understanding of the Gospel of John," in *History and Theology*, 1–23; originally published in *The Conversation Continues:*

Studies in Paul and John in Honor of J. Louis Martyn, ed. Robert Fortna and Beverly R. Gaventa (Nashville: Abingdon, 1990), 275–94.

70. *History and Theology*, 29.

71. Ibid., 49.

72. Ibid., 138.

73. Ibid., 140.

74. Ibid., 143.

75. This was previously published in J. Louis Martyn, *The Gospel of John in Christian History: Essays for Interpreters* (New York: Paulist, 1979), 90–121.

76. In addition to this chapter on the history of the Johannine Community, *The Gospel of John in Christian History* includes two other significant essays. In "'We Have Found the Messiah': A View of Christ Formulated Very Early in the Life of the Johannine Community" (pp. 9–54) Martyn detects an early source used by John in which Jesus is identified with Elijah. In "Persecution and Martyrdom: A Dark and Difficult Chapter in the History of Johannine Christianity" (pp. 55–89) he investigates the evidence for the persecution and execution of members of the Johannine community (John 16:2). On the basis of a careful study of the Pseudo-Clementine literature, Martyn finds evidence of an independent Jewish-Christian tradition confirming the charge against the Jews who had believed in Jesus (John 8:31).

77. J. Louis Martyn, *Galatians: A New Translation with Introduction and Commentary*, AB 33A (New York: Doubleday, 1997).

78. Ibid., 23.

79. Ibid., 42.

80. Ibid., 97–105.

81. Ibid., 99.

82. Ibid., 99.

83. Ibid., 101.

84. Ibid., 105.

85. Ibid., 117–26.

86. Ibid., 180–86.

87. See p. 546, n. 100 above.

88. *Galatians*, 200.

89. Ibid., 208–11.

90. Ibid., 211.

91. Ibid., 240–45.

92. Ibid., 245.

93. Ibid., 263–75.

94. Ibid., 302–6.

95. Ibid., 324–28.

96. Ibid., 327.

97. Ibid, 378–83.

98. Ibid., 382.

99. Ibid., 447–57.

100. Ibid., 455.

101. Ibid., 502–14.

102. Ibid., 506.

103. Ibid., 512.

104. Ibid., 524–36.

105. J. Louis Martyn, *Theological Issues in the Letters of Paul* (Nashville: Abingdon, 1997).

106. Ibid., 77–84.

107. Ibid., 82.

108. Ibid., 89–110.

109. Ibid., 110.

110. Ibid., 161–75.

111. See pp. 284–89 above.

112. *Theological Issues*, 209–30.

113. Ibid., 224.

114. For biographical information see "Keck, Leander E.," *DAR* 4: 219; Brevard S. Childs, "Leander Keck: A Tribute," in *The Future of Christology: Essays in Honor of Leander E. Keck* (Minneapolis: Fortress Press, 1993), xix–xxi; "Foreword to the Series," in David Friedrich Strauss, *The Christ of Faith and the Jesus of History*, trans. and ed. Leander E. Keck (Philadelphia: Fortress Press, 1977), vii–viii; "Personal Musings" in Leander E. Keck, *The Church Confident* (Nashville: Abingdon, 1993), 15.

115. Childs, "Leander Keck," xix. As a theological educator Keck has been committed to the life and work of the church. This is seen, for example, in his book *The Church Confident* (Nashville: Abingdon, 1993), based on his Beecher Lectures at Yale (1992). Also important is Keck's *Bible in the Pulpit: The Renewal of Biblical Preaching* (Nashville: Abingdon, 1978).

116. For bibliography see Grace Pauls, "Works by Leander E. Keck," in *Future of Christology,* 239–46.

117. Leander E. Keck, *Taking the Bible Seriously* (Nashville: Abingdon, 1962), 7. Throughout his career Keck has been a skilled practitioner and staunch defender of the historical-critical method. The issue is directly addressed in his essay, "Will the Historical-Critical Method Survive? Some Observations," in *Orientation by Disorientation: Studies in Literary Criticism and Biblical Literary Criticism, Presented in Honor of William A. Beardslee*, ed. Richard A. Spencer (Pittsburgh: Pickwick, 1980), 115–27.

118. Ibid., 34.

119. Ibid., 95.

120. Leander E. Keck, *The New Testament Experience of Faith* (St. Louis: Bethany, 1976).

121. Related to his work on early Christian history is Keck's popular introduction to Acts, *Mandate to Witness: Studies in the Book of Acts* (Valley Forge, PA: Judson, 1964).

122. Leander E. Keck, *Paul and His Letters*, 2nd ed., PC (Philadelphia: Fortress Press, 1988).

123. *Paul and His Letters*, 29.

124. Ibid., 43.

125. Ibid., 49.

126. Ibid., 68.

127. Ibid., 70.

128. Ibid., 73.

129. Ibid., 82.

130. Ibid., 93.

131. Ibid., 102–3.

132. Ibid., 116.

133. Ibid., 122.

134. Ibid., 158. Keck, with Victor Paul Furnish, also co-authored *The Pauline Letters* (Nashville: Abingdon, 1984), an introduction written for the non-specialist.

135. Leander E. Keck, *Romans*, ANTC (Nashville: Abingdon, 2005).

136. Ibid., 13.

137. Ibid., 32.

138. Ibid., 33–34.

139. Ibid., 35.

140. Ibid., 37.

141. Ibid., 38.

142. Ibid., 45.

143. Ibid., 52.

144. Ibid., 113.

145. Ibid., 180.

146. Ibid., 184.

147. Ibid., 187.

148. Ibid., 188.

149. Ibid., 194.

150. Ibid., 280.

151. Ibid., 285.

152. Ibid., 286.

153. Ibid., 286–87.

154. Ibid., 289.

155. David Friedrich Strauss, *The Christ of Faith and the Jesus of History*, trans. and ed. Leander E. Keck (Philadelphia: Fortress Press, 1977).

156. Leander E. Keck, *A Future for the Historical Jesus: The Place of Jesus in Preaching and Theology* (Nashville: Abingdon, 1971).

157. Ibid., 20.

158. Ibid., 35.

159. Ibid., 48.

160. Ibid., 71.

161. Ibid., 106.

162. Ibid., 114.

163. Ibid., 127.

164. Ibid., 177.

165. Ibid., 181.

166. Ibid., 211.

167. Ibid., 214–15.

168. Ibid., 228.

169. Ibid., 231.

170. Ibid., 233.

171. Ibid., 238.

172. Ibid., 240.

173. Ibid., 244.

174. Ibid., 249.

175. Ibid., 262.

176. Leander E. Keck, *Who is Jesus? History in Perfect Tense* (Columbia, SC: University of South Carolina Press, 2000).

177. Ibid., x.

178. Ibid., 8.

179. Ibid., 58.

180. Ibid.

181. Ibid., 81.

182. Ibid., 89.

183. Ibid., 98.

184. Ibid., 112.

185. Ibid., p 124.

186. Ibid., p 130.

187. Ibid., p 139.

188. Ibid., 142.

189. Ibid., 144.

190. Ibid., 148.

191. Ibid., 155.

192. Ibid., p. 160.

193. Ibid., 162.

194. Ibid., 166.

195. Ibid., 169.

196. Ibid., 171.

197. Ibid., 177.

198. Ibid., 182.

199. Leander E. Keck, "Toward a Renewal of New Testament Christology," *NTS* 32 (1986): 362–77. An example of the careful tradition-historical and redaction-critical analysis that undergirds Keck's christological research is seen in his essay, "Mark 3:7-12 and Mark's Christology, *JBL* 84 (1965): 341–58.

200. For biographical information see "Furnish, Victor Paul," *DAR* 4: 141; Michael Patrick Cullinan, *Victor Paul Furnish's Theology of Ethics in Saint Paul: An Ethic of Transforming Grace*, Tesi Accademia Alfonsiana 3 (Rome: Editiones Academiae Alfonsianae, 2007), 33–68; "Preface," in *Theology and Ethics in Paul and His Interpreters: Essays in Honor of Victor Paul Furnish*, ed. Eugene H. Lovering, Jr. and Jerry L. Sumney (Nashville: Abingdon, 1996), ix–x; "Acknowledgments," in Victor Paul Furnish, *Theology and Ethics in Paul* (Louisville: Westminster John Knox, 2009), xix.

201. "Acknowledgments," in *Theology and Ethics*, xix.

202. "Preface," *Essays in Honor of Victor Paul Furnish*, ix.

203. Victor P. Furnish, *Theology and Ethics in Paul* (Louisville: Westminster John Knox, 2009). For the setting of Furnish's book within the context of major works on NT ethics, see the informative bibliographical essay by Wendell L. Willis, "Bibliography: Pauline Ethics, 1964–1994," in *Essays in Honor of Victor Paul Furnish*, 306–19. See also David G. Horrell's chapter, "Approaches to Pauline Ethics: From Bultmann to Boyarin," in his *Solidarity and Difference: A Contemporary Reading of Paul's Ethics* (London: T & T Clark, 2005), 7–46; in the introduction Horrell writes: "Despite the wealth of publications dealing with Paul's letters, and many studies of specific aspects of Paul's ethics, there have been surprisingly few book-length attempts to deal with his ethics as a whole. Victor Paul Furnish's *Theology and Ethics in Paul*, published in 1968, remains a significant landmark in this respect" (p. 1). For a complete bibliography of Furnish's publications (through 2004) see Cullinan, *Furnish's Theology of Ethics*, 343–62.

204. Willis, "Bibliography," 307.

205. See "Appendix: A Survey of Nineteenth- and Twentieth-Century Interpretations of Paul's Ethic," *Theology and Ethics*, 242–79. Furnish's competence in the history of the discipline is evident in other works; see, e.g., his "The Jesus-Paul Debate: From Baur to Bultmann," in *Paul and Jesus: Collected Essays*, ed. Alexander J. M. Wedderburn, JSNTSup 37 (Sheffield: JSOT Press, 1989), 17–50; "The Historical Criticism of the New Testament," *BJRL* 56 (1974): 336–70.

206. For a complete summary and critique of the book see Cullinan, *Furnish's Theology of Ethics*, 122–86.

207. *Theology and Ethics*, xvii.

208. Ibid., 66.

209. Ibid., 75.

210. Ibid., 82.

211. See pp. 49–50 above.

212. *Theology and Ethics*, 110.

213. Ibid., 112.

214. Ibid., 114.

215. Ibid., 126.

216. Ibid., 132.

217. Ibid., 136.

218. Ibid., 146.

219. Ibid., 162.

220. Ibid.

221. Ibid., 169.

222. Ibid., 180.

223. Ibid., 187.

224. Ibid., 194.

225. Ibid., 212.

226. Ibid., 231.

227. Ibid., 214.

228. Ibid., 217.

229. Ibid., 225.

230. Ibid., 235.

231. Ibid., 237.

232. Victor P. Furnish, *The Love Command in the New Testament* (Nashville: Abingdon, 1972). For a review and critique of this book, see Cullinan, *Furnish's Theology of Ethics*, 187–244.

233. *Love Command*, 19.

234. Ibid., 44.

235. Ibid., 66.

236. Ibid., 116.

237. Ibid., 138.

238. Ibid., 154.

239. This book includes an appendix on "New Testament Words for Love" (pp. 219–31). This thoroughly-researched and incisively written piece should be widely read by NT exegetes. It carefully corrects popular notions about terms for love in the NT, notably ἀγαπᾶν and ἀγάπη. Among other things, Furnish demonstrates that these terms are not "distinctive" Christian words but have a long history of secular use in Greek literature. In Rev 3:19, where conventional wisdom would expect ἀγαπῶ, the text actually has φιλῶ. Furnish believes the two verbs are probably used synonymously in John 21:15-17.

240. Victor P. Furnish, *The Moral Teaching of Paul: Selected Issues*, 3rd ed. (Nashville: Abingdon, 2009).

241. Ibid., 26.

242. Furnish has participated in study commissions and lectured widely on the topic. His other publications on the issue include: "The Bible and Homosexuality," in *Homosexuality in Search of Christian Understanding*, ed. Leon Smith (Nashville: Discipleship Resources, 1981), 6–19; "The Bible and Homosexuality: Reading the Texts in Context," in *Homosexuality in the Church: Both Sides of the Debate*, ed. Jeffrey S. Siker (Louisville: Westminster John Knox, 1994), 18–35; "What Does the Bible Say about Homosexuality?" in *Caught in the Crossfire: Helping the Church Debate Homosexuality*, ed. Sally B. Geis and Donald E. Messer (Nashville: Abingdon, 1994) 57–66.

243. Ibid., 140.

244. Ibid., 163.

245. Victor P. Furnish, *II Corinthians: Translation with Introduction, Notes and Commentary*, AB 32A (Garden City, NY: Doubleday, 1984).

246. For a summary of Furnish's historical-critical view of the Pauline epistles, see his book, written for the non-specialist and co-authored with Leander E. Keck, *The Pauline Letters* (Nashville: Abingdon, 1984). Furnish wrote sections on the setting, sources, and center of Paul's gospel.

247. *II Corinthians*, 201.

248. Ibid., 248.

249. Ibid., 294.

250. Ibid., 296.

251. Ibid., 333.

252. Ibid., 550.

253. Victor P. Furnish, *1 Thessalonians, 2 Thessalonians*, ANTC (Nashville: Abingdon, 2007).

254. Ibid., 106. In regard to 2 Thessalonians the crucial question is authenticity. Furnish carefully summarizes the issues and concludes that Paul was not the author.

255. In *The Conversation Continues: Studies in Paul and John, in Honor of J. Louis Martyn*, ed. Robert T. Fortna and Beverly R. Gaventa (Nashville: Abingdon, 1990), 19–34.

256. "Paul the Theologian," 26.

257. Ibid., 29.

258. Victor P. Furnish, *The Theology of the First Letter to the Corinthians* (Cambridge: Cambridge University Press, 1999).

259. Ibid., 86.

260. Ibid., 125. Furnish's book, *Jesus According to Paul* (Cambridge: Cambridge University Press, 1993) can also be understood as an exposition of Pauline theology. Although this small book (written for the general reader) gives considerable attention to Paul's understanding of the Jesus tradition, it puts major emphasis on Paul's Christology.

261. *Furnish's Theology of Ethics*, 321–42.

262. For biographical information see "Betz, Hans Dieter," *DAR* 4: 32; Hans Dieter Betz, "Mein Weg in die neutestametliche Wissenschaft," in *Neutestamentliche Wissenschaft: Autobiographische Essays aus der Evangelischen Theologie*, ed. Eve-Marie Becker (Tübingen: Francke, 2003), 41–48; Franklin I. Gamwell, J. Albert Harrill, Elizabeth Asmis, and François Bovon, "Hans Dieter Betz: A Tribute," *Criterion* 39, no. 2 (2000): 2–11; Adela Yarbro Collins, "Introduction," in *Ancient and Modern Perspectives on the Bible and Culture: Essays in Honor of Hans Dieter Betz* (Atlanta: Scholars, 1998), 1–4; "Editors' Preface," Adela Yarbro Collins and Margaret M. Mitchell, eds., *Antiquity and Humanity: Essays on Ancient Religion and Philosophy, Presented to Hans Dieter Betz on His 70th Birthday* (Tübingen: Mohr Siebeck, 2001), xi–xiii.

263. Another major scholar teaching at Chicago during the second half of the twentieth century is the erudite Robert M. Grant, who has made major contributions to the study of early Christian literature. Mention should also be made of Norman Perrin, who taught at Chicago from 1964 until his untimely death in 1976; Perrin made important contributions to the study of the life and teaching of Jesus.

264. Retirement did not mean the termination of scholarly activity. For example, Betz published another contribution to his long list of works of the history of religion: *The "Mithras Liturgy": Text, Translation, and Commentary*, STANT 18 (Tübingen: Mohr Siebeck, 2003).

265. "Editors' Preface," xi.

266. Adela Yarbro Collins, "Introduction," 3.

267. For bibliography, see "Hans Dieter Betz Bibliography (to October 2000)" in *Antiquity and Humanity*, 501–12. Besides the major works reviewed here, Betz has produced a large number of essays, some of which are published in collections: four volumes of *Gesammelte Aufsätze*, published from 1990 to 2009 (Tübingen: Mohr Siebeck); *Essays on the Sermon on the Mount*, trans. L. L. Welborn (Philadelphia: Fortress Press, 1985), (German ed.: *Studien zur Bergpredigt* [Tübingen: Mohr Siebeck, 1985]). Betz also edited important works that make major contributions to the understanding of Hellenistic backgrounds: *Plutarch's Theological Writings and Early Christian Literature*, SCHNT 3 (Leiden: Brill, 1976); *Plutarch's Ethical Writings and Early Christian Literature*, SCHNT 4 (Leiden: Brill, 1978); *The Greek Magical Papyri in Translation, Including the Demotic Spells*, 2d ed., with updated bibliography(Chicago: University of Chicago Press, 1996). Betz also edited volumes of more general interest: *Christology and a Modern Pilgrimage: A Discussion with Norman Perrin* (Claremont, CA: New Testament Colloquium, 1971); *The Bible as a Document of the University* (Chico, CA: Scholars, 1981).

268. Hans Dieter Betz, *Lukian von Samosata und das Neue Testament; religionsgeschichtliche und paränetische Parallelen. Ein Beitrag zum Corpus Hellenisticum Novi Testamenti*, TU 76 (Berlin: Akademie, 1961).

269. Hans Dieter Betz, *Nachfolge und Nachahmung Jesu Christi im Neuen Testament*, BHT 37 (Tübingen: Mohr [Siebeck], 1967).

270. Ibid., 168.

271. Hans Dieter Betz, *Galatians: A Commentary on Paul's Letter to the Churches in Galatia*, Hermeneia (Philadelphia: Fortress Press, 1979); German trans.: *Der Galaterbrief: ein Kommentar*

zum Brief des Apostels Paulus an die Gemeinden in Galatien, trans. Sibylle Ann (Munich: Kaiser, 1988).

272. *Galatians,* 7.

273. Ibid., 28.

274. Ibid., 64–66.

275. Ibid., 71.

276. Ibid., 81–83.

277. Ibid., 103–4.

278. Ibid., 104.

279. Ibid., 109.

280. Ibid., 112.

281. Ibid., 117–18.

282. Hans Dieter Betz, *2 Corinthians 8 and 9: A Commentary on Two Administrative Letters of the Apostle Paul,* Hermeneia (Philadelphia: Fortress Press, 1985); German trans.: *2. Korinther 8 und 9: Ein Kommentar zu zwei Verwaltungsbriefe des Apostels Paulus,* trans. Sibylle Ann (Gütersloh: Kaiser, 1993).

283. Hans Dieter Betz, *Der Apostel Paulus und die sokratische Tradition. Eine exegetische Untersuchung zu seiner "Apologie," 2 Korinther 10–13,* BHT 45 (Tübingen: Mohr Siebeck, 1972). A précis of this work is presented in English translation: Hans Dieter Betz, *Paul's Apology in II Corinthians 10–13 and the Socratic Tradition,* ed. Wilhelm Wuellner, Center for Hermeneutical Studies in Hellenistic and Modern Culture (Berkeley, CA: Center for Hermeneutical Studies, 1975).

284. *2 Corinthians 8 and 9,* xii.

285. This view had been proposed earlier by Günther Bornkamm; see p. 149 above.

286. *2 Corinthians 8 and 9,* 134.

287. Hans Dieter Betz, *The Sermon on the Mount: A Commentary on the Sermon on the Mount, including the Sermon on the Plain (Matthew 5:3–7:27 and Luke 6:20–49),* Hermeneia (Philadelphia: Fortress Press, 1995).

288. Ibid., 44.

289. Ibid., 70.

290. Ibid.

291. Ibid., 88.

292. Ibid., 146.

293. Ibid., 198–328.

294. Ibid., 214.

295. Ibid., 223.

296. Ibid., 224.

297. Ibid., 239.

12

Epilogue

This is not a conclusion. The report has ended; the history moves on. No progress has been completed, no goal achieved. The study of the NT continues in each age according to the needs of the time. Although lessons have been learned from the past, NT research does not advance cumulatively or by the paradigm shifts of Thomas Kuhn's scientific revolutions. NT research uses elements of scientific method, but it is not a science. It deals in ideas, beliefs, traditions—the lives and hopes of humans.

What are some of the lessons learned in the recounting of the history? Fundamental is the study of the sources. Since the eighteenth century the sources used in NT research have multiplied exceedingly. At that time no one could have predicted the discovery of hundreds of scrolls in Judean caves or a jar containing codices in the Egyptian dessert (chap. 4). As a result of the first discovery, scholars were supplied with a multitude of texts in Aramaic, previously represented by a relatively small number of manuscripts. Manuscripts of the OT, a thousand years older than the extant manuscripts, provided the source for new critical texts, the basis for better translations. The Dead Sea Scrolls also provided firsthand information about a Jewish sect parallel in time to another sect that came to be called the Christian church.

The codices found near Nag Hammadi offered new information about the development of early Christianity, especially Christianity beyond the borders of orthodoxy. Whereas earlier knowledge had come mainly from their orthodox opponents, now firsthand information was available from the "heretics" themselves. Among the texts were documents formerly known only from secondhand reports. The newly-discovered material included a full text of the Gospel of Thomas, a collection of sayings reminiscent of the hypothetical Q and possibly preserving early, independent tradition about the teachings of Jesus (Robinson and Koester). The direct data about Gnosticism supplied new ammunition for the battle over pre-Christian Gnosticism, an issue important for Bultmann and his friends (and foes).

The twentieth century also saw the development of devices for the preservation and analysis of this extensive source material. Digital photography and computer technology made possible the collection and facsimile reproduction of manuscripts. Where once it was necessary to travel to libraries and distant monasteries to study texts, now all extant manuscripts can be copied and collected in a single center like the Institut für Neutestamentliche Textforschung at Münster (chap. 4). Whereas concordances were formerly produced by scholars laboriously listing and tabulating words, now scholars can make sophisticated searches by touching a key on the personal computers on their desks.

Important developments have been made—here it is possible to speak of progress—in textual criticism (chap. 4). In contrast to Westcott and Hort, who listed not a single papyrus, the 27th edition of the Nestle-Aland text cites over a hundred papyri. New ways of collating the multitude of manuscripts, like the "Claremont Profile Method" and Münster's "test-passages" method, have been developed. The application of these methods has contributed to the ongoing effort to publish critical editions that attend to virtually all the extant variants—the International Text Critical Project and the *Editio Critica Maior*. As in other areas surveyed in this volume, textual criticism has become sensitive to the social and ideological dimensions: how the development of the text has been shaped by the beliefs and practices of the people who copied and used it (Ehrmann, Epp). Most innovative is the rejection of the ideal of the "original text," now replaced by the view that the text is a process (Parker).

Attention has been given to linguistics and grammar. The Blass-Debrunner grammar that had become standard in Germany was translated into English, and Robert Funk produced a grammar of his own, making use of the insights of modern linguists. Virtually every commentary reviewed in this volume, from Taylor to Betz, has attended to the language and grammar of the NT texts. Attention has also been given to the nature of NT language, especially its poetic and mythic character (Bultmann, the Bultmann School, Knox, Minear, Betz). Several scholars have given attention to ancient rhetoric, for example, in the study of parables. However, the use of classical rhetoric as the key to investigating NT documents is a distinctive contribution of Betz.

Historical backgrounds, as in the earlier history of religion school, hold a prominent place. The import of the OT for understanding the NT is again and again emphasized. The tension between the alternative contexts—Jewish vs. Hellenistic—continues, though the lines have blurred (Hengel). A tendency with the more "conservative" scholars (Jeremias, Bruce, Dunn), but also with the more "liberal" (Martyn, Keck) is to emphasize the Jewish context. Stress on the Hellenistic backgrounds (and Gnosticism) is found all the way from Dodd to Betz, and especially with Bultmann and his followers, who still attend the history of religion school. In regard to Jewish backgrounds, a "new perspective" has been proposed (Davies, Sanders, Dunn). Most important, the old caricature of Judaism as a legalistic foil for free and vital Christianity has been abolished. Archaeology, a discipline long used to illuminate the historical context of early Christianity, has spawned new methods. Again, the social emphasis of the "new archaeology" has moved beyond the steps of Jesus to the daily lives of persons in Galilean villages (chap. 4).

The discipline of Introduction, once designated "higher criticism," is represented in this volume primarily by two examples (others have been mentioned, including Marxsen, Brown, and Cullmann): the work of Kümmel (for some years standard in Germany, replaced by the *Introduction* of Udo Schnelle) and the two volumes of German-American Helmut Koester. These works follow the traditional pattern, although Koester insists that early Christian literature should not be limited to the books of the NT canon. On critical decisions the two scholars agree on major points: the adoption of the Two-Document Hypothesis (2HD), the acceptance of seven authentic Pauline letters (plus 2 Thessalonians and Colossians, according to Kümmel), Acts as a secondary source for the life and thought of Paul, and the Catholic Epistles as pseudonymous. The twentieth century saw the development of redaction criticism, a method that complemented form criticism. Whereas form criticism emphasized the function of the gospel writers as collectors of tradition, redaction criticism affirmed their work as authors: literary composers with convictions of their own.

The traditional way of understanding early Christian tradition—as the work of anonymous reporters and the collection of early written fragments—was challenged; a larger role was assigned to the oral tradition—a tradition direct from Jesus to select witness to faithfully written Gospels (Gerhardsson). Also challenged was the majority solution to the Synoptic problem, the 2DH. Some (advocates of the Two-Gospel Hypothesis) attacked the priority of Mark while others (advocates of the Farrer-Goulder Hypothesis) pleaded for dispensing with Q. Most scholars were not persuaded, and the 2DH survived the storm and prevailed, but with much less self-confidence. In the mean time, advocates of the existence of Q explored the document in detail, detecting various strata in the document and reconstructing the evolving Q community and its theology. While the majority remain convinced of the existence of the Q document(s), most did not believe a hypothetical document could sustain the sort of precise analysis the Q scholars advanced.

The Gospel of John remained a battlefield as the twentieth century produced a shelf of superb books on the Fourth Gospel. Dodd's two volumes are significant. In the first he presents numerous Hellenistic parallels; in the second he detects an independent historical tradition. Bultmann's magisterial commentary surmises three major sources, used in an innovative gospel that was later rearranged and domesticated by an ecclesiastical redactor. Käsemann made the bold suggestion that John betrays a veiled docetism. Virtually opposite is the view of Hengel, who thinks the tradition contained in the Fourth Gospel had its source in John the Elder, a Palestinian eyewitness of events in the life of Jesus. Schnackenburg's multivolume commentary (4 vols. in German; 3 in English translation) makes a major contribution to Johannine research. He tends to be conservative, detecting the original source of the tradition in John, the "Beloved Disciple"; the background is primarily found in the OT and Judaism; John is a theological gospel, but not without historical significance. Brown's monumental two-volume commentary also supports the idea of independent tradition, enlisted in the service of profound theology. Brown, along with others (Cullmann, Martyn), offered a hypothetical history of the Johannine community that produced the Gospel, Epistles, and Revelation. Barrett published an excellent commentary (essentially a collection of notes) on the Greek text of John. Unique in the history of Johannine research is Martyn's imaginative presentation of the Gospel as a two-level drama.

Making use of many of the subdisciplines, scholars have engaged in extensive exegesis of the NT documents. Their work was prefaced by reflection on hermeneutics, the philosophical question concerning the essential nature of interpretation. This question had been raised by Barth and especially by Bultmann's method of demythologizing. It was more fully explored by members of the Bultmann school, the advocates of the "new hermeneutic," inspired by the philosophy of the "later" Heidegger. This question emerged again in the work of Cullmann, Knox, and especially Minear, who viewed the NT with the eyes of faith. Dunn discusses the issue, and, for Schüssler Fiorenza hermeneutics is of crucial importance. Regardless of hermeneutical presuppositions, scholars reviewed in this volume—from Taylor to Betz—composed a large library of commentaries. Some of these are mammoth in size: Barrett's two-volume commentary on Acts, Dunn's two-volume *Romans*, Betz's massive volume on the Sermon on the Mount. A distinctive kind of work is Brown's two-volume *Death of the Messiah*, a commentary on the passion narrative of all four Gospels. Along with the major commentaries on the Fourth Gospel, the twentieth century witnessed the publication of other significant commentaries: Taylor's *Mark*, Käsemann's *Romans*, Martyn's *Galatians*, Furnish's *2 Corinthians*.

The major subjects of NT research are Jesus and Paul. Work on Jesus reviewed in Chapter 1 (Taylor and Manson) is reminiscent of the nineteenth century: the "liberal" Jesus is the center of Christianity, but the life of this Jesus was driven by his messianic consciousness, his full awareness of his role as Suffering Servant and Son of Man. Cadbury, by way of contrast, warned of the peril of modernizing Jesus, and conversely of the danger of archaizing ourselves. Bultmann's Jesus was "bearer of the word," and Bornkamm, despite his disclaimers, almost produced a biography. Jeremias (and Funk) gave attention to the parables. Scholars explored and disagreed about Jesus' understanding of the kingdom: present (Dodd), future (Sanders), present and future (Kümmel and many others). Sanders, reminiscent of Schweitzer, recognized the importance of apocalyptic for understanding the life of Jesus. With Funk, the strident skepticism of scholars like Reimarus was revived. In contrast is the informed and nuanced approach of Keck. For Schüssler Fiorenza, Jesus is Miriam's child, the prophet of Sophia who welcomed women into his community. Life of Jesus research reached a high point with Meier. His massive volumes, composed with careful attention to context, criteria of authenticity, and exegetical detail, constitute a monument to historical-critical research.

Paul, too, was given much attention in the century. He was brought to the center with Barth's *Romans* and kept there by Bultmann, though nudged by a Paulinized John. For Käsemann the theocentric apocalyptic Paul with his doctrine of justification was clearly the center. Bornkamm's popular *Paul* is a genuine biography, but extensive attention is given to the apostle's theology. Davies rejected the idea of justification as the center and depicted Paul in the garb of the rabbis. Sanders also rehabilitated Paul, discovering in the traditional Lutheran view the seeds of a malevolent anti-Judaism. Bruce presents a masterful portrait of Paul—his life, letters, and theology—thoroughly researched, lucidly written. The old notion of Paul as the second founder of Christianity has been laid to rest. Paul, however, is viewed as the first, and for some (Dunn, Martyn, Keck) the NT's most important theologian; others (Sanders, Knox) were less enthusiastic.

NT research in the twentieth century was preoccupied with biblical theology. This, of course, was instigated by Barth, whose shadow extended over the century. But attention was given to Christology by Taylor, who scarcely tipped his hat to Barth. With Bultmann, NT theology was practiced by a scholar skilled in the disciplines of historical criticism. Bultmann's anthropocentric theology was replaced by the theocentric apocalyptic of

Käsemann. Jeremias, with his notion that the *ipisissma vox* of Jesus could be recovered, presented a unique Christology, by implication the Christology of Jesus himself. Similar is Hengel's notion that the "messianic secret" has its origin with Jesus. NT theology took special (but not new) shape with Cullmann's history of salvation. For Cullmann the theology of the NT traced a timeline that extended from creation to the consummation, with Christ the midpoint and decisive event. For Minear the view of history was more complex: a cosmic battle, a transcendent reality, perceived by the eyes of faith, explicated by myth and symbol.

Dunn's most important book is on the theology of Paul, viewed in the context of the OT and Judaism: indeed, a Judaism that Paul understood better than the Jews. For Dunn (as for others like Cullmann, Brown, and Keck), the center of NT theology was Christology, explicated by titles preserved in the biblical record (according to Keck, a dubious method). Knox, with his usual sensitivity, produced a trilogy of small books on Christology, wary of exaggerating the divinity of Christ, stressing the importance of understanding Christ in the context of the Christian community. The theological ethic of Paul is thoughtfully explicated by Furnish. Some of the larger questions—the nature of revelation, the authority of the Bible—that had been posed by the biblical theologians (Barth, Bultmann, the Bultmann school) were given attention (by Dodd, Jeremias, Marxsen, Schnackenburg, Brown, Knox, Cullmann, Minear, Bruce, Dunn, Schüssler Fiorenza, Keck). These scholars provided a variety of answers, but the questions continue as an ongoing concern. Attention was given to canon and canon within the canon (Käsemann, Marxsen); Knox notes the role of a heretic in the development of the canon, and Koester appreciates noncanonical literature, whereas Bruce affirms the role of the Spirit in the collection of the canonical books.

In the twentieth century the historical-critical method has come under attack. The method has, nevertheless, survived, and indeed prevailed.[1] The attack, in the main, has charged historical criticism with failure to accomplish goals it never (or should never have) promised. The notion that all the historical-critical and exegetical problems could be solved, given time and effort, is a grand illusion. The belief that the life of Jesus, the theology of Paul, the history of the early church could eventually be reconstructed and finally explicated is misguided. History is not that kind of discipline. Equally mistaken is the supposition that skilled practitioners of the historical method could be completely objective. The lack of objectivity is evident in the fact that capable scholars, using the same method, have produced different results. Absolute objectivity is impossible, but within a discipline like history a consensus of fundamental practices and procedures makes possible a high degree of objectivity.[2] Within this limited objectivity there is a dialectic that acknowledges that objective knowledge involves the subjectivity of the knower. Everyone, of course, subscribes to Bultmann's oft-quoted opinion that exegesis without presuppositions is impossible.[3] However, this dictum does not mean that "anything goes"; some presuppositions are less possible than others. Like Bultmann, the one who presupposes must base his/her presuppositions on some epistemological or ontological ground, an issue that needs ongoing attention.

A major promise of the historical method in its early days was the liberation of the Bible from the domination of ecclesiastical authority: a democratizing of the study of the Bible. Despite the suspicions of the Jesus Seminar, this goal has largely been achieved. Indeed, it is striking that scholars of the most hierarchical authority of all—the Roman Catholic Church—have embraced historical criticism and become some of its most accomplished practitioners. However, the NT that escaped ecclesiasticism faces a more subtle threat—the scholarly captivity of the Bible. As this chapter has demonstrated, the discipline of NT research has become increasingly complex. The complete NT scholar should be a master of several ancient languages, skilled in the various sub-disciplines of textual criticism and archaeology, conversant with the history of Judaism and Greco-Roman culture, expert in linguistic and rhetorical criticism, sensitive to theological issues—and more. A perusal of this book suggests that some indeed are able historical-critical-exegetical virtuosi. The solution to the problem is not to take the Bible from the scholars and give it back to the people. Without historical scholarship the Bible remains mute. The text of the NT is the product of historical research. The translation of the Bible is accomplished by scholars. Without knowledge of the historical context, interpretation of the NT is moribund. What is needed is not less historical scholarship but continued research at the highest level, translated into the language of the common people. Some of the scholars reviewed in this volume have effectively done both. It is not necessary to be a professional biblical scholar to understand the Bible, but understanding the Bible requires the results of biblical scholarship.

And so the basic method—the collection and analysis of sources, the formulation of hypotheses, the rational testing of the hypotheses, and the synthesizing composition—proceeds. In the twentieth century attention has been given to social concerns, and methods from the social sciences have been appropriated; these do not replace but merely complement the historical-critical method. But why is a historical understanding of the NT important? Would it be more appropriate, for example, to read the Bible as a devotional book, enriching the spiritual and moral lives of the readers? The historical critic cannot restrict the uses of the Bible; after all, the Bible is the church's book. However, the historical scholar will insist that historical criticism is essential to understanding the NT according to its essential character. For some—I speak for myself—this insistence has a theological ground: Christianity is a historical religion; it is not a religion of the book but a religion of the person. The NT is the record of the revelation of God in a historical person. To understand that book and that revelation, historical research is necessary. The Word became flesh in history; the Word continues to live in historical witness.

Notes

1. See Leander E. Keck, "Will the Historical-Critical Method Survive? (see ch. 11, n. 171 above). Keck reviews and answers the charges of critics, including Walter Wink, Roland Fry, and Hans Frei. See also Joseph A. Fitzmyer, *The Interpretation of Scripture: In Defense of the Historical-Critical Method* (New York: Paulist, 2008).

2. See Allan Megill, *Historical Knowledge, Historical Error: A Contemporary Guide to Practice* (Chicago: University of Chicago Press, 2007), 107–24.

3. Rudolf Bultmann, "Is Exegesis without Presuppositions Possible?" in *Existence and Faith: Shorter Writings of Rudolf Bultmann*, ed. Schubert M. Ogden (New York: Meridian, 1960), 289–96.

Select Bibliography

GENERAL WORKS

Barton, John, ed. *The Cambridge Companion to Biblical Interpretation*. Cambridge: Cambridge University Press, 1998.

Bray, Gerald. *Biblical Interpretation: Past and Present*. Downers Grove, IL: InterVarsity, 1996.

Duling, Dennis C. *Jesus Christ Though History*. New York: Harcourt Brace Jovanovich, 1979.

Epp, Eldon J., and George W. MacRae, eds. *The New Testament and Its Modern Interpreters*. SBLBMI. SBLCP. Atlanta: Scholars, 1989.

Fuller, Reginald H. *The New Testament in Current Study*. New York: Scrib-ners, 1962.

Frey, Jörg. *Die johanneische Eschatologie, Bd. 1: Ihre Probleme im Spiegel der Forschung seit Reimarus*. WUNT 96. Tübingen: Mohr Siebeck, 1997.

Harrisville, Roy A., and Walter Sundberg, eds. *The Bible in Modern Culture: Baruch Spinoza to Brevard Childs*. 2d ed. Grand Rapids: Eerdmans, 2002.

Hyatt, J. Philip, ed. *The Bible in Modern Scholarship: Papers Read at the 100th Meeting of the Society of Biblical Literature, December 28–30, 1964*. Nashville: Abingdon, 1965, 2000

Kümmel, Werner Georg. *The New Testament: The History of the Investigation of Its Problems*. Translated by S. McLean Gilmour and Howard C. Kee. Nashville: Abingdon, 1972.

Larsson, Tord. *God in the Fourth Gospel: A Hermeneutical Study of the History of Interpretations*. ConBNT 35. Stockholm: Almqvist & Wiksell, 2001.

Lührmann, Dieter. *An Itinerary for New Testament Study*. Philadelphia: Trinity Press International, 1989.

Morgan, Robert, with John Barton. *Biblical Interpretation*. Oxford: Oxford University Press, 1988.

Macquarrie, John. *Twentieth Century Religious Thought*. New ed. Harrisburg, PA: Trinity Press International, 2002.

Neill, Stephen, and N. T. Wright. *The Interpretation of the New Testament: 1861–1986*. 2nd ed. Oxford: Oxford University Press, 1989.

O'Neill, J. C. *The Bible's Authority: A Portrait Gallery of Thinkers from Lessing to Bultmann*. Edinburgh: T & T Clark, 1991.

697

Porter, Stanley E., ed. *Dictionary of Biblical Criticism and Interpretation*. London: Routledge, 2007.

Reventlow, Henning Graf. *Epochen der Bibelauslegung: Band IV: Von der Aufklärung bis zum 20. Jahrhundert.* Munich: Beck, 2001. ET: *History of Biblical Interpretation: Vol. 4: From the Enlightenment to the Twentieth Century*. Translated by Leo G. Perdue. SBLRBS 63. Atlanta: SBL, 2009.

Riches, John. *A Century of New Testament Study*. Cambridge: Lutterworth, 1993.

Rogerson, John W., Christopher Rowland, and Barnabas Lindars, eds. *The History of Christian Theology. Volume 2: The Study and Use of the Bible*. Grand Rapids: Eerdmans, 1988.

Rogerson, John W., and Judith M. Lieu, eds. *The Oxford Handbook of Biblical Studies*. Oxford: Oxford University Press, 2006.

Sandys-Wunsch, John. *What Have They Done to the Bible?: A History of Modern Biblical Interpretation*. Collegeville, MN: Liturgical, 2005.

Schmithals, Walter. *Johannesevangelium und Johannnesbriefe: Forschungsgeschichte und Analyse.* BZNW 64. Berlin: de Gruyter, 1992.

Soulen, Richard N. *Sacred Scripture: A Short History of Interpretation*. Louisville: Westminster John Knox, 2009.

Weaver, Walter P. *The Historical Jesus in the Twentieth Century, 1900–1950*. Harrisburg, PA: Trinity Press International, 1999.

Wilder, Amos N. "New Testament Studies, 1920–1950: Reminiscences of a Changing Discipline." *JR* 64 (1984): 432–51.

Willoughby, Harold R., ed. *The Study of the Bible Today and Tomorrow*. Chicago: University of Chicago Press, 1947.

Yarbrough, Robert W. *The Salvation Historical Fallacy? Reassessing the History of New Testament Theology*. Leiden: Deo, 2004.

Yarchin, William. *History of Biblical Interpretation: A Reader*. Peabody, MA: Hendrickson, 2004.

THE ZENITH OF CRITICISM

VINCENT TAYLOR

Taylor, Vincent. *The Atonement in New Testament Teaching*. 2d ed. London: Epworth, 1945.

———. *Behind the Third Gospel: A Study of the Proto-Luke Hypothesis*. Oxford: Clarendon, 1926.

———. *The Cross of Christ: Eight Public Lectures*. London: Macmillan, 1956.

———. *The Epistle to the Romans*. London: Epworth, 1955.

———. *Forgiveness and Reconciliation: A Study in New Testament Theology*. London: Macmillan, 1941.

———. *The Formation of the Gospel Tradition: Eight Lectures*. 2d ed. London: Macmillan, 1957.

———. *The Gospel According to Mark: The Greek Text with Introduction, Notes, and Indexes*. 1952. Repr. London: Macmillan, 1957. 2d ed. New York: St. Martins, 1966. Repr. Grand Rapids: Baker, 1981.

———. *The Gospels: A Short Introduction*. 7th ed. London: Epworth, 1952.

———. *The Historical Evidence for the Virgin Birth*. Oxford: Clarendon, 1920.

———. *Jesus and His Sacrifice: A Study of the Passion-Sayings in the Gospels*. London: Macmillan, 1937.

———. *The Life and Ministry of Jesus*. New York: Abingdon, 1955.

———. *The Names of Jesus*. London: Macmillan, 1953.

———. *The Passion Narrative of St Luke: A Critical and Historical Investigation*. Ed. Owen E. Evans. Cambridge: Cambridge University Press, 1972.

———. *The Person of Christ in New Testament Teaching*. London: Macmillan, 1958.

———. *The Text of the New Testament: A Short Introduction*. London: Macmillan, 1961.

HENRY J. CADBURY

Cadbury, Henry J. *Behind the Gospels*. PHP 160. Wallingford, PA: Pendle Hill, 1968.

———. *The Book of Acts in History*. New York: Harper & Brothers, 1955.

———. *The Eclipse of the Historical Jesus*. PHP 133. Wallingford, PA: Pendle Hill, 1964.

———. *Jesus: What Manner of Man*. New York: Macmillan, 1947.

———. *The Making of Luke-Acts*. New York: Macmillan, 1927. Reprints: London: SPCK, 1958; Peabody, MA: Hendrickson, 1999.

———. *The Peril of Modernizing Jesus*. New York: Macmillan, 1937.

———. *A Quaker Approach to the Bible*. Guilford, NC: Guilford College, 1953.

———. *The Style and Literary Method of Luke*. HTS 6. Cambridge, MA: Harvard University Press, 1920.

Bacon, Margaret Hope. *Let This Life Speak: The Legacy of Henry Joel Cadbury*. Philadelphia: University of Pennsylvania Press, 1987.

Parsons, Mikeal C., and Joseph B. Tyson, eds. *Cadbury, Knox, and Talbert: American Contributions to the Study of Acts*. SBLBSNA. Atlanta: Scholars, 1992.

THOMAS W. MANSON

Manson, T. W. *The Beginning of the Gospel*. London: Oxford University Press, 1950.

———. *The Church's Ministry*. London: Hodder & Stoughton, 1948.

———. *Ethics and the Gospel*. New York: Scribners, 1960.

———. *Jesus and the Non-Jews*. London: Athlone, 1955.

———. *Ministry and Priesthood: Christ's and Ours*. London: Epworth, 1958.

———. *On Paul and John: Some Selected Theological Themes*. Ed. Matthew Black. SBT 38. Naperville, IL: Alec R. Allenson, 1963.

———. *The Servant-Messiah*. Cambridge: Cambridge University Press, 1953.

———. *Studies in the Gospels and Epistles*. Ed. Matthew Black. Manchester: Manchester University Press, 1962.

———. *The Teaching of Jesus: Studies of Its Form and Content*. 2d. ed. Cambridge: Cambridge University Press, 1963.

CHARLES HAROLD DODD

Dodd, Charles Harold. *According to the Scriptures: The Sub-Structure of New Testament Theology*. London: Nisbet, 1952.

———. *The Apostolic Preaching and Its Developments: Three Lectures with an Appendix on Eschatology and History*. New York: Harper, 1935. Repr. New York and Evanston: Harper & Row, 1964.

———. *The Authority of the Bible*. New York and London: Harper & Brothers, 1929; 2d ed. 1938. Repr. New York: Harper & Brothers, 1958.

———. *The Bible and the Greeks*. London: Hodder & Stoughton, 1935. Repr. 1954.

———. *The Bible To-Day*. Cambridge: Cambridge: University Press; New York: Macmillan, 1947. Repr. 1956, 1965.

———. *The Epistle of Paul to the Romans*. MNTC. New York: Harper and Brothers, 1932.

———. *The Founder of Christianity*. New York: Macmillan; London: Collier-Macmillan, 1970.

———. *Gospel and Law: The Relation of Faith and Ethics in Early Christianity*. Cambridge: Cambridge University Press, 1951.

———. *Historical Tradition in the Fourth Gospel*. Cambridge: Cambridge University Press, 1963.

———. *History and the Gospel*. New York: Scribner's, 1938. Rev. ed. London: Hodder and Stoughton, 1964.

———. *The Interpretation of the Fourth Gospel*. Cambridge: Cambridge University Press, 1953.

———. *The Johannine Epistles*. MNTC. New York: Harper & Brothers, 1946.

———. *The Meaning of Paul for Today*. London: Swarthmore Press, 1920. Repr. New York: Meridian, 1957.

———. *More New Testament Studies*. Manchester: Manchester University Press; Grand Rapids: Eerdmans, 1968.

———. *New Testament Studies*. Manchester: Manchester University Press, 1953.

———. *The Parables of the Kingdom*. Rev. ed. New York: Scribners, 1961.

———. *The Present Task in New Testament Studies*. Cambridge: Cambridge University Press, 1936.

Dillistone, Frederick William. *C. H. Dodd: Interpreter of the New Testament*. Grand Rapids: Eerdmans, 1977.

THE NEW BIBLICAL THEOLOGY

KARL BARTH

Barth, Karl. *Anselm: Fides Quaerens Intellectum: Anselm's Proof of the Existence of God in the Context of his Theological Scheme*. Translated by Ian W. Robertson. London: SCM, 1960.

———. *Die Auferstehung der Toten: Eine akademische Vorlesung über 1. Kor. 15*. 4th ed. Zollikon-Zürich: Evangelischer Verlag, 1953. ET: *The Resurrection of the Dead*. Translated by H. J. Stenning. New York: Revell, 1933. Repr. New York: Arno, 1977.

———. *Christ and Adam: Man and Humanity in Romans 5*. Translated by T. A. Smail. New York: Macmillan, 1968.

———. *Church Dogmatics: The Doctrine of the Word of God* I/1. Translated by Geoffrey W. Bromiley. Edinburgh: T & T Clark, 1975.

———. *Church Dogmatics: The Doctrine of the Word of God* I/2. Translated by George T. Thomson and Harold Knight. Edinburgh: T & T Clark, 1956.

———. *Church Dogmatics: The Doctrine of God* II/2. Ed. Geoffrey W. Bromiley and Thomas F. Torrance. Translated by George T. Thomson. Edinburgh: T & T Clark, 1957.

——. *Church Dogmatics: The Doctrine of Reconciliation* IV/1. Ed. Geoffrey W. Bromiley and Thomas F. Torrance. Translated by George T. Thomson. Edinburgh: T & T Clark, 1956.

———. *Dogmatik im Grundriss.* Munich: Kaiser, 1947. ET: *Dogmatics in Outline.* Translated by George T. Thomson. New York: Philosophical Library, 1949.

——. *Einführung in die evangelische Theologie.* Zürich: Evangelischer Verlag, 1962. ET: *Evangelical Theology: An Introduction.* Translated by Grover Foley. New York: Holt, Rinehart and Winston, 1963.

——. *Erklärung des Johannes Evangelium.* Zürich: Theologischer Verlag, 1976. ET: *Witness to the Word: A Commentary on John 1: Lectures at Münster in 1925 and at Bonn in 1933.* Ed. Walther Fürst. Translated by Geoffrey W. Bromiley. Grand Rapids: Eerdmans, 1986.

———. *Erklärung des Philipperbief.* Munich: Kaiser, 1927. ET: *The Epistle to the Philippians.* Translated by James W. Leitch. Richmond, VA: John Knox, 1962. Repr., *The Epistle to the Philippians: 40th Anniversary Edition.* Louisville: Westminster John Knox, 2002.

——. *The Epistle to the Romans.* Translated from the 6th ed. by Edwyn C. Hoskyns. London: Oxford University Press, 1933.

——. *How I Changed My Mind: Introduction and Epilogue by John D. Godsey.* Richmond, VA: John Knox, 1966.

——. *The Humanity of God.* Richmond, VA: John Knox, 1961.

——. *Kurze Erklärung des Römerbriefes.* Munich: Kaiser, 1941. ET: *A Shorter Commentary on Romans.* Richmond, VA: John Knox, 1959.

——. *The Word of God and the Word of Man.* Translated by Douglas Horton. New York: Harper & Brothers, 1957.

Jaspert, Bernd, ed. *Karl Barth–Rudolf Bultmann Letters 1922–1966.* Translated by Geoffrey W. Bromiley. Grand Rapids: Eerdmans, 1981.

Bakker, Nicolaas T. *In der Krisis der Offenbarung: Karl Barths Hermeneutik, dargestellt an seiner Römerbrief-Auslegung.* Neukirchen-Vluyn: Neukirchener Verlag, 1974.

Bourgine, Benoît. *L'Herméneutique Théologique de Karl Barth.* BETL 171. Leuven: Leuven University Press, 2003.

Burnett, Richard E. *Karl Barth's Theological Exegesis: The Hermeneutical Principals* [sic] *of the Römerbrief Period.* WUNT 2/145. Tübingen: Mohr Siebeck, 2001.

Busch, Eberhard. *Karl Barth: His life from letters and autobiographical texts.* Translated by John Bowden. Philadelphia: Fortress Press, 1976.

Cunningham, Mary Kathleen. *What is Theological Exegesis? Interpretation and Use of Scripture in Barth's Doctrine of Election.* Valley Forge, PA: Trinity Press International, 1995.

Demson, David E. *Hans Frei and Karl Barth: Different Ways of Reading Scripture.* Grand Rapids: Eerdmans, 1997.

Ford, David. *Barth and God's Story: Biblical Narrative and the Theological Method of Karl Barth in the "Church Dogmatics."* Frankfurt: Peter Lang, 1981.

Lindemann, Walter. *Karl Barth und die kritische Schriftauslegung.* TF 54. Hamburg-Bergstedt: Herbert Reich, 1973.

McGlasson, Paul. *Jesus and Judas: Biblical Exegesis in Barth.* AARAS 72. Atlanta: Scholars, 1991.

Runia, Klaas. *Karl Barth's Doctrine of Holy Scripture.* Grand Rapids: Eerdmans, 1962.

Trowitzsch, Michael, ed. *Karl Barths Schriftauslegung.* Tübingen: Mohr Siebeck, 1996.

Weber, Otto. *Karl Barth's Church Dogmatics: An Introductory Report on Volumes I:1 to III:4.* Translated by Arthur C. Cochrane. London: Lutterworth, 1953.

Webster, John. *Barth.* London: Continuum, 2000.

RUDOLF BULTMANN

Bultmann, Rudolf. *Der Begriff der Offenbarung im Neuen Testament.* Tübingen: Mohr Siebeck, 1929. ET: "The Concept of Revelation in the New Testament." In *Existence and Faith,* 58–91.

———. *Das Evangelium des Johannes.* KEK. Göttingen: Vandenhoeck & Ruprecht, 1941. ET: *The Gospel of John: A Commentary.* Translated by G. R. Beasley-Murray, Rupert W. N. Hoare and John K. Riches. Philadelphia: Westminster, 1971.

———. *Exegetica: Aufsätze zur Erforschung des Neuen Testaments.* Ed. Erich Dinkler. Tübingen: Mohr Siebeck, 1967.

———. *Exegetische Probleme des zweiten Korintherbriefes.* Darmstadt: Wissenschaftliche Buchgesellschaft, 1963.

———. *Existence and Faith: Shorter Writings of Rudolf Bultmann.* Translated by Schubert M. Ogden. New York: Meridian, 1960.

———. *Glauben und Verstehen.* Gesammelte Aufsätze. 4 vols. Tübingen: Mohr Siebeck, 1933–65. English selections : *Faith and Understanding I.* Ed. Robert W. Funk. Translated by Louise Pettibone Smith. New York: Harper & Row, 1966. *Essays Philosophical and Theological.* Translated by James C. G. Greig. New York: Macmillan, 1955.

————. *Jesus.* Berlin: Deutsche Bibliothek, 1926. ET: *Jesus and the Word.* Translated by Louise Pettibone Smith and Erminie Huntress Lantero. New York: Scribner's, 1934. Repr. 1958.

————. *Jesus Christ and Mythology.* New York: Scribners, 1958. German ed.: *Jesus Christus und die Mythologie: Das Neue Testament im Licht der Bibelkritik.* Gütersloh: Mohn, 1964.

————. *New Testament and Mythology and Other Basic Writings.* Edited and translated by Schubert M. Ogden. Philadelphia: Fortress Press, 1984.

————. *The Presence of Eternity: History and Eschatology.* Gifford Lectures 1955. New York: Harper & Brothers, 1957. Repr. New York: Harper, 1962.

————. *Theologie des Neuen Testaments.* 2d ed. NThG. Tübingen: Mohr Siebeck, 1954. ET: *Theology of the New Testament.* Translated by Kendrick Grobel. 2 vols. New York: Scribner's, 1951, 1955. Repr. Waco, TX: Baylor University Press, 2007. 9th [German] ed. Otto Merk. Tübingen: Mohr Siebeck, 1984.

————. *What Is Theology?* Ed. Eberhard Jüngel and Klaus W. Müller. Translated by Roy A. Harrisville. FTMTh. Minneapolis: Fortress Press, 1997.

————. *Der zweite Brief an die Korinther.* Ed. Erich Dinkler. KEK. Göttingen: Vandenhoeck & Ruprecht, 1976. ET: *The Second Letter to the Corinthians.* Translated by Roy A. Harrisville. Minneapolis: Augsburg, 1985.

Bartsch, Hans Werner, ed. *Kerygma und Mythos.* 6 vols. Hamburg: Herbert Reich, 1948. English selections from vols. 1–5: *Kerygma and Myth.* Translated by Reginald H. Fuller. 2 vols. London: SPCK, 1953, 1962.

Bornkamm, Günther, and Walter Klaas, eds. *Mythos und Evangelium: Zum Programm R. Bultmanns.* 3d ed. ThEH 26. Munich: Kaiser, 1953. ET: *Kerygma and History: A Symposium on the Theology of Rudolf Bultmann.* Translated and edited by Carl E. Braaten and Roy A. Harrisville. New York: Abingdon, 1966.

Fergusson, David. *Bultmann.* Collegeville, MN: Liturgical, 1992.

Hammann, Konrad. *Rudolf Bultmann: Eine Biographie.* 2d ed. Tübingen: Mohr Siebeck, 2009.

Hobbs, Edward C., ed. *Bultmann, Retrospect and Prospect: The Centenary Symposium at Wellesley.* HTS 35. Philadelphia: Fortress Press, 1985.

Hohmeier, Friedebert. *Das Schriftverständnis in der Theologie Rudolf Bultmanns.* AGThL13. Berlin: Lutherisches Verlagshaus, 1964.

Jaspert, Bernd, ed. *Bibel und Mythos: Fünfzig Jahre nach Rudolf Bultmanns Entmythologisierungsprogramm.* KVR 1560. Göttingen: Vandenhoeck & Ruprecht, 1991.

———. *Rudolf Bultmanns Werk und Wirkung*. Darmstadt: Wissenschaftliche Buchgesellschaft, 1984.

Johnson, Roger A. *The Origins of Demythologizing: Philosophy and Historiography in the Theology of Rudolf Bultmann*. SHR 28. Leiden: Brill, 1974.

Jones, Gareth. *Bultmann: Towards a Critical Theology*. Cambridge: Polity Press, 1991.

Kay, James F. *Christus Praesens: A Reconsideration of Rudolf Bultmann's Christology*. Grand Rapids: Eerdmans, 1994.

Kegley, Charles W., ed. *The Theology of Rudolf Bultmann*. New York: Harper and Row, 1966.

Körner, Johannes. *Eschatologie und Geschichte: Eine Untersuchung des Begriffes des Eschatologischen in der Theologie Rudolf Bultmanns*. TF 13. Hamburg: Herbert Reich, 1957.

Lorenzmeier, Theodor . *Exegese und Hermeneutik: Eine vergleichende Darstellung der Theologie Rudolf Bultmanns, Herbert Brauns und Gerhard Ebelings*. Hamburg: Furche, 1968.

Macquarrie, John. *An Existentialist Theology: A Comparison of Heidegger and Bultmann*. New York: Harper & Row, 1965.

Malet, André. *The Thought of Rudolf Bultmann*. Translated by Richard Strachan. Garden City, NY: Doubleday, 1971.

Marlé, René. *Bultmann et l'interprétation du Nouveau Testament*. Théologie 33. Aubier: Montaigne, 1956.

Ogden, Schubert M. *Christ Without Myth: A Study Based on the Theology of Rudolf Bultmann*. New York: Harper & Row, 1961.

Pausch, Eberhard Martin. *Wahrheit zwischen Erschlossenheit und Verantwortung: Die Rezeption und Transformation der Wahrheitskonzeption Martin Heideggers in der Theologie Rudolf Bultmanns*. Berlin: de Gruyter, 1995.

Painter, John. *Theology as Hermeneutics: Rudolf Bultmann's Interpretation of the History of Jesus*. Sheffield: Almond, 1987.

Schmithals, Walter. *Die Theologie Rudolf Bultmanns: Eine Einführung*. Tübingen: Mohr Siebeck, 1967. ET: *An Introduction to the Theology of Rudolf Bultmann.* Translated by John Bowden. Minneapolis: Augsburg, 1968.

Smith, Dwight Moody. *The Composition and Order of the Fourth Gospel: Bultmann's Literary Theory*. New Haven: Yale University Press, 1965.

Wolf, Herbert C. *Kierkegaard and Bultmann: The Quest of the Historical Jesus*. Augsburg Publishing House Theological Monograph. Minneapolis: Augsburg, 1965.

The Bultmann School

Ernst Käsemann

Käsemann, Ernst. *Exegetische Versuche und Besinnungen.* 2 vols. Göttingen: Vandenhoeck & Ruprecht, 1960, 1965. English translations: *Essays on New Testament Themes.* Translated by W. J. Montague. SBT 41. London: SCM, 1964. *New Testament Questions of Today.* Translated by W. J. Montague. Philadelphia: Fortress Press, 1969.

——. *Jesu letzter Wille nach Johannes 17.* Tübingen: Mohr Seibeck, 1966. ET: *The Testament of Jesus: A Study of the Gospel of John in the Light of Chapter 17.* Translated by Gerhard Krodel. Philadelphia: Fortress Press, 1968. 3d rev. [German] ed. Tübingen: Mohr Siebeck, 1971.

——. *Kirchliche Konflikte.* Vol. 1. Göttingen: Vandenhoeck & Ruprecht, 1982.

——. *Die Legitimität des Apostels: Eine Untersuchung zu II Korinther 10–13.* Darmstadt: Wissenschaftliche Buchgesellschaft, 1956.

——. *Leib und Leib Christi: Eine Untersuchung zur paulinischen Begrifflichkeit.* BHT 9. Tübingen: Mohr Siebeck, 1933.

——. *Paulinische Perspektiven.* Tübingen: Mohr Siebeck, 1969. ET: *Perspectives on Paul.* Translated by Margaret Kohl. Philadelphia: Fortress Press, 1971.

——. *An die Römer.* HNT 8a. Tübingen: Mohr Siebeck, 1973. ET: *Commentary on Romans.* Translated and edited by Geoffrey W. Bromiley. Grand Rapids: Eerdmans, 1980.

——. *Der Ruf der Freiheit.* 3d ed. Tübingen: Mohr Siebeck, 1968. ET: *Jesus Means Freedom.* Translated by Frank Clarke. Philadelphia: Fortress Press, 1970.

——. *Das wandernde Gottesvolk: Eine Untersuchung zum Hebräerbrief.* 3d ed. FRLANT. Göttingen: Vandenhoeck & Ruprecht, 1959. ET: *The Wandering People of God: An Investigation of the Letter to the Hebrews.* Translated by Roy A. Harrisville and Irving L. Sandberg. Minneapolis: Augsburg, 1984.

Ehler, Bernhard. *Die Herrschaft des Gekreuzigten: Ernst Käsemanns Frage nach der Mitte der Schrift.* BZNW 46. Berlin: de Gruyter, 1986.

Gisel, Pierre. *Vérité et histoire: La Théologie dans la modernité Ernst Käsemann.* Paris: Beauchesne, 1977.

Schmitz, Hermann-Josef. *Frühkatholizismus bei Adolf von Harnack, Rudolph Sohm und Ernst Käsemann.* Düsseldorf: Patmos, 1977.

Way, David. *The Lordship of Christ: Ernst Käsemann's Interpretation of Paul's Theology.* OThM. Oxford: Clarendon, 1991.

Zahl, Paul Francis Matthew. *Die Rechtfertigungslehre Ernst Käsemanns*. SThK 13. Stuttgart: Calwer, 1996.

GÜNTHER BORNKAMM

Bornkamm, Günther. *Bibel—Das Neue Testament: Eine Einführung in seine Schriften im Rahmen der Geschichte des Urchristentums*. Stuttgart: Kreuz, 1971. ET: *The New Testament: A Guide to Its Writings*. Translated by Reginald H. Fuller and Ilse Fuller. Philadelphia: Fortress Press, 1973.

———. *Early Christian Experience*. Translated by Paul L. Hammer. New York: Harper & Row, 1969. (Selections from *Das Ende des Gesetzes* and *Studien zu Antike und Urchristentum*).

———. *Das Ende des Gesetzes: Paulusstudien*. Gesammelte Aufsätze 1. BEvT 16. Munich: Kaiser, 1958.

———. *Geschichte und Glaube*. Part 1. Gesammelte Aufsätze 3. BEvT 48. Munich: Kaiser, 1968.

———. *Geschichte und Glaube*. Part 2. Gesammelte Aufsätze 4. BEvT 53. Munich: Kaiser, 1971.

———. *Gesetz und Schöpfung im Neuen Testament*. Tübingen: Mohr Siebeck, 1934.

———. "Jesus: The Christ and Christology." *The New Encyclopedia Britannica*. 15th ed. Chicago: Encyclopedia Britannica, 1974. 22: 336–46.

——— . *Jesus von Nazareth*. 11th ed. Stuttgart: Kohlhammer, 1977. ET: *Jesus of Nazareth*. Translated by Irene and Fraser McLuskey, with James M. Robinson. New York: Harper & Brothers, 1960.

———. *Mythos und Legende in den apokryphen Thomas-Akten: Beiträge zur Geschichte der Gnosis und zur Vorgeschichte des Manichäismus*. FRLANT 49. Göttingen: Vandenhoeck & Ruprecht, 1933.

Paulus. Stuttgart: Kohlhammer, 1969. ET: *Paul*. Translated by D. M. G. Stalker. New York: Harper & Row, 1971.

———. *Studien zu Antike und Urchristentum*. Gesammelte Aufsätze 2. BEvT 28. Munich: Kaiser, 1959.

———. *Studien zum Matthäus-Evangelium*. Ed. Werner Zager. WMANT 125. Neukirchen-Vluyn: Neukirchener Verlag, 2009.

———, Gerhard Barth, and Heinz Joachim Held. *Uberlieferung und Auslegung im Matthäusevangelium*. 4th ed. WMANT 1. Neukirchen: Neukirchener Verlag, 1965. ET: *Tradition and Interpretation in Matthew*. Translated by Percy Scott. Philadelphia: Westminster, 1963.

JAMES M. ROBINSON

Robinson, James M. *Kerygma und historischer Jesus.* 2d ed. Zürich: Zwingli, 1967.

———. *A New Quest of the Historical Jesus: And Other Essays.* Philadelphia: Fortress Press, 1983.

———. *Das Problem des Heiligen Geistes bei Wilhelm Herrmann: Inaugural-Dissertation zur Erlangung der Doktorwürde der Theologischen Fakultät der Universität Basel.* Marburg/Lahn: Universitäts-Buchdruckerei, 1952.

———. *The Problem of History in Mark: And Other Marcan Studies.* Philadelphia: Fortress Press, 1982. German trans.: *Das Geschichtsverständnis des Markus-Evangeliums.* Translated by Karlfried Fröhlich. ATANT 30 Zürich: Zwingli, 1956.

New Discoveries, Archaeology, Textual Criticism

NAG HAMMADI

Bianchi, Ugo, ed. *The Origins of Gnosticism: Colloquium of Messina, 13–18 April 1966.* SHR 12. Leiden: Brill, 1967.

Dart, John. *The Jesus of Heresy and History: The Discovery and Meaning of the Nag Hammadi Gnostic Library.* San Francisco: Harper & Row, 1988.

Doresse, Jean. *The Secret Books of the Egyptian Gnostics: An Introduction to the Gnostic Coptic Manuscripts Discovered at Chenoboskion.* Translated by Philip Mairet. New York: Viking, 1960.

Filoramo, Giovanni. *A History of Gnosticism.* Translated by Anthony Alcock. Oxford: Basil Blackwell, 1990.

Franzmann, Majella. *Jesus in the Nag Hammadi Writings.* Edinburgh: T & T Clark, 1996.

Gärtner, Bertil. *The Theology of the Gospel according to Thomas.* Translated by Eric J. Sharpe. New York: Harper & Brothers, 1961.

Grant, Robert M. *Gnosticism and Early Christianity.* New York: Columbia University Press, 1959.

Haenchen, Ernst. *Die Botschaft des Thomas-Evangeliums.* Berlin: Alfred Töpelmann, 1961.

Hedrick, Charles W., and Robert Hodgson, Jr., eds. *Nag Hammadi, Gnosticism, & Early Christianity.* Peabody, MA: Hendrickson, 1986.

Helmbold, Andrew K. *The Nag Hammadi Gnostic Texts and the Bible.* Grand Rapids: Baker, 1967.

Jonas, Hans. *Gnosis und spätantiker Geist. Erster Teil: Die mythologische Gnosis: Mit einer Einleitung zur Geschichte und Methodologie der Forschung*. 3d ed. FRLANT 33. Göttingen: Vandenhoeck & Ruprecht, 1964.

———. *The Gnostic Religion: The Message of the Alien God and the Beginnings of Christianity*. 2d ed. Boston: Beacon, 1963.

King, Karen L. *What is Gnosticism?* Cambridge, MA: Harvard University Press, 2003.

Krause, Martin, ed. *Essays on the Nag Hammadi Texts: In Honour of Pahor Labib*. NHS 6. Leiden: Brill, 1975.

———. *Gnosis and Gnosticism: Papers read at the Seventh International Conference on Patristic Studies (Oxford, September 8th–13th 1975)*. NHS 8. Leiden: Brill, 1977.

Layton, Bentley, ed. *Nag Hammadi Codex II,2-7: Together with XIII,2, Brit. Lib. Or.4926(1), and P. Oxy. 1, 654, 655*. Vol. 1. NHS 20. Leiden: Brill, 1989.

Lelyveld, Margaretha. *Les Logia de la vie dans l'Évangile selon Thomas: A la recherche d'une tradition et d'une rédaction*. NHS 34. Leiden: Brill, 1987.

Ménard, Jacques-É. *L'Évangile selon Thomas*. NHS 5. Leiden: Brill, 1975.

———, ed. *Les Textes de Nag Hammadi: Colloque du Centre d'Histoire des Religions (Strasbourg, 23–25 octobre 1974)*. NHS 7. Leiden: Brill, 1975.

Pagels, Elaine. *Beyond Belief: The Secret Gospel of Thomas*. New York: Random House, 2003.

Patterson, Stephen J. *The Gospel of Thomas and Jesus*. FF. Sonoma, CA: Polebridge, 1993.

Pearson, Birger A. *Gnosticism, Judaism, and Egyptian Christianity*. SAC. Minneapolis: Fortress Press, 1990.

Perkins, Pheme. *Gnosticism and the New Testament*. Minneapolis: Fortress Press, 1993.

Robinson, James M. *Nag Hammadi: The First Fifty Years*. OPIAC 34. Claremont, CA: Claremont Graduate School, 1995.

Robinson, James M., ed. *The Facsimile Edition of the Nag Hammadi Codices: Introduction*. Leiden: Brill, 1984.

———. *The Nag Hammadi Library in English*. Translated and Introduced by Members of the Coptic Gnostic Library Project of the Institute for Antiquity and Christianity, Claremont, California. 3d ed. San Francisco: Harper, 1990; Leiden: Brill, 1996.

Rudolph, Kurt. *Die Gnosis: Wesen und Geschichte einer spätantiken Religion*. 2d ed. Göttingen: Vandenhoeck & Ruprecht, 1980. ET: *Gnosis: The Nature and History of Gnosticism.* Translated by Robert McLachlan Wilson. San Francisco: Harper & Row, 1983.

Schenke, Hans-Martin. *On the Compositional History of the Gospel of Thomas.* OPIAC 40. Claremont, CA: Claremont Graduate School, 1998.

Scholer, David M., ed. *Gnosticism in the Early Church.* SEC 5 New York: Garland, 1993.

Tröger, Karl-Wolfgang, ed. *Gnosis und Neues Testament: Studien aus Religionswissenschaft und Theologie.* Berlin: Evangelische Verlagsanstalt, 1973.

Turner, John D., and Anne McGuire, eds. *The Nag Hammadi Library after Fifty Years: Proceedings of the 1995 Society of Biblical Literature Commemoration.* NHMS 44. Leiden: Brill, 1997.

Tuckett, Christopher M. *Nag Hammadi and The Gospel Tradition: Synoptic Tradition in the Nag Hammadi Library.* Studies of the New Testament and Its World. Ed. John Riches. Edinburgh: T & T Clark, 1986.

Williams, Michael Allen. *Rethinking "Gnosticism": An Argument for Dismantling a Dubious Category.* Princeton: Princeton University Press, 1996.

Wilson, Robert McLachlan, ed. *Nag Hammadi and Gnosis: Papers read at the First International Congress of Coptology (Cairo, December 1967).* NHS 14. Leiden: Brill, 1978.

Zöckler, Thomas. *Jesu Lehren im Thomasevangelium.* NHMS 47. Leiden: Brill, 1999.

DEAD SEA SCROLLS

Abegg, Martin, Jr., Peter Flint, and Eugene Ulrich, eds. *The Dead Sea Scrolls Bible: The Oldest Known Bible, Translated for the First Time into English.* San Francisco: HarperCollins, 1999.

Betz, Otto, and Rainer Riesner. *Jesus, Qumran and the Vatican: Clarifications.* New York: Crossroad, 1994.

Braun, Herbert. *Qumran und das Neue Testament.* 2 vols. Tübingen: Mohr Siebeck, 1966.

Brooke, George J. *The Dead Sea Scrolls and the New Testament.* Minneapolis: Fortress Press, 2005.

Charlesworth, James H., ed. *Jesus and the Dead Sea Scrolls.* ABRL. New York: Doubleday, 1992.

———, ed. *John and the Dead Sea Scrolls.* New York: Crossroad, 1990.

Collins, John J. *Apocalypticism in the Dead Sea Scrolls.* Literature of the Dead Sea Scrolls. London: Routledge, 1997.

———. *Beyond the Qumran Community: The Sectarian Movement of the Dead Sea Scrolls.* Grand Rapids: Eerdmans, 2010.

———. *The Scepter and the Star: Messianism in Light of the Dead Sea Scrolls.* 2d ed. Grand Rapids: Eerdmans, 2010.

Davies, Philip R., George J. Brooke, and Phillip R. Callaway. *The Complete World of the Dead Sea Scrolls.* London: Thames & Hudson, 2002.

Davila, James R., ed. *The Dead Sea Scrolls as Background to Postbiblical Judaism and Early Christianity: Papers from an International Conference at St. Andrews in 2001.* STDJ 46. Leiden: Brill, 2003.

Evans, Craig A., and Peter W. Flint, eds. *Eschatology, Messianism, and the Dead Sea Scrolls.* Studies in the Dead Sea Scrolls and Related Literature. Grand Rapids: Eerdmans, 1997.

Fitzmyer, Joseph A. *The Dead Sea Scrolls and Christian Origins.* Studies in the Dead Sea Scrolls and Related Literature. Grand Rapids: Eerdmans, 2000.

Flint, Peter W., and James C. VanderKam, eds. *The Dead Sea Scrolls after Fifty Years: A Comprehensive Assessment.* 2 vols. Leiden: Brill, 1998–99.

Fujita, Neil S. *A Crack in the Jar: What Ancient Jewish Documents Tell Us About the New Testament.* New York: Paulist, 1986.

Golb, Norman. *Who Wrote the Dead Sea Scrolls? The Search for the Secret of Qumran.* New York: Scribner, 1995.

Herbert, Edward D., and Emanuel Tov, eds. *The Bible as Book: The Hebrew Bible and the Judaean Desert Discoveries.* London: British Library, 2002.

Kugler, Robert A., and Eileen M. Schuller, eds. *The Dead Sea Scrolls at Fifty: Proceedings of the 1997 Society of Biblical Literature Qumran Section Meetings,* SBLEJL 15. Atlanta: Scholars, 1999.

Lim, Timothy H., ed. *The Dead Sea Scrolls in Their Historical Context.* Edinburgh: T & T Clark, 2000.

Magness, Jodi. *The Archaeology of Qumran and the Dead Sea Scrolls.* SDSSRL. Grand Rapids: Eerdmans, 2002.

Martínez, Florentino García, ed. T*he Dead Sea Scrolls Translated: The Qumran Texts in English.* 2d ed. Translated by Wilfred G. E. Watson. Leiden: Brill; Grand Rapids: Eerdmans, 1996.

——— and Eibert J. C. Tigchelaar, eds. *The Dead Sea Scrolls Study Edition.* 2 vols. Leiden: Brill; Grand Rapids: Eerdmans, 2000.

Murphy-O'Connor, Jerome, and James H. Charlesworth, eds. *Paul and the Dead Sea Scrolls.* New York: Crossroad, 1990.

Parry, Donald W., and Stephen D. Ricks, eds. *Current Research and Technological Developments on the Dead Sea Scrolls: Conference on the Texts from the Judean Desert, Jerusalem, 30 April 1995.* STDJ. Leiden, Brill, 1996.

Stegemann, Hartmut. *The Library of Qumran: On the Essenes, Qumran, John the Baptist, and Jesus.* Grand Rapids: Eerdmans, 1998.

Stendahl, Krister, and James H. Charlesworth, eds. *The Scrolls and the New Testament.* New York: Crossroad, 1992.

Tov, Emanuel, ed. *Discoveries in the Judaean Desert.* 39 vols. Oxford: Clarendon, 1955–2002.

VanderKam, James, and Peter Flint. *The Meaning of the Dead Sea Scrolls: Their Significance for Understanding the Bible, Judaism, Jesus, and Christianity.* San Francisco: HarperCollins, 2002; paper 2004.

Van der Ploeg, Johannes P. M., et al., eds. *La Secte de Qumrân et les origines du Christianisme.* Paris: Desclée de Brouwer, 1959.

Vermes, Geza, ed. *The Complete Dead Sea Scrolls in English.* Rev. ed. London: Penguin, 2004.

———. *An Introduction to the Complete Dead Sea Scrolls.* Minneapolis: Fortress Press, 1999.

Wise, Michael O., Martin Abegg, Jr., and Edward Cook, *The Dead Sea Scrolls: A New Translation.* San Francisco: HarperSanFrancisco, 1996.

ARCHAEOLOGY

Abrahamsen, Valerie A. *Women and Worship at Philippi: Diana/Artemis and Other Cults in the Early Christian Era.* Portland, ME: Shell, 1995.

Bakirtzis, Charalambos, and Helmut Koester, eds. *Philippi at the Time of Paul and after His Death.* Harrisburg, PA: Trinity Press International, 1998.

Bardtke, Hans. *Bibel, Spaten und Geschichte.* Göttingen: Vandenhoeck & Ruprecht, 1967.

Bartlett, John R., ed. *Archaeology and Biblical Interpretation.* London: Routledge, 1997.

Batey, Richard A. *Jesus and the Forgotten City: New Light on Sepphoris and the Urban World of Jesus.* Grand Rapids: Baker, 1991.

Blaiklock, E. M. *The Archaeology of the New Testament.* Grand Rapids: Zondervan, 1970.

Bormann, Lukas. *Philippi: Stadt und Christengemeinde zur Zeit des Paulus.* NovTSup 78. Leiden: Brill, 1995.

Chancey, Mark A. *Greco-Roman Culture and the Galilee of Jesus.* SNTSMS 134. Cambridge: Cambridge University Press, 2005.

———. *The Myth of a Gentile Galilee.* SNTSMS 118. Cambridge: Cambridge University Press, 2002.

Charlesworth, James H., ed. *Jesus and Archaeology* Grand Rapids: Eerdmans, 2006.

Crossan, John Dominic, and Jonathan L. Reed. *Excavating Jesus: Beneath the Stones, Behind the Texts.* Rev. ed. San Francisco: Harper, 2001.

DeVries, LaMoine F. *Cities of the Biblical World.* Peabody, MA: Hendrickson, 1997.

Dowley, Tim, ed. *Discovering the Bible: Archaeologists Look at Scripture.* Grand Rapids: Eerdmans, 1986.

Downey, Glanville. *Ancient Antioch.* Princeton: Princeton University Press, 1963.

Edwards, Douglas R., ed. *Religion and Society in Roman Palestine: Old Questions, New Approaches.* New York: Routledge, 2004.

———, and C. Thomas McCollough, eds. *Archaeology and the Galilee: Texts and Contexts in the Graeco-Roman and Byzantine Periods.* SFSHJ 143. Atlanta: Scholars, 1987.

Elliger, Winfried. *Paulus in Griechenland: Philippi, Thessaloniki, Athen, Korinth.* StBS 92/93. Stuttgart: Katholisches Bibelwerk, 1978.

Finegan, Jack. *The Archaeology of the New Testament: The Life of Jesus and the Beginning of the Early Church.* Rev. ed. Princeton: Princeton University Press, 1992.

———. *The Archaeology of the New Testament: The Mediterranean World of the Early Christian Apostles.* Boulder, CO: Westview, 1981.

Freyne, Sean. *Galilee and Gospel: Collected Essays.* WUNT 125. Tübingen: Mohr Siebeck, 2000.

———. *Galilee, Jesus, and the Gospels: Literary Approaches and Historical Investigations.* Philadelphia: Fortress Press, 1988.

———. *Jesus, a Jewish Galilean: A New Reading of the Jesus Story.* London: T & T Clark, 2004.

Gregory, Timothy E., ed. *The Corinthia in the Roman Period.* JRASup 8. Ann Arbor: Cushing-Malloy, 1993.

Harrison, Roland K. *Archaeology of the New Testament.* New York: Association, 1964.

Holum, Kenneth G., Robert L. Hohlfelder, Robert J. Bull, and Avner Raban, *King Herod's Dream: Caesarea on the Sea.* New York: W. W. Norton, 1988.

Hoppe, Leslie J. *What Are They Saying About Biblical Archaeology?* New York: Paulist, 1984.

Horsley, Richard A. *Archaeology, History, and Society in Galilee: The Social Context of Jesus and the Rabbis.* Valley Forge, PA: Trinity Press International, 1996.

Koester, Helmut, ed. *Ephesos: Metropolis of Asia: An Interdisciplinary Approach to Its Archaeology, Religion, and Culture.* HTS 41. Valley Forge, PA: Trinity Press International, 1995.

Lampe, Peter. *Die stadtrömischen Christen in den ersten beiden Jahrhunderten: Untersuchungen zur Sozialgeschichte.* 2d ed. WUNT 2d series 18. Tübingen: Mohr Siebeck, 1989. ET: *From Paul to Valentinus: Christians at Rome in the First Two Centuries.* Translated by Michael Steinhauser. Edited by Marshall D. Johnson. Minneapolis: Fortress Press, 2003.

Lanci, John R. *A New Temple for Corinth: Rhetorical and Archaeological Approaches to Pauline Imagery.* New York: Peter Lang, 1997.

Levine, Lee I., ed. *The Galilee in Late Antiquity.* New York: Jewish Theological Seminary of America, 1992.

Mare, W. Harold. *The Archaeology of the Jerusalem Area.* Grand Rapids: Baker, 1987.

Meeks, Wayne A., and Robert L. Wilken. *Jews and Christians in Antioch in the First Four Centuries of the Common Era.* SBLSBS 13. Missoula: Scholars, 1978.

Meyers, Eric M., ed. *Galilee through the Centuries: Confluence of Cultures.* DJS 1. Winona Lake: Eisenbrauns, 1999.

Murphy-O'Connor, Jerome. *St. Paul's Corinth: Texts and Archaeology.* 3d ed. Collegeville, MN: Liturgical, 2002.

Pilhofer, Peter. *Philippi: 1 Die erste christliche Gemeinde Europas.* WUNT 87. Tübingen: Mohr Siebeck, 1995.

Portefaix, Lilian. *Sisters Rejoice: Paul's Letter to the Philippians and Luke-Acts as Received by First-Century Philippian Women.* ConBNT 20. Stockholm: Almqvist & Wiksell, 1988.

Reed, Jonathan L. *Archaeology and the Galilean Jesus: A Re-examination of the Evidence.* Harrisburg, PA: Trinity Press International, 2000.

Richard, Suzanne, ed. *Near Eastern Archaeology: A Reader.* Winona Lake: Eisenbrauns, 2003.

Snyder, Graydon F. *Ante Pacem: Archaeological Evidence of Church Life Before Constantine.* Macon, GA: Mercer University Press, 1985.

Unger, Merrill F. *Archaeology and the New Testament.* Grand Rapids: Zondervan, 1962.

Wilkinson, John. *Jerusalem as Jesus Knew It: Archaeology as Evidence.* London: Thames and Hudson, 1978.

Yamauchi, Edwin M. *The Archaeology of New Testament Cities in Western Asia Minor.* Grand Rapids: Baker, 1980.

Zetterholm, Magnus. *The Formation of Christianity in Antioch: A Social-Scientific Approach to the Separation between Judaism and Christianity.* London: Routledge, 2003.

TEXTUAL CRITICISM

Aland, Barbara, and Joël Delobel, eds. *New Testament Textual Criticism, Exegesis, and Early Church History: A Discussion of Methods.* Kampen: Kok Pharos, 1994.

Aland, Kurt. *Kurzgefasste Liste der griechischen Handschriften des Neuen Testaments.* 2d revised and enlarged ed. ANTF 1. Berlin: de Gruyter, 1994.

———, ed. *Repertorium der griechischen christlichen Papyri: I. Biblische Papyri: Altes Testament, Neues Testament, Varia, Apokryphen.* PTS 18. Berlin: de Gruyter, 1976.

———. *Studien zur Überlieferung des Neuen Testaments und Seines Textes.* ANTF 2. Berlin: de Gruyter, 1967.

Aland, Kurt, and Barbara Aland. *The Text of the New Testament: An Introduction to the Critical Editions and to the Theory and Practice of Modern Textual Criticism.* Translated by Erroll F. Rhodes. 2nd. rev. and enlarged ed. Grand Rapids: Eerdmans, 1989.

American and British Committees of the International Greek New Testament Project, eds. *The New Testament: The Gospel According to St. Luke. Part One, Chapters 1–12.* Oxford: Clarendon, 1984.

———. *The New Testament: The Gospel According to St. Luke. Part Two, Chapters 13–24.* Oxford: Clarendon, 1987.

Black, David Alan, ed. *Rethinking New Testament Textual Criticism.* Grand Rapids: Baker, 2002.

Colwell, Ernest C. *Studies in Methodology in Textual Criticism of the New Testament.* NTTS 9. Grand Rapids: Eerdmans, 1969.

Comfort, Philip Wesley. *The Quest for the Original Text of the New Testament.* Grand Rapids: Baker, 1992.

Denaux, Adelbert, ed. *New Testament Textual Criticism and Exegesis: Festschrift Joël Delobel.* BETL 161. Leuven: University Press, 2002.

Duplacy, Jean. *Où en est la critique textuelle du Nouveau Testament?* Paris: Gabalda, 1959.

Ehrman, Bart D. *Misquoting Jesus: The Story Behind Who Changed the Bible and Why.* San Francisco: Harper, 2005.

———. *The Orthodox Corruption of Scripture: The Effect of Early Christological Controversies on the Text of the New Testament.* New York: Oxford University Press, 1993.

———. *Studies in the Textual Criticism of the New Testament.* Leiden: Brill, 2006.

———, and Michael W. Holmes, eds. *The Text of the New Testament in Contemporary Research: Essays on the* Status Quaestionis. A Volume in Honor of Bruce M. Metzger. SD 46. Grand Rapids: Eerdmans, 1995.

Epp, Eldon Jay. *Junia: The First Woman Apostle.* Minneapolis: Fortress Press, 2005.

———. *Perspectives on New Testament Textual Criticism: Collected Essays, 1962–2004.* NovTSup 116. Leiden: Brill, 2004.

———. *The Theological Tendency of Codex Bezae Cantabrigiensis in Acts.* SNTSMS 3. Cambridge: Cambridge University Press, 1966.

———, and Gordon D. Fee, eds. *Studies in the Theory and Method of New Testament Textual Criticism.* SD 45. Grand Rapids: Eerdmans, 1993.

———. *New Testament Textual Criticism: Its Significance for Exegesis: Essays in Honor of Bruce M. Metzger.* Oxford: Clarendon, 1981.

Finegan, Jack. *Encountering New Testament Manuscripts: A Working Introduction to Textual Criticism.* Grand Rapids: Eerdmans, 1974.

Greenlee, J. Harold. *Introduction to New Testament Textual Criticism.* Rev. ed. Peabody, MA: Hendrickson, 1995.

Hodges, Zane C., and Arthur L. Farstad, eds. *The Greek New Testament According to the Majority Text.* Nashville: Nelson, 1982.

Metzger, Bruce M. *Chapters in the History of New Testament Textual Criticism.* NTTS 4 Grand Rapids: Eerdmans, 1963.

———. *The Early Versions of the New Testament: Their Origin, Transmission, and Limitations.* Oxford: Clarendon, 1977.

———, and Bart D. Ehrman. *The Text of the New Testament: Its Transmission, Corruption, and Restoration.* 4th ed. New York: Oxford University Press, 2005.

Parker, David C. *The Living Text of the Gospels.* Cambridge: Cambridge University Press, 1997.

_____, and Christian-Bernard Amphoux, eds. *Codex Bezae: Studies from the Lunel Colloquium, June, 1994.* NTTS 22. Leiden: Brill, 1996.

Sturz, Harry A. *The Byzantine Text-Type and New Testament Textual Criticism.* Nashville: Nelson, 1984.

Taylor, David G. K., ed. *Studies in the Early Text of the Gospels and Acts: The Papers of the First Birmingham Colloquium on the Textual Criticism of the New Testament.* SBLTCS 1. Atlanta: SBL, 1999.

Vaganay, Leon. *An Introduction to New Testament Textual Criticism.* 2d rev. ed. Christian-Bernard Amphoux. Translated by Jenny Heimerdinger. Cambridge: Cambridge University Press, 1991.

Vogels, Heinrich Joseph. *Handbuch der Kritik des Neuen Testaments.* 2d ed. Bonn: Peter Hanstein, 1955.

Wisse, Frederik. *The Profile Method for the Classification of Manuscript Evidence as Applied to the Continuous Greek Text of the Gospel of Luke.* SD 44. Grand Rapids: Eerdmans, 1982.

Zimmermann, Heinrich. *Neutestamentliche Methodenlehre: Darstellung der historisch-kritischen Methode.* Stuttgart: Katholisches Bibelwerk, 1967.

HISTORICAL BACKGROUNDS: JUDAISM

INTRODUCTIONS, TEXTS, AND TRANSLATIONS

Charlesworth, James H., ed. *The Old Testament Pseudepigrapha.* 2 vols. Garden City, NY: Doubleday, 1983, 1985.

———. *The Old Testament Pseudepigrapha and the New Testament: Prolegomena for the Study of Christian Origins.* Harrisburg, PA: Trinity Press International, 1998.

Kümmel, Werner G., ed. *Jüdische Schriften aus hellenistisch-römischer Zeit.* 6 vols. Gütersloh: Mohn, 1973–99.

Nickelsburg, George W. E. *Ancient Judaism and Christian Origins: Diversity, Continuity, and Transformation.* Minneapolis: Fortress Press, 2003.

———. *1 Enoch: A Commentary on the Book of 1 Enoch, Chapters 1–36; 81–108.* Ed. Klaus Baltzer. Hermeneia. Minneapolis: Fortress Press, 2001.

———. *Jewish Literature Between the Bible and the Mishna: A Historical and Literary Introduction.* Philadelphia: Fortress Press, 1981.

_____. *Resurrection, Immortality, and Eternal Life in Intertestamental Judaism and Early Christianity: Expanded Edition.* HTS 56. Cambridge, MA: Harvard University Press, 2006.

JOACHIM JEREMIAS

Jeremias, Joachim. *Abba: Studien zur neutestamentlichen Theologie und Zeitgeschichte.* Göttingen: Vandenhoeck & Ruprecht, 1966.

——. *Die Abendmahlsworte Jesu.* 3d ed. Göttingen: Vandenhoeck & Ruprecht, 1960. ET: *The Eucharistic Words of Jesus.* Translated by Norman Perrin. New Testament Library. London: SCM, 1966.

——. *The Central Message of the New Testament.* New York: Scribner's, 1965.

——. *Die Gleichnisse Jesu.* 8th ed. Göttingen: Vandenhoeck & Ruprecht, 1970. ET: *The Parables of Jesus.* Rev. ed. translated by S. H. Hooke. New York: Scribner's, 1963.

——. *Golgotha.* ΑΓΓΕΛΟΣ: Archiv für neutestamentliche Zeitgeschichte und Kulturkunde 1. Leipzig: Pfeiffer, 1926.

——. *Jesu Verheissung für die Völker.* Stuttgart: Kohlhammer, 1959. ET: *Jesus' Promise to the Nations.* Translated by S. H. Hooke. Philadelphia: Fortress Press, 1982.

——. *Jesus and the Message of the New Testament.* Ed. K. C. Hanson. Minneapolis: Fortress Press, 2002.

——. *Jerusalem in the Time of Jesus: An Investigation into Economic and Social Conditions in the New Testament Period.* Translated by F. H. and C. H. Cave. Philadelphia: Fortress Press, 1969.

——. *Die Kindertaufe in den ersten vier Jahrhunderten.* Göttingen: Vandenhoeck & Ruprecht, 1958. ET: *Infant Baptism in the First Four Centuries.* Translated by David Cairns. Philadelphia: Westminster, 1960.

——. *Neutestamentliche Theologie: Erster Teil: Die Verkündigung Jesu.* Gütersloh: Mohn, 1970. ET: *New Testament Theology: The Proclamation of Jesus.* Translated by John Bowden. New York: Scribners, 1971.

——. "παῖς θεοῦ in Later Judaism in the Period after the LXX." *Theological Dictionary of the New Testament.* Edited by Gerhard Kittel. Translated by Geoffrey W. Bromily. Grand Rapids: Eerdmans, 1967, 5: 677–717. Repr.: Walther Zimmerli and Joachim Jeremias. *The Servant of God.* Rev. ed. SBT 20. London: SCM, 1965.

——. *The Prayers of Jesus.* Philadelphia: Fortress Press, 1978.

——. *Das Problem des historischen Jesus.* Stuttgart: Calwer, 1960. ET: *The Problem of the Historical Jesus.* Translated by Norman Perrin. Philadelphia: Fortress Press, 1964.

——. *The Sermon on the Mount.* Translated by Norman Perrin. Philadelphia: Fortress Press, 1963.

———. *Die theologische Bedeutung der Funde am Toten Meer.* Göttingen: Vandenhoeck & Ruprecht, 1962.

MATTHEW BLACK

Black, Matthew. *An Aramaic Approach to the Gospels and Acts.* 3d ed. Oxford: Clarendon, 1967.

———. *The Book of Enoch or I Enoch: A New English Edition: With Commentary and Textual Notes.* SVTP 7. Leiden: Brill, 1985.

———. *Romans.* NCB. Greenwood, SC: Attic, 1973.

———. *The Scrolls and Christian Origins.* New York: Scribner's, 1961.

W. D. DAVIES

Davies, W. D. *Christian Engagements with Judaism.* Harrisburg, PA: Trinity Press International, 1999.

———. *Christian Origins and Judaism.* London: Darton, Longman & Todd, 1962.

———. *The Gospel and the Land: Early Christianity and Jewish Territorial Doctrine.* Berkeley: University of California Press, 1974.

———. *Invitation to the New Testament: A Guide to Its Main Witnesses.* Garden City, NY: Doubleday, 1966.

———. *Jewish and Pauline Studies.* Philadelphia: Fortress Press, 1984.

———. *Paul and Rabbinic Judaism: Some Rabbinic Elements in Pauline Theology.* 4th ed. Philadelphia: Fortress Press, 1980.

———. *The Setting of the Sermon on the Mount.* Cambridge: Cambridge University Press, 1964.

E. P. SANDERS

Sanders, E. P. *The Historical Figure of Jesus.* London: Penguin, 1993.

———. *Jesus and Judaism.* Philadelphia: Fortress Press, 1985.

———. *Jewish Law from Jesus to the Mishnah: Five Studies.* London: SCM; Philadelphia: Trinity Press International, 1990.

———. *Judaism: Practice and Belief: 63 BCE–66 CE.* London: SCM, 1992. Repr. Valley Forge, PA: Trinity Press International, 1994. Repr. Eugene, OR: Wipf & Stock, 2004. Repr. London: SCM, 2005.

———. *Paul and Palestinian Judaism: A Comparison of Patterns of Religion.* Philadelphia: Fortress Press, 1977.

———. *Paul, the Law, and the Jewish People.* Philadelphia: Fortress Press, 1983.

———. *The Tendencies of the Synoptic Problem.* SNTSMS 9. Cambridge: Cambridge University Press, 1969.

——— and Margaret Davies. *Studying the Synoptic Gospels.* London: SCM; Philadelphia: Trinity Press International, 1989.

Martin Hengel

———. *The Atonement: The Origins of the Doctrine in the New Testament.* Translated by John Bowden. Philadelphia: Fortress Press, 1981.

———. *Between Jesus and Paul: Studies in the Earliest History of Christianity.* Translated by John Bowden. Philadelphia: Fortress Press, 1983.

———. *The Four Gospels and the One Gospel of Jesus Christ: An Investigation of the Collection and Origin of the Canonical Gospels.* Translated by John Bowden. Harrisburg, PA: Trinity Press International, 2000. German ed.: *Die vier Evangelien und das eine Evangelium von Jesus Christus.* WUNT 224. Tübingen: Mohr Siebeck, 2008.

———. *The "Hellenization" of Judaea in the First Century after Christ.* In collaboration with Christoph Markschies. Translated by John Bowden. London: SCM, 1989.

———. *The Johannine Question.* Translated by John Bowden. London: SCM; Philadelphia: Trinity Press International, 1989. Expanded German ed.: *Die johanneische Frage: Ein Lösungsversuch.* Tübingen: Mohr Siebeck, 1993.

———. *Judaica et Hellenistica: Kleine Schriften I.* With Roland Deines, Jörg Frey, Christoph Markschies, and Anna Maria Schwemer. WUNT 90. Tübingen: Mohr Siebeck, 1996.

———. *Judaica, Hellenistica et Christiana: Kleine Schriften II.* With Jörg Frey and Dorothea Betz. WUNT 109. Tübingen: Mohr Siebeck, 1999.

———. *Juden, Griechen und Barbaren: Aspekte der Hellenisierung des Judentums in vorchristlicher Zeit.* StBS 76. Stuttgart: Katholisches Bibelwerk, 1976. ET: *Jews, Greeks and Barbarians: Aspects of the Hellenization of Judaism in the pre-Christian Period.* Translated by John Bowden. Philadelphia: Fortress Press, 1980.

———. *Judentum und Hellenismus: Studien zu ihrer Begegnung unter besonderer Berücksichtigung Palästinas bis zur Mitte des 2 Jh. v. Chr.* 2 vols. 2d ed. WUNT 10. Tübingen: Mohr Siebeck, 1973. ET: *Judaism and Hellenism: Studies in their Encounter in Palestine during the Early Hellenistic Period.* Translated by John Bowden. 2 vols. Philadelphia: Fortress Press, 1974.

———. *Nachfolge und Charisma: Eine exegetisch-religionsgeschichtliche Studie zu Mt 8.21f und Jesu Ruf in die Nachfolge.* BZNW 34. Berlin: de Gruyter, 1968. ET:

The Charismatic Leader and His Followers. Translated by James C. G. Greig. Edited by John Riches. Edinburgh: T & T Clark, 1996.

———. *Der unterschätze Petrus: Zwei Studien.* Tübingen: Mohr Siebeck, 2006. ET: *Saint Peter: The Underestimated Apostle.* Translated by Thomas H. Trapp. Grand Rapids: Eerdmans, 2010.

———. *Paulus und Jakobus: Kleine Schriften III.* WUNT 141. Tübingen: Mohr Siebeck, 2002.

———, in collaboration with Roland Deines. *The Pre-Christian Paul.* Translated by John Bowden. London: SCM; Philadelphia: Trinity Press International, 1991.

———. *Der Sohn Gottes: Die Entstehung der Christologie und die jüdisch-hellenistische Religionsgeschichte.* Tübingen: Mohr Siebeck, 1975. ET: *The Son of God: The Origin of Christology and the History of Jewish-Hellenistic Religion.* Translated by John Bowden. Philadelphia: Fortress Press, 1976.

———. *Studien zur Christologie: Kleine Schriften IV.* Ed. Claus-Jürgen Thornton. WUNT 201. Tübingen: Mohr Siebeck, 2006.

———. *Studies in Early Christology.* Edinburgh: T & T Clark, 1995.

———. *Die Zeloten: Untersuchungen zur Jüdischen Freiheitsbewegung in der Zeit von Herodes I. bis 70 n. Chr.* 2d ed. AGSU 1. Leiden: Brill, 1976. ET: *The Zealots: Investigations into the Jewish Freedom Movement in the Period from Herod I until 70 A.D.* Translated by David Smith. Edinburgh: T & T Clark, 1989.

——— and Ulrich Heckel, eds. *Paulus und das antike Judentum.* WUNT 58. Tübingen: Mohr Siebeck, 1991.

——— and Anna Maria Schwemer. *Paulus zwischen Damaskus und Antiochien: Die unbekannten Jahre des Apostels.* Tübingen: Mohr Siebeck, 1998. ET: *Paul Between Damascus and Antioch: The Unknown Years.* Translated by John Bowden. Louisville: Westminster John Knox, 1997.

DEVELOPMENTS IN HISTORICAL CRITICISM

WERNER GEORG KÜMMEL

Kümmel, Werner Georg. *Das Bild des Menschen im Neuen Testament.* Zurich: Zwingli, 1948. Repr.: *Römer 7 und Das Bild des Menschen im Neuen Testament: Zwei Studien.* Munich: Kaiser, 1974. ET: *Man in the New Testament.* Translated by John J. Vincent. Rev. ed. Philadelphia: Westminster, 1963.

———. *Jesus der Menschensohn?* Wiesbaden: Steiner, 1984.

———. *Das Neue Testament: Geschichte der Erforschung seiner Probleme.* 2d ed. Freiburg: Alber, 1970. ET: *The New Testament: The History of the Investigation of Its Problems.* Translated by S. McLean Gilmore and Howard C. Kee. Nashville: Abingdon, 1972.

———. *Das Neue Testament im 20. Jahrhundert: Ein Forschungsbericht.* StBS 50 Stuttgart: Katholisches Bibelwerk, 1970.

———. *Römer 7 und die Bekehrung des Paulus.* UNT 17. Leipzig: Hinrichs, 1926. Repr. Lexington, KY: ATLA, 1965.

———. *Die Theologie des Neuen Testaments nach seinen Hauptzeugen: Jesus, Paulus, Johannes.* 2d ed. Göttingen: Vandenhoeck & Ruprecht, 1972. ET: *The Theology of the New Testament: According to its Major Witnesses: Jesus—Paul—John.* Translated by John E. Steely. Nashville: Abingdon, 1973.

———. *Verheißung und Erfüllung: Untersuchungen zur eschatologischen Verkündigung Jesu.* 3d ed. ATANT 6. Zürich: Zwingli, 1956. ET: *Promise and Fulfilment: The Eschatological Message of Jesus.* 2d ed. Translated by Dorothea M. Barton. SBT 23. London: SCM, 1961.

Grässer, Erich, Otto Merk, and Adolf Fritz, eds. *Heilsgeschehen und Geschichte: Gesammelte Aufsäze 1933–1964, 1965–76.* 2 vols. MTS 3/16. Marburg: Elwert, 1965, 1978.

HELMUT KOESTER

Koester, Helmut. *Ancient Christian Gospels: Their History and Development.* Philadelphia: Trinity Press International, 1990.

———, ed. *Ephesos: Metropolis of Asia: An Interdisciplinary Approach to Its Archaeology, Religion, and Culture.* HTS 41. Valley Forge, PA: Trinity Press International, 1995.

———. *Introduction to the New Testament.* 2d ed. Vol. 1: *History, Culture, and Religion of the Hellenistic Age.* Vol. 2: *History and Literature of Early Christianity.* New York: de Gruyter, 1995, 2000.

———. *From Jesus to the Gospels: Interpreting the New Testament in Its Context* Minneapolis: Fortress Press, 2007.

———. *Paul and His World: Interpreting the New Testament in Its Context.* Minneapolis: Fortress Press, 2007.

———, ed. *Pergamon: Citadel of the Gods: Archaeological Record, Literary Description, and Religious Development.* HTS 46. Harrisburg, PA: Trinity Press International, 1998.

———. *Synoptische Überlierferung bei den apostolischen Vätern.* TU 65. Berlin: Akademie Verlag, 1957.

Bakirtzis, Charalambos, and Helmut Koester, eds. *Philippi at the Time of Paul and after His Death.* Harrisburg, PA: Trinity Press International, 1998.

Robinson, James M., and Helmut Koester. *Trajectories through Early Christianity.* Philadelphia: Fortress Press, 1971. Repr. Eugene, OR: Wipf & Stock, 2006.

HANS CONZELMANN

Conzelmann, Hans. *Der erste Brief an die Korinther.* KEK 5/11. Göttingen: Vandenhoeck & Ruprecht, 1969. ET: *1 Corinthians: A Commentary on the First Epistle to the Corinthians.* Translated by James W. Leitch. Hermeneia. Philadelphia: Fortress Press, 1975.

———. *Grundriss der Theologie des Neuen Testaments.* 2d ed. Munich: Kaiser, 1968; ET: *An Outline of the Theology of the New Testament.* Translated by John Bowden. New York: Harper & Row, 1969.

———. *Heiden, Juden, Christen: Auseinandersetzungen in der Literatur der hellenistisch-römischen Zeit.* Tübingen: Mohr Siebeck, 1981. ET: *Gentiles, Jews, Christians: Polemics and Apologetics in the Greco-Roman Era.* Translated by Eugene Boring. Minneapolis: Fortress Press, 1992.

———. *Jesus: The Classic Article from RGG³ Expanded and Updated.* Translated by J. Raymond Lord. Edited by John Reumann. Philadelphia: Fortress Press, 1973.

———. *Die Mitte der Zeit: Studien zur Theologie des Lukas.* 3d ed. BHT 17. Tübingen: Mohr Siebeck, 1960. ET: *The Theology of Luke.* Translated by Geoffrey Buswell. New York: Harper & Brothers, 1960.

WILLI MARXSEN

Marxsen, Willi. *Anfangsprobleme der Christologie.* 2d ed. Gütersloh: Mohn, 1964. ET: *The Beginnings of Christology: A Study in Its Problems.* Translated by Paul J. Achtemeier. Philadelphia: Fortress Press, 1969.

———. *Die Auferstehung Jesu von Nazareth.* Gütersloh: Mohn, 1968. ET: *The Resurrection of Jesus of Nazareth.* Translated by Margaret Kohl. Philadelphia: Fortress Press, 1970.

———. *"Christliche" und christliche Ethik im Neuen Testament.* Gütersloh: Mohn, 1989. ET: *New Testament Foundations for Christian Ethics.* Translated by O. C. Dean, Jr. Minneapolis: Fortress Press, 1993.

———. "Christology in the New Testament." *IDBSup,* 146–56.

———. *Einleitung in das Neue Testament: Eine Einführung in ihre Probleme.* 3d ed. Gütersloh: Mohn, 1964. ET: *Introduction to the New Testament: An Approach to its Problems*. Translated by Geoffrey Buswell. Philadelphia: Fortress Press, 1960.

———. *Der Evangelist Markus: Studien zur Redaktionsgechichte des Evangeliums*. 2d ed. FRLANT 67. Göttingen: Vandenhoeck & Ruprecht, 1959. ET: *Mark the Evangelist: Studies on the Redaction History of the Gospel*. Translated by James Boyce, Donald Juel, and William Poehlmann with Roy A. Harrisville. Nashville: Abingdon, 1969.

———. *Das Neue Testament als Buch der Kirche*. Gütersloh: Mohn, 1966. ET: *The New Testament as the Church's Book*. Translated by James E. Mignard. Philadelphia: Fortress Press, 1972.

THE SYNOPTIC PROBLEM

Dungan, David L. *A History of the Synoptic Problem: The Canon, the Text, the Composition, and the Interpretation of the Gospels*. ABRL. New York: Doubleday, 1999.

Foster, Paul, Andrew F. Gregory, John S. Kloppenborg, and Jozef Verheyden, eds. *New Studies in the Synoptic Problem: Oxford Conference, April 2008: Essays in Honour of Christopher M. Tuckett*. BETL 239. Leuven: Peeters, 2011.

Tuckett, Christopher M. *The Revival of the Griesbach Hypothesis: An Analysis and Appraisal*. Cambridge: Cambridge University Press, 1983.

WILLIAM R. FARMER

Farmer, William Reuben. *The Gospel of Jesus: The Pastoral Relevance of the Synoptic Problem*. Louisville: Westminster John Knox, 1994.

———. *Jesus and the Gospel: Tradition, Scripture, and Canon*. Philadelphia: Fortress Press, 1982.

———. *The Last Twelve Verses of Mark*. Cambridge: Cambridge University Press, 1974.

———. *Maccabees, Zealots, and Josephus: An Inquiry into Jewish Nationalism in the Greco-Roman Period*. New York: Columbia University Press, 1956. Repr. Westport, CT: Greenwood, 1973.

———. *The Synoptic Problem: A Critical Analysis*. New York: Macmillan, 1964. Repr. Dillsboro, NC: Western North Carolina, 1976.

McNicol, Allan J., ed., with David L. Dungan and David Peabody. *Beyond the Q Impasse—Luke's Use of Matthew: A Demonstration by the Research Team of the International Institute for Gospel Studies*. Valley Forge, PA: Trinity Press International, 1996.

Peabody, David B., ed., with Lamar Cope and Allan J. McNicol. *One Gospel from Two: Mark's Use of Matthew and Luke: A Demonstration by the Research Team of the International Institute for Renewal of Gospel Studies*. Harrisburg, PA: Trinity Press International, 2002.

MICHAEL GOULDER

Goulder, Michael D. *The Evangelists' Calendar: A Lectionary Explanation of the Development of Scripture*. London: SPCK, 1978.

———. *Luke: A New Paradigm*. 2 vols. JSNTSup 20. Sheffield: Sheffield Academic Press, 1989.

———. *Midrash and Lection in Matthew*. London: SPCK, 1974.

Goodacre, Mark S. *The Case Against Q: Studies in Markan Priority and the Synoptic Problem*. Harrisburg, PA: Trinity Press International, 2002.

———. *Goulder and the Gospels: An Examination of a New Paradigm*. JSNTSup 133. Sheffield: Sheffield Academic, 1996.

———. *The Synoptic Problem: A Way Through the Maze*. London: Sheffield Academic, 2001.

Goodacre, Mark, and Nicholas Perrin, eds. *Questioning Q: A Multidimensional Critique*. Downers Grove, IL: InterVarsity, 2004.

Rollston, Christopher A., ed. *The Gospels According to Michael Goulder: A North American Response*. Harrisburg, PA: Trinity Press International, 2002.

RESEARCH ON Q

Kloppenborg, John S. *Excavating Q: The History and Setting of the Sayings Gospel*. Edinburgh: T & T Clark, 2000.

———. *The Formation of Q: Trajectories in Ancient Wisdom Collections*. SAC. Philadelphia: Fortress Press, 1987.

———. *Q, The Earliest Gospel: An Introduction to the Original Stories and Sayings of Jesus*. Louisville: Westminster John Knox, 2008.

———. *Q Parallels: Synopsis, Critical Notes, and Concordance*. FF. Sonoma, CA: Polebridge, 1988.

Robinson, James M., Paul Hoffmann, and John S. Kloppenborg, eds. *The Critical Edition of Q: Synopsis including the Gospels of Matthew and Luke, Mark and Thomas with English, German, and French Translations of Q and Thomas*. Hermeneia. Minneapolis: Fortress Press, 2000.

———. *The Sayings Gospel Q in Greek and English: with Parallels from the Gospels of Mark and Thomas*. BETL 30. Leuven: Peeters, 2001.

Roman Catholic Scholarship

Prior, Joseph G. *The Historical Critical Method in Catholic Exegesis.* TGST 50. Rome: Gregorian University Press, 1999.

Robinson, Robert Bruce. *Roman Catholic Exegesis Since* Divino Afflante Spiritu*: Hermeneutical Implications.* SBLDS 111. Atlanta: Scholars, 1988.

Rudolf Schnackenburg

Schnackenburg, Rudolf. *Gottes Herrschaft und Reich: Eine biblisch-theologische Studie.* Freiburg: Herder, 1959. ET: *God's Rule and Kingdom.* Translated by John Murray. New York: Herder and Herder, 1963.

———. *Die Johannesbriefe.* HTKNT 3,13. Freiburg: Herder, 1975. ET: *The Johannine Epistles.* Translated by Reginald and Ilse Fuller. New York: Crossroad, 1992.

———. *Das Johannesevangelium.* 4 vols. HTKNT. Freiburg: Herder, 1965–75. ET: *The Gospel According to St. John.* 3 vols. HTKNT 4 New York: Herder and Herder, 1968; Seabury, 1980; Crossroad, 1982.

———. *Der Brief an die Epheser.* EKKNT. Cologne: Benziger, 1982. ET: *Ephesians: A Commentary.* Translated by Helen Heron. Edinburgh: T & T Clark, 1991.

———. *Mattäusevangelium.* 2 vols. Würzburg: Echter, 1985, 1987. ET: *The Gospel of Matthew.* Translated by Robert R. Barr. Grand Rapids: Eerdmans, 2002.

———. *Die Person Jesu Christi im Spiegel der vier Evangelien,* HTKNTSup 4. Freiburg: Herder, 1993. ET: *Jesus in the Gospels: A Biblical Christology.* Translated by O. C. Dean, Jr. Louisville: Westminster John Knox, 1995.

———. *Schriften zum Neuen Testament: Exegese in Fortschritt und Wandel.* Munich: Kösel, 1971.

———. *Die sittliche Botschaft des Neuen Testaments.* HTKNTSup 1, 2. Freiburg: Herder, 1986.

Raymond E. Brown

Brown, Raymond E. *The Birth of the Messiah: A Commentary on the Infancy Narratives in the Gospels of Matthew and Luke.* New Updated ed. ABRL. New York: Doubleday, 1993.

———. *The Churches the Apostles Left Behind.* New York: Paulist, 1984.

———. *The Community of the Beloved Disciple.* New York: Paulist, 1979.

———. *The Death of the Messiah: From Gethsemane to the Grave: A Commentary on the Passion Narratives in the Four Gospels.* 2 vols. ABRL. New York: Doubleday, 1994.

———. *The Epistles of John.* AB 30. Garden City, N.Y: Doubleday, 1982.

———. *The Gospel According to John.* 2 vols. AB 29. Garden City, NY: Doubleday, 1966, 1970.

———. *An Introduction to the New Testament.* ABRL. New York: Doubleday, 1997.

———. *An Introduction to New Testament Christology.* New York: Paulist, 1994.

———. *New Testament Essays.* Milwaukee: Bruce, 1965.

———. *The* Sensus Plenior *of Sacred Scripture.* Baltimore: St. Mary's University, 1955.

———. *The Virginal Conception and the Bodily Resurrection of Jesus.* New York: Paulist, 1973.

Fogarty, Gerald P. *American Catholic Biblical Scholarship: A History from the Early Republic to Vatican II.* SBLCPS. San Francisco: Harper & Row, 1989.

John P. Meier

Meier, John P. *Law and History in Matthew's Gospel: A Redactional Study of Mt. 5:17-48.* AnBib 71. Rome: Biblical Institute Press, 1976.

———. *A Marginal Jew: Rethinking the Historical Jesus. Vol. 1: The Roots of the Problem and the Person.* ABRL. New York: Doubleday, 1991.

———. *Vol. 2: Mentor, Message, and Miracles.* New York: Doubleday, 1994.

———. *Vol. 3: Companions and Competitors.* New York: Doubleday, 2001.

———. *Vol. 4: Law and Love.* AYBRL. New Haven: Yale University Press, 2009.

The Development of Scholarly Societies

Society of Biblical Literature

Attridge, Harold W., and James C. VanderKam, eds. *Presidential Voices: The Society of Biblical Literature in the Twentieth Century.* SBLBSNA 22. Atlanta: SBL, 2006.

Hyatt, J. Philip, ed. *The Bible in Modern Scholarship: Papers Read at the 100th Meeting of the Society of Biblical Literature, December 28–30, 1964.* Nashville: Abingdon, 1965.

"Journal of Biblical Literature: 125th Anniversary: Commemorative Essays." *JBL* 125 (2006): 151–212.

Saunders, Ernest W. *Searching the Scriptures: A History of the Society of Biblical Literature, 1880–1980.* SBLBSNA 8. Chico, CA: Scholars, 1982.

CATHOLIC BIBLICAL ASSOCIATION

Fogarty, Gerald P. *American Catholic Biblical Scholarship: A History form the Early Republic to Vatican II.* SBLCPS. San Francisco: Harper & Row, 1989.

Jensen, Joseph. "Y2K Plus 4." *CBQ* 66 (2004) *Supplement,* 14–16.

Osiek, Carolyn. "Catholic or catholic: Biblical Scholarship at the Center." *Presidential Voices: The Society of Biblical Literature in the Twentieth Century.* Ed. Harold W. Attridge and James C. VanderKam. SBLBSNA 22. Atlanta: SBL, 2006, 325–42.

Rossiter, Francis S. "Forty Years Less One: An Historical Sketch of the C.B.A. (1936–1975." *CBQ* 66 (2004) *Supplement,* 1–13.

STUDIORUM NOVI TESTAMENTI SOCIETAS

Barrett, C. K. "*New Testament Studies:* 1954–2004." *NTS* 50 (2004): 1–4.

Black, Matthew. "Foreword." *NTS* 1 (1954–55): 1–4.

Boobyer, G. H. "Studiorum Novi Testamenti Societas." *NTS* 1 (1954–55): 66–70.

ROBERT W. FUNK AND THE JESUS SEMINAR

Borg, Marcus J. *Jesus in Contemporary Scholarship.* Harrisburg, PA: Trinity Press International, 1994.

Funk, Robert W. *A Beginning-Intermediate Grammar of Hellenistic Greek.* 3 vols. 2d ed. SBS 2. Missoula: SBL, 1973.

———. *A Credible Jesus: Fragments of a Vision.* Santa Rosa, CA: Polebridge, 2002.

———. *Honest to Jesus: Jesus for a New Millennium.* San Francisco: HarperSanFrancisco, 1966.

———. *Language, Hermeneutic, and Word of God: The Problem of Language in the New Testament and Contemporary Theology.* New York: Harper & Row, 1966.

———. *Jesus as Precursor.* SBLSSup 2. Philadelphia: Fortress Press, 1975.

———. *New Gospel Parallels: Vol. 1, The Synoptic Gospels. Vol. 2, John and the Other Gospels.* FF. Philadelphia: Fortress Press, 1985.

———. *Parables and Presence: Forms of the New Testament Tradition.* Philadelphia: Fortress Press, 1982.

———. *The Poetics of Biblical Narrative.* FF. Sonoma, CA: Polebridge, 1988.

———, Roy W. Hoover, and the Jesus Seminar. *The Five Gospels: The Search for the Authentic Words of Jesus: New Translation and Commentary.* San Francisco: HarperSanFrancisco, 1997.

———, and the Jesus Seminar. *The Acts of Jesus: The Search for the Authentic Deeds of Jesus.* San Francisco: HarperSanFrancisco, 1998.

———, Bernard Brandon Scott, and James R. Butts. *The Parables of Jesus: Red Letter Edition.* Sonoma, CA: Polebridge, 1988.

Johnson, Luke Timothy. *The Real Jesus: The Misguided Quest for the Historical Jesus and the Truth of the Traditional Gospels.* San Francisco: HarperSanFrancisco, 1996.

Miller, Robert J. *The Jesus Seminar and its Critics.* Santa Rosa, CA: Polebridge, 1999.

Pearson, Birger A. *The Gospel According to the Jesus Seminar.* OPIAC 35. Claremont, CA: Institute for Antiquity and Christianity, 1996.

Scrimgeour, Andrew D. *Just Call Me Bob: The Wit and Wisdom of Robert W. Funk.* Santa Rosa, CA: Polebridge, 2007.

Scott, Bernard Brandon, ed. *Jesus Reconsidered: Scholarship in the Public Eye.* Santa Rosa, CA: Polebridge, 2007.

THEOLOGICAL AND HERMENEUTICAL DEVELOPMENTS

OSCAR CULLMANN

Cullmann, Oscar. *Die Christologie des Neuen Testaments.* Tübingen: Mohr Siebeck, 1957. ET: *The Christology of the New Testament.* Translated by Shirley C. Guthrie and Charles A. M. Hall. Philadelphia: Westminster, 1959. French trans.: *Christologie du Nouveau Testament.* 3d ed. Neuchâtel: Delachaux et Niestlé, 1968.

———. *Christus und die Zeit: Die urchristliche Zeit- und Geschichtsauffassung.* 3d rev. ed. Zollikon-Zürich: Evangelischer Verlag, 1962. ET: *Christ and Time: The Primitive Christian Conception of Time and History.* Rev. ed. Translated by Floyd V. Filson. London: SCM, 1962.

———. *The Early Church: Studies in Early Christian History and Theology.* Ed. A. J. B. Higgins. Philadelphia: Westminster, 1956.

———. *Heil als Geschichte: Heilsgeschichtliche Existenz im Neuen Testament.* Tübingen: Mohr Siebeck, 1965. ET: *Salvation in History.* Translated by Sidney G. Sowers. NTL. London: SCM, 1967.

————. *Immortality of the Soul or Resurrection of the Dead? The Witness of the New Testament*. New York: Macmillan, 1958.

————. *Petrus: Jünger, Apostel, Märtyrer: Das historische und das theologische Petrusproblem*. 2d rev. ed. Zürich: Zwingli, 1960. ET: *Peter: Disciple, Apostle, Martyr: A Historical and Theological Study*. Translated by Floyd V. Filson. Philadelphia: Westminster, 1953. Repr. Waco, TX: Baylor University Press, 2011.

————. *Les Premièrs confessions de foi chrétiennes*. Paris: Presses Universitaires de France, 1943. German translation: *Die ersten christlichen Glaubensbekenntnisse*. Zollikon-Zürich: Evangelischer Verlag, 1943. ET: *The Earliest Christian Confessions*. Translated by J. K. S. Reid. London: Lutterworth, 1949.

————. *La signification de la Sainte-Cène dans le christianisme primitif*. Paris: Presses Universitaire de France, 1936. ET: "The Meaning of the Lord's Supper in Primitive Christianity." *Essays on the Lord's Supper*. Ecumenical Studies in Worship 1. Richmond, VA: John Knox, 1958.

————. *The State in the New Testament*. New York: Scribner's, 1956.

————. *Die Tauflehre des Neuen Testaments: Erwachsenen- und Kindertaufe*. Zürich: Zwingli, 1948. French ed.: *Le Baptême des enfants et la doctrine biblique du baptême*. Neuchâtel: Delachaux & Niestlé, 1948. ET: *Baptism in the New Testament*. Translated by J. K. S. Reid. SBT 1. London: SCM, 1950.

————. *Urchristentum und Gottesdienst*. Zürich: Zwingli, 1950. ET: *Early Christian Worship*. Translated by A. Stewart Todd and James B. Torrance. SBT 10. London: SCM, 1953.

————. *Vorträge und Aufsätze, 192--1962*. Ed. Karlfried Fröhlich. Tübingen: Mohr Siebeck, 1966.

Dorman, Theodore Martin. *The Hermeneutics of Oscar Cullmann*. San Francisco: Mellen Research University Press, 1991.

Frisque, Jean. *Oscar Cullmann: Une théologie de l'hisoire du salut*. Cahiers de l'actualité religieuse 11. Tournai: Casterman, 1960.

Schlaudraff, Karl-Heinz. *"Heil als Geschichte"? Die Frage nach dem heilsgeschichtlichen Denken, dargestellt anhand der Konzeption Oscar Cullmanns*. BGBE 29. Tübingen: Mohr Siebeck, 1988.

JOHN KNOX

Knox, John. *Chapters in a Life of Paul*. Rev. ed. Macon, GA: Mercer University Press, 1987.

————. *The Church and the Reality of Christ*. New York: Harper & Row, 1962.

———. *Criticism and Faith.* London: Hodder and Stoughton, 1953.

———. *The Death of Christ: The Cross in New Testament History and Faith.* New York: Abingdon, 1958.

———. *The Early Church and the Coming Great Church.* New York: Abingdon, 1955.

———. "The Epistle to the Romans: Introduction and Exegesis." *Interpreter's Bible* 9: 355–668.

———. *The Humanity and Divinity of Christ: A Study of Pattern in Christology.* Cambridge: Cambridge University Press, 1967.

———. *Limits of Unbelief.* New York: Seabury, 1970.

———. *Marcion and the New Testament.* Chicago: University of Chicago Press, 1942.

———. *Myth and Truth: An Essay on the Language of Faith.* Charlottesville: University Press of Virginia, 1964.

———. *Philemon Among the Letters of Paul: A New View of Its Place and Importance.* Rev. ed. New York: Abingdon, 1959.

———. *A Trilogy Comprising: The Man Christ Jesus, Christ the Lord, On the Meaning of Christ.* New York: Harper & Brothers, 1958.

PAUL S. MINEAR

Minear, Paul S. *And Great Shall Be Your Reward: The Origins of Christian Views of Salvation.* YSR 12. New Haven: Yale University Press, 1941.

———. *Christian Hope and the Second Coming.* Philadelphia: Westminster, 1954.

———. *Eyes of Faith: A Study in the Biblical Point of View.* Rev. ed. St. Louis: Bethany, 1966.

———. *The Gospel According to Mark.* LBC 17. Atlanta: John Knox, 1962.

———. *Horizons of Christian Community.* St. Louis: Bethany, 1959.

———. *I Saw a New Earth: An Introduction to the Visions of the Apocalypse.* Washington: Corpus Books, 1968.

———. *Images of the Church in the New Testament.* Philadelphia: Westminster, 1960.

———. *John: The Martyr's Gospel.* New York: Pilgrim, 1984.

———. *The Kingdom and the Power: An Exposition of the New Testament Gospel.* Philadelphia: Westminster, 1950. Repr. 2004.

———. *New Testament Apocalyptic.* Nashville: Abingdon, 1981.

———. *The Obedience of Faith: The Purposes of Paul in the Epistle to the Romans.* SBT 2d Series 19. Naperville, IL: Alec R. Allenson, 1971.

F. F. BRUCE

Bruce, Frederick Fyvie. *The Acts of the Apostles: The Greek Text with Introduction and Commentary.* 3d ed. Grand Rapids: Eerdmans, 1990.

——. *Biblical Exegesis in the Qumran Texts.* Grand Rapids: Eerdmans, 1959.

——. *The Canon of Scripture.* Downers Grove, IL: InterVarsity, 1988.

——. *The Defence of the Gospel in the New Testament.* Grand Rapids: Eerdmans, 1959.

——. *The Epistle to the Galatians: A Commentary on the Greek Text.* NIGTC. Grand Rapids: Eerdmans, 1982.

——. *The Gospel of John: Introduction, Exposition and Notes.* Grand Rapids: Eerdmans, 1983.

——. *Jesus: Past, Present, and Future: The Work of Christ.* Downers Grove, IL: InterVarsity, 1979.

——. *The New Testament Development of Old Testament Themes.* Grand Rapids: Eerdmans, 1968.

——. *The New Testament Documents: Are They Reliable?* London: InterVarsity, 1961.

——. *New Testament History.* London: Nelson, 1969.

——. *Paul: Apostle of the Heart Set Free.* Grand Rapids: Eerdmans, 2000.

——. *In Retrospect: Remembrance of Things Past.* Grand Rapids: Eerdmans, 1980.

——. *Second Thoughts on the Dead Sea Scrolls.* 2d ed. Grand Rapids: Eerdmans, 1961.

——. *The Teacher of Righteousness in the Qumran Texts.* London: Tyndale, 1957.

——. *Tradition Old and New.* Grand Rapids: Zondervan, 1970.

CRITICAL, EXEGETICAL, AND THEOLOGICAL ACCOMPLISHMENTS: EUROPE

C. K. BARRETT

Barrett, C. K. *A Commentary on the Epistle to the Romans.* HNTC. New York: Harper, 1957.

——. *A Commentary on the First Epistle to the Corinthians.* HNTC. New York: Harper, 1968.

——. *A Commentary on the Second Epistle to the Corinthians.* HNTC. New York: Harper, 1973.

———. *A Critical and Exegetical Commentary on The Acts of the Apostles*. 2 vols. ICC. London: T & T Clark, 2004.

———. *From First Adam to Last: A Study in Pauline Theology*. New York: Scribner's, 1962.

———. *The Gospel According to John: An Introduction with Commentary and Notes on the Greek Text*. 2d ed. Philadelphia: Westminster, 1978.

———. *Jesus and the Gospel Tradition*. London: SPCK, 1967.

———. *New Testament Background: Selected Documents*. San Francisco: Harper and Row, 1989.

———. *Paul: An Introduction to His Thought*. Louisville: Westminster John Knox, 1994.

JAMES D. G. DUNN

Dunn, James D. G. *Baptism in the Holy Spirit: A Re-examination of the New Testament Teaching on the Gift of the Spirit in Relation to Pentecostalism Today*. SBT 2d Series 15. London: SCM, 1970.

———. *Christianity in the Making*. Vol. 1, *Jesus Remembered*; Vol. 2, *Beginning from Jerusalem*. Grand Rapids: Eerdmans, 2003, 2009.

———. *Christology in the Making: A New Testament Inquiry into the Origins of the Doctrine of the Incarnation*. 2d ed. Grand Rapids: Eerdmans, 1989.

———. *The Epistle to the Galatians*. BNTC. Peabody, MA: Hendrickson, 1993.

———. *Jesus and the Spirit: A Study of the Religious and Charismatic Experience of Jesus and the First Christians as Reflected in the New Testament*. Philadelphia: Westminster, 1975.

———. *The New Perspective on Paul*. Rev. ed. Grand Rapids: Eerdmans, 2008.

———. *The Partings of the Ways: Between Christianity and Judaism and their Significance for the Character of Christianity*. 2d ed. London: SCM, 2006.

———. *Romans 1–8*. WBC 38A. *Romans 9–16*. WBC 38B. Dallas: Word, 1988.

———. *The Theology of Paul the Apostle*. Grand Rapids: Eerdmans, 1998.

———. *The Theology of Paul's Letter to the Galatians*. Cambridge: Cambridge University Press, 1993.

———. *Unity and Diversity in the New Testament: An Inquiry into the Character of Earliest Christianity*. 3d. ed. London: SCM, 2006.

BIRGER GERHARDSSON

Gerhardsson, Birger. *The Ethos of the Bible*. Translated by Stephen Westerholm. Philadelphia: Fortress Press, 1981.

———. "Illuminating the Kingdom: Narrative Meshalim in the Synoptic Gospels." In *Jesus and the Oral Gospel*. Ed. Henry Wansbrough. JSNTSup 64. Sheffield: JSOT Press, 1991, 266–309.

———. *Memory and Manuscript: Oral Tradition and Written Transmission in Rabbinic Judaism and Early Christianity*. Translated by Eric J. Sharpe. Grand Rapids: Eerdmans, 1998.

———. *The Mighty Acts of Jesus According to Matthew*. Lund: Gleerup, 1979.

———. *The Reliability of the Gospel Tradition*. Peabody, MA: Hendrickson, 2001.

———. *The Testing of God's Son (Matt 4:1-11 & Par): An Analysis of an Early Christian Midrash*. Translated by John Toy. ConBNT 2:1. Lund: Gleerup, 1966.

CRITICAL, EXEGETICAL, AND THEOLOGICAL ACCOMPLISHMENTS: NORTH AMERICA

ELISABETH SCHÜSSLER FIORENZA

Schüssler Fiorenza, Elisabeth. *The Book of Revelation: Justice and Judgment*. 2d ed. Minneapolis: Fortress Press, 1998.

———. *Bread Not Stone: The Challenge of Feminist Biblical Interpretation*. Boston: Beacon, 1984.

———. *But She Said: Feminist Practices of Biblical Interpretation*. Boston: Beacon, 1992.

———. *Democratizing Biblical Studies: Toward an Emancipatory Educational Space*. Louisville: Westminster John Knox, 2009.

———. *Jesus: Miriam's Child, Sophia's Prophet: Critical Issues in Feminist Christology*. New York: Continuum, 1995.

———. *Jesus and the Politics of Interpretation*. New York: Continuum, 2000.

———. *In Memory of Her: A Feminist Reconstruction of Christian Origins*. New York: Crossroad, 1992.

———. *The Power of the Word: Scripture and the Rhetoric of Empire*. Minneapolis: Fortress Press, 2007.

———. *Priester für Gott: Studien zum Herrschafts- und Priestermotiv in der Apocalypse*. NTAbh 7. Münster: Aschendorff, 1972.

———. *Rhetoric and Ethic: The Politics of Biblical Studies*. Minneapolis: Fortress Press, 1999.

———. *Transforming Vision: Explorations in Feminist The*logy*. Minneapolis: Fortress Press, 2011.

Ng, Esther Yue L. *Reconstructing Christian Origins? The Feminist Theology of Elisabeth Schüssler Fiorenza: An Evaluation.* Carlisle: Paternoster, 2002.

J. LOUIS MARTYN

Martyn, J. Louis. *Galatians: A New Translation with Introduction and Commentary.* AB 33A. New York: Doubleday, 1997.

———. *The Gospel of John in Christian History: Essays for Interpreters.* New York: Paulist, 1979.

———. *History and Theology in the Fourth Gospel.* 3d ed. NTL. Louisville: Westminster John Knox, 2003.

———. *Theological Issues in the Letters of Paul.* Nashville: Abingdon, 1997.

LEANDER E. KECK

Keck, Leander E. *A Future for the Historical Jesus: The Place of Jesus in Preaching and Theology.* Nashville: Abingdon, 1971.

———. *Mandate to Witness: Studies in the Book of Acts.* Valley Forge, PA: Judson, 1964.

———. *The New Testament Experience.* St. Louis: Bethany, 1976.

———. *Paul and His Letters.* 2d ed. PC. Philadelphia: Fortress Press, 1988.

———. *Romans.* ANTC. Nashville: Abingdon, 2005.

———. *Taking the Bible Seriously.* Nashville: Abingdon, 1962.

———. *Who is Jesus? History in Perfect Tense.* Columbia: University of South Carolina Press, 2000.

VICTOR PAUL FURNISH

Furnish, Victor Paul. *II Corinthians: Translation with Introduction, Notes and Commentary.* AB 32A. Garden City, NY: Doubleday, 1984.

———. *The Love Command in the New Testament.* Nashville: Abingdon, 1972.

———. *The Moral Teaching of Paul: Selected Issues.* 3d ed. Nashville: Abingdon, 2009.

———. *Theology and Ethics in Paul.* Louisville: Westminster John Knox, 2009.

———. *The Theology of the First Letter to the Corinthians.* Cambridge: Cambridge University Press, 1999.

———. *1 Thessalonians, 2 Thessalonians.* ANTC. Nashville: Abingdon, 2007.

Cullinan, Michael Patrick. *Victor Paul Furnish's Theology of Ethics in Saint Paul: An Ethic of Transforming Grace.* Tesi Accademia Alfonsiana 3. Rome: Editiones Academiae Alfonsianae, 2007.

HANS DIETER BETZ

Betz, Hans Dieter. *Der Apostel Paulus und die sokratische Tradition: Eine exegetische Untersuchung zu seiner "Apologie," 2 Korinther 10–13.* BHT 45. Tübingen: Mohr Siebeck, 1972.

———. *2 Corinthians 8 and 9: A Commentary on Two Administrative Letters of the Apostle Paul.* Hermeneia. Philadelphia: Fortress Press, 1985. German trans.: *2. Korinther 8 und 9: Ein Kommentar zu zwei Verwaltungsbriefe des Apostels Paulus.* Translated by Sibylle Ann. Gütersloh: Kaiser, 1993.

———. *Galatians: A Commentary on Paul's Letter to the Churches in Galatia.* Hermeneia. Philadelphia: Fortress Press, 1979. German trans.: *Der Galaterbrief: ein Kommentar zum Brief des Apostels Paulus an die Gemeinden in Galatien.* Translated by Sibylle Ann. Munich: Kaiser, 1988.

———. *Lukian von Samosata und das Neue Testament: religionsgeschichtliche und paränetische Parallelen: Ein Beitrag zum Corpus Hellenisticum Novi Testamenti.* TU 76. Berlin: Akademie Verlag, 1961.

———. *Nachfolge und Nachahmung Jesu Christi im Neuen Testament.* BHT 37. Tübingen: J. C. Mohr (Paul Siebeck), 1967.

———. *The Sermon of the Mount: A Commentary on the Sermon on the Mount, including the Sermon on the Plain (Matthew 5:3–7:27 and Luke 6:20–49).* Hermeneia. Philadelphia: Fortress Press, 1995.

Index of Subjects

Index of Names

Index of Scripture

John